D0162814

Accounting Theory

Accounting Theory

Eldon S. Hendriksen
Michael F. van Breda
Southern Methodist University

Fifth Edition

IRWIN

Chicago • Bogotá • Boston • Buenos Aires • Caracas
London • Madrid • Mexico City • Sydney • Toronto

© RICHARD D. IRWIN, INC., 1965, 1970, 1977, 1982, and 1992

Sponsoring editor: Ron M. Regis
Project editor: Paula M. Buschman
Production manager: Carma W. Fazio
Designer: Larry J. Cope
Compositor: Bi-Comp, Inc.
Typeface: 10/12 Times Roman
Printer: R. R. Donnelley & Sons Company

Library of Congress Cataloging-in-Publication Data

Hendriksen, Eldon S.

    Accounting theory / Eldon S. Hendriksen, Michael F. van Breda. — 5th ed.

      p.   cm.

    Includes bibliographical references and index.

    ISBN 0-256-08146-8   **ISBN 0-256-11269-X Int'l Ed.**

    1. Accounting.   I. Van Breda, Michael F.   II. Title.

HF5625.H45   1991

657–dc20   91–27330

Printed in the United States of America
5 6 7 8 9 0 DOC 8 7 6

Preface

This fifth edition, like its predecessors, is designed to provide a frame of reference for junior, senior, and graduate courses in financial accounting and financial accounting theory; seminars on financial accounting standards and issues; and seminars on the theory of income and asset valuation. Those who wish to obtain a good understanding of financial accounting standards or want a general survey of financial accounting theory and those who wish to study for the theory section of the Uniform CPA Examination should also find this book useful.

It is assumed that the reader has a knowledge of the basic structure of accounting. Experience has shown, however, that mature students who have not studied accounting can understand the subject matter with concurrent additional formal or independent study of this basic structure. A background in finance or economics can also lead into this book.

A general frame of reference has been used to evaluate the many areas of financial accounting theory and practice. The frame of reference includes a number of theories that are not necessarily consistent with each other and that may lead to different conclusions. Evaluations are made at three basic levels:

1. The structural level—the relationships between and within procedural systems and financial reports.
2. The semantic interpretation level—the relationships of descriptions and measurements to real-world phenomena.
3. The pragmatic level—the reactions of all individuals affected by accounting reports, including users (individually and in aggregate) and producers of accounting information.

Emphasis is placed on the inductive-deductive and the capital market approaches in the evaluations, although other approaches are discussed where appropriate. In some cases, the several viewpoints resulting from the different approaches are criticized without attempting to suggest a solution or the best alternative. In other cases, the authors have expressed their own views and presented supporting evidence based on a priori logic and empirical findings where available. In all cases, suggested solutions are tentative and subject to change as new evidence becomes available.

The first eight chapters of this edition develop the foundations of accounting theory. They include an introductory chapter, including a section on methodology, two chapters on the development of accounting, a chapter on how generally accepted accounting principles have evolved, a chapter describing the elements of financial reporting, a chapter on capital market theory, another on decision theory, and one on accounting regulation.

The next three chapters examine the income statement. They include two chapters on income measurement and one on revenues and expenses. A chapter on reporting for price changes emphasizes their effect on income determination, but also discusses the problems of asset measurement under conditions of changing prices, including the use of current costs. This is followed by eight chapters on the statement of financial position, each growing more specific than the last. Assets are treated first, then liabilities, and finally equity. The final chapter discusses the disclosure of relevant information to investors, creditors, and other interested readers of financial statements.

A revolution has occurred in accounting in the years in which this book has appeared. Where once inductive-deductive reasoning was dominant, today empirical studies cast in a pragmatic framework are the rule. This edition has sought to reflect this change by expanding its coverage of recent research, while not neglecting the contributions of earlier researchers in accounting. Among the basic changes in this edition are:

1. Greater use of the FASB's Conceptual Framework to unify material throughout the book.
2. The addition of two chapters to cover the early history of accounting and the search for accounting principles, respectively.
3. The addition of a section on ethics to the chapter on decision making.
4. Added stress on the importance of cash flows by integrating it with the capital-maintenance approach to income measurement, allowing the revenue-expense approach to income measurement to be given its own chapter.
5. The combination in one chapter of the recognition and classification of assets and liabilities, permitting one to survey the statement of position as a whole before examining its components.
6. Giving asset measurement its own chapter, allowing the chapter on inventory to be folded into the chapter on current assets.
7. Separating pensions from income taxes, enabling each to be treated at more length.
8. The addition of much new end-of-chapter material, including a number of new cases.

At the close of each chapter is a list of selected readings on specific parts of the chapter. These articles and sections of books have been selected on the basis of their quality, accessibility, readability, and ability to present the several sides of controversial topics. Because of the rapid expansion of the literature relevant to these topics, the selections represent only a sample. Students are encouraged to make use of the many readings available including those that will become available after the publication of this book. There is no substitute for wide reading in the area of accounting theory to obtain an understanding and balanced evaluation of the many different points of view found in the literature.

Also at the end of each chapter is a group of questions classified by topic. Many of these were selected from the theory section of the Uniform CPA Examination. We wish to express our appreciation to the officers of the American Institute of Certified Public Accountants for their kind permission to reprint these questions. Other questions, especially some cases, are used by kind permission of their authors. Those authors are recognized in footnotes to these cases. The remaining questions and cases were prepared by the authors for this edition.

We wish to express our appreciation to the many students and colleagues who have made comments on this and previous editions. We think especially of people like Willard J. Graham and Robert N. Anthony who contributed greatly to earlier editions. For this edition we are grateful to the Accounting Theory class at Southern Methodist University and its teaching assistants Melissa Chandler, David Kennedy, Mark Kohlbeck, and Mitch Mulvehill, who made many helpful comments on the manuscript. We are especially grateful to Professors Noel Addy, Tom Barton, Tom Burns, Michael Dugan, Joe Icerman, Gordon May, Lillian Mills, R. D. Nair, Thomas Sullivan, and Michael Vetsuypens, for commenting in detail on the manuscript. All their comments were most helpful, although for special reasons we may not have incorporated all of the ideas suggested. Whatever faults remain are our responsibility.

We wish to express particular gratitude to Dr. J. Leslie Livingstone for his encouragement over many years. Most of all, we are indebted to our wives, Kathleen and Nancy, for their patience and support.

Our hope is that you, our readers, will enjoy using this book as much as we have enjoyed writing it. We like to think that this book belongs to all of us. We would be delighted to hear from you so that we might continue to edit it in ways that you would find most helpful.

Eldon S. Hendriksen
Michael F. van Breda

Contents in Brief

Contents

Development Costs. Software. Brand Names. Push-Down Accounting. Noncurrent Investments: *Noncurrent Marketable Equity Securities. The Equity Method for Unconsolidated Subsidiaries.*

Chapter 1

Introduction and Methodology of Accounting

CHAPTER OBJECTIVES

After studying this chapter, you will be able to:

Sketch various approaches to the development of accounting theories: tax, legal, ethical, economic, behavioral, and structural.

Explain the different levels of accounting theories: syntactic, semantic, and pragmatic.

Define various classifications of accounting theories: positive versus normative, empirical versus nonempirical, deductive versus inductive.

Outline the means of verifying accounting theories.

CHAPTER OVERVIEW

Approaches to Accounting Theory

Accountants have tried numerous approaches to solve questions like that of revenue recognition. Six approaches are outlined: tax, legal, ethical, economic, behavioral, and structural.

Classifying Accounting Theories

Accounting theory itself may be variously classified: by its level (syntactic, semantic, pragmatic); by its reasoning (deductive, inductive); or by its stance (normative, positive).

Theory Verification

Each approach to defining accounting theory requires a different method of verification.

Conclusion

Each of the approaches described in this chapter has its place in accounting theory and will be used in inquiring into the nature of accounting, providing a framework for evaluating, developing, explaining, and predicting practice.

Alleghany Beverages Corporation (ABC), a Maryland-based soft drink bottling company, found itself in the early 1970s locked in an acrimonious debate with its auditors over its financial reporting. The company had formed a fully owned subsidiary, Valu Vend, to install soft-drink vending machines. The company recorded the sale of these machines as they were delivered to Valu Vend's clients. More precisely, as ABC explained it in a footnote to the 10-K:

> Valu Vend sells its machines under conditional sales contracts. Under these contracts, a purchaser is required to make a $50 down payment and to pay the balance in equal monthly installments over a 48-month period after purchase. Under moratorium plans, the first of such monthly payments may begin 120 days or 210 days after the date of purchase, but all payments are completed within 48 months after purchase.
>
> The machines are sold to distributors and through the distributors to other purchasers, who may have their own locations for the machines. Each distributor appointee is required to warehouse and distribute beverages in his marketing territory and to establish sales and maintenance organizations.

A letter to the shareholders (slightly shortened here) tells the rest of management's side of the story:

> The Company has found it necessary to replace its auditors, Alexander Grant & Company. Our internal accounting staff had been working closely with Alexander Grant throughout the year, and had determined to adopt the accrual method of accounting, which is the method used in our industry. On March 2nd, we were informed by the Baltimore office of Grant that we must defer earnings from our Valu Vend subsidiary. During a long discussion, we were requested to provide supporting information from similar companies. This was done and our accounting method was substantiated.
>
> After much additional research and many meetings, on March 18, the Baltimore Grant office once again was prepared to return to the accrual method of accounting with substantially the same figures we had reported preliminarily. A meeting was held at the Grant main offices in Chicago on March 21st, and we were informed that they would not accept our accrual accounting and proposed a hybrid approach which was unacceptable to us. We had no choice but to recommend to our Board that Grant be terminated.

The issue at stake here is one of the most fundamental in accounting theory: When should revenue be recognized? The question the participants were forced to ask was a simple one, even if the answer was hard to come by. Could one treat the sale of a vending machine the same as one treated the sale of a bottle of pop? Is it appropriate to recognize a sale at the time of delivery when it is a conditional sale? Should the size of the deposit affect one's decision? And what does one do about the fact that the sales are not to the ultimate customer but to an intermediary?

The case raises a number of interesting points regarding accounting theory. First, it points out that theoretical issues are not just matters of "theory." They have very practical implications for both management and the auditors. In this case, the refusal to recognize Valu Vend's revenues at the point of delivery would have meant a 30 percent drop in sales for ABC. This might have prevented them from raising a loan in the marketplace, which would have stymied their expansion plans. From the auditors' point of view, an unjustifiable refusal to provide an unqualified opinion could lead to a breach of contract suit from the company; an agreement to provide an unqualified opinion could lead to a class action suit from irate shareholders, if things turned sour. In every case, the lives and the livings of a variety of people are intimately affected by the outcome of questions such as these. In short, the application of theory can matter.

Second, the case demonstrates that accounting theory is often a matter of professional judgment made by individuals involved with specific cases. It is not only the members of the Financial Accounting Standards Board (FASB) who are obliged to theorize; practicing accountants are often required to exercise their own judgments in theoretical issues. Theoretical issues are seldom completely settled by accounting authorities. Some of their guidelines, it is true, are quite detailed, but many leave a great deal of discretion to management and to the local auditors. Many theoretical issues, therefore, are decided at the local level. As the FASB put it:

> Accounting choices are made at two levels at least. At one level they are made by the Board or other agencies that have the power to require business enterprises to report in some particular way or, if exercised negatively, to prohibit a method that those agencies consider undesirable. . . . Accounting choices are also made at the level of the individual enterprise. As more accounting standards are issued, the scope for individual choice inevitably becomes circumscribed. But there are now and will always be many accounting decisions to be made by reporting enterprises involving a choice between alternatives for which no standard has been promulgated or a choice between ways of implementing a standard.[1]

Revenue recognition is a classic example of a broad rule which requires professional judgment at the local level. As one textbook defined the rule:

> Revenue should be recognized in the earliest period in which (1) the entity has performed substantially what is required in order to earn income and (2) the amount of income can be reliably measured.[2]

In many industries, the first part of this definition is assumed to occur at the time of delivery. In the case of Alleghany Beverages, the vending machines had been delivered. The second requirement was clearly met in management's judgment. Why then the dispute? Apparently, Alexander Grant was uncomfortable with the claim that delivery in this case was substantial performance. Who was right? And who should determine who is right?

Should the FASB or the SEC provide more specific guidelines to avoid cases like this? Arguments go both ways. Some argue strongly, as we shall see later, that managers, left to themselves, will come to resolutions that are perfectly satisfactory to all concerned. Others feel that it is the role of the accounting professional to make judgments like these. Take choice away, they say, and accountants are just clerks. Still others feel that the case makes it patently clear that managers and auditors cannot be left to set rules on their own. Managers will want to manipulate earnings, they say; accountants need the sanction of accounting standards to resist. A laissez-faire approach, they argue, results either in a proliferation of alternatives or in the selection of the weakest of several alternatives.* The jury is still out on who has the best of these arguments.

Arguments aside, the imposition of accounting procedures by an official body seems to be the direction in which most countries are moving, particularly the United States, with the Financial Accounting Standards Board. For example, in the case of real estate accounting, revenue recognition rules have been stated in almost excruciating detail in *SFAS 66*.

APPROACHES TO ACCOUNTING THEORY

Numerous approaches have been taken in an attempt to resolve knotty problems in accounting like the one raised by ABC. The paragraphs which follow outline some of the more common: tax, legal, ethical, economic, behavioral, and structural. Several of these approaches are enlarged on in subsequent chapters. Exhibit 1-1 on page 10 summarizes the points made in this section.

A Tax Approach

The approach favored by many newcomers to accounting is to ask what the Internal Revenue Service (IRS) has to say on the subject. For instance, one might ask whether the IRS would permit ABC to recognize revenue at this point; alternatively, would it prohibit it?

---

* This is said to follow Gresham's Law, named after the 16th century English financier, Sir Thomas Gresham, who suggested that good money tends to drive out bad.

The first and most obvious dilemma with this approach is that it begs the question of how the IRS arrived at its conclusion. When one explores the theoretical origins of tax accounting, one rapidly finds that the objectives of tax accounting are very different from those of financial reporting. The IRS is not so much interested in measuring the income of a company as establishing a base for tax purposes. As a result, the conclusions of tax accounting are irrelevant for our purposes.

This is not to say that the various income tax acts have not had a major impact on accounting practice in many areas. They were important in bringing the average accounting practice up to the standards of the better companies at the time. This created an improvement in general accounting practices and in maintaining consistency. Also, the provision for depreciation included in the 1909 Excise Act and in subsequent acts gave rise to the use of systematic depreciation methods, the search for better depreciation concepts, and the use of more appropriate methods for calculating depreciation costs.

In addition, the requirements in the 1918 Act making inventories mandatory where necessary for the determination of income brought about widespread discussion relating to the appropriate methods of valuation. The acceptance in the early regulations of cost or market, whichever is lower, in the valuation of inventories led to a general adoption of this procedure and to discussions regarding the propriety of the concept. Finally, as the next section shows, court cases regarding tax law have had considerable influence upon the development of accounting concepts.

Regrettably, income tax rules have had adverse effects on accounting theory and principles in many areas. The tendency to accept income tax provisions as accepted accounting principles and practices is unfortunate. The following are examples:

1. Any depreciation method acceptable for tax purposes is acceptable for accounting purposes also, regardless of whether or not it follows good accounting theory in the situation.

2. LIFO must be used for financial reporting purposes if it is used in the tax return.

3. Items that otherwise might be capitalized in financial reports are charged to expense following the treatment in the tax return where the company seeks to obtain the earliest possible tax deduction.

4. Since the tax law does not permit it, no provision is generally made in financial reports for "accruing" repair and maintenance expenses except indirectly and haphazardly through accelerated depreciation.

In summary, the effect on accounting of taxation of business incomes in the United States and in other countries has been considerable, but it has been primarily indirect in nature. The tax laws themselves have not pioneered in accounting thought. While the revenue acts did hasten the adoption of good accounting practices and thus brought about a more critical analysis of accepted accounting procedures and concepts, they have also been a deterrent to experimentation and the acceptance of good theory.

CHECKPOINTS
---

1. List three positive influences tax accounting has had on financial reporting.
2. Give one example of where tax accounting and financial reporting differ, and one where they are the same.
3. What negative influences has tax accounting had on financial reporting?

A Legal Approach

A second common approach of newcomers to accounting to analyzing situations such as that in the ABC case is to suggest getting a legal opinion. Surely, some say, a sale should be recognized when legal title passes. Unfortunately, this does not solve the problem as easily as one might hope since generally title passes when the court litigating a particular case decides that it has. A case in point is the litigation in which Pennzoil claimed that Texaco had snatched Getty Oil away from them after a legal sale between Getty and Pennzoil had been concluded. Texaco responded that a handshake did not constitute a legal sale or, in other words, a passage of legal title. Most observers of the case seemed to agree with Texaco. The Texas courts, however, continued to find for Pennzoil. Eventually, Texaco settled out of court for $3 billion. Had there been a sale? Arguments still rage on both sides in this case.

Much case law involves the nature of income. Consider, for instance, the case of Eisner v. Macomber heard in the U.S. Supreme Court in 1920. The issue was whether a stock dividend was income or not. Charles Evans Hughes, appearing for the defendant, declared that:

> It is of the essence of income that it should be realized. Potentiality is not enough. . . . Income necessarily implies separation and realization. The increase of the forests is not income until it is cut. The increase in the value of lands due to the growth and prosperity of the community is not income until it is realized. Where investments are concerned, there is no income until there has been a separate, realized gain. . . .[3]

Since there was no cash, he argued, there was no income. The argument was accepted by a majority of the Court.*

Another intriguing case was James v. United States. This involved a man who embezzled $738,000 from his employer over the years 1951

---

* Justice Brandeis, in his dissent, pointed out that, if stock dividends were to go tax free, management would issue all dividends in stock, leaving stockholders to cash them in.

through 1954. The IRS took him to court because he failed to pay income tax on his ill-gotten gains.[4] Justice Whittaker took James's side, arguing that he had no income, since an embezzler acquires "not a semblance of right, title, or interest in his plunder." What he took, said the judge, was more in the nature of a loan! Following this logic, does this mean that a company involved in drug smuggling earns no income because it obtains no legal right to the monies it acquires? Should it, therefore, be exempt from income tax?*

The FASB, in establishing a Conceptual Framework for accounting, investigated the use of law to establish accounting principles. They noted that in many situations there are economic as well as legal issues. "Lawyers and judges look at property and related concepts in much the same way that accountants and businessmen look at assets and have many of the same difficulties with definition."[5] That they do not always arrive at the same conclusion often reflects the fact that lawyers are usually interested in income available for tax or income available for dividends and not income in the sense of an increment in value or a measure of operational efficiency.[6] In summary then, while law certainly provides numerous examples that can stimulate thinking on questions of accounting theory, it is seldom the deciding factor.†

CHECKPOINTS

1. Define the term *legal title*. When does legal title pass when you purchase a car? When is a sale typically taken?
2. Define the term *realization*. Why might attorneys have placed so much emphasis on realization as a measure of profit?

An Ethical Approach

A third approach asks whether there is an ethical solution to the ABC dilemma? Is there something management *ought* to be doing? Is this something more than just following a set of generally accepted accounting procedures? In asking these questions in a separate section, there is no implication that other approaches have no ethical content, nor does it imply that ethical theories necessarily ignore all other concepts. Fundamental ethical questions are at the heart of all modern theory building.[7]

---

* The question is actually moot since the government has the right to impose taxes on anything it chooses.

† Organizations governed by regulatory accounting are exceptions to this general rule.

The ethical approach to accounting theory places emphasis on the concepts of justice, truth, and fairness. Interestingly, every one of these concepts has found its way into the Conceptual Framework created by the FASB. Considerations such as the absence of bias and representational faithfulness are both considered necessary characteristics of a reliable accounting system. Neutrality, meaning that information should not be colored so as to influence behavior in a particular direction, is an essential feature of standard setting. Ethical considerations, in other words, have a pervasive influence on all of accounting.

In this particular case, one might begin by asking whether management was being fair to the shareholders by recording these transactions at this point. Or, one might ask the reverse question: Would management have been fair not to recognize revenue at this point? One might also ask whether the management of ABC was being truthful, although truth in accounting is difficult to define and apply.

Many seem to use the term *truth* to mean "in accordance with the facts," which is equivalent to the concept of "representational faithfulness," defined in Chapter 5. However, not all who refer to truth in accounting have in mind the same definition of facts. Some refer to accounting facts as data that are objective and verifiable. Thus, historical costs represent accounting facts to them. For others, the term *truth* is used to refer to the valuation of assets and expenses in current economic terms. For example, one practitioner claimed that financial statements display the truth only when they disclose the *current* value of assets and the profits and losses accruing from changes in values, although the increases in values should be designated as realized or unrealized.[8]

Many associate the term *truth* with propositions or statements that they believe to be established principles. For example, many consider the recognition of a gain at the time of the sale of an asset to be a reporting of "true" conditions. These same people feel that reporting an appraisal increase in the value of an asset, prior to sale as ordinary income, lacks truthfulness. Thus, the established rule regarding revenue recognition is used as a guide to determine the truth—not the other way around. This makes the truthfulness of the financial reports depend on the fundamental validity of the accepted rules and principles on which the statements are based. This is an inadequate foundation for measuring truthfulness.

CHECKPOINTS

---

1. What does the term *fair* mean in an auditor's report? Does this correspond with the term *fair* in ordinary discourse?
2. What do you mean by the word truthful in ordinary discourse? Does this correspond with the way you think about truth in accounting?

Economic Approaches

In hopes of settling issues like those raised by ABC, accountants have long attempted to interpret accounting concepts in terms of economic concepts. In recent years, there has been a veritable explosion of research exploring the correspondence between economic interpretations and accounting data. The following sections lay out three different avenues in taking an economic approach to accounting: the macroeconomic, the microeconomic, and the corporate social.

Macroeconomics. A macroeconomic approach attempts to explain the effect of alternative reporting procedures on economic measurements and economic activities at a level broader than the firm, such as an industry or the national economy. What effect, if any, would there be on the economy if every company recognized revenue at the point that ABC's management would like to?

Some want to go further than explanations and argue that one of the objectives of accounting should be to direct the behavior of firms and individuals toward the implementation of specific national economic policies. For example, some argue that national economic objectives require accounting reports that will permit and even encourage higher dividends and larger capital expenditures during slack economic periods and discourage investments during periods of inflation.

While most countries implement macroeconomic policies through monetary and fiscal policies and direct controls, some countries, notably Sweden, do attempt to base accounting concepts and practices on macroeconomic goals.[9] One of the effects of this approach is that the objective of reporting stable earnings from year to year legitimizes the use of reserves and flexible depreciation policies. How this would help ABC's management is unclear.

Microeconomics. A microeconomic approach to accounting theory attempts to explain the effect of alternative reporting procedures on economic measurements and economic activities at the level of the firm. Modern accounting theory, which is founded in microeconomics, therefore focuses on the enterprise as an economic entity with its main activities affecting the economy through its operations in markets. This is the view adopted by the FASB in its Conceptual Framework. This approach takes as its fundamental premise that financial information has inevitable *economic consequences*. The exact form these consequences take is not always easy to determine and is subject to some dispute.[10]

More is said on this approach in Chapters 6 through 8. Suffice it to say for now that accounting theorists in this area tend to argue that, as long as the full facts *are* disclosed, it matters little *how* they are disclosed. They would probably feel that the recognition issues in the ABC case were irrelevant to the marketplace, because there had been full disclosure of the facts. Any remaining interest in the issue would revolve around why management was interested in a higher rather than a lower income number. What, they would wonder, was management's real motivation?

Corporate Social Accounting.   The microeconomic view of accounting does not necessarily encompass all the effects companies have on society. The costs of environmental pollution, unemployment, unhealthful working conditions, and other social problems are not normally reported by a firm, except to the extent that their costs are borne directly by the firm through taxation and regulation. Corporate social accounting seeks to address these issues.

One prominent example of an attempt to include both social accounting and macroeconomic objectives within a theory of corporate reporting is provided in the *Corporate Report,* a discussion paper published by the Institute of Chartered Accountants in England and Wales.[11] One of the report's proposals is the publication of a value-added statement which allocates revenues, net of the cost of materials, to employees, creditors, and shareholders.[12] These groups are often referred to collectively as the *stakeholders* of the company. Proponents of stakeholder analysis argue, with some justification, that orthodox accounting with its emphasis on shareholders, is really a subset of social accounting with its emphasis on the broader group of stakeholders.

Recognition of the wider role that corporations play is also found in the enterprise theory of equity discussed in Chapter 19. In addition, the FASB formally recognized in their Conceptual Framework that there are many parties other than present owners interested in financial informa-

---

EXHIBIT 1-1   Questions to Ask

Tax	What is the tax situation?
Legal	What is required by law? Are there any specific regulations covering this industry?
Ethical	What is the right thing to do? Is this fair presentation?
Economic	What effect will this accounting procedure have on the economy? What effect will this choice of accounting procedure have on shareholders? Is there full disclosure of the facts behind the procedure? What effect will this have on other stakeholders?
Behavioral	Why does management want to make this choice?
Structural	Is there a specific rule covering this situation? What is the definition of revenue? What is GAAP? What are others doing in the industry?

---

tion. They include creditors, consumers, labor unions, trade unions, teachers, and, yes, students. Modern accounting theory too, as will be discussed in Chapter 8, recognizes that information itself is a public good with many of the same qualities as externalities, such as pollution. Financial statements and unwanted noise, for example, are both free goods to the recipients. A market for each is difficult, if not impossible, to establish.

Much work, though, remains to be done in developing a complete theory of social accounting. Interest has been relatively low in the past, perhaps because organized labor, although a major stakeholder in companies, has not played a large role in the United States in the establishment of accounting policy. This situation might change in the future if America moves more in line with European experience.[13] Additionally, as theorists come to terms with the public-good nature of financial information, they may well develop techniques to deal with other public goods that form the basis for the concerns of social accounting.

Note that here, as elsewhere, ethics play an important role. The entity approach favored by the FASB assumes not only that firms *do,* but also that they *should,* maximize their profits. The reason for the latter is the economic theorem that, in a market economy, this leads to an ethically desirable outcome known as *Pareto Optimality.** Social accountants respond with the claim that public goods invalidate this result, requiring a broader ethical approach to be taken. The point at this stage is not to take sides but to make the reader aware that ethical issues confront the accounting theorist at every point.

CHECKPOINTS

1. Contrast macroeconomics with microeconomics.
2. Why is it not unreasonable to describe traditional accounting as a subset of social accounting?
3. Define the term *stakeholder* and contrast it with the term *shareholder*.

A Behavioral Approach

An alternative to the economic approach is to rely on the insights of psychology and sociology in the development of accounting theories. The focus in this approach is on the relevance of information being communicated to decision makers and the behavior of different individuals or

---

* This is described in Chapter 4.

groups as a result of the presentation of accounting information. In the case of ABC, the question might concern what impact the early recognition of profit, together with the disclosure of the controversy, might have on decisions being made by shareholders.

The most important users of accounting reports presented to those outside the firm are generally considered to include stockholders, other investors, creditors, and government authorities; however, behavioral theories can also take into consideration the effects of external reports on the decisions of management and the feedback effect of the actions of accountants and auditors. Thus, behavioral theories attempt to measure and evaluate the economic, psychological, and sociological effects of alternative accounting procedures and reporting media.

The behavioral approach to accounting theory has stimulated a search among both academic and practicing accountants for basic objectives of accounting and for answers to questions such as: Who are the users of published financial statements? What is the nature of the specific information wanted by the several user groups? Can common needs be found for the presentation of general-purpose statements or should specific needs be met?* How do investors, creditors, and managers react to different accounting procedures and presentations?

CHECKPOINTS

---

1. Define the behavioral approach to accounting theory. Contrast it with the microeconomic approach.
2. List questions asked by accounting behavioralists.

A Structural Approach

The classical approach in accounting to solve problems like those raised by ABC might be called "structural" because it focuses on the structure of the accounting system itself. Most reasoning in this approach, particularly at the local level, is by analogy. It attempts to treat like with like. The judgment as to the most appropriate point at which to recognize a particular event is typically based on the moments chosen to record other events. In other words, accountants attempt to classify similar transactions similarly or, more formally, to seek *consistency* in recording and reporting transactions. It is only when they encounter a transaction which

---

* Technically, no information is needed to make a decision, but information might be wanted because of uncertainties. The term *needs* is used here because of common usage.

does not fit into a previous mold that they are forced back to more basic principles.

The whole process is reminiscent of the first week in Principles of Accounting. Most readers will be able to recall the anxious search, in those early days of learning accounting, for what names to put on journal entries. How should one classify a purchase of pencils? Should it be treated the same way as the purchase of widgets? What should go into supplies and what into inventory?

It is clear from the ABC case that both auditors and management took a structural approach. Consistency was the first line of argument for the company and its critics. They had used delivery as the point at which they recognized sales in all their previous dealings. They planned to continue to use it in the belief that the new sales were similar to the old. The arguments from the auditors seem to have been that the transactions were different enough that a parallel could not be drawn. The principle of consistency was not disputed, simply the specific application.

This process of classifying like data with like and then summarizing them "in specific groupings (accounts and ledgers) and further summarizing the groupings into reports and statements" has been called "compacting."[14] Illinois professor A. C. Littleton described this process as similar to that of statisticians.[15] Both accountants and statisticians aggregate numbers to arrive at totals or averages. Both must be concerned with classifying things correctly. It is senseless to average temperatures over a year when one is trying to establish the average summer temperature. Similarly, accountants should classify economic events correctly to arrive at meaningful financial statements.

In 1941, the Committee on Terminology of the American Institute of Accountants (AIA), the forerunner of the American Institute of Certified Public Accountants (AICPA), captured this compacting process in a widely quoted definition:

> Accounting is the art of recording, classifying, and summarizing in a significant manner and in terms of money, transactions, and events, which are in part, at least, of a financial character, and interpreting the results thereof.[16]

Broader definitions of accounting are in vogue today, but the process of "recording, classifying, and summarizing" is still the heart of accounting.

CHECKPOINTS

1. The AIA defined accounting as an art. How do you distinguish art from science? Why do you think they did not speak of the science of accounting?
2. Think back on the accounting you learned before entering this class. How much of it was based on a structural approach to accounting?

How much of it was based on economic theory? How much on the behavior of users? Provide an example of each approach from your own experience.

CLASSIFYING ACCOUNTING THEORIES

Regardless of the approach one takes to solving accounting problems, one is always left with the question: How can one tell whether one's solution is correct? That leads to a second question: What does one mean by a correct solution in this context? Answers to these questions depend not only on the approach one has taken, but also on the form one's reasoning has taken. Three ways of classifying the way people reason are discussed in the sections that follow. They are followed by a discussion of how one might determine correctness given the pattern of reasoning. More formally, we discuss how theories might be classified and then verified.* Exhibit 1-2 on page 19 summarizes the classification of accounting theories.

Theory as Language

A first classification relies on the notion that accounting is a language. Many call it the language of business. Theorists suggest that there are three questions that should be asked about a language and the words and phrases that make up that language:

1. What *effect* will the words have on listeners?
2. What *meaning*, if any, do the words have?
3. Do the words make *logical* sense?

Answers to each of these questions form part of the study of a language. *Pragmatics* is the study of the effect of language; *semantics* is the study of the meaning of language; and *syntactics* is the study of the logic or grammar of the language. Both the behavioral and the economic approaches alluded to above are primarily pragmatic in style, while the structural approach is primarily syntactic. Although it is fair to say that almost all current research into accounting is pragmatic in its orientation, semantics and syntactics are also important in accounting theory. Semantics is important because ideally financial information has economic or physical content that is agreed to by both the producers and the users of the

---

* This section draws heavily on the ''Report of the Committee on Accounting Theory Construction and Verification,'' *The Accounting Review* (Supplement 1971), pp. 37–45.

information. Syntactics is important in accounting because ideally one piece of financial information relates logically to another.

Accounting numbers and classifications vary with respect to the degree of interpretation that can be inferred by the reader of accounting reports. For example, the item *cash* in the statement of financial condition is fairly well understood to mean what accountants intend it to mean. On the other hand, the classification *deferred charges* has no specific interpretation apart from the structural processes that gave rise to it. The role of theories that emphasize semantics is to find ways to improve the interpretation of accounting information in terms of human observations and experience. The FASB, in particular, is working steadily to rid the balance sheet of items lacking in semantic content.

Despite the efforts of the FASB, and hard as it is for newcomers (and the general public) to accept, many accounting concepts still have no semantic content. Consider again the ABC case and the question of when they should recognize revenue. Realize that no flashing light goes off in the real world telling accountants that the great moment of recognition has arrived. A signature on a contract is a real event, the delivery of a vending machine is a real event, the payment for the machine is a real event, but the moment of a ''sale'' is simply the moment at which a bookkeeper decides to record the transaction, no more and no less. Recognition of sales, expenses, assets, and liabilities are all syntactic in origin. There is no semantic counterpart to which one can point.

CHECKPOINTS

1. Define the terms *syntactic*, *semantic*, and *pragmatic* as they apply to theory.
2. Consider one element in a balance sheet, such as inventory or accounts payable, and define it syntactically, semantically, and pragmatically.
3. Assets are sometimes said to be possessions of the company. What level of definition is this?

Theory as Reasoning

The second means of classifying the form of the theoretical debate is to ask whether the arguments flow from generalizations to specifics (deductive reasoning) or whether they flow from specifics to generalizations (inductive reasoning). In accounting, the generalizations are often termed *postulates*. From these, accountants hope to deduce *accounting principles* that will provide a basis for concrete or practical *applications*. With the deductive method, practical applications and rules are deduced from the postulates and not from observing practice. With the inductive method, principles are induced from best current practice.

Deductive Reasoning.   Objectives are an important part of the deductive process, because different objectives can require entirely different structures and result in different principles. For instance, the basic objectives of tax accounting are different from those of financial accounting. This is one of the main reasons why rules for determining taxable income are different in many respects from the generally accepted practice for the determination of financial income. Sometimes, though, despite differences in objectives, cost-benefit considerations demand a compromise. For instance, it is likely that individual users have different objectives in mind when using accounting data. It does not seem feasible, though, to set up an entirely different set of principles for every user! Instead, as a compromise, a general-purpose statement is produced.

A more precise method of formulating the logic in deductive reasoning is found in the *axiomatic* or mathematical approach to accounting theory. In this method, mathematical symbols are given to certain ideas and concepts. The framework is provided in the form of mathematical models utilizing matrix algebra or symbolic logic. Constraints can be applied in the form of mathematical expressions. Therefore, starting with basic postulates and rules of logical inference, theorems can be formulated and tested through mathematical operations. Thus, the axiomatic method can provide a very rigorous application of the deductive method.

One of the main disadvantages of the deductive method is that, if any of the postulates and premises are false, the conclusions may also be false. Also, it is thought to be too far removed from reality to be able to derive realistic and workable principles or to provide the basis for practical rules. But these criticisms generally stem from a misunderstanding of the purpose and meaning of theory. It is not necessary for theory to be entirely practical for it to be useful in establishing workable procedures. The main purpose of theory is to provide a framework for the development of new ideas and new procedures and to help in making choices among alternative procedures. If these objectives are met, it is not necessary that theory be based completely on practical concepts or that it be restricted to the development of procedures that are completely workable and practical in terms of current technology. In fact, many of the currently accepted principles and procedures are general guides to action rather than specific rules that can be followed precisely in every applicable case.

Inductive Reasoning.   The process of induction consists of drawing generalized conclusions from specifics. A typical inductive argument begins with a set of particular examples, claims that these examples are representative of some greater whole, and infers some generalization about that whole. Usually, but not always, the specifics are based upon practical experiences such as the outcomes of experiments. Sciences that rely on experience are termed *empirical*. Experimental sciences are empirical by definition. Mathematics is inherently nonempirical. Accounting theory that collects financial data to induce its conclusions can be considered empirical. The structural approach, on the other hand, is typically nonempirical.

Just because the observers look only at raw data does not mean that they do not need some initial postulates and concepts. By merely choosing what to observe they are reflecting preconceived notions of what might be relevant. By restricting themselves to the financial data of a firm, for example, they are drawing on certain postulates regarding the environment of accounting. Furthermore, if they restrict themselves to observing only financial transactions, they may only confirm existing practice. Induction and deduction, therefore, are really complementary. Almost all theories will include some elements of both deductive and inductive reasoning.

The advantage of the inductive approach is that it is not necessarily constrained by a preconceived model or structure. Researchers are free to make any observations they may deem relevant. The main disadvantage of the inductive process is that observers are likely to be influenced by subconscious ideas of what the relevant relationships are and what data should be observed. Another disadvantage of the inductive approach is that, in accounting, the raw data are likely to be different for each firm. Relationships may also be different, making it difficult to draw generalizations.

CHECKPOINTS

1. Contrast the terms *deductive* and *inductive*.
2. Contrast the terms *empirical* and *nonempirical* as they apply to accounting theory.
3. Why is it that accounting theory remains so controversial?

Theory as Script

Both inductive and deductive theories may be descriptive (*positive*) or prescriptive (*normative*.) Descriptive theories attempt to set forth and explain what and how financial information is presented and communicated to users of accounting data. Normative theories attempt to prescribe what data ought to be communicated and how they ought to be presented; that is, they attempt to explain what *should* be rather than what *is*. Inductive theories, by their nature, are usually positive; but it does not follow that deductive theories are necessarily normative. One can begin with generalizations about how the world is perceived to be and draw from that specific deductions that are intended to be wholly descriptive.

The question in the case of Alleghany Beverages of which revenue recognition method to use is a prescriptive or normative one for the participants because they are seeking an answer to what they should do. We could ask a more descriptive or positive question: Why did management want to accrue earnings? One answer might be that management was simply trying to do the theoretically correct thing (whatever that might be); another, more cynical answer perhaps, might be that management was trying to puff up earnings to impress shareholders and creditors. Whether they were or not is an empirical question.

Accounting theorists are interested in answers to both kinds of questions: the normative one that attempts to discover the best way of accounting for a transaction, and the positive one that attempts to discover how management and others decide which is the best way for them. The answers to these sorts of questions, together with the attempt to find these answers, constitute the subject of accounting theory.

CHECKPOINTS

1. Define the *structural* approach. Why is it so closely associated with a positive approach to accounting theory?
2. Why are positive theories sometimes criticized?
3. Explain why a positive approach to theory is associated with inductive reasoning.

THEORY VERIFICATION

Verification may be defined as establishing the acceptability, or the truth, of a theory. All theories should be logically sound, but beyond that the nature of verification will depend on the nature of the theory being verified. Normative theories are judged one way; positive theories another.

Normative theories, including the theory of verification itself, are judged by the reasonableness of their assumptions. Ideally, the assumptions on which a normative theory is based, and the grounds on which they might be judged acceptable, are stated clearly in the theory. Others may then reject the normative conclusions by refusing to accept the assumptions, but the basis of disagreement is then well defined.

Descriptive theories are evaluated in two different ways depending on whether they have empirical content or not. Syntactic theories are de-

EXHIBIT 1-2   Classifying Theories

Theory
Descriptive or Prescriptive
(positive vs. normative)

Reasoning	*Language*
1. Deduction (Is it logically sound?)	1. Syntactics (What are the rules?)
2. Induction (What evidence is there?)	2. Semantics (What does it mean?)
	3. Pragmatics (What effect will it have?)

scriptive theories which have no empirical content. They are confirmed by logic alone. For instance, the equation $2(y + 3) = 2y + 6$ is true because of the agreed-upon rules of mathematics. Similarly, gross margin will be $500 if revenue is $800 and cost of goods sold is $300, not because of any empirical observations, but because of the agreed-upon rules of accounting. Many accounting propositions fall into this category and are true for syntactical reasons only. Consider, by way of a further example, the question of whether a particular item, such as a dry hole, is an asset or not. One might argue as follows:

All assets have value to a company.
A dry oil well has no value to a company.
Therefore, the dry well cannot be an asset.

This is a perfectly valid conclusion but we do need to be aware that the validity of our reasoning is completely independent of the meaning of the word *asset*. We can substitute nonsense words without affecting the truth of the conclusion. For instance, we could have simply said that if all bzrs have eechs, then x cannot be a bzr if it does not have an eech! Much reasoning in accounting, particularly in the structural approach, is syntactical in nature. It may be logically true but it lacks empirical content.

Semantic theories, on the other hand, are descriptive theories that do have empirical content. Since they are intended to say something about the real world, their truth depends upon observation. For instance, that there is $56.23 in petty cash can be verified only by examination. Verification of semantic theories can be obtained from research studies which determine whether users of accounting information understand the information producers' intended meaning, within the context of relevant theory.

Pragmatic theories are also descriptive theories with empirical content. Pragmatic theories emphasize the usefulness of accounting to investors and others. Their verification depends not so much on their truth as on their value to users. In other words, one does not verify a pragmatic accounting theory as such, but rather its use. This, as will become apparent in the chapters that follow, has been the path taken by modern accounting theorists.

Tests of descriptive theories are often cast in the form of predictions. For instance, the theory of gravity enables scientists to predict how falling bodies will behave and tests can be done to verify that they do indeed behave as predicted. The result, if the test is repeated sufficiently to satisfy observers, is said to be confirmation of the theory. On the other hand, if the theory fails to predict, or if anomalies are discovered, it is said to lack confirmation—or even be refuted.[17]

Several authors have taken issue with this description of the scientific process. Thomas Kuhn, for instance, suggests that science proceeds by establishing what he terms *paradigms,* which may be defined as frameworks for generating research questions. Scientists do not so much confirm or refute theories as find them more or less useful in provoking thoughtful questions about the nature of our world. They are discarded when they are no longer useful in generating questions.[18]

Others have rejected an approach to verification based purely on predictions on grounds that predictions, in the social sciences particularly, are frequently unreliable because of their behavioral implications. For instance, the prediction of an economic depression may cause the government to take actions that may actually create or deepen the depression (such as hoarding or panic selling of securities). A theory that could lead to the prediction of business failure could actually bring about such a failure if people believed the prediction. By denying funds to a firm having difficulties, investors and creditors could cause the firm to go into bankruptcy. Accountants are not unaware of this possibility with traditional accounting procedures, and more accurate predictions could even multiply these concerns. Therefore, the ability to predict cannot be the only consideration in the development of theories in accounting.

The use of predictions as the main criterion for the evaluation of accounting theory is also complicated by the fact that accounting theories are typically a blend of various forms of theorizing. Their confirmation, therefore, takes place at several levels:

1. Assumptions regarding the real world must be tested for correspondence between the statement and observable phenomena.
2. The interrelationship of the statements in the theory must be tested for logical consistency.
3. If any of the premises are based on value judgments, they should be accepted or rejected based on their correspondence to one's own value judgments.

4. If there is inconclusive empirical verification, the conclusions of the theory or the hypothesis must be subjected to independent empirical verification.

CHECKPOINTS

---

1. How might one verify accounting theory?
2. Why is verification so important to accounting theory?

CONCLUSION

Accounting theory, as described in this book, focuses on the set of principles which underlie and, presumably, are supportive of accounting practice: those generally accepted accounting principles (GAAP) to which auditors attest whenever they sign an opinion. It must be said at once, though, that accounting principles are only one force shaping accounting practice. Politics, economics, and law are among many powerful forces which contend with purely theoretical considerations to shape practice. Accounting theory, in addition to developing principles, also seeks to understand these forces.

Restating all this more formally, and drawing on the definition of theory as found in Webster's dictionary, accounting theory may be defined as a coherent set of hypothetical, conceptual, and pragmatic principles forming a general frame of reference for inquiring into the nature of accounting.[19] The definition is deliberately broad so as to encompass both the more traditional view of theory as a general frame of reference for the evaluation and development of sound accounting practices, and the more modern view of theory as a general frame of reference by which accounting practice can be explained and predicted.

An immediate caveat to this definition is that, while a single general theory of accounting may be desirable, accounting as a science is still in too primitive a stage for such a development. The best that can be accomplished in this developmental stage is a set of theories (models) and sub-theories that may be complementary or competing. But even this can be valuable. As Italian historian, Guglielmo Ferrero, once said,

> theory, which gives facts their value and significance, is often very useful, even if it is partially false, because it throws light on phenomena which no one has observed, it forces examination, from many angles, of facts which no one has hitherto studied, and it produces the impulse for more extensive and more productive researches. . . .[20]

The truth of this will become apparent as one examines the many different approaches to theory that have been developed.

Simple questions, like when does one recognize a sale, form the core of accounting theory. From the very start of their studies in the discipline, accounting students have been grappling with questions like this—in other words with theoretical issues. As a result, most accounting students, unwittingly perhaps, bring a great deal of theoretical knowledge to a theory class. Accounting theory does not so much add new knowledge as systematize knowledge the reader already has.

CHECKPOINTS

1. What is accounting theory? What are its objectives?
2. Is it important to have a definition of accounting theory? Why?

SUMMARY

Accounting theory has been defined as a coherent set of logical principles that:

1. Provides a better understanding of existing practices to practitioners, investors, managers, and students.
2. Provides a conceptual framework for evaluating existing accounting practices.
3. Guides the development of new practices and procedures.

Numerous approaches to developing such a theory have been outlined in this chapter: tax, law, ethical, economic, behavioral, and structural. Each of the several approaches to accounting theory has some merit in helping to establish and evaluate accounting principles and procedures. Economic and behavioral approaches help set the stage for explaining the environment within which accounting operates and for selecting what data should be reported. The ethical approach provides fundamental objectives in establishing accounting standards. The social accounting and macroeconomic approaches add to the controversies of theory development and application, and so on.

Three levels of theory—syntactic, semantic, and pragmatic—were seen to exist and three ways of classifying theories were discussed: empirical versus nonempirical, inductive versus deductive, and normative versus positive. No approach to accounting theory relies completely on a single method. This book favors an eclectic approach making use of those approaches and those levels as are most appropriate at the time. The aim of this book is to provide readers with a coherent set of logical principles for the evaluation and development of sound accounting practices in their professional lives.

The following chapter presents the historical development of accounting theories in the belief that a historical perspective provides a better understanding of the several theories currently in circulation and why accounting is what it is today. One of the first steps to understanding the traditional, structural approach to accounting is an examination of the objectives, fundamentals, concepts, and elements on which it is based. These are found in Chapter 5, along with a discussion of the FASB's Conceptual Framework. Chapter 6 presents a discussion of capital markets theories and their relationship to accounting information, while Chapter 7 presents a discussion of research related to the individual decision processes. Research findings are presented and discussed in later chapters relating to the specific topics.

PROBLEMS AND CASES

LIFO and the GNP

The widespread shift from FIFO to LIFO for inventory valuation purposes in 1974 had the effect of reducing the measured gross national product. Although the effect of inflation on inventory profits is removed by an inventory valuation adjustment, the adjustment did not allow for this shift. Some economists were concerned that this artificial reduction of reported GNP would have the effect of reducing consumer demand if it led consumers to anticipate a more severe recession than they otherwise might expect.

Required:

Should the APB at the time have outlawed the use of LIFO for macroeconomic reasons? Discuss.

Alleghany Beverages Corporation

The brief facts presented about Alleghany Beverages in the text provide endless food for thought. You are asked to present a number of possible solutions to the case, each emanating from the various approaches to theory discussed in this chapter. Specifically, you might consider the following issues among others.

   1. How might you arrive at a deductive solution to their situation? How would this differ from an inductive solution? Was the company's argument that accrual accounting was industry practice inductive or deductive? What other evidence might you gather? Is inductive reasoning always based on observations?

   2. Are there ethical considerations in this case? Would one method have been fairer than the other? Given that everything we know about the transaction was disclosed in the company's financial reports and proxy statements, had the company not fulfilled all its ethical obligations?

3. Efficient-market theories suggest that full disclosure, even if it is narrative, should be sufficient. Apparently, the auditors disagreed. What is your position?

4. Outline a syntactic, semantic, and pragmatic avenue to a solution. What would you need to do or to know for each?

Six Flags Over Texas

On June 30, 1969, Great Southwest Corporation (GSC) sold an amusement park in Dallas called Six Flags Over Texas to a group of private investors. The footnote describing this transaction read as follows:

> On June 30, 1969, Great Southwest Corporation sold all of the property and equipment of Six Flags Over Texas, an amusement park, for $40,000,000, resulting in a gain of $17,530,170. Upon completion of the sale, the purchaser, Six Flags Over Texas Fund Ltd., contributed the amusement park to a limited partnership in which Six Flags Over Texas, Inc., a wholly owned subsidiary of Great Southwest Corporation, is the General Partner and operator. As partial consideration for the sale, the Company received a 6½ percent mortgage note in the amount of $38,031,585 which is secured by the amusement park. The note is payable in annual principle installments of $1,094,331 beginning in March 1971 and is subject to optional prepayments without penalty.

Required:

Should this be recognized as a sale? If so, in what amount? Provide reasons for your answer.

Elmo Company (November 1973)

Part a. Elmo Company operates several plants at which limestone is processed into quicklime and hydrated lime. The Bland plant, where most of the equipment was installed many years ago, continually deposits a dusty white substance over the surrounding countryside. Citing the unsanitary condition of the neighboring community of Adeltown, the pollution of the Adel River, and the high incidence of lung disease among workers at Bland, the state's Pollution Control Agency has ordered the installation of air pollution control equipment. Also, the Agency has assessed a substantial penalty, which will be used to clean up Adeltown. After considering the costs involved (which could not have been reasonably estimated before the Agency's action), Elmo decides to comply with the Agency's orders, the alternative being to cease operations at Bland at the end of the current fiscal year. The officers of Elmo agree that the air pollution control equipment should be capitalized and depreciated over its useful life, but they disagree over the period(s) to which the penalty should be charged.

Required:

Discuss the conceptual merits and reporting requirements of accounting for the penalty as a:

1. Charge to the current period.
2. Correction of prior periods.
3. Capitalizable item to be amortized over future periods.

Part b. Elmo's Davis Plant causes approximately as much pollution as Bland. Davis, however, is located in another state, where there is little likelihood of governmental regulation, and Elmo has no plans for pollution control at this plant. One of Elmo's officers, Mr. Pearce, says that uncontrolled pollution at Davis constitutes a very real cost to society, which is not recorded anywhere under current practice. He suggests that this "social cost" of the Davis Plant be included annually in Elmo's income statement. Further, he suggests that measurement of this cost is easily obtained by reference to the depreciation on Bland's pollution control equipment.

Required:

1. Is Mr. Pearce necessarily correct in stating that costs associated with Davis's pollution are entirely unrecorded? Explain.
2. Evaluate Mr. Pearce's proposed method of measuring the annual "social cost" of Davis's pollution.
3. Discuss the merit of Mr. Pearce's suggestion that a "social cost" be recognized by a business enterprise.

PRIMARY SOURCES

Those interested in learning more about the topics covered in this chapter might begin by consulting the following sources. Each has numerous excellent citations.

Belkaoui, Ahmed. *Accounting Theory,* 2nd ed. San Diego: Harcourt, Brace Jovanovich, 1985.

Kam, Vernon. *Accounting Theory.* New York: John Wiley & Sons, 1986.

Most, Kenneth S. *Accounting Theory,* 2nd ed. Columbus: Grid Publishing, Inc., 1982.

Wolk, Harry I.; Jere R. Francis; and Michael G. Tearney. *Accounting Theory,* 2nd ed. Boston: Kent Publishing Co., 1989.

SELECTED ADDITIONAL READINGS

In addition to the works cited in the primary sources and the endnotes to this chapter, the reader is referred to the following authors:

General Methodology

American Accounting Association. "Report of the Committee on Foundations of Accounting Measurement." *The Accounting Review,* Supplement, 1971, pp. 37–45.

American Accounting Association. "Report of the Committee on Accounting Theory Construction and Verification." *The Accounting Review,* Supplement, 1971, pp. 53–63.

American Accounting Association. Committee on Concepts and Standards for External Financial Reports, *Statement on Accounting Theory and Theory Acceptance* (1977).

Beams, Floyd A. "Indications of Pragmatism and Empiricism in Accounting Thought." *The Accounting Review,* April 1969, pp. 382–88.

Caplan, Edward. "Accounting Research as an Information Source for Theory Construction." *The Accounting Review,* Supplement, 1972, pp. 437–44.

Devine, Carl Thomas. *Essays in Accounting Theory,* vol. 3 (Privately published, 1971), pp. 1–80.

Hakansson, Nils. "Normative Accounting Theory and the Theory of Decision." *International Journal of Accounting,* Spring 1969, pp. 33–48.

Kam, Vernon. "Judgment and the Scientific Trend in Accounting." *Journal of Accountancy,* February 1973, pp. 52–57.

Kuhn, T.S. *The Structure of Scientific Revolutions,* 2nd ed. University of Chicago Press, 1970.

Larson, Kermit. "Implications of Measurement Theory on Accounting Concept Formulation." *The Accounting Review,* January 1969, pp. 38–47.

McDonald, Daniel L. *Comparative Accounting Theory.* Reading, Mass.: Addison-Wesley, 1972.

Mattessich, Richard. "Methodological Preconditions and Problems of a General Theory of Accounting." *The Accounting Review,* July 1972, pp. 469–87.

Popper, Karl R. *The Logic of Scientific Discovery.* London: Hutchinson & Co., 1959.

Sterling, Robert R. "An Explication and Analysis of the Structure of Accounting, Part One." *Abacus,* December 1971, pp. 137–52; and "Part Two." *Abacus,* December 1972, pp. 145–62.

Sterling, Robert R., and Richard E. Flaherty. "The Role of Liquidity in Exchange Valuation." *The Accounting Review,* July 1971, pp. 441–56.

Yu, S.C. *The Structure of Accounting Theory.* Gainesville, Fla.: University of Florida Press, 1976.

Pragmatic Theories

Demski, Joel S. "Choice among Financial Reporting Alternatives." *The Accounting Review,* April 1974, pp. 221–32.

Hawkins, David F. "Behavioral Implications of Generally Accepted Accounting Principles." *California Management Review,* Winter 1969, pp. 13–21.

Hofstedt, Thomas R. "Some Behavioral Parameters of Financial Accounting." *The Accounting Review,* October 1972, pp. 679–92.

Hofstedt, Thomas R. "The Processing of Accounting Information: Perceptual Biases." *Behavioral Experiments in Accounting.* Edited by Thomas J. Burns. Columbus: College of Administrative Science, The Ohio State University Press, 1972, pp. 285–315.

Normative Deductive Theories

Bedford, Norton M. "The Impact of A Priori Theory and Research on Accounting Practice," in *The Impact of Accounting Research on Practice and Disclosure.* Edited by A. Rashad Abdel-khalik and Thomas F. Keller. Durham, N.C.: Duke University Press, 1978, pp. 2–31.

Langenderfer, Harold Q. "A Conceptual Framework for Financial Reporting." *Journal of Accountancy,* July 1973, pp. 46–55.

Pellicelli, Georgio. "The Axiomatic Method in Business Economics: A First Approach." *Abacus,* December 1969, pp. 119–31.

Tippet, Mark. "The Axioms of Accounting Measurement." *Accounting and Business Research,* Autumn 1978, pp. 266–78.

Normative Theories

Demski, Joel S. "The General Impossibility of Normative Accounting Standards." *The Accounting Review,* October 1973, pp. 718–23.

Hakansson, Nils H. "Normative Accounting Theory and the Theory of Decision." *International Journal of Accounting Education and Research,* Spring 1969, pp. 33–47.

Predictive Ability

American Accounting Association. "Report of the Committee on Corporate Financial Reporting." *The Accounting Review,* Supplement 1972, pp. 525–28.

Ashton, Robert H. "The Predictive-Ability Criterion and User Prediction Models." *The Accounting Review,* October 1974, pp. 719–32.

Beaver, William H.; John W. Kennelly; and William M. Voss. "Predictive Ability as a Criterion for the Evaluation of Accounting Data." *The Accounting Review,* October 1963, pp. 675–83.

Greenball, M. N. "The Predictive-Ability Criterion: Its Relevance in Evaluating Accounting Data." *Abacus,* June 1971, pp. 1–7.

Libby, R. "Accounting Ratios and the Prediction of Failure." *Journal of Accounting Research,* Spring 1975, pp. 150–61.

Louderback, Joseph G. III. "Projectability as a Criterion for Income Determination Methods." *The Accounting Review,* April 1971, pp. 298–305.

Revsine, Lawrence. "Predictive Ability, Market Prices, and Operating Flows." *The Accounting Review,* July 1971, pp. 480–89.

Revsine, Lawrence. *Replacement Cost Accounting.* Englewood Cliffs, N.J.: Prentice Hall, 1973, pp. 86–138.

The Events Approach

Benbasat, Izak, and Albert S. Dexter. "Value and Events Approaches to Accounting: An Experimental Evaluation." *The Accounting Review,* October 1979, pp. 735–49.

Johnson, Orace. "Toward an 'Events' Theory of Accounting." *The Accounting Review,* October 1970, pp. 641–53.

Lieberman, Arthur Z., and Andrew B. Whinston. "A Structuring of an Events-Accounting Information System." *The Accounting Review,* April 1975, pp. 246–58.

Revsine, Lawrence. "Data Expansion and Conceptual Structure." *The Accounting Review,* October 1970, pp. 704–11.

Sorter, George H. "Events Approach to Basic Accounting Theory." *The Accounting Review,* January 1969, pp. 12–19.

Ethical Approaches

Arnett, Harold E. "The Concept of Fairness." *The Accounting Review,* April 1967, pp. 291–97.

Burton, John C., ed. *Corporate Financial Reporting: Ethical and Other Problems.* AICPA, 1972, esp. pp. 17–27, 73–86, and 107–32.

Pattillo, James W. *The Foundations of Financial Accounting,* particularly Ch. 3. Baton Rouge: Louisiana State University Press, 1965.

Spacek, Leonard. *A Search for Fairness in Financial Reporting to the Public.* Chicago: Arthur Andersen & Co., 1969, particularly pp. 27–38 and 349–56.

Corporate Social Accounting Approach

American Accounting Association. "Report of the Committee on Accounting for Social Performance." *The Accounting Review,* Supplement 1976, pp. 38–69.

American Institute of Certified Public Accountants. *The Measurement of Corporate Social Performance.* AICPA, 1977.

Anderson, John E., and Alan W. Frankle. "Voluntary Social Reporting: An Iso-Beta Portfolio Analysis." *The Accounting Review,* July 1980, pp. 467–79.

Burton, Eric James, and Manuel A. Tipgos. "Toward a Theory of Corporate Social Accounting: A Comment and Reply." *The Accounting Review,* October 1977, pp. 971–73 and 977–83.

Dierkes, Meinolf, and Raymond A. Bauer, eds. *Corporate Social Accounting.* New York: Praeger Publishers, 1973.

Estes, Ralph. *Corporate Social Accounting.* New York: John Wiley & Sons, 1976.

Ingram, Robert W. "An Investigation of the Information Content of (Certain) Social Responsibility Disclosures." *Journal of Accounting Research,* Autumn 1978, pp. 270–85.

Jensen, Robert E. *Phantasmagoric Accounting: Research and Analysis of Economic, Social, and Environmental Impact of Corporate Business.* AAA Studies in Accounting Research, 1976.

Ramanatham, Kavasseri V. "Toward a Theory of Corporate Social Accounting." *The Accounting Review,* July 1976, pp. 516–28.

Spicer, Barry H. "Investors, Corporate Social Performance and Information Disclosure: An Empirical Study." *The Accounting Review,* January 1978, pp. 94–111.

Tinker, Anthony M.; Cheryl Lehman; and Marilyn Neimark. "Marginalizing the Public Interest: A Critical Look at Recent Social Accounting History," in *Behavioral Accounting Research: A Critical Analysis.* Edited by K.F. Ferris. Columbus: Century VII Publishing Co., 1988.

Macroeconomic Approach

Enthoven, Adolf J. H. Accountancy and Economic Development Policy. New York: American Elsevier Publishing, 1973.

Mueller, Gerhard G. "Accounting within a Macroeconomic Framework." *International Accounting.* New York: MacMillan, 1967, Ch. 1.

Verification of Accounting Theories

American Accounting Association. "Report of the Committee on Accounting Theory Construction and Verification." *The Accounting Review,* Supplement 1971, pp. 53–79.

Gonedes, Nicholas J. "Perception Estimation and Verifiability." *International Journal of Accounting Education and Research,* Spring 1969, pp. 63–73.

Schrader, William J., and Robert E. Malcolm. "A Note on Accounting Theory Construction and Verification." *Abacus,* June 1973, pp. 93–98.

Sterling, Robert R. "On Theory Construction and Verification." *The Accounting Review,* July 1970, pp. 444–57.

Williams, Thomas H., and Charles H. Griffin. "On the Nature of Empirical Verification in Accounting." *Abacus,* December 1969, pp. 143–78.

ENDNOTES

1. Financial Accounting Standards Board, *Statements of Financial Accounting Concepts,* No. 2 (FASB, May 1980), pars. 6 & 7.
2. Robert N. Anthony and James W. Reese, *Accounting: Text and Cases* (Homewood, Ill.: Richard D. Irwin, 1983), p. 132.
3. Eisner v. Macomber, 252 U.S. 189 (1920).
4. James v. U.S., 366 U.S. 213 (1961).
5. Financial Accounting Standards Board Discussion Memorandum, *An Analysis of Issues Related to Conceptual Framework for Financial Accounting and Reporting: Elements of Financial Statements and Their Measurement* (FASB, December 1976), pars. 116–123.
6. Henry Rand Hatfield, *Accounting, Its Principles and Problems* (reprinted by Scholars Book, 1971, originally printed in 1927), p. 250.
7. James W. Pattillo, *The Foundation of Financial Accounting* (Baton Rouge: Louisiana State University Press, 1965), p. 11.

8. Kenneth MacNeal, *Truth in Accounting* (Philadelphia: University of Pennsylvania Press, 1939), p. 203.

9. F. D. S. Choi and G. G. Mueller, *International Accounting* (Englewood Cliffs, N.J.: Prentice Hall, Inc., 1984), pp. 89–91.

10. Stephen A. Zeff, "The Rise of Economic Consequences," *The Journal of Accountancy,* December 1978, pp. 56–63.

11. *The Corporate Report* (London, Eng.: Accounting Standards Steering Committee of the Institute of Chartered Accountants of England and Wales, 1975).

12. Gary K. Meek and Sidney J. Gray, "The Value Added Statement: An Innovation for U.S. Companies?" *Accounting Horizons,* June 1988, pp. 73–81.

13. William H. Beaver, *Financial Reporting: An Accounting Revolution* (Englewood Cliffs, N.J.: Prentice Hall, 1967), p. 8.

14. James W. Pattillo, *Foundation of Financial Accounting,* p. 41.

15. A. C. Littleton, *The Structure of Accounting Theory,* American Accounting Association Monograph No. 5 (AAA, 1958).

16. American Institute of Accountants, "Review and Resume," *Accounting Terminology Bulletin No. 1* (New York: AIA, 1953), par. 9.

17. Karl Popper, *Conjectures and Refutations* (Basic Books, 1965).

18. Thomas S. Kuhn, *The Structure of Scientific Revolution* (Chicago: University of Chicago Press, 1962).

19. Webster's *Third New International Dictionary,* Unabridged (Springfield, Mass.: G. & C. Merriam, 1961), p. 2371.

20. Gugliemo Ferrero, *Les Lois psychologiques du symbolisme,* p. viii; used by Karl Jung on the flyleaf introducing Part I of *Symbols of Transformation* (Collected Works, vol. 5, New York: Pantheon Books, 1956), p. 2.

Chapter 2

Four Thousand Years of Accounting

CHAPTER OBJECTIVES

After studying this chapter, you will be able to:

Explain what social, cultural, and technological antecedents were necessary for the invention of accounting.

Describe the major contributions that non-Western civilizations made to the invention of accounting.

Identify the major differences and similarities between the system of accounting that was in place at the turn of the twentieth century and that in place today.

Relate developments in accounting to developments in society.

Appreciate the ancient, noble, and multicultural origin of accounting and its importance to our society.

CHAPTER OVERVIEW

The Renaissance

The earliest double-entry bookkeeping systems are found in Northern Italy and date back to the 14th century. Brother Lucas Pacioli codified these systems in an appendix to a book published in Venice in 1494.

Accounting's Antecedents

Accounting flowered in a soil made rich by centuries of learning, trade with the East, inventions like the lateen sail, printing, and a new number system. Much of this was brought to Europe from China and India by Arab scholars.

The Age of Stagnation

Relatively few developments occurred in accounting in the next several centuries. This period was marked by great explorations such as that of the Americas by Columbus and by the onset of the Industrial Revolution.

The Rise of the Profession

Accounting professionals began making their appearance in the late 18th century. The English and Welsh Institute of Chartered Accountants was founded in 1880. The American Institute followed in 1887.

The Future of Accounting

Accounting developed in response to upheavals in the environment, new discoveries, and technological advances. There is no reason to believe that accounting will not continue to evolve in response to changes that we are experiencing in our times.

Accounting is a product of the Italian Renaissance. The forces that led to that renewal of the human spirit in Europe were the same forces that created accounting. Some even argue that those forces would not have progressed to shape our world today were it not for the invention of double-entry bookkeeping, which provided a framework within which private capitalism could develop and generate the wealth which sustained the artist, the musician, the priest, and the writer.[1] The story of accounting is the story of our age; in many ways, accounting itself tells that story since accounting records are in fact part of the raw materials of historians. We learn much about men like Isaac Newton and John Wesley from the account books they kept. As the novelist Josephine Tey said, "Truth is not in accounts but in account books."* Accounting, properly understood, can lay fair claim, then, to being one of the liberal arts.

This chapter seeks to tell the story of accounting by relating it to the world which gave it birth. It begins with the first modern accounting records that have been found, dating back some 600 years. The story leading up to the Renaissance is recounted in an effort to explain why accounting was invented at this particular point in time. The hope is that

---

* "Real history is written in forms not meant as history. In Wardrobe accounts, in Privy Purse expenses, in personal letters, in estate books. If someone, say, insists that Lady Whosit never had a child, and you find in the account book the entry: 'For the son born to my lady on Michaelmas eve: five yards of blue ribbon, fourpence halfpenny' it's a reasonably fair deduction that my lady had a son on Michaelmas eve." *The Daughter of Time* (New York: Collier Books, 1951), pp. 90–91.

students will leave this section aware of the origins of the ancient and noble art they practice, proud to call themselves accountants, and conscious of how much our heritage owes to the great civilizations of Africa and Asia. The chapter continues with the Age of Exploration and the Industrial Age, and their impact on the world of business and of accounting in particular. The chapter concludes with the rise of the public accounting profession in Britain, Europe, and America as the first wave of industrialization crested across the globe.

THE RENAISSANCE

We do not know who invented accounting. We do know, though, that double-entry bookkeeping systems gradually began to make their appearance during the 13th and 14th centuries in several trading centers in northern Italy. The first record of a complete system of double-entry bookkeeping is found in the municipal records of the city of Genoa, Italy, for the year 1340.[2] Earlier fragments are found in the accounts of Giovanni Farolfi & Company, a firm of merchants in Florence dating from 1299–1300, and in those of Rinieri Fini & Brothers, who traded at fairs that were famous in their day in the Champagne area of France.[3] Exhibit 2-1 indicates the location of many of the places mentioned in this chapter.

The first codifier of accounting was a Franciscan friar by the name of Brother Luca Pacioli who spent most of his life as a teacher and scholar at the Universities of Perugia, Florence, Pisa, and Bologna. He ended his illustrious career teaching mathematics at the University of Rome, a prestigious post to which he was called by Pope Leo X.* Among his many friends were several popes, the mathematician and architect Leon Battista Alberti, and, closest of all, Leonardo da Vinci. This was the Renaissance and Pacioli was one of its true products.

The book Pacioli wrote was called the *Summa de Arithmetica, Geometrica, Proportioni et Proportionalita*. It appeared in 1494 in Venice—just two years after Columbus landed in America and only a few years after the first printing presses were set up in Venice, thus indicating the importance of the work. His *Summa* was primarily a treatise on mathematics, but it included a section on double-entry bookkeeping called *Particularis de Computis et Scripturis*. This section was the first published material describing the double-entry bookkeeping system and giving us insight into the reasoning behind the accounting records. His comments on accounting are still as relevant and fresh as when they were written almost 500

---

* The link between accounting and mathematics continued into the 19th century with the publication of *The Principles of Double-Entry Bookkeeping* by Arthur Cayley (1821–1895), a professor of mathematics at Cambridge University, England.

EXHIBIT 2-1 Europe and the Near East

years ago. For instance, hear him on the subject of what to do after making up a trial balance:

> So as to make everything more clear in the said closing you will make this other comparison, viz., you shall summarize on a sheet of paper all the debit items of Ledger+ and place them on the left-hand side, and summarize all the credit items and place them on the right, and then these last sums you will resummarize and make one total of all the debit items which shall be called sum total, and thus you will make one total also of all the credit items which will also be called sum total; but the first will be called the sum total of debits, and the second the sum total of the credits. Now if these two sum totals are equal, that is, so much in one as in the other, viz., that of the debit and the credit, you will infer that your Ledger has been well kept . . . and closed for the reason that was stated above in Chapter 14; but if one of the said sum totals exceeded the other it will denote that there is an error in your Ledger which, with diligence, it will be best for you to find with the ability of the intellect God has given you, and with the artifice of reason which you will have learnt well, and which, as we said in the commencement is extremely necessary to the good merchant; otherwise, not being a good accountant in your affairs, you will feel your way forward like a blind person, and much loss can arise therefrom. . . .[4]

As the accounting historian A. C. Littleton said, one is struck on reading sections like this how little we have added to accounting in the intervening years.[5]

That is not to say that there have been no changes. Some of those changes make for interesting contrasts between the practices of the Italian cities and current methods and theory:

1. During the period extending to the 16th century, the primary objective of accounting was to provide information for the owner—usually a single proprietor. As a result, accounts were held in secrecy and there was no external pressure, as there is today, for accuracy or uniform standards of reporting.

2. Partly as a result of the first point, generally no clear distinction was made between the personal and the business affairs of a proprietor, that is, today's entity concept was not well developed. There were exceptions, though, and it was not infrequent to find a merchant keeping a set of books for his home and another for his shop.[6]

3. The concepts of the accounting period and the going-concern nature of the business enterprise were lacking. Most business ventures were of short duration, or continuing only until a specific trading objective had been reached. As a result, profit was calculated only on completion of the venture. Without the concept of periodic profit, there was no need for accruals and deferrals. As fixed assets played only a small part in the affairs of businessmen, there was no need to calculate depreciation. For those businesses which were organized for longer periods of time, there was still little need for periodic computation of profit, because the owners were in personal contact with the affairs of the business.

4.   The fourth characteristic stems from the lack of a single stable monetary unit. Without some common denominator, double-entry bookkeeping is impossible; with the many monetary units in existence during the medieval period, double-entry was possible but awkward. As a result, entries in the journal, also known as the Memorial or Day Book, were quite descriptive including details about goods such as their weight, size, and measurement, as well as their price. The FASB's recent proposals for disclosures about financial instruments appear to indicate that early accountants were 500 years ahead of their time!

Summary

To summarize, by 1494 when Pacioli's book appeared, almost all of the machinery of bookkeeping, as we know it today, was in place. When Congress mandated the creation of the Securities and Exchange Commission in 1934 to regulate accounting, it was not creating a new information system; on the contrary, it was merely seeking to regulate a system that had flourished on its own for over five centuries. Given that management, with the aid of managerial accountants, presumably had created adequate accounting systems without the aid of government intervention, a real question arises as to whether this intervention is really necessary. The debate on this topic has been vigorous and is addressed in later chapters. For now, it is sufficient to simply be aware of the ancient history of the discipline.

The Origin of Words

Debits, credits, journal entries, ledgers, accounts, trial balances, balance sheets, and income statements all date back to the Renaissance. Accounting, therefore, can claim as noble a lineage as many of the liberal arts. Accounting students can take pride in their heritage. Part of this heritage is a rich vocabulary, almost all of which dates back to this period and much of which is fascinating in its origin. Debts, debtors, debentures, and debits, for instance, all derive from the base *debere*, to owe, which contracts to the *dr* used in journal entries. Credits come from the same root as the word *creed* meaning something in which one believes, such as the Christian statement of belief known as the Apostles' Creed. It can also mean people in whom one believes, like creditors—by lending them money one has reposed one's trust in them. The Latin origin is *credere,* which contracts to the *cr* used in journal entries.

Taxes in early England provide another example. They were collected on a table covered with a cloth divided into squares. Counters were placed in one square to indicate monies owed; goods and monies paid were placed in an adjacent square in a primitive visual form of double-entry bookkeeping. The cloth, being checkered, led to the English equivalent of the American Internal Revenue Service becoming known as the Exchequer. When government notes were later issued they became known as exchequer bills or cheques for short—spelled *checks* in the United States!

CHECKPOINTS

1. List the differences between present accounting and that practiced in 14th century Italy.
2. List three major changes that you think have occurred in accounting since the days of Luca Pacioli.

ACCOUNTING'S ANTECEDENTS

But why Italy? And why the 14th century? The following tells a strange and wonderful story of how it was that accounting finally flowered at this time and in this place. As the story is told, it rapidly becomes apparent that accounting was the product of many hands and many lands. The story of accounting reveals just how cosmopolitan our ancestors were. Accounting's history quickly shows that our own culture is almost entirely derivative from that of others. The story also serves to underline the fact that mankind has made its greatest intellectual and social strides in periods of peace and tolerance.

Early Civilizations

Long before Europe emerged from huts and skins, sophisticated economies had risen in the Middle and the Far East. The Shang dynasty in China can date itself back as far as 1600 BC, while records of a sophisticated culture in India date from as early as 2300 BC. The great pyramids of Egypt, the earliest of which was built 4,000 years ago, attest to the great age of that civilization. The learning of these ancients reached its apex in classical Greece. Philosophers like Plato and Aristotle, writers like Homer and Sophocles, and mathematicians like Euclid and Pythagoras still influence our thinking. And more than two millenia after his death, doctors continue to pledge to uphold the oath of Hippocrates.

It was one of Aristotle's pupils, Alexander the Great, who was to establish the largest empire known to the ancient world—second only to the British empire in extent. In 332 BC he founded the city of Alexandria where the most extraordinary library of the ancient world was subsequently gathered. By 235 BC it already contained over 500,000 manuscripts—a literal treasure trove. It was there, in the early part of the second century, that Claudius Ptolemy, one of the world's greatest scholars, developed his astrological theories. He wrote a book called the *Almagest,* which shaped world thinking on astronomy for centuries and from which we derive the zodiacal signs such as Aquarius, Aries, and Pisces.[7]

Numerous accounting records date from these very early days. For example, Egyptian farmers on the banks of the Nile paid the bailiffs grain and flax for the use of irrigation water. Receipts were given to farmers by drawing pictures of the measures of grain on the walls of the farmers' houses.[8] Archaeologists believe that the clay tokens that abound in the Mesopotamian region were similarly used for accounting purposes. Sophisticated accounting systems appear to have been in place in China as early as 2000 BC and tantalizing references indicate a familiarity with double-entry bookkeeping in Rome at the beginning of the Christian era. More controversially, some even claim that the Romans were familiar with the concept of depreciation.[9]

Barely a hundred years after Ptolemy had completed his great work, a shortage of land in north and central Europe caused thousands of Vandals and Goths to attack the Roman Empire. Rome was sacked in AD 410 and "vandalized" in AD 455. Huns under the leadership of Attila poured out of Russia, forcing the northern European tribes even further westward. Angles and Saxons invaded England, laying the foundation of the Anglo-Saxon culture. In the confusion and turmoil that followed, the knowledge of the Greeks vanished. By AD 646, when Arabs reached Alexandria, the great library there had been completely destroyed by unknown hands. What civilization was left clung to the cliffs of Ireland. The western world had entered the Dark Ages.

The Arabic Influence

Then in far away Mecca, a little village in modern Saudi Arabia, the prophet Muhammad was born. A series of visions beginning in 610 led him to write the Qur'an and so found Islam. Within a century of his death, his followers had conquered much of Northern Africa and the Middle East, and had penetrated into Europe, before being stopped by Charlemagne and his immediate predecessors. In particular, Spain was wrested from the Visigoths in 711 and Sicily became an Arab province. Jerusalem was captured, and between 685 and 705 the great shrine known as the Dome of the Rock was built on the place where Solomon's temple had rested. Muslims had even spread as far as India.

In 765 the leaders of Islam, the Abbasid caliphate, transferred the capital of the Islamic empire to the newly founded city of Baghdad in modern Iraq. There, in one of those curious accidents of fate that transform our lives, the second caliph, Al-Mansur, fell ill. Members of his court, in search of a cure, discovered the monastery of Jundi Shapur, 150 miles to the south. This monastery was inhabited by followers of Nestorius, a former Patriarch of Constantinople who had been banished by the Council of Ephesus in 431 for preaching heresy. The Nestorians had taken copies of a number of the ancient manuscripts into exile with them and so, almost miraculously, Greek learning had been preserved after all.

The result was the establishment in Baghdad of the greatest center of learning of the first millenium. It was to this institution that the Arabs brought back from India one of the great discoveries of the human mind: the concept of zero. Alexander the Great had taken his armies all the way to India. The Indians were as fascinated by astrology as the Greeks and rapidly absorbed all the West had to teach them including, at a later stage, the teachings of Ptolemy. Now, centuries later, India returned the favor to the West by providing scholars at Baghdad with their extensions of Ptolemy's work. The combination of Syriac and Indian texts encouraged a Jewish scholar, Jacob ben Tarik, to found a school of astrology at Baghdad. At this school Musa Al-Khwarizmi, the greatest of all Arab mathematicians and the librarian to the sick caliph, wrote his text *Al-Jabr Wa'l Mugabala* from which we derive the term al-jabra or algebra. Central to his work was the Indian discovery of the concept of zero and along with it the notion of place value which had enabled Indian scholars to develop the system of numerals we use today. We take all this so much for granted that it is difficult to appreciate how sophisticated is the notion of a number *zero* being more than empty nothingness.* We also forget how inconvenient arithmetic was before the development of place value.

This knowledge was not confined to Baghdad but spread across the African littoral to Spain, where the last of the Umayyad caliphs had fled after the Abbasids had taken over the leadership of Islam. The new learning, drawing as it did on so many cultures, promoted great tolerance. Jews, like Samuel ibn Nagdela, rose to high office in the courts of the caliphs.[10] Arabs, Jews, and Christians worked amicably together at the universities of Cordoba, Seville, Malaga, and Granada, making them the intellectual centers of Europe. Among the visitors at Cordoba was Gilbert, Archbishop of Ravenna,† who was among the first to introduce the Hindu-Arabic numeral system to Europe. The 12th century English scholar, Adelard of Bath, was another visitor to Cordoba, returning to

---

* There is evidence that both the Baylonians and the Mayans developed the concept of zero. No other nations are known to have been so sophisticated in their mathematical thinking—not even the Greeks.

† Gilbert later became Pope Sylvester II.

England with a copy of Euclid which shaped English mathematics teaching for centuries afterward. But the golden age of Moorish Spain did not last long. By 1085, Toledo had fallen to Christian armies. The great Jewish philosopher, Maimonides, fled from Spain to Egypt, where he was to become physician to Saladin, the vizier of Egypt. Saladin was the conqueror of Jerusalem against whom Robin Hood's Richard I of England battled. In 1258, Baghdad fell to the invading Mongols led by Kublai Khan.

Individuals and cities were lost but not the learning. There were men like Leonard Fibonacci of Pisa (ca 1180–1250), who grew up in North Africa where, as a child, he learned both the language and the mathematics of the Arabs. On the family's return to Pisa, he wrote *Liber Abacci* which did much to popularize the Arabic system of numerals in Europe. Reaction to the numbers was not always favorable, however. The Church considered their use heresy, and in 1299 their use was banned in Florence. The ban did not last long, however. By the time Pacioli wrote his book, he was instructing his readers to use Arabic numerals except for headings where ". . . you will first write down in the Ledger the year in the old way; that is, alphabetically thus: MCCCCLXXXXIII . . . you will say thus: 'let us use the ancient letters, if only for the sake of more beauty'."[11] Many of us still do the same today. And each time we write a check out in letters as well as Arabic numerals, we are unconsciously carrying forward a centuries-old distrust of the newfangled numbers.

Technological Advances and Socioeconomic Changes

The East provided more than book learning. At the battle of Samarkand in 751, the Arab armies captured a paper mill from the Chinese. Soon, Xativa, a town south of Valencia, became the paper manufacturing center for Europe. Gunpowder, invented by the Chinese in the ninth century, was exploited for the purposes of war by the Mongols and soon made its way to Europe. In 1180 Alexander Neckham, foster brother to King Richard and Abbot of Cirencester, described a compass that was in use in China. Less than a century later, Alfonso the Wise, Spanish king of Castile and Leon, had made its use compulsory for navigation.

The biggest advance, though, was the invention of a triangular sail known as the lateen sail, which by 1250 had supplanted the square sail of the Romans. The square sail was ideal when the wind was behind one but was otherwise relatively useless. The lateen sail made sailing into the wind possible. Before its invention, trade was limited to sailing in one direction at one time of the year and sailing back at another time; the lateen made year-round travel a reality. This sail, together with the sternpost rudder, probably derived through the Arabs from the Chinese, made possible the invention of the Portuguese caravel—the ship that took

Bartholomew Diaz to the Cape of Good Hope in 1488 and the predecessor of the carrack that carried Columbus to America. Exhibit 2-2 shows the lateen sail and the sternpost rudder very clearly. Dhows, the modern survivors of these old ships, still ply Arab waters.[12]

The ships provided the means of transportation, but the immediate call for that transportation resulted from the capture of Jerusalem by the Turks in 1079. This capture caused Pope Urban II, just 16 years later, to declare a holy war known to us as the First Crusade. From the close of the 11th century to the latter part of the 13th century, succeeding crusades provided the impetus for the development of trade, primarily between the Italian cities and the East. The Crusaders needed ships and supplies, and they brought back products from the East that served to stimulate the demand for such items. Silks, spices, and dyestuffs flowed into Europe; salt, timber, grain, and wool flowed out. Merchants in ports like Genoa, Amalfi, and Venice grew rich on the trade.

EXHIBIT 2-2   A Portuguese Caravel[13]

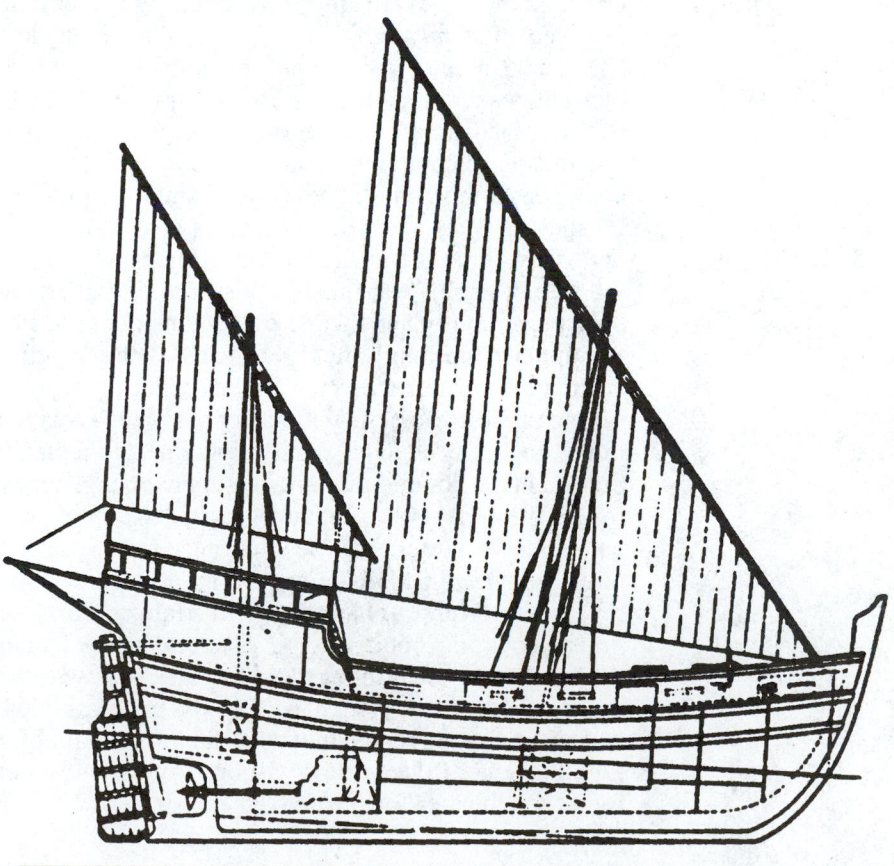

As trade expanded and wealth accumulated, individual trading was replaced largely by trading through agencies and partnerships. The use of partnerships permitted the risks of the long sea voyages to be shared and allowed the wealth of the capitalist to be combined with the daring of younger traders.

In the silent partnership, known as the *commenda,* the capital furnished by the silent partner (the *commendator*) was like a loan to the active partner (the *tractator*), an arrangement which avoided the payment of interest, a practice of which the Church disapproved at that time. The partnership was, therefore, important in the development of accounting because it led to the recognition of the firm as a separate entity distinct from the owners. The agency relationship was important because it required accountability. It was also important in the later development of the corporation since the liability of the commendator was typically limited to the amount invested.

One tragic side effect of the increase in trade was the ease with which disease could travel the known world. Sailors returning to Marseilles from Caffa on the Black Sea in 1347 brought back with them a bacterial infection known as *pasteurella pestis,* or bubonic plague, which was to strike Europe in an epidemic that became known as the Black Death. Within an incredibly short time the disease had spread across the whole of Europe. Before it had run its course, one-third of Europe's population was wiped out by the plague. What was a disaster of devastating proportions for some was a moment of great opportunity for others. Farms, homes, and businesses were abandoned by the dying. Estates were left to the fortunate survivors. A shortage of labor forced wages up. The feudal system fell into decay as peasants left in search of higher wages. A money economy began to replace the old obligations of class. Private property began to supplant the jointly held tenancies of the Middle Ages. In short, the foundations of our society were being laid.

One of the curious side effects of the plague was a tremendous increase in the cost of producing manuscripts due to the deaths of so many of the literate in the community. As so often happens, necessity drove invention for, in the early 1400s, Johannes Gensfleisch, better known by his maternal name of Gutenberg, revolutionized the world by the invention of movable type. In 1457 the first book, a psalter, was published by Gutenberg's ex-partner, Johann Fust, in Mainz. Thirty-seven years later the first accounting book was published. Venice had by then become the world's center of printing. Leading the way was Aldus Manutius who, before his death in 1515, had printed a translation of every Greek author known so that never again would the destruction of one library mean the potential end of the world's wisdom. And so it was in Venice that Pacioli found a publisher for his text.

Antecedents Summarized

This, then, was the world in which accounting saw its birth. As Littleton noted, it was a world in which a number of events, which he called antecedents, had converged.[14] One set of antecedents was the ability of expression: the art of writing, the development of arithmetic, and the widespread use of money as a common denominator. Another set was institutional in nature and included the concept of private property, the development of credit, and the accumulation of capital. Of these antecedents, the joint venture and the partnership, as institutions to facilitate the accumulation and use of capital, were probably the most potent influences in creating the need for the concept of the accounting entity and the necessity to compute profits. Fourteenth-century Italy was the fortunate country in which these events converged. It was the recipient of the accumulated wisdom of generations of scholars from Mesopotamia, Egypt, India, and the Middle East. Political upheavals and disease had destroyed an old social order and had laid the foundations of a new. Modern accounting, therefore, is as much a product of the rebirth of Europe that we call the Renaissance as the art of Michelangelo, Da Vinci, and Titian.

Debits and Credits

But why specifically double-entry bookkeeping? The duality concept that is so often used to justify double entry merely requires that two sides to each transaction be recognized. This could just as easily be done in a single column using pluses and minuses as in two columns using debits and credits. For instance, when using cash to purchase inventory why not simply place a positive number in the inventory column and a negative number in the cash column of a spreadsheet? Why talk about debiting the one while crediting the other? Why all the complex machinery? The curious fact is that, although the inventors of accounting had concepts like money, equity, and expense with which to work, they had no negative numbers at their disposal! Negative numbers were known to occur but as late as 1544, mathematicians like the German Michael Stifel thought of them as absurd and fictitious. In fact, they were not used in mathematics until the 17th century.[15] The T account was developed, therefore, to show increases on one side and decreases on the other. The balance was derived by using a "subtraction-by-opposition" technique or, as Pacioli put it, by seeing whether "he has beaten his credit . . . with his debit."[16] In other words, the whole machinery of debits and credits is an incredibly ingenious solution to a nonexistent problem!

CHECKPOINTS

---

1. Rank Littleton's three antecedents for the introduction of double-entry bookkeeping in the order of importance as you perceive them.
2. List three contributions made by non-European cultures to Europe that made the invention of double-entry bookkeeping possible.
3. Compare the technological advances made at the time of the Renaissance with those of this century.

THE AGE OF STAGNATION

Starting with the close of the 15th century, the Italian cities began to decline both politically and as the centers of trade. With the discovery of the New World and the opening of new trade routes, the centers of commerce moved to Spain and Portugal and then to Antwerp and the Netherlands. It was natural, then, that the Italian system of double-entry bookkeeping should spread to these other countries. Writers like the Dutch mathematician, Simon Stevin, popularized Pacioli's ideas in his book *Vorstelicke Boukhouding* published in Leyden in 1607 and later translated into French. Little change was made in the bookkeeping techniques; however, the writings began to show a change. According to Peragallo, during the period from 1458 to 1558,

> writers were intent on setting forth the mechanics of bookkeeping as developed by business. No one attempted to develop a theory of double entry and no one went beyond the bookkeeping needs of the mercantile firm. In the second cycle, extending from 1559 to 1795, a new element appeared—the critique of bookkeeping. This was also the period when double entry extended its field of application to other types of organizations, such as monasteries and the state. With the critique and the widening sphere of bookkeeping, began theoretical research into the subject.[17]

Historian Raymond de Roover called the period from 1494 up to 1800 a period of stagnation for accounting.[18] This characterization is a little unfair since this period began as an age of exploration and ended as an age of revolution. The world was transformed and accounting was shaped with it.

The Age of Exploration

The Age of Exploration was prompted by the power of the Italian city-states, which prevented the rest of Europe from participating in the Mediterranean trade. The Portuguese showed the way by traveling down the coast of Africa in their frail caravels. In 1492, just two years before Pacioli's book appeared, Christopher Columbus sailed west in a Spanish carrack, the successor to the caravels. Appropriately enough, Columbus had been born in Genoa, the site of the earliest accounting records known to us. And, even more appropriately, he was accompanied on his voyage by an auditor appointed by the Spanish court to "keep tabs on Columbus' swindle sheet when he started to figure the cost of gold and spices he would accumulate."[19] Vasco da Gama, Ferdinand Magellan, John Cabot, and many others were to follow Diaz and Columbus in exploring the world.

Joint Stock Companies. The financial needs of the voyages of these great explorers led to the development of the joint stock company, which was to have considerable significance for accounting. These companies might be seen as extensions of the Italian *commenda*s and forerunners of modern corporations. Individuals joined together in financing a venture, each being given shares of stock in proportion to their investments. At the end of the venture, the stockholders were supposed to be paid out in total, hence the term *terminating stock*.

One of the first joint stock companies to be formed was the English East Indies Company in 1600.* An immediate dilemma was that often there was not enough cash at the end of a voyage to pay out the stockholders, who were then offered shares in the next voyage in lieu of cash: the forerunner of the stock dividend. When terminating stock was laid upon terminating stock, it necessitated some extremely complex accounting. It was proposed, therefore, that investments in stock be made jointly for several voyages. This proved just as unsatisfactory from an accounting standpoint. On October 19, 1657, a new charter was sealed allowing for permanent stock to be issued that would be a joint investment in all voyages for the indefinite future. One effect of the movement from terminating to permanent stock was a growing practice of balancing the profit and loss at the end of each year rather than at the end of each venture. By 1673, the Code of Commerce in France required that a balance sheet be drawn up at least every two years by every business.[20] With the provision of transferability, the world of the investor, the primary user of modern financial reporting, was established.[21]

---

* "Queen Elizabeth I was a considerable shareholder in the syndicate which had financed (Drake's) expedition: Out of her share she paid off the whole of England's foreign debt, balanced her budget, and found herself with about 40,000 pounds in hand. This she invested in the Levant Company, which prospered. Out of the profits of the Levant Company, the East India Company was founded; and the profits of this great enterprise were the foundation of England's subsequent foreign investment." (J. M. Keynes, "Economic Possibilities for Our Grandchildren," *Saturday Evening Post*, October 11, 1930, p. 160, quoted in Littleton, *Accounting Evolution to 1900*, p. 209.)

South Sea Bubble.   Joint stock companies were to come to a spectacular end. Few investment opportunities existed in the early 18th century. Those that did drew crowds of investors who flocked to participate in new issues, causing their share prices to double or even triple. The best known of these was the South Sea Company, supposedly formed to profit from the slave trade between Africa and South America. One says "supposedly" because no prospectuses and no financial statements were ever issued. Inevitably, the paper castles that had been erected collapsed, costing the British royal family and many other wealthy nobles hundreds of thousands of pounds in losses, equivalent to many millions today.* As a result, stock certificates were banned in Britain for over a century.

The Industrial Revolution

The Age of Stagnation ended with the second development of great importance for accounting in this period: the onset of the Industrial Revolution. It is hard to pinpoint an exact date when this revolution began or to trace its precise causes. Its origin probably lay in a period of good weather in Britain that permitted a series of good harvests, causing food prices to fall, and in turn allowing society to enjoy better nutrition and health. Simultaneously, an appreciation of the basics of personal hygiene caused a decline in the plague after four centuries of death. The population, and hence the demand for goods, soared. Manufacture rose to meet the demand and inventions began to transform the workplace.† To supply the increasing demand and sustain the growing population, larger farms and factories (earlier called "manufactories") requiring more equipment became common. More capital was a necessity and banks sprang up to finance the need. By 1800, there were 80 banks in London alone and as many as 400 in the country. In 1773, the London Stock Exchange was created, followed shortly by the New York Stock Exchange in 1792.‡

The 19th century and early 20th century saw a tremendous expansion in industry, particularly in the United States and England. As just one example, the annual production of steel in the United States increased from about 20,000 tons in 1867 to about 24 million tons in 1914 and to about 56 million tons in 1929. Mechanical inventions of the 18th century were

---

* Given the nature of their proposed business, there is some poetic justice in this financial debacle.

† The word *manufacture* derives from *manu-*, meaning hand, and *factor,* meaning work, so originally it meant handwork. Only later did machines replace hands. Some of the more amazing machines were Kay's flying shuttle (1733), Hargreaves' spinning Jenny (1764), and Watts' steam engine (1769).

‡ Pride of first place goes to the Amsterdam Exchange (1602). The Paris Bourse (1726) was followed closely by Philadelphia (1746).

perfected and placed in widespread use in the 19th century. Cartwright's power loom, for example, was patented in 1787, but it was not entirely successful in its practical applications until some 30 years later. Trade also expanded, partly as a result of the doctrines of Adam Smith's *Wealth of Nations,* published in 1776, which helped establish freer trade and led to the commercial treaty negotiated between France and Great Britain in 1786.

Effects on Accounting.　The effects on accounting were both direct and indirect. For instance, the advent of the factory system and mass production resulted in fixed assets becoming a sizable cost in the production and distribution process, making the concept of depreciation more important. As the need for management information regarding the costs of production and the costs to be assigned to inventory valuations grew, so did the need for cost accounting systems. Large requirements of capital, necessitating the separation of the investor and the manager, meant that one of the major objectives of accounting became reporting to absentee owners. Financial information, which had been provided mainly for managerial uses, was increasingly required by stockholders, investors, creditors, and the government. Thus, income as a return to investors had to be distinguished from a return of capital to the owners. Large requirements of capital also led to the creation of the corporation and, in due course, to mandatory audits.

Summary

Thus, by the close of the 19th century several changes had shaped the accounting system laid out by Pacioli into a form more suited for the needs of the large industrial corporations that characterize our world.

1. Early forms of companies had been invented and distinguished from their owners.
2. Stock in these companies had been created.
3. The distinction between capital and income was known.
4. The concept of a going concern had been launched.
5. Stock exchanges were active.
6. Industry and trade were growing.

It was time for an accounting profession to stride onto the scene.

CHECKPOINTS

1. What was the Age of Stagnation and what ended it?
2. What effects did the Age of Exploration have on accounting?

3. List three effects that the Industrial Revolution had on the development of accounting.
4. Distinguish terminating stock from permanent stock.

THE RISE OF THE PROFESSION

With the onset of the Industrial Revolution, accounting specialists began to make their appearance. Edinburgh led the way, listing seven accountants in its 1773 city directory. By the beginning of the 19th century, there were still fewer than 50 public accountants recorded in the directories of all of the large cities of England and Scotland. These numbers were to grow rapidly as a result of the passage of the Companies Act in 1844, which required audited balance sheets. A similar act in 1862, dubbed the "accountant's friend," provided for the use of accountants in the case of bankruptcies, which were to provide much of the early work for accountants. This act led Justice Quain in 1875 to complain that, "The whole affairs in bankruptcy have been handed over to an ignorant set of men called accountants, which was one of the greatest abuses ever introduced into the law."[22] A Society of Accountants was formed in Edinburgh in 1854 under a royal charter which entitled them to style themselves as "chartered accountants." Other local societies followed quickly until, in 1880, the Institute of Chartered Accountants in England and Wales was approved by Queen Victoria.*

American Institute of CPAs

The industrialization of America was accompanied by huge inflows of capital from abroad and particularly from Great Britain, the leading economic power at the time. It was natural, therefore, that British chartered accountants should find their way to the United States as auditors. Both Price Waterhouse & Co. and KPMG Peat Marwick can trace their roots back to Britain. Haskins and Sells (now part of Deloitte & Touche) was among the oldest of the all-American firms, being founded by Charles Waldo Haskins and Elijah Watt Sells in 1895. By 1887, the American profession, albeit small in number, had grown confident enough to form the American Association of Public Accountants, the forerunner of

---

* Green, *History and Survey of Accountancy,* p. 139, reports that the first society of accountants was formed in Venice in 1581.

the modern American Institute of Certified Public Accountants, with the *Journal of Accountancy* as its flagship publication. However, it would be 50 years before the profession would take the lead in setting financial reporting policies, and it would be 100 years before it could claim the 290,000 members it has today—a far cry from its 10 founders.

The AAPA was by no means the only accounting organization in America. Independent state societies sprang up all over the country. The first legal recognition of their members came in the state of New York in 1896 which permitted individuals to style themselves Certified Public Accountants on obtaining a certificate from the regents of the university of the state. Other states passed similar CPA laws in the following decade. The effect was that one could be a CPA without being a member of the AAPA. Equally, one could be a member of the AAPA without being a CPA. Resolving this conflict was not easy because the legal recognition of accountants was seen as a states' rights issue. In addition, many feared the domination of the New York State society. Mindful of the debate, the AAPA reorganized in 1917 as The American Institute of Accountants (AIA) with stricter educational requirements for admission; however, the possession of a CPA certificate was still not mandatory. Four years later a breakaway group formed The American Society of Certified Public Accountants with the only criterion for admission being the possession of a state-issued certificate. For 15 years, while the most momentous events in the regulation of accounting were taking place, these two organizations attempted to represent American accountants. Eventually, in 1936, the two organizations merged, keeping the Institute's name but adding to its requirements the possession of a "valid and unrevoked certified public accountant certificate." It would not be until 1957 that the AIA added the term "certified" and became The American Institute of Certified Public Accountants (AICPA). The long and arduous battle that many fought for appropriate educational requirements for practice as certified public accountants has added interest today as accountants in many states seek to implement a 150 hour rule.

Public accounting was not the only area of accounting to organize: Others in the United States included the National Association of Cost Accountants, later to become the National Association of Accountants (NAA); the American Association of University Instructors, later to become the American Association of Accountants (AAA); and the Controllers Institute of America, later to become the Financial Executives Institute (FEI). Two international organizations, the International Accounting Standards Committee (IASC) and the International Co-ordination Committee for the Accountancy Profession (ICCAP) have been organized in an attempt to attain some degree of uniformity in accounting for multinational corporations and for other firms that have shareholders or other interests in more than one country.

National Association of Accountants

The NAA was created in 1919 to represent the interests of management accountants. Its secretary for many years, Dr. Stuart C. Macleod, insisted that the NAA should be primarily an educational vehicle, which it has remained to this day. In 1972 it founded the Institute of Management Accounting, which manages the education necessary for examinations leading to the Certificate of Management Accounting (CMA). Still less well known than the CPA certificate, it is slowly gaining a good reputation as an excellent alternative for those not going into public accounting. Since its inception, the association also has sponsored a number of research studies in the cost accounting area which have provided management with a basis for selecting the best practice for their businesses. The association also publishes a monthly journal called *Management Accounting*.

American Accounting Association

The American Association of University Instructors in Accounting was established in 1916, changing its name in 1935 to the American Association of Accountants (AAA). From the start, this organization sought to encourage and sponsor research and to develop accounting principles and standards and seek their endorsement in practice. The general approach of the executive committee was that of suggesting broad, basic principles upon which corporate financial statements could be based. Their objective was to see financial statements that were sufficiently uniform and understandable to justify opinions regarding the financial condition and progress of the firm. This broad approach was adopted primarily because of the limited resources of the Association and because of the theoretical orientation of its members. It sponsors two main journals, the older of which is *The Accounting Review;* the younger is *Accounting Horizons*. In addition, it has sponsored numerous research studies, sponsored several journals representing particular interests of the members, and published a number of monographs over the years. Many of these studies are referenced throughout this book.

CHECKPOINTS

This section introduced a number of organizations active in developing accounting. Write each of their acronyms out in full and briefly describe the nature of the organization.

1. AAPA	3. AIA	5. NAA	7. AICPA
2. AAA	4. FEI	6. IASC	8. ICCAP

THE FUTURE OF ACCOUNTING

In the 500 years since Pacioli wrote his book, accounting itself has remained virtually constant. Pacioli would feel remarkably comfortable with the accounting systems that he would encounter today. There would be a variety of financial instruments that would puzzle him, no doubt, but once it was explained that these were simply new forms of credit to be entered on the right side of the balance sheet, he would have no difficulty.

Meanwhile, the world has undergone an information revolution which should have affected accounting dramatically. Instead, somewhat like in the Industrial Revolution, there has been a delay between the inventions and the applications. Textbook writers still explain how debits are found on the left and credits on the right and teach students the subtraction-by-opposition technique that was made obsolete in arithmetic three centuries ago. Programmers then faithfully seek to reflect these medieval ideas on the modern computer screen. Accounting has still to take hold of the new inventions which promise to transform financial reporting as we know it.

Instead of ledgers there will be databases of which financial data will be only a part. Managers will have immediate access to these databases using query routines based on expert systems. A simplified version of these databases will be telephoned to users for transfer onto their laser-operated compact disks, which will contain a generic analysis package that will provide users with menus enabling them to choose the type of financial statement that they want. Companies will not have to choose one revenue recognition method, for example, but will be able to provide a variety of methods to shareholders for their analysis. Dynamic graphics of all kinds will be available, making it possible for users to track the growth of the company visually across the screen. Hypertext will be built in so that users can delve into the level of background information appropriate for the analysis they want to undertake. With all this information at the fingertips of investors, there truly will have been a revolution in accounting. All that is needed to make it a reality is the application of available technology.

CONCLUSION

As the story of accounting has unfolded in this chapter, several things should have become apparent. First, accounting is not a newcomer to the business scene. Early records go back thousands of years. Second, accounting is not synonymous with public accounting. Virtually all its early development was related to the information requirements of management, not investors. Third, accounting is not the creation of white, Anglo-Saxon, Protestant males. Its development depended crucially on events in Africa, in India, in Iraq, in Iran, and elsewhere. Accounting is truly a product of the world. Fourth, accounting is the product of an extraordinary intellectual collaboration between Jews, Christians, and Muslims; it is truly a multicultural endeavor. Fifth, the development of accounting was stimulated by technological changes that were at least as dramatic as those of our day and age.

The period covered in this chapter, from the earliest beginnings of accounting to the late 19th century, is particularly fascinating to today's accounting theorist, because it is the period when accounting was unregulated. One is able, therefore, to get some idea of what accounting might be like in the absence of government regulation.

Its terms and techniques stand as a living reminder that we are the children of our ancestors, that we are one world, and that the richest intellectual times have always occurred in periods when cultures shared their heritages, as in Moorish Spain. The poorest intellectual times have been when dictators have attempted to thwart mankind's natural curiosity.

SUMMARY

This chapter tells the story of accounting from its earliest beginnings to the end of the 19th century. Records of financial transactions exist from 4,000 years ago but it was not until 14th-century Italy that the double-entry system of bookkeeping that we use today was initiated. The chapter traced why it was that modern accounting saw its birth in Italy. That development was attributed to a series of advances in mathematics brought to Europe by the Arabs from India, a variety of technological advances derived mostly from China, and the breakdown of the feudal system in Europe under the weight of war and disease.

In the centuries since its invention, the basic technology of accounting has changed very little, although various aspects of it, particularly financial reporting, have. For instance, as trading ventures gave way to permanent companies and as more capital was needed for industrial ventures, so owners' equity and income accounts grew in importance and accounting began to make periodic reports to owners. Few public companies existed until the 19th century, when incorporation by registration became possible. The British tied incorporation to a mandatory annual audit but no such requirement was made in the United States. The British audit led to the emergence of the accounting profession in the country. English and Scottish accountants came to the United States to audit companies in which the British had invested, leading to the emergence of an accounting profession in this country.

All of these developments took place in a largely laissez-faire environment. This period came to an abrupt end in 1929 with the crash of the stock market and the subsequent depression. The next chapter takes up the story of the role accountants, and particularly public accountants, have played in developing accounting in the 20th century. A further chapter deals specifically with the history and form of regulation that has arisen in the United States to control financial reporting.

QUESTIONS

1. In light of this chapter, discuss in what sense we might speak of "Western" civilization.

2. Draw up a bicolumnar time chart listing major events in world history in one column and developments in accounting in the other. Attempt to project your chart into the future.

3. As a class project building on the special interests of members in the class, draw up time charts for art, music, science, mathematics, and medicine, and compare them with a time chart of major developments in accounting.

4. Many feudal estates were run by women while the men were off fighting their interminable wars. Explore the feminist literature for evidence of the particular contribution women made to the early development of accounting.

5. Compare and contrast the accounting for medieval trading ventures with that for modern consulting or construction contracts. In what way does project-type accounting simplify financial reporting?

6. Is double-entry bookkeeping possible in a communist country such as China? Why or why not?

7. Eugene H. Flegm, Deputy Assistant Comptroller at General Motors Corporation, is very critical of the current dominance of public accountants. He reminds his readers that accounting "evolved essentially as managerial accounting." It is, he says, "an ancient art, which developed from a basic need for a disciplined system of record-keeping and analysis of transactions and not as an offshoot of the economist's search for a definition of intrinsic wealth and value. It is important to keep this genesis in mind."

Required:

Do you agree with Mr. Flegm's reading of the historical record? Discuss why management accountants might feel the historical record to be so important.

8. A. C. Littleton commented: "We may note how different accounting is from the bookkeeping practices of the 15th century, how broad its modern field, how closely refined its definitions and concepts. But it is seldom realized that we have added little to the structure but a body of theory; outside the technique of auditing, cost finding, and budgeting, moderns have contributed relatively little on the practical side. And all of this—the best and most that can be shown—can not compare, as a real contribution, with the first steps taken so long ago."

Required:

Discuss the changes that you think have occurred in accounting since those "first steps taken so long ago."

9. In writing this chapter, the authors selected particular events that they believed were important for telling the story of accounting. One reason for making this selection was space. Another reason was that these events appeared to be significant for understanding material later in the book. Accounting is often compared to history.

Required:

Do accountants select particular events? If you agree that they do, then in what ways do they select those events? Do they choose those events in light of what they expect the rest of the financial story of the company to be?

10. A. C. Littleton provides the following account drawn from a textbook written by Gotlieb in 1546.

1545		*1545*	
To close this trade or account everything on hand on July 17 is found to be the following:		To close this trade or account everything that I am obligated to pay on July 17 is found to be the following:	
to money	2,229.10.3	my capital	2,000. 0.0
to debts	20. 0.0	other creditors	44.16.0
to goods	16. 0.0		
		Both together make	2,044.16.0
		These deducted from the left side gives the profit gained	220.14.3
Together this wealth is	2,265.10.3	Makes together with the profit mentioned	2,265.10.3

Required:

Convert this to a modern-style balance sheet. In what ways does Gotlieb's version differ from yours? In what ways is it similar? Are there any advantages or disadvantages to Gotlieb's presentation over yours?

SELECTED ADDITIONAL READINGS

The literature on accounting history is voluminous. The references below, together with those in the text, will at best give the interested reader a foothold into that literature. The *Accounting Historians Journal* is particularly recommended as a source of further material.

Early Accounting History

American Accounting Association. "Report of the Committee on Accounting History." Supplement to *The Accounting Review*, 1970, pp. 53–64.

Chatfield, Michael. *A History of Accounting Thought*. Rev. ed. New York: Robert E. Krieger Publishing, 1977.

De Roover, Raymond. "New Perspectives on the History of Accounting." *The Accounting Review*, July 1955, pp. 405–20.

Frishkoff, Paul. "Capitalism and the Development of Bookkeeping: A Reconsideration." *The International Journal of Accounting* 5, no. 2, pp. 29–38.

Keister, Orville. "Commercial Record-Keeping in Ancient Mesopotamia." *The Accounting Review*, April 1963, pp. 371–76.

Lee, Geoffrey Alan. "The Development of Italian Bookkeeping, 1211–1300." *Abacus*, December 1973, pp. 137–55.

Lee, Geoffrey Alan. "The Coming of Age of Double Entry: The Giovanni Farolfi Ledger of 1299–1300." *The Accounting Historians Journal*, Fall 1977, pp. 79–96.

Littleton, A. C., and V. K. Zimmerman. *Accounting Theory: Continuity and Change*. Englewood Cliffs, N.J.: Prentice Hall, 1962.

Littleton, A. C., and Basil S. Yamey, eds. *Studies in the History of Accounting*. Homewood, Ill.: Richard D. Irwin, 1956.

Peloubet, Maurice E. "The Historical Background of Accounting." In *Modern Accounting Theory*. Edited by Morton Backer. Englewood Cliffs, N.J.: Prentice Hall, 1966, pp. 5–27.

Peragallo, Edward. *Origin and Evolution of Double-Entry Bookkeeping*. New York: American Institute Publishing Company, 1938.

Williams, John J. "A New Perspective on the Evolution of Double-Entry Bookkeeping." *The Accounting Historians Journal*, Spring 1978, pp. 29–39.

Winjum, James O. "Accounting and the Rise of Capitalism: An Accountant's View." *Journal of Accounting Research*, Autumn 1971, pp. 333–50.

Yamey, Basil. "Accounting and the Rise of Capitalism: Further Notes on a Theme by Sombart." *Journal of Accounting Research*, Autumn 1964, 117–36.

Development of Accounting Theory before Mid-1930s

Carey, John L. *The Rise of the Accounting Profession*, vol. 1. AICPA, 1969.

Daniels, Mortimer B. *Corporation Financial Statements*. Ann Arbor: University of Michigan, 1934.

Previts, Gary John, and Barbara Dubis Merino. *A History of Accounting in America*. New York: John Wiley & Sons, 1979.

ENDNOTES

1. Werner Sombart, *Der Moderne Kapitalismus,* 6th ed., vol. II (Munich: Dunker & Humblot, 1924), pp. 118–19. For a dissenting view see Basil Yamey, "Accounting and the Rise of Capitalism: Further Notes on a Theme by Sombart," *Journal of Accounting Research,* Autumn 1964, p. 132.

2. Raymond de Roover, "The Development of Accounting Prior to Luca Pacioli according to the Account-Books of Medieval Merchants." In *Studies in the History of Accounting.* Edited by A. C. Littleton and B. S. Yamey. Homewood, Ill.: Richard D. Irwin, 1956, p. 115.

3. Geoffrey Alan Lee, "The Coming of Age of Double Entry: The Giovanni Farolfi Ledger of 1299–1300," *The Accounting Historians Journal* 4, no. 2, pp. 79–96.

4. Frater Luca Pacioli, *An Original Translation of the Treatise on Double-Entry Book-keeping* by Pietro Crivelli for the Institute of Book-keepers. New York: Harper & Row, 1924, p. 100.

5. A. C. Littleton, *Accounting Evolution to 1900.* New York: American Institute Publishing Co., 1933, p. 77.

6. Wilmer L. Green, *History and Survey of Accountancy.* New York: Standard Text Press, 1930, p. 101.

7. James Burke, *Connections.* Boston: Little, Brown, 1978, p. 21.

8. Bertil Nystromer, *Four Thousand Years in the Office,* National Office, Management Association, Stockholm, Sweden, 1940. Reprinted in the *World of Business,* vol. 1, Harvard Business School. New York: Simon & Schuster, 1962, p. 62.

9. From Lyndon Lamarr, *Rate Making for Public Utilities.* New York: McGraw-Hill Book Co., 1923, p. 51 quoting from *Drexel Institute Monograph* by C. J. Tilden, February 16, 1916.

10. James Parkes, *A History of the Jewish People.* Middlesex, England: Pelican Books, 1964, pp. 48–53.

11. Pacioli, *An Original Translation,* p. 36.

12. James Burke, *Connections,* p. 25.

13. Research for design by Portuguese Sail Training Association. Replica built by Samuel & Filhos, Vila do Conde, Portugal, launched June 17, 1987, to celebrate Dias 1488–1988, organized by the National Festival Committee, Cape Town, South Africa, and currently on display at the Diaz Museum in Mossel Bay, South Africa where Diaz made his first landing.

14. A. C. Littleton, *Accounting Evolution to 1900.* For a fascinating example of how history repeats itself, read "East of Eden" in *The Economist,* August 12, 1989, on how Eastern Europe is currently seeking to develop the same antecedents as a precondition to a switch to capitalism.

15. Florian Cajori, *A History of Mathematics,* 2nd ed. New York: MacMillan, 1922, pp. 139–41.

16. Pacioli, *An Original Translation,* p. 84.

17. Edward Peragallo, *Origin and Evolution of Double-Entry Bookkeeping.* New York: American Institute Publishing Co., 1938, p. 54.

18. Raymond de Roover, "New Perspectives on the History of Accounting," *The Accounting Review*, July 1955, p. 418.

19. Alistair Cooke, *America*. New York: Alfred A. Knopf, Inc., 1973, pp. 32–33. Accountants prefer the less descriptive title of "expense account."
20. Witt Bowden, Michael Karpovich, and Abbott P. Usher, *An Economic History of Europe since 1750*. New York: American Book Co., 1937, p. 36.
21. James O. Winjum, *The Role of Accounting in the Economic Development of England: 1500–1750*. Champaign: Center for International Education and Research in Accounting, University of Illinois, 1972, p. 214.
22. James Don Edwards, *History of Public Accounting in the United States*. Michigan State University Press, 1960, p. 14.

Chapter 3

The Century of the CPA

CHAPTER OBJECTIVES

After studying this chapter, you will be able to:

Recount the origin of the Financial Accounting Standards Board and its predecessors.

Contrast the organization of the Financial Accounting Standards Board with that of the Committee on Accounting Procedure and the Accounting Principles Board.

Summarize the role of the Securities and Exchange Commission in setting accounting standards.

Describe the origin of auditing in the United States and in Great Britain.

Describe the importance of the concept of uniformity in the history of accounting standard setting and contrast it with the concept of flexibility.

CHAPTER OVERVIEW

The Origin of Regulation

Financial regulation in America began with the railroads in 1887, the year of the founding of the AICPA. It spread to other industries in an attempt to control the giant trusts.

The Crash of 1929

The crash led to the creation of the Securities and Exchange Commission in 1934 and the setting of accounting standards by the Committee on Accounting Procedures in 1938.

The Postwar Boom

The increased participation of ordinary investors in the stock market led to increased demands for uniformity of procedures to permit comparisons and to the formation of the Accounting Principles Board (APB) in 1959.

The Modern Era

An inability to resolve fundamental issues in financial reporting led to the replacement of the APB by the Financial Accounting Standards Board, which is independent of the AICPA and has a full-time board.

Conclusion

In the century since the founding of what is today the AICPA, the numbers and influence of CPAs have grown dramatically.

The period since 1887 might be called the "Century of the Certified Public Accountant" because it is this branch of the profession that has dominated accounting in the United States. So much so that many see public accountants and accountants as one and the same. This dominance is quite astonishing when one considers how long accounting has been in existence and that for most of those thousands of years it was performed by managerial accountants for managers. It is a reminder of how recent our industrial age is, with its myriads of investors, and the resultant need for auditors.

This period could also be called the "Century of Financial Regulation," because for the better part of 100 years the U.S. government has sought to control the flow of financial information. This is equally astonishing when one considers that for thousands of years accounting went completely unregulated. What makes it even more remarkable is that almost all the empirical evidence gathered by academics in the past 20 years indicates that regulation of financial markets is less necessary than regulation of the airline industry, the telephone industry, or the trucking industry, all of which have been deregulated in recent years!

The chapter begins with the railroads and the first government regulatory bodies. From there it moves into the 1930s, tracing the birth of generally accepted accounting principles and the rise of the Securities and Exchange Commission. English experience is used to highlight the peculiarities of the American experience in financial regulation. The drive to uniformity that characterized the postwar years and the reason for that drive in the search for comparability forms the next section. The chapter then leads into the origin, the subsequent history, and the shape of the FASB, which currently has the responsibility for determining GAAP. A short time line of the events covered in this chapter appears in Exhibit 3-1. The chapter concludes with a brief overview.

EXHIBIT 3-1 Century of the CPA

1830		Liverpool-Manchester railroad opens in Great Britain.
1844	Joint Stock Companies Act in Great Britain.	
1886	First meeting of AAPA on December 22.	
1887	AAPA incorporated in New York on August 20.	Formation of the ICC.
1890	Sherman Antitrust Act.	
1906	Hepburn Act permitting ICC to establish uniform accounting rules.	
1914	Clayton Antitrust Act. Creation of FTC. Creation of FRB.	Outbreak of WW I. Opening of Panama Canal.
1916	AAPA becomes AIA.	
1917	*Uniform Accounting* issued by FRB.	
1919		End of WW I.
1926	NYSE requires unaudited annual reports.	
1929	Stock market crash.	
1933	NYSE requires audited annual reports. Truth-in-Securities Act. Glass-Steagal Banking Act.	Franklin Roosevelt becomes President.
1934	Creation of SEC.	
1936	CAP created by AIA.	
1959	APB formed.	
1965	Rule 203 issued.	
1971	Failed attempt to reissue substance of APB 2.	
1973	APB replaced by FASB. *ASR 150* released.	

THE ORIGIN OF REGULATION

Regulation in America began with the railroads. Invented in Great Britain, the railway age began with the opening of the Liverpool and Manchester line in 1830. The greatest development of railways came there in the 1840s, and by 1870 about three-fourths of the country's mileage had been completed. In the United States, on the other hand, railroad construction had its greatest growth from 1878 to 1893, when the massive migrations of Americans across the continent led to a literal frenzy of railroad building.[1] Numerous disputes broke out as railroad barons expropriated farmland for their lines. Also, during the early period of the railroad industry in the United States it was not uncommon for promoters to pay huge dividends out of capital during the early life of a firm. Investors, believing that these dividends were indicative of the future income of the firm, paid high prices for the stock, only to find later that the huge dividends could not be continued without jeopardizing the future operations of the firm. When this became known, the market price of the stock would fall, creating huge losses for long-term investors who were the permanent stockholders.

Interstate Commerce Commission

Individual states attempted to protect their citizens against the activities of the railroad companies, but eventually in 1886, in the case of the Wabash, St. Louis, and Pacific Railroad Company versus Illinois, the Supreme Court held that commerce originating or ending beyond the boundaries of a state was beyond the power of that state to regulate. A year later, Congress established the first federal regulatory agency, the Interstate Commerce Commission (ICC), with specific authority to regulate railroads.[2] The Hepburn Act of 1906 gave the ICC the authority to establish a uniform accounting system for use in establishing appropriate rail rates, thereby setting the stage for the century of regulation of accounting. In particular, that first charter to establish a "uniform" accounting system has haunted accounting ever since.[3]

Railroads were not the only sector of the economy to be experiencing growth and consolidation, causing great concern for many. John D. Rockefeller and the Standard Oil Company led the way by creating a virtual monopoly in the oil business. Other monopolies followed in cottonseed oil (1884); linseed oil (1885); lead, whiskey, and sugar (1887); matches (1889); tobacco (1890); and rubber (1892). Household names like Armour and Swift controlled the beef industry, the Guggenheims the copper industry, the McCormicks the farm equipment business, and the Dukes the tobacco industry. A small handful of fabulously wealthy and often quite ruthless men ran the country between them. Congress responded by passing the Sherman Antitrust Act in 1890. The Act proved relatively ineffectual as companies maneuvered around it, and as the Supreme Court found in favor of the monopolies in several key decisions.

Creation of American Association of Public Accountants

This was the world in which the early American accountants and their colleagues visiting from Britain found themselves. In October 1886, James T. Anyon arrived in New York from London to join the firm of Barrow, Wade, Guthrie & Company.* Edward Guthrie visited the firm in December 1886, and the two of them called a meeting of interested parties to set in motion an organization similar to the recently founded English Institute. (Chapter 2 tells of the founding of the English Institute.) Six or seven attended the first meeting on December 22, 1886. The following day the 10 then present voted to form the American Association of Public Accountants (AAPA), the forerunner to the AICPA. A year later on August 20, 1887, just six months after the founding of the ICC, the AAPA was incorporated in the state of New York with the eight Americans signing the certificate; the two Britons were not permitted by state law to sign.[4]

From its inception, the new organization was determined to influence accounting standards. For instance, as early as 1894 the AAPA adopted a resolution recommending that the order of presentation in the balance sheet should be from the most to the least liquid—clearly indicating an emphasis on providing information for creditors. (British accounting, influenced in its early years more by reporting to investors, reverses the order and continues to show owners' equity in the top left corner and cash in the bottom right of a balance sheet.) A second example came in 1910 when a committee of the Association was appointed to formulate definitions of technical accounting terms in order to give uniformity to their meaning. The AAPA also attempted to make its influence felt in the area of income taxes.

Federal Trade Commission

Dissatisfaction with the inability of the government, despite the passage of the Sherman Antitrust Act, to control the growth of big business brought Woodrow Wilson to power in 1913 on the slogan of a "New Freedom" for the people. Within a year he had enacted the Clayton Antitrust Act. This Act greatly strengthened the government's attack on

---

* This was the first accounting firm in the United States.

monopolies, specifically outlawing interlocking directorates. That same year he created the Federal Trade Commission (FTC) to oversee the provisions of the Act. It had specific authority to investigate any practices that might lead to restraint of trade, and to issue "cease and desist" orders. Also, in 1914, the year that saw the start of World War I and the opening of the Panama Canal, the Federal Reserve Board (FRB) was formed, which, for the first time, created a publicly controlled central banking system in the country.

Within three years the new regulatory bodies perceived a need for standardization in the preparation of financial statements submitted to bankers for credit purposes. The FTC took the lead by, as one writer put it, dropping a bomb on the fledgling accounting profession. It suggested that the FRB maintain a register of accountants considered acceptable to practice before the Board and the Commission. The specter of government regulation of accountants caused an immediate flurry of activity, with the eventual outcome being the publication by the Federal Reserve Board in 1917 of a pamphlet entitled *Uniform Accounting*. The title was chosen in deference to the wishes of Edward N. Hurley, chairman of the FTC at the time. It was wholly inappropriate since the pamphlet said nothing about uniformity or about accounting; it was really an auditing document. The acquiescence of the AAPA in the unfortunate title left as a legacy "the belief held outside the profession that 'uniformity' was *the* solution to all accounting problems."[5] The title was changed a year later to the more descriptive *Approved Methods for the Preparation of Balance-Sheet Statements*, but the damage had already been done.

The significance of the 1917 document for students of accounting lies in its being the first formal statement of acceptable practice produced by American accountants, even though issued by an outside body.* It also marks the beginning of the curious relationship that the governing body of private accountants has had with government regulators ever since.[6] The pamphlet reappeared in 1929 under yet another title: *Verification of Financial Statements*. The 1929 revision was to serve as the official basis for audits of companies listed on the New York Stock Exchange from 1933 onward.

Regulation in Britain

Regulation in Britain took a somewhat different path. As the last chapter pointed out, joint stock companies had risen and fallen with devastating effect in the 17th century. One result was the complete banning of such

---

* The document was essentially the internal audit procedures manual in use at Price Waterhouse, written a few years previously by John C. Scobie (John L. Carey, *The Rise of the Accounting Profession*, vol. 1, New York: AICPA, 1969, p. 133.)

companies in the so-called Bubble Act of 1719. Early in the 19th century, the corporate form of organization was recognized as the most successful means of managing the new enterprises spawned by the Industrial Revolution. In 1825 the Bubble Act was repealed and corporations were permitted to once again obtain charters by direct negotiation with the Crown. Few businesses, though, sought incorporation by this means.

Meanwhile, in 1811 back in the United States, an act was passed enabling manufacturing companies to incorporate simply by registration. The first modern statute permitting incorporation for any lawful business in the United States appeared in Connecticut in 1837. Once this new system of incorporation became available, the number of incorporations increased rapidly. Pressure was placed on the British legislature to make a similar scheme available. Their unfortunate experience with the South Sea Bubble led the British in the Joint Stock Companies Act of 1844 to permit incorporation by registration only if shareholders would accept unlimited liability. (General registration with limited liability was not introduced until the Act of 1855 and in the more complete Companies Act of 1862.*) As a further safeguard, the Act provided for the periodic balancing of the accounts and the presentation of a "full and fair" balance sheet to stockholders. To ensure that such information was disclosed, the Act called for auditors, each of whom had to have at least one share in the company. These auditors were then permitted:

> to employ such accountants and other persons as they may think proper, at the expense of the company, and they shall either make a special report on the said accounts, or simply confirm the same; and such report or confirmation shall be read together with the report of the directors at the ordinary meeting.[7]

In other words, the auditors were not unlike a modern audit committee availing themselves of the services of a public accounting firm.† In short, as Littleton put it, "the audit was an instrument for the shareholders' control over the discharge of the responsibilities which they had delegated."[8]

The British Companies Act was not materially altered until 1908. During this period, the general principle with regard to accounting matters was basically one of noninterference. In the Acts of 1900 and 1908, a trend was started toward the requirement of increasing amounts of specific and general financial disclosures in annual reports of corporations in the United Kingdom and in other countries influenced by the British laws. The 1929 Companies Act introduced sweeping changes, including a requirement that an income statement be disclosed.

---

* Europe, with its medieval commendas, had known limited liability at least as far back as 1408 in Florence.

† The term *audit* (= *audio*) derives from the practice centuries ago, before managers were literate, of accountants reading the accounts to them aloud.

The significant point to emerge from this brief survey of English experience is that their history led to a policy of regulation by disclosure. This is very different from the policy of regulation by uniformity that has dominated American experience. The policy of disclosure was accompanied by an audit, which was lacking in the uniform approach of Americans. The audit requirement led to the earlier development of the accounting profession in Britain than in the United States. As a result, British accountants were a dominant influence in early American accounting.[9]

CHECKPOINTS

---

1. What is the ICC? the FTC? the FRB? When were they founded?
2. What was the South Sea Bubble? (Hint: Review Chapter 2.)
3. List three ways in which the original British auditors differ from today's auditors.

THE CRASH OF 1929

The crash of the New York stock market in 1929 left shock waves which continue to reverberate 60 years later. The decade leading up to 1929 was a good one—too good it would appear in retrospect. The ending of the Great War in 1919 released a pent-up demand for consumer goods, plants, and equipment, which fueled an investment boom. The rapid expansion of new industries such as radios, telephones, motion pictures, and, above all, the automobile added to the boom. Car production alone increased from 485,000 in 1913, through 1,934,000 in 1919, to 5,622,000 in 1929. Unofficial unemployment figures went as low as 3.3 percent. Prices were stable and even declined slightly. Labor productivity increased substantially. Investment on the New York Stock Exchange increased dramatically with average turnover rising fourfold from 1922 through 1929. These were some of the best years the American economy has ever had.

Then in the space of two short months the boom collapsed and the Great Depression was ushered in. The first break in the stock market on September 5 was attributed to the dire predictions of Roger Babson, a respected financial advisor from Wellesley, Massachusetts. In the weeks that followed, government officials and so-called experts tried to allay the public's fears—in vain because on Monday, October 21, and again on Black Thursday, October 24, the market, in record breaking levels of trading, dropped hundreds of millions of dollars in value. That Friday, Herbert Hoover solemnly announced that "the fundamental business of the country . . . is on a sound and prosperous basis." The market responded on Tuesday, October 29, by plummeting almost perpendicularly. By the end of the day vast fortunes were wiped out, stockholders had lost $15 billion, more than one suicide was reputed to have occurred, and a great economy lay in ruins.[10]

The Great Depression was ushered in with all its concomitant misery and deprivation that statistics simply cannot fully capture. Private investment dropped 90 percent. Production fell 56 percent. Arthur Andersen & Co. reported a drop of over one third in its fees between 1929 and 1932.[11] As one business after another closed its doors, millions found themselves out of work, pushing unemployment figures to over 24 percent. Tax collections declined to the point where even school teachers and city employees could not be paid.[12] Soup lines lengthened across the country. More than 9,000 banks shut their doors in this period until by March 9, 1933 all the banks in the country were closed.[13]

To this day, the causes of the crash (and its effects) remain controversial. At the time, business was severely criticized for its perceived role. Accountants did not escape from this criticism unscathed. Adolph Berle, a Columbia University law professor and Gardiner Means, an economist, wrote an extraordinarily influential book that laid out the consequences, as they saw them, of industrial power and wealth being concentrated in the hands of a very few. They attributed this concentration of power, at least in part, to the lack of uniformity in accounting practices and claimed that: "So long as accounting standards are not hardened and the law does not impose any specific canons, directors and their accountants may frame their figures, within limits, much as they choose." They laid the blame in this regard on "the fact that accountants themselves have as yet failed to work out a series of standard rules."[14]

Auditor's Reports Required

The New York Stock Exchange (NYSE) was among the first to react to the crash. In a speech before the convention of the American Institute of Accountants in September 1930, J. M. B. Hoxsey, executive assistant of the Committee on Stock List of the NYSE, severely criticized the lack of uniformity in accounting practice.* He was especially critical of practice in the areas of depreciation and consolidation, where no rules existed at the time. He complained that companies were not even disclosing which methods they were using. He pointed out that many companies still refused to release their revenue numbers on grounds that it would give advantage to competitors. In addition, he accused firms of being ultraconservative in undervaluing their inventory and in taking excessive depreci-

---

* The AAPA became the AIA in 1916.

ation charges. (This was justified by firms as a necessary part of reporting to creditors.) He ended his speech with a plea for the provision of adequate, understandable information for stockholders, arguing that this information should avoid misleading the stockholders and should aid them in determining the true value of their investments.[15]

The implicit criticism of accountants was a little unfair because several years earlier the AIA (the predecessor of the AICPA) had attempted fruitlessly to draw the NYSE into conversation. Also, the NYSE itself had been relatively lax in its listing requirements. Although it was organized as early as 1792 to facilitate the exchange of corporate securities and governmental bonds, it did not attempt to obtain financial statements from listed companies until about 1866.[16] That met with little success until, in 1900, it requested that all companies applying for listing on the Exchange agree to publish annual reports of their financial condition and operating results. This agreement was expanded in 1926 to require all listed companies to publish and submit to stockholders an annual financial report prior to the annual meeting. These statements were not required to be audited, however.

The AIA responded immediately to Hoxsey's speech by creating a Special Committee on Cooperation with Stock Exchanges under the chairmanship of George O. May, chairman of the AIA. One immediate result was a requirement by the NYSE that after July 1, 1933, 89 years after a similar provision in Britain, all companies seeking listing with the NYSE would have to furnish financial statements bearing the certificate of accountants "qualified under the laws of some state or country."[17] These audits were required to comply with the Federal Reserve Board's *Verification of Financial Statements* published in 1929 and to provide an opinion on fairness, consistency, and, for the first time, conformity with "accepted accounting practices."

The New Deal

Despite the manifest response of accountants and the NYSE, many felt that business leaders were not doing enough. This was not completely untrue—many believed that the country had simply moved into the down phase of a temporary business cycle. On July 2, 1932, Franklin Delano Roosevelt, the Democratic nominee for president, went to Chicago to make his acceptance speech and pledged himself "to a new deal for the American people." Herbert Hoover, a probusiness Republican, was swept from office. On March 4, 1933, in an inaugural speech delivered in drenching gusts of rain outside the east wing of the Capitol, the new president began his inaugural speech by asserting his "firm belief that the only thing we have to fear is fear itself." After laying the blame for the Depression squarely at the feet of business, whom he described, using powerful biblical imagery, as "unscrupulous moneychangers desecrating the temple of America," he demanded that the time had come to "restore that temple to the ancient truths," claiming that the "measure of the restoration (would lie) in the extent to which we apply social values more noble than mere monetary profit."[18]

With that, Roosevelt's famous first 100 days in office began. The Emergency Banking Act, enabling the banks to reopen, was passed first on March 9 after just four hours of discussion by Congress. The Truth-in-Securities Act of 1933, requiring the registration of securities offered for public sale and containing provisions against false representations and other fraudulent activities, followed on May 26. The Glass-Steagal Banking Act, creating the Federal Deposit Insurance Corporation (FDIC) and authorizing the 100 percent insurance of bank deposits under $10,000, came on June 16. In three short months then, the financial world of laissez-faire had been transformed into one of intense regulation.[19]

The vast and swift political changes that were sweeping the country caught the accounting profession, which had no strategy for dealing with the proposed legislation, off guard. The situation was further complicated by the existence of two major organizations representing public accountants, the Institute and the Society, and by the lack of leadership from the organization representing management accountants. (The story of these two organizations is told in Chapter 2.) Adding to concerns was the fear that accountants would be exposed to hostile cross examination because many perceived them to be responsible for the crash. As a result, the Institute did not appear at any of the hearings. One outcome was that the first draft of the Truth-in-Securities Act made no mention of auditors at all and later discussions seemed to suggest that government auditors would be appointed. Fortunately, Colonel Arthur H. Carter, senior partner of Haskins and Sells and president of the New York Society of Certified Public Accountants, saved the day for the profession by appearing before a Senate committee and persuading them that audits performed by private accountants were essential for the proper functioning of the Act.[20]

The Securities and Exchange Commission

On June 26, 1934, the Securities and Exchange Commission (SEC) was created by an act of Congress which set up this independent regulatory agency of the U.S. government to administer the Truth-in-Securities Act of 1933, the Securities Exchange Act of 1934, and several other acts. (The 1933 Act was originally administered by the Federal Trade Commission.) The 1934 Act provides for the registration of securities with the SEC before they may be sold to the public (with certain exemptions). The Act provides for the disclosure of specific financial and other information by means of a registration statement and a prospectus, both of which are available for inspection by the public. In addition, the information available to the public must be kept up to date by periodic financial statements and other information filed by the company. Many of these requirements are found in Regulation S-X. Should the financial statements contain a qualification, the SEC will issue a deficiency notice which will ultimately lead, if unresolved, to the delisting of the company's stock and the suspension of trading in that stock.[21]

The Commission has broad powers to prescribe accounting procedures and the form of accounting statements used in filings. From 1936 to 1938, the Commission engaged in heated controversy regarding whether or not the Commission itself should promulgate a set of accounting principles to be followed by all firms in their filings. Due in large part to the persuasiveness of the chief accountant of the SEC, Carmen Blough, and over the dissent of then SEC commissioner and later Supreme Court Justice William O. Douglas, the Commission decided in 1938 to permit the profession to lead the way in the formulation of accounting principles. This policy was issued in the form of *Accounting Series Release No. 4 (ASR 4)*, which stated that the Commission would accept only financial statements prepared in accordance with accounting principles which have "substantial authoritative support" or in accordance with rules, regulations, or other official pronouncements of the Commission or the chief accountant. This action established the policy of relying on generally accepted principles and practices as developed in the private sector by the accounting profession.

Committee on Accounting Procedure

This relationship between the accounting profession and government regulators, which has been a peculiar feature of American accounting, began with the Committee on Accounting Procedure (CAP), founded in 1936 by the AIA. Little was done until 1938 when, in a series of speeches, Carmen Blough threatened that the SEC would prescribe accounting principles if the profession did not respond more swiftly. The AIA responded by expanding the committee's membership from 7 to 21 and by authorizing it to issue pronouncements on matters of accounting principle and procedure. The CAP continued to meet until 1959 and issued 51 bulletins. Eight were subsequently consolidated into *Accounting Terminology Bulletin No. 1*, "Review and Resume"; 31 were consolidated into *Accounting Research Bulletin No. 43*. None bore any particular relationship to the other; some were even inconsistent with one another, reflecting the piecemeal approach of the Committee. One should not be too critical, though, because the Committee did magnificent work in ridding accounting of the worst excesses that characterized financial reporting in the 1920s.

CHECKPOINTS

---

1. What was the CAP? When was it founded? What were its official pronouncements known as?
2. Name at least one pronouncement of the CAP that is still in effect.
3. What is the SEC? When were the securities acts that created it passed?

THE POST-WAR BOOM

The end of World War II in 1945 released a pent-up demand for goods and services by consumers that caused the economy to surge ahead. Jobs boomed and wealth grew. This was the era of bobby-socks and poodle skirts; of Middle America moving out to the suburbs; of "Father Knows Best" on television; and of the Big Band sound with Benny Goodman, Frank Sinatra, and Bing Crosby. Universities prospered as servicemen and -women were able to return to school under the G.I. Bill of Rights. The newly found prosperity of middle-class America persuaded many people to invest in the stock market. In 1940 there were an estimated 4 million stockholders; by 1962 that number had risen to 17 million. Providing these shareholders with appropriate information for their investment decisions was perceived to be a matter of national importance. The standard investment advice given to investors at the time as to how to determine the appropriate stock price of a company was that they should multiply the company's earnings by a price-earnings ratio (PE ratio).

The company's earnings number is a key part of the PE approach to investment because this is the base which is multiplied to arrive at an estimate of the share price. Accounting was seen, therefore, as vitally important. Investors naturally enough expected that higher earnings per share would indicate a better company. Instead, as they were to discover, differences in earnings often meant no more than a different way of accounting for an event. Stated otherwise, differences in accounting earnings were discovered to be as much a matter of definition as of economic substance.

Accounting Alternatives

One problem was that numerous reporting alternatives were open to management at the time. For instance, in 1963, in response to a request from Congress, the SEC was obliged to list areas that could lead to material differences. The long list they drew up is shown in Exhibit 3-2.

EXHIBIT 3-2   Accounting Alternatives

---

1. Valuation of inventories (FIFO versus LIFO, still an option today).
2. Depreciation and depletion (tax versus book, "useful lives," a major option today).
3. Income tax allocation (later partially resolved by *APB 11* and *SFAS 96*).
4. Pensions (later partially resolved by *APB 8* and *SFAS 87*).
5. Research and development costs (later resolved by *SFAS 2*).
6. Goodwill (later resolved by *APB 17*).
7. Time of realizing income (still largely unresolved).
8. All-inclusive versus an operating concept of income statement (still a major issue today as a result of *SFAS 52*).
9. Intercorporate investments (still a question today).
10. Long-term leases (resolved by *SFAS 13*).
11. Principles of consolidation (largely resolved by *SFAS 94*).
12. Business combinations (largely resolved by *APB 16* and *17*).
13. Income measurement in finance companies (resolved by *APB 13*).
14. Intangible costs in the oil and gas industries (still an issue today).[22]

Price Level Adjustments

The relatively serious burst of inflation that accompanied the boom also seriously affected comparability and lead to a debate on "price-level depreciation." Later chapters pick up the details of this debate. In outline, the concern was that with rising prices regular depreciation was not sufficient to cover the replacement cost of plant and equipment. The sum of the annual depreciation charges equals the original cost of the asset. In periods of price stability, the replacement cost equals the original cost; in periods of inflation the replacement cost is greater. A grant from the Rockefeller Foundation funded a five-year study of the problem.[23] Published in 1952, the report recommended that financial statements be adjusted for changes in the general price level. That doughty fighter, George O. May, by now retired, led the argument in favor of adjusting depreciation to "current dollars," but the SEC and public opinion were not in favor of the change so it was duly tabled to be picked up again by the FASB and the SEC 20 years later.

Earning Power Debate

To add to the confusion of investors, a vigorous debate was raging on the appropriate definition of earnings. The AIA argued that the real measure of interest to stockholders was the expected "earning power" of the firm, defined as the firm's ordinary income, excluding extraordinary gains and losses, determined consistently from year to year and uniformly across firms. This was also termed the "current operating income" of the company. The concept of current operating income is not unreasonable; however, the dilemma is that management has been tempted on numerous occasions to call all gains ordinary and all losses extraordinary in an attempt to puff up the potential earning power of the company. Such practices led the SEC and the AAA to call for an "all-inclusive" measure of income, that is, income including all gains and losses, thus preventing management from manipulating the earnings per share number.

Calls for Comparability

As a result of these debates on the most appropriate definition of income, the call went out for uniformity in accounting: the same call that the FTC had made to accountants in 1917. Powerful voices were to press the argument. One of the most powerful was Leonard Spacek, senior partner of Arthur Andersen, who launched a campaign for "comparability." In speech after speech, he denounced the profession, arguing that:

> Comparisons between two companies in the same industry, and to a greater extent between two companies in different industries and between entire industries, are so arbitrary as to be not only worthless, but dangerous.[24]

He attributed this lack of comparability to the inability of the Committee on Accounting Procedure to withstand the pressures of industry. In August 1957, in a speech before the annual convention of the American Accounting Association, he called for the creation of an Accounting Court of Appeals where arguments could be heard, decisions rationally made, and the plethora of reporting alternatives limited.[25] Gradually, he felt, case law would create the conceptual framework for accounting that was sorely needed.

In 1957 the AAA added its voice to the pressure for comparability, although not necessarily for uniformity, by issuing its third revision of *Tentative Principles*, now called *Accounting and Reporting Standards*. It noted that:

> Because the effective use of financial statements involves interperiod and intercompany comparisons, comparability of data over time and among companies is important. The principal barriers to such comparability are distortions resulting from price fluctuations and variations in accounting methods.[26]

However, it added:

> Uniformity of accounting method is neither expected nor necessarily desirable, but reasonable comparability of reported data is essential. . . . When alternative practices in common use give materially different results, the practice

adopted should be stated and the data required to achieve reasonable comparability should be supplied.[27]

This paragraph was added possibly because of the criticism the 1936 edition received for its apparent support of uniformity.[28]

Formation of the Accounting Principles Board

In October 1957, Alvin R. Jennings, the president of the AICPA, responded to these calls for comparability by proposing a new organization to examine basic accounting assumptions, identify "best" principles, and devise new methods to guide industry and the accounting profession.[29] As a result of Jennings' speech, a Special Committee on Research Programs was appointed in December 1957. Its report of December 1958 recommended replacing the Committee on Accounting Procedure with an Accounting Principles Board (APB) and an Accounting Research Division (ARD), both of which were formed in 1959.

The objectives of the APB were to advance the written expression of generally accepted accounting principles, narrow the areas of difference in appropriate practice, and lead in discussions of unsettled and controversial issues. Its official pronouncements were intended to be based primarily on the extensive studies of the Accounting Research Division; its conclusions were to be supported by reasoning; and its opinions were to include minority dissents by members of the Board. The Board was to be composed of 18 to 21 members, selected primarily from the accounting profession but also including representatives of industry, the academic community, and the government (all members of the Institute, however). This last requirement raised the question of whether financial reporting standards should be set by accountants or by users and, if by accountants, whether management accountants should be allowed to participate.

The Turbulent Sixties

Events were to outrun the profession. The relative calm of the 50s was replaced by the turbulence of the 60s with flower children, Elvis Presley, the Beatles, and, dominating everything, the war in Vietnam. John F. Kennedy became the 35th president of the United States in 1960. The economy was struggling, so, to stimulate investment in new factories and machinery, his administration enacted an Investment Tax Credit. Put very simply, when businesses purchased qualifying assets, they were entitled to a reduction in their taxes equal to a percentage of the cost of the new assets. Arguments raged furiously on how one should account for this. Some said that the tax rebate should be shown as a straight reduction in income tax expense. This "flow-through" method gave an immediate boost to reported net income. Others said that, in effect, the tax credit had lowered the cost of the new asset, the benefits of which would be felt over the life of the asset. Accordingly a "deferred" method should be used in which the benefits of the tax credit were taken over the life of the asset. In December 1962 the APB, in only its second opinion and by the narrowest of voting margins, ruled in favor of the deferred method.

The argument was bitter and long. *APB Opinion No. 2 (APB 2)*, which was issued with a considerable minority dissent, was not well received by professional accountants. Several Big Eight accounting firms announced that they would not abide by the Board's decision. The SEC added fuel to the fire by issuing *ASR 96* in which it announced that it would accept both the deferral method and the flow-through method. The resulting confusion forced the APB to reconsider its position and release an amendment (*APB 4*) permitting several alternatives, including the immediate reduction of income tax expense. The loss of face for the new organization was devastating and resulted in much soul searching.

In the belief that the theoretically correct method should rule, the APB made a second attempt in 1971 to mandate the deferral method in the context of *APB 11*, "Accounting for Income Taxes." Opposition from the Internal Revenue Service and others resulted in a clause in the Revenue Act of 1971 specifically providing "that no taxpayer shall be required to use any particular method of accounting for the credit for purposes of financial reports subject to the jurisdiction of any federal agency or reports made to the federal agency."[30] This statement caused the APB to withdraw its recommendation prior to the final draft in order to restudy the case, pointing out the difficulty in resolving conflict in accounting arising from diverse objectives and diverse origins of concepts accepted as valid accounting theory.

Authoritative Opinions

The Opinions of the Accounting Principles Board and effective Accounting Research Bulletins of the former Committee on Accounting Procedure, up to this point, were enforced primarily through the prestige of the Institute. This situation was changed by the investment tax credit controversy. To avoid similar cases in future, where firms simply refused to abide by AICPA rulings, the Council of the Institute adopted recommendations that after 1965 all departures from APB Opinions and effective Accounting Research Bulletins should be disclosed in footnotes to financial statements or in audit reports of members. That is, all Opinions of the APB were considered to constitute substantial authoritative support for generally accepted accounting principles—thus for the first time adding

---

EXHIBIT 3-3   Rule 203

A member [of the AICPA] shall not express an opinion that financial statements are presented in conformity with generally accepted accounting principles if such statements contain any departure from an accounting principle promulgated by the body designated by Council to establish such principles [currently the FASB] which has a material effect on the statements taken as a whole, unless the member can demonstrate that due to unusual circumstances the financial statements would otherwise have been misleading. In such cases his report must describe the departure, the approximate effects thereof, if practicable, and the reasons why compliance with the principle would result in a misleading statement.

---

substance to *ASR 4*, dating back to 1938. Rule 203, with the replacement of the APB by the FASB, is still in force today. (See Exhibit 3-3.)

While the Institute recognizes that there might be other sources of authoritative support, the decision in these cases rests with the reporting member. If individual accountants decide that the principle or procedure does not have substantial authoritative support, they are required to handle the situation in accordance with the Code of Professional Ethics of the Institute. If they decide that it does have support outside official pronouncements, they are required to disclose such departure if material. A failure to disclose is considered to be substandard reporting and is referred to the Practice Review Committee of the Institute. The activities of this committee are concerned with educating the reporting members and encouraging them to comply with the above recommendations. The committee also publishes bulletins periodically to encourage self-discipline among Institute members through education.

CHECKPOINTS

---

1. What was the APB? When was it founded? What were its official pronouncements known as?
2. What is Rule 203 and what is its effect?
3. List three pronouncements of the APB that are still in effect.

THE MODERN ERA

The APB came under almost continuous attack during most of its life for its inability to fulfill its mission to narrow the areas of difference and inconsistency in accounting practice and advance financial reporting in new problem areas. Much of the initial attack came from the accounting profession itself, as typified by Spacek's comments.[31] The writings of "Abe" Briloff, Professor of Accounting at Baruch College, during this period also had a considerable impact in bringing the abuses of financial reporting in these areas to the attention of the financial community.[32] But pressures also came from the SEC and other government agencies. Many predicted that if the APB did not accelerate its progress in establishing accounting principles, the SEC would take the initiative in doing so.[33]

Formation of the Financial Accounting Standards Board

Both the AICPA and the AAA proposed studies on the most effective organization structure for establishing accounting principles. They also wanted to determine the basic objectives of financial accounting, which they hoped would serve as a guide in the establishment of principles. In December 1970, the president of the Institute called a special conference to discuss the establishment of accounting principles. This special conference, consisting of representatives from 21 accounting firms, proposed that two studies be sponsored by the Institute. One study would explore the means by which accounting principles should be established. The other study would review the objectives of financial statements.* Following the approval of these proposals by the board of directors of the Institute, a seven-man group under the chairmanship of Francis M. Wheat, a one-time SEC commissioner, was appointed in March 1971 to study the establishment of accounting standards.

The report of the Wheat Study Group was submitted to the AICPA in March 1972 and adopted by the AICPA Council in June.[34] Its recommendations led in 1973 to the demise of the Accounting Principles Board and to the establishment on July 1 of the Financial Accounting Foundation (FAF), separate from all other professional bodies, the Financial Accounting Standards Board (FASB), and the Financial Accounting Standards Advisory Council (FASAC). The relationship among these three groups is diagrammed in Exhibit 3-4.

Structure and Function

The principal duties of the Foundation, which meets quarterly, are to appoint the members of the FASB and FASAC and to raise the funds for their operations. It is also responsible for appointing the members of the

---

* The Accounting Objectives Study is discussed in Chapter 5.

Government Accounting Standards Board. Thirteen of the trustees of the Foundation represent a variety of interested organizations:

American Accounting Association	1 trustee
American Institute of CPAs	4 trustees
Financial Analysts Federation	1 trustee
Financial Executives Institute	2 trustees
National Association of Accountants	1 trustee
Securities Industry Association	1 trustee
Various governmental accounting groups	3 trustees

EXHIBIT 3-4   The Structure of the Board's Constituency Relationships

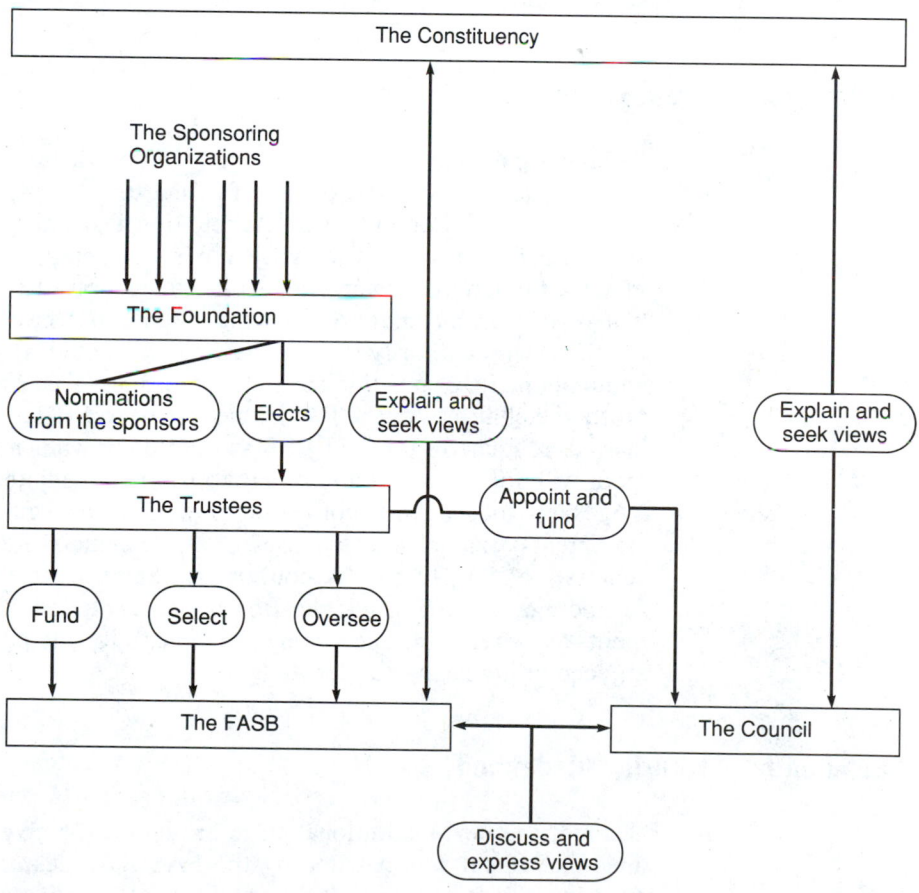

Source: *The Structure of Establishing Financial Accounting Standards.* Report of the Structure Committee, Financial Accounting Foundation, April 1977, p. 48.

Two are appointed by the trustees themselves, and the sixteenth is the senior elected official of the AICPA.

The Financial Accounting Standards Board itself consists of seven full-time members with a background mix that includes "major experience in public accounting, in business or industry, as a user of financial information, and as an accounting educator."[35] Its stated mission is to "establish and improve standards of financial accounting and reporting for the guidance and education of the public including issuers, auditors, and users of financial information."[36] The Financial Accounting Standards Advisory Council has a minimum of 20 members. The Council assists the Standards Board by maintaining contact with business and the accounting profession, by suggesting new issues, by pressing or delaying old issues, and by acting as a sounding board on tentative positions taken by the Board. The Board also draws on the services of a full-time, closely associated research staff.

An Independent Body

Several significant things had to occur to permit the transition from the APB to the FASB. First, the AICPA had to relinquish its primary role, begun with the Committee on Accounting Procedure, in the setting of accounting standards. The AICPA has not relinquished its role completely, though. The year prior to the formation of the FASB, it established the 15-member Accounting Standards Executive Committee (AcSEC) with authority to issue industry audit guides, accounting guides, and statements of position (SOPs). According to Dennis Beresford, currently the chairman of the FASB, the role of AcSEC is "to offer guidance in areas too narrow for the FASB's attention or when a Board pronouncement will not be sufficiently timely to solve immediate problems."[37] The FASB has subsequently converted several of these guides and SOPs into statements: examples include *SFAS 63*, "Financial Reporting by Broadcasters," and *SFAS 66*, "Accounting for Sales of Real Estate." In *SFAS 32* and again in *SFAS 83*, the Board also endorsed AcSEC pronouncements as "preferable accounting principles" for the purpose of justifying an accounting change under *APB 20*.

"Substantial Authority" Redefined

Second, the new institutional structure had to be given some authority. This movement was initiated by the FASB's Rules of Procedure which gave the APB's opinions, to the extent that they had not been superseded or amended, the force of an FASB statement. The AICPA then amended *Rule 203* to give FASB pronouncements official recognition by Certified Public Accountants.[38] The state Boards of Public Accountancy provided another source of authority for the FASB through their licences to accountants to practice in their states. Each enforces compliance with GAAP as set by the FASB through its ethics regulations. State regulation of the profession is also the means by which companies which are not SEC registrants are forced into compliance with GAAP. The Securities and Exchange Commission added their recognition through the following endorsement of the FASB which appeared in *Accounting Series Release No. 150* issued in December 1973:

> the Commission intends to continue its policy of looking to the private sector for leadership and improving accounting principles and standards. . . . [Consequently,] principles, standards and practices promulgated by the FASB in its Statements and Interpretations will be considered by the Commission as having substantial authoritative support, and those contrary to such FASB promulgations will be considered to have no such support.

The SEC did add that it will "continue to identify areas where investor information needs exist and will determine the appropriate methods of disclosure to meet these needs," so the SEC did have some reservations in its endorsement of the FASB. At least government regulation in the United States has not placed rigid controls on the presentation of general financial statements or on the variety of accounting procedures in use. Rigid controls would have stifled the development of accounting theory, and the progress in accounting practice stemming from new ideas in theory.

Due Process

A third change was the introduction of a very deliberate process for arriving at a new standard. The process is outlined in Exhibit 3-5.[39]

The process, in brief, begins with the selection of an item for review. This is possibly the most important step of the process and is a long and

---

EXHIBIT 3-5   Steps in the FASB's Due Process

Preliminary evaluation

Admission to agenda

Early deliberations
(discussion memorandum)

Tentative resolution
(exposure draft)

Further deliberations
(hearings)

Final resolution
(standard)

---

arduous task that involves many different organizations. At least four selection criteria are used:

1. The pervasiveness of the problem, i.e., the extent of the diversity of practice, the number of persons and interest groups affected, and whether the problem is likely to persist or is transitory.

2. The availability of possible solutions and the probability that one of them will materially improve financial reporting.

3. Technical feasibility, i.e., the availability of possible solutions and the state of other Board prospects that could have a bearing on the problem in question.

4. Practical considerations such as the political acceptability of an improved solution to a problem and possible reactions from the SEC or Congress.[40]

An item, once selected, is made the subject of a task force. Often a discussion memorandum will result from the early deliberations and be sent to interested parties across the country for comments. The subsequent reaction is folded into an exposure draft which will again be circulated for comment. Finally, a statement will emerge. Single copies of all these documents are available on request at no cost from the FASB's Publication Office. Subscriptions to these documents are maintained by most accounting libraries. Articulate, well-reasoned responses are welcomed by the Board. The discussion memoranda are of particular interest for students of accounting because they usually lay out the pros and cons of each issue in full.

Emerging Issues Task Force

Given the length of the process, the FASB deemed it necessary to establish a group to attempt to resolve pressing issues rapidly. Accordingly, it created a 16-person permanent Emerging Issues Task Force (EITF) whose chairman is the FASB's Director of Research and Technical Activities. Most of its members are high-level technical experts drawn from accounting firms. Significantly, the SEC's chief accountant is in attendance at each meeting. If a consensus can be reached, the solution is deemed to have authoritative support. If consensus cannot be reached and the problem is considered to fulfill the FASB's other criteria, the issues will be placed on the Board's agenda for later resolution. The EITF's conclusions appear regularly in the *Journal of Accountancy;* a subscription to their decisions is also available from the FASB.

Government Accounting Standards Board

A Government Accounting Standards Board (GASB) was established in 1984 to parallel the FASB and, like it, to report to the Financial Accounting Foundation. The GASB has five members, of whom two serve full-time and three serve part-time. These board members are appointed to five-year terms by the FAF acting in consultation with the Governmental Accounting Standards Advisory Council (GASAC) which, in turn, parallels the FASAC. From the start, sensitive issues of jurisdiction arose. The initial agreement was that the GASB would rule on issues affecting state and local governments, while all other institutions would remain the responsibility of the FASB. Standards set by the prior organization, the National Council on Governmental Accounting (NCGA), would be binding in the absence of a ruling by the GASB. Where neither the GASB nor the NCGA had ruled, the rules of the FASB would hold. In words that now appear prescient, Wharton professor David Solomons wrote:

> It is conceivable that at some time in the future a municipal transportation and a private transportation system, a state university and a private university, may find themselves having to follow divergent accounting standards. It is to be hoped that the two boards, working in close proximity to each other as they do, will be able to avoid such an undesirable state of affairs.

During 1989, as a result of a five-year review, the FAF recommended that the FASB should become, in effect, the senior standard-setting body. A threat by governmentally owned entities to establish a separate standard-setting body led to a brief, but tense, standoff until the recommendation was abandoned.

Ongoing Dissent

One of the difficulties with the APB was that it was composed only of members of the AICPA (including industry and academic members) and was appointed and financed by the Institute. The hope in creating the FASB was that a change to a semi-independent organization with a broader base of support and full-time members would overcome some of these difficulties, but many problems persist. In fact, despite both the efforts to broaden the participants and the institution of elaborate mechanisms to ensure full due process with each issue, controversies continue. Many of the controversies regarding accounting policy relate to a basic philosophy of the Board that reported earnings should highlight differences in risk rather than obscure them through allocations or averaging, and that similar situations should be reported in similar ways. Industry has frequently opposed this policy and lobbied against exposure drafts and statements in oral and written presentations to the Board and to Congress and federal agencies in a number of cases. The adverse consequences perceived by corporate executives include anticipated increases in the cost of capital resulting from a greater fluctuation in reported earnings. As a result of this opposition, the FASB has changed its position on several exposure drafts and reversed itself on a few Statements.[41]

More recently, criticism has focused on the volume of standard setting. While the formation of the FASB was particularly significant, because it moved the locus of standard setting from the hands of the profession more closely into the hands of the user community, it has not seemed to slow the production of regulations. The CAP produced 51 bulletins; the APB issued 31 opinions; by contrast the FASB has issued over 100 statements. Rising complaints from the business community about the sheer quantity of new rules, sometimes described as "accounting indigestion" and "standards overload" have led the FASB to strengthen the role of the FAF in determining the FASB's agenda. Whether this will satisfy the critics, only time will tell.

Broader issues have also impinged on the Board's activities. For instance, a major controversy exploded on the scene in the last years of the Nixon era. During the Watergate investigations in 1973, it was discovered that 17 major companies, including names like Gulf Oil, Lockheed, and Northrop, had made illegal political contributions. The SEC began an investigation to discover whether financial reporting provisions had been broken in the process. Tension heightened when the chairman of United Brands leaped to his death from the 44th floor of the Pan Am building rather than face disgrace. Congressman John E. Moss, chairman of the House committee with oversight responsibilities over the SEC, began an investigation into the effectiveness of the SEC itself. The sole witness heard by the committee was a long-time critic of accounting, Professor Briloff, who recommended, among other things, that the SEC set accounting standards in future. Not surprisingly, the Moss report condemned the profession, and in particular the FASB, claiming that it had "accomplished virtually nothing toward resolving fundamental problems plaguing the profession. These include the plethora of optional 'generally accepted' accounting principles. . . ." They concluded that "to the maximum extent practicable, the SEC should prescribe by rule a framework of *uniform* accounting principles. . . ." History appeared about to repeat itself.

In December 1976, after a year of investigation, a Senate committee under the chairmanship of Senator Lee Metcalf issued a staff report entitled *The Accounting Establishment* which was even more critical of the profession, if that were possible. They claimed that "the Financial Accounting Foundation (FAF) is the non-profit corporation organized by the AICPA and co-sponsored by . . . other private interest groups to operate the Financial Accounting Standards Board (FASB), which sets accounting standards. . . . None of these private interest groups is suited to control the setting of accounting standards which affect the Federal Government and the public." Their recommendation was that Congress itself, not the SEC which they felt was too closely aligned with the accounting profession, establish accounting objectives which would lead to "*uniform and meaningful accounting standards.*" (emphasis added)[42]

The AICPA, understandably afraid that accounting would be swept from the private sector, reacted swiftly. In September 1977 it separated its membership into two groups: the SEC Practice Section and the Private Companies Practice Section. The Institute also established a Public Oversight Board (POB) to exercise oversight of the SEC Practice Section and, simultaneously, instituted peer reviews. Whether this would have satisfied the two leading critics of accounting was never put to the test. Congressman Moss did not return to Congress and Senator Metcalf died in 1978. The Foreign Corrupt Practices Act was passed in December 1977, outlawing bribery of foreign officials and mandating internal financial controls, but with that the interest of Congress appeared to wane. However, memory of how swiftly the private sector can lose its financial responsibilities remains.

CHECKPOINTS

1. How many members does the FASB have? When was it founded? What are its official pronouncements known as?
2. What is the GASB? What is its role?
3. What is the EITF? What is its role?
4. Briefly describe the role of the FAF and its relationship to the FASB.

CONCLUSION

What might one conclude, then, from this recounting of the first century of the AICPA and the regulation of financial reporting which has accompanied it? It is probably fair to say that it has been a dramatic history. When the period began, industrial capitalism was in its infancy. Powerful trusts strode like colossi across the economic scene. Little financial information was provided the general public; there was little expectation that the titans of industry would supply details about their fiefdoms. Yet, less than a century later, a "people's capitalism" was to arise in which ordinary folk would be encouraged to invest in corporations by the provision of relatively copious financial information. That this transformation occurred is partly due to the extraordinarily skillful and dedicated leadership of members of the accounting profession. To name one or even a few would be to slight a legion.

It is also a curious history, though, in which leaders of the profession, politically averse to government regulation and believers in the virtues of private enterprise, found themselves drawn into widespread and pervasive *self*-regulation in order to avoid what they perceived to be the greater evil of *external* regulation. The process continues to this day. The resulting institutional relationship in which the AICPA and the FASB effectively do the bidding of the government and, by so doing, draw off criticism which would otherwise flow to the SEC, is so familiar as to have lost its shock value.

It is a history in which standards have tended to be set reactively rather than proactively. From the outset, accountants have found themselves having to respond to threats of more regulation and increasing uniformity. Seldom have they had the luxury of being able to take the lead. In particular, events have driven accounting away from May's original concept of regulation by disclosure to regulation by uniformity. There are no signs that the pressure for uniformity will abate. On the contrary, companies in other countries, more hedged by government regulation, have never enjoyed this flexibility. It would appear, therefore, that as the globe continues to shrink and accounting standards tend to draw closer to one another, the drive to uniformity might increase rather than decrease. Whether the end result will really be more information for shareholders or simply a more convenient system for bureaucratic enforcement of accounting rules remains to be seen.

SUMMARY

This chapter picks up the story of accounting approximately where the last chapter left off. Its primary focus is on the growth and development of the institutions that are responsible for accounting's regulation: the AICPA (1887), the SEC (1934), the CAP (1936), the APB (1959), and the FASB (1972). It traces the origin of regulation back to the monopolies that were spawned in the late 1800s. Government regulation in that era produced a system of uniform accounting which was originally rejected by public accountants but reluctantly accepted in the 50s and 60s under pressure from the public and the SEC.

The chapter notes that the period since 1887, when the AICPA was founded, has been a momentous one for accounting and accountants. The year the AICPA was formed was also the year that financial regulation began in the railroad sector under the ICC. That regulation was extended to other sectors of the economy in 1914 with the establishment of the FTC, which was intended to control and prevent the abuses of monopoly power. The stock market crash in 1929 led to the creation of the SEC in 1934 to oversee financial reporting. The SEC gave authority to set standards to the private sector in 1938: Subsequently the CAP (1933–59), the APB (1959–72), and the FASB (1972–present) have attempted to fill that mandate.

The choice of organizations consisting primarily of public accountants to set standards for the regulation of accounting ensured that the profession would dominate the private aspect of the regulatory process. Both the CAP and the APB were directly under the control of the AICPA. Neither permitted non-CPAs to participate in the process except by submission of comments. By contrast, the FASB is independent of the AICPA, and its members today primarily represent the user community.

Regulation of accounting began with a call for more uniformity in accounting. Initially, accountants resisted the call, opting for flexibility accompanied by full disclosure. In the decades since, companies have been reluctant to make full disclosure of their accounting practices while, of course, still preferring flexibility. Pressure has mounted, therefore, for uniformity in accounting often concealed in a call for comparability.

The century of the CPA, therefore, has been characterized by three things:

1. Intense regulation quite distinct from the previous centuries of laissez-faire.
2. Domination of the field by public accountants as opposed to managerial accountants.
3. Increasing pressure to move to a uniform accounting system.

Chapter 8 focuses its attention on the nature and problems of regulation. It concludes that one way to legitimize regulation is to provide a theoretical framework from which regulations might be deduced. Chapter 4 homes in on the search for accounting principles to provide this framework. The chapter picks up the story in 1933 when the first GAAP-driven auditor's report appeared and explains how theorists have attempted to define just what generally accepted accounting principles are. Chapter 5 describes the Conceptual Framework that the FASB has developed—the most recent attempt to provide a theoretical constitution for accounting.

QUESTIONS

1. Make a time line showing key dates in accounting from 1887 to 1987. Attach to it what events you can from your other reading. (You might want to fill in the dates when your parents and grandparents were born.) Can you interpret what was happening in accounting at the time in light of the other events?

2. Imagine that you are an accounting historian writing in the 21st century about the late 1980s to early 1990s. What do you think that they will say?

3. The modern development of much business education in the United States dates from the return of GIs to university campuses after the Second World War. Research the history of your business school to see whether there is any relationship at your institution.

4. Pick one of the topics listed in Exhibit 5-1 and read the relevant statement on the subject by the FASB. In what ways did that statement limit the alternatives open to management? How, in your opinion, did those limitations improve the quality of financial reporting?

5. The chapter noted the increasing pressure for uniformity in financial reporting that has been a distinguishing feature of regulation in accounting. Bertrand N. Horwitz and Richard Kolodny comment that "some observers believe that the underlying reason for uniformity is that auditors prefer to operate in a tightly structured environment which minimizes judgment and, thus, the risk of legal liability. . . . An examination of the positions behind the 'uniformity versus flexibility' debate reveals that a major concern has been whether possible legal liabilities would be less under uniformity than under practices which permit alternatives."[43]

a. Based on what you know of accounting, do you agree or disagree with this claim?
b. Are you aware, from your reading in other courses, of specific cases affecting accountants? If so, can you trace the impact they had on financial reporting?
c. Is there any current litigation affecting accountants of which you are aware? If so, what effect do you think it will have on accounting?
d. If you have done an auditing course, or are doing a concurrent auditing course, can you analyze the effect changing perceptions of accountants' legal liability might have had on financial reporting standards in this century?

6. Auditing, and in particular the auditors' report, changed quite dramatically in this century. Consider the following list of reports, noting the dates in which each was being published. Compare these reports to the events of this chapter and see to what extent each reflects the changes discussed in this chapter. What caused the most recent change in auditors' reports to occur?

Statement 1:
We have audited the books and accounts of the ABC Company for the year ended December 31, 1915, and we certify that, in our opinion, the above balance sheet correctly sets forth its position as at the termination of that year and that the accompanying profit and loss account is correct.

Statement 2:
We have examined the accounts of the ABC Company for the year ended December 31, 1931. In our opinion the accompanying balance sheet and statement of profit and loss set forth the financial condition of the company at December 31, 1931, and the results of its operations for the year ended that date.

Statement 3:
We have made an examination of the balance sheet of the ABC Company as at December 31, 1933, and of the statement of income and surplus

for the year 1933. In connection therewith, we examined or tested accounting records of the company and other supporting evidence and obtained information and explanations from officers and employees of the company; we also made a general review of the accounting methods and of the operating and income accounts for the year, but we did not make a detailed audit of the transaction.

In our opinion, based upon such examination, the accompanying balance sheet and related statement of income and surplus fairly present, in accordance with accepted principles of accounting consistently maintained by the company during the year under review, its position at December 31, 1933, and the results of its operations for the year.

Statement 4:

We have examined the balance sheet of the ABC Company as of February 28, 1941, and the statement of income and surplus for the fiscal year then ended, have reviewed the system of internal control and the accounting procedures of the company, and, without making a detailed audit of the transactions, have examined or tested accounting records of the company and other supporting evidence, by methods and to the extent we deemed appropriate. Our examination was made in accordance with generally accepted auditing standards applicable in the circumstances and it included all procedures which we considered necessary.

In our opinion, the accompanying balance sheet and related statements of income and surplus present fairly the position of the ABC Company at February 28, 1941, and the results of its operations for the fiscal year, in conformity with generally accepted accounting principles applied on a basis consistent with that of the preceding year.

PRIMARY SOURCES

Those interested in learning more about the topics covered in this chapter might begin by consulting these sources. Each has numerous excellent citations.

Briloff, Abraham J. *Unaccountable Accounting*. New York: Harper & Row, 1972.

Carey, John L. *The Rise of the Accounting Profession*. New York: American Institute of Certified Public Accountants, 1970.

Edwards, James Don. *History of Public Accounting in the United States*. East Lansing: Michigan State University Press, 1960.

Miller, Paul B.W., and Rodney Redding. *The FASB: The People, the Process, & the Politics*. Homewood, Ill.: Richard D. Irwin, 1986.

Previts, Gary John, and Barbara Merino. *A History of Accounting in America*. John Wiley & Sons, Inc., 1979.

SELECTED ADDITIONAL READINGS

In addition to the works cited in the primary sources and the footnotes in the chapter, the reader is referred to the following authors:

Securities and Exchange Commission

Blough, Carmen. "Development of Accounting Principles in the United States," *Berkeley Symposium on the Foundations of Financial Accounting*. Berkeley: Schools of Business Administration, University of California, 1967, pp. 1–14.

Burton, John C. "Some General and Specific Thoughts on the Accounting Environment." *Journal of Accountancy*, October 1973, pp. 40–46.

Chatov, Robert. *Corporate Financial Reporting*. New York: The Free Press, 1975.

King, Earle C. "SEC May Take Exception to Financial Statements Reflecting Application of Bulletin No. 32," letter to Carmen G. Blough dated December 11, 1947. *Journal of Accountancy*, January 1948, p. 25.

Pines, J. Arnold. "The Securities and Exchange Commission and Accounting Principles." *Law and Contemporary Problems*, Autumn 1965, pp. 727–51.

Previts, Gary John. "The SEC and Its Chief Accountants: Historical Impressions." *Journal of Accountancy*, August 1978, pp. 83–91.

Rappaport, Louis H. *SEC Accounting Practice and Procedure*. 2nd ed. New York: Ronald Press, 1963, chaps. 2 and 3.

Skousen, K. Fred. *An Introduction to the SEC*. 4th ed. Cincinnati: South-Western Publishing Co., 1987.

Sprouse, Robert T. "The SEC-FASB Partnership." *Accounting Horizons*, December 1987, pp. 92–95.

Committee on Accounting Procedure

"History of the Accounting Procedure Committee—from the Final Report." *Journal of Accountancy*, November 1959, pp. 70–71.

Accounting Principles Board

Meyer, Philip E. "The APB's Independence and Its Implications for the FASB." *Journal of Accounting Research*, Spring 1974, pp. 188–96.

Moonitz, Maurice. "Obtaining Agreement on Standards in the Accounting Profession." *Studies in Accounting Research, No. 8*. AAA, 1974.

Rockness, Howard O., and Loren A. Nikolai. "An Assessment of APB Voting Patterns." *Journal of Accounting Research*, Spring 1977, pp. 154–67.

Sprouse, Robert T., and Detlev F. Vagts. "The Accounting Principles Board and Differences and Inconsistencies in Accounting Practice: An Interim Appraisal." *Law and Contemporary Problems*, Autumn 1965, pp. 706–26.

Trueblood, Robert M. "Ten Years of the APB: One Practitioner's Appraisal." *Tempo*, Touche Ross, September 1969, pp. 4–8.

Financial Accounting Standards Board

Brown, Paul R. "A Descriptive Analysis of Select Input Bases of the Financial Accounting Standards Board." *Journal of Accounting Research*, Spring 1981, pp. 232–46.

Newman, D. Paul. "Coalition Formation in the APB and the FASB: Some New Evidence on the Size Principle." *The Accounting Review*, October 1981, pp. 897–909.

Newman, D. Paul. "An Investigation of the Distribution of Power in the APB and FASB." *Journal of Accounting Research*, Spring 1981, pp. 247–62.

Schuetze, Walter P. "The Early Days of the FASB." *World*, Peat, Marwick & Mitchell, Summer 1979, pp. 34–39.

Wishon, Keith. "Plugging the Gaps in GAAP: The FASB's Emerging Issues Task Force." *Journal of Accountancy*, June 1986, pp. 96–105.

ENDNOTES

1. Harold Pollins, "Aspects of Railway Accounting before 1868," in A. C. Littleton and B. Yamey, *Studies in the History of Accounting* (London: Sweet & Maxwell, Ltd., 1956), p. 332.
2. Thomas K. McCraw, "Regulatory Agencies," *Encyclopedia of American Economic History*. Edited by Glenn Porter. (New York: Scribners, 1980).
3. For more details on the links between GAAP and regulation see the Financial Accounting Standards Board Discussion Memorandum, *An Analysis of Issues Related to Effect of Rate Regulation on Accounting for Regulated Enterprises,* FASB, December 31, 1979.
4. James Don Edwards, *History of Public Accounting in the United States* (East Lansing: Michigan State University Press, 1960), pp. 52–57.
5. Gary John Previts and Barbara Dubis Merino, *A History of Accounting in America* (John Wiley & Sons, 1979), p. 189.
6. "Uniform Accounting" also appeared in the June 1919, issue of *Journal of Accountancy,* pp. 401–33 and in *Canadian Chartered Accountant,* July 1917, pp. 5–33.
7. Joint Stock Companies Act, 1845 (Sec. 108).
8. For evidence that voluntary audits preceded this date, see Ross L. Watts & Jerold L. Zimmerman, "Agency Problems, Auditing, and the Theory of the Firm: Some Evidence," *Journal of Law & Economics,* October 1983, pp. 613–33.
9. The current state of accounting regulation in Britain is described in Michael Bromwich, *The Economics of Accounting Standard Setting* (Englewood Cliffs, N.J.: Prentice Hall, 1985).
10. Burton G. Malkiel, *A Random Walk down Wall Street,* 4th ed. (New York: W.W. Norton & Co., 1985).
11. Arthur Andersen, "The First Fifty Years," quoted in John L. Carey, *The Rise of the Accounting Profession,* vol. 1 (New York: AICPA, 1969), p. 154.

12. Allan Nevins and Henry Steele Commager, *A Pocket History of the United States,* 6th rev. ed. (New York: Pocket Books, 1976), p. 414.

13. Robert Aaron Gordon, *Economic Instability and Growth: The American Record* (New York: Harper & Row, 1974).

14. Adolph A. Berle, Jr. and Gardiner C. Means, *The Modern Corporation and Private Property* (New York: Jovanovich, Harcourt, Brace, 1932), pp. 182–83 quoted in Flegm, pp. 70–71.

15. J. M. B. Hoxsey, "Accounting for Investors," *Journal of Accountancy,* 50 (October 1930), pp. 251–84.

16. B. Bernard Greidinger, *Preparation and Certification of Financial Statements* (New York: Ronald Press, 1950), p. 6.

17. Carey, *Rise of the Accounting Profession,* vol. 1, p. 169.

18. Janet Podell and Steven Anzovin, *Speeches of the American Presidents* (New York: The H. W. Wilson Company, 1988).

19. Glenn G. Munn, Encyclopedia of Banking and Finance, 8th revised and expanded ed. by F. L. Garcia (Boston: Bankers Publishing Company, 1983).

20. Carey, *Rise of the Accounting Profession,* vol. 1, pp. 182–92.

21. Eugene H. Flegm, *Accounting* (New York: John Wiley & Sons, 1984), p. 79.

22. Carey, *Rise of the Accounting Profession,* vol. 2, p. 110. Also Flegm, *Accounting,* pp. 87–88.

23. *Changing Concepts of Business Income* (New York: Macmillan, 1952).

24. Carey, *Rise of the Accounting Profession,* vol. 1, p. 77.

25. Leonard Spacek, "The Need for an Accounting Court," *The Accounting Review,* July 1958, pp. 368–79.

26. American Accounting Association, *Accounting and Reporting Standards Underlying Corporate Financial Statements and Supplements* (Madison, Wis: AAA, 1957).

27. Ibid.

28. Carey, *Rise of the Accounting Profession,* vol. 2, p. 9.

29. Alvin R. Jennings, "Present-Day Challenges in Financial Reporting," *Journal of Accountancy,* January 1958, pp. 28–34.

30. Flegm, *Accounting,* p. 96.

31. For example, see "A Search for Fairness," in *Financial Reporting to the Public,* selected addresses by Leonard Spacek (Chicago: Arthur Andersen & Co., 1969).

32. See Abraham J. Briloff, *Unaccountable Accounting* (New York: Harper & Row, 1972) and his articles in *Barron's* and *Forbes* and in several accounting journals during the 1960s.

33. See, for example, Robert N. Anthony, "Showdown on Accounting Principles," *Harvard Business Review,* May–June 1963, pp. 99–106.

34. *Establishing Financial Accounting Standards:* Report of the Study on Establishment of Accounting Principles (New York: AICPA, 1972).

35. *Report of the Special Review Committee to the Board of Trustees* (Financial Accounting Foundation, July 25, 1985), pp. 18–19.

36. *Facts about FASB*, October 1983, p. 1 quoted in Solomons, *Making Accounting Policy,* pp. 34–35.

37. Dennis R. Beresford, "Emerging Problems: How the Profession Is Coping," *Journal of Accountancy,* February 1981, pp. 57–60.

38. Under AICPA Rules of Conduct, Rule 203 as amended, May 1973 and May 1979.
39. Paul B. W. Miller and Rodney Redding, *The FASB: The People, the Process, & the Politics* (Homewood, Ill.: Richard D. Irwin, 1986), p. 59.
40. David Solomons, *Making Accounting Policy* (Oxford University Press, 1986), p. 36.
41. For example, see FASB Exposure Draft, "Financial Reporting in Units of General Purchasing Power" of December 31, 1974; Exposure Draft "Constant Dollar Accounting" of March 2, 1979; and FASB Statement No. 33, "Financial Reporting and Changing Prices" of September 1979.
42. Quoted in Flegm, *Accounting,* pp. 142–50.
43. "The Economic Effects of Involuntary Uniformity in the Financial Reporting of R&D Expenditures," *Journal of Accounting Research,* Supplement 1980, p. 42.

Chapter 4

The Search for Principles

CHAPTER OBJECTIVES

After studying this chapter, you will be able to:

Trace the development of accounting thought over the past 50 years.

Contrast the various meanings of the word *principles*.

Define what is meant by *generally accepted accounting principles*.

Analyze the impact the small investor has had on the development of accounting practice.

Define what is meant by a postulate in accounting.

Define what a standard is and how it differs from a principle.

Explain why the search for principles was so frustrating.

CHAPTER OVERVIEW

The Search Begins

The attempt to define *generally accepted accounting principles* is traced from the invention of the term in the 1930s to the end of World War II.

The Search Quickens

The end of World War II brought increasing prosperity, an emphasis on investing this new wealth in the stock market, and a renewed emphasis on sound financial reporting.

The Search Shifts

By the late 1960s, it was apparent that *principles* were hard to define and the search turned to a consideration of *standards,* which were seen as less pretentious.

The Search in Retrospect

Principles are difficult to define because of the inherent complexity of accounting theory. Their implications are sometimes difficult to sustain because of the economic consequences that flow from accounting information.

Conclusion

Broad concepts, whether called principles, postulates, or standards, are a necessary part of accounting. Nevertheless, it must never be forgotten that as a social science, accounting depends upon the wisdom, judgment, and integrity of accountants.

Every audited financial statement today is accompanied by an auditor's report attesting to its compliance with "generally accepted accounting principles." But what exactly are these principles? Are they the same that one finds in a "Principles of Accounting" text? And who decides what principles are accepted and how widely they must be accepted before they are considered to be generally accepted? What happens if these principles are required by the SEC, say, but not approved by practicing accountants, as has happened? Do they then conflict with generally accepted accounting principles? What happens when the SEC's chief accountant concludes that "procedures so generally followed among accountants as to constitute substantial precedent are not always fundamentally sound?"[1] And, just why do we need these principles in the first place? These questions have never been answered satisfactorily and have set the stage for an ongoing debate on just what precisely constitutes generally accepted accounting principles (GAAP), just what exactly the term *principles* means, and how these principles might be derived, if at all.

This chapter outlines that debate as it has developed over the past 50 or 60 years. The first section relates how the word came to be chosen and the subsequent efforts to give it meaning. The second section develops an approach to theory building which uses the concept of postulates. The third section turns to the more recent approach based on objectives and standards. The rest of the chapter is a critical overview of the theoretical framework developed by the FASB. Later chapters develop at more length the revolutionary developments in theory which have taken place in the past two decades.

THE SEARCH BEGINS*

The precise nature of accounting principles was a matter for debate from the very start as Exhibit 4-1 shows. The word *principle* derives from the Latin *principe*, meaning first in the sense of elementary. Since the first texts accounting students encounter are elementary, the term *Principles of Accounting* is wholly appropriate. What we study in a first accounting course are its principles in the sense of the material being first in time and first in terms of difficulty. However, these topics are not necessarily the principles of the subject in the sense of being first in logic or the subject's foundation stones. One learns, for instance, a great deal of mathematics in school and in college without ever touching the deep philosophical questions which form the foundations of that subject. Many use probability tables in statistics without ever delving into the precise nature of uncertainty. The same is true for accounting. Principles of Accounting might be a first course, but it is hardly a course in the fundamental truths of accounting. For a study of these, as opposed to an introduction to the elements of its practice, one must turn to a course in accounting theory.

First Efforts

Many individuals and groups began work in the 1930s on elucidating what they thought should be meant by accounting principles. First out of the block, somewhat to the chagrin of the AIA, was the American Accounting Association (AAA). Under the leadership of Michigan professor William Paton, who was appointed the first research director of the AAA at the start of 1936, the AAA published in June 1936 the first of what would be a series of brief monographs on the principles of accounting. The 1936 edition was entitled *A Tentative Statement of Accounting Principles Underlying Corporate Financial Statements*.[5] Its expressed hope was that it would be possible "to agree upon a foundation of underlying considerations which will tend to eliminate random variations in accounting procedure resulting not from the peculiarities of individual enterprises, but rather from the varying ideas of financiers and corporate executives as to what will be expedient, plausible, or persuasive to investors at a given point of time." In particular, the Association sought to eliminate the confusion arising from the revaluation of assets up and down according to changes in price levels and expected business conditions by emphasizing the cost basis of accounting. Some saw in this action an attempt to impose a uniform system on accounting; it really just reflected the distrust of

---

* The title of this chapter derives from one in Stephen Gilman's *Accounting Concepts of Profit* (1939). It was also used as the title of Reed Storey's monograph (1964).

academics for the subjective judgments of financial managers. A review of the accounting practices of the time certainly provides a good basis for their distrust; unfortunately, distrust does not necessarily lead to good accounting theory.

Four years after the appearance of the Tentative Statement, Paton and Illinois professor A. C. Littleton, both members of the 1936 Executive Committee of the American Accounting Association, published *An Introduction to Corporate Accounting Standards*.[6] The intention of the authors

---

EXHIBIT 4-1   The Nature of Principles

Gilbert Byrne, in his prize-winning and influential paper presented at the Fiftieth Anniversary Celebration of the American Institute of Accountants (AIA) in 1937, insisted that principles were fundamental truths.[2] Or, as Webster's *New International Dictionary* puts it: "A fundamental truth; a comprehensive law or doctrine, from which others are derived, or on which others are founded; a general truth; an elementary proposition or fundamental assumption; a maxim; an axiom; a postulate."

George May was to respond swiftly to Byrne's suggestion that principles should be fundamental truths, arguing that the more appropriate definition was one from the Oxford dictionary, reading: "A general law or rule adopted or professed as a guide to action; a settled ground or basis of conduct or practice." He claimed that this was the meaning that the AIA committee intended when it used the term.[3] One has to give credence to May's interpretation both because he essentially wrote the report and because this connotation corresponds most closely with the examples of principles that were attached to May's letter of September 22, 1932.* Freely transcribed, these read:

1. Profit shall not be recognized before a sale occurs.
2. All expenses should be charged to the income statement and not to retained earnings.
3. The retained earnings of a new acquisition, earned prior to acquisition, may not be added to the retained earnings of the acquirer, that is, the purchase method rather than the pooling method should be used.
4. Dividends on treasury stock are not income to the company although treasury stock may be treated as an asset.
5. Loans to related parties should be segregated from other loans.[4]

These so-called principles are not Byrne's broad underlying truths. They are much more in the nature of May's rules. In fact, these principles presuppose the existence of the whole set of fundamentals that form the body of accounting: They assume debits and credits, balance sheets and income statements, and so on. Nevertheless, they do give some rather fascinating insight into the way the known body of accounting was being manipulated at the time.

---

* The background to this letter is described in the last chapter and in Chapter 8.

was to present a framework of accounting theory conceived to be a "coherent, coordinated, and consistent body of doctrine" which would support the principles enunciated in the 1936 statement. Significantly, they avoided the word *principles*, replacing it with the word *standards* because they felt the former suggested "a universality which obviously cannot exist in a service institution such as accounting." The monograph is considered by many to be a classic and has sold tens of thousands of copies. It is particularly noteworthy for its development of the concept of matching costs to revenues, the process taught to every accounting student for over 50 years now. See Exhibit 4-2 for Littleton's description of the meaning of matching.

Subsequent editions of the AAA's 1936 statement did not make substantive changes in the content but, rather fascinatingly, the title kept changing, indicating each time the current state of academic theory. The 1941 edition, for instance, dropped the adjective *tentative* in the title, while the 1948 edition substituted the term *concepts and standards* for the term *principles*. The series ran its course in 1957 in a document summarizing all the previous work. Here, for the first time, the Association allowed that value was an appropriate measure for assets and equal to the "sum of the future market prices of all streams of service to be derived, discounted by probability and interest factors to their present worths."[8]

The precise impact of these statements is hard to determine because, due to limited resources and the theoretical orientation of the members, the general approach was that of establishing broad basic principles rather

---

EXHIBIT 4-2   Matching Expenses with Revenues

Littleton defined matching in these words:

The central problem of accounting is to bring into association, in the present, the revenues identified with the present and their related costs, and to bring into association, in the future, the revenues identified with the future and their related costs. In solving this problem, those who use accounting are, in effect, matching enterprise efforts and accomplishments. Some efforts are effective in the present; they are measured by the costs (effort) currently deductible from revenue (accomplishment); they are the revenue costs of the present. Other efforts are expected to be effective in the future; they are measured by the costs that are deferred as being revenue costs of the future (assets). Some efforts prove ineffective in the present and are judged unlikely to be effective in the future; they are measured by the costs that must be currently deducted from revenue as recognized losses. The fundamental problem of accounting therefore is to cut through a continuing stream of costs and correctly assign portions to the present and to the future. . . .[7]

This view was to dominate accounting thought for several decades.

---

than specific rules; however, many members of the AAA served, and continue to serve, on rule-making committees where the broad principles were applied. Among the changes induced by altering theoretical perspectives was the nature of the presumed user group. The definition of this group has tended to broaden over the years. There has also been a consistent recommendation of the all-inclusive concept of income, partly as a result of that distrust of academics of the individual judgments of accountants and managements of corporations alluded to above. This judgment coincided with the views of the SEC and ultimately won out as the ruling view.

Early Foundations

The AAA's *Tentative Statement on Accounting Principles*, described in the previous section, did not appear in a vacuum. Paton himself had written a doctoral thesis which was published under the title of *Accounting Theory* in 1922. The book is radical even by today's standards. In it he espouses the "liberal view that, ideally, all bona fide value changes in

---

EXHIBIT 4-3　Paton's Postulates

According to Paton, only if "the accountant sees clearly the foundation upon which she (or he) is standing" will she avoid "improper applications and erroneous general conclusions." Toward that end he listed six postulates together with their limitations:

1. The *existence of a distinct business entity*: This is universally assumed even though in reality it is only a figure of speech.
2. The *continuity of this entity*: The assumption of a going concern is largely one of convenience.
3. The *balance-sheet equation*: The equality occurs only because we "plug" whatever gaps might exist by adjusting the owners' equity accounts.
4. The *monetary* postulate: This is the unfounded assumption that "a statement of assets and liabilities in dollars and cents is a complete representation of the financial condition of the enterprise on the date of the statement."
5. The *cost* postulate: This is the equally unfounded assumption that "cost gives actual value for purposes of initial statement."
6. The *revenue recognition* postulate: This assumes that "net revenue or profit suddenly appears, full-blown, on some specific occasion, commonly that of the sale," which is clearly not true.

Never before, and seldom since, has an author so succinctly and so beautifully captured the limitations of historical cost accounting. As with Pacioli, Paton's acerbic comments read as freshly today as when they were written.

---

either direction, from whatever cause, should be reflected in the accounts. . . ."[9] "It is above all important," he says, "that the accountant's statements present as accurate a picture of *current* data in terms of the actual dollar as of the date of the statement."[10] He is equally insistent that by "no reasonable line of analysis can the interest paid to the bondholder be classed with operating expense while the return to the stockholder is treated as a distribution of net revenue," that is, what we now call net income.[11] The book ends with its list of postulates appearing in Exhibit 4-3, which he describes as the basic assumptions of accounting.

Paton was not the only one to make an early and notable contribution to the literature. Stanford professor John Canning made a valuable contribution to accounting theory in his *Economics of Accountancy*.[12] The subtitle, "A Critical Analysis of Accounting Theory," helps explain his contribution. While Canning acknowledged in his preface that he drew from the writings of Cole, Hatfield, McKinsey, Montgomery, Paton, Stevenson, and Sprague, he also compared then-current accounting thought with economic theory, particularly with that set forth by the American economist Irving Fisher. The two most important areas discussed by Canning were asset valuation and income measurement. His comments on these areas and his definitions of assets and liabilities, rooted as they are in economics, are still quoted today in FASB discussion memoranda and appear in later chapters of this book.

The Rise of the Investor

The most important shift in basic accounting thought coming out of these writings and the discussions of the late 1920s and early 1930s was the change in the objective of accounting from that of presenting information to management and creditors to that of providing financial information for investors and stockholders. The pressure for this change in objective came from the financial sector and stock exchanges rather than from accountants. The rapid growth in the widespread ownership of corporations, particularly during the first few years following World War I, created new needs for accounting information. The average number of shares listed on the New York Stock Exchange in 1900 was about 60 million, compared with 180 million in 1917 and 1,212 million in 1930 (unadjusted for stock splits).[13]

The change in the objective of financial statements led to:

1. A de-emphasis of the balance sheet as a statement of values.
2. A consequent increased emphasis on the income statement and a uniform concept of income.
3. A need for full disclosure of relevant financial information, by present-

ing more complete financial statements and increasing the use of foot-notes.

4. An emphasis on consistency in reporting, particularly with respect to the income statement.

There is also evidence of an increasingly arbitrary use during this period of deferrals of losses and income items to permit a smoothing of income from one year to the next. These actions led to the attempts in the 1930s to establish better standards for the presentation of the income statement.

These changes are evident in the literature and in the pronouncements of several interested organizations before and after 1930. It is interesting to note that these changes in accounting thought were not the direct result of the stock market crash of 1929 nor the Great Depression of the 1930s, but rather they were the result of institutional changes which had begun much earlier and to which accountants had not yet adapted. Of course they were made more urgent by the events of the period.

Other Notable Attempts

In 1938, at the request of the Haskins & Sells Foundation, Harvard professor Thomas Henry Sanders, California professor Henry Rand Hatfield, and Yale Law School professor Underhill Moore published *A Statement of Accounting Principles,*[14] which purported to "set forth the principles and rules of accounting which dictate what should appear in a balance-sheet and an income statement and in the accounts from which they are compiled." The content of the monograph reveals that the authors were more concerned with accepted practices—practices which deviate quite radically in certain instances from accepted practice today. For instance, the authors would permit companies to defer losses by placing them on the balance sheet as assets and amortize them slowly over time. They also would permit companies to record bond discounts as assets.[15] It was practices such as these which caused the FASB to set its face so firmly against deferred assets and liabilities. The authors do devote a small section of the monograph to what they call *conventions*, which they describe as "hardened practices" underlying the preparation of balance sheets. They include the historical-cost basis for assets and the going-concern concept as two examples of conventions. For all its faults, this monograph is a fascinating repository of accounting practice at the time and an important source of data for positive research in accounting.[16]

Stephen Gilman's *Accounting Concepts of Profit,* the first comprehensive discussion of accounting theory since the shift in emphasis from the balance sheet to the income statement point of view, effectively closes this period of accounting theory development.[17] He attempts to sort out the terminological tangle caused by the introduction of the word *principles* into the audit report. He distinguishes between rules, which can be made, and principles, which cannot. He suggests that the term *doctrine* more accurately describes the "teachings" of accountants. He also points out that many books which describe themselves as Principles of Accounting do not even have the word *principles* in the index.[18] But in the end the problem of how to define generally accepted accounting principles was seen to lie deeper than mere semantics. The debate over words hid a far more serious issue: who was to determine the disclosure of financial information and by what means.

CHECKPOINTS

1. What do you think a principle is? How does your own definition compare with that of May and Byrne? On whose side are you?
2. Explain in your own words why Paton and Littleton preferred the term *standards* to the term *principles*.
3. What did Paton mean by the term *postulate*? How does this compare with Byrne's use of the word *principle*?
4. What impact did returning GIs have on accounting and why?
5. Why did the AAA in 1936 think principles were important?

THE SEARCH QUICKENS*

The search for broad accounting principles was renewed immediately after the war. Again, the AAA led the way by releasing its 1948 revision of the Tentative Principles now relabeled *Accounting Concepts and Standards*.[19] The AIA's Committee on Accounting Procedures also resumed its work and by 1953 had issued 17 new bulletins. As before, though, they were piecemeal in approach and not intended to forward the search of broad principles. Also, they were not binding on the membership of the AIA. They were required only to find *substantial authority* for the practices they selected.

The Accounting Research Division

In 1959, acting on the recommendations of the Special Committee on Research Programs, the Institute was reorganized to advance "the writ-

---

* This section of the chapter relies heavily on John L. Carey, *The Rise of the Accounting Profession,* vol. II (AICPA, 1970).

ten expression of what constitutes generally accepted accounting principles, for the guidance of its members and of others.''[20] One of the objectives of the reorganization was to be able to attack the broad problems of financial accounting at four levels:

1. Establishment of basic postulates.
2. Formulation of broad principles.
3. Development of rules or other guides for the application of principles in specific situations.
4. Research.

A permanent accounting research staff was recruited to carry out the research program with the intent that the results of its efforts, ''as adopted by the [Accounting Principles] Board, should serve as the foundation for the entire body of future pronouncements by the Institute on accounting matters, to which each new release should be related.''[21]

California professor Maurice Moonitz, the newly appointed research director and a disciple of J. B. Canning, whose work was mentioned earlier, was commissioned to produce *Accounting Research Study No. 1 (ARS 1)* on the basic postulates in accounting.[22] Some examples of postulates appear in Exhibit 4-4. Moonitz and Robert T. Sprouse, then a professor at Stanford and later to become a member of the Financial Accounting Standards Board, were subsequently commissioned to produce *Accounting Research Study No. 3 (ARS 3)* on the subject of principles of accounting.[23] Some examples of principles appear in Exhibit 4-5.

Postulates in *ARS 1* were seen as basic assumptions or fundamental propositions concerning the economic, political, and sociological environment in which accounting must operate.[24] As the American Institute of Certified Public Accountants (AICPA) put it in 1958:

> Postulates are few in number and are the basic assumptions on which principles rest. They necessarily are derived from the economic and political environment and from the modes of thought and customs of all segments of the business community. The profession, however, should make clear their understanding and interpretation of what they are, to provide a meaningful foundation for the formulation of principles and the development of rules or other guides for the application of principles in specific situations.[25]

It was argued then that, if principles of accounting were actually just rules, it should be possible to deduce them from the more basic assumptions called *postulates*.[26]

The response to these two studies, which appeared in 1961 and 1962, respectively, was swift and fairly dramatic. They were issued with a loose insert stating that they were not acceptable to the Board because they were too different from generally accepted accounting principles at the time. Comments from individual Board members were published at the end of the studies. Leonard Spacek, managing partner of Arthur Andersen, commented that there was only one postulate. He summed this up as

---

EXHIBIT 4-4   *ARS 1* and Postulates

Examples of postulates in *ARS 1* included assertions about the environment such as:

Economic activity is carried on through specific units or entities. Any report on the activity must identify clearly the particular unit or entity involved.

It also included assertions about the accounting process such as:

The results of the accounting process are expressed in a set of fundamentally related financial statements which articulate with each other and rest upon the same underlying data.

And, finally, there were also a number of normative postulates characterized by the use of the word "should," such as:

Accounting reports should disclose that which is necessary to make them not misleading.

The basic criteria for selecting postulates were that:

1. They had to be relevant to the development of accounting logic; that is, they had to serve as a foundation for the logical derivation of further propositions.
2. They had to be accepted as valid by the participants in the discussion as either being true or providing a useful starting point as an assumption of accounting logic. It was not seen as necessary that the postulates be true or even realistic. For example, it was argued, the assumption in economics of a perfectly competitive society has never been strictly true, but it has provided useful insights into the working of the economic system.

---

the need for fairness "to all segments of the business community."[29] William W. Werntz, who had been chief accountant of the SEC, went further, saying that he thought "it would be a disservice for this study to be published in its present form."[30] Florida professor Harvey Deinzer later argued that he could see no connection between the postulates and the principles.[31]

As a result of the rejection of *ARS 1* and *3*, Paul Grady was commissioned to produce a review of existing accounting principles. This study appeared in *Accounting Research Study No. 7 (ARS 7)* titled an "Inventory of Generally Accepted Accounting Principles for Business Enterprises." The purposes of this study were to discuss the basic concepts of accepted accounting principles, to summarize accepted principles and practices, and to summarize the pronouncements of the Accounting Principles Board and its predecessor committee. Like other statements before it, *ARS 7* rejected the imposition of a single uniform system of accounting, instead emphasizing diversity in accounting as a basic concept. One major

---

EXHIBIT 4-5   *ARS 3* and the Principle of Revenue Recognition

---

Among the principles, which were purportedly derived from the postulates of *ARS 1,* was the assertion that:

Profit is attributable to the whole process of business activity. Any rule or procedure, therefore, which assigns profit to a portion of the whole process should be continuously re-examined to determine the extent to which it introduces bias into the reporting of the amount of profit assigned to specific periods of time.[27]

Justification for this principle was grounded on a passage from a book written by George O. May two years after his retirement and subtitled *A Distillation of Experience.* In it, he confesses to the dubious nature of the revenue realization principle as propounded by his own committee 10 years earlier:

The problem of allocation to particular short periods obviously offers great difficulty— indeed, it is the point at which conventional treatment becomes indispensable, and it must be recognized that some conventions are scarcely in harmony with the facts. Manifestly, when a laborious process of manufacture and sale culminates in the delivery of the product at a profit, that profit is not attributable, except conventionally, to the moment when the sale or delivery occurred. The accounting convention which makes such an attribution is justified only by its demonstrated practical utility.[28]

ARS 3's acceptance of May's argument was one of the factors that led to its rejection.

CHECKPOINTS

1. Several examples of postulates are provided in this chapter. Pick one and see what, if anything, in accounting you can deduce from it. If you cannot deduce something, can you exclude something, that is, is there something that we do not do because of the postulate?
2. Explain what you understand by the term *matching.* Use an example such as wages to make your point clear. Compare your explanation with that of Littleton, May, and the authors of *ARS 3.*
3. Compare the various definitions of revenue recognition provided in this chapter. How comfortable are you with the position of the authors in *ARS 3?*
4. Why were the recommendations of the research division of the APB rejected?

difference between this study and *ARS 1* and *3* was the emphasis on inductive and pragmatic methods instead of the deductive method.

   While this study had greater acceptance by the accounting profession than did *ARS 1* and *3*, it did not lead to a statement of broad principles of accounting. Accordingly, accounting research studies continued to be ad hoc studies without a common foundation supporting them. Each study was based on the researcher's basic fundamental concepts and his findings in the specific area. In fact, according to Ohio professor Thomas Burns, only a little more than a third of the APB's Opinions could be linked even casually with prior research studies.[32]

THE SEARCH SHIFTS

Attacks on the postulate/principle approach began to mount from other directions. Berkeley professor William Vatter questioned the entire enterprise.[33] He argued first that before one could begin to address any issues in accounting, one had to establish an aim or purpose. He suggested, therefore, that objectives, instead of postulates, are the primary blocks in building an accounting theory. Principles, he then argued, were the means by which objectives could be achieved. They would be subject to "conventions," such as an agreement to make annual financial reports; and to "doctrines," such as the desirability of consistency in reporting. Postulates in such a framework were just "fillers" to complete broken chains of logic. In a perfect theory, he said, there would be no postulates.

A Statement of Basic Accounting Theory

Vatter's attack on the postulate/principle approach was reflected in a new document to appear from the American Accounting Association in 1966, entitled *A Statement of Basic Accounting Theory* and known by its acronym, ASOBAT. It began with an assertion that accounting is "the process of identifying, measuring, and communicating economic information to permit informed judgments and decisions by users of the information." ASOBAT thereby stamped itself as the first of the new statements of accounting theory to be user-oriented. That is not to say that accounting was not perceived as user-oriented prior to this. Paton, for instance, as early as 1922 insisted that "The function of accounting and explanations of accounting principles and procedure must be stated immediately in terms of the needs and purposes of the owners. . . ."[34] Nevertheless, ASOBAT was the first statement to insist that the desires of the user should be put ahead of the views and opinions of the experts, that is, the accountants who prepare the reports. To determine user desires, the presumed objectives of accounting were listed (see Exhibit 4-6 for details).

Other lists of objectives have been drawn up since, but they all essentially come down to the same set—and face the same problem: how to link user objectives to the development of principles, and how to link the

---

EXHIBIT 4-6   ASOBAT

Objectives
1. Making decisions concerning the use of limited resources, including the identification of crucial decision areas, and determination of objectives and goals that is, decisions by shareholders, creditors, and others about investment.
2. Effectively directing and controlling an organization's human and material resources, that is, decisions by management about the company.
3. Maintaining and reporting on the custodianship of resources, that is, the stewardship or custodial function of management.
4. Facilitating social functions and controls, that is, facilitating the operations of organized society for the welfare of all.

Standards
1. Relevance, that is, it must be usefully associated with the action it is designed to facilitate.
2. Verifiability, that is, qualified individuals working independently should arrive at the same result.
3. Freedom from bias, that is, it should not favor one set of users at the expense of another.
4. Quantifiability, that is, measurement should be possible although not necessarily monetary measurement.

Guidelines
1. Appropriateness to expected use.
2. Disclosure of significant relationships.
3. Inclusion of environmental information.
4. Uniformity of practice within and among entities.
5. Consistency of practices over time.

---

provision of accounting information with the "welfare of all." The link between objectives and principles is notoriously weak, especially when users are heterogeneous. For instance, do creditors want the same information as investors? Do sophisticated investors want the same information as naive investors? Do we even know? The existence of heterogeneous users with widely varying utility functions also poses an enormous theoretical social welfare problem that ASOBAT did not attempt to address. Not unimportantly, the list was noteworthy for reintroducing management's desires for financial information.

ASOBAT attempted to circumvent the difficulties of determining the desires of particular investors by suggesting that the provision of financial information should be subject to four *standards* or *criteria*. These were to be accompanied by five *guidelines*. (The FASB now terms all of these *qualitative characteristics*.) The committee concluded that the only way this new approach could be realized was by *data expansion*, that is, by reporting multiple measures and several income numbers "to meet a reasonably wide range of needs." In particular, the statement recommended the presentation of both historical and current costs, with separate columns showing the presentation of the statement in terms of each. In addition, the recommended statement would show net gains separately from current cost valuations and purchasing power gains on net debt before arriving at "net income" but following "net income after federal income taxes on a transaction basis." The problem with this approach is that it rapidly leads to information overload, the technical term for users being overwhelmed by too much data.[35,36]

ASOBAT was far more influential than the AAA Statements which preceded it. The user orientation has continued to dominate accounting standard setting, as has the use of objectives. Interestingly, the statement appeared about the same time as the first edition of this book. The observant reader will notice numerous passages that echo ASOBAT. Echoes will also be heard in *APB Statement No. 4* and in the FASB's Conceptual Framework. For all that, this was the last attempt by the AAA to participate in standard setting. Paton's impetus had run its course.

APB Statement No. 4

The AICPA, dissatisfied with its previous attempts at establishing theory, recommended that, at the earliest possible time, the Board should, among other things, set forth the objectives of accounting, enumerate and describe basic concepts and accounting principles, and define words and phrases used in accounting, including the terms *present fairly* and *generally accepted accounting principles*.[37] Five long years later, in response to this directive, the Board published *APB Statement No. 4*, "Basic Concepts and Accounting Principles Underlying Financial Statements of Business Enterprises."[38] The Statement is summarized in Exhibit 4-7. The new statement adopted the user approach made fashionable by ASOBAT and defined accounting in paragraph 9 as:

> a service activity . . . (whose) function is to provide quantitative information, primarily financial in nature, about economic entities that is intended to be useful in making economic decisions.

The nature of these economic decisions is spelled out in a chapter dealing with the economic environment within which accounting finds itself.* The Statement develops the notion of arms-length transactions between profit-maximizing units in a private-market economy so as to justify the use of market prices in financial statements.

After reaffirming that the objective of accounting is to provide financial information "that is useful in making economic decisions," the Statement asserts that, to achieve this goal, various *qualitative objectives* must be met: Information must be relevant, understandable, timely, and so on.

---

* For more details, see Chapter 7.

EXHIBIT 4-7 *APB Statement No. 4*

1. Objectives:

1A. General	To provide reliable information about economic resources and obligations and changes in those resources and obligations; to assist in estimating earning potential of an enterprise.
1B. Qualitative	Relevance; understandability; verifiability; neutrality; timeliness; comparability; completeness

2. Basic Features — Accounting entity; going concern; measurement of economic resources and obligations; time periods; measurement in terms of money; accrual; exchange price; approximation; judgment; general-purpose financial information; fundamentally related financial statements; substance over form; materiality

3. Basic Elements — Assets; liabilities; owners' equity; revenue; expenses; and net income

4. Principles:

4A. Pervasive	Initial recording of assets and liabilities; revenue realization; expense recognition: cause and effect, systematic and rational allocation, immediate recognition; unit of measure.
4B. Modifying Conventions	Conservatism; emphasis on income; application of judgment
4C. Broad Operating	Selecting; analyzing; measuring; classifying; recording; summarizing; adjusting; communicating
4D. Detailed	Rules found in practice.

The FASB was to adopt these qualitative objectives almost in their entirety in SFAC 2 but rename them *qualitative characteristics.*

The Statement then lists 13 *features* of accounting such as the focus on the entity and the assumption of a going concern. Paton had called these *postulates;* the FASB terms them *fundamentals.* The APB then claimed, without providing much evidence, that these fundamentals result in the *pervasive principles* that supposedly make up GAAP. The APB defined GAAP, itself, as:

> the conventions, rules, and procedures necessary to define accounting practice at a particular time.[39]

Included in the pervasive principles were the practices of recording assets at cost, recognizing revenue at the point of sale, and the process of matching costs to revenues. These principles, in association with the modifying conventions of conservatism and materiality, supposedly lead to a long list of operating principles and a series of definitions of elements of financial statements, such as assets.

APB Statement No. 4 is an important document. Major portions of it have been incorporated in the FASB's Conceptual Framework. The bulk of what was not explicitly incorporated, such as some of the features of accounting, continues to represent "the most authoritative formulation of GAAP available."[40]

That is not to say that the Statement is without its critics. First, many condemned it because it was, by its own admission, primarily descriptive and not prescriptive. The definitions of the elements of financial statements received particularly severe criticism because they lacked semantic content. Assets, for instance, were defined as:

> economic resources of an enterprise . . . (and) certain deferred charges that are not resources . . . that are recognized and measured in conformity with generally accepted accounting principles.[41]

Thus, the definitions are not expressed in terms of real-world objects or events. Second, justification for various assertions is lacking. For instance, the Statement makes the assumption, without evidence, that traditional financial accounting statements satisfy the common needs of many user groups. Third, there is no clear relationship between the objectives, the basic elements of financial accounting, and the pervasive and detailed principles. For example, no evidence or logic is presented to show that the pervasive principle that:

> assets and liabilities are measured by the exchange prices at which the transfers take place[42]

follows from the primary qualitative objective of relevance. Nor is there any logical relationship between the broad operating principle that:

> costs of some assets are charged to expense immediately on acquisition[43]

is derived from the pervasive principle that assets are measured at cost.

Additionally, a complete theory should contain descriptive statements that are verified empirically or at least are verifiable. When normative statements are made, the basis for the judgment should be given. Neither of these conditions is found in *Statement No. 4*. While it is conceded that generally accepted accounting principles:

> become generally accepted by agreement (often tacit agreement) rather than by formal derivation from a set of postulates or basic concepts. . . .[44]

the Statement does not indicate the basis for establishing when agreement exists. What percentage of disagreement would deny a specific practice the right to be included among GAAP? Apparently, the authors of the

Statement were in doubt themselves, since many of the principles of financial statement presentation are stated in normative terms without presenting the basis for the judgment in each case.

In summary, *Statement No. 4* is not a theory of accounting practice nor a clear statement of generally accepted accounting principles. In the words of California professor George Staubus, the Statement is "a fine set of objectives of financial accounting juxtaposed against a set of principles that clearly fall short of what is needed to meet the objectives."[45] But the APB should not be criticized too severely for attempting to do what is currently impossible. Accounting theory has not arrived, and may never arrive, at a stage where a grand theory can be formulated. Considerably more work is necessary in the specific areas where theory formulation and verification can take place.

The Conceptual Framework

The ink was barely dry on *APB Statement No. 4* when the APB was disbanded and the Financial Accounting Standards Board (FASB) was formed. After considering the history of the search for principles, the Wheat committee, which proposed the formation of a new standard-setting organization, noted that:

> "Accounting principles" has proven to be an extraordinarily elusive term. To the non-accountant (as well as to many accountants) it connotes things basic and fundamental, of a sort which can be expressed in few words, relatively timeless in nature, and in no way dependent upon changing fashions in business or the evolving needs of the investment community. Yet the APB (despite the prominence in its name of the term "principles") has deemed it necessary throughout its history to issue opinions on subjects which have almost nothing to do with "principles" in the usual sense.[46]

The committee concluded that one of the reasons for the difficulty accountants had had in establishing accounting principles was that:

> the word "principles" was a slightly pretentious term in accounting. I think we know what principles are in the natural sciences. But accounting arrangements are clearly man-made. There is no one "right" way of proceeding . . . . It isn't anything derived from an inquiry into fundamental truths any more than a decision to drive on the right side of the road is in the United States or on the left is in Britain. It's just a convenient way of doing things. And this is true of many of the rules that must be issued by a body like the [FASB].[47]

The committee, therefore, proposed that the term *principles* be replaced by the term *standards*, defined as "solutions to financial accounting problems." They felt the new term would be "more descriptive of the majority of the Board's pronouncements as well the great bulk of its ongoing effort."[48] The committee also suggested that the new organization be called an accounting *standards* board and not an accounting *principles* board. In short, the long search for principles seemed to have come to a rather inglorious end.

It was more of a shift, though, than an end, because in many ways the search has continued under a different title. For instance, the new Board, almost immediately after its founding, began to search for accounting objectives much like its predecessors had searched for postulates. This work was done in a series of Statements of Financial Accounting Concepts (SFACs) known as the Conceptual Framework.* Almost all of the concepts that were developed under the rubric of principles and postulates have found their way into the framework, albeit under different titles. In fact, one might argue that the changes were semantic only, but this argument probably underestimates the vast changes that have occurred in accounting in the past two decades.

Some have likened the Conceptual Framework to a constitution, not unlike the Constitution of the United States. The analogy suggests an intent to set forth broad goals and policies that have general agreement among almost all interested parties. These broad goals and policies then should serve as a foundation for the establishment of a cohesive set of accounting standards. Almost inevitably, given the controversy that surrounds the U.S. Constitution, the Conceptual Framework has come under a great deal of fire. For instance, New York professor Lee Seidler contended that there are "no conceptual frameworks in the social sciences" and that to claim one merely demonstrates "the vanity of ignorance."[49] In a similar vein, Arthur Young partner Dale Gerboth argued that "the fundamental error of the Conceptual Framework [is] the mistaken notion that it is possible to avoid, minimize, or control debate on basic issues by prior agreement on abstract principles."[50] The origin of such criticism is the subject of the next section.

CHECKPOINTS

---

1. Explain in your own words why some feel that postulates are the starting point for establishing accounting rules while others feel that objectives are more appropriate. What is your own opinion?
2. What do you feel are the primary objectives of accounting? How does your list compare with that in ASOBAT?
3. How would you define an objective? Do the qualitative objectives in *APB 4* fit your definition? If not, where would you place them?
4. Do you agree with the Wheat committee that the search for principles should be abandoned in favor of a search for standards? Explain your position.

---

* The Conceptual Framework is described in depth in the next chapter.

THE SEARCH IN RETROSPECT

The search for principles, as this chapter has demonstrated, has been long, frustrating, and even futile in the eyes of some. Fifty years of intense effort by many very talented and dedicated professionals has produced little more than a few high-sounding phrases to accompany a system invented 500 years ago. As a result, the term *generally accepted accounting principles* (GAAP), despite its appearance in every auditor's report, is as empty of meaning today as it was when it was first coined. There is still no consensus on what constitutes a principle, how principles relate to postulates, nor on how either can be used to derive accounting standards. In practice, all the term GAAP means is those rules that have been sanctioned through Rule 203 of the AICPA. In other words, GAAP means no more than accounting practices with substantial authority. This is a procedural definition, not a semantic one.

The lack of a consensus on accounting principles was the subject of a committee report commissioned by the American Accounting Association in 1973 entitled *Statement on Accounting Theory and Theory Acceptance* (SATTA). The authors concluded that "a single universally accepted basic accounting theory does not exist at this time."[51] They, therefore, sought to explain why the accounting community has been unable to achieve theoretical closure. Their explanations are the subject of this and later chapters.

Accounting Theory Is Complex

The lack of progress accountants have made in establishing a set of principles may be attributed to the extreme difficulty of the task that accountants have set for themselves. Economists have been content to develop their theories in a stylized world containing numerous simplifying assumptions, such as the free availability of information to all participants in the market. Accountants are prevented from making these assumptions, because with them there is no reason for accounting to be done at all. Stated otherwise, in the typical perfect market that inhabits economic textbooks, there is no room for accounting. One has to relax the assumptions to find a reason for accountants. The result is a very complex economic model.

The complexity of the analysis has led to ongoing disagreements on the precise objective(s) of accounting and the nature of the economic environment in which it operates. Initially, accounting in the United States focused on creditors, then it assumed a stewardship role toward investors, and more recently it has sought to provide information for investment decisions. Each change of objective implies a change in principles. Then, during the 1960s, a number of academic researchers claimed that they had found statistical evidence that the stock markets are efficient in the sense that they swiftly impound all available information into the prices of stocks. The result was the Efficient-Market Hypothesis, which is discussed in Chapter 6. Their claims were disputed by skeptics who pointed to a variety of situations where the market appeared to have ignored or misinterpreted information that seemingly was public. More is said on this issue in later chapters. Suffice it to note for now that a conclusive agreement, either way, would be a major determining factor in defining accounting principles. While disagreement reigns on facts, such as market efficiency, inevitably there will be disagreement over principles.

Accounting Has Economic Consequences

A second cause of the difficulties accountants have had in arriving at fundamental principles may be attributed to the fact that accounting is a pragmatic discipline—it exists because it is thought to be useful. The postulates/principles approach tends to focus on accounting as a theoretical system akin to mathematics, ignoring, or at least downplaying, the role of the user, that is, the pragmatic aspect of the subject. In terms of information theory, the postulates/principles approach tends to analyze the signal more than the nature of the receiver or the transmitter of the signal. At one level, one could say that the postulate/principle approach is a partial one because it ignores some of the most important features of accounting, such as the user and the producer. In particular, the approach ignores the *economic consequences* that information has for individuals and organizations. Accounting systems are not purely abstract structures, nor is the debate over accounting rules purely theoretical in the sense of being without practical significance. In other words, accounting matters. Purely theoretical arguments tend to get swept away in the perceived implications for affected parties.

Examples of both direct and indirect economic consequences from accounting rules abound. For instance, if one is obliged by a new standard to disclose a poorer financial situation than was expected, existing shareholders might be hurt as the share price falls. Also, the bonuses of many top managers, which are based on reported income, would fall. In addition, many corporations have debt covenants with their creditors which force repayment of debt if net income falls below a particular level or if debt-to-equity ratios rise too high. Any change in accounting rules, therefore, can have a series of quite significant economic impacts on a wide variety of people. There is also a direct cost in the form of audit fees, printing costs, and so on, to the preparer of financial statements. Companies who perceive few benefits from an accounting rule might be reluctant to bear this cost. This was true of accounting for inflation, for example, which was subsequently abandoned because its cost outweighed its perceived benefits. It is, thus, not unreasonable for there to be much dispute over accounting rules and the principles that would support them.

In a world in which financial rules are perceived to have economic consequences, one can reasonably expect the debate over these rules to be phrased in economic rather than theoretical terms—and in specific rather than global terms. In such situations, principles, postulates, and conceptual frameworks are of limited value. This is not to say that they are completely useless. The language and the terminology are extremely valuable intellectual exercises. So are the definitions and the framing of concepts which help to sharpen thinking about accounting. But they all tend to give way to the force of economic arguments.

Truth or Consequences?

Whether common practice is desirable is a matter of some dispute. One can make a strong case that, even though it might be important to heed economic consequences in the standard-setting process, they should not be permitted to influence the standard itself. Consider the simple matter of traffic lights: A red light is an inconvenience to those in a hurry and may even cause economic harm to those stopped, but no one seriously suggests changing the "stop-on-red" rule on grounds of the economic consequences it has for a few. Instead, impatient drivers are asked to consider the broader interest of society in having an orderly flow of traffic. Many, of course, do attempt to beat the red light, but they simply emphasize how important it is that, as a body politic, we agree to abide by certain traffic conventions.

In like vein, the FASB has argued that accounting standards should be measured not by their immediate effect on individuals, but in terms of the value to society as a whole of having a reliable financial information system. This idea was reaffirmed recently when the FASB responded to criticisms for requiring the amortization of goodwill for financial reporting purposes in the United States when it is not a universal requirement throughout the world. In the words of the critic:

> Would-be purchasers of U.S. firms are burdened by accounting rules that favor foreign buyers (since) of the major industrial nations, only the United States requires its companies to amortize, or write off, goodwill against earnings but doesn't allow tax deductions.[52]

He urged the FASB to repeal its amortization requirement to enable U.S. corporations to have a level playing field with foreign buyers. The FASB was quite adamant that this treatment would not be appropriate. The chairman of the FASB, Dennis R. Beresford, responded that:

> Once again, an easy accounting "fix" is proposed as a solution for a difficult economic problem, overlooking the fact that accounting rules are intended not

to influence behavior but to provide relevant, reliable information on which economic decisions can be based with a reasonable degree of confidence.

To which, he added more generally:

> The article helps to raise a much broader question about the objective of accounting standards in the marketplace. Should the objective of accounting standards be to manipulate behavior and affect economic or social change, or to provide relevant and reliable information? I believe that most serious observers would agree that the purpose of accounting standards is to improve the quality of financial reporting, not to cure perceived economic or social problems.[53]

While it is true that the FASB and its predecessor have bent to the winds of economic consequences on several occasions, it is equally true that this is not the FASB's policy. As it put its case in its description of the term *neutrality*, "accounting information cannot avoid affecting behavior, nor should it." But, "accounting information must report economic activity as faithfully as possible, without coloring the image it communicates for the purpose of influencing behavior in *some particular direction*."

Such a perspective would be less difficult to maintain were accounting rules more easily and directly derived from the Conceptual Framework. Unfortunately, like *APB Statement No. 4* before it, there are few logical connections between specific practices and general theory. Standard setting remains, therefore, in a relatively unsettled state. In such a situation, it is surely true that:

> The key to accounting objectivity, both in setting standards and in practice, lies where it has always lain: in the values—in the integrity and personal responsibility—of those who practice accounting. With those values, accounting has all it needs to attain the highest degree of objectivity the profession is capable of attaining. Without those values, objectivity of any kind is beyond reach. Now, when accounting is being challenged as never before, it must take its direction not from its concepts, but from its values; it must find its security not in its intellectual structure, but in its professional conduct; in short, it must attend not to the book of accounting, but to the behavior of accountants.[54]

In short, accounting is not a mechanical exercise nor a set of rules that can be applied by a computer. It is at best a social science. Some would say it is still an art. It requires, and will continue to require, the considered judgments of responsible professionals.

CHECKPOINTS

1. What was the purpose of the FASB's Conceptual Framework?
2. List three reasons why it is so difficult to build such a framework?

SUMMARY

All audited financial statements have to be in accordance with *generally accepted accounting principles*. But, as this chapter has shown, those principles have proved to be very elusive. This phenomenon can be attributed to the sheer complexity of theorizing about financial reporting, and to the fact that accounting has economic consequences for its users, that is, some benefit and some lose financially when a new standard is promulgated. As a result, the choice of accounting standards and the principles used to justify them is as much a political choice as a technical choice. This chapter has traced accountants' growing awareness of this point and the evolution of the search for principles into a search for accounting standards. The previous chapter tells essentially the same story but explains how the fruitlessness of the search for principles caused successive regulatory bodies, such as the Committee on Accounting Procedure and the Accounting Principles Board, to fail. Later chapters provide more details as to why it has been so difficult to establish accounting theory. These chapters also raise the question of what kind of body would be most appropriate for setting accounting standards—and what form those standards should take ideally.

QUESTIONS

1. The term *standards* has been used in different ways by different authors. Collect and compare the different meanings. With which one are you most comfortable?

2. Compare and contrast the two definitions of accounting in this section and the one in the first chapter.

3. One of the themes in the development of accounting in this century has been the swing from a balance sheet orientation to an income statement back to a balance sheet orientation. Trace these changes from the origins of accounting to the present, noting when, and for what reasons, these changes occurred.

4. The chapter noted the move from principles to standards from the APB to the FASB. What significance was there in the move from the Committee on Accounting *Procedures* to the Accounting *Principles* Board?

5. Explain why the authors of ASOBAT allowed "deferred costs" as assets. Why has the FASB sought to eliminate them?

6. What does the term "substantial authority" mean? (You might want to check your auditing text in answering this question.)

7. How would you feel as a user if the term "in accordance with GAAP" was replaced by the term "in accordance with PSA," that is, in accordance with practices that have substantial authority?

8. How does your definition of principles correspond with that of *ARS 7*, p. 23, which said principles are in "the category of conventions or rules developed by man from experience to fulfill the essential and useful needs and purposes in establishing reliable financial and operating information control for business entities"?

9. Chapter 1 describes the rejection of the economic consequences argument by the FASB in the case of goodwill. Discuss in light of this chapter.

10. Sanders, Hatfield, and Moore suggested that losses be capitalized and amortized over time. Is this ever appropriate?

11. The notion of all-inclusive income is treated in this chapter and the last. Explain why it has been such an important part of the development of accounting.

12. Do we need principles in accounting? Do you agree with the 1936 position of the American Accounting Association? Why?

13. Australian professor Louis Goldberg commented that: "While the label 'principles' may have been forsaken in the course of discussion over the next half-century, the substance of what was being sought has not changed fundamentally; accountants are still looking for a security blanket of theory to protect them from misinterpretation of accounting 'circumstances' or 'situations.' " Discuss.[55]

THE NVF COMPANY

During 1968, NVF, a manufacturing company, sought to acquire Sharon Steel Corporation. As part of the deal, NVF offered the shareholders of Sharon Steel a $70 subordinated debenture with a 5 percent coupon rate in place of their shares in Sharon. By March 1969, approximately 86 percent of Sharon's shares had been tendered. The market rate of interest at the time was considerably higher than the coupon rate, causing the debentures to be issued at a sizable discount. NVF's financial statements for December 31, 1989, showed these debentures at their full face value of $93,886,000 among the liabilities and the associated discount called deferred debt expense in the amount of $51,881,0000 among the assets. This was perfectly consistent with GAAP at the time.

Required:

1. Do you agree with this treatment of the discount? Explain the grounds for your opinion. Do any of the principles, postulates, concepts, criteria, or standards discussed in this chapter help you in arriving at your conclusion?

2. Present GAAP requires that the discount be treated as a contra-liability. What led to the change in method? Have the principles of accounting changed since 1969 or has our interpretation of those principles changed?

3. Can you create an argument for why treating a discount as an asset might be satisfactory?

PRIMARY SOURCES

Those readers interested in pursuing in more depth, the topics raised in this chapter might begin by consulting the following texts.

Carey, John L. *The Rise of the Accounting Profession*, vols. 1 and 2 (AICPA, 1969 and 1970).

Moonitz, Maurice "Obtaining Agreement on Standards in the Accounting Profession." *Studies in Accounting Research No. 8* (AAA, 1974).

Storey, Reed K. *The Search for Accounting Principles—Today's Problems in Perspective* (AICPA, 1964).

Zeff, Stephen A. *Forging Accounting Principles in Five Countries: A History and an Analysis of Trends.* Accounting Lectures 1971 (Champaign, Ill.: Stipes Publishing, 1972).

SELECTED ADDITIONAL READINGS

In addition to the works cited in the endnotes to this chapter, the reader is referred to the following authors:

APB Statement No. 4

Ijiri, Yuji. "Critique of the APB Fundamentals Statement." *Journal of Accountancy*, November 1971, pp. 43–50.

Schattke, R. W. "An Analysis of Accounting Principles Board Statement No. 4." *Accounting Review*, April 1972, pp. 233–44.

Staubus, George J. "An Analysis of *APB Statement No. 4.*" *Journal of Accountancy*, February 1972, pp. 36–43.

Development of Alternative Theory Approaches

American Accounting Association Committee on Concepts and Standards for External Financial Reports. *Statement on Accounting Theory and Theory Acceptance* (AAA, 1977).

Chambers, Raymond J. "Canning's *The Economics of Accountancy*—After 50 Years." *The Accounting Review*, October 1979, pp. 764–75.

Danos, Paul. "A Revolution in Accounting Thought? A Comment." *The Accounting Review*, July 1977, pp. 746–47.

Hakansson, Nils H. "Where We Are in Accounting. A Review of *Statement on Accounting Theory and Theory Acceptance*." *The Accounting Review*, July 1978, pp. 717–25.

Kapnick, Harvey. "Accounting Principles—Concern or Crisis?" *Financial Executive*, October 1974, pp. 23–25, 64.

Mattessich, Richard. "On the Evolution of Theory Construction in Accounting: A Personal Account." *Accounting and Business Research*, Special Accounting History Issue (1980), pp. 158–73.

Wells, M. C. "A Revolution in Accounting Thought." *The Accounting Review*, July 1976, pp. 471–82.

Wells, M. C. "A Revolution in Accounting Thought? A Reply." *The Accounting Review*, July 1977, pp. 748–50.

Whittington, Geoffrey. "Pioneers of Income Measurement and Price-Level Accounting: A Review Article." *Accounting and Business Research*, Spring 1980, pp. 232–40.

Postulates

Deinzer, Harvey T. *Development of Accounting Thought* (New York: Holt, Rinehart & Winston, 1965).

Lambert, Samuel J., III. "Basic Assumptions in Accounting Theory Construction." *Journal of Accountancy*, February 1974, pp. 41–48.

Mautz, R. K. "The Place of Postulates in Accounting." *Journal of Accountancy*, January 1965, pp. 46–49.

Metcalf, Richard W. "The Basic Postulates in Perspective." *The Accounting Review* 39, January 1964, pp. 16–21.

Popoff, Boris. "Postulates, Principles and Rules." *Accounting and Business Research*, Summer 1972, pp. 182–93.

ENDNOTES

1. Carman G. Blough, "The Need for Accounting Principles," *The Accounting Review,* March 1937, pp. 30–37.
2. Gilbert Byrne, "To What Extent Can the Practice of Accounting Be Reduced to Rules and Standards," *Journal of Accountancy,* November 1937, pp. 364–79.
3. George O. May, "Principles of Accounting," *Journal of Accountancy,* December 1937, pp. 423–25. The AICPA in *ARB 7,* 1940, not surprisingly, adopted May's definition rather than Byrne's.
4. These five principles may be found today in full in Chapter 1 of Accounting Research Bulletin No. 43.
5. *The Accounting Review,* June 1936, pp. 187–91.
6. W. A. Paton and A. C. Littleton, *An Introduction to Corporate Accounting Standards,* American Accounting Association Monograph No. 3 (AAA, 1940).
7. Quoted in Eugene Flegm, *Accounting* (New York: John Wiley & Sons, 1984), p. 32.
8. American Accounting Association, "Accounting and Reporting Standards for Corporate Financial Statement," *The Accounting Review,* October 1957, pp. 536–46.

9. W. A. Paton, *Accounting Theory* (1922). (Accounting Studies Press reprint, 1962), p. vii.
10. Ibid., p. 429.
11. Ibid., p. 267.
12. John B. Canning, *The Economics of Accountancy* (New York: Ronald Press, 1929).
13. *New York Stock Exchange Fact Book,* 1959, p. 38.
14. American Institute of Accountants, 1938.
15. Ibid., pp. 75–77.
16. Mortimer B. Daniels, *Financial Statements,* American Accounting Association Monograph No. 2 (AAA, 1939) is another useful source of data on this period.
17. Stephen Gilman, *Accounting Concepts of Profit* (New York: Ronald Press, 1939).
18. Ibid., pp. 169–88.
19. American Accounting Association, "Accounting Concepts and Standards Underlying Financial Statements," *The Accounting Review,* October 1948, pp. 339–44.
20. "Report to Council of the Special Committee on Research Program," *Journal of Accountancy*, December 1958, p. 62.
21. Ibid., p. 67.
22. Maurice Moonitz, "The Basic Postulates of Accounting," *Accounting Research Study No. 1* (New York: AICPA, 1961), pp. 51–53.
23. Maurice Moonitz and Robert T. Sprouse, *A Tentative Set of Broad Accounting Principles for Business Enterprises* (New York: AICPA, 1962), pp. 6–7.
24. *Accounting Terminology Bulletin No. 1* (pp. 10–11) published under the title *Review and Resume* adopted a different approach claiming that "accounting postulates are derived from experience and reason; after postulates so derived have proved useful, they become accepted as principles of accounting."
25. *Journal of Accountancy,* December 1958, p. 63.
26. Raymond J. Chambers, "Why Bother with Postulates?" *Journal of Accounting Research*, Spring 1963, pp. 3–15.
27. *ARS 3,* p. 55.
28. George O. May, *Financial Accounting* (New York: Macmillan, 1943), p. 30.
29. *ARS 1*, p. 57.
30. *ARS 3*, p. 79.
31. Harvey T. Deinzer, *Development of Accounting Thought* (New York: Holt, Rinehart & Winston, 1965), chap. 9.
32. From a quotation in Moonitz, *Obtaining Agreement on Standards in the Accounting Profession* (American Accounting Association Studies in Accounting Research No. 8, 1974), p. 27.
33. William J. Vatter, "Postulates and Principles," *Journal of Accounting Research,* Autumn 1963, pp. 179–97.
34. W. A. Paton, *Accounting Theory,* 1922; reprinted by Accounting Studies Press, 1962, p. 16.
35. Lawrence Revsine, "Data Expansion and Conceptual Structure," *The Accounting Review,* October 1970, pp. 704–11.
36. Henry Miller, "Environmental Complexity and Financial Reports," *The Accounting Review,* January 1972, pp. 31–37.

37. ''Summary of the Report of the Special Committee on Opinions of the Accounting Principles Board,'' *Journal of Accountancy,* June 1965, p. 12.
38. *Accounting Principles Board Statement No. 4,* ''Basic Concepts and Accounting Principles Underlying Financial Statements of Business Enterprises'' (New York: AICPA, 1970).
39. *APB Statement No. 4,* par. 138.
40. David Solomons, *Making Accounting Policy* (Oxford University Press, 1986).
41. Ibid., par. 132.
42. Ibid., pars. 145 and 88.
43. Ibid., par. 181.
44. Ibid., par. 139.
45. George J. Staubus, ''An Analysis of *APB Statement No. 4*,'' *Journal of Accountancy,* February 1972, p. 43.
46. *Establishing Financial Accounting Standards: Report of the Study on Establishment of Accounting Principles* (AICPA, March 1972), p. 13.
47. James Nolan, ''Wheat Study Members Assess Product,'' *The Journal of Accountancy,* June 1972, p. 18.
48. FASB Discussion Memorandum, *Conceptual Framework for Accounting and Reporting: Consideration of the Report of the Study Group on the Objectives of Financial Statements* (FASB: June 6, 1974).
49. Lee J. Seidler, ''No Accounting for the FASB's Draft on Recognition and Measurement,'' *Accounting Issues* (Bear, Stearns & Co., April 9, 1984), p. 13.
50. Dale L. Gerboth, ''The Conceptual Framework: Not Definitions but Professional Values,'' *Accounting Horizons,* September 1987, pp. 1–8.
51. American Accounting Association, *Statement on Accounting Theory and Theory Acceptance* (AAA, 1977).
52. Sanford Pensler, ''Accounting Rules Favor Foreign Bidders,'' *The Wall Street Journal,* March 24, 1988.
53. Dennis R. Beresford, Letters to the Editor, *The Wall Street Journal,* March 26, 1988.
54. Gerboth, *Accounting Horizons.*
55. Louis Goldberg, ''Foreword to A. A. Fitzgerald on the 'Principles of Accounting','' *Accounting Historians Journal,* Spring 1988, pp. 119–24.

Chapter 5

The Conceptual Framework

CHAPTER OBJECTIVES

After studying this chapter, you will be able to:

Distinguish financial reporting from financial accounting.

List and define the elements of the FASB's Conceptual Framework for financial accounting and reporting.

List and critique the objectives of financial reporting as they are currently understood by the FASB.

Discuss and apply the qualitative characteristics which, according to the FASB, make information useful, relating each characteristic to the others in the set.

Define the fundamental concepts of financial accounting and explain their significance for setting accounting standards.

CHAPTER OVERVIEW

Hierarchy of Elements

The FASB has proposed a Conceptual Framework as a basis for setting accounting standards. An annotated diagram is shown explaining the relationship between the various elements in the framework.

The Objectives of Accounting

The main objective of financial reporting is to support shareholders and others in their financial decisions by assisting them in predicting corporate cash flows.

Qualitative Characteristics

Information that is useful for this purpose is deemed to have a number of characteristics, such as relevance and reliability. It should provide more benefits than costs, be understandable, and permit comparisons across companies.

Fundamentals

Fundamental concepts underpinning accounting include the notion of the entity, the going concern, periodicity, conservatism, and the monetary unit as the basis for measurement.

Conclusion

Objectives, qualitative characteristics, and fundamentals form part of a Conceptual Framework with which accounting standards should be consistent. They also provide the necessary terminology in which financial reporting issues may be discussed.

The previous chapter told the story of the search for generally accepted principles. It also told how the search for principles changed to a search for a conceptual framework of which standards were an important part. This chapter lays out the details of the FASB's Conceptual Framework. This appeared, as Exhibit 5-1 shows, in six separate statements over a period of seven years at an estimated cost to the FASB running into millions of dollars. In a discussion memorandum that preceded the Conceptual Framework, the FASB described it as a *constitution* on which

---

EXHIBIT 5-1   The Conceptual Framework

SFAC 1 (November 1978)	The objectives of accounting for business enterprises. The objectives in this statement (and those in *SFAC 4*) lean heavily on the list of objectives developed by the Trueblood Committee.[2]
SFAC 2 (May 1980)	The qualitative characteristics of financial information.
SFAC 3 (December 1980)	Definitions of the elements of financial statements for business enterprises. This statement was superseded by *SFAC 6*, which encompassed not-for-profit organizations as well as business enterprises.
SFAC 4 (December 1980)	The objectives of accounting for nonbusiness enterprises.
SFAC 5 (December 1984)	Definitions of concepts such as recognition, realization, and measurement for business enterprises giving guidance on what should be included in financial statements and when. Measurement rules relating to questions of recognition are discussed.
SFAC 6 (December 1985)	*SFAC 6* replaced *SFAC 3* by defining the elements of financial statements for all enterprises.

standards would be based much as the laws of the land derive from the U.S. Constitution.[1] The choice of words is not insignificant, because it underlines the political nature of accounting standard setting.

The chapter begins with a diagram of the framework. It then continues with a discussion of three of the major features of the framework:

1. The objectives of accounting.
2. The qualitative characteristics of useful accounting information.
3. The fundamental concepts in accounting.

The remaining parts of the framework are discussed in subsequent chapters.

THE HIERARCHY OF ELEMENTS

A discussion memorandum on the work of the Study Group on the Objectives of Financial Statements, also called the Trueblood Committee after its chairman, appeared in 1974. A diagram from its appendix is reproduced in Exhibit 5-2. This diagram seeks to tie together the various parts of the Conceptual Framework.[3] In the chapter which follows, these various parts are discussed in some detail.

The terms in the hierarchy shown in Exhibit 5-2 were defined by the FASB in the following way:

1. *Objectives* are "something toward which effort is directed, an aim or end of action, a goal." These objectives were the subject of *SFAC 1*.

2. *Information needed* "involves identification of the broad categories of financial accounting information needed by users. For example, several objectives specified in the Objectives Study deal with specific types of financial statements perceived to be necessary to meet the information needs of users." This element is similar to the general objectives in *APB Statement No. 4*.

3. *Qualitative characteristics* "are attributes of accounting information which tend to enhance its usefulness. Such qualitative characteristics might be expected to be

    a. Able to withstand the test of time.
    b. Pervasive—that is, apply to all accounting entities.
    c. Implementable—that is, capable of application and susceptible to objective verification."

This element is similar to the qualitative objectives in *APB Statement No. 4*. These characteristics were the subject of *SFAC 2*.

4. *Fundamentals* "are the basic concepts underlying the measurement of transactions and events and disclosing them in a manner meaningful to users of accounting information. . . . Such fundamentals might include the definitions of an accounting entity, assets, liabilities, income,

EXHIBIT 5-2   Hierarchy of Elements in a Conceptual Framework for Financial Accounting and Reporting

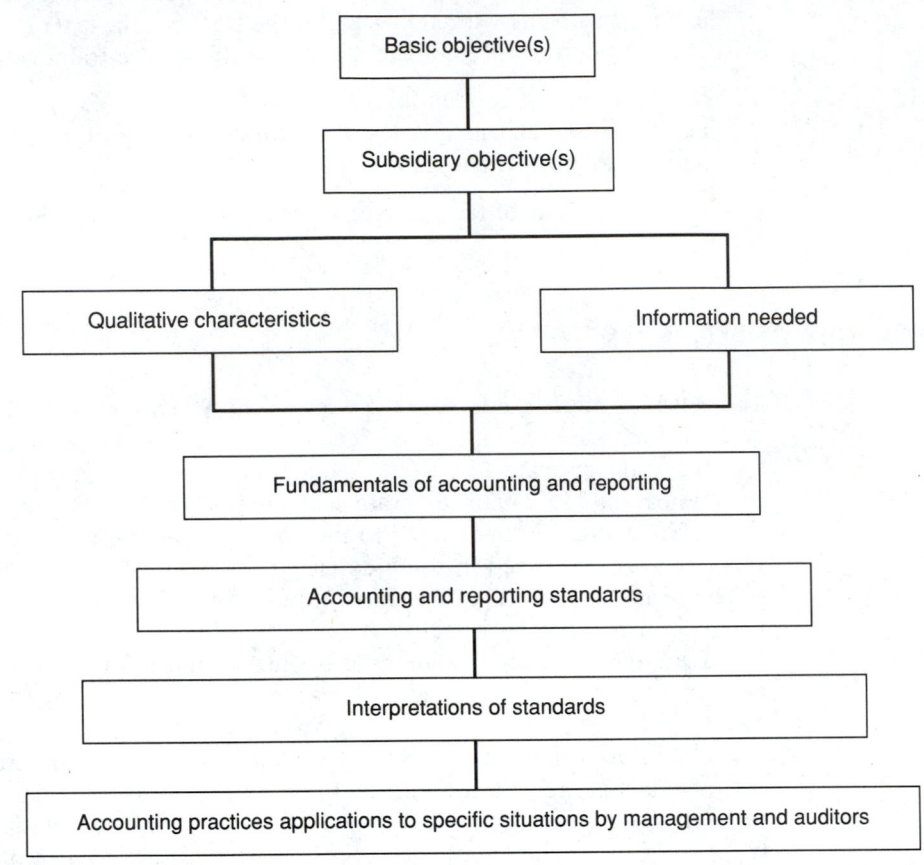

revenue, expense, realization, and others.'' These fundamentals were treated in *SFAC 5* and *6*.

    5.   *Standards* ''represent general solutions to financial accounting problems.''

    6.   *Interpretations* ''clarify, explain, or elaborate upon the accounting and reporting standards as an aid to their application in accounting practices.''

    7.   *Practices* are ''the means to attain the basic objective(s) of financial statements.''

    This chapter seeks to develop in detail several parts of the framework, leaving other parts to be dealt with in later chapters. Specifically, this chapter focuses on the supposed objectives of accounting and the qualitative characteristics that are believed to enhance the usefulness of ac-

EXHIBIT 5-3   Financial Reporting[5]

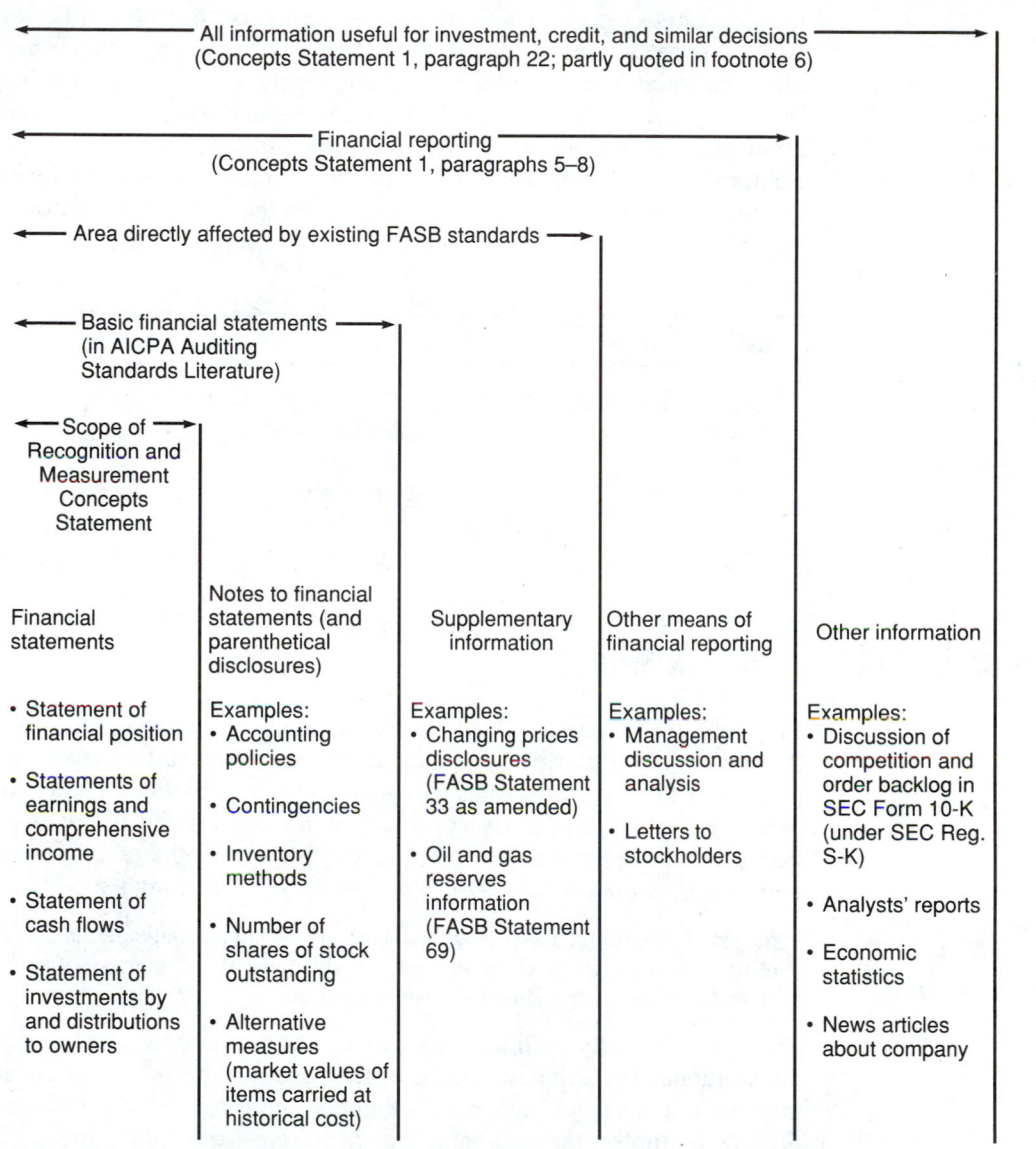

counting information. This chapter also speaks to some of the fundamental concepts used in accounting, such as going concern. Later chapters deal with the nature of the environment and the elements of financial statements, such as assets and liabilities. Standards and their interpretations are the focus of several still later chapters. It is interesting and important to note at the outset that this is a Conceptual Framework for financial *reporting* and not financial *accounting*. The distinction is illustrated in Exhibit 5-3. As the FASB explained it, ". . . some useful information is better provided by financial statements and some is better provided, or can only be provided, by means of financial reporting other than financial statements."[4] Examples of such other reporting include supplementary statements such as on inflation or oil and gas reporting, management discussions and analysis in the annual report, and letters to stockholders. The acceptance of other relevant sources of financial information is a significant departure from prior thinking that all material information was required to be reflected in the financial statements themselves.

CHECKPOINTS

1. List the six statements that form the Conceptual Framework.
2. What are the seven elements that form the Conceptual Framework's hierarchy?
3. Define, in your own words, each of the elements in the hierarchy.

THE OBJECTIVES OF ACCOUNTING

The earliest approach to defining the objectives of accounting focused on the computation and presentation of net income resulting from specific realization and matching rules with a balance sheet that relates the current period to future periods. Accordingly, emphasis was on the data collection process and the format of financial statements. For example, *Accounting Terminology Bulletin No. 1* defined accounting as:

> the art of recording, classifying, and summarizing in a significant manner and in terms of money, transactions and events which are in part at least, of a financial character, and interpreting the results thereof.[6]

The main difficulty with an emphasis on the accounting process and the conventional reporting structure is that accounting terms, such as net income and revenue, and measurements, such as historical cost, have little or no interpretational significance to real-world phenomena. These terms are the artifacts of accountants and, although it may be possible for such artifacts to be useful in making predictions of real-world phenomena, the evidence does not support the validity of making the structure of accounting its basic objective.

Later pronouncements emphasized the semantic approach, which focused on the measurement and reporting of wealth in terms familiar to an economist. *APB Statement No. 4,* for instance, stated the general objective of financial reporting as the provision of reliable financial information about economic resources and obligations of a business enterprise.[7] In a similar vein, *Accounting Research Study No. 1* said the objective of accounting is:

1. To measure the resources held by specific entities.
2. To reflect the claims against and the interests in those entities.
3. To measure the changes in those resources, claims, and interests.
4. To assign the changes to specifiable periods of time.
5. To express the foregoing in terms of money as a common denominator.[8]

These definitions serve as a basis for an emphasis on the balance sheet and the income statement as measurements of wealth and changes in wealth.[9]

A basic difficulty with the application of semantic objectives has been an inability to define them clearly enough to permit agreement on either an appropriate selection of the items to be included, or their measurement.

The FASB, while not rejecting the semantic and the syntactic approaches, places primary emphasis on the pragmatic approach. *SFAC 1* was entitled "Objectives of Financial Reporting by Business Enterprises." As noted above, this statement was based largely on a report drawn up by an AICPA committee under the chairmanship of Robert M. Trueblood.[10] The Trueblood Report, in turn, was based in large part on the objectives that were laid out in *APB Statement No. 4*.[11] There is considerable history, therefore, behind the FASB's objectives. The FASB summarized the objectives appearing in that statement in the following manner:

> Financial reporting should provide information that is useful to present and potential investors and creditors and other users in making rational investment, credit, and similar decisions. The information should be comprehensible to those who have a reasonable understanding of business and economic activities and are willing to study the information with reasonable diligence.
>
> Financial reporting should provide information to help present and potential investors and creditors and other users in assessing the amounts, timing, and uncertainty of prospective cash receipts from dividends or interest and the proceeds from the sale, redemption, or maturity of securities or loans. Since investors' and creditors' cash flows are related to enterprise cash flows, financial reporting should provide information to help investors, creditors, and others assess the amounts, timing, and uncertainty of prospective net cash inflows to the related enterprise.
>
> Financial reporting should provide information about the economic resources of an enterprise, the claims to those resources (obligations of the enterprise to transfer resources to other entities and owners' equity), and the effects of transactions, events, and circumstances that change its resources and claims to those resources.

Not all were convinced by the FASB's objectives. Some argued that they added nothing new.[12] Others argued that the FASB's objectives did not point, as claimed, to a goal or an end other than the one we have already achieved, that is, dropping the word *should* from the objectives leaves them as a quite reasonable description of reality.[13] The problem this creates is that they fail to guide any improvements in accounting. Still others, as noted below, believe that accounting's role is to attest, not to predict. More recently, a school of thought suggests that business can be likened to a game in which accountants are scorekeepers. In such a world, accounting has no meaning other than as a scoring system agreed upon by the participants. All these critics, though, are quick to acknowledge that it is easier to criticize than to construct a set of objectives.

Another line of argument sees accounting as "an ideological weapon in social conflict over the distribution of income and wealth."[14] This suggests that deciding who should be favored in preparing financial statements is a political as much as a technical question. Political questions are normally addressed by elected officials such as members of Congress. Accountants are seen to be usurping the political process and are criticized for focusing on certain, relatively privileged members of society such as shareholders and bankers, leaving the vast bulk of society out of its calculations. The underlying argument is that if the current standard-setting arrangements in the United States, and in other countries, are intended to protect the public interest, then the public needs fuller consideration in the establishment of accounting's objectives.

A third line of criticism is that, while the focus on users may be appealing at first, it is not free of its own difficulties. In particular, it leaves unresolved three important questions:

1. Which users should be considered?
2. How similar are the objectives of different users?
3. Should the wishes of management be considered?

User Groups

The first problem is defining the primary user group. Some argue that this is management itself.[15] Others favor employees, or customers, or the public. The FASB maintains that stockholders, other investors, and creditors are the primary users of accounting.

They conclude from their assumptions about the primary user group that financial reporting should be useful for making investment, credit, and similar decisions. Critics respond that such decisions are based upon a variety of forward-looking data which are largely economic in nature and that the role of accounting is only to "attest" to these data.[16] In other words, the critics claim that the feedback value of accounting information is more important than the predictive value.[17]

The FASB tightened their focus on investors even further by stating that:

> The objectives stem primarily from the informational needs of external users who lack the authority to prescribe the financial information they want from an enterprise and therefore must use the information that management communicates to them.[18]

In other words, their focus is on the smaller investor.

This emphasis on "external users who lack the authority" in *SFAC 1* has been criticized on grounds that the efficient-market hypothesis, discussed in a later chapter, suggests that stock market prices are established by the actions of sophisticated investors.* If this is the case, the objective of financial reporting should not be to provide information for the investor with limited authority and ability, but rather to make publicly available information that might otherwise be used to earn monopoly returns by those who have access to this private or inside information.

User Objectives

Each of the user groups could have very different objectives for financial reporting. For instance, managers and their auditors often differ in their perception of appropriate objectives for accounting. There are also differences within groups. For example, the managers of many smaller businesses, along with their auditors, have been known to feel that the standard-setting process is biased toward the objectives of the larger companies. Similarly, many not-for-profit managers feel the standard-setting process is biased toward the objectives of for-profit businesses. This variety of viewpoints suggests the desirability of the presentation of either different reports for different users, or of a considerable amount of information, much of which might be irrelevant to any specific user.

If one adopts the idea of producing a series of *special-purpose* reports, one must select information relevant to the various prediction and decision models of the users. It may be possible to establish which decision models are in use by finding out how users actually make the decisions and what information they want. This procedure may not lead to the best results, though, because users are limited by the accounting information now available. Also, they may not be using the best models based on information that might be made available to them.

The FASB and the AICPA acknowledge the force of the arguments in favor of special-purpose reports, but argue in return that users have enough in common that a set of *general-purpose* statements are sufficient. As *APB Statement No. 4* stated:

---

* A discussion of the efficient-market hypothesis appears in Chapter 6.

The emphasis in financial accounting on general-purpose information is based on the presumption that a significant number of users need similar information. General-purpose information is not intended to satisfy specialized needs of individual users.[19]

Stated otherwise, general-purpose statements attempt to satisfy the needs of the largest number of users possible.

Accountability

Yet another difficulty in establishing appropriate objectives for financial reporting is that users are only one side of the information equation. Information has the potential to affect the behavior of both users and suppliers. One must consider both parties to the transmission of that information, therefore. Stated otherwise, one has to take the objectives of the suppliers of information into account as well as those of the recipients. If nothing else, one must take the cost of supplying information into consideration. Carnegie professor Yuji Ijiri attempts to capture the various parties concerned in a model of *accountability* in which he describes an accountor, an accountee, and an accountant. He notes that in:

> an accountability-based framework, the objective of accounting is to provide a fair system of information flow between the accountor and the accountee. . . . Based on the underlying accountability relation, the accountee has a certain right to know; at the same time this framework recognizes that the accountor also has a right to protect privacy. More information about the accountor is not necessarily better. Better perhaps from the standpoint of the accountee but not necessarily so from the overall accountability relation.[20]

It is interesting to see the ethical consideration of fairness introduced in Chapter 1 making its reentry here.

Summary

Discussions of accounting objectives can focus on one of three levels of accounting theory: the syntactic, semantic, and pragmatic levels.* The syntactic focuses on the syntax or grammar of accounting; the semantic focuses on its meaning; and the pragmatic focuses on its use. The FASB's objectives are essentially pragmatic in tone.

The Conceptual Framework's objectives, despite all the time, effort, and money poured into them, have not resolved the questions which haunt accounting theory. One can make assertions as to the types of users and the uses to which they put information, but without evidence it is hard

---

* See Chapter 1 for further discussion of these three levels.

to make these assertions conclusive. As a result, the framework has not been the driving force in establishing standards that its proponents had hoped. Instead, it has tended to languish. Terms are drawn from it in which to couch arguments, but the arguments remain essentially political—as its critics predicted.

CHECKPOINTS

---

1. Summarize the three objectives of financial reporting according to the FASB.
2. Briefly distinguish between syntactic, semantic, and pragmatic objectives.
3. Contrast the user view of accounting with the accountability view. Is one a subset of the other? Explain.
4. Who are the primary users of financial statements according to the FASB?

QUALITATIVE CHARACTERISTICS

Qualitative characteristics were defined earlier as those properties of information necessary to make it useful.[21] The Board suggested a number of different qualitative characteristics in the framework. Exhibit 5-4 illustrates how these characteristics are related.

The Board distinguished between *user-specific* and *decision-specific* qualities. The former classification focuses on qualities related to a user. For instance, knowledgeable users might find some information irrelevant because they are already aware of it. Sophisticated users might find complex information more relevant than novices. Thus, the nature of the user is a key determinant in deciding what information to release. Because the intelligibility or understandability of proposed information is dependent on the nature of the user, this characteristic is classified as user-specific.

On the other hand, a characteristic such as timeliness is independent of users, because all users want timely information. Other information is specific to a particular decision. For example, variable costs are often more relevant to volume-related decisions than fixed costs. This too is a decision-specific property. In fact, as a general statement relevance is by definition related to a decision. Reliability, too, is a decision-specific characteristic.

In the sections that follow, each of the Board's proposed qualitative characteristics is discussed. Note that there are two main headings: relevance and reliability. Both are associated with comparability. All three

EXHIBIT 5-4   A Hierarchy of Accounting Qualities

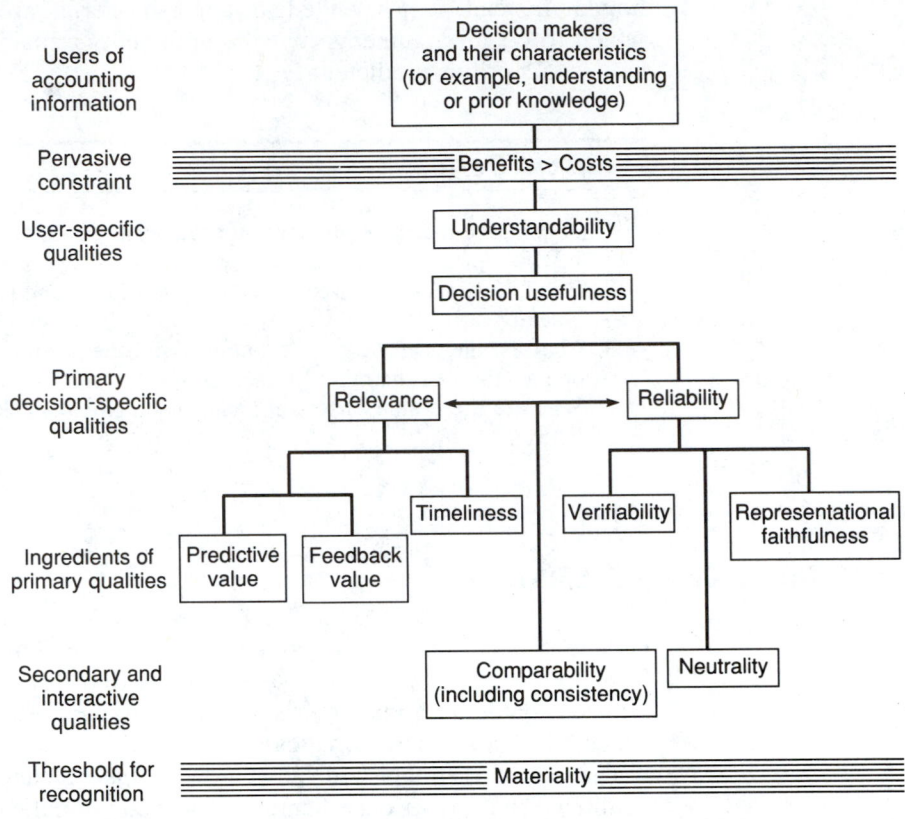

are subject to understandability and to the basic criterion that benefits should exceed costs.

Benefits and Costs

Information must be cost-beneficial, that is, its benefits must exceed its costs. Despite its seeming simplicity, a cost-benefit analysis of accounting information is exceedingly difficult to do; it may even be impossible.[22] As the FASB noted:

Most of the costs of providing financial information fall initially on the preparers, while the benefits are reaped by both preparers and users. Ultimately, the costs and benefits are diffused quite widely. The costs are mostly passed on to the users of information and to the consumers of goods and services. The benefits also are presumably passed on to consumers by assuring a steady supply of goods and services and more efficient functioning of the marketplace. But, even if the costs and benefits are not traced beyond the preparers and users of information, to say anything precise about their incidence is difficult.[23]

So difficult, in fact, that some would feel it a lost cause to even attempt to do a cost-benefit analysis. Nevertheless, the Board pressed on, saying:

> Despite the difficulties, the Board does not conclude that it should turn its back on the matter, for there are some things that it can do to safeguard the cost-effectiveness of its standards. Before a decision is made to develop a standard, the Board needs to satisfy itself that the matter to be ruled on represents a significant problem and that a standard that is promulgated will not impose costs on the many for the benefit of a few.[24]

Events during 1989, such as the Business Roundtable's complaints about the actions of the FASB and the subsequent decision to use the FAF more actively to respond to such complaints, indicate that a cost-benefit equilibrium may be harder to achieve than the Board at first acknowledged.[25] We return to this issue in Chapter 8, where we note again the user-specific character of cost-benefit analysis.

The Board then turned its attention back to the primary issue in its objective statements: how to ensure that financial reporting be most useful for making investment decisions; that is, it turned to decision-specific considerations. It began by asserting that usefulness as a function of two basic characteristics: relevance and reliability. Each of these terms is discussed in detail below.

Relevance

Relevance has been variously defined. At its most basic, relevant information is information that has a bearing on the matter at hand. Information can have a bearing in at least three ways: by affecting goals, by affecting understanding, and by affecting decisions. (See Exhibit 5-5.) Each way provides a definition of relevance.

A decision-relevant concept was the primary standard in ASOBAT, where it was suggested that:

> Relevance . . . requires that the information must bear upon or be usefully associated with actions it is designed to facilitate or results desired to be produced.[26]

The FASB also put itself firmly on the side of decision relevance when it defined the term as the capacity of information "to make a difference" in a decision.[27]

The FASB went on to argue in the next paragraph that this difference would be accomplished by "helping users to form predictions about the

---

EXHIBIT 5-5 Relevance

Goal relevance	Attained when information enables goals of users to be achieved.
	Difficult to determine when met because goals are subjective.
Semantic relevance	Attained when receiver of information understands the intended meaning of the information reported.
	An essential prerequisite but not an ultimate objective.
Decision relevance	Attained when information facilitates decisions made by users.
	This is the ultimate objective of the FASB.

---

outcome of past, present, and future events or to confirm or correct prior expectations.'' These two roles of information have been referred to as the *predictive value* and the *feedback value* of information, respectively. In addition, if information is to be helpful, it must be *timely*, that is, referring back to Exhibit 5-4 we have relevance as a function of:

Predictive value.

Feedback value.

Timeliness.

Predictive Value.   The concept of *predictive value* is derived from investment valuation models and is defined by the FASB in the glossary to *SFAC 2* as:

> The quality of information that helps users to increase the likelihood of correctly forecasting the outcome of past or present events.

If accounting data are to be relevant for decision making by investors, they must provide input into investors' decision models. And since only expectations of future objects and events are relevant for these decision models, it follows that if accounting data are to be relevant, they must provide or permit predictions of future objects or events. However, the emphasis on prediction leaves several questions unanswered:

1. What objects or events are or should be included in investors' decision models?
2. What relationships should be assumed or sought between accounting data and the inputs into decision models?
3. What alternative sets of accounting data and what alternative accounting procedures best meet the predictive ability criterion?

Before the predictive ability test can be applied, there must be some knowledge of what decision models are in use or what decision models investors should be using. The former can be studied through descriptive theories of investors and market reactions to accounting data. The main difficulty with using descriptive models is that investors are limited by the information made available to them. Therefore, it is difficult to evaluate the effect of alternative accounting data or procedures. The normative approach has the advantage of permitting freedom to select alternative accounting procedures and accounting data not previously reported. Normative theories, however, are always difficult to evaluate and must always be subject to change as new information is obtained.

As suggested by the 1969–71 American Accounting Association Committee on Corporate Financial Reporting, there are at least four ways by which accounting data can be related to the inputs of decision models: by direct prediction, by indirect prediction, by the use of lead indicators, and as corroborative evidence. The roles of each are summarized in Exhibit 5-6.[28]

The predictive ability concept has considerable potential for future development of relevant financial reporting. However, several major obstacles stand in the way at the present time. A major obstacle is the lack of tested normative (or even descriptive) investor decision models with a sufficient description of the model inputs.

EXHIBIT 5-6   Predictive Value

Direct	Provision of forecasts by management; for example, projected cash flows.
	Potential misuse and liability, in the case of inaccurate forecasts, constrain their use.
Indirect	Provision of past data; for example, past cash flows to enable users to predict future cash flows.
	Assumes high correlation between past and future events, which may not be justified.
Lead indicators	Provision of data whose movements precede the movements in the objects or events being predicted; for example, increasing debt-equity ratios might precede a deterioration in cash flows.
	Assumes indicators that led turning points in the past will do so in the future.
Corroborating information	Provision of accounting data which may be used to predict other data; for example, an increase in the return on assets may reflect increased managerial efficiency that may herald increased cash flows.
	Assumes the relationship between accounting data and other data is known.

A second obstacle is the lack of understanding of the relationship between accounting data and relevant objects or events that may be inputs into decision models. It is improper to assume that a given concept of income, for example, is a relevant predictor just because it permits a prediction of future values of itself. Accounting income is an artifact derived from the formal accounting structure and is relevant for prediction purposes only if it is also a good substitute or surrogate for a relevant input into the decision models. At the present time, the complexities of the business environment, the lack of understanding of the relationships of past and future measurements of objects and events, and the inability to formulate reliable normative or descriptive decision models make the predictive ability test a difficult one.

Feedback Value.   Information also has an important role to play in confirming or correcting earlier expectations. Decisions are seldom made in isolation. Information about the outcome of one decision is often a key input into making the next decision. This kind of information is often called *feedback*. It is often illustrated by a thermostat, which does not only "decide" at what temperature to set a room but continues to seek feedback by monitoring the room so as to adjust the temperature when needed. Accounting ideally performs a similar service for investors, enabling them to adjust their investment strategies over time.

Timeliness.   Information cannot be relevant if it is not timely, that is, it must be available to a decision maker before it loses its capacity to influence decisions. Timeliness does not guarantee relevance, but relevance is not possible without timeliness. Timeliness, therefore, is an important constraint on the publication of financial statements. The accumulation, summarization, and subsequent publication of accounting information should be as rapid as possible to ensure the availability of current information in the hands of the users. Timeliness also implies that financial statements should be presented at frequent intervals so as to reveal changes in the firm's situation that may in turn affect the user's predictions and decisions.

Relevance, Information, and Data.   The concept of relevance enables one to make a useful distinction between information and data. Data can be defined as measurements or descriptions of objects or events. If these data are already known, or are of no concern to the person to whom they are communicated, they cannot be information. Information can be defined as data that have a surprise effect on the receiver. Furthermore, information should reduce uncertainty, communicate a message to the decision maker that has a value greater than its cost, and potentially evoke a response in the decision maker.[29] It follows that a starting point in the selection of data for presentation is to ensure that they are at least information; otherwise they cannot be relevant.

When accounting data included in financial statements have already been obtained by the users from other sources, they do not contain surprise characteristics and, therefore, are not information (e.g., dividend announcement dates or data relating to economic conditions published in the financial press). If this is the case and if there is any cost to their inclusion, such data should be omitted from the financial statements. Furthermore, some information may be obtainable from alternative sources at a lower total social cost (including the cost to the user of obtaining the information separately). When this is the case, consideration should be given to excluding such information from accounting reports and permitting the alternative source to provide the information.

CHECKPOINTS

---

1. Contrast feedback value and predictive value. Can information be both?
2. Contrast information and data.
3. Compare goal relevance and decision relevance.

Reliability

Reliability, the other major decision-specific characteristic, was defined in *SFAC 2* as:

> The quality of information that assures that information is reasonably free from error and bias and faithfully represents what it purports to represent.

Reliability, said the FASB, is a function of:

Representational faithfulness.

Verifiability.

Neutrality.

Each of these terms is discussed in the sections that follow.

Representational Faithfulness. If one is to depend on information, it is essential for the information to report faithfully the phenomena that it purports to represent. For example, to use the FASB's own illustration:

> A spelling test is administered orally to a group of students. The words are read aloud by the tester, and the students are required to write down the test words. Some students, though they can usually spell well, fail the test. The reason, it turns out, is that they have hearing problems. The test score purports to measure ability to spell, whereas it, in fact, is partly measuring aural acuity. The test score lacks true representational faithfulness.[30]

In light of this illustration, the FASB defined *representational faithfulness* as:

> Correspondence or agreement between a measure or description and the phenomenon that it purports to represent (sometimes called validity).

The difficulty with this definition is that many of the measures used in accounting have no economic interpretation. The price paid for an asset at the time of its purchase may have been a meaningful exchange price, but its depreciated value 10 years later has no significant meaning at all. It is faithful only to the mechanics that created it in the first place. One cannot verify the result; at best, one can check the inputs to its computation and recompute it to test for arithmetical accuracy. In such circumstances, representational faithfulness has a more limited meaning which is better captured by the term verifiability.

Verifiability. The word *verify* derives from the Latin *verus* meaning truth. To verify something means to establish its truth. Truth seems to imply that the measurement has an existence separate from the person making the measurement. Thus, an absence of subjective valuation and personal bias is assumed. However, particularly in accounting, an important question is whether or not a measurement can exist independent of the measurer.

The existence of an external transaction does not automatically imply that an objective measure of the transaction exists. The accountant must still determine the value of what is given up and the value of what is received. Value, like beauty, may be in the eye of the beholder.

In an attempt to escape the dilemma of the interaction between the measurer and the measured, some have placed emphasis on the evidence, rather than on the measurement, and suggested that information is verifiable when objective evidence can be found to support it.[31] The difficulty with this approach is that the selection of the evidence to be used may be subject to personal bias.

A third approach was developed, therefore. In this approach, measurements are verifiable if they can be corroborated by the intersubjective consensus of qualified experts. *Accounting Research Study No. 1*, for example, states that verifiable "means . . . unbiased; subject to verification by another competent investigator."[32] ASOBAT defined verifiability similarly as that attribute of information which allows qualified individuals working independently of one another to develop essentially similar measures or conclusions from an examination of the same evidence.[33] These were the definitions drawn on by the FASB when it defined *verifiability* in the glossary to *SFAC 2* as:

> The ability through consensus among measurers to ensure that information represents what it purports to represent or that the chosen method of measurement has been used without error or bias.

The astute reader will note how the FASB has attempted to cover both the situation where an interpretation can be given to a measure and the situation where only a method exists. The concept of verifiability may be illustrated as follows:

First, one notes that, even if several investigators use the same or similar methods of measurement of an attribute and base their measurements on similar evidence, it is still probable that they will provide a range of values. If the measurements are free from personal bias, it is probable, although not necessary, that a frequency distribution of these measurements will produce a symmetrical curve. For any given number of observations or measurements, then, the degree of objectivity or verifiability may be said to depend upon the dispersion of the measurement values around a mean or average figure. This definition of verifiability is demonstrated by the two measurement procedures in Exhibit 5-7, which result in the same average value.

Measurement procedure A is more verifiable than procedure B, since any measurement value x_1 has a greater probability of being close to the mean value $\bar{x}$ by using procedure A than by using procedure B. Thus, verifiability is a relative concept. Very few procedures will result in values upon which many accountants would have complete agreement. Although verifiability cannot be obtained unless the measurements are relatively free from personal bias, measurement errors and differences in interpretation may also result in the loss of verifiability.

Note that the relative degree of verifiability alone does not determine the reliability of the measurement procedure in describing accurately the attribute under consideration. Even the mean value $\bar{x}$ may fail to measure the attribute accurately.

EXHIBIT 5-7   Verifiability

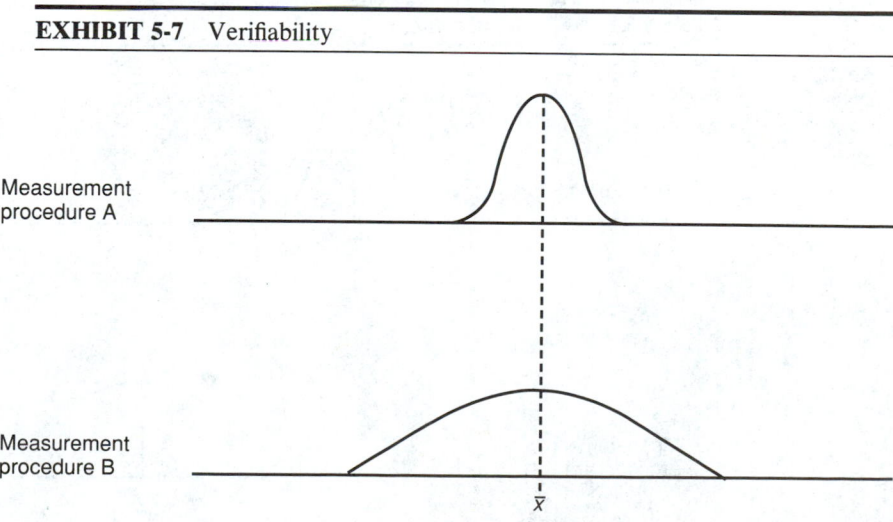

Measurement procedure A

Measurement procedure B

$\bar{x}$

Neutrality.   Bias, said the FASB, is "the tendency of a measure to fall more often on one side than the other of what it represents instead of being equally likely to fall on either side."[34] Freedom from bias then represents the ability of the measurement procedure to provide an accurate description of the attribute under consideration. The concept is most easily illustrated by the diagrams in Exhibit 5-8.

Bias is determined by the relative deviation of the mean value $\bar{x}$ determined by the measurement procedure and the alleged, or "true," value x^* of the attribute. Therefore, measurement procedure C is more verifiable than D, and procedure D is less biased than C because the mean value produced lies closer to the alleged value x^*.

For example, historical cost is not likely to be free from bias in measuring the current market value of an asset if prices have changed radically since the date of acquisition. On the other hand, a procedure that adjusts historical cost for changes in the specific prices of that class of asset may be less verifiable, but result in less bias. When a true value for an attribute cannot be determined, the difference between the mean value $\bar{x}$ and the alleged value x^* must be based upon expert judgment, taking into consideration the logical relationship between the measurement procedure and the attribute being measured.[35]

The term *neutrality* is closely related, but not identical, to the term *freedom from bias*. Neutrality means that one is not biased toward a predetermined result. Neutrality is particularly important for the FASB, because it has decided as a matter of policy not to allow its standards to be used to seek a particular economic or political goal. This is not to say that accounting does not have economic consequences; it does mean that the

---

EXHIBIT 5-8   Bias

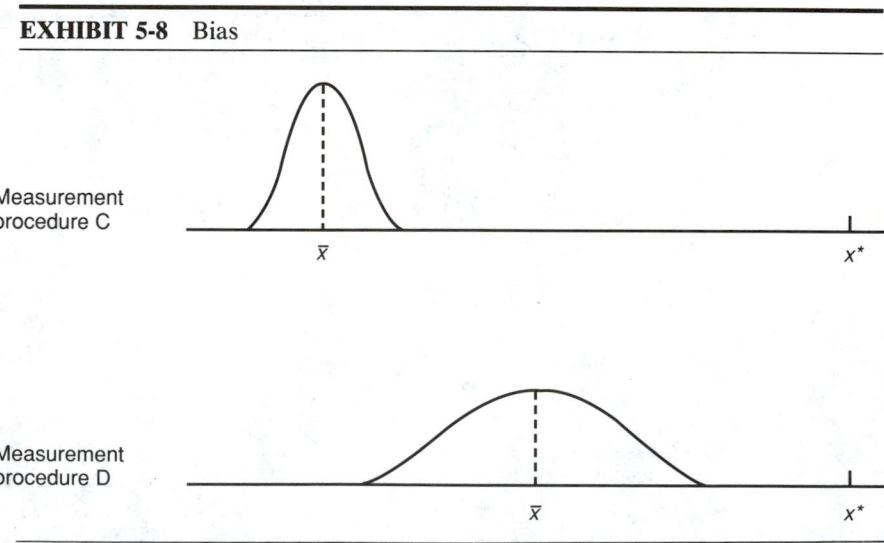

Measurement procedure C

Measurement procedure D

FASB is determined not to seek particular economic consequences.*
Whether, though, neutrality can be achieved remains a relatively controversial matter.

CHECKPOINTS

---

1. Compare representational faithfulness with verifiability.
2. Contrast neutrality and freedom from bias.
3. Compare relevance and reliability. Can information be both?

Comparability

The Board claimed that the usefulness of information is greatly enhanced
when it is presented in such a fashion that one is able to compare one
entity with another—or with the same entity over time. *Comparability*
was then defined as that

> quality of information that enables users to identify similarities in and differ-
> ences between two sets of economic phenomena.

The former depends in part upon uniformity; the latter on consistency.

Uniformity. The term *uniformity* implies that like events are being accounted for identically. Accounting theorists Harry Wolk, Jere Francis,
and Michael Tearney distinguish between *finite* uniformity and *rigid* uniformity. They define the latter as "prescribing one method for generally
similar transactions, even though relevant circumstances may be
present."[36] Accounting for research and development costs is an example
of rigid uniformity in accounting. Finite uniformity permits relevant circumstances to be considered. Accounting for loss contingencies, which
permits different treatment according to the degree of probability, is offered as an example of finite uniformity in accounting.

Uniformity among firms in their financial reporting is frequently
thought to represent a desirable goal for its own sake. That is, the goal of
uniformity frequently encourages the presentation of financial statements
by different firms using the same accounting procedures, measurement
concepts, classifications, and methods of disclosure, as well as a similar
basic format in the statements. As used in this context, the concept is
rightfully criticized; the objective should be comparability, not strict or
rigid uniformity. The primary objective of comparability should be to

---

* For more discussion of economic consequences, see pages 161–7 in Chapter 4.

facilitate the making of predictions and financial decisions by creditors, investors, and others. It may be defined as the quality or state of having enough like characteristics to make comparison appropriate. The main opposition to uniformity is based on the claims that:

1. It would infringe on the basic rights and freedoms of management.
2. It would place accounting in a straitjacket of rules and procedures that would make financial statements less comparable.
3. It would stifle progress and prevent desirable changes.

On the other hand, the arguments for some degree of uniformity are that:

1. The wide variety of acceptable practices makes comparability among different firms impossible or at least difficult.
2. The freedom of management to choose their own methods may introduce the possibility of bias through manipulation of reported information to suit the purposes of those who control the reports.
3. If the private sector does not take steps to achieve greater uniformity, it may be imposed by the SEC or some other governmental agency.

Narrowing the areas of difference in financial reporting among firms may be desirable as an objective of accounting policy; however, it can be only one of the means of achieving the basic goals of moving toward an optimum level of social and economic welfare. If diverse procedures or methods of disclosure are found to provide greater or even equal benefits, the firms are likely to choose the methods that are least costly or that have the more favorable economic consequences for themselves. Since it is impossible to anticipate all of the possible economic consequences, there is some merit in permitting each firm to make some choices so long as investors and creditors are not harmed. At a minimum, accounting standards should require finite uniformity only.

Consistency.   Consistency, as with many of the terms used in this chapter, has been variously defined. It has been used to refer to the use of the same accounting procedures by a single firm or accounting entity from period to period, the use of similar measurement concepts and procedures for related items within the statements of a firm for single period, and the use of the same procedures by different firms. This latter meaning of the term was considered above in the discussion of uniformity, and the term *consistency* will be applied to the first two meanings only.

Consistency in the use of accounting procedures over time is required because of the difficulty of making predictions based on time-series data that are not measured and classified in the same way over time. If different methods or measurement procedures are used, it is difficult to project trends or discern the effects from period to period on the firm caused by external factors (changes in economic conditions, actions of competitors, etc.) or separate the fluctuations caused by internal and external economic factors. For instance, if assets were valued at cost in some periods and at replacement cost in others, both the fluctuations from period to period and the trend may be distorted, especially if price changes are significant over time.

However, care must be taken in the use of the concept of consistency. For instance, while the continued use of historical costs may be consistent in one sense, all it produces in times of changing prices is an aggregate of very dissimilar costs. The result is a number that is actually inconsistently measured from one period to the next. Also, consistency should not be used to prevent a change to a method that provides more accurate or more useful information for predictions or decision making. When a change is made, however, the effect of the change should be stated clearly so that users of the data can take the change into account in their decisions. Of course, disclosure is not necessary if the change would not affect any of the decisions likely to be based on the accounting data.

According to *APB Opinion No. 20*, an accounting change includes a change in an accounting principle, an accounting estimate, or in the reporting entity. It states further that once adopted, an accounting principle should not be changed unless the new method can be justified as being preferable. Changes should be disclosed in the period in which the change is made. Only a few types of changes should be reported by restating the financial statements of prior years.[37]

Consistency can, and should, be interpreted more broadly to mean disclosure, each period, of all relevant information necessary for users to make predictions. Consistency then becomes one means to achieve relevance and is not a goal in its own right.[38] As with uniformity, consistency of disclosure is more important than consistency of procedures.

CHECKPOINTS

1. What factors make financial information comparable?
2. Compare consistency with uniformity.

Materiality

Materiality, which is described by the FASB as a pervasive characteristic, is very similar to the concept of relevance in many respects. As indicated above, the concept of relevance implies that all information should be presented that may aid in the prediction of the types of information required in the decision processes or that may aid directly in the making of decisions. But materiality has also been used in a positive sense to determine what should be disclosed for general, undefined uses. That is, information may be considered to be material (and thus disclosure is necessary) if the knowledge of this information may be significant to the users of accounting reports. According to *SFAC 2*, the basic nature of materiality is that

> it is probable that the judgment of a reasonable person relying upon the report would have been changed or influenced by the inclusion or correction of the item.[39]

Materiality may be looked upon also as a constraint determined by the inability of the specific users to handle large masses of detail. Financial information that may be relevant for investment and other decisions can generally be made available in considerable detail, particularly with the widespread use of computers and other communication devices. One of the responsibilities of the accountant in financial reporting is to summarize this mass of data in such a way that it will be meaningful to the users of the reports. Too much data can be just as misleading as too little. If too much is presented, the relevant items are buried, and the reader must base decisions on inadequate data, in which case the decisions are not likely to be sound. Just as too little information does not promote good predictions and decisions, information that is replete with insignificant details may also detract from good prediction and decision making. Thus, materiality places a restriction on what should be disclosed.

Materiality may relate to the significance of value changes, to corrections of errors in prior reports, or to the several means of disclosure of quantified data and relevant descriptions or qualifications of these data. These changes, corrections, and descriptions should be considered material if they are large enough or significant enough to influence the decisions of the users of financial reports.

The types of items where materiality may be involved in the decision to disclose or not include the following:

1. Quantitative data, such as items affecting net income and asset valuation.
2. The extent of aggregation or itemization of quantitative data in the formal statements.
3. Quantitative data that cannot be estimated accurately enough to be included in the statements.
4. Quantitative features that must be disclosed by descriptive phrases or sentences.
5. Special relationships between the firm and particular individuals or groups affecting the rights and interests of other individuals or groups.
6. Relevant plans and expectations of management.

Materiality regarding the measurement of accounting data is assumed throughout this book.

CHECKPOINTS

---

1. Define materiality.
2. Contrast relevance and materiality.
3. Look back at the diagram in Exhibit 5-4 that lays out the qualitative characteristics that make information useful. Briefly define each characteristic in your own words.

FUNDAMENTALS

Featured in the hierarchy of elements listed in Exhibit 5-2, but not appearing in the Conceptual Framework, are some concepts and elements underlying the measurement of transactions that the FASB termed *fundamentals*. The elements of financial statements, that is, assets, liabilities, and so on, are discussed in detail in subsequent chapters. This section treats those basic concepts which are truly fundamental to accounting but which are not discussed elsewhere. The list is long, so the focus here is on a few key concepts. The basis for much of the discussion is drawn from *APB Statement No. 4*, which appeared shortly before the Conceptual Framework and was the Accounting Principles Board's last attempt to create a framework for its deliberations.

Entity

A definition of the accounting entity is significant because it defines the area of interest and thus narrows the possible objects and activities and their attributes that may be selected for inclusion in financial reports. Furthermore, the entity concept may aid in determining how best to present information regarding the entity. Thus, relevant features may be disclosed and irrelevant features that cloud the basic information may be omitted.

One approach to the definition of the accounting entity is to determine the economic unit that has control over resources, accepts responsibilities for making and carrying out commitments, and conducts economic activity. Such an accounting entity may be either an individual, a partnership, or a legal corporation or a consolidated group engaged in carrying out either profit-seeking or not-for-profit activity.[40] An alternative approach is to define the entity in terms of the area of economic interest of particular individuals, groups, or institutions.[41] In this approach, the boundaries of an economic entity are identifiable:

1. By determining the interested individual or group.
2. By determining the nature of that individual's or that group's interest.[42]

Thus, this approach is oriented to the interests of the users of financial reports.

Both approaches may lead to the same conclusions, but the latter, more user-oriented approach may lead to a selection of different information than the former, economic-activity approach. Additionally, the user approach may extend the boundaries of the entity to include some environmental activity, such as attempts to improve sociological relations within the enterprise or within the community, and information regarding the social responsibilities of the enterprise.

The concept of the accounting entity may include the legal enterprise, a division of the enterprise, or a "super-enterprise," such as a consolidation of several interrelated firms. The choice of the appropriate entity and the determination of its boundaries depend upon the objectives of the reports and the interests of the users of the reported information. The nature of the entity and the interests in it may be classified according to proprietary, entity, funds, or enterprise theories. These theories are discussed in Chapter 22.

Going Concern

An assumption generally made regarding the nature of the relevant accounting entity is that most economic units are organized for operation over an indefinite period of time. Therefore, it is frequently argued that it is a logical step to recognize that the entity should be viewed as remaining in operation indefinitely under normal circumstances (the traditional going-concern postulate). As generally applied, the continuity postulate assumes that the accounting entity will continue in operation long enough to carry out its *existing* commitments.[43] Some argue that, since commitments are of varying time periods, new commitments will have to be made continually into the future to carry out all commitments, thus, in effect, making the continuity assumption one of *indefinite* life.[44] Others argue that a going concern is simply a firm that is adapting itself by the sale of its assets in the ordinary course of its business, that is, it is in orderly liquidation as opposed to forced liquidation.[45] *SAS 59* goes in another direction and defines the expected life of a concern as a reasonable "period of time not to exceed one year from the date of the financial statement."

The reason for including the concept of *continuity* in the set of fundamentals at all is generally to support the benefits theory of valuation, or in some cases to support the use of historical costs as opposed to liquidation values.[46] As indicated earlier, the objective of financial reporting is to permit investors and others to make predictions. Information regarding a specific firm should be presented in such a way that users of financial reports can make their own assessments regarding the future of the enterprise. Therefore, in the authors' opinion, the continuity postulate should not be interpreted to be either a status quo assumption, or a justification for historical cost, or even the benefits concept, in the valuation of assets. However, it is a relevant assumption, leading to the presentation of information regarding resources and commitments and operational activity, such as the sales of goods and services over several years, or even for one year, on the ground that such information may aid in the prediction of future operational activities. Continuity assumes some connection between the past and the future, although not necessarily that the future will be a repetition of the past.* *SAS 59* seeks to fulfil this information objective by requiring an explanatory paragraph from the auditor when there is substantial doubt about the entity's ability to continue as a going concern for a reasonable period of time.[47]

Periodicity

The concept of *periodicity* refers to the fact that accountants measure income over regular calendar periods, such as a year, a quarter, or a month. As Luca Pacioli noted, "Books should be closed each year, especially in a partnership, because frequent accounting makes for long friendships." The significance of the concept lies in the fact that income is relatively easily measured over the full life of a project—in general, lifetime income is equal to the cash earned over the life of the project. It is a considerably more difficult problem to determine income before the end of a project. Consider, by way of illustration, the buccaneer setting sail from London for the New World. When the ship returns, the total income for the voyage is the cash value of the sale of the booty less the amount invested at the outset less depreciation on the ship. But what income has the buccaneer earned if December 31, the financial year-end, happens to fall while the ship is still in mid-Atlantic?

Uncertainty and Conservatism

Uncertainty in accounting arises from two main sources. First, accounting generally relates to entities that are expected to have continuity of existence into the future. Since allocations are frequently made between

---

* The precise meaning of continuity came back to haunt the FASB in setting *SFAS 96* and is discussed again in that setting.

past and future periods, assumptions must be made regarding the logic of these allocations on the basis of expectations regarding the future. Although some of these assumptions and expectations regarding allocations may be validated in later periods, many allocations can never be verified completely.

Second, accounting measurements are frequently assumed to represent monetary expressions of wealth that require estimates of uncertain future amounts. The reliability of these estimates may vary considerably: No monetary quantification of wealth can be known with certainty. Thus, any measurement based on estimates can only be tentative. However, this does not mean that estimates and predictions should not be made as accurately as possible if they are relevant. But it does imply that measurements based on past estimates should be scrutinized closely and adjusted as new and more reliable estimates become possible.

The general constraint of uncertainty has served as the basis for the traditional accounting concept of conservatism. As it is generally stated, the concept of conservatism is a constraint on the presentation of data that may otherwise be reliable and relevant. To understand conservatism in accounting, we should try to understand the conditions that give rise to it and point out the element of truth in the constraint, if indeed there is any.

The term *conservatism* is generally used to mean that accountants should report the lowest of several possible values for assets and revenues and the highest of several possible values for liabilities and expenses. It also implies that expenses should be recognized sooner rather than later and that revenues should be recognized later rather than sooner. Therefore, net assets are more likely to be valued below current exchange prices than above them, and the computation of income is likely to result in the lowest of several alternative amounts. Thus, pessimism is assumed to be better than optimism in financial reporting.

One of the arguments for conservatism is that the accountant's tendency toward pessimism is assumed to be necessary to offset the overoptimism of managers and owners. Entrepreneurs are naturally optimistic about their own enterprises. This optimism tends to be reflected in both the selection and emphasis in accounting reports. Through the pressure of creditors and other users of financial reports, the accountants of the 19th century were continually under pressure to refrain from reflecting this optimism in their reports. Thus, many of the traditional tenets in accounting were supported by conservatism, and many of these concepts permeate accounting practice today.

A second argument for conservatism is that overstatement of profit and valuations is more dangerous for the business and its owners than understatement. That is, the consequences of loss or bankruptcy are much more serious than the consequences of a gain. Therefore, it is argued, there is no reason for the measurement and recognition rules for losses to be the same as for gains when the consequences are different.[48] The basis, presumably, for this argument is that the accountant is in a better position to evaluate risk than is the investor or creditor. However, the evaluation of risk and the preference or aversion for it are subjective judgments, which cannot be assumed by the accountant. Instead of applying conservatism, the objective of financial reports should be to provide adequate information to permit users to make their own evaluations of risk.

A third argument for conservatism is based upon the assumption that the accountant has access to much more information than can be communicated to investors and creditors and that the accountant is faced with two types of risk in doing an audit. On the one hand, there is the risk that what is reported may turn out subsequently to be untrue. On the other hand, there is the risk that what is not reported may subsequently turn out to be true. Conservatism implies that the penalties of disclosure are greater than the penalties of nondisclosure.[49] The objection to this practice is that there is no basic evidence that the consequence of the one risk is so much greater than the consequence of the other to justify this bias in accounting reports. The accountant should attempt to balance these risks as much as possible and provide information for a proper evaluation of the risk whenever possible.

Conservatism is, at best, a very poor method of treating the existence of uncertainty in valuation and income. At its worst, it results in a complete distortion of accounting data. The main danger is that, because conservatism is a very crude method, its effects are capricious. Therefore, conservatively reported data are not subject to proper interpretation even by the most informed readers. Conservatism also conflicts with the objective to disclose all relevant information, and with consistency to the extent to which that is a relevant constraint. It can also lead to a lack of comparability because there can be no uniform standards for its implementation. The authors believe, therefore, that conservatism has no place in accounting theory. Deliberate understatements may lead to poor decisions just as frequently as do overstatements.

Monetary Unit

Although accounting data are not limited to measurement in terms of a monetary unit, accounting reports have traditionally included primarily financial information. And in many cases, the monetary unit provides the best measurement unit, particularly where aggregation is necessary or desirable. However, the monetary unit has its limitations as a method of communicating information. The most serious limitation or constraint is due to the fact that the value of the monetary unit is not stable over time. Since many predictions and decisions must rely on valid comparisons of accounting data over time, the lack of a stable monetary unit means that accounting data based on past exchange prices must be translated into current monetary values in order to be relevant and reliable for making appropriate predictions and decisions. In other words, the measurement constraint of instability of the measuring unit requires some modification in the use of exchange prices of different time periods expressed in terms of money. The problems resulting from this instability and the effect on the derivation of accounting principles are discussed at greater length in Chapter 12.

CHECKPOINTS

1. Define, in your own words, each of the fundamental concepts: *entity, going concern, monetary unit,* and *periodicity*.
2. Explain how conservatism was a response to uncertainty and why it is an inadequate response.
3. What is the most serious limitation of using money as the basis for measurement in accounting?
4. Do the concepts of *conservatism* and *freedom from bias* conflict? Explain.

CONCLUSION

The Conceptual Framework remains the most current attempt to establish a constitution for resolving issues in setting accounting standards. Other countries, such as Britain and Canada, have explored the idea, but to date none has followed the example of the United States. The lack of imitators may reflect New York professor Lee Seidler's earlier contention that there are "no conceptual frameworks in the social sciences."[50] This is not to say that attempts to draw up conceptual frameworks are completely useless. The language and the terminology are all extremely valuable intellectual exercises—they provide what they are supposed to provide: a conceptual framework within which fruitful debate can take place about standards. What it has not done, what it should never have been expected to do, is to provide a single statement from which standards could be derived without further debate.

SUMMARY

This chapter provides an overview of the Conceptual Framework for Financial Accounting and Reporting that was developed by the FASB between 1972 and 1985. It discusses the five statements which cover the framework (one was superseded); the elements that make up the framework (objectives, qualitative characteristics, and fundamental concepts); the qualitative characteristics (relevance and reliability); and the fundamental concepts (entity, going concern, periodicity, conservatism, and the monetary unit). Discussion of the elements of financial statements (assets, liabilities, revenues, expenses) and of other fundamental concepts such as revenue recognition and matching are left to later chapters.

Financial reporting was seen as more encompassing than financial accounting since it can include supplemental data. The essential objective of financial reporting is the provision of information to enable investors, particularly those who lack authority to specify what information they want, to predict the future cash flows of the enterprise. For this information to be useful it should be relevant (i.e., it should be timely and have predictive and feedback value) and it should be reliable (i.e., it should be representationally faithful, verifiable, and neutral). Later chapters use these concepts in showing how the FASB has attempted to develop accounting standards.

QUESTIONS

Multiple Choice

1. (M87#1) According to the FASB Conceptual Framework, predictive value is an ingredient of

	Relevance	*Reliability*
a.	Yes	No
b.	Yes	Yes
c.	No	Yes
d.	No	No

2. (N86#1) According to the FASB Conceptual Framework, which of the following relates to both relevance and reliability?

	Consistency	*Verifiability*
a.	Yes	Yes
b.	Yes	No
c.	No	Yes
d.	No	No

3. (N84#1) Under Statement of Financial Accounting Concepts No. 2, which of the following relates to both relevance and reliability?

   a. Timeliness.
   b. Materiality.
   c. Verifiability.
   d. Neutrality.

4. (M83#2) Under Statement of Financial Accounting Concepts No. 2, feedback value is an ingredient of the primary quality of

	Relevance	*Reliability*
a.	No	No
b.	No	Yes
c.	Yes	Yes
d.	Yes	No

5. (M84#1) Under Statement of Financial Accounting Concepts No. 2, timeliness is an ingredient of the primary quality of

- *a.* Reliability.
- *b.* Relevance.
- *c.* Verifiability.
- *d.* Representational faithfulness.

PROBLEMS

1. The FASB's objectives focus on private enterprise. For an objective which points to a new and different goal, but one which is not necessarily acceptable, one might turn to the English Corporate Report. Their list, which parallels the FASB's in most respects, also includes as an objective:

> Evaluating the economic function and performance of the entity in relation to society and the national interest and the social costs and benefits attributable to the entity.[51]

What sets this objective off from the FASB's is the stress placed upon social costs and benefits as opposed to private costs and benefits. With growing concerns in society about pollution and the like, is this a foretaste of things to come?

2. Nicholas Dopuch and Shyam Sunder, professors at the University of Chicago at the time of writing this, said

> We should not be surprised if auditors, like everyone else, seek to maximize their own wealth through participation in the accounting process. If the provision of economically useful information implies greater exposure to the risk of being sued without corresponding benefits of higher compensation, they will not see the provision of economically useful information (however defined) as *their* objective of the financial accounting process.[52]

Required:

Discuss this view in the light of determining who the users of accounting are and whether they have an objective in common.

3. Arthur Andersen & Co. stated that:

. . . the overall purpose of financial statements is to communicate information concerning the nature and value of the economic resources of a business enterprise, the interests of creditors and the equity of owners in the economic resources, and the changes in the nature and value of those resources from period to period.[53]

Required:

Compare and contrast this objective with those of the FASB. Is this a pragmatic, a semantic, or a syntactic objective?

4. Ernst & Ernst (later Ernst & Whinney and now Ernst & Young) was sharply critical of the Conceptual Framework and is quoted as having said:

The proposed objectives of financial statements are narrowly directed to benefit investors, a single, special interest, with inadequate consideration of the effect this might have on the total economy or on other interests in financial reporting.[54]

Required:

Discuss their concerns. You might begin by listing the other interests and how they might conflict with those of investors. What response could you make in defense of the FASB's position?

5. Many of the concerns of the FASB in regard to financial reporting such as relevance and reliability could be expressed with regard to standardized tests such as the SATs, GMATs, and GREs.

Required:

Based on your personal experiences with these tests, sketch out a "conceptual framework" that would guide the use and disclosure of the results and use of these tests. You might want to consider questions such as: Is a score of 1,330 materially different from a score of 1,340? Do the tests have predictive value? Are the tests reliable? Are they relevant?

6. The current objectives of financial reporting in the United States are directed toward investors. Should they be, in your opinion? Can you make a case for more social reporting? Can you make a case for no social reporting? What do you think the ethical obligations of corporations are in this regard?

7. "Information that is not reliable has no place in financial statements. If it appears anywhere, it should be in the notes or in management's discussion." Discuss the pros and cons of this statement.

8. Companies typically report a higher income figure to their shareholders than to the tax authorities. One way to achieve this is to use accelerated depreciation for tax purposes but straight-line depreciation for financial reporting purposes. The effect is to shift a portion of the tax burden from the current year to future years.

What assumptions are we making when we assume that the burden shifted to the future years will be paid?

9. It has been pointed out that accounting earnings can differ between companies despite similar situations for at least three reasons:[55]

1. Management has open to it several generally accepted accounting alternatives such as FIFO and LIFO.
2. Management has to choose parameters within a given accounting alternative such as the length of an asset's life or the size of the provision for bad debt.
3. Business judgments such as when to retire an asset or when to purchase a new asset will vary across managements.

For these reasons, some question whether comparability through uniformity can ever be achieved. Chapter 8 notes that George O. May initially had preferred more complete disclosure as the better route to comparability.

Required:

Discuss the impact on comparability of the alternatives open to management.

CHEROKEE INDUSTRIES

Cherokee Industries are furniture manufacturers with sales of some $120 million a year. During 1989, the company wanted to establish an additional line of credit with the Grand Alliance Bank to permit them to expand. In preparing the financial statements for the bank, Tom Hansen, one of the partners of Crockett & Hansen, a firm of auditors in Atlanta, Georgia, tried to persuade Don Walker, vice president of Finance, to bring his accounting procedures more into line with those of the industry. Cherokee was a private company and had, to a large extent, followed its own accounting policies over the years. Hansen's feeling was that restating the financials would permit the bank to more easily compare Cherokee with its competitors, and so it would make a strong line of credit more likely. As Hansen explained to Walker:

"Let's assume that Grand Alliance wants to compare ratios between your company and that of your industry. For example, they may be using your current ratio or your debt-equity ratio to evaluate their risk in being your creditor. Or they may want to use your rate of return on assets as a basis for figuring the present values of the cash flows that Cherokee might generate. It would surely be desirable that your ratios be as comparable as possible to others in the industry. If you're going to get them comparable, you will have to use information computed by uniform procedures in those situations in which there is no evidence that one procedure is better than another."

Hansen went on to say: "We like to tell our clients that differences in procedures used by the various firms within an industry are permissible only if conditions in the firms are not alike. Choose procedures providing the most accurate or most reliable data, but where there is little difference in the various procedures, get into line with your industry and adopt a uniform procedure."

Walker was not persuaded: "We have always argued that all relevant information for Cherokee should be presented to permit our investors and creditors to make predictions for Cherokee. With all the information we provide them, our investors and creditors can make their own estimates of the present value of the firm and evaluate our risk. Frankly, Tom, I just don't believe that banks should do ratio analysis like that. The only sensible comparisons between companies should be made at an aggregate level. In other words, I maintain that their estimates of present values and risk should be used in making the final comparisons, rather than relying on comparisons of detailed information regarding the firms. If I'm right, accountants should be concerned with presenting relevant information for each firm, rather than being concerned with presenting comparable detailed data.

"Of course, I agree that it is still important that predictions be based on equally reliable data. And I will also allow that some general standards are necessary regarding the choice of information to be presented, the degree of detail to be presented, and the selection of measurement concepts and procedures relevant for specific users in their making of predictions and decisions. However, in the end, I believe that uniformity of *disclosure* is more important than uniformity of *procedures* if the goal is to improve the information available to efficient capital markets."

Required:

With whom do you agree most, Tom Hansen or Don Walker?

PRIMARY SOURCES

Those interested in learning more about the topics covered in this chapter might begin by consulting these sources. Each has numerous excellent citations.

American Institute of Certified Public Accountants, Accounting Principles Board, *Basic Concepts and Accounting Principles Underlying Statements of Business Enterprises,* APB Statement No. 4 (AICPA, 1970).

Anthony, Robert N. *Tell It Like It Was* (Homewood, Ill.: Richard D. Irwin, 1983).

Financial Accounting Standards Board, Discussion Memorandum of the issues related to the *Conceptual Framework for Financial Accounting and Reporting: Elements of Financial Statements and Their Measurement* (FASB, December 2, 1976).

Financial Accounting Standards Board, *Statements of Financial Accounting Concepts* (Homewood, Ill.: Richard D. Irwin, 1987).

Flegm, Eugene H. *How to Meet the Challenges of Relevance and Regulation* (New York: John Wiley & Sons, 1984).

Solomons, David. *Making Accounting Policies* (New York: Oxford University Press, 1986).

SELECTED ADDITIONAL READINGS

In addition to the works cited in the primary sources and the footnotes in the chapter, the reader is referred to the following authors:

Postulates

Deinzer, Harvey T. *Development of Accounting Thought* (New York: Holt, Rinehart & Winston, 1965).

Ijiri, Y. "Three Postulates of Momentum Accounting." *Accounting Horizons,* March 1987, pp. 25–34.

Lambert, III. "Basic Assumptions in Accounting Theory Construction." *Journal of Accountancy,* February 1974, pp. 41–48.

Mautz, R. K. "The Place of Postulates in Accounting." *Journal of Accountancy,* January 1965, pp. 46–49.

Metcalf, Richard W. "The Basic Postulates in Perspective." *The Accounting Review,* January 1964, pp. 16–21.

Popoff, Boris. "Postulates, Principles and Rules." *Accounting and Business Research,* Summer 1972, pp. 182–93.

Continuity

Devine, Carl Thomas. "Entity, Continuity, Discount, and Exit Values." *Essays in Accounting Theory* 3 (1971), pp. 111–35.

Fremgren, James M. "The Going Concern Assumption. A Critical Appraisal." *The Accounting Review,* October 1968, pp. 649–56.

Mutchler, J. F. "A Multivariate Analysis of the Auditor's Going-Concern Opinion Decision." *Journal of Accounting Research,* Autumn 1985, pp. 668–82.

Sterling, Robert R. "The Going Concern. An Examination." *The Accounting Review,* July 1968, pp. 481–502.

Yu, S. C. "A Reexamination of the Going Concern Postulate." *International Journal of Accounting, Education, and Research,* Spring 1971, pp. 37–58.

Objectives

Anton, H. R. "Objectives of Financial Accounting. Review and Analysis." *Journal of Accountancy,* January 1976, pp. 40–51.

Beaver, William H., and Joel S. Demski. "The Nature of Financial Accounting Objectives: A Summary and Synthesis." *Studies on Financial Accounting Objectives, Supplement to Journal of Accounting Research,* 1974, pp. 170–87.

Goetz, B. E., and J. G. Birnberg. "A Comment on the Trueblood Report." *Management Accounting,* April 1976, pp. 18–20.

Govindarajan, V. "The Objectives of Financial Statements: An Empirical Study of the Use of Cash Flow and Earnings by Security Analysts." *Accounting, Organizations, and Society,* 1980, pp. 457–78.

Kenley, W. John, and George J. Staubus. "Objectives and Concepts of Financial Statements." *Accounting Research Study No. 3* (Melbourne: Accountancy Research Foundation, 1972).

Sterling, Robert R. "Decision-Oriented Financial Accounting." *Accounting and Business Research,* Summer 1972, pp. 198–208.

Williams, Jan Robert. "Differing Opinions on Accounting Objectives." *CPA Journal,* August 1973, pp. 651–56.

Relevance

Chambers, R. J. "Usefulness—The Vanishing Premise in Accounting Standard Setting." *Abacus,* December 1979, pp. 71–92.

Martin, Alvin. "An Empirical Test of the Relevance of Accounting Information for Investment Decisions." *Empirical Research in Accounting. Selected Studies,* 1971, pp. 1–31.

Shwayder, Keith. "Relevance." *Journal of Accounting Research,* Spring 1968, pp. 86–97.

Materiality

Barlev, Benzion. "On the Measurement of Materiality." *Accounting and Business Research,* Summer 1972, pp. 194–97.

Bernstein, Leopold A. "The Concept of Materiality." *The Accounting Review,* January 1967, pp. 86–95.

Estes, R., and D. D. Reames. "Effects of Personal Characteristics on Materiality Decisions: A Multivariate Analysis." *Accounting and Business Review,* Autumn 1988, pp. 291–96.

Frishkoff, Paul. "An Empirical Investigation of the Concept of Materiality in Accounting." *Empirical Research in Accounting. Selected Studies. Journal of Accounting Research,* 1970, pp. 116–37.

Hostrum, G. L., and W. F. Messier. "A Review and Integration of Empirical Research on Materiality." *Auditing: A Journal of Practice and Theory,* Fall 1982, pp. 45–63.

Jennings, M.; D. C. Kneer; and P. M. J. Reckers. "A Reexamination of the Concept of Materiality: Views of Auditors, Users and Officers of the Court." *Auditing: A Journal of Practice and Theory,* Spring 1987, pp. 104–15.

Morris, M. H., and W. D. Nichols. "Consistency Exceptions: Materiality Judgments and Audit Firm Structure." *The Accounting Review,* April 1988, pp. 237–54.

Ro, B. T. "An Analytical Approach to Accounting Materiality." *Journal of Business Finance and Accounting,* Autumn 1982, pp. 397–412.

Rose, J.; W. H. Beaver; S. Becker; and G. Sorter. "Toward an Empirical Measure of Materiality." *Empirical Research in Accounting: Selected Studies. Journal of Accounting Research,* 1970, pp. 138–56.

Steinbart, P. J. "Materiality: A Case Study Using Expert Systems." *The Accounting Review,* January 1987, pp. 97–116.

Timeliness

Chambers, A. E., and S. H. Penman. "Timeliness of Reporting and the Stock Price Reaction to Earnings Announcements." *Journal of Accounting Research,* Spring 1984, pp. 21–47.

Courtis, J. K. "Relationships between Timeliness in Corporate Reporting and Corporate Attributes." *Accounting and Business Research,* Winter 1976, pp. 45–56.

Gilling, Donald M. "Timeliness in Corporate Reporting. Some Further Comment." *Accounting and Business Research,* Winter 1977, pp. 34–36.

Givoly, D., and D. Palmon. "Timeliness of Annual Earnings Announcements: Some Empirical Evidence." *The Accounting Review,* July 1982, pp. 486–508.

Keller, S. B. "Reporting Timeliness in the Presence of Subject to Audit Qualifications." *Journal of Business, Finance, and Accounting,* Spring 1986, pp. 117–24.

Whittred, G., and I. Zimmer. "Timeliness of Financial Reporting and Financial Distress." *The Accounting Review,* April 1984, pp. 287–95.

Zeghal, D. "Timeliness of Accounting Reports and Their Informational Content on the Capital Market." *Journal of Business, Finance, and Accounting,* Autumn 1984, pp. 367–80.

Accounting Measurement

Ashton, Robert H. "Objectivity of Accounting Measures. A Multirule-Multimeasurer Approach." *The Accounting Review,* July 1977, pp. 567–75.

Dewhirst, John F. "Dealing with Uncertainty." *Canadian Chartered Accountant,* August 1971, pp. 139–46.

Ijiri, Yuji. *The Foundations of Accounting Measurement* (Englewood Cliffs, N.J.: Prentice Hall, 1967).

"Report of the Committee on Foundations of Accounting Measurement." Supplement to *The Accounting Review,* 1971, pp. 3–48.

"Report of the Committee on Accounting Valuation Bases." Supplement to *The Accounting Review,* 1972, esp. pp. 556–68.

Understandability

Fertakis, J. P. "On Communication, Understanding, and Relevance in Accounting Reporting." *The Accounting Review,* October 1969, pp. 680–91.

Morton, J. R. "Qualitative Objectives of Financial Accounting: A Comment on Relevance and Understandability." *Journal of Accounting Research,* Autumn 1974, pp. 288–98.

ENDNOTES

1. Financial Accounting Standards Board, *Scope and Implications of the Conceptual Framework Project* (Stamford: FASB, December 2, 1976), p. 2.
2. Financial Accounting Standards Board Discussion Memorandum, *Conceptual Framework for Accounting and Reporting* (Stamford, Conn.: FASB, June 6, 1974), p. 15.
3. *Report of the Study Group on the Objectives of Financial Statements,* "Objectives of Financial Statements" (AICPA, October 1973).
4. *SFAC 1,* par. 5.
5. American Institute of Accountants, *Accounting Terminology Bulletin No. 1,* "Review and Resume" (New York: AIA, 1953), par. 9.
6. *SFAC 5,* par. 8.
7. *APB Statement No. 4,* p. 33.
8. Maurice Moonitz, "The Basic Postulates of Accounting," *Accounting Research Study No. 1* (AICPA, 1961), p. 23.
9. Robert T. Sprouse and Maurice Moonitz, "A Tentative Set of Broad Accounting Principles for Business Enterprises," *Accounting Research Study No. 3* (AICPA, 1962), p. 53.
10. American Institute of Certified Public Accountants, Study Group on the Objectives of Financial Statements, *Objectives of Financial Statements* (AICPA, 1973).
11. American Institute of Certified Public Accountants, Accounting Principles Board, *Basic Concepts and Accounting Principles Underlying Statements of Business Enterprises,* APB Statement No. 4 (AICPA, 1970).
12. Kenneth S. Most and A. L. Winters, "Focus on Standard Setting: From Trueblood to the FASB," *Journal of Accountancy,* February 1977, pp. 67–75.
13. Nicholas Dopuch and Shyam Sunder, "FASB's Statements on Objectives and Elements of Financial Accounting: A Review," *The Accounting Review,* January 1980, p. 11.
14. Tony Tinker, Cheryl Lehman, and Marilyn Neimark, "Marginalizing the Public Interest: A Critical Look at Recent Social Accounting History," *Behavioral Accounting Research: A Critical Analysis.* Edited by Kenneth R. Ferris (Columbus, Ohio: Century VII Publishing Company, 1988), pp. 117–43. This article contains an extensive bibliography.
15. Eugene H. Flegm, *Accounting* (New York: McGraw-Hill, 1984), p. 234.
16. Ibid., p. 223.
17. Also see Robert N. Anthony, *Tell It Like It Was* (Homewood, Ill.: Richard D. Irwin, 1983).
18. *SFAC 1,* par. 28.
19. *APB Statement No. 4,* p. 20.
20. Yuji Ijiri, "On the Accountability-Based Conceptual Framework of Accounting," *Journal of Accounting and Public Policy,* Summer 1983, p. 75.
21. Don W. Vickrey, "Normative Information Qualities: A Contrast between Information-Economics and FASB Perspectives," *Abacus,* September 1985,

pp. 115–29, provides some useful theoretical insights into these qualitative characteristics.

22. Joel S. Demski, "The General Impossibility of Normative Accounting Standards," *The Accounting Review,* October 1973, pp. 718–23.

23. *SFAC 2,* par. 136.

24. *SFAC 2,* par. 143.

25. For a response to these complaints, see Dennis Beresford, "What's Right with the FASB," *Journal of Accountancy,* January 1990, pp. 81–85.

26. Committee to Prepare a Statement of Basic Accounting Theory, *A Statement of Basic Accounting Theory* (AAA, 1966), p. 7.

27. *SFAC 2,* par. 46.

28. American Accounting Association, "Report of the Committee on Corporate Financial Reporting," *The Accounting Review,* supplement to vol. 47, 1972, pp. 526–27.

29. Errol R. Iselin, "The Objectives of Accounting in an Accounting Theory Based on Deductive Methodology," *University of Queensland Papers* (St. Lucia, Australia: University of Queensland Press, 1971), p. 22.

30. *SFAC 2,* par. 69.

31. W. A. Paton and A. C. Littleton, *An Introduction to Corporate Accounting Standards* (AAA, 1955), pp. 18–21.

32. Moonitz, "The Basic Postulates," p. 42.

33. Committee to Prepare a Statement of Basic Accounting Theory, p. 10.

34. *SFAC 2,* par. 77.

35. The AAA Committee on Accounting Valuation Bases suggested that, since the true value cannot be known, an alternative is to measure the displacement (bias) of the present measure from the next best measure that can be regarded as the challenger. Committee on Accounting Valuation Bases, "Report of the Committee on Accounting Valuation Bases," *The Accounting Review,* supplement to vol. 47, 1972, p. 563.

36. Harry I. Wolk, Jere R. Francis, and Michael G. Tearney, *Accounting Theory,* 2nd ed. (Boston: PWS-Kent, 1989), p. 237. The discussion leading up to this definition is insightful.

37. APB Opinion No. 20, "Accounting Changes" (AICPA, 1971).

38. For some empirical support of consistency, see Andrew M. McCosh, "Accounting Consistency—Key to Stockholder Information," *The Accounting Review,* October 1967, pp. 693–700.

39. *SFAC 2,* par. 132.

40. This is the basic view of Moonitz, "The Basic Postulates," p. 22; and of *SFAC 1,* pars. 9–12.

41. This approach is that selected by the AAA 1964 Concepts and Standards Research Study Committee on the Business Entity Concept, "The Entity Concept," *The Accounting Review,* April 1965, pp. 358–67.

42. Ibid., p. 358.

43. For one argument, see Richard Mattessich, *Accounting and Analytical Methods* (Homewood, Ill.: Richard D. Irwin), pp. 44–45.

44. Robert R. Sterling, "The Going Concern: An Examination," *The Accounting Review,* July 1968, pp. 481–502.

45. Raymond J. Chambers, *Accounting Evaluation and Economic Behavior* (Englewood Cliffs, N.J.: Prentice Hall), p. 218.
46. Chambers used it to buttress his arguments for current cash equivalents in measuring assets.
47. John E. Ellingsen, Kurt Pany, and Peg Fagan, "*SAS no. 59:* How to Evaluate Going Concern," *Journal of Accountancy,* January 1989, pp. 24–31.
48. See Eugen Schmalenbach, *Dynamic Accounting,* English trans. (London: Gee & Co., 1959), pp. 81–82.
49. See Arthur L. Thomas, *Revenue Recognition* (Ann Arbor: University of Michigan Press, 1966), pp. 53–54; and Carl Thomas Devine, "The Rule of Conservatism Reexamined," *Journal of Accounting Research,* Autumn 1963, pp. 137–38.
50. Lee J. Seidler, "No Accounting for the FASB's Draft on Recognition and Measurement," *Accounting Issues* (Bear, Stearns & Co., April 9, 1984), p. 13.
51. Accounting Standards Committee, *The Corporate Report* (ASC, 1975), p. 78.
52. Dopuch & Sunder, "FASB's Statements: A Review," p. 13.
53. Arthur Andersen & Co., *Accounting Standards for Business Enterprises Throughout the World* (Chicago: Arthur Andersen & Co., 1974), p. 13.
54. Flegm, *Accounting,* p. 213.
55. Dean E. Graber and Bill D. Jaravazin, "The FASB—Eliminator of 'Managed Earnings,'?" *The Financial Analysts Journal,* March/April 1979, p. 73.

Chapter 6

The Economic Environment of Accounting

CHAPTER OBJECTIVES

After studying this chapter, you will be able to:

Define the potential users of accounting information and distinguish their preferences for information.

Characterize the nature of the economy within which accountants provide financial reporting and trace the impact of this economy on the nature of accounting.

Define the term *market efficiency* in its three forms, strong, semistrong, and weak.

Describe the implications of market efficiency for financial reporting.

Outline the market-based approach to accounting and its significance for explaining current accounting practice.

CHAPTER OVERVIEW

A Private Economy

Accounting in the West occurs in the framework of private, capitalist economies permitting the use of exchange prices as measures of economic value. Users of accounting are many and varied but appear to have a common interest in predicting future cash flows.

Capital Markets

Empirical analysis demonstrates that American stock markets are semistrong-efficient. The meaning of efficiency, the various forms of efficiency, and the implications of efficiency are discussed.

Asset Valuation

Two capital market valuation models are presented: the capital asset pricing model and the option pricing model. Each has been used in research to determine the impact of financial statements on capital markets. Some of the implications of this research are summarized.

Conclusion

Research, by definition, is fluid and subject to change in the light of new findings. Currently, though, it appears that capital markets react remarkably swiftly and intelligently to the publication of new information.

The objectives of financial reporting, says the FASB, "stem largely from the needs of those for whom the information is intended, which in turn depends significantly on the nature of the economic activities and decisions with which users are involved."[1] An understanding of the economic, legal, political, and social environment is essential, therefore, in setting standards.

A second reason why an understanding of the environment of accounting is so important to accountants is that it is the environment that provides the accountant with the prices that are used to measure the assets and the equities which appear on balance sheets. The general rule of accounting is to enter the item at its equivalent cash value. For many items this value is known and poses no problem. Difficulties, though, present themselves when the cash paid covers the cost of two or more assets, such as buildings and the land on which they rest. How much should go to the land; how much to the buildings? The problem is no less difficult when one incurs two obligations wrapped in one contract: An example is convertible debt. Here the firm has an obligation to pay interest but it also has an obligation to provide the creditor with shares if certain conditions are later met. In effect, it has a certain liability and a contingent common stock. How does one divide the cash price between the two? To solve problems like this, one needs economic models of how prices are set. Stated otherwise, one needs pricing theory.

Researchers have examined the environment of accounting from several different angles. They have considered the nature of the economic system and listed the potential users of accounting within that system, asking who uses accounting, why, and what are their preferences. They have extensively researched the nature of the financial markets, which appear to be the primary targets of accounting information. In addition, they have examined the nature of the political system, analyzing in depth the form and effect of contracts, both implicit and explicit, between the various users of financial information. This chapter examines the world of accounting from the economic perspective; the next examines the political context.

The first part of the chapter describes the potential user community, their diverse interests, and their possible common interest in information about cash flows. Shareholder analysis is contrasted with stakeholder analysis as a means to highlight some of the implications of how one views the economic environment. The second section introduces research into financial markets and asks what financial information might be desired in this world. The meaning and implications of market efficiency are explored here. The third section discusses the pricing of assets in capital markets and how these pricing models have been used to tackle issues in accounting. A brief conclusion follows.

A PRIVATE ECONOMY

The U.S. economy may be characterized as essentially private, that is, for the most part, private individuals, rather than the state, own businesses.[2] Another characteristic is that businesses produce goods and services for exchange instead of consumption by their producers. The processes generating these goods and services tend to be long and complex. Few owners of large public companies are directly engaged in the production process, leaving this to managers and their employees under the ultimate direction of a board of directors. It is the directors' task to report on the affairs of the company to the shareholders at regular intervals. Apart from the initial and subsequent offerings of capital, shareholders do not trade with the company, but with one another. Nevertheless, the price of the shares presumably reflects the earnings prospects of the company. Government intervenes directly and indirectly in this economy, but the main engine driving the economy remains the search for profit by individual investors through their shares in companies.

To a greater or lesser extent the above characterization of the economy is true for most economies which practice modern for-profit accounting; however, it is not universally true. The upheavals in Eastern Europe during 1989 highlighted for many the differences between a private and a state-run economy. Things that one tends to take for granted in the one economy do not exist in the other. Who owns a firm is not well established in communist countries, making a definition of owners' equity extremely difficult. There is also an absence of private property, making the definition of an asset moot. And with only government-controlled markets, prices can hardly be claimed to measure value in any normal sense of that word. These are not just theoretical difficulties but real problems, as accounting firms are discovering as they seek to set up business in Eastern Europe![3]

The characterization of the economy as private and capitalist leads the FASB to suggest that "the function of financial reporting is to provide information that is useful to those who make economic decisions about business enterprises and about investments in or loans to business enterprises."[4] The potential list of those making economic decisions is long but includes owners, lenders, suppliers, employees, and management. Each is seen to have made an investment in the enterprise and, therefore, to have an interest in the outcome of that investment: Owners expect dividends, lenders expect interest, suppliers expect payment, and employees and management expect salaries and wages. The enterprise must generate enough cash to provide the desired return on the investments these groups have made. The FASB thus concludes that there is "a common interest of various potential users in the ability of an enterprise to generate favorable cash flows."[5] Thus, "financial reporting should provide information to help investors, creditors, and others assess the amounts, timing, and uncertainty of prospective net cash inflows to the related enterprise."[6]

Despite the attempt to define investors as broadly as possible, the FASB's approach does stress the primary role of the owner. For example, in their section on management they claim that financial reporting should provide information that is "useful to managers and directors in making decisions in the interests of owners"; and "about how management of an enterprise has discharged its stewardship responsibility to *owners* (stockholders) for the use of enterprise resources entrusted to it [our italics]."[7] This emphasis on the primary role of ownership is not surprising given the nature of a private economy which the FASB assumes exists. It also coincides with the thrust of the Securities Acts of 1933 and 1934. To the extent that other groups are considered, their interests are assumed to be in common with those of owners, that is, user interests are assumed to be relatively homogeneous.

The assumption that users have a common interest has drawn implicit criticism from several sources. Stanford professor William Beaver, for example, tabulates the various users of accounting information, breaking them into the five main groups shown in Exhibit 6-1: investors, information intermediaries, regulators, management, and auditors. Each of these groups is then divided into subgroups. Investors, for instance, are distinguished by the extent of their activity in the marketplace, the degree to which they are diversified, and the level of their sophistication, among other things. Investors who adopt a buy-and-hold strategy and those who keep a diversified portfolio may have no desire for firm-specific information. As a result, they may consider it a waste of society's resources to provide such information. Similarly, investors who defer their investment decisions to financial intermediaries, such as their brokers, may also reject the provision of more financial information directly to them.

EXHIBIT 6-1   Constituencies in the Financial Reporting Environment

---

    I. Investors
        A. Diversified vs. Undiversified
        B. Active vs. Passive
        C. Professional vs. Nonprofessional
    II. Information Intermediaries
        A. Financial Analysts
        B. Bond Rating Agencies
        C. Stock Rating Agencies
        D. Investment Advisory Services
        E. Brokerage Firms
    III. Regulators
        A. FASB
        B. SEC
        C. Congress
    IV. Management
        A. Large vs. Small Firms
        B. Publicly vs. Closely Held Firms
    V. Auditors
        A. National vs. Local Firms
        B. SEC Practice vs. Non-SEC Practice

Beaver concludes that users are heterogeneous rather than homogeneous.[8] As the multiperson decision theory section in Chapter 7 underlines, heterogeneous demands raise difficult and perplexing questions for regulators.

Shareholders versus Stakeholders

Critics of the FASB argue that the FASB's emphasis on owners does not pay full compliment to the complexity of the modern economy. They point to the following facts:

1. Pension funds and other large financial intermediaries own most of the shares in public companies so that individual ownership has become more distant.
2. Leveraged buyouts have increased the liability section of the balance sheet to the point where creditors might be able to exercise more control than shareholders.
3. Government agencies control vast sections of the economy in most countries.

They ask whether one can continue to build one's theories around the views of 19th-century economists who were the first to distinguish between capitalists and workers or, equivalently, between owners and employees; who saw managers as paid agents of the owners not very much different from other employees; and whose list of creditors consisted only of banks and trade suppliers.[9]

Those who adopt a broader view tend to argue that all organizations, not just public companies, have an obligation to report not simply to *shareholders* but to everyone with a "stake" in the company—the *stakeholders*. In other words, churches, universities, charitable organizations, cities, states, private companies, and public companies should provide reports to everyone who has an interest in them. The general public is considered to have a fundamental interest in information about social organizations because they "exist with the general consent of the community, are afforded special legal and operational privileges, they compete for resources of manpower, material, and energy and they make use of community-owned assets such as roads and harbors."[10] Proponents of this view would not limit financial reporting to traditional financial statements but would include detailed reports on employment for the benefit of employees, and of transactions between the company and government bodies so that the public could assess its role in the economy. This might even include information about contributions to political campaigns, and it would be required of all enterprises—public or private, for profit or not for profit—regardless.

This view is clearly controversial. The point here is not to take a stance but simply to stress that one's view of how the economy works does affect one's view of the appropriate nature of the information that should flow from enterprises to their constituents. The following paragraphs explore the characteristics of a private economy in more depth. At each point the implications of these characteristics are traced for the optimal design of accounting systems.

CHECKPOINTS

1. Briefly describe the economy within which you find yourself. Name two other countries with similar economies and two with dissimilar economies.
2. List the five major groups into which Beaver divides potential users of accounting. In what other way might one classify users?
3. How might managers differ from shareholders in their demand for financial reporting? In what ways might banks differ from shareholders?

SECURITY MARKETS

The fact that markets aggregate individual preferences makes them potential indicators of society's demand for information. This result has led to much research into the way markets work. The securities market, in which the holdings of shareholders are traded, is of particular interest to accountants.* This is also known as the capital market since it is the market in which equity capital is raised. The New York Stock Exchange is especially interesting because of its size and dominance in the United States. Studies of other markets followed.

Accounting researchers were particularly interested in capital markets because observations of market reactions to accounting information offered a means of testing accounting theories that had been lacking in the past. One of the dilemmas of an emphasis on usefulness of information to individual users is the difficulty of testing hypotheses empirically. Usefulness of information to individual investors is largely a matter of individual decision-making processes. Even if measurements of subjective personal utilities could be made, aggregation for even specific classes of investors would be difficult. So, if the objective is to predict what accounting information may be most useful to individual investors, a real-world test is extremely difficult, if not impossible. The market test seemed to offer a way out of this by enabling researchers to focus on the impact of investors as a whole on the market.

The market approach changes the focus of theory from the welfare of the individual investor to that of the welfare of society. The change is most easily demonstrated by an example. Intrinsic-value theories assume that an objective of accounting is to provide information to help the investor find underpriced securities—that is, where the intrinsic value is greater than current market price. If this does occur, the result of a securities transaction would be a transfer of wealth from one individual to another. But, under the market approach, one notes that the investor purchasing the undervalued security would gain, and the investor selling the security would lose. There is no increase in wealth to society, therefore. Stated otherwise, what in one approach is of value to an individual has no value in another approach when the focus is the market.

More generally, a market-based approach to theory suggests two objectives for accounting. First, information is necessary to permit an optimal allocation of resources among producers. An optimal allocation will occur when producers are able to obtain the necessary capital funds to attain a maximum gross national product with a given amount of resources. This definition of optimal allocation may be qualified in order to include social

---

* Documents, such as share or bond certificates, which ensured payment by a debtor, gave the creditor a sense of security and were termed *securities*.

welfare and other goals. However defined, though, the point is that the information going to a securities market is important in the allocation of resources.

Second, information is necessary to permit investors to hold security portfolios that are optimal with respect to the risk-return preferences of the investors within the framework of the security prices existing in the market. Stated otherwise, information is necessary for the establishment of security prices that reflect risk and return relationships. It is also necessary for individual investors to obtain portfolios that reflect their own preferences in obtaining a maximum rate of return with a given degree of risk.

Market Efficiency

How to achieve these objectives has been an ongoing research effort for almost 25 years. An early finding was that price changes on capital markets were uncorrelated. Chicago finance professor Eugene Fama suggested that this lack of correlation was because markets are efficient in the sense that the prices of the securities on these markets fully reflect all available information in an unbiased manner.[11] No relevant information is ignored by the market. This has become known as the Efficient-Market Hypothesis (EMH). In its theoretical form, the sufficient conditions for an efficient market are:

1. There are no transaction costs in the trading of securities.
2. All available information is equally available to all traders without cost.
3. All traders have homogeneous expectations regarding the implications of available information.

These conditions are sufficient for the theoretical model, but they are not necessary in order to obtain an approximation of an efficient market in the real world. All that is really necessary for market efficiency is that all available information be impounded in security prices immediately, or with a minimum of delay, and in an unbiased manner. In other words, whenever new relevant information regarding a specific security appears that alters the expectations of investors, the equilibrium price of the security should be reached swiftly and appropriately. It should be kept in mind that it is the relative prices that will change with new information regarding specific securities. The level of securities prices is a result of a number of general economic factors, including the prevailing rate of interest, the rate of inflation, and expectations regarding general economic conditions—although individual securities may be affected differently by each of these factors. A competitive securities market is sufficient for these adjustments to occur, that is, a market in which prices of securities are free to move in such a way that they will reach equilibrium when the supply and demand for each security are equal.

It follows, almost by definition, that a market may be said to be efficient with respect to a particular piece of information if it is impossible to make abnormal profits by trading on the basis of that piece of information.[12] It is not sufficient to point to cases where excessive profits were earned to overturn the finding of efficient markets because the definition is statistical, that is, it applies on average only. Some will lose and some will gain: It is only on average that there are no abnormal gains. This is not unlike tossing a coin: The chances of winning and losing are identical.

Fama's definition of market efficiency, while intuitively appealing in many ways, is also fraught with problems. How can one tell when information is fully reflected in a security price? If one says abnormal profits may not be earned, then one has to define abnormal profits. Problems such as these led Beaver to propose a more workable, but also controversial, definition that the market is efficient "with respect to an information system if and only if the prices act as if everyone observes the signals from that information system."[13] Stated more fully, the test involves the "creation" of a second economy identical to the one that actually exists except that everyone in the second economy has access to the information under discussion. If prices in the second (full-knowledge) economy are identical to those in the real economy, then one can say the real economy is efficient with respect to that piece of information.

An example illustrates the definition. Canadian professor Ross Archibald examined the behavior of the stock prices of individual companies before and after they had switched depreciation methods for financial accounting purposes.[14] They had made no changes in their depreciation methods for tax purposes. He discovered that stock prices did not react to these changes. Since these changes do not appear to affect the cash flow of the companies, this is the result one would expect—assuming, of course, that investors knew and understood the economics of the company. Stated otherwise, real market prices behaved as one would expect in an identical economy where everyone was aware that changes in financial depreciation are essentially cosmetic only. As a result, one can conclude that the market is efficient with respect to depreciation changes.

There are actually two parts to efficiency: the first relates to the speed with which the market reacts; the second relates to the propriety of the response. The evidence with regard to speed appears to be relatively conclusive: Markets react to new information with remarkable swiftness and even anticipate accounting information. For example, research shows that in many cases the market reaction to new information is complete within a matter of hours.[15] Research also indicates that, by the time annual earnings are released, approximately 85 to 90 percent of the information is already impounded in the share price. The evidence is not quite as clear with regard to propriety. Initial studies supported the concept but more recent work, some of which is described later, has begun to evoke a few doubts as to its complete truth. A partial reason for doubts lies in defining what a proper response would be. This is particularly difficult to do in a world where opinions are divided, that is, a world of heterogeneous beliefs.

Even if beliefs were homogeneous, one would still have to cope with the possibility of multiple layers of responses. For instance, while at a first level of analysis a change in financial depreciation may have no cash flow implications, at another level the change might signal a revision in the prospects of the company: A switch from accelerated to straight-line depreciation might be an attempt to cover up declining earnings. Such signals do have information content. In this case, no response from investors indicates an inefficient rather than an efficient market with respect to financial depreciation. The researcher's problem is deciding which argument to make.

Researchers face two other sources of difficulty in investigating market efficiency. First, almost all the tests rely on theoretical pricing models to distinguish the normal from the abnormal. The tests are, therefore, joint tests of market efficiency and the model. Since these models are themselves still being developed, market efficiency results must be treated as tentative. Second, a "true" price against which one can test divergences does not exist. Security prices are simply reflections of public sentiments about the future, based on available information. As either sentiment or information changes, so prices must change. If sentiment changes abruptly, so will prices. In and of itself, a collapse such as occurred in October 1987 does not prove the market to be inefficient. The reverse, unfortunately, is also true: It is hard, if not impossible, to prove market efficiency. Its real test, though, lies in the value of its consequences.

Analyzing whether the market is truly efficient or not would be easier if we understood more completely how information is processed by individuals, aggregated across individuals, and impounded in security prices. In particular, we know relatively little about the role of financial intermediaries in disseminating information, despite the importance assigned them in several documents.[16] We know equally little about the relative costs of impounding information from different sources into security prices. Much research remains to be done. As a first step in this research program, but only a first step, potential information has been divided into three broad categories: that which can be derived from simply watching security prices; that which is publicly available, which includes security prices; and all information which includes prices, publicly available information, and also "insider" information. This gives rise to an analysis of three forms of market efficiency: the weak, the semistrong, and the strong. Each is discussed in the following sections along with its implications.

The Weak Form of the EMH

The weak form of the EMH states that security prices fully reflect information implied by the historical sequence of prices. Sufficient research has been conducted that this hypothesis is now generally accepted as being confirmed. Earlier studies of what was known as the random walk theory found that security price changes are random with respect to the information available before the change. That is, excess gains cannot be obtained merely by a knowledge of past security prices.

The importance of this form of the EMH for accounting is that it implies that new information is impounded immediately in security prices. If the new information were reflected in prices gradually over time, one price change would be an indication of the size and direction of the next price change. Only if the market adjustment to new information is instantaneous would the price changes be independent, which has been proven to be the case. Since this form of the EMH does not have further relevance for accounting, we must look further at studies relating information to securities markets.

The Strong Form of the EMH

At the other end of the spectrum, the strong form of the EMH states that all *available* relevant information is reflected in security prices. That is, security prices fully reflect privileged (insider) information as well as all publicly available information. However, the evidence to date has not shown this hypothesis to be true. Therefore, it may be assumed that the market is inefficient with respect to insider information and that excess earnings could be obtained by trading on the basis of such information. This assumption is difficult to prove, however, for several reasons. First, there are laws in the United States prohibiting certain individuals (such as financial analysts and corporate officers) and firms from trading on the basis of privileged insider information. But even the laws are not clear regarding what can be considered insider information and what is public information. Second, by definition insider information is not available to the public and is difficult, therefore, to observe and study. Third, it is not clear how insider information could be fully reflected in security prices, since it is available to only a small segment of the market participants.

On a priori grounds, insider information could become impounded in security prices in at least two ways:

1. If those obtaining insider information trade on the basis of such information, the additional demand alone for the security would increase the price until the information became public or no longer relevant. But if those trading on such information had limited resources, the effect on the market price would be minimal. As the number of individuals using such information increases, the information can at some point be considered to be public. So it is difficult to assess on either a priori grounds or empirically the effect of insider information on security prices.

2. A second way the insider information could affect security prices is really associated with the first way. If those known to possess, or likely to possess, insider information increase the volume of their trades in that security significantly, other participants in the market will assume that there is positive or negative information available to those individuals thought to possess such information; thus, the other participants will react to the information without knowing precisely what it is. In this way, at least, the implications of the insider information become public and are impounded in the market. The difficulty is that those using the insider information will already have obtained a competitive advantage and will have been at least temporarily able to earn excess returns.

The implications of the strong form of the EMH for accounting are that, if accounting is to serve a social function, it should attempt to make relevant financial information available publicly as soon as possible in order to minimize the possibility for the use of insider information. When insider information is used to the advantage of specific individuals, other participants in the market lose. The effect is a transfer of wealth from some investors to others. And since prices do not reflect this information immediately, the allocation of resources is less than optimal. Furthermore, individual investors are not able to evaluate securities properly in order to obtain optimal portfolios.

The Semistrong Form of the EMH

The semistrong form of the EMH takes a position between the weak and the strong forms. It states that security prices reflect all *publicly available* information. This includes information regarding current and previous security prices, but it excludes insider information. If the market is efficient in the semistrong form, new information publicly available will be impounded in stock prices instantaneously and in an unbiased manner. Alternatively defined, the market is semistrong efficient if security prices behave as if everyone were aware of publicly available information. The depreciation study quoted above is an example of where the market did react as one might expect if it were semistrong efficient.

A number of research studies have supported the EMH in the semistrong form so that it is now fairly generally accepted for the securities markets in the United States and in several other countries; however, an increasing number of anomalies have begun to appear in recent years, casting some doubt on the theory.[17] Many of these anomalies appear to be related to stocks which are traded less often or where information is more difficult to interpret. Others are more difficult to understand and must await further research. Stanford professor George Foster, for instance, discovered that well-known critic of accounting "Abe" Briloff was able to drive security prices to permanent new lows through articles he wrote that appeared in *Barrons*. Given that Briloff's information for his articles had appeared in the financial press before, this is a puzzling result. Despite these anomalies, we will continue for now to assume that the market is semistrong efficient partly because no well-articulated alternatives exist at present and partly because the balance of the evidence continues to favor efficiency.[18]

Some Implications for Accounting

Perhaps the most provocative implication of the semistrong form of the EMH is that fundamental analysis is not necessarily a profitable activity. Fundamental analysis, that is to say the examination of financial ratios based on publicly available financial statements, for identifying undervalued securities has a long history and continues to be practiced by many investors and their advisors.[19] If, however, the market is efficient with respect to such information, this activity cannot produce more profit than a simple buy-and-hold strategy. The only exception to this involves market makers who are interpreting new information just as it becomes publicly available. This usually occurs far in advance of the release of financial reports. One cannot infer from this that fundamental analysis is socially useless: In fact, it would appear to be the swift analysis of financial information that makes the market efficient in the first place.

Other Sources Exist.   One reason why the market is semistrong efficient is that accounting is only one source (and possibly not the major source) of publicly available information regarding firms and their securities. Industrywide and general economic information may have special implications for a specific firm. News reports and articles in financial journals may also provide insights into a firm. Other sources include corporate press releases and interviews of corporate officials by financial analysts, major investors, or representatives of public groups. However, most information relating directly to the specific firm will come originally from the firm itself, and much of this will come from the accounting department, although it may not first be made public through accounting reports.

The result may be that, by the time accounting financial reports are published, the information contained in the reports will already have become public information or have been anticipated. For example, the press frequently publishes revenue and earnings amounts before the publication of financial statements. In other cases partial information, such as production or employment data, may become available from time to time, thus permitting financial analysts to forecast fairly accurately the earnings, and earnings-per-share, numbers before they are fully computed. The result is that security prices will react to the information as soon as it becomes public, or is anticipated, and no further adjustment may be necessary at the time the financial statements are published.

This last appears to suggest that, if the securities markets do not react to financial accounting reports at the time they are published, they must be irrelevant. This is not necessarily true; it may still be possible that the reports are relevant. Financial reports may at least confirm information published by other sources and confirm or refute forecasts made on the basis of other information. This permits financial analysts and investors to evaluate the reliability of other sources and forecasts. Also, financial accounting may be relevant to individual investors if we relax the assumption of homogeneous expectations. If investors form different expectations regarding the relative riskiness of different securities, they may use accounting information to aid in forming their own expectations in order to obtain optimal portfolios, even though they are unable to earn excess returns based on the market's expectations.

An efficient securities market does not react differently to alternative sources of the same information. We cannot assume that just because the information is included in published financial statements, the information somehow has a special impact on security prices. There may be a difference, however, in the cost and effort incurred by the investor in obtaining and using the information. The question, therefore, becomes which source provides the information to the investor at the lowest cost, where cost includes the expense of processing the information. It may be that financial statements provide data processed in a sufficiently uniform manner that this is the least-cost source. It may also be that investors find it costly to disaggregate the information found in financial statements and turn, therefore, to other sources.[20] For example, the fact that formal inflation accounting has been abandoned in the United States indicates that investors are able to get this same information more cheaply from another source—or create it themselves at lower cost.[21]

Investors Are Protected.   Market efficiency in the semistrong form does not imply that all investors will understand and immediately take into account all new information. A corollary to this is that not all investors need to believe that the market is efficient for it to be efficient. It is sufficient that there be enough informed or professional analysts and investors to react to new information quickly. If the information is incorrectly interpreted, there will be investors available to take advantage of the situation, and potential excess earnings will disappear quickly, if not immediately. That is, when new information becomes available, both buyers and sellers of securities will adjust their expectations accordingly, and transactions will take place at the new equilibrium price. The investor who, through lack of knowledge or because of deliberate action, does not take the new information into account does not gain or lose by buying or selling at the market price.[22] However, the market will be efficient only if enough investors use the new information in an attempt to earn superior returns. That is, they must react as if the market were not efficient.

Markets Are Sophisticated.   Another implication of the semistrong form of the efficient-market hypothesis is that the market cannot be fooled by accounting gimmicks or tricks. The *functional fixation* principle is that investors associate the value of securities with certain accounting numbers, such as earnings per share, regardless of how the numbers are computed or the informational content of the numbers. That is, investors are functionally fixated on the numbers, rather than on the information. Thus they may make incorrect evaluations of security return and risk. But this principle is inconsistent with an efficient market, although it may be consistent with the intrinsic-value theory. With an efficient market, it is the publicly available information that is impounded in the security price, not the accounting number itself. A sufficient number of investors will see through the accounting numbers, and the security prices will be based on the best information for evaluating return and risk. It follows from the preceding discussion that accounting procedures based on arbitrary allocations and changes in accounting procedures that do not reflect the amount, timing, or probability of future cash flows to or from the firm would not provide information to securities markets and thus would not affect security prices. The market will react only to information that will affect expectations regarding return and risk. In other words, an efficient market will utilize only information that has semantic interpretation.*

Some Misconceptions

Several misconceptions have arisen around the nature and implications of market efficiency. First, the term should not be confused with efficient portfolios, productive efficiency, or the efficient allocation of resources. A certain amount of information is necessary and assumed for these other concepts of efficiency. However, market efficiency (in the semistrong form) assumes only that all publicly available information is impounded in security prices. If there were no published financial reports and no accounting information available, the market could still be efficient. Public information available from other sources could not be used to gain abnormal returns. However, the securities market structure of prices—and possibly the variability of prices—would differ.

---

* This was the basis for disallowing the capitalization of self-insurance in *SFAS 2*.

A second misconception is that, by observing market reactions to alternative accounting procedures, it is possible to assess the desirability of one as opposed to another procedure. Stated differently, changes in security prices do not provide conclusive evidence regarding the preferences of investors for alternative accounting procedures.[23] Very briefly, the reason that security prices cannot be used alone in assessing alternative accounting procedures is that the value of the information is not included in the security prices. Because the information is publicly available at no cost to the investors, no one would be willing to pay for the information (the *free-rider* concept). This is not to say, however, that the effects of alternative accounting procedures cannot be assessed by using security prices in an efficient-market setting.

Finally, it needs to be stressed that market efficiency does not imply clairvoyance on the part of the market. All it implies is that the market reflects the best guesses of all its participants based on the knowledge available at the time. New information appears all the time that proves the market was incorrect. In fact, by definition, the market will not react unless it learns something that it did not know the day before. One cannot prove the market inefficient, therefore, by looking back, using the benefits of hindsight and pointing to places where the market was incorrect. Market efficiency simply asserts that prices are appropriately set based on current knowledge; practical evidence shows that with hindsight the market is always incorrect.

Historical Costs

Market efficiency is thought by some to be unrealistic and even of academic interest only. It is worthwhile, therefore, to pause for a moment to consider an old and fundamental concept of accounting that makes little sense in the absence of efficient markets: the *cost* concept which suggests that assets should be entered on the books at the cost of the asset. As this concept is typically explained:

> historical costs are presumed to represent objective measurements of prices in arm's length transactions. . . . The cost incurred in acquiring an asset therefore may be assumed to represent the market value of the asset at the time of its acquisition.[24]

A moment's thought reveals that this can be true only in a competitive economy: A single, relatively powerless consumer making a purchase from a powerful, giant retail chain cannot possibly arrive at a price that reflects market value in the sense it is being used in this quotation.

A second rationale for the use of acquisition costs lies in the objectives of financial reporting as laid out earlier in this chapter. The assertion was made that the function of financial reporting is to disclose information regarding prospective cash flows. Assets should be entered, therefore, at an amount that indicates their cash flow potential. This is generally measured by the present value of the future cash flows. It is a well-known theorem of capital budgeting that cost and present value equate when the discount rate being used is the internal rate of return. Stated otherwise, when an asset is entered at the appropriate cost, it implicitly reveals the rate the enterprise can expect to earn in its use. It is a simple matter to show that the appropriate cost is that generated in an arm's-length transaction in a perfectly competitive economy. This last is why *SFAS 57* obliges companies to disclose whether there are any related party transactions—the existence of such relationships may not allow a competitively set price to emerge.

But as the argument on efficient markets pointed out earlier, it is the existence of competition in security markets that leads to market efficiency in the first place. Market efficiency and perfect competition are virtually synonymous terms. In short, for arm's-length transactions to produce measures of assets that are of any interest, an efficient market for that asset is required. Thus, the historical-cost concept, which requires efficiency in all asset markets, imposes far stronger requirements on the nature of the economy than market efficiency as espoused by those studying security markets alone!

CHECKPOINTS

---

1. Define in your own words the meaning of market efficiency.
2. Briefly distinguish three forms of market efficiency.
3. List three implications of market efficiency.
4. List three nonimplications of market efficiency.

VALUING SECURITIES

The efficient-market hypothesis explains the effect of relevant information on security prices. However, to test for market efficiency or for the relevancy of information, a theoretical model is needed to explain what factors or parameters determine security prices in equilibrium. Such a model could have a very large number of parameters, because a large number of factors could affect security prices. There is considerable merit, however, in a model that has few parameters and yet a high degree of predictability.[25] One of the models developed—the Capital Asset Pricing Model (CAPM)—has the characteristics of having only two parameters—risk and return—and a satisfactory degree of predictability. Before describing the model, it is necessary to look at portfolio theory, upon which the model is based.

Portfolio Theory

Portfolio theory is based upon two basic assumptions regarding investment decisions under uncertainty:

1. Investors are risk-averse and prefer a greater return for a given level of risk or a lower risk for a given level of return.
2. Security returns are normally distributed.

The second assumption is important because it implies that security returns can be measured by the mean of their distribution and that risk can be measured by their variance. Since every investor can invest in several securities, it is the portfolio risk and return that are important, rather than the risk and return of the individual securities.

The portfolio return is the mean of the returns of the individual securities; but the variance (measure of risk) of the portfolio is not the same as the mean of the variances of the individual securities. This is so because the correlation between the individual securities in the portfolio affects the portfolio variance. For example, consider two ocean waves. If they come together exactly, they reinforce each other; if they move in exactly opposite directions, they cancel one another out. In general, they combine somewhere in between as some parts reinforce and some parts cancel. Exhibit 6-2 illustrates the point.

In the first panel, the two waves move opposite one another, canceling out the variance of the individual securities; in the second, the waves work against each other at times and with one another at other times.

EXHIBIT 6-2   Variance and Covariance

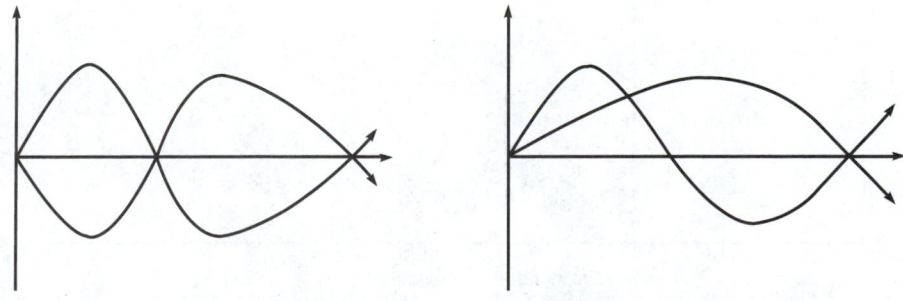

Formally, if a sum of money is invested in a portfolio in the proportions w_i, then:

$$\text{Mean } (\tilde{R}_p) = \sum_{i=1}^{n} w_{ip} \text{ Mean } (\tilde{R}_i) \tag{1}$$

$$\text{Variance } (\tilde{R}_p) = \sum_{i=1}^{n} w_{ip}^2 \text{ Variance } (\tilde{R}_i) +$$

$$\sum_{i=1}^{n} \sum_{j=1}^{n} w_{ip} w_{jp} \text{ Covariance}(\tilde{R}_i \tilde{R}_j) \tag{2}$$

It may be shown that the variance of the portfolio will be at a maximum when there is perfect correlation between the securities within the portfolio. The more the correlation between the securities drops below one, the less the portfolio variance. But choosing securities that imperfectly correlate with one another is precisely what one does when diversifying.

Through diversification, therefore, an individual investor can obtain a lower level of (portfolio) risk for the same return. Since diversification is readily available to all investors, the market will not pay a price for the risk borne by those investors who do not (by choice or otherwise) diversify. We attempt to demonstrate this in Exhibit 6-3.

EXHIBIT 6-3   The Efficient Portfolio Curve

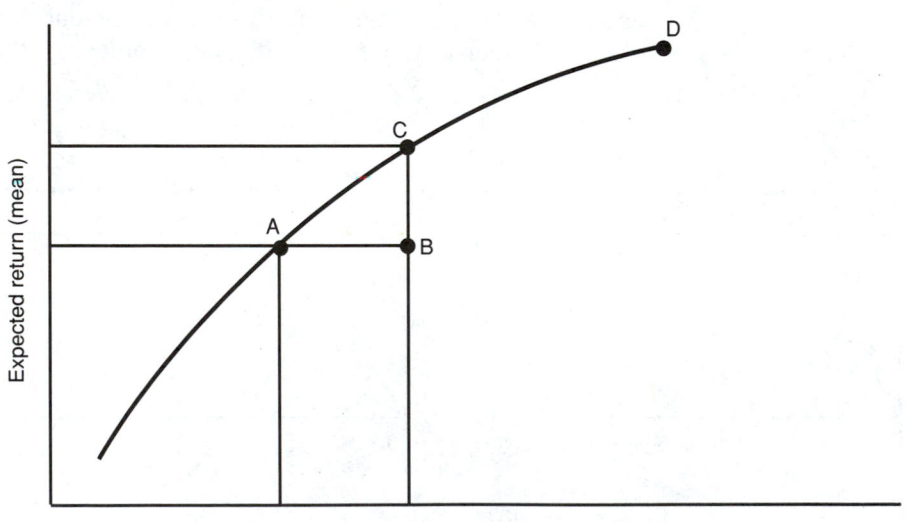

An investor with portfolio B can reduce the amount of risk by (moving to the left) the amount BA and still maintain the same return, that is, remain on the same level. As an alternative, she could invest in such a way as to increase the return to C with the same risk as at B, that is, she could move vertically up by the amount BC. The curve ACD represents the highest expected return for a given level of risk or the lowest risk for a given level of return. This is referred to as the *efficient frontier,* and any portfolio on the curve is an efficient portfolio. A portfolio under the curve is less preferable than one on the curve. The market values portfolios A, C, and D equally. That is, the market is indifferent regarding the combinations of risk and return represented by portfolios on the curve. An individual investor, however, may have a preference for a specific risk and return combination, and other investors will have other preferences, depending on their personal degree of aversion to risk and their income and wealth situation.

The market as a whole can be thought of as a portfolio of securities expanded until it includes all securities, weighted by the value of each security priced in equilibrium. This is known as the *market portfolio*. If all investors are able to borrow and lend at a riskless rate of interest, they can replicate all possible mixes of risk and return simply by holding a suitable combination of riskless debt and the market portfolio. This is illustrated in Exhibit 6-4.

EXHIBIT 6-4 The Capital Asset Pricing Model

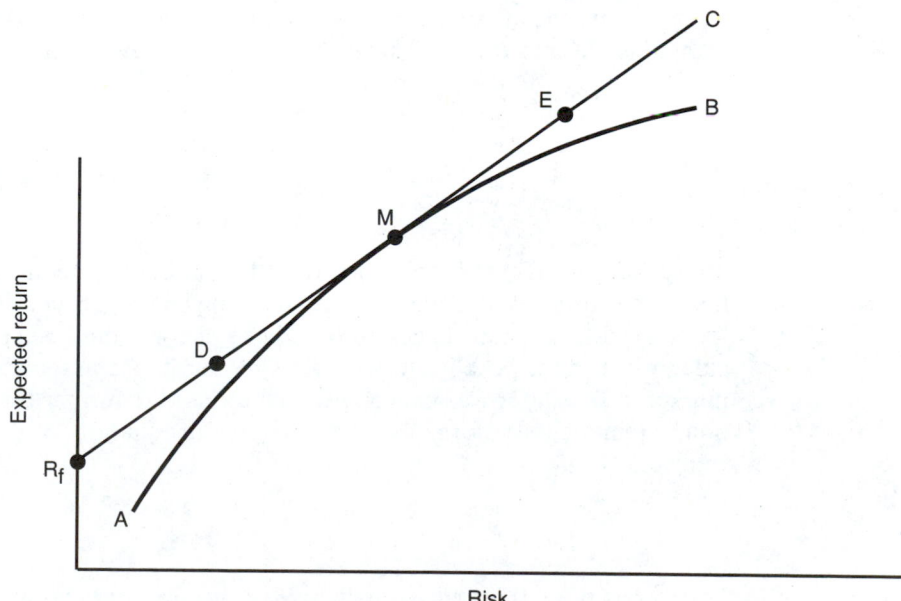

The riskless rate (R_f) is earned when risk is zero, that is, at the far left of the graph. From this point as one moves to the right, the increase in risk is associated with an increase in return, that is, D, M, E, and C are points with increasing risk as well as increasing return. The curve AB is the efficient portfolio frontier described in Exhibit 6-3. The line RC, also known as the *capital market line,* is a tangent to the efficient portfolio at the point M.

Consider now an investor who begins by investing his savings in a portfolio with risk at M. He then borrows at the riskless rate and invests his borrowings in purchasing more shares in his portfolio, M. The result is that he can leverage himself to where his total portfolio places him at point E. This is a higher return than he could have earned by investing in the market alone. A more risk-averse investor might lend some of the money generated by his portfolio at the riskless rate. This would take him down to point D. Again, note that the combination of riskless debt and portfolio produces a higher return for less risk that the original portfolio alone. Given the benefits that flow to all, it might be reasonable to assume that everyone will invest in M (and leverage themselves up or down the market line). The result is that M will be the total market portfolio.

Stated otherwise, given the benefits of diversification and of leveraging one's investments, one arrives at a relatively simple, but ultimately extremely powerful description of how investors might be expected to behave. It is this simple diagram that has led to a revolution in both finance and accounting. In particular, it has provided researchers with a model whereby they might begin to establish a base for evaluating security-price mechanisms. In particular, the slope of the line, its *beta,* provided considerable insight into the mechanism governing risk evaluation.

The Market Model*

Many factors affect the return and risk of an individual security. Stanford finance professor William F. Sharpe, building on earlier work by his mentor Harry Markowitz, suggested that these factors could be split into two categories: those peculiar to the company and those associated with the market.[26] The latter was called systematic risk; the former the specific or nonsystematic risk. Formally, one can write an equation for the security's return as:

$$\tilde{R}_{it} = \alpha_i + B_i \tilde{R}_{Mt} + \tilde{\varepsilon}_t$$

---

* The next two sections are relatively technical and may safely be skipped by those unfamiliar with this material. The argument is taken up again on page 267.

where

$\tilde{R}_{it}$ = rate of return on asset i for period t

$\tilde{R}_{Mt}$ = rate of return on all securities in the market for period t

$\tilde{\varepsilon}_t$ = random noise in the process for period t.

This is known as the market model or the characteristic equation. It corresponds to the capital market line shown in Exhibit 6-4.

The major assumption of the market model is that the variations in individual securities are largely due to marketwide factors. This enables one to replace all the individual factors by a single market factor.* As one diversifies, the nonsystematic risk, measured by $\alpha_i + \varepsilon_i$ then disappears, leaving one with the systematic risk only, measured by $B_i \tilde{R}_{Mt}$. The systematic risk of an individual security, therefore, is the effect that security has on the riskiness of a well-diversified portfolio. This effect is measured by the coefficient that precedes the market return, which has come to be known in the financial literature by its name of *beta*.† A stock that is twice as volatile as the market will have a beta of 2; one that is 40 percent less volatile than the market, a beta of 0.6; and so on.

The Capital Asset Pricing Model

Harvard finance professor John Lintner, Norwegian professor Jan Mossin, William Sharpe, and others later extended this work to arrive at a model of equilibrium prices for securities trading in an efficient market. This is known as the Capital Asset Pricing Model (CAPM). They showed that the expected return for an individual security is equal to the return on a riskless asset plus the relative risk (referred to as beta) of the security times the excess of the expected market portfolio return over the return on a riskless asset. This is expressed in the following formula:

$$E(\tilde{R}_i) = R_f + \beta_i[E(\tilde{R}_M) - R_f] \tag{3}$$

where

$E(\tilde{R}_i)$ = the expected return on security i

R_f = the return on a riskless security

$E(R_M)$ = the expected return on the market portfolio

B_i = the relative risk of security i

where beta is measured by the ratio of the covariance of the security returns with the market portfolio returns to their variance.

---

* Technically speaking, the pairwise covariances between individual securities in a portfolio variance equation are replaced with a smaller set of covariances with the market portfolio.

† Both Markowitz and Sharpe won Nobel prizes for their work in this area.

In words, according to the CAPM, the relative risk of an individual security (beta) is measured by the covariance of the security returns with the market portfolio returns. It is a measure of the sensitivity of the returns of an individual security or portfolio to the variability of returns of the market portfolio. That is, the beta for the market portfolio is one, since the covariance of any distribution with itself is unity. Any security with a risk (measured by the covariance) greater than that of the market portfolio would have a beta greater than one; conversely, any security with risk less than that of the market portfolio would have a beta less than one. The only difference between the return on an individual asset or portfolio and the market portfolio is due to the positive linear relationship that exists between the expected return of a security and its beta.

Sufficient conditions for the CAPM to hold are that the securities market be complete and perfectly competitive with zero transaction costs, that investors are risk-averse, that security returns are normally distributed, and that all investors have common investment horizons and identical beliefs about the means, variances, and covariances of securities in the future. These assumptions have been relaxed in later discussions, but they were important for development of the theory.

Some Implications of the CAPM

The efficient-market hypothesis and the capital asset pricing model imply that relevant new information will have an immediate effect on the price of a security by either altering expectations regarding the average return on the security or altering the expectations regarding the security's beta. If all investors' expectations are homogeneous, a change in the price of the security relative to the prices of all securities in the market is an indication that the new information has an effect on market expectations. Therefore, one of the important implications of the CAPM is that it provides a means of testing the effect of making new information publicly available.

Within the restrictive assumptions of the CAPM, an individual investor should hold a portfolio with a beta risk of one (the market portfolio beta) and borrow or lend at the riskless rate in order to attain the appropriate risk level in accordance with his/her preference or aversion for risk. If we relax the assumption that the investor has an unlimited ability to borrow and lend at the riskless rate, the best that one could do would be to move to the efficient portfolio frontier through diversification. The beta for each security must be known in order to establish the beta for the portfolio and adjust the portfolio appropriately for personal risk preferences.

One of the difficulties with an interpretation of the implications of the CAPM is that the risk and return concepts are ex ante or expectations and risk is associated with the uncertainty of future returns. However, most measurements of the mean return and beta are ex post, computed from a past period of 60 months in many cases. There is some evidence that future values of beta can be estimated on the basis of past long-term measurements of beta; however, it is the expected values of returns and beta that determine the relative prices of securities. If we relax the assumption that all investors have the same expectations regarding the mean and distribution of future returns, information that will aid individual investors in making their personal expectations is just as important as information directed toward the market as a whole. There is some evidence that some of the traditional accounting partial measures of risk, such as financial leverage (debt-to-equity ratios), operating leverage (the ratio of fixed-to-variable expenses), and liquidity, are associated with the market measures of beta, and thus with future expectations of beta.[27]

One of the main advantages of the capital asset pricing model and the supporting efficient-market hypothesis and portfolio theory is that it is empirically testable. However, the assumptions and the statistical techniques used limit the validity of the tests and the conclusions that can be reached. Also, research on the effect of accounting on capital markets can provide only a partial answer to questions regarding the validity of accounting measures, the degree of relevance of accounting information, and the choice of alternative accounting procedures. Policy-making decisions should include many other factors, including the political preferences of certain groups, social implications, and the relative costs and benefits of presenting information in financial reports.

Using the CAPM

The importance of the capital asset pricing model for accountants is that it provides a means of establishing what the return on a security should be. Simple observation of prices from day to day on the NYSE give one the actual returns being earned on this security. Subtracting the one from the other yields what is known as the *abnormal* return, that is, the difference between what the security did earn and what it should earn based on the CAPM. Algebraically, the abnormal return is:

$$e_t = \tilde{R}_t - E(\tilde{R}_t)$$

Summing these returns over time gives one an indication of the value of the information one is using to earn an above-average return.

This approach was used by two Australian researchers, Ray Ball and Phil Brown. The question they addressed in their paper was whether one could use annual earnings-per-share numbers to earn abnormal returns. Their test was simple. They assumed that they had knowledge of earnings per share one year in advance. If the future earnings per share were up on this, they invested in the stock; if the future earnings per share were down compared with the present, they sold the stock short. They then used the preceding equation to compute the abnormal return, if any, that they could have earned if it were possible to get earnings-per-share information in advance.

Exhibit 6-5 illustrates their result. The graph begins one year in advance. Positive abnormal returns, shown by the steeply rising curve, are earned in the period prior to the actual release of the earnings per share at

EXHIBIT 6-5   Association between Annual Earnings Changes and Security Returns

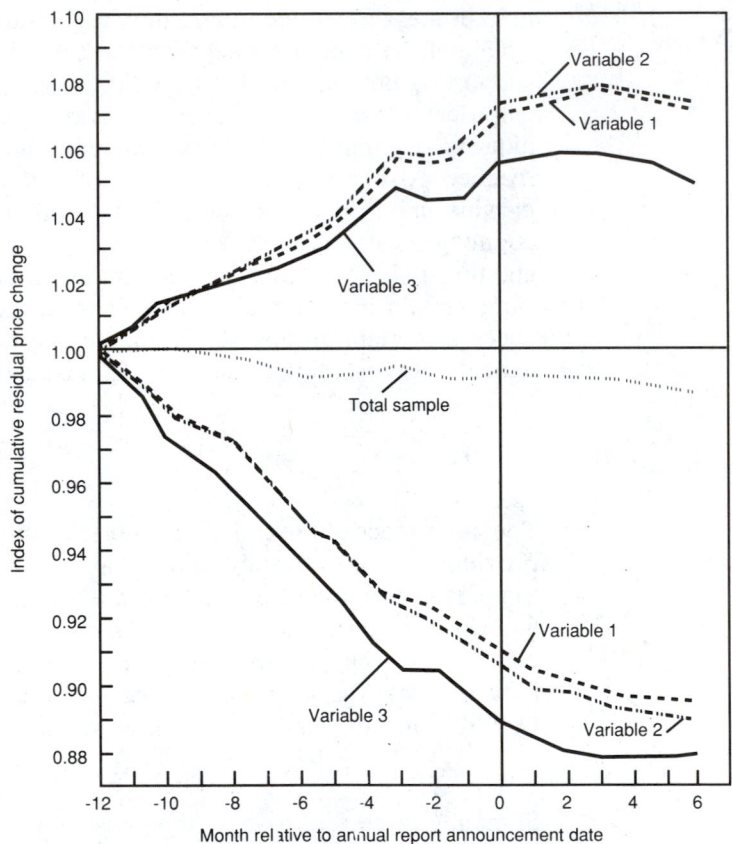

Monthly residual price change for positive and negative residual earnings changes. The top set of lines represents the cumulative residual price change associated with positive residual earnings changes measured three ways (i.e., variables 1 through 3). The bottom set of lines represents the cumulative residual price changes associated with negative residual earnings changes measured three ways. The cumulative residual price changes start with a hypothetical portfolio of 1.00 (e.g., $1) twelve months prior to the announcement. The graph shows the value of that portfolio over time.

Source: Ball and Brown (1968), Figure 1, p. 169.

the time denoted zero by investing in the stock. Negative abnormal returns, shown by the steeply falling curve, are earned in the same period by going short in the stock. After release of the information, the curves flatten out—not entirely, but considerably by comparison with the rise and fall before the release date.

In other words, if one can get a preview of earnings numbers, one is able to earn abnormal returns. If one knows in advance that earnings are going to rise (fall), then on average one can benefit by buying (selling) shares. Getting this information in advance is difficult, if not impossible. When it is possible it is usually illegal, so this result does not benefit investors directly. But it does provide evidence of the potential usefulness of earnings numbers. Just as interesting is the virtual disappearance of abnormal returns once the information becomes publicly available. This confirms the semistrong form of market efficiency with respect to earnings per share.

A series of tests then followed as to whether the market was able to interpret accounting numbers correctly. Archibald's study, referred to earlier, was the first of many to suggest that the market did not react to changes in accounting numbers if they were not accompanied by changes in the underlying cash flow stream. Other studies seemed to show that the market did react if it perceived that the cash flow stream was being affected. As already noted, the dilemma that accounting researchers encounter is determining whether or not a change in accounting is associated with a change in cash flow.

Option Pricing

Capital asset pricing theory concerns itself with the expected risk and return on common stock. However, there are many different kinds of securities in the market other than common stock. The introduction to this chapter mentioned convertible debt; preferred stock comes to mind immediately; and those familiar with the modern investment scene will know that it is filled with Bulls and Bears, TIGRS, and LIONS, and all kinds of other exotica.* Most of these are hybrid securities, that is, they are combinations of simpler securities. Convertible debt is an example, being a mixture of debt and owners' equity. One kind of security that has been widely studied in recent years, because it is a basic ingredient in so many hybrid securities, is the "option." This section of the chapter discusses their nature, their valuation, and some implications for accounting of the option pricing model.

There are several kinds of options. Call options give an investor the

* These are just some of the names that have been given to some of the securities currently being offered to investors by various financial intermediaries.

right to buy a share some time in the future at a prespecified price known as the exercise price. A put option is the mirror image of a call option; it gives the investor the right to sell a share some time in the future at a prespecified price. Stock options given to executives in lieu of salary are one example of a call option. If the stock rises above the exercise price, the executive is able to buy at a discount and realize a profit. Convertible debt is another example—if the price of the company's stock rises there is an incentive for the creditor to convert to stock.

The value of a simple call option, exercisable only at its expiration date and paying no dividends, can never be less than zero. One would not exercise one's right to purchase the share if it did not exceed the exercise price. Once the share price gets above the exercise price, the value of the option rises linearly with the share price, that is, if the exercise price is $25 and the value of the share is V_s, the value of the option at expiration date will be the greater of $(V_s - 25)$ or zero. The value of the option prior to its expiration date will be greater because prior to expiration there is always the possibility that the share price will rise—remember there is no downside risk because the holder of the option can always walk away. The greater the volatility of the share, the higher the value of the option!

These simple insights led two finance professors, Myron Scholes of Chicago and Fisher Black of MIT, to develop a model for the equilibrium pricing of options corresponding to the capital asset pricing model for common stock. Given a number of assumptions that are similar to those underlying the CAPM, they were able to show that the equilibrium price (V_0) of a call option on a single share is given by the equation:

$$V_0 = V_s N(d_1) - \frac{E}{e^{rt}} N(d_2)$$

where

> V_s = the current price of the stock
> E = the exercise price of the option
> e = 2.71828
> r = the short-term interest rate continuously compounded
> t = the length of time in years to the expiration of the option
> $N(d)$ = the value of the cumulative normal density function, with

$$d_1 = \frac{\ln(V_s/E) + (r + 1/2\sigma^2)t}{\sigma \sqrt{t}}$$

$$d_2 = \frac{\ln(V_s/E) + (r + 1/2\sigma^2)t}{\sigma \sqrt{t}}$$

where

> ln = the natural logarithm
> σ = the standard deviation of the annual rate of return on the stock continuously compounded

Research on this model continues apace. The model itself has been programmed into hand-held calculators and into personal computers to enable investors to determine the appropriate price for their investments. Its implications for accounting are several.

Some Implications

First, both the CAPM and the option pricing model affirm that it is measures of risk that are, or should be, of most interest to shareholders. Accounting, as it is currently taught, tends to place more emphasis on the measurement of net income and asset values, that is, on return. Both security pricing models question that emphasis. Unlike the CAPM, though, the options pricing model shows a need for information about total risk—not just the beta of a security. It is the total volatility of the share that drives the price of the option. Second, both models provide accountants with a potential vehicle for determining the appropriate weighting to give the components of hybrid securities as they are entered in financial statements. Third, the two models provide accountants with a framework within which they can derive a theory for how best to report on equities. The FASB is currently engaged in developing such a framework. More is said on the subject in the section on hybrid securities in Chapter 19.

CHECKPOINTS

---

1. Explain the implications of portfolio theory for investors.
2. What does beta mean?
3. What did the Ball and Brown study, described in the chapter, show about the information content of annual accounting earnings?
4. What is an option? What implications does option theory have for accounting theory?

CONCLUSION

Numerous empirical studies have been done in the past two decades using the insights of market efficiency, the capital asset pricing model, and the option pricing model. The initial hope was that it would be possible, by examining the effect of accounting numbers on security prices, to determine the most useful way to present to shareholders the results of the company's business. It is fair to say that the initial high hopes that were held for this line of research have been somewhat dampened. This is not to say that a knowledge of such effects is not important in setting accounting standards or in the establishment of accounting policy for a specific firm. However, a number of other factors, such as public opinion and political realities, must be considered in the establishment of a social policy regarding accounting information.

Several general results appear to have emerged. First, there is evidence that the market does react to the release of accounting information. Second, there is evidence that accounting numbers can be used in estimating the beta risk of a company. Third, despite the difficulties in interpreting the results of the different studies, the market does appear to be able to interpret accounting numbers appropriately. This last result, along with evidence on the speed of reaction of the market to new information, suggests that sophisticated professionals who are trading actively in the market set prices. As a result, fears that the market may not be able to understand particular standards appear to be unwarranted.

The market gains its efficiency mostly through the supply of financial information outside of financial reports. Financial reports and other published financial information derived from accounting data may be the most economical way to provide such information to securities markets. However, alternative sources do exist and the relative cost of these sources should be considered in establishing accounting policy. Professional financial analysts and managers of institutional and mutual funds obtain information directly by interviews with the executives or employees of the corporations or through management's press releases. Pressures to transfer the disclosure of much of this information may result only in the transfer of the information-gathering costs from the financial analysts to the firms and their stockholders. On the other hand, information relevant to all investors for the establishment of efficient portfolios may be produced at a lower cost by the firm than the cost to investors of obtaining the information indirectly by purchasing it from brokers, investment analysts, or investment advisors. Several types of costs should be considered:

1. The direct costs of producing and publishing the information.
2. The costs of producing and publishing the information by alternative sources.
3. The costs of interpreting and evaluating the information incurred by investors and other decision makers.
4. The costs that would be incurred by investors if they had to search for the information themselves.
5. Such indirect costs as the adverse effects of published information on the efficient operation of the firm.[28]

Published accounting information is produced and distributed at a cost to the firm (and indirectly to stockholders and possibly others) and is received without charge by the investor (with a few exceptions, such as financial libraries and special financial services). A reduction of the costs to the firm would provide a social benefit if the published information is irrelevant, if it is not used by any investors or the market, or if the information is provided more timely and at no additional cost by some other source. That is, accounting information produced and published at a material additional cost should be eliminated if no benefit for the information can be found or even assumed to exist.

In summary, it can be assumed that the allocation of resources will be improved by any increase in the amount of information impounded in market prices. But this does not mean that it is possible to state a preference for one set of accounting procedures over another on the basis of the association with market prices. Several other factors must be considered in evaluating accounting policy, including the costs of producing and distributing the information, the costs of alternative sources, and the costs of analyzing the information by investors and analysts.

SUMMARY

This chapter has provided an outline of the environment within which accounting operates, in the belief that before one can account for something, one must understand what it is for which one is attempting to account. Briefly this chapter concluded that:

1. Accounting in the Western world operates within essentially private, capitalist economies. The influence of governments exists, but is relatively limited.
2. The users of accounting in this economy are diverse, but they may have a common interest in the prediction of future cash flows.
3. Stock markets in these economies appear to be semistrong efficient.
4. Stock markets appear to process news releases relatively swiftly and intelligently.

These statements appear to be accepted by most observers as a fair description of the environment of accounting. Nevertheless, one should bear in mind that research in this area is ongoing and that as a result opinions could easily change in light of new evidence.

QUESTIONS

1. State whether each of the following assertions is true or false. Provide your reasons.

a. Investors prefer to invest in less-risky companies.
b. Diversified companies are less risky.

c. Diversification is desirable even when stocks are perfectly correlated.
d. Stocks with a negative beta have expected returns less than the risk-free rate of interest.
e. The expected return on a stock with a beta of 2 is twice that of the expected return on the market.

2. Given that the risk-free rate is 5 percent and that the market rate is 15 percent, what will the expected return be on a company whose beta is:

a. 1
b. 0
c. 1.2
d. −0.2
e. What is the beta of the stock whose expected return is 0.5?

CHRYSLER CORPORATION

Lynn Townsend, chairman of the board of Chrysler Corporation, sent the company's shareholders a typewritten copy of the audited financial statements in February 1971. Accompanying these statements was a letter, extracts from which appear below:

> Sales of Chrysler Corporation and consolidated subsidiaries throughout the world in 1970 totaled $7.0 billion, compared with $7.1 billion in 1969. Operations for the year resulted in a net loss of $7.6 million or $0.16 a share, compared with net earnings of $99.0 million or $2.09 a share in 1969.
>
> Net earnings for 1969 are restated to reflect a retroactive change in the company's method of valuing inventories, from a LIFO (last-in, first-out) to a FIFO (first-in, first-out) basis, as explained in the notes to the financial statements. The LIFO method reduces inventory values and earnings in periods of rising costs. The rate of inflation in costs in 1970 and for the projected short-term future is so high that significant understatements of inventory values and earnings result. The use of the LIFO method in 1970 would have reduced inventory amounts at December 31, 1970, by approximately $150 million and did reduce inventory amounts reported at December 31, 1969, by approximately $110 million. Also, the use of the LIFO method in 1970 would have increased the loss for the year by approximately $20.0 million, and its use in 1969 reduced the earnings as reported for that year by $10.2 million. The other three U.S. automobile manufacturers have consistently used the FIFO method. Therefore the reported loss for 1970 and the restated profit for 1969 are on a comparable basis as to inventory valuation with the other three companies. Prior years' earnings have been restated to make them comparable.

The footnote alluded to in this letter added that, as a result of these changes, the Net Earnings Retained for Use in the Business at December 31, 1969 and 1968 had been increased by $53.5 million and $43.3 million, respectively.

A footnote tax expense noted that their taxes on income shown in the consolidated statement of net earnings include the following:

	1970	1969
Currently payable:		
U.S. taxes (credit)	$(81,800,000)	$50,000,000
Other countries	44,300,000	36,300,000
Deferred taxes	16,100,000	(6,000,000)
As previously reported		80,300,000
Adjustment in deferred taxes for change in inventory valuation		11,400,000
Total taxes on income (credit)	$(21,400,000)	$91,700,000

The change in inventory valuation resulted in a reduction in income taxes allocable to the following year of approximately $56 million at December 31, 1969.

Required:

   1.   Why do you think Chrysler changed its method of accounting for inventories?
   2.   What benefits did Chrysler gain by switching? What was the cost of the switch?
   3.   In light of what you know from this chapter about market efficiency, would you recommend this change?
   4.   Duke professor William E. Ricks did an empirical study of the market's response to 400 switches from FIFO to LIFO in 1974. He concluded that, "LIFO adopters suffered negative abnormal return performance during the period surrounding their annual earnings announcements."[29] In brief, the market interpreted the decrease in earnings as a result of the switch as bad news. In light of this finding, how would you have advised Mr. Townsend to act?

ANGLO AMERICAN

Anglo American Corporation of South Africa Limited (Anglo) is South Africa's leading mining financial house. It was established in 1917 by Sir Ernest Oppenheimer. The initial capital to develop gold mines on the East Rand was raised in England and the United States—hence the name—Anglo American.

   In 1987 it launched an employee shareholder scheme to give its employees, and in particular its black employees, a stake in the company. This is not entirely altruistic because the company is concerned about its possible

The Financial Report

Anglo's business year (this is normally called the financial year) begins on April 1 of one year, and ends on March 31 of the next. The profit statement of Anglo for the financial year which began on April 1, 1987 and ended on March 31, 1988 is set out below, with the figures for the previous year shown in the right-hand column:

	1988 (millions of rands)	1987 (millions of rands)
Anglo's income was earned from these sources		
Dividends from investments	923	853
Anglo's share of trading profits of its subsidiary companies	199	319
Interest and fees earned after deducting Anglo's operating expenses	420	478
	1,542	1,650
Anglo paid out		
Interest on money lent to us	191	231
Prospecting expenditure on the search for new mining ventures	108	72
Taxes	206	316
	505	619
Leaving a profit of	1,037	1,031
Anglo also accounts for its share of the profits of its associate companies not paid out as dividends	772	472
Giving a total profit of	1,809	1,503
The profit was used		
By Anglo to pay dividends to its shareholders	516	514
By Anglo to provide for future business expansion	521	517
	1,037	1,031
By Anglo's associate companies to provide for future business expansion	772	472
	1,809	1,503

The profit of R1,037 million earned by Anglo and its subsidiaries was only slightly better than the profit earned in the previous year. This was mainly because of the lower trading profits from the subsidiary companies, which were due in part to lower profits earned by the gold mines arising from the strike of last year. However, the profits of Anglo's associate companies improved compared with the previous year.

Of this profit, R516 million will be paid out in dividends to those people who own shares in Anglo. The rest of the profit will be kept in Anglo to pay for future expansion, thus helping to increase the value of Anglo to the benefit of all its shareholders. After paying dividends to their own shareholders, Anglo's associate companies also retained R772 million of profits which will be used to finance expansion of their own businesses.

nationalization after the government of that country moves into the hands of the black majority. By July 22, 1988, employees owned 571,559 shares worth approximately R33 million. (At this time, the South African rand is worth about 40 American cents.) In addition to the normal financial reports, the company prepared a special report for its employee shareholders. The income statement is reproduced on the previous page.

1. Do you think that this report is well tailored for its intended users?

2. Would you alter the presentation of the income statement in any way?

3. Would you suggest that the company send this same report to its shareholders, the majority of whom know less about the company than its employees?

4. Compared to a regular income statement with which you are familiar, is this sufficient for investment purposes? If not, what would you add? If it is, why do we prepare more complex statements?

SELECTED ADDITIONAL READING

The literature in this area is so voluminous these days, also so much of it is technically beyond the average reader of this text, that it did not seem worthwhile to provide a list of papers for further reading. Instead, we have contented ourselves with providing some other texts and some review papers that cover the material in this chapter in more depth. These have numerous references that the interested reader can use to extend their understanding in particular areas of interest.

Ball, Ray, and George Foster. "Corporate Financial Reporting: A Methodological Review of Empirical Research." *Journal of Accounting Research,* Supplement 1982, pp. 161–234.

Beaver, William F. *Financial Reporting: An Accounting Revolution* (Englewood Cliffs, N.J.: Prentice Hall, 1989).

Dyckman, Thomas R., and Dale Morse. *Efficient Capital Markets and Accounting: A Critical Analysis,* 2nd ed. (Englewood Cliffs, N.J.: Prentice Hall, 1986).

Foster, George. *Financial Statement Analysis,* 2nd ed. (Englewood Cliffs, N.J.: Prentice Hall, 1986).

Griffin, Paul A. *Usefulness to Investors and Creditors of Information Provided by Financial Reporting: A Review of Empirical Accounting Research* (Financial Accounting Standards Board, 1982).

Lev, Baruch, and James A. Ohlson. "Market-Based Empirical Research in Accounting: A Review, Interpretation, and Extension." *Journal of Accounting Research,* Supplement 1982, pp. 249–332.

Ricks, William E. "Market Assessment of Alternative Accounting Methods: A Review of the Empirical Evidence." *Journal of Accounting Literature,* Spring 1982, pp. 59–99.

ENDNOTES

1. *SFAC 1,* par. 9.
2. This part of the chapter reflects the thinking of the FASB in *SFAC 1.*
3. "East of Eden," *The Economist,* August 12, 1989, is a fascinating survey of the difficulties of starting a capitalist society.
4. *SFAC 1,* par. 16.
5. *SFAC 1,* par. 30.
6. *SFAC 1,* par. 37.
7. *SFAC 1,* pars. 52 & 50.
8. William H. Beaver, *Financial Reporting* (Englewood Cliffs, N.J.: Prentice Hall, 1989), p. 16.
9. This view goes back at least as far as A. A. Berle, Jr. and G. C. Means, *The Modern Corporation and Private Property* (New York: Commerce Clearing House, 1932).
10. Accounting Standards Steering Committee, *The Corporate Report* (Institute of Chartered Accountants of England and Wales, 1975), par. 2.36.
11. Eugene Fama, "Efficient Capital Markets: A Review of Theory and Empirical Work," *Journal of Finance,* May 1970, pp. 383–417.
12. Michael C. Jensen, "Some Anomalous Evidence Regarding Market Efficiency," *Journal of Financial Economics,* June–September 1978, p. 95–102.
13. William H. Beaver, *Financial Reporting,* p. 135. Also see William H. Beaver, "Market Efficiency," *The Accounting Review,* January 1981, pp. 23–37.
14. T. R. Archibald, "Stock Market Reaction to the Depreciation Switch-Back," *The Accounting Review,* January 1972, pp. 22–30.
15. James Patell and Mark Wolfson, "The Intraday Speed of Adjustment of Stock Prices to Earnings and Dividend Announcements," *Journal of Accounting and Economics,* June 1984, pp. 223–52.
16. See, for example, *The Wheat Report*, "Disclosure to Investors: A Reappraisal of Administrative Policies under the '33 and '34 Securities Acts." (Brown & Co., 1969), p. 52.
17. For a discussion of supporting evidence and some evidence that questions efficiency, see Thomas R. Dyckman and Dale Morse, *Efficient Capital Markets and Accounting: A Critical Analysis,* 2nd ed. (Englewood Cliffs, N.J.: Prentice Hall, 1986).
18. George Foster, "Briloff and the Capital Markets," *Journal of Accounting Research,* Spring 1979, pp. 262–74.
19. The classic text in the field is Benjamin Graham and David L. Dodd's, *Security Analysis* (New York: McGraw-Hill, 1934).
20. For more insight into the aggregation question in accounting, see George Sorter, "An 'Event' Approach to Basic Accounting Theory," *The Accounting Review,* January 1969, pp. 12–19.
21. William H. Beaver, Andrew Christie, and Paul A. Griffin, "The Information Content of SEC Accounting Series Release No. 190," *Journal of Accounting and Economics,* June 1980, pp. 127–57.
22. This raises a question as to whether the SEC needs to protect naive investors.
23. Nicholas J. Gonedes and Nicholas Dopuch, "Capital Market Equilibrium, Information Production, and Selecting Accounting Techniques: Theoretical Framework and Review of Empirical Work," Studies on Financial Account-

ing Objectives: 1974, supplement to vol. 12 of the *Journal of Accounting Research,* pp. 48–120.

24. Financial Accounting Standards Board, An Analysis of Issues Related to *Conceptual Framework for Financial Accounting and Reporting: Elements of Financial Statements and Their Measurement* (FASB, 1976), par. 404.

25. Steven A. Ross proposed an alternative model with more parameters called the Arbitrage Pricing Model in "The Arbitrage Theory of Capital Asset Pricing," *Journal of Economic Theory,* December 1976, pp. 341–60.

26. For a fuller treatment of this work, see William F. Sharpe, *Portfolio Theory and Capital Markets* (New York: McGraw-Hill, 1970).

27. See, for example, John S. Bildersee, "The Association between a Market-Determined Measure of Risk and Alternative Measures of Risk," *The Accounting Review,* January 1975, pp. 81–98.

28. The economic consequences of publishing information is discussed in Chapter 8.

29. William E. Ricks, "The Market's Response to the 1974 LIFO Adoptions," *Journal of Accounting Research,* Autumn 1982, pp. 367–87.

Chapter 7

Making Decisions

CHAPTER OBJECTIVES

After studying this chapter, you will be able to:

Define what is meant by the usefulness of information to individuals.

Compare the different approaches to defining decision usefulness.

Distinguish the several roles of accounting information.

Discuss the assumptions underlying normative models of individual decision making.

Describe the role of fairness in financial reports.

Describe some of the findings of research into how people actually make decisions.

Discuss the implications of human information processing research for the design of accounting systems.

CHAPTER OVERVIEW

A Prescriptive Approach

Accounting theorists, building on the work of economists, have developed a theory of how rational individuals should make decisions. The theory encompasses uncertainty and situations involving more than one person. In essence, decision makers are assumed to maximize their expected utility functions and to revise their priors in accordance with Bayes Theorem.

A Descriptive Approach

Positive accountants have used the prescriptive approach to develop hypotheses about behavior at an aggregate level. Behavioral accountants have examined the assumptions of the prescriptive approach. Empirical evidence is somewhat conflicting—it supports the prescriptive approach at the aggregate level, but not at the individual level.

An Ethical Approach

The prescriptive approach depends on utilitarian theory for its ethical foundations. Rights theory and justice theory provide useful alternatives. Ethics define acceptable decisions and are, therefore, an important aspect of decision theory.

Decision making plays a central role in accounting theory. Its importance has been stressed time and again in definitions of accounting. For instance, the American Accounting Association said accounting is " . . . the process of identifying, measuring, and communicating economic information to permit informed judgments and *decisions* by users of the information."[1] The Accounting Principles Board claimed that the function of accounting is " . . . to provide quantitative information, primarily financial in nature, about economic entities that is intended to be useful in making economic *decisions*."[2] And the FASB asserted that the role of financial reporting in the economy is "to provide information that is useful in making business and economic *decisions*."[3],*

It is apparent, therefore, that we need to study how users of accounting information make decisions. If we could determine how this takes place, we might be able to deduce what information would be of most value to them. For instance, as Chapter 3 pointed out, during the 1960s a price-earnings (PE) ratio approach to investment became popular. To compute a PE ratio, investors needed an appropriate earnings-per-share number. The APB obliged by issuing *Opinion No. 15,* which laid out the details of how the earnings-per-share computation should be done. It also insisted that the result appear on the face of the income statement because of its importance to investors.[4] By contrast, the FASB appears to have concluded that most investors are using a net-present-value model. As a result, they have stressed cash flows in their statement of objectives for financial reporting.[5]

In studying the decisions that users make, and the impact those decisions have on the provision of information, accounting theorists have adopted a two-pronged strategy. One is to ask how people should make decisions, that is, a *normative* approach; the other is to ask how people actually do make decisions, that is, a *positive* approach. In the first, one typically starts with an economic model and attempts to deduce what information is necessary to make it work. In the second, one studies how

---

* Emphasis added in each case.

individuals make use of financial data that are provided. It is important to study the positive approach, because it gives insight into the information that is most useful. It is equally important to study the normative approach, because many financial accounting standards are based on the deductive logic from normative decision models.

This chapter attempts to give an overview of the research that has been done using both the prescriptive and the descriptive approaches. (It is an overview only and presumes some familiarity with the details from your other classes.) It begins with an analysis of the assumptions underlying the decision tools, such as present-value analysis, that are taught in typical business programs. It continues with the normative model that many accounting researchers use today. The chapter proceeds to a discussion of the field of behavioral accounting in which the question of how people actually do make decisions is researched. That leads into a section on ethics which addresses the question of what is the right decision in a broader framework than is traditional. In particular, we ask what would be fair.

A PRESCRIPTIVE APPROACH

How should people make decisions? This is an old question and has been answered at a variety of levels. There are the partial models of decision making familiar to business students; there are the more general economic models that academic researchers study in an attempt to provide underpinnings for the partial models; and then there are the still broader philosophical issues that question one's approach to analyzing decisions. This section addresses the first two of these questions; the section on ethics addresses the third question.

Partial Analysis

Most accounting students will be familiar with a variety of decision tools that form the staple diet of a typical BBA course. Examples of such tools are cost-volume-profit analysis, relevant cost analysis, regression analysis, linear programming, and cost allocation models. These tools are called partial models because they attempt to analyze only one piece of a large problem. Most of these models fall into the normative category since they are offered to the student as examples of how decisions should be made. They are often accompanied by discussions of how managers fail to use these models, that is, by descriptions of the models that managers actually appear to be using. Many of these models also assume certainty, although some analyses end by saying that one should consider issues of risk.

Perhaps the most widely used of all these models is present-value analysis, which became popular in the professional literature of finance in the

1960s.[6] A typical problem presents a student with a series of cash flows over time, asks the students to discount them at a rate of interest that is usually provided and which is typically standard across each of the cash flows, and then calls for the student to select that cash flow producing the highest net present value. Risk is taken into consideration by adjusting the interest rate to a required rate for a given level of risk. Alternatively, the expected dividend stream is adjusted by using a certainty equivalent (the amount the investor would be willing to take with certainty now instead of waiting for the outcome).

Simplified decision models involve a host of assumptions of which the user is usually unaware. They include the presence of constant risk across projects (or the absence of risk); the ability to substitute cash flow for utility in the computations (or the risk-neutral stance of the decision maker); the ability to break the cash flow into periodic segments; and the ability to separate the investment from the financing decision. The intent here is not to take the reader through a Ph.D. course in the assumptions underlying such models, but to make the point that no decision models are assumption-free. Usually the simpler the model, the more "horrifying" the assumptions that have to be made to make the model work. As the British economist Lord Keynes once commented, "practical men, who believe themselves to be quite exempt from any intellectual influences, are usually the slaves of some defunct economist."[7]

Many, although not all, of these tools are used widely in practice. The fact that managers may not use all of the models espoused by academics is a matter of interest to researchers. One reason may be that simpler models work just as well as more complex models in the face of the rough data that are often all that one has. Thus, practice underlines the often-stated maxim that the purpose of modeling is not realism, but prediction. That being the case, one can fall back on models which, while admittedly unrealistic in parts, enable one to gain some insight into what information might be preferred by users. Another reason some models are not used may be a function of education. Managers use models that they learned in school; new models take time to diffuse into the community. The rate of diffusion of new ideas is itself a matter of research.[8] A third reason is probably the fact that some of the models that have been developed are not rich or complex enough to capture those facets of decisions that are of interest to managers. This suggests that, as models are further developed, they might diffuse more widely in the community.

CHECKPOINTS

1. Give three examples of partial decision analysis.
2. Explain why the models used are called partial models.

Choice Theory

The purpose of a general theory of decision making is to provide a setting within which one can examine the assumptions underlying models, like those examined above. It should also provide a framework within which one might develop new models. Such a general theory of decision making begins with the notion of actions which are open to individuals; outcomes or consequences of their actions; and preference functions that determine how they will choose among the actions open to them. Textbooks often describe consequences in cash flow terms, but they could be perfectly general. For example, when President Truman was considering whether to permit the dropping of the bomb on Hiroshima, there was a whole range of international and long-lasting consequences that had to be considered. Such consequences are sometimes called *scenarios*. A change in any one detail in a scenario produces a new consequence from the point of view of general choice theory.

Economists typically assume that people's preferences are complete and transitive, that is, they have an opinion on everything in their choice set, and they can order these preferences. For instance, everyone is assumed to have a definite opinion on automobile manufacturers. Those who prefer Ford to Chrysler and Chrysler to General Motors are expected to prefer Ford to General Motors. At a given point in time the transitivity assumption is probably relatively trivial, but over a period of time it assumes that people's preferences are stable, which is a considerably larger assumption. Advertising, for one, has as its aim the disturbing of people's preference functions.

Individuals are assumed to sort through all the alternatives open to them and to choose those actions which are most preferable. For example, an individual might be considering where to save $1,000. The following alternatives are open:

Actions	*Consequences*
Save with a bank at 5% interest	$1,050
Save with a money fund at 8% interest	$1,080

Notice how every action has a known consequence because we have assumed a world of perfect certainty. Individuals are assumed to do the computations necessary to determine the consequences and to base their preferences on them. In this case, they should choose the money fund.

Given a finite set of alternatives, the assumptions of a complete and transitive preference function are sufficient to enable one to provide a numerical measure of an individual's preferences, that is, the more-preferred consequences can be given higher weights than the less-preferred ones. For example, on an ex post basis one might give the money fund a weight of 8 and the bank a weight of 5 to indicate that the fund is preferred to the bank. These measures form the basis of utility theory in which each individual is assumed to behave as if he or she has a built-in set of weights, termed a *utility function,* guiding him or her to those consequences with the highest utility. (The measures were once called *utils*.) Choice theory then reduces to maximizing utility.

Utility functions enable one to treat other aspects of decision making. For instance, a typical assumption is that one's utility for a product declines as one accumulates more of it—the first hot fudge sundae tastes better than the third or fourth. This assumption enables theorists to model observed consumer behavior that shows a preference for collections of different items rather than single items, that is, a sundae and a coke rather than two sundaes.

Carnegie-Mellon professor and Nobel prizewinner Herbert Simon questioned the optimization assumption in traditional choice theory. He suggested that if search is costly, individuals might satisfice rather than optimize. They would achieve this by taking the first "satisfactory" consequence.[9] For instance, individuals might deposit money in a bank at 5 percent interest because they lack the time to find a money fund that pays a higher rate of interest. While Simon's work is undoubtedly more realistic, it is also logically inconsistent in this particular context, because in a world of perfect certainty there can be no costly searches. This follows because everything is already known or instantaneously available. This points up a major dilemma for accounting theorists seeking to understand decisions: The simple world described above assumes that all is known. If this were true, accountants would not be needed.

Information Economics

To find a theoretical home for accountants, one has to "enrich" the choice model by adding additional further layers of complexity. In particular, it is necessary to build into the model the uncertainty in the world. We do this by introducing the concept of states of the world that are descriptions of possible outcomes. To continue our previous example, in an uncertain world the economy might rise or fall in the year ahead. Each of these possibilities constitutes a possible state of the world. Our investor's choice then might look like this:

	States	
Acts	*Economy Rises*	*Economy Falls*
Save with bank	$1,050	$1,050
Save with money fund	$1,080	$1,030

Actions no longer have known consequences because uncertainty now intervenes. Economists analyze situations like this by attaching a probability to each state and computing the expected value of each action. Say one thinks the likelihood of the economy rising is 80 percent and of its falling 20 percent. The expected value of each action is then:

Save with bank:	80% × $1,050 + 20% × $1,050 = $1,050
Save with money fund:	80% × $1,080 + 20% × $1,030 = $1,070

It has been shown that this methodology, that is, people maximizing the expected value of their actions, can be justified if the following four conditions are met.

1. Preferences are complete and transitive.
2. Given identical outcomes, the one with the higher probability will be selected.
3. Complicated gambling situations can be broken down into simpler ones. This is called the *no-fun-in-gambling* assumption.
4. There exists a certain gamble to which the individual will be indifferent. This is called the *certainty-equivalent* assumption.[10]

Given these assumptions, we have a model of choice that includes uncertainty. There is, therefore, now a logical necessity for a theory of information that can explain how this uncertainty might be resolved. Early work in the area of information analysis under the heading of information economics concentrated on how information enabled individuals to revise the probabilities they attached to the possible occurrence of various states. This is called the *predecisional* role of information because it provides a value for information prior to one's making a decision. For instance, continuing the same example, our investor might suspect that an economic report about to be released would lead to a reversal of the probability estimates. The new expected values are then:

Save with bank:	20% × $1,050 + 80% × $1,050 = $1,050
Save with money fund:	20% × $1,080 + 80% × $1,030 = $1,040

One could reasonably expect the investor, aware of the potential risk, to pay up to $10 (i.e., $1,050 − 1,040) for this information to avoid being stuck with the wrong choice. More generally, the expected value of information is measured by the increase in value one might expect from having that information.*

---

* This revision process is assumed to occur through the working of Bayes Theorem.

The expected utility approach can be extended to the consideration of an entire information system, for example, to the question of whether one should purchase an ongoing subscription to the economic report. Assume, for simplicity's sake, that the report enables one to predict exactly each year how the economy will behave. With that information one will be able to invest in the bank in bad times and in the money fund in good times. If one can assume that good times occur 80 percent of the time, and bad times 20 percent, then over time one can expect to make:

$$80\% \times \$1,080 + 20\% \times \$1,050 = \$1,074$$

Without the information, and sticking to the strategy of investing in the money fund only, one could expect to make:

$$80\% \times \$1,080 + 20\% \times \$1,030 = \$1,070$$

One should pay, therefore, no more than $4 per year for this service.

Risk Aversion.   Cash values were used in the above examples. Given certain assumptions about human behavior, one could have substituted utility functions. This substitution enables us to refine the concept of attitudes to risk. The risk-neutral are assumed to be indifferent to it; the risk lovers are the gamblers; the risk-averse seek to avoid it. For instance, consider individuals presented with the following options:

A: $1,000 for sure

B: A 50/50 chance of either $500 or $1,500

Risk lovers will choose B; the risk-averse will choose A; the risk-neutral will be indifferent. At first glance one might assume that everyone is risk-averse, but the millions who gamble against the odds each day cannot be risk-averse—the expected value of entering a state lottery is considerably less than the cost of playing. The same is true for insurance: the cost of coverage exceeds the expected value of that coverage. The difference between the expected value of a lottery and the price that one is prepared to pay for it is called the *risk premium*. Risk lovers are prepared to pay for the privilege of gambling, presumably because they derive nonmonetary pleasure from it.

Contributions.   Information economics has sharpened accountants' views of what makes information valuable by stressing the relationship of information to its users: It is from their utility functions and only from their utility functions that a value for information arises. By contrast, the FASB stresses a series of qualities that supposedly give information value: These include characteristics such as relevance, timeliness, and reliability, all of which were discussed in Chapter 5. Thus far, research in the area of information economics has shown no necessary connection between the value of information and these qualities. This does not imply that no connection can ever be found; merely that information economics has not found one to date.

The information economics approach has also proved valuable in simply stressing the fact of uncertainty. Most accounting proceeds as though the world were perfectly certain. Depreciation expense, just to name one instance, is computed each period as though the life of the asset were a given instead of a guess. Information economics was certainly not the first to insist that accountants pay more attention to the uncertainties inherent in accounting. New York professor Richard Brief, for instance, argued more than a decade ago that accountants would not be fulfilling their responsibilities completely until they acknowledged how uncertain their estimates were in financial statements.[11] Information economics has taken a lead role in making this important point ever since its establishment.

Unfortunately, positive, generalizable findings in the area of information economics have been disappointingly few. It can be shown, for instance, that when information is free, more information is preferable to less. More information is defined in terms of "fineness." One information set is said to be finer than another if one contains all the information contained in the other. For instance, a detailed list of expenses is finer than a single total of expenses. The preferability of a finer information set holds only for free information that can be discarded if "useless." It may fail if one has to pay for it. It is also apparent from our preceding numerical example that information has no value unless it changes, or might change, one's choices. Apart from these two facts, not much more can be said at a general level about decisions. Still more structure has to be added to wring more insights out of the model.

CHECKPOINTS

1. Define risk premiums. How might one use the concept?
2. Define fineness and explain when and how finer information sets are preferable.
3. What makes predecisional information valuable?

Agency Theory

One way in which more insights can be gained from information economics is to extend the model from a single individual to two individuals. One of these individuals is an *agent* for another called a *principal*—hence the title of agency theory. The agent contracts to perform certain duties for the principal; the principal contracts to reward the agent. An analogy may be drawn between owners of a business and the management of that business.

Owners are called *information evaluators* in this particular context; their agents are called *decision makers*. The information evaluators are assumed to be responsible for choosing the information system. Their choice must be made in such a way that the decision makers make the best decisions in the owners' interests in light of the information available to them. In other words, the actions are those of the agent, while the utility function of ultimate interest is that of the principal. The problem is made more complex by the need to consider the agent's utility function as well because this is what drives the agent's actions.[12]

Given that principals will always be interested in the outcomes generated by their agents, agency theory provides the underpinning for an important role for accounting in providing information after an event: a so-called *postdecisional* role. This role is often associated with the stewardship role of accounting in which an agent reports to a principal on the events of the past period. This is what gives accounting its feedback value in addition to its *predictive* value.*

Several insights are available from this model and its extensions. These extensions relate mostly to the way the two parties share risk and information. For example, in the standard economic story, risk-averse owners are assumed to carry the risk of the business, while managers act as risk-neutral agents. The dilemma of this story is that it can be shown, using the machinery of agency theory, that if management is indifferent to risk, but owners are risk-averse, then management and not owners will carry the risk—for a fee. This rather spoils the story that capitalists are rewarded by profits because they bear all the risk! Economists have responded by assuming that managers are risk-averse too. It is the interplay of relative risk aversion between managers and owners that creates some of the most interesting issues in agency theory for accountants. Information is one means to reduce uncertainty, giving accountants an important role in risk sharing between managers and owners.

Information Asymmetries. Recent work in the area of agency theory has focused on the problems engendered by incomplete information, that is, when not all states are known to both parties and, as a result, when certain consequences are not considered by both. Such situations are known as *information asymmetries*. For example, owners may not know managers' preferences, making it difficult for them to do the computation referred to above.

---

* See Chapter 5 for more discussion of these two terms.

A particular example of incomplete information exists in agency theory when an owner is unable to observe all the actions of the manager. These actions may differ from those the owners would have preferred, either because the manager has a different set of preferences, or because the manager is deliberately attempting to shirk or to cheat the owners. This creates what is known as a *moral hazard* problem. One possible solution is for the owners to hire a firm of auditors to check on what management is doing. Another is to provide management with incentives, such as shares in the company, to align their preferences with the owners.

The secondhand car market was the subject of a celebrated paper illustrating the nature of information asymmetries.[13] The seller of a secondhand car knows more about the car than the buyer; if the seller does not share the information about the expected future of the car, it may not be possible to agree on a price, because the buyer will offer an average price for the car, while the seller might want top dollars. Even if the seller does share information, the buyer may be suspicious from previous purchases of secondhand cars. The buyer may discount the information the seller provides, even though it is true. In the extreme, information asymmetries can lead to a complete breakdown of the market as good cars are withheld, because one cannot persuade buyers of their value, leaving only "lemons" for sale. This problem is called *adverse selection* because of the poor selection of cars that can result.

One possible solution to adverse selection is for the seller to hire an independent "auditor" to check the car, and to provide the buyer with a certificate as to its quality. Another possible solution is for the government to regulate the sale of secondhand cars by insisting that all sellers provide a prescribed list of information to would-be buyers. They also might prohibit those with superior knowledge from exploiting that knowledge at the expense of the less knowledgeable, that is, by banning insider trading. A third possible solution lies in the marketplace itself. If good cars are being offered at a discount, there is an incentive for sophisticated car buyers to step in and arbitrage the market. Competition between sophisticated arbitragers could lead to appropriate market prices being set.

In a variation on the same theme, it could be argued that sellers of good cars have a natural incentive to disclose as much information about their cars as possible. Buyers could infer, therefore, that those who were unwilling to disclose had only inferior cars to sell. If this could be shown to occur, there would be no cause for auditing, regulation, or arbitration. The analogy between the secondhand car market, on the one hand, and companies and their accountants, on the other, should be clear. It is interesting in this light to ponder on why accounting today is so heavily regulated. More is said on this subject in Chapter 8 on Regulation, where possible reasons for failures in the market are discussed.

CHECKPOINTS

---

1. Give an example of a principal-agent setting. Explain how the principal might select an information system for use by the agent.
2. Define moral hazard and adverse selection. What is their significance for accountants?
3. In what ways does agency analysis extend the work of information economics?
4. Explain why an agent might want to be audited.

Multiperson Decision Theory

Thus far our discussion of decision making and the resulting demand for information has focused on choices taken in isolation—even in agency theory one is focusing on an individual owner choosing an information system. What, if anything, can be said about choices by collections of individuals? The reason for our interest in this question is that policymakers like the FASB presumably attempt to take into account the desires of all their constituents. Technically speaking, they attempt to aggregate individual utility functions.

One common way to attempt to capture the will of the people is by majority vote. Consider, however, the following scenario. A student senate is called to vote on whether to recommend the building of a new student union. Some feel strongly it should include a pub; others feel equally strongly that it should be "dry." Another group feels that it is a waste of time. The preferences among the three groups for the three options run as follows where the numbers correspond to rankings:

Groups	I	II	III
A: Union with pub	1	2	3
B: Union without pub	2	3	1
C: No union	3	1	2

Given these rankings, a union with a pub is preferred to a union without a pub by groups II and III; the union without a pub is preferred to no union at all by groups I and II. This suggests that a union with a pub will be the choice. But, an examination of the rankings shows that groups II and III both prefer no union at all to a union with a pub! Denoting preferred by the greater than sign we have:

$$A > B \text{ and } B > C \rightarrow A \text{ is the choice of the majority.}$$

In fact, if one had arranged the vote slightly differently, so that the union with a pub was compared to no union at all in the first round, a vote of the no union at all against the union without a pub would have resulted in the choice of the latter! A check of the rankings shows that:

$$C > A \text{ and } B > C \rightarrow B \text{ is the choice of the majority.}$$

In other words, one can determine the outcome simply by arranging the order of the votes. Majority votes are not conclusive, therefore. Alternatively stated, majority votes do not lead to an aggregate utility function that can then be used by regulators to determine whether a particular decision would meet the desires of the populace. They might vote today for A over B and for B over C, but they might also vote for C over A if it is presented in an appropriate order.

Such strategies, sometimes called *log rolling,* are well known to politicians who specialize in parliamentary procedure. They utilize their expertise to guide legislation through the voting process to gain the result they desire. Stanford economist and Nobel prizewinner Kenneth Arrow demonstrated that voting strategies can be generalized to the rather startling result that,

a. If everyone's vote is to count, and
b. Only available opportunities are to be considered, an appropriately rational group preference function cannot be constructed unless,
c. Everyone is unanimous, or
d. Group preferences are dictated by one person.[14]

Stated otherwise, given these assumptions it is impossible to arrive at a utility function that will consistently reflect society's wishes.

This rather disconcerting result has drawn the attention of many researchers who have sought to escape Arrow's strictures. In particular, Yale professor Joel Demski translated its strictures into terms appropriate for accounting.[15] At the outset it must be appreciated that the theoretical problem is more severe than the practical. Both individuals and societies make inconsistent choices all the time, blissfully unaware that academics consider that irrational. The theoretical problem is genuinely severe, though, because it does hamper our ability to develop models of group behavior in the decision-making area. As a result, research into society's information requirements is slowed, and regulators lack theoretical justification for their necessary actions.

Arrow's theorem is particularly awkward for a body like the FASB, since it suggests that, despite all their best efforts to be democratic, they will inevitably impose their own wishes on their constituents, unless they can build unanimous consent for their proposals—a very unlikely event. The Conceptual Framework, though, was an attempt to do this. It began by listing the large number of potential users, such as investors, creditors, managers, government, employees, and the public. It then suggested that all these potential users are "generally interested" in the ability of a business enterprise "to generate favorable cash flows because their decisions relate to amounts, timing, and uncertainties of expected cash flows."[16] They concluded that users were homogeneous and would have identical preferences for types of accounting information. The last chapter suggested that this is too optimistic; potential users are a more heterogeneous group than the FASB might prefer. The FASB, therefore, has not escaped Arrow's theorem.

A DESCRIPTIVE APPROACH

The previous section focused on attempts to construct a normative model for decision making involving utility theory. This section focuses on attempting to understand how decisions are really made. The discussion centers on two of the questions that researchers have considered:

1. How do companies decide which information to release? How, in other words, do they decide their financial reporting policies?
2. How do individuals process the information they receive in making their decisions? Do processing techniques differ systematically across individuals?

There have been two major thrusts in accounting research in attempting to answer these questions. One approach draws on the psychological literature and seeks to understand how individuals use given sets of information. It is known broadly as *behavioral accounting*—the two branches of behavioral accounting that are of particular interest here are *human information processing* and *cognitive theory*. The other approach draws on the literature on information economics, agency theory, and efficient markets to build hypotheses for how accounting standards are set. This approach tends to deal with individuals in the aggregate. It is more concerned with the decisions of organizations than with those of particular users. It has chosen to call itself *positive accounting*.

The title has been severely criticized for several reasons. One is that it appears to imply that other areas of accounting research such as behavioral accounting are not equally positive or descriptive in their approach. The other is that it seems to suggest that it is an entirely non-normative approach to accounting when, in fact, it is based upon a number of quite stringent normative judgments about individual behavior.[17] The theory assumes, for instance, that individuals are utility maximizers, with all the assumptions that involves. In particular, work is assumed to have negative utility. None of these assumptions has been proven. The point is not to dispute this view of the world or to decry the very real contributions of positive accounting. It is merely to stress that "positive accounting" is only one avenue of positive research and that it is as normative in its own way as are other areas of research in accounting.

There is, as yet, little integration between behavioral and positive accounting. They differ in the level of analysis—the one examines aggregate behavior, the other individual behavior. We lack, almost entirely, a model of how individual decisions are aggregated to produce corporate decisions. They differ also in their assumptions about the cognitive abilities of human beings. The standard economic model makes much use of rationality and assumes that human beings have unlimited computational powers in maximizing their utility. The standard behavioral model is more inclined to accept irrational behavior because it takes as its premise that human beings have quite limited computational powers. Behavioralists tend to accuse economic theorists of being unrealistic. Economists claim that the only criterion by which a model should be judged is its predictive power. The most unrealistic models may be quite acceptable, therefore. Behavioralists reject this argument in favor of the need for greater understanding. In short, the two approaches have been quite antagonistic toward each other. This has led to some quite spirited arguments between accounting researchers. This section attempts to describe the thrusts of each approach and their implications for accounting.

Corporate Reporting Policies

As already noted, one of the questions that accounting researchers have attempted to explore empirically is how companies select the accounting procedures they use. Of course, to a certain extent these choices are made for them by the FASB, but there are still sufficient alternatives left at management's discretion to make it an interesting question. Positive accountants have made this question their particular preserve. They found their hypotheses on the normative decision theory discussed in the previous section. From this they have produced a series of relatively provocative hypotheses that they have tested. For the most part these hypotheses appear, at this stage, to be supported by the data.

The language used in positive accounting is that of contracts or covenants. Investors, consumers, management, employees, and others are assumed to enter into explicit or implicit contracts with each other. For these contracts to be of any interest, one must assume that they are costly to construct and destruct, or else the parties would make and break them with impunity. The questions then become:

1. Which parties to the contract reap the return?
2. Which parties bear the risks?
3. On what outcomes are these results based?

Since contracts establish rights, this approach is sometimes referred to as the *property rights* theory of economics.

One of the particularly important contributions of positive accounting has been its timely reminder that contracts are drawn in the context of markets. And if the efficient market is to be believed, some of these markets are remarkably sophisticated. As a result, problems that an individual principal might have in monitoring a contract, because of an information asymmetry, might be resolved by market forces. Equally, individual investors are not making their decisions in isolation, but in the company of a host of other investors. One result is that a decision not to invest does not ensure the status quo, because others are investing all the time. Another result is that solutions to various investment problems must be sought in association with already present market forces.

Contracts between Management and Owners.   One area that has been widely studied in positive accounting involves contracts between management and owners.[18] This area is very closely related to that of agency theory. Owners are understandably concerned that management make decisions that are consistent with the wishes of the owners, that they are honest and efficient, and that their decisions produce for management the greatest increase in value possible. One way to motivate management to do this is to give management shares in the company. Another possibility is to give managers performance bonuses attached to the share price. One also observes performance bonuses for managers that are a function of accounting numbers such as net income and revenue. The use of accounting numbers enables performance to be tied more closely to specific components of net income such as increasing revenue or decreasing expenses. But if it is to be in the interests of owners, increases in net income should generate increases in market value. This is not always true.

Managers who are rewarded for high net income numbers have a clear incentive to increase those numbers by either deciding to manipulate given rules or, more interestingly for accounting theory, by deciding on accounting rules that favor them. Specifically, one can expect managers whose performance bonuses are tied to net income to manipulate or choose accounting rules that will increase income in this period at the expense of later periods. This is called the *bonus plan hypothesis*. Taking a "big bath" is an example of manipulating the rules: In this process, managers write off everything they can when earnings are down so as to increase the probability of positive net incomes in the future. Choosing straight-line depreciation rather than accelerated depreciation is an example of deciding on an accounting rule.

Contracts between Management and Creditors.   Another area that has been widely studied concerns debt covenants. It can be shown that a utility-maximizing management, particularly if they have shares in the company, may not always make decisions in the best interests of debt holders. Creditors, therefore, often ask management to sign a contract protecting the interests of the creditor. For instance, management has a natural incentive to issue new debt that is senior to old debt, because this action, by lowering the risk of the new debt, lowers its price. The seniority of the debt, while of no personal interest to management, is of great interest to debt holders who will want to write contracts with management to ensure that this does not happen.

As with the bonus hypothesis, management also has an incentive to shift income from future periods to the present because this decreases the debt-to-equity ratio. This is described as the *debt/equity* hypothesis. Many debt covenants take the form of holding certain financial ratios above a certain level. For instance, the corporation may be required by its creditors to keep its current ratio (i.e., its current assets to current liabilities) above a certain level.

Contracts between Management and Society.   Positive accountants have studied the relationships between corporations and the various political bodies, and the effect this has on corporate decisions. They have hypothesized that large and, therefore, politically visible firms have an incentive to defer income to future periods. This is known as the *size* hypothesis. This hypothesis goes in the opposite direction from the bonus and the debt/equity hypotheses. It suggests that large firms will base their accounting-related decisions on income-reducing strategies in an attempt to avoid being noticed by politicians. The hypothesis appears to be true for very large firms and, in particular, the oil and gas industry.

Positive accountants have said relatively little about contracts between management and the general public and management and employees. Clearly, it would be possible to extend the theory to take into consideration questions such as whether management is bound to provide safe working conditions for employees or whether management is bound to avoid polluting the atmosphere by its activities and how, if at all, these contracts affect decisions related to financial reporting. It may be, for instance, that social policy could be advanced by obliging management to include estimates of external costs in their annual statements. The Corporate Report that was referred to earlier, for instance, could be discussed in this context.

Individual Financial Analysis

The second question to draw the attention of accounting researchers has been how users analyze the information they receive in making their decisions. A related question is whether the processing methods in use differ systematically across individuals. For instance, do sophisticated investors use a different information set than unsophisticated investors? These questions are potentially important because if companies knew more precisely what information investors and others want and use, they could design their financial reports more specifically to facilitate their decision making. Unfortunately, experimental results are still fragmentary and confusing, with only a few apparently conclusive findings.

One finding that does appear to emerge consistently is that individuals have a limited ability to process information. The evidence in this regard appears to be unassailable. Some would even consider the matter self-evident. Limitations reveal themselves in a variety of ways.

One line of research has examined the ability of individuals to cope with increasing quantities of data. The general finding is that decisions improve with increased information until a point is reached where the information provided becomes too great for the individual to analyze. At that point, where the individual begins to experience what is termed *information overload,* decision making begins to deteriorate again.[19] A related finding is that individuals appear to prefer a limited amount of information on which to make a decision. This may be the result of the fact that most people's short-term memory is limited to carrying no more than seven items.[20] Thus, people tend to omit information, claiming that it is insignificant or irrelevant. They also tend to use information in aggregated form. This accounts, in part, for the popularity of indexes, such as stock price indexes, and earnings and earnings-per-share figures.

The point at which overload occurs varies among individuals. It is also mitigated by the use of technical assistance such as computers. More importantly still, it must be recognized that people seldom make decisions in isolation. Generally they are part of an organization where the role of each individual is to make inputs into a joint decision. The organizational literature is replete with discussions of how decisions made by leaders of corporations depend on the nature of the information fed them by their subordinates, by the structure of the organization, by the performance measurement system, and by the strategic thrust of the organization.[21] The information overload problem does not go away, therefore, but the concept does have to be translated to an organizational level.

Studies have revealed also that people who rely on subjective statistical procedures act in a biased manner.[22] For example, people feel more comfortable selecting their own random numbers for state lotteries. They also prefer betting on coins before they are tossed rather than afterwards. Studies have shown too that individuals attribute greater certainty to unreliable information than is warranted.[23] They respond more to vivid events such as stories about prominent individuals. Also, individuals tend to base estimates and predictions on recent or available observations, even though these may be neither representative of long-run conditions nor reflect objective probabilities. For instance, a run of heads often persuades people to call heads. In other words, individuals do not appear to be making decisions in line with the normative theories outlined in the first section of this chapter.[24]

Given that individuals are limited in their abilities to process information in a complex environment with uncertain probabilities regarding future events, it is natural that they should wish to simplify the complexity of the situation as they perceive it and reduce the uncertainty. They typically achieve this by using rules of thumb or what are termed *heuristics*. One heuristic that has drawn the attention of accounting researchers is termed *anchoring*.

Anchoring.   It has been observed that individuals select particular pieces of information as a starting point and, using other available information, make adjustments to form predictions.[25] For example, an investor might use the prior period's earnings or earnings per share for an anchor, add to it current information about specific economic conditions for the firm, and then make a prediction of the current year's earnings. As a second example, a couple attempting to place a value on their home might use the original cost as an anchor and then make adjustments for changes in building costs and selling prices of homes in the neighborhood.

The difficulty with the anchoring process is that individuals generally fail to adjust fully to the new information, that is, they do not follow Bayes' rule in revising their prior probabilities. If an upward adjustment is required in light of new information, the estimate or prediction is likely to be lower than is realistically warranted. On the other hand, if the new information indicates a downward adjustment, the prediction is likely to be too high. This concept is important for accounting because, generally, individuals are not aware of this bias, and most persons do not know that they are using an anchoring process.

What then can be done in publishing financial reports to reduce the anchoring bias? First, it is important that accounting numbers have semantic interpretation. If the economic events measured by the accounting numbers are correctly understood by investors, there should be less opportunity for anchoring bias. Second, this appears to provide an argument for the use of current market prices as much as possible instead of historical costs. The older the information that may be used as an anchor, the greater the adjustment process and, therefore, the greater the likelihood of bias. These suggestions are made with considerable caution, however, since there has not been sufficient research on the anchoring bias in accounting to know how it can be eliminated or even reduced.

Functional Fixation.   Perhaps as a result of anchoring, individuals tend to display behavior known as *functional fixation*.[26] This means that individuals assume that the symbols, aggregations, or surrogates that they are using in making judgments regarding the future maintain the same meaning and relevance over time, regardless of changes in what they represent or in the way they are computed. In accounting, it implies that investors use accounting numbers (such as earnings per share) consistently over time without making full adjustments for changes in accounting techniques. For example, if the firm changes from capitalization of R&D expenses to current expensing, functional fixation on the reported earnings would result in an incorrect judgment, since the change in reported earnings resulting from the accounting change would not reflect fundamental economic changes (assuming no income tax effect). The general finding is that investors do adapt to the changes in accounting procedures over time, but they do not readily change the way they interpret the meaning and importance of the earnings figure in making a judgment regarding the value of the firm.

These findings are significant for financial reporting because they imply that consistency in the use of accounting procedures is important. When material changes in procedures are made, figures computed under both methods should probably be reported during the adaptation period. There is also an implication that accounting classifications and aggregations should permit as much semantic interpretation as possible, that is, accounting numbers should be interpreted in terms of economic realities wherever possible. A third implication is that decomposition of financial data may be desirable in order to avoid functional fixation on aggregate figures, which may fail to disclose fundamental economic relationships.

Conclusion.   Modeling "realistic" human behavior is extremely difficult—mathematical models do not deal easily with irrational behavior or even with behavior that exhibits bounded rationality. In spite of the difficulties of studying individual decision processes that can guide accounting policy, there are many reasons for learning as much as possible about individual decision making in an accounting context. These include:

1. The possibility of improving the quality of individual decisions and decreasing the cost of processing information by both accountants and investors.
2. The possibility of improving the set of information available to the individual and to the market, although the relationship to the market is unclear at this time.

These objectives may improve the allocation of resources in the economy as well as improve the welfare of individuals. As a first approximation, improving the welfare of individuals is desirable if in so doing the welfare of no one else is decreased (Pareto optimality). Three methods of reaching these goals are discussed in the following paragraphs.

1.   Research on individual decision processes may provide clues regarding what information should be included in financial reports. There may be no limit to the amount of information that can be utilized by the market as a whole, but individuals do have limitations; therefore, it may prove desirable to publish different statements for different groups of investors. The capital asset pricing model can be used to test the effect on security prices of certain information, but there must be some means of determining which information to publish before the market test can be made. Making a random selection of potentially relevant information would be an expensive way to proceed. Therefore, a knowledge of individual decision processes would permit improvements in the set of information provided to decision makers. Although the market may be efficient with the existing set of information (or with any set), an alternative set may provide an improvement in the allocation of resources and minimize the possibility of monopoly returns through the use of insider information.

2. The capital asset pricing model assumes a given state of technology in the use of information. That is, the ability of decision makers to use information is assumed to be constant. Research on the individual decision-making process might improve this ability. By improving the quality of investment decisions, resource allocation would also be improved, and investors would be better off because they would be holding portfolios closer to the optimum. The education of investors in the new technology would take time, but the market would react to the new methods quickly, because some investors would attempt to exploit the new opportunities immediately. However, there is evidence that learning is not efficient, which raises a question regarding the ability of the market to utilize new technology.[27]

3. A third method of improving the quality of investment decisions and reducing the cost of processing the information is the possibility of constructing investment decision models that would take the available information and process it as the investor would do. This could lead to lower processing costs for the investor and to greater consistency in the quality of the decisions. However, many problems now prevent these models from becoming reality. Much more research is needed before models can be constructed to fit different individuals and to account for changes over time in the variables and their weights that are taken into consideration by the individual investor.

A Synthesis

What emerges in this section is considerable conflict between the way people actually make decisions and the way that normative theory describes rational behavior. For instance, a disturbing characteristic of functional fixation is that, on the face of it, it is inconsistent with rational behavior. Rationality suggests that one should not react to accounting changes that have no substantive economic implications. But there are grounds for believing that the gap between the two approaches may be more apparent than real.

First, behavioral studies are done at an individual level. Heuristics are descriptions of potential biases in the individual investment decision process. Market studies are done at an aggregate level. There is no current way to know how individual biases work out in the aggregate to affect a market price. It is possible that the biases are offsetting in the aggregate so that the market does reflect fundamental economic relationships. In short, because the one analysis is done at the individual level and the other at the aggregate level, they do not necessarily speak to one another. This does not imply that the anchoring bias is unimportant for accounting at the aggregate level. The biases may affect individual welfare and permit a less than optimum distribution of securities among investors.

Second, there are also considerations of cost. As noted above, many contracts are signed on the basis of accounting numbers. Managerial bonuses, for instance, are often based on net income. These contracts, because they are costly to make, are not necessarily changed when accounting rules are changed. This being the case, what appears at first glance to be functional fixation might simply reflect the realities of the individual's economic situation. Stated otherwise, what has no substantive economic implications for a company might still have substantive economic implications for an individual.

The conflict should not be discounted entirely, though. There are two quite distinct views of human behavior present in the studies discussed in this section. One begins with a rational human being with superhuman computational powers, but then allows that there are costs to doing those computations. The other begins with a less rational and very fallible human being, relying on rules of thumb—regardless of costs. Science proceeds by rejecting theories. That means that theories have to be stated in such a way that they can be rejected by evidence. If we attempt too much synthesis, we run the danger of so blurring our theories that they become impossible to reject. Science then becomes dogma.

In this regard, it might be noted that positive accounting has tended to be associated with the so-called Chicago school of economics which has been politically conservative and opposed to government intervention.* Much of their work has appeared to their critics as special pleading. The approach, though, has the potential to be a great deal broader because in its essence it simply distinguishes "research aimed at explanation and prediction from research whose objective was prescriptive."[28] It could include, therefore, the insights of behavioral accountants as laid out in this chapter. It could also include the insights of radical accountants such

---

* The section on ethics suggests that they are modern-day Whigs.

as Baruch professors Marilyn Neimark and Tony Tinker, and Hofstra professor Cheryl Lehman.[29] This would mean dropping those normative behavioral and political assumptions that are part of present positive accounting in favor of a thorough-going positive approach to all phases of analysis. The result could be a unified field of accounting research whose only commitment is to follow the evidence wherever it leads.

CHECKPOINTS

1. Briefly describe what information processing characteristics of users have been found by behavioral accounting researchers.
2. Explain the interrelationship between fineness and information overload.
3. Explain the significance of satisficing in the light of what we know about human decision making.

AN ETHICAL APPROACH[30]

How to make the right decision, or as Socrates phrased it, "How one should live," predates business and constitutes the field of ethics. Ethical theorists have suggested many ways to guide decisions. These approaches have been summarized in two broad categories: the "deontological" which focuses on the motive to achieve the end and the "teleological" which focuses on the end itself. Deontologists are sometimes said to stress what is right, while teleologists stress what is good. Deontologists argue that bad motives can never be justified by good ends, while teleologists argue that bad ends vitiate good motives.

Utilitarianism

Traditional neoclassical economics of the kind that we have been discussing is based on utility theory, which is an example of teleological theory since it focuses almost completely on the consequences of our actions. In its classical form, utilitarians suggest that one should act so as to maximize one's utility. Loosely speaking, one should maximize one's happiness. In its most general form, one's utility can include concern for others. As used in most economic theories, though, one's utility is based on one's own interests only. This "extremely important restriction on the preferences of consumers is referred to as the condition of *selfishness of preferences*" by economists; ethicists call it *egoism*.[31] Even more restrictively, most commonly utility is assumed to be simply a function of personal wealth. Clearly, this imposes a limitation on what economic models can say about total well-being. This is typically handled (like risk) by a stricture at the end of a problem that the user is advised to take "qualitative factors" into consideration.

In this view, the role of regulators is to maximize the utility of all members of society. An immediate dilemma is the difficulty, if not the impossibility, of comparing individual utilities. This has led economists to suggest the concept of Pareto optimality. This is the point at which it is not possible to improve the situation of one individual without harming that of another. The argument goes that as long as one can improve the situation of one without harming another, one should do so, that is, there will be unanimous consent to move to Pareto optimality but dissent thereafter. This suggests that regulators will find assent from society as long as they are moving to a Pareto optimal point but can expect much argument thereafter.

Pareto optimality leaves a number of unsolved problems in its wake. For instance, although it can be shown that in a perfectly competitive economy, individuals will trade to a Pareto-optimal point in a process Adam Smith named the "invisible hand," the precise Pareto-optimal point that one reaches is a function of one's starting point. If Robinson Crusoe has all the fish and Man Friday all the bread, they can be expected to trade until each has some of both; however, no amount of trading can improve the situation if Robinson Crusoe has all the fish and all the bread and Man Friday nothing. This latter situation is as Pareto optimal as the first, yet many find it an unsatisfactory definition of utility maximization. A second problem emerges from the first: There is no guarantee that society will prefer a Pareto-optimal solution. It may be that society would want to equalize the fish and bread across the population. Stated otherwise, Pareto optimal solutions might not be socially preferable.

This last is particularly problematic for accounting. It appears that few decisions that the FASB has to face involve choices that will improve the lot of some in society and hurt the lot of none. Most choices involve the provision of information that has the potential to transfer wealth from one group to another. Financial reporting, in other words, has definite economic consequences. It is these consequences which cause groups to lobby before the FASB in favor of, or against, various proposals. As Rice professor Stephen Zeff noted, questions such "as accounting for research and development costs, self-insurance and catastrophe reserves, development-stage companies, foreign currency fluctuations, leases, the restructuring of troubled debt, domestic inflation and relative price changes, and the exploration and drilling costs of companies in the petroleum industry" have each provoked intensive lobbying.[32] In many cases, the "Basis for Conclusions" section of the relevant standard describes some of these efforts and the attention the FASB paid to an economic consequences argument.

Another problem for accounting with a strictly utility approach to information is that there is, indeed there can be, no sense of objective truth in this setting. Instead, information is a commodity to be traded like any other good. To quote Yale professor Joel Demski:

> The basic premises (of information economics) are that (1) information is a commodity whose acquisition, like that of other commodities, constitutes a problem of economic choice, and (2) one can obtain insight into this vague problem by viewing information issues within the formal structure of the economics of uncertainty, or decision theory.[33]

Given that there is a great diversity of preferences on commodities like cars and clothes, it is not surprising to those who hold this view of information that there is no consensus here either. Others feel more uncomfortable with this conclusion.

Human Rights

An alternative approach to addressing questions regarding what financial information to provide potential users begins with deontological theory which, it will be recalled, ignores consequences. Deontological theories have been subdivided in a variety of different ways. The most useful distinctions for our purposes contrast theories of human rights on the one hand with theories of justice on the other. Rights theorists maintain that we all have natural rights simply as a result of being human beings. Among them is the right to know. Government has an obligation to disclose its actions to the public, not because it necessarily increases social welfare, but simply because it is the right of voters. By the same token, the public has a right to financial information about companies, because they exist only with the consent of that public. This approach led the English Accounting Standards Steering Committee to conclude that:

> the fundamental objective of corporate reports is to communicate economic measurements of and information about the resources and performance of the reporting entity useful to those having reasonable rights to such information.
>
> A reasonable right to information exists where the activities of an organization impinge or may impinge on the interest of a user group . . . .[34]

Rights theorists argue that only "practical considerations of cost and confidentiality" should limit this fundamental right to know.

Neutrality.   The language of rights enables one to reexamine some of the stances that the FASB has taken. For instance, one of the FASB's dilemmas is that many of its standards have economic consequences for its constituents, adverse for some, positive for others. Despite this, the FASB has continued to maintain that its role is to supply information that is neutral and unbiased.[35] This seeming contradiction can be resolved in the context of rights theory rather than utility theory. It may never be possible to issue standards that affect utilities equally; however, it may always be possible to issue standards that affect the right to know equally.

Justice and Fairness

The concept of justice forms the other branch of the deontological approach to ethics. Justice theorists maintain that right actions should be guided not by their ends, nor by the rights of individuals, but by whether they are inherently just, that is, by whether they are fair or not. As that term is generally used in an auditor's report, fairness simply means that an auditor has applied officially established accounting principles; however, several notable accountants have used it in a broader setting. Accounting theorist DR Scott, for instance, sought to ground accounting standards in the following principles:

1. Justice—equitable treatment should be accorded to all interests involved in the financial situation covered by the accounts.
2. Truth—accounts must not be made a means of misrepresentation.
3. Fairness—accounting rules, procedures, etc., should not serve a special interest.[36]

Maurice Moonitz, research director of the APB, quotes Scott approvingly, noting that the usefulness approach to accounting can easily lead to accounting being trapped by special-interest groups such as "the business community, or the regulatory agencies, or investors, or tax collectors."[37]

Louisiana State professor James Patillo later asserted that the "major objective of financial accounting is to give a financial representation of the relative economic rights and interests of the segments of the economy. The basic standard in achieving this objective is fairness to all parties or economy segments."[38] Arthur Andersen & Co., not surprisingly given the leadership in that firm of Leonard Spacek, said "financial statements must be fair to all users and should provide the basis for resolving these conflicting interests in a manner that recognizes lawfully established economic rights and interests."[39] It is interesting to consider from this perspective that a balance sheet is really a list of a company's ethical rights (its assets) and its ethical obligations (its liabilities).*

Contracts.   The language of rights and justice has the potential for providing much insight into the demand for accounting information. It has already been noted that companies exist only by consent of the public. Some described this consent in terms of a contract, both implicit and

---

* Credit derives from *credere,* to believe, which also gave us the religious word *creed.* When one lends money to another, one does so in the belief that one will be repaid. *Credere* underlines the ethical covenant involved in doing business.

explicit, between a company and its stakeholders. Modern accounting theory makes much use of this concept, but does so in the context of egoistic utilitarianism. Parties to a contract are assumed to maximize their self-interest. This is assumed to lead individuals to seek to minimize their efforts for a given level of reward where minimization includes shirking where feasible. Owners and managers seek to monitor this behavior so as to maximize their own rewards while minimizing their own efforts in this regard.

An alternative approach to contract theory takes a fairness approach. It notes that a company's obligations are defined by the terms of its contracts with its stakeholders. Violating any of these contracts would be a violation of the principle of fairness. In this view contracts are not kept because of utilitarian considerations, but because one would be breaking an agreement to do otherwise. Breaking an agreement is equated by justice theorists to breaking one's promises. If keeping one's promises, regardless of the costs or benefits in a particular case, is considered desirable by society, then one can expect contracts to be honored regardless of whether they are being monitored or not. In utilitarian terms, honesty may be an inexpensive substitute for auditing!

A Positive Approach to Ethics

The words *morals* and *ethics* derive from the Latin *mores* and the Greek *ethos,* respectively, and simply mean customs—that is, the way people do behave. Today, ethics is invariably treated in terms of how one should behave—and doesn't. But the origin of the word reminds us that there is a positive aspect, too. Ethics can be a study of the customs that actually do rule people's behavior. Economic theory, based as it is on utilitarianism, tends to downplay customs for partly historical reasons.

Utilitarianism is the product of a political group in England who were dubbed *Whigs* by their opponents, the *Tories*. The Tories represented the establishment at the time. The community and authority, including that present in the monarchy, were seen by the Tories as the source of moral authority. The Whigs, who rejected the monarchy, sought to place the source of moral authority in the individual. It was essential for their political agenda that customs be excluded totally. This 300-year-old political debate continues to drive much of today's discussion of how decisions are and should be made. As noted earlier, positive accounting is largely the product of political conservatives, the modern descendants of 17th-century Whigs. It is not surprising, therefore, that most of their research produces results that are mostly negative about the role of government.

With the benefit of hindsight, we should now be able to see that decisions are affected by both social customs *and* individual calculations. It is a matter of common observation that individual choices are constrained by the customs of their environment. There are many alternatives which go unexamined in making decision-related computations, because they are either illegal or unfashionable. One can explain this in utilitarian terms by saying that the cost of going against the fashion is too great, but this would seem a complicated way of simply acknowledging that there are things that one simply does not do. These constraints are often the result of decisions based on questions of what is right, or what is just. Ethics, therefore, often provides a framework within which decisions are made.

Customs are not the only factors to constrain computations. Sigmund Freud, for instance, provided much insight into how lust and power swirl in the subconscious to drive many decisions. By the time Freud had produced his theories, the foundations of modern economic theory had already been laid and much productive work was being done using normative decision theory as its underpinning. There was no obvious need to introduce Freud into this model—unless one were in advertising or entertainment when the new theories added a potent explanation of how and why consumers choose products. Academics might have downplayed sex appeal in favor of rational computations; the business community has not. The extent to which these drives can be exploited are themselves subject to ethical standards, that is, a community's sense of what is right and wrong at a given point in time, regardless of the wealth involved.

Ethics, therefore, has a potentially important role to play in furthering our understanding of the nature of accounting. However, a study of the role of ethical theory in accounting is still in its infancy. This section has done no more, therefore, than alert the reader to the assumptions that are inherent in the use of the utilitarian model, and to the possible insights that can be gained from other ethical theories. Further research in this area is needed.

CHECKPOINTS

1. Distinguish teleological from deontological approaches to ethics. Is agency theory teleological or deontological?
2. Define Pareto optimality in your own words. Why does the concept lack usefulness for accounting?
3. List some of the rights that you as a student have. What gives you those rights? For instance, does the university have a right to enter your dorm room at any time of the day or night without warning?
4. What does the term *fair* mean when used by children on a playground? What does the term *fair* mean when accountants use it in an auditor's report?

SUMMARY

Understanding how decisions are made (positive theory) and formulating ways in which they should be made (normative theory) have been seen as important for accountants. Some of the objectives of studying individual decision making in an accounting context include:

1. A possible improvement in the ability of financial information to portray accurately the real events or objects (the predictive significance of the information set).
2. An understanding of how the amount, type, and format of financial accounting information affect the judgments or predictions of the investor or analyst (cue usage).
3. An understanding of the ability of the decision maker to respond accurately to a perception of the environment (response accuracy).
4. An understanding of how individuals deal with complexity in decision making and an understanding of the effect of the different styles of decision making on how information is used (the behavioral factors).

Normative theory has provided numerous insights into the role of information in the decision process, both from a predictive standpoint prior to a decision and after a decision for monitoring or feedback purposes. At the individual level, the theory suggests that predecisional information will have value only if it can engender a possible change of action and that more information is preferred to less, provided it is free. At the agency-principal level, the theory shows how risk might be shared in accordance with individual risk preferences, and the role of postdecisional information. At the group level, the theory shows that group preferences for information sets may be hard to come by.

A number of studies in the positive theory of how individuals handle uncertainty have concluded that individuals are poor intuitive statisticians. That is, when faced with a complex environment with uncertain probabilities, individuals tend to be biased in their estimates and judgments and use simplifying rules (heuristics) that make the task less difficult, but the results less accurate. Examples include the concepts of anchoring and functional fixation.

Research approaches to human information processing that have received attention in accounting literature include the lens model, the probabilistic judgment (Bayesian) approach, and the cognitive complexity/ cognitive style approach. These research methods have their origin in the literature of psychology and related fields, and the capital market theories have been based upon studies in economics and finance. Both directions of research have proven to be significant for an understanding of financial accounting, including its production and final use, and for aiding in the development of accounting policy and the establishment of standards. However, research in the area of human information processing is still in its infancy, and much has to be done before definitive conclusions can be reached.

One of the basic problems yet to be solved is what is the direct relationship between capital market theories and individual decision making. The former suggests that the market is efficient and that in equilibrium, securities prices are in an optimum relationship to each other within the limits of available public information. Research on individual behavior suggests that all individual decisions are suboptimal. How can aggregate decisions be optimal if all of the individual decisions are suboptimal? The answer to this question lies in future research. We can only speculate that either the market is not as efficient as it has been thought to be, or a sufficient number of individual decisions are optimal or have been made optimal with the aid of sophisticated models or unbiased heuristics.

QUESTIONS

1. Some accounting theorists feel investors' emphasis on a price-earnings ratio is misguided. Should accountants provide information in accordance with how people actually do make decisions, even if they are perceived to be misguided by some, or should accountants provide the information that our best theoretical models say should be needed? Is the FASB's assertion that the objectives of financial reporting are based on "the informational needs of external users who lack the authority to prescribe the financial information they want from an enterprise" helpful in resolving this issue?[40]

2. The FASB has said that:

> Cost benefit considerations may indicate that information understood or used by only a few should not be provided. Conversely, financial reporting should not exclude relevant information merely because it is difficult for some to understand or because some investors or creditors choose not to use it.[41]

Required:

In your view, and in the light of the discussion in the chapter, should the FASB be permitted to provide information that is understandable by only a few even if the benefit to those few outweighs the cost?

3. In *SFAS 87,* the FASB regretfully acknowledged that the recent statement on pension accounting was not the final word; that would await further development of thinking among managers about pensions—*SFAS 87* merely represents current thinking.

Required:

Explain how this illustrates how accounting policymakers have to take both positive and normative approaches into consideration.

4. It was pointed out here and in Chapter 1 that positive decision models are evaluated in terms of their predictive power only—unrealistic assumptions are irrelevant so long as the model has predictive power. Normative models, on the other hand, must be evaluated in terms of their realism. The assumptions underlying the tools taught business students, therefore, present an intriguing situation because these are normative models that, by having gained widespread usage, have become positive models. Does one, therefore, attack them for their admittedly unrealistic assumptions?

5. The AICPA says that "Principles of the Code of Professional Conduct of the American Institute of Certified Public Accountants express the profession's recognition of its responsibilities to the public, to clients, and to colleagues." An example of such a Principle appears below:

Article III—Integrity

> *To maintain and broaden public confidence, members should perform all professional responsibilities with the highest sense of integrity.*

.01 Integrity is an element of character fundamental to professional recognition. It is the quality from which the public trust derives and the benchmark against which a member must ultimately test all decisions.

.02 Integrity requires a member to be, among other things, honest and candid within the constraints of client confidentiality. Service and the public trust should not be subordinated to personal gain and advantage. Integrity can accommodate the inadvertent error and the honest difference of opinion; it cannot accommodate deceit or subordination of principle.

.03 Integrity is measured in terms of what is right and just. In the absence of specific rules, standards, or guidance, or in the face of conflicting opinions, a member should test decisions and deeds by asking: "Am I doing what a person of integrity would do? Have I retained my integrity?" Integrity requires a member to observe both the form and the spirit of technical and ethical standards; circumvention of those standards constitutes subordination of judgment.

.04 Integrity also requires a member to observe the principles of objectivity and independence and of due care.

Required:

a. Are these principles closer to those of Mr. Byrne or Mr. May? [Hint: You may want to review Chapter 4 at this point.]

b. How would you classify the ethics in this article? For instance, are they based on deontological or teleological theories?

c. The Code of Professional Conduct was used by the AICPA to exclude a number of practices that it deemed unethical. Among these were practices such as "offering clients a discount for referring a prospective client." On August 9, 1990 the AICPA entered into a final consent agreement with the FTC which provides that the "AICPA may not interfere if its members wish to engage in any of the following activities:

  1. Accepting contingent fees from nonattest clients.

  2. Accepting disclosed commissions for products or services supplied by third parties to nonattest clients.

  3. Making or accepting disclosed payments for referring potential clients to a CPA.

  4. Using trade names.

Required:

In your opinion were these unethical practices? Does this mean that accountants are now being permitted to be unethical? Lay out the possible grounds on which the AICPA felt they were unethical practices.[42]

  6. Kenneth MacNeal, author of *Truth in Accounting*, laid out the ethical issues that he saw facing accountants in the following manner:

"Prior to 1933, the usual form of unqualified certificate employed by auditors read, with minor variations, as follows:

> We certify that the above balance sheet is, in our opinion, a correct statement of the financial condition of the Company as of December 31, 1931, and that the accompanying profit and loss statement is correct.

In this usage Webster's *Unabridged Dictionary* defines "correct" as meaning "conforming to fact or truth." . . . On April 7, 1934, subsequent to conferences with representatives of the American Society of Certified Public Accountants, the Federal Trade Commission announced that its original regulations had been amended and accountants need not thereafter certify to a belief in the truth of their statements. The accounting profession thereupon changed its form of unqualified certificate . . . .

The accounting profession is not dishonest. Its individual members probably possess as high a degree of personal integrity as the members of any calling in the world today. Yet, upon the passage of a law which would make accountants responsible for material untruths, their profession, without a single important exception, felt impelled to change its form of certificate from one which states that its financial statements are true, to a form of certificate which omits any mention of truth but merely states that such financial statements *truly and fairly reflect the application of accepted accounting practices to the facts disclosed.*"[43]

Required:

Do you agree with his assessment of audited statements? Explain your view.

PRIMARY SOURCES

Those interested in learning more about the topics covered in this chapter might begin by consulting these sources each of which has numerous excellent citations:

Ashton, Robert H. *Human Information Processing in Accounting.* Studies in Accounting Research No. 17 (American Accounting Association, 1982).

Beauchamp, Tom L., and Norman E. Bowie. *Ethical Theory and Business,* 2nd ed. (Englewood Cliffs, N.J.: Prentice Hall, 1983).

Beaver, William S. *Financial Reporting: An Accounting Revolution,* 2nd ed. (Englewood Cliffs, N.J.: Prentice Hall, 1989).

Demski, Joel S. *Information Analysis,* 2nd ed. (Reading, Mass.: Addison-Wesley, 1980).

Libby, R. *Accounting and Human Information Processing: Theory and Applications* (Englewood Cliffs, N.J.: Prentice Hall, 1981).

Watts, Ross L., and Jerold L. Zimmerman. *Positive Accounting Theory* (Englewood Cliffs, N.J.: Prentice Hall, 1986), pp.179–99.

SELECTED ADDITIONAL READINGS

In addition to the works cited above and in the footnotes, the reader is referred to the following authors:

Information Economics, Agency Theory, and Positive Accounting

Baiman, Stanley. "Agency Research in Managerial Accounting: A Survey." *Journal of Accounting Literature,* 1982, pp. 154–210.

Demski, Joel S., and Gerald A. Feltham. *Cost Determination: A Conceptual Approach* (Ames: The Iowa State University Press, 1976).

Demski, Joel S., and David M. Kreps. "Models in Managerial Accounting." *Journal of Accounting Research Supplement,* 1982, pp. 117–48.

Griffin, Paul A. *Usefulness to Investors and Creditors of Information Provided by Financial Reporting: A Review of Empirical Accounting Research* (Financial Accounting Standards Board, 1982), pp. 99–134.

Hilton, R. W. *Probabilities Choice Models and Information.* Studies in Accounting Research No. 24 (American Accounting Association, 1985).

Hilton, R. W. "Integrating Normative and Descriptive Theories of Information Processing." *Journal of Accounting Research,* Autumn 1980, pp. 477–505.

Kelly, Lauren. "Positive Theory Research: A Review." *Journal of Accounting Literature,* Spring 1983, pp. 111–50.

Behavioral Accounting

Ashton, Robert H., ed. *The Evolution of Behavioral Accounting Research: An Overview* (New York: Garland Press, 1984).

Atkinson, Anthony A. "Truth-Inducing Schemes in Budgeting and Resource Allocation." *Cost and Management,* May–June 1985, pp. 38–43.

Einhorn, H. J., and R. M. Hogarth. "Behavioral Decision Theory: Processes of Judgment and Choice." *Journal of Accounting Research,* Spring 1981, pp. 1–31.

Libby, Robert, and Barry L. Lewis. "Human Information Processing Research in Accounting: The State of the Art." *Accounting, Organizations and Society,* 1977, pp. 245–68.

Slovic, Paul. "Psychological Study of Human Judgment: Implications for Investment Decision Making." *The Journal of Finance,* September 1972, p. 787.

Swieringa, Robert J., and Karl E. Weick. "Management Accounting and Action." *Accounting, Organizations and Society,* 1987, pp. 293–308.

Ethics

Bowie, Norman E. *Business Ethics* (Englewood Cliffs, N.J.: Prentice Hall, 1982).

Donaldson, Thomas, and Patricia H. Werhane. *Ethical Issues in Business,* 3rd ed. (Englewood Cliffs, N.J.: Prentice Hall, 1988).

Mintz, Stephen M. *Cases in Accounting Ethics and Professionalism* (New York: McGraw-Hill, 1990).

Newton, Lisa H., and Maureen M. Ford. *Taking Sides: Clashing Views on Controversial Issues in Business Ethics and Society* (Guildford, Conn.: The Dushking Publishing Group, Inc., 1990).

ENDNOTES

1. *A Statement of Basic Accounting Theory* (American Accounting Association, 1966), p. 1.
2. APB Statement No 4, *Basic Concepts and Accounting Principles Underlying Financial Statements of Business Enterprises* (AICPA, 1978), par. 9.
3. Financial Accounting Standards Board, *Statement of Financial Accounting Concepts No. 1* (FASB, 1978), par. 9.
4. For empirical evidence on the information content of earnings-per-share numbers, see William Kross, Gordon Chapman, and Kenneth H. Strand, "Diluted Earnings per Share and Security Returns: Some Additional Evidence," *Journal of Accounting, Auditing, and Finance,* 1980, pp. 36–46.
5. Financial Accounting Standards Board, *Statement of Financial Accounting Concepts No. 1* (FASB, 1978), par. 25.
6. See, for example, Alexander A. Robichek and Stewart C. Myers, *Optimal Financing Decisions* (Englewood Cliffs, N.J.: Prentice Hall, 1965), Chap. 6; and Eugene M. Lerner and William T. Carleton, *A Theory of Financial Analysis* (New York: Harcourt Brace Jovanovich, 1966), Chap. 7.
7. John Maynard Keynes, *The General Theory of Employment, Interest, and Money* (New York: Harbinger Books Harcourt Brace Jovanovich, 1964; originally published in 1936), p. 383.

8. For some recent examples of work being done in this area see: Vijay Mahajan, Eitan Muller, and Rajendra K. Srivasta, "Determination of Adopter Categories by Using Innovative Diffusion Models," *Journal of Marketing Research,* February 1990, pp. 37–51; and Alan D. Mayer and James B. Goes, "Organizational Assimilation of Innovations: A Multilevel Contextual Analysis," *Academy of Management Journal,* December 1988, pp. 897–924.

9. Herbert A. Simon, *Models of Man, Social and Rational* (New York: John Wiley & Sons, 1957).

10. John von Neumann and Oscar Morgenstern, *Theory of Games and Economic Behavior* (Princeton, N.J.: Princeton University Press, 1947).

11. Richard P. Brief, "The Accountant's Responsibility in Historical Perspective," *The Accounting Review,* April 1975, pp. 285–97.

12. For more information, see Joel S. Demski, *Information Analysis,* 2nd ed. (Reading, Mass.: Addison-Wesley, 1980), pp. 85–99.

13. G. Akerlof, "The Market for 'Lemons': Quality Uncertainty and the Market Mechanism," *The Quarterly Journal of Economics,* August 1970, pp. 488–500.

14. Kenneth J. Arrow, *Social Choice and Individual Values* (New York: John Wiley & Sons, 1963).

15. Joel S. Demski, "The General Impossibility of Normative Accounting Standards," *The Accounting Review,* December 1973, pp. 718–23.

16. Financial Accounting Standards Board, *Statement of Financial Accounting Concepts No. 1* (FASB, 1978) par. 25.

17. For more details of this criticism read Charles Christenson, "The Methodology of Positive Accounting," *The Accounting Review,* January 1983, pp. 1–22.

18. Michael C. Jensen and William H. Meckling, "Theory of the Firm: Managerial Behavior, Agency Costs and Ownership Structure," *Journal of Financial Economics,* October 1976, pp. 305–60 is the seminal paper in this area.

19. Doug Snowball, "Information Load and Accounting Reports: Too Much or Just Right?" *Cost and Management,* May–June 1979, pp. 22–28.

20. G. A. Miller, "The Magical Number Seven, Plus or Minus Two: Some Limits on Our Capacity for Processing Information," *Psychological Review,* March 1956, pp. 81–97.

21. For an overview of this literature, see J. Leslie Livingstone and Michael F. van Breda, "Strategy, Structure, and Budgeting," in *Management Planning and Control.* Edited by Kenneth R. Ferris and J. Leslie Livingstone (Columbus, Ohio: Century VII Publishing Co., 1987).

22. Robert J. Swieringa, Michael Gibbins, J. Lawson, and J. Sweeney, "Experiments in the Heuristics of Information Processing," *Studies on Human Information Processing in Accounting,* Supplement to *Journal of Accounting Research,* 1976, pp. 159–87.

23. Ian R. C. Eggleton, "Patterns, Prototypes, and Predictions: An Exploratory Study," *Studies on Human Information Processing in Accounting,* Supplement to the *Journal of Accounting Research,* 1976, pp. 68–131.

24. For a critical review of some of these studies, see Carol Eger and John Dickhaut, "An Examination of the Conservative Information Processing Bias in an Accounting Framework," *Journal of Accounting Research,* Autumn 1982, pp. 711–23.

25. Edward J. Joyce and Gary C. Biddle, "Anchoring and Adjustment in Probabi-

listic Inference in Auditing,'' *Journal of Accounting Research,* Spring 1981, pp. 120–45.

26. A. Rashad Abdel-Khalik and Thomas F. Keller, *Studies in Accounting Research No. 16,* ''Earnings or Cash Flows: An Experiment on Functional Fixation and the Valuation of the Firm,'' (AAA, 1979), p. 50.

27. Hillel J. Einhorn, ''A Synthesis: Accounting and Behavioral Science,'' *Journal of Accounting Research,* Supplement 1976, p. 197.

28. Ross L. Watts and Jerold L. Zimmerman, ''Positive Accounting Theory: A Ten Year Perspective,'' *The Accounting Review,* January 1990, p. 148.

29. Tony Tinker, Cheryl Lehman, and Marilyn Neimark, ''Marginalizing the Public Interest: A Critical Look at Recent Social Accounting History,'' in *Behavioral Accounting Research.* Edited by Ken Ferris (Columbus, Ohio: Century VII Publishing Co., 1988), pp. 117–43.

30. This section leans heavily on Tom L. Beauchamp and Norman E. Bowie, *Ethical Theory and Business,* 3rd ed. (Englewood Cliffs, N.J.: Prentice Hall, 1988), pp. 1–48.

31. James Quirk and Rubin Saposnik, *Introduction to General Equilibrium Theory and Welfare Economics* (New York: McGraw-Hill, 1968), p. 16.

32. Stephen A. Zeff, ''The Rise of 'Economic Consequences','' *Journal of Accountancy,* December 1978, pp. 56–63.

33. Joel Demski, *Information Analysis,* 2nd ed. (Reading, Mass.: Addison-Wesley, 1980), p. 2.

34. Accounting Standards Steering Committee, *The Corporate Report* (The Institute of Chartered Accountants in England and Wales, July 1975).

35. For details of the FASB's closely reasoned arguments in this regard read the Financial Accounting Standards Board, *Statements of Financial Accounting Concepts No. 2* (FASB, 1980) pars. 98–110.

36. DR Scott, ''The Basis of Accounting Principles,'' *The Accounting Review,* December 1941, pp. 341–49.

37. Maurice Moonitz, *The Basic Postulates of Accounting,* ARS 1 (AICPA, 1961), p. 4.

38. James W. Patillo, *The Foundation of Financial Accounting* (Baton Rouge: Louisiana State University Press, 1965), p. 9.

39. *Objectives of Financial Statements for Business Enterprises* (Arthur Andersen & Co., 1972), p. 8. Interestingly, the 1984 revision of this book makes no mention of fairness.

40. *SFAC 1,* par. 28.

41. Ibid., par. 36.

42. Principles of Professional Conduct, *AICPA Professional Standards.*

43. Kenneth MacNeal (1939), *Truth in Accounting* (New York: Scholars Book Co., 1970), pp. 20–22.

Chapter 8

Setting Accounting Policy

CHAPTER OBJECTIVES

After studying this chapter, you will be able to:

Define accounting policy.

Compare the arguments in favor of regulation of accounting policy with those against.

Describe the effect that accounting policies have on different users of financial reports.

Interpret the arguments seen in accounting journals and in the financial press on the appropriate role of government in setting accounting standards.

Contrast accounting regulation in the United States with that in other countries.

CHAPTER OVERVIEW

The Alternatives

The manner in which a company reports its finances constitutes its accounting policies. Some policies are set by regulatory authorities such as the SEC and the FASB; others are set by the company itself. How much policy is mandated by authorities varies from one country to another. How much policy should be mandated is a matter of considerable debate.

Social and Economic Consequences of Accounting Policy

The way in which accounting policies are set tends to be controversial partly because policies have economic consequences for companies and users. The nature and extent of these consequences is a topic of much current research.

Accounting Regulation: Pros and Cons

Proponents of regulation point to failures in the marketplace that make government intervention essential. Critics of regulation argue that even if the failures do exist, government regulation has proved ineffective.

Managing Accounting Policy

The authors conclude that some accounting policies can be settled on technical grounds; other policies can be settled by compromise. The few policies that remain a matter of debate should be settled by the political system, because of their potential effect on the welfare of individuals.

Accounting policy is the body of accounting standards, opinions, interpretations, rules, and regulations used by companies in their financial reporting. Accounting policies of a specific company include ''the methods of applying those principles that are judged by the management of the entity to be the most appropriate in the circumstances to present fairly financial position, changes in financial position, and results of operations in accordance with generally accepted accounting principles and that accordingly have been adopted for preparing the financial statements.''[1]

Some policy choices are made by specific firms within the alternatives available to them. For example, firms can choose whether to use FIFO or LIFO for inventory measurement purposes.[2] Other choices are made by government or by private bodies with the authority to establish enforceable policies. For example, the FASB determined that long-term receivables and payables should be entered at their present value. Choices made by government and by authoritative private bodies constitute the regulation of accounting policy. This chapter addresses two fundamental questions:

1. Who should make accounting policy?
2. How should accounting policy be made?

Chapters 2 and 3 laid out the historical record—what it was that Congress found in 1933, how they responded, and what has happened since. This historical record is important because it is to history that both proponents and opponents of regulation invariably turn for support of their respective positions. This chapter presents those positions and seeks to discuss the merits of the many different ways in which accounting has been administered.

The chapter begins by laying down, as a backdrop to the arguments that follow, the various existing alternatives for setting accounting policies and discusses some of the economic consequences of financial reporting. It then sets out some of the arguments that are typically made for and against regulation, such as the supposed need for uniformity and comparability and the need to protect the public interest. The chapter then switches to an analysis of the nature of regulation, asking whether the objectives of regulation could not be achieved equally well through the marketplace. The arguments are strong but currently unpersuasive to the general public, apparently, because financial reporting continues to be regulated. The chapter, therefore, shifts to how one might best regulate financial reporting: privately, publicly, or by constitution. The chapter closes by arguing that the FASB's structure and procedures are well suited to address the issues and problems raised by regulation.

THE ALTERNATIVES

It is useful to recognize, at the very outset, the different ways in which accounting policy has been set. In the United States, for instance, the SEC and the FASB are the major regulators of accounting policy. But there are numerous other organizations that seek to establish accounting standards. They include, but are not limited to, the Government Accounting Standards Board, the Railway Accounting Standards Board, the United Nations Centre for Transnational Corporations, the Federal Government Procurement and Taxation Departments, the National Association of Accountants. Each of these has a different role, a different structure, and a different philosophy toward accounting policymaking.

Policymaking at the Company Level

Historically, the first major effort in the United States at formal standard setting dates back to 1929. As noted in Chapter 3, the AIA responded immediately to the concerns of the NYSE in the aftermath of the 1929 crash by creating a Special Committee on Cooperation with Stock Exchanges under the chairmanship of George O. May, chairman of the AIA. The correspondence between this committee and the Committee on Stock List of the NYSE was issued on January 21, 1934, in a pamphlet entitled *Audits of Corporate Accounts*.[3] The correspondence begins with a letter from the AIA to the NYSE dated September 22, 1932, in which George May laid out his suggestions for the improvement of financial reporting by public companies. A profound and insightful letter, it is important because it laid the foundations for financial reporting in the United States. It is prophetic because its recommendations are only now, almost 60 years later, beginning to be understood and accepted.

He began with a call for the public to be educated in the significance and the limitations of financial reports. This reflected his long-held convictions that accounting statements are not facts and that accountants are not engaged in a fact-finding mission. In particular, he rejected the analogy of Harvard professor William Ripley that balance sheets are like photographs both because one cannot take a picture of history and because it suggests an accuracy about accounting that is completely missing. He abhorred the practice at the time of "certifying" that financial statements were "correct." Rather, he said, accounting statements are matters of opinion on which accountants are called to exercise their judgment. He pressed his case by arguing that the real value of assets is a function of their earning power. The latter lies in the future and can be determined only by judgment, ensuring that asset values can be opinions only.

Opinions, he said, do not lend themselves to the straitjacket imposed by the type of uniform accounting thrust on the railways by the ICC. Far better that every corporation be:

> . . . free to choose its own methods of accounting within the very broad limits to which reference has been made, but require disclosure of the methods employed and consistency in their application from year to year. . . . Within quite wide limits, it is relatively unimportant to the investor what precise rules or conventions are adopted by a corporation in reporting its earnings if he knows what method is being followed and is assured that it is followed consistently from year to year.[4]

These limits, he said, should be set by requiring corporations to follow "certain broad principles of accounting which have won fairly general acceptance," thereby providing the language for the auditors' report that has become so familiar.

He concluded with three action plans for the NYSE. First, public corporations should be obliged to disclose a detailed statement of accounting methods being used. (An example of appropriate disclosure was attached to the letter.) Second, corporations should attest that they have followed these methods consistently. Third, auditors should attest that the corporation was following its own disclosed accounting methods. This is almost precisely the approach to financial reporting favored by accounting theoreticians of all stripes today.

One result of May's letter, as the section on auditors' reports in Chapter 3 noted, was a requirement by the NYSE that after July 1, 1933, 89 years after a similar provision in Britain, all companies seeking listing with the NYSE would have to furnish financial statements bearing the certificate of accountants "qualified under the laws of some state or country."[5]

The importance of the letter lies in the framework which May set for financial reporting. He argued for relative freedom in determining the most appropriate way to communicate a company's financial situation. In other words, he argued in favor of leaving accounting policy decisions to the discretion of individual companies.* The price for this freedom was full disclosure and guarding this disclosure was to be a universal acceptance of certain broad principles. Since this was standard practice in the United Kingdom, it is apparent that May was drawing on his British heritage in establishing this framework.

Two problems soon made themselves manifest. Companies and their accountants revelled in the freedom that May had won for them; unfortunately, they were not prepared to pay the price of full disclosure of their accounting methods. Few, if any, companies provided their shareholders with the details. Second, it was to prove extremely difficult, if not impossible, to arrive at these broad, universally accepted principles. (The story of the search for these elusive principles was told in Chapter 4.) Instead, the AIA found itself creating a series of detailed rules that earned itself the title of a "piecemeal" approach to accounting. In one of the great enigmas of accounting history, it was George O. May who led the way down the piecemeal lane. As Reed Storey put it, "the program proposed by the special committee on cooperation with the stock exchanges (George O. May, chairman) was essentially eviscerated by the committee on accounting procedure (George O. May, the active head)."[6]

Policymaking above the Company Level

Whatever the strengths and weaknesses of May's proposals, as a practical matter they were killed by the collapse of the economy in the wake of the stock market crash. By 1933, the population was calling for stronger medicine than just disclosure. The result was two major pieces of legislation affecting accounting, the Truth-in-Securities Act of 1933 and the Securities Exchange Act of 1934; and the creation on June 26, 1934, of the Securities and Exchange Commission, in the belief that supervision of financial institutions would "contribute to a more efficient capital market" by "giving investors more confidence" that they were getting the whole story. They also hoped to encourage "the development of better tools of analysis and more responsibility on the part of the professional analyst."[7] Less than five years after its creation, the SEC delegated much of its standard setting to the private sector: initially the Committee on Accounting Procedures, later the Accounting Principles Board, and today the Financial Accounting Standards Board.

Delegation has not meant withdrawal, though, because throughout its life the SEC has made its influence on accounting felt. It has done so primarily through comments on drafts of APB Opinions and FASB State-

---

* Lest this seem too shocking, let us remind ourselves that internal accounting policies are set entirely by management.

ments and concurrences with drafts of Opinions and Statements prior to their publication. However, the Commission has also had a direct influence through the publication of Regulation S-X, Accounting Series Releases (ASRs) of the Commission or the Chief Accountant, and other official decisions. In a few cases, the SEC has overruled an Opinion or a Statement and threatened to act alone if necessary. For example, the APB had considered expressing an opinion regarding the classification of deferred income taxes relating to installment receivables, but in deference to the retail industry it had not decided whether to require uniform classification in this case. Upon the petition of Arthur Andersen & Co., the Commission went ahead and issued *ASR 102,* specifying that the deferred income taxes should be classified consistently with the classification of the related accounts receivable. Manuel Cohen, the chairman of the Commission at the time, commented later that:

> A formal expression of opinion by the Commission seemed called for, and we obliged . . . . I do not believe it will be necessary for us to use that device with great frequency—although the option is always open to us.[8]

The reassurance notwithstanding, the threat of being overruled always has to be in the minds of accounting committees.

As another illustration of its influence, the SEC took an early stand in opposition to the write-up of asset values. This stand is one of the reasons for the strong support for the cost basis of accounting in the United States. As a result of this stance, the APB was frustrated in its attempt to issue an opinion regarding the recognition of portfolio gains and losses from the holding of marketable securities. The SEC's position may be attributed in part to vigorous opposition from the insurance industry, but it was also in line with the Commission's long-standing position against the use of fair values.[9]

The SEC has even published interpretations of APB Opinions. In 1973, for instance, the SEC issued *ASR 146* as an interpretation of *APB 16.* Not only was this action opposed by the Institute's AcSEC but one of the large CPA firms brought suit against the SEC on grounds that:

1. The subject should be dealt with by the FASB because the SEC should not interpret a pronouncement that it has not accepted.
2. If the SEC is the appeal body, it should not be able to overrule the FASB by an administrative decree.
3. The SEC should be required to follow appeal procedures, including exposure drafts and hearings.

The CPA firm's complaint held that the SEC violated the Administrative Procedures Act by failing to give public notice and permitting hearings or comment prior to issuing the release. The case failed and the SEC has continued to use its considerable powers to influence accounting.

The SEC has overridden FASB pronouncements on certain occasions and has taken the initiative on others. For example, in 1978 the SEC issued *ASRs* 253 and 258, prescribing a form of full-cost accounting for oil and gas producers as an acceptable alternative to the successful-efforts method. Previously, the FASB had required the use of the successful-efforts method (*SFAS 19*). But, as a result of the action of the SEC, the FASB issued *SFAS 25* in 1979, which suspended the required use of successful-efforts accounting.

Stanford professor Charles Horngren likened the relationship between the SEC and public accountants to that between top management and lower management.[10] Although the SEC, with the power to determine accounting principles, has delegated this duty through the principle of decentralization to the CAP, and later the APB and the FASB, as top management it has retained the power to set constraints and exert veto power. John Burton, once chief accountant of the SEC, disagrees with Horngren and argues that the two organizations "are in partnership and that our best interests are served in an atmosphere of mutual nonsurprise."[11] He believes that the "SEC does not view itself as being in a position of absolute authority and the FASB working for it."[12]

Evidence of this sense of partnership between the SEC and the FASB was demonstrated when the SEC took the initiative in 1976 in requiring the disclosure of certain replacement-cost information (*ASR 190*) but deleted this requirement in 1979 (*ASR 271*) when the FASB issued *SFAS 33*, "Financial Reporting and Changing Prices." Another indication that the SEC was innovative and cooperative in the 1970s and 1980s was the trend toward requiring soft data (information that cannot be audited in the traditional manner), such as current cost information, information regarding oil and gas reserves, interim information data, and proposals for forecast information. Soft data are issued with "safe-harbor" provisions protecting accountants; an example of such a provision is found in *ASR 203* relating to current cost information required by *ASR 190*.[13] Time will tell whether this cooperative attitude continues.

International Comparisons[14]

Other countries also regulate accounting policies but the nature of that regulation differs significantly from one country to another. In some countries, such as Great Britain and The Netherlands, accounting policy setting is less structured, not as detailed, and certainly less formal. On the other hand, in many other European countries accounting tends to follow uniform codes laid down by law that make for much more structure than in the United States. The growing cooperation of European nations and the promise of an economic community in 1992 has led to much work being done to harmonize these different policies. Much remains to be done.

A major difference exists with regard to the purpose of the accounts. It is part of an Anglo-Saxon tradition that financial reports are for the benefit of investors, creditors, and others. Most other countries place a greater emphasis on tax accounting. In West Germany, for instance, the Stock Corporation Law of 1965 effectively required that financial reporting be in accordance with tax accounting. This means that income is not necessarily a measure of earnings power, but simply the smallest permissible with tax law. The EEC's Fourth Directive requires that financial reports be prepared in accordance with the traditional Anglo-Saxon requirement of *true and fair*. Ultimately, this should bring European accounting into line with that in the United States and other English-speaking countries.

The process by which accounting standards are set also differs substantially. The British, for instance, have established an Accounting Standards Committee (ASC) that is not unlike the APB in its process and structure. Its due process rules are considerably less well developed than the FASB's, which led to criticism that its rules were being set by accountants for accountants, and in virtual secrecy. Unlike the FASB, the recommendations that the ASC produces are subject to the approval of the professional accounting bodies before they can be issued as *Statements of Standard Accounting Practice (SSAPs)*. Standard setting is time consuming, therefore, but it does mean that the standards that are eventually issued do have wide acceptance. This process has also meant that considerably fewer standards are issued than in the United States. Many would feel that this is a blessing.

The Canadians also have an Accounting Standards Committee which again resembles the APB. Since the passage of the Canada Business Corporations Act of 1975, the standards mandated by the Canadians have the automatic force of law. In this they differ sharply from the British ASC, which has no authority beyond that of the profession and the stock exchanges. While in the United States standards are not law, the SEC does provide a measure of legal enforcement of FASB standards.

In addition to these national bodies, accounting policies are also being established on an international level through the International Accounting Standards Committee (IASC). This body was established in 1973 by representatives of the professional bodies of most of the developed nations and has since grown to represent virtually the entire international community. Compliance with its standards is limited to the acceptance of the standards, on a voluntary basis, by the representing professional accounting societies and by other organizations and governmental agencies within represented countries. The FASB, being independent of the AICPA, is not a member of the IASC and has no obligation, therefore, to harmonize its standards with those of the international committee. Nevertheless it does keep in close touch with the IASC.

EXHIBIT 8-1   Alternative Systems for Setting Accounting Policies in the
United States

Regulation by:	Technically	Politically
1. Government		Congress
2. Government agency	SEC	
3. Private bodies	FASB	
4. Disclosure		

Alternatives Summarized

The wide array of alternative systems that exist both within one country and across different countries indicates that there is no single, good solution as to how best to set accounting policies. The lack of a solution reflects the technical and political difficulties that attend accounting standard setting. Nevertheless, one can distinguish four basic systems in place across the world: regulation by government, by government agency, by private bodies, and by companies themselves. The first could also be described as a top-down system; the last as a bottom-up system. The middle two are a compromise between these two extremes. Mixtures of these four occur also.

In addition, in some systems accounting standards are set on essentially political grounds. The tax system, in most countries, is an example of a politically determined set of accounting standards. In other systems, accounting standards are set on primarily technical grounds. This corresponds to the structural approach described in Chapter 1. Most systems are a blend of these two.

The various possibilities result in the eight potential systems shown in Exhibit 8-1. In the sections which follow, the merits of the various alternatives are discussed. How should financial reporting be structured? Should corporations be free to determine their own accounting policies? Should they be constrained in their choices? If so, should these constraints be imposed by Congress, a governmental regulatory body like the SEC, or a private body like the FASB? Should financial disclosure be voluntary? Should organizations other than public corporations be required to make financial disclosures? Answers to such questions are far from settled among academics and are equally unsettled in practice.

SOCIAL AND ECONOMIC CONSEQUENCES OF ACCOUNTING POLICY

All decisions regarding accounting policy should have economic consequences. If there were no economic consequences, there would be no reason for the policy decision. The desired consequences include an improvement in the information available to investors and other users with

---

EXHIBIT 8-2   Economic Consequences

Users	*Economic Consequences*
Investors and creditors	Financial decisions.
	Cost of gathering and analyzing financial information.
	Cost of drawing up and later, perhaps, having to revise contracts based on accounting numbers.
Corporations	Cost of publishing financial reports.
	Changes in company's share price through new information or differences in volatility of earnings numbers.
Management	Behavior of management.
National	Allocation of resources.
Other	Policies of regulatory commissions.
	Public perceptions of companies.

---

the result of permitting sounder economic decisions or a reduction in the information-gathering costs for users. Through the securities markets, better decisions should result in an allocation of resources closer to the optimum and an opportunity for an improvement in portfolio selections. If decisions are not altered and if information costs to users are not reduced, this is evidence that the policy decision was not desirable.

Users Affected

As the opening section in Chapter 6 noted, many users are affected by accounting policies. Some of these policies may alter the economic wealth or cash flows of users directly. Other policies may affect the behavior of individuals such as customers, employees, and the general public toward the enterprise. Still other policies that are perceived to affect national goals may draw the attention of Congress or administrative agencies. Exhibit 8-2 summarizes the users affected and some of the effects of accounting policies.

Some consequences are direct and obvious. Others are more indirect and, as a result, less obvious. For instance, the fact that many contract, equity relationships, and legal covenants of credit arrangements are frequently expressed in terms of accounting numbers or financial statement ratios means that accounting policy changes will affect the meaning of these numbers and ratios.* This alters the economic relationships from

---

* For more on contracts, see the section on corporate reporting policies in Chapter 7.

what was originally intended. For example, the capitalization of long-term leases may affect the debt-equity ratio and thus affect relationships that are tied to this ratio. It can be argued that the contracts and financial arrangements can be adjusted to take into consideration the new meanings of the accounting numbers and ratios. However, this cannot be accomplished quickly, so the effect may be significant for a long time.

Some consequences are heavily disputed. For instance, one of the common arguments against new accounting policies, or the elimination of current practices, is that the change would lower the market price of corporate stocks or bonds. Generally, corporate executives prefer procedures that tend to smooth reported income because, they assert, the more volatile the reported income, the greater will be the investors' perception of risk and the lower the price of the securities. For example, some financial executives opposed the required expensing of research and development costs because of the effect on reported income and the potential effect on security prices. However, a number of research studies have concluded that the securities markets are efficient and that they cannot be fooled by changing accounting procedures.* This suggests an absence of economic consequences.

Other studies contradict this result. For example, in an early study Israeli professor Baruch Lev concluded that the FASB Exposure Draft eliminating the full costing method for oil and gas companies did result in lower security prices, particularly for those firms using full costing.[15] According to capital market theories, there should have been no effect on security prices. These unexpected conclusions can possibly be explained by the fact that there may have been a real effect on the firms' financial operations. For example, outstanding contracts and debt covenants may have been adversely affected, or it may have been expected that the reduced reported earnings would result in lower dividends. But it is also possible that investors did react to the change even though there was no economic effect on the firms. Whatever the precise mechanism, these studies suggest the presence of economic consequences.

Positive accounting, discussed in more depth in the section on corporate financial reporting in Chapter 7, seeks to build a theoretical framework within which these consequences can be more closely examined. One line of argument suggests that managers' preferences for specific accounting policies may result from the way they perceive the effect of the policies on their own interests. Management compensation and bonuses are frequently based on reported accounting numbers, such as corporate net income. If a new policy is likely to reduce their own compensation, they are likely to oppose the change. The otherwise desirable policy

---

* Market efficiency is discussed at length in Chapter 6. In this context, it means that market prices impound all available information.

change may have the side effect of causing an unanticipated change in their compensation and thus cause an unanticipated transfer of wealth. Even if compensation is not affected directly, managers still may oppose a policy that reduces reported earnings on grounds that such a decrease might reflect on their abilities and threaten their job security. Using arguments such as this, one may then examine empirically the economic consequences of accounting policy.

Another subtle effect associated with economic consequences is the feedback effect known as *information inductance*.[16] Information that is published has an intended effect on the behavior of the receiver, but it may also have an effect on the decisions and actions of the sender. Measurement and disclosure requirements may cause management to take certain actions to offset the perceived or anticipated effect of the information requirement, even though the actions may not be in the interests of either management or the firm. For example, it was claimed that the required reporting of foreign currency gains and losses would cause multinational firms to engage in uneconomical hedging transactions. It was also claimed that the required elimination of self-insurance reserves would result in the purchase of insurance that was not in the best interests of the firm.

Given the economic consequences that flow from accounting policies, it is not surprising that the establishment of standards is attended by controversy. For top-down approaches to establishing accounting policies, the existence of these economic consequences can pose formidable problems. Policymakers, like the FASB, may want to take into account the desires of all their constituents and the effects of their policies on them. But with so many parties affected in so many different ways by financial reporting, it is hard for them ever to be sure that they are acting in the "public interest." Technically speaking, it is extremely difficult, if not impossible, to aggregate individual utility functions.*

CHECKPOINTS

---

1. Can you think of any other economic consequences of accounting other than those in Exhibit 8-1?
2. In each category of economic consequences listed in Exhibit 8-1, provide one or more specific examples known to you from your reading.
3. Explain the implications of Arrow's theorem for accounting regulation. (Hint: Reread the relevant section of Chapter 7 for details on Arrow's theorem.)

---

* The nature of these difficulties was addressed in Chapter 7 in the section on multiperson decision theory.

ACCOUNTING REGULATION: PROS AND CONS

Regulation of accounting policy is a hotly disputed topic. No empirical evidence was produced in 1934 that regulation of accounting by the SEC would achieve the goals set for it and little has accumulated since. There is some evidence that Congress in creating the SEC mistook accounting for auditing—and auditing for fraud detection.[17] The historical record suggests that the real concern of Congress was, and still is, financial fraud, which neither financial reporting nor auditing is intended to catch. There is abundant evidence since, that regulation of financial reporting has not brought financial fraud to a halt. This raises a serious question for accountants and students of accounting: Was the action of 1934 appropriate? Why not return to the situation of the 1920s when freedom of choice in the United States was almost complete?* Indeed, is the present structure of regulating financial reporting in the interest of the American public?

Market Failures

The classic economic argument for regulation is that the market has broken down in some way. In the case of accounting, regulation is deemed necessary because the market is thought to have failed in some way to produce the socially optimal amount of information. Regulation is called for, therefore, to protect the "public's interest."

The classic argument for government regulation, and the one that led to the creation of the Federal Trade Commission in 1914, involves monopolies. The lack of competition present when monopolies exist enables them to price their goods high. As a result, demand is lower than it would be in a competitive economy. The market is said to have failed in the sense that an optimal quantity of goods is not supplied. Companies are considered by some to have a natural monopoly in information about themselves. One deduces that less information than is desirable reaches users. More generally, an *information asymmetry* is said to occur when one party to a transaction has more information than another. A market failure is predicted as the inevitable outcome.†

Public Goods and Free Riders.   A second argument for government regulation is the existence of a *public good,* defined as one that can be

---

* The primary exception was in the regulation of public service companies. Government regulation of the railroads began in the 19th century, and regulation of public utilities by state commissions began about 1907.

† Information asymmetries are discussed in more detail under the heading of agency theory in Chapter 7.

enjoyed by one individual without affecting the enjoyment of others. The classic example is national defence. By their very nature, public goods are not easily, if at all, traded in a market place. Hence, they are traditionally managed by government.

Beekeepers are sometimes used to illustrate the problem. Besides the honey, which is produced from their standpoint as a by-product, bees provide great benefit to the world by pollinating flowers. Because the beekeeper does not reap these benefits, but does pay all their costs, she will keep fewer hives than she would if she could reap all the rewards. Accounting information is similarly suspected of being underproduced in a free market, because producers pay the costs, while users reap the benefits.

Accounting information is considered a public good because the use of it by one investor does not prevent it from being used by others.* In particular, noninvestors have as much access to accounting information as investors. If one tried to make investors pay for financial statements, one would have to deal with the problem of the so-called *free riders:* those individuals who enjoy the benefits without paying.

Opponents of regulation note that the publication of financial information is not entirely without benefit to firms, since it is to their advantage to have an orderly capital market in which to obtain capital funds, and it is to the advantage of the stockholders to see that there is a market for their shares. Therefore, even without regulation, firms might be willing to incur costs in order to publish financial information. In addition they point to the indisputable fact that many investors do pay financial analysts for financial information—despite the existence of free riders.

The historical record shows that many companies did make substantive voluntary disclosures before the 1930s. The difficulty was that the financial reports were in some cases very brief and infrequent, that is, they were underproduced because not all the rewards were captured.

To illustrate, consider the reporting of depreciation in early financial statements. The inadequacy of depreciation in income statements is evident from the findings of the Federal Trade Commission in 1915–16, which showed that out of 60,000 successful corporations doing business in excess of $100,000 a year, fully one half did not include depreciation at all. In some cases, income statements were omitted entirely, and in many other cases the income statement was completely inadequate by failing to disclose revenue or by a failure to classify expenses. In some cases, the net income figure reported was even erroneous because of the direct charge to surplus of depreciation and other expenses. Similar difficulties

---

* This is a matter of dispute because if one investor trades to an equilibrium on the basis of this information, its value is greatly reduced for the next.

were encountered with balance sheets which in some cases omitted important items and in other cases did not disclose the basis for valuations.[18] The counterargument to this is that companies might have been producing the information that investors really desired—not the information that regulators think they desire.

Comparability and Credibility.   A lack of comparability is a third argument sometimes used to support regulation. Comparability of disclosure between firms is often claimed to be necessary so as to facilitate the making of predictions and financial decisions by creditors, investors, and others and in order to avoid a market failure. As the section on comparability in Chapter 5 notes, uniformity is typically the vehicle through which comparability is sought. Uniformity is thought to simplify the process of comparing different companies, thereby reducing the search costs of users. It has been suggested also that limiting management's flexibility may increase the reliability of inferences users make based on this information.[19]

Uniformity is also believed to increase the credibility of financial reports. This is typically accompanied by the claim that the availability of many alternatives permits firms to report their financial performance in the best light by using what is referred to as *creative accounting*.[20] If two companies experiencing similar circumstances report them in two very different ways, what can one infer about truth and fairness in accounting? Would this mean that there is a variety of truths in accounting? Where two companies do experience circumstances that are essentially identical, the argument is impeccable. The dilemma is that circumstances are seldom so similar that one cannot suggest a reason for an alternative means of reporting.

The implicit claims here are twofold. First, it is believed that comparability can best be achieved by uniformity and, second, that managers left to their own devices would produce nonuniform disclosures that were not comparable. Critics of regulation respond to the first by pointing out that if the aim is for users to make sound financial decisions, then the provision of all relevant information is probably more important than the provision of the same information. For example, there is no virtue in requiring the same disclosure from banks and automobile producers. If industries should be treated on their respective merits, why not individual companies? Critics respond to the second claim by pointing out that those companies that did make disclosures before 1929 provided balance sheets and income statements that were quite similar. Proponents of regulation, undoubtedly, would say that they were not similar enough and could quote many examples of differences in the treatment of items within these statements. A list of the many accounting alternatives that were open to management appears in Exhibit 3-1 in Chapter 3.

Regulation: Cure or Curse?

To all the arguments in favor of regulation, critics respond with an anecdote concerning a king, who it is said, organized a singing competition. Two finalists were presented to him for his ultimate choice. After he had heard the first singer, he presented the prize to the second. The public is like the king because when they do not like the market they choose regulation without any consideration as to whether it can do any better. This is known as the *grass is greener* fallacy.* Critics suggest several reasons, in addition to Arrow's theorem, why the grass may not be greener on the other side of the fence. Three are described here: regulations are conceived in crises, regulators are captured by regulatees, and regulators are necessarily reactive rather than proactive.†

Crisis Oriented.　Theorists note that almost invariably the onset of regulation occurs in response to an identifiable crisis. Financial regulation of corporations in the United States can properly be said to have begun with the stock market crash of 1929, a classic example. Each crisis is typically accompanied by much recrimination—understandably, because many people lose a great deal of money in the typical crisis. The perception is that most often it is the "little guy" who gets hurt in these crises. In the case of financial collapses, many believe it is the small investor who is hurt. The large investor is perceived as more sophisticated, better diversified, and so more able to ride the storm. The mere survival of a few large investors, when many smaller investors are losing, is often interpreted as the "big guy" profiting from the troubles of others. Those who profit, even in relative terms, by weathering a storm are often suspected of having created the storm for their own gain. The result is an appeal to the government to protect the smaller investor. Invariably, the response has been government regulation, which steps in to protect the "public interest."

There is a special irony in this in the case of financial regulation. Research into the workings of capital markets, as described in the section on capital markets in Chapter 6, shows that, for the most part, capital markets are efficient, in the sense that prices reflect all available information in an unbiased manner. The research, described in that chapter, concludes that the only appropriate investment strategy is to purchase a diversified portfolio of shares. This done, the investor, whether sophisticated or naive, is guaranteed a return consistent with the risk of that

---

* The dilemma with this argument is that it works both ways.

† A fourth argument, that regulators are privately, rather than publicly, motivated is not discussed here.

portfolio. In short, the public needs protection from failing to diversify, not from the market itself, nor from a lack of detailed financial information.

The rule of regulation following economic disaster has the curious result that the specific nature of the disaster tends to color the resulting regulation. American accounting, in its conservatism, is truly a child of the Great Depression. The 1929 collapse of the stock market, as Chapter 3 indicated, was attributed in large part to unsound accounting practices such as the writing up of asset values to market. There was no evidence that unsound accounting was to blame but the claim stuck, forcing firms into the absurd position of even reporting historical values on marketable securities that are traded regularly. The regulation of British accounting began in a different era and is much more permissive when it comes to revaluing property.

Capture Theory.   The dilemma that regulatory bodies face is that they are required to fulfil this charter each year. It may be that, in any given year, there really is no overwhelming need for regulation. It may even be that the need for regulation of a particular industry has passed entirely. Unfortunately, the internal politics of the regulatory body seldom permits it to avoid regulation at that point. Regulation, therefore, tends to develop its own momentum—a momentum based on past actions. Almost inevitably, the groups who demanded the formation of the regulatory body fade away, leaving only the regulated involved. Who still remembers with any passion, for instance, the issues that forged the ICC? What emerges is a regulatory body that is "captured" by the very forces that it was meant to control. The regulator now serves the interests of the regulated by creating a protected cartel. Many suggest that the SEC is a notable exception to this general rule.

Reactionary.   Critics also note that regulation is reactive rather than proactive, that is, regulators are always fighting the last battle. The APB, for instance, did not manage to agree on appropriate rules for managing poolings until the investment boom that spawned them was over. *SFAS 96* was designed to deal with the reductions of the tax rate contained in the Tax Reform Act of 1986. Currently the FASB is attempting to set standards for complex financial instruments when, it might be argued, the surge of new instruments, which generated the demand for new standards, has diminished considerably. Finally, it must be confessed that after more than a half century of regulatory experience, the SEC was not able to prevent the stock market crash of 1987. It was only after the crash that it attempted to produce regulations to cover the use of program trading which was thought to be the source of the crash.

Conclusion

Conclusions must be guarded because research continues actively in the area of regulation. It seems though that the ultimate outcome will be mixed, bringing victory to neither side. Many managements seem willing and able to make their own accounting policies and to provide full disclosure to users of the reasons for their choices. Some managements are more reluctant to disclose such information and appear to take unfair advantage of any flexibility that is provided them. The result of such a situation will be some regulation, but not a lot.

CHECKPOINTS

1. List three reasons why accounting should be regulated.
2. List three reasons why accounting should not be regulated.
3. Explain what is meant by capture theory.

MANAGING ACCOUNTING POLICY

What then might one conclude about the establishment of accounting standards? First, it must be recognized that accounting information is only one source of financial information for individuals and markets. Accounting policy should take these alternative sources into account and permit nonaccounting sources to provide the information where it can be made available more efficiently and at a lower cost to the firm and the investors combined.

Second, it is apparent that accounting policy cannot be limited to the prescribing of measurement methods, disclosure rules, and forms of presentation, because of the economic and social consequences relating to alternative decisions. Accounting policy must take into consideration the costs and benefits, both direct and indirect, of financial information. The FASB, as noted in the section on benefits and costs in Chapter 5, does this explicitly as part of the desirable qualities of information. This is not to say that economic consequences should determine accounting policies, but simply that accounting regulators need to be aware of the politics of standard setting.

Third, it cannot be limited to specific groups such as the preferences of management, accountants, individuals, or the market, or the interests of other special groups in society. Difficult as it may be, a national accounting policy must take into consideration the broader social welfare. This is not to say that the particular interests of investors should be ignored nor does the FASB try to do that. The inevitable consequence of a need to take the wider world into account is that accounting must become part of the purview of a national government, even if only indirectly.

Government by the People

Any suggestion that Congress regulate accounting standards invariably sets off alarm bells among practising accountants in the United States. Yet in most countries in the world, accounting standards are established by law and are, therefore, the direct responsibility of government. This is the situation in the United Kingdom, for instance, where a series of Companies Acts have been passed over the years. This is also the situation in Canada and most European nations. There is no obvious sign that these countries have suffered irreparable harm as a result. In fact, it can be argued that, in the case of the United States, Congress should always be central to the accounting policy process.

Impositions of standards which are not in the interests of management implicitly redistribute wealth away from management. In the democratic tradition, it is the role of a government, duly elected by the people, to redistribute wealth in accordance with the majority vote of the people. Accountants have no constitutional right to increase the wealth of some at the expense of others. Economic consequences lead, therefore, ineluctably, to the necessity of turning standard setting in accounting over to government. How government should do that redistribution is a matter of considerable debate. But, once one accepts the fact that accounting has potential economic consequences, then one has to admit government as a necessary partner in the establishment of accounting standards.

There is a direct analogy here to law. Courts are entitled to settle cases within the law and on the basis of precedent from similar cases. But courts, in the United States, are not supposed to set the law. That is the function of government. Opinions vary on how loosely or how tightly existing laws may be interpreted, but no one disputes the essential foundation of the law in the will of the people. What holds for law, holds for accounting. The FASB derives its authority from the SEC, which is a duly appointed body of Congress. The FASB, therefore, is duly responsible to Congress and through Congress to the American body politic.

Delegating Authority to Act. Having claimed a central role for government, however, one must immediately add that the government's role need not take the form of direct regulation. It could, and probably should, take the form of a mandate from government to certain bodies to act on its behalf. This appears to be the situation that has evolved in the United States where Congress formed a regulatory agency, the SEC, responsible to it. The SEC in turn has delegated its authority to a private organization, the FASB, on the implicit understanding that the FASB will carry out the wishes of the SEC.

However, Congress can never delegate all its responsibilities. Whenever opposing interests come into conflict, democracy demands that the decision be turned back for a vote. One example where this occurred concerned the oil and gas industry. The FASB was asked by Congress for a single method of accounting so as to promote uniformity. The FASB obliged in December 1977 by selecting successful efforts as the only permissible method in *SFAS 19*.

Many claims were made that adverse economic consequences would flow from requiring the successful-efforts method. From a national policy point of view, they centered on the possible effects on competition, since it was mostly the smaller oil and gas producers that were using the full-costing method. It was claimed that the restriction on using the full-costing method would have an adverse effect on the ability of these firms to raise capital and compete with the larger firms. Another argument was that it created a disincentive to risk taking in the exploration for oil and gas. The opposition was led by an important segment of industry, the Justice Department, and the Federal Trade Commission, and the SEC required a reversal by the FASB in 1979. *SFAS 25* permits both methods.[21] This can be interpreted as an unfortunate willingness on the part of Congress to bend to the interests of powerful interest groups. It should be interpreted as the appropriate response of a democratically elected body.

Delegation by Charter. Government regulation, whether direct or indirect, also need not address the redistribution of wealth at every point. Instead, it can provide agencies with a political mandate that presumably represents the will of the people. In the case of the United States, the essential mandate that Congress appears to have given accountants through the SEC is to create an accounting system, characterized by uniformity and comparability, regardless of its impact on wealth. For instance, the opening line to the charter given the Committee on Accounting Procedure was to "narrow differences and inconsistency in accounting practice . . . ." This was enforced by threats from the SEC that "the Commission would prefer to have the profession itself take the necessary steps to reduce these differences, but if the profession did not do so, the Commission had the authority and would."[22]

Role of FASB

Seen in this light, the role of regulators such as the FASB becomes clearer. In the first place, they are to formalize policies which are acceptable to all parties. These may already be in place. In many cases, organizations simply want to know how to account for a transaction. There are no disputes involved. In the second place, the FASB is to discover the desire of the body politic so as to align itself with the public interest. Its task is then to persuade its various constituents of the desirability of policies that are in that interest. If a consensus fails to develop at this point, then the FASB should be obliged to transfer the issue to Congress, through the offices of the SEC, for resolution.

An analogy is sometimes drawn between setting accounting standards and establishing laws. Laws, too, have distributive effects. They are established, therefore, by Congress, subject to the overarching rule of the U.S. Constitution and to the oversight of the courts. A direct parallel between law and accounting was drawn when the Conceptual Framework was described as a constitution. Accounting standards would not necessarily be derived directly from the Conceptual Framework, any more than new laws are derived directly from the Constitution, but they would have to be consistent with the Framework in the same way that law has to be consistent with the Constitution.

It is not surprising, in light of this analogy, that some have suggested establishing a U.S. Court of Accounting Appeals. As proposed by Arthur Andersen senior partner Leonard Spacek, the court would have consisted of five members appointed by the president of the United States. It would have had "jurisdiction over the accounting rules of . . . the Securities and Exchange Commission, the Federal Power Commission, the Civil Aeronautics Board, and the Federal Communications Commission . . . . The full judicial process of petitions for redress (of an accounting rule), oral arguments, briefs, and so on would be used to resolve the disputes that arose."[23] The proposal never made much progress, but its very suggestion by an accountant as distinguished as Mr. Spacek gives some insight into the turmoil in accounting in the 60s.

Politics versus Principles.   The debate over accounting standards is often cast in terms of politics versus principles. FASB board member David Mosso put it this way:

> Rules of conduct call for a political process. Bargaining, horsetrading, logrolling, clout—describe it as you will, it is a power game. The stake in the game is business income and the object is to report it when you want it. The standards-setters in this environment try to write rules only when rules can't be avoided, and then to write them so the power is balanced. Balancing the power forces may lead to rules that favor a single interest group or it may lead to rules that create or preserve a stalemate. Logical consistency and economic reality cannot be overriding objectives. Income determination is the image, political power is the reality.
>
> Rules of measurement, on the other hand, call for a research process of observation and experimentation—a trial and error search for the dimensions of

business income. The object is to report it when it is. The standards-setter tries to write rules that link the reporting of income to the period in which it arises. It doesn't matter whether the business is large or small, rich or poor, volatile or stable—if the income is there, report it, if not, don't.[24]

These comments suggest that the political approach is diametrically opposed to the technical approach. But what this chapter has argued is that the one is supportive of the other. It is indeed the role of the FASB to undertake research and to write rules of measurement. But this role was given to it by the political process.

There have been times, and there will again be times, when rules of measurement produce economic consequences that lie outside the zone of what is acceptable to one or other group of users. Once those users have exhausted the technical process, they have a right, in a democratic society, to seek relief through the political process. The passage, therefore, from measurement to politics, and back, is not an indicator of failure in the standards-setting process, but a natural outcome of the fact that standards have consequences.

The Search for Consensus.   The key to the success of the FASB is its ability to build consensus. Arrow's theorem is particularly awkward for a body like the FASB since it suggests that, despite all their best efforts to be democratic, they will inevitably impose their own wishes on their constituents, unless they can build unanimous consent for their proposals. As noted above, this consensus need not hold for specific outcomes, merely for process. It is sufficient that all agree on how accounting standards are to be set and to agree to abide by the outcomes.

The need for consensus was appreciated early. That much is clear from the choice of the phrase *generally accepted accounting principles*. What was less clear was by whom these principles had to be accepted. The thought was to establish a consensus by laying an intellectual foundation on which individual firms could shape their own practices accompanied by complete disclosure of their policies. Accountants, being the experts, were the natural people to call on to establish that foundation. The first committees consisted almost exclusively of senior partners in accounting firms. The APB, although not quite as exclusive, was limited to members of the AICPA. In short, there was no overt recognition that acceptance should mean acceptance by the community at large—or even by a more immediate user group. It was not until the formation of the FASB that users, represented by nonaccountants, were allowed a voice in the establishment of accounting rules.

Consensus is sought by an elaborate system of due process described in the section of that name in Chapter 3, sending out discussion memoranda, exposure drafts, holding public hearings, and so on. Consensus was also sought through a Conceptual Framework project which was intended to lay a foundation on which specific standards could be established logically. Chapter 5 describes the framework in some detail.

CHECKPOINTS

1. Contrast what is meant in the chapter by delegation of authority to act with delegation by charter.
2. How has the FASB sought to establish a consensus for its standards?
3. In what circumstances can the FASB's mechanism be expected to fail?

CONCLUSION

The purpose of national accounting policies is to narrow the areas of differences among firms in the disclosure, measurements, and method of presentation of financial information in financial statements and financial reports and to change the quantity and quality of information in published financial reports. The effect of accounting policies established by the FASB, SEC, or other bodies is, therefore, to limit the number of choices and the amount of discretion available to individual firms in their financial statements and reports.

The standards which ultimately emerge are typically based on what might be called the three Ps of standard setting: precedents set previously, precepts that guide the standard setter, and pressure from the wider community. In tabular form these three bases are:

Precedents	Precepts	Pressures
Customs	Principles	Politics
Conventions	Pronouncements	Community

The FASB and other similar standard-setting bodies often are under enormous stress because of the need to reconcile these three elements. The process of establishing accounting policy is made more difficult because of the complexities in the economic and social environment in which it must operate.

Accounting theories and their verification through research do provide some guidelines. However, no accounting theories or research methods have been able to provide conclusive evidence that a single alternative is socially superior to all others. In addition to accounting theories, policy-makers must take into consideration the social, economic, and political consequences of their decisions. Accounting theories and accounting research, therefore, can contribute to policymaking, but only as one of many economic and social considerations.

SUMMARY

The establishment of accounting policies determining the amount and type of information disclosure, measurement rules and procedures, and the form of presentation of financial statements and financial reporting is a complex process. The main responsibility for accounting policy was granted to the SEC by Congress in 1934 for corporations whose securities are publicly traded. The FASB was formed as an independent agency in the private sector to establish accounting policy enforced by the AICPA on its members. But the support of the FASB by the SEC has given it considerably greater authority. Even with regulation, however, accounting policies must still be formulated by the AICPA, professional accounting firms, and the reporting enterprises.*

Traditionally, accounting policy has been based on generally accepted practice and inductive-deductive logic in an attempt to narrow the areas of differences. Research, particularly in the areas of capital markets and human information processing, does provide some assistance in meeting the objectives of accounting policy to improve social and economic welfare. Other social and economic consequences should also be considered in accounting policy decisions in relationship to the costs and benefits of the policies. Economic consequences that affect specific industries, individuals, or corporations must be placed in this broader context. However, because of these economic consequences, there is an attempt through lobbying and other means to place the establishment of accounting policy in the political arena. These political pressures cannot be ignored, and individuals and corporations should have an opportunity to be heard; but accounting policy should not be established by the political process alone. Technical considerations including the results of theory and research should be of primary importance with the objective of producing the greatest benefit to society.

---

* The FASB in *SFAS 32* declared the specialized accounting and reporting principles contained in AICPA Statements of Position (SOPs) and Guides on Accounting and Auditing Matters to be preferable accounting principles for purposes of justifying a change in accounting principles (under *APB 20*).

QUESTIONS

1. Two years before his death, Mr. May commented on the nature of GAAP, as he and the original committee had understood the term and its application. He said:

> It must be remembered that the plan called for a fairly full disclosure of the methods of accounting adopted by each listed company. It is often forgotten that this was a part of the program and that the certificate was designed for use only by listed companies which furnished the required details. It is, I think, widely used today in cases in which it is not appropriate because there is no source from which even a general idea of the principles can be gained.[25]

Required:

Do you agree with Mr. May that unlisted companies should not be permitted to issue statements certified in accordance with GAAP?

2. *APB 22,* "Disclosure of Accounting Policies" said that:

> The Board concludes that information about the accounting policies adopted by a reporting entity is essential for financial statement users. When financial statements are issued purporting to present fairly financial position, changes in financial position, and results of operations in accordance with generally accepted accounting principles, a description of all significant accounting policies of the reporting entity should be included as an integral part of the financial statements.

This is typically disclosed in a "Summary of Significant Accounting Policies" at the head of the footnotes. Three examples of the details that were disclosed in various Annual Reports about inventory policy follow:

> Crude oil and refined product inventories are valued at the lower of cost or market value. Cost of such inventories is determined under the first-in, first-out method for approximately two-thirds of the inventories, and the remaining inventories are valued using the average method. (Amerada Hess, 1979)
>
> Inventories are valued at the lower of cost or market. Certain domestic inventories are valued using the LIFO method, while other inventories are generally valued using the FIFO method. (General Mill, 1986)
>
> Inventories of new and reusable material and supplies are stated at lower of cost or market with cost determined on a first-in, first-out or average cost basis. In the cases of certain large individual items, however, cost is determined on a specific identification basis. Non-reusable material is carried principally at estimated salvage value. (Ameritech, 1988)

Required:

Do you consider this disclosure sufficient for financial analysis? Do you think this would have satisfied George May? What suggestions can you make for improved disclosure, if any? Would disclosure be improved if all companies were obliged to use one method of inventory accounting only?

3. The opening paragraph asked whether the actions of 1933 and 1934 by Congress were appropriate. Also, whether the present structure of regulating financial reporting is in the interest of the American public. What is your own feeling now that you have read this and the preceding chapters?

UNION CARBIDE

Prior to 1980, Union Carbide calculated depreciation for financial reporting purposes using the straight-line method. In addition, the company estimated the useful lives of its assets using the U.S. Treasury Asset Depreciation Range (ADR) system. For tax purposes, Union Carbide used an accelerated depreciation method, along with the minimum ADR guideline lives, thereby obtaining the lowest tax liability.

In 1980, however, the company abandoned the ADR guidelines and adopted longer depreciable lives for a substantial portion (i.e., 70 percent) of its assets. While the change did not impact the depreciation on the firm's buildings and transportation equipment, it did impact machinery and equipment.

	ADR Guideline Lives (years)	Revised Lives (years)
Machinery and equipment in:		
Chemicals and plastics	11	17
Gases and related areas	11	15
Metals and carbons	10,12,14,18	15,20
Batteries, home and automotive	11,12	13,15

The overall effect of this change was to increase the average life of the company's assets by 35 percent.

At a presentation to security analysts, Union Carbide controller Peloubet stated that the ADR guidelines were unrealistically short, and thus tended to distort reported financial results. Moreover, the new depreciable lives were now comparable to those used by the company's leading competitors, Dow Chemical and E.I. du Pont de Nemours & Co.

Although the accounting change did achieve greater comparability in depreciable lives between Union Carbide and its competitors, increased comparability in depreciation method was not enhanced. Specifically, while Union Carbide retained its use of the straight-line method, Dow Chemical and du Pont utilized accelerated depreciation methods.

Required:

    1. Why would a company adopt longer depreciable lives for its assets?

    2. Should a company be allowed to choose its own lives or should it use lives laid down by the government? If one company cares for its assets more than another, should it be permitted to use longer lives?

    3. What factors do you think Congress might consider in setting depreciable lives on assets for tax purposes? Are they based solely on their useful life or does Congress take into consideration issues such as the need for more tax dollars? If depreciable lives for tax purposes are biased by tax considerations, does their use provide information that is representationally faithful?

(Case prepared by Kenneth R. Ferris from publicly available data.)

PRIMARY SOURCES

Those interested in learning more about the topics covered in this chapter might begin by consulting these sources, each of which has numerous excellent citations.

Bromwich, Michael. *The Economics of Accounting Standard Setting* (Englewood Cliffs, N.J.: Prentice Hall, 1985).

Carey, John L. *The Rise of the Accounting Profession* (New York: AICPA, 1969).

Kelly-Newton, Lauren. *Accounting Policy Formulation* (Reading, Mass.: Addison-Wesley, 1980).

McCraw, Thomas K. *Prophets of Regulation* (Cambridge, Mass.: Belknap Press, 1984).

Solomons, David. *Making Accounting Policy* (New York: Oxford University Press, 1986).

SELECTED ADDITIONAL READINGS

Accounting Policy-Standard Setting

Abdel-Khalik, A. Rashad, ed. *Government Regulation of Accounting, Accounting Series No. 11* (University Presses of Florida, 1980).

Bromwich, Michael. "The Possibility of Partial Accounting Standards." *The Accounting Review,* April 1980, pp. 288–300.

Demski, Joel. "Choice among Financial Reporting Alternatives." *The Accounting Review,* April 1974, pp. 221–32.

May, Robert G., and Gary L. Sundem. "Research for Accounting Policy. An Overview." *The Accounting Review,* October 1976, pp. 747–63.

Merino, Barbara Dubois, and Marilyn Dale Neimark. "Disclosure Regulation and Public Policy: A Sociohistoric Reappraisal." *Journal of Accounting and Public Policy,* Fall 1982, pp. 33–57.

Moonitz, Maurice. "Obtaining Agreement on Standards in the Accounting Profession." *Studies in Accounting Research No. 8* (AAA, 1974).

Puxty, A. G.; Hugh C. Wilmott; David J. Cooper; and Tony Lowe. "Modes of Regulation in Advanced Capitalism: Locating Accountancy in Four Countries." *Accounting, Organizations, and Society,* 1987, pp. 273–91.

Sterling, Robert R., ed. *Institutional Issues in Public Accounting* (Houston, Tex.: Scholars Book Co., 1974).

Tinker, Anthony. "Theories of the State and State Accounting: Economic Reduction and Political Voluntarism in Accounting Regulation Theory." *Journal of Accounting and Public Policy,* Spring 1984, pp. 55–74.

Zeff, Stephen A. *Forging Accounting Principles in Five Countries* (Champaign, Ill.: Stipes Publishing Co., 1972).

Uniformity and Comparability

Hendriksen, Eldon S. "Toward Greater Comparability through Uniformity of Accounting Principles." *New York Certified Public Accountant,* now *CPA Journal,* February 1967, pp. 105–15.

Merino, Barbara D., and Teddy L. Coe. "Uniformity in Accounting. A Historical Perspective." *Journal of Accountancy,* August 1978, pp. 62–69.

Miller, Paul B.W. "A New View of Comparability." *Journal of Accountancy,* August 1978, pp. 70–77.

Revsine, Lawrence. "Toward Greater Comparability in Accounting Reports." *Financial Analysts Journal,* January–February 1975, pp. 45–51.

Simmons, John K. "A Concept of Comparability in Financial Reporting." *The Accounting Review,* October 1967, pp. 680–92.

Sterling, Robert R. "A Test of the Uniformity Hypothesis." *Abacus,* September 1969, pp. 37–47.

Sterling, Robert R. "Uniformity in Financial Accounting." *Law and Contemporary Problems,* Autumn 1965.

Economic Consequences of Accounting Policy

American Accounting Association. Report of the Committee on *The Social Consequences of Accounting Information* (AAA Committee Reports, 1978).

Benston, George J. "The Economic Consequences of Financial Accounting Statements," in *FASB Economic Consequences of Financial Statements.* Selected Papers (July 1978), pp. 161–252.

Chow, Chee W. "Empirical Studies of the Effects of Accounting Regulation on Security Prices: Findings, Problems and Prospects." *Journal of Accounting Literature,* Spring 1983, pp. 73–109.

Dhaliwal, Dan S. "The Effect of the Firm's Capital Structure on the Choice of Accounting Methods." *The Accounting Review,* January 1980, pp. 78–84.

Holthausen, Robert W., and Richard W. Leftwich. "The Economic Consequences of Accounting Choice: Implications of Costly Contracting and Monitoring." *Journal of Accounting and Economics,* August 1983, pp. 77–117.

Lev, Baruch. "The Impact of Accounting Regulation on the Stock Market. The Case of Oil and Gas Companies." *The Accounting Review,* July 1979, pp. 485–503.

Rappaport, Alfred. "The Economic Impact of Financial Accounting Standards—Implications for the FASB." *1976 Accounting Research Convocation. Emerging Issues* (University of Alabama, 1977), pp. 113–28.

Wyatt, Arthur R. "The Economic Impact of Financial Accounting Standards," *1976 Accounting Research Convocation. Emerging Issues* (University of Alabama, 1977), pp. 129–38.

Zeff, Stephen. "The Rise of Economic Consequences." *Journal of Accountancy,* December 1978, pp. 56–63.

The Impact of Politics on Accounting Policy

Gerboth, Dale L. "Research, Intuition, and Politics in Accounting Inquiry." *The Accounting Review,* July 1973, pp. 475–82.

Horngren, Charles T. "The Marketing of Accounting Standards." *Journal of Accountancy,* October 1973, pp. 61–66.

Solomons, David. "The Politicization of Accounting. The Impact of Politics on Accounting Standards." *Journal of Accountancy,* November 1978, pp. 65–72.

Watts, Ross, and Jerold L. Zimmerman. "Toward a Positive Theory of Determination of Accounting Standards." *The Accounting Review,* January 1978, pp. 112–34.

Watts, Ross, and Jerold L. Zimmerman. "The Demand for and Supply of Accounting Theories. The Market for Excuses." *The Accounting Review,* April 1979, pp. 273–305.

Financial Accounting Standards Board

Beaver, William H. "What Should Be the FASB's Objectives? *Journal of Accountancy,* August 1973, pp. 49–56.

Dopuch, Nicholas, and Shyam Sunder. "FASB's Statements on Objectives and Elements of Financial Accounting. A Review." *The Accounting Review,* January 1980, pp. 1–21.

Johnson, Steven B., and David Solomons. "Institutional Legitimacy and the FASB." *Journal of Accounting and Public Policy,* Fall 1984, pp. 165–83.

Moonitz, Maurice. *Studies in Accounting Research No. 8.* "Obtaining Agreement on Standards in the Accounting Profession" (AAA, 1974), pp. 80–87.

Puro, Marsha. "Audit Firm Lobbying before the Financial Accounting Standards Board: An Empirical Study." *Journal of Accounting Research,* Autumn 1984, pp. 624–46.

Securities and Exchange Commission

Benston, George J. "Required Disclosure and the Stock Market. An Evaluation of the Securities Act of 1934." *American Economic Review,* March 1973.

Phillips, Susan M., and J. Richard Zecher. *The SEC and the Public Interest* (Cambridge, Mass.: MIT Press, 1981).

Pines, J. Arnold. "The Securities and Exchange Commission and Accounting Principles." *Law and Contemporary Problems. Uniformity in Financial Accounting,* Autumn 1965, pp. 727–51.

Previts, Gary John. "The SEC and Its Chief Accountants. Historical Impressions." *Journal of Accountancy,* August 1978, pp. 83–91.

Rappaport, Louis H. *SEC Accounting Practice and Procedure.* 3rd ed. (New York: Ronald Press, 1972).

International Accounting

Arpan, Jeffrey S., and Lee H. Radebaugh. *International Accounting and Multinational Enterprises,* 2nd ed. (New York: John Wiley & Sons, 1985).

Bromwich, Michael, and Anthony G. Hopwood, eds. *Accounting Standards Setting: An International Perspective* (London: Pitman, 1983).

Burton, John C., ed. *The International World of Accounting: Challenges and Opportunities* (Reston, Va.: Council of Arthur Young Professors, 1981).

Choi, Frederick D. S., and Gerhard G. Mueller. International Accounting (Englewood Cliffs, N.J.: Prentice Hall, 1984).

Evans, Thomas G.; Martin E. Taylor; and Oscar Holzmann. *International Accounting and Reporting* (New York: Macmillan, 1985).

Holzer, H. Peter. *International Accounting* (New York: Harper & Row, 1984).

Nobes, Christopher, and Robert Parker. *Comparative International Accounting,* 2nd ed. (Oxford: Philip Allan, 1985).

ENDNOTES

1. Accounting Principles Board, Opinion 22, *Disclosure of Accounting Policies,* April 1972, par. 6.
2. Ibid., par. 8.
3. AIA, *Audits of Corporate Accounts,* 1934. Reprinted in G. O. May, *Twenty-Five Years of Accounting Responsibility, 1911–1936* (New York: AIA, 1936), pp. 119–20.
4. Ibid., pp. 116–17.
5. Carey, J. L. *The Rise of the Accounting Profession* (New York: American Institute of Certified Public Accountants, 1970), vol. 1, p. 169.
6. Reed K. Storey, *The Search for Accounting Principles* (New York: AICPA, 1964), p. 28.
7. John C. Burton, "An Interview with John C. Burton," *Management Accounting,* May 1975, pp. 19–23.
8. Carey, *The Rise of the Accounting Profession,* vol. 2, p. 131.
9. Charles T. Horngren, "Accounting Principles: Private or Public Sector?" *Journal of Accountancy,* May 1972, p. 63.
10. Ibid., p. 38.

11. "Paper Shuffling and Economic Reality," an interview with John C. Burton, *Journal of Accountancy,* January 1973, p. 26.

12. John C. Burton, "Some General and Specific Thoughts on the Accounting Environment," *Journal of Accountancy,* October 1973, p. 41.

13. For a fuller discussion of changes in SEC policies over the years, see Gary John Previts, "The SEC and Its Chief Accountants: Historical Impressions," *Journal of Accountancy,* August 1978, pp. 38–91.

14. This section relies heavily on David Solomons, *Making Accounting Policy* (New York: Oxford University Press, 1986), pp. 53–65.

15. Baruch Lev, "The Impact of Accounting Regulation on the Stock Market: The Case of Oil and Gas Companies," *Accounting Review,* July 1979, pp. 485–508.

16. See Prem Prakash and Alfred R. Rappaport, "Information Inductance and Its Significance for Accounting," *Accounting, Organizations and Society,* 1977, pp. 29–38.

17. Eugene H. Flegm, *Accounting: How to Meet the Challenges of Relevance and Regulation* (New York: Ronald Press, 1984), p. 5.

18. W. Z. Ripley, *Main Street and Wall Street* (Boston: Little, Brown & Co., 1927), p. 190.

19. Joshua Ronen, "The Dual Role of Accounting: A Financial Economic Perspective," in *Handbook of Financial Economics.* Edited by James L. Bicksler (Amsterdam: North-Holland, 1979), pp. 425–26.

20. See, for example, "Paper Profits: Slick Accounting Ploys Help Many Companies Improve Their Income—By Proper or Improper Means They 'Manage' Earnings for the Desired Effect," *The Wall Street Journal,* June 20, 1980, p. 1.

21. Lev, "Impact on the Stock Market," p. 487.

22. W. W. Cooper and Yuri Ijiri, eds. *Eric Louis Kolher* (Reston, Va.: Reston Publishing Co., 1979), p. 37.

23. Eugene H. Flegm, *Accounting* (John Wiley & Sons, 1984), p. 89.

24. David Mosso, *Viewpoint* (Stamford, Conn.: FASB, January 26, 1978).

25. George O. May, "Generally Accepted Principles of Accounting," *The Journal of Accountancy,* January 1959, p. 24.

Chapter 9

Cash, Capital, and Income

CHAPTER OBJECTIVES

After studying this chapter, you will be able to:

Derive entity cash flows from a cash flow statement.

Contrast different definitions of income.

Compute the market-based income of an enterprise.

CHAPTER OVERVIEW

Objective of Cash Flow Information

The primary objective of accounting, according to the FASB, is to provide investors and others with information useful for assessing the amount, timing, and uncertainty of prospective cash flows. These cash flows are assumed to form the basis for estimating the market value of debt, equity, and other financial instruments issued by the firm.

Presentation and Prediction

Given the importance of cash flows, the FASB mandated the presentation of a cash flow statement in annual reports. The statement falls into three sections: operations, investments, and financing. The last of these corresponds broadly to what this chapter defines as *entity cash flow*.

Income Measurement

Income may be defined as an increase in well-being. In the case of an enterprise, this may be operationalized as entity cash flow plus the change in value of the enterprise. Different definitions of value lead to various definitions of income.

Capital and income are two of the most basic concepts in accounting. Both are ultimately dependent on underlying cash flows. In the final analysis, therefore, cash flows into and out of a business enterprise are the most fundamental events upon which accounting measurements are based and upon which investors and creditors are assumed to base their decisions.

Accountants tend to equate the term *capital* with the book value of the holdings of common shareholders. Likewise, they tend to equate the term *income* with the net income accruing to common shareholders. This chapter broadens that usage to the way in which those terms are more commonly used by economists. Capital, broadly defined as in this chapter, is the value of all the monies lent to an enterprise. This includes all loans, all preferred stock, all common stock, and any other financial instruments that the enterprise may have issued. We will speak of all these financial instruments as *equity*—the holdings of common shareholders are termed *owners' equity*. By analogy, the term *income* will refer in this chapter to the amount earned by *all* equity holders, that is, the holders of both owners' equity and liabilities. This is sometimes termed *entity income* to distinguish it from the concept of *net income,* which is that income accruing to the holders of owners' equity. Stated otherwise, entity income is earnings before interest expense is deducted from net income.

Cash attains its significance in the relationship between capital and income because it represents purchasing power that can be transferred readily in an exchange economy to any individuals or organizations for their own specific needs in acquiring goods and services desired by them and available in the economy. By far the most significant method of transferring cash (claims for purchasing power) is the bank check, or other means of instructing a bank to transfer bank credit from one individual or organization to another. Currency and coins represent merely a small fraction of the total means of transferring cash to and from a business firm.

With only a very few exceptions, business firms acquire rights to goods and services in order to produce other goods and services for sale to customers, with the intent of distributing interest and dividends to long-term investors. Very seldom do stockholders receive benefits from the firm in a form other than cash.

Most accounting measurements, therefore, are based upon past, present, or expected flows of cash. Revenues are generally measured in terms of the net cash expected to be received from the sale of goods or services. Expenses are generally measured in terms of the cash paid, or expected to be paid, for goods and services used by the firm. Accruals represent the allocation to the current period of expected future cash receipts or cash disbursements for services. Deferrals represent the allocation to current and future periods of past cash receipts and cash disbursements for goods and services.

The theoretical measurements of assets, liabilities, and income are also based heavily on actual and expected cash flows. As will be discussed in Chapter 14 on asset measurement, the present value of an asset is frequently defined as the discounted expected net receipts to be derived from an asset. Liabilities can be measured in terms of the discounted amount to be paid in the future. Income, as will be apparent from this chapter, can be similarly defined in terms of changes in expected cash flows.

Income and balance sheet items measured on the accrual basis are usually proposed, and accepted, on the basis that they provide useful measurements of firm efficiency and relevant information for the prediction of future firm activity and dividend payments. Because of the deliberate and inherent biases created by the use of allocation procedures and historical transaction prices, there is some doubt that traditional accounting methods are adequate to report the complex economic activities of today. One way of avoiding some of these biases is to emphasize the reporting of cash flows, supplemented by other information and appropriate classifications to permit users of financial statements to make their own predictions regarding the future. Historical cash flow information as well as budgeted cash flows may provide relevant information, either alone or as supplements to conventional financial reports, for investors and creditors in their evaluation of the firm and in their predictions of expected dividend payments.

Although few advocate the complete replacement of the traditional income statement and balance sheet by a cash flow statement, many suggest a preference for certain procedures on the basis of their avoidance of allocations to several periods that appear to be arbitrary in nature. Others have a preference for income flows on the basis of their approximation of cash flows. For example, the use of direct costing of inventories, the flow through method of treating interperiod tax differences (nonallocation), and the tax reduction method of handling the investment tax credit have all been advocated in the past, at least in part, because they are more closely related to the actual cash flows. Still others use cash flows to argue against some of the stances taken by the FASB. For instance, General Motors controller Eugene Flegm argues that one of the reasons for "the rejection of current value theories by managerial accountants is . . . its subjective, non-cash orientation." He goes on to say:

> The creation of "paper profits or losses" through the subjective determination of the sales or liquidation value of a company's net assets at different points in time, unrelated to realized cash, would leave management with "profits" without perhaps the cash to pay dividends or to reinvest.[1]

Flegm is not saying that managers believe that value is unimportant; merely that they believe that values should not be permitted to dominate the computation of income, which they believe should be more closely tied to realized cash.

With the issuance of *SFAS 95*, the disclosure of cash flow information to investors was mandated by the FASB. This chapter develops a theoretical framework within which the provision of cash flow information can be seen to fall logically and naturally. The first part of the chapter lays out the reasons for disclosure. The second and third sections discuss potential uses of disclosure, including the use of cash in the computation of income.

THE OBJECTIVE OF CASH FLOW INFORMATION

SFAC 1 noted that the primary objective of accounting is to enable shareholders and others to form expectations regarding future cash flows. In the words of the FASB:

> Financial reporting should provide information to help present and potential investors and creditors and other users in assessing the amounts, timing, and uncertainty of prospective cash receipts from dividends or interest and the proceeds from the sale, redemption, or maturity of securities or loans.[2]

This objective derives from a normative discounted cash flow valuation model—essentially the same model used in capital budgeting. Those who lend money to an enterprise, whether they are holders of common stock or preferred stock, or creditors, do so in the expectation of getting a return on their money that is not less than the market rate of interest for an investment with equivalent risk. Stated otherwise, the present value of the cash flow stream that is expected to be generated by the investment should not be less than the cash that is to be invested, that is, the net present value should be greater than zero. We can write this algebraically, using the following notation:

CF_j = cash flow in year j

r = market rate of interest (assumed constant)

V_0 = present value of the investment at time 0, the start

I = cost of the proposed investment at the start

A potential investor will lend money only if

$$V_0 \geq I \qquad (1)$$

where

$$V_0 = \sum_{j=1}^{\infty} \frac{CF_j}{(1 + r)^j} \qquad (2)$$

Restating equations (1) and (2) in words, investors will not place their monies in a project unless the discounted present value of expected cash flows is at least as great as the cost of the investment.

The key issue now becomes what information should be provided to investors and creditors to enable them to establish the expected value of their own investments so that they might make correct investment decisions. The ideal is the future cash flows that will accrue to each individual. But future cash flows cannot be projected with certainty, and providing individual statements is not cost effective. So the typical surrogate is to provide information about past cash flows of the enterprise as a whole ($ENCF_j$). These past cash flows serve as a basis for forecasting future cash flows. Each individual is then free to estimate his or her own share of the total entity cash flow. As the FASB noted:

> The prospects for those cash receipts [i.e., the cash received by individuals] are affected by an enterprise's ability to generate enough cash to meet its obligations when due and its other cash operating needs, to reinvest in operations, and to pay cash dividends. . . . Thus, financial reporting should provide information to help investors, creditors, and others assess the amounts, timing, and uncertainty of prospective net cash inflow to the related enterprise.[3]

Rewriting equation (2) at the enterprise level yields:

$$TV_0 = \sum_{j=1}^{\infty} \frac{ENCF_j}{(1 + r)^j} \tag{3}$$

where

TV_j = total value of the enterprise at time j

$ENCF_j$ = entity cash flow expected in period j

Thus, a major reason for the provision of historical cash flow statements at the enterprise level is to permit shareholders, both major and minor, and creditors to value the enterprise as a going concern. This value may then be fed into the investment model of individual investors and creditors. As the expectations of investors and creditors regarding the enterprise's future change, so one can expect their estimates of the value of the enterprise to change.

The relationship between the entity cash flow of an enterprise and the corresponding cash flows remitted to investors and creditors can be expressed in the form of a cash flow identity.

Entity cash flows	$\equiv$	Cash flows to and from lenders	$+$	Cash flows to and from majority shareholders	$+$	Cash flows to and from minority shareholders

One may rewrite this identity for each period j as:

$$ENCF_j \equiv LCF_j + SHCF_j + MICF_j \qquad (4)$$

where

LCF = Lender cash flows (net)

$SHCF$ = Majority shareholder cash flows (net)

$MICF$ = Minority shareholder cash flows (net)

In other words, the cash generated by the enterprise is identically equal to the sum of the net cash flows of each of the participants in the cash flows. Combining equations (3) and (4) yields:

$$\sum_{j=1}^{\infty} \frac{ENCF_j}{(1 + r)^j} \equiv \sum_{j=1}^{\infty} \frac{LCF_j}{(1 + r)^j} + \sum_{j=1}^{\infty} \frac{SHCF_j}{(1 + r)^j} + \sum_{j=1}^{\infty} \frac{MICF_j}{(1 + r)^j} \qquad (5)$$

In words, the value of the enterprise as a whole is identically equal to the value of the holdings of the lenders, the majority shareholders, and the minority shareholders.

Present Values and Market Values

In situations where companies are traded, the market establishes a price at which investors and creditors may sell and buy their rights to their expected cash flows. For instance, investors may trade their shares on stock exchanges; creditors may trade their holdings in markets for debt such as the bond market. The prices of these stocks, bonds, and other financial instruments are readily available for public companies on a daily basis in the financial press.

If an investment were worth more than its cost, the investor would earn more than the market rate of interest over the life of the investment. The rate earned is often termed the *internal rate of return*, or the *effective rate*. In the case of investments made in securities on the major financial markets, such as the purchase of shares on the NYSE, considerations of market efficiency suggest that competition between investors will force the rate earned on investments in these markets to the risk adjusted market rate. In these cases value is equal to cost. Stated otherwise, the efficient market hypothesis requires that at all times:

$$V_0 = I \qquad (6)$$

In other words, the price of the investment is at all times equal to the present value of the expected cash flows. That is to say, knowledge of expected future cash flows is what permits the market to set prices of shares in a company. This is true for all the various financial holdings in the company such as bank notes, mortgages, bonds, common stock, preferred stock, warrants, and so on. When equation (6) holds, we may then say that:

$$TV_j = TMV_j \tag{7}$$

where

TMV_j = the total market value of the firm

In words, the discounted value of future expected cash flows is equal to the market value of the firm established by arm's-length trading. We may therefore rewrite the identity in equation (5) as:

$$TMV_0 \equiv MV^{(d)}_0 + MV^{(e)}_0 + MV^{(mi)}_0 \tag{8}$$

or

$$
\begin{array}{ccccc}
\text{Total market} & & \text{Market} & & \text{Market value} \\
\text{value of} & \equiv & \text{value} + & \text{value} + & \text{of minority} \\
\text{enterprise} & & \text{of debt} & \text{of equity} & \text{interests}
\end{array}
$$

This result sheds further light on why the provision of information about future cash flows is so important. Estimates of the amount and timing of future cash flows are the critical ingredients in the pricing model. Estimates of risk are essential to establishing the appropriate market rate at which to discount the flows. The more effective the financial disclosure, the more accurate are the expectations that are formed about the amounts and timing of future cash flows. The more accurate the expectations, the more efficient is the pricing of the investment. Inefficiently priced securities that reflect overly optimistic expectations will cause wealth losses to investors when the expected cash flows fail to materialize.

Net Income as a Predictor of Cash. Accounting net income is frequently claimed to be an indication of the ability of the firm to pay dividends. And, indeed, where management elects to base their dividends strictly on a fixed fraction of net income, then projected net income is all an investor needs to estimate a future dividend. However, the dividend decision must take into consideration many other factors, such as the availability of cash; the opportunities and objectives of the firm with respect to capital growth and expansion; and the policies of the firm regarding external financing, as well as the ability of the firm to obtain outside funds. But one of the great deficiencies of reported net income as a predictor of future dividends is that it may be considerably biased, because of the inability in many cases to obtain a proper matching of expenses with revenues, and because of the arbitrary nature of allocation procedures. The use of cash flows as a predictor of future dividends, therefore, avoids the biases of reported net income, except to the extent that the timing of certain cash receipts and disbursements can be altered by management.

Liquidity, Solvency, and Financial Flexibility

Thus far, the discussion of cash flow information has emphasized the provision of information to help investors and creditors predict cash flows likely to be distributed in the form of dividends and interest and repayment of principal, and to evaluate probable risk. Information regarding solvency and financial flexibility helps in meeting these goals by permitting better predictions of the probabilities of future returns, rather than just predictions of expected values. The probabilities of insolvency and bankruptcy on the one hand and a very high return on the other are important in the evaluation of total risk.

An additional objective in the presentation of data regarding cash flows is to permit an evaluation of liquidity and firm solvency. *Liquidity* is the relative ability to convert assets into cash, sometimes referred to as the nearness of assets to cash. It also refers to the relationship between a firm's short-term liabilities and its cash and near-cash items. *Solvency* is a broader term referring to the ability of a firm to obtain cash, or have cash available, for whatever purpose the business requires. More specifically, solvency is the ability of a firm to pay its debts when they become due. *Financial flexibility* is the ability of a firm to obtain cash on short notice in order to meet unforeseen contingencies, or to take advantage of favorable opportunities. All three concepts are related, but financial flexibility is a broader concept than solvency, and solvency is broader than liquidity.

The importance of solvency is that it is necessary for firm continuity. Insolvency may lead to bankruptcy, forced liquidation, and the loss of claims by both stockholders and creditors. However, even in the absence of bankruptcy, insolvency may lead to a restructuring of debt and equity claims, resulting in a loss to both stockholders and creditors.

But solvency itself is not necessary to cause losses to stockholders and creditors. The mere threat of insolvency may cause the equity and credit markets to react by a reduction in the market price of shares and certificates of indebtedness and an increase in the costs of additional borrowing and new equity. The reason for the reaction of market prices to a threat of insolvency is that it creates an increase in risk—the risk of complete or partial loss of equity or credit claims.

Since liquidity refers to asset characteristics, a discussion of the presentation of liquidity information is also found in Chapter 13.* It is suffi-

---

* See the section on classification in Chapter 13.

cient for now to note that liquidity information is part of the information necessary to evaluate solvency and financial flexibility. These broader concepts require not only information regarding the ability to convert existing assets into cash, but also information regarding the commitments and expectations relating to future cash receipts and disbursements.

CHECKPOINTS

1. What is the primary objective of accounting?
2. What are the objectives of providing cash flow information to users of financial statements?
3. Define entity cash flow.
4. Under what circumstances are present values likely to equal market values?
5. Distinguish the terms *liquidity, solvency,* and *financial flexibility*.

THE PRESENTATION AND PREDICTION OF CASH FLOW INFORMATION*

As already noted, the primary objective of accounting is to present data that will:

1. Help the investor or creditor predict the amount of cash likely to be distributed in the future in the form of dividends or interest and in the form of liquidation distributions or repayment of principal.
2. Aid in the evaluation of risk. The term *risk*, in this context, includes both the expected variability of future returns and the probability of insolvency or bankruptcy.

Data that will enable users to form predictions about expected distributions of cash by the firm are key, therefore. However, the cash distribution decisions of the firm each period are based on many complex factors. In particular, what portion of that cash flow will go to servicing shareholders and what to servicing creditors will depend on debt financing policies represented, perhaps, by a target debt-to-equity ratio. Taken as a whole, though, cash distribution in the long run must reflect cash flow generating capacity. Investors and creditors, therefore, may be able to obtain assistance in the prediction of future dividend levels if they have information regarding the following types of flows:

---

* This section has benefited considerably from conversations with Professor Gerald Lawson.

1. Cash flows relating to the basic current operations of the enterprise.
2. Recurring or occasional cash flows unrelated to current operations, but arising from either unexpected events or the desire to maintain a good environment for the firm in the future.
3. Cash flows required to increase operating facilities and inventories, or obtained from their sale when not needed for future operations.
4. Cash obtained from, or repaid to, bondholders and stockholders as a part of firm financing.
5. Payments of interest and dividends to investors with priority claims, such as preferred stockholders.

These five requirements, together with the tax implications of each, form the basis for the format of cash flow statements seen in practice today. This format includes the following three sections:

1. A statement of operating receipts and payments.
2. A statement of financing activities.
3. A statement of investing activities.

These three sections have now been mandated by *SFAS 95*. An example of the format that the FASB prefers appears in Exhibit 9-1.

This format is not without its critics. Many firms still appear to prefer an indirect format that begins with net income and adds back adjustments to income to convert it to operating cash. The authors believe this approach conceals more than it reveals and would prefer it be discarded. Others prefer to place several items in the FASB's format in other classifications. In particular, some prefer to treat interest paid as part of investing activities and dividends received as part of investing activities rather than part of operating activities. The FASB acknowledged that different classifications might be desired, and required that sufficient detail be provided within the statement to permit users to make their own rearrangements.

There is some dispute also about the nature of cash equivalents which should be used. The FASB suggested these be limited to short-term, highly liquid investments with a maturity limit of three months. By contrast, the Accounting Standards Committee of the Canadian Institute of Chartered Accountants defines cash equivalents more broadly as short-term investments less short-term borrowings.[4] The Board acknowledged that any choice was arbitrary, and suggested that whatever definition is used in the statement of cash flows be consistent with that in the balance sheet—and that management disclose the nature of its choice.

Traditionally, noncash transactions, such as the purchase of property financed by a mortgage, have appeared in cash flow and funds flow statements. This treatment is based on the assumption that cash flows in from a mortgage and then out to purchase land. The FASB has suggested that such transactions now be disclosed in a footnote on grounds that doing

EXHIBIT 9-1   Statement of Cash Flows—The Direct Method

COMPANY M
CONSOLIDATED STATEMENT OF CASH FLOWS
FOR THE YEAR ENDED DECEMBER 31, 19X1
Increase (Decrease) in Cash and Cash Equivalents

Cash flows from operating activities:		
Cash received from customers	$13,850	
Cash paid to suppliers and employees	(12,000)	
Dividend received from affiliate	20	
Interest received	55	
Interest paid (net of amount capitalized)	(220)	
Income taxes paid	(325)	
Insurance proceeds received	15	
Cash paid to settle lawsuit for patent infringement	(30)	
Net cash provided by operating activities		$1,365
Cash flows from investing activities:		
Proceeds from sale of facility	600	
Payment received on note for sale of plant	150	
Capital expenditures	(1,000)	
Payment for purchase of Company S, net of cash acquired	(925)	
Net cash used in investing activities		(1,175)
Cash flows from financing activities:		
Net borrowings under line-of-credit agreement	300	
Principal payments under capital lease obligation	(125)	
Proceeds from issuance of long-term debt	400	
Proceeds from issuance of common stock	500	
Dividends paid	(200)	
Net cash provided by financing activities		875
Net increase in cash and cash equivalents		1,065
Cash and cash equivalents at beginning of year		600
Cash and cash equivalents at end of year		$1,665

otherwise is confusing. By contrast, Canadian standards still require their inclusion in the statement itself.[5] The precise positioning of the disclosure is probably moot given the findings of the efficient market theory.

Entity Cash Flow

The bottom line in *SFAS 95* is the change in cash and cash equivalent holdings of the enterprise, otherwise known as the change in *liquidity*. In this case, it is $1,065. Such changes are primarily due to speculative and precautionary motives and may be thought of as investments in the financial security of the firm. Entity cash flow, the number we seek, is cash generated by the enterprise through operations, less the cash earned or invested in the disposal and acquisition of property, less the cash invested in (withdrawn from) the security of the enterprise, that is, the increase (decrease) in liquidity. Using the FASB's illustration in Exhibit 9-1, one has:

$$\text{Net cash provided by operating activities} = \$1,365$$

$$\text{Net cash used in invested activities} = \$1,175$$

$$\text{Net cash used in increasing liquidity} = \$1,065$$

Entity cash flow, defined as operating cash less cash invested less increase in liquidity is, therefore, $(875) = $1,365 − 1,175 − 1,065.

This cash flow is distributed among two groups of users in this particular example. It goes to shareholders and to debtholders. One may write:

$$SHCF_j = \$300 \ (= \$500 - 200)$$

$$LCF_j = \$575 \ (= \$300 - 125 + 400)$$

In other words, the cash generated from operations of $1,365 less the cash spent on investments of $1,175, less the increase in liquidity of $1,065 equals the cash inflow from creditors of $575, plus the cash inflow from shareholders of $300. In short:

$$\$1,365 - 1,175 - 1,065 = (300) + (575)$$

Both sides represent entity cash; the left focuses on the cash generated, the right on the cash distributed.*

As noted above, some cash flow theorists believe that a few of the items in the FASB's formulation of cash flows should be reclassified. In particular, they would treat interest and dividends received from affiliates as part of investments, and interest paid as part of the lender cash flow stream. They, therefore, would revise the numbers in the following manner:

Original	$1,365	− 1,175	− 1,065 =	(300) +	(575)
Dividend received	(20)	20			
Interest received	(55)	55			
Interest paid	220				220
Revised	$1,510	− 1,100	− 1,065 =	(300) +	(355)

---

* Note that the sign on the right is reversed to match the sign on the left.

In words, under this formulation, cash from operations excludes interest paid of $220, interest received of $55, and dividends received of $20. Cash spent on investing activities includes dividends received of $20 and interest received of $55. Net cash flows from investors includes dividends paid by the enterprise to investors; net cash flows from lenders includes interest paid by the enterprise to lenders.

Prediction of Future Cash Flows

One of the difficulties in using historical cash flows as a predictor of future cash distributions is that many cash flows, including dividends, are interdependent. For example, available cash or expected cash receipts may be used for capital expenditures or for the repayment of debt, as well as for the payment of dividends. Therefore, plans and expectations of management as well as other information, such as a statement of the resources and commitments of the firm, should supplement the cash flow information.

Dividends to common stockholders can be looked on as that amount available after the above expected flows are predicted. However, as indicated above, many of these flows are interrelated, and consideration should also be given to the needs of the firm for holding cash or increasing its cash holdings. In addition to the knowledge of past cash flows, the investor should have information regarding the philosophy, or attitudes, of the firm regarding the payment of dividends, and regarding the investment, or reinvestment, of cash available, or obtainable by additional financing.

In making predictions regarding future cash flows from operations, it is important to start with historical information classified according to the behavioral characteristics of the cash flow requirements. For example, ideally the various types of cash flows relating to operations would be classified according to major product groups or product categories, so that predictions could be made regarding future demand for the products and regarding special cost relationships related to specific product groups. Geographic distribution of source and sales of products may also be significant, particularly where foreign countries are involved. Furthermore, ideally, classifications of cash flows would permit a prediction of changes in future cash flows that are related to other known or predictable variables. Much of this detail is not currently available in reported cash flow statements.

Other relationships, though, are easier to detect. For instance, committed cash flows should be classified separately from cash flows that are variably related to the quantity of sales or production. For example, operating cash flows for the last five years, expressed in constant dollars, may give some indication of the rate of growth of end-product markets or the level of operating cash flows that can be expected in the future, in the case of a company whose market share has been changing over time.

One of the most difficult of cash requirements to predict is that needed for capital expenditures. Depreciation, as generally computed for measuring income, is not relevant for this purpose because replacements are not necessarily related to either the cost of the items acquired in the past, or to periodic allocations of this cost. Although capital expenditure patterns in the past may provide some guide to the future, expectations of management regarding its plans and opportunities can greatly assist this prediction. The desirability of disclosing such expectations was underlined by the FASB which wrote:

> Management knows more about the enterprise and its affairs than investors, creditors, or other "outsiders" and can often increase the usefulness of financial information by identifying certain transactions, other events, and circumstances that affect the enterprise and explaining their financial impact. Moreover, financial reporting often provides information that depends on, or is affected by, management's estimates and judgment.[6]

Discussions of such information are now a required feature of the section in the annual report labeled *Management's Discussion and Analysis*.[7]

Future capital expenditure will typically be a function of the age structure of existing assets and the need (if any) to create additional capacity to accommodate the operating cash flows that are expected to grow in the future.

In attempting to predict a sequence of future capital expenditures, a distinction between replacement and growth capital expenditures can be made. *Replacement expenditures* are principally a function of the age structure and expected useful service lives of existing assets, that is, the existing asset stock will cause particular replacement cycles. *Growth expenditures* are a function of anticipated sales volume growth, including that of new or contemplated products, and the degree of utilization of existing capacity. Thus, the greater the amount of idle capacity, the more distant is the need for additional capacity for any given expected rate of sales volume growth.

The use of historical cash flow information to make predictions regarding future dividends is, therefore, a complex process. However, as recent empirical studies have shown, the reliability of making predictions that take cash flow information into account is greater than predictions made from historical income data alone.[8] Because of the increase in predictability, the presentation of historical cash flow information in external financial reports has been mandated.*

---

* The reverse is also true. Conventional net income appears to have information content beyond that contained in cash flows. Releasing both cash and income numbers is, therefore, the most desirable.

CHECKPOINTS

---

1. What classifications does the FASB use in its suggested format for a cash flow statement?
2. Define shareholder cash flows.
3. Define lender cash flows.
4. List three factors that are helpful in predicting investing cash flows.

INCOME MEASUREMENT

Accountants frequently refer to two economic concepts based on real-world observations as logical starting points for a definition of a concept of accounting income. These two economic concepts are the change in well-being and the maximization of profit under specified conditions of market structure, product demand, and input costs. These concepts are implicit in the FASB's assertions that:

> Comprehensive income is the change in equity of a business enterprise during a period . . . .[9]
> The test of success (or failure) of the operations of an enterprise is the extent to which the cash returned exceeds (or is less than) the cash spent (invested) over the long run.[10]

The former is the concept of *capital maintenance*, and the latter is a form of the *profit maximization* concept. Economists have attempted to refine these concepts as saying something about real-world observations, even though they disagree among themselves regarding their significance. However, economists have not been very helpful in solving the measurement problems surrounding these concepts. As a result, accountants have chosen to apply precise rules for income measurement regardless of how close they may come to measuring the economists' concepts. This section explores the various concepts of capital maintenance and the alternative methods that have been suggested for their measurement. Practical and conceptual limitations are also presented. In particular, this section demonstrates how the measurement of income relates to the provision of information regarding cash flows.

Capital versus Income

In the language of the American economist Irving Fisher, *capital* is a *stock* of wealth at an instant of time.[11] *Income* is a *flow* of services through time. *Capital* is the embodiment of future services, and *income* is the enjoyment of these services over a specific period of time. With these definitions, it does not seem possible to confuse the two terms. The one relates to the amount in the reservoir at any one time, and the other refers to the amount flowing out of the reservoir during a period of time.

When these terms are related to a business enterprise, however, they take on slightly different meanings. In the above definition, income is the enjoyment derived from the use of capital; however, a business enterprise does not exist for the purpose of its own enjoyment. Its purpose is to provide a flow of wealth for the benefit of its owners. Whereas capital is still thought of as the *stock* of wealth that can provide future services, income is thought of as the *flow* of wealth or service in excess of that necessary to maintain a constant capital.

These terms are broadened still further in the enterprise concept of income. Now, capital consists of all monies provided by external parties to the enterprise, that is, it includes share capital and debt capital. Income is then the income accruing to all providers of monies to the firm, that is, it includes interest accruing to creditors and earnings accruing to minority shareholders.

Care should be taken here to distinguish the term *comprehensive income* from the term *entity income* as used in this chapter. The former refers to the income accruing to common shareholders only and was introduced by the FASB to cover some items such as prior period adjustments which, although reported as a change in retained earnings, might better be considered as part of income in this period. Comprehensive income is comprehensive only with respect to common shareholders. The term *entity income* refers to the income accruing to the enterprise as a whole. It includes interest income, minority shareholder income, income to preferred shareholders—and comprehensive income to common majority shareholders.

Regardless of the precise definition, the concern throughout is to distinguish income, sometimes referred to as a return *on* capital, from a return *of* capital. The distinction is important for two reasons. First, changes in the capital of the enterprise may affect the amount of future flows to residual equity holders (such as the holders of common stock) and thus the value of their equity at any point in time. Second, changes in enterprise capital may affect the relationships among the various equity holders, including the holders of debt and preferred stock.

Holders of equity are interested not only in how much they can expect to receive from the enterprise during the following period, but also in the net changes in the ability of the enterprise to provide future flows. Investor (and lender) interest is focused not only on the ability of the firm to maintain dividends, but in many cases on its growth potential. The knowledge of these changes is even more important when the ownership rights to these future flows are transferred frequently during the life of the enterprise. During the early period of the railroad industry in the United States, it was not uncommon for promoters to pay huge dividends out of capital during the early life of the firm. Investors, believing this to be the true income of the firm, paid high prices for the stock, only to find later that the ability to pay dividends in the future was being eroded because of these huge early dividends. Equity requires that both buyers and sellers of common stock have adequate information to make expectations regarding the current and future dividends of the firm.

With the separation of ownership and control in most large corporations, accounting also has the responsibility to report on the stewardship of the management group entrusted with the proper use of the invested capital. A proper distinction between income and changes in capital is one of the means of determining the extent to which management has carried out the function of operating the enterprise for the benefit of the owners.

The concept of wealth maintenance is also important to bondholders, preferred stockholders, and the providers of short-term credit. All of these equity holders are interested in the probability of repayment at some future date. The prospect of repayment is greater if the total invested capital of the enterprise is maintained at a constant level or permitted to increase. The prospect of repayment is less if the capital is diminished, either through losses, or by the payment of dividends in excess of earnings. The creditors cannot always be protected against losses, but if they are properly notified, they may be able to protect their position before it is too late. To a certain extent, creditors are protected legally, and often contractually, from the impairment of invested capital by the payment of dividends in excess of earnings.

The various classes of equity holders are also interested in the return on their investment, whether it be contractual (as interest on debt) or dependent on earnings (as dividends on preferred and common stock). Since invested capital reflects, in part, the ability of the firm to continue the payment of a return to equity holders in the future, changes in the amount of invested capital are vital in decisions regarding the future flow of this return to any class of equity holders.

The concepts of capital and income, however, are not clearly formulated. *Capital* can be defined in terms of the current monetary unit or a monetary unit of constant value; in physical terms; in terms of capacity to produce goods and services; or in terms of the future expectations regarding future flows to stockholders. The measurement difficulties in separating capital and income are even greater. These conceptual and measurement difficulties are discussed in the following section.

The Wealth Maintenance Concepts of Income

The Scottish economist Adam Smith was the first to define *income* as that amount that can be consumed without encroaching upon capital. English economist and Nobel prizewinner Sir John Hicks elaborated upon this by saying that income is the amount that a person can consume during a period of time and be as well off at the end of that time as at the beginning.[12] Stated alternatively, income, according to Smith and Hicks, is the surplus after the maintenance of well-offness, but before consumption.

For example, if the net assets of the firm were valued at $80,000 at the end of the period and $76,000 at the beginning, income would be $4,000 in the absence of capital transactions and the payment of dividends. If additional capital stock in the amount of $11,000 had been sold and if dividends in the amount of $8,000 had been paid during the period, the net income would have been $1,000. In other words:

$$\text{Income} = (\$8,000 - \$11,000) + (\$80,000 - \$76,000)$$

Algebraically, where W represents well-offness:

$$INC_j = CF_j + (W_j - W_{j-1}) \tag{9}$$

The nature of income to emerge from this formulation depends on the definition one gives to W_j and how one measures it. A variety of options has been proposed. None has received universal acceptance. This lack of acceptance reflects a lack of agreement as to the precise meaning of the term *well-offness*. A fundamental problem is whether, and to what extent, to include psychic benefits in the definition. One may be wealthy but in poor health; alternatively, one may be "rich" in one's children. Organizations, of course, do not suffer either psychic joys or sorrows. The lack of applicability of psychic benefits to organizations and the difficulty of application to individuals have caused most authors to limit the concept of well-offness to tangible wealth. Several methods of valuing this wealth include:

1. Valuation of the firm by using input values (either historical or current cost) for nonmonetary assets and adding the present cash value of monetary assets and subtracting liabilities.
2. The aggregation of the selling prices of the several assets of the firm less the summation of the liabilities.
3. Capitalization of the expected future net stream of cash or services to be received over the life of the firm.
4. Valuation of the firm on the basis of the current stock market prices applied to the total stock outstanding.

Each of these approaches is discussed in the sections that follow. In this discussion, we assume for argument's sake that the general value of money remains constant over time and that meaningful measurements of wealth can be obtained and expressed in money terms. The measurement of well-offness during periods of price-level changes is discussed in Chapter 12 on inflation.

Individual versus Entity Income. The formulation of income in equation (9) focuses attention on the individual. One can extend it to the enterprise by simply noting that:

NI of majority shareholders
$$= \text{(Dividends} - \text{capital contributions)} + \text{Change in majority shareholder wealth}$$
$$= SHCF_j + \Delta\, MASHW_j \tag{10}$$

NI of minority shareholders
$$= \text{(Dividends} - \text{capital contributions)} + \text{Change in minority shareholder wealth}$$
$$= MICF_j + \Delta\, MISHW_j \tag{11}$$

NI of debt holders or lenders
$$= \text{(Interest} - \text{new borrowings} + \text{repayments)} + \text{Change in debt-holder wealth}$$
$$= LCF_j + \Delta\, LW_j \tag{12}$$

These three income streams combine to form the total income of the enterprise (defined on a before interest, before minority shareholder basis.) In other words, one may write entity income (*ENINC*) as

$$\begin{aligned} ENINC_j = {} & SHCF_j + \Delta\, MASHW_j \\ & + MICF_j + \Delta\, MISHW_j \\ & + LCF_j + \Delta\, LW_j \end{aligned} \tag{13}$$

But the three cash flow terms on the right combine to form entity cash flows so we may rewrite equation (13) as

$$ENINC_j = ENCF_j + \Delta\, [MASHW_j + MISHW_j + LW_j] \tag{14}$$

This can be rewritten as:

$$ENINC_j = ENCF_j + \Delta\, ENW_j \tag{15}$$

where

ENW = wealth of all investors and creditors in the entity.

As already noted, the exact nature of the income term on the left depends on the way in which the entity wealth (*ENW*) is measured on the right. However, entity cash flows (*ENCF*) are completely independent of the way in which wealth is measured and constant across all formulations of income. This universality of entity cash flows across all income formulations underlines once again the importance of the provision of cash flow information to investors and creditors by an enterprise. This is particularly true as the world moves toward an integrated global economy.

Historical Input Prices

An assumed concept of wealth maintenance similar to that accepted in practice is the use of input prices in terms of either historical costs or current costs (less depreciation where necessary). The wealth-maximization formulation of income that is most familiar to readers in this regard involves income to majority shareholders only:

$$NI = \text{Dividends} + \Delta \text{ Retained earnings} \qquad (16)$$

By including capital contributions one can convert this to read

$$NI = (\text{Dividends} - \text{Capital contributions})$$
$$+ \Delta \text{ Net worth} \qquad (17)$$

$$= SHCF_j + \Delta NW_j$$

By adding interest expense, borrowings and lendings, and minority income to both sides, one can further expand this last equation to read

Entity income = Net cash paid to lenders
+ Net cash paid to minority shareholders
+ Net cash paid to majority shareholders
+ Change in book value of holdings of lenders, minority shareholders, and majority shareholders

$$= LCF_j + MICF_j + SHCF_j + \Delta ENNW_j \qquad (18)$$

where

$$ENNW = \text{Entity net worth}$$

$$= \text{Book value of owners' equity plus debt} \qquad (19)$$

But the three cash flow terms on the right combine to form entity cash flows so we may rewrite equation (18) as:

$$\text{Entity income} = ENCF_j + \Delta ENNW_j \qquad (20)$$

It should be emphasized that although this appears to have the same structure as other capital maintenance concepts, it is not subject to real-world interpretation because of its reliance on depreciation allocations and the accounting concept of realization.* In other words, the entity income derived here is simply an expansion of conventional accounting income. It does not include changes in wealth due to fluctuations in value in the marketplace—except to the extent that these are recognized in the writing down of inventory, for instance. The resulting income computa-

---

* See Chapters 11 and 15 for further discussion of the lack of real-world interpretation of these concepts.

tion is based on structural rules rather than reality. It is discussed here because it is frequently described as financial capital maintenance with income representing the difference between beginning and ending valuations.

In the absence of price changes, real invested capital is assumed to be maintained if the assets at the end of the period, expressed in terms of input prices (costs), are equal to the total input prices of the assets at the beginning of the period. Income is reflected in an increase in these values adjusted for capital transactions and dividend payments. This income results from the conversion of input prices into market values by the process of sale and exchange. Cash and receivables are received in exchange for the assets valued at cost. Therefore, some of the asset values at the end of the period as well as some at the beginning (the monetary assets) are expressed in terms of market values (output prices).

Current Input Prices

When the inputs are expressed in terms of current values, the computation of income is the same as with historical costs, but the income resulting includes holding gains and losses arising from price changes—whether or not these holding gains and losses have been realized through sale or exchange.

Algebraically, one has:

$$\text{Entity income (current input basis)} = ENCF_j + \Delta\ ENCV_j \qquad (21)$$

where

ENCV = Entity value in terms of current input prices.

That is, the income will include gains and losses from the holding of assets as well as the normal operating profit.[13] By expressing the asset values at the beginning of the period in terms of end-of-period input costs, some of these gains and losses can be eliminated; but, unless adjustments are made for changes in input values of costs incurred during the period, capital gains and losses will still be included.

Maintenance of Constant Purchasing Power

Economists often contend that income should be measured in real terms, rather than in nominal terms. Algebraically, they suggest:

$$\text{Entity income (constant purchasing power basis)} = ENCF_j + \Delta\ ENCPV_j \qquad (22)$$

where

ENCPV = Entity value in terms of constant purchasing power.

When changes in the general level of prices occur, the measurement of income by comparing capital values at different times in terms of the monetary unit at each time results in measurements that do not represent changes in real capital. Therefore, many suggestions have been made for the adjustment of capital values so that income can be measured in terms of a constant purchasing power or in terms of a constant value of the monetary unit. These suggestions and the problems involved in making adjustments for changes in the purchasing power of money are discussed at greater length in Chapter 12 on inflation.

Current Cash Equivalents

As another alternative to the capitalization of a firm, the firm's capital can be defined as the sum of the money or cash equivalent of all assets less the sum of the money equivalent of the liabilities. In other words:

Entity income (current cash equivalent basis)
$$= ENCF_j + \Delta\ ENMVA_j \tag{23}$$

where

$ENMVA$ = Entity value in terms of market value of individual assets.

The current cash equivalent can be defined as the market selling price or realizable price of the assets held by the firm.[14] This is the price that would be reached in an orderly liquidation. By computing the net assets computed in a similar fashion at the beginning of the period, and adjusting for capital transactions, the income for the period can be determined.[15]

The value of the firm determined by the summation of market prices is assumed to be relatively objective or verifiable, because these prices depend upon the expectations of others outside the firm. Note that these are opportunity cost values. They represent values for which the existing assets could be exchanged in the market. The value of the firm as a whole would normally be greater than the sum of the market prices of the specific assets, because if it were not, the owners of the firm would be better off by selling its assets in the market. This difference is due, in part, to the exclusion of goodwill and other intangibles that do not have market prices separate from tangible asset prices. However, it may also be due to the evaluations of expectations, the selections of discount factors, and the adjustments for risk, as well as costs involved in the sale and transfer of specific assets.

In addition to the verifiability of current cash equivalents, the computation of income by comparing changes in the market prices of assets and liabilities has the advantage of providing a better basis for judging the alternatives open to management. But it provides a limited basis for the prediction of future changes because it does not disclose the nature of the changes arising in prior periods.

A major disadvantage of using market valuations of individual assets is the lack of a ready market for many of the assets owned by a firm. For many items of plant and equipment, the only market prices available would probably represent liquidation or forced-sale values rather than the price that could be obtained in organized markets. As a result, the income would be similar to the income that would be obtained if the firm were liquidated at the end of each period and then started over with the liquidation valuations for the next period. Also, in cases such as the underground pipe lines of chemical companies, an exit value simply does not exist even though the company may have enormous value as a going concern.

Capitalization

The most frequently suggested measure of net assets from a theoretical perspective is to capitalize the value of the expected cash distributions to stockholders by the firm during the remaining life of the enterprise, including the final amount expected to be paid at liquidation. This was the measure used at the start of this chapter to motivate the FASB's insistence that the prediction of future cash flows is the primary objective of accounting and was captured in equation (2). If the investment is being made for a finite number of years, in the expectation not only of a return over these years, but also repayment of capital at the end, then equation (2) can be rewritten as:

$$V_0 = \sum_{j=1}^{n} \frac{CF_j}{(1 + r)^j} + \frac{V_n}{(1 + r)^n} \tag{24}$$

For a single period, this can be rewritten as

$$V_0 = \frac{CF_1}{(1 + r)} + \frac{V_1}{(1 + r)} \tag{25}$$

Reordering equation (25) yields

$$V_1 = (1 + r)V_0 - CF_1 \tag{26}$$

In words, the value of one's investment can be expected to grow with the rate of interest, but decrease with the amount of cash that is consumed. Reordering this in accordance with our general definition of income, one finds that

$$\text{Income} = CF_1 + (V_1 - V_0) = rV_0 \tag{27}$$

In other words, the ex ante income of an individual can be computed by combining the cash flow that the individual expects to receive from the company with the expected change in the value of that individual's holdings, where the values are established by discounting future expected cash flows. At the enterprise level we have:

$$\text{Entity income} = ENCF_1 + (TV_1 - TV_0) = rTV_0 \qquad (28)$$

In other words, the ex ante income of the enterprise can be computed by combining the enterprise's expected cash flow with the expected change in its total value. Both the individual and the enterprise formulations can be converted from ex ante to ex post by focusing on realized cash flows.

The income computed by this method is seldom the same as accounting net income. As computed here, income is the excess after market value has been maintained. Accounting net income is the excess after net book values are maintained. The former is sometimes termed *economic income*. Accounting net income is at best an approximation of economic income.

A Numerical Example.   As an example, let us assume certainty and the following cash distributions during a life of five years for a firm:

Year	Cash Flow (net)
1	$100
2	300
3	200
4	400
5	500

In the case of certainty, the appropriate discount rate would be the risk-free interest rate (assumed to be 5 percent in this case) and the present value of the firm at the start would be $1,261. Present values are computed as follows:

Beginning of First Year	End of First Year
$\$100 \times 0.9524 \left[\left(\frac{1}{1.05}\right)\right] = \$\ \ 95$	$\$300 \times 0.9524 \left[\left(\frac{1}{1.05}\right)\right] = \$\ \ 286$
$300 \times 0.9070 \left[\left(\frac{1}{1.05}\right)^2\right] = \ \ \ 272$	$200 \times 0.9070 \left[\left(\frac{1}{1.05}\right)^2\right] = \ \ \ 181$
$200 \times 0.8638 \left[\left(\frac{1}{1.05}\right)^3\right] = \ \ \ 173$	$400 \times 0.8638 \left[\left(\frac{1}{1.05}\right)^3\right] = \ \ \ 346$
$400 \times 0.8227 \left[\left(\frac{1}{1.05}\right)^4\right] = \ \ \ 329$	$500 \times 0.8227 \left[\left(\frac{1}{1.05}\right)^4\right] = \ \ \ \underline{411}$
$500 \times 0.7835 \left[\left(\frac{1}{1.05}\right)^5\right] = \ \ \underline{392}$	$\$1,224$
$\$1,261$	

At the end of the first year the capitalized value of the remaining cash distributions would be $1,224 and the net income for the first year would be computed as follows:

Cash distributed at the end of the first year	$ 100
Capitalized value at the end of the first year of the cash flows for the remaining years	1,224
Total value of the firm at the end of the first year assuming no distributions to stockholders	1,324
Less: Capitalized value at the beginning of the year	1,261
Income for year	$ 63

This income of $63 represents the increase in the total value of the firm during the year. It equals 5 percent of the initial capitalized value of $1,261. It represents, in effect, interest on the capital invested. If the cash distribution each year is greater than the income (interest), the income would decline each year. In the case cited, the incomes for each of the five years would be $63, $61, $42, and $24. If the cash distributed to stockholders each year is equal to the income and the remaining available cash reinvested by the firm in projects that will yield 5 percent, then both the income and the capitalized value of the firm will remain constant into the future. Finally, note that periodic income is not directly proportional to the cash distributions in each year. One must include the change in value to convert from income to cash and vice versa.

Capitalization under Uncertainty.   Two cases present themselves here. In the first, markets are said to be *complete*. Formally, this means that trades can be made in all commodities and in all states of the world. In the second, markets are said to be *incomplete*. In other words, trades cannot be made for certain goods or in certain states of the world. When the latter case occurs, and some feel this is the normal case, it becomes technically infeasible to define an ex ante enterprise income number on a capitalized value basis. The essence of the problem is that in the absence of a market there can be no agreement on the value of future benefit streams of assets.

It remains possible for each individual to make a personal estimate of income. In the absence of certainty, the future cash payments represent expected values of probability distributions. For example, if the subjective estimates of the cash dividend for the first year are either $120 with a probability of 0.6 or $70 with a probability of 0.4, the expected value would be $100.* The number of probable values could be few or many, including all possible values of the monetary unit. Each value would be assigned a probability value such that the sum of all probabilities is one. Note that the expected value is subjective because of the necessity of estimating the possible values and because of the assignment of subjective probability values to these.

In the case of uncertainty, most authors define the appropriate rate as the subjective required rate for investments of equal risk or the target rate of return, also known as the opportunity cost. In what follows, a subjective rate is simply assumed in order to focus on the income concepts. Therefore, in the absence of changes in expectations, and if the actual cash distribution in the first year is equal to the expected cash payment, income as computed in the above example is equal to the subjective rate of return multiplied by the beginning (or average) capitalized value. Edwards and Bell call this *subjective profit*, because it is defined as the interest at the target rate on the subjective value of the firm's assets at the beginning of the period.[16]

But if the anticipations at the end of the period have changed since the beginning of the period, the ex post subjective profit for this period will differ from the anticipated or ex ante subjective profit. While the anticipated subjective profit is based on the subjective value of the firm's assets at the beginning of the period, the actual or ex post subjective profit includes changes in the subjective value of the assets at the end of the period.[17]

A Numerical Example.   For example, if the cash flow during the first period is $100 as anticipated, but at the end of the period, and cash flows for the following four periods are now expected to be $400 a year instead of $300, $200, $400, and $500, the income for the first year would be computed as follows:

Cash distributed at the end of the first year	$ 100
Capitalized value at the end of the year of remaining expected cash flows of $400 a year for four years	1,418
Total value of the firm at the end of the year	1,518
Less: Capitalized value at the beginning of the year	1,261
Income for year	$ 257

----

* The expected value of the cash flow would be computed as follows:

$$\$120 \times 0.6 = \$72$$
$$70 \times 0.4 = \underline{\quad 28}$$
$$\$100$$

This income of $257 is made up of the following:

Anticipated subjective profit	$ 63
Increase in subjective value of the firm	194
Total income	$ 257

There is some question as to whether the increase in subjective value of the firm of $194 is really income. One contention is that this change in expectations is really an adjustment of the original value of the firm, which was in error at the beginning of the year. In fact, one argument is that with the current expectations at the end of the year, the value at the beginning of the year should have been $1,446 instead of $1,261. Therefore, the net change in capitalized value can be analyzed as follows:

Subjective profit or interest (5% × $1,446)	$ 72
Adjustment of original subjective value ($1,446 less $1,261)	185
Total increase in capitalized value	$257

If, on the other hand, the expectations regarding future cash flows do not change, but the cash receipt for the first year is $130 instead of $100 as anticipated, the income for the period would be as follows:

Cash distributed at the end of the first year	$ 130
Capitalized value at the end of the year of remaining expected cash flows (unchanged)	1,224
Total value of the firm at the end of the year (before dividend payment)	1,354
Less: Capitalized value at the beginning of the year	1,261
Income for year	$ 93

This income of $93 is made up of the following:

Anticipated subjective profit (interest)	$ 63
Increase in the cash distributed over that expected	30
Total income	$ 93

Conclusion. The capitalization of future cash flows approach to defining income yields a number of very useful concepts. For instance, it demonstrates that:

1. The main part of income is subjective interest on the capitalized value of the firm. This is a function of time, the expected interest rate, and the expected cash flows in the future. The expected cash flows are due to either current or future production and sales efforts.
2. The changes in expectations regarding future cash flows arise because of changes either in the appraisal of management's efficiencies or deficiencies, or in expectations regarding economic conditions (such as changes in tastes). They may also be due to general optimism or pessimism.
3. The difference between the actual cash available for distribution and that expected may be due to windfall gains and losses from external causes or miscalculations in original expectations.

Conventional accounting practice recognizes some of these concepts, but generally rejects most of them. In a few cases, such as the recognition of interest on investments, the accrual concept requires the reporting of income on the basis of time alone. Actual cash receipts in excess of the expected amount are traditionally included in ordinary income or classified as extraordinary losses. However, accounting practice does not require the actual receipt of the cash for this recognition; changes in anticipated cash flows may be recorded when they become fairly certain and the amount is verifiable, such as when an asset is sold under a contract requiring payment at a later date. Other changes in expectations, however, are generally denied recognition.

While the capitalization concept has merit as an economic concept of income, it has some specific conceptual and practical disadvantages for accounting purposes. The practical disadvantages arise primarily from the subjective nature of the expectations. Even an accountant, independent in judgment, is likely to be overly optimistic—or overly pessimistic—in the eyes of management, stockholders, or other users of the financial reports. A better approach is to provide adequate information to permit each user of accounting statements to apply his or her own judgment regarding expectations of future cash flows and the selection of an appropriate discount factor to arrive at his or her own subjective estimate of profit.

Many argue that the capitalization concept is also deficient on the following grounds:

1. Expectations regarding future cash flows cannot be converted into single values or certainty equivalents without knowing the risk preferences of the users of the information. Furthermore, it is said, the adjustment for risk, by including it in the subjective discount rate, is conceptually inappropriate.

2. Emphasis is placed upon the time factor and expected cash flows; all other economic events and activities are ignored.

3. The income measurement does not disclose whether it is due to commendable actions of management or only to fortuitous circumstances;

that is, it does not provide information useful for measuring management efficiency.

4. The value of the firm is determined by discounting all expected cash flows indefinitely into the future, many of which have no relationship to current or past activity.

5. It places the cart before the horse. Net cash flows of future periods must be predicted accurately in order to compute current income. In a world of certainty, there would be no reason to compute periodic income, as this would be known in advance; and under conditions of uncertainty, expected cash flows are used to determine current income. However, one of the objectives of measuring current income is thought to be to permit the users of financial reports to make reliable predictions of future cash flows. Since predictions must be based at least in part on current and past economic activity, the users of financial data should be given some measurements of past activity in order to make their own predictions or evaluate the predictions of others.

6. Finally, in a world of uncertainty, expectations are dependent at least in part on the state of optimism or pessimism existing at the time. A consistent treatment of uncertainty from one period to another would be difficult to accomplish.*

Market Valuation of the Firm

It was noted in the section on values and prices that, in efficient markets, the price of the shares of an enterprise (and likewise the price of its debt) equals the present value of the expected cash flows. In other words, the market may be used as a substitute for capitalizing future cash flows. Note that the market value being used here is that for the entire firm, not just for its individual assets, as was the case when basing wealth on current cash equivalents. In addition, the market value addressed here is the value in use, not the value in exchange. Stated otherwise, the value of the entire enterprise derived by using market prices is in general the value of the enterprise as a going concern. Where it is not, the enterprise should be in the process of liquidating its individual assets.

The market value of the enterprise that is of interest is the total market value. Stated otherwise, it is the market value of all the liability and owners' equity items on a statement of financial position. In other words:

$$TMV_j = MV_j \text{ (debt)} + MV_j \text{ (owners' equity)}$$
$$+ MV_j \text{ (minority interests)} \quad (30)$$

---

* For a further discussion of valuation on the basis of discounted expected cash flows, see Chapter 14.

For publicly listed companies these values are freely available in publications such as *The Wall Street Journal* and from sources such as *Moody's*. The entity income number which results is an ex post formulation and may be written as:

$$ENINC_j = ENCF_j + \Delta TMV_j \qquad (31)$$

The advantages of using market values are several. First, the expectations of the market are substituted for the expectations of individuals. A verifiable valuation is obtained, therefore, that is based on the market's evaluation of future cash flows to stockholders. This is different from the capitalization method because the opportunity rate of return and the adjustment for risk in the market may be different from the accountant's subjective discount rate.

Second, it is the only measure of capital that is semantically interpretable, that is, one can point to an actual market price as the source of this measure. The use of market values in computing income is also representationally faithful in the sense that it represents the essence of the relationship between the suppliers of capital and the corporation: The suppliers provide the corporation with capital; it distributes cash to them in the form of dividends, interest, and repayment of loans; and, in addition, the market causes fluctuations in the value of the suppliers' holdings. Finally, the use of market values provides an explicit, broadly defined model of the financial relationship between a company and its investors. The entity cash flow can be attributed to the efforts of the enterprise; the change in value is attributable to the market. The two together form income to the investor. Conceptually, this is the most meaningful way to define income.

Some have argued that the quoted market price represents the price of only a few shares and that, therefore, it does not imply that all shares could be purchased at that price. However, it is standard practice to equate the marginal price with the total price in such situations. Others have argued that stock prices are affected by external and capricious factors. They conclude that verifiability may be offset by a lack of freedom from bias. However, the results of the efficient market theory contradict this conclusion because they indicate that market prices are set swiftly and without bias.

Of course, this method of estimating income works only when a market value is available. In other words, it works best with publicly traded companies. For private companies, a separate estimate of market value is necessary to make the computation of income possible. In fact, accountants in Europe spend a great deal of their time valuing companies as going concerns. The European Economic Community has actually produced an accounting standard on going concern valuations.

A Numerical Example.   An estimate of the total market value of E-Systems is shown in Exhibit 9-2 for 1987 through 1989. The cash flows to shareholders and equity holders were drawn from their reported cash flow

EXHIBIT 9-2　E-Systems, Inc. and Subsidiaries 1988–89

	1988	1989
Cash flows: Year to March 31		
Lender cash flow	2,214	43,485
Shareholder cash flow	13,133	11,739
Entity cash flow	15,347	55,224

	1987	1988	1989
Market values as at December 31			
Interest-bearing debt	130,977	157,832	171,263
Owners' equity	816,805	903,763	958,452
Total entity market value	947,782	1,061,595	1,129,715

Lender income 1988 = 2,214 + (157,832 − 130,977) = 29,069
Lender income 1989 = 43,485 + (171,263 − 157,832) = 56,916

Shareholder income 1988 = 13,133 + (903,763 − 816,805) = 100,091
Shareholder income 1989 = 11,739 + (958,452 − 903,763) = 66,428

Entity income 1988 = 15,347 + (1,061,595 − 947,782) = 129,160
Entity income 1989 = 55,224 + (1,129,715 − 1,061,595) = 123,344

Lender return 1988/87 = 29,069/130,977 = 22.19%
Lender return 1989/88 = 56,916/157,832 = 36.06%

Shareholder return 1988/87 = 100,091/816,805 = 12.25%
Shareholder return 1989/88 = 66,428/947,782 = 7.01%

Entity return 1988/87 = 126,160/ 947,782 = 13.31%
Entity return 1989/88 = 123,344/1,061,595 = 11.62%

	1988	1989
Reported net income	74,570	82,984
Interest expense	9,058	10,226
Entity income (conventional)	83,628	93,210

statements and the notes to those statements. The shareholder cash flows were computed as follows:

	1988	1989
Common stock dividends	15,431	15,483
Less: Proceeds from exercise of stock options	2,298	3,744
Net: Shareholder cash flow:	13,133	11,739

The entity cash flows, as noted earlier, are essentially derived by combining the reported cash flow from operations with the cash spent on equipment and the change in liquidity. An additional refinement shown here is to transfer all interest expense, including that on leases, to the debt-holder section. The result is as follows:

	1988	1989
Cash flow from operations as reported	$58,624	$76,626
Less: Net cash used by investing activities	50,716	62,040
Add back: Interest payments	7,350	9,505
Add back: Lease expense	17,463	20,451
Less: Capital portion	995	3,556
Less: Increase in liquidity	16,379	(14,238)
Entity cash flow	$15,347	$55,224

In the absence of minority shareholders, subtracting the shareholder cash flow from the entity cash flow leaves the cash flow to debt holders of $2,214 and $43,485, respectively.

The market value of equity was computed by multiplying the number of shares outstanding by their year-end stock price. The market value of most of the debt was assumed to be approximately equal to its face value. The market value of the lease obligations was computed by discounting the reported future lease payments at the AAA bond rating. The combination of these numbers forms the value of debt appearing in Exhibit 9-2. A sensitivity analysis was performed on these computations and showed the results to be reasonably insensitive within the range of possible assumptions.

Combining the cash flows and the market values enables one to determine the ex post economic income for the two years. Note that these numbers give a slightly different picture of the company from the conventional net income numbers provided for the same period. For instance, conventional income shows an increase; value-based income shows a decrease. Also, by comparing the incomes with the value of the holdings generating those incomes, one can see that the return to debt holders greatly exceeds that to shareholders. Why this should be so bears further analysis—analysis which is beyond the scope of this text.

The point, here, is simply to note that the presentation of cash flow statements enables users not only to see what past cash flows were, but also to estimate what past incomes were, using value-based, capital-maintenance driven concepts.

CHECKPOINTS:

---

1. Explain the wealth-maintenance concept of income in your own words.
2. How does entity income differ from conventional net income.
3. List one advantage and one disadvantage of using market prices for individual assets and liabilities in measuring income.
4. How will the use of market prices for individual assets and liabilities differ from the use of the market price of the total enterprise?
5. Explain how income might be computed in the context of capitalized values.

CONCLUSION

Although in the long run the income statement and cash flow statement are related to the same information, in the short run they represent different information and different concepts. This much is clear from empirical results which show that cash and income both have incremental information content over one another. This suggests at least two things.

First, cash flows should be disclosed. Second, the presentation of historical cash flows should not be considered a part of the presentation or computation of net income. That is, revenues and expenses should not be computed according to specific procedures on the grounds that these procedures result in amounts that are more closely related to the actual cash flows. For example, the flow-through method of presenting interperiod tax differences and the direct costing of manufactured goods are occasionally proposed as valid because they reflect more closely the actual cash flows. These methods may be relevant for other reasons, as discussed elsewhere in this book, but they should not be included in the income statement merely because they reflect cash flows. This simply duplicates information already disclosed in the cash flow statement.

Individual historical cash flow statements, like individual income statements, should be analyzed with care. Because of the leads and lags between cash receipts and disbursements on the one hand and the operational activities giving rise to these cash flows on the other, a cash flow statement for a single period may have little significance in predicting future cash flows. A comparison of cash flows over several periods is necessary to begin to observe the behavior of recurring flows and to predict the likelihood and frequency of nonrecurring flows.

In this regard, proper classification of cash flows could assist readers of financial statements. Receipts and disbursements relating to the recurring activities of the enterprise could be classified by product groups and according to whether they are committed or discretionary. Capital expenditures could be classified in such a way that the effect on future cash flows could be predicted. That is, major expenditures that are nonrecurring or discretionary could be classified in such a way that the reader could predict whether the effect will be a replacement or continuation of existing operations, an improvement in efficiency that will reduce future annual expenditures, or an addition to capacity that will permit an expansion of future receipts.

Finally, users of cash flows should be aware that, occasionally, significant transactions are carried out without a transfer of cash. For example, common or preferred stock may be exchanged for additional capacity or for new businesses, as in the acquisition of an operating firm to continue as a subsidiary. In these cases, supplementary information should be provided to indicate the extent to which the cash flows in the future are likely to be different from the cash flows in the past. Furthermore, supplementary information should be presented whenever new contracts or changes in contracts, such as pension commitments or long-term leases, will affect future cash flows.

SUMMARY

The primary objective of accounting, according to the FASB, is to provide investors and others with information useful for assessing the amount, timing, and uncertainty of prospective cash flows. The assumption is that these cash flows are being used to estimate the market value of debt, equity, and other financial instruments issued by the firm. Information about liquidity and solvency is also important in this regard because it provides evidence as to the uncertainty of the prospective cash flows.

SFAS 95 mandates the presentation of a cash flow statement in annual reports. The statement falls into three sections: operations, investments, and financing. The last of these corresponds broadly to what this chapter defines as *entity cash flow*, that is, the net cash transferred between the enterprise and its financiers. This might also be termed its net external financing.

Income is defined as the surplus after the maintenance of well-being. In the case of an enterprise, well-being is operationalized as the value of the enterprise. In other words, income to shareholders may be defined as the net cash flow, that is, dividends less new capital plus the change in value of the shares of the enterprise. By varying the definition of value, a variety of different definitions of income may be derived. Each of these is related to the concept of *capital* or *wealth maintenance*. In the next chapter, income is discussed more from the viewpoint of matching.

The wealth-maintenance concept of capital requires an evaluation of total or specific assets and liabilities at the beginning and end of each period. The change in the assets and liabilities over the period are combined with the cash generated by the enterprise to yield the income of the entity for the period. The precise measure of income achieved by this approach depends on the manner in which assets and liabilities are evaluated. Conventional income relies on historical cost measures of assets and liabilities. Economic income relies on the total market value of the entity. Other alternatives include measurements based on expectations regarding future cash flows, or on market prices of assets.

The capital-maintenance approach to income measurement has many strengths, but a practical disadvantage is that the most relevant of the measures of capital, the total market value of the entity, is available only for public companies. Another limitation is that the method provides no income information on specific operational activities of the firm. Nevertheless, where market values are available, or where they can be adequately simulated, the approach is an extremely powerful adjunct to conventional income numbers and a useful consequence of providing cash flow numbers.

QUESTIONS

Multiple Choice

1. [M89#26] In a statement of cash flows, receipts from sales of property, plant, and equipment and other productive assets should generally be classified as cash inflows from

a. Operating activities.
b. Financing activities.
c. Investing activities.
d. Selling activities.

2. [M89#27] In a statement of cash flows, interest payments to lenders and other creditors should be classified as cash outflows for

a. Operating activities.
b. Borrowing activities.
c. Lending activities.
d. Financing activities.

Discussion

3. [November 1977] What effect, if any, would each of the following seven items have upon the preparation of a statement of cash flows prepared in accordance with generally accepted accounting principles?

1. Accounts receivable—trade.
2. Inventory.
3. Depreciation.
4. Deferred income tax credit from interperiod allocation.
5. Issuance of long-term debt in payment for a building.
6. Payoff of a current portion of debt.
7. Sale of a fixed asset resulting in a loss.

4. Erik's Retail Hardware (November 1972)

Mr. Erik, owner of Erik's Retail Hardware, states that he computes income on a cash basis. At the end of each year he takes a physical inventory and computes the cost of all merchandise on hand. To this he adds the ending balance of accounts receivable because he considers this to be a part of inventory on the cash basis. Using this logic he deducts from this total the ending balance of accounts payable for merchandise to arrive at what he calls inventory (net).

The following information has been taken from his cash basis income statements for the years indicated:

	1981	1980	1979
Cash received	$173,000	$164,000	$150,000
Cost of goods sold: Inventory (net),			
January 1	$ 8,000	11,000	3,000
Total purchases.	109,000	102,000	95,000
Goods available for sale	117,000	113,000	98,000
Inventory (net), December 31	1,000	8,000	11,000
Cost of goods sold	116,000	105,000	87,000
Gross margin.	$ 57,000	$ 59,000	$ 63,000

Additional information is as follows for the years indicated:

	1981	1980	1979
Cash sales	$151,000	$147,000	$141,000
Credit sales	24,000	18,000	14,000
Accounts receivable, December 31 . . .	8,000	6,000	5,000
Accounts payable for merchandise,			
December 31	33,000	20,000	13,000

Required:

    a. Without reference to the specific situation described on preceding page, discuss the various cash basis concepts of revenue and income and indicate the conceptual merits of each.

    b. 1. Is the gross margin for Erik's Retail Hardware being computed on a cash basis? Evaluate and explain the approach used with illustrative computations of the cash-basis gross margin for 1980.

        2. Explain why the gross margin for Erik's Retail Hardware shows a decrease while sales and cash receipts are increasing.

    5. In each of the situations outlined below, determine the accounting and the economic income. Evaluate each on grounds of relevance, reliability, and so forth.[18]

a. Two investors each have $1,000 to invest. One buys $1,000 worth of stock A; the other buys $1,000 worth of stock B. By the end of the year both stocks have doubled in price. The first investor sells out just before December 31 and reinvests the $2,000 he gets from the sale in stock B. The second investor continues to hold his block of stock, which is also worth $2,000 at the start of the year. Thus, both start equal, with $1,000 each in cash; they also finish equal, both holding equal quantities of stock B worth $2,000.

b. A manager of a large corporation is considering a deal which will bring in $1 million in cash. It is conservatively estimated that the firm has built up $10 million of goodwill over the years. The deal is contingent on the firm leaving the market in which it has established its goodwill.

c. An investor holds a perpetual bond which pays $10 if, on the toss of a coin, it comes down heads, and nothing if it comes down tails. The market rate of interest is 5 percent.

d. An investor holds a 20-year bond which pays $10 if, on the toss of a coin, it comes down heads, and nothing if it comes down tails. The market rate of interest is 5 percent.

e. Suppose that, at the end of five years, the perpetual bond begins to pay $12 on heads but continues to pay nothing on tails. The market rate remains at 5 percent.

BABCOCK COLLEGE*

The trustees of Babcock College met to study the latest financial figures of the university. To their dismay they discovered there had been a net shortfall in cash of $280,000 despite increased borrowings from the bank

---

* This case was prepared by Michael F. van Breda. Copyright © Michael F. van Breda, 1986.

EXHIBIT 9-3   Babcock College

Cash Flow Statement for Year
Ended December 31, 1986

Receipts

Tuition	$3,520
Government Grants	1,500
Endowment Receipts	650
Donations Received	350
Notes Payable	400
Total	$6,420

Expenditures

Operations	$4,350
Plant Restoration	1,250
Financial Aid	1,100
Total	$6,700
Change in Cash	$(280)

totalling $400,000. A detailed cash flow may be found in Exhibit 9-3. After much discussion, it was decided by a narrow vote that it would be necessary to raise fees by 10 percent if no further information came to light.

James Brown, Jr., one of the dissident trustees, was not happy with the financial data presented to the meeting. He felt that although cash flow was clearly critical, it was not enough to simply look at a cash flow statement. As president of Brown Engineering, he was used to seeing balance sheets and income statements as well as cash flow statements. The following day he called David Church, vice-president of administration at Babcock, and asked him to supply one of Brown's young associates, Jack Cooper by name, with sufficient data to prepare such statements.

Jack Cooper returned from his visit to Church's office with the balance sheet for December 31, 1985, shown in Exhibit 9-4. He also came away with the following information pertinent for December 31, 1986:

Tuition Receivables had risen by $80,000. A large donation of $1 million had been pledged but had not yet been received; Church expected the check to be deposited sometime in early January. As part of a cost-cutting measure, inventories had been cut $110,000. A further $300,000 of securities had been acquired as part of the college's endowment. Accounts Payable had risen to $575,000. It also appeared that the value of the Endowment Securities portfolio had risen $1 million since the start of the year.

EXHIBIT 9-4   Babcock College

Statement of Financial Position as
of December 31, 1985

Cash	$ 1,610
Tuition Receivable	60
Donations Receivable	400
Inventories	280
Endowment Securities	8,000
Buildings and equipment	15,500
Total Assets	$25,850
Accounts Payable	$ 375
Notes Payable	2,790
Fund Balances	22,685
Total Liabilities	$25,850

Required:

Based on the information that Jack Cooper has been able to glean, should the trustees increase tuition? Your answer should include the development of balance sheets and income statements.

EDWARD CHABLIS*

Edward Chablis has just finished planting a new vineyard on 100 acres of land which he leases for $15,000 a year. He has asked you to assist him in determining the value of his vineyard operation.

The vineyard will bear no grapes for the first five years (1–5). In the next five years (6–10) Edward estimates that the vines will bear grapes that can be sold for $40,000 each year. For the next 20 years (11–30) he expects the harvest will provide annual revenues of $60,000. But during the last 10 years (31–40) of the vineyard's life he estimates that revenues will decline to $50,000 per year.

During the first five years the annual cost of pruning, fertilizing, and caring for the vineyard is estimated at $4,000; during the years of production, 6–40, these costs will rise to $6,000 per year. The relevant market

---

* This case was written by Professor Marvin L. Carlson. It is based in part on a case which has appeared in a number of sources over the years. It was designed to be used as the basis for class discussion rather than to illustrate either effective or ineffective handling of an administrative situation.

rate of interest for the entire period is 8 percent. Assume that all receipts and payments are made at the end of each year.

Objectives:

1. Sue Bonfield has offered to buy Edward's vineyard business at the beginning of year 1 by assuming the 40-year lease. On the basis of the current value of the business, what is the minimum price Edward should accept?

2. Assuming that the cash flows for year 1 took place as estimated and that there was no change in expectations for the future,

a. What was the economic income for year 1?
b. What was the accounting income for year 1?
c. How do you explain the difference between economic and accounting income in year 1?

3. (Ignore the information in Part 2. Return to the facts of the original case.) As it turned out, cash outflows for year 1 were actually $6,000 due to an unexpected attorney's fee of $2,000, paid on December 31, 19X1. The attorney was engaged to clear up an ambiguity in the lease which Chablis holds. The basic terms of the lease were unaffected. The attorney employed was the attorney who drafted the original lease for Chablis.

a. What was the ex post economic income for the first year of operations?
b. Analyze the ex post economic income determined above into its expected income and unexpected gain (loss) components.

PRIMARY SOURCES

Those interested in pursuing the topics raised in this chapter might begin by consulting the following sources.

Financial Accounting Standards Board. *FASB Discussion Memorandum: An Analysis of Issues Related to Reporting Funds Flows, Liquidity, and Flexibility* (Stamford, Conn.: FASB, 1980).

Heath, Loyd C. *Accounting Research Monograph No. 3.* "*Financial Reporting and the Evaluation of Solvency* (AICPA, 1978).

Jaedicke, Robert K., and Robert T. Sprouse. *Accounting Flows: Income, Funds, and Cash* (Englewood Cliffs, N.J.: Prentice Hall, 1965).

Sorter, George, et al. "Earning Power and Cash Generating Ability." *Accounting Objectives Study Group, Objectives of Financial Statements, Vol. 2 Selected Papers* (1974), pp. 110–16.

SELECTED ADDITIONAL READINGS

Cash Flow Concepts and Reporting

Brennan, M. J. "Approach to the Valuation of Uncertain Income Streams." *Journal of Finance,* June 1973, pp. 661–74.

Drtina, Ralph E., and James A. Largay III. "Pitfalls in Calculating Cash Flow from Operations." *The Accounting Review*, April 1985, pp. 314–26.

Ijiri, Yuji. "Cash-Flow Accounting and Its Structure." *Journal of Accounting, Auditing and Finance,* Summer 1978, pp. 331–48.

Jones, Colin J. "Accounting Standards—A Blind Alley?" *Accounting and Business Research,* Autumn 1975, pp. 273–79.

Lawson, G. H. "Cash-Flow Accounting." *Accountant,* October 1971; November 1971, pp. 536–89; 620–22.

Lawson, G. H. "The Measurement of Corporate Performance on a Cash Flow Basis: A Reply to Mr. Egginton." *Accounting and Business Research,* Spring 1985, pp. 99–112.

Lee, T. A. "A Case for Cash Flow Reporting." *Journal of Business Finance,* Summer 1972, pp. 27–36.

Lee, T. A. "A Note on Users and Uses of Cash Flow Information." *Accounting and Business Research,* Spring 1983, pp. 103–6.

Lee, T. A. "Cash Flow Accounting, Profit and Performance Measurement: A Response to a Challenge." *Accounting and Business Research,* Spring 1985, pp. 93–97.

Lee, T. A., and A. W. Stark. "Ijiri's Cash Flow Accounting and Capital Budgeting." *Accounting and Business Research*, June 1987, pp. 125–31.

Salamon, Gerald L. "Cash Recovery Rates and Measures of Firm Profitability." *The Accounting Review*, April 1982, pp. 292–302.

Funds Concepts

Anton, Hector R. *Accounting for the Flow of Funds* (Boston, Mass.: Houghton Mifflin, 1968).

Buzby, Stephen L., and Haim Falk. "A New Approach to the Funds Statement." *Journal of Accountancy*, January 1974, pp. 55–61.

Giese, J. W., and T. P. Klammer. "Achieving the Objectives of APB Opinion No. 19." *Journal of Accountancy,* March 1974, pp. 54–61.

Grinnell, D. Jacque, and Corine T. Norgaard. "Reporting Changes in Financial Position." *Management Accountant*, September 1972, pp. 15–22.

Heath, Loyd C. "Let's Scrap the 'Funds' Statement." *Journal of Accountancy*, October 1978, pp. 94–103. See also James A. Largay III, Edward P. Swanson, and Max Block, "The 'Funds' Statement: Should It Be Scrapped, Retained, or Revitalized?" Replies by Loyd C. Heath, *Journal of Accountancy,* December 1979, pp. 88–97.

Ketz, J. Edward, and James A. Largay III. "Reporting Income and Cash Flows from Operations." *Accounting Horizons*, June 1987, pp. 9–17.

Mason, Perry. "Cash Flow Analysis and the Funds Statement." *Accounting Research Study No. 2,* 1961.

Nurnberg, Hugo. "APB Opinion No. 19, Pro and Con." *Financial Executive*, December 1972, pp. 58–71.

Rosen, L. S., and Don T. DeCoster. " 'Funds' Statements: A Historical Perspective." *The Accounting Review*, April 1982, pp. 124–36.

Sorter, George H. "The Emphasis on Cash and Its Impact on the Funds Statement—Sense and Nonsense." *Journal of Accounting, Auditing and Finance*, Spring 1982, pp. 188–94.

Thomas, Barbara S. "Deregulation and Cash Flow Reporting: One Viewpoint." *Financial Executive*, January 1983, pp. 20–24.

Yu, S. C. "A Flow of Resources Statement for Business Enterprises." *The Accounting Review*, July 1969, pp. 571–82.

Liquidity, Solvency, and Financial Flexibility

Backer, M., and M. L. Gosman. *Financial Reporting and Business Liquidity* (New York: National Association of Accountants, 1978).

Fadel, Hisham, and John M. Parkinson. "Liquidity Evaluation by Means of Ratio Analysis." *Accounting and Business Research,* Spring 1978, pp. 101–7.

Heath, Loyd C., and Paul Rosenfield. "Solvency: the Forgotten Half of Financial Reporting." *Journal of Accountancy*, January 1979, pp. 48–54.

Empirical Research

Beams, Floyd A., and Robert H. Strawser. "Preferences for Alternative Presentations of the Statement of Changes in Financial Position." *Massachusetts CPA Review*, November–December 1973, pp. 14–18.

Gombola, Michael J., and J. Edward Ketz. "A Note on Cash Flow and Classification of Patterns of Financial Ratios." *The Accounting Review*, January 1983, pp. 105–14.

Gonedes, Nicholas J. "The Significance of Selected Accounting Procedures: A Statistical Test." *Empirical Research in Accounting: Selected Studies* (supplement to Journal of Accounting Research, 1969), pp. 90–123.

Largay, James A., III, and Clyde P. Stickney. "Cash Flows, Ratio Analysis and W. T. Grant Company Bankruptcy." *Financial Analysis Journal*, July–August 1980, pp. 51–54.

Louis Harris and Associates Inc. *A Study of the Attitudes toward and an Assessment of the Financial Accounting Standards Board* (Louis Harris and Associates, Inc., 1980).

ENDNOTES

1. Eugene Flegm, *Accounting: How to Meet the Challenges of Relevance and Regulation* (New York: John Wiley & Sons, 1984), p. 193.
2. *SFAC 1,* par. 37.
3. *SFAC 1,* par. 37.

4. *CICA Handbook,* Section 1540, par. 03.

5. *CICA Handbook,* Section 1540, par. 20.

6. *SFAC 1,* par. 54, in part.

7. See *Accounting Series Release 279* (SEC Financial Reporting Release No. 501) issued in 1980 and Regulation S-K, Item 303.

8. See, for instance, Robert M. Bowen, David Burgstahler, and Lane A. Daley, "The Incremental Information Content of Accrual versus Cash Flows," *The Accounting Review,* October 1987, pp. 723–47. Also G. Wilson, "The Relative Incremental Information Content of Accruals and Cash Flows: Combined Evidence at the Earnings Announcement and Annual Report Date," *Journal of Accounting Research,* Supplement 1986, pp. 165–200.

9. *SFAC 6,* par. 70.

10. *SFAC 1,* par. 39.

11. Irving Fisher, *The Nature of Capital and Income* (New York: Macmillan, 1906), p. 52.

12. J. R. Hicks, *Value and Capital* (Oxford: Clarendon Press, 1946), p. 172.

13. *SFAS 33*, par. 100. (Subsequently superseded by *SFAS 89.*)

14. See Raymond J. Chambers, *Accounting, Evaluation and Economic Behavior* (Englewood Cliffs, N.J.: Prentice Hall, 1966), p. 92.

15. Ibid., pp. 112–14.

16. Edgar O. Edwards and Philip W. Bell, *The Theory and Measurement of Business Income* (Berkeley and Los Angeles: University of California Press, 1961), pp. 38–44.

17. David Solomons, "Economic and Accounting Concepts of Income," *Five Monographs on Business Income* (Study Group on Business Income, 1950).

18. All these examples are taken from David Solomons, "Economic and Accounting Concepts of Income."

Chapter 10

Income Concepts for Financial Reporting

CHAPTER OBJECTIVES

After studying this chapter, you will be able to:

Contrast the three levels of income concepts.

Distinguish income determined by the transactions approach from income determined by the activities approach.

Compare the terms *comprehensive income, net income,* and *earnings.*

Explain the effects of prior-period adjustments, extraordinary items, cumulative accounting changes, and discontinued operations on income.

CHAPTER OVERVIEW

Introduction

The provision of an income measure as an indicator of enterprise performance is the primary focus of modern financial reporting. This chapter examines various approaches to defining and measuring net income.

Concepts of Income

Income can be approached syntactically, that is, through the rules that define it; semantically, that is, through its relationship to underlying economic realities; or pragmatically, that is, through its use by investors regardless of how it is measured or what it means. Each approach is examined in this chapter.

Defining Income

The various objectives of income reporting suggest different definitions of net income and different audiences to be addressed. The polar extremes are current operating and all-inclusive income. The FASB's definition of comprehensive income is an all-inclusive concept.

The accrual concept of income continues to come under challenge as a fundamental measurement; however, from an informational perspective, it does describe accounting activity.[1] On the basis of efficient capital market assumptions, empirical research supports the view that accounting income does have information content.[2] Whether it is from a desire for a single measurement of income or from the recognition of the information included in the computation of accounting income, practicing accountants continue to emphasize the role of income measurement, and financial analysts continue to demand its measurement and publication. For example, *SFAC 1* states that "the primary focus of financial reporting is information about an enterprise's performance provided by measures of earnings and its components."[3] This demand for income measurement is also supported by the preliminary findings of a laboratory experiment by Pankoff and Virgil, which concluded that there was rather close agreement among analysts that earnings per share and sales were the most important of normally available information items.[4] However, they also concluded that earnings per share had very little, if any, general impact on the expectations of all but a few analysts.[5] This chapter examines several concepts of income at the structural (syntactical), interpretive (semantic), and behavioral (pragmatic) levels. It seeks to evaluate the various attempts to define the concept of accounting income.

The following are some of the criticisms of accounting income in its traditional form:

1. The concept of accounting income has not yet been clearly formulated.
2. There is no long-run theoretical basis for the computation and presentation of accounting income.
3. Generally accepted accounting practices permit inconsistencies in the measurement of periodic income of different firms.
4. Price-level changes have modified the meaning of income measured in terms of historical dollars.
5. Other information may prove more useful to investors and stockholders for the making of investment decisions.

Recognizing that the measurement of income has considerable conceptual and practical problems, several suggestions have been made to provide solutions. The following five major positions are probably representative of the suggestions regarding the problem of income measurement:

1. Much discussion has centered on an attempt to improve the reporting of what may be called accounting income by focusing on transaction data and the accrual process.
2. Others support a single operational concept of income that can be used as an indication of the firm's ability to pay dividends.
3. One belief is that future progress in accounting theory depends upon agreement on a single concept of income that will conform more closely to what is referred to as economic income.
4. Some writers subscribe to the idea that several concepts of income should be measured and reported for different purposes.
5. Several suggestions have been made to the effect that all measurements of income are deficient and that they should be superseded by other measures of economic activity.

The concepts of income on the syntactic, semantic, and pragmatic levels are discussed in this chapter following a discussion of the objectives of income reporting. The previous chapter discussed the concept of income primarily in terms of capital maintenance. The theory and measurement of the several elements making up accounting income, that is revenues and expenses, gains and losses, are discussed in the next chapter.

INTRODUCTION

A knowledge of different measurements of a firm's net income may be useful for different purposes, but there is thought to be an advantage in the general acceptance of one all-pervasive concept of net income for external reporting purposes. However, a close analysis of the various concepts and objectives of net income indicates clearly that a single concept cannot serve all purposes equally well if, indeed, it can serve any purpose well. At least two choices are possible—a single concept that meets most of the objectives fairly well or several net income figures clearly labeled to serve the several objectives. Disadvantages and difficulties in both of these choices are discernible in the following discussion.

The primary objective of income reporting is to provide useful information to those who are most interested in financial reports. But more specific objectives must be spelled out in order to obtain a clearer understanding of income reporting. One of the basic objectives assumed to be most important for all users of financial reports is the need to distinguish between invested capital and income—between the stocks and flows—as a part of the descriptive process of accounting. More specific objectives include:

1. The use of income as a measurement of the efficiency of management.
2. The use of historical income figures to aid in predicting the future course of the business or future dividend distributions.

3. The use of income as a measurement of accomplishment and as a guide to future managerial decisions.

Each of these objectives is discussed at greater length in the following paragraphs. Other objectives not discussed include the use of income as a base for taxation, the use of income as a means of regulating firms vested with a public interest, and the use of income figures by economists in evaluating the allocation of resources.

INCOME CONCEPTS AT THE SYNTACTIC LEVEL

Although accountants give lip service to the real-world interpretation of accounting income (generally economic income), or its behavioral impact (either its predictive ability or its general relevance in decision processes), they generally base principles and rules on premises that may not be related to real-world phenomena or behavioral effects. For example, the Study Group on the Objectives of Financial Statements said that "earnings . . . are based on conventions and rules that should be logical and internally consistent, even though they may not mesh with economists' notions of income."[6] The conventions and rules are made logical and consistent by being based on premises and concepts that have been developed from existing practice. However, such concepts as realization, matching, accrual basis, and cost allocations can be defined only in terms of precise rules, because they do not have real-world counterparts.

Accountants have used these terms so often and for so long that they tend to accept them as having interpretation in the real world. It is difficult to accept the fact that they have no significance outside of their limited role in the logic of the accounting structure. This lack of significance may be one reason why many students have difficulty grasping the meaning of accounting concepts; they try to give interpretive significance to concepts that have no relationship to real objects and events. The lack of interpretive significance of some accounting terms does not mean that all accounting concepts lack interpretive significance. Many concepts, such as product sales, are based on external transactions or other observable events. But accounting income is the summation of many positive and negative items, many of which do not have interpretive content; if any one or more of these items lack interpretive significance and are material, the resulting net income will also lack interpretive significance, even though it may contain information for capital markets.

SFAC 1 assumed that accounting income is a good measure of a firm's performance and that accounting income can be used to predict future cash flows. Other writers assume that accounting income is relevant in a general way for the decision models of investors and creditors. However, these assumptions have not been proven to have empirical validity.

Bedford, on the other hand, contends that readers of income reports should realize that the meaning of accounting income can be understood only by knowing how the income was measured (operationalism). That is, the readers should understand the operations used by the accountant to produce the income amount.[7]

The Transactions Approach to Income Measurement

The transactions approach to income measurement is the more conventional approach used by accountants. It involves the recording of changes in asset and liability valuations only as these are the result of transactions. The term *transactions* is used in the broad sense to include both internal and external transactions. External transactions arise from dealing with outsiders and transfer of assets or liabilities to or from the firm. Internal transactions arise from the use or conversion of assets within the firm. Changes in values are excluded if they arise from changes in market valuations or changes in expectations alone. To the extent that asset valuations are adjusted at the end of the period to take these changes into consideration, there is a deviation from the pure transactions approach; this adjustment represents an application of the annual inventory method implicit in the capital-maintenance approach.

To the extent that new market valuations replace the input (cost) valuations when an external transaction takes place, income is recognized when the external transaction occurs. Internal transactions could lead to valuation changes, but only those that result from the use or conversion of assets are usually recorded. When conversions take place, the value of the old asset is usually transferred to the new asset. Therefore, the transactions approach lends itself readily to the concept of recognition at the time of sale or exchange and to the cost convention in accounting.

The main advantages of the transactions approach are:

1. The components of net income can be classified in several ways, such as by product or class of customer, in order to obtain more useful information for management.
2. The income arising from the various sources such as from operations and from external causes can be reported separately to the extent that they can be measured.
3. It provides a basis for determining the types and quantities of assets and liabilities existing at the end of the period. Other valuation methods can then be applied more easily to this inventory.
4. Business efficiency requires the recording of external transactions for other reasons.
5. The various statements can be made to articulate with each other, which is assumed to permit greater understanding of the underlying data.

The general procedure is to record revenues and expenses as they arise from external transactions. The problems of timing and valuation are present in the recording of each transaction, but the main problem is focused upon the proper matching of expenses with the related revenue reported during the specific period. These problems are discussed in the next chapter. The several concepts of net income computed by the different methods of determining capital maintenance, as discussed in the previous chapter, can be incorporated into the transactions approach by making adjustments to revenues and expenses when each transaction is recorded and by making adjustments to asset valuations at the end of each period. Thus, current accounting practice is a combination of capital-maintenance concepts of income, operations concepts, and the transactions-based approach to income measurement.

The Activities Approach to Income Measurement

The activities approach to income differs from the transactions approach in that it focuses on a description of the activities of a firm rather than on the reporting of transactions. That is, income is assumed to arise when certain activities or events take place, rather than only as a result of specific transactions. For example, activity income would be recorded during the planning, purchasing, production, and sale processes, as well as during the collection process. In its application, it is merely an expansion of the transactions approach, since it starts with the transaction as a basis for measurement. The main difference is that the transactions approach is based on the reporting process that measures an external event—the transaction; the activities approach is based on the real-world concept of activity or event in a broader sense. Both approaches, however, fail to reflect reality in the measurement of income because they both are dependent upon the same structural relationships and concepts that have no real-world counterpart.

One of the assumed advantages of the activities approach is that it permits the measurement of several different concepts of income, which can be used for different purposes. Income arising from the production and sale of merchandise involves different types of evaluations and predictions than does the income arising from buying and selling securities or from holding assets for expected capital gains. The efficiency of management can be measured better if the components of income are classified according to the different types of operations or activities that are subject to more or less control by management. Furthermore, the classification of income components by types of operations permits better predictions because of the different behavioral patterns of the different types of activities.

CHECKPOINTS

---

1. Explain in your own words what a syntactic, or a structural, approach to net income means.
2. How well does the syntactic concept of income meet the primary objective of income measurement?
3. Compare the transactions approach to the activities approach to income measurement. What are the advantages and disadvantages of each?
4. When is income recognized in the transactions approach?
5. When is income recognized in the activities approach?

CONCEPTS OF INCOME AT THE SEMANTIC LEVEL

As Chapter 9 notes, accountants rely on two economic concepts in defining income. The first, the change in well-being, was discussed in the last chapter. The second, the maximization of profit under specified conditions of market structure, product demand, and input costs, is the subject of this section of this chapter.

Income as a Measurement of Efficiency

The efficient operation of an enterprise affects both the current dividend stream and the use of the invested capital for providing a future dividend stream. Therefore, all equity holders, but particularly the common stockholders, are interested in the efficiency of management. The present equity holders can take the necessary steps to obtain a new management if the present management is not operating efficiently, or they may provide for incentives or bonuses to efficient managements. Prospective stockholders will attempt to evaluate the efficiency of management before investing or placing a value on the stock of the firm. In either case, a measurement of the efficiency of the firm provides a basis for decisions. This objective of measuring the efficiency of a firm is reflected in *SFAC 1*. It states that "Financial Reporting should provide information about an enterprise's financial performance during a period."[8]

Efficiency has a real-world referent at least in concept. One of its interpretations is that it represents the relative ability to obtain the maximum output with a given amount of resources, a constant output with the use of a minimum amount of resources, or an optimum combination of resources together with a given demand for the product (and therefore price) to permit a maximum return to owners. However, with this concept of income as a goal, how could a measurement of past income provide a basis for determining the efficiency of a firm? *Efficiency* is a relative term and has meaning only when compared with an ideal or some other base. It also depends on whether the goal of the firm is to maximize income or to provide a fair or reasonable return on investment. If the capital employed by the firm is constant from year to year, the income figure itself may be useful as a measure of efficiency of the firm. The income of the current year can then be compared with prior years, and some judgment would have to be made as to whether the income of any year has reached, exceeded, or fallen short of the proper goal. However, if the capital invested changes from year to year, the income must be compared with some changing magnitude, such as invested capital or total revenue.

When net income is divided by invested capital, the result is called the rate of return on investment. This return can be computed by dividing the net income to stockholders by the stockholders' equity—the rate of return on stockholders' investment—or by dividing the net income plus interest (net of taxes) by the total capitalization of the firm, including long-term debt and stockholder equity—the rate of return on total equity. In either case, a measurement of the efficient utilization of the capital employed in the enterprise is thought to be obtained. But, again, the criterion of efficiency depends upon the standard used. The rate of return for prior years, the rate of return earned by other firms, an arbitrary rate, or a market-determined rate might be used as the standard. In each case, the validity of the return on investment as a measure of efficiency depends upon employing both an appropriate measure of income and an appropriate measure of capital employed in the business.*

Another base for comparing income is the total revenue of the period. Although the total revenue of the period can be measured more accurately than the capital invested, using total revenue as a base has some definite disadvantages. A comparison of the net income to sales for several years is valid only if capacity utilization is the same each year or if the failure to utilize capacity is considered a part of the inefficiency of management. Comparisons with other firms are even more difficult to make. Only if the capital turnover (sales divided by capital) is the same for several firms would the ratio of income to sales be comparable. As this is not likely, this ratio is not valid for interfirm comparisons.

Accounting versus Economic Income

Both producers and users of accounting information have sought for many years to give net income economic content. The primary focus of their attempts has been to establish a relationship between the return on investment and the internal rate of return. This formed the basis for what

---

* The use of ROIs in estimation theory, discussed below, has been severely criticized. These criticisms do not necessarily invalidate its use as a measure of efficiency.

was called *estimation theory* in which the emphasis was on the presentation of reported income that would permit investors to predict the internal rate of return for the firm as a whole and thus predict future cash flows and the firm's present value.[9]

Both returns are measures of the efficiency with which assets are being used, but the two are defined very differently. The return on investment (ROI) is simply:

$$ROI = \frac{NI}{TA} \tag{1}$$

where

NI = Net income

TA = Total assets employed at cost

The internal rate of return is that rate which equates present value of the expected future cash flow from the assets with the cost of those assets, that is, it is the return (r) which emerges from the equation

$$TA = \sum_{n=1}^{\infty} \frac{\text{Net cash flow}}{(1 + r)^n} \tag{2}$$

These two equations can be manipulated to show that:

Accounting net income
$$= \text{Revenue} - \text{expenses} - \text{accounting depreciation}$$

Economic net income
$$= \text{Revenue} - \text{expenses} - \text{economic depreciation}$$

Therefore, the difference between the two income numbers is attributable to the different methods of depreciation. Accountants use straight-line (SL) or accelerated (AD) depreciation methods; economists use the interest method (I). The relationship between these methods is illustrated in Exhibit 10-1. Note how the interest method works exactly opposite to the accelerated depreciation methods.

In theory, then, it looks as if companies could be persuaded to use the interest method; accounting measures would coincide with economic measures. This comfortable conclusion does not hold because the parameters that the model is holding constant are not constant in the real world. Inflation changes the cost of the asset; expected changes in the inflation rate affect the discount rate; supply and demand factors affect the risk of the company; and so on. In short, the analysis is changing constantly. This would require accountants to be remeasuring net income every day to keep it in tune with economic reality.

A moment's thought reveals that this is what investors are doing. The results of their analyses and reanalyses are revealed in the fluctuations in

EXHIBIT 10-1   Relationship between Different Depreciation Methods

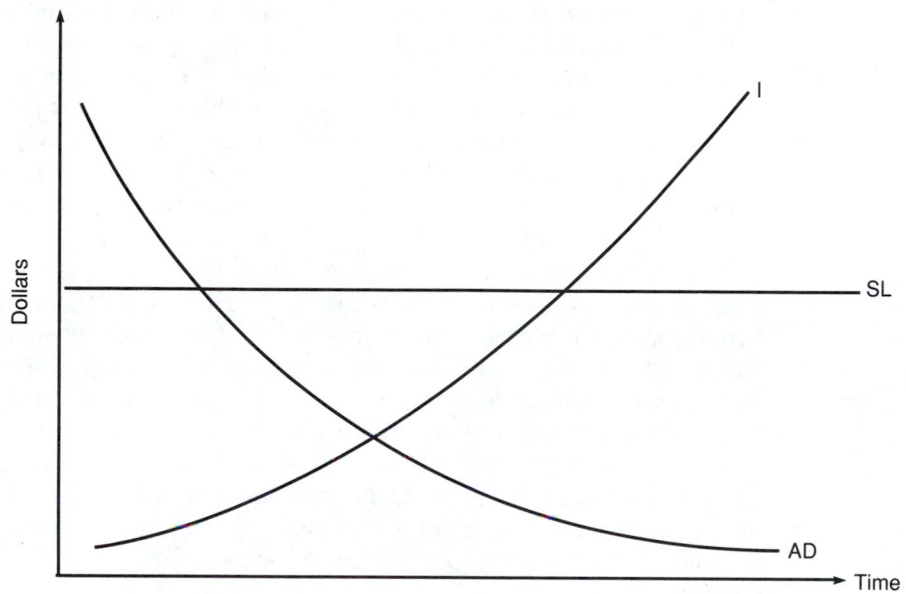

the company's share price from day to day. Why then ask accountants to compute economic income when the market is doing it already? The conclusion must be that accountants are in business, not to compute economic income, but to provide information to the marketplace to enable investors to compute economic income. In the extreme, as the previous chapter noted, one could simply provide cash flow information and leave all further computations of economic income to investors.

Multiperson Income

The previous section attributed the difficulties in giving corporate income an economic interpretation to what might be considered technical difficulties. There are deeper problems, though. Almost all analyses of accounting income in relationship to economic income are done in the context of certainty. In other words, all the facts of a situation are assumed to be known to everyone. For instance, present-value analysis typically begins by assuming a single discount rate. In reality, of course, there are dozens of different rates.

In a world of certainty, not only is everything known, but everyone is in agreement on the facts—because they are facts. In such a world, as Chapter 7 noted, there would be no need for accountants. Investors would already know all that accountants could tell them. To begin to create a role for accountants, one has to introduce uncertainty into the analysis. New York professor and accounting historian Richard Brief notes that historically and in practice "an effort was made to minimize uncertainty-related problems by arguing that the accountant's main responsibility was for 'prosaic facts' and 'dry realities.' This did not work in practice because uncertainty is at the very heart of the 'idea of profit as a return for risk bearing.' "[10] Excluding uncertainty works equally poorly in theoretical analysis; however, including uncertainty makes theoretical models very difficult to analyze.

In an attempt to deal with these difficulties, researchers have distinguished one case where markets are said to be *perfect* and *complete*. Broadly stated, in a perfect and complete world, investors no longer know which state of the world will occur in the future, but they remain agreed on the characteristics of each potential state, and they are agreed on the range of possible states. As a simple illustration, one may not know which way a coin will fall, but all will agree it will be heads or tails. This agreement on the potential outcome enables bets to be taken on the spin of a coin. Stated more generally, perfect and complete markets enable contracts to be entered into and, it can be shown, a meaningful net income number to be computed.

Reality is, of course, a lot more complex. For one thing, as Chapter 8 pointed out, there are a number of information asymmetries, where one party knows more than another. Trading, in such situations, can break down. Consider, for instance, the effect on betting on a coin if some insist that the coin might land on its side. Until agreement can be reached on the likelihood of this possibility, all bets will be off. In such a world, markets are said to be *incomplete*. In an uncertain and incomplete world, consensus on the "facts" is not possible—because there are no facts as such, only opinions, estimates, and guesses. In such a world, corporate net income cannot be defined to the mutual agreement of all. One can give it, at best, a syntactic definition. That is to say, one can agree only on how it was computed, not what it means. Whether this rather discouraging result, which it should be noted is related to Arrow's theorem, will continue to stand the scrutiny of time will have to await the judgment of future researchers.

CHECKPOINTS

1. Define what is meant by efficiency in the context of defining income.
2. How might efficiency be measured? What problems affect this measurement?
3. Compare the concept of efficiency described in this chapter with the concept of capital maintenance described in the last chapter.

CONCEPTS OF INCOME AT THE PRAGMATIC LEVEL

Pragmatic concepts of income relate to the decision processes of investors and creditors, the reactions of securities prices in organized markets to income reporting, the capital expenditure decisions of management, and the feedback reactions of management and accountants. This approach was introduced in Chapter 6, which spoke of behavioral studies at the individual level in accounting, the efficient-market theory, and the empirical studies done in the area of accounting and capital markets, and in Chapter 8, which spoke of how positive accounting is extending this work into the area of regulation. This work is drawn into the discussion that follows.

The sections which follow can do more than briefly introduce the pragmatic approach to the concept of income as reported in the literature. So much work has appeared in this area in the last two decades that it is impossible to give an adequate discussion of each of them or even provide a complete list of the many approaches suggested in the literature. The interested reader is advised to pursue the suggested readings at the end of this chapter for more details.

Income as a Predictive Device

SFAC 1 states that investors, creditors, and others are concerned with assessing the prospects for enterprise net cash inflows, but that they often use earnings to help them evaluate earning power, predict future earnings, or assess the risk of investing in or lending to the enterprise.[11] Thus, there is an assumed relationship between reported income and cash flows, including cash distributed to owners.

Many researchers have sought to provide evidence for the FASB's assumptions. One line of research asks what specific numbers are preferred by investors and others in assessing the enterprise's prospects. Such numbers are termed *summary indicators* because they purport to summarize the relative success or failure of an enterprise. Earnings per share is one such indicator and has received much attention in academic research. One line of research has examined its value in predicting bankruptcies.

The current value of a firm and the value of a share of stock in the firm are dependent upon the expected future stream of distributions to stockholders. Based on these expectations, a current stockholder may decide to either sell the shares or continue to hold them. An investor who is not currently a stockholder may decide either to purchase shares in the firm or to invest the capital elsewhere. Thus, expectations regarding future distributions are paramount in these investment decisions. If there is a relationship between reported income and dividend distributions, investors may focus their attention on their expectations regarding future incomes of the firm. For many firms, income predictions are assumed to be more relevant in predicting the future market price of stock than are predictions of short-term dividend distributions, and long-term distributions are assumed to be dependent upon retained income and growth factors. Therefore, expectations of future incomes are thought to be used by many investors as a main factor in predicting future dividend distributions, and expected dividends are an important factor in placing a current value on shares of stock or on the entire firm.

Bondholders and short-term creditors are also interested in the future income. The greater the expectation of income for the firm, the greater the expectation that the creditors will receive their annual return and also the greater the expectation that they will receive payment of the principal when the debt matures.

Can a knowledge of past incomes aid in the prediction of future incomes and thus in the current value of the firm? One study concluded that past values of accounting income computed on the basis of historical costs provide a better predictor of future values of the same series than do past values of income computed on the basis of current costs. Both models were shown to be superior to general price-level adjusted income.[12] However, the study suggests that both concepts of income can be useful in predicting future values of the same series, particularly on an industry basis. However, projection assumes either that the future values being predicted are good surrogates for a meaningful concept of income that has real-world significance, or that the projected accounting concept of income is relevant in the decision processes of investors. There is no evidence that either of these conditions prevails. However, since many investors believe that a prediction of future reported incomes is relevant to an evaluation of a firm's stock in buy-sell decisions, many writers suggest that there is some validity in the presentation of a measurement of income that will permit projections of future income. It is this concept of predictive ability that has led to arguments for the smoothing of periodic income.[13] Whereas smoothing is advocated as appropriate also for internal measurement and control, its defense for external reporting purposes rests on the assumption that income is an indicator of future cash flows and that capital asset values are related to the expected stream of future cash flows, including a future sale price of the security. In the authors' opinion, smoothing hides more information than it discloses. Information regarding variability of activity from year to year is relevant in an evaluation of risk and therefore in the decision process.

Managerial Decision Making.   The formal financial statements are directed primarily to the external users of accounting data, but accountants must also furnish management with the tools and raw material required for control and for good decisions. Just as the investor is interested primarily in future dividend flows, so also is management interested primarily in what will happen in the future. Decisions can affect future events only. But management is not so interested in predicting future dividends as it is in making decisions to meet its goals regarding current and future cash flows.

To the extent that income is used by management for decision and control purposes, care should be taken to ensure that the arbitrariness of allocations and matching are minimized or made neutral. Neutrality is achieved only if the decisions are not affected by the allocations and matching procedures applied in the measurement of income. If this cannot be avoided, income should not be used as a basis for managerial decisions.

Managements do react, however, to what they consider the behavior of investors and creditors to reported income. Even though the reported income is based only in the accounting structure, the feedback phenomenon will affect the choice of accounting methods by management.[14] For example, many firms believe that the price of their shares will be maximized if the net income grows at a constant rate each year. Consequently, they choose available accounting policies and procedures to report income that meets this goal or report earnings-per-share figures that will create the greatest demand for their stock.[15] The smoothing of reported income figures over time is frequently a goal based on the premise that investors will pay more for stock if the reported income deviates very little over time from a constant or growth trend than if the reported income varies widely from year to year.

The Capital Market Approach

The previous section examined the potential of income to assist individual users. This section examines the potential impact of earnings numbers on the securities market as a whole.* A huge amount of research has been done in this area, some of which was reported in Chapter 6. The essential findings in this area are fascinating and have caused a revolution in accounting thought if not, as yet, in practice.

Direct and indirect observations suggest that reported earnings per share and projected earnings per share have a direct impact on the market price of common shares and are in demand by individual investors even though the efficient-market hypothesis implies that individuals cannot gain by a knowledge of this information. However, in the semistrong form of the efficient-market hypothesis (security prices fully reflect all publicly available information about the firm) the use of the information content of reported income is assumed on the basis of market reactions to this infor-

---

* Researchers in this area tend to use the terms *earnings* and *net income* interchangeably.

mation. Several empirical studies have suggested that reported earnings per share or projected earnings per share do have a direct impact on the market price of common shares.

The first evidence of the relationship between accounting earnings and security prices was provided by Australian professors Ray Ball and Philip Brown, who were at the University of Chicago at the time.[16] That study was described in Chapter 6. Their results, essentially that security prices move in the same direction as accounting earnings, have been confirmed many times since. This may be because securities are responding to the same events as earnings. Alternatively, it may be because earnings convey information to the securities market. At the very least, the market behaves *as if* earnings conveyed information. Some may feel that this is a rather obvious and not very exciting result. It was, though, the first real evidence to which accountants were able to point to demonstrate that accounting numbers were informative. As such it was an extremely important study.

The correlation between earnings and prices is imperfect. Part of the reason for the lack of a perfect correlation is that prices are capturing a much wider set of information than simply accounting earnings. For instance, prices respond to things as exotic as rumors of war and as mundane as changes in the rate of interest on Treasury bills. Another reason for the lack of a perfect correlation is that some fluctuations in accounting earnings result from changes in accounting rules that may have no immediate economic implications. For example, a switch in financial depreciation methods has no effect on pretax cash flows. (Clouding the picture is the possibility that the change in methods may have been induced by an expected decline in cash flows. For instance, companies sometimes extend the lives of their assets to boost declining income.)

The possibility that the market can be fooled by changes in accounting, such as extending asset lives, has been the subject of much research. The essential outcome of this research is that the market is not easily misled. There are exceptions, referred to in the literature as *anomalies*. Many of these exceptions involve situations where it is hard to decide whether there is an economic impact or not. For instance, an oil company may decide to decrease its net income number to lower its profile and so to avoid the prospect of increased regulation. Teasing out the implications of such situations requires much careful detective work on the part of the researcher.

A key aspect of research into the impact of accounting earnings on capital markets is determining the information content of earnings numbers. A number by itself says nothing. It is the deviation of that number from what was expected that conveys information. For example, IBM's stock price rose recently on an announcement of a fall in their earnings. The reason for the rise was that the decline in earnings was smaller than expected. In other words, measured against expectations, there was a rise in earnings.

Building an earnings expectations model requires an understanding of how earnings behave over time, for example, one needs to know what is called their *time-series properties,* that is, their statistical properties from one period to the next. Early work showed that earnings per share follows a random walk, that is, accounting earnings have the same appearance as the results of flipping coins. From a predictive standpoint, this means that our best guess of next year's earnings per share is this year's earnings per share. (Later work showed that there was a slight upward drift that had to be considered as well.) This result surprised most observers, because it destroyed the notion of "growth" stocks. It also seemed to imply that apparently good management, as measured by a few years of steady growth, may be no more than a lucky string of beads. Needless to say, this implication is highly controversial—and overstated. The result, though, does confirm that company managements, no matter how good, are at the mercy of the environment.

The Contractual Approach View of Income

As discussed in Chapter 8, reported accounting income has become a basis for many legal and contractual relationships in society; to this extent, it has behavioral implications even though it may not have semantic interpretation. The role played by earnings in a wide range of contracts gives much insight into the way earnings can be expected to behave. For instance, one hypothesis addressed in Chapter 8 suggests that companies that are close to their debt covenant limits will choose accounting methods that boost net income, and thereby increase the equity number in the debt-to-equity ratio.

The strength of the contractual approach is that it does not demand semantic interpretation of accounting earnings. Proponents of the approach argue that society can agree to play by any rules that it chooses regardless of whether they make sense or not. This position is considered extreme by some who argue that all theories should in the long run be based on concepts that have interpretive significance; pragmatic theories of income cannot be valid in the long run without a real-world concept of income and a verification of their behavioral implications. To illustrate this point consider the 1938 radio program that depicted a landing in New Jersey of men from Mars. Many people who had not heard the beginning of the program thought it was real, and the result was near-panic. Theories of handling a panic could be applied immediately, but the long-run solution was to convince people that the Martians were fictitious.

CHECKPOINTS

---

1. According to *SFAC 1*, what is the primary interest of investors?
2. Why are investors thought to be interested in income measures?
3. How does managerial interest in income differ from that of investors?
4. Why does management want to smooth the growth of income over time?
5. What is the role of income in capital market studies?

WHAT SHOULD BE INCLUDED IN INCOME?

The computation of income by an annual valuation of the firm as done in Chapter 9 raises important questions regarding the proper valuation methods that provide the most meaningful measurement of net income. A more important limitation of the annual valuation procedure is the inability to reveal the nature and composition of income necessary in meeting the objective of predictability discussed earlier in this chapter. The transactions approach, on the other hand, makes it possible to record changes when specific events occur and to summarize these changes in financial statements according to the nature of the firm's activities.

One of the major objectives of business enterprise is the maximization of the dividend flow to stockholders over the entire life of the enterprise, or the maximization of the liquidation value or market value of the enterprise at the end of its life, or at intermediate points, or some combination of these. All economic changes are relevant for an evaluation of the overall success or failure of the enterprise over its lifetime. But the more common objectives of income measurement require a measurement of income for shorter periods of time in order to provide a means of control and a basis for decisions of stockholders, creditors, and management on a continuing or periodic basis. The overall measurement of income for the entire life of the enterprise does not provide the information when it is most useful, nor does it describe the causes of success or failure. Success may be the result of good fortune or efficient management. The sources or causes of income are thus important in a proper evaluation of the progress of the firm. But some accountants held that the figure called "net income for the period" should include all recorded economic events and that income arising from specific sources should be labeled properly. This controversy has led to two basic concepts of income—the current operating concept and the all-inclusive concept of income—and an intermediate position required in *APB 30* and *SFAS 16*.

The Current Operating Concept of Income

The current operating concept of income focuses on the measurement of the efficiency of the business enterprise. The term *efficiency* relates to the effective utilization of the firm's resources in operating the business and earning a profit. In the broad economic sense, it relates to the proper combination of the factors of production—land, labor, capital, and management. An evaluation of relative efficiency, however, requires a comparison with a given standard or ideal. Evaluation is necessarily subjective, but as a starting point comparisons can be made with the results of previous periods and with the incomes of the other firms or industries.

In computing income, particular emphasis is placed on the terms *current* and *operating*. Only those value changes and events that are controllable by management and that result from decisions of the *current* period should be included. However, this statement must be qualified to include the use of factors acquired in a prior period but used in the current period. Each period is not a separate economic experience. Most of the capital equipment and even the services of most of the workers will have been obtained or contracted for in prior periods. The decisions of the current period involve the proper use and combination of these factors. The changes that should be excluded are those that actually arose in prior periods but were not recognized or recorded previously. For example, equipment that is discovered to be obsolete in the current period may have become obsolete in prior periods. The decision to abandon its use in the current period may be the result of efficient management and, therefore, this is not an operating event of the current period. Likewise, recognition of an error in the computation of a prior period's income is not a reflection on the efficiency of management in the current period. But one note of caution—errors in the computation of income for prior periods do affect the evaluation of the efficiency of management in those prior periods.

The second aspect of this concept is that the relevant changes arise only from *normal* operations, enabling a better comparison to be made with other operations. Also, the relative efficiency of management shows up better. While nonoperating activities may also be affected by managerial efficiency, it is more difficult to obtain a standard with which to measure the period results. At a minimum the results of operating and nonoperating activities should be separated. It is also frequently suggested that nonoperating activities should be reported separately because they are nonrecurring. This argument is really a different reason for separate classification, and is discussed more fully below. If nonrecurring items arise from normal operations, the current operating performance concept of income should include them to provide a good measure of the firm's earning power and a means of projecting and evaluating income trends.

Proponents of the current operating concept suggest that the resulting reported net income is more meaningful for interperiod and interfirm comparisons and for making predictions. They also suggest that, although classification of operating and nonoperating items may be difficult, the trained accountant is in a better position to make this classification than outsiders or nonaccountants. There should be full disclosure of noncurrent and nonoperating items, but financial analysts and other users of accounting data frequently emphasize one figure for the net income for the year. Thus, it is proposed that, if only one figure is quoted, the current operating net income is more useful as a measure of current operating performance.

The All-Inclusive Concept of Income (Comprehensive Income)

The all-inclusive concept of income is defined as the total change in proprietorship recognized by the recording of transactions or the revaluation of the firm during a specific period, except for dividend distributions and capital transactions. This is the concept referred to by the FASB as *comprehensive income*. Comprehensive income is broader than net income because it includes:

> certain other changes in net assets (principally certain holding gains and losses) that are recognized in the period, such as some changes in market values of investments in marketable equity securities classified as noncurrent assets, some changes in market values of investments having specialized accounting practices for marketable securities, and foreign currency translation adjustments.[17]

Net income, on the other hand, contains certain items that are not, strictly speaking, current. Specifically, net income (and comprehensive income) include:

> effects of certain accounting adjustments of earlier periods that are recognized in the period, such as the principal example in present practice—cumulative effects of changes in accounting principles. . . .[18]

The FASB has chosen to describe a concept of income that reflects only current times by the term *earnings*. One therefore has the following hierarchy:

Earnings = Current operating income + nonrecurring items

Net income = Earnings
   + cumulative effect on prior years of a change in accounting principle

Comprehensive income = Net income
           + cumulative prior period adjustments
                   + remaining nonowner changes in equity

The term *nonowner changes* is intended to exclude capital transactions such as dividends and the receipt of new capital.

All changes in the retained earnings section of the stockholders' equity should arise from either net income, dividend distributions, appropriations of net income, or the return of appropriations to "free" retained earnings. If a classification of operating and nonoperating or recurring and nonrecurring items is desirable, it should be made in the income statement before arriving at the figure labeled "net income for the period."

Proponents of the all-inclusive concept of income claim the following reasons for this measurement of income:

1. The annual reported net incomes, when added together for the life of the enterprise, should be equal to the total net income of the enterprise. It is claimed that the charges resulting from extraordinary events and from corrections of prior periods tend to exceed the credits, resulting in an overstatement of the net income for a series of years if these are omitted.

2. The omission of certain charges and credits from the computation of net income lends itself to possible manipulation or smoothing of the annual earnings figures. This fear has been well founded over the years.[19]

3. An income statement that includes all income charges and credits recognized during the year is said to be easier to prepare and more easily understood by the readers. It is not subject to the personal judgments of management or the accountants preparing the statement. This claim is based on the assumption that accounting statements should be as verifiable as possible; several accountants working independently on the same figures should be able to arrive at similar results.

4. With full disclosure of the nature of income changes during the year, the reader of the statements is assumed to be more capable of making appropriate classifications to arrive at an appropriate measurement of income than are the accountants and management, who cannot anticipate the specific needs of the users.

5. The distinction between operating and nonoperating charges and credits is not clear-cut. Transactions classified as operating by one firm may be classified as nonoperating by another firm. Furthermore, items classified as nonoperating in one year may be classified as operating by the same firm in a subsequent year. This reclassification, in itself, leads to inconsistencies in making comparisons among different firms or over several periods for the same firm. But the definition of operating income becomes even more clouded when we look beyond the trees and see that some extraordinary events are really ordinary and expected over a longer period of time and that the frequent occurrence of "nonoperating" events may be normal to business operations. The family can budget its entire income for the normal family requirements, such as food, housing, clothing, and entertainment; special items such as medical bills, car repairs, and semiannual payments for property taxes are not normal expenditure items in any one single month. If the budget, however, does not include provisions for these extraordinary items, the family may soon be in financial difficulties. Each item may be extraordinary for any single month, but as a group, the extraordinary items become normal.

A major difference between the current operating and the all-inclusive concepts of income is in the assumed objective for reporting net income. While the current operating net income emphasizes the current operating performance or efficiency of the firm and the possible use of this figure for predicting the future performance and earning power, the proponents of the all-inclusive net income claim that both the operating efficiency and the prediction of future performance can be improved if they are based on the entire historical experience of the firm over a series of years. Because the useful lives of assets usually extend over many periods and because income-producing transactions are not at uniform stages of completion at the end of each period, the net income of a single period is, at best, an estimate based on good judgment. Because of this necessarily subjective nature of accounting, the net income of a single period is tentative and always subject to verification at later dates.

Recurring and Nonrecurring Income

The proponents of the current operating performance concept of income frequently claim that operating items are generally defined as recurrent features of business operations and that nonoperating items are generally considered to be irregular and unpredictable. However, this is not necessarily true. Many items may be operating in nature, but not necessarily recurring. The necessity to pay overtime labor rates during a rush period and the acquisition of raw materials under extremely fortunate circumstances are both operating events, but are possibly nonrecurring. On the other hand, some nonoperating events are recurring in nature. Annual floods in unavoidable hazardous areas may result in nonoperating charges, but they are recurring in nature.

A net income figure based on recurring events is generally more useful to investors in predicting possible future income and dividend flows. Recurring nonoperating events are just as important as those recurring events that are the result of normal operations. The distinction between operating and nonoperating, however, is more useful for measuring management efficiency. The assumption upon which this statement is based is that operating events tend to be more controllable than nonoperating events. This assumption may be disputed in many instances, however.

The advantage of classifying income charges and credits as recurring or nonrecurring is based upon the improved usefulness of the resulting net income figure in the making of predictions by investors. It is probably more difficult for outsiders to distinguish between recurring and nonrecurring events than it is for them to distinguish between operating and nonoperating items.

The disadvantages of the classification and reporting of recurring income are similar to the disadvantages of the current operating concept of income. These disadvantages can be readily recognized in the above discussion of the all-inclusive concept of income.

Prior-Period Adjustments

As new information appears, changes are inevitable. *APB 20* distinguished three kinds of changes: changes in principle, changes in estimates, and changes in the reporting entity. Discovered errors cause changes but are not in themselves accounting changes as defined in the Opinion. Examples of changes in principles include a switch from one inventory method to another or from one depreciation method to another. Changes in estimates include a revision of the estimated useful life of an asset, or the amount to be set aside for warranty expenses. When a change in estimate accompanies a change of principle, it is the change in estimate that is assumed to be the fundamental cause.

The main issue at stake in establishing this Opinion was whether companies should revise statements of earlier periods for changes made in this period. In other words, the question was whether prior-period adjustments should be permitted. Two of the changes were relatively uncontroversial. Changes in entity clearly require a restatement of earlier periods to permit comparisons with the new entity's current financial statements. Therefore, changes of estimates refer to the future and are treated on a prospective basis. The difficult issue is a change in principle. Guidance on this issue was provided by paragraph 23 of *APB 9*, since superseded by *SFAS 16*, which stated that:

> Adjustments related to prior periods—and thus excluded in the determination of net income for the current period—are limited to those material adjustments which
>
> *a.* Can be specifically identified with and directly related to the business activities of particular prior periods.
> *b.* Are not attributable to economic events occurring subsequent to the date of the financial statements for the prior period.
> *c.* Depend primarily on determinations by persons other than management.
> *d.* Were not susceptible of reasonable estimation prior to such determination.

Such adjustments are rare in modern financial accounting. The two exceptions noted in the Opinion were discovered errors and the treatment of certain deferred tax amounts.

The authors of *APB 20,* driven by their consensus that all-inclusive income was desirable, agreed that prior-period adjustments should remain rare. The cumulative effect of a change in principle was, therefore, required to be shown in the income statement of the current period, as part of net income. The only exceptions allowed are:

a. A change from the LIFO method of inventory pricing to another method.
b. A change in the method of accounting for long-term construction-type contracts.
c. A change to or from the "full cost" method of accounting that is used in the extractive industries.
d. A change from retirement-replacement-betterment accounting to depreciation accounting.

These continue to be treated as prior-period adjustments on grounds that the benefits outweigh the perceived costs. The nature of, effect of, and justification for, the change must also be disclosed.

The FASB tightened the noose on prior-period adjustments in *SFAS 16,* which stated that, with only two exceptions, all items of profit and loss recognized during an annual period must be included in the computation of the annual earnings.[20] The one exception related to deferred income taxes and was removed by *SFAS 96.*[21] The remaining exception is the correction of an error in the financial statements of a prior period. An *error* is defined as a mathematical mistake, a mistake in the application of accounting principles, or oversight or misuse of facts that existed when the financial statements were prepared.

The FASB apparently attempted to leave little room for judgment regarding classification as a prior-period adjustment. Thus, the emphasis is on objectivity and verifiability of the reported net income, rather than on its predictability. In adopting *SFAS 16,* the FASB came very close to the adoption of the all-inclusive concept of income for annual reporting purposes. One wonders why they were not completely consistent. Corrections of estimations and measurements of prior periods are included in the reported income of the current period; therefore, there appears to be no reason why corrections of errors should not also be included in the computation of reported income. It might be better to follow an all-inclusive concept completely, rather than follow it for some items and exclude others on the basis of the current operating concept.

Following the implications of the efficient-market hypothesis, disclosure of prior-period corrections is sufficient to impound the information in the market prices. It does not really matter whether the items are disclosed in the income statement or in the statement of retained earnings. However, it can be argued that the income statement is a primary statement and that disclosure within that statement is more prominent than disclosure within the retained earnings statement. On the other hand, it can be argued that, because of possible functional fixation on the net income figure, noncurrent items should be excluded if it can be done objectively without permitting manipulation of reported income.

Extraordinary Items

APB 30 defined an extraordinary item as including events and transactions that are both infrequent (or nonrecurring) and unusual (or not related to normal operations). Both criteria must be met in the classification of extraordinary items. The only exception to this general rule is the gain or loss on the extinguishment of debt, which is treated as an extraordinary item. Items that are infrequent but not unusual, or vice versa should be shown as a separate line in income from operations. An example of the treatment of an extraordinary item (and a change in accounting principle) is shown in Exhibit 10-2.

The objective of the approach in *APB 30* apparently was to restrict the use of this classification to unusual times that may affect predictability, but will not permit the use of management discretion in determining the

---

EXHIBIT 10-2   Disclosure of Extraordinaries

TOSCO CORPORATION

	(DEC)($000s)		
	1988	1987	1986
Income (loss) before extraordinary items	$55,238	$27,822	$(56,420)
Extraordinary (charge) gain from early retirement (1988) and refinancing (1986) of debt, net of income tax effects	(1,806)		74,000
Extraordinary credit—utilization of net operating loss carryforwards	36,994	25,133	
Net income	90,426	52,955	17,580

Notes to Consolidated Financial Statements

7 (In part): Long-Term Debt

During 1988, Tosco retired $51,040,000 of its Bonds at a premium of $3,130,000. The premium paid has been classified as an extraordinary item in Tosco's statement of income. As the income tax benefit related to the premium paid on the Bonds of $1,324,000 was largely offset by the reduced utilization of federal and state net operating loss carryforwards, the effect on Tosco's net income was approximately equal to the premium paid. The purchase of the Bonds will reduce Tosco's interest expense by approximately $6,400,000 per year.

---

computation of net income before extraordinary items. However, the theoretical reasons for this separate classification are not clear. Since unusual items that do recur are included in the computation of net income before extraordinary items, this partitioning of net income does not reflect current operating income. Furthermore, since most items that are nonrecurring but of a normal nature are not separately disclosed, the ability to meet the predictability objective is weakened. For example, a significant nonrecurring increase in an operating item would be included in the results of normal operations. Therefore, the separation of extraordinary items from other income statement items does not result in a separation of recurring and nonrecurring items, nor a separation of operating from nonoperating activities. However, an emphasis on behavioral characteristics of at least some items is a step in the right direction. Nevertheless, a movement toward a greater recognition of the separate disclosure of recurring and nonrecurring items is apparent.[22] The purpose would be to permit greater evaluation of the components of net income, rather than an emphasis on the bottom-line amount. This movement is consistent with the efficient-market thesis and also might minimize the effect of functional fixation.

Discontinued Operations

Discontinued operations are covered by the provisions of *APB 30,* whose intent was to classify items in such a way as to give the reader the sense of what income might reasonably be expected from ongoing operations. The company is to segregate the net-of-tax income or loss earned by the discontinued operation in the current period and prior to the *measurement date,* defined as the date on which management commits itself to a formal plan to dispose of the operation. The income or loss earned by the discontinued operation in the period between the measurement date and the disposal date is part of the gain or loss, after tax, on sale of the operation. If this is estimated to be a loss, that estimate should be shown. An example of the treatment of discontinued operations is shown in Exhibit 10-3.

The intent of the statement is noble. However, in practice, the problem of determining what should be included in the discontinued operation and what in continuing operations is so great as to make interpretation of the result extremely difficult. The information content of this separation is, therefore, highly uncertain. In particular, in what is colloquially known as the *big bath theory,* management is often suspected of writing-off into the discontinued segment as much of their future expenses as possible. Unburdening future revenues of expenses almost guarantees that future income will show an improvement.

EXHIBIT 10-3   Discontinued Operations

SPS TECHNOLOGIES, INC.

	1988	*(DEC)($000s)* 1987	1986
Earnings from continuing operations	$18,980	$14,515	$15,045
Discontinued operations—Loss from operations (net of income tax benefits of $1,500 in 1988, $3,161 in 1987, and $2,153 in 1986)	(2,449)	(3,623)	(2,260)
Estimated loss on disposal (net of income tax benefit of $3,640)	(5,940)		
Earnings before extraordinary item and cumulative effect of change in accounting policy	10,591	10,892	12,785

Notes to Consolidated Financial Statements

5. Discontinued Operations

   The Company adopted a formal plan to discontinue operations of the materials handling segment and seek a buyer for its Hartman Systems Division during the third quarter of 1988. During 1987, the Company sold all of the assets, net of certain liabilities, associated with its Hallowell product line, which previously was included in the materials handling segment. The total consideration received for Hallowell, less costs associated with the sale, approximated the net book value of the assets sold. The net assets and operating results of the materials handling segment, including those of the Hallowell product line, are shown separately in the accompanying financial statements. Prior years have been reclassified for comparative purposes.

   The estimated loss on disposal of the segment was $5,940,000 (net of income tax benefits of $3,640,000), consisting of a loss on the disposal of assets of $3,145,000 and a provision of $2,795,000 for expected operating losses during the phase-out period through September 30, 1989. Net sales of the segment were $6,774,000, $33,308,000 and $35,099,000 in 1988, 1987 and 1986, respectively.

   A summary of the net assets of the materials handling segment at December 31, 1988 and 1987, which have been reclassified as net assets of discontinued operations, is as follows:

	1988	*1987*
Current assets	$4,323,000	$9,106,000
Other assets	1,394,000	1,685,000
Current liabilities	(1,828,000)	(2,827,000)
Net assets of discontinued operations	$3,889,000	$7,964,000

Disclosure

Given the great number of different categories that now appear in an income statement, some agreement on the order of presentation was necessary to facilitate their interpretation. A composite income statement might look as follows:

Earnings from continuing operations
Less: Provision for income taxes, on continuing operations
Plus: Equity in net earnings of unconsolidated subsidiaries
Less: Income from discontinued operations, net-of-income tax benefit
Plus: Estimated loss on sale of discontinued operations, net of income tax
Extraordinary item (description), net-of-income tax
Cumulative effect of accounting change, net-of-income tax
Net income

Usually, there will be a series of intermediate earnings numbers, each of which will be described. For instance, the penultimate line might read "Earnings prior to the cumulative effect of accounting change."

Net Income to Whom?

Stemming from the proprietary approach to accounting, net income has usually been assumed to mean net earnings or net profits accruing to current stockholders or owners of the business. However, there may be valid reasons for the presentation of a net income figure that represents net earnings to a narrower or broader group of recipients.

The Value-Added Concept of Income.   Broadly speaking, it is possible to view the enterprise as having a large group of claimants or interested parties, including not only owners and other investors, but also employees and landlords of rented property. This view is called the *value-added* approach.[23] In economic terms, value added is the market price of the output of an enterprise less the price of the goods and services acquired by transfer from other firms. Thus, all employees, owners, creditors, and governments (through taxation) are recipients of the enterprise income. This enterprise income is the total pie that can be divided among various contributors of factor inputs to the enterprise in the production of goods and services. How this pie is divided is usually subject to contractual agreements and bargaining. An example of such a statement appears in Exhibit 10-4.

The value-added concept becomes most meaningful when it is applied to the very large corporations that affect the lives of thousands of individuals and have a general social and economic significance beyond the narrow interests of the owners or stockholders. The value-added income includes wages, rent, interest, taxes, dividends paid to stockholders, and undistributed earnings in this concept. It does not necessarily accrue to the owners alone, but also to all of the other recipients or claimants of corporate value added. Only in the case of liquidation do common stock-

EXHIBIT 10-4

**1985 Value-Added Statement
(Sources and Disposal of Value Added)
Imperial Chemical Industries**

	1985 £m	1984 £m	Percentage Change
Sources of Income:			
Sales turnover	10,725	9,909	+8%
Royalties and other trading income	142	116	+22%
Less: materials and services used	(7,560)	(6,845)	+10%
Value added by Manufacturing and Trading Activities	3,307	3,180	+4%
Share of profits less losses of related companies and amounts written off investments	56	71	−21%
Total Value Added	3,363	3,251	+3%
Disposal of Total Value Added:			
Employees*			
Pay, plus pension and national insurance contributions, and severance costs	1,835	1,647	
Profit-sharing bonus†	48	58	
	1,883	1,705	+10%
Governments‡			
Corporate taxes	308	373	
Less: grants	(28)	(28)	
	280	345	−19%
Providers of Capital			
Interest cost of net borrowings	122	100	
Dividends to stockholders	214	186	
Minority shareholders in subsidiaries	52	56	
	388	342	+13%
Re-investment in the Business			
Depreciation and provisions in respect of extraordinary items	514	460	
Profit retained	298	399	
	812	859	−5%
Total Disposal	3,363	3,251	

NOTES:

* The average number of employees in the Group worldwide increased by 3 percent. The number employed in the U.K. decreased by 2 percent.

† 1985 U.K. bonus rate 8.1p per £1 remuneration (1984 10.1p).

‡ Does not include tax deducted from the pay of employees. Income tax deducted from the pay of U.K. employees under PAYE amounted to £157m in 1985 (1984 £148m).

This table, which is used for calculating the bonus under the Employees' Profit-Sharing Scheme, is based on the audited historical cost accounts; it shows the total value added to the cost of materials and services purchased from outside the Group and indicates how this increase in value has been disposed of.

holders have residual claims. In the long run, the retention of earnings provides for a growth in the firm's capital, which through increased productivity may provide increased flows of income to all recipients. If the corporation is assumed to have perpetual or indefinite life, the stockholders may never receive the direct and sole benefit from the retention of earnings in the business.

Enterprise Net Income.   According to the 1957 statement of the American Accounting Association, " . . . interest charges, income taxes, and true profit-sharing distributions are not determinants of enterprise net income."[24] One might conclude, then, that these items are distributions of net income, rather than deductions before arriving at net income. One might also conclude that stockholders, holders of long-term debt, and governments are beneficiaries of the corporation.

This concept of net income has an advantage from the point of view of separating the financial aspects of the corporation from the operating. The net income to the enterprise is an operating concept of net income. Interest to debt holders and earnings to stockholders are financial in nature. Income taxes are neither financial nor strictly operating; and their exclusion from the computation of enterprise net income has some merit because they do not represent controllable input costs. But the treatment of governments as beneficiaries of the corporation when employees and other groups are excluded is of dubious merit from a logical point of view.

Net Income to Investors.   In accordance with the entity concept of the business enterprise, both stockholders and holders of long-term debt are considered equally as investors of permanent capital. With the separation of ownership and control in the large corporation, the differences between stockholders and debt holders are no longer as important as they once were. The main differences arise in the priorities of claims against income and against assets in liquidation. With the emphasis on the observed indefinite life of most large corporations, the claims in liquidation become less important. When we observe the claims against income more closely, we find that the differences between many bond issues and some preferred stock issues are quite fuzzy. Holders of income bonds, for example, may have less security in their claim against income than some holders of cumulative preferred stock, and holders of convertible bonds may obtain rights in undistributed earnings by converting their interests to common stockholder claims.

In the entity concept, income to investors includes the interest on debt, dividends to preferred and common stockholders, and the undivided remainder. This concept of income has considerable merit for several purposes:

1. The decisions regarding the sources of long-term capital are financial rather than operating matters. Therefore, the net income to investors reflects more clearly the results of operations.
2. Because of differing financial structures, comparisons among firms can be made more readily by using this concept of income.
3. The rate of return on total investment computed from this concept of income portrays the relative efficiency of invested capital better than does the rate of return to stockholders.

In the computation of net income to investors, income taxes are treated as expenses. This is the treatment recommended by the APB and adopted by the FASB.[25] It is the authors' opinion that this is the realistic position. The government is not a beneficiary of the corporation in the same way that investors are. The corporation does receive direct benefit from the government, although not in direct proportion to the amount of the tax. The right to operate in a viable economy and to obtain the protection of the courts and protection from external force and violence are only a few of these benefits. Furthermore, corporate income *after* taxes is more stable—by industries—than income before taxes; income taxes seem to be "passed on" much as other expenses.[26] Also, both investors and managers seem to make most of their decisions on the basis of income after taxes.

Net Income to Stockholders. The most traditional and accepted viewpoint of net income is that it represents the return to the owners of the business. Although this concept has its firm foundation in the proprietary approach, many authors apply it to the entity approach and consider the accounting profit of the entity to be a liability to the owners.[27] Implicit in the statements of the FASB is the concept that net income accrues to all stockholders. *SFAC 1* emphasized the predictive nature of reported earnings. It states, for example, that in addition to being used to evaluate management's performance, reported earnings may be used to predict future earnings, to predict the long-term earning ability of the enterprise, or to evaluate the risks of investing in or lending to the enterprise.[28]

The concept of net income to shareholders also has its support in the field of economics. Although the definition of *economic profits* is different from that of *accounting profits,* economists usually treat accounting profits statistically as the total return to the entrepreneurs in their various roles as managers, investors of capital, risk takers, and rentiers. It may or may not be desirable, but it is a realistic fact that the users of accounting statements usually interpret net income to mean the return to shareholders.

Net Income to Residual Equity Holders.   In financial statements presented primarily for stockholders and investors, the net income available for distribution to common stockholders is usually thought to be the most important single figure in the statements. Net income per share of common stock and dividends per share are the most commonly quoted figures in financial news, along with the market price per share. Therefore, there is pragmatic support for presenting statements from which the net income to residual equity holders can readily be obtained.

In a profitable enterprise with indefinite life, the residual equity holder would be the common stockholder or an investor who can become a common stockholder through conversion or exercise of other rights. But there is always the possibility that through reorganization, or because of default in the payment of preferred claims, one of the other groups of investors—preferred stockholders or bondholders—might become the residual equity holders. Therefore, the priorities in the claims to income are important to all groups. The residual net income indicates the degree of security of the priority claims as well as the amount available for distribution to the residual claimants.

The holders of common stock and the prospective buyers of common stock are interested primarily in the future flow of dividends, but knowl-

EXHIBIT 10-5   Summary of Net Income Classifications by Income Recipients

Income Concept	*Income Included*	*Income Recipients*
Valued-added	Selling price of firm's product less cost of goods and services acquired by transfer	All employees, owners, creditors, and governments
Enterprise net income	Excess of revenues over expenses; all gains and losses. Expenses do not include interest charges, income taxes, and true profit-sharing distributions	Stockholders, bondholders, and governments
Net income to investors	Same as enterprise net income, but after deducting income taxes	Stockholders and holders of long-term debt
Net income to shareholders	Net income to investors less interest charges and profit-sharing distributions	Stockholders (preferred and common)
Net income to residual equity holders	Net income to shareholders less preferred dividends	Current and potential common stockholders unless priority payments cannot be met

edge of the net income available and the financial policy of the corporation may provide useful information to common stockholders in their evaluation of the firm and in their prediction of the total amount of annual dividend distributions in the future. However, in order to predict the amount of dividends he or she may receive in the future, an investor must also predict the number of shares that will be outstanding in each period. To the extent that there are outstanding senior stock or debt securities convertible into common shares or stock options, warrants, or agreements for the sale of common stock at less than market prices, a potential dilution of earnings per share and dividends per share exists. *APB 15* recognized this potential dilution and recommended that supplementary pro forma computations of earnings per share should be presented, showing what the earnings per share would have been if the conversions or options had been executed. The computation of earnings per share when potential dilution is present is discussed at greater length in Chapter 20.

Thus, although it is possible to view current net income as the return to current outstanding stockholders, potential residual equity holders must be taken into consideration in predictions regarding future earnings and dividends per share. Furthermore, if current net income is not distributed to current stockholders, the amount added to retained earnings may be shared by these potential holders of common stock.

Exhibit 10-5 summarizes the several concepts of corporate income classified by the income recipients. Note that the value-added concept requires the recognition of income during production, as all product values are expressed in terms of selling prices. The other concepts are more liberal in their acceptance of the several methods of income recognition.

CHECKPOINTS

1. What is meant by the term *lifetime income*? How does this differ from the term *periodic income*?
2. Contrast the concepts of current operating income with that of all-inclusive income.
3. Compare the terms *normal, recurring,* and *operating*.
4. What are the presumed advantages of the all-inclusive income approach to income measurement?
5. Under what conditions would flood damage be considered an extraordinary item for financial reporting purposes?
6. Under what conditions can an item legitimately be considered a prior-period adjustment?

SUMMARY

The concept of income most appropriate for reporting financial operations of business enterprises is determined largely by the objectives of the intended recipients of the summarized accounting data and the interpretive content of the reported amount. A concept useful for one group of individuals or for one purpose may not be the best choice for another. The main questions regarding the choice of an appropriate concept of income are:

1. What are the major objectives of income reporting?
2. What are the basic elements of each of the several income concepts, and how well do they meet the objectives?
3. What types of changes should be included in or excluded from the computation of net income?
4. Who are the major income recipients?

This last question is, of course, related to the objectives of income reporting.

A common objective of income reporting was that it should be the result of rules and procedures that are logical and internally consistent. It was assumed that if users of financial statements understand these rules, they would be able to interpret the meaning of income. Since accounting income was based, and still is in many respects, on such concepts as revenue realization and the matching of expenses with revenues, it was generally assumed that the major activities of the firm could be measured and reported as well as aggregate firm activity.

A necessary long-run objective of an income concept is that it should be related to real-world observations. Two basic interpretive concepts are:

1. *The wealth maintenance concept:* This is assumed by many to be the most basic because it derives its support from economic theory. Changes in the capitalized value of expected cash receipts serve as the foundation of the concept; however, current market prices and similar alternatives are frequently justified on the basis that they represent surrogates (reasonable acceptable substitutes) for current value.

2. *The efficiency concept:* Net income and its components are frequently used as measures of the efficiency of management. Efficiency has interpretive meaning in the economic sense of the optimum utilization of limited resources.

As a third major objective, income should be evaluated on the basis of behavioral dimensions. One behavioral characteristic is predictive ability. The net incomes of several periods may be useful for making predictions regarding the future operations of a firm if proper care is taken to include other relevant factors. Investors may be interested in predicting future incomes or future dividends and share prices. Other groups may wish to make predictions regarding the solvency or other characteristics relevant to decisions regarding relationships with the firm. A similar characteristic is the assumption that income should be closely tied to cash or funds flows. Cash flow activity is considered more relevant in investment decisions than attempts to measure value changes directly. The concept was discussed at greater length in Chapter 9. Other behavioral characteristics include managerial decision making, the relationship of income changes to market prices, and the demand for income figures by investors regardless of their lack of interpretive content.

A final argument is that all concepts of income are both theoretically and practically unsound in the presentation of relevant information to investors and others. That is, they either lack the necessary real-world interpretation or they are not relevant because they lack the necessary behavioral characteristics. Alternative information systems are suggested that may permit the readers of statements to select the relevant data and make their own predictions regarding the value of the firm and other evaluations necessary in their decision making.

What should be included in the computation of net income is dependent upon which of the several objectives are considered to be the most relevant. Income based on the maintenance of capital requires the inclusion of all changes during the period. A report on stewardship should emphasize those changes that are controllable by management. For predictive purposes, changes that are recurring and changes with distinct behavioral characteristics should be disclosed along with these characteristics. The separation of extraordinary items and the exclusion of certain corrections of prior periods suggested in *APB 30* are steps in this direction, but they are inadequate to fulfill this objective. Management is interested primarily in those operating changes that are variable or controllable and are thus relevant for managerial planning and decisions. Because of these several uses for reported income and income components and the different types of information needed for each use, it has been suggested that several concepts of income should be reported. A single concept of income may serve several purposes at least partially, but it is not likely to serve all objectives equally well.

From a broad social and economic point of view, all income generated by the firm should be reported as income. But the division of this income among the income recipients should be reported as well as the total generated. More complete information can probably be presented if the residual net income is restricted to a few income recipients. In any case, the report of net income should state to whom the income accrues. If a broad classification, such as net income to the enterprise, is used, the division of this income should also be presented. Furthermore, when a dilution of income per share is likely because of outstanding convertible securities, warrants, or grants, the probable effect of such a dilution should also be presented.

Conventional accounting practice has tended to emphasize a single net income to stockholders or to the entity. But the computation of this net income has been based on an eclectic approach. One of the major difficulties with discussions regarding alternative accounting procedures is that the writers do not usually indicate the basic concepts of income that they have in mind; therefore, many arguments are fruitless, since the opposing statements are based on different premises without a clear indication of these premises, nor a clear discussion of the basic concepts upon which the arguments rest. A critical analysis of conventional accounting practices regarding valuation procedures and in terms of the various concepts of income will be found in the following chapters.

MULTIPLE CHOICE QUESTIONS

Comprehensive Income

1. [M89#1] According to the FASB's Conceptual Framework, comprehensive income includes which of the following?

	Operating Income	*Investments by Owners*
a.	Yes	No
b.	Yes	Yes
c.	No	Yes
d.	No	No

2. [N86#1] According to the FASB's Conceptual Framework, earnings

a. Are the same as comprehensive income.
b. Exclude certain gains and losses that are included in comprehensive income.
c. Include certain gains and losses that are excluded from comprehensive income.
d. Include certain losses that are excluded from comprehensive income.

3. [M85#1] Under Statements of Financial Accounting Concepts, comprehensive income includes which of the following?

	Gains	*Gross Margin*
a.	No	No
b.	No	Yes
c.	Yes	No
d.	Yes	Yes

Recurring versus Nonrecurring Transactions and Events

4. [M89#23] An extraordinary item should be reported separately on the income statement as a component of income

	Before Discontinued Operations of a Segment of a Business	Net-of-Income Taxes
a.	No	No
b.	No	Yes
c.	Yes	Yes
d.	Yes	No

5. [N88#31] When a segment of a business has been discontinued during the year, the disposal should

a. Exclude operating losses of the current period up to the measurement date.
b. Exclude operating losses during the phase-out period.
c. Be an extraordinary item.
d. Be an operating item.

6. [M88#28] A gain or loss from a transaction that is unusual in nature and infrequent in occurrence should be reported separately as a component of income

a. Before cumulative effect of accounting changes and after discontinued operations of a segment of a business.
b. After cumulative effect of accounting changes and after discontinued operations of a segment of a business.
c. Before cumulative effect of accounting changes and before discontinued operations of a segment of a business.
d. After cumulative effect of accounting changes and before discontinued operations of a segment of a business.

Accounting Changes

7. [M89#24] The cumulative effect of changing to a new accounting principle should be recorded separately as a component of income after continuing operations for a change from the

a. Straight-line method of depreciation for previously recorded assets to the sum-of-the-years'-digits method.
b. LIFO method of inventory pricing to the FIFO method.

c. Percentage-of-completion method of accounting for long-term construction-type contracts to the completed-contract method.

d. Cash basis of accounting for vacation pay to the accrual basis.

8. [N88#32] The cumulative effect of changing to a new accounting principle on the amount of retained earnings at the beginning of the period in which the change is made should be included in net income of

	Future Periods	*The Period of Change*
a.	No	No
b.	Yes	No
c.	Yes	Yes
d.	No	Yes

DISCUSSION QUESTIONS

Accounting Changes

1. [May 1988] There are various types of accounting changes, each of which is required to be reported differently.

Required:

a. What type of accounting change is a change from the sum-of-the-years'-digits method of depreciation to the straight-line method for previously recorded assets? Under what circumstances does this type of accounting change occur?

b. What type of accounting change is a change in the expected service life of an asset arising because of more experience with the asset? Under what circumstances does this type of accounting change occur?

c. With respect to a change in accounting principle,
   1. How should a company calculate the effect?
   2. How should a company report the effect? Do not discuss earnings per share requirements.

d. With respect to a change in accounting principle,
   1. Why are accounting principles, once adopted, normally continued?
   2. What is the rationale for disclosure of a change from one accounting principle to another?

Discontinued Operations and Extraordinaries

1. [May 1987] Lynn Company discontinued operations of a segment of its business in the middle of the year. The segment was operating at a loss from the beginning of the year. At the measurement date, a loss is expected from the proposed sale of the segment. This expected loss includes operating losses during the phase-out period, which will extend into next year.

In addition, Lynn had one of its manufacturing plants destroyed by an earthquake during the year. The loss is properly reported as an extraordinary item.

Required:

a. How should Lynn report discontinued operations of a segment of its business on its income statement for this year? Do not discuss earnings per share requirements.
b. What are the criteria for classification as an extraordinary item?
c. How should Lynn report the extraordinary loss from the earthquake on its income statement for this year? Do not discuss earnings per share requirements.

THE SHEEPHERDERS*

Part I

In the high mountains of Chatele, two sheepherders, Deyonne and Batonne, sit arguing their relative positions in life, an argument which has been going on for years. Deyonne says that he has 400 sheep while Batonne has only 360 sheep. Therefore, Deyonne claims, he is much better off. Batonne, on the other hand, argues that he has 30 acres of land while Deyonne has only 20 acres; then too, Deyonne's land was inherited while Batonne had given 35 sheep for 10 acres of land 10 years ago, and this year he gave 40 sheep for 10 acres of land. Batonne also observes that of Deyonne's sheep 35 belong to another man and he merely watches over them. Deyonne counters that he has a large one-room cabin that he built himself. He claims that he has been offered three acres of land for the cabin. Besides these things, he has a plow, which was a gift from a friend and is worth a couple of goats; two carts which were given him in trade for a poor acre of land; and an ox which he had acquired for five sheep.

Batonne goes on to say that his wife has orders for five coats to be made of homespun wool, and that she will receive 25 goats for them. His wife has 10 goats already, 3 of which have been received in exchange for 1 sheep just last year. She has an ox which she acquired in a trade for three sheep. She also has one cart which cost her two sheep. The Batonne's

* Originally published in *Accounting Education: Problems and Prospects,* ed. James Don Edwards (American Accounting Association, 1974), pp. 365–69.

Copyright Marvin Carlson, Southern Methodist University, and J. Warren Higgins, University of Connecticut, 1990.

two-room cabin, even though smaller in dimensions than Deyonne's, should bring him two choice acres of land in a trade. Deyonne is reminded by Batonne that he owes Tyrone three sheep for bringing up his lunch each day last year.

Objective:

By studying the situation carefully, see what solution you can offer these men. Specify any assumptions which you find necessary to make.

THE SHEEPHERDERS

Part II

A year has elapsed since you solved Part I of the Sheepherders Game. After studying your solution to Part I, Deyonne and Batonne grudgingly accepted your opinion as to their relative wealths at the end of last year. The passage of time has not diminished their penchant for argument, however. Now they're arguing about who had the largest *income* for the year just ended.

Deyonne points out that the number of sheep which he personally owns at year-end exceeds his personal holdings at the beginning of the year by 80, whereas Batonne's increase was only 20. Batonne replies that his increase would have been 60 had he not traded 40 sheep during the year for 10 acres of additional land. Besides, Batonne points out that he exchanged 18 sheep during the year for food and clothing, whereas Deyonne exchanged only 7 for such purposes. The food and clothing has been pretty much used up by the end of the year.

Batonne is happy because his wife made five coats during the year (fulfilling the orders she had at the beginning of the year) and received 25 goats for them. She managed to obtain orders for another five coats (again for 25 goats)—orders on which she has not begun to work. Deyonne points out that he took to making his own lunches this year; therefore he does not owe Tyronne anything now. Deyonne was very upset one day last year when he discovered that his ox had died of a mysterious illness. Both men are thankful, however, that none of the other animals died or was lost.

Except for the matters reported above, each man's holding at the end of the current year are the same as his holdings at the end of last year.

Objective:

What solution can you offer the two men as to which had the greatest income for the year?

PRIMARY SOURCES

Readers interested in the topics raised in this chapter might want to consult the following texts. Each has numerous references.

Bedford, Norton M. *Income Determination Theory: An Accounting Framework* (Reading, Mass.: Addison-Wesley, 1965).

Lee, T. A. *Income and Value Measurement: Theory and Practice* (Baltimore, Md.: University Park Press, 1975).

SELECTED ADDITIONAL READINGS

Accounting Concepts of Income

Barlev, Benzion, and Haim Levy. "On the Variability of Accounting Income Numbers." *Journal of Accounting Research,* Autumn 1979, pp. 305–15.

Beaver, William H., and Joel S. Demski. "The Nature of Income Measurement." *The Accounting Review,* January 1979, pp. 38–46.

Bedford, Norton M. "Income Concept Complex: Expansion or Decline." In *Asset Valuation and Income Determination.* ed. Robert R. Sterling (Lawrence, Kans.: Scholars Book, 1971), pp. 135–44.

Frishkoff, Paul. *Reporting of Summary Indicators: An Investigation of Research and Practice* (FASB, 1981).

Philips, G. Edward. "The Accretion Concept of Income." *The Accounting Review,* January 1963, pp. 14–25.

Sprouse, Robert T. "The Importance of Earnings in the Conceptual Framework." *Journal of Accountancy,* January 1978, pp. 64–71.

Economic Concepts of Income

Alexander, Sidney S. "Income Measurement in a Dynamic Economy." Revised by David Solomons and reprinted in *Studies in Accounting Theory.* ed. W. T. Baxter and Sidney Davidson (Homewood, Ill.: Richard D. Irwin, 1962), pp. 126–200.

Barton, A. D. "Expectations and Achievements in Income Theory." *The Accounting Review,* October 1974, pp. 664–81.

Demski, Joel S. "The General Impossibility of Normative Accounting Standards." *The Accounting Review,* October 1973, pp. 718–23.

Gonedes, Nicholas J. "Corporate Signaling, External Accounting, and Capital Market Equilibrium: Evidence on Dividends, Income, and Extraordinary Items." *Journal of Accounting Research,* Spring 1978, pp. 26–79.

Shwayder, Keith. "A Critique of Economic Income as an Accounting Concept." *Abacus,* August 1967, pp. 23–35.

Shwayder, Keith. "The Capital Maintenance Rule and the Net Asset Valuation Rule." *The Accounting Review,* April 1969, pp. 304–16.

Solomons, David. "Economic and Accounting Concepts of Income." *The Accounting Review,* July 1961, pp. 374–83.

Van Breda, Michael F. "Integrating Capital and Operating Budgets." *Sloan Management Review,* Winter 1984, pp. 49–58.

Income as a Measure of Efficiency

Amey, L. R. *The Efficiency of Business Enterprises* (New York: Augustus M. Kelley, 1970).

Glautier, W. E. "Theoretical Considerations of Accounting Profit with Particular Reference to the Assessment of Operating Efficiency." *Journal of Business Finance,* Summer 1972, pp. 5–14.

Predictive Ability

Albrecht, W. Steve; Larry L. Lookabill; and James C. McKeown. "The Time-Series Properties of Annual Earnings." *Journal of Accounting Research,* Autumn 1977, pp. 226–44.

Foster, George. "Quarterly Accounting Data: Time-Series Properties and Predictability Results." *The Accounting Review,* January 1977, pp. 1–21.

Griffin, Paul A. "The Time-Series Behavior of Quarterly Earnings: Preliminary Evidence." *Journal of Accounting Research,* Spring 1977, pp. 71–83.

Lorek, Kenneth. "Predicting Annual Net Earnings with Quarterly Earnings Time-Series Models." *Journal of Accounting Research,* Spring 1970, pp. 190–204.

Louderback, Joseph G. III. "Projectability as a Criterion for Income Determination Methods." *The Accounting Review,* April 1971, pp. 298–305.

Watts, Ross, and Richard W. Leftwich. "The Time Series of Annual Accounting Earnings." *Journal of Accounting Research,* Autumn 1977, pp. 253–71.

Income and Capital Market Theories

Basu, S. "The Effect of Earnings Yield of Assessment of the Association between Annual Accounting Income Numbers and Security Prices." *The Accounting Review,* July 1978, pp. 599–625.

Beaver, William H. "The Information Content of Annual Earnings Announcements." *Journal of Accounting Research,* Empirical Research in Accounting: Selected Studies, 1968, pp. 67–92.

Firth, Michael. "Impact of Earnings Announcement on the Share Price Behavior of Similar-Type Firms." *The Economic Journal,* June 1976, pp. 296–306.

Hoskin, Robert E., and William E. Ricks. "Evidence on the Incremental Information Content of Additional Firm Disclosures Made Concurrently with Earnings." *Journal of Accounting Research,* Supplement, 1986, pp. 1–32.

Extraordinary Items

Barnea, Amir; Joshua Ronen; and Simcha Sadan. "The Implementation of Accounting Objectives: An Application to Extraordinary Items." *The Accounting Review,* January 1975, pp. 58–68.

Barnea, Amir; Joshua Ronen; and Simcha Sadan. "Classificatory Smoothing of Income with Extraordinary Items." *The Accounting Review,* January 1976, pp. 110–22.

Bernstein, Leopold A. "Extraordinary Gains and Losses—Their Significance to the Financial Analyst." *Financial Analysts Journal,* November–December 1972, pp. 49–52, 88–90.

Bernstein, Leopold A. *Accounting for Extraordinary Gains and Losses* (New York: Ronald Press, 1967), especially chaps. 1, 2, 3, and Appendix B.

Carroll, Thomas J. "The Accountants' Extraordinary Dilemma." *World,* Summer 1974, pp. 14–19.

Most, Kenneth S. "A Proposal for the Abolition of 'Extraordinary Events' and Transactions." *Singapore Accountant,* 1974, pp. 23–29.

Ronen, Joshua, and Simcha Sadan, *Smoothing Income Numbers: Objectives, Means, and Implications* (Reading, Mass.: Addison-Wesley, 1981).

Snaveley, Howard J., and Allan H. Savage. "Clean Surplus vs. Current Operating Performance—Gaps in *APB Opinion No. 9.*" *New York Certified Public Accountant,* February 1970, pp. 124–29.

Estimation Theory

Brief, Richard P., and Joel Owen. "A Reformulation of the Estimation Problem." *Journal of Accounting Research,* Spring 1973, pp. 1–15.

Brief, Richard P., and Joel Owen. "Present Value Models and the Multi-Asset Problem." *The Accounting Review,* October 1973, pp. 690–95.

Jarrett, Jeffrey E. "Notes on the Estimation Problem in Financial Accounting." *Journal of Accounting Research,* Spring 1972, pp. 108–12.

Return on Investment

Stauffer, T. A. "The Measurement of Corporate Rates of Return: A Generalized Foundation." *Bell Journal of Economics and Management Science,* 1971, pp. 434–69.

Van Breda, Michael F. "The Misuse of Accounting Rates of Return: A Comment." *American Economic Review,* June 1984, pp. 507–8.

Van Breda, Michael F. "Accounting Rates of Return under Inflation." *Sloan Management Review,* Summer 1981, pp. 15–28.

ENDNOTES

1. See, for example, William H. Beaver and Joel S. Demski, "The Nature of Income Measurement," *The Accounting Review,* January 1979, pp. 38–46.
2. See Ray Ball and Philip Brown, "An Empirical Evaluation of Accounting Income Numbers," *Journal of Accounting Research,* Autumn 1968, pp. 159–78.
3. *SFAC 1,* par. 43.
4. Lyn D. Pankoff and Robert L. Virgil, "Some Preliminary Findings from a Laboratory Experiment on the Usefulness of Financial Accounting Informa-

tion to Security Analysts,'' *Journal of Accounting Research,* Empirical Research in Accounting: Selected Studies, 1970, p. 22.

5. Ibid., p. 23.
6. American Institute of Certified Public Accountants, *Report of the Study Group on the Objectives of Financial Statements,* ''Objectives of Financial Statements'' (October 1973), p. 22.
7. Norton Bedford, ''The Income Concept Complex: Expansion or Decline,'' in *Asset Valuation,* ed. Robert Sterling (Lawrence, Kans.: Scholars Book, 1971), p. 142.
8. *SFAC 1,* par. 42.
9. For more details on estimation theory, see Richard P. Brief and Joel Owen, ''A Reformation of the Estimation Problem,'' *Journal of Accounting Research,* Spring 1973, pp. 1–15.
10. Richard P. Brief, ''The Accountant's Responsibility in Historical Perspective,'' *The Accounting Review,* April 1975, pp. 285–97.
11. *SFAC 1,* pars. 43 and 46.
12. Dale Buckmaster, Ronald M. Copeland, and Paul E. Dascher, ''The Relative Predictive Ability of Three Accounting Income Models,'' *Accounting and Business Research,* Summer 1977, pp. 177–86.
13. See, for example, Carl R. Beidleman, ''Income Smoothing: The Role of Management,'' *The Accounting Review,* October 1973, p. 653. Smoothing can be defined as the use of alternative procedures and measurements to minimize variability of accounting income.
14. Prem Prakash and Alfred Rappaport, ''Information Inductance and Its Significance for Accounting,'' *Accounting, Organizations, and Society,* 1977, pp. 29–38.
15. For many examples of the misuse of accounting to influence and even deceive investors, see Abraham J. Briloff, *Unaccountable Accounting* (New York: Harper & Row, 1972), and Anthony Sampson, *The Sovereign State of ITT* (New York: Stein & Day, 1973), p. 142.
16. See, for example, Ray Ball and Philip Brown, ''An Empirical Evaluation of Accounting Income Numbers,'' *Journal of Accounting Research,* Autumn 1968, pp. 159–78.
17. *SFAC 5,* par. 42.
18. Ibid.
19. See Briloff, *Unacceptable Accounting,* pp. 178 and 194–95.
20. *SFAS 16,* par. 10. Special exceptions are made for prior interim periods of the current year.
21. Application of *SFAS 96* was deferred at the time of writing until after December 15, 1991.
22. See, for example, *FASB Discussion Memorandum,* ''Reported Earnings,'' (July 31, 1979) and *SFAC 6,* par. 220.
23. Michael F. Morley, *The Value-Added Statement: A Review of Its Use in Corporate Reports* (London: Gee & Co., 1978).
24. Committee on Accounting Concepts and Standards, *Accounting and Reporting Standards for Corporate Financial Statements and Preceding Statements and Supplements* (AAA, 1957), p. 5.

25. *APB 11,* par. 13 and *SFAS 96,* par. 206.
26. See Marian Krzyzaniak and Richard A. Musgrave, *The Shifting of the Corporation Income Tax* (Baltimore: John Hopkins Press, 1963), pp. 65–66.
27. See, for example, Stephen Gilman, *Accounting Concepts of Profit* (New York: Ronald Press, 1939), p. 598.
28. *SFAC 1,* par. 47.

Chapter 11

Revenues and Expenses, Gains, and Losses

CHAPTER OBJECTIVES

After studying this chapter, you will be able to:

Define the nature of revenue, determine what should be included under the heading of revenue, and measure it appropriately.

Distinguish recognition of revenue from its realization and determine when, in general, revenue should be recognized.

Define the nature of expenses, determine what should be included under the heading of expense, and measure it appropriately.

Determine when an expense should be recognized.

Distinguish gains and losses from each other and from revenues and expenses.

CHAPTER OVERVIEW

Revenues and Gains

Revenues may be defined most generally as the product of an enterprise. They are typically measured in terms of current exchange prices. They should be recognized after a critical event or once the selling process has been substantially accomplished. In practice, this usually means that revenues are recognized at the point of sale. Gains are distinguished from revenues and expenses by being more peripheral to the primary activities of the enterprise.

Expenses and Losses

Expenses are the costs incurred to generate those revenues. They should be recognized at the same time as the revenues that they generate. An association between revenues and expenses is often difficult to determine, so a variety of relatively arbitrary rules are used for expense recognition. Expenses are measured in both historical and current exchange prices. Losses are more peripheral to the primary activities of the firm. Their recognition and measurement, though, are the same as those of expenses.

Industry-Specific Rules

The motion picture industry and the real estate industry provide two examples of how detailed rules have been set for specific areas. Whether this level of detail in a standard is desirable or not is debatable.

Revenues are the lifeblood of an enterprise. Without revenues, there are no earnings. Without earnings, there is no enterprise. Given its importance, it has been surprisingly difficult to define revenue as an accounting element in its own right. What is true for revenues is true for expenses, which are equally difficult to define. Ideally, it should be possible, given that revenues and expenses are elements of income, to draw a definition of revenue from the two preceding chapters. It should also be possible to determine the most appropriate moment to recognize revenues and expenses from definitions of income. In practice, that has proved hard to do.

Many, including the FASB, resort to definitions that are independent of a definition of income and rely instead upon changes in assets and liabilities. The result is that income tends to emerge from definitions of revenues and expenses rather than the other way around. What is worse, from a theoretical standpoint, is that revenue and expense recognition tends to follow common practice rather than best practice, let alone theory. These difficulties would be merely academic were revenues and expenses not such an important ingredient in the measurement of corporate performance. Companies frequently have used the weakness in the definitions to claim disputable amounts as revenue and thus boost their income. Similarly, companies have found accounting loopholes which they use to avoid reporting items as expenses of a particular period.

The chapter begins with a discussion of revenues. The discussion suggests that determining the precise nature of revenues should precede questions of how to measure them and when to recognize them. A similar discussion then follows for expenses. Gains and losses are then distinguished from each other and from revenues and expenses in each section. Two industry-specific examples are used to close the chapter. In each section, the link between revenues, expenses, and income is stressed.

REVENUES AND GAINS

The nature, the measurement, and the timing of revenue are fascinating problems of accounting theory. In practice, revenue definitions are often associated with specific accounting procedures, certain types of value changes, and assumed or implicit rules for determining when revenue should be reported. This practice makes separating a definition of revenue from the valuation and timing problems a difficult task. Since a clear understanding of each component of revenue is necessary, this chapter attempts to disentangle the concept of revenue by asking the following questions:

1. What is the nature of revenue?
2. What should be included in the term *revenue*?
3. How should revenue be measured?
4. When are revenues incurred and when should they be reported for accounting purposes?

The Nature of Revenue

At its most basic, revenue is an increase in income. Like income, it is a flow process—the creation of goods or services by an enterprise during a specific interval of time.[1] Paton and Littleton called this creation of goods and services the *product* of the enterprise.[2] Notice that the definition of revenue as the product of the enterprise does not dictate either the amount or the timing of recognition of the revenue and, thereby, of income. Generally, revenue is expressed in monetary terms, although the measurement of revenue under this concept is open for discussion without changing the nature of revenue being measured.

Several similar definitions also state that revenue is the product of the enterprise, but add that the product must leave the firm before it can be called revenue (an *outflow* concept). For example, the Committee on Accounting Concepts and Standards of the American Accounting Association defined revenue in the 1957 statement as follows:

> Revenue . . . is the monetary expression of the aggregate of products or services transferred by an enterprise to its customers during a period of time.[3]

An immediate criticism of this addition is that it precludes the use of the percentage-of-completion method in which revenue is recognized before a product or service is transferred.*

The FASB attacked the problem of defining revenue from the opposite direction. They focused on the cash received at the point of sale or later, if a credit sale, and defined revenue in terms of the *inflow* of assets into the firm as a result of sales of goods and services. In their words:

> Revenues are inflows or other enhancements of assets of an entity or settlements of its liabilities (or a combination of both) from delivering or producing goods, rendering services, or other activities that constitute the entity's ongoing major or central operations.[4]

This definition has been faulted on several grounds. First, it confuses the product with the payment received for that product. In other words, critics say, it confuses the *measurement* and *timing* of the revenue with the revenue *process* itself. Of course, assets are generally increased, or liabilities decreased, at the time of sale of goods or services. And it is true that the amount of revenue is traditionally determined by the monetary measurement of the assets received. So their definition is in accord with traditional practice. The problem is that their definition does not permit as broad a perspective of the measuring and timing processes as the product approach.

The inflow approach also requires a careful statement of which inflows should be considered revenues and which should not. Assets may increase and liabilities decrease for many reasons, of which revenue is only one. For instance, payments made in advance, such as those made when purchasing season tickets, are inflows of assets and an activity that is part of the entity's central operations. Yet these inflows are not revenues. Revenues may also be reported before an actual inflow of assets occurs. In fact, it may be argued that all credit sales take place before there is an inflow of assets. The sale, at best, creates an asset, namely accounts receivable; accounts receivable does not create the sale. The FASB's definition, therefore, is not entirely satisfactory.

To avoid the criticisms of the last paragraph, revenue is sometimes defined in terms of its effect on stockholders' equity. This was the approach taken in *APB Statement No. 4*, where revenue was defined as:

> gross increases in assets or gross decreases in liabilities recognized and measured in conformity with generally accepted accounting principles that result from those types of profit-directed activities . . . of an enterprise that can change owners' equity. . . .[5]

---

* One response might be that the percentage-of-completion method should be disallowed!

Now it is true that the revenue account has a credit balance and is closed at the end of the accounting period to retained earnings through the revenue and expense summary account. Therefore, revenue does have the effect of increasing the stockholders' equity. However, all that this approach does is relate revenue to double-entry bookkeeping. It adds nothing to our understanding of its basic nature. In addition, it has the disadvantage of defining revenue in terms of a residual. Stockholders' equity is itself undefined, except as the difference between assets and liabilities. Furthermore, there are several reasons for increases in stockholders' equity not associated with revenue. For instance, donated property causes a gross increase in assets and affects owners' equity, yet it is usually not considered to be revenue.*

Thus, in the opinion of the authors, the definition of revenue as the product of the enterprise is superior to the outflow concept, and the outflow concept is superior to the inflow concept. The product concept is neutral with respect to both timing and measurement; the inflow concept, as it is generally proposed, avoids neither. The product approach tends to be ignored, though, because revenue is traditionally associated with a transaction instead of being viewed as something that is being created over time and recognized only at a point in time. More important, though, than whether revenue is an inflow or an outflow, is the fact that revenue is *not* a cash flow. This is a key insight in accounting that relates directly to consumption theory in classical economics.

The FASB's definition introduces a second theme into this discussion of the nature of revenue. Their definition attempts to define revenue in terms of assets and liabilities. In other words, the FASB attempts to define the income statement in terms of changes in the balance sheet. This is rather like attempting to define nuclear particles in terms of their effects on X-ray plates. Many argue that this confuses the measurement of revenue with a definition of revenue. There can be no effect of revenue on assets or liabilities until revenue has been recognized; revenue cannot be recognized until it is defined. The attempt to define it in terms of its effects, therefore, involves circular reasoning. Circular or not, the asset-liability approach to revenue (and to expense) definition is currently favored by the FASB.

What Should Be Included in the Term Revenue?

Many argue that it is necessary to distinguish revenues from gains. A variety of attempts have been made to do this, most of which have ended with rather arbitrary results. The view expressed in this book is that a

---

* Again, the argument can be made that perhaps donated property should be treated as revenue.

better understanding of accounting may be obtained by ignoring this distinction while maintaining sufficient classifications by type of revenue to help the user understand the operations of the enterprise. The authors prefer to make a distinction between the wealth-producing activities of the firm and unexpected transfers of wealth arising from gifts or windfalls. Stated otherwise, all activities, whether major or minor, that relate to the *wealth-producing* activities of the firm would be included in the general category *revenue*. The result would be a more comprehensive view of revenue. Among those who take such a comprehensive view of revenue is the APB in *Statement No. 4*. In addition to sales and services, it included in revenue the sale of resources other than products, such as plant and equipment and investments.[6] Paton and Littleton also allowed that, although the "flow of accomplishment" was the primary source of revenue, the entire range of goods and services furnished by the enterprise, regardless of the relative amount of a particular item, should be included in revenue.[7]

The FASB, however, preferred a narrower definition of revenues. Their definition of revenues stated that they result from "the enterprise's ongoing major or central operations." This last was included to distinguish revenues from gains, which were defined as "increases in equity (net assets) from peripheral or incidental operations."[8] Gains for most companies, therefore, would include profits on activities such as the occasional sale of land and other property, as well as increases in equity resulting from donations and other windfalls. The FASB acknowledges that this definition does not permit fine distinctions, but argues that, since the distinction is important for display purposes only, fine distinctions are not necessary.

Most gains will appear in the income statement—and, therefore, are increases in income. Gifts to the enterprise are an exception. They may be classified as either capital or income, depending on the intent of the donor, the circumstances surrounding the gift, and one's definition of income. In a few cases, the intent of a gratuity may be to increase the income of the firm, as in the case of "conscience payments," or extra payments to show gratitude for special services received. But, in the case of contributions in aid of construction required before service can be supplied to some public-utility customers, and in the case of special donations to attract a firm to a community, the intent is to provide permanent capital. GAAP, therefore, credits them directly to an equity account.

How Should Revenue Be Measured?

Revenue, however defined, is best measured by the exchange value of the product or service of the enterprise. This exchange value represents the cash equivalent, or the present discounted value of the money claims to be received eventually from the revenue transaction. In many cases, this amount is simply the price established in a cash transaction with the customer. However, where necessary, appropriate allowance must be made for the necessity to wait for final collection. A cash sale for $100 produces $100 of revenue, but a similar sale permitting the same payment a year later produces less than $100 of revenue because of the necessity to compute the present value of the latter amount.

Gains are treated similarly to revenues, except that related costs are offset immediately to provide a net gain. In the sale of assets not usually traded by the firm, these costs include the value of the assets sold plus the direct costs of sale. The allocation of income taxes to the transaction will be discussed in Chapter 20.

The criterion that revenue should be measured by the present value of the money or money equivalent finally to be received implies that all returns, trade discounts, and other reductions of the billed prices should be deducted from the revenue resulting from the specific transactions. Stated otherwise, they should be treated as the reductions of revenues that they are, and not as expenses. The treatment of cash discounts and losses resulting from uncollectible accounts may not be quite so clear. However, as the next paragraph demonstrates, they should also be treated as reductions from billed prices and not as expenses.

Cash discounts are granted, in part, to equate the value of the money received within the discount period with the present discounted value of the money that would be received under the granted credit terms. But one of the main purposes of the cash discounts is to reduce bad debt losses by encouraging people to pay early or in cash. If the cash discount rates were set rationally, sellers would be indifferent as to whether they received the net discounted price, or the gross price less a normal expectation of bad debt losses. Cash discounts and expected bad debt losses are, therefore, similar in nature and should be treated similarly. Cash discounts expected to be taken and bad debt losses expected to be incurred should be deducted directly from gross revenue. Their traditional treatment as expenses does not result in a different amount of reported net income but, as will be apparent after reading the next section on expenses, they do not have the basic characteristics of expenses. If the degree of homogeneity within classifications in the income statement is increased, each category, such as net revenue, will be a better representation of real-world observations.

All of the above is subject to the usual caveat of materiality. When the waiting period is short, the discount may be ignored for three pragmatic reasons:

1. At low discount rates the amount of the discount is small and does not materially affect the total revenue valuation. For example, if the claim is to be paid in 60 days, the amount of the discount at an annual rate of 10 percent would be less than 2 percent of the revenue.

2. Because interest is classified as part of total revenue, the main effect is that of timing. Interest should be recorded subsequent to the recording of the revenue from the initial transaction. However, if the interest is not material in amount, including it in the sales revenue would have little effect on total revenue for the period.

3. If revenues are not discounted, the classification of revenue arising from waiting (interest) would be lost and included in the classification of revenue arising from the sale of the product or service. However, if the implicit interest is not material in amount, little useful information is lost by the failure to classify it separately.*

Materiality, therefore, tends to blur theoretical niceties.

When Are Revenues Recognized?

The general rules for recognition in accounting are that the item meet the definition of the element and that it be measurable, relevant, and reliable. In the present context, an item should be recognized as revenue of an enterprise when it is part of the product of the organization, when it can be measured, when it has predictive or feedback value, and when it can be reliably verified. The FASB gave suggestions for revenue recognition that were specific to revenue. Revenue, it said, should not be recognized until it is:

a. Earned.
b. Realized or realizable.

Given that revenue is a part of income, the rules for revenue recognition are part of the rules for income recognition. Key, therefore, to understanding when income should be recognized is a determination when it has been earned and realized.

Earning Revenue. From an economic point of view, earning is a continuous process. The product of the enterprise appears gradually as raw materials are assembled and changed in form or processed by the application of labor and capital equipment. The transportation of raw materials to the plant, and of the finished product to the market, are also part of the earning process in an economic sense. Likewise, storage, either as a part of the production process, or as a necessary requirement of meeting market demand, is also a part of the service provided by a firm. Strictly speaking, therefore, revenues should be recognized continuously over the entire product cycle. The percentage-of-completion method is an example where this is actually done in practice.

---

* Receivables arising from revenue transactions are exempt from the discounting requirements of *APB Opinion No. 21* if they are due within one year.

EXHIBIT 11-1   International Business Machine (IBM) Revenue Recognition
Policies, 1988

Revenue is recognized from sales or sales-type leases when the product is
shipped, from software when the program is shipped or as monthly license fees
accrue, from support services (primarily maintenance services) over the contractual period or as the services are performed, from rentals under operating
leases in the month in which they accrue, and from financing at level rates of
return over the term of the lease or receivable.

The cost of continually accumulating revenues prevents the universal
use of continuous recognition in practice. Instead, accountants have
searched for a single point at which revenues might legitimately be said to
have been earned. Several different approaches have been suggested as a
basis for establishing this point. Exhibit 11-1 illustrates some of these
points. *ARS 3* offered a general rule for recognition, stating that:

> Revenues should be identified with the period during which the major economic
> activities necessary to the creation and disposition of goods and services have
> been accomplished, provided objective measurements of the results of those
> activities are available. These two conditions, i.e., accomplishment of major
> economic activity and objectivity of measurement, are fulfilled at different
> stages of activity in different cases, sometimes as late as time of delivery of
> product or the performance of a service, in other cases, at an earlier point of
> time.[9]

The authors are in general agreement with this view that revenue should
be acknowledged and reported when the major economic activities are
accomplished if its measurement is verifiable and free from bias.

An alternative to the reporting of revenue at the time of accomplishment of the major economic activities is the *critical event* (or crucial
event) concept of revenue reporting.[10] The critical event approach recognizes revenue as soon as uncertainty has been sufficiently resolved. This
approach suggests that sufficient resolution occurs when the most critical
decision is made or when the most difficult task is performed. This moment could be when the contract is signed, which would be ahead of the
major accomplishments. It could be at the time when the services are
performed, which is the moment when most of the sales work is complete.
In cases where uncertainty is high, the point of resolution could be still
later in the process, such as when the cash is finally collected. This last
case would indicate the use of the installment method.

An extension of the critical event concept is found in a 1964 AAA
monograph, *The Realization Concept*. It was suggested there that some of
the revenue should be recognized later if additional economic functions or
activities are to take place subsequently. The committee rejected the
reporting of income on the basis of costs incurred, but it implied that the

value added by the firm should be allocated to more than one point in time. In their view, even if the value added by the firm is reported at a single point in time, the amount of revenue represented by the value added by other economic factors should be reported at a later time if, in fact, the services provided by these factors follow the main point of recognition. This suggestion has not been adopted, nor has that of the 1974 AAA committee that proposed to circumvent the difficulties of determining the critical event through the use of probabilistic measurements of revenue.[11]

Realization.   The term *revenue realization* was used by accountants for many years to refer to the recording of revenue. One of the difficulties with the realization concept was that the term meant different things to different people.[12] The general view, however, was that realization represented the reporting of revenue when an exchange or outflow of product had occurred. That is, goods or services must have been transferred to a customer or client, giving rise to either the receipt of cash or a claim to cash or other assets. In this view, realization could not take place by the holding of assets or as a result of the production process alone. Thus, the term *realization* came generally to mean the reporting of revenue when it was validated by a sale.* The reporting of revenue before or after the point of sale was generally considered an exception to the realization rule. The problem with the way the term realization came to be used is that what should have been left as a question of when to "realize" revenue was already answered in the definition, namely at the point of sale.

To avoid this problem, the FASB now prefers the use of the word *recognition* to refer specifically to the recording of an element. In other words, now when one is questioning whether it is appropriate to report an asset, a liability, income, a revenue, or an expense in the financial statements, one is discussing recognition. The FASB has now reserved the term *realization* to mean "the process of converting noncash resources and rights into money."[13] Since realization typically occurs at the point of the sale, this is a change in usage, but not in meaning.

Realizability, then, means the ability to convert claims into cash. So one condition of recognition is that the product has been sold for cash or credit. Assets, such as corn and wheat, that "have (i) interchangeable (fungible) units and (ii) quoted prices available in active markets that can rapidly absorb the quantity held by the entity without significantly affecting the price," are an exception to this rule. These assets are readily converted and may be considered realizable before an actual sale.[14]

---

* Paton and Littleton, however, stated that the dominant view was that realization includes the test of ". . . validation through the acquisition of liquid assets." Paton and Littleton, *Corporate Accounting Standards*, p. 49.

The effect of the rule that revenue not be recognized until realized is that many of the income recognition possibilities discussed in the previous two chapters are excluded. In particular, it excludes many of the capital-maintenance approaches that are based on changes in value, on grounds that these value changes are unrealized.

Recognizing Gains.   The timing of the recognition of gains, and specifically gains resulting from increases in the value of assets, should be identical to the timing of the recognition of revenues. However, accountants generally have held more closely to the realization concept. That is, usually they have not recognized gains until an exchange or sale has taken place. Most accountants require that a reversal in the increase in value be almost impossible before making recognition.[15] From a theoretical point of view, this requirement is an extreme position. The most probable outcome in uncertain situations should be recorded, rather than limiting recognition to only those cases that are certain. Also, using a double standard for the recognition of gains and losses is inconsistent; both should be recognized on the same basis of probability. Aside from pure conservatism, accountants are reluctant to record appreciation for two reasons:

1. The uncertain and possibly ephemeral nature of the increase in value.
2. The fact that an increase in value does not give rise to liquid resources that can be used for the payment of dividends.

This emphasis on liquid resources or cash flows may be relevant for some types of decisions, but not for the measurement of most concepts of income. For income determination, relative certainty and verifiable measurements are the relevant criteria.

There has been one shift in the traditional approach to recognizing gains. For investments in marketable securities, the recording of losses and recoveries from losses, arising from material changes in market prices, became acceptable in accounting practice because both verifiability and liquidity are present, even though the change had not been validated by a sale or exchange in which the firm is a party. But if land increases in value, it is generally thought inappropriate in the United States (but not in some other countries) to increase the recorded valuation above cost. However, to the extent that verifiable measurements can be obtained regarding the changes in the market price of land, changes in its price may be just as relevant in the determination of income as are changes in the value of bonds or investments in marketable securities. The economic gain or loss is not more real just because the securities or land are sold and the proceeds used to reacquire securities or land of the same type. The opportunity to do so, however, may be relevant information regarding the firm, even though the intent is not to sell.

Summary

To summarize then, GAAP dictates that revenue and, therefore, income should be recognized in accounting statements when the following criteria have been met:

1. Economic value must have been added by the firm to its product.
2. The amount of the revenue must be measurable.
3. The measurement must be verifiable and relatively free from bias.
4. It must be possible to estimate related expenses with a fair degree of accuracy.

In general, accounting statements are improved if the revenue is reported at the earliest possible point after the value increase can be measured. In practice, a variety of points are recognized. These are briefly described below and summarized in Exhibit 11-2.

EXHIBIT 11-2

Time of Reporting	*Criteria*	*Examples*
During production	Establishment of a firm price based on contract or general business terms or existence of market prices at various stages of production.	Accruals; long-term contracts; accretion
At completion of production	Existence of a determinable selling price or stable market price. No substantial cost of marketing.	Precious metals, agricultural products, services
At time of sale	Established price for the product. Reasonable method for estimating amount collectible. Estimation of all material-related expenses.	Most merchandise sales
At time of cash collection	Impossible to value assets received with fair degree of accuracy. Additional material expenses are likely, and these cannot be estimated with a fair degree of accuracy at the time of sale.	Installment sales; exchange for fixed assets without verifiably determined value

Reporting Revenue during Production

There are numerous cases where revenue is recognized during production. The bulk of these cases involve services where recognition during production is general practice. Examples include rent, interest, commissions, and personal services performed on a time basis. In each of these examples the basic criteria for revenue reporting are met. The services are usually performed on a time basis and the performance of services may be assumed to be crucial. The amount of the revenue has been established by prior contract or agreement. Related expenses are usually determinable simultaneously with the revenue. In addition, a valid claim arises against the customer, client, or tenant even though the amount is not billed and payment is not required until a later date.

Long-Term Contracts. A second accepted application of the reporting of revenue during production is the recognition of revenue on long-term contracts, usually with the percentage-of-completion method. The general acceptance in this case is based primarily on pragmatic grounds. Firms usually object to publication of financial statements showing no income for a year during which the firm had spent considerable effort in obtaining partial completion of a contract that would have permitted a reasonable profit with a fair degree of certainty. The procedure can be justified, though, on grounds that earning has occurred, uncertainty regarding the selling price is minimized because the total price is known, and uncertainty regarding collection is usually not very great, particularly if the buyer is a governmental unit or a large established corporation.

The percentage-of-completion method that is typically used compares the costs incurred in a specific accounting period with the total estimated costs for the project. This is termed the *cost-to-cost* method. The expected profit on the contract is then allocated to each period on the basis of these costs. This procedure has two difficulties, which make the resulting periodic income suspect at best:

1. The total costs of the project may be difficult to estimate with accuracy. This is particularly so where excavation and weather conditions may present unknown hazards. If the actual costs of completion differ from the estimated costs, the net income of each period will have been affected.

2. It assumes that the firm's profit is earned as costs are incurred. But an important part of the firm's contribution may come from the planning stage, before large costs are incurred. Furthermore, many of the costs involve work performed by subcontractors and are not the result of the firm's contribution. An alternative might be to include only those costs included in the concept of value added. But the assumption that each dollar of cost produces the same amount of revenue implies that the value added by the firm is related to the use of other economic factors, an assumption that is conceptually unacceptable.

Accretion.   Related to the reporting of revenue during production is the recognition of increased values arising from natural growth or an aging process. This natural growth or aging over time is just as much a part of the production process from an economic point of view as the process of changing the form of commodities. In an economic sense, then, accretion gives rise to revenue. Examples include growing timber, nursery stock, and livestock, and the aging of certain liquors and wines.

The revenues or income from accretion can be recognized only by making comparative inventory valuations. This recognition is not the result of transactions. Therefore, it does differ from the cases of revenue reporting during production discussed so far. But this does not affect the logic of reporting the increases in asset measurement. The limitations of using this method relate primarily to the difficulty of determining the present discounted value, because it depends upon expectations regarding future market prices and expectations regarding future costs of providing for growth and future costs of harvesting and getting the product ready for market.

Reporting Revenue at the Completion of Production

When a product is completed, one of the former uncertainties—the cost of production—can now be computed with a fair degree of accuracy. The selling price and the additional costs of selling and delivering may still remain uncertain. But when they can be estimated reliably, there is good justification for reporting the revenue at this time. The main consideration should be the ability to obtain reliable, verifiable measurements of revenue and *additional costs*. For most commodities, the lack of a stable market price is a major stumbling block for the general acceptance of the recognition of revenue at the completion of production.

According to *APB Statement No. 4,* revenue may be reported at the completion of production under the above criteria only for "precious metals that have a fixed selling price and insignificant marketing cost."[16] Similar treatment is acceptable for agricultural, mineral, and other products only if the firm is unable to determine appropriate approximate costs. In all cases, however, the sales prices should be reduced by the estimated costs of disposal. Note that the lack of cost measurement is not a basic standard for using market prices; rather it is an extenuating circumstance under which market prices are permitted.

Reporting Revenue at the Time of Sale

For many years delivery has been the general rule for the reporting of revenue. The uncertainties regarding the final measurement of revenue are minimal at the time of delivery, but they are not eliminated. Accepted business practice may permit the return of all or a part of the merchandise, thus canceling the sales contract. Failure to collect the sale price is often a possibility, the likelihood of which may depend upon the credit rating of the customer. Also, additional expenses may arise, many of which are unexpected. These would include abnormal collection charges and expenses of meeting express or implied customer warranties. However, usually the uncollectible accounts and the additional expenses may be estimated from past experience.

Reporting Revenue Subsequent to Sale

Delaying the reporting of revenue, beyond the time when a valid claim against customers arises and the basic activity regarding such sale of products or services has been accomplished, can be justified only if one of the two following criteria is met:

1. If it is impossible to measure the assets received in the exchange with a fair degree of accuracy.
2. If additional material expenses directly associated with the transaction are likely and if they cannot be estimated with a fair degree of accuracy.

Situations in which recognition may be deferred beyond the point of sale include sales with recourse and installment sales.

Sales with Recourse. The FASB, basing its conclusions on Statement of Position 75-1, recommended in *SFAS 48,* "Revenue Recognition When Rights of Return Exists," that when a seller is exposed to the risks of ownership through return of the property, the revenue should not be recognized currently unless *all* of the following conditions are met:

a. The seller's price to the buyer is substantially fixed or determinable at the date of sale.
b. The buyer has paid the seller, or the buyer is obligated to pay the seller and the obligation is not contingent on resale of the product.
c. The buyer's obligation to the seller would not be changed in the event of theft or physical destruction or damage to the product.
d. The buyer acquiring the product for resale has economic substance apart from that provided by the seller.

e. The seller does not have significant obligations for future performance to directly bring about resale of the product by the buyer.

f. The amount of future returns can be reasonably estimated.

If the transaction passes this long list, provision must be made for any costs or losses that may be expected relating to possible future returns consistent with *SFAS 5.** Florida International professor and accounting theorist Kenneth Most observes perceptively that "the FASB's definition of revenue was of no assistance in this problem area; it was not even mentioned in the statement."[17] So much, perhaps, for definitions.

Installment Sales.   The most often quoted example of justifiable deferral of revenue reporting is the case of installment sales. Usually these are justified on grounds that collection is said to be doubtful because the customers who enter into these installment contracts often overextend themselves and therefore are poor risks. Billing and collection expenses subsequent to the time of sale are usually large, and warranty expenses may also enter into the picture. These arguments are usually quite weak. However, there are situations, such as in real estate sales, when the installment method might be justified.

The position of the Accounting Principles Board in *Opinion No. 10* was that " . . . revenues should ordinarily be accounted for at the time a transaction is completed, with appropriate provision for uncollectible accounts"; and in the absence of circumstances where the sale price is not reasonably ensured, it concluded that the installment method of recognizing revenue is not acceptable. A footnote, however, weakened this position by recognizing exceptional cases in which there may be no reasonable basis for estimating the degree of collectibility. In the authors' opinion, this exception is not warranted because installment sales probably would not be made under such conditions.

Cost-Recovery Method.   A modification of the installment basis has often been suggested for highly speculative ventures where cash collections are received in installments and where the collection of the final installments may be doubtful. Under these circumstances, the final net income or loss cannot be determined until all collections have been received. Accordingly, the first installments are considered to be a return of invested costs, and income is recorded only after all costs have been recovered. After all costs have been recovered, all additional installments are treated as income. A good example is where a bond is in default and payments of principal and interest are made as cash becomes available through liquidation of the mortgaged property or through other means.

---

* Lists like this give some clues to the accounting games that managements must have been playing.

Because of the uncertainty regarding future payments under the bond contract, all collections, whether considered payments of principal or interest by the trustee, are treated as a return of the bond investment until such investment has been fully recovered.

CHECKPOINTS

1. Define, in your own words, the nature of revenues. Are you more comfortable with the notion of revenue as an inflow, an outflow, or a product?
2. What is the advantage of distinguishing gains from revenues? Can you relate your answer to the objectives of financial reporting?
3. In your opinion, should cash discounts be treated as an offset to revenue or as an expense?
4. Distinguish the critical event approach to revenue recognition from the substantial accomplishment approach. Do you have a preference?
5. Contrast recognition with realization as the FASB uses those terms.
6. When should revenue be recognized according to the FASB?
7. When should gains be recognized? Is this the same rule as for revenues?

EXPENSES AND LOSSES

Like the term *revenue,* the term *expense* is also a flow concept. Expenses, though, represent the unfavorable changes in the resources of the firm, that is, the decreases in income. However, not all unfavorable changes in resources are expenses. More precisely defined, expenses are the using or consuming of goods and services in the process of obtaining revenues. Economists speak of the labor, the material, and the capital that go into producing goods and services as *factors.* Expenses are the expirations of factor services related either directly or indirectly to the producing and selling of the product of the enterprise. For instance, depreciation expense represents the use of a capital asset in the production of a good or the provision of a service. When service expirations result in a product still held by the enterprise, but on which revenue has not been reported, the factor services are embodied in an asset in an account termed *work-in-process.* Final expiration of the factor services traditionally does not occur until the assets are transferred out of the firm when they form part of cost of goods sold.

All the comments made earlier about defining revenues apply equally to defining expenses. For instance, it is true that expenses do reduce the stockholders' equity in the firm, and that expenses are often defined in this context. Nevertheless, it cannot be a satisfactory solution to define one element in terms of another, which is itself undefined. Expenses therefore, like revenues, should not be defined solely in terms of their effect on stockholders' equity.

Similarly, expenses should not be defined in terms of cost expirations or cost allocations. These terms are simply descriptions of the structural model for the measurement of accounting income; they do not reflect real-world observations. Also like revenue, the definition of expenses should not be confused with the valuation of expenses. These are distinct problems. Expenses are measured by the valuation of the goods or services used or consumed, but this measurement does not define the expense.

Finally, the same criticisms can be made of the FASB's definition of expenses that were made of their definition of revenues. Their definition focuses on the flow of assets out of the enterprise to pay for the factors of production. This contrasts with other definitions of expenses that focus on the inflow of factors into the enterprise to permit production. Specifically, the Board defines expenses as:

> outflows or other using up of assets or incurrences of liabilities (or a combination of both) from delivering or producing goods, rendering services, or carrying out other activities that constitute the entity's ongoing major or central operations.[18]

First, the definition confuses the effect of expenses with expenses themselves. Second, it does not specify clearly enough what outflows should be considered. There are many outflows of assets that are part of an entity's central operations that have nothing to do with expenses. For example, the repayment of a loan taken out to finance the production of goods is not traditionally considered an expense, yet it fits this definition quite adequately. The authors prefer, therefore, the older AICPA definition of expenses as "all expired costs which are deductible from revenues."[19]

The questions arising with respect to the term *expense* are similar to the questions asked regarding *revenue*. They are:

1. What should be included in expenses?
2. How should expenses be measured?
3. When are expenses incurred and when should they be reported for accounting purposes?

And, as noted in the case of revenues, these questions are intimately related to identical questions regarding income—more particularly, decreases in income.

What Should Be Included in Expenses?

Many argue that losses should be excluded from expenses in the same way as gains are excluded from revenues. The FASB has followed this approach. Expenses, it says, relate to the major or central operations of

---

EXHIBIT 11-3   Hercules Incorporated Nonrecurring Operating Expenses,
                    1988

Nonrecurring operating expenses represent items of expense which by their
nature are considered operating expenses of the corporation, but do not relate
directly to current ongoing business activity. They include an early retirement
incentive program for salaried employees at substantially all domestic locations
($25,548) in 1988; environmental cleanup costs for a previously owned idle
facility ($20,000) and a write-down of an acquisition overprice ($11,056) in
1987; and a retirement incentive program ($5,500), inventory write-offs ($7,767)
and environmental cleanup of an inactive facility ($4,991) in 1986. [All numbers
in thousands.]

---

the firm. Losses result from transactions or events that are peripheral or
incidental to the operations of the enterprise. Other authorities define
expenses broadly to include the expiration of both operating and nonoperating costs. For example, the 1948 statement of the American Accounting
Association defined expenses as consisting of both operating costs and
losses. Whatever one's approach to expenses and losses, it should be
consistent so that revenues and expenses are appropriately related. Exhibit 11-3 provides an illustration of what one company included in expenses, albeit nonrecurring expenses.

   If one accepts the broad definition of revenues as the product of the
enterprise, then expenses are the costs incurred to generate those revenues. A corollary of this definition of expenses is that asset expirations or
asset reductions not related to the process of providing goods or services
to customers or clients should be classified as losses rather than as expenses. As with the FASB's approach, this ensures that revenues and
expenses are appropriately related.

   One should also distinguish between expenses and offsets to revenue.
As noted in the section on revenues, sales returns and allowances, sales
discounts, and bad debt losses are all more appropriately treated as reductions of gross revenues than as expenses. None of them represents the use
of goods or services to generate revenues; each represents a reduction of
the amount to be received in exchange for the product. Proponents of
treating cash discounts and bad debt losses as expenses claim that they
represent alternatives to other expenses such as collection expense and
interest expense. In the opinion of the authors, however, it does not seem
logical to classify an item on the basis of an alternative action.

   One should also make a careful distinction between expenses and offsets to capital or stockholders' equity. Asset expirations and obligations
incurred in relation to capital transactions should not be classified as
expenses, but shown as reductions of capital or one of its components.
Costs incurred in the sale of capital stock, for example, are not expenses,

but reductions of the amount of capital received by the corporation. Thus we see that the use of goods and services is not a sufficient definition of expenses. The objective of obtaining revenue must also be present, although the relationship to revenue might be quite indirect, as in the case of expenditures necessary to service debt.

The term *loss,* therefore, should be restricted to mean the expiration or write-off of costs not related to revenues of any period, not just, as the FASB has it, costs that are peripheral to the main activities of the enterprise. For a loss to have real-world interpretation, it should reflect a decline in market value or other observable measurement of value at the time of the sale or abandonment of property, or at the time of whole or partial destruction by casualty. Losses result from extraneous and exogenous events that are not anticipated as necessary in the process of producing revenues. If they were anticipated, they possibly could have been avoided; if they were necessary in the production of revenues, they should be included among the expenses. To the extent that value expirations represent corrections of the expenses of prior periods, they should not be included among the losses, but separately classified as prior-period corrections. Given the strictures of *SFAS No. 16,* though, this separation is usually very difficult to make in practice. Unforeseen declines in value represent losses; but if they had been foreseen, should they have been included in the expenses? The answer to this question is not always clear. In some cases, if the decline in value had been foreseen, the asset would not have been acquired; in this case the recognition of the decline is clearly a loss.

How Should Expenses Be Measured?

Measurement of the goods and services used in the operations of the enterprise does not have a simple solution. This is so because the objectives for such measurement are not clearly defined. Those measurements currently found acceptable are determined in large part by the income concept applied. Many of the controversial discussions regarding the appropriate measurement do not lead to solutions, primarily because the proponents of the different viewpoints have in mind different objectives or different income concepts, which generally are not clearly stated.

According to those who define expenses as decreases in the net assets of the firm, a logical measurement is the value of the goods and services at the time they are used in the operations of the enterprise. Expenses in this view are the unfavorable aspects of revenue operations and represent the economic sacrifices to obtain the revenue. The term *value* has many meanings, but it is usually used in this context to represent the exchange price of the goods or services or their opportunity cost. On the other hand, those who emphasize the reporting of cash flows of the enterprise usually suggest that expenses should be measured in terms of transactions to which the firm is a part and measured by the past, current, or future cash expenditures. In either view of income, the purpose is to measure the amounts assignable to the current period and to defer to future periods those amounts that represent transformations of goods or services to be used in future periods. The most common measurements of expenses are:

1. Historical cost.
2. Current measurements, such as replacement cost.
3. Opportunity costs of current cash equivalents.

The measurement of losses is similar to the measurement of expenses, except that any proceeds are offset directly to reflect a net amount.

Historical Cost.   The conventional method of measuring expenses and losses is in terms of the historical cost to the enterprise. The main reason for adhering to historical costs is that they are assumed to be verifiable, since they represent cash outlays by the firm. Some claim that historical costs represent the exchange value of the goods and services at the time they were acquired by the enterprise. An essential feature of this argument is that management considered the value of the goods and services to be at least as great as the cost at the time of acquisition, or they would not have been acquired. Given that there is no real evidence that the firm would have acquired the goods and services if it had to pay a higher price for them, the best evidence available indicates that they were worth just what they cost the firm, no more and no less.* If the goods and services turn out to be worth more than the historical cost, the excess represents a gain to the firm that will be included in aggregate income at the time revenue is reported, if the expense is then reported at historical cost. The opposite is the case if the goods and services are subsequently worth less than cost.

Historical cost, as represented by the book value or other recorded value, is usually used in computing gains and losses, for several reasons. Probably the most significant of these reasons is that making a distinction between a true gain or loss and a correction of prior periods is not important. However, if the increase in value is due in part to the changing value of the monetary unit, cost is not appropriate; a part of the increase in value represents a restatement of the capital of the firm, rather than an increase in retained earnings. This concept is discussed further in Chapter 12.

The main disadvantages of historical cost are that it frequently does not represent a relevant measurement of the goods and services used in attempting to meet the objectives of the external users of financial reports,

---

* For an additional discussion of cost, see Chapter 14.

and that it does not permit a separation of operating activity from gains and losses arising from fortuitous purchases or unpredictable price changes. Consider, for instance, a building destroyed by fire before the end of its useful life. This represents a loss to the firm (to the extent that it is uninsured), even though it may be fully depreciated in the accounts; the most sensible measure of the loss would appear to be its current value, not its historical cost. Logically, depreciation for prior periods should be adjusted and a loss recorded in the amount of its current value. However, since all this will have no net effect on total stockholders' equity when using the traditional structural approach, accountants may prefer to refrain from attempting a measurement of the loss in favor of disclosure in some other way.

Determining Cost.   What is meant by *cost* and what should be included in the term? Basically, cost is measured by the current value of the economic resources given up or to be given up in obtaining the goods and services to be used in operations—this is the value in exchange. When cash is paid or agreed to be paid for merchandise, supplies, and personal services, the measurement of cost is fairly definite. The cash paid or agreed to be paid represents the exchange value determined by the market price or by agreement between the buyer and seller. The cash represents the monetary value of claims to economic resources given up by the buyer.

When economic resources other than cash or claims to cash are given up in the exchange, however, the problem of valuation still remains. A possible solution can be found in the market prices of the goods and services acquired, or in the market prices of the goods given up in the exchange. If the goods or services given up were acquired previously for cash or its equivalent, this original cost may now be assumed to be the cost of the newly acquired goods and services. Because this latter cost is considered more verifiable than the current market price of either the goods received or the goods given up, accountants usually prefer it, but its relevance is suspect. Suppose, for example, that a plot of land is exchanged for a piece of equipment to be used in the business. The original cost of the land would be considered the basis for valuing the expense of using the equipment, but such cost may have little relevance to current conditions or objectives.

The complexities of cost determination will be discussed more fully in the following chapters. The following situations suggest some of the problems that are relevant in the measurement of expenses in terms of cost:

1. The total agreed price may be payable at a deferred date, in which case the discounted price may be the appropriate measurement of the expense.
2. The appearance of joint costs may permit no adequate solution to the measurement of the several types of expenses.

3. A cost price that is not the result of an arm's-length transaction may be less valid than other methods of measurement.
4. The aggregate cost price should include all of the costs necessary to acquire the goods or services, not only the invoice or quoted price.

Current Prices.   As revenue is usually measured in terms of the current prices received for the product, it is frequently argued that the expenses matched against this revenue should also be measured in terms of the current prices of the goods and services used or consumed. Income resulting from the sale transaction is the excess of the cash or claims received over the amount of the resources used. Thus, the measurement of expenses in terms of current prices has the advantage of distinguishing between:

1. The income arising from the transaction.
2. The gains or losses arising from the holding of assets prior to use.

Holding assets for a period prior to use (or allocation to expense) may result from a deliberate decision to speculate or from the necessity to acquire goods and services early. The gains and losses occurring may arise from price changes, deterioration, obsolescence, or other factors. When the acquisition of goods or services prior to use is necessary and the loss of deterioration is also necessary and can be anticipated, this reduction in value should be included in the measurement of the expense; it is a necessary part of the revenue operations of the firm.

Current prices can be obtained to represent either a current liquidation (sale) price or a replacement cost. A current liquidation price or current equivalent may be relevant in the measurement of expense because it represents the opportunity cost to the firm in using the specific asset. Furthermore, this measurement of the expense does not require speculation regarding the future possibility of replacement. If there is a good market in which the item can be purchased and sold with little loss, the liquidation price may be particularly relevant. On the other hand, the current replacement cost represents the acquisition price at the time of use. Therefore, the replacement cost may permit a better prediction of the results of future firm activity—if there is likely to be continuity of the past into the future. One of the difficulties with the use of a replacement cost is that there may not be a current price available for the same type of goods or services previously acquired, or there may be no verifiable measurement of such a price.

Many expenses are contracted for or obtained currently, so that cost is not far removed from the current price. Those cases where the costs may be materially different from the current prices comprise primarily the valuation of inventories and fixed assets. These problems are discussed more fully in Chapters 12 and 14. In the following discussion of the timing of expenses, reference will be made primarily to costs, but it should be recognized that the term *current prices* could be substituted for costs at any point.

When Are Expenses Incurred?

By definition, an expense is incurred when goods or services are consumed or used in the process of obtaining revenue. The timing or reporting of expense is brought about by recording this activity in the accounts or including it in financial reports. Reporting of the expense may coincide with the activity of using the goods or services; or it may follow the activity; or, in unusual circumstances, it may precede the activity.

When expenses should be reported is determined, in part, by the approach to income being proposed either explicitly or implicitly. The definition of income as changes in values generally suggests that expenses should be reported whenever there is a decrease in value or when there is no apparent benefit or value to be received in the future arising from the use of those goods or services. The concept of income that emphasizes cash flows leads to the conclusion that expenses should be reported as close to the actual cash expenditure as is reasonable. Traditional accrual accounting is somewhat between these two extremes, but it leans toward the value concept in that it suggests that input (cost) prices should be retained until an increase in value is reported by the substitution of the exit (sales) prices. That is, expense should be recognized in the period in which the associated revenue is recognized. This is the matching process—the timing of revenue reporting comes first, followed by the reporting of related expenses in the same period. Only in unusual cases are revenues deferred until expenses can be measured or identified.

The criteria for the recognition of losses are similar to the criteria for the recognition of period expenses. Losses cannot be matched with revenue, so they should be recorded in the period in which the fact that a given asset will provide less benefit to the firm than indicated by the recorded valuation becomes fairly definite.

In the case of a sale of assets not traded normally, and in the case of a loss by fire or other catastrophe, the timing of the event is fairly definite. However, when the decline in value is gradual over several periods, determining exactly when the loss occurs is difficult. The asset may be sold or abandoned eventually; but if the asset has lost its usefulness, withholding recognition of the loss until the final disposition is unreasonable. Reporting should occur as soon as it appears quite probable that the asset has lost its usefulness, and that this loss of usefulness is not likely to be reversed in the future.

In no case should a loss be deliberately carried forward to later periods. If the loss is fairly definite, and if the amount of the loss can be measured reasonably well, it should be recorded as soon as it is ascertainable. For example, when equipment is replaced, the undepreciated cost should not be added arbitrarily to the cost of the new asset. Also, when bonds are refunded, the unamortized discount and call premium represent a change in the value of the bonds and should be written off rather than carried forward and allocated over the life of the new bonds.*

The Matching Concept.   If income were reported gradually over the entire operating process of the firm, the measurement of the net assets of the firm would be increased as value was added by the firm. In this case, there would be no necessity for a matching concept. However, because revenue and expense transactions are reported separately, and because the acquisition and payment for goods and services usually do not coincide with the sales and collection processes related to the same product of the enterprise, matching has come to be considered a necessity, or at least a desirable convention. The leads and lags in the acquisition and use of, and payment for, goods and services are assumed to be the reason for accruals or deferrals in order to match the expenses with associated revenue.

As defined by the 1964 AAA committee on the matching concept, matching is the process of reporting expenses on the basis of a cause-and-effect relationship with reported revenues. The committee advocated that costs (defined as product and service factors given up) should be related to revenues realized within a specific period on the basis of some discernible positive correlation of such costs with the recognized revenues.[20] That is, the measurement of net income should represent the excess of revenues, reported during a period, over the expenses associated with those revenues and reported during that same period. A proper matching occurs only when a reasonable association is found between the revenues and expenses. The timing of expenses, therefore, requires:

1. Association with revenues.
2. Reporting in the same period as the related revenue is reported.

Matching expenses with revenues thus requires a proper association between the two. All expenses, by definition, are incurred as a necessary part of the revenue operation. This does not mean, however, that revenue will always result; expenses may be incurred without resultant revenue. Several calls by a salesman may be necessary before a sale is made; but all calls should be included in the expenses, as they are necessary in the revenue operations. In fact, even if no sales were made the calls should nevertheless be included in the operating expenses. As another example,

---

* For an extended discussion of the treatment of unamortized bond discount at the time of refunding, see Chapter 16.

normal breakage of merchandise should be classified as an expense even though they cannot be associated with particular revenues. The display of merchandise that permits this breakage is necessary in the revenue process. This requires the classification of an expense.

The association of expenses with revenues is, therefore, a difficult step. In fact, in some cases, no association may be possible. This difficulty has led accountants to establish specific rules and procedures, or to establish basic criteria for the timing of expenses. These basic criteria are established by drawing a distinction between direct expenses or product costs and indirect or period expenses. Direct expenses are usually reported in the period in which the goods or services are used. Indirect expenses are reported in the period in which they are incurred. Where expenses provide benefits over several periods, such as with prepaid insurance, the cost is systematically and rationally amortized over those periods.

Costs are frequently carried forward to be matched with future revenues on the ground that they are assumed to benefit some future periods. The argument is that, if the use of goods and services does not benefit the current period and does not represent a loss, it must benefit future periods and, therefore, it should be allocated to future periods in order to match the expenses with the associated revenue. For instance, it was considered appropriate to capitalize the costs of organizing a firm in order to charge these costs against the revenues of future periods. In 1975, the FASB, in *Statement No. 7*, required that start-up costs of development-stage enterprises be presented in the same way as for established enterprises. The argument in favor of expensing these costs immediately is that, since there is no specific revenue associated with the expense, the matching process does not apply. The result of deferring the cost is merely the smoothing of income by spreading the expense over several years. The information provided to users of financial statements is not improved by such allocations. Another example would be the deferral and allocation of basic research and development expenditures which cannot be associated directly with any specific revenues. Even though these expenditures may benefit many periods, there may be no method of applying the matching concept in a meaningful and relevant way. Accordingly, the FASB required in *SFAS 2* that research and development expenses be charged against income currently.

The Asset/Liability Approach.   The matching concept has been heavily criticized by some for failing to provide useful rules for determining the point at which expenses should be recognized. The FASB has thus increasingly made use of the asset/liability approach in which it essentially determines first whether an item is an asset. If the item fails that test, then it is classified as an expense or a loss. The most thoroughgoing application of this approach may be found in *SFAS 96* on deferred income taxes. The income tax liability is determined directly, as is the deferred income tax payable. The change in these two balance sheet accounts, together with the amount of tax actually paid to the Internal Revenue Service and other taxing authorities, determines tax expense. Stated otherwise, tax expense is the residual. More is said on this particular subject in Chapter 20.

Reporting Expenses

To conclude this section on expenses, four final points need to be made. The choice between the all-inclusive and the current operating concept of income as discussed in the previous chapter dictates how important the distinction is between expenses or losses; but it does not help settle how to define each. The all-inclusive concept of income includes all expenses and losses recognized during the current period; there is no need to differentiate between the two in the computation of net income. On the other hand, the current operating concept excludes from the computation of net income all losses, and all those expenses actually incurred in a prior period, but not recognized until the current period. Deciding on which approach yields the most meaningful concept of net income does not define expenses, although it may help to clarify one's thinking.

The classification of expenses as "selling," "administrative," or "cost of goods sold" may be useful for analytical purposes within the firm, such as establishing functional responsibilities. However, for external reporting purposes, this distinction serves no particular useful function. The reader of financial reports is neither better able to make predictions by using this classification nor able to evaluate the contributions of the several functions. Although each classification may represent the use of goods or services at different times in the enterprise operating process, their elements are all just expenses. The "cost of goods sold" is an expense just as much as sales representatives' salaries.

The order of the expenses in an income statement is also irrelevant. In particular, one should avoid the temptation to assign priorities to expenses; all are equal in the determination of income. Expenses are not recovered in preferential order. Cost of goods sold is not more important than administrative expenses. Income measurement is not meaningful until all expenses have been subtracted from the total revenues.

Last, a classification of expenses that might be useful to investors and others in making predictions and in evaluating current management decisions would be one that describes the behavioral nature of the expenses. That is, expenses should be classified and described according to whether they are variable or fixed in nature with respect to production, sales volume, or some other factor. There may also be an advantage in describing their relationship to cash flows. Items that result from cash expenditures of a prior period have a different effect upon the firm than expenses resulting from current or future cash outflows.

Summary

The rules for recognizing expenses are summarized by the FASB in this manner:

Expenses and losses are generally recognized when an entity's economic benefits are used up in delivering or producing goods, rendering services, or other activities that constitute its ongoing major or central operations or when previously recognized assets are expected to provide reduced or no further benefits.

Consumption of economic benefits during a period may be recognized either directly or by relating it to revenues recognized during the period:

a. Some expenses, such as cost of goods sold, are matched with revenues—they are recognized upon recognition of revenues that result directly and jointly from the same transactions or other events as the expenses.

b. Many expenses, such as selling and administrative salaries, are recognized during the period in which cash is spent or liabilities incurred for goods and services that are used up either simultaneously with acquisition or soon after.

c. Some expenses, such as depreciation and insurance, are allocated by systematic and rational procedures to the periods during which the related assets are expected to provide benefits.

An expense or loss is recognized if it becomes evident that previously recognized future economic benefits of an asset have been reduced or eliminated, or that a liability has been incurred or increased, without associated economic benefits.[21]

CHECKPOINTS

1. Define, in your own words, the nature of expenses.
2. What is the advantage of distinguishing losses from expenses? Can you relate your answer to the objectives of financial reporting?
3. In your opinion, should bad debt "expense" be shown as an offset to revenue? How does treating it as an expense affect the gross margin?
4. Is advertising an expense or an offset of revenue? Relate your answer to the discussion of cash discounts and bad debts in the section on revenue.
5. Provide two reasons for using historical costs to measure expenses. Why are current costs recommended by some?
6. When should expenses be recognized?
7. When should losses be recognized? Is this the same rule as for expenses?

INDUSTRY-SPECIFIC RULES

Some American corporations have a regrettable tendency to treat accounting principles as boundaries of acceptable practice against which they should press as hard as possible, rather than standards which they should seek to uphold in the interest of the general public. Nowhere is this tendency more evident than in the area of revenue recognition. The rules are broad and require judgments made in good faith. Instead, many have sought to bend these rules for personal gain. The most egregious example of this manipulation of accounting rules for personal gain occurred in the savings and loan industry. The FASB, as a result, has been forced to write extremely detailed rules in an attempt to outlaw that which good judgment should have prohibited in the first place. In the sections which follow, two examples of industry-specific rules are examined to illustrate the incredibly detailed nature of some rules the FASB has been forced to make.

Each of the statements from which these illustrations are drawn was based on prior Accounting Guides and Statements of Position drawn up by the AICPA to provide guidance to auditors. *SFAS 66*, "Accounting for Sales of Real Estate," for instance, was drawn from AICPA Industry Accounting Guides, *Accounting for Profit Recognition on Sales of Real Estate* and *Accounting for Retail Land Sales;* AICPA Statement of Position 75-6, *Questions Concerning Profit Recognition on Sales of Real Estate,* and 78-4, *Application of the Deposit, Installment, and Cost Recovery Methods in Accounting for Real Estate.* Thus, they form an example of how the AICPA and the FASB have continued to work together to set accounting standards. At the time of writing, no standard exists on revenue recognition in the computer software industry. Instead, GAAP is based on an AICPA Issues Paper 87-1, *Software Revenue Recognition.* The FASB has asked the AICPA to convert this into a Statement of Position, which will be the first step, presumably, in producing a statement on the issue.

Motion Pictures

Movie producers earn a return on their investment by licensing to others the right to exhibit their films. Two major categories of licencees exist: theaters and television. Producers generally license films to theaters on the basis of a percentage of box office revenues. *SFAS 53* permits the licensor to earn revenue from theaters only on the dates when the movie is exhibited. The rights to films are effectively sold to television, creating a different set of rules. Specifically:

> A licensor shall recognize revenue from a license agreement for television program material when the license period begins *and* all of the following conditions have been met:

    a. The license fee for each film is known.

    b. The cost of each film is known or reasonably determinable.

    c. Collectibility of the full license fee is reasonably ensured.

    d. The film has been accepted by the licensee in accordance with the conditions of the license agreement.

    e. The film is available for its first showing or telecast. Unless a conflicting license prevents usage by the licensee, restrictions under the same license agreement or another license agreement with the same licensee on the timing of subsequent showing shall not affect this condition.

Ordinarily, when the conditions specified in [the preceding] paragraph(s) are met, both the licensee and the licensor are contractually obligated under a noncancelable license agreement and are able to perform in compliance with all the significant terms of the license agreement. If significant factors raise doubt about the obligation or ability to perform under the agreement, revenue recognition shall be delayed until such factors no longer exist.

Some would say all this is inherent in the critical event concept and should not need to be spelled out in this manner!

Real Estate Sales

The rules of revenue recognition for real estate are even more detailed. In fact, they became so cumbersome that the FASB was obliged to draw up flowcharts to enable readers to follow them. Consider, for instance, the accompanying flowchart for retail land sales. The full accrual method of accounting for revenue, that is, the simple recognition of revenue, is allowed only when all of the following conditions have been met (the paragraph numbers correspond to the numbers in Exhibit 11-4):

1. *Expiration of refund period.* Many retail land sales are accompanied by a "cooling-off" period in which buyers may ask for a refund of their deposits and subsequent payments. This period must have passed.

2. If this condition is not met, the deposit method should be used, that is, payments are treated as deposits and booked as liabilities until the period has expired.

3. *Sufficient cumulative payments.* The buyer must have made payments greater than or equal to 10 percent of the contract sales price.

4. If this condition is not met, the deposit method should be used.

5. *Collectibility of receivables.* The seller's bad debt experience should not exceed 10 percent. Alternatively, the buyer's down payment should exceed 20 percent.

6. *Nonsubordination of receivables.* The buyer should not be able to take out a second mortgage on the land that is senior in payment to the first mortgage.

EXHIBIT 11-4 Accounting for Sales of Real Estate

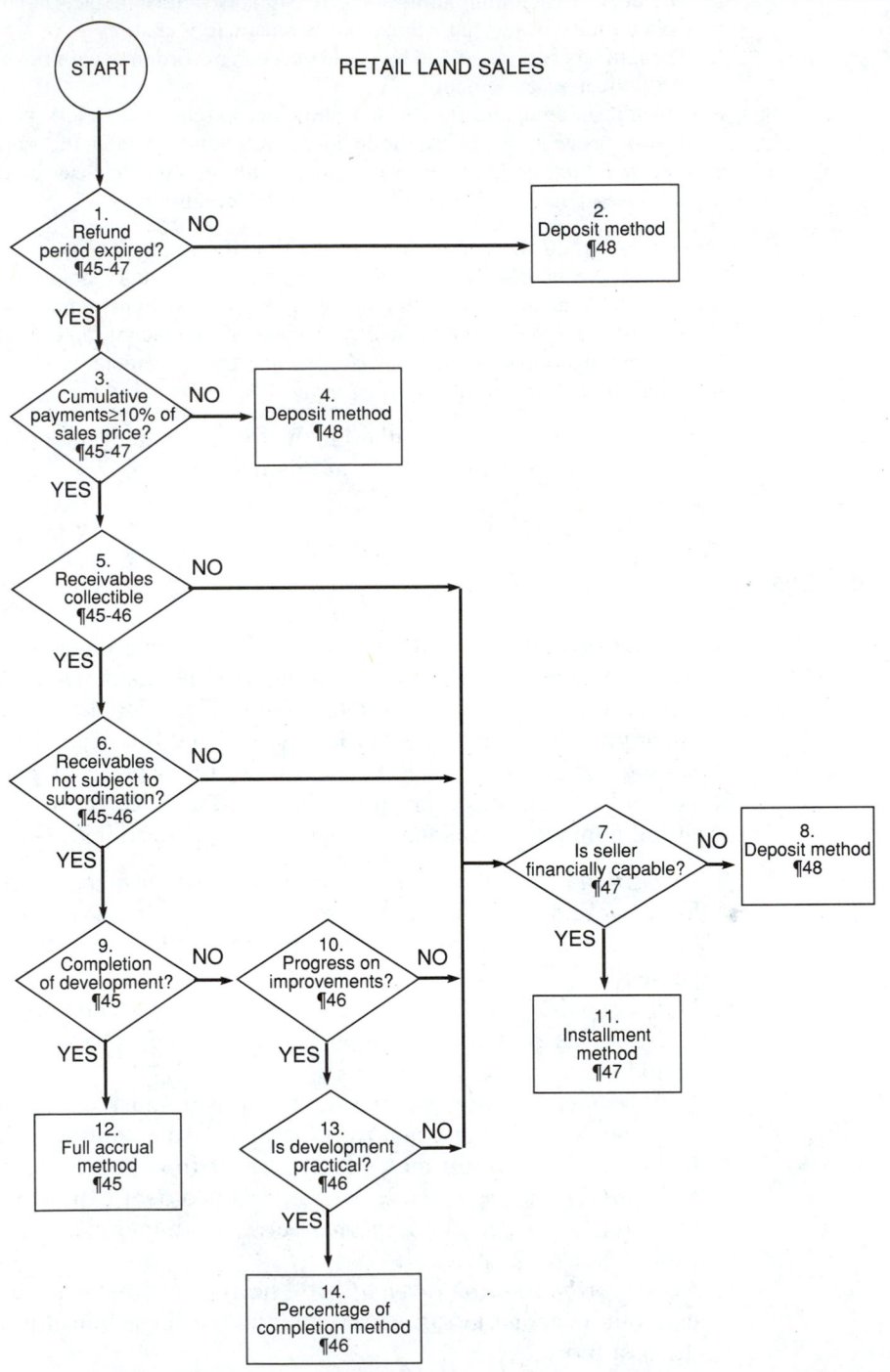

7. If either of these last two conditions is not met, the question then turns to the financial capability of the seller. If the seller is financially strong, the installment method of recognizing revenue is required (11); if not, the deposit method is used (8).
8. Use deposit method.
9. *Completion of development.* The final condition for use of the full accrual method is that the seller not be obliged to develop the sold lots any further.
10. If the development on the sold lots is incomplete, but there is evidence of progress and a reasonable expectation exists that the land can be developed for the purposes represented, then the percentage-of-completion method may be used. If either of these two conditions is not met, the question turns back to the financial capability of the seller as addressed in (7) above.

The response of one of the Board members to this statement is worth quoting in full:

> Mr. Walters dissents to the issuance of this Statement primarily because he objects to incorporating these complex, rigid, and detailed rules into accounting standards. Entirely aside from the conceptual merit of these rules, which is at least debatable, he believes the Board should focus at a level [consistent with the rules of recognition laid out in the Conceptual Framework.] Beyond that, he believes the accounting profession can serve its members by offering more specific *guidance* for applying the standards in particular specialized areas, but such detailed and arbitrary guidelines should not be dignified as accounting standards. To do so debases accounting standards and inevitably will diminish the stature and effectiveness of the accounting profession, whose strength and purpose arise from applying broad accounting and reporting objectives and standards to specific circumstances with professional judgment and objectivity. That judgment is the hallmark of a true profession.

To which the authors say, Amen.

MULTIPLE CHOICE QUESTIONS

Revenues and Gains

1. [M89#14] According to the cost recovery method of accounting, gross profit on an installment sale is recognized in income

a. After cash collections equal to the cost of sales have been received.
b. In proportion to the cash collection.
c. On the date the final cash collection is received.
d. On the date of sale.

2. [M89#16] Under a royalty agreement with another enterprise, a company will receive royalties from the assignment of a patent for four years. The royalties received in advance should be reported as revenue

a. In the period received.
b. In the period earned.
c. Evenly over the life of the royalty agreement.
d. At the date of the royalty agreement.

3. [N87#16] When should an anticipated loss of a long-term contract be recognized under the percentage-of-completion method and the completed-contract method, respectively?

	Percentage-of-Completion	*Completed-Contract*
a.	Over life of project	Contract complete
b.	Immediately	Contract complete
c.	Over life of project	Immediately
d.	Immediately	Immediately

4. [M87#26] A company uses the percentage-of-completion method to account for a four-year construction contract. Progress billings sent in the second year that were collected in the third year would

a. Not be included in the calculation of the income recognized in the second, third, or fourth year.
b. Be included in the calculation of the income recognized in the second year.
c. Be included in the calculation of the income recognized in the third year.
d. Be included in the calculation of the income recognized in the fourth year.

Expenses and Losses

5. [N88#27] A research and development activity for which the cost would be expensed as incurred is

a. Engineering follow-through in an early phase of commercial production.
b. Design, construction, and testing of reproduction prototypes and models.
c. Troubleshooting in connection with breakdowns during the commercial productions.
d. Periodic design changes to existing products.

6. [N87#21] An employer offered for a short period of time special termination benefits to some employees. The employees accepted the offer, which provided for immediate lump-sum payments and future payments at the end of the next two years. The amounts can be reasonably estimated. The amount of expense recognized this year should include

a. One-third of the lump-sum payments and one-third of the present value of the future payments.
b. Only the lump-sum payments.
c. The lump-sum payments and the total of the future payments.
d. The lump-sum payments and the present value of the future payments.

DISCUSSION QUESTIONS

Revenue Reporting

1. (March 1986) Village Company Village Company is accounting for a long-term construction contract using the percentage-of-completion method. It is a three-year fixed-fee contract that is presently in its first year. The latest reasonable estimates of total contract costs indicate that the contract will be completed at a profit. Village will submit progress billings to the customer and has reasonable assurance that collections on these billings will be received in each year of the contract.

Required:

a. 1. What is the justification for the percentage-of-completion method for long-term construction contracts?
   2. What facts in the situation above indicate that Village should account for this long-term construction contract using the percentage-of-completion method?
b. How would the income recognized in each year of this long-term construction contract be determined using the cost-to-cost method of determining percentage of completion?
c. What is the effect on income, if any, of the progress billings and the collections on these billings?

2. (November 1974) Revenue Recognition The earning of revenue by a business enterprise is recognized for accounting purposes when the transaction is recorded. In some situations, revenue is recognized approximately as it is earned in the economic sense. In other situations, however, accountants have developed guidelines for recognizing revenue by other criteria; such as, at the point of sale.

Required (ignore income taxes):

a. Explain and justify why revenue is often recognized as earned at time of sale.
b. Explain in what situations it would be appropriate to recognize revenue as the productive activity takes place.
c. At what times, other than those included in *a* and *b* above, may it be appropriate to recognize revenue? Explain.

3.   **(May 1970) Bonanza Trading Stamps**   Bonanza Trading Stamps, Inc., was formed early this year to sell trading stamps throughout the Southwest to retailers to distribute the stamps gratuitously to their customers. Books for accumulating the stamps and catalogs illustrating the merchandise for which the stamps may be exchanged are given free to retailers for distribution to stamp recipients. Centers with inventories of merchandise premiums have been established for redemption of the stamps. Retailers may not return unused stamps to Bonanza.

The following schedule expresses Bonanza's expectations as to percentages of a normal month's activity which will be attained. For this purpose, a normal month's activity is defined as the level of operations expected when expansion of activities ceases or tapers off to a stable rate. The company expects that this level will be attained in the third year and that sales of stamps will average $2 million per month throughout the third year.

Month	Actual Stamp Sales (percent)	Merchandise Premium Purchases (percent)	Stamp Redemptions (percent)
6th.	30	40	10
12th.	60	60	45
18th.	80	80	70
24th.	90	90	80
30th.	100	100	95

Bonanza plans to adopt an annual closing date at the end of each 12 months of operations.

Required:

a. Discuss the factors to be considered in determining when revenue should be recognized in measuring the income of a business enterprise.
b. Discuss the accounting alternatives that should be considered by Bonanza Trading Stamps, Inc., for the recognition of its revenues and related expenses.
c. For each accounting alternative discussed in *b* above, give balance

sheet accounts that should be used and indicate how each should be classified.

4. (November 1971) Southern Fried Shrimp Southern Fried Shrimp sells franchises to independent operators throughout the Southeastern part of the United States. The contract with the franchise includes the following provisions:

> The franchisee is charged an initial fee of $25,000. Of this amount $5,000 is payable when the agreement is signed and a $4,000 noninterest-bearing note is payable at the end of each of the five subsequent years.

> All of the initial franchise fee collected by Southern Fried Shrimp is to be refunded and the remaining obligation canceled if, for any reason, the franchisee fails to open his franchise.

> In return for the initial franchise fee Southern Fried Shrimp agrees to (1) assist the franchisee in selecting the location of the business, (2) negotiate the lease for the land, (3) obtain financing and assist with building design, (4) supervise construction, (5) establish accounting and tax records, and (6) provide expert advice over a five-year period relating to such matters as employee and management training, quality control, and promotion.

> In addition to the initial franchise fee the franchisee is required to pay to Southern Fried Shrimp a monthly fee of 2 percent of sales for menu planning, recipe innovations, and the privilege of purchasing ingredients from Southern Fried Shrimp at or below prevailing prices.

Management of Southern Fried Shrimp estimates that the value of the services rendered to the franchisee at the time the contract is signed amounts to at least $5,000. All franchisees to date have opened their locations at the scheduled time, and none has defaulted on any of the notes receivable.

The credit ratings of all franchisees would entitle them to borrow at the current interest rate of 10 percent. The present value of an ordinary annuity of five annual receipts of $4,000 each discounted at 10 percent is $15,163.

Required:

a. Discuss the alternatives that Southern Fried Shrimp might use to account for the initial franchise fee, evaluate each by applying generally accepted accounting principles to this situation, and give illustrative entries for each alternative.

b. Given the nature of Southern Fried Shrimp's agreement with its franchisees, when should revenue be recognized? Discuss the question of revenue recognition for both the initial franchise fee and the additional monthly fee of 2 percent of sales and give illustrative entries for both types of revenue.

c. Assuming that Southern Fried Shrimp sells some franchises for $35,000 which includes a charge of $10,000 for the rental of equipment for its useful life of 10 years, that $15,000 of the fee is payable immediately and the balance on noninterest-bearing notes at $4,000 per year, that no portion of the $10,000 rental payment is refundable in case the franchisee goes out of business, and that title to the equipment remains with the franchisor; what would be the preferable method of accounting for the rental portion of the initial franchise fee? Explain.

Expenses, Costs, and Losses

5. **(November 1975) Expense Recognition** An accountant must be familiar with the concepts involved in determining earnings of a business entity. The amount of earnings reported for a business entity is dependent on the proper recognition, in general, of revenue and expense for a given time period. In some situations, costs are recognized as expenses at the time of product sale; in other situations, guidelines have been developed for recognizing costs as expenses or losses by other criteria.

Required:

a. Explain the rationale for recognizing costs as expenses at the time of product sale.

b. What is the rationale underlying the appropriateness of treating costs as expenses of a period instead of assigning the costs to an asset? Explain.

c. In what general circumstances would it be appropriate to treat a cost as an asset instead of as an expense? Explain.

d. Some expenses are assigned to specific accounting periods on the basis of systematic and rational allocation of asset cost. Explain the underlying rationale for recognizing expenses on the basis of systematic and rational allocation of asset cost.

e. Identify the necessary conditions in which it would be appropriate to treat a cost as a loss.

6. **(November 1970) Kwik-Bild Corporation** Kwik-Bild Corporation sells and erects shell houses. These are frame structures that are completely finished on the outside, but are unfinished on the inside except for flooring, partition studding, and ceiling joists. Shell houses are sold chiefly to customers who are handy with tools and who have time to do the interior wiring, plumbing, wall completion and finishing, and other work necessary to make the shell houses liveable dwellings.

Kwik-Bild buys shell houses from a manufacturer in unassembled packages consisting of all lumber, roofing, doors, windows, and similar materials necessary to complete a shell house. Upon commencing operations in a new area, Kwik-Bild buys or leases land as a site for its local warehouse, field office, and display houses. Sample display houses are erected at a total cost of from $3,000 to $7,000, including the cost of the unassembled packages. The chief element of cost of the display houses is the unassembled packages, since erection is a short, low-cost operation. Old sample models are torn down or altered into new models every three to seven years. Sample display houses have little salvage value because dismantling and moving costs amount to nearly as much as the cost of an unassembled package.

Required:

a. A choice must be made between (1) expensing the costs of sample display houses in the period in which the expenditure is made and (2) spreading the costs over more than one period. Discuss the advantages of each method.
b. Would it be preferable to amortize the cost of display houses on the basis of (1) the passage of time or (2) the number of shell houses sold? Explain.

STIRLING HOMEX CORPORATION*

In 1967, the Stirling Homex Corporation was founded by David and William Stirling. The two brothers had pioneered the concept of modular housing, which employed many of the mass-production techniques developed in the automobile industry. Because of the substantial savings in labor cost due to mass production, the company estimated that it could build a modular home, exclusive of land, at a cost of between $16,000 and $25,000.

Because of low construction costs and the ability to erect entire housing projects on site in very short periods of time, the company developed close ties with federal, state, and local housing authorities that were in search of ways to provide housing for low-income groups. In 1968, for example, the company constructed a 275-unit housing project in Rochester, New York, in just 36 hours. Two years later, the company won a U.S. Department of Housing and Urban Development (HUD) contract to construct a 13-story apartment building in Memphis, Tennessee. Shortly thereafter, the company also announced that it had a "tentative under-

---

* This case was prepared by Kenneth R. Ferris and M. Edgar Barrett. The idea for the case is taken from an earlier case (Stirling Homex 9-173-193) written by Professor Barrett while at the Harvard Business School. Copyright © 1985 by M. Edgar Barrett and Kenneth R. Ferris. All rights reserved to the authors.

standing" with the Greater Gulfport (Mississippi) Housing Development Corporation to build over $100 million of modular housing for moderate and lower income families.

In February 1970, Stirling Homex went public. The offering prospectus reported earnings of $1 million on sales of $10 million for fiscal year 1969. The public offering opened on the market at $16.50 per share. By mid-March, the stock was selling in excess of $51 per share.

The 1971 annual report provided more good news: Stirling Homex would market its products to a broader consumer spectrum—hotels, motels, colleges and universities, and to private consumers. During the same year the company reported that it had also doubled its manufacturing facilities and created the U.S. Shelter Corporation, a wholly owned subsidiary to provide construction and permanent financing for its customers. As anticipated, record earnings per share ($0.37) were achieved in 1971 (see financial statements, Exhibits 1–5).

On July 10, 1972, however, the Stirling Homex Corporation filed for bankruptcy under Chapter 10 of the Federal Bankruptcy Act. When the company collapsed, some 10,000 modular units were found sealed in plastic and stored in fields around the United States; the value of the units ranged between $35 million and $65 million. Full payment, however, existed for only 900 of those units. The back-log of uninstalled modules had grown from 3,500 as of April 1971, to 6,700 at December 1971, to over 9,000 units as of July 1972. Evidence gathered in the months following the July bankruptcy filing raised questions concerning the firm's method of recognizing revenue.

Revenue Recognition

Stirling Homex Corporation recognized revenue from the sale of many of its modular units when production was completed. The company did this in those cases where the unit was assigned to a specific contract and if there was an identified site plan and a financially capable purchaser. The company did not, however, require progress payments from its buyers or demand that the housing site itself be approved by the purchaser. Some of these "contracts" were in the form of "letters of intention to buy" from various institutions. These tentative buyers included public housing authorities, whose final decisions were often delayed by such things as the necessity of seeking voter approval through public referenda.

According to corporate insiders, the company's profit margin came primarily from the production of modular units. Revenues from installation operations, on the other hand, were recognized on a percentage-of-completion basis and were allocated on an estimated break-even point. Neither the February 1970 offering prospectus nor the July 1970 annual report provided a breakdown of revenues and costs between production and installation. The 1970 annual report stated that "contracts generally provided for payment upon completion and receipt of all approvals necessary for occupancy, or for payment upon completion of each respective phase." Because most of its receivables were due from public housing authorities, no provision for doubtful accounts was considered necessary.

Epilogue

In July 1975, the Securities and Exchange Commission released the results of its investigation of the Stirling Homex Corporation:

> The consolidated statements of income of Stirling Homex for the seven-month period ended February 28, 1971, included in the registration statement for the preferred stock and the consolidated statements of income of Stirling Homex for the year ended July 31, 1971, contained in the Annual Report to Shareholders and Annual Report on Form 10-K for such fiscal year were false and misleading in that among other things:
>
> - All modular sales of $12,493,000 for the February 28, 1971, period and $25,292,600 out of total modular sales of $29,482,271 for the July 31, 1971, period were improperly recorded in that the purported sales were not supported by required financing commitments.
> - Installation sales were overstated by approximately $3,723,000 out of a total reported installation sales of $5,137,000 for the February 28, 1971, period and $2,443,000 out of total installation sales of $7,200,000 for the July 31, 1971, period through the inclusion of sales from projects for which there were no commitments of financing and through Stirling Homex's improper reporting of approximately $1,000,000 as of February 26, 1971, and approximately $2,000,000 as of July 31, 1971, of excess installation costs as "cost overruns" reimbursable to the company.
> - General, administrative, and other expenses were materially understated by approximately $832,000 as of February 28, 1971, and approximately $1,000,000 as of February 28, 1971, and approximately $1,000,000 as of July 31, 1971, as a result of the improper capitalizing of such expenses. Additionally, certain other expenses and construction costs were improperly capitalized.

On January 29, 1977, David and William Stirling were found guilty on nine counts of fraud; they were sentenced on March 11, 1977.

EXHIBIT 1

STIRLING HOMEX CORPORATION
Consolidated Balance Sheet July 31, 1971
With Comparative Figures for 1970

	1971	1970
Assets		
Current assets:		
Cash (Note 11)	$ 3,196,457	$ 2,778,077
Preferred stock proceeds receivable (Note 2)	19,000,000	—
Receivables (Notes 1 and 3)	37,845,572	15,486,119
Inventories (Note 5):		
Raw materials, work in process and salable merchandise at lower of cost (first-in, first-out) or replacement market	2,614,200	2,167,603
Land held for development or sale, at cost	1,878,343	1,583,621
Prepaid expenses and other current assets	226,530	124,765
Total current assets	64,761,102	22,140,185
Investment in unconsolidated subsidiary (Note 1)	1,134,579	—
Long-term receivables (Note 4)	4,225,349	541,124
Property, plant, and equipment at cost, less accumulated depreciation and amortization: 1971—$733,705; 1970—$230,921 (Notes 6 and 8)	9,426,941	5,245,745
Deferred charges, less accumulated amortization: 1971—$586,011; 1970—$153,894 (Note 7)	2,558,792	944,109
	$82,106,763	$28,871,163

Liabilities and Stockholders' Equity		
	1971	1970
Current liabilities:		
Current portion of long-term debt (Note 8)	$ 295,630	$ 333,036
Notes payable to banks-unsecured (1971—6 to 6 1/2%; 1970—8 to 8 1/2%) (Note 11)	37,700,000	11,700,000
Accounts payable	4,025,254	2,480,834
Due to unconsolidated subsidiary (Note 1)	76,894	—
Accrued expenses and other liabilities	577,377	232,819
Current and deferred income taxes (Note 9)	3,528,125	1,387,338
Total current liabilities	46,203,280	16,134,027
Long-term debt (Note 8)	236,588	496,489
Deferred income taxes (Note 9)	2,098,767	587,265
Option deposit on land contract (Note 5)	235,000	—
Stockholders' equity:		
$2.40 cumulative convertible preferred stock (Note 2): Authorized 500,000 shares, $1.00 par value; shares subscribed: 1971—500,000 (aggregate involuntary liquidation value—$20,000,000); 1970—none	500,000	—

EXHIBIT 1   (*continued*)

	1971	1970
Common stock (Notes 2 and 10)		
Authorized 15,000,000 shares, $0.01 par value; shares issued:		
1971—8,909,200; 1970—8,897,400	$ 89,092	$ 88,974
Additional paid-in capital (Note 2)	26,554,453	8,446,738
Retained earnings	6,370,333	3,117,670
	33,513,878	11,653,382
Less treasury stock at cost (60,000 shares)	180,750	—
Total stockholders' equity	33,333,128	11,653,382
Commitments and contingencies (Note 11)	$82,106,763	$28,871,163

See accompanying Notes to Consolidated Financial Statements.

EXHIBIT 2

STIRLING HOMEX CORPORATION
Consolidated Statement of Income
Year Ended July 31, 1971, with Comparative Figures for 1970

	1971	1970
Revenues:		
Manufacturing division—trade (Note 3)	$29,482,271	$16,492,770
Installation division (Note 3):		
Trade	7,230,878	5,601,357
Affiliate	—	459,941
Equity in undistributed net income of subsidiary (Note 1)	134,579	—
Total revenues	36,847,728	22,554,068
Cost and expenses:		
Cost of sales:		
Manufacturing division	17,729,078	9,919,327
Installation division	6,601,413	5,240,388
Administrative and selling expenses	4,048,113	2,390,604
Interest expense	1,838,461	648,181
Total costs and expenses	30,217,065	18,198,500
Income before federal and state income taxes	6,630,663	4,355,568
Federal and state income taxes (Note 9):		
Current	368,000	1,965,982
Deferred	3,010,000	354,397
	3,378,000	2,320,379
Net income	$ 3,252,663	$ 2,035,189
Average common shares outstanding (Note 12)	8,881,938	8,649,483
Earnings per common share (Note 12)	$ 0.37	$ 0.24

See accompanying Notes to Consolidated Financial Statements

EXHIBIT 3

STIRLING HOMEX CORPORATION
Consolidated Statement of Changes in Financial Position
Year Ended July 31, 1971, with Comparative Figures for 1970

	1971	*1970*
Source of working capital:		
Net income	$ 3,252,663	$ 2,035,189
Expenses not requiring outlay of working capital:		
Depreciation and amortization	529,116	220,227
Amortization of deferred charges	432,117	133,288
Deferred income taxes (noncurrent)	1,511,502	184,776
Undistributed net income of finance subsidiary	(134,579)	—
Working capital provided from operations	5,590,819	2,573,480
Net proceeds from sales of stock:		
Public offering of common stock	—	5,985,715
Private sale of common stock	—	516,500
Common stock issued under qualified stock option plan	37,200	—
Public offering of preferred stock	18,570,633	—
Long-term borrowings	51,402	124,677
Decrease in long-term receivables	10,000	43,421
Option deposit received on land contract	235,000	—
Total source of working capital	24,495,054	9,243,793
Application of working capital:		
Purchase of treasury stock	180,750	—
Additions to property, plant, and equipment	4,710,312	4,422,506
Additions to deferred charges	2,046,800	735,093
Reduction in long-term debt	311,303	3,052,140
Increase in noncurrent portion of long-term receivables	3,694,225	—
Investment in unconsolidated subsidiary	1,000,000	—
Total application of working capital	11,943,390	8,209,739
Increase in working capital	$12,551,664	$ 1,034,054
Change in working capital:		
Increase in current assets:		
Cash	$ 418,380	$ 1,357,917
Preferred stock proceeds receivables	19,000,000	—
Receivables	22,359,453	12,286,631
Inventories	741,319	1,236,215
Prepaid expenses and other current assets	101,765	34,973
	42,620,971	14,915,736

EXHIBIT 3   (*continued*)

	1971	1970
Increase in current liabilities:		
Current portion of long-term debt and notes payable to banks . .	$25,962,594	$10,721,700
Accounts payable and accrued expenses	1,888,978	2,155,635
Due to unconsolidated subsidiary	76,894	—
Current and deferred income taxes	2,140,787	1,004,347
	30,069,253	13,881,682
Increase in working capital	$12,551,664	$ 1,034,054

During the year ended July 31, 1971, the company assigned $4,650,000 of its accounts receivable, without recourse, to an unconsolidated subsidiary for which that subsidiary paid $4,650,000 to the company. See Note 1.
See accompanying Notes to Consolidated Financial Statements.

EXHIBIT 4

STIRLING HOMEX CORPORATION
Consolidated Statement of Additional Paid-in Capital and Retained Earnings
Year Ended July 31, 1971, with Comparative Figures for 1970

	1971	1970
Additional paid-in capital:		
Balance at beginning of period	$ 8,446,738	$1,949,813
Excess of proceeds over par value of 400,000 shares of common stock issued in public offering (less expenses of $118,285)	—	5,981,715
Excess of proceeds over par value of 129,000 shares of common stock issued in private sales (less applicable expenses)	—	515,210
Excess of proceeds over par value of 500,000 shares of preferred stock issued in public offering (less expenses of $429,367) (Note 2)	18,070,633	—
Excess of proceeds over par value of 11,800 common shares issued under stock options (Note 10).	37,082	—
Balance at end of period	$26,554,453	$8,446,738
Retained earnings:		
Balance at beginning of period	$ 3,117,670	$1,082,481
Net income	3,252,663	2,035,189
Balance at end of period	$ 6,370,333	$3,117,670

See accompanying Notes to Consolidated Financial Statements.

EXHIBIT 5

STIRLING HOMEX CORPORATION
Notes to Consolidated Financial Statements July 31, 1971

---

1. Principles of Consolidation

The consolidated financial statements included the accounts of the Company and its subsidiaries except for U.S. Shelter Corporation, its financing subsidiary (all of which are wholly owned). The Company carries its investment in all subsidiaries at equity in the underlying net assets. On consolidation, all significant accounts and transactions with consolidated subsidiaries have been eliminated.

The following are condensed financial statements of the unconsolidated financing subsidiary:

Balance Sheet
July 31, 1971
Assets

Cash	$ 5,171
Accounts receivable—unbilled (Note *a*)	4,950,000
Other assets	24,593
Due from parent company	76,894
	$5,056,658

Liabilities and Stockholders' Equity

Notes payable—bank (7%) (Note *b*)	$3,750,000
Payables, accruals, and other liabilities	172,079
Stockholders' equity	1,134,579
	$5,056,658

Statement of Income
From Date of Incorporation
(September 25, 1970) to July 31, 1971

Finance income	$ 544,946
General and administrative expenses	
(including interest expense of $54,917)	263,367
	281,579
Federal and state income taxes—current	147,000
Net income	$ 134,579

Notes:

a. Accounts receivable includes $4,650,000 relating to accounts assigned to U.S. Shelter by the Company for which U.S. Shelter remitted cash.

b. The subsidiary has obtained an unsecured $15,000,000 line of credit from a bank. These funds are being used in financing transactions involving customers of the Company. The Company has not guaranteed the line of credit.

2. Preferred Stock Offering

On July 29, 1971, the Company, through its underwriters, offered 500,000 shares of $2.40 cumulative convertible preferred stock to the public at $40 per share. Net proceeds of $19,000,000 after deducting an underwriting discount, were received by the Company on August 5, 1971. Additional paid-in capital has been credited with the net proceeds received less the par value of the stock issued ($500,000) and expenses related to the offering ($429,367).

EXHIBIT 5 (*continued*)

The preferred stock is nonvoting except for certain defined events which would significantly affect the preferred stockholders' equity interests. The preferred shares are convertible into 1,379,310 common shares subject to adjustment in certain events, including stock split-ups and stock dividends. At its option, the Company may redeem the preferred stock at an initial price of $50 per share, as of August 1, 1971, ranging downward annually to $40 per share as of August 1, 1981 and thereafter.

3. Receivables

The Company enters into various modular housing sales contracts which contain an allocation of the sales price between modules (based on published price lists) and installation work. Sales of modules (Manufacturing Division) are recognized when units are manufactured and assigned to specific contracts. Installation work (Installation Division) is recorded on the percentage of completion method. The contracts generally provide for payment upon completion and receipt of all approvals necessary for occupancy, or for payment upon completion of each respective phase. "Unbilled" receivables represent recorded sales on contracts in process for which billings will be rendered in the future in accordance with the contracts. Receivables consist of:

	July 31, 1971	July 31, 1970
Contract receivables:		
Billed	$10,382,626	$10,559,145
Unbilled	24,633,799	4,626,370
Total	35,016,425	15,185,515
Income tax refund receivable (Note 9)	2,498,672	—
Current portion of long-term receivables (Note 4)	12,500	17,500
Other receivables	317,975	283,104
	$37,845,572	$15,486,119

Substantially all sales are to local housing authorities and sponsors who qualify for financial assistance from Federal agencies of the U.S. Government or who have made arrangements for long-term financing. In light of this, no provision for doubtful accounts is considered necessary.

See the condensed financial statements of U.S. Shelter Corporation in Note 1 for information with respect to receivables assigned by the Company to U.S. Shelter Corporation.

4. Long-Term Receivables

Long-term receivables consist of:

	July 31, 1971	July 31, 1970
Mortgages receivable:		
Mortgage due June 1, 1974—payments of $2,500 due quarterly with interest at the prime commercial rate in effect on the interest payment date	$ 241,624	$256,624
Mortgage due June 30, 1975—payments of $25,000 due June 30, 1973, and June 30, 1974, and the balance due June 30, 1975. Interest payable annually at the prime commercial rate in effect on the interest payment date	302,000	302,000
	543,624	558,624
Less installments due within one year (Note 3)	12,500	17,500
	531,124	541,124
Long-term portion of contract receivables—unbilled	3,694,225	—
	$4,225,349	$541,124

The mortgage notes are secured by mortgages on the property sold.

EXHIBIT 5 (*continued*)

5. Inventories

Inventories of the Company consist of the following:

	July 31, 1971	July 31, 1970
Raw materials	$1,439,960	$ 963,664
Work in process	1,001,632	139,531
Salable merchandise.	172,608	1,064,408
	$2,614,200	$2,167,603

Land held for development or sale is recorded at cost plus real estate taxes, mortgage interest, and other related carrying costs. The Company has entered into a contract to sell a parcel of the land with costs of $673,017 for a sale price of $2,100,000. The Company has received nonrefundable payments of $235,000 which have been accounted for as an option deposit.

6. Property, Plant, and Equipment

Property, plant, and equipment consist of the following:

	Useful Life	July 31, 1971	July 31, 1970
Land and land improvements	20 years	$ 1,136,499	$1,002,067
Buildings	10 and 45	4,822,055	1,702,924
Machinery, equipment, and tools	2–10	1,735,396	1,071,515
Furniture, fixtures, and office equipment.	5–10	942,131	500,951
Other	1–15	135,952	27,998
Construction in progress		1,388,613	1,171,211
		10,160,646	5,476,666
Less accumulated depreciation and amortization . . .		733,705	230,921
		$ 9,426,941	$5,245,745

The straight-line method of depreciation is used for all depreciable assets. Depreciation for the years ended July 31, 1971, and 1970 is $529,116 and $220,227, respectively.

7. Deferred Charges

The unamortized balance of deferred charges consist of:

	Amortization Period	Unamortized Balance July 31, 1971	Unamortized Balance July 31, 1970
Patents pending and trademarks	Legal life	$ 171,680	$ 88,660
Training and professional development	3 years	491,641	148,636
Research and development	5	671,897	84,496
Project and production start-up costs.	2–5	844,028	503,539
Property acquisition costs.	(a)	379,546	118,778
		$2,558,792	$944,109

a. Expenditures in connection with property acquisition will be added to the cost of property subsequently acquired.

In the event of project abandonment or other circumstances causing a loss of value to deferred items, the related unamortized costs are charged to current operations.

EXHIBIT 5 (*continued*)

8. Long-Term Debt
Long-term debt consists of the following:

	July 31, 1971	*July 31, 1970*
Mortgages maturing at various dates through December 31, 1976, and bearing interest at rates ranging from 4 3/4% to 6%	$433,176	$704,615
Installment contracts and lease purchase agreements maturing at various dates through August 1974.	89,042	124,910
	532,218	829,525
Less payments due within one year	295,630	333,036
	$236,588	$496,489

Land, buildings, and equipment with a net book value of $2,223,803 and $2,232,091 as of July 31, 1971, and July 31, 1970, respectively, are encumbered under the above agreements.

9. Income Taxes
Deferred taxes relate principally to manufacturing division and installation division sales, depreciation, deferred costs, and capitalized costs. None of the Company's tax returns have been examined by the Internal Revenue Service. The tax refund included in Note 3 relates to refundable advance tax payments and the planned amendment of the prior year's tax returns.

10. Stock Options
The Company has a qualified stock option plan in effect whereby options to purchase shares of common stock may be granted to officers and key employees at not less than the fair market value on the date of grant. During February 1971, authorized shares under the plan were increased from 400,000 to 900,000 shares. Options expire five years after the date of grant and are exercisable in cumulative installments of 20% after one year. A summary of activity for the year ended July 31, 1971, follows:

	Option Price per Share		
	From	*To*	*Shares*
Options outstanding at July 31, 1970	$ 3.00	$16.50	399,300
New options granted	15.13	22.00	275,500
Less: Options exercised	3.00	12.00	(11,800)
Cancellations	3.00	19.25	(61,900)
Options outstanding at July 31, 1971	3.00	22.00	601,000
Options outstanding at July 31, 1971 which are currently exercisable	3.00	16.50	58,360

No entries are recorded with respect to options until exercised at which time the excess of the option price over the par value of common stock is credited to additional paid-in capital.

11. Commitments and Contingencies
An action has been brought to enjoin the use of the word *Homex* by the Company. In the opinion of legal counsel, the plaintiff will be unsuccessful in obtaining the relief which it seeks.

A former shareholder of restricted shares of Company common stock has brought an action against the Company and another party, a broker. It is claimed that the Company refused, in concert with the other

EXHIBIT 5   *(concluded)*

defendant, to permit the transfer of plaintiff's stock except at a price substantially below its alleged market price. Compensatory damages in the amount of $1,575,000 and treble damages are alleged. In the opinion of management, the suit can be successfully defended in the option of counsel, the claim for treble damages is without merit.

The Company is engaged in other disputes involving claims which, in the aggregate, are insignificant compared to the Company's net worth.

Construction of a manufacturing plant in Mississippi is expected to be commenced in the latter part of 1971 at an approximate cost of $4,900,000. In a contract with the Company, Harrison County (where the plant site is located) has agreed to take the steps necessary to authorize the issuance and sale of tax-exempt industrial revenue bonds in an amount necessary to meet the cost of constructing and equipping the plant. The contract also provides for a 30-year lease to the Company of the completed facility and the related land. Semiannual payments in respect of the bonds will be based on principal and interest requirements; an additional $36,325 is due annually for the land. Options to purchase the plant and the land are provided for during and at the end of the lease term. If the bond offering is not consummated, the Company will arrange to finance the cost of the facility itself.

At July 31, 1971, the Company had leases on various equipment and office facilities with terms ranging from two to six years. Minimum annual rentals under such leases amount to approximately $404,000.

Notes payable consist of 90 day unsecured notes to 11 banks bearing interest at a rate 1/2% above the respective bank's best rate on the date of issue. The Company is required to maintain average annual compensating cash balances at each of these banks equal to approximately 15% to 20% of the outstanding indebtedness to such bank.

12.   Earnings per Share

Earnings per common share are based on the weighted average number of common shares outstanding during the periods presented after giving retroactive effect to the four-for-one stock split effected in February 1970. The preferred stock is not considered a common stock equivalent in accordance with *Opinion 15* of the Accounting Principles Board of the American Institute of Certified Public Accountants. In addition, the effect of the preferred stock offering, for the fiscal year ended July 31, 1971, on a fully diluted earnings per share calculation is insignificant. Stock options outstanding have not been included in these computations since the effect of their inclusion would be insignificant.

Accountants' Report

The Board of Directors and Stockholders
Stirling Homex Corporation

We have examined the consolidated balance sheet of Stirling Homex Corporation and consolidated subsidiaries as of July 31, 1971, and the related statements of income, additional paid-in capital and retained earnings, and changes in financial position for the year ended. Our examination was made in accordance with generally accepted auditing standards, and accordingly included such tests of the accounting records and such other auditing procedures as we considered necessary in the circumstances. The financial statements for the year ended July 31, 1970, included for comparative purposes, were examined by other accountants.

In our opinion, such financial statements present fairly the consolidated financial position of Stirling Homex Corporation and consolidated subsidiaries at July 31, 1971, and the results of their operations and changes in their financial position for the year then ended, in conformity with generally accepted accounting principles applied on a basis consistent with that of the preceding year.

Rochester, New York
September 15, 1971   PEAT, MARWICK, MITCHELL & COMPANY

Questions

1. Comment on the "fairness" of Stirling Homex's method of recognizing revenue and its allocation of profit between the manufacturing and installations divisions.
2. Comment on Note 7 in Exhibit 5.
3. What other financial reporting issues are present in this case? List and comment briefly.

PRIMARY SOURCES

Those interested in pursuing the topics related in this chapter could do no better than consult three monographs prepared for the FASB to guide their own thinking in the development of the Conceptual Framework.

Ijiri, Yuji. *Recognition of Contractual Rights and Obligations* (Stamford, Conn.: FASB Research Report, 1980).

Jaenicke, Henry R. *Survey of Present Practices in Recognizing Revenues, Expenses, Gains, and Losses* (Stamford, Conn.: FASB Research Report, 1981).

Johnson, Todd, and Reed K. Storey. *Recognition in Financial Statements: Underlying Concepts and Practical Conventions* (Stamford, Conn.: FASB Research Report, 1982).

SELECTED ADDITIONAL READINGS

The Timing of Revenue Reporting

American Accounting Association, 1964 Concepts and Standards Research Committee. "The Realization Concept." *The Accounting Review,* April 1965, pp. 312–22.

American Accounting Association, 1972–73 Committee on Concepts and Standards. "External Reporting." *The Accounting Review,* Supplement to 1974, pp. 203–22.

Horngren, Charles T. "How Should We Interpret the Realization Concept?" *The Accounting Review,* April 1965, pp. 323–33.

Installment Accounting

Cerf, Alan Robert. "Accounting for Retail Land Sales." *The Accounting Review,* July 1975, pp. 451–65.

Scott, Richard A., and Rita K. Scott. "Installment Accounting: Is It Inconsistent?" *Journal of Accountancy,* November 1979, pp. 52–58.

The Matching of Expenses and Revenues

American Accounting Association 1964 Concepts and Standards Research Committee. "The Matching Concept." *The Accounting Review,* April 1965, pp. 368–72.

Liao, Shu S. "The Matching Concept and Cost Allocation." *Accounting and Business Research*, Summer 1979, pp. 228–36.

Most, Kenneth. "The Rise and Fall of the Matching Principle." *Accounting and Business Research*, Autumn 1977, pp. 286–90.

Whittred, G. P. "Accounting for the Extractive Industries: Use of Abuse of the Matching Principle?" *Abacus*, December 1978, pp. 154–59.

ENDNOTES

1. See George J. Staubus, "Revenue and Revenue Accounts," *Accounting Research,* July 1956, pp. 284–94. Reprinted in Sidney Davidson, David Green, Jr., Charles T. Horngren, and George H. Sorter, *An Income Approach to Accounting Theory: Readings and Questions* (Englewood Cliffs, N.J.: Prentice Hall, 1964), pp. 78–88.
2. W. A. Paton and A. C. Littleton, *An Introduction to Corporate Accounting Standards, American Accounting Association Monograph No. 3* (AAA, 1940), p. 46.
3. AAA Committee on Accounting Concepts and Standards, *Accounting and Reporting Standards for Corporate Financial Statements and Preceding Statements and Supplements* (AAA, 1957), p. 5.
4. *SFAC 6*, par. 78.
5. American Institute of Certified Public Accountants, *APB Statement No. 4,* "Basic Concepts and Accounting Principles Underlying Financial Statements of Business Enterprises" (New York: AICPA, 1970), par. 134.
6. *APB Statement No. 4*, par. 148.
7. Paton and Littleton, *Corporate Accounting Standards*, p. 47.
8. *SFAC 6*, par. 82.
9. Sprouse and Moonitz, "Broad Accounting Principles," p. 47.
10. See John H. Myers, "The Critical Event and Recognition of Net Profit," *Accounting Review*, October 1959, pp. 528–32; and the 1964 Concepts and Standards Research Study Committee, "The Realization Concept," *Accounting Review*, April 1965, p. 316.
11. See, for example, the suggested probabilistic reporting suggested in the *AAA Committee on Concepts and Standards—External Financial Reporting*, "Report of the 1973–74 Committee," pp. 219–22.
12. For example, see Charles T. Horngren, "How Should We Interpret the Realization Concept?" *The Accounting Review*, April 1965, p. 325.
13. *SFAC 6*, par. 143.
14. *SFAC 5*, pars. 63 and 83.
15. See, for example, Floyd W. Windal, "The Accounting Concept of Realization," *The Accounting Review*, April 1961, p. 256.
16. *APB Statement No. 4*, Chap. 7, par. 10. Reconfirmation of this position is provided by *SFAC 5,* par. 84e.
17. Kenneth S. Most, *Accounting Theory,* 2nd ed. (Columbus, Ohio: Grid Publishing, Inc., 1982), p. 429.

18. *SFAC 6,* par. 80.
19. American Institute of Certified Public Accountants, *Accounting Terminology Bulletin No. 4,* "Cost, Expense and Loss" (New York: AICPA, July 1957), par. 3.
20. American Accounting Association, 1964 Concepts and Standards Research Study Committee, "The Matching Concept," *The Accounting Review,* April 1965, p. 369.
21. *SFAC 5,* pars. 85–87.

Chapter 12

Reporting the Effects of Price Changes

CHAPTER OBJECTIVES

After studying this chapter, you will be able to:

Compare the different kinds of price changes that occur in an economy, tracing the causes and effects of each on monetary and nonmonetary items.

Adjust financial statements to allow for price changes and interpret supplementary statements that show the effects of price changes.

Relate the effects of changing prices to the effects of foreign currency fluctuations.

CHAPTER OVERVIEW

The Nature of Price Changes

Prices reflect the exchange value of goods and services in an economy. They change for a variety of reasons, including changes in the supply of money, changes of consumers' tastes, and technological changes.

The Monetary and Nonmonetary Classifications

Price changes affect monetary and nonmonetary items differently because monetary items are denominated in fixed quantities of dollars or other currencies, while nonmonetary items can fluctuate in nominal terms.

Restating for Purchasing Power Changes

Methods have been developed to restate balance sheets and income statements in such a way as to reflect both general and specific changes in prices. The relevance of doing these restatements is unclear given that users have expressed no firm opinion in favor of price-adjusted statements.

Accounting for Current Costs

Focusing on current costs, which are the prices that would be paid for an asset at balance sheet date, raises questions of capital maintenance. Similar concepts were treated in Chapter 9.

Foreign Currency Translations

Assets and liabilities held in foreign countries involve issues of changing prices because they are subject to foreign currency fluctuations.

Inflation has become an important and constant fact of life in almost all countries of the world. The changing value of the monetary currency is now well recognized among accountants, but there is considerable disagreement regarding the theoretical and practical means of adjusting for it.

In 1976 the SEC mandated in *ASR 190* that certain disclosures regarding replacement costs be made by large enterprises. Three years later the FASB produced its own standard on the subject, which it labeled an experiment. *SFAS 33* required special disclosures by certain large firms. In particular, it required certain large enterprises to present (the terms the FASB uses are defined in the chapter):

1. Income from continuing operations restated for the effect of general inflation.
2. The purchasing power gain or loss on net monetary items.
3. Income from continuing operations on a current cost basis.
4. The current cost amounts of inventory and property, plant, and equipment at the end of the fiscal year.
5. Increases or decreases in current cost amounts of inventory and property, plant, and equipment, net of inflation.[1]

The FASB did not specify, however, the relationship of these disclosures to the basic financial statements.

In 1983 the FASB issued a call for comments on whether the experiment should continue. As a result of that survey, *SFAS 89* was issued encouraging, but now not requiring, a continuation of the supplementary disclosures required by *SFAS 33*. In effect, the official experiment had ended. Many reasons were provided as to why price-level adjusted statements were no longer to be required. They all reduce, essentially, to a perceived lack of relevance of the data, partly because analysts can make their own adjustments and partly because of the decline in inflation rates.

Differing rates of inflation among countries also cause exchange rates to fluctuate. This requires adjustments to be made when accounting for transactions between different countries and when consolidating the statements of foreign subsidiaries into those of the parent. These effects of inflation were first addressed by the FASB in October 1975 in *SFAS 8*. This statement drew very heavy and ongoing criticism from the business community. Eventually, in December 1981, *SFAS 8* was replaced by *SFAS 52*. Criticism since has been comparatively muted.

At the heart of the debate on how to account for unstable monetary units caused by price changes is a measurement constraint embedded in the structural approach to accounting theory. When financial measurements are based on historical prices, or when comparisons are made of price aggregates among different years, the usual assumed relationships in financial statements are altered. The ideal would be to take a radical approach and establish a new structure of accounting that would avoid comparisons and aggregations of prices of different years. Instead, the only proposals that have proved acceptable to accountants and the business community simply modify or restate traditional accounting measurements.

The purpose of this chapter is to analyze the alternative methods of accounting for price changes. The first two sections discuss the nature of price changes and the importance of monetary and nonmonetary classifications. The third section discusses the purchasing-power approach. It should be emphasized that the purchasing-power approach includes both the restatement for general purchasing-power changes and the restatement to reflect specific purchasing power as these are competing alternatives. The fourth section discusses current value accounting, including the use of both current costs and replacement costs as surrogates for current input values. Foreign currency translations are discussed in the final section because they represent restatements of the monetary unit and because exchange rates are related to the relative changes in prices in the separate countries.

The main objective of purchasing-power accounting is to restate the unit of measure into a common denominator. That is, the restatement is a scale adjustment and not a substitution of one measurement for another. For example, I could say that I traveled 1,000 miles in the United States and 1,000 kilometers in Europe, a total of 2,000 miles and kilometers. The latter, of course, is meaningless because it reflects the summing of two different scales of measurement. If I wished to restate this into a single scale of measurement, I could say that I traveled a total of 1,620 miles or 2,610 kilometers. Likewise, the summation of historical costs incurred at different periods of time represents the aggregation of different scales of measurement.[2] The restatement of historical costs for changes in purchasing power is assumed to result in figures measured in terms of the same scale of measurement.

An important observation regarding purchasing-power accounting is that the major objective is to improve the measurement system in the structural framework of the accounting process. Although the behavioral impact of price-level-adjusted accounting information is not fully understood at the present time, some studies have supported the hypothesis that price-level-restated data do contain information not included in traditional financial reports.[3]

THE NATURE OF PRICE CHANGES

Prices reflect the exchange value of goods and services in the economy. These goods and services include the several factors of production and items at intermediate stages of production, items held for speculative purposes, and goods and services acquired for consumption purposes. In general, these prices can be classified as either input prices (prices of factors of production or of goods and services at intermediate stages, acquired for further production or resale) or output prices (prices of goods and services sold as the product of the enterprise).

Price changes occur only when the prices of goods or services are different from what they were previously in the same market. The fact that a firm buys a commodity in its input market at one price and sells it to its customers at a higher price does not mean that the price of the commodity has changed. A price change occurs only if a price increases or decreases in either an input or an output market, or both.

Price changes can be classified as one of three types, although these classifications are interdependent and not mutually exclusive. These are:

1. General price changes.
2. Specific price changes.
3. Relative price changes.

General price changes reflect increases or decreases in the value of the monetary unit. They may be caused by changes in the supply or velocity of money that are greater or less than the changes in the total supply of goods and services in the economy, by an imbalance in the total supply and demand of goods and services in general, or by changes in world prices of basic commodities. Specific price changes occur for several reasons, including changes in tastes of consumers, technological improvements, speculation, and natural or artificial changes in the supply of particular products or as a result of changes in the value of money. Relative price changes reflect the change in the structure of prices or the change in the price of one commodity relative to the prices of all goods and services. General and relative price changes are both reflected in changes in the prices of specific goods. Although it is difficult, if not impossible, to separate the two effects on specific prices, they are different economic phenomena conceptually.

General Price-Level Changes

A general price-level change occurs as a result of a change in the value of the monetary unit during periods of inflation and deflation. In the absence of structural or relative price movements, all prices would move together by the same percentage. However, if prices are moving at different rates, which is the usual case, a measure of general price changes can be obtained only by computing an average or index of prices to express the general level of current prices compared with some base period. The ratio of the current index of prices to the base-period index expresses the relative change in all prices included in the index. The reciprocal of this ratio expresses the change in the value of the dollar or the change in *purchasing power*. For example, if the price index increased from 100 to 200, prices would have doubled, but the purchasing power of the dollar would have decreased to one-half its previous level.

The term *purchasing power* refers to the ability to buy goods and services with a given quantity of money (e.g., one dollar) compared with what the same quantity of money could have purchased at an earlier date. To obtain a good comparison of the purchasing power of money at two different dates, the goods and services available at the two dates must be the same or similar. Since the types and qualities of goods and services available change considerably over time, good comparisons of purchasing power cannot be obtained over several decades.

General purchasing power refers to the ability to buy all types of goods and services available in the economy, and it is measured by changes in the general price level. *Specific purchasing power* refers to the ability to buy specific goods and services at different dates. Thus, specific purchasing power can be measured by changes in specific prices. In between the concepts of general purchasing power and specific purchasing power are many concepts relating to the ability to buy certain goods and services that may be purchased by specific groups of individuals or that may be used for certain purposes. For example, the Consumer Price Index of the U.S. Bureau of Labor Statistics (CPI-U) measures the average change in prices of a specific "market basket" of goods and services bought by all urban consumers. Therefore, this index can be used to measure the ability of these individuals to maintain their level of living by purchasing the "basket" of goods and services usually acquired by them. However, the CPI-U was selected by the FASB for use in complying with *Statement 33* because it is fairly well understood and is broad enough to be considered a general index, rather than a specific one. In a like manner, it is also possible to measure the purchasing power of business enterprises to buy the goods and services usually acquired by them. These concepts of specific purchasing power (purchasing power for certain groups) are discussed at greater length below in the discussion of the choice of a proper index.

Specific Price Changes

In the absence of general price movements or changes in the value of the monetary unit, a change in the price of a specific commodity represents a change in its exchange value. Changes in prices in an input market result in increases or decreases in costs or expenses of the firm, and changes of prices in the output market result in a shift in revenues (assuming that the price change does not affect the quantity sold). In the traditional transactions approach to accounting, the original transaction price of goods or services acquired is matched with the revenue associated with the period or the goods sold. Changes in the specific input prices of goods sold are, therefore, included in the computation of the reported net income for the period. A more relevant matching is thought to be obtained by reporting as expenses the current prices of the goods used in the process of obtaining revenue. This matching of the current input prices with the current output (revenue) prices is thought to be more relevant as a measure of operating efficiency and as a better basis for predicting the results of future transactions.

Although there is no general agreement regarding the nature of the changes in specific prices of goods held by a firm, one view is that an increase in prices results in a holding gain, and a decrease results in a holding loss. According to this view, these should be included in the computation of the income of the firm because they represent changes in the value of the stockholders' equity (the net assets of the firm). However, most authors would not include these holding gains and losses in the computation of operating income because it is thought that they do not result from the normal recurring activities of the firm. That is, profit from normal operations is assumed to be the excess of selling price (or other determined revenue) over the current input price (current cost) of the product of the enterprise less other operating expenses.

The cost convention in accounting reports no change in value of assets until revenue is reported, usually at the time of sale. If current costs are used, holding gains and losses may be reported as prices change, although these gains and losses may be classified as either realized or unrealized.[4] For example, if a commodity was purchased for $100 and sold for $150 at a time when its current input price (replacement cost) was $120, the operating gross profit is $30 and the holding gain is $20. If the increase in the input price had occurred in a prior period, Edwards and Bell would consider the $20 to be realizable cost savings (unrealized) in the earlier period, but realized in the current period when the item is sold.[5]

Current costs represent current exchange prices, and thus their use results in a deviation from the historical cost basis. An objection is frequently made regarding the use of current costs, on the ground that a subjective value is substituted for a verifiable exchange price (historical cost). However, verifiability may still be present in those cases where the current exchange prices are obtained from well-organized markets. Furthermore, while some verifiability may be lost in the use of current costs rather than historical costs, the former are likely to be more relevant in meeting the objectives of the users of financial reports. However, current input prices can be assumed to represent current costs to the firm only if the firm generally purchases the same types of assets and is continuing to do so. If the firm is not purchasing the same type of asset, there is no evidence that it would acquire the asset in use at the current price, and therefore the current price of an asset acquired earlier at a lower price may not represent the relevant price, either in evaluating the firm's activities or in making predictions regarding the future.

Relative Price Changes

In the usual situation, prices of goods and services are moving at different rates, and some even in different directions. The extent to which specific prices move at a different rate or in a different direction from an index of all prices represents a relative price change. That is, if all prices increase by 20 percent and the price of product A increases by 32 percent, the relative price increase of product A is 10 percent (132/120 − 1.00).

In traditional accounting, with the use of historical costs, no price changes are isolated for separate reporting; all price changes are included in income as a result of transactions. The accounts and statements can be adjusted for general price-level changes without making adjustments for specific price changes, in which case costs and expenses would be adjusted for changes in the value of money and the price-level effect of these restatements would be excluded from the income calculation. But holding gains and losses resulting from relative price changes would not be measured or separated from reported net income.

If current prices are used instead of historical costs, net operating income can be computed without including any of the effects of price changes. But holding gains and losses cannot be measured unless the accounts are adjusted for both specific price changes and changes in the general price level. That is, the full effect of relative price changes cannot be measured and disclosed unless the accounts are adjusted for changes in the value of money and for changes in specific prices.

CHECKPOINTS

---

1. Distinguish the three types of price change from one another.
2. Explain in your own words what is meant by the term *purchasing power*.
3. What circumstances cause holding gains to occur?

THE MONETARY AND NONMONETARY CLASSIFICATIONS

Monetary assets are claims to a fixed quantity of the monetary unit (e.g., dollars) representing general purchasing power. Although prices of goods and services may change, claims expressed in a given number of dollars remain unchanged, but the purchasing power, or ability to convert these claims into goods and services, is altered. Monetary assets include cash; contractual claims to a specific amount of money in the future, such as accounts and notes receivable; and investments that pay a fixed amount of interest or dividends and will be repaid at a fixed amount in the future, although the date of repayment need not be specified—as in the case of preferred stock.

Convertible debt and convertible preferred stock are hybrid items that may be monetary or nonmonetary, depending on the circumstances. If the market price of the common stock into which they may be converted has increased sufficiently, the market will value the convertible securities in terms of the common stock equivalents. Therefore, investments in convertible securities should be classified as monetary or nonmonetary, depending on whether the market values them as debt or equity securities.

Monetary liabilities represent obligations to pay a fixed amount of dollars at some time in the future, regardless of what happens to the value of the monetary unit. They also include obligations to pay a fixed number of dollars, even though the exact amount is not known for certain. The important criterion is that the amount to be paid does not depend upon changes in the value of the monetary unit. These include accounts and notes payable; accruals, such as wages and interest payable; and long-term obligations payable in a fixed sum. Such items as rents and royalties received in advance are nonmonetary because they represent amounts payable in goods and services whose prices may fluctuate. As with investments in convertible securities, convertible debt should not be classified as a monetary liability. In most cases, where there is a possibility of future conversion, convertible debt should be treated as equity because it is not likely to be retired by the payment of a fixed number of dollars. *SFAS 33,* however, suggested that convertible debt should be classified as monetary until it is converted.

Nonmonetary assets, on the other hand, include those items whose prices in terms of the monetary unit may change over time, or claims to a variable amount of the monetary unit representing a predetermined amount of purchasing power. They include all rights to goods and services and all other rights to future benefits other than claims or rights expressed in terms of a fixed dollar value at some future time. Nonmonetary liabilities include the obligation to provide given amounts of goods and services or an equivalent amount of purchasing power, even though the payment might be in the form of cash. For example, an obligation to pay cash equal to the price of a given quantity of goods or services would be nonmonetary in nature.

The difficulty in defining monetary and nonmonetary assets and liabilities arises basically because the distinction is arbitrary. Only in a very extreme case would the price of an asset change by exactly the same percentage as the change in the general price level. On the other hand, it is possible that the price of an asset or the number of dollars to be exchanged for a claim may increase or decrease by a very small percentage in relation to the change in general prices. For example, a contract could call for the repayment of x number of dollars plus one-tenth of the percentage change in general prices. Thus, if a claim for $100 comes due after a period when general prices increased by 10 percent, the amount of the claim would be $101. Is this not more closely related to a monetary claim than one that is nonmonetary by the above definitions? For those who say that this is not a realistic case, let us look at claims to foreign currency and claims payable in a foreign currency. *SFAS 33* classified them as monetary, but suggested that claims to foreign currency are technically nonmonetary. It is true that a U.S. firm may not necessarily receive the same number of dollars when the claims are converted as when they were established; but, like claims to domestic currency, they may result in purchasing-power gains and losses. Therefore, they may be monetary or nonmonetary; the choice is arbitrary.

Gains and Losses on Monetary Items

Inflation is known to be beneficial to debtors and detrimental to creditors. Increased price levels usually mean increased dollar incomes, making repayment of debt easier in terms of the economic sacrifice involved. If A borrows $1,000 from B and repays it after a period during which the price level has increased by 60 percent, A has an economic gain and B has an economic loss. Although A repays $1,000, this represents only five-eighths (62.5 percent) of the purchasing power it had when borrowed. From the point of view of capital maintenance, if A has held the value of the borrowed money in the form of assets that have increased in monetary value with the price level, A will have realized a gain of $600 by selling the asset and repaying the loan. The creditor will have sustained a loss of $600 in purchasing power.

The gain or loss from the holding of net monetary assets by a firm is not so easily evaluated. Normally a firm will have cash and receivables in excess of monetary current liabilities. With a positive net monetary current position, an economic loss occurs as price levels increase and an economic gain occurs as price levels fall. During periods of inflation, the purchasing power of this working capital is not maintained. In fact, if the volume of business remains constant in real terms, working capital must usually be increased.

A gain or loss also occurs because of the holding of long-term monetary assets, such as long-term receivables and investments in government bonds and preferred stocks, and because of outstanding long-term debt. If the long-term debt exceeds the long-term monetary assets, an economic gain will occur when the price level rises, and vice versa when the price level falls.

The computation of the purchasing power gains or losses on monetary items involves two distinct steps:

1. The amount of the claim is first restated for the change in the purchasing power of the dollar during the accounting period, or during the period it was held or outstanding if for less than a year.
2. This restated amount is then compared with the current value of the asset or liability at the end of the period or at the time the item was reduced. The difference is the gain or loss in purchasing power.

This computation is similar to the restatement of nonmonetary items for changes in the value of money and a subsequent revaluation for changes in specific prices. However, monetary items are already expressed in current terms, so the computation is necessary only to measure the gain or loss arising from changes in their value expressed in terms of purchasing power.

Writers on this subject are not in agreement on the nature of this gain or loss or on the method of disclosing it in financial reports. Because it is similar to the holding gain or loss on nonmonetary items, one view is that it should be included in the computation of net income but not in income from operations. This is in accord with the financial capital maintenance concept and was preferred by the Board in the Exposure Draft. In *SFAS 33*, however, the Board expressed no preference, in the hopes of encouraging experimentation.

The fact that these gains and losses have no counterpart in conventional accounting has been responsible for much of the disagreement on the subject. Traditional accounting concepts and principles emphasize the allocation of costs to expenses and the recognition of gains through realization only at the time of external transactions. The discussions regarding the use of current costs and the recognition of holding gains and losses are not entirely comparable to the gains and losses on monetary items because the former refer primarily to nonmonetary assets, and the latter do not even appear unless adjustments are first made for changes in the value of money.

An alternative view suggested by Deupree is that the purchasing-power gain from holding liabilities (during periods of general price-level increase) represents a reduction in the cost of the assets acquired with the debt financing.[6] As an adjustment of the cost of assets, these credits (or debits in the case of deflation) should be taken into income as the assets are allocated to expenses, by depreciation or otherwise, or when they are sold. This view holds that the cost of an asset should be measured by the amount of cash finally paid for the asset, rather than the amount intended to be paid at the time of acquisition. It also holds strictly to the realization rule that the difference between this cost and the revenue against which it is matched should not be recognized until the asset is allocated to expense or sold.

Another interpretation is that, because of the rapid turnover of monetary working capital items, the purchasing-power gains and losses on these items can be considered to be realized as they occur, but that the purchasing-power gains and losses from the holding of long-term debt should not appear in the current operating statement until they are realized through payment of the bonds.[7]

Another view is that, from the point of view of the enterprise, the gains and losses on long-term debt are not a determinant of income, but rather an adjustment of the total equity of the firm—a shift from the bondholders' equity to the stockholders' equity. During periods of price-level increases, stockholders gain and bondholders lose, but the enterprise as a whole is not affected by the existence of the long-term debt. Therefore, if the income statement shows the income to the enterprise before interest on long-term debt, the purchasing power loss on the long-term debt should not be included. But in showing net income to stockholders, the gain or loss should be included. Since most income statements are prepared with the latter objective, the gain or loss on the long-term debt should be included. However, since the equity of the *enterprise* is relevant for some comparisons, a distinction should be made between the gains and losses on monetary working capital and the gains and losses on the long-term debt.

Some of the difficulties in reporting the purchasing-power gains and losses on monetary items relate to the logic of the structural framework of accounting. First, the arbitrary distinction between monetary and nonmonetary items weakens a structure that is already weak in terms of precise definitions. Second, the basic objective of purchasing-power restatements is to utilize a consistent scale of measurement, not to measure changes in values of specific items. Since nonmonetary items are not stated at current values, the valuation of monetary items at current values is inconsistent. That is, monetary items are restated for the change in purchasing power and then restated again back to the nominal value that may approach current value; nonmonetary items are restated only for the change in purchasing power. A partial explanation is that traditional accounting also recognizes changes in the value of some items that are measured in terms of exit prices.

From the point of view of real-world interpretation, the purchasing-power gains and losses are also deficient. A significant deficiency in the interpretation of such gains and losses arises from the fact that many future monetary commitments are made with the expectation of continuing inflation. In this case, protection against inflation may be included in the price of the goods exchanged giving rise to the monetary claim, in the rate of interest, or in the final amount to be paid. For example, if a one-year note requires repayment by the debtor of $100 plus 16 percent (including an expected price-level increase of 10 percent), there may be no purchasing-power loss if the actual increase in the general price level turns out to be 10 percent. The reporting of a $10 purchasing-power loss from holding the monetary asset may permit a wrong interpretation of the advantage or disadvantage of holding that asset. The situation becomes more complex when the firm is able to compensate for anticipated price changes by altering its costs and prices. Problems of interpretation also arise because measurement of the purchasing-power gains or losses depends to a large extent upon the timing of the increases or decreases of monetary assets or liabilities. With a large number of transactions during the year relating to monetary assets and liabilities, a considerable difference in the amount of the reported purchasing-power gain or loss may result from shifting the dates at which the changes in the monetary items are assumed to occur.

As indicated in Chapter 9, the presentation of income as representing changes in the value of the firm to stockholders is subject to many theoretical and practical difficulties. Since the value of a firm is dependent upon expectations regarding future cash flows and the individual utility preferences of stockholders, accounting reports can provide only the bases for making predictions and evaluating risk. Changes in the value of the firm as a whole cannot be measured by summing the changes in exchange prices or purchasing power of specific assets and liabilities. Furthermore, since purchasing-power gains and losses are measured by the use of general purchasing-power indexes, this measurement may be relevant to neither the firm nor the stockholder, as both may be interested in the ability to purchase specific goods and services, although this possibility has not been verified by adequate research. This concept is discussed later.

Another objection to reporting purchasing-power gains and losses in income is the assumption that they are not relevant to most decisions of investors and other users of external reports. For example, if prices were rising, a firm could borrow money in order to pay a cash dividend or purchase treasury stock and thus report a purchasing-power gain arising from the existence of the liability. But such a gain may not be relevant to a description of the assumed basic activities of the firm, nor to predictions by investors of the firm's future. Likewise, holding cash acquired by the sale of preferred stock may permit the firm to acquire operational assets that may significantly improve the income of the firm in the future; the presentation of a purchasing-power loss on the holding of this cash while awaiting the proper opportunity may be deceptive with respect to the advisability of such a transaction and the future expectations regarding the firm. Therefore, it is likely that a separate reporting of purchasing-power gains and losses does not provide information because of their interrelationship with all other activities of the firm.

CHECKPOINTS

1. Distinguish monetary from nonmonetary assets, giving an example of each.
2. Distinguish monetary gains and losses from holding gains and losses.
3. How do monetary gains and losses relate to nominal interest rates?

RESTATING FOR PURCHASING POWER CHANGES

The Restatement of Nonmonetary Items

Nonmonetary assets acquired in one period and held for sale or use in a later period can be measured in terms of the exchange prices existing when the assets were acquired or in terms of the exchange price at the date of reporting or some other date. These measurements are called nominal dollars because they represent the number of dollars at the date of measurement, and they cannot logically be compared with similar measurements at other dates. Only if the measurements are stated in terms of prices at the same date or if they are restated for changes in the purchasing power of money are they expressed in constant units. When they are restated in terms of changes in the value of money, they are referred to as constant dollars. When historical costs are restated for changes in the value of money, the result is referred to as historical cost/constant dollar information. When current costs are restated for comparative purposes or to express the amounts at other than the measurement date, the result is current cost/constant dollar information.

A frequent argument for the use of the historical cost/constant dollar approach has been that it retains the objectivity of historical costs, whereas the use of current costs substitutes a less objective measurement base—a current value. However, objectivity is maintained if current market prices for similar assets are obtained. If estimates are made, the resulting values are less objective. In evaluating the two measurement systems—historical cost/constant dollar and current cost/constant dollar—consideration should be given to the relevance and verifiability of the resulting amounts and the information content for security markets.

The restatement for changes in the general purchasing power is an improvement in the structural framework only. It leads to real-world interpretations only if the general price level and the specific prices move together in such a way that the general price-level restatement can be considered a surrogate for the specific prices.[8]

Price-Level Restatement Models

The following examples are drawn from the discussions initiated by Chambers.[9] The models assume a basic classification of assets and liabilities as monetary and nonmonetary, a transactionless interval, and either a general price-level change or changes in the prices of specific items or both.

General Price-Level Restatements. Let us assume a firm with net monetary assets M, total nonmonetary assets N, and residual equity R, all expressed in dollars at time t_0*:

$$M_0 + N_0 = R_0 \tag{1}$$

Assume also that restatements are to be made by the use of an index of changes in the general level of prices p, representing the change in the general price level such that $p = (P_1/P_0 - 1)$ where P_1 = the price index at t_1, and P_0 = the price index at t_0. Then the restatement of the financial condition of the firm in terms of prices at t_1 is as follows†:

$$M_0(1 + p) + N_0(1 + p) = R_0(1 + p) \tag{2}$$

By multiplication we have:

$$M_0 + M_0 p + N_0 + N_0 p = R_0 + R_0 p \tag{3}$$

---

* Nonmonetary liabilities are assumed to be negligible.

† Note that, for simplification, it is assumed that there are no changes in the net monetary assets (M) or in the nonmonetary assets (N) and that no depreciable assets are included.

and because the amount of net monetary assets (M) remains constant from t_0 to t_1, we subtract M_0p from both sides and change M_0 to M_1:

$$M_1 + (N_0 + N_0p) = (R_0 + R_0p) - M_0p \tag{4}$$

($N_0 + N_0p$) represents the original price of the nonmonetary assets expressed in terms of a common dollar at t_1 and ($R_0 + R_0p$) represents the stockholders' equity at t_0 restated in terms of the purchasing power of the dollar at t_1. It can be assumed that stockholders would be as well off at t_1 as at t_0 if $R_1 = R_0 + R_0p$. Since the dollar amount of monetary assets (M) cannot increase merely because of the increase in the general price level, R_1 is less than $R_0 + R_0p$ by the amount of M_0p; thus M_0p represents the purchasing-power loss from the holding of net monetary assets while prices in general are rising. (M_0p would represent a gain if $M < 0$ or if $p < 0$.)

We can expand upon the above example by separating the net monetary assets (M) into two parts, net monetary current assets C and net monetary long-term debt L, such that $M = C - L$. Substituting in equation (1), we have at t_0:

$$C_0 - L_0 + N_0 = R_0 \tag{5}$$

and multiplying all expressions by ($1 + p$), we have at time t_1:

$$C_0(1 + p) + N_0(1 + p) - L_0(1 + p) = R_0(1 + p) \tag{6}$$

or:

$$C_0 + C_0p + N_0 + N_0p - L_0 - L_0p = R_0 + R_0p \tag{7}$$

Because both C and L remain constant from time t_0 to t_1 (that is, $C_0 = C_1$ and $L_0 = L_1$), we must subtract C_0p from both sides, add L_0p to both sides of the equation, and change C_0 to C_1 and L_0 to L_1:

$$C_1 + (N_0 + N_0p) - L_1 = (R_0 + R_0p) + L_0p - C_0p \tag{8}$$

If income is measured by the net change in the purchasing power of the residual equity, L_0p represents a gain from the outstanding debt during the period, and C_0p represents the loss from holding monetary current assets from time t_0 to t_1. The argument that L_0p and C_0p are not gains and losses from a structural point of view can be supported only on the basis of a different concept of income. For example, under the transactions concept of income these are not part of income because they do not represent the results of activity on the part of the firm.

Another argument that the gain on long-term debt (L_0p) is not a part of the income for the period is based on the assumption that capital invested in the firm includes both debt and residual equity capital, $R + L$. Therefore, capital is maintained if $R_1 + L_1$ at time t_1 is equal to ($R_0 + R_0p$) + ($L_0 + L_0p$). Any loss to bondholders is equal to the purchasing power gain to stockholders, but the effect on the firm as a whole is neutral.[10]

Restatements for Specific Price Changes. If assets are restated for the price changes of individual assets rather than for changes in general purchasing power, each nonmonetary asset must be adjusted by the rate of change in its specific price, s_i; net monetary assets are not restated because their specific prices in dollars do not change. Since each nonmonetary asset or group of similar assets N_i must be adjusted separately, equation (1) should be restated as follows:

$$M + \sum_{i=1}^{k} N_i = R \tag{9}$$

where

$$\sum_{i=1}^{k} N_i = N_i + N_2 \ldots N_k$$

By adjusting the nonmonetary assets for the rate of specific price changes (s_i), we obtain the following equation:

$$\sum_{i=1}^{k} N_i(1 + s_i) = \sum_{i=1}^{k} N_i + \sum_{i=1}^{k} N_i s_i \tag{10}$$

where

$$\sum_{i=1}^{k} N_i(1 + s_i) = N_1(1 + s_i) + N_2(1 + s_2) \ldots N_k(1 + s_k)$$

so that the exchange price at time t_0 of each nonmonetary asset in the total set owned by the firm from asset N_1 to asset N_k is adjusted by the specific price change (s_i) relating to each asset.

Therefore, by adding $\sum_{i=1}^{k} N_i s_i$ to each side of equation (9) and combining as indicated in equation (10), we obtain the following equation:

$$M_0 + \sum_{i=1}^{k} N_{0i}(1 + s_i) = R_0 + \sum_{i=1}^{k} N_{0i} s_i \tag{11}$$

The effect of equation (11) is to show on the left side all net assets at their current prices, and on the right side the total residual equity at the time period t_0, plus the increase in the prices of specific nonmonetary assets. Mathews argues that this adjustment results in no gain or loss to the firm because the specific purchasing power of the net assets is the same as it was at the beginning of the period.[11]

Gynther proposes similar adjustments for changes in the prices of specific nonmonetary assets, but he suggests that the purchasing-power loss from the holding of net monetary current assets should be reported.[12] However, he recommends that the gains or losses on monetary current items should be computed by using the price indexes of the goods generally acquired by these monetary assets. That is, the firm can maintain its capital only if it maintains its purchasing power in terms of the specific goods it generally purchases. This position has some merit, as discussed later.

Relative Price Changes.   If there is no change in the general purchasing power of the dollar, the increase in residual equity indicated in equation (11) represents a holding gain, according to some proponents of general price-level adjustments. That is, the firm is assumed to be as well off at the end of the period as at the beginning if $R_1 = R_0 + R_0p$, but if $p = 0$, $R_0p = 0$; thus, the increase in the prices of specific nonmonetary assets permits the firm to be better off at the end of the period in terms of its ability to use its resources to purchase goods and services in general. The entire specific price changes in this case are assumed to be relative price changes.

If the prices of the specific goods held by the firm change at a different rate from the rate of change of general prices, the differences between the two rates represent the relative price change. For example, if the specific price of asset N_i has increased by the rate s_i and if this rate is greater than p, the increase in the general level of prices is such that $s_i > p$ and the holding gain due to the relative price increase would be $N_i(s_i - p)$. This result is obtained by subtracting the price of the specific asset N_i at t_0 adjusted for changes in the general price level from the current price of the asset at t_1. Thus:

$$N_i(1 + s_i) - N_i(1 + p) = N_i + N_is_i - N_i - N_ip$$
$$= N_is_i - N_ip = N_i(s_i - p)$$

The current price of the specific asset can then be approximated as the sum of the price of the asset N_i at time t_0 adjusted for the change in the general level of prices and the relative price change of this asset. Thus:

$$N_i(1 + p) + N_i(s_i - p) = N_i + N_ip + N_is_i - N_ip = N_i + N_is_i \quad (12)$$
$$= N_i (1 + s_i)$$

Therefore, for the entire firm, the nonmonetary assets can be expressed in terms of the current specific prices by adjusting first for changes in the general level of prices and then adding the relative price changes to both sides of the equation. This can be computed as follows, starting with equation (9):

$$M_0 + \sum_{i=1}^{k} N_{0i} = R_0 \quad (9)$$

and adjusting both sides by the change in the level of general prices, we obtain:

$$M_0(1 + p) + \sum_{i=1}^{k} N_{0i}(1 + p) = R_0(1 + p) \qquad (13)$$

By multiplication, and subtracting $M_0 p$ from both sides, we have:

$$M_0 + \sum_{i=1}^{k} N_{0i}(1 + p) = R_0 + R_0 p - M_0 p \qquad (14)$$

Then by adding the relative price changes to both sides, we reach the following equation:

$$M_0 + \sum_{i=1}^{k} N_{0i}(1 + p) + \sum_{i=1}^{k} N_{0i}(s_i - p)$$

$$= (R_0 + R_0 p) - M_0 p + \sum_{i=1}^{k} N_{0i}(s_i - p) \qquad (15)$$

Since $(R_0 + R_0 p)$ is necessary at time t_1 to maintain the residual equity in terms of a constant general purchasing power, $M_0 p$ represents the loss in purchasing power from the holding of a constant amount of monetary items and $\sum_{i=1}^{k} N_{0i}(s_i - p)$ represents the gains arising from the increase in relative prices of nonmonetary assets.

Since the practical application of equation (15) leaves much to be desired, a similar application suggested by Chambers has considerable merit, although it does not permit the separation of purchasing-power gains and losses on monetary items and the gains and losses from the holding of nonmonetary assets.[13] Chambers' suggestion can be interpreted as follows:

By combining the general and relative price adjustments of nonmonetary assets on the left side of equation (15) and expanding the right side, we obtain:

$$M_0 + \sum_{i=1}^{k} N_{0i}(1 + s_i) = (R_0 + R_0 p) - M_0 p + \sum_{i=1}^{k} N_{0i} s_i - \sum_{i=1}^{k} N_{0i} p \quad (16)$$

and, since $M_0 p + \sum_{i=1}^{k} N_{0i} p = R_0 p$, we can substitute $R_0 p$ in equation (16) and obtain the following:

$$M_0 + \sum_{i=1}^{k} N_{0i}(1 + s_i) = (R_0 + R_0 p) + \left[\sum_{i=1}^{k} N_{0i} s_i - R_0 p \right] \qquad (17)$$

Therefore, according to equation (17), nonmonetary assets need to be adjusted only for specific price changes, and the income effect of the general and specific price changes is measured by adding the sum of the increases in the specific price changes of nonmonetary assets and subtracting a capital adjustment $(R_0 p)$ so that the total adjustment is

$$\left[\sum_{i=1}^{k} N_{0i} s_i - R_0 p \right]$$

This net adjustment to income could, of course, be positive or negative, depending upon the relative rates of change of s_i and p.

Equation (17) is significant because it points out the major difference between those who propose adjustments for specific price changes only and those who propose adjustments for general and relative price changes. If the $+R_0 p$ and the $-R_0 p$ on the right side of equation (17) are canceled, we have equation (11), which represents the adjustments necessary according to those who propose the adjustment for specific price changes only. However, the interpretation is different, because the adjustment for specific price changes in equation (11) is assumed to represent an adjustment of capital, whereas in equation (17) it is a part of the adjustment of income. Therefore, the differences between the proponents of specific price adjustments only and the proponents of adjustments for general and relative price changes are primarily based on the assumptions regarding the nature of the firm and the objectives of financial reporting.

An Evaluation of Price-Level Restatements

Some of the main controversies regarding price-level restatements center around the following questions:

1. Are the procedures and measurement techniques feasible?
2. Are the resulting accounting structures logical and internally consistent?
3. Are the resulting statements subject to meaningful interpretations? In other words, do they have real-world significance?
4. What is the behavioral impact of price-level restatements? Are they relevant for the decision models of investors and creditors?
5. Do the benefits of the information provided by price-level restatements exceed the costs of computing and reporting the data?

Alternative approaches to price-level restatements must be evaluated in terms of all of these questions. The following evaluations are intended to place them in proper perspective, although final answers cannot be given at this time because of a lack of sufficient empirical research on this subject.

General Purchasing Power. Most of the proposals and studies for restating financial statements using a single price index have made explicit or assumed statements that the index should measure the changes in prices in general, reflecting changes in general purchasing power or changes in the general value of the dollar.

General purchasing power, as measured by a general index of prices, shows the general tendency of all prices of goods and services in the economy to rise or fall or remain constant on the average as appropriately weighted, and reflects changes in the value of money. No index of all prices in the economy has ever been computed, and none is likely to be computed, but several available indexes may be used as close approximations.

The Gross National Product Implicit Price Deflators produced by the U.S. Department of Commerce are probably the best currently compiled indexes of the general level of prices in the United States. They are computed by dividing the current dollar series of the GNP by the corresponding constant dollar series, and therefore reflect all exchange prices in the economy. However, because the index does not generally reflect secular quality improvements and the emergence of superior products, the index does not provide a good comparison for years not close to each other. The Consumer Price Index for All Urban Consumers was selected by the FASB in *SFAS 33* because of its widespread use and because it is generally understood by most people, as well as its broad base in the economy.

From a structural point of view, the general purchasing-power system appears to be logical and consistent with two exceptions: (1) The distinction between monetary and nonmonetary items is arbitrary, and (2) monetary items are restated twice—once for the change in general purchasing power and again for the restatement back to a nominal or current value—but nonmonetary items are restated only for general purchasing-power changes. It should be recognized, however, that only the scale of measurement is changed. The structure continues to have all of the deficiencies of historical cost accounting.

From an interpretational point of view, it is assumed that general purchasing power is generally understood as a standard resource that can be used to acquire any or all types of goods and services in the economy.[14] The interpretation, however, is not intended to represent current values, but merely the historical cost restated for changes in general purchasing power. However, interpretation remains difficult because historical cost represents the number of dollars paid for a specific item, but the restated amount does not represent the amount that would have been paid for the item if the current price level and the current price structure were then known. And since it is not intended to be a surrogate for current value, there is difficulty in attaching any current market or utility valuation interpretation to it.

One of the major criticisms of general purchasing-power restatements is that the concept is too broad. Individuals and corporations think of purchasing power in terms of the items they usually buy or might be interested in buying or selling. With a general purchasing-power concept, it is assumed that the investor had a free choice to spend money in the economy in any way at the time of the investment, and that when the capital is recovered through the sale of product or services the investor will again have the freedom to spend the money in any way. That is, the operating cycle of the business is assumed to flow from cash to nonmonetary assets and back to cash, and the cash is then available to the investor for general spending. This is a single-venture concept that is not relevant to large corporate enterprises. An alternative way of looking at it is to assume that the firm is continually making choices to invest and reinvest its capital in the economy for all types of goods and services. However, the intentions and technical resources generally limit the types of goods and services that it will purchase.

From a behavioral point of view, the evidence of relevance for investment decisions is not conclusive. As a result of an empirical study, Petersen suggested that "... if one accepts the notion that published financial information is an input to the investment decision, some impact on that choice is suggested."[15] In another study of securities price behavior, it was concluded that price-level restated data do contain information not available in traditional statements.[16] However, as a result of research in the United Kingdom, Morris concluded that there is very little indication that the market has responded to information provided by inflation-adjusted earnings figures.[17] This lack of strong supporting relevance of general price-level restatements may result from several factors, including the following: (1) the inability to define investment decision models; (2) the impounding of information in market prices from other sources in accord with the efficient-markets hypothesis; and (3) the lack of interpretability of the restated data. Further research may, of course, prove otherwise.

Purchasing Power of Stockholders.   One of the earliest concepts of purchasing power is that capital is maintained only if the ability of stockholders to purchase a given quantity and quality of consumers' goods and services is held constant. For example, Sweeney held the view that the cost-of-living index was the ideal, and this concept has been implied by many other writers. The adoption of the CPI-U by the FASB in *SFAS 33* may have been influenced by this reasoning but, as indicated above, there are several other reasons for using the CPI-U as a measure of general purchasing power. It is generally claimed that investors buy production goods only because they hope to obtain, eventually, more consumption goods than they could have had by consuming rather than investing. However, this is unrealistic for two reasons: (1) Large corporations usually intend to continue in business indefinitely rather than liquidate so that stockholders can consume their investments. (2) Stockholders do not usually liquidate their holdings in order to consume the amount of the investment. Although investors are constantly liquidating their holdings, it is more common for stockholders to reinvest their savings and consume only the income from the investments than it is for them to consume the amounts invested in corporate stocks.

Investment Purchasing Power of the Firm. The postulate of continuity assumes that the firm will continually reinvest its assets in order to maintain its *invested capital*. Thus, the operating cycle of the business is from nonmonetary assets to cash to nonmonetary assets. However, continuity of life does not imply that the firm must replace specific assets. But it does mean that the firm should maintain its purchasing power to acquire investment goods.

Investment purchasing power can be looked at from at least three different views:

1. The ability of the firm to reinvest in an equal quantity of investment goods in general.
2. The ability of the firm to reinvest in capital goods generally purchased by all firms in the industry.
3. The ability to reinvest in investment goods similar to those it has acquired in the past.

Each of these views is a relevant description of some parts of the economy. Some firms diversify their investment over time and actually move from one industry to another or branch out into different industries. Other firms remain in the same industry but change the composition of their investment to keep up with technological innovations and to produce new products. And many firms do reinvest in capital goods and inventories similar to those they have had in the past.

The first view—general investment purchasing power—may reflect a dynamic economy, such as in the United States. Although there are some institutional frictions to movement, many firms do branch out into different industries, and accounting data should indicate when this is desirable. Adjustments for price-level changes in this case require the use of an overall investment price index. No such comprehensive index is now available, but an approximation could be obtained by combining the implicit price deflators for the "other new construction" and "producers' durable equipment" segments of GNP and adjusting for changes in the prices of inventories. A single-investment index for the economy has the advantage of uniformity among firms and ease of application once the index is determined.

The second view—industry investment purchasing power—is a logical interpretation because firms do generally reinvest in the same industry. However, it would require a different investment index for each industry. A major practical difficulty in applying this approach is the fact that many firms produce a wide variety of products, so it is impossible to determine exactly in which industries they operate.

The third view—purchasing power relating to the past behavior of a specific firm—may be a good approximation of firm investment purchasing power because firms do maintain continuity of operations over time. However, technological changes in methods of production and in products require firms to alter their investment mix constantly.

From an interpretational point of view, it appears that the greater the correspondence between the investment index and specific movement in prices, the greater will be the interpretability of the data. That is, the individual measurements will then reflect valuations closer to current values. However, the use of an investment index has the advantage over specific revaluations in that the resulting valuations are less subjective and are not as easily manipulated for personal or firm advantage. While considerable research is necessary to determine its feasibility, interpretability, and relevance for investment decisions, the investment purchasing power concept is appealing as a method of capturing the best of both worlds—general purchasing-power revaluations and specific replacement purchasing-power revaluations.

CHECKPOINTS

1. Provide a brief critique of the concept of *general purchasing power*.
2. Distinguish the purchasing power of stockholders from the investment purchasing power of the firm.
3. List the three aspects from which investment purchasing power may be viewed.

ACCOUNTING FOR CURRENT COSTS

Current costs reflect the prices that must be paid for an asset or its use at the date of the balance sheet or the date of the use or sale if that asset is not already owned. For inventories, current cost is the current acquisition price of the merchandise or the current cost to produce it. For plant, equipment, and other property, the best measure of current cost is the used asset price of a similar asset in the same condition and of the same age as the asset owned. If there is a competitive market for used plant and equipment, with many buyers and sellers, the price in this market may reflect the current value of the asset to the firm if its expectations can be assumed to be similar to the expectations of other firms in the industry. If the market is not highly competitive or if the asset is used for different purposes, the used equipment price is not relevant except as an indication of what the firm could obtain for the asset in liquidation.

In the absence of used asset markets, the current cost may be approximated by using the acquisition cost of an identical new item purchased in current established markets less accumulated depreciation for a period equal to the age of the asset in use. If identical assets are not available, the cost of an asset that will provide the equivalent service capacity may be substituted. This price, however, must be adjusted for technological changes in either operating efficiency or in product quality. A reproduction cost may be substituted for a current replacement cost, but a reproduction cost is not relevant if the asset cannot be produced efficiently with current production tools and methods. The reproduction cost of vintage automobiles, for example, is in excess of the cost of new automobiles that are greatly superior to the former models.

An alternative to the use of market prices is the application of specific cost indexes to the historical cost of the specific asset. Although this may provide an acceptable approximation of current cost, technological changes in production of the asset and obsolescence should be taken into consideration. If the asset could be reproduced currently with technologically superior methods, the current cost might be overstated if broad cost indices are applied to the historical costs. On the other hand, if the equivalent service is obtainable by using newer and more efficient equipment, the current value of the old equipment may be little more than its scrap value or its unallocated historical cost, even though replacement cost has increased considerably. Unless the accumulated depreciation is adjusted for this obsolescence, the recording of obsolete equipment at its replacement cost (estimated by using price indexes) less normal depreciation has the effect of delaying the recognition of the loss in value until the period of use, at which time depreciation would be excessive as a measurement of the value of the asset's service contribution to the product. *SFAS 33* requires that current costs should not exceed recoverable amounts measured by the net realizable value for items to be sold or the value in use for other assets. The value in use is the discounted value of future expected cash flows. Since the future cash flows cannot be measured for most assets, an indication that value in use is less than current cost would be evident if the firm would not replace an existing asset because of its high operating costs.

Capital-Maintenance Concepts

As discussed in Chapter 9, one of the interpretations of accounting income is that it is based on the concept of capital maintenance. That is, *income* is defined as the amount a firm could distribute to its stockholders and be as well off at the end of the period as it was at the beginning. However, the term *well off* has several interpretations relevant for accounting for price changes. These include financial capital maintenance, general purchasing-power capital maintenance, and physical capital maintenance.

In the financial capital-maintenance concept, income results from the increase in the number of nominal dollars representing capital. The traditional historical cost/nominal dollar approach is a financial capital-maintenance concept because revenues must exceed historical costs before income can be reported. Likewise, the current cost/nominal dollar approach may be based on a financial capital-maintenance concept. However, increases in the prices of assets held during a period result in holding gains, and decreases result in holding losses. The current cost at the beginning of the period is subtracted from the current cost of the same asset at the end of the period to arrive at the holding gain or loss, as described above. In the financial capital-maintenance concept, these holding gains and losses are included in the determination of income for the period.

The historical cost/constant dollar approach is based on the general purchasing-power capital-maintenance concept. Income is the excess of the capital at the end of the period over the capital at the beginning, both expressed in terms of a constant general purchasing power of the dollar. Accordingly, restatements of nonmonetary assets and liabilities are not included in income, but the purchasing-power gains and losses on monetary items are included. In the current cost/constant dollar approach, current costs at the beginning of the period are restated in terms of a constant purchasing power at the end of the period, and the difference between this and the current cost of the asset at the end of the period is a holding gain or loss. This is the relative price change discussed above (also referred to as the change in current costs net of inflation).* In the financial capital-maintenance concept, these holding gains and losses should be included in the income computation.

In the physical capital-maintenance approach, also referred to as the operating capability approach, it is assumed that capital is maintained if the firm is able to replace its assets with assets of the same type or if it is able to maintain the capacity to produce a constant supply of goods and services. Firms may not necessarily replace specific assets or even continue to produce the same goods and services, but the use of current costs (or restatements by the use of specific indexes) may in the aggregate be an acceptable surrogate for the physical capacity purchasing power of the firm. The major difference between the physical capital-maintenance concept and the financial capital-maintenance concept is that in the former the holding gains and losses are not included in income. Instead, they are considered to be adjustments to stockholders' equity. An alternative is to consider the holding gains and losses to be restatements of equity with the thought that equity is restated for changes in the specific purchasing power of the firm. In the current cost/constant dollar approach, the hold-

---

* See above, pp. 420–22.

ing gains and losses arising from the relative price changes are likewise excluded from the computation of income.

Although there are doubts regarding the logic of including purchasing-power gains and losses on monetary items in the computation of income, as discussed above, many writers include them even under the physical capital-maintenance concept. Gynther, for example, recommended that gains and losses on monetary items be computed by using specific indexes representing the price changes of the goods for which the monetary items are held. For example, gains and losses on accounts receivable might be computed by using an index of the prices of merchandise generally purchased by the firm. For cash items, an index of the prices of merchandise generally purchased by the firm, representing changes in the prices of supplies, wages, and operating expenses, might be·used.[18] This approach is consistent with the physical capital-maintenance approach, but a broader index would probably be more appropriate because monetary assets are not generally held for specific purchases, and monetary liabilities do not generally finance specific items. Because of the similarity of purchasing-power gains and losses on monetary items and holding gains and losses net of inflation for nonmonetary items, logic is on the side of excluding them from income and considering them to be adjustments of equity. However, *SFAS 33* specifies that both purchasing-power gains and losses on monetary items and the changes in current costs net of inflation should not be included in income. But no disposition is suggested in order to permit greater experimentation.

An Evaluation of Accounting for Current Costs

Current costs are claimed to have several advantages over the historical cost concept. Among them are the following:

1. The current cost represents the amount the firm would have to pay currently to obtain the asset or its services; therefore, it represents the best measure of the value of the inputs being matched against current revenues for predictive purposes.
2. It permits the identification of holding gains and losses, thus reflecting the results of asset management decisions and the impact of the environment on the firm not reflected in transactions.
3. The current cost represents the value of the asset to the firm if the firm is continuing to acquire such assets and if value has not been added to the asset by the enterprise.
4. The summation of assets expressed in current terms is more meaningful than the addition of historical costs incurred at different time periods.
5. It permits the reporting of current operating profit, which may be used to predict future cash flows.

With respect to the second objective, the emphasis is on the distinction between trading and price facets of business operations to provide better information for management decisions and a better measure of managerial efficiency. However, it can be argued that this separation of income into holding gains and losses and current operating profit is artificial because, since efficient buying is a part of operations, it is impossible to separate the two effects that arise jointly from the same decision.

The fifth objective assumes on theoretical grounds that current operating profit of one year is a good indicator of the operating profit of the succeeding year, which, in turn, is a surrogate for that year's distributable operating flow.[19] The distributable operating cash flows, in turn, may permit the prediction of potential future dividend contributions.

One of the disadvantages of the current cost concept is that some objectivity has been lost; unless the assets currently sold in the market are identical in all respects to the assets held, some subjectivity must be applied in transferring current exchange prices to the owned assets. Also, current costs might not represent the current value to the enterprise. If the firm were required to pay the current costs, it might be economically advantageous to acquire other asset forms instead. The present value of the benefits to be provided by the asset may not be equal to the current or replacement cost of the asset. This is particularly true when technological changes have occurred in the demand for the product. For example, if the demand for a product has declined significantly, the specialized equipment required for its production will have declined in service value to the firm; the depreciated cost of acquiring similar equipment is not a good measure for the service value to the firm.

From an interpretational point of view, the current cost concept appears to be more relevant than the general purchasing-power concept. That is, costs related by the use of specific indexes or replaced by current cost measurements are probably closer to current values than are historical costs adjusted for general purchasing-power changes. However, the use of conventional allocation and amortization procedures applied to the current costs of new items weakens the potential correspondence between the resulting figures and current values.

From a behavioral point of view, recent research has found little empir-

---

CHECKPOINTS

1. Define the term *current cost*. How might it be approximated?
2. Distinguish the maintenance of financial capital from the maintenance of physical capital.
3. What are the advantages and disadvantages using current costs?

ical evidence supporting the existence of information content for current cost information.[20] Additional research may prove otherwise as more empirical data become available.

FOREIGN CURRENCY TRANSLATIONS

In those cases in which it is desirable to aggregate assets or liabilities or transactions expressed in different currencies, the amounts expressed in the different currencies should be translated into terms of the currency of the country in which most of the readers of the financial statements reside. The need for translation generally occurs when the statements of a branch or subsidiary are consolidated with a domestic parent corporation or when the statements of an independent foreign corporation are translated for use in a different country.

The translation of foreign currency measurements is not the same problem as the restatement of dollar amounts for changes in the price level. In the former an actual exchange rate does exist at a specific point in time, but it is impossible to exchange purchasing power at one time with purchasing power at another time. However, some of the concepts relating to restatements for price changes are also relevant in the translation of foreign currencies. For example, one of the purposes of foreign currency translation is to be able to obtain meaningful sums of amounts originally expressed in different currencies—similar to the objective of restating historical dollar amounts for the changes in the value of the dollar. The financial and physical capital-maintenance concepts are also relevant for both foreign currency translations and price-level restatements in deciding whether the so-called gains and losses are elements of income or of stockholders' equity.

In making foreign currency translations, the two basic questions relate to the decision regarding which exchange rate to use and the decision regarding the nature of the gain or loss on the translation. Several approaches have been suggested, including the following:

1. The monetary/nonmonetary approach.
2. The current/noncurrent approach.
3. The temporal approach.
4. The current approach.
5. The net-investment approach.

The monetary/nonmonetary approach is similar to the historical cost/constant dollar approach to price-level restatements. Monetary assets and monetary liabilities are expressed in current terms and therefore should be translated by using the exchange rate at the date of the balance sheet. When monetary assets are held or monetary liabilities are outstanding during the periods when the exchange rate changes, gains or losses from the translation arise. These gains and losses are assumed to be realized because the amounts are monetary and, therefore, they should be reported in the income statement. This is similar to the purchasing-power gains and losses on monetary items resulting from general price-level restatements. The nonmonetary assets and liabilities are translated at the exchange rates prevalent at the dates of acquisition. That is, the assumption is made that the historical cost in dollars or other domestic currency of the parent firm is the equivalent number of dollars that would have been needed to purchase the foreign currency which, in turn, was used to acquire the asset. A decline in the exchange rate of the foreign currency subsequent to the date of acquisition does not result in a loss by this method because the historical cost in equivalent dollars has not changed. One of the difficulties with this approach is that the monetary/nonmonetary classification is arbitrary, as discussed above.

A second approach is based on the current/noncurrent classification. Current items are translated at the current rate because they relate to the current operations of the firm. However, it is argued that, by reporting the changes in exchange rates applied only to current items, the resulting gains and losses reflecting the exposure to foreign exchange risk are over-stated. That is, the assets, current and noncurrent, operate as a hedge against the risk from having liabilities outstanding and vice versa.

The temporal method is a modification of both of the above approaches. Under the temporal method, the exchange rate for translation purposes is determined by the measurement basis employed in the accounting system. That is, items reported in terms of historical costs are translated at historical exchange rates; items reported in terms of current prices or future expected prices are translated at the current exchange rate. This method appears to be in accord with the structural procedures of the historical cost accounting system. However, it is not logical because foreign exchange gain and losses are related to the accounting procedures used and not to economic reality. Therefore, the readers of financial statements are not provided with any interpretation of existing economic relationships.

The net investment approach views the business of a foreign subsidiary or division as an investment with a return measured by the net income of the foreign operation, which accrues to the benefit of the parent. That is, in concept, the foreign operation is treated as a separate entity rather than as a part of the operations of the parent. Therefore, all assets and liabilities should be translated in terms of the exchange rate at the date of the balance sheet (the current approach). Income statement items would be translated at the exchange rates existing at the dates for which the operating transactions are reported, generally the average for the year. It is the net investment that is assumed to be exposed to the risks of the changes in exchange rates. Whether or not the effects of changes in exchange rates should be reported as gains or losses depends on the view of the net investment and the assumptions regarding the exposure to risk. If the investment is assumed to be relatively permanent in nature, the argument is that no gains or losses occur so long as the investment is not converted into the domestic currency; that is, no gain or loss occurs until the investment is liquidated, at which point the gains or losses are assumed to be realized.

Economic theory supports the view that, over relatively long periods, most assets and liabilities are not exposed to exchange gains and losses. Assuming perfect and complete markets, the Purchasing Power Parity theory states that changes in equilibrium exchange rates are proportional to changes in the ratio of similar combinations of nonmonetary assets in two countries. For monetary assets and monetary liabilities, the Fisher Effect refers to the proposition that changes in exchange rates are reflected in the relative differential in interest rates in the two countries. If these propositions are valid over long periods, a net investment would not be exposed to exchange risks and, therefore, exchange gains and losses should not be reported.[21] Transactions in a foreign currency that will be completed in a relatively short time, however, are subject to exchange risks, and the exchange gains and losses should be reported as income statement items.

Adjustments for current costs and for price-level changes in a foreign country are relevant in the reporting of foreign operations, particularly in those cases in which there is an intent to continue such foreign operations. That is, the purchasing power in the specific or general goods and services in the foreign country is relevant to external financial reporting if operations are expected to continue in that country. Changes in the prices of the specific or general goods and services of the country of the parent company are relevant only when cash is remitted to the parent company.

When foreign currency translations are made at the rates of the historical dates in the strict historical cost tradition, the amounts expressed in the foreign currency are first translated into U.S. dollars and then restated for changes in the general purchasing power of the dollar. However, when the translations are made using current rates, the assets and liabilities should be restated first for changes in the price level of the foreign country and then translated into the domestic currency. This latter procedure carries the weight of logic and also provides measurements that are more meaningful from an interpretational point of view.

SFAS 8 versus SFAS 52

The FASB, after much public debate, issued *SFAS 8* in October 1975. The statement essentially required companies to use the temporal method. Any gains or losses on fluctuations in exchange rates were taken into the income statement. An immediate, ongoing outcry followed, primarily motivated by the impact that these gains and losses had on income statements. It appears that many managers are uncomfortable with accounting procedures that cause income to fluctuate in ways beyond their control.

The FASB revisited, therefore, the topic of foreign currency translations and eventually devised the notion of a *functional currency*. This is defined as the currency in which the company's subsidiary runs its business. Thus, a French subsidiary that is run by the American head office will have the dollar as its functional currency. If that French subsidiary is effectively run by an Italian office, the lire will be its functional currency.

The FASB then mandated a two-step translation process. All nonfunctional currencies are to be translated into their respective functional currencies using the temporal method. The functional currencies, though, are translated into the dollar using the net investment approach. In other words, all assets and liabilities are translated at the current exchange rate. Income statement items are translated at a weighted average for the period. Equity is translated at the historical rate. The key addition is that any gains and losses computed on this method are taken into a balance sheet account. In other words, as long as all of a company's foreign subsidiaries are run in a relatively independent fashion, there will be no impact on the income statement. The compromise appears to have been satisfactory because the previously loud level of complaints has been muted. Whether the compromise is theoretically sound is a matter of ongoing debate.

CHECKPOINTS

1. Why is the monetary/nonmonetary method of foreign currency translation like the cost/constant dollar method of inflation accounting?
2. Which exchange rate is used in the temporal method?
3. Briefly describe in your own words the purchasing power parity theory.

PROBLEMS AND QUESTIONS

Restatements for General Price-Level Changes

1.   (November 1973) Barden Corp., a manufacturer with large investments in plant and equipment, began operations in 1938. The company's history has been one of expansion in sales, production, and physical facilities. Recently, some concern has been expressed that the conventional financial statements do not provide sufficient information for decisions by investors. After consideration of proposals for various types of supplementary financial statements to be included in the 1982 annual report, management has decided to present a balance sheet as of December 31, 1982, and a statement of income and retained earnings for 1982, both restated for changes in the general price level.

Required:

a. On what basis can it be contended that Barden's conventional statements should be restated for changes in the general price level?

b. Distinguish between financial statements restated for general price-level changes and current value financial statements.

c. Distinguish between *monetary* and *nonmonetary assets* and *liabilities,* as the terms are used in general price-level accounting. Give examples of each.

d. Outline the procedures Barden should follow in preparing the proposed supplementary statements.

e. Indicate the major similarities and differences between the proposed supplementary statements and the corresponding conventional statements.

f. Assuming that in the future Barden will want to present comparative supplementary statements, can the 1982 supplementary statements be presented in 1983 without adjustment? Explain.

2. Proponents of price-level restatement of financial statements state that a basic weakness of financial statements not adjusted for price-level changes is that they are made up of "mixed dollars."

Required:

a. What is meant by the term *mixed dollars,* and why is this a weakness of unadjusted financial statements?

b. Explain how financial statements restated for price-level changes eliminate this weakness. Use property, plant, and equipment as your example in this discussion.

Purchasing-Power Gains and Losses

3. **(May 1970)** Although cash generally is regarded as the simplest of all assets to account for, certain complexities can arise for both domestic and multinational companies.

Required:

a. Unrealized and/or realized gains or losses can arise in connection with cash. Excluding consideration of price-level changes, indicate the nature of such gains or losses and the context in which they can arise in relation to cash.

b. 1. How might it be maintained that a gain or a loss is incurred by holding a constant balance of cash through a period of price-level change?

2. Identify and give a justification for the typical accounting treatment accorded these gains or losses.

4.   (May 1977) Asset measurement is a concept that involves the valuation of pricing of the future service of an asset. Receivables are particular assets that represent future claims to fixed amounts of monies.

Required:

a. Discuss how the asset measurement concept is applied to receivables (short term and long term).

b. Describe how a company that has a significant amount of receivables during an inflationary period sustains a "general price-level loss." Include in your answer an example of how such a "loss" would be computed when a $100,000 receivable exists at the beginning and end of a year that had an inflation rate of 10 percent.

5.   (November 1977) Price-level adjusted financial statements are prepared in an effort to eliminate the effects of inflation or deflation. An integral part of determining restated amounts and applicable gain or loss from restatement is the segregation of all assets and liabilities into monetary and nonmonetary classifications. One reason for this classification is that price-level gains and losses for monetary items are currently matched against earnings.

Required:

What are the factors that determine whether an asset or liability is classified as monetary or nonmonetary? Include in your response the justification for recognizing gains and losses from monetary items and not for nonmonetary items.

Current Costs

6.   (May 1978) Advocates of current value accounting propose several methods for determining the valuation of assets to approximate current values. Two of the methods proposed are replacement cost and present value of future cash flows.

Required:

Describe each of the two methods cited above and discuss the pros and cons of the various procedures used to arrive at the valuation for each method.

Current Costs and General Price-Level Restatements

7. **(May 1978)** The financial statements of a business entity could be prepared by using historical cost or current value as a basis. In addition, the basis could be stated in terms of unadjusted dollars or dollars restated for changes in purchasing power. The various permutations of these two separate and distinct areas are shown in the following matrix:

	Unadjusted Dollars	*Dollars Restated for Changes in Purchasing Power*
Historical cost	1	2
Current value	3	4

Block number 1 of the matrix represents the traditional method of accounting for transactions in accounting today, wherein the absolute (unadjusted) amount of dollars given up or received is recorded for the asset or liability obtained (*relationship between resources*). Amounts recorded in the method described in block number 1 reflect the original cost of the asset or liability and do not give effect to any change in value of the unit of measure (*standard of comparison*). This method assumes the validity of the accounting concepts of a going concern and stable monetary unit. Any gain or loss (including holding and purchasing-power gains or losses) resulting from the sale or satisfaction of amounts recorded under this method is deferred in its entirety until sale or satisfaction.

Required:

For each of the remaining matrix blocks (2, 3, and 4) respond to the following questions. *Limit your discussion to nonmonetary assets only.*

Complete your discussion for *each matrix block* before proceeding to the discussion of the next matrix block.

a. How will this method of recording assets affect the relationship between resources and the standard of comparison?

b. What is the theoretic justification for using each method?

c. How will each method of asset valuation affect the recognition of gain or loss during the life of the asset and ultimately from the sale or abandonment of the asset? Your response should include a discussion of the timing and magnitude of the gain or loss and conceptual reasons for any difference from the gain or loss computed using the traditional method.

8. **(May 1981)** Financial reporting should provide information to help investors, creditors, and other users of financial statements. *FASB 33* required large public enterprises to disclose certain supplementary information.

Required:

a. Describe the historical cost/constant dollar method of accounting. Include in your discussion how historical cost amounts are used to make historical cost/constant dollar measurements.

b. Describe the principal advantage of the historical cost/constant dollar method of accounting over the historical cost method of accounting.

c. Describe the current method of accounting.

d. Why would depreciation expense for a given year differ using the current cost method of accounting instead of the historical cost method? Include in your discussion whether depreciation expense is likely to be higher or lower using the current cost instead of the historical cost method of accounting in a period of rising prices, and why.

Foreign Currency Translations

9. (May 1978) The Financial Accounting Standards Board discusses certain terminology essential to both the translation of foreign currency transactions and foreign currency financial statements. Included in the discussion is a definition of and distinction between the terms *measure* and *denominate*.

Required:

Define the terms *measure* and *denominate* as discussed by the Financial Accounting Standards Board, and give a brief example that demonstrates the distinction between accounts measured and accounts denominated in a particular currency.

10. (May 1978) There are several methods of translating foreign currency transactions or accounts reflected in foreign currency financial statements. Among these methods are current/noncurrent, monetary/nonmonetary, current rate, and the temporal method.

Required:

a. Define the temporal method of translating foreign currency financial statements.

b. Explain why the temporal method and the current rate method would result in significantly different amounts of translation gains and losses.

c. Explain why translation gains and losses are deferred under the net investment approach.

SENOR VALDEZ (A)

Juan Valdez lives high in the Pyrenees near the city of Pamplona, capital of Navarre in northern Spain. He makes his living by making and selling wooden wheelbarrows to farmers in the surrounding district. Many of his children have moved away to other parts of the country. One has even emigrated to the United States and is a student at SUNY-Buffalo in upstate New York.

Senor Valdez has two wheelbarrows in stock, both of which he made for P5,000. (The currency in Spain is known as the peseta—Pta or P for short.) He sells his wheelbarrows for P7,500 for a profit of P2,500. His balance sheet prior to the last sale simply showed P105,000 in cash and P10,000 in inventory. His balance sheet after the sale showed P112,500 in cash and P5,000 in inventory.

Unfortunately, the price of the wood he needs for making the wagons has risen substantially. Juan's wife Conchita, who does his bookkeeping, realizes that the next wagon will cost him P6,000 to make. What troubles her is that when he has replaced the wagon he has just sold, they will have only P106,500, not the P107,500 that they normally have. Since their cash will have increased only P1,500, she wonders whether she would be right to register a profit of P2,500 on the sale.

Required:

a. Draw up an opening and a closing balance sheet for Senor Valdez using conventional accounting methods. Also draw up an income statement showing the profit of P2,500 on the sale. Reconcile your income statement to your change in owner's equity.

b. What accounting changes would you suggest that Senor Valdez make given that the cost of wheelbarrows has risen 20 percent? Can you reconcile his cash increase of P1,500 with the income statement?

c. Restate Senor Valdez's closing balance sheet in current cost terms. What effect does this have on his equity? Can you reconcile the change in owner's equity with the income statement?

SENOR VALDEZ (B)

Senor Valdez and his wife are relatively independent people. They raise most of their own food. About the only things they buy are wood for his wheelbarrows and flour for making bread. The cost of flour has gone up too. Previously they paid P10 for a kilo of flour; now they have to pay P12 for that same kilo.

Required:

a. Restate in real terms the opening and closing balance sheets that you derived in part (A) of this case. More specifically, restate them in terms of the purchasing power they represent in terms of bread. For instance, at the start of the year the cash on hand would have purchased 10,500 kilos of flour and the inventory would have purchased 1,000 kilos. His opening equity might be written K11,500. What is his closing equity position?

b. Reconcile the real change in equity with his income statement restated in real terms.

c. Discuss the differences between the conventional profit shown in part (A) with the real profit computed here.

SENOR VALDEZ (C)

All the Valdez children are grown up and independent except for their youngest son Enrico, who is a student at SUNY-Buffalo in upstate New York. Conchita Valdez usually sets aside any profits made from the sale of wheelbarrows and sends it across to Enrico to help him while he is still at school. The exchange rate has hovered around 100 pesetas to the American dollar for some time. Enrico, therefore, typically would get $25 each time a wheelbarrow was sold. With the rise in the price of wood and flour in Pomplano, his mother is no longer sure what she can afford to send him. On top of that, the exchange rate has gone to 120 pesetas to the dollar.

She starts to write him a letter explaining why the dollar check is so much smaller this time. She decides to put the facts in terms of dollars so that he will better understand the background. Converting the opening cash balance to dollars is relatively easy: she simply divides by 100 and tells him that they began with $1,050 on hand. But then she isn't quite sure what to do about the closing cash balance—or the income statement.

Required:

a. Explain first why the exchange rate has risen from 100 to 120.

b. Help Senora Valdez draw up a dollar version of the business in Spain. Be explicit as to whether you are dealing with a functional or a nonfunctional currency.

c. Reconcile the dollar check received by Enrico Valdez from his mother with the dollar profit you show for the business.

ALPHA COMPANY

Alpha Company began business five years ago. They are a small, but fairly capital-intensive assembler of specialized stereo equipment which they sell to cognoscenti.

Sales have been fairly good and, as Exhibit 12-1 shows, they have risen steadily each year. Their return on equity (net income after tax divided by capital plus retained earnings) has also shown a steady increase.

As a result of their success, they opened a second plant—identical to the Boston office, but on the West Coast. Results for this operation are shown in Exhibit 12-2. Comparative results for 19X5 have proved disap-

EXHIBIT 12-1   Boston Office

	19X5	*19X4*	*19X3*	*19X2*	*19X1*
Cash	1221	928	662	420	200
Inventory	200	200	200	200	200
Gross book value	1000	1000	1000	1000	1000
(accumulated depreciation)	(1000)	(800)	(600)	(400)	(200)
	1421	1328	1262	1220	1200
Capital	1200	1200	1200	1200	1200
Retained earnings	221	128	62	20	0
	1421	1328	1262	1220	1200
Revenue	1464	1331	1210	1100	1000
Cost of sales	732	666	605	550	500
Expenses	346	333	321	310	300
Net income (before taxes)	386	332	284	240	200
Tax	193	166	142	120	100
Net income (after taxes)	193	166	142	120	100
Dividend	100	100	100	100	100
Additions to retained earnings	93	66	42	20	0
Return on equity	13.3%	12.5%	11.3%	9.8%	8.3%

pointing, however. The California operation, for example, has a return on equity of only 8.6 percent versus the 13.3 percent being earned by the Boston office.

The California manager has been asked to explain her poor performance. Assuming that the annual rate of inflation has been a steady 10 percent since 19X1, can you help her?

Required:

a. Calculate the cost of replacing Boston's plant at the end of 19X4 and 19X5. Compare this with California's gross book value.

b. Should the book value of one or both firms be adjusted for inflation? If so, what effect does the adjustment have on their return? If not, how, if at all, would you compare the performance of these two offices?

c. Speak to someone who works for or manages a real-world company. Ask how they measure performance. Do they:

1. Adjust for inflation?
2. Calculate returns on a different basis? Not at all?
3. Compare actuals with a budget only?

d. If companies do not adjust their performance reports for inflation, should they?

EXHIBIT 12-2   California Office

	19X5	19X4
Cash	526	200
Inventory	266	266
Gross book value	1331	1331
(accumulated depreciation)	(266)	0
	1857	1797
Capital	1797	1797
Retained earnings	60	—
	1857	1797
Revenue	1464	
Cost of sales	732	
Expenses	412	
Net income (before taxes)	320	
Tax	160	
Net income (after taxes)	160	
Dividend	100	
Additions to retained earnings	60	
Return on equity	8.6%	

PRIMARY SOURCES

Those students interested in pursuing the topics raised in this chapter in more depth might begin by consulting the following sources. Each has numerous references to other papers.

Alhashim, Dhia D., and Jeffrey S. Arpan. *International Dimensions of Accounting,* 2nd ed. (Boston: PWS-Kent Publishing Co., 1988).

Lorensen, Leonard. "Reporting Foreign Operations of U.S. Companies in U.S. Dollars." *Accounting Research Study No. 12,* AICPA, 1972.

Nobes, Christopher, and Robert Parker, eds. *Comparative International Accounting,* 3rd ed. Englewood Cliffs, N.J.: Prentice Hall, 1991.

Revsine, Lawrence. *Replacement Cost Accounting.* Englewood Cliffs, N.J.: Prentice Hall, 1973.

Whittington, Geoffrey. *Inflation Accounting: An Introduction to the Debate.* Cambridge University Press, 1983.

SELECTED ADDITIONAL READINGS

General Price-Level Restatements

Devon, Philip C. "Price-Level Reporting and Its Value to Investors." *Accounting and Business Research,* Winter 1978, pp. 19–24.

Gill, Charles W., and S. Thomas Moser. "Inflation Accounting at the Crossroads." *Journal of Accountancy,* January 1979, pp. 70–78.

Griffin, Paul, ed. *Financial Reporting and Changing Prices: The Conference.* FASB, 1979.

Ijiri, Yuji. "The Price-Level Restatement and Its Dual Interpretation." *Accounting Review,* April 1976, pp. 227–43.

Staubus, George J. "The Effects of Price-Level Restatements on Earnings." *Accounting Review,* July 1976, pp. 574–89.

Vickrey, Don W. "General Price-Level Adjusted Historical Cost Statements and the Ratio-Scale View." *Accounting Review,* January 1976, pp. 31–40.

The Choice of an Appropriate Price Index

Bromwich, Michael. "Individual Purchasing Power Indices and Accounting Reports." *Accounting and Business Research,* Spring 1975, pp. 118–22.

Ma, Ronald, and M. C. Miller. "Inflation and the Current Value Illusion." *Accounting and Business Research,* Autumn 1976, pp. 250–63.

Staubus, George J. "Price-Level Accounting: Some Unfinished Business." *Accounting and Business Research,* Winter 1975, pp. 42–47.

General versus Specific Price Changes

AICPA Task Force. *The Accounting Responses to Changing Prices: Experimentation with Four Models.* AICPA, 1979.

Rosenfeld, Paul. "Confusion between General Price-Level Restatement and Current Value Accounting." *Journal of Accountancy,* October 1972, pp. 63–68.

Sterling, Robert R. "Relevant Financial Reporting in an Age of Price Changes." *Journal of Accountancy,* February 1975, pp. 42–51.

Vancil, R. F. "Inflation Accounting—The Great Controversy." *Harvard Business Review,* March–April 1976.

Accounting for Current Costs

Arnold, Donald F., and Ronald J. Huefner. "Measuring and Evaluating Replacement Costs: An Application." *Journal of Accounting Research,* Autumn 1977, pp. 245–52.

Bromwich, Michael. "The General Validity of Certain 'Current' Value Asset Valuation Bases." *Accounting and Business Research,* Autumn 1977, pp. 242–49.

Lemke, Kenneth W. "The Achilles Heel of Sandilands." *CA Magazine,* September 1976, pp. 37–42.

McKeown, James C., ed. *Inflation and Current Value Accounting.* Urbana: Board of Trustees of the University of Illinois, 1979.

Prakash, Prem, and Shyam Sunder. "The Case against Separation of Current Operating Profit and Holding Gains." *Accounting Review,* January 1979, pp. 1–22.

Revsine, Lawrence. *Replacement Cost Accounting.* Englewood Cliffs, N.J.: Prentice Hall, 1973, esp. Chap. 5.

Revsine, Lawrence. "Technological Changes and Replacement Costs: A Beginning." *Accounting Review,* April 1979, pp. 306–22.

Samuelson, Richard A. "Should Replacement Cost Changes Be Included in Income?" *Accounting Review,* April 1980, pp. 254–87.

Monetary Items

Bradford, William D. "Price-Level Restated Accounting and the Measurement of Inflation Gains and Losses." *Accounting Review,* April 1974, pp. 296–305.

Gringyer, John R. "Holding Gains on Long-Term Liabilities—An Alternative Analysis." *Accounting and Business Research,* Spring 1978, pp. 130–48.

Heath, Loyd C. "Distinguishing between Monetary and Nonmonetary Assets and Liabilities in General Price-Level Accounting." *Accounting Review,* July 1972, pp. 458–68.

Kaplan, Robert S. "Purchasing Power Gains on Debt: The Effect of Expected and Unexpected Inflation." *Accounting Review,* April 1977, pp. 369–78.

Behavioral and Empirical Studies

Abdel-khalik, A. Rashad, and James C. McKeown. "Disclosure of Estimates of Holding Gains and the Assessment of Systematic Risk." *Journal of Accounting Research,* Supplement, 1978, pp. 46–77.

Baran, Arie; Josef Lakonishok; and Aharon Ofer. "The Information Content of General Price Level Adjusted Earnings: Some Empirical Evidence." *Accounting Review,* January 1980, pp. 22–35.

Beaver, William H., and Wayne R. Landsman. FASB Research Report. *Incremental Information Content of Statement 33 Disclosures* (Stamford, Conn.: FASB, 1983).

Berliner, Robert W. "Do Analysts Use Inflation-Adjusted Information? Results of a Survey." *Financial Analysts Journal,* March/April 1983, pp. 65–72.

Bublitz, Bruce; T. Frecka; and J. McKeown. "Market Association Tests and FASB Statement No. 33 Disclosures: A Reexamination." *Studies on Accounting Earnings and Security Valuation: Current Research Issues, Journal of Accounting Research,* Supplement 1985, pp. 1–23.

Deberg, Curtis L., and Keith A. Shriver. "The Relevance of Current Cost Data: A Review and Analysis of Recent Studies." *Journal of Accounting Literature,* 1987, pp. 55–87.

Frishkoff, Paul. *Financial Reporting and Changing Prices: A Review of Empirical Research* (Stamford, Conn.: FASB, 1982).

Hillison, William A. "Empirical Investigation of General Purchasing Power Adjustments on Earnings per Share and the Movement of Security Prices." *Journal of Accounting Research,* Spring 1979, pp. 60–73.

Ketz, J. Edward. "The Effect of General Price-Level Adjustments on the Predictive Ability of Financial Ratios." *Journal of Accounting Research,* Supplement 1978, pp. 273–84.

Ketz, J. Edward. "The Validation of Some General Price Level Estimation Models." *Accounting Review,* October 1978, pp. 952–60.

Lustgarten, Stephen. "The Impact of Replacement Cost Disclosure on Security Prices: New Evidence." *Journal of Accounting and Economics,* October 1982, pp. 121–41.

Parker, James E. "Impact of Price-Level Accounting." *Accounting Review,* January 1977, pp. 69–96.

Short, Daniel G. "The Impact of Price-Level Adjustment in the Context of Risk Assessment." *Journal of Accounting Research,* Supplement 1978, pp. 259–72.

Swanson, Edward P., and Keith A. Shriver. "The Accounting-for-Changing-Prices Experiment: A Valid Test for Usefulness?" *Accounting Horizons,* September 1987, pp. 69–77.

Tweedie, David, and Geoff Whittington. *The Debate of Inflation Accounting* (New York: Cambridge University Press, 1984).

Foreign Currency Translation

Aliber, R. Z., and C. P. Stickney. "Accounting Measures of Foreign Exchange Exposure: The Long and Short of It." *Accounting Review,* January 1975, pp. 44–57.

Clarke, F. L. "A Note on Exchange Rates, Purchasing Power Parities, and Translation Procedures." *Abacus,* June 1977, pp. 60–66.

Dukes, Roland E. *An Empirical Investigation of the Effects of Financial Accounting Standard No. 8 on Security Return Behavior* (Stamford, Conn.: FASB, 1978).

Houston, Carol Olson, and Gerhard G. Mueller. "Foreign Exchange Rate Hedging and *SFAS 52*—Relatives or Strangers?" *Accounting Horizons,* December 1988, pp. 50–57.

Huefner, Ronald J.; J. Edward Ketz; and James A. Largay III. "Foreign Currency Translation and the Cash Flow Statement." *Accounting Horizons,* June 1989, pp. 66–75.

Lorensen, Leonard. "Reporting Foreign Operations of U.S. Companies in U.S. Dollars." *Accounting Research Study No. 12* (AICPA, 1972).

Norris, D. "Improved Foreign Exchange Disclosure for the Investor." *Financial Analysts Journal,* March–April 1977, pp. 17–20.

Patz, Dennis H. "A Price Parity Theory of Translation." *Accounting and Business Research,* Winter 1977, pp. 14–24.

Shank, John K, and Gary S. Shamis. "Reporting Foreign Currency Adjustments: A Disclosure Perspective." *Journal of Accountancy,* April 1979, pp. 59–65.

Wyman, Harold E. "Analysis of Gains or Losses from Foreign Monetary Items: An Application of Purchasing Power Parity Concepts." *Accounting Review,* July 1976, pp. 545–58.

Ziebart, David A. "Exchange Rates and Purchasing Power Parity: Evidence Regarding the Failure of SFAS No. 52 to Consider Exchange Risk in Upper-Inflationary Countries." *International Journal of Accounting,* Fall 1985, pp. 39–51.

ENDNOTES

1. *Invitation of Comment: Supplementary Disclosures about the Effects of Changing Prices* (Stamford, Conn.: FASB, December 27, 1983), p. 15.

2. See Maurice Moonitz, *Changing Prices and Financial Reporting* (Champaign, Ill.: Stipes Publishing, 1974), esp. Ch. 2, pp. 5–21.

3. See, for example, Arie Baran, Josef Lakonishok, and Aharon R. Ofer, "The Information Content of General Price Level Adjusted Earnings: Some Empirical Evidence," *Accounting Review,* January 1980, pp. 22–35.

4. Edgar O. Edwards and Philip W. Bell, *The Theory and Measurement of Business Income* (Berkeley and Los Angeles: University of California Press, 1961), esp. pp. 111–15.

5. Ibid.

6. See also Arthur Andersen & Co., *Accounting and Reporting Problems of the Accounting Profession,* 2nd ed. (Chicago, 1962), pp. 16–17. Russell Morrison holds a similar view, except he offsets current liabilities against the current monetary assets and considers only the gains and losses from the holding of long-term debt as adjustments of the cost of assets. See AICPA, "Reporting the Financial Effect of Price-Level Changes," *Accounting Research Study No. 6* (1963), pp. 250–51.

7. See Perry Mason, *Price-Level Changes and Financial Statements—Basic Concept and Methods* (AAA, 1956), fn., pp. 23–24.

8. See Yuji Ijiri, "Theory of Accounting Measurement," *Studies in Accounting Research No. 10* (AAA, 1975), p. 115.

9. R. J. Chambers, *Towards a General Theory of Accounting* (Adelaide: University of Adelaide, 1961) and *Accounting, Evaluation and Economic Behavior* (Englewood Cliffs, N.J.: Prentice Hall, 1965), pp. 223–27.

10. See, for example, R. S. Gynther, *Accounting for Price-Level Changes: Theory and Procedures* (Oxford: Pergamon Press, 1966), p. 140.

11. R. L. Mathews, "Price-Level Changes and Useless Information," *Journal of Accounting Research,* Spring 1965, p. 143.

12. Gynther, *Accounting for Price-Level Changes,* p. 156.

13. Chambers, *Accounting, Evaluation,* p. 246.

14. See, for example, Paul Rosenfield, "GPP Accounting—Relevance and Interpretability," *Journal of Accountancy,* August 1975, pp. 52–59.

15. Russell J. Petersen, "A Portfolio Analysis of General Price-Level Restatement," *Accounting Review,* July 1975, p. 532.

16. Arie Baran, Josef Lakonishok, and Aharon R. Ofer, "The Information Content of General Price-Level Adjusted Earnings: Some Empirical Evidence," *Accounting Review,* January 1980, pp. 22–35.

17. R. C. Morris, "Evidence of the Impact of Inflation Accounting on Share Prices," *Accounting and Business Research,* Spring 1975, p. 90.

18. Gynther, *Accounting for Price-Level Changes,* pp. 252–53.

19. Lawrence Revaine, *Replacement Cost Accounting* (Englewood Cliffs, N.J.: Prentice Hall, 1973), p. 137.

20. See, for example, A. Rashad Abdel-khalik and James C. McKeown, "Disclosure of Estimates of Holding Gains and the Assessment of Systematic Risk," *Journal of Accounting Research,* Supplement 1978, pp. 46–77.

21. See, for example, Robert Z. Aliber and Clyde P. Stickney, "Accounting Measures of Foreign Exchange Exposure: The Long and Short of It," *Accounting Review,* January 1975, pp. 44–57.

Chapter 13

The Statement
of Financial Position

CHAPTER OBJECTIVES

After studying this chapter, you will be able to:

Define the essential characteristics of assets and liabilities.

Distinguish assets from economic resources and liabilities from economic obligations.

Distinguish liabilities from owners' equity.

Discuss the various objectives of classification of statements of financial position.

Define contingent liabilities and discuss their treatment.

CHAPTER OVERVIEW

Ripley's Photograph

The statement of financial position, also known as the balance sheet, is one of the central reports prepared by accountants. An early accountant, William Ripley, likened it to a still photograph of the enterprise with its assets on one side and its liabilities and equities on the other.

Assets and Liabilities

Assets are essentially stores of future benefits; liabilities are essentially claims against those benefits. A variety of rules distinguish accounting assets and liabilities from the broader set of economic resources and obligations.

Recognition

Resources and obligations are recognized in financial statements as assets and liabilities only when they meet the relevant definition, are measurable, relevant, and reliable.

Classification

Classification of assets and liabilities is necessary for meaningful financial reporting. Whatever classification is used, though, inevitably obscures some relationships while highlighting others, thereby furthering some objectives at the expense of others.

Is Mickey Mouse an asset? Michael Eisner, president of the Disney Corporation, was recently quoted saying that characters like Mickey Mouse and Donald Duck are the only real assets that the company has.[1] Most people would concur with that statement. It comes as quite a surprise then to discover that neither Mickey nor Donald, nor any of the other characters so well known to so many, can be found on the balance sheet of the Disney Corporation.

Disney is not alone in having major resources that do not appear on its financial statements. In most companies there are major economic resources that are not shown as assets. For instance, accountants do not recognize self-created goodwill, the ability to raise loans, research and development in progress, employee skills and dedication, or employee loyalty. These are all very potent corporate resources, but they do not appear in financial statements. Similarly, many corporate obligations are excluded. For example, companies currently do not show the full extent of their pension obligations and none of their obligations under postretirement contracts. Whether these various resources and obligations should appear on balance sheets is the main topic of this chapter.

The chapter begins with a discussion of what is meant by a statement of financial position or a balance sheet. It points out that there are two approaches to defining balance sheets: the *revenue-expense* or *indirect* method, and the *asset-liability* or *direct* method. The asset-liability method is currently favored by the FASB. The chapter then moves on to a discussion of assets and liabilities and their definitions. Conditions for entering resources and obligations on financial statements are then introduced and the reasons for the typical classification of a balance sheet are treated. The chapter concludes with a discussion of whether the definitions in this chapter are sufficient to determine which resources and obligations companies should recognize in their financial statements. Chapters 16, 17, and 18 discuss in more depth the nature of the individual asset categories in common use. Chapters 19 and 20 discuss the nature of individual liability categories. Chapters 21 and 22 treat the nature of owners' equity.

RIPLEY'S PHOTOGRAPH

The presentation to stockholders and other investors at regular intervals of a summary of the resources and the obligations of a company in the form of a *statement of financial position* is one of the major objectives of accounting. The statement is more colloquially known as the *balance sheet.** Assets are shown equal to equities in a balance sheet. Recall, however, Michigan professor William Paton's comment in Chapter 4 that assets are equal to equities only because accountants make them so. Also recall Harvard professor William Ripley's concept of the balance sheet as a still photograph, giving us a picture of a company at a point in time. The balance sheet is sometimes referred to as a statement of stocks as opposed to a statement of flows. It is also compared to measuring the water *in* a dam as opposed to measuring the water flowing *over* the dam.

The older approach to creating a balance sheet is called the *asset-liability* method. In this approach one simply lists the assets and the liabilities of the company. The difference between the two constitutes the residual interest of the owners and is what makes the two sides balance. If one entered the owners' equity in the company at its true market value, the balance sheet would not balance. In cases when owners' equity is entered at market, such as when one acquires another company, a plug on the left side of the balance sheet is created called goodwill.† Proponents of the asset-liability approach claim that the valuation concepts that the approach includes make the statement more useful for investment decisions.

The asset-liability approach requires a definition of what constitutes an asset and what constitutes a liability. For instance, does one include leased equipment, computer software, or brand names among the assets? Does one include future pension payments or unsettled claims from litigation among the liabilities? And if one has decided to include a particular item, when does one include it? Does one have to have completed the software before it becomes an asset? Do pension obligations have to vest before they can be liabilities? In short, which elements does one recognize and when does one recognize them?

An alternative approach that became popular in this country in the early part of the 20th century stressed the income statement. We can call

---

* It has been suggested that the term *balance sheet* derives from the fact that the statement lists the balances found in a ledger rather than from the fact that the two sides balance.

† Some, including *ARS 12,* argue that the plug should be a contra to owners' equity.

this the *revenue-expense* approach to defining a balance sheet. Instead of asking whether an asset "Accounts Receivable" exists, the key question is whether an income item denoted "Revenue" exists. If there is revenue, an accounts receivable has to follow—assuming that not all sales are for cash. These distinctions may seem to be simply flip sides of the same question. The asset-liability and revenue-expense approaches are different, though, and can lead to different answers.

In the income-based approach to accounting, the balance sheet becomes a residual statement—a step between two income statements. As such, the balance sheet often provides little information because it lacks interpretability. Balance sheets are sometimes said to be a point of arrival and departure in the accounting process, but when derived by the revenue-expense approach they are related more closely to the past than to the future. Monetary accounts, such as cash and receivables, may represent current purchasing power or expectations of future funds flows, but the nonmonetary accounts, such as inventory and equipment, reflect only past costs and residuals resulting from past amortization and expensing procedures.

In spite of these deficiencies, a number of claims have been made in favor of residual-type balance sheets. First, it is claimed that the conventional balance sheet provides accountability for the dollars invested by the owners. Actual dollars invested can be traced either through enterprise operations or through residual valuations at the end of the period. Thus, fraud and embezzlement can be detected more readily than if other valuation concepts had been substituted.

A second set of claims relates to the function of the position statement as a summary of the nature of the operations of the enterprise and the nature of the monetary assets and unused services of the firm. It is argued that the process of determining value is too subjective and that the best that can be accomplished is a fairly complete disclosure of the economic relationships by the use of adequate terminology and descriptions. It is also argued that the nature of operations of the firm can be disclosed by the use of supplementary statements, such as a cash flow statement.

Third, it is claimed that history has shown that, when subjective valuations are permitted in the balance sheet, not only does the balance sheet become less informative, but the income statement also becomes distorted. Thus, it is better to have one statement—the income statement—objectively determined and understandable than to have both statements misleading and failing in comparability. In the view of the authors, these claims are completely inadequate in supporting the residual balance sheet. For one thing, it would be relatively simple to reconcile the subjective and the objective. For another, with the provision of cash flow statements, the reader has one completely objective statement on which to rely.

CHECKPOINTS

---

1. Distinguish the asset-liability approach from the revenue-expense approach in defining a statement of financial position.
2. What is a residual balance sheet? List three reasons in its favor.
3. List three reasons for the FASB's preference for the asset-liability approach.

ASSETS AND LIABILITIES

If accounting theory is to provide the proper guidelines for the development of accounting thought and accounting principles, there is considerable merit in an explicit definition of assets and liabilities and an analysis of their basic nature. A discussion of the classification and valuation of assets and liabilities may be of help in this analysis, but the initial emphasis should be on the characteristics that are common to all assets and liabilities. Several attempts have been made to tackle the problem in this way. Most recently, the FASB defined assets in *SFAC 6* as:

> probable future economic benefits obtained or controlled by a particular entity as a result of past transactions or events.[2]

They defined liabilities in that same statement in parallel fashion as:

> probable future sacrifices of economic benefits arising from present obligations of a particular entity to transfer assets or provide services to other entities in the future as a result of past transactions or events.[3]

The strengths and weaknesses of the FASB's definitions become apparent only when compared with the definitions preceding them and in the context of practices that they both permit and effectively prohibit.

Canning's Definitions

Stanford professor John Canning was one of the first to attempt comprehensive definitions of the elements of balance sheets. He defined an asset as:

> any future service in money or any future service convertible into money . . . the beneficial interest in which is legally or equitably secured to some person or set of persons. Such a service is an asset only to that person or set of persons to whom it runs.[4]

He defined a liability as:

> a service, valuable in money, which a proprietor [a holder of assets] is under an existing legal (or equitable) duty to render to a second person (or a set of persons) . . .[5]

The great virtue of these two definitions is that they permit semantic interpretations, that is, a reasonable person could decide whether an item was an asset or a liability by examining its economic and legal character. The FASB has followed Canning in attempting to provide semantic definitions.

APB Statement No. 4

Canning's definitions follow the asset-liability approach outlined above. In the years between Canning and the FASB, considerable emphasis was placed on the determination of income. As a result, many of the subsequent discussions of assets have stressed their nature as unallocated costs or as amounts to be carried forward to future periods, that is, they provided definitions related to the revenue-expense approach. For example, *APB Statement No. 4* defined assets as:

> economic resources of an enterprise that are recognized and measured in conformity with generally accepted accounting principles [including] certain deferred charges that are not resources.[6]

The emphasis in this definition is clearly on the amount carried forward in a trial balance, with the main objective being the computation of periodic income. As a result, a number of deferred charges, being unexpired costs, found their way onto the balance sheet as assets. As the APB put it, assets "also include certain deferred charges that are not resources but that are recognized and measured in conformity with generally accepted accounting principles." *SFAC 6*'s definition effectively prohibited these deferred charges. In like vein, *APB Statement No. 4* defined liabilities as:

> economic obligations of an enterprise that are recognized and measured in conformity with generally accepted accounting principles.[7]

The reason for this essentially syntactical definition of liabilities was that, in the traditional accounting model, credits tended to follow debits. The reporting of a liability was dependent upon the importance of recognizing the other side of the transaction or event—the accrual of an expense, the recognition of a loss, or the receipt by the firm of specific assets. The first of these, the accrual of an expense, was generally thought to be the most important, because it directly affected the computation of current income. If the firm had received services and used them in current operations, accruing the liability was necessary in order to include the expense in the determination of net income. Likewise, the reporting of an extraordinary loss was required in order to disclose the effect of the event on nonoperating income; a related liability then had to be recorded to complete the transaction. When specific assets were received by the firm and recorded, a related liability had also to be recorded in order to present a balanced statement of financial position.

The result of this approach was that a variety of deferred credits found their way onto balance sheets. One example is self-insurance. Companies would make a charge to income to cover future losses in somewhat the same way as they would to cover future claims against warranties. The credit side of the entry for a warranty expense is "Estimated Liability under Warranties"; the credit side of the insurance expense might be similarly labeled "Estimated Liability under Insurance." At the time that an actual repair or refund is made under the terms of a warranty, the company charges it to the estimated liability account rather than to income. Precisely the same was done in the case of losses that the company believed were covered by their self-insurance. However, the situations are not the same. Warranties are payable to someone other than the company; self-insurance merely recompenses oneself. In other words, self-insurance of one's own property is not an obligation of one entity to transfer resources to another entity.

The APB specifically permitted such deferred credits, saying that "liabilities also include certain deferred credits that are not obligations but that are recognized and measured in conformity with generally accepted accounting principles."[8] *SFAC 6,* on the other hand, effectively prohibited self-insurance and similar deferred credits. It did this by approaching the nature of liabilities directly, and by giving them a semantic interpretation. Liabilities, in the eyes of the FASB, are not simply the credit side of "real" debits but "real" obligations in their own right.

Accounting Terminology Bulletins

Lest one forget, *APB Statement No. 4* represented real progress when it was issued. In *ATB 1,* which appeared in 1953, assets were essentially defined as debit balances carried forward upon a closing of books while liabilities were defined as credit balances carried forward—except those credit balances that represented owners' equity.[9] These definitions were almost entirely structural in their emphasis. Those of the APB laid much greater stress on interpretability while those of the FASB have a pragmatic cast to them. The FASB's definitions reflect its concern that financial reporting be useful to investors, creditors, and others.

Three Essentials of Assets

According to the FASB, an asset has three essential characteristics:

1. It embodies a probable future benefit that involves a capacity, singly or in combination with other assets, to contribute directly or indirectly to future net cash inflows.
2. A particular entity can obtain the benefit and control others' access to it.
3. The transaction or other event giving rise to the entity's right to or control of the benefit has already occurred.[10]

If just one of these characteristics is missing, one may not recognize an accounting asset.

A Probable Future Benefit.   There must exist some specific right to future benefits or service potentials. Rights and services that have expired cannot be included. Also, the rights must have a positive benefit; rights with zero or negative potential benefits are not assets. For instance, if a building has lost its service value its only value lies in salvage of its materials. If the cost of removal is equal to or greater than the salvage value of the materials, the building has no value and should not appear as an asset. If the cost of removal is greater than the salvage value, the valuation of the land on which it is sited should be reduced to avoid showing a negative asset. On the other hand, the fact that the future value of a right or service potential may be uncertain does not remove it from the definition of assets. The uncertainty affects the valuation, but it changes the nature of the item only if the uncertainty is so great that the expected future benefit is zero or negative.

Control.   The rights must accrue to a specific individual or firm. The right to benefit from driving on public highways does not result in an asset. The right must permit the exclusion of others, although in some cases the right may be shared with specific firms or individuals. Carnegie professor Yuji Ijiri placed considerable emphasis on control criteria in his definition of assets.[11] That is, according to him, assets are resources under the control of the entity. However, control can be interpreted broadly enough to include the ability of the firm to exercise its rights. Australian professor Raymond Chambers also defined assets as means under the control of an entity. To fit his measurement scheme, he further stressed the severable nature of the assets, that is, that it must be possible to transform or utilize the rights to an asset so that it can be exchanged and thereby have exchange value.[12] The effect of this is to exclude many intangibles that have value only in conjunction with another asset. This view remains controversial.

There must be a legally enforceable claim to the rights or services or some other evidence that receipt of the future benefits is probable. Services that may be withdrawn at will by some other firm or individual or by the government without compensation should not be included as assets. This does not mean, of course, that the firm must have a formal legal title or even a formal contract. In most cases, the accountant must rely upon the apparent intent of those who may have an interest in the asset rather than on the strict legality of the right.

This characteristic often has to be given syntactical content. Consider, for instance, the sale of land which, if recognized, would lead to a receivable for the seller. The sales contract surely indicates probable future economic benefits to be derived by the seller. But if the purchaser has not put down a sufficient deposit, defined in purely syntactical terms by fixed percentages of the fair value in *SFAS 66,* then the seller is not deemed to have control of the resource, that is, the potential receivable, and, therefore, an accounting asset, does not exist.

Transactions and Other Events. The economic benefits must be the result of past transactions or events. Assets should not include benefits that will arise in the future but that currently do not exist or are not under the control of the entity at the present time. However, the necessity of this criterion is arguable because if economic benefits do exist and are under the control of the entity, they must have arisen from some past event. The key here is whether the event satisfies accountants as sufficient. For instance, as soon as a company signs a contract, it has established a probable future economic benefit which it controls. Even though an event has occurred, accountants do not consider it sufficiently significant. Significance, in most cases, is structurally defined, that is, a certain process has been completed. Since it lacks semantic content, accounting assets often lack interpretability, despite the FASB's efforts.

Summary. In summary, the authors believe that assets should be defined as service potentials or rights to prospective benefits under the control of an organization. This definition does not mention the need for a preceding transaction on grounds that this stipulation has been used to exclude resources that should be reported for a proper interpretation of the position of a company or organization. It also does not include the need for a preceding event on grounds that this stipulation is too vague to form a restriction. In particular, there is a strong pragmatic case to be made for including some estimate of the value of resources such as Mickey Mouse on the balance sheets of the Disney Company—despite the lack of a transaction.

The definition's emphasis is deliberately all-inclusive and permits the problem of measurement to be treated separately. Finally, one should note that all assets are fundamentally identical, regardless of the conventional classification. Both inventory and intangibles provide rights to future benefits. The classification does not change their nature as assets.

Three Essentials of Liabilities

According to the FASB, a liability has the following three essential characteristics:

1. It embodies a present duty or responsibility to one or more entities that entails settlement by probable future transfer or use of assets at a specified or determinable date, on occurrence of a specified event, or on demand.
2. The duty or responsibility obligates a particular entity, leaving it little or no discretion to avoid the future sacrifice.
3. The transaction or other event obligating the entity has already happened.[13]

If just one of these characteristics is missing, one may not recognize an accounting liability.

A Present Obligation.   The first of the three essential characteristics is really a complex amalgam of several different stipulations. The first stipulation is that a liability be a present obligation. Stated otherwise, next year's expenses are not a liability of this year. In particular, insurance companies are no longer permitted by this requirement to accrue reserves against future catastrophes. The second stipulation is that the obligation be between entities. This, we have already noted, excludes self-insurance of one's own property. This stipulation also prevents a company from establishing a reserve for the acquisition of future property. The third stipulation is that there be a time or event at which the liability will be settled. In other words, one may not include an entirely open-ended obligation as a liability. In particular, this stipulation distinguishes owners' equity from liabilities.

Several potential characteristics were deliberately omitted. For instance, the settlement was not limited to cash so as not to exclude companies which are paid in advance for their products. The unearned revenue account which this transaction creates is a liability which is settled by an asset, that is, by the delivery of the product. Second, the nature of the settlement was not limited to the transfer of assets. This omission was necessary to avoid excluding symphony orchestras, opera houses, theaters, and sports franchises which sell subscription tickets in advance of a season. The receipt of the cash generates a liability that will be satisfied by providing customers with the promised entertainment. In other words, the liability will be settled by the provision of services or the use of assets.

The requirement states that a settlement point be known but it does not state that the identity of the payee be known before the time of settlement if the future payment or transfer of assets is probable. A case in point is the accrual of warranty obligations at the time of sale. Experience indicates that there will be claims within a period specified in the sales contract. Experience, though, cannot indicate precisely who will claim.

The stipulations also do not limit the liability to one individual only. It is possible for a single transaction to generate obligations to more than one party, as in the case of warranties. In particular, transactions between two parties have the interesting ability to generate a liability to third parties. One example is the royalties that are payable to a third party because of a sale of merchandise to a second party. Another example is the taxes that are payable to the government on the sale of goods.

Legal, Equitable, or Constructive Obligations. The second essential characteristic of a liability is that it leave the obligor little or no discretion to settle. This statement does not require, however, that the company be legally obliged. In fact, the FASB specifically included equitable as well as constructive obligations as potential liabilities. Equitable obligations are sometimes called moral obligations. They arise from ethical or moral, rather than legal, constraints. For example, a business might feel ethically bound to satisfactorily complete repairs on a customer's car, even though the legal obligation extends only to a refund of the customer's money. Constructive obligations are inferred from custom. For instance, if a company typically gives its employees vacation pay each year, it might be inferred that this practice represents an obligation of the company. Neither equitable nor constructive obligations are necessarily enforceable by legal means; nevertheless, both parties may regard them as binding obligations.

The narrowest position has been that only legal obligations or debts should be included as accounting liabilities. Canning's definition, on the other hand, specifically includes equitable obligations. However, Canning did not present examples of equitable duties that should be included. Presumably he would include amounts intended to be paid for damages sustained or services received when there is no legal obligation to make such payment. He would also probably include amounts to be paid to maintain goodwill and business confidence, such as refunds for damaged or returned merchandise when no legal obligation exists to make such refunds.

The broader approach to liability definition can raise difficulties for accountants. Equitable and constructive obligations arise from social or moral sanctions, or from custom. Generally, it is appropriate, and often more conservative, to follow custom and traditional business practices; however, the legality of such obligations is difficult to determine in many cases and may require a court decision. Also, social and moral obligations, particularly as companies cross national borders, are sometimes hard to determine. Their inclusion can leave the accountant, therefore, in the untenable position of having to make moral judgments.

Transactions and Other Events.   The third essential characteristic of a liability, according to the FASB, is that it be preceded by a "transaction or other event." An event is defined as "a happening of consequence to an entity."[14] A transaction is defined as a "particular kind of event, namely, an external event involving a transfer of something of value (future economic benefit) between two (or more) entities."[15] Limiting liabilities to situations where there had been a prior transaction would have taken us back in time to where credits followed debits. On the other hand, the addition of the term "other events" to the stipulation loosens the definition considerably. Some argue that it renders this aspect of the definition useless, since almost anything can be claimed to be an "event."

One might argue that the conditions giving rise to the obligation are less important than a semantic interpretation of the obligation itself. If an obligation does in fact exist, recording it as a liability regardless of how it arose is important. From the point of view of the users of financial statements, the effect of the obligation on future cash requirements is surely more important than the past transactions or events which gave rise to the liability. Given the looseness of the third essential characteristic, dropping it might make little difference as to which liabilities are recognized.

Eliminating the third characteristic, though, would force changes in many arguments that have been made for the exclusion or inclusion of particular obligations. For instance, self-insurance was not excluded on grounds that it was a liability to refund oneself, but on grounds that no preceding event had occurred. Accruals by insurance companies against catastrophes were excluded for the same reason: the event had yet to occur. As we have seen, though, multiple grounds exist for excluding these potential obligations as liabilities. Therefore, creating more conclusive arguments based on those other grounds should be possible.

Summary.   In summary, from an interpretive point of view, liabilities might be defined as obligations or duties of the enterprise to provide money, goods, or services to a person, firm, or outside organization at some time in the future. Like the definition of an asset, and for the same reason, this definition omits mention of the need for a preceding transaction. Also like the definition of assets, this definition permits problems of measurement to be treated separately. In particular, it does not exclude the recognition of loss contingencies as liabilities, by entering them at their expected value. Some such scheme appears to be desperately needed in light of the savings and loan debacle where billions of dollars of loan guarantees were not reported as possible liabilities because default was deemed to be remote.

CHECKPOINTS

---

1. List the factors in common between the various definitions of assets in this section. List the factors that distinguish them.
2. List the factors in common between the various definitions of liabilities in this section. List the factors that distinguish them.
3. List the three essentials of assets and the three essentials of liabilities.

RECOGNITION

When a resource or an obligation appears on a statement of financial position, it is said to be *recognized*. Recognition does not automatically follow definition: one cannot record an element when one cannot measure it. To be able to recognize a liability, for instance, it must be measurable. But simply because a liability cannot be measured does not mean that it is not a liability—it remains an unrecognized liability.

Many argue that there is little distinction between recognizing a resource or obligation and disclosing it in the footnotes. They argue that as long as the related events are disclosed, users can interpret them and incorporate them into their prediction models. The FASB responded to this argument in *SFAS 87*:

> Some respondents agreed that better information about net periodic pension cost and the pension obligation is needed but argued that the information would be just as useful if it were disclosed in the footnotes and, therefore, that changes in the basic financial statements (changes that they believed would be costly) were not necessary. The Board is aware that costs are involved for both preparers and users whenever changes are made in accounting principles, but in the Board's view it is important that elements qualifying for recognition be recognized in the basic financial statements. Footnote disclosure is not an adequate substitute for recognition. The argument that the information is equally useful regardless of how it is presented could be applied to any financial statement element, but the usefulness and integrity of financial statements are impaired by each omission of an element that qualifies for recognition. Further, although the "equal usefulness" argument may be valid for some sophisticated users, the Board does not believe it holds for all or even most other users. Finally, if the argument were valid, the consequences of recognition would not be different from those of not recognizing but disclosing the same information; it is obvious from their arguments that many who assert that disclosure would be equally useful believe recognition would have different consequences.[16]

Contingent Liabilities

The question of recognition is well illustrated by loss contingencies. According to *SFAS 5*, a contingency is defined as:

an existing condition, situation, or set of circumstances involving uncertainty as to possible . . . gain . . . or loss . . . to an enterprise that will ultimately be resolved when one or more future events occur or fail to occur. Resolution of the uncertainty may confirm the . . . incurrence of a liability.[17]

Putting the definition of a contingency together with that of a liability, a loss contingency might be defined as a probable future sacrifice of economic benefits arising from present obligations of a particular entity to transfer assets or provide services to other entities in the future as a result of past transactions or events where the settlement depends upon one or more future events that have some probability of occurrence. *SFAS 5* says that such loss contingencies should be recognized as liabilities if:

1. They meet the definition of a liability.
2. The probability of the occurrence of the future event is relatively high.
3. The contingent loss can be reasonably estimated.

Loss contingencies should not be recognized in financial statements, but disclosed in a footnote if the probability of occurrence of the future event is only reasonably possible. No mention need be made of the contingency if one deems the probability of its occurrence to be remote.

Obligations under warranties are an example of contingent liabilities because an event, failure of the product, has yet to occur. They are recognized because the probability is high that some payments will be required, even though the total amount must be estimated. A legal suit against the company for damages, however, will not be recognized as a contingent liability if it appears most likely that the firm will win the case. If it is probable that the firm will lose the case, a contingent liability exists: the problem is in estimating the expected value of the damages to be awarded. Accountants may not be able to estimate the most probable amount of damages so the best disclosure may be provided by a full description in a footnote or elsewhere.

If an actual obligation exists but has a range of probable values, the expected value should be listed as the estimated amount of the liability on the balance sheet. If a range only is known, the minimum of the range should be shown. Only if the range is broad and if an estimated single value would be misleading is it preferable to omit the obligation from the list of liabilities and present a description, in a footnote or otherwise, indicating the range of probable values.

A distinction should be based on whether or not an expected value would be meaningful to readers of the financial reports as a representation of the approximate most probable (modal) value and the extent to which the expectations must be subjective. If an obligation has a 90 percent chance of being $100,000 and a 10 percent chance of being zero, the expected value would be $90,000, and this would be a meaningful representation of the liability, particularly if the probabilities are based on past experience. On the other hand, if the obligation has a 90 percent chance of being zero and a 10 percent chance of being $100,000 the expected value would be $10,000; but this may not be as meaningful as a description of the probable amount to be paid. That is, if the most probable (modal) value of the obligations is positive, a liability exists and the amount should be estimated. If the obligation has a high probability of being zero, it should be disclosed in a footnote.

Summary

Similar recognition rules apply to all assets and liabilities. In general, for an asset or a liability to be recognized, the resource or the obligation must meet the definition of an asset or a liability. It must be measurable. In addition, the element must meet the test of relevance and reliability.[18] As Chapter 18 points out, one of the major reasons that so many intangibles are not recognized is that their measurement is unreliable. And, as noted in Chapter 21, this has also been one of the major arguments used against recognizing postretirement benefits.

CHECKPOINTS

---

1. What is the meaning of the word *recognized*?
2. What criteria must an economic resource meet to be recognized in a statement of financial position?
2. To facilitate international trade, banks issue *letters of credit*. These guarantee that a supplier in one country will get paid by purchaser in another country. How should the bank record these letters, if at all?
4. To enable students to raise loans to pay for their educational expenses, the government stands surety for them at the bank. How should the government record this surety, if at all?

CLASSIFICATION

Classification is necessary for the study and communication of relevant information in all of the physical and social sciences. Accounting is no exception. The classification of the resources and commitments of a firm into appropriate categories is needed in order to present interpretable summaries of accounting information that can be understood and analyzed by investors and other users of financial statements in their decision processes.

If unclassified data were presented to those interested in the firm, they would be forced to make their own summaries; the mind can cope with only a reasonable amount of data at one time. But if the summaries and classifications are performed for them, a choice is made for them regarding what information is important and what is not important, and what items should be emphasized more than others.

In the paragraphs which follow, the possible objectives of classification are treated first. That is followed by a brief discussion of the criticisms that have been leveled against the prevalent use of a current-noncurrent classification. An alternative classification is offered based on valuation bases. The section closes with a discussion of when it is permissible to offset current liabilities against current assets.

Objectives of Classification

Readers of external reports have different objectives and different backgrounds regarding their knowledge of the firm. Summaries and classifications necessarily omit some information and relationships that may be of value to specific readers or groups of readers. Thus, the principal guidelines for summaries and classifications are an important part of accounting theory. Developing these guidelines requires knowledge of who the intended readers are and what information they desire. It follows that balance sheet classification should attempt to meet certain specific objectives. Among the many objectives identified by accounting theorists, one finds the following:

Presentation of solvency to creditors.

Description of enterprise operations.

Illumination of the accounting process.

Highlighting of valuation methods.

Illumination of management's intentions.

Prediction of cash flows.

Each of these is discussed in the sections that follow.

Presentation of Liquidity to Creditors.   The earliest objective of balance sheet classifications was the presentation to creditors of information showing the solvency of the firm, that is, the probability of obtaining repayment in case the firm is liquidated. The primary test of the security of their loans was the liquidity of specific assets and their availability for the payment of debts, particularly those debts falling due within the following year. This emphasis on the liquidity of assets and on the order in which debts would become payable stemmed from the lack of other reliable operating data, and from the fact that creditors (particularly short-term creditors) represented the major group demanding financial information.

The ordering of balance sheets in terms of liquidity led to an increasing distinction between current and noncurrent elements and to the concept of working capital as the difference between current assets and current liabilities.* Initially, a current asset or liability was one which would be realized in cash within one year—the so-called *one-year rule*.

Today, the objectives of financial reporting have broadened considerably, and the statement of financial position has become only one of several financial reports. But current accounting practice and thought still carry many of the earlier ideas and practices. Assets and liabilities are still generally classified according to their relative liquidity, and the time period of a year is still the general rule in the classification of many assets and liabilities as current.

Description of Enterprise Operations.   It has long been recognized that the balance sheet should provide information about operations as well as information about liquidity. For example, Charles Sprague, one of the early leaders of American accounting, wrote as early as 1907 that:

> The arrangement of items in the balance sheet is of some importance especially if the list is voluminous. . . . In our example the order of availability has been followed, or, as it might be termed, the order of liquidation. . . . In an industrial enterprise where it was thought that productivity or earning power was more important than readiness in debt-paying, it might be that the fixed plant was entitled to the first place among the assets and that the cash on hand would be placed at the end as the least productive of assets.[19]

As noted in Chapter 3, British practice is to arrange the balance sheet in reverse order of liquidity, thereby reflecting the predominant interests of shareholders in operations rather than the interests of creditors in liquidation.

The current classification as a description of operations has also long been established in governmental fund accounting. Current assets and current liabilities are often set up as a separate fund, in either the accounts or the statements or both. The term *fund* is used in this situation to refer to a segregation of assets and liabilities for a given purpose as a specific unit of operations or as a center of interest. Berkeley professor William Vatter has suggested that the current classification is also very appropriate in the application of fund theory to general financial accounting.[20]

The concept of working capital as a partial description of enterprise operations gained considerable popularity in the 1940s and is commonly employed in the United States today. The concept originated in the authoritative literature in *ARB 43*, where its authors were attempting to develop a definition of working capital related to the operating cycle of a business and not tied to the narrower *one-year* definition. They defined

---

* *SFAS 6*, par. 7 notes that, for certain industries, such as broker-dealers and finance, real estate, and stock life insurance enterprises, the distinction between current and noncurrent is irrelevant and may be ignored.

the *operating cycle* as the time it takes to convert cash into the product of the enterprise and then to convert the product back into cash again. The concept of an operating cycle permits an operational demarcation between short-term and long-term commitments. Plant and equipment items are omitted from the current asset classification because their turnover period covers many product turnover periods.

Illumination of the Accounting Process.   Accounting classifications have often been established because of their convenience in the bookkeeping process. The deferred charge classification, for example, has often been used as a resting place for unallocated debits. As a result, such items as unamortized discount on bonds payable, discount on preferred stock, and losses carried forward have found a place among the assets of published balance sheets. As has already been noted, classifications based on accounting procedures have come under heavy fire in recent years.

Classification according to the accounting process, however, is not necessarily entirely irrelevant to the readers of published financial statements. It may be meaningful to draw a distinction between those items that will be disposed of through charges and credits to income and those items that will result directly or indirectly in cash flows. Gilman called the former items "deferred charges and credits to revenue" and the latter items "deferred charges and credits to cash."[21] Deferred charges to cash include receivables, marketable securities, and long-term investments; deferred charges to revenue include prepaid expenses, plant and equipment, and inventories. Most liabilities are deferred credits to cash, but obligations to provide goods or services are considered deferred credits to revenue.

The main difficulty with this objective is that it is an attempt to explain the results of technical accounting procedures and it is, therefore, nontheoretical in nature. Because of its lack of logical orientation, the use of deferred charges and deferred credits permits the application of procedures that have no logical basis, or at least do not permit an explanation of the meaning of the deferral. Therefore, the classifications of deferred charges to revenue and deferred credits to revenue are highly objectionable.*

Highlighting of Valuation Methods.   It has been suggested that assets should be classified according to their valuation basis, that is, assets valued according to current costs would be segregated from assets valued on a historical cost basis. Most of the valuation concepts discussed in the

---

* See Chapter 19 for a discussion of the meaning of the term *deferred credits* and Chapter 18 for a discussion of *deferred charges* and the objections to this terminology and classification.

previous chapter are used in published financial statements, and very often many of the concepts are used in the same balance sheet. From a theoretical point of view, an eclectic procedure is not necessarily objectionable, as the valuation concept chosen should depend upon the available evidence, the degree of uncertainty in each case, and an attempt to approach the most relevant concept of income. But groupings of assets and liabilities that include different valuation concepts may be misleading to even informed readers of published statements.

A grouping of assets according to valuation concepts includes the following classifications:

1. Cash and expected cash receipts (properly discounted when appropriate).
2. Assets valued in terms of current or expected sales prices (output prices).
3. Assets valued in terms of current costs (input prices).
4. Assets valued in terms of historical costs or costs restated to adjust for changes in the general level of prices.

Other classifications may be used when appropriate. The main advantage of classification according to valuation concepts is that it provides better interpretation of the balance sheet and its relationship to the income statement and funds flow statement. In the authors' opinion, however, adequate disclosure of valuation procedures can be obtained by parenthetical notations and in other ways, rather than through the groupings of assets.

Insight into Management's Thinking.   Another possible objective in classifying assets and liabilities is to give users insight into management's intentions regarding whether or not to recommit funds for use in operations. Current assets in the aggregate may be just as permanent as the investment in noncurrent assets, but the opportunity for reinvestment in current operations occurs within the current operating cycle of the business. However, once assets are committed by management for investment in specific long-term forms, they should not be classified as current assets given this objective. For example, cash, securities, or other assets committed by management for the later acquisition of plant and equipment, or for other noncurrent uses, should not be included among the current assets.

The commitment need not be legally binding on management, but it should be explicit. The investment is not intended to become available for the current operations of the business, nor for investment opportunities other than that for which it is allocated. It is necessary, but not sufficient, that the current assets be capable of being converted readily into cash or other monetary assets; they must also be free of commitment for long-term uses.

The concept of "working capital" that emerges from considering re-commitments refers to the net investment required in a business enterprise to maintain the day-to-day operations, as opposed to the investment that is committed for a longer period. This has sometimes been called *circulating capital*. The investment in assets committed for long periods includes land, plant, and equipment that provide the facilities for enterprise operations; generally, they provide services and wear out gradually, but some assets represent indefinite commitments. The investment in working capital, on the other hand, is in a continual process of change through daily transactions. Because the short-term liabilities are not generally thought of as providing permanent invested capital but are closely related to the financing of the working assets, the term *working capital* is used to mean the excess of current assets over current liabilities.

A major criticism of using intent as a means of classification is that it is frequently difficult to determine and may be subject to change. As a result, investments are frequently classified as current because of the intent to convert them when and if needed for current operations, even though there may be very little expectation that they will ever be needed. Furthermore, there is also an inclination to classify investments as current because of a desire to make the working capital position appear more favorable.

Prediction of Cash Flows.   As indicated in Chapter 5, the presentation of information that will permit prediction of the future cash flows of the firm should be one of the objectives of financial reporting. The current-noncurrent classification by itself is unlikely to permit predictions of future cash flow. Working capital is, after all, merely a net figure obtained by subtracting some of the liabilities from some of the assets, without a necessary relationship between the two classifications of their components. Furthermore, the net figure has little meaning as either a homogeneous grouping of net resources or as a margin or buffer available for the protection of creditors. The current classification includes both monetary and nonmonetary items, which should be measured with different objectives in mind or with different degrees of reliability, even if an attempt is made to make them homogeneous. The description of working capital as a buffer assumes that current liabilities will be paid from resources classified as current, and that the current assets will not be required for other purposes having priority over the payment of the current liabilities; since neither of these assumptions is realistic, the presentation of working capital as a net figure is of doubtful relevance in financial reporting.

No classification of resources and commitments alone can permit predictions of future cash flows, but a classification may be relevant when it is associated with historical and budgeted cash flow information. Such a classification should provide information regarding the likely timing of conversions of resources into cash, or their availability for conversion and the timing of the payment of obligations.

Critiques

The current-noncurrent classification of balance sheets that is almost universal today has received a torrent of criticism over the years. These criticisms have come regardless of whether the classification was based on the one-year or the operating rule. Arguments against its use include problems in using it to describe operations, in defining the operating cycle, in the static nature of working capital, and the loss of relevance in the presence of cash flow statements and changes in the user community.

Operations and the Operating Cycle.   As a device for describing the operations of the firm, the current-noncurrent classification is defective. Such assets as interest receivable do not arise from the same type of operations as accounts receivable and inventories, but they are all grouped together as current assets. Among the current liabilities, dividends payable does not arise from the same type of operations as accounts payable, and from an operational point of view, the current portion of long-term debt is not dissimilar to the remainder of the long-term debt.

The current-noncurrent classification is also criticized for its assumption that working capital items are closely related to current operations, and that long-term assets and liabilities are related to the long-term planning functions of the organization. This distinction is also reflected in the classifications in the income statement; expenses related to the use of current resources are often classified separately from the amortization and depreciation of long-term assets. And it is also clearly reflected in the cash flow statement; cash provided from operations is classified separately from cash obtained from other sources.

In most firms, though, there is little relationship between working capital and current operations. Cash flows becoming available for payment of liabilities may be as closely related to the use of long-term resources as to the sale of inventories. This is particularly true in the service industries, where inventories may be relatively small or nonexistent and current obligations will be paid from the revenues derived from the use or leasing of depreciable assets.

The Operating Cycle.   This difficulty is compounded by the way the operating cycle concept is applied in practice. Generally, if it is less than one year, the one-year rule still applies; the result is that the current asset classification does not disclose consistently the frequency of the circulation of assets. But even if the operating cycle criterion were applied consistently, there would still be some major difficulties because of the complexity of many business enterprises and the resultant inability to determine the length of the operating cycle. Thus, although the frequency of circulation of assets may be relevant to the prediction of cash flows, the ability to tie this information to the income and cash flow information is difficult when all current assets are classified as if they had the same frequency of circulation.[22]

Working Capital Is Static.   The presentation of working capital may provide some valid information to the grantors of short-term credit because it indicates the degree of protection or the amount of buffer carried by long-term creditors and stockholders. However, neither the amount of working capital nor the working capital ratio is necessarily a good indication of the ability of the firm to pay current liabilities as they come due. This is because working capital is a static concept, and debt-paying ability is dynamic. Cash becoming available for the paying of debt arises primarily from operations, not from the liquidation of particular assets. Cash and other liquid assets available at a particular balance sheet date are likely to be used in operations for the payment of liabilities not yet incurred at balance sheet date (e.g., current payroll), rather than being held for the payment of the balance sheet liabilities as they mature. Stated otherwise, the ability of a firm to meet its debts as they mature depends primarily on the outcome of projected operations; the pairing of current liabilities with current assets assumes that the latter will be available for the payment of the former.

Furthermore, nonliquid current assets become liquid sequentially (i.e., from raw material inventories to work in process to finished inventories to accounts receivable to cash), and current liabilities become due simultaneously or at dates that are unrelated to each other. Therefore, if revenues are contracting, the liquidation of assets through normal operations will be delayed, but the due dates for liabilities will not change.[23] This type of situation presents a good argument for the valuation of current assets in terms of current cash equivalents.

Lack of Relevance.   It is also argued that the classification of assets and liabilities as current and noncurrent as a method of presenting the solvency of the firm is less important today than earlier for several reasons:

1.   Other statements, particularly the income statement and the cash flow statement, may provide better information regarding expectations of solvency.

2.   External financial reports are used more by investors and other groups than by creditors.

3.   Corporations are generally considered to be more permanent in nature and more stable than were most of the 19th-century firms.

4. The widespread use of some valuation procedures, such as LIFO, has made the working capital ratio less meaningful than it once was.

5. The demand by creditors and others for a "favorable" working capital ratio forces managements to take certain actions, such as the payment of current liabilities immediately preceding the balance sheet date, and places pressure on accountants to permit reclassifications to make the working capital appear favorable, even though in so doing, the operations and solvency of the firm are not affected.

6. Business enterprises are becoming highly complex, so that no predetermined working capital ratio can be deemed to be necessary for adequate solvency.

7. The increased entry of many firms into the service industries has made the solvency of firms less dependent upon resources classified as current.

The last reason is particularly relevant for the parents of financial service companies. As noted earlier, financial service companies are not

---

EXHIBIT 13-1 Consolidated Balance Sheet (dollars in millions except per share amounts)

	December 31,	
	1990	*1989*
Assets		
Cash and cash equivalents	$ 3,688.5	$ 5,625.4
Other marketable securities	4,132.9	4,587.9
Total cash and marketable securities (Note 11)	7,821.4	10,213.3
Finance receivables—net (Note 12)	90,116.2	92,354.6
Accounts and notes receivable (less allowances)	5,731.3	5,447.4
Inventories (less allowances) (Note 1)	9,331.3	7,991.7
Contracts in process (less advances and progress payments of $2,353.1 and $2,630.7) (Note 1)	2,348.8	2,073.3
Net equipment on operating leases (less accumulated depreciation of $2,692.6 and $3,065.9)	5,882.0	5,131.1
Prepaid expenses and deferred charges	4,751.6	3,914.7
Other investments and miscellaneous assets (less allowances)	7,252.5	5,050.2
Property (Note 1)		
Real estate, plants, and equipment—at cost (Note 14)	67,219.4	63,390.7
Less accumulated depreciation (Note 14)	38,280.8	34,849.7
Net real estate, plants, and equipment	28,938.6	28,541.0
Special tools—at cost (less amortization)	7,206.4	5.453.5
Total property	36,145.0	33,994.5
Intangible assets—at cost (less amortization) (Notes 1 and 6)	10,856.4	7,126.3
Total assets	$180,236.5	$173,297.1

EXHIBIT 13-1   (*continued*)

	December 31,	
	1990	*1989*

Liabilities and Stockholders' Equity

Liabilities		
Accounts payable (principally trade)	$ 8,824.4	$ 7,707.8
Notes and loans payable (Note 15)	95,633.5	93,424.8
United States, foreign, and other income taxes (Note 9)	3,959.6	5,671.4
Other liabilities (Note 16)	38,255.2	28,456.7
Deferred credits (including investment tax credits—$723.0 and $915.4)	1,410.1	1,403.9
Total liabilities	148,082.8	136,664.6
Stocks subject to repurchase (Notes 1 and 17)	2,106.3	1,650.0
Stockholders' equity (Notes 3, 4, 5, and 17)		
Preferred stocks ($5.00 series, $153.0; $3.75 series, $81.4)	234.4	234.4
Preference stocks (E $0.10 series, $1.0; H $0.10 series, $1.0 in 1989)	1.0	2.0
Common stocks		
$1-2/3 par value (issued, 605,592,356 and 605,683,572 shares)	1,009.3	1,009.5
Class E (issued, 100,220,967 and 48,830,764 shares)	10.0	4.9
Class H (issued, 34,450,398 and 35,162,664 shares)	3.5	3.5
Capital surplus (principally additional paid-in capital)	2,208.2	2,614.0
Net income retained for use in the business	27,148.6	31,230.7
Subtotal	30,615.0	35,099.0
Minimum pension liability adjustment (Note 6)	(1,004.7)	—
Accumulated foreign currency translation and other adjustments	437.1	(116.5)
Total stockholders' equity	30,047.4	34,982.5
Total liabilities and stockholders' equity	$180,236.5	$173,297.1

Reference should be made to the Notes to Financial Statements.

General Motors Operations with GMAC on an Equity Basis

	December 31,	
	1990	*1989*

Assets

Consolidated balance sheet (dollars in millions)		
Current assets		
Cash and cash equivalents	$ 3,491.3	$ 5,455.7
Other marketable securities	1,115.2	1,615.0
Total cash and marketable securities	4,606.5	7,070.7

General Motors Operations with GMAC on an Equity Basis   (*concluded*)

	December 31,	
	1990	*1989*
Accounts and notes receivable		
Trade	16,691.1	18,037.4
Nonconsolidated affiliates	2,998.0	3,758.8
Inventories	9,331.3	7,991.7
Contracts in process	2,348.8	2,073.3
Prepaid expenses and deferred income taxes	3,968.0	2,374.4
Total current assets	$ 39,943.7	$41,306.3
Equity in net assets of nonconsolidated affiliates	9,752.2	9,000.1
Other investments and miscellaneous assets	6,692.7	5,761.8
Property	36,034.7	33,895.2
Intangible assets	10,355.5	6.801.7
Total assets	$102,778.8	$96,765.1

Liabilities and Stockholders' Equity

Current liabilities		
Accounts payable	$ 8,188.8	$ 7,659.2
Loans payable	3,117.8	2,301.7
Income taxes payable	1,148.5	706.4
Accrued liabilities	15,851.5	13,409.2
Stocks subject to repurchase	822.0	—
Total current liabilities	$ 29,128.6	$24,076.5
Long-term debt	4,614.5	4,254.7
Payable to GMAC*	12,918.0	14,460.5
Capitalized leases	309.3	311.0
Other liabilities	23,027.6	15,584.3
Deferred credits	1,449.1	1,445.6
Stocks subject to repurchase	1,284.3	1,650.0
Stockholders' equity	30,047.4	34,982.5
Total liabilities and stockholders' equity	$102,778.8	$96,765.1

*For marketing and financial reasons, GM has assumed part of the dealer inventory financing previously provided by GMAC. To help support these receivables, General Motors entered into a financing agreement with GMAC through 1996 which provides that GMAC will extend loans to GM up to a maximum of $17 billion which bear interest at floating market rates. GMAC services these receivables for General Motors for a fee. This financing agreement ensures that GMAC's ongoing funding activities continue, and returns to GMAC the approximate amount of interest and fees it would have earned had it retained the dealer inventory financing business. At December 31, 1990, $12,718.0 million of such loans were outstanding at a rate of 10.0%, compared with $14,328.0 million at a rate of 10.5% a year earlier. Interest and fees paid by GM to GMAC totaled $1,233.7 million in 1990, $1,469.2 million in 1989, and $1,042.5 million in 1988.

required to make a distinction between current and noncurrent. Under *SFAS 94,* companies are required to consolidate all their majority-owned subsidiaries. Previously, manufacturing companies did not consolidate their financial service subsidiaries on grounds that the result would be misleading. The effect of the new standard has been to create a new kind of financial-manufacturing company. Some of these hybrids have elected not to make a distinction between current and noncurrent elements.

An example is General Motors in its consolidation with its finance subsidiary GMAC [Exhibit 13-1]. Its statement of financial position for 1990 appears alongside: it is shown unclassified with GMAC consolidated and classified with GMAC treated on the equity basis, that is, as an investment.

Alternatives. Because of these difficulties regarding the interpretation of the operating cycle and because of the lack of evidence regarding the relevance of the current asset classification to any specific user's needs, many believe that other methods of classifying assets should be investigated. It has already been suggested that the balance sheet be classified on the basis of valuation method. Another alternative that has been suggested is to:

1. Present a classification of the liabilities based on the type of credit source available to the firm.
2. Disclose supplemental information regarding the amount and timing of expected cash receipts and cash disbursements related to specific assets and obligations.[24]

Liabilities would be classified as either spontaneous or negotiated; that is, as either originating from the normal operations of the firm, such as normal trade credit and accruals, or from the specific negotiations of the firm with banks and other financial lending institutions for either short- or long-term loans. This classification would be relevant because the former sources are fairly automatic, and the latter require negotiation and the lender's evaluation of the financial position of the firm. Information regarding the amount and timing of cash receipts and disbursements would include schedules classifying receivables and payables by due dates and schedules showing the amount and timing of interest, lease, and other periodic receipts or disbursements related to the financing contracts.

Vatter has suggested instead that special statements be prepared to reveal the state of liquidity of a company.[25] Such a statement should show the expected sources of cash in liquidation and the special restrictions regarding the use of particular assets or sources of cash. In the conventional balance sheet, the pairing of current assets with current liabilities leads to the false assumption that, in liquidation, the short-term creditors necessarily have some priority over the current assets and that only the excess is available to long-term creditors. A solvency statement should show the specific priorities that do exist and the rights of all general creditors, regardless of whether they are short term or long term in nature.

Offsetting Liabilities against Assets

Accountants have usually been careful to avoid the offsetting of assets against liabilities in balance sheet presentations. Even though specific funds are available for the payment of specific liabilities, both should be shown on the balance sheet as separate items. The intent to use specific resources does not justify the offsetting. But in a few cases, the offsetting may be justified. When justified, a *right to setoff* is said to exist. Technical Bulletin 88-2 issued by the FASB described this right as:

> a debtor's legal right, by contract or otherwise, to discharge all or a portion of the debt owed to another party by applying against the debt an amount that the other party owes to the debtor.[26]

Conditions for justification may be summarized as follows:

1. There must exist a legal right of offset or an agreed unconditional setoff. A receivable and a payable to the same firm would be a good example. But a negotiable note payable to Firm A cannot be offset against a receivable from Firm A without an unconditional agreement to that effect, because otherwise the right of offset would not be legally binding on the holder in due course.
2. There must be an intent to apply the right of offset. If the items will be treated as other assets and liabilities, the offsetting would not be descriptive of the circumstances.
3. The amount offset against a liability cannot be greater than the amount of the liability and vice versa.

As a general principle, assets and liabilities should not be offset except where a specific right of setoff exists.[27] Cash and other assets, for example, should not be offset against taxes payable. The only exception is when the purchase of certain securities is in substance an advance payment of taxes and the securities are specifically designated by the relevant governments as being acceptable for the payment of taxes owing to them.

Two major exceptions to this general principle exist—both sanctioned by the FASB. The first concerns pensions, where companies have the right to offset the pension obligation with the pension fund, leaving a net pension obligation. The second concerns the use of the equity method in accounting for a parent's investment in a subsidiary. The effect of the equity method is to offset the assets and liabilities of the subsidiary. Whether these situations are sufficiently different to provide theoretical justification for ignoring the general rule on offsetting is moot.

CHECKPOINTS

---

1. List the possible objectives of a classified balance sheet.
2. Why is the current–noncurrent classification of assets and liabilities not as important today as it used to be?
3. In what circumstances can a current asset be offset against a current liability?
4. Contrast the operating cycle approach to defining working capital with the one-year rule.
5. Distinguish deferred charges and credits to revenue from deferred charges and credits to cash. Give an example of each.

CONCLUSION

This chapter has provided definitions of assets and liabilities and has discussed three supposedly essential characteristics of each. It has discussed the requirements of recognition and talked about the typical classification of statements of financial position. The chapter has also noted the changing view of the balance sheet in this century from a residual statement to an independent statement. In doing so, it has followed the path laid out in Chapter 4—that is, it has followed the search for broad, fundamental principles, in this case in the form of definitions, that will direct the search for solutions in specific situations. Whether these definitions will provide definitive answers to the difficult recognition questions faced by accountants is a matter of dispute.

Even within the context of the Conceptual Framework, the FASB admitted that there were elements appearing in financial statements that were neither assets nor liabilities—nor part of owners' equity. These so-called *valuation accounts* include things like the estimate of uncollectible receivables, the premium on a bond receivable, or the discount on a bond payable. These "valuation accounts," said the FASB, are neither assets nor liabilities in their own right but part of the related asset or liability. While this may accord with common sense in most cases, it is uncomfortable from a theoretical standpoint to have essentially undefined elements in a system.

Professors Sunder and Dopuch attack the definitions from another angle. They argue that the definitions are so broad as to be unlikely to settle any major disputes regarding particular issues. Specifically, they claim that:

The FASB's definition of liabilities is so general that at this stage we cannot predict the Board's position on deferred taxes. However, those who favor the recognition of deferred taxes can adopt a somewhat board interpretation of the FASB's definition of liabilities to justify the inclusion of deferred taxes as an element of financial statements, particularly at the individual asset level. In contrast, those who do not could take the FASB's statements literally and just as easily argue against the inclusion of deferred taxes.[28]

In numerous discussions, the existence of deferred credits on balance sheets was held up as a major shortcoming of accounting since they were not real obligations. Stanford professor and later FASB member Robert Sprouse, in a memorable article, tore into the existence of deferred credits which he labeled "what-you-may-call-its!"[29] The FASB continued the same theme, specifically claiming that proponents of the definition of liabilities espoused in this chapter would "reject the deferred method of interperiod tax allocation . . . because they believe that the method creates . . . liabilities that do not represent economic . . . obligations. . . ."[30] Less than 20 years later, as is discussed in a later chapter, the FASB adopted the liability approach to deferred income taxes and decided, as a result, that deferred income taxes were not just deferred credits, not just "what-you-may-call-its," but true liabilities. Much ink was spilled, therefore, to little purpose.

With hindsight, it appears that the definition followed rather than led the cases. The definition provided an excuse for what accountants wanted to do anyway. This evolution is not necessarily a bad thing. This is precisely how the law advances. Perhaps the real problem is that we have attempted to put too much faith in abstract definitions, forgetting the discussion in Chapters 4 and 8 regarding the way accounting theory informs, but does not determine, accounting policy.

SUMMARY

Statements of financial position are summaries of the resources and obligations of a company. The elements of a statement of financial position are assets, liabilities, and owners' equity with the last being defined as a residual, that is, as the difference between assets and liabilities. The FASB defined assets as probable future economic benefits obtained or controlled by a particular entity as a result of past transactions or events. They defined liabilities as probable future sacrifices of economic benefits arising from present obligations of a particular entity to transfer assets or provide services to other entities in the future as a result of past transactions or events. Each is recognized when it is measurable, relevant, and reliable. Classification of assets and liabilities is necessary to provide investors with a means of interpreting what would otherwise be voluminous data.

DISCUSSION QUESTIONS

1. **(May 1977)** Three *independent, unrelated* statements follow regarding financial accounting. Each statement contains some unsound reasoning.

Statement 1

One function of financial accounting is to measure a company's net earnings for a given period of time. An earnings statement will measure a company's true net earnings if it is prepared in accordance with generally accepted accounting principles. Other financial statements are basically unrelated to the earnings statement. Net earnings would be measured as the difference between revenues and expenses. Revenues are an inflow of cash to the enterprise and should be realized when recognized. This may be accomplished by using the sales basis or the production basis. Expenses should be matched with revenues to measure net earnings. Usually, variable expenses are assigned to the product, and fixed expenses are assigned to the period.

Statement 2

One function of financial accounting is to accurately present a company's financial position at a given point in time. This is done with a statement of financial position, which is prepared using historical-cost valuations for all assets and liabilities except inventories. Inventories are stated at first-in, first-out (FIFO), last-in, first-out (LIFO), or average valuations. The statement of financial position must be prepared on a consistent basis with prior years' statements.

In addition to reflecting assets, liabilities, and stockholders' equity, a statement of financial position should, in a separate section, reflect a company's reserves. The section should include three different types of reserves: depreciation reserves, product warranty reserves, and retained earnings reserves. All three of these types of reserves are established by a credit to the reserve account.

Statement 3

Financial statement analysis involves using ratios to test past performance of a given company. Past performance is compared to a predetermined standard, and the company is evaluated accordingly. One such ratio is the current ratio, which is computed as current assets divided by current liabilities, or as monetary assets divided by monetary liabilities. A current ratio of 2 to 1 is considered good for companies, but the higher the ratio, the better the company's financial position is assumed to be. The current ratio is dynamic because it helps to measure fund flows.

Required:

Identify the areas that are not in accordance with generally accepted accounting principles or are untrue with respect to the financial statement analysis discussed in each of the statements and explain why the reasoning is incorrect. Complete your identification and explanation of each statement before proceeding to the next statement.

2. The FASB in the Discussion Memorandum that preceded the Conceptual Framework posed the following question to users of financial reports: Which of the following alternative definitions or modifications of definitions should comprise the substance of a definition of asset for a conceptual framework for financial accounting and reporting?

A-1. Assets are financial representations, broadly defined. Assets represent cash and future economic benefits expected to eventuate, directly or indirectly, in net cash inflows to a particular enterprise as a result of a past transaction or event affecting the enterprise.

A-2. The same as A-1, with an added limitation: Items that do not represent exchangeable or serveable economic resources of an enterprise are not its assets.

A-3. Same as A-1, with the following addition: Assets also include certain "deferred charges" that do not represent economic resources of the enterprise but are required to match costs and revenues properly to measure periodic earnings.

A-4. Same as A-1 or A-2, with the following addition: Balance sheets include, in addition to assets, certain "deferred charges" representing "incomplete allocations of resources and obligations"; they are not assets but are required to match costs and revenues properly to measure periodic earnings.

A-5. Assets comprise a business enterprise's cash; its rights or claims to receive cash, goods, or services; and other items whose costs (historical costs, replacement costs, or opportunity costs) are to be deducted from its revenues of future periods to measure earnings for those periods.

A-6. Assets are the uncommitted or liquid capital (cash, receivables, temporary investments, and the like) and the committed capital (inventories, building, tools, and the like) which "are, in effect, charges against future revenue" in a balance sheet that is a "statement of the sources and composition" of enterprise capital.

How would you have responded to the FASB's question?

3. The FASB in the Discussion Memorandum that preceded the Conceptual Framework posed the following question to users of financial reports: Which of the following alternative definitions or modifications of definitions should comprise the substance of a definition of liabilities for a conceptual framework for financial accounting and reporting?

L-1. Liabilities are financial representations of obligations of a particular enterprise to transfer economic resources to other entities in the future as a result of a past transaction or event affecting the enterprise.

L-2. Same as L-1, with an added limitation: Items that do not represent legally binding obligations to transfer economic resources in the future are not liabilities.

L-3. Same as either L-1 or L-2, with the following addition: Liabilities also include certain "deferred credits" and "reserves" that do not represent obligations to transfer economic resources but are required to match costs and revenues properly to measure periodic earnings.

L-4. Same as either L-1 or L-2, with the following addition: Balance sheets include in addition to liabilities certain "deferred charges" representing "incomplete allocations of resources and obligations"; they are not liabilities but are required to match costs and revenues properly to measure periodic earnings.

L-5. Liabilities are "sources of enterprise capital" in a balance sheet that is "a statement of sources and composition" of enterprise capital. How would you have responded to the FASB's question?

4. A recent article questions whether the resources used by government bodies are assets as the FASB defines that term. The article points out that resources used by government have some features not found in companies.

a. They have a social, rather than commercial, purpose. In particular, they are provided without the prospect of generating positive cash inflows.

b. They are available for the direct use of the community at large. Office furniture, motor vehicles, and EDP equipment held by government agencies are not community assets as they are meant to be used by management, not the public at large.

c. They are not saleable, either because there is no market (as is frequently the case in the nonprofit sector) or because management is prevented, in the community interest, from selling them.[31]

Required:

Discuss whether, in your view, government resources should be excluded from the definition of assets. Consider resources such as the national parks in your answer. Should the definition of assets be broadened to include these resources? If so, how? If not, what do you suggest governments include when drawing up statements of financial position?

5. The FASB in *SFAS 47* defined *take-or-pay contracts* as agreements between a purchaser and a seller that provides for the purchaser to pay specified amounts periodically in return for products or services. The purchaser must make specified minimum payments even if he does not take delivery of the contracted products or services. The FASB provided the following situation as an example:

> To assure a long-term supply, one of the company's subsidiaries has contracted to purchase half the output of an ammonia plant through the year 2005 and to make minimum annual payments as follows, whether or not it is able to take delivery (in thousands):

19X2 through 19X6 ($6,000 per annum)	$ 30,000
Later years	120,000
Total	150,000
Less: Amount representing interest	(65,000)
Total at present value	$ 85,000

In addition, the subsidiary must reimburse the owner of the plant for a proportional share of raw material costs and operating expenses of the plant. The subsidiary's total purchases under the agreement were (in thousands) $7,000; $7,100; and $7,200 in 19X9, 19X0, and 19X1, respectively.

    a. In your opinion, is it sufficient to simply disclose this contract in a footnote or should it be recognized in the financial statements themselves?

    b. How does a consideration of *SFAS 5,* Contingent Liabilities, affect your answer to part *a?*

    c. What is the difference between a lease and a take-or-pay contract in terms of financial obligation? How does this comparison affect your answer to part *a?*

    6.   Cope Company is a manufacturer of household appliances. During the year, the following information became available:

- Probable warranty costs on its household appliances are estimated to be 1 percent of sales.
- One of its manufacturing plants is located in a foreign country. There is a threat of expropriation of this plant. The threat of expropriation is deemed to be reasonably possible. Any compensation from the foreign government would be less than the carrying amount of the plant.
- It is probable that damages will be received by Cope next year as a result of a lawsuit filed this year against another household appliances manufacturer.

Required:

In answering the following, do not discuss deferred income tax implications.

    a. How should Cope report the probable warranty costs? Why?

    b. How should Cope report the threat of expropriation of assets? Why?

    c. How should Cope report this year the probable damages that may be received next year? Why?

7. Spackenkill Company is a manufacturer of household appliances. During the year, the following information became available:

• Potential costs due to the discovery of a safety hazard related to one of its products—These costs are probable and can be reasonably estimated.
• Potential costs of new product warranty costs—These costs are probable but cannot be reasonably estimated.
• Potential costs due to the discovery of a possible product defect related to one of its products—These costs are reasonably possible and can be reasonably estimated.

Required:

a. How should Spackenkill report the potential costs due to the discovery of a safety hazard? Why?

b. How should Spackenkill report the potential costs of warranty costs? Why?

c. How should Spackenkill report the potential costs due to the discovery of a possible product defect? Why?

GARLAND CREATIONS, INC.

Sandy Lawson was determined to own her own company after completing her MBA. As an accomplished seamstress, she had always had a little business on the side making clothes for friends and specialty stores. The success of the Cabbage Patch dolls convinced her that there was money in stuffed toys. She decided that there was an unexploited niche for a family of animals, each having its own personality.

She took the savings of $7,044 that she had accumulated over the years and with $263 worth of materials set out to realize her dreams. Her family was very supportive and lent her $6,000 on a short-term note. She used $3,000 of this to purchase the specialized sewing equipment that she needed to make the animals.

From her years in the clothing business, she managed to find a supplier willing to let her have 90-days' credit and invested in a further $7,364 of materials. Her own car was on its last legs so she purchased a good secondhand pickup truck for $6,600, which she financed through a bank with a $1,600 deposit. One of the family had an unused garage where she could set up her equipment. Installation of the equipment cost her $1,053. A year's insurance to cover the equipment cost a further $1,000. A variety of different supplies necessary to get her operations off the ground absorbed another $963.

---

*This case was prepared by Michael F. van Breda. Copyright © 1988 by Michael F. van Breda.

By the end of the first six months she had made a substantial payment to her supplier, leaving a balance owing in the account of $3,726. Sales had gone well bringing in a very welcome and reassuring inflow of cash totaling $12,325. She attributed these sales partly to the advertisement that she had run in a trade magazine that had cost her $2,442.

Although she had not been able to repay her family or the bank any of the capital that they had lent her, she had paid the family $360 in interest. Wages had totalled $10,697.

While everyone else headed off for New Year's Eve parties, Sandy Lawson sat down at her desk to determine how well her business had done in the first six months of its life. She had worked extremely hard making stuffed toy animals and was proud of the different personalities that she had been able to create. They surrounded her on all sides as she pored over the numbers.

The results, as she figured them, were very pleasing to her. They appear in Exhibits 13-2 and 13-3.

1. Using the description of events in the case and the financial statements provided, replicate her analysis of the transactions involved. Do this using the equation method or using journal entries and T-accounts as is most comfortable for you.
2. Where you believe it appropriate, adjust her accounting to better reflect the events. Revise her statements accordingly.
3. Comment on how well the business has done.

EXHIBIT 13-2

GARLAND CREATIONS
Income Statement
For six months ended 12/31/1987

Revenue		$12,325
Opening inventory	$ 263	
Purchases	7,364	
Wages	10,697	
Prepaid expenses	2,053	
Supplies	963	
Total	21,340	
Less: Closing inventory	16,005	
Cost of goods sold		5,335
Gross margin		6,990
Advertising expenses		2,442
Interest expense		360
Net income		$ 4,188

EXHIBIT 13-3

GARLAND CREATIONS
Balance Sheet
As of 12/31/1987

Cash	$ 616
Inventory	16,005
Current assets	$16,621
Equipment	3,000
Truck	6,600
Total assets	$26,221
Accounts payable	$ 3,726
Notes payable	6,000
Current liabilities	$ 9,726
Bank loan	5,000
Capital	7,307
Retained earnings	4,188
Total equities	$26,221

PRIMARY SOURCES

Those interested in learning more about the topics covered in this chapter might begin by consulting these sources. Each has numerous excellent citations.

Financial Accounting Standards Board, "Conceptual Framework for Financial Accounting and Reporting: Elements of Financial Statements and their Measurement," *FASB Discussion Memorandum* (Stamford, Conn.: FASB, 1976).

Ijiri, Yuji. *Recognition of Contractual Rights and Obligations* (Stamford, Conn.: FASB Research Report, 1980).

Ijiri, Yuji. *Theory of Accounting Measurement* (American Accounting Association, 1975).

Johnson, Todd, and Reed K. Storey. *Recognition in Financial Statements: Underlying Concepts and Practical Conventions* (Stamford, Conn.: FASB Research Report, 1982).

SELECTED ADDITIONAL READINGS

Definitions

Dieter, Richard, and Arthur R. Wyatt. "Get If Off the Balance Sheet." *Financial Executive,* January 1980, pp. 42–48.

Kirk, Donald J. "On Future Events: When Incorporated into Today's Measurements?" *Accounting Horizons,* June 1990, pp. 86–92.

Working Capital

Dun, L. C. "Working Capital—A Logical Concept." *Australian Accountant,* October 1969, pp. 461–64.

Heath, Loyd C. "Is Working Capital Really Working?" *Journal of Accountancy,* August 1980, pp. 55–62.

Hunter, Robert D. "Concept of Working Capital." *Journal of Commercial Bank Lending,* March 1972, pp. 24–30.

Lemke, Kenneth W. "The Evaluation of Liquidity: An Analytical Study." *Journal of Accounting Research,* Spring 1970, pp. 47–77.

Current Assets and Current Liabilities

Cramer, Joe J. "Incompatibility of 'Bad Debt Expense' with Contemporary Accounting Theory." *The Accounting Review,* March 1972, pp. 596–98.

Heath, Loyd. "Financial Reporting and the Evaluation of Solvency." *Accounting Research Monograph No. 3* (New York: AICPA, 1978).

Heath, Loyd, and Paul Rosenfield. "Solvency: The Forgotten Half of Financial Reporting." *Journal of Accountancy,* January 1979, pp. 48–54.

Huizingh, William. *Working Capital Classification* (Ann Arbor: Bureau of Business Research, Graduate School of Business Administration, University of Michigan, 1967).

Public Assets

Mautz, Robert K. "Monuments, Mistakes and Opportunities." *Accounting Horizons,* June 1988, pp. 123–28.

Mautz, Robert K. "Financial Reporting: Should Government Emulate Business?" *Journal of Accountancy,* August 1981, pp. 53–60.

ENDNOTES

1. Peter Waldman and Richard Turner, "Shamu Is the Big Prize Buyer of Sea World Will Get for Its Money," *The Wall Street Journal,* August 28, 1989, p. A1.
2. *SFAC 6,* par. 25.
3. *SFAC 6,* par. 35.
4. John B. Canning, *The Economics of Accountancy* (New York: Ronald Press, 1929), p. 22.
5. Ibid., pp. 55–56.
6. *Accounting Principles Board Statement No. 4,* "Basic Concepts and Accounting Principles Underlying Financial Statements of Business Enterprises" (AICPA, 1970), par. 132.
7. *Accounting Principles Board Statement No. 4,* "Basic Concepts and Accounting Principles Underlying Financial Statements of Business Enterprises" (AICPA, 1970), par. 132.

8. *APB Statement No. 4,* par. 132.
9. Accounting Terminology Bulletin No. 1, pars. 26–27.
10. *SFAC 6,* par. 26.
11. Yuji Ijiri, *The Foundations of Accounting Measurement* (Englewood Cliffs, N.J.: Prentice Hall), p. 70.
12. Raymond J. Chambers, *Accounting, Evaluation and Economic Behavior* (Englewood Cliffs, N.J.: Prentice Hall, 1966), p. 103.
13. *SFAC 6,* par. 36.
14. *SFAC 6,* par. 135.
15. Ibid., par. 137.
16. *SFAS 87,* par. 116.
17. FASB Statement No. 5, "Accounting for Contingencies," par. 1.
18. *SFAC 5,* par. 62.
19. Charles E. Sprague, *The Philosophy of Accounts* (New York: Ronald Press, 1907), p. 32. Reprinted by Scholars Book Company, Lawrence, Kansas, 1927.
20. William J. Vatter, *The Fund Theory of Accounting and Its Implications for Financial Reports* (Chicago: University of Chicago Press, 1947), p. 60.
21. Stephen Gilman, "Accounting Principles and the Current Classification," *The Accounting Review,* April 1944, p. 114.
22. See William Huizingh, *Working Capital Classification* (Ann Arbor: Bureau of Business Research, Graduate School of Business Administration, University of Michigan, 1967), p. 109.
23. Robert D. Hunter, "Concept of Working Capital," *Journal of Commercial Bank Lending,* March 1972, pp. 24–30.
24. Loyd C. Heath, "Is Working Capital Really Working?" *Journal of Accountancy,* August 1980, pp. 55–62; and Loyd C. Heath, *Financial Reporting and the Evaluation of Solvency,* Accounting Research Monograph No. 3 (New York: AICPA, 1978).
25. Vatter, *Fund Theory,* p. 58.
26. *FASB Technical Bulletin No. 88.2,* par. 2.
27. *APB Statement No. 4,* par. 198.
28. Nicholas Dopuch and Shyam Sunder, "FASB's Statements on Objectives and Elements of Financial Accounting: A Review," *The Accounting Review,* January 1980, p. 8.
29. Robert T. Sprouse, "Accounting for What-You-May-Call-Its," *The Journal of Accountancy* 122, no. 4 (October 1966), pp. 45–53.
30. "Conceptual Framework for Financial Accounting and Reporting: Elements of Financial Statements and Their Measurement," *FASB Discussion Memorandum,* December 2, 1976, par. 54.
31. June Pallot, "The Nature of Public Assets: A Response to Mautz," *Accounting Horizons,* June 1990, pp. 79–85.

Chapter 14

Assets and Their Measurement

CHAPTER OBJECTIVES

After studying this chapter, you will be able to:

Define the different bases that have been proposed for asset measurement.

Compare input measures with output measures; current measures with past measures; and future measures with current measures.

Trace the effect of different uses on the choice of particular asset measurements.

Explain the impact of different accounting objectives on the choice of asset measures.

CHAPTER OVERVIEW

The Measurement Process

Measurement consists of attaching a numerical quantity to a characteristic or attribute of some object, such as an asset, or an activity, such as production.

Input Measures

Input measures represent the acquisition costs of assets in organized markets. They can be taken from past, current, or future markets.

Output Measures

Output measures represent the disposal values of assets in organized markets. They can be taken from past, current, or future markets.

Lower-of-Cost-or-Market Measures

The lower-of-cost-or-market rule creates neither input nor output measures but has a long history that, presumably, indicates its perceived value to users.

Objectives of Measurement

The choice of asset measures must be guided by the objectives of financial reporting derived from either the structure of accounting, the desire to be able to interpret financial statements in economic terms, or from its value to users.

A furious debate has raged for decades on how best to measure assets. The debate can be complex and confusing but the main battle lines can be drawn between what might be called the historians and the futurists. The historians tend to favor historical costs because they supposedly tell the company's story better, while the futurists tend to favor current costs because they better reflect the company's future. Historians often, though not always, tend to place the measurement of income as central to accounting. For them, the balance sheet is a statement of residual amounts to be carried forward to future periods. Valuation of assets, therefore, is at best indirect. Futurists tend to make the balance sheet the central focus and level income to be derived as a second order of business. The FASB termed these two approaches the *revenue-expense* and the *asset-liability* views.

To illustrate, consider the debate about the use of LIFO and FIFO. The LIFO method is often favored by historians because in periods of inflation it leads to a more appropriate measure of the gross margin; its disadvantage is that it leaves a less appropriate measure of inventory on the balance sheet. Futurists tend to favor FIFO because it provides a better measure of asset value on the balance sheet; its disadvantage is that it creates a less appropriate measure of cost of goods sold. Note how the one argument stresses the balance sheet, while the other stresses the income statement.

The debate has spawned a wide variety of different potential asset measures. The number reflects the variety of uses to which accounting is put, since each use suggests a different measure. As a result, although there is a definite advantage in the general acceptance of one all-pervasive concept, a close analysis of patterns of usage indicates that a single-valuation concept cannot serve all purposes equally well. The appropriate concept in each case requires the knowledge of who will use the information and for what purpose.

This chapter defines the process of measurement in terms of attaching values to attributes. The strengths and weaknesses of six different asset measures are discussed. These measures are then reexamined in light of the several objectives of financial reporting and the desirable qualitative characteristics of accounting information. The appropriate valuation of liabilities will be discussed in a later chapter.

THE MEASUREMENT PROCESS

Measurement in accounting is the process of assigning meaningful quantitative monetary amounts to objects or events related to an enterprise and obtained in such a way that they are suitable for aggregation (such as the total valuation of assets) or disaggregation as required for specific situations.[1] Examples of objects include receivables, plant and equipment, and long-term debt; examples of activities include sales of goods and services and dividend payments. Before measurement can take place, however, a specific *attribute* to be measured must be selected. In the case of receivables, the selected attributes might include the number of dollars to be received and the expected date of collection. Attributes of plant and equipment might include physical capacity to produce, resource outlay at the time of acquisition, or resources necessary to replace the assets currently.

Measurement is usually thought of in monetary terms. It should not be forgotten that nonmonetary data, such as productive capacity in tons or numbers of employees, may often be relevant for certain predictions and decision making. For instance, one objective in the description of measurement of plant and equipment items is to provide an indication of the amount of physical quantities or productive capacities held by the firm, as well as some indication of their relative ages and expected future lives. It is unlikely that aggregate dollar figures can provide this information. Accountants have recognized for many years the need for presentation of information such as this. They have frequently placed it in the footnotes or elsewhere in the financial statements.

Since assets have several attributes, the measurement and publication of more than one attribute may be relevant to investors and other users of financial statements. Therefore, valuation concepts can be complementary to each other as well as competitive with one another. In many cases, one measure is used to represent another. For example, historical cost under certain circumstances may be relevant as a surrogate for the current cost of an asset. Current cost may, in turn, be a surrogate for the present value of future cash flows, which is the real attribute we wish to measure.

EXHIBIT 14-1 Measurement Bases		
	Input Values	*Output Values*
Past	Historical costs	Past selling prices
Current	Replacement costs	Current selling price
Future	Expected costs	Expected realizable value

Exchange Prices

Since goods and services are generally exchanged in terms of money, it follows logically that exchange prices (market prices) should be relevant to external reporting. Further, since economic decisions can affect only current and future outcomes, current and future exchange prices are potentially as relevant as past exchange prices. All three types of exchange prices must be examined, therefore.

Exchange prices are drawn from markets. But there are two markets in which the firm operates and, therefore, two types of exchange prices or values—output values and input values. Output values reflect the funds received by a firm, based particularly on the exchange price for the firm's product or output. Input values reflect some measure of the consideration given up in obtaining the assets used by a firm in its operations—the inputs. There are, therefore, six major categories of exchange values. These are summarized in Exhibit 14-1.

It might be thought ideal to use only one of these six categories in accounting. As a practical matter, accounting uses all of them at various times. The question is not so much which measure to use, but when to use it. Consider merchandise inventory, for example. When first purchased it is entered at cost—current at the time of purchase, but rapidly dated thereafter. When the inventory is finally sold, it is effectively revalued to its selling price—and renamed accounts receivable. The question is when, if at all, one should do that revaluation. Some argue that it should await the point of sale; others argue that revaluation should follow unexpected bursts of inflation; and so on.

Revaluing Assets

A graphical illustration of the revaluation process appears in Exhibit 14-2. All possibilities begin at the same point: the input cost of the asset when purchased. All possibilities end at the same point: the output cost of the asset when the revenue process is complete. In between, several possible paths are shown. One assumes the asset is revalued at the delivery point;

EXHIBIT 14-2   Revaluing Assets

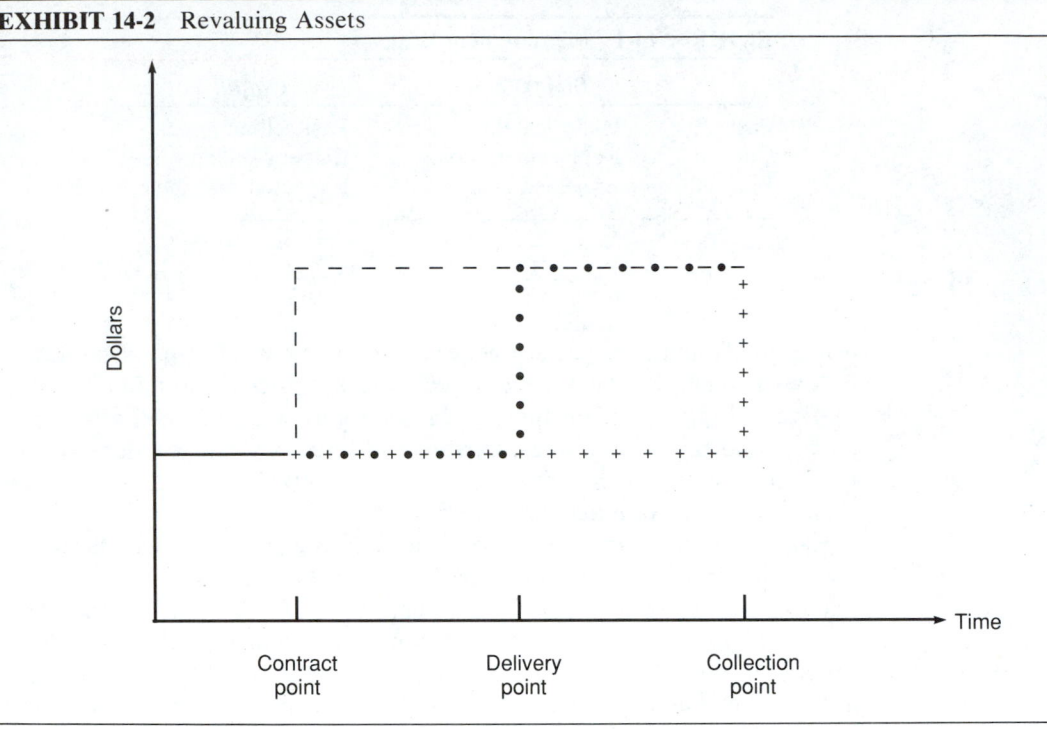

another assumes the asset is revalued at the final cash collection point; a third assumes the asset is revalued continuously over the period; and a fourth assumes the asset is revalued when a firm contract is signed with the buyer even though no delivery has yet taken place. A key point to emerge is that made in the last paragraph. It is not a question of *whether* to restate an asset in output prices, it is simply *when* to do it.

When assets are revalued, new measurement bases are necessary. Traditionally, accounting has looked to the transactions or exchanges directly affecting the accounting entity itself for its exchange prices. However, if it is determined that costs other than transactions costs are relevant, it may be necessary to use exchanges between other entities for the measurement of goods and services for a specific accounting entity. For example, if current costs and appraisal value are deemed relevant in certain circumstances, as has been suggested, then one may need to get these costs from another company's transactions, or from appraisals based on another company's transactions.[2] In other words, it may be necessary to broaden the set of information used in asset measurement.

CHECKPOINTS

---

1. What do accountants mean by the term *attributes*?
2. What do accountants mean by measurement?
3. Why might future exchange prices be more relevant than past exchange prices?

INPUT MEASURES

Input measures represent the amount of cash, or the value of other consideration, paid when an asset or its service enters the firm by an exchange or conversion. Input values can be based on past exchanges, current exchanges, or expected future exchanges.

Historical Input Costs

Historical cost is defined as the aggregate price paid by the firm to acquire ownership and use of an asset, including all payments necessary to obtain the asset in the location and condition required for it to provide services in the production or other operations of the firm. When assets other than cash are given in exchange, the cost should be the current selling price of the asset being given up, rather than its book value or other input value, because the asset is no longer being held for the value of its future services, it any; however, accountants often go back to the original monetary payment for the asset given up in the exchange.

Cost as a valuation concept for nonmonetary assets has its main advantage in the fact that it is verifiable: it is the price in a realized transaction. The cost that results from an arm's-length transaction agreed upon by the buyer and seller in a free economy represents the minimum value of the asset to the buyer. It is possible that the firm may occasionally pay more than it should for an asset, but it is usually assumed that prudent judgment was used and that the firm could not have obtained the same asset or service elsewhere for a lower total cost.

A stronger assumption than minimum value is sometimes made, that is, that cost represents the actual value of the asset to the firm at the time of acquisition. The argument in favor of this assumption is frequently based on the concept of the value of the asset to a going concern.[3] The firm is assumed to have a life long enough to be able to receive the service benefits to be provided by the asset. But this cannot be proved, since all factors of the enterprise are used jointly in providing the cash available for distribution to investors. Cost is at best a minimum value, therefore.

One of the main disadvantages of historical cost valuation is that the value of the asset to the firm may change over time; after long periods of time it may have no significance whatever as a measure of the quantity of resources available to the enterprise, the value of its future services, or its current market price. Even if prices remained constant, it is unlikely that the expectations regarding future services would remain constant. Expectations may change because of greater certainty as the remaining life of the asset becomes shorter, or because of changes in technology, or in economic conditions. Price changes affect the relevancy and comparability of historical costs applied to noncurrent assets to a greater extent than costs applied to current assets. This is because of the longer period from the date of acquisition to the average period of use. The longer this period, the greater the cumulative effect of price changes since the date of acquisition.

Cost is more easily defined than measured. Very often it is not represented by a single exchange price but includes many sacrifices of economic resources necessary to obtain the asset in the form, location, and time in which it can be useful to the operations of the firm. All of these sacrifices should be included in the concept of cost valuation. Identifying all the sacrifices can be extremely difficult in a world of complex interactions. For example, in clearing land for a building, how much of the cost belongs to the building and how much to the land? A similar problem is encountered in a production setting where cost is determined by a series of allocations that are rarely adequate in reflecting causal relationships. It should be recognized also that the term *cost* is used in many senses and for various purposes. In some cases, such as in speaking of marginal costs, or relevant costs, cost includes only a part of the total sacrifices.

Further insight into the meaning of cost is provided by three variations of historical input cost found in the literature. These are prudent costs, standard costs, and original costs.

Prudent Costs.   The concept of *prudent costs* states that only those costs that would normally be paid for property by reasonably prudent management should be included in measuring an asset or an activity. This concept has been used by public utility regulators as a method of placing the public interest ahead of the interests of promoters, management, and stockholders. For example, the Texas Utilities nuclear plant at Glen Rose cost $9.1 billion to build. The cities covered by this plant claimed that $8 billion of that cost were due to the "incompetence and mismanagement of TU people." As a result, they claim, these costs should not be passed on to customers but should be paid for by shareholders. The Public Utility Commission in Austin, Texas, will decide whether these costs were indeed prudent.[4] The definition of a prudent cost is clearly of more than theoretical interest to both customers and investors, therefore.

The prudent cost concept is also applicable to the general valuation of assets. For example, the prudent cost concept suggests that costs of production should include only the normal direct costs of material and labor and the normal indirect costs that can be allocated to the product on the basis of logical association. Normal wasted material and normal idle labor time are logical costs of production, but excessive material waste and abnormal amounts of idle time are not costs of production: they are losses to the firm. What are normal and what are abnormal uses of resources depends, of course, on the production standards of the firm. But, within given limits, necessary production costs can be determined from existing engineering and institutional standards of performance.

Similar concepts of cost can be applied to the acquisition of retail merchandise. Normal costs of transportation, storage, and handling should be included as a part of total inventoriable costs. But excessive costs of shipping, because of the acquisition of inefficient lot sizes, or excessive costs due to reshipping or rehandling, should be excluded from inventory valuations. The mere fact that a cost is incurred does not justify including it in the initial asset value.

That said, it must be acknowledged that the concept is difficult to apply, because it requires the use of value judgments in determining what costs are excessive and what costs are required. In general, the costs intended to be incurred by management at the time of the initial commitment can be assumed to be based on prudent judgment unless evidence is clearly to the contrary. Unanticipated additional costs should be excluded because evidence is lacking that management would have agreed to incur these costs initially.

Standard Costs.   The term *standard costs* applies to valuations on the basis of what costs should be under certain assumptions regarding the desired level of productive efficiency and capacity utilization. Valuation on the basis of standard costs is an input valuation concept based on the appropriate exchange prices of the proper quantities of goods and services necessary for production of the product. Although standard costs have their primary significance as a managerial tool of cost control, they also provide a useful concept of valuation for produced assets.

A major advantage of the standard cost concept is that, as with prudent costs, the costs of inefficiencies are omitted. A product is not worth more because of the existence of idle capacity. The costs of inefficiency and idle capacity are losses incurred by the firm in the current or past periods. They should not be carried forward to future periods to be matched against future revenues and they cannot be converted into future funds flows.

From a valuation point of view, however, standard costs are not necessarily superior to actual costs. An efficiently produced product is not necessarily worth less than one produced under less-efficient methods. The value of a product to the firm depends more on its future service potential or expected sales price than upon either what it cost or what it should have cost. Thus, since the standard cost concept is an input exchange value, it has many of the disadvantages of other input valuations.

The appropriateness of the standard cost concept of a good measure of input exchange values depends in large part on the type of standard cost chosen and the way it is applied. Ideal standards may be useful for managerial purposes, but they tend to understate asset valuations because they tend to exclude some normal costs of inefficiency and idle capacity. Current standards that take these normal inefficiencies into account may be more appropriate; but there is always a difficulty in keeping them current by incorporating changes in prices and production methods.

AICPA Bulletin No. 43 states that "standard costs are acceptable if adjusted at reasonable intervals to reflect current conditions so that at the balance sheet date standard costs reasonably approximate costs computed under one of the recognized bases."[5] Such recognized bases include average cost and FIFO. The implication is that standard cost should not be used to reflect current replacement costs. However, it is the authors' opinion that one of the major advantages of standard costs in the valuation of inventories is that they can be used to reflect current production costs under efficient and normal conditions.

Original Costs.   As used in public utility regulation, the term *original cost* refers to the cost of property to the firm first devoting it to public service. Any amounts paid in excess of the original cost less accumulated depreciation in the purchase by a second firm must be classified separately and disposed of by methods approved by the utility commission. They cannot be charged, though, to ordinary operating expenses because these are used in the rate-making process. The logic behind this concept is that customers should not be required to pay rates that permit a utility to earn excessive profits by selling its property, whereas it could earn only a reasonable return by holding it. Because of the absence of competition in the selling of utility property, a buying firm would not be encouraged to pay the lowest price possible if it were permitted to pass whatever it paid along to its customers. There is considerable truth in this position during periods of stable prices; however, the equity involved becomes clouded when prices are rising rapidly.

While the original cost concept has some merit in the process of utility rate making, there is little merit to its application in the competitive sector of the economy. The cost of secondhand equipment can be assumed to represent a bargained price and, therefore, the current market price of the asset. The cost paid by the original purchaser is no longer of interest.

Exceptions do exist: original cost is used in cases where there is no arm's-length transaction, or where there is deemed to be a pooling of interest rather than a purchase.

Current Input Costs

Current costs represent the exchange price that would be required today to obtain the same asset or its equivalent. If a market exists in which similar assets are bought and sold, an exchange price can be obtained and associated with the asset owned; this price represents the maximum value to the firm (unless net realizable value is greater), except for very short periods until a replacement can be obtained. It should be noted, however, that this current exchange price is a cost price only if it is obtained from quotations in a market in which the firm acquires its assets on services; it cannot be obtained from quotations in the market in which the firm usually sells its assets or services in the normal course of its operations, unless the two markets are coincident.

Current standards reflect what a product should cost to produce under current conditions of prices and technology and with a desired standard of efficiency. Current standard costs, therefore, resemble replacement costs, with the exception that costs of inefficiency and idle capacity are excluded. However, replacement costs may also exclude some costs that are unnecessary in the production process. The main difference is that standard costs are determined independently of past production techniques, on a scientific basis, while current replacement costs may be computed by applying current factor prices to past production techniques.[6]

Current cost has become an important valuation basis in accounting, particularly for presenting information regarding the effect of inflation on an enterprise. In many situations, current cost is an appropriate measure of fair value, either in establishing an initial acquisition price (as in certain exchanges or nonmonetary assets), or in establishing a maximum value (as in determining the present value of a capital lease for the lessee).[7] Critics who favor the use of historical cost until at least the point of sale point out some disadvantages of using current costs:

1. Current costs or quotations are not available for seasonal and style items and for goods produced by obsolete methods. Estimates of the current input values of these items may, therefore, be subjective in nature.
2. Changes in current costs do not always reflect changes in current selling prices. Values do not necessarily change because of changes in costs.
3. Increases in costs would result in gains recorded in the current period

even though they have not been realized through sale.[8] For example, an increase in labor costs would appear to be profitable in the current period even though sales prices have remained stable.

4. Gains and losses caused from changes in specific input prices would be included in the net income from operations unless the cost of sales, as well as the ending inventory, is valued in terms of costs current at the time of sale.

For the most part, proponents of maintaining historical input costs for assets up to the point of realization have won the day. Exceptions do exist, though. One is marketable securities in which the portfolio is moved down to current market value and then restored to original cost with movements in the market and regardless of realization.

Appraisal Value.   The term *appraisal value* refers to an estimated value of current costs or current values using systematic procedures. Whether an input or an output value is obtained depends on the objective of obtaining the appraisal. If an appraisal is obtained for the fixed assets of a going concern, it should represent an estimate of current replacement or reproduction cost less depreciation to the date of appraisal. Therefore, if the objective is properly stated, an appraisal value should represent the current input value of the asset to the firm.

The main advantage of obtaining an appraisal value is that, since it is usually computed by someone outside of the firm, it is considered to be more objective than replacement costs computed by the firm itself. The main disadvantage of appraisals is that they can be obtained only at periodic intervals and, therefore, they become out of date, just as do historical costs.

Fair Value.   The term *fair value* has been used primarily in the public utility field to refer to the total amount on which the investors are entitled to earn a fair return. The courts have held that the computation of fair value should include all pertinent facts, including the prudent past costs and reproduction costs.[9] Public utility firms have claimed that it should include primarily replacement costs. Fair value, therefore, is not a specific valuation basis that can be applied to financial statements generally. It is, rather, a combination of valuation bases determined by the commissions and courts for a specific purpose.

Net Realizable Value Less a Normal Markup.   When replacement costs are not available, they can sometimes be estimated by subtracting a normal gross profit margin from the net realizable value (estimated selling price less additional expected incremental costs).* Before this procedure

---

* Net realizable values are discussed in more detail later under output costs.

can result in a good approximation of current costs, however, there must be a direct relationship between costs and selling prices. If these do not move together, the result will not be an approximation of current costs. The normal markup assumed must also apply to the specific items in question as well as to the original items from which they were derived.

Net realizable value less a normal markup is also occasionally suggested as a measure of the net value of the inventory to the firm when this value is below historical cost and current cost. The assumption is that a loss should be recorded currently and the normal profit should be permitted when the goods are sold. However, this is an incorrect usage of the concept. While this method is often used in the valuation of used equipment received by an equipment dealer as trade-ins on new equipment, it must be recognized that the trade-in allowance does not necessarily represent cost. In most cases, valuation at net realizable value alone would be more appropriate.

Net realizable values are also useful in those cases where the firm would not have acquired the items if it had to do so at current prices. For example, if merchandise is acquired at a low price because of a liquidation of a supplier's stock, or for other special reasons, the current replacement cost in the regular markets may be irrelevant. The net realizable value of the merchandise, in this case, is dependent on the expected sales prices, and this is more relevant than the current cost. Also, the trading margin representing the difference between the expected sales price and the current cost lacks significance either to the firm or to readers of financial statements.

Discounted Future Input Costs

If the price, under the terms of the contract, is to be paid later, the cost of the asset should be the present discounted value of the contractual obligation. However, short delays in payment may be ignored because the discount is usually immaterial. The discounted future cost concept has also been recommended in cases where the firm has the alternative of purchasing the services as required, rather than in a lump sum. One might rent a building rather than purchase it; one might hire temporary labor instead of contracting for full-time labor. But, once the firm has made the advance commitment, it no longer has the alternative of purchasing services separately, making the comparison more hypothetical than real. Further, even if the discounted future costs were equal to the value of the asset at the date of acquisition, this identity of discounted future expected costs of equivalent services and the current value of the asset to the firm is not likely to persist in subsequent periods. Therefore, the discounted future cost concept has all the disadvantages of historical cost plus the limitations applicable to the discounted service potential concept.

CHECKPOINTS

---

1. Define, in your own words, the three main categories of input values.
2. What are the major advantages and disadvantages of historical cost accounting?
3. Compare prudent, standard, and original costs.
4. Compare net realizable value with replacement cost.

OUTPUT MEASURES

Output prices represent the amount of cash, or the value of other consideration, received when an asset or its service leaves the firm by an exchange or conversion. It follows that the discounted expected cash receipt value of assets is the measurement of most interest when using output measures. When the product of the enterprise is generally sold in an organized market, the current market price may be a reasonable estimate of the actual selling price in the near future. If, however, the product is not expected to be sold within a short period, the current market price (used as a substitute for the expected sales price) should be appropriately discounted. Accounts receivable is an example of a nonmonetary asset measured at a current exchange output value. Bonds receivable is an example of an asset measured at its discounted future value.

It has been argued that whenever assets have exchange prices that are likely to be received at specific future periods, they should be treated similarly to receivables. Under this approach, inventory would be entered at its sales price, not at its cost price. The use of output prices has been sanctioned when the asset is readily realizable. Examples include marketable securities, precious metals, and certain agricultural products. Such assets have "quoted prices available in an active market that can rapidly absorb the quantity held by the entity without significantly affecting the price."[10] A further requirement is that there is little expected delay in receiving the sale price in cash, so that any interest (discount) is not a material factor in the measurement of income. A similar situation may exist where there is a delivery contract with little delay in collection. In these cases, the firm's product is completed and any additional effort is negligible. In such circumstances, the selling price is the best measure not only of the revenue, but also of the funds to be received in exchange for the goods.

Net Realizable Values

It has been suggested that whenever output values are being used in the measurement of inventory and additional costs of production or expenses of selling are anticipated, these costs should be subtracted from the current sales price to obtain an approximation of the current valuation. This current valuation is referred to as the *net realizable value*. This ensures that the additional costs of completion or sale and collection are recorded in the period in which the revenue is reported. Net realizable value is, therefore, defined as the current output price less the current value of all additional anticipated incremental costs and expenses (exclusive of tax effects) relating to completion, sale, and delivery of the merchandise. Additional expenses of collection should also be deducted, if material.

One of the major difficulties with the net realizable value concept is that it is usually quite difficult to estimate the additional out-of-pocket costs necessary to complete, sell, and deliver the product. As an alternative, a normal gross margin is frequently deducted from the selling price to be sure that all possible additional costs are taken into account; but this may approximate an input value if the additional expected costs are not large.[11]

Another difficulty with the net realizable value concept is that the net income from the transaction is reported before all of the activities of the firm relating to the sale have been accomplished. If it can be assumed that value is added by the firm throughout the entire period during which activities relating to the sale are performed by the firm, some income will have been reported before it has been "earned." An alternative is to deduct from net realizable value the normal operating income to the various activities. Ideally this could be accomplished by making the allocation on the basis of the value added by the firm in the several activities, but an allocation on the basis of total costs incurred and expected might be a reasonable alternative in many cases. Because of these difficulties of measurement and the arbitrariness of the allocations, this refinement should probably remain a theoretical ideal rather than a practical goal.

Current Cash Equivalents

Ordinarily output prices refer to prices in normal exchange markets. It has been suggested, however, that prices should be drawn from other markets. For example, it is often argued that creditors are interested in the liquidation value of a company. Two cases are discussed below: liquidation in orderly markets and liquidation in disorderly markets.

The term *current cash equivalent* was proposed by Australian professor Raymond Chambers as a single measurement concept for all assets, representing their present realizable prices.[12] It represents the amount of cash or generalized purchasing power that could be obtained by selling each asset under conditions of orderly liquidation, which may be measured by quoted market prices for goods of a similar kind and condition. The current cash equivalent represents, therefore, the position of the firm in relation to its adaptive behavior to the environment.*

One of the major difficulties with the current cash equivalent concept is that, if it is strictly interpreted, it provides justification for excluding from the position statement all items that do not have a contemporary market price. For example, nonvendible specialized equipment, as well as most intangible assets, would be written off at the time of acquisition, because of an inability to obtain a current market price. However, Chambers modified the procedures somewhat to provide approximation of the current cash equivalents by the use of specific price indexes and by making subjective depreciation computations.

From the authors' point of view, the main deficiency in using the current cash equivalent concept for all assets is that it does not take into consideration the relevancy of the information to the prediction and decision needs of the users of financial statements, although it does provide the investor with contemporary information regarding the financial position of the firm and some alternatives available to it.

Liquidation Values

Liquidation values are similar to current output prices and to current cash equivalents, except that they are obtained from different market conditions. Current output prices assume normal selling operations and usually a normal profit, and current cash equivalents assume at least orderly liquidation. The concept of *liquidation values* assumes a forced sale, either to regular customers at greatly reduced prices or to other firms or dealers, usually at prices considerably below cost. The application of liquidation values usually results in the writing down of asset valuations and the recognition of losses. Because they are not realistic under normal circumstances, liquidation values should be used only under two main circumstances:

1. When merchandise or other assets have lost their normal usefulness, have become obsolete, or have otherwise lost their normal market.
2. When the firm expects to discontinue business in the near future, so that it will not be able to sell in its normal market.

---

* Current cash equivalents are assumed to be a contemporary property of all assets, relevant for all actions in markets, and thus uniformly relevant at a point in time. Their use avoids the necessity to aggregate past, present, and future prices.

Discounted Future Cash Receipts or Service Potentials

When expected cash receipts require a waiting period, the present value of these receipts is less than the actual amount expected to be received. The longer the waiting period, the smaller is the present value. Conceptually, the present value is determined by the process of discounting. But discounting involves not only an estimate of the opportunity cost of the money, but also an estimate of the probability of receiving the expected amount. The longer the waiting period, the greater the uncertainty that the amount will be received.

Although the discounted cash flow concept has validity in the valuation by an investor of an entire firm, or in the valuation by owners of single ventures, it is of doubtful validity when applied to separate assets of a firm, for the following reasons:

1. The expected cash receipts generally depend upon subjective probability distributions that are not verifiable by their nature.
2. Though opportunity discount rates might be obtainable, the adjustment for risk preference must be evaluated by management or the accountants, and it might be difficult to convey the meaning of the resultant valuation to the readers of financial statements.
3. When two or more factors, such as human resources and physical assets, contribute to the product or service of the firm and the subsequent cash flows, a logical allocation to the separate service factors is generally impossible. It has been suggested that the marginal net receipts associated with the asset can be used, but the sum of the individual marginal net receipts is not likely to add to the total net receipts from the product or service.
4. The discounted value of the differential cash flows of all of the separate assets of the firm cannot be added together to obtain the value of the firm. This is partly due to the jointness of the contributions of the separate assets, but it is also due to the fact that some assets, such as intangibles, cannot be separately identified.

In spite of these difficulties, the discounted cash flow concept has some merit as a valuation concept for single ventures where there are no joint factors requiring separate accounting or where the aggregation of assets can be carried far enough to include all of the joint factors. But it is also appropriate for monetary assets where waiting is the primary factor determining the net benefit to be received in cash by the firm. For example, if a note receivable is fairly certain of being collected and if the timing of the payments is specified by contract, the discounted value of the note represents the amount of cash that the firm would be indifferent to holding as compared to holding the note.

CHECKPOINTS

1. Define, in your own words, the three major categories of output values.
2. What are the major advantages and disadvantages of output value over input values?
3. What difficulties does one encounter using net realizable values?
4. Why are discounted future cash receipts not used more?

LOWER-OF-COST-OR-MARKET MEASURES

The lower-of-cost-or-market valuation procedure is neither an output nor an input valuation concept, but a mixture of the two concepts. The term *market* may refer to either an output or an input price. When the concept is applied to inventories, the term market usually refers to replacement cost (an input concept), but it may refer to selling price or net realizable value (output concepts) under certain conditions. When it is applied to the valuation of investments in securities, market usually refers to the selling price, although in this case the costs and selling prices are obtained from the same market; the difference between the two is represented primarily by the costs of buying and selling. However, since securities are not usually purchased with the purpose of selling in a different market at a higher price, both the cost and selling price of securities can be considered output prices.

The lower-of-cost-or-market concept has a long history in accounting, going back to the 19th century and before. One of the reasons for its early prominence is the early emphasis on the balance sheet as a report to creditors. Without a reliable report on which to base expectations regarding future operations, creditors emphasized the lowest probable conversion value of assets. Thus, a policy of conservatism was adopted with regard to balance sheet valuations.* The valuations presented in the statements could be assumed to be worth at least as much as stated.

With the change in emphasis to the income statement, the lower-of-cost-or-market rule took on new meaning. It was now the income that would be conservatively stated. By reducing asset valuations at the end of a period because of a fall in prices, the net income for the period would be smaller. All possible losses would be included in the current income determination, but all probable gains would be deferred until the usual recognition at the time of sale or later. The recognition of gains is based on

---

* See Chapter 5 for more details on the doctrine of conservatism.

different criteria than the recognition of losses. Gains are not recognized until there is little or no possibility of their being reversed, but losses are recognized whenever there is some available evidence that they might occur.

There is some question as to whether the cost-or-market rule is a basic accounting concept or merely an accepted accounting procedure. It does not use any valuation concept different from the concepts discussed above, but because it does not apply any one of the valuation concepts consistently, it can be considered a different concept at least in its application, or it can be considered an eclectic application of various valuation concepts. Regardless of the level of dignity ascribed to the method, it has been vigorously criticized for many years in discussions of accounting theory. Many believe the lower-of-cost-or-market concept is unacceptable in accounting theory for the following reasons:

1. As a method of conservatism, it tends to understate total asset valuations. Individual asset valuations may also be understated, but because valuations are not increased above acquisition cost in those cases where future service or sales values have increased, the total valuations tend to be understated whenever the cost-or-market concept is applied. This understatement may not harm creditors, but it is deceiving to stockholders and potential investors, and management is kidding itself if it believes its own statements.

2. The conservatism in asset valuations is offset by an unconservative statement of net income in a future period. A lower asset valuation in the current period will result in a larger reported profit or smaller loss in some future period when the asset valuation is charged off as an expense. Because gains are not reported currently, the resulting net income will be less useful as a predictive device or as a measure of efficiency.

3. While the cost-or-market concept can be applied consistently from year to year, it is internally inconsistent. No single valuation concept is used consistently; one valuation concept may be applied one year and another concept the next year. Also, there is no consistent application of valuation concepts to a single asset classification in the same year.

4. A less convincing argument is that the cost-or-market rule applies to decreases in costs as well as to diminished utility due to deterioration, obsolescence, or decreased earning capacity. There may not be any changes in net realizable value just because costs have changed.

Its most amazing attribute is that it has found so many followers for so many years. It has even maintained formal recognition by the American Institute of Certified Public Accountants, the American Accounting Association, the Securities and Exchange Commission, the Institute of Chartered Accountants in England and Wales, and other associations and agencies. The acceptance of the cost-or-market concept by the FASB is stated as follows:

A departure from the cost basis of pricing the inventory is required when the utility of the goods is no longer as great as its cost. If the utility of goods is impaired by damage, deterioration, obsolescence, changes in price levels, or other causes, a loss shall be reflected as a charge against the revenues of the period in which it occurs. The measurement of such losses shall be accomplished by applying the rule of pricing inventories at cost or market, whichever is lower. This provides a practical means of measuring utility and thereby determining the amount of the loss to be recognized and accounted for in the current period.[13]

In this context, the term *market* is used to mean replacement cost, with net realizable value as an upper limit and net realizable value less a normal profit margin as a lower limit.

CHECKPOINTS

---

1. Define what is meant by the lower-of-cost-or-market rule.
2. Provide two reasons why the rule is theoretically weak.

OBJECTIVES OF MEASUREMENT

The choice of a particular measurement base is influenced by the objectives of asset measurement. Since some form of valuation is necessary in the accounting process, the objectives of valuation are, in large part, the same as the objectives of accounting. They also fall into the same three categories that were discussed in Chapter 5: syntactic, semantic, and pragmatic.

Syntactic Objectives

Selection is affected in the first place by one's approach to asset measurement. As previous chapters have pointed out, in the traditional accounting structure the balance sheet became a step between two income statements, and asset valuation became a process of computing how much to carry forward to future periods. More recently, there has been strong support for a statement of financial position that is defined independently of the income statement, that is, for an asset-liability as opposed to a revenue-expense approach.

Measurement and Matching.   The conventional approach to accounting remains the revenue-expense approach. In this approach, the objective of asset measurement is to obtain a basis for the computation of the gross operating margin and the income from all transactions. Income is defined as the difference between total revenues and the *input* value of all expenses associated with these revenues or with the period. It follows that nonmonetary assets should be measured in terms of input values until they are allocated to expenses and either matched with product revenues or charged to a specific period. Monetary assets, on the other hand, are typically measured in terms of net realizable values.

In its most conservative form, the only event that is recognized is imminent realization of revenue that defines the point of sale. This forms a justification for the use of historical costs from the time of acquisition to the point of sale. No other event occurs before sale to generate profit or loss and, therefore, to change the value of the asset. In other words, matching provides the justification for a historical cost balance sheet.

With changes in the value of the monetary unit, some allow that a better measure of ongoing income may be obtained by restating the historical costs in terms of dollars representing the same purchasing power as the current revenue. Others argue that a separation of current operating income from holding gains and losses obtained by valuing the inputs in terms of current replacement costs is also useful. This separation may be achieved in one of two ways:

1. The emphasis may be placed on the valuation of the inputs as they expire. For example, the cost of goods sold may be valued on a current basis, by the use of LIFO or current replacement cost. This leaves the ending inventories in terms of residuals.
2. The nonmonetary assets may be restated at the balance sheet date or periodically during the year, permitting matching at current costs as these assets expire. An unexpected burst of inflation that raises the current input price of the asset above its original input price might prompt such a revaluation. Such revaluations result in a holding gain.[14]

The main difficulty with using the matching process as a basis for determining asset valuations is that many enterprise activities do not lend themselves to accurate matching. As a result, many allocations of asset valuations to products or expenses are arbitrary in nature. The valuations carried forward have no particular relationship to specific current benefits; therefore, the values remaining have no particular relationship to future benefits. This has led to the adoption of many procedures that cannot be supported on logical grounds. The use of the deferred charge classification and the allocation of the cost of intangibles are examples that cast considerable doubt on the usefulness of the matching concept to provide relevant information to investors and other interested parties.

Measurement and Accretion. According to the accretion concept, income accrues to a firm as asset valuations increase (or as liability valuations decrease) in the absence of capital transactions. An example is an interest-bearing loan. Interest is debited to the loan and credited to interest income each period regardless of realization. Thus, income results from increasing valuations from input values to output values or from increasing discounted net realizable values to cash values when the revenues have been earned—at the completion of production or at the time of sale. The discounted net realizable values may then be increased to cash values when the receivables are collectible or converted into cash.

Note that the objective of valuation in this concept is to approach the output values and cash values as soon as the basic services have been performed by the firm and as soon as verifiable measurements can be obtained. By so doing, income is recorded on an accretion basis. The income may be separated into realized and unrealized elements, but this is not necessary to meet the objectives of this approach. The accretion approach results in an all-inclusive concept of income, but the extraordinary gains and losses can be reported separately by combining this with the transactions approach.

The importance of this approach to valuation is that the emphasis is on recognizing and recording all changes in value based on the best evidence of the final output value or the amount of cash finally to be received. Thus, net realizable value should take precedence over input values; current replacement cost may be closer to net value to the firm than historical cost; and historical cost may be relevant if it represents the current value to the firm. The type of valuation selected depends on whether or not the basic services have been performed by the firm, the verifiability and relative freedom from bias of the valuation procedure, the relative certainty of the expected conversion to cash, and the ability to measure related expenses. The objective of the valuation, however, remains: to measure the increment in specific asset valuations, rather than to present the value of the firm as a whole to the investors or to any other group.

It can be argued that manufacturing inventories are effectively treated on an accretion basis. Inventories appear at various stages in the operating process of a business. In some cases they appear at the beginning of the process, as raw material or as a semifinished product with considerable economic activity still required before they can be transferred to customers. Costs are added to inventories as they pass through this process, independent of any outside transactions. It is only when inventory reaches the finished goods stage that the accretion process stops.

CHECKPOINTS

---

1. Contrast matching and accretion. What implications, if any, does each have for the valuation of assets?
2. What is the difference in total income earned under the different approaches to income measurement discussed in this section? How is that income recognized?

Semantic Objectives

The advent of the APB and the publication of documents such as *ARS 3* and ASOBAT strengthened support for financial statements that would present clearly interpretive measurements of the resources and obligations of a firm at a specific time as well as permit interpretive measurements of changes in financial position over time.[15] In particular, there was a strong feeling that historical cost valuation lacks interpretation (unless specific costs are associated with specific dates). Current replacement costs were preferred because they permit greater interpretation, if the valuations are taken from prices existing in markets.

There was also a growing sense that accountants should search for improved alternative methods of measuring and presenting both monetary and nonmonetary data. For example, it might be possible to present data showing probability intervals and ranges (in probabilistic form), in addition to single-valued data (in deterministic form). Also, it may be desirable, as the authors of ASOBAT suggested, to present multiple values representing different attributes of objects and activities if they are all found to be relevant. In addition, consideration should be given to the presentation of budget data as evidence of management's plans and expectations.

One way to achieve semantic objectives is to ensure that all measures used in accounting are representationally faithful. This term was described in Chapter 5 as the "correspondence or agreement between a measure or description and the phenomenon that it purports to represent." For example, *SFAC 1* suggests that one of the objectives of accounting is to provide a relative measurement of the resources available to the firm in the generation of future receipts. This argues for the abandonment of historical costs, which fail in this regard. Changes over time mean that historical costs of assets no longer represent even the minimum value of discounted cash flows. Current costs permit greater interpretation, if the valuations are taken from prices existing in markets.

Pragmatic Objectives

Pragmatic objectives focus on the usefulness, or the relevance, of accounting. Relevance was defined in the Conceptual Framework as "the capacity of information to make a difference in a decision by helping users to form predictions about the outcomes of past, present, and future events or to confirm or correct prior expectations."[16]

According to the Conceptual Framework, the primary users of accounting are investors interested in "assessing the amounts, timing, and uncertainty of prospective cash receipts."[17] The most obvious means to achieve this is by the direct provision of estimates of future cash flows, but this is not always feasible. An alternative is to provide a history of past cash flows but this is bedeviled by the fact that cash flows tend to be lumpy. The FASB concluded that an alternative means to providing information about future cash flows is to "provide information about an enterprise's economic resources, obligations, and owners' equity," that is, balance sheets.[18] In addition, the user should be given information regarding "the enterprise's performance provided by measures of earnings and its components," that is, income statements.[19]

In the case of inventory, for example, cash flows can be predicted from two points of view. First, inventory supports the inflow of cash through its sale in the ordinary course of business. Second, under normal circumstances inventory has an effect on the amount of cash required during the subsequent period to acquire the merchandise that will be sold during the period. The inventory should be measured in ways that will aid in the prediction of both the inflows of cash from sales and the outflows required for the acquisition of the merchandise. One way to achieve this is by the use of *net realizable values*. This is in line with the arguments in *ARS 3* which state that ". . . inventories which are readily salable at known prices with negligible costs of disposal, or with known or readily predictable costs of disposal, should be measured at net realizable value."[20] They suggest further that this should not be an exception to usual acceptable valuation procedures, but should be considered ". . . in keeping with major objectives of accounting."[21]

For a statement of financial position to provide information relevant to a prediction of future cash flows, it should include quantitative measurements of resources and commitments for comparisons with other periods or with other firms. The quantities of resources available to the firm, however, are relevant to predictions only if they are related to the cash flows likely to be generated by the firm. That is, valuations of assets held by the firm can provide relevant information only if the investor can detect some relationship between such measurements and expected cash flows. In some cases, the relevant attribute of available resources may be measured in terms of *current replacement costs*. In other cases, the best measure may be the *current output values,* or some other available measurement.

Others argue that *future costs* are the most relevant. They note that most nonmonetary assets represent goods or services acquired in advance. These goods or services are usually acquired in advance because:

1. It is less costly to acquire them in large quantities.
2. Some assets (e.g., a building or equipment) by their nature represent a stream of future services that cannot be acquired separately.
3. It is often desirable to purchase future services (e.g., leasehold) in order to be sure that they will be available when they are needed.
4. It is often desirable to obtain rights to property to protect other investments, such as leasehold improvements.

In all these cases, it is the equivalent cost of the service at the time of use that is the most relevant valuation concept, not the cost at the time of purchase or acquisition. Following this argument, the most relevant cost is the present value of the services that the asset can be expected to deliver, that is, the discounted value of the *future costs.* It should be noted that this is a cost concept; the discounted amounts are input exchange prices, not output service values.

In the case of purchased long-term plant and equipment, the prediction of future cash flows is a difficult assignment under the best of circumstances because the conventional depreciation methods and balance sheet valuations are inadequate as measurements of plant and equipment services used during a period and measurements of the service potentials remaining at the end of the period. This is partly the result of an inability to identify specific items or services used during the accounting period and the quantity of services remaining unused at the end of the period. Information that indicates either implicitly or explicitly the productive capacity, estimated lives, operating efficiency, and cash requirements for replacement should be relevant. When plant and equipment are leased, at least some requirements are specified in the lease contract so that better information regarding some of the expected cash flows can be presented.

Using normative investment models, it may be assumed that an objective of asset valuation is to provide information that will permit the prediction of future cash outflows necessary to acquire similar resources in the future in the continuation of business operation and to permit the prediction of future cash receipts. Current replacement costs obtained from existing markets may reflect the cash outflows required to duplicate the existing facilities.[22] Thus, as a prediction of future cash outflows, current input costs, and expected future input prices should be more significant than past input valuations.

Despite these arguments in their favor, current output costs have not found favor in general-purpose financial statements. One can speculate on the reasons why. Presumably, those who want information on future cash flows are able to generate it at lower cost from other sources. Also, since most contracts are specified in historical input terms, this may make the provision of this information more important than that of current output numbers. In addition, it may be that the expected future cash flows are just so uncertain that the use of input valuations offers an acceptable substitute to users.

Relevance for Creditors.   Creditors also have an interest in future cash flows—especially those available when the firm is approaching bankruptcy. As Chapter 3 noted, in the early part of the 20th century and before, one of the major objectives of the balance sheet was the presentation of financial information to creditors. Because of the lack of reliable information, creditors had to rely heavily on any indication of the security of the loan. *Liquidation values* were thus considered more important than other valuation concepts, and the doctrine of conservatism gained a strong influence in reporting. But if the probability of enterprise continuity is good, current output values are probably more important than liquidation values for an evaluation of the enterprise by creditors. Current debt will generally be paid from funds becoming available to the firm in the future rather than the forced sale of assets now held. However, if it should become apparent that a firm will not have continuity of existence, the expected conversion values may be at or close to forced liquidation levels.

Relevance for Equity Holders.   According to traditional accounting concepts, the invested capital of a firm is equal to the valuation of the net assets of the enterprise. This figure cannot represent the value of the firm as a whole to the equity holders, but it is possible that the accounting statements may be able to give the equity holders some information regarding their relative rights and risks. Commonly, several classes of equity holders are represented in the capital structure of a firm, including some whose rights may change through the conversion of bonds into stock, or of one class into another, or by the exercise of warrants. Many of these relationships cannot be described by single measurements or even in quantitative terms, but certain valuation procedures may provide at least partial information, such as the relative amount of buffer that may exist for the protection of equity holders with priority rights.

Relevance for Managers.   For managerial purposes, the valuation process should provide information relevant to the making of operating decisions. But the information required by management is not necessarily the same as that required by investors and creditors. Investors and creditors are interested primarily in predicting the future course of the business from an evaluation of the past and from other information, but management must continually make decisions that determine the future course of action. Therefore, management has greater need for information regarding valuations arising from different courses of action. For example, managements must occasionally compare the benefits of using assets in the firm with their liquidation values. Also, opportunity costs, marginal or differential costs, and present values from expected differential cash flows are relevant for many types of management decisions. But just because they are relevant to managerial decisions does not necessarily mean that they are also relevant to the decisions of investors and creditors. Therefore, these valuations do not need to be reported in the position statement; they can be made readily available to management in supplementary reports.

Reliability. Reliability is often presented as the main justification for historical cost and the main argument against all its competitors. Input values are preferred to output values for the same reason: they are believed to be more verifiable, possibly because they do not permit the reporting of revenue before it is "realized." In other words, one may agree that exchange prices (market prices) are relevant to external reporting and that, since economic decisions can affect only current and future outcomes, current and future exchange prices on the face of it are more relevant than past exchange prices. But one can still argue that constraints, such as the existence of uncertainty and a desire for objectivity and verifiability, make current market prices more reliable than future prices and, in many cases, past exchange prices more reliable than current prices.* The historical cost of an asset, being based on one or more transactions, has the supreme advantage of being verifiable. One may conclude, on grounds of reliability, therefore, that past exchange prices, that is, historical cost, are preferable.

Relevance and reliability sometimes appear to be opposites: one can have one or the other, but not both. This is not necessarily true. Many contracts are set in terms of past exchange prices. Past exchange prices are as relevant, therefore, for external reporting as current and future reporting. Reliability and relevance, thus, go hand in hand in many cases.

---

* These constraints are discussed in Chapter 5.

CHECKPOINTS

---

1. Contrast syntactic, semantic, and pragmatic objectives.
2. List two methods that have been suggested for improving matching in periods of changing prices.
3. Briefly explain the concept of accretion.
4. Provide a semantic argument against historical costs.
5. How can inventory measures be used to improve the prediction of future cash flows?
6. When are relevance and reliability supportive of one another?

CONCLUSION

In the valuation of assets, there is no single concept or procedure that is ideal in the presentation of the statement of financial position, in the determination of income, or in the presentation of other information relevant to the decisions of investors, creditors, and other users of financial statements. From a structural point of view, historical cost valuation is frequently assumed to be the ideal insofar as it is based on double-entry bookkeeping, which requires the recording of all resource changes and permits their subsequent identification.[23] However, formal structures can also be devised for other valuation concepts.

Accounting, as a result, is eclectic in nature, choosing output values in some cases and input values in others. Although output values may be better conceptually for the presentation of the financial statements, in many situations input values are thought to be more appropriate because they may represent the maximum value to the firm or because an output market does not exist, making it impossible to obtain exchange output values.

The problem is that we really don't know what measures users would like. For example, while theory suggested that inflation-adjusted numbers would be preferred by many users, practice revealed that they were not used. Alternatively, the information might have been available elsewhere at a lower cost, making its provision in the financial statements irrelevant. As a result, *SFAS 33,* "Financial Reporting and Changing Prices," which introduced these numbers on an experimental basis, was eventually abandoned.

Exhibit 14-3 summarizes the various asset valuation concepts and the general conditions under which they may be applicable.

EXHIBIT 14-3

Valuation Concept	Conditions Where Applicable*
Exchange output values:	When reliable evidence of output values is available as an indication of future cash receipts.
1. Discounted future expected cash receipts or service potentials.	When expected cash receipts or the equivalent are known or can be estimated with a high degree of certainty and when the waiting period is relatively long.
2. Current output values.	When current sales prices represent the future output price.
3. Current cash equivalents.	When the best alternative is orderly liquidation.
4. Liquidation values.	When the firm is not likely to be able to sell its product in the usual marketing channels or it is not likely to be able to utilize normal expected service values.
Exchange input values:	When reliable evidence of output values is not available or as an indication of future cash requirements.
5. Historical cost.	As a measure of current input value when acquired recently.
6. Current input costs.	When verifiable evidence of current input values can be obtained.
7. Discounted future costs.	When future services of known or estimated cost are purchased in advance instead of being acquired when needed.
8. Standard costs.	When they represent current costs under normal conditions of efficiency and capacity utilization.

* Assuming an objective of the prediction or future cash receipts or future cash requirements.

SUMMARY

Measurement in accounting is the process of assigning monetary amounts to objects or activities related to an enterprise. Typically, these monetary amounts are based on market prices that obtain in arm's-length transactions. There are a variety of markets and periods from which such prices could be drawn. A major line may be drawn between markets in which assets are acquired and markets in which they are disposed, the so-called wholesale and retail markets. These two markets, together with the period in which the measurement is made, namely past, present, or future, provide a wide range of possible measures for use in accounting. This range is further widened by concepts such as standard costs.

There is general agreement that assets should be entered at their acquisition (entry) price and removed at their disposal (exit) price. The disagreements revolve around what value to use between entry and exit. Some favor no revaluations unless the asset is sold. Others suggest that revaluations should be made to take into consideration events such as inflation, the signing of sales contracts, and so on. Still others would defer revaluation to exit prices until cash has been received for the asset.

Selecting which measure to use involves a careful consideration of the objectives of measurement in accounting. Some argue that measurement should simply follow the logic of historical cost accounting, others that measures should be chosen which have economic meaning. Still others would base their choice on the use to which the numbers are to be put. In many cases, the most relevant measure may not be reliable enough for a general-purpose statement. In all cases, asset measurement should be a function of the overall purposes of financial reporting.

DISCUSSION QUESTIONS

1. *Newsweek* reported that the state of Oregon was attempting to develop a set of rankings that would enable them to set priorities on who would receive health care. The dilemma faced by the state is that it does not have enough money to cover all those that need its services. Some rationing of services is deemed necessary—but how should it be done? The state's current answer is a scale based on costs, benefits, and an estimate of the resulting quality of life. Cheaper procedures yielding high benefits are preferred. One key to the system is clearly the measurement of costs: what accountants determine to be a costly procedure will receive a low ranking, other things being equal. Accountants, therefore, become very important people in such a system.

Required:

Use what you learned about measurement in your cost accounting courses to illustrate how rankings might be made to vary tremendously. (Hint: Consider different allocation schemes.)[24]

2. *Forbes* reported that, between 1986 and 1988, the Dow Jones Industrials wrote off over $10 billion against assets which were considered to be "impaired."[25] One example of an impaired asset is discussed in *SFAS 5* which states:

In some cases, the carrying amount of an operating asset not intended for disposal may exceed the amount expected to be recoverable through future use of that asset even though there has been no physical loss or damage of the asset or threat of such loss or damage. For example, changed economic conditions may have made recovery of the carrying amount of a productive facility doubtful. The question of whether, in those cases, it is appropriate to write down the carrying amount of the asset to an amount expected to be recoverable through future operations is not covered by this Statement.

Required:

How would you suggest that business account for impaired assets? How does one determine when an asset has been impaired? If it later appears that the asset was not permanently impaired, would you permit (or require that) business return the asset to its original carrying amount?

3. *Forbes* reported that The Hydraulic Company, the largest investor-owned water utility company in Connecticut, owns 20,000 acres of potentially prime residential property. Some of this land was purchased in the 1880s by the utility's second chief executive, Phineas T. Barnum of Barnum & Bailey fame, for around $1,000 per acre. In 1986, when the article was written, choice lots in that area were selling for over $100,000 each![26]

Required.

Make a case for why the land should be kept on the books at its original acquisition cost. What is the pragmatic effect of using the historical cost?

HOMEBUYING

Professor Tom Tunks was seeking to explain the ins and outs of assets to his students. Consider, he said, an example that is literally close to home: finding a place to live. The price that we are prepared to pay for a particular home (or for the rental of an apartment, as the case may be) is a function of many things. Certainly we find ourselves with bricks, mortar, a roof, and a yard—all of which need constant attention. More importantly, though, we have shelter, privacy, warmth, coolness, and one hopes, a healthy environment. We also have a neighborhood. For those with children the quality of the schools in the district is usually very important. For those who hate driving in peak times, close access to the office or the ability to drive across town or to travel by public transportation are equally important. We may end by debiting our personal balance sheets with the term "House" but really we have purchased a stream of intangible benefits. Once settled into one's new home, one finds its value changes over time for many different reasons, most of which have little to do with one's own actions. If a new school is added to the district, if our neighbors paint their homes and mow their lawns, if trees grow older, the value of the house is almost certain to increase. Another way of saying this is that our stream of (intangible) benefits increases in value.

What, finally, he asked, does this example teach us about the nature of assets? Does it shed any light on whether to include intangibles on a balance sheet?

METOLIUS ACRES *

It was early January 1984, and Ernest Gmur was trying to sort out his notes in respect to a central Oregon farm property called Metolius Acres. Herr Gmur hoped to be able to construct several sets of pro forma financial statements for the farm prior to continuing his discussions with a local realtor.

While his interest in the farm was primarily focused upon potential capital gains, he did want to have some idea of how well it might do as an operating farm. He knew that the investors he represented, through the Lucerne Investors Group of Zug, Switzerland, would expect a thorough analysis on his part.

Background

Herr Gmur had settled upon Metolius Acres as his prime purchase prospect after a three-day tour of farm property in central Oregon. He had been aided in his search by Ken Morrow, a local realtor. Gmur and Morrow had driven by a score of properties, actually visiting four or five of them in person. Metolius Acres, a 1,500-acre wheat farm with river frontage and a view of the Cascade Mountains struck him as being the most attractive prospect.

Unfortunately, the data that Mr. Morrow had been able to put together about the farm were neither complete nor well organized. Gmur understood that this was due to the fact that the farm in question was not actively on the market. Morrow, being a reasonably resourceful realtor, had gathered all of his data from sources external to the farm. A friend of his who managed the adjoining farm, an extension agent for the state university, and an employee of the local grain elevator had all supplied useful data.

Earlier that morning, Morrow had dropped by at Gmur's rented condominium with the following data:

Land Value.   Farms of similar size and condition are currently selling for $3,000 per acre. This would imply a value of $4.5 million.

Residential Buildings.   The residential portion of the buildings appear to be worth about $100,000.

Farm Buildings and Equipment.   Based on data from an adjoining farmer, the farm buildings and equipment appear to be worth about $150,000 and $200,000, respectively.

---

* This case was prepared by Professor M. Edgar Barrett. Copyright © 1979 and 1984 by M. Edgar Barrett.

Inventory.   Metolius Acres held title to 28,000 bushels of wheat at the local grain elevator as of December 31, 1983. This was in contrast to the fact that there had been none held there by the farm on January 1, 1983.

Sales.   The farm sold 140,000 bushels of wheat to the elevator operator during 1983. It appeared that this was their only sales outlet.

Prices.   The elevator operator had paid, on average, $3.60 per bushel for its 1983 purchases. The closing bid, on December 31, had been $3.95.

Operating Expenses.   The local agricultural extension agent had provided the following pro forma estimates for a wheat farm of about this size:

Seed, fertilizer, and chemicals	$ 0.415
Machinery rentals, with operator	0.116
Other costs.	0.094
Variable cost per bushel	$ 0.625
Salaries and wages	$ 54,000
Property taxes	26,000
Other expenses, including transient labor	28,000
Total annual costs	$108,000

After some questioning, Morrow opined that farm buildings and residential buildings should probably be depreciated over a 25-year life. Farm equipment, he thought, should be viewed as having a five-year life. Further, he thought, the farm's inventory—computed on a direct cost basis— could easily be financed by short-term debt. A cash balance of $10,000 should easily cover any routine cash needs.

As he started out the door, he added: "I assume, of course, that you're aware that most farms around here prepare income statements based on the assumption that revenue should be recognized when the wheat is harvested. Thus, you'll need to include the last 28,000 bushels in your sales computations."

Gmur told Morrow that this made no sense to him. "Besides," he said, "How could you bookkeep such a thing?"

Morrow, much to Gmur's surprise, responded to that aspect of the question quite quickly. "That's no problem. You can either revalue the inventory, or set up an unbilled accounts receivable account, whichever you prefer. Either way you'd reflect some profit on this winter wheat."

Required:

1. Prepare two pro forma income statements for 1983. The first should be based on normal accrual accounting, while the second should follow Morrow's advice.

2. Prepare two pro forma balance sheets for Metolius Acres as of December 31, 1983, based on the same assumptions as above.

3. Prepare two pro forma funds flow statements for 1983 based on similar assumptions.

4. Based on the case data, what should Gmur be prepared to pay for Metolius Acres?

Note: For purposes of the first three questions, you may assume that the following estimates of value, as of January 1, 1983, had been made available to you:

a. Land value	.$ 2,750 per acre
b. Residential buildings	90,000
c. Farm buildings	140,000
d. Farm equipment	190,000

You may also assume that there were no capitalized expenditures during 1983 in respect to the above four items. Finally, you may prepare the pro forma financial statements on the assumption that the farm had been purchased—at market value—on January 1, 1983.

PRIMARY SOURCES

Those interested in learning more about the topics covered in this chapter might begin by consulting these sources. Each has numerous citations.

Anthony, Robert N. *Tell It Like It Was* (Homewood, Ill.: Richard D. Irwin, 1983).

Edwards, Edgar O., and Philip W. Bell. *The Theory and Measurement of Business Income* (University of California Press, 1961).

Financial Accounting Standards Board, *Conceptual Framework for Financial Accounting and Reporting: Elements of Financial Statements and Their Measurement* (FASB Discussion Memorandum, 1976).

Ijiri, Yuji. *The Foundations of Accounting Measurement* (Englewood Cliffs, N.J.: Prentice Hall, 1967).

Staubus, George. "An Induced Theory of Accounting Measurement." *The Accounting Review*, January 1985, pp. 53–75.

Sterling, Robert R. "Costs (Historical versus Current) versus Exit Values." *Abacus,* 1981, pp. 93–129.

SELECTED ADDITIONAL READINGS

Asset Measurement and Valuation

American Accounting Association Committee on Accounting Valuation Bases. "Report of the Committee on Accounting Valuation Bases." *The Accounting Review,* Supplement 1972, pp. 535–73.

Barret, M. Edgar. "Proposed Bases for Asset Valuations." *Financial Executive,* January 1973, pp. 12–17.

Penman, Stephen H. "What Net Asset Value? An Extension of a Familiar Debate." *The Accounting Review,* April 1970, pp. 333–46.

Sprouse, Robert T. "Balance Sheet—Embodiment of the Most Fundamental Elements of Accounting Theory." *Foundations of Accounting Theory* (Gainesville: University of Florida Press, 1971), pp. 90–104.

Staubus, George J. "Measurement of Assets and Liabilities." *Accounting and Business Research,* Autumn 1973, pp. 243–62.

Sunder, Shyam. "Accuracy of Exchange Valuation Rules." *Journal of Accounting Research,* Autumn 1974, pp. 286–96.

Walker, R. G. "Asset Classification and Asset Valuation." *Accounting and Business Research,* Autumn 1974, pp. 286–96.

Historical Costs

Ijiri, Yuji. *A Defense for Historical Cost Accounting* (Lawrence, Kans.: Scholars Book, 1971), pp. 1–14.

Ijiri, Yuji. "The Significance of Historical Cost Valuation." *The Foundation of Accounting Measurement* (Englewood Cliffs, N.J.: Prentice Hall, 1967), pp. 64–67.

Ijiri, Yuji. *Historical Cost Accounting and Its Rationality* (Vancouver: Canadian Certified General Accountants' Research Foundation, 1981).

Mautz, Robert K. "A Few Words for Historical Cost." *Financial Executive,* January 1973, pp. 23–27, 64.

Current Costs

See Chapter 12 on inflation.

Value to the Enterprise

Brief, Richard P., and Joel Owen. "Present Value Models and the Multi-Asset Problem." *The Accounting Review,* October 1973, pp. 690–95.

Bromwich, Michael. "The Use of Present Value Valuation Models in Published Accounting Reports." *The Accounting Review,* July 1977, pp. 587–96.

Chambers, Raymond J. "Asset Management and Valuation." *Cost and Management,* March–April 1971, pp. 30–35.

Peasnell, K. V. "A Note on the Discounted Present Value Concept." *The Accounting Review,* January 1977, pp. 186–89.

Warrell, C. J. "The Enterprise Value Concept of Asset Valuation." *Accounting and Business Research,* Summer 1974, pp. 220–26.

Wright, F. K. "Relationship between Present Value and Value to the Owner." *Journal of Business Finance,* Summer 1973, pp. 19–25.

Market Values

Backer, Morton, assisted by Richard Simpson. *Current Value Accounting* (New York: Financial Executive Research Foundation, 1973), pp. 690–95.

Beidleman, Carl R. "Valuation of Used Capital Assets." *Accounting Research Study No. 7* (AAA, 1973). For a review, see Carl R. Beidleman, "Determinants of Second-Hand Asset Values." *Accounting and Business Research,* Spring 1974, pp. 102–15.

Bromwich, Michael. "Asset Valuation with Imperfect Markets." *Accounting and Business Research,* Autumn 1975, pp. 242–53.

Chambers, Raymond J. "Evidence for a Market-Selling Price Accounting System." In *Asset Valuation and Income Determination.* Edited by Robert R. Sterling (Lawrence, Kans.: Scholars Book, 1971), pp. 74–96.

Edwards, Edgar O. "The State of Current Value Accounting." *The Accounting Review,* April 1975, pp. 235–45.

King, Alfred M. "Fair Value Reporting." *Management Accounting,* March 1975, pp. 25–30.

Parker, James E. "Testing Comparability and Objectivity of Exit Value Accounting." *The Accounting Review,* July 1975, pp. 512–24.

Net Realizable Values and Replacement Costs

Benjamin, James. "Accuracy of the Period-End Method for Computing the Current Cost of Materials Used." *Abacus,* June 1973, pp. 73–80.

Cadenhead, Gary M. "Net Realizable Value Redefined." *Journal of Accounting Research,* Spring 1970, pp. 138–40.

Petri, Enrico. "Holding Gains and Losses as Cost Savings: A Comment on Supplementary Statement No. 2 on Inventory Valuation." *Accounting Review,* July 1973, pp. 483–88.

Revsine, Lawrence. *Replacement Cost Accounting* (Englewood Cliffs, N.J.: Prentice Hall, 1973).

Revsine, Lawrence. "A Test of the Feasibility of Preparing Replacement Cost Accounting Statements." *Objectives of Financial Statements, Vol. 2, Selected Papers* (AICPA, 1974), pp. 229–44.

The Lower-of-Cost-or-Market Rule

Holmes, William. "Market Value of Inventories—Perils and Pitfalls." *Journal of Commercial Bank Lending,* April 1973, pp. 30–35.

Parker, R. H. "Lower of Cost and Market in Britain and the United States: An Historical Survey." *Abacus,* December 1965, pp. 156–72.

Comparative Valuation Studies

Bedford, Norton, and James C. McKeown. "Comparative Analysis of Net Realizable Value and Replacement Costing." *The Accounting Review,* April 1972, pp. 333–38.

McKeown, James C. "Comparative Application of Market and Cost Based Accounting Models." *Journal of Accounting Research,* Spring 1973, pp. 62–99.

ENDNOTES

1. An emphasis on quantitative measurement is found in the postulates of *Accounting Research Study No. 1,* as one of the basic standards of *A Statement of Basic Accounting Theory,* and in the *Statements of Financial Accounting Concepts.*
2. See the Study Group on the Objectives of Financial Statements, *Objectives of Financial Statements* (AICPA, October 1973), p. 36 for such a suggestion.
3. See the discussion of continuity above, pp. 64–66.
4. Bridgette Y. Rose, *Dallas Times Herald,* June 23, 1990, p. A–17.
5. *ARB 43,* Ch. 4, par. 6, fn. 3.
6. Carr Thomas Devine, *Inventory Valuation and Periodic Income* (New York: Ronald Press, 1942), p. 59.
7. See Chapter 12 for more on accounting for current costs.
8. Except when the increase is considered to be a capital adjustment resulting from inflation. See Chapter 9.
9. J. Rhoads Foster and Barnard S. Rodey, *Public Utility Accounting* (Englewood Cliffs, N.J.: Prentice Hall, 1951), pp. 27–29.
10. *SFAC 5,* pars. 83 (b) and 84 (e).
11. See above, p. 710.
12. Chambers, Accounting Evaluation, p. 92.
13. FASB, *Accounting Standards: Current Text* I78.109.
14. See, for example, Edgar O. Edwards and Philip W. Bell, The Theory and Measurement of Business Income (Berkeley and Los Angeles: University of California Press, 1961); Committee on Concepts and Standards—Inventory Measurement, AAA, "A Discussion of Various Approaches to Inventory Measurement," supplementary statement no. 2, *Accounting Review,* July 1966, pp. 700–14; and Lawrence Revsine, *Replacement Cost Accounting* (Englewood Cliffs, N.J.: Prentice Hall, 1973).
15. See, for example, *Statements of Financial Accounting Concepts Nos. 2* and *6.*
16. *SFAC 2,* glossary.
17. *SFAC 1,* par. 37.
18. *SFAC 1,* par. 41.
19. *SFAC 1,* par. 43.
20. Robert T. Sprouse and Maurice Moonitz, "A Tentative Set of Broad Accounting Principles for Business Enterprises," *Accounting Research Study No. 3* (AICPA, 1962), p. 27.
21. Ibid., p. 28.
22. See Lawrence Revsine, *Replacement Cost Accounting,* p. 84.
23. See, for example, Yuji Ijiri, "A Defense for Historical Cost Accounting," in *Asset Valuation and Income Determination.* Edited by Robert R. Sterling (Lawrence, Kans.: Scholars Book, 1971). p. 13.

24. Melinda Beck, Nadine Joseph, and Mary Hager, "Not Enough for All People," *Newsweek,* May 14, 1990, pp. 53–55.

25. Penelope Wang, "You Know It When You See It," *Forbes,* July 25, 1988, p. 84.

26. Allan Dodds Frank, "Found Money," *Forbes,* August 11, 1986, p. 82.

Chapter 15

Depreciation and Maintenance

CHAPTER OBJECTIVES

After studying this chapter, you will be able to:

Compare the various definitions of depreciation that have been proposed in the literature.

Justify on the basis of a decline in service potential why one method of depreciation might be preferable to another.

Explain the advantages of a neutral allocation system.

Evaluate management's choice of a particular asset life and depreciation method.

CHAPTER OVERVIEW

Rational and Systematic Allocation

Accounting depreciation is the rational and systematic allocation of the original cost of an asset (less scrap value, if any) over the expected useful life of that asset. The process involves allocation only, so periodic depreciation expense lacks semantic interpretation.

Decline in Service Potential

Not content with this lack of interpretation, many accountants have sought to explain depreciation procedures in terms of a decline in service potential. Proponents then attempt to use the pattern of decline to justify different methods of depreciation.

Repairs and Maintenance

Repairs and replacements are intended to maintain the service potential of an asset. This link suggests that depreciation can be measured by the amount of maintenance necessary to keep an asset at its original service potential.

The Return on Investment

Most discussions of depreciation focus on assets in isolation, but companies are really collections of assets. The closer the company is to a steady state, the more similar various methods of depreciation become. At the limit, all depreciation methods produce exactly the same depreciation expense at the aggregate level.

In the traditional accounting structure, depreciation refers to the process of allocating the input valuation, usually the original or restated cost, of plant and equipment to the several periods expected to benefit from their acquisition and use.* The main emphasis of the depreciation process is generally on the computation of a periodic charge to be "matched" with the revenues reported in each period. This charge will be allocated either to expense as a period cost, or to the cost of a product. Seldom is the balance sheet valuation given much attention, except in consideration of the total amount to be allocated to future periods.

The most serious difficulty with depreciation is that no allocation method is fully defensible.[1] That is, defending one allocation method as being superior to all others is impossible. An additional difficulty is that before a pattern or formula for allocating the original or restated valuation (less scrap value) to periodic expenses or product costs can be applied, certain estimates must be made. These estimates include the following:

1. The valuation (cost or other basis) of the asset when acquired, or a restatement of this at a subsequent date.
2. The expected service life of the asset.
3. The scrap value or liquidation value at the end of the service life.

The last two (and in some cases the first) of these are ex ante measurements of uncertain future values. Although the estimates may be based on multiple probabilities, their reduction to single values is at best a difficult problem. The difficulty is partly the result of the complex interaction of benefits derived from assets used in association with others. It is also

---

* As stated in Chapter 8, *allocation* in accounting is the process of partitioning a set and of assigning the resulting subsets to separate classifications or periods of time.

partly the result of the little-understood relationship between costs and benefits at the individual asset level.

These estimates, even if they can be made, shift over time. The conventional application of depreciation methods, however, is static. It generally proceeds as if the estimates were constant over time. Therefore, even if an allocation procedure could be logically defended, it would be irrelevant to financial reporting because of the estimation difficulties involved.

To gain an appreciation of just some of the difficulties, consider the case of Blockbuster Entertainment. This Dallas-based company, founded in 1985, is a large and growing retail chain that leases videotapes. At its founding, the firm discovered that videotapes were being depreciated by members of the industry over periods ranging from nine months to five years! The company apparently decided to take the average of the industry and depreciate all its tapes on a straight-line basis over a period of 36 months. Less than two years later, in September 1987, Blockbuster announced that the firm would begin to make a distinction between "hits" and "classics." Hits, it claimed, have a life of eight months on average with 75 percent of the rentals derived in the first three months; classics, such as *Gone with the Wind,* last for an indeterminate time. In the third quarter of 1987, therefore, the company switched its hits to straight-line depreciation over nine months. Less than six months later, in January 1988, in an apparent response to a request by the SEC that the industry adopt standard depreciation policies, the company switched again. Now all films will be depreciated over three years—with no salvage values. New-release feature films, however, will be depreciated on an accelerated basis; base-stock films will be depreciated on a straight-line basis.

But which of today's hits will be tomorrow's classics? Which new-release features will turn out to be base stock? How many movies will not last even as long as three years? Which movies, if any, will later be rediscovered? Have we any guarantees that the industry will not find it necessary to adopt new rules a year from now? Would any one of their tapes be rented out if they did not have thousands of other titles in stock? Questions like these point to the ultimate dilemma of all methods of depreciation: no conclusive reason exists for picking any one method. The dilemma is not that there are *no* solutions; rather it is that there are *too many* solutions, none of which is fully defensible.[2] That is, defending one depreciation method as being superior to all others is not possible. Some have gone so far as to suggest that all depreciation methods are arbitrary and do not result in measurements that can be defended within reasonable limits. Therefore, because no depreciation procedure can be relevant for income reporting, they would abandon depreciation entirely and replace it with alternative reporting methods.*

---

* Those familiar with management accounting will know that one is advised to ignore depreciation in most managerial decisions.

Regardless of these difficulties, researchers and writers on the subject of depreciation continue to attempt to defend depreciation procedures on the basis of economic interpretation. They also attempt defenses on behavioral grounds primarily relating to the relevance of the depreciation figures for decision making. This real-world interpretation is frequently assumed to be derived from one of the following concepts:

1. A measurement of the decline in the value of the asset (restated for general or specific price changes).
2. An allocation of the cost or other basis according to the benefits expected to be received in each period.

Attempts to defend depreciation on behavioral grounds include estimation theory and purpose utility.

This chapter begins with a discussion of the traditional view of accounting depreciation as simply a rational and systematic allocation of costs. It notes that many researchers have sought to escape the confines of this approach by giving semantic interpretation of depreciation. The next section discusses the major efforts that have occurred in defining depreciation as the decline in service potential of the asset. This definition provides a framework within which alternative depreciation methods may be evaluated. This framework leads into a discussion of repair, replacement, and maintenance policy, which is seen to be a major determinant of depreciation and, perhaps, even a source of measurement of depreciation. The chapter closes with a note on how the usual focus on individual assets obscures what is happening at the aggregate level. This is the level seen by the user and, therefore, the only level that is relevant in financial reporting.

RATIONAL AND SYSTEMATIC ALLOCATION

As early as 1942, the AIA's Committee on Terminology noted that accountants use the term *depreciation* in a specialized sense which differs not only from the colloquial, but also from the way the term is used in engineering, and in a way that is far removed from the root meaning of the word itself. The Latin *pretium* means price or value—hence "de-pretium" means a decline in price or value. Ignoring this origin of the word, the Committee settled on a definition of *depreciation* as a systematic and rational method of allocating costs to periods in which benefits are received.[3] As the Committee put it:

> Depreciation accounting is a system of accounting which aims to distribute the cost or other basic value of tangible capital assets, less salvage (if any), over the estimated useful life of the unit (which may be a group of assets) in a systematic and rational manner. It is a process of allocation, not of valuation.[4]

They added to this the rider that:

> Depreciation for the year is the portion of the total charge under such a system that is allocated to the year. Although the allocation may properly take into account occurrences during the year, it is not intended to be a measurement of the effect of all such occurrences.

In other words, the Committee was at pains to point out that annual depreciation has little semantic interpretation. At best, the annual allocation is simply a fraction of the total depreciation cost.

In particular, annual depreciation, as accountants use that term, is not, as the U.S. Supreme Court suggested, the "loss which takes place in a year."[5] As *ARB 16* (p. 142) said, depreciation is not an "attempt to measure the exhaustion which actually takes place within a given period." This position was later reaffirmed by *ARB 20* (p. 165), which stated, ". . . annual depreciation, or depreciation for the year, is the portion of the estimated total depreciation that is allocated to the year, and as already noted, this amount has no necessary relation to either the occurrences within the year or the changes in value during the period."

The AIA's definition is static, meaning that the initial cost or other value is not changed during the life of the asset: the sum of all depreciation charges is equal to the initial value less any salvage value. The definition does not suggest how the cost or other value should be distributed; any allocation procedure that is systematic and rational is perfectly sufficient. However, the requirement that the method be rational probably means that it should be reasonably related to the expected benefits in each case.

The AIA's definition of depreciation is as interesting for what it excludes as for what it includes. It does not include, for instance, a decline in the value of assets even though that would seem to be the understanding most people have of the word. The definition thereby excludes value declines due to price changes; that is, *depreciation,* as accountants use the term, is not the opposite of what they mean by *appreciation.* It also excludes a decline in value due to obsolescence and the exhaustion of an asset's useful life. Finally, the definition excludes computations of the replacement cost of the asset, since the focus of amortization is on the existing asset only.

The Committee on Terminology, after reviewing the various meanings that depreciation did not have for accountants, added wistfully that a great deal of confusion and much misapprehension could have been avoided if a term such as *amortization* had been used in place of *depreciation.* But, by 1942, the term was already too embedded in the accountant's vocabulary to be removed.[6]

The IRS fared better than the accounting profession because it abandoned the use of the word *depreciation* many years ago. The term did appear in the 1909 and the 1913 Tax Acts, but was discarded in the 1916

Act. Instead, the IRS, at the urging of accountants, uses the lengthier, but more precise, "reasonable allowance for the exhaustion, wear and tear of property used in the trade or business, including a reasonable allowance for obsolescence."[7]

The most common "rational and systematic method" is straight-line depreciation. The great virtue of this method is that it is simple to apply and easy to understand. Other commonly used methods are sum-of-the-years' digits and double-declining balance. Neither of these two methods pretends to have any theoretical content. They are simply methods allowed by the IRS to provide favorable tax treatment to companies. Their only virtue is that they permit companies to defer their taxes.

Given the conclusion that amortization is nothing more than an allocation of costs over the life of the asset, there seems to be little more to add. However, researchers have not been willing to leave the matter there. A vast literature has arisen explaining why certain methods should be used and what the effect of other methods would be—usually harmful. This literature is reviewed with the warning that, in the conclusion to this chapter, we will return to the conclusion of this section: accounting amortization is simply the division of the total cost into portions. There is no theoretical basis for preferring any one method over any other. In short, absent tax reasons, use the simplest method at all times—usually straight-line depreciation.

CHECKPOINTS

1. What is the usual understanding of the word *depreciation?*
2. What do accountants mean by the word *appreciation?*
3. Why is annual depreciation expense less interpretable than the total depreciation expense over the life of the asset?
4. Why do many argue that straight-line depreciation is the best alternative?

DECLINE IN SERVICE POTENTIAL

The definition of *depreciation* as a systematic and rational method of allocating costs to periods is purely syntactic. The resulting allocation has no real-world connotations. As already noted, this definition suggests no means of computing appropriate numbers. The definition is silent also on how to choose among depreciation methods such as straight line and double-declining balance. In an attempt to provide support for choosing particular methods of depreciation, researchers and writers on the subject of depreciation have made frequent attempts to define depreciation in economic or behavioral terms, primarily relating to the relevance of the depreciation figures for decision making.

Some of the proposals that have emerged from these writings have shaded into definitions of depreciation rejected in the *Accounting Terminology Bulletins* and have evoked considerable controversy. Invariably, these proposals involve either an examination of depreciation's cause or its supposed relationship to benefits that are received from the use of the asset. Often, the benefits are defined as the services one can expect to reap from the asset. The cause is usually specified as a decline in asset value resulting from wear and tear and obsolescence of an asset on its "irresistible march to the junk heap."[8]

The 1957 Committee on Concepts and Standards of the American Accounting Association asserted that depreciation could be interpreted as the decline in service potential of the long-term assets. The Committee added that the decline in service potential may be the result of physical deterioration, consumption through use, or loss in economic value because of obsolescence or change in demand.[9] Under their definition, the asset represents a storehouse of services that can be released over the life of the asset. Whenever a portion of these services expires through use, wear and tear, or other cause, the quantity of service potential declines. Thus, a portion of the cost of the asset should be transferred to an expense, another asset, or a loss account. This approach was also taken in *ARS 3,* which stated that:

> Depreciation accounting is the process of allocating the cost or other basis of the services rendered by items of plant and equipment to the products or periods that used those services.[10]

SFAC 6 also states that wear and tear from use is a major cause of depreciation.[11]

Definitions based on service potential are static, but less so than those conventional approaches based on the concept of rational and systematic allocation. The service potential definitions do recognize that the loss in service potential may be irregular. These definitions also recognize that depreciation is subject to many factors that could not be foreseen when the asset was acquired. The conventional approach assumes that the conditions anticipated at the time of acquisition will continue without material change over the expected life of the asset. All definitions, though, are based on single-valued expectations regarding the total expected quantity of potential service or the expected life of the asset.

Decline in Physical Services

The primary notion in these definitions is that of physical services available for the use or consumption of the holder of the asset. Surrogates for expected services include the number of units that will be produced over its life; the number of hours, days, or months that the asset is expected to be in operation; the kilowatt hours of electric power that will be used in production; or some other intermediate unit of production input or output. At this level of analysis, depreciation is based strictly on physical usage. For example, a truck may be expected to operate for 100,000 miles during its lifetime. If it accumulates 20,000 miles in its first year, 20 percent of its cost will be charged to depreciation. The result is a variable depreciation expense.

For many types of assets, the assumption of a variable depreciation expense is reasonable, particularly if the physical wear and tear is more important than economic obsolescence, or if the expected services can normally be expected to be obtained before obsolescence sets in. Accordingly, if an asset's services are not used in one year, no depreciation should be recorded because no decline in service value occurs. This approach is similar to the expense of using a coal pile; if no coal is used while the plant is idled, or shut down temporarily, no charge is made for coal during that period. Even though obsolescence may be a significant factor in determining the expected life of an asset, the activity method of depreciation may be appropriate if the obsolescence can be anticipated and if the approximate usage to be obtained from the asset can be estimated. Under these conditions, the cost of the asset can be assumed to represent the purchase of a given number of service units, and the allocation of the cost to these units is then reasonable. The main objective of depreciation applied in this case is the allocation of input costs to each service unit; the measurement of the decline in service value may be of secondary importance.

A major question that arises is whether the total costs should be allocated over all the potential services, or over just the services that the firm anticipates using in operations. An asset is usually acquired with certain services in mind. Therefore, allocating the initial input cost less salvage, if any, over the period of anticipated use can be logical. For example, a crane could be acquired for a specific contract. Its total cost less salvage should be assigned to the contract—even though it is used for only a few days and remains idle for the rest of the time. If this process is the most economical way of getting the job done, there is no reason why the total cost should not be assigned to the anticipated use.

In other cases, an asset may be acquired with the anticipation of using it only 3 or 4 years out of 10. If utilizing the services in all years is not feasible, there is some logic in charging depreciation only in the years of anticipated use. It was for this purpose that the asset was acquired, and to insist on depreciation in every year is not consistent with the pattern of expected benefits. On the other hand, if an asset is acquired for use and forced to remain idle for one of many reasons, depreciation should be recorded if the service units expected to be obtained during the period of idleness cannot be obtained in a latter period. A charge should be made for the services expired, even though they serve no benefit to the firm; however, the depreciation charge may be shown as a loss, rather than as a charge to current operations.

Pricing These Services: Historical or Current Cost?

The allocation of physical services has been the focus thus far. Arriving at a price for the services for purposes of depreciation is necessary.* If the original cost of the asset is the base, the services are priced at their original cost. Furthermore, if the price is determined by dividing the total expected services into the total cost, then the approach is similar to the straight-line method in the sense that it assigns an *equal* amount to each unit of service. However, there is no basis for assuming equal costs per unit of service. Furthermore, because of the necessity of waiting for the later units of service, the total service value does not, in fact, decline uniformly, unless interest is assumed to be zero.

The 1964 AAA Committee on Concepts and Standards—Long-Lived Assets also defined depreciation as an expiration of service potential of the asset. The committee stated, however, that "depreciation must be based on the *current* cost of restoring the service potential consumed during the period (emphasis added)."[12] *ARS 3* also suggested that current replacement costs are more significant than historical costs, particularly when some significant event occurs in the organization of the firm. The authors of *ARS 3* assumed that depreciation represents an allocation of current costs, and that the depreciation charge for a specific period is the current cost of the services consumed in that period. These definitions are based on a decline in the value (the service potential) of the asset, but are also related to the capital-maintenance concept. This approach is developed further later.

One problem with a current cost approach is that it very rapidly brings one to a definition of depreciation as a decline in value, one which was rejected earlier. This is not to say that a value-based definition is not appropriate—merely that it is different from pure cost allocation. Also, once one has accepted value depreciation, why should one not introduce value appreciation? This is what the authors of *ARS 3* did, bringing down a firestorm of criticism on their heads.

The advantages and disadvantages of current costs are discussed further in Chapter 14. One should keep in mind that nonmonetary assets, by their very nature, represent large blocks of potential services. The use of current costs, therefore, does not alleviate the problem of making allocations to specific periods.

---

* As *ARB 16*, p. 138, succinctly noted, accounting depreciation, unlike engineering depreciation, corresponds to wages, not labor, that is, to a dollar rather than a physical quantity.

The Net Revenue Contribution Approach

A modification of the production method is allocation on the basis of revenue. For major components, this method may be a good approximation of use, and it has the added advantage of taking into consideration changes in revenue per unit. But this approach has all the other disadvantages of the production method. Furthermore, it is inapplicable in those cases in which goods are produced for stock and where overall revenue cannot be reasonably attributed to specific assets. Notice that an allocation on the basis of revenue does not justify an allocation on the basis of net income; none of the objectives of depreciation is met by using income as a basis for allocation.

A variation of the revenue method defines the cost of services using the so-called *net revenue contribution* as a surrogate for the cost of the services. Net revenue contribution is defined as the revenue generated by the asset less the operating expenses, including maintenance and repair costs. The total cost of the asset is then allocated in proportion to the net revenue contribution received each period.* An example illustrates one approach which uses a constant depreciation cost-to-contribution ratio. The ratio can be computed by the following formula:

$$m = \frac{C}{\sum_{t=1}^{n} R_t} \tag{3}$$

where

m = The ratio of historical cost to the total expected net revenue contribution.

C = The cost or other basis (less scrap value) of the asset.

R_t = The expected net revenue contribution in each year (t) during the life of the asset.

Depreciation in each year can be computed as follows:

$$D_t = mR_t$$

where D_t is the depreciation allocated to year t.

Assume that an asset costs $2,025 and that the net revenue contributions are expected to be $500, $600, $1,000, $400, and $500, respectively, for each of the five years. Assuming no scrap value, the ratio would be 0.675 (computed by dividing $2,025 by $3,000). The depreciation for each of the five years would be as shown in Exhibit 15-1.

---

* No depreciation is allocated to years in which the net revenue is negative.

EXHIBIT 15-1 Computation of Depreciation Based on a Constant Ratio of Cost to Expected Net Revenue Contribution

Year	*(1)* Expected Net Revenue Contribution	*(2)* Ratio	*(3)* Depreciation
1	$ 500	0.675	$ 338
2	600	0.675	405
3	1,000	0.675	675
4	400	0.675	270
5	500	0.675	337
	$3,000		$2,025

A major advantage of the approach is its simplicity. It has the additional virtue of ensuring that annual net income from the asset has the same pattern as the net revenue contribution. The net revenue contribution in the second year, for instance, is one-fifth of the total, that is, 600/3,000. The net income in each period is the net revenue contribution less depreciation. This is $195 in the second year and $975 in total. The method ensures that the net income in the second year is one-fifth of the total. The importance of this approach is that depreciation, which is so ill defined, is not permitted to destroy the relationships among numbers which are perhaps better defined. The allocation is said to be *neutral*.[13]

The net revenue contribution method may be used to justify various commonly used forms of depreciation. A flat net revenue contribution stream may be used to justify the use of straight-line depreciation; a declining contribution may be used to justify the use of accelerated depreciation.

For an asset such as a hotel, the revenues may be greater when it is newer and more prestigious than when it is older. Eventually, it may be converted into an office building and provide an entirely different type of service with lower revenues. If variable costs can also be estimated, the net revenue contributions from the entire hotel may be used as a rough guide for the allocation of all specific assets associated with the net revenues from operating the hotel. Also, recomputing the net revenue contribution pattern expected for the remaining life of the asset is possible at any time during its life so that the actual ratios used in computing the depreciation may come close to the final ex post ratio. To this extent, it may be possible for external users of financial statements to predict future relationships, but only if the ratio of cost to net revenue contributions is relatively constant for additional investments by the firm.

One of the disadvantages of the net revenue contribution approach is that it may cause the rates of return on invested assets to vary widely because it does not adjust for the timing of the net revenue contributions. Interactions among the several assets and other factors used by the firm are not eliminated even if the ratios are computed from groups of assets. Another major disadvantage is that this method does not escape the need to make arbitrary allocations. The determination of the contribution is the result of two allocation processes. First, the total revenues of the firm must be allocated to specific periods of time. Second, the total revenues of each period must be allocated to specific assets or asset classes.

Measuring either the ex ante or ex post net revenue contributions in the several periods during the use of an asset is rarely possible, because of the many interactions of the production functions and their inputs. Most defenses of depreciation methods merely assume the plausibility of certain patterns and amounts of revenue contributions. The association of these net revenue contributions to real-world observations has been made only in very general terms or indirectly by observing market prices of used assets.

Pros and Cons

The advantage of the service potential approach to depreciation is that allocation can be adapted to unanticipated changes in the pattern of use. This adaptability is particularly useful in those cases where the decline in the expected future benefits is more closely related to use than to obsolescence and the passage of time.

There are several disadvantages, though. First, as noted by many, including the FASB, the causes of depreciation, such as wear and tear, in any given period cannot normally be measured. Thus, no traceable relationship exists between the allocations and specific revenues or the periods to which they are charged. There is no reason to believe that a truck or a car yields exactly the same service every mile. Consider, for example, the miles driven by a salesman to a filling station. These miles are, strictly speaking, valueless. With no obvious relationships on which to build, allocations may result in capricious charges to income, which are not likely to be relevant to the predictions and decisions of investors and other external users of financial reports. Since no causal relationship can be specifically identified, and the relationship to benefits is at best indirect, the FASB leaves depreciation where it found it, that is, as a systematic and rational allocation of costs to periods in which the assets are assumed to be used.

Second, even if one could identify the services being used, one would still have to attach a cost or value to each unit of service. There is no reason for the rate at which services are being used to be flat, which is what this method assumes. Semantic interpretation in terms of the exhaustion of the store of physical services does not produce, therefore, a nonarbitrary measurement of depreciation.

Furthermore, both the choice of a measure of the physical service of the asset and the allocation of cost to each service unit are likely to be based upon expediency rather than logic. The service unit is likely to be some measure that is readily available, such as direct labor hours or units of production, and each unit of such service is usually assumed to provide equal benefit value, or net revenue contribution. Different costs can be assigned to different service units, but it is seldom possible to do so in a logical manner, except by resorting to an alternative cost of obtaining the same services or by making expectations regarding changes in total revenues. Taking changes in variable costs or cost savings into account is generally difficult.

Two other problems, typically encountered in the use of the services or production method, as it is typically applied, are:

1. No consideration is usually given to increasing repair and maintenance costs, decreasing operating efficiencies, or declining revenues.
2. Uncertainties regarding the quantity of services that the asset is capable of producing can be taken into consideration by using the expected value based on engineering probability estimates, but the probability of early obsolescence is more difficult to anticipate.

Finally, one must not forget that accounting depreciation is simply a means of amortizing the cost of an asset over its useful life. The term has no further meaning. If one wishes to let net income move in the same direction as the net revenue contribution, then there is logic in using straight-line depreciation when net revenue is constant, an accelerated method when net revenue is declining, and an increasing-charge method when net revenue is increasing. In doing this, one is ensuring an arithmetical outcome—nothing more. One must not, as Justice Jackson once said, allow our ardent quest for certitude to persuade us ". . . to pay an irrational reverence to a technique which uses symbols of certainty, even though experience again and again warns us that they are delusive."

CHECKPOINTS

1. How did the FASB define an asset? (Hint: Review Chapter 12.)
2. Provide a definition of depreciation based on the service potential of the asset.
3. How might one price the services provided by an asset? (Hint: Review Chapter 14.)
4. Define net revenue contribution.
5. Using the net revenue contribution approach, provide a justification for the use of accelerated methods of depreciation.

REPAIRS AND MAINTENANCE

It is useful at this point to reexamine the nature of the assets that are being depreciated since we tend to discuss depreciation in terms of a single asset. We overlook the fact that most assets are actually combinations of other assets. Consider, for instance, a truck. It can be considered a single item but it can equally be viewed as an assembly of major parts, such as a frame, an engine, and a transmission. Each of these consists of a variety of more minor parts such as the carburetor, the engine valves, and so on. When we speak of the decline in service potential of that truck, we could equally be speaking of the decline in service potential of the parts which make up the truck, but which are themselves assets. Furthermore, one can interpret the decline in service potential of the asset as a whole to be a function of the decline in service potential of each of its parts.

Accounting for Collections of Assets

Assets are often pooled for ease of accounting. Pools of similar assets are known as *groups*; pools of dissimilar assets are known as *composites*. New individual assets are added to the pool at cost. Old assets are removed from the pool at a net book value equal to their disposal value, that is, no profit or loss is recognized on their disposal.

Accounting for a truck, although not usually viewed in this light, is really a variation of accounting for a composite of assets. Replacing a wheel on a truck is not very different from replacing a truck in a pool of motor vehicles. As replacement parts are needed, so they are added to the truck. The old parts, which typically have no residual value, are simply scrapped. Where they do have scrap value, that value is credited back to the cost of the truck.

As parts of the truck deteriorate, so the truck's ability to deliver its services is hindered. Its service potential, therefore, declines. This decline in service potential was defined earlier as depreciation. However, what if each of the parts of the truck was replaced when it became worn? The asset would remain at all times in its original condition and no decline in its service potential would occur. Stated otherwise, instead of depreciation, one would incur maintenance expenses. Looked at in this light, depreciation represents the maintenance the company is unwilling or unable to do. Depreciation due to wear and tear is no different than the cost of repairing and replacing parts. This analysis led the 1964 AAA Committee on Concepts and Standards—Long-Lived Assets to define depreciation as the "cost of restoring the service potential consumed during the period."[14] While this cost may be hard to estimate, it remains true that depreciation "is always closely related to a maintenance policy that is assumed to be in force in respect of the property to which it relates."[15]

A method of depreciation that does use the link between maintenance and depreciation is called the *replacement* method. When a firm has a large number of similar assets, the decline in service potential of the pool can be approximated by the cost of current replacements. This cost is used in place of a depreciation expense. (The *retirement* method uses the historical cost of the assets being replaced in place of depreciation expense.) In a large mature firm, replacements occur regularly and provide a good substitute for depreciation charges. The cost of the original asset is retained as the book value of the asset in use regardless of the change in costs at the time of replacement. A modification of this method requires the use of a reserve account and a periodic charge to depreciation during the early years of the life of the enterprise until the replacements reach a relatively constant level.

The replacement method is generally considered obsolete, but it is still used by railroads for ties, rails, tie plates, and ballast. It is also used in the trucking industry for tires. Its current counterpart in general financial accounting is the charging of the cost of ordinary repairs to expense as they occur, while continuing to carry the original cost of the replaced parts in the total cost of the main asset.

One of the difficulties in estimating depreciation on this basis is that the treatment of maintenance cost depends in part upon the manner in which assets are pooled or aggregated. If each component is depreciated separately on the basis of its own expected life, the replacement of a component requires the retirement of the old component and the installation of a new one. For example, if the tires on a truck are depreciated separately, they would be depreciated over their individual expected lives and written off when they are replaced; the new tires would then be capitalized and depreciated over their expected lives. On the other hand, if the tires are treated as part of the truck, their replacement might well be treated as an ordinary repair and expensed. One has to distinguish, therefore, between replacement of components of the original asset and new components. Making this distinction is not always easy. Despite the practical problems, the conceptual link between depreciation and maintenance remains valuable.

One must also distinguish between foregone repairs and increases in other costs. Repairs and maintenance can frequently be delayed or minimized, with the result that other operating expenses, such as fuel and labor costs, may increase. Thus, if the value of the output of the asset remains constant, the net contribution of the asset declines. This decline in net contribution also occurs as a result of an increasing number of repairs as the asset grows older. Frequent repairs curtail the time available for production or use, and thus diminish the output of the equipment. The several concepts of depreciation based on service contributions require that this decline in output potential be taken into consideration.

Asset Lives

Absent economic obsolescence and a replacement policy, the life of an asset, such as a truck, is the life of the first critical part that fails. Without repair and replacement policies in place, the physical life of an asset is equal to the shortest physical life of its critical parts—a worn tire would mean the end of the truck. Worn tires, though, are usually repaired or replaced. In so doing, the life of the truck asset is extended until some other part fails and needs repair or replacement. In some cases, assets can be preserved almost indefinitely for historical or cultural reasons; but the cost of doing so is generally greater than the cost of replacement with a new asset. Furthermore, obsolescence usually makes such continued maintenance uneconomical. The point is that, within certain broad limits, the life of an asset is not a given, but is determined by the repair and replacement policy of the company. A truck which is regularly maintained by having parts replaced and repaired whenever they fail will have a longer life than one that is neglected. Maintenance and repair policies, therefore, determine, in part, the life of an asset.

The reverse holds too: a company's repair and replacement policy is a function of the expected life of the asset. For instance, repair and maintenance costs can be reduced to a minimum whenever the economic life of an asset is expected to be quite short. For example, if specialized equipment is to be used for the completion of a specific contract and abandoned upon the termination of the contract, the most economical level of repair and maintenance expenditures would be the minimum necessary to keep the equipment operating only until the end of the contract. Usually, then, the life of an asset is determined by what may be considered an optimum level of repair and maintenance expenditures, or by economic obsolescence, whichever is the shorter.

One effect of this close connection between maintenance policies and the life of an asset is that, if repair or maintenance expenditures are delayed or curtailed below those required to obtain the expected economic life of the asset, the current depreciation allocation should be increased accordingly.

Budgeting for Repairs

The term *maintenance* generally refers in this context to the normal upkeep of property in an efficient operating condition. Maintenance is frequently considered to include normal, recurring repairs. The term *repair* refers to the restoration of an asset without increasing its expected service life capacity. However, repairs may be of two general types: (1) the adjustment of a machine or working parts and the labor necessary to restore a damaged or worn component to its original condition and (2) the replacement of one or more parts of an asset with new parts without replacing the entire asset. Maintenance expenses and repairs of the first type may increase over the life of an asset because of the increasing need for adjustment and care when items of plant and equipment become worn through use or age. This increase is partly a function of replacement policies. If some of the components are replaced every year or two and if others are replaced at longer intervals, there will be a bunching of replacements in the later years of the asset's life. This bunching results in increasing repair expenses as the asset ages.

Accountants have occasionally recommended that repair costs should be equalized over the life of an asset by setting up a budgetary reserve. The need for this allocation or equalization of repair costs is based on the assumption that the annual depreciation charge represents an allocation of the original cost of the asset only, without regard to the timing of repairs. The recommendation usually requires an estimation of the total repair costs during the life of the asset and an allocation to each period by setting up an allowance or reserve for repairs. This allowance account is usually classified as a liability reserve. However, it does not have the usual characteristics of a liability, because it is based on the occurrence of a future event.

A better alternative to treating budgeted repair costs as a liability would be to treat them as a contra to the related asset account, similar to the treatment of accumulated depreciation. This treatment is more logical, because it represents an additional allocation of costs of the parts with lives shorter than that of the major components. Therefore, it is depreciation and could just as well be credited to the accumulated depreciation account. When repairs are actually incurred, they would be debited to the allowance for repairs account or the accumulated depreciation account. This procedure is similar, therefore, to the treatment of major repairs. Although it would be more precise to write off an asset and capitalize the repair costs, determining the cost of the item being replaced is usually too difficult. But this procedure also has the same limitations as the similar method suggested for handling major repairs.

Capital Maintenance

The view of assets as composites can lead one to look on a company as a giant asset with all its component parts, such as walls, roofs, machines, and delivery vans being replaced on a more or less regular basis. Under the going-concern concept, the firm is assumed to have an indefinite life. As a result, at the firm level there is no depreciation. Instead, there is the continual expense of replacing and repairing the parts. Of course, management can elect not to restore a part. When that happens, the service potential of the firm, as a whole, is reduced. Equally, management can elect to add parts, thus increasing the service potential of the firm as a whole.

The composite view of assets leads in turn to a definition of depreciation in terms of capital maintenance. This concept of depreciation, which is broader than that of decline in service potential, says that income emerges only if the invested capital at the end of the period exceeds the invested capital at the beginning (assuming no capital transactions or dividend payments during the period). The definitions of the FASB, the AAA statement, and the AAA committee all rely on the maintenance approach, but the concept of capital to be maintained is slightly different in each case. The FASB's definition requires that the original monetary investment be maintained (financial capital maintenance) at least by the end of the asset's life; recovery of original cost may occur over the life of the asset in any rational manner. The AAA definition of depreciation requires that the service potential, or its equivalent in terms of the original cost of services, be maintained. The AAA committee definition emphasizes the maintenance of operating capacity or physical capital maintenance. In none of these cases, however, is actual replacement or equivalent replacement necessary; the failure to maintain physical capital or dollar capital because of a loss or for other reasons does not deny the existence of the depreciation.

The advantage of the capital-maintenance concept is that it permits the recognition of changes in the value of the dollar and in specific replacement values. The capital to be maintained can be interpreted as the original investment expressed in terms of a common dollar, or it can be expressed in terms of the current replacement values at the beginning or end of the accounting period.

The main disadvantage of the capital-maintenance concept is that it results in a failure to permit a separation of operating income from extraordinary gains and losses. Unless other criteria are introduced, it does not provide a basis for determining normal operating depreciation separately from abnormal losses of service potential. The concept also requires that one specify more precisely what definition of capital is to be used. Therefore, the concept is not a precise definition that can be used as a specific guide; rather, it is only a broad guide subject to further interpretation.

Inventory Method.   Probably the earliest method of recognizing depreciation was a capital-maintenance method. It revalued the assets periodically or at the termination of a venture. The inventory valuation was based on either the valuation of the asset to the new venture or on the cost of the asset adjusted for any loss in productive efficiency. The first basis may be determined by a liquidation value or by a current market price. The second valuation basis results in what is called observed depreciation, which is based on the change in engineering efficiency of the asset rather than the decline in service potential.

The use of a liquidation value or current market price is advantageous, because it permits a real-world interpretation and avoids the necessity for arbitrary allocations. However, the decline in these prices does not represent what is normally thought of as depreciation because it includes gains and losses due to market factors. The use of observed depreciation is usually thought to be inadequate, because it does not take into consideration such economic facts as expected obsolescence.

Although the inventory method is obsolete, it is occasionally applied in one of several forms for reasons of convenience. For example, it is often used in depreciating tools. An inventory is taken at the end of each period and valued on the basis of its physical condition. The depreciation expense is computed by subtracting this inventory valuation from the sum of the beginning inventory and the cost of tools acquired during the period.

CHECKPOINTS

1. Distinguish composite depreciation from group depreciation.
2. In what ways does maintenance policy affect the life of an asset?
3. Define depreciation in terms of maintenance expenses.
4. How will increasing repair costs affect the net revenue contribution? Assume that it is otherwise constant.
5. Define the concept of "depreciating" the enterprise as whole.

RETURN ON INVESTMENT

By far the most common form of depreciation involves what might be called *time-based depreciation*. These are allocation methods that allocate costs to periods and not to services. The major example of this approach is straight-line depreciation; double-declining balance is another example. The basic assumption underlying these methods is that depreciation is a function of time rather than use. Obsolescence and deterioration over time are considered to be determining factors in the decline in service potential, as opposed to physical wear and tear caused by use. Thus, the service potential of the asset is assumed to decline by a set amount each period. The total cost of the services used in any period is assumed to be the same regardless of the extent of use.

The Single-Asset Case

Time-based methods, as is often noted, can give the appearance of a rising rate of return on invested capital (ROI). For example, take the case where straight-line depreciation is used, and the asset generates a constant stream of income. Consider, specifically, a machine that is acquired at a cost of $6,000 and is expected to last three years with no scrap value. Assume that straight-line depreciation is used. Also assume that the investment provides a constant net revenue stream (total revenues less all operating costs other than depreciation) of $2,400. Net income, which is net revenue less depreciation, is $400, therefore. The return on investment is successively:

$$\text{Year one:} \quad 400/6,000 = 6.67\%$$

$$\text{Year two:} \quad 400/4,000 = 10.00\%$$

$$\text{Year three:} \quad 400/2,000 = 20.00\%$$

More sophisticated analyses, which track the disposition of the cash flows each year, can be done, but this simple analysis makes the point: As the net book values decrease, so, all other things being equal, the return on investment increases.

The concern is that false conclusions may be drawn during each three-year period. An upward trend is apparent but not real. Projections based on this trend would be erroneous. Furthermore, this kind of analysis can lead to the erroneous belief that only a technologically vastly improved machine with considerable operating capacity could challenge the existing asset before the end of its physical life. Like a one-horse carriage, the existing machine would be used until it finally fell apart, or the horse died.

The Multiple-Asset Case

The analysis that has just been done assumes that a company has a single asset only. Alternatively, the company is assumed to have purchased all its assets at a single point in time. This assumption is completely unrealistic. Instead, most companies have collections of assets that have been accumulated over a period of time. Consider a company that purchases one new asset a year for $6,000. Assume, as before, that these assets have a life of three years and that they have no scrap value. Assume further to make a point, any depreciation pattern: say $2,500, $1,500, and $2,000. The only stipulation is that the three numbers must sum to $6,000.

After three years, the company will have three assets: one that is brand-new, one that is a year old, and one that is two years old. Denote these A_0, A_1, and A_2. A three-year-old asset is worthless. During the fourth year (and in every year thereafter) the assets will each grow one year older and be amortized by one year's depreciation. The following pattern emerges:

A_0 becomes A_1, generating depreciation of $2,500

A_1 becomes A_2, generating depreciation of $1,500

A_2 becomes A_3, generating depreciation of $2,000

Total depreciation for the year is $6,000

The depreciation is equal to the cash needed to acquire a new asset now that the oldest asset has died. On acquisition of this new asset, the cycle repeats itself. Companies in this situation are said to be in a *steady* or a *stationary state*.

The book value of these three assets is $6,000; $3,500; and $2,000 for a total of $11,500. With three assets in hand, each generating net revenues of $2,400, the return on assets is ($7,200 − $6,000)/$11,500 or 10.43 percent. This return equals none of those computed above but, not surprisingly, it is approximately equal to their average.

Several key points emerge from this analysis for companies that are in a steady state:

1. All depreciation methods yield the same total depreciation.
2. The total depreciation is constant over time.
3. The net book value and the gross book value are constant over time.
4. Presupposing that income is steady, the return on investment (defined here as income divided by net book value) is constant.

Stating these points a little differently, companies that are in a steady state will be completely indifferent between the choice of one time-based depreciation method and another. The choice matters only to companies that are not in a steady state, such as new, fast-growing companies.

It is true that steady state companies are rare; as rare as companies that have only one asset. Most companies lie somewhere between these two extremes. Larger companies tend to approximate a steady state. Newer companies that are growing are further away from a steady state. Any analysis of the effect of depreciation methods, therefore, should use both extremes and then look for reality somewhere in between.

The growth to a steady state is also interesting. It can be demonstrated that, in certain circumstances in the passage to a steady state, the rate of return oscillates with a decreasing amplitude until the steady state target is reached. In short, one must beware of generalizing from the single-asset to the multiple-asset case when discussing the effect of depreciation.

Measuring Profitability

The fact that the return on investment, or the return on assets, settles down to a long-run constant as companies move to a steady state has interested many researchers. What, if anything, does this return tell us about the profitability of the company? More precisely, what can we tell about the rate of profit? The rate of profit is usually associated with the internal rate of return (IRR). In this particular case, a three-year net revenue stream of $2,400 per year from an asset costing $6,000 yields an internal rate of return of 9.70 percent. This return is equal to none of the computations preceding. In other words, the return on investment is not a measure of profitability.

Note further that the return on investment can be increased by speeding up depreciation. For example, if, instead of $2,500, $1,500, and $2,000 we use $3,500, $1,500, and $1,000, the total net book value will be the sum of $6,000, $2,500, and $1,000, for a total of $9,500. The return on investment, in this case, is ($7,200 − $6000)/$9,500 or 12.63 percent. If companies can increase their return on investment by manipulating their depreciation schedules, then maximizing a return on investment is not a very reliable measure of maximizing profitability.

Unfortunately, there are few substitutes for return on investment. The user is obliged, therefore, to rely on ROI numbers, bearing in mind always that if management has not been consistent in its treatment of assets, any changes in ROI may simply reflect bookkeeping changes.

The Interest Method

One method that ensures that the return on investment is equal to the internal rate of return is called the *interest method*. This is favored in the amortization of long-term receivables and payables but is seldom used in the case of capital assets. The method is of interest, though, because it sets a standard against which the bias of ROIs away from the IRR can be measured.

The interest method is based on the present value computations used in capital budgeting. The formula for computing the present value at time t_0 is as follows:

$$V_0 = \sum_{t=1}^{R} \frac{C_t}{(1 + i)^t} \tag{1}$$

where

V_0 = The present value at time 0

C_t = The incremental cash flow in each period t

i = The opportunity rate of return or the cost of capital

As indicated in Chapter 6, if i is assumed to be the opportunity rate of capital for a riskless investment, the discounted cash flow for each period should be adjusted by a risk-preference factor. However, in much of the literature, i is assumed to represent the cost of capital. The limitations of these assumptions are also discussed in Chapter 6.

By equating the historical cost (or other input valuation) with the present value of the asset in equation (1), and by substituting the internal rate of return for the opportunity rate or the cost of capital, we obtain the following equation:

$$BV = \sum_{t=1}^{R} \frac{C_t}{(1 + r)^t} \qquad (2)$$

where

BV = The cost of the asset—its initial book value

r = The internal rate of return

Solving equation (2) for r yields an internal rate of return of 9.7 percent in the illustration used in the previous paragraph. By assuming that this rate is constant during the life of the asset, the depreciation for each year can be computed for each year. This is demonstrated in Exhibit 15-2. The method is identical to that used for long-term receivables and payables, such as bonds.

The interest method, also known as the sinking-fund method or the annuity method, has been used by public utility firms. Typically they charge depreciation with the annuity portion, and charge interest expense on the increasing accumulated depreciation (equal to a hypothetical sinking fund). This method is particularly relevant when the utility's rates are computed by using an undepreciated cost as the rate base. One of the most relevant arguments for the sinking-fund method is that it permits a public utility to earn a constant rate of return on its total investment when its revenue is held constant through regulation.

The main arguments against using the interest method to compute depreciation on assets are that:

1. Very few assets can be expected to provide services with a constant or increasing value.
2. Repair and maintenance costs usually increase.
3. Operating efficiency usually declines over the asset's life.

EXHIBIT 15-2   Computation of Depreciation Based on the Interest Method

Start of Year	*Book Value of Asset at Start of Year*	*Earnings = 9.70% of Book Value at Start*	*Depreciation = Net Revenue of $2,400 Less Earnings*	*Return on Investment*
1	6,000	582	1,818	582/6,000 = 9.70%
2	4,182	406	1,994	406/4,182 = 9.70%
3	2,188	212	2,188	212/2,188 = 9.70%
4	0			

Interest methods are not better than methods such as straight-line depreciation. They do take into consideration one additional factor—the rate of return—but they still omit more factors than they include.

CHECKPOINTS

---

1. What key points about depreciation emerge when one focuses on groups of assets in steady state?
2. Compare the depreciation expense which arises in steady state with the depreciation that arises when using the replacement method.
3. What is the key difference between the interest method and all other methods of depreciation?
4. What two major problems does one encounter when attempting to measure profitability by using the return on investment?

SUMMARY

Accountants have long recognized that plant and equipment have limited lives and that some consideration must be made in the accounts for the inevitable necessity to dispose of once-productive assets. During the 19th century and the early part of the 20th century, most of the firms that treated the problem at all did so by a periodic revaluation of the assets or by charging either replacements or retirements to current expense. Later efforts focused on periodic depreciation as a means of systematically allocating the cost of an asset over its life.

Many seem to want to reject the dismal conclusion that depreciation is no more than cost allocation and want to find a meaning for depreciation. The most sustained effort at interpretation starts with the definition of an asset as a store of services and suggests that depreciation is best thought of as a decline in this store. The store of services may decline in one of four ways.

1. In accordance with activity or use, yielding activity-based methods of depreciation.
2. Evenly over time, yielding straight-line or constant charge methods.
3. Increasingly over time, yielding increasing charge methods.
4. Decreasingly over time, yielding decreasing charge methods such as sum-of-the-years' digits.

Part of the reason for the decline in services is wear and tear. Repair and maintenance policies are designed to keep an asset in working order, and thus to slow the decline in the store of services. Asset lives depend, therefore, in part on maintenance policies. The reverse holds too—companies tend to neglect assets which are expected to have a short life.

Wear and tear is not the only cause of a decline in the store of services. Obsolescence, caused by either technological advances or changes in public taste, is another major factor. Given the numerous factors that affect the decline in services, determining the size of the decline in a particular period is exceedingly difficult. In addition, before the service flow can be used in accounting, it has to be priced or valued. Pricing service flows poses another very difficult problem. Some have suggested that they be valued at current prices, others at historical cost. Still others have argued that the cost of replacing services should be used as the estimate of depreciation. Yet another group has claimed that the cost of maintenance to keep the asset at its original working capacity is best. Some have argued that the interest method should be used because that method best matches the change in value. None of these solutions is perfect. The conclusion of most observers, therefore, is to use the simplest depreciation method for financial reporting purposes whenever possible. That is usually the straight-line method.

DISCUSSION QUESTIONS

Nature of Depreciation

1. Discuss the following quotation, which is taken from *ARB 16*, p. 138.

Exhaustion is constantly being restored in part as well as being retarded by current maintenance, and it is generally recognized that in defining depreciation there must be an exclusion from the costs or losses from exhaustion in respect of costs chargeable to maintenance. Immediately, a question arises whether the exclusion should be the cost of exhaustion which is, in fact, restored by current maintenance, or the cost of exhaustion which would be restored by adherence to an established standard of maintenance. The definitions of [many assumed current maintenance.] . . . However, depreciation schemes are normally formulated on the basis of assuming a standard of maintenance . . . .

2. Should depreciation be related only to gradual declines in service potential or should it include sudden, sharp, and unexpected declines? In other words, does the wear and tear alluded to by the FASB include only that due to normal actions of the elements or does it include damage that results from "storms, fires, and floods?"

3. Discuss the following question taken from *ARB 16*, p. 140.

The question whether depreciation as an accounting term should in normal times be so interpreted as to include a decline in profitability to a subnormal standard such as has occurred in relation to much railroad property is one of great theoretical interest and does not seem to have been adequately discussed. It is illogical and erroneous to write off property which is still earning profits, though of an obsolete type, but not to write off property that, though up-to-date in type, is not earning profit.

4. Should a building that was in use but is now being held for sale continue to be depreciated?

5. **(May 1972)** Depreciation continues to be one of the most controversial, difficult, and important problem areas in accounting.

Required:

a. 1. Explain the conventional accounting concept of depreciation accounting; and
   2. Discuss its conceptual merit with respect to (*a*) the value of the asset, (*b*) the charge(s) to expense, and (*c*) the discretion of management in selecting the method.
b. 1. Explain the factors that should be considered when applying the conventional concept of depreciation to the determination of how the value of a newly acquired computer system should be assigned to expense for financial reporting purposes. (Income tax considerations should be ignored.)
   2. What depreciation methods might be used for the computer system?

6. **(May 1976)** Property, plant, and equipment (plant assets) generally represent a material portion of the total assets of most companies. Accounting for the acquisition and usage of such assets is, therefore, an important part of the financial reporting process.

Required:

a. Distinguish between revenue and capital expenditures, and explain why this distinction is important.
b. Briefly define depreciation as used in accounting.
c. Identify the factors that are relevant in determining the annual depreciation, and explain whether these factors are determined objectively or whether they are based on judgment.
d. Explain why depreciation is usually shown in the sources of funds section of the statement of changes in financial position.

Depreciation Methods

7. If depreciation is the cost associated with the exhaustion of physical services, why does one use relatively arbitrary methods like sum-of-the-years' digits?

8. Provide a semantic justification for Blockbuster's switch from three years to nine months in their depreciation policy on video hits. In your opinion, why did the SEC allow them to return to the three-year depreciation policy they had on all their tapes?

9. What assumptions are necessary to justify straight-line depreciation?

10. (November 1988) At the beginning of the year, Patrick Company acquired a computer to be used in its operations. The computer was delivered by the supplier, installed by Patrick, and placed into operation. The estimated useful life of the computer is five years, and its estimated residual (salvage) value is significant.

During the year, Patrick received cash in exchange for an automobile that was purchased in a prior year.

Required:

a. 1. What costs should Patrick capitalize for the computer?
   2. What is the objective of depreciation accounting? Do not discuss specific methods of depreciation.
b. What is the rationale for using accelerated depreciation methods?
c. How should Patrick account for and report the disposal of the automobile?

11. (May 1987) Deskin Company purchased a new machine to be used in its operations. The new machine was delivered by the supplier, installed by Deskin, and placed into operation. It was purchased under a long-term payment plan for which the interest charges approximated the prevailing market rates. The estimated useful life of the new machine is 10 years, and its estimated residual (salvage) value is significant. Normal maintenance was performed to keep the new machine in usable condition.

Deskin also added a wing to the manufacturing building that it owns. The addition is an integral part of the building. Furthermore, Deskin made significant leasehold improvements to office space used as corporate headquarters.

Required:

a. What costs should Deskin capitalize for the new machine? How should the machine be depreciated? Do not discuss specific methods of depreciation.
b. How should Deskin account for the normal maintenance performed on the new machine? Why?
c. How should Deskin account for the wing added to the manufacturing building? Where should the added wing be reported on Deskin's financial statements?
d. How should Deskin account for the leasehold improvements made to its office space? Where should the leasehold improvements be reported on Deskin's financial statements?

12. (November 1985) Gehl Company purchased significant amounts of new equipment this year to be used in its operations. The equipment was delivered by the suppliers, installed by Gehl, and placed into operation. Some of it was purchased for cash with discounts available for prompt payment. Some of it was purchased under long-term payment plans for which the interest charges approximate prevailing rates. As a result, Gehl is studying its capitalization and depreciation policies.

Required:

a. What costs should Gehl capitalize for the new equipment purchased this year?
b. What factors cause the equipment to lose its future economic benefit?
c. What factors should be considered in computing the equipment's depreciation expense?
d. What theoretical justifications are there for the use of accelerated depreciation methods?

13. (November 1966) During examination of the financial statements of the Fendo Company, your assistant calls attention to significant costs incurred in the development of EDP programs (i.e., software) for major segments of the sales and production scheduling systems (not R&D).

The EDP program development costs will benefit future periods to the extent that the systems change slowly and the program instructions are compatible with new equipment acquired at three- to six-year intervals. The service value of the EDP programs is affected almost entirely by changes in the technology of systems and EDP equipment and does not decline with the number of times the program is used. Since many system changes are minor, program instructions frequently can be modified with only minor losses in program efficiency. The frequency of such changes tends to increase with the passage of time.

Required:

a. Discuss the propriety of classifying the unamortized EDP program development costs as
1. A prepaid expense.
2. An intangible fixed asset with limited life.
3. A tangible fixed asset.
b. Numerous methods are available for amortizing assets that benefit future periods. Each method (like a model) presumes that certain conditions exist and, hence, is most appropriate under those conditions.
   Discuss the propriety of amortizing the EDP program development costs with
1. The straight-line method.
2. An increasing-charge method (e.g., the annuity method).

3. A decreasing-charge method (e.g., the sum-of-the-years'-digits method).
4. A variable-charge method (e.g., the units-of-production method).

14. (November 1973)   The Norvell Company manufactures electrical appliances, most of which are used in homes. Company engineers have designed a new type of blender which, through the use of a few attachments, will perform more functions than any blender currently on the market. Demand for the new blender can be projected with reasonable probability. In order to make the blenders, Norvell needs a specialized machine, which is not available from outside sources. It has been decided to make such a machine in Norvell's own plant.

Required:

a. Norvell's plant may be operating at or below capacity. Compare and contrast the problems in determining the cost to be assigned to the machine at these different levels of operations.
b. 1. Discuss the effect of projected demand in units for the new blenders (which may be steady, decreasing, or increasing) on the determination of a depreciation method for the machine.
   2. What other matters should be considered in determining the deprecial method? *Ignore income tax considerations.*

SAINT PATRICK AND THE FASB*

"Is nothing sacred?" asked Austin Bennet, priest in the Roman Catholic diocese of Brooklyn and accounting practices chairman of the U.S. Catholic Conference. He was responding acerbically to the exposure draft of a proposed standard to be promulgated by the FASB requiring not-for-profit organizations to depreciate their assets. (This appeared later as *SFAS 93*.)

"I'm not the only one who feels this way. Listen to Jack Gary, who should know because he was at the Treasury Department for many years. He wrote to the FASB saying, 'depreciating churches would be like depreciating the Pyramids and the Sphinx of Egypt, and the Sistine Chapel at the Vatican. While their reproduction value could be estimated, it would undoubtedly be prohibitive.' As Mr. Gary said, figuring depreciation on assets like these is 'the acme of futility.'"

"Our cathedrals last for centuries and often gain in value with age. Just appraising them would cost us millions of wasted dollars."

---

* The basis for this case, and its quotes are drawn from "Is Nothing Sacred?" by Lee Berton, *The Wall Street Journal,* April 16, 1987, pp. 1 and 13.

Colleagues chimed in to say that requiring their churches to depreciate their assets would reduce their income and, as a result, cause fund-raising, financial-reporting, and borrowing woes. It could even, they added, impair the financial health of some of their churches. On top of that, depreciating an institution like St. Patrick's Cathedral, which has been around for years, would be irrelevant.

Harold Bennett, president and treasurer of the Southern Baptist Convention, provided another argument against depreciation. "As some Southern communities change their character, so does the value of the churches," he said. "Our depreciation values would have to change every year."

Harry Bullen, project manager at the FASB, responded that things don't last forever. "The Parthenon may still be there, but its roof has fallen in. Physical assets that are exhaustible should be depreciated."

Ronald Bossio, another project manager at the FASB added, "In looking at all nonprofit assets, we had to be evenhanded. Church properties can wear out; therefore, they should be depreciated. I can see quibbling about the Pyramids, because their useful life is so long the costs per year would be immaterial. But not most churches. Even St. Patrick's Cathedral in Manhattan has parts that must be replaced and other parts that can be salvaged."

Father Laurence, pastor of St. Vincent de Paul Roman Catholic Church in Baltimore, and a former consultant to the FASB, agreed. "Depreciation helps show what it costs to maintain and repair a church." It fits, they both pointed out, with *SFAC 6,* which stated in paragraph 104:

> Unless a not-for-profit organization maintains its net assets, its ability to continue to provide services dwindles; either future resource providers must make up the deficiency or services to future beneficiaries will decline. For example, use of an asset such as a building to provide goods or services to beneficiaries consumes part of the future economic benefits or service potential constituting the asset, and that decrease in future economic benefits is one of the costs (expenses) of using the asset for that purpose.

To which, Father Laurence added, "I guess I accept depreciation for churches because I like Rubik's cube."

Msgr. Bennet responded that, "Father Laurence is entitled to his opinion, but he speaks only for himself. He has no official accounting status in the Catholic Church."

Further support for Msgr. Bennet's position came from Robert Anthony, professor emeritus of management control at Harvard Business School, and an expert on accounting by nonprofit groups. "Depreciating cathedrals and churches is stupid. It would be like trying to compare the cost per soul saved among churches," he said.

Professor Anthony went on to point out that in his book, *Should Business and Nonbusiness Accounting Be Different?* he agreed that depreciation was necessary for all organizations on assets acquired from operating resources. However, he also showed that depreciation on contributed assets should not be allowed to affect income.[16] One way to do that, a way that is required by *IASC 20,* is to record contributed revenue exactly equal to the amount of depreciation. Another way is to simply ignore depreciation on such assets.

Representatives from the FASB responded that there was no basis in theory for treating assets differently depending on their source of acquisition. To follow Professor Anthony's suggestion would be to destroy comparability, they said.

"That may be," said Msgr. Bennet. "But the board is on the verge of causing more trouble for American Churches than all the sinners in their congregations."

Required:

a. Should churches, such as St. Patrick's, and other not-for-profit organizations be required to depreciate their assets?
b. Review the general objectives of depreciating assets. Are these objectives applicable to nonprofits?
c. Should distinctions be made based on whether assets were acquired from operating resources or contributed?
d. What base should be used for these assets?

SELECTED ADDITIONAL READINGS

Readers interested in pursuing the topics raised in this chapter might begin by perusing the following texts. Each contains numerous references to other work.

Edwards, Edgar O., and Philip W. Bell. *The Theory and Measurement of Business Income* (Berkeley: University of California Press, 1967), esp. Ch. 6.

Livingstone, J. Leslie, and Thomas J. Burns. *Income Theory and Rate of Return* (Columbus: The Ohio State University, 1971).

Thomas, Arthur L. *Studies in Accounting Research No. 9.* "The Allocation Problem: Part Two" (AAA, 1974).

Concepts of Depreciation

Bennett, Anthony H. M. "Depreciation and Business Decision Making." *Accounting and Business Research,* Winter 1972, pp. 3–28.

Burt, Oscar R. "Unified Theory of Depreciation." *Journal of Accounting Research,* Spring 1970, pp. 28–57.

Grinyer, J. R. "A New Approach to Depreciation." *Abacus,* March 1987, pp. 43–54.

Johnson, Orace. "Two General Concepts of Depreciation." *Journal of Accounting Research,* Spring 1968, pp. 29–37.

Lamden, Charles W.; Dale L. Gerboth; and Thomas W. McRae. *Accounting for Depreciable Assets* (AICPA, 1975).

Lev, Baruch, and Henri Theil. "A Maximum Entropy Approach to the Choice of Asset Depreciation." *Journal of Accounting Research,* Autumn 1978, pp. 286–93.

Lowe, Howard. "The Essentials of a General Theory of Depreciation." *The Accounting Review,* April 1963, pp. 293–301.

McIntyre, Edward V. "Present Value Depreciation and the Disaggregation Problem." *The Accounting Review* (January 1977), pp. 162–71.

NAA Management Accounting Practices Committee. "Fixed Asset Accounting: The Allocation of Costs." *Management Accounting,* January 1974, pp. 43–49.

Nurnberg, H. "Depreciation in the Cash Flow Statement of Manufacturing Firms: Amount Incurred or Amount Expensed." *Accounting Horizons,* March 1989, pp. 95–101.

Peasnell, K. V. "The CCA Depreciation Problem—An Analysis and Proposal." *Abacus,* December 1977, pp. 123–40.

Wright, F. K. "Toward a General Theory of Depreciation." *Journal of Accounting Research,* Spring 1964, pp. 80–90.

Depreciation Methods, Economic Life, and Salvage Values

Coughlan, Joseph D., and William K. Strand. *Depreciation: Accounting, Taxes, and Business Decisions* (New York: Ronald Press, 1969).

Ijiri, Yuji, and Robert S. Kaplan. "Probabilistic Depreciation and Its Implications for Group Depreciation." *The Accounting Review,* October 1969, pp. 743–56.

Mullen, Louis E. "Spotlight on Estimated Economic Life of Depreciable Assets." *CPA Journal,* August 1973, pp. 662–66.

Depreciation and Allocation

Callen, Jeffrey L. "Financial Cost Allocations: A Game Theoretic Approach." *The Accounting Review,* April 1978, pp. 303–8.

Eckel, Leonard G. "Arbitrary and Incorrigible Allocations." *Accounting Review,* October 1976, pp. 764–77.

Lewis, W. Arthur. "Depreciation and Obsolescence as Factors in Costing." In *Studies in Accounting.* Edited by W. T. Baxter and S. Davidson (Institute of Chartered Accountants in England and Wales, 1977), pp. 210–33.

Meyers, S. L. "A Proposal for Coping with the Allocation Problem." *Journal of Accountancy,* April 1976, pp. 52–56.

Thomas, Arthur L. "Useful Arbitrary Allocations." *The Accounting Review,* July 1971, pp. 472–79.

Thomas, Arthur L. "Arbitrary and Incorrigible Allocations: A Comment." *The Accounting Review,* January 1978, pp. 263–69.

Capital Maintenance

Edwards, Edgar. "Depreciation and the Maintenance of Real Capital." In *Depreciation and Replacement Policy.* Edited by J. L. Meij (Eindhoven: North-Holland, 1961), pp. 46–136.

Milburn, J. Alex. "Discussion." In *Maintenance of Capital: Financial versus Physical*. Edited by Robert R. Sterling and Kenneth W. Lemke (Scholars Book Co., 1982), pp. 95–103.

Nichols, Donald. "Operating Income and Distributable Income under Replacement Cost Accounting: The Long-Life Asset Replacement Problem." *Financial Analysts Journal,* January–February 1982, pp. 68–73.

Sterling, Robert R. "Limitations of Physical Capital." In *Maintenance of Capital: Financial versus Physical*. Edited by Robert R. Sterling and Kenneth W. Lemke (Scholars Book Co., 1982), pp. 3–58.

Return on Investment

See Chapter 10.

Empirical Research

Archibald, T. Ross. "Stock Market Reaction to the Depreciation Switchback." *The Accounting Review,* January 1972, pp. 22–30.

Barefield, Russel M., and Eugene E. Comiskey. "Depreciation Policy and the Behavior of Corporate Profits." *Journal of Accounting Research,* Autumn 1971, pp. 351–58.

Comiskey, Eugene E. "Market Response to Changes in Depreciation Accounting." *The Accounting Review,* April 1971, pp. 279–85.

Holthausen, R. W. "Evidence on Effect of Bond Covenants and Management Compensation Contracts on Choice of Accounting Techniques: Case of the Depreciation Switch-Back." *Journal of Accounting and Economics,* March 1981, pp. 73–109.

Kim, M., and G. Moore. "Economic vs. Accounting Depreciation." *Journal of Accounting and Economics,* April 1988, pp. 111–26.

Staubus, George J. "Statistical Evidence of the Value of Depreciation Accounting." *Abacus,* August 1967, pp. 3–22.

ENDNOTES

1. See Arthur L. Thomas, "The Allocation Problem: Part Two," *Studies in Accounting Research No. 9* (AAA, 1974), p. 2.
2. Ibid.
3. *Accounting Research Bulletin No. 16* (New York: AIA, October 1942).
4. *Accounting Terminology Bulletin No. 1,* "Review and Resume" (1953), p. 25.
5. United States Supreme Court, in Lindheimer v. Illinois Bell Telephone Company, 292 U.S. 151 (1934) as quoted in *Accounting Research Bulletin No. 16* (October 1942), p. 136.
6. *Accounting Research Bulletin No. 20* (November 1943), p. 166.
7. A. P. Richardson, "Editorial," *Journal of Accounting* (March 1930), p. 165.
8. Henry Rand Hatfield, *Modern Accounting* (New York: Appleton-Century-Crofts, 1919), p. 121.
9. AAA Committee on Accounting Concepts and Standards, *Accounting and Reporting Standards for Corporate Financial Statements and Preceding Statements and Supplements* (AAA, 1957), pp. 4, 6.

10. Robert T. Sprouse and Maurice Moonitz, *Accounting Research Study No. 3,* "A Tentative Set of Broad Accounting Principles for Business Enterprises" (New York: AICPA, 1962), p. 34.
11. *SFAC 6,* par. 149.
12. AAA Committee on Concepts and Standards—Long-Lived Assets, "Accounting for Land, Buildings, and Equipment," Supplementary Statement No. 1, *The Accounting Review,* July 1964, p. 696.
13. See, for example, Orace Johnson, "Two Concepts of Depreciation," *Journal of Accounting Research,* Spring 1968, pp. 29–37.
14. Committee on Concepts and Standards-Long Lived Assets, p. 696.
15. *ARB 16,* p. 143.
16. Robert N. Anthony, *Should Business and Nonbusiness Accounting Be Different?* (Harvard Business School Press, 1989), esp. pp. 38 and 64.

Chapter 16

Current Assets

CHAPTER OBJECTIVES

After studying this chapter, you will be able to:

Determine what should be included in the various categories of current assets.

Provide a theoretical justification for the amount at which to record the various categories of current assets.

Contrast the treatment of current and noncurrent marketable equity securities.

CHAPTER OVERVIEW

Introduction

The previous three chapters dealt with assets in the broad. This and the next deal with specific categories of assets. This chapter deals with current assets and investments not giving the investor control over the investee; the next deals with tangible noncurrent assets such as plant and equipment. The third chapter in the series deals with other noncurrent assets and intangibles such as goodwill.

Monetary Current Assets

Monetary current assets are claims to a fixed number of dollars that will be realized within the operating cycle or within one year, whichever is longer. The category includes cash, accounts receivable, and notes receivable. Each has relatively specific rules for what items will be included in that category. Each should be entered at the present value of the cash that will be realized, adjusted for uncertainty.

Nonmonetary Current Assets

Nonmonetary assets are claims that cannot be converted into a currently known fixed number of dollars. This includes marketable equity securities, prepaids, and inventories. Like cash and receivables, they will be realized within the operating cycle or a year, whichever is longer. Also like monetary current assets, they are bound by a number of rules that determine which transactions will be charged to that category and which will not. Inventories, particularly, present difficult and challenging theoretical problems in deciding what should be included and at what cost.

Current assets include some of the most manipulable accounts in the financial reporting system. The point at which revenue is recognized directly affects not only profitability, but also the size of accounts receivable. How much of this period's operating costs are attributed to inventory and not to this period's expense has a major impact on the gross margin and, therefore, on a company's profitability. The amount capitalized directly affects the size of inventory. In short, the effects of the accrual system of accounting are seen most clearly in the current assets of an enterprise.

Current assets, and to a lesser extent current liabilities, are also the link between the income statement and the cash flow statement. A rise in accounts receivable indicates that not all the revenue that has been claimed was collected in cash. Financial analysts say that the wider the gap, the lower the quality of earnings. Likewise, a rise in inventory indicates that not all purchases have been sold. A sharp rise in inventory can indicate that the firm is having difficulties. Cash is being spent on acquiring inventory, but cash is not being generated from selling that inventory.

Understanding the behavior of current assets is key, therefore, to understanding the total operations of the company. It is through this understanding that one gains insight into the quality of the earnings and into the source and direction of cash flows. It is through these insights that one forms a basis for developing expectations about the size, timing, and uncertainty of future cash flows.

The chapter begins by defining current assets. It distinguishes between monetary and nonmonetary current assets and discusses the nature of the various classifications found in each category. The treatment of long-term monetary investments is contrasted with that of short-term monetary investments. Similarly, the treatment of short- and long-term marketable securities is contrasted. In both cases, one is dealing with investments that do not give the investor a controlling interest in the investee companies. Chapter 18 discusses the situation when the investing company does have a controlling interest.

In this and the other related chapters, keep in mind the fundamental relationships between the problems of valuation, income determination, and cash flows; but do not be bound by the limits of the double-entry accounting structure when discussing the development of theoretical accounting concepts and their application to the communication of relevant accounting information. In the traditional accounting structure, some of the concepts discussed in Chapter 11 relating to the reporting of revenues and gains and losses may dictate the valuation concept applied. At other times, however, the guidelines for valuation applied in practice seem to dictate the timing and classification of revenues, gains, and losses. The following discussion attempts to evaluate the objectives and keep the process of valuation, income determination, and the presentation of cash flows in proper balance.

CURRENT ASSETS

The term *current assets* is defined as "cash and other assets or resources commonly identified as those which are reasonably expected to be realized in cash or sold or consumed during the normal operating cycle of the business."[1] This compares with earlier, much narrower definitions such as " . . . those assets which in the regular course of business will be converted into cash and those assets acquired with a view to their availability for conversion into cash."[2] As Chapter 13 noted, the one-year rule was common in the application of these earlier definitions. Two other changes that have occurred in the definition of current assets are:

1. A greater emphasis on expectations or intent to convert rather than the availability for conversion, particularly with respect to marketable securities.
2. A broadening of the scope of current assets to include prepaid expenses (items to be consumed).

One reason to include prepaid expenses in the definition is that, if they had not been acquired, they would require the use of current assets in the normal operations of the business. In this regard, they are the same as inventories; both would require the use of current funds if they had not been acquired previously. A more important reason for the inclusion of prepaids is that they represent resources committed for only a short period—the current operating cycle. Like inventories, they result in current funds becoming available for recommitment through the sale of the product or services and the collection of the proceeds. However, the reporting of prepaid expenses is a product of the traditional accounting structure. Little economic interpretation can be obtained from this information, and it is doubtful that it can be helpful to investors in their prediction and decision activities.

MONETARY CURRENT ASSETS

Monetary current assets are claims to a fixed number of dollars of general purchasing power becoming available and intended to be used in current operations with the operating cycle of the business or one year, whichever is the longer. These include money in its various forms and claims to money. The claims generally are represented by formal or informal contracts specifying that a second party pay the firm a given sum of money at a specified date or within a specific time period (possibly implied from general business practice).

Money

Cash and the various other forms of money are expressed in terms of their current value, which is definite. Therefore, any gains or losses resulting from the exchange of other assets for the given amount of cash or money forms should have been recognized; no gain or loss should be recognized from the holding of cash and money forms except possibly in consideration of purchasing-power gains and losses during periods of price-level change, as discussed in Chapter 12 on inflation. Holdings of convertible foreign currency or moneys should be expressed in terms of their domestic equivalent at the balance sheet date.

Receivables

Since the cash from receivables is not available until after a waiting period, the receivable is not worth its maturity value (the amount finally due under the contract). Strictly speaking, therefore, all receivables and monetary securities should be valued in terms of the discounted value of the cash to be received in the future.* In most cases, the amount of interest (discount) is small and, therefore, not material in the computation of the firm's net income for the year. As a result most receivables are entered at their maturity value—for noninterest-bearing receivables this is the same as their face value.[3]

Unless it is specifically stated, the rate of interest or discount that should be used is the market rate for credit of equal risk. There is some merit in using the firm's cost of capital rate or its internal rate of return, because these represent an approximation of the opportunity cost of the money to the firm. However, the actual differential cost of granting credit

---

* This holds regardless of *APB 21*'s caveat that it does not apply to trade receivables, for instance.

to customers may be very low or even negative because of the possible loss of product revenue if credit were not granted. For interest-bearing receivables, the rate used is usually the stated interest rate. Since the discounted value of interest-bearing receivables is their face value, they are entered correctly at their face value. Interest on these receivables will then accrue in an interest receivable account. Long-term receivables, such as investments in bonds, should be accounted for using the interest method detailed in Chapter 18.[4]

Generating Cash from Receivables.   Firms sometimes have need of cash before their receivables mature. Several options are open to them in this case. They may sell their receivables to a finance house. The company may agree to make good a default on the receivables when they are said to have been sold (or discounted) *with recourse*. All risk may be transferred to the purchaser when the receivables are sold *without recourse*. Selling trade receivables without recourse is called *factoring*. Selling trade receivables with recourse is called *assigning*. Selling notes receivable, usually done with recourse, is called *discounting*. Alternatively, a company may simply borrow against its receivables by *pledging* them as collateral for a loan.

Borrowing and selling without recourse are perfectly straightforward transactions. Sales *with* recourse raise the question of whether a sale has indeed taken place or whether the transaction is in substance a loan. *SFAS 77* stated that a sale could be considered to have taken place when *all* of the following conditions had been met:

1. The transferor surrenders control of the future economic benefits embodied in the receivables. (Control, they added, has not been surrendered if the transferor has an option to repurchase the receivables at a later date.)
2. The transferor's obligation under the recourse provisions can be reasonably estimated.
3. The transferee cannot require the transferor to repurchase the receivables except pursuant to the recourse provisions.

If any of these conditions is not met, the transaction is effectively accounted for as a loan with the amount received from the transfer of the receivables shown as a liability.

Two members of the Board vigorously dissented from *SFAS 77*, arguing that all transfers of receivables are simply alternative means of financing. All should be treated as one would a simple borrowing where an asset was being used as collateral. They note that *SFAS 48*, discussed in Chapter 11, disallowed a sale when the right of return existed. Recourse, they contend, is equivalent to a right of return. *SFAS 77*, therefore, is not consistent with *SFAS 48*. The authors agree.

In the case of discounting notes receivable with recourse, it is common practice to net the liability, equal to the amount of money received from the finance house, against the note receivable adjusted for accrued interest. Any difference is treated as interest expense or revenue. This treats discounting as a sale with recourse. It is difficult to sustain the notion that companies engage in trading notes receivable, though. Discounting notes with recourse, even more than selling receivables with recourse, is simply another means of financing one's business. To be consistent with *SFAS 77*, therefore, the monies received should generate a liability. Any final adjustment, on the maturity of the note, should be treated as a gain or a loss, not as a revenue or expense.

Allowance for Bad Debts.   An important factor in the proper valuation of receivables is the treatment of the uncertainty of collection. As indicated in Chapter 11, revenue should be measured by the expected amount to be collected. The *direct* method in which uncollectible accounts are written off against income has no basis in theory, therefore. In the *allowance* method, revenue is adjusted by accruing a valuation account known as the *allowance for doubtful accounts*. Two methods are in common use: an estimate based on the accounts receivable, and an estimate based on the credit sales for the year.

The estimate of the allowance for doubtful accounts is most accurate when it is based on the age and characteristics of the outstanding accounts at the balance sheet date and the probabilistic expectations of collectibility. On the other hand, the ''bad debt loss'' (reduction of revenue) associated with the revenue of the current period is more accurate when it is based on an estimated percentage of the revenue of the period. In the former procedure, the allowance for bad debts is determined directly and the bad debt loss is a residual; in the latter procedure, the allowance for bad debts is the residual. Theory dictates that both should be placed in proper perspective. For income statement purposes, the percentage of revenue based on statistical analysis of past experience adjusted for current conditions should be used. The valuation of the receivables in the balance sheet, however, should be based on expectations regarding the specific composite of accounts existing at the balance sheet date.[5] Technically, any differences between the two methods would represent corrections of prior periods. The commonly accepted procedure of adjusting the current year's charge to bad debt losses for any errors of estimation in prior years is not consistent with the current operating concept of income, unless the amounts involved are clearly immaterial.

As discussed in Chapter 11, revenue should be reported whenever there is verifiable evidence of the value of the asset received in exchange for the product. Since a receivable is generally expressed in money terms, there is a verifiable measure of valuation, and the revenue should have been reported at the time of sale or before; after the period of sale, any effect on net income should arise only from interest (implicit or actual) during the waiting period or from corrections for errors in the estimation of uncollectible amounts. These errors, typically from the collection of a previously deemed uncollectible account, cause a reversal of the write-off of the accounts receivable and an increase in the allowance.

The Installment Basis.   The Accounting Principles Board, in *Opinion No. 10*, stated that the installment method of reporting revenue is not acceptable except when the collection of the sales price is not reasonably assured. As indicated in Chapter 11, this exception is not generally justi- fied. Collection statistics are available for most types of loans if a firm has not obtained its own experience data. One instance where the installment method has been sanctioned involves real estate sales. If the transfer of property does not meet the conditions laid down in *SFAS 66* for it to be recognized as a normal sale, several alternatives are permitted. One of those alternatives is the installment method, which is required if the " . . . recovery of the cost of the property is reasonably assured if the buyer defaults."[6]

When the installment basis is justified, the deferred gross profit account should be treated as a valuation account to accounts receivable rather than as deferred income. The nature of installment sales is to defer the reporting of income until the cash has been received. Thus, at the time of the sales, the receivable takes the place of the product inventory, and the receivable should be valued in terms of the valuation of the product (the input value), rather than in terms of the present value of the receivable (the output value). Treating the deferred gross profit as a liability does not affect the computation of net income on the installment basis, but it does distort the asset and liability relationships.

When the revenue from installment sales is reported at the time of sale for accounting purposes, but at the time of collection for income tax purposes, a deferred tax credit arises.* *APB 11* requires that the deferred tax credit relating to installment sales be classified as a current liability when the related installment receivable is classified as current, and as noncurrent when the related receivable is classified as noncurrent. (*SFAS 96*'s requirements are similar in effect.) This paired classification is based on the assumption that the collection of the receivable will result in a tax liability payable in the same year that the receivable is collected. Al- though there is a time lag for payment of the tax after collection of the receivable, the assumption that both relate to the same operating cycle is basically correct. However, there is theoretical support in this case for

---

* See Chapter 19 for a more complete discussion of income tax allocation.

presenting the installment receivable at a valuation net of the expected tax, as the specific obligation to pay the tax arises only when the receivable is converted into cash.

Monetary Investments

Monetary securities (such as bonds receivable and notes receivable) with known maturity dates and values should be treated similarly to accounts receivables. That is, they should be entered at their net present value where the discount factor is based upon prevailing market rates. Typically this is done by establishing a valuation account for the premium or discount. They should also be adjusted for uncertainties of collection but this is usually negligible. Interest, based on the market rate, should be accrued in an interest receivable account with the difference between the interest accrued and the interest received charged to the valuation account.

Under conventional accounting procedures, securities (when held for current working capital purposes) are generally recorded on the basis of the lower-of-cost-or-market method. Since the FASB has not specified the procedures for reporting monetary investments classified as current, it is presumed that they may be included in portfolios of marketable equity securities for which the portfolio lower-of-cost-or-market method (discussed in the following section) is followed. However, the use of current market prices for the valuation of all securities classified as current assets is common in special industries and as supplementary information for many other firms.

The argument for the use of the lower-of-cost-or-market method in this context has been that cost is generally the most relevant basis for measuring the gains or losses realized when the securities are sold. If market price rises above cost, the increase in value is not generally recorded, because it is thought that this gain is unrealized in the technical sense of the word, and because it is possibly ephemeral in nature and may disappear before the asset is sold. If the market value of the securities is less than cost, however, it is thought that the loss should be recorded and the securities should not be shown in the balance sheet in excess of their current realizable value.* This treatment of unrealized gains and losses is not consistent with the findings of efficient market theory as outlined in Chapter 6. There is a strong case to be made based on empirical evidence for the use of market prices at all times. In addition, there are many advantages for the use of current market prices for all marketable securities including the following:

---

* See Chapter 14 on asset measurement for a more complete discussion of the lower-of-cost-or-market rule.

1. Market values are as verifiable as cost in most cases (except where the market is "thin"), and they provide more useful information to investors.
2. They provide better information regarding the effects of holding securities. The gains and losses from holding securities are just as important as the gains and losses from selling them.
3. When identical securities are acquired at different prices, it seems reasonable that they should be given identical values.
4. Current assets are more homogeneous when all items are expressed in terms of current values. Thus, the investment classification permits a better interpretation of these resources and is more likely to be meaningful in aiding the prediction of cash flows.

Noncurrent Investments.   Chapter 18 deals with noncurrent investments in securities in which the company controls more than 20 percent of the voting stock. Chapter 19 deals more specifically with the interest method in the case of noncurrent liabilities. This section summarizes the treatment of noncurrent monetary investments as a useful contrast, at this point, to the treatment of current monetary investments.

When long-term marketable corporate bonds are acquired at a premium or discount and held as temporary investments, the maturity value does not reflect the amount that will be received when the bonds are sold. Therefore, the amortization of the premium or discount is not appropriate. Current market quotations are better not only because the bonds are expected to be sold in the near future, but also because the current market price reflects changes in the market rate of interest, while amortization assumes a constant rate.

When corporate bonds or notes are held as long-term investments, the accepted procedure is to amortize the discount or premium over the remaining life of the bonds using what is termed the *interest method*. The current market price or the lower of cost or market is not generally considered applicable in this case because there is no intent to convert the bonds into cash until the maturity date. However, *APB 21* states that when bonds or notes are received in exchange for property or services that do not have an established exchange price, the notes should be recorded initially at the discounted present value using current implicit interest rates. This is assumed to be equivalent to a market rate at the date of acquisition, but the valuation is not changed when interest rates change. This is based on the traditional historical cost accounting structure and the assumption that gains and losses resulting from temporary fluctuations in bond prices and interest rates tend to offset each other over the life of the bond or note because of the fixed-dollar maturity value. But, since amortization procedures assume a constant rate of interest, the reporting of current market prices or present values provides a better base for interpreting of the economic resources of the firm. Long-term and short-term investments should not be valued on different bases. Consistency of reporting within the firm and uniformity among firms should permit a better interpretation of a firm's resources and an improvement in the evaluation of investment decisions.

NONMONETARY CURRENT ASSETS

Nonmonetary current assets are rights or claims that cannot be converted into a currently known quantity of dollars at a specific future date. The most common examples are investments in common stock of other corporations, product inventories, and prepaid expenses. These items have a common characteristic different from monetary assets in that their current value cannot be estimated by discounting a future maturity value and adjusting for the uncertainties of collection. But they do not have homogeneous characteristics among themselves. Marketable investments in common stocks are similar to monetary investments in that they may be converted directly into cash when such funds are needed for current operations. The conversion of inventories into cash requires the sale through the marketing operations of the business and through the final collection of receivables. Prepaid expenses are not converted directly into cash; the benefits are received by the firm through their use in current operations. From a procedural point of view, however, inventories and prepaid expenses are usually treated alike as amounts to be allocated to expense in the future.

Marketable Equity Securities

SFAS 12 requires that all marketable equity securities, whether current or noncurrent, be reported on a portfolio lower-of-cost-or-market basis.* The application of the lower-of-cost-or-market rule to a portfolio, rather than to each security, is consistent with portfolio theory. That is, the relevant return to the firm is the return on the portfolio, since an investor is not rewarded for the failure to diversify.

Declines in the market price of the current portfolio are reported in the income statement as unrealized holding losses; increases in market prices of the portfolio to the original cost of the portfolio are reported in the income statement as recoveries of losses. Declines and recoveries are recorded in a valuation account which, because of nonrecognition of gains above previous losses, will never have a debit balance. Limiting increases

---

* The lower-of-cost-or-market rule is discussed in more depth in Chapter 14.

in market prices to the previously recognized decrease was adopted on grounds that the reversal in prices represents a change in the accounting estimate of the unrealized loss reported previously—not an unrealized gain.[7]

Reporting the reversal of the unrealized holding loss is an improvement over the conventional lower-of-cost-or-market rule, but its general application to the valuation of the portfolio is still objectionable for the same reasons as indicated earlier. However, this objection is reduced by the requirement that the aggregate cost and market value of each portfolio be disclosed in the body of financial statements or in notes and that information regarding the gross unrealized gains and the gross unrealized losses also be presented. But a case similar to that presented above for monetary investments can be made for reporting marketable equity securities at current market prices and the full recognition of all holding gains and losses.

Temporary investments are generally held as secondary cash reserves. Therefore, dividend and interest income on these investments and gains and losses from holding and selling them are incidental to the main operations of the business. While interest income is accrued and recorded in the period in which it is earned, dividend income is not. Dividend income is generally recognized when it is declared, because the stockholder has no legal claim before that time, and because of the uncertainty of the amount that will be declared, if any. However, if expectations regarding payment of dividends are good, there is no theoretical reason why dividends could not be estimated and accrued. The validity of recording the accrued dividend asset and the resulting income depends more on the validity of the estimate than on the legal right to receive the dividend.

When the cost basis is used for several identical lots of marketable securities acquired at different prices, a question arises regarding measurement of the gains or losses when some of the securities are sold. The realized gains and losses are computed by taking the difference between original cost and the current net selling price. But how should we select the relevant cost? Is it the specific cost of the certificates sold, or should the cost be computed on the basis of a FIFO or LIFO flow concept or on the basis of an average cost? One encounters the same problem selecting the relevant cost in computing cost of goods sold based on inventory. Of course, if the securities are all valued at current market prices, the problem does not exist; all lots are then valued in terms of the same prices.

Noncurrent Marketable Securities. Chapter 18 deals with investments in securities in which the company controls more than 20 percent of the voting stock. Because much of the above discussion is also relevant for long-term investments in common stocks where the holding is less than 20 percent, those investments are addressed here. Such limited investments may be held for a variety of reasons, such as providing permanent financing to suppliers or customers, or obtaining diversification of the firm's investment. Where the balance sheet is not classified into current and noncurrent categories, all marketable equity investments should be treated as noncurrent.

SFAS 12 requires the noncurrent investments in equity securities to be classified separately and valued on the basis of the lower-of-cost-or-market rule applied to the portfolio in the same way that it is applied to the current portfolio, with the exception that the accumulated changes in the valuation allowance are included in the equity section of the balance sheet instead of showing the current changes in the income statement. Securities that are reclassified from the noncurrent to the current portfolio must be transferred at the lower of cost or market. If market is below cost, market becomes the new basis and the difference is charged to income as a realized loss. In effect, a transfer is equivalent to a sale and repurchase. If the decline in market value is considered to be other than temporary, the write-down is to be reported as a realized loss.*

The Board acknowledged that the treatment of unrealized gains between current and noncurrent portfolios was inconsistent. They adopted the rule on grounds that to do otherwise raised larger issues about asset values that they felt unable to settle within this statement. In particular, as two dissenting Board members pointed out, the statement makes the recognition of an unrealized gain depend not on the difference between market and cost but on irrelevancies such as:

1. Whether the security is classified in the balance sheet as a current or a noncurrent asset.
2. Whether unrealized losses on marketable securities have previously been recognized in net income in prior periods.
3. Whether in a given accounting period an enterprise has unrealized losses in some securities that offset unrealized gains in others.[8]

All of these irrelevancies could be solved at a stroke by simply recognizing all marketable equity securities at their market value at all times. There is little reason not to mark to market, given that these securities are marketable, making their market prices readily and objectively accessible.[9]

Prepaid Expenses

Prepaid expenses are benefits to be received by the firm in the future in the form of services. They include such items as office and factory supplies, prepaid rent, unexpired insurance, prepaid interest, and prepaid taxes.

---

* More is said on this subject under the heading of "Noncurrent Investments" in Chapter 18.

Although the various prepaid expenses have some common characteristics for classification purposes, they also have some major differences. Some represent specific tangible assets (e.g., supplies), others represent the right to use assets owned by others (e.g., prepaid rent), and still others are related quite closely to other assets or liabilities. Stanford professor John Canning asserted that prepaid taxes and prepaid insurance are really valuation accounts relating to the specific assets for which they are incurred.[10] A building for which taxes and insurance have been prepaid is worth more than a building for which no taxes or insurance have been prepaid. There is some merit in this argument, but the presentation of these items as additions to plant and equipment would not necessarily provide better information to investors. Taxes and insurance must be paid at current intervals unrelated to the life span of the plant and equipment.

The procedures for allocating the prepaid expenses to periods depend primarily on the type of asset to be amortized. Tangible assets, such as supplies, are normally transferred to expenses as they are consumed or used. Prepayments that relate to a specific period—such as prepaid rent, unexpired insurance, and prepaid taxes—are normally charged off to costs or expenses on the basis of the passing of time, similar to the straight-line method of depreciation. In both cases, the objective is to allocate the cost, or other basis of valuation, to the periods in which the goods or services are used or when the benefits are received by the firm.

As indicated in Chapter 11, under the matching rule, expenses should be recorded in the period in which the related revenue is reported. Thus, when prepaid expenses are associated with the production process, the amounts are transferred to product costs. In most other cases, however, prepaid expenses cannot be associated directly with revenue. Therefore, indirect or period matching must be used; they must be charged to expenses in the period in which they are used or in which the services are received by the firm.

In the case of supplies, costs are usually identified with specific items, and these are then charged to expense when the items are used. The methods for cost identification are similar to the problem of inventories. Current values may provide useful information for some purposes, but costs are generally adequate as a measurement of supplies used because:

1. The costs are generally recent exchange prices, so they will usually represent close approximations of current values.
2. The differences between costs and current values are usually not material in relationship to net income.

When price levels are changing rapidly, however, restatements should be made, as suggested in Chapter 12 on inflation.

As indicated above, for prepayments of services to be received on a time basis, the straight-line method of amortization is the method most commonly found in practice. The assumption is that the services are to be received continually over a specific period and that the final benefits are received in these same periods. While this assumption may not necessarily be true, the short period over which the prepayments are to be allocated and the immaterial effect of different allocation methods are convincing pragmatic reasons for the use of a simple allocation procedure.

The theory involved in evaluating amortization procedures is similar to the theory for the evaluation of depreciation procedures, discussed in Chapter 15. One observation, though, should be made at this point. The argument for straight-line depreciation on the basis of a similarity of plant and equipment to prepaid expenses is not valid. Straight-line amortization may not be appropriate for either, but its use in the amortization of prepaid expenses, given the short life of most prepaids, is of less concern in meeting the basic objectives of financial reporting.

Inventories

The term *inventories* includes merchandise destined for sale in the normal course of business, and materials and supplies to be used in the process of production for sale. Excluded from this category are supplies that will be consumed in nonproducing operations; securities held for resale, but incidental to the operations of the firm; and plant and equipment in use or awaiting final disposition upon termination of use. In the traditional definition, inventories are current assets, because they will normally be converted into cash or other assets within the operating cycle of the business. Obsolete and unsalable merchandise, however, if material in amount, should be excluded from this classification, unless it can be disposed of in available markets within normal selling periods.

Inventories are usually thought of as stocks of merchandise, although accounting for the flow of merchandise is usually considered more important. In the traditional accounting structure, the stocks at the end of one period are interrelated with the flows of that period, even though they may be residually determined. The valuation of the stocks, therefore, is affected by matching the input values with revenues for the period preceding the balance sheet date, and it may also be affected by the matching process of prior periods.

In the valuation process, inventories are different from both monetary assets and prepaid expenses. Monetary assets represent amounts of purchasing power available, or to become available at some time in the future. The current value of monetary assets can be computed, therefore, by discounting the expected cash receipts or conversions. Prepaid expenses, on the other hand, represent services to be received by the firm in the process of obtaining its revenue. Generally, there is no possible way to determine the value of these services in terms of the additional revenue to be generated by them. They can be valued only in terms of their acquisition value—a current or past cost. Inventories, however, are between the two extremes. They are not monetary assets, because the amount of cash or liquid resources to be generated by their sale is usually dependent upon expectations regarding future price changes; but even when prices can be predicted accurately, the timing of the future cash receipts may also be uncertain, making estimates of present values difficult. The validity of output prices for inventories also depends on the amount of additional direct expenses and the use of joint resources and joint activities of the firm required in selling the goods and collecting the proceeds. In this regard, they are similar to prepaid expenses. But, generally speaking, the present value of merchandise can be estimated more readily from expected future cash flows than can prepaid expenses.

Input Values. As applied to inventories, input values may be defined as some measurement of the resources used to obtain the inventory in its present condition and location. When the consideration given for the inventory is cash or its equivalent, the interpretation of the input value is fairly clear. However, when merchandise is manufactured, the input value of the inventory represents a summation of the valuations of resources used in production and other resources assignable to the product. Because of the necessity for allocations of resource valuations to periods and the reallocation to departments and products, interpreting the final input valuation of the product is difficult. Furthermore, the use of allocation procedures diminishes the possibility that the inventory valuations will be relevant in the prediction of cash flows or directly in investment decision models.

In the traditional accounting structure, the differences between the input values and the output value of the product sold, generally referred to as the gross profit or gross margin, should represent the nonproduct input values of the firm plus the profit or minus the net loss to the firm. The effect of all input valuation methods is to defer the recognition of revenue and net income until a later period. This delay in the recognition of revenue is justified whenever considerable services are yet to be performed by the firm or whenever verifiable output values cannot be obtained.

Input values are generally expressed in terms of historical costs.[11] The validity of historical costs rests on the assumption that they represent the input value of the resources obtained at the time of acquisition or use in the process of production. They are measured by the net monetary payment made in the past or to be made in the future in the acquisition of the goods or services. If payment is to be made in the distant future, the amount to be paid should be discounted to obtain the present cost. Theory, therefore, suggests that, subject to the usual caveat of materiality, inventory costs should be measured net of all trade, quantity, and cash discounts. This is the so-called *net* method. Cash discounts subsequently not taken should be recorded as Purchase Discounts Lost with the opposing credit going to Accounts Payable.*

When nonmonetary assets are exchanged for current goods or services, the current value of the nonmonetary assets represents the cost of the goods or services acquired; but accountants generally go back to the original monetary payment for the asset given up in exchange. Thus, historical cost generally means the monetary consideration paid in the acquisition or production of merchandise, including all services necessary to obtain the merchandise in a salable state.

Care must be taken, however, to exclude from historical cost, payments not intended or anticipated by the buyer at the time of the purchase decision. For example, repairing unexpected water damage done to goods in transit should be treated as an expense, not as part of the cost of the goods. Costs should include only that amount which the purchaser considered the item to be worth to him at the time of purchase. The mere fact that a cost is incurred does not justify including it in the initial asset value.

What Should Be Included?   Cost is a measure of the value of inputs necessary in the acquisition of material or merchandise in its present condition and location. The value of the inputs, in turn, is measured by the value of the consideration given up in acquiring them. The questions still to be answered, however, are these: What costs can be considered necessary? What costs can be associated with merchandise and, therefore, with future revenue? What costs should be considered expenses?

What costs are necessary is a matter of judgment. The accountant must use either an engineering standard or some other basis for comparison in making this judgment. *ARB 43* suggests that the concept of normality can be used as an acceptable basis:

> under some circumstances, items such as idle facility expense, excessive spoilage, double freight, and re-handling costs may be so *abnormal* as to require treatment as current period charges rather than as a portion of the inventory.[12]

An American Accounting Association committee, on the other hand, suggested that only costs *reasonably traceable* to the product should be included in acquisition costs.[13]

There is some similarity between the costs of normality and traceability. Many of the abnormal costs cannot be traced to specific products. For example, the costs of idle capacity and excessive spoilage of raw materials or finished products cannot be traced to the production of specific products. They are not costs of producing anything. But, presumably,

---

* Cash discounts not taken are often treated as an interest expense on grounds that they are offered to encourage early payment. But see Chapter 11 on why cash discounts may not be a financing charge.

costs of inefficiency in production can be traced to the product even though they are abnormal in nature. Thus, the AAA Committee concept of cost is somewhat broader than that of the AICPA. Although the concept of traceability is an important aspect of cost assignment, abnormal costs are not really input values, but rather losses to the firm.

The substitution of current replacement costs for historical costs does not avoid the problem of determining what costs are necessary. Costs expressed in current terms must still be classified as normal or abnormal, and as traceable or not traceable to specific products. Current costs, however, require a closer focus on the necessary costs of production or acquisition. The substitution of current costs of inefficient production for historical costs of efficient production is not an improvement in valuation procedures.

The second basic question—what costs should be associated with the inventory valuation and thus be matched with future revenues—is an even more difficult problem. *ARB 43* is not explicit on this point. It states that general and administrative expenses should not be included in product costs unless they are clearly related to production. It also states that ". . . the exclusion of all overheads from inventory costs does not constitute an accepted accounting procedure."[14] But this does not define what overhead costs should be included. The ambiguous nature of this statement has resulted in the proponents of both full absorption costing and direct costing claiming formal acceptance by the AICPA. Certainly full costing is acceptable, as there is no requirement that any normal manufacturing overhead be excluded from costs. On the other hand, the proponents of direct costing claim that, since it includes variable overhead costs, direct costing is an acceptable method.

The question of which costs should be included in the measurement of inventories has generally been answered within the historical cost accounting structure on the basis of the matching concept. That is, costs are allocated to the inventory if there is an assumed association between such costs and the revenues of future periods. This allocation, however, is necessarily arbitrary and is generally resolved by the use of allocation rules applied consistently. Thus, the accounting structure can be designed to be consistent with either variable costing or full costing. The choice must be made on other than structural logic.

In an attempt to attain economic interpretation of product costs, it can be assumed that, as long as costs are current, they represent value to the firm because the inventory could not be obtained without incurring the costs. While generalizations are always subject to exceptions and modifications, it is probably safe to state that costs should be added to inventory valuations to the point at which the merchandise is in the proper condition and location for sale or transfer to customers. In addition to specific manufacturing costs, this would include necessary costs of shipping, storage, and handling in bringing the merchandise to the store, display room, or warehouse. The inability to trace some of these costs, however, may necessitate their treatment as period expenses. If the turnover period is short and if these costs are not a substantial part of acquisition costs, inventory valuation and income determination will not be materially affected by the treatment of these costs as period expenses. Costs incurred in selling the product and in shipping the merchandise to customers, in many cases, can also be considered as increasing the inventory valuation. But since the selling prices should be available at this time, a better economic interpretation could be obtained by using the net realizable value.

From the point of view of using the inventory valuations as predictive indicators and as inputs into decision models, it would appear that variable costs might be more appropriate because they are more closely associated with cash flows and because they avoid the use of most arbitrary allocations required for full costing. Little is known about decision models, but under certain assumptions it appears that the classification of costs by their behavior and predictive ability might be more relevant than classification by product association.

CHECKPOINTS

1. What distinguishes monetary from nonmonetary assets? Give two examples of each.
2. At what value, theoretically, should accounts receivable be stated? Why does this, strictly speaking, make the installment method unnecessary?
3. Contrast the treatment of monetary investments with marketable equity securities. Are they consistent?
4. Distinguish the different types of prepaid expenses that occur.
5. Contrast the concept of normal costs with that of traceable costs in determining which costs should be charged to inventory.

THE ROLE OF ECONOMIC CONSEQUENCES

Chapter 8 points out that financial reporting has economic consequences for an enterprise and for society at large. These consequences are particularly noticeable in the case of current assets and, as a result, there has been much research into and debate about the nature, the implications, and the effects of these consequences. Two areas are discussed in this section: valuation of assets by financial institutions and the choice of LIFO versus FIFO in inventory valuation.

Marketing to Market

As noted above, *SFAS 12* requires companies under their jurisdiction to keep their investment portfolios at market values as long as market value does not exceed the original cost. Financial institutions tend to follow a different pattern. Banks distinguish between a trading portfolio and an investment portfolio. They keep the former at market value (regardless of original cost); they keep the latter at original cost (regardless of market) unless there is a permanent impairment in its value. Savings and loans and insurance companies follow a similar pattern, although their terminology varies somewhat.

On September 10, 1990, Richard C. Breeden, chairman of the SEC, made a speech that has been described as containing the "most significant initiative in accounting principles development in over 50 years."[15] Its significance lay in his testimony that all financial institutions be required to report all of their financial investments at market value. The basis for his testimony was that historical costs are no longer relevant in the new world in which we find ourselves. He did not argue, but others have, that if the savings and loan industry had been required to show its investments at market value, the parlous state of their loans might have been recognized earlier and the final debacle avoided. In other words, these critics claim that the failure to record assets at market value has had enormous and malign economic consequences.

This book has long called for marketable securities to be shown at fair value. What it has not done, and what Mr. Breeden is doing, is to call for all securities, whether marketable or not, to be shown at fair value. The dilemma, which the SEC acknowledges, is that we do not know as yet whether the benefits of determining fair value will exceed the costs of determining it in the case of nonmarketable securities. The effect of Mr. Breeden's testimony, though, is to provide considerable impetus for the cost-benefit relationship to be researched. The FASB, the AICFA, and the SEC have already met to coordinate their actions in this regard.

One of the other potential consequences of the call for assets to be marked to market is a change in the nature of regulation. Arthur Wyatt, former FASB board member, comments that:

> regulation historically has been based in part on the magnitude of capital, or shareholders' equity. Any accounting which artificially enhances capital is subverting the intent of the regulation. Up to now, regulators have used (and misused) accounting in order to make it appear that capital adequacy standards had been met. Mark-to-market accounting will force regulators to focus more attention on their own capital adequacy guidelines and reduce the artificiality of the regulatory process.

The call to mark to market, therefore, could bring a revolution to the regulation of accounting.

LIFO versus FIFO

It is an old truism that, in times of inflation, corporate taxes will be lower if an enterprise uses LIFO instead of FIFO. The choice of an accounting method has considerable economic consequences, therefore, and consequences whose effects are apparent—or so it would seem. It is somewhat of a puzzle, therefore, that so many companies have elected *not* to switch to LIFO. A survey of 213 companies provided some insight into management's reasons for not switching: 73 percent of the respondents said that, due to particular circumstances of their company, or their industry, LIFO produced no benefits. Another 12 percent said they were precluded from using it for regulatory reasons. The remainder cited problems with the high cost of managing LIFO, possible problems with the IRS, and the effect that lower earnings would have on the company.[16]

These reasons are somewhat surprising at first. Common wisdom has it that the stock market will reward handsomely those companies that switch to LIFO and, thereby, increase the after-tax cash flow of the company. An early study confirmed that market prices did indeed rise after a switch to LIFO.[17] But then a series of studies of LIFO switches during 1974–75 showed the opposite: market prices fell after the switch.[18] On the face of it, this kind of reaction shows that the market does not understand the benefits of LIFO.

Much research has followed these unexpected results. Some have suggested that they might be due to factors such as management's bonuses being tied to reported net income.[19] Stanford professor George Foster, after surveying some of this research, concluded that a "reliable body of evidence has not emerged from this literature, in part due to the severe problems associated with this research."[20] For example, one researcher has argued that the anomalous findings were due to the improper choice of dates on which the market was supposed to hear about the switch.[21] Other researchers have noted with some surprise that the tax savings from the use of LIFO are much smaller than is generally thought.[22] Research in the area continues.

SUMMARY

Previous chapters have provided the basic definition of assets, discussed their broad classification, how to measure them, and when to recognize them. This chapter treats the recording of current assets. The next two chapters treat plant and equipment, intangible assets, and noncurrent investments.

The general rule for recording all assets is to enter them at the present value of their maturity value adjusted for uncertainty. This is subject to the usual caveats of materiality and conservatism—specifically, assets should not be entered above their net realizable values. Cost accumulation ceases once an asset is available for sale or use.

Application of the general rule is automatic for cash. Accounts receivable is entered at the discounted value of the amount to be received at maturity adjusted by an allowance for doubtful accounts. Monetary securities (such as bonds and notes receivable) follow the general rule directly. Marketable securities also follow the general rule, except that they are handled at the portfolio level. Like other nonmonetary assets, inventories are entered at their accumulated costs subject to the market test of net realizable values.

MULTIPLE CHOICE QUESTIONS

Receivables and Accruals

1. [M86#8] When the allowance method of recognizing bad debt expense is used, the entries at the time of collection of a small account previously written off would

a. Increase net income.
b. Decrease the allowance for doubtful accounts.
c. Have no effect on the allowance for doubtful accounts.
d. Increase the allowance for doubtful accounts.

2. [M83#12] A method of estimating bad debts that focuses on the income statement rather than the balance sheet is the allowance method based on

a. Direct write-off.
b. Aging the trade receivable accounts.
c. Credit sales.
d. The balance in the trade receivable accounts.

Monetary Investments

3. [M87#3] On July 1, 1986, a company received a one-year note receivable bearing interest at the market rate. The face amount of the note receivable and the entire amount of the interest are due on June 30, 1987. The interest receivable account would show a balance on

a. July 1, 1986, but not December 31, 1986.
b. December 31, 1986, but not July 1, 1986.
c. July 1, 1986, and December 31, 1986.
d. Neither July 1, 1986, nor December 31, 1986.

4. [M86#7] A 90-day 15 percent interest-bearing note receivable is sold to a bank with recourse after being held for 60 days. The proceeds are calculated using an 18 percent interest rate. The amount credited to notes receivable at the date of the discounting transaction would be

a. The same as the cash proceeds.
b. Less than the face value of the note.
c. The face value of the note.
d. The maturity value of the note.

5. [N83#8] On July 1, 1983, a company received a one-year note receivable bearing interest at the market rate. The face amount of the note receivable and the entire amount of the interest are due on June 30, 1984. When the note receivable was recorded on July 1, 1983, which of the following were debited?

	Interest Receivable	*Unearned Discount on Note Receivable*
a.	Yes	No
b.	Yes	Yes
c.	No	No
d.	No	Yes

Nonmonetary Investments

6. [M86#4] The valuation allowance for a marketable equity securities portfolio included in current assets should be a component of

a. Current liabilities.
b. Noncurrent liabilities.
c. Noncurrent assets.
d. Current assets.

7. [N88#2] The amount by which the aggregate cost of a marketable equity securities portfolio exceeds its aggregate market value should be reported as a valuation allowance when the portfolio is included

	As a Current Asset	*In an Unclassified Balance Sheet*
a.	Yes	No
b.	Yes	Yes
c.	No	Yes
d.	No	No

8. [N83#5] A security in a current marketable equity securities portfolio is transferred to a noncurrent marketable equity securities portfolio. The security should be transferred between the corresponding portfolios at

a. The book value at date of transfer if higher than the market value at date of transfer.
b. The market value at date of transfer, regardless of its cost.
c. Its cost, regardless of the market value at date of transfer.
d. The lower of its cost or market value at date of transfer.

Inventories

9. [N88#6] According to the net method, which of the following items should be included in the cost of inventory?

	Freight Costs	Purchase Discount Not Taken
a.	Yes	No
b.	Yes	Yes
c.	No	Yes
d.	No	No

PROBLEMS AND DISCUSSION QUESTIONS

1. (**November 1977, amended**) The Financial Accounting Standards Board issued its *Statement No. 12* to clarify accounting methods and procedures with respect to certain marketable securities. An important part of the statement concerns the distinction between noncurrent and current classification of marketable securities.

Required:

a. Why does a company maintain an investment portfolio of current and noncurrent securities?
b. What factors should be considered in determining whether investments in marketable equity securities should be classified as current or noncurrent, and how do these factors affect the accounting treatment for unrealized losses?
c. What is the effect on the valuation allowance of noncurrent marketable equity security when it is reclassified as a current marketable equity security?

d. In your opinion, does the difference in treatment of current and noncurrent marketable equity securities make theoretical sense? Explain your opinion.

e. Discuss briefly the logic for making an adjustment in the valuation allowance because of the reclassification from noncurrent to current.

2. Assume the allowance method is being used for handling doubtful accounts in accounts receivable. Using I (increase), D (decrease), N (no effect), complete the following table by inserting in each column the effect of the transaction listed on each line. The first line is completed by way of example.

	Net Income	*Working Capital*	*Accounts Receivable*	*Allowance for Doubtful Accounts*
The initial recognition of a bad debt	D	D	N	D
Specific account receivable is collected				
Account previously written off is collected				
Account previously written off becomes collectible				
Specific uncollectible account is written off				

3. **(November 1964)** Due to calamitous earthquake losses the Morgan Company, one of your client's oldest and largest customers, suddenly and unexpectedly became bankrupt. Approximately 30 percent of your client's total sales have been made to the Morgan Company during each of the past several years.

The amounts due from Morgan Company—none of which is collectible—equal 25 percent of total accounts receivable, an amount that is considerably in excess of what was determined to be an adequate provision for doubtful accounts at the close of the preceding year.

Required:

How would your client record the write-off of the Morgan Company receivable if it is using the allowance method of accounting for bad debts? Justify your answer.

4. **(May 1971)** One of your corporate clients operates a full-line department store that is dominant in its market area, is easily accessible to public and private transportation, has adequate parking facilities, and is near a large permanent military base. The president of the company seeks your advice on a recently received proposal.

A local bank, in which your client has an account, recently affiliated with a popular national credit card plan and has extended an invitation to your client to participate in the plan. Under the plan, affiliated banks mail credit card applications to persons in the community who have good credit ratings regardless of whether they are bank customers. A recipient who wishes to receive a credit card completes, signs, and returns the application and installment credit agreement. Holders of cards thus activated may charge merchandise or services at any participating establishment throughout the nation.

The bank guarantees payment to all participating merchants on all presented invoices that have been properly completed, signed, and validated with the impression of credit cards that have not expired or been reported stolen or otherwise canceled. Local merchants, including your client, may turn in all card validated sales tickets or invoices to their affiliated local bank at any time and receive immediate credits to their checking accounts of 96.5 percent of the face value of the invoices. If card users pay the bank in full within 30 days for amounts billed, the bank levies no added charges against them. If they elect to make their payments under a deferred payment plan, the bank adds a service charge, which amounts to an effective interest rate of 18 percent per annum on unpaid balance. Only then do local affiliated banks and the franchiser of the credit card plan share in these revenues.

The 18 percent service charge approximates what your client has been billing customers who pay their accounts over an extended period on a schedule similar to that offered under the credit card plans. Participation in the plan does not prevent your client from continuing to carry on its credit businesses as in the past.

Required:

a. What are (1) the positive and (2) the negative financial—and accounting—related factors that your client should consider in deciding whether to participate in the described credit-card plan? Explain.

b. If your client does participate in the plan, which income statement and balance sheet accounts may change materially as the plan becomes fully operative? (Such factors as market position, sales mix, prices, markup, etc., are expected to remain about the same as in the past.) Explain.

5. Paragraphs 21 through 23 of *International Accounting Standard No. 2* state:

.21 The historical cost of manufactured inventories should include a systematic allocation of those production overhead costs that relate to putting the inventories in their present location and condition. Allocation of fixed production overhead to the costs of conversion should be based on the capacity of the facilities. If fixed production overhead has been entirely or substantially excluded from the valuation of inventories on the grounds that it does not directly relate to putting inventories in their present location and condition, that fact should be disclosed.

.22   Overheads other than production overhead should be included as part of inventory cost only to the extent that they clearly relate to putting the inventories in their present location and condition.

.23   Exceptional amounts of wasted material, labour, or other expenses should not be included as part of inventory cost.

Required:

To what extent do these requirements coincide with GAAP in the United States? Will American practice be consistent with this standard? Will international practice always be consistent with American standards?

6.   (November 1972) The Jonesville Company maintains capacitors used in radios, television sets, and rockets. Some orders are filled from inventory; others are for capacitors that are specially made to customer specifications as to size, lead wires, voltage, and tolerance.

When manufacturing a custom order, the Jonesville Company intentionally produces more capacitors than are ordered by the customer. These extra capacitors are carried at no value in the Jonesville Company inventory, since all costs of the job are charged to cost of goods sold at the time that the order is shipped. The extras are kept:

1. To replace any capacitors that may be returned as rejects that currently constitute 20 percent of all units sold.
2. To fill any subsequent orders from the customer for additional units of the same item.

Since there is no market for the unused custom manufactured capacitors, any that remain in inventory for two years are destroyed.

Jonesville warrants the replacement of defective capacitors returned by the purchaser. Often three to six months elapse between delivery of the order and receipt of the defectives.

Jonesville predicts that its production capacity is adequate so that no sales would be lost in future periods, even though it did not have the extras on hand to cover subsequent orders of custom manufactured capacitors.

Required:

a. What are the conceptual merits of Jonesville carrying the custom-manufactured extras held for replacement of defectives at:

1. No value? Explain.
2. Marginal or incremental cost? Explain.
3. Full cost? Explain.

b. What are the conceptual merits of Jonesville carrying the custom manufactured extras held for subsequent sale at:

1. No value? Explain.
2. Marginal or incremental cost? Explain.
3. Full cost? Explain.

c. What disclosure, if any, should Jonesville make for its obligation to replace defective capacitors? Explain.

7. John Stephens, owner of Stephens Inc., a manufacturer of small parts for lawnmowers and somewhat of a literary buff, stumbled across an old accounting text in a secondhand bookstore. Leafing through it he was intrigued to discover mention of a "base stock" method for handling inventory accounting. As described in the text, the method argues that part of inventory, the base stock, is a permanent investment of the firm and, therefore, should be treated as a noncurrent asset. Amounts held in excess of the normal are recorded on the basis of an average cost; first-in, first-out; or last-in, first-out.

As a noncurrent asset, no profit or loss arising from changes in prices should be recognized until the base stock is finally sold, presumably when the firm is liquidated. Current operating profit is assumed to arise from purchases and sales in excess of the normal base inventory. The text suggested that the base inventory be written down at the time of acquisition to an amount below that to which any future replacement cost could be expected to fall.[23] The amount of the write-down was considered to be a capital adjustment charged to retained earnings. Mr. Stephens is most intrigued with the method, which makes sense to him, and he asks you to implement it. Explain what you see as the strengths and weaknesses of the method.

8. The following example illustrates the use of the lower-of-cost-or-market rule in accounting. In each of the cases say which value should be used for measuring inventory.

			Market	
				Net Realizable Value less Normal
		Replacement	Net Realizable Value	Profit Margin
Case	Cost	Cost	(ceiling)	(20 percent) (floor)
A	$1.00	$1.04	$1.20	$0.96
B	1.00	0.96	1.10	0.88
C	1.00	0.80	1.05	0.84
D	1.00	0.92	0.90	0.72

9. The authors of *ARS 3* stated that ". . . inventories which are readily salable at known prices with negligible costs of disposal, or with known or readily predictable costs of disposal, should be measured at net realizable value."[24] They suggested further that this should not be an exception to usual acceptable valuation procedure, but rather, it should be considered ". . . in keeping with the major objectives of accounting."[25] *ARB 43*, on the other hand, stated that "only in exceptional cases may inventories properly be stated above cost."[26] According to this source, cost is the primary basis for inventory valuation.

As might be expected, the conditions prescribed by *ARB 43* are more restrictive than those prescribed in *ARS 3*, which provided two necessary conditions.

1. Inventories must be "readily salable at known prices."
2. Additional costs must be known or readily predictable.

These conditions are consistent with the objective of recognizing revenue whenever it has been earned as a result of the firm's activities and whenever it can be measured objectively. The term *known prices*, however, should not be interpreted as known with certainty. Even government-controlled prices may be subject to change. But the amount of the anticipated revenue (based on current sales prices) should be readily determinable with a reasonable degree of certainty.

The conditions required by *ARB 43* for stating inventories above cost are as follows:

1. Immediate marketability at quoted prices.
2. Interchangeability of units.
3. Deduction of additional expenditures to be incurred in disposal.
4. Difficulty or inability to estimate appropriate costs.

Required:

a. Compare the conditions laid down by Sprouse and Moonitz with those laid down by *ARB 43*.

b. Could these conditions be used to support the SEC's call for companies to mark to market?

SELECTED ADDITIONAL READINGS

Readers interested in pursuing the topics raised in this chapter might begin by reviewing the readings listed in Chapters 13 and 16. A few readings specific to this chapter, and additional to those in the Endnotes, are listed below.

Barden, Horace G. "The Accounting Basis of Inventories." *Accounting Research Study No. 13* (AICPA, 1973).

Buckley, John W., and James R. Goode. "Inventory Valuation and Income Measurement: An Improved System." *Abacus,* June 1976, pp. 34–48.

Chasteen, Lanny Gordon. "Empirical Study of Differences in Economic Circumstances as a Justification for Alternative Inventory Pricing Methods." *The Accounting Review,* July 1971, pp. 504–8.

Chasteen, Lanny Gordon. "Economic Circumstances and Inventory Method Selection." *Abacus,* June 1973, pp. 22–27.

Dhaliwal, D.; G. Salamon; and E. Smith. "The Effect of Owner versus Management Control on the Choice of Accounting Methods." *Journal of Accounting and Economics,* July 1982, pp. 41–53.

Hoffman, Raymond A., and Henry Gunders. *Inventories: Control, Costing, and Effect upon Income and Taxes,* 2nd ed. (New York: Ronald Press, 1970).

Hunt, H., III. "Potential Determinants of Corporate Inventory Accounting Decisions." *Journal of Accounting Research,* Autumn 1985, pp. 448–67.

Morse, D., and G. Richardson. "The LIFO/FIFO Decision." *Journal of Accounting Research,* Spring 1983, pp. 106–27.

Ricks, W. "The Market's Response to the 1974 LIFO Adoptions." *Journal of Accounting Research,* Autumn 1982, pt. I, pp. 367–87.

ENDNOTES

1. *ARB 43*, Ch. 3A, par. 4.
2. Thomas Henry Sanders, Henry Rand Hatfield, and Underhill Moore, *A Statement of Accounting Principles* (New York: American Institute of Accountants, 1938), p. 70.
3. See *APB 21,* par. 3 for other exceptions to the general rule of discounting all receivables and payables.
4. *APB 21,* par. 15.
5. See *SFAS 5,* particularly pars. 22 and 23.
6. *SFAS 66,* par. 22.
7. *SFAS 12,* par. 29c.
8. *SFAS 12.* Dissenting statement.
9. For a strong argument in this regard, see William H. Beaver, "Accounting for Marketable Equity Securities: Some Empirical Results." *Journal of Accountancy,* December 1973, pp. 58–64.
10. John B. Canning, *The Economics of Accountancy* (New York: Ronald Press, 1929), p. 37.
11. *ARB 43,* Ch. 4, par. 4 states that historical cost is the primary basis of measurement for inventories in financial accounting.
12. *ARB 43,* Ch. 4, par. 5.
13. Committee on Concepts and Standards—Inventory Measurement, AAA. "A Discussion of Various Approaches to Inventory Measurement," Supplementary Statement no. 2, *The Accounting Review,* July 1966, pp. 700–14.
14. *ARB 43,* Ch. 4, par. 5.
15. See Arthur Wyatt, "The SEC Says: Mark to Market!" *Accounting Horizons,* March 1991, pp. 80–84 on which this section draws heavily.

16. M. H. Granof and D. G. Short, "Why Do Companies Reject LIFO?" *Journal of Accounting, Auditing and Finance,* Summer 1984, pp. 323–33.

17. Shyam Sunder, "Relationship between Accounting Changes and Stock Prices: Problems of Measurement and Some Empirical Evidence," *Journal of Accounting Research,* Supplement 1973, pp. 1–45.

18. For instance, see G. Biddle and F. Lindahl, "Stock Price Reactions to LIFO Adoptions: The Association between Excess Returns and LIFO Tax Savings," *Journal of Accounting Research,* Autumn 1982, pt.II, pp. 551–88.

19. R. Abdel-Khalik, "The Effect of LIFO-Switching and Firm Ownership on Executive's Pay," *Journal of Accounting Research,* Autumn 1985, pp. 427–47.

20. George Foster, *Financial Statement Analysis*, 2nd ed. (Englewood Cliffs, N.J.: Prentice Hall, 1986), p. 157.

21. Francis L. Stevenson, "New Evidence on LIFO Adoptions: The Effects of More Precise Event Dates," *Journal of Accounting Research*, Autumn 1987, pp. 306–16.

22. Nicholas Dopuch and Morton Pincus, "Evidence on the Choice of Inventory Accounting Methods: LIFO versus FIFO." *Journal of Accounting Research,* Spring 1988, pp. 28–59.

23. Carl Thomas Devine, *Inventory Valuation and Periodic Income* (New York: Ronald Press, 1942), p. 92.

24. Robert T. Sprouse and Maurice Moonitz, "A Tentative Set of Broad Accounting Principles for Business Enterprises," *Accounting Research Study No. 3* (AICPA, 1962), p. 27.

25. Ibid., p. 28

26. *ARB 43,* Ch. 4, par. 15.

Chapter 17

Plant and Equipment: Purchased and Leased

CHAPTER OBJECTIVES

After studying this chapter, you will be able to:

Determine which costs should be included in the initial valuation of plant and equipment.

Contrast the treatment of purchased, self-constructed, and leased assets with respect to their initial valuation.

Provide a theoretical justification for certain repairs and maintenance costs to be expensed and for others to be capitalized.

Use and critique the criteria provided by the FASB for the capitalization of leases by lessees and lessors.

CHAPTER OVERVIEW

Introduction

This chapter deals with problems that are particularly associated with the reporting of plant and equipment. Some of these problems are independent of how the asset was acquired; others are related specifically to whether the asset was self-constructed, purchased, or leased.

Their Nature and Cost

Plant and equipment, like all assets, are entered at figures that include all costs necessary to make them useful. Particular problems encountered with self-constructed assets are whether, and how much, interest and manufacturing overhead to include in the cost of the asset. Another unique set of problems involves the acquisition of plant and equipment either through a nonmonetary exchange or by outright donation.

Leases

Long-term, noncancelable leases often appear to be disguised installment purchases. The FASB has suggested a number of criteria by which one might judge when the lease is in substance a sale. A better, and simpler, approach might be to require the capitalization of all long-term commitments.

Capital and Revenue Expenditures

Subsequent to the installation, costs associated with the asset, such as repairs and maintenance, should be expensed. Additions, improvements, and betterments that increase the benefits the asset will deliver, either by extending its life or by increasing its efficiency, should be capitalized.

Two major retail chains are in head-to-head competition. To permit them to grow, they need to borrow increasing sums of money from banks and other lenders. One returns a pretax return on assets that is 50 percent higher than the other. The chain with the lower return on assets also has a debt-to-equity ratio that is almost three times higher than that of its competitor! At first glance, the more profitable company, which also has lower financial leverage, is the preferred company. Analysis reveals that a major reason why its figures look better is that it leases its stores rather than purchases them. As a result, it shows no mortgages payable among its debts, and fewer assets to pull down its return.

Should companies be permitted to report their assets in such different ways? Should companies be required to capitalize all their leases? On what basis does one argue for doing this? Is it on the basis of comparability? What then if after one has capitalized the lease, one discovers that these are all new leases whereas the other chain has mostly older stores. The return on assets is then upward biased in favor of the chain with assets purchased before their current cost rose with inflation. Should one force both companies to report at current cost? And, what does one do about the chain that constructs its own stores—what costs should be included in their construction estimates to ensure comparability?

These are the questions that this chapter seeks to address in conjunction with other chapters on similar topics. The specific question addressed in this chapter is the cost of a newly acquired asset. At first glance, the answer is obvious: it is the cash paid for the asset. More broadly, it is the resources that are given up to acquire the asset. But which resources does one count when an asset is not purchased but is constructed by the firm?

And, as already noted, even more difficult to answer, is what resources to include when the asset is not purchased, but leased. These questions have provided so many difficult issues for accountants that the topics in this chapter have the distinction of drawing more financial standards than any other topics.

In the first part of this chapter the nature and costing of plant and equipment are examined. Particular attention is paid to the problems of assets that are acquired through nonmonetary transactions and assets that are self-constructed. The chapter then addresses the question of leased assets. It outlines the FASB's suggestions for when leased assets should be capitalized on the books of lessees and lessors. The chapter closes by considering the problems of when to capitalize the various kinds of repair and maintenance costs.

THEIR NATURE AND COST

Although all assets have some basic common characteristics, plant and equipment have some additional characteristics which may be summarized as follows:

1. The assets represent physical goods held to facilitate the production of other goods or to provide services to the firm or its customers in the normal course of operations.
2. They all have a limited life, at the end of which they must be abandoned or replaced. This life may be an estimated number of years determined by wear and tear caused by the elements, or it may be variable, depending on the amount of use and maintenance.
3. The value of the assets stems from the ability to enforce the exclusion of others in obtaining the legal property rights to their use rather than from the enforcement of contracts.
4. They are all nonmonetary in nature; the benefits are received from the use or sale of services rather than from their conversion into known quantities of money.
5. In general, the services are to be received over a period longer than a year or the operating cycle of the business. However, there are some exceptions. For example, a building or a piece of equipment is not reclassified as current when it has less than a year of remaining life. In a few cases, such as tools, some items may have an original life less than the operating cycle of the business.

As with inventories, regardless of whether historical costs or current costs are used, there is the problem of what should be included in the cost of the plant and equipment. When plant and equipment are acquired initially by purchase or when they are produced under contract, the initial cost is the total value of the resources given up to acquire the asset, install it at the proper location, and place it in the condition necessary for its intended service. Questions arise, however, regarding the measurement of the value of what is given up, the treatment of expenditures made subsequent to the initial installation, and the computation of costs of assets constructed by the firm intending to use them. The problems affect not only the input value of the plant and equipment, but also the periodic depreciation and the amounts charged directly to the current expense.

The initial cost of plant and equipment is definite only when a single asset is acquired for a cash price at the time that it becomes available for use. In a "basket" purchase, the total price may be definite, but the allocation to specific assets is a matter of judgment. The solution generally suggested is to allocate the total cost among the specific assets in the ratio of the appraised value of each, or in the ratio of the book values carried by the previous owner. The former assumes that any saving or excess payment should apply proportionately to all of the assets acquired. The latter assumes that the excess (or deficiency) over the previous owner's book value should apply proportionately. Both are arbitrary allocations, but they have the advantage of at least providing an answer to an extremely difficult problem. There is no reason to believe that the initial value to the firm is necessarily in the ratio of the appraised values. But this method is preferred to the second method because the allocation on the basis of book values to the previous owner results in a perpetuation of errors and differences arising from price changes during the period that the assets were held by the previous owner.

When nonmonetary assets must be destroyed and removal costs must be incurred to make space for the new asset being constructed, the costs of the new asset should include the liquidation selling price of the old asset plus the removal costs. These both represent costs that could have been avoided by not constructing the new asset; and it can be assumed that the value of the new asset is at least as great as its total cost—including the liquidation price and removal cost of the old asset net of the tax effect—or the new asset would not have been constructed.

In general, the initial cost should include the cash price plus freight and installation costs. Trade discounts and cash discounts should be deducted. When a cash discount is allowed but not taken, there is a question as to whether the invoice price represents the cost, or whether the net price allowed should be recorded and the allowed cash discount shown as a loss. Some argue that the invoice price is the correct cost because it represents the amount actually paid. Others prefer to record the net price that could have been paid because it represents the prudent cost to the firm. Although the latter is logical, it leads to the conclusion that the lowest cost should always be recorded because it is the prudent cost to the firm.[1] In many cases, this is a reasonable conclusion, but there are frequently valid reasons why the lowest initial cost is not the most favorable price to the firm in the longer run.

Nonmonetary Exchanges

APB 29 states that, in general, a nonmonetary asset obtained by exchanging a nonmonetary asset for it should be recorded at the fair value of the asset given up.[2] This is equivalent to valuing an acquired nonmonetary asset at the cash paid for it. This same concept applies to the acquisition of a nonmonetary asset in exchange for equity securities of the enterprise; that is, the asset should be recorded at the fair value of the stock given in exchange. However, in a nonreciprocal transfer* or when the fair value of the asset given up is not determinable within reasonable limits, the fair value of the nonmonetary asset received should be used as the basis of the acquired asset. In the case of a donation, the credit should be to a donated capital account, not to retained earnings since no earnings have taken place. The discovery of a previously unknown natural resource belonging to a corporation would be treated similarly.

In most cases, it can be assumed that the exchange is the result of arm's-length negotiation, so that the fair value of the asset received is equal to the fair value of the asset surrendered. This use of fair value is consistent with the concept that nonmonetary assets should be recorded at their cost to the enterprise, which in this case is the fair value of the asset exchanged. Fair value is the amount that could be obtained for a similar asset of the same age and condition. It is also assumed that the exchange is equivalent to the sale of the one asset and the purchase of the other.

Two exceptions to the above rule are made by *APB 29*. One exception is when neither the fair value of the asset surrendered nor the fair value of the asset received are determinable within reasonable limits. Presumably, the asset received would be recorded in the amount of the carrying value of the asset given up. However, the carrying value merely perpetuates an error in the valuation of one asset into the valuation of another. Although no measurement estimate may be ideal, an estimate of fair value based on the evidence available is better than no estimate.

A second exception is an exchange transaction that does not result in the culmination of the earning process. One type of exchange transaction is the exchange of assets held for sale in the same line of business. Another type is the exchange of nonmonetary productive assets of the same general type and that perform the same function. For these exchanges, if the fair value of the asset given up is less than the carrying value, the asset received should be recorded at fair value and a loss should be recorded. However, if the fair value is greater than the carrying value, *APB 29* states

---

* A *nonreciprocal transfer* is defined as a transfer of assets in one direction, such as a contribution to the firm, a donation of assets to the firm, or a transfer of assets to stockholders.

that the asset received should be recorded at the carrying amount of the asset transferred, or the sum of the monetary consideration and the carrying amount of the asset given up. No gain should be recorded. In the case of monetary consideration received in addition to the nonmonetary asset, a pro rata share of the gain should be recorded and the asset received would be recorded at the carrying value of the asset given up, plus the gain recognized, minus the monetary consideration received.

This second exception is also of doubtful validity. The purpose of the rule was to prevent firms from reporting gains when there was, in substance, no real change in the quantity or type of assets held. A lack of culmination of the earnings process is not a sufficient guide in this case, because, as discussed in Chapter 11, earnings are reported at many different times before the final collection of cash from the sale of products. Furthermore, if the fair value is interpreted to mean the price in a market in which the nonmonetary asset can be bought and sold, the gain or loss resulting from the use of fair value represents a holding gain or loss, and not operating income. Since current costs are assumed to be relevant to users of accounting information, it appears that fair value would be relevant in all exchanges and that all holding gains and losses should be recorded at the time of the transaction if not on a continuing basis.

Interest on Construction

Assets constructed for a firm's own use present the problem of whether or not to capitalize interest on the funds invested during the time required to get them ready for their intended use. Four general proposals are:

1. Capitalize no interest.
2. Capitalize only interest actually paid for funds borrowed for the specific purpose.
3. Capitalize all interest on borrowed capital regardless of the reason for the borrowing.
4. Capitalize interest on all funds invested regardless of whether the funds are obtained from borrowing or from equity sources.

The first proposal, that no interest should be capitalized, is based on the interpretation that it is not a cost of construction, but rather a financial charge. Since financial charges are generally debited to expense in the period that they are incurred, a deferral is assumed to result in the overstatement of current income during the period of construction or, if there are no sources of income during this period, the deferral would result in the failure to show a loss that is assumed to be real. Another basic argument is that interest could be avoided by financing the construction with stockholders' equity rather than with debt equity. But this does not eliminate the cost of using money; it merely shifts the burden to the stockholders and permits a deferral of actual payment since undeclared dividends are not contractual obligations of the firm.

The second proposal, to capitalize only the actual interest paid, is based on the assumption that interest is a cost of production, but that only amounts actually paid represent costs. Charging interest on funds provided by owners is assumed to result in unrealized income and the valuation of assets in excess of cost. Interest on ownership is rejected also because it is subjectively determined and its final realization is uncertain. But the uncertainty of the present value of the asset is the same, regardless of how it is financed. Thus, there is little justification for adding interest in one case and not in the other. It is difficult to argue that a building is more valuable simply because it was constructed with borrowed funds rather than funds acquired by the sale of stock. Furthermore, since funds are generally commingled, there is no way of determining what proportion of the asset is financed by debt equity and what proportion by stockholders' equity, except, perhaps, in a new firm.

The third proposal avoids the problem of deciding how much of the investment was financed by debt and how much by equity. The entire investment is assumed to arise from debt, but with the limitation that the total interest capitalized should not exceed the total interest cost incurred during the period. The interest, therefore, represents an opportunity cost—the amount that could have been avoided by not borrowing or by using the funds to reduce outstanding debt. This is the approach selected by the FASB in *SFAS 34* and illustrated in Exhibit 17-1. One of the advantages of this approach is that the interest capitalized represents a cost to the firm consistent with basic historical cost accounting methods. However, it does not lead to comparable results by different firms producing similar assets but different capital structures. Also, there is an opportunity cost for using funds obtained from equity sources; the different treatment of debt and equity sources leads to valuations that are inconsistent and not comparable.

The fourth proposal, that interest should be charged for all funds used is based primarily on the assumption that it represents an economic cost. From a logical point of view, this is the best procedure, although it is not generally accepted in the United States. The total cost of the asset is the value of the goods and services given up in order to acquire it. Interest represents the service value of the money invested in the acquisition of the asset before its use. Since this money is not used for current operations, but rather for future operations, a deferral of the implicit interest is appropriate. The argument that it should not be recorded because it represents unrealized income is tied more closely to the realization rules than to the basic principle that income should be reported during the entire period of production.

The main application of the fourth proposal is in the area of public utilities. The primary reason for its use in this situation arises from the fact that the income of a utility is regulated on the basis of its total

---

EXHIBIT 17-1   Georgia Pacific Footnote Disclosure of Interest Capitalization

The Corporation capitalizes interest on projects when construction takes considerable time and entails major expenditures. Such interest is charged to the property, plant, and equipment accounts and amortized over the approximate life of the related assets in order to properly match expenses with revenues resulting from the facilities. Interest capitalized, expensed, and paid was as follows:

	Year ended December 31		
(Millions)	*1988*	*1987*	*1986*
Total interest costs	$222	$134	$147
Interest capitalized	(25)	(10)	(9)
Interest exposure	$197	$124	$138
Interest paid	$164	$116	$136

The Corporation defers net operating costs on new construction projects during the start-up phase and amortizes the deferral over five years. The amounts deferred, which were not material in 1988, 1987, and 1986, are included in the property, plant, and equipment accounts.

---

capitalization. If a normal rate of return is permitted only on revenue-producing assets in use, there would be no opportunity for the firm to earn any income on investments necessary during the construction period before assets are placed in operation. The common practice of crediting the interest expense, however, implies that the construction was financed with debt equity. As indicated above, generally no specific allocation can be made.

Overhead on Self-Constructed Assets

When plant and equipment are constructed by the firm that will use the asset, the accumulation of costs is little different from the costing of manufacturing products. Labor and material cost can usually be assigned directly to the fixed asset being constructed. The main difficulty comes in the allocation of joint overhead costs to the asset and to the normal production. At least four proposals are frequently made to handle this problem:

1. Assign no overhead to the fixed asset.
2. Assign the incremental overhead.
3. Assign overhead equal to the amount that would have been assigned to the production that is curtailed because of the production.

4. Assign a proportionate share of overhead to the construction on the basis of the procedure that is used for the assignment to normal production.

The first proposal, the assignment of no overhead to the asset constructed, is based on the assumption that overhead is primarily a fixed expense, that it is chargeable only to the normal operations of the current period, that an allocation of overhead to the plant and equipment results in an overstatement of the net income for the current period, and that allocation of overhead to the plant and equipment results in an overstatement of the net income for the current period. In general, the assumption that all overhead is fixed is false; the construction of fixed assets practically always results in some increase of total overhead costs. To the extent that this is true, the second proposal (to assign the increase in overhead costs to the constructed asset) is far superior to the first. The incremental costs are the minimum that should be assigned to the constructed asset. All of the incremental costs are incurred to benefit future periods rather than current operations. However, if there is evidence that such costs result from errors or inefficiencies, they represent a loss to be recognized in the current period.

The arguments for charging only incremental costs to the constructed asset are similar to the arguments for direct costing of inventories. The main argument is that the allocation of fixed overhead results in additional income in the current period because of the construction. That is, the net income in the current period would have been smaller if the overhead had been charged to current operations. This capitalization of fixed overhead appears to be inconsistent to those who advocate that income should reflect sales effort only and not production or construction effort. The second argument for direct costing—that there is no benefit to future periods if there is likely to be excess capacity in later years—is less convincing in this situation. Plant and equipment, unlike inventories, must be constructed in anticipation of many years' use. They cannot be constructed piecemeal only as services are needed. Therefore, the failure to construct a needed fixed asset in the current year may result in a lower total income in the following year.

One of the strongest arguments for charging only variable costs to the construction is that, if normal production and sales are not curtailed by the construction (the most likely situation), there is no evidence that management would have been willing to incur additional costs. Thus, there is no evidence that management considered the constructed asset to have a value greater than the variable costs incurred. But this is only the minimum value; the subjective value to the firm based on expectations of future benefits is probably much greater than the variable costs. Should accountants take the conservative position and include only those costs that represent clear evidence of future value, or should they exclude costs only when there is good evidence that they do not represent the value of future benefits?

The third proposal, to assign overhead equal to that which would have been allocated to curtailed production, seems plausible on the surface. The remaining overhead allocated to current production is no different than it would have been if the construction had not been undertaken, and it appears to represent service capacity that would have been utilized under normal conditions. But it is a cost based on what would have been allocated if an alternative course of action had been chosen. This is not a true opportunity cost, because it is not based on a service value given up to obtain the construction.

The proposal to allocate a full share of all overhead to the constructed asset is an appropriate full-costing procedure. If the amount of overhead allocated to the constructed asset represents the input value of services actually used, the capitalization is logical on the basis that it represents the input value of future service benefits. If there is an expectation of future benefits in the form of either larger revenues or smaller costs, capitalization is assumed to provide a better matching of revenues and expenses in future periods and a better measurement of the net income from operations during the construction period. Whether there is excess capacity to handle the construction is not the determining factor in the capitalization decision, although the argument for capitalization is weaker if facilities are used that would otherwise have been idle. The important consideration is the expectation of future benefits.

CHECKPOINTS

1. List the specific characteristics of plant and equipment.
2. To what account should the costs of tearing down an old building in preparation for a new one be charged?
3. In general, at what value should a nonmonetary asset that has been swapped for another nonmonetary asset be entered?
4. What are the arguments for capitalizing overhead on self-constructed assets?
5. What is the argument against capitalizing interest on the total cost of a project?

LEASES OF PLANT AND EQUIPMENT

Plant and equipment are occasionally rented or leased to other firms or individuals for short periods, extending from a day to a year or more. In these cases, the lessor usually takes care of the maintenance of the property and pays the recurring expenses related to the property, such as taxes and insurance. These recurring expenses are called *executory costs*. In addition, the lessor must continually enter into new lease contracts during the life of the property. Therefore, the rental revenues are part of the operating revenues of the lessor. The maintenance, tax, and insurance expenses, as well as depreciation on the leased property, should be included in its operating expenses. Reporting the leased plant and equipment in the financial statements is no different than reporting plant and equipment used in manufacturing or in providing services to customers. From the lessee's point of view, the lease results in a rental expense, which is recorded as the services are received or when payment is made.

Many argue that there are circumstances, such as when the lease contract permits the leased asset to be transferred to the lessee at the end of the lease, or when the lease covers a long period, or when the lease is noncancelable, that the lease is in substance a credit sale by the lessor and a purchase of property on an installment basis by the lessee. Various reasons are offered for wanting to structure the sale and purchase of an asset as a lease. One common reason that is given for leasing is the desire of the lessee to avoid showing a large payable in the balance sheet. Leases, if correctly structured, enable lessees to engage in *off-balance sheet financing*. Another common reason given is that, although the lessee wants to purchase, it lacks the capital to purchase the asset outright or even to put a sufficient deposit on the asset. A third reason that is sometimes given is that the lessor, by not transferring title to the lessee, is able to earn certain tax benefits, which it can pass on to the lessee if it so chooses. In each case, the intent of the buyer/lessee is to take final possession of the asset from the seller/lessor, but the transaction is being disguised. This is not to say that no perfectly legitimate leases exist— many do.

An obvious example of a lease having basic financing and purchase characteristics is the case in which a manufacturer finances the acquisition of equipment by one of its customers. Title may pass to the customer at the end of the finance term, which may extend to the end of the useful life of the asset. An alternative scenario involves a finance company (the equity holder) that pays the manufacturer for the equipment in exchange for title to it. The finance company receives an installment note from the customer, who receives the right to use the property for what may be almost the entire useful life of the asset. Most people feel that the financing company has simply financed the acquisition of an asset.

Broadly speaking, in cases where the lease is in effect a purchase, the lessee should record the equipment leased at its fair value and show a lease payable in the same amount. By analogy, and subject to the usual rules of conservatism, the lessor should treat the lease as a sale. In a sales-type lease, the difference between the fair value of the asset and its cost should be shown as normal profit. In a direct-financing lease, there is no profit. In both cases, the lessor should show interest revenue as one would on an installment sale. The whole procedure is generally referred to as the *capitalization* of leases and leases treated as purchases are termed *capital* leases. More details about capitalization follow in a later section.

Defining Capital Leases

Determining the point at which a simple rental changes over to become a purchase has proven extremely difficult. What if the lease is only for two years? Or five? Or ten? There is a gray area in which it is hard to decide how to define the transaction. The result is that more standards have been written, and continue to be written, on leases than any other single topic. The Committee on Accounting Procedure produced one standard, the Accounting Principles Board produced five standards, and the Financial Accounting Standards Board has issued eight to date, not counting a number of technical bulletins.

The first attempt to draw a line was made by the Committee on Accounting Procedure in October 1949 in *ARB 38,* which subsequently became Chapter 14 of *ARB 43,* which said: "Where it is clearly evident that the transaction involved is in substance a purchase, the 'leased' property should be included among the assets of the lessee with suitable accounting for the corresponding liabilities. . . ."[3] This statement rather begs the question. In practice, the prime means for determining whether the transaction was in substance a purchase was whether a bargain purchase option existed.

APB 5, "Reporting of Leases in Financial Statements of Lessees" issued in 1964 and *APB 7,* "Accounting for Leases in Financial Statements of Lessors" issued in 1966 were the main attempts by the Accounting Principles Board to deal with the difficulties of determining when leases should be capitalized. These statements introduced the terms *operating* and *financing leases* into general usage, but did not significantly change the general approach laid out in *ARB 38.* Significantly, though, the criteria used in *APB 5* and *APB 7* for determining when a lease was to be capitalized differed. As a result, a transaction could be capitalized on the lessee's books but not on the lessor's books, or vice versa.

The SEC was highly critical of reporting requirements and pressured the FASB to review them. *SFAS 13* resulted. The FASB set out in this statement its own criteria by which one might judge when a lease was sufficiently like a purchase to warrant treatment as an installment purchase by the lessee.* It argued that at least one of the following should be present:

---

* *SFAS 13* has been amended or had paragraphs superseded on numerous occasions. Changes to *SFAS 13* are found in standards 17, 22, 23, 26, 27, 28, 29, 71, 91, 94, and 98.

1. The property title will be transferred to the lessee by the end of the lease term or under a bargain purchase option.
2. The term of the lease is at least 75 percent of the economic life of the property, unless the term begins within the last 25 percent of this life.
3. At the inception of the lease, the present value of the minimum lease payments, as defined below, equals or exceeds 90 percent of the fair value of the leased property to the lessor (reduced by any related investment tax credit to be used by the lessor). As with the second criterion, this criterion is not relevant if the lease term begins within the last 25 percent of the life of the property.[4]

The first criterion is the most obvious in that passage of title effectively defines the transaction as a purchase. The second criterion suggests that, if one has had the use of the asset for almost its entire life, one has in effect bought it. The third suggests that, if one pays an amount virtually equal to the fair value of the asset, one might as well have purchased it outright. In each case, the lease is equivalent to a purchase.

Restating the FASB's position, these three criteria are applied under the assumption that the basic characteristics of a purchase include the transfer to the purchaser by the seller of the risks and benefits to be obtained from owning and using the property during its expected life, including the obligation to pay for its benefits. But the only semantically interpretable dividing line in the criteria offered by the FASB is that, if the unguaranteed residual value is relatively small, the risk and benefits of ownership are transferred and, therefore, the lease should be capitalized. As a result, the determination of when a lease transfers a sufficient amount of the risk and benefits to classify it as a capital lease is based upon a series of arbitrary criteria such as 75 percent of the life and 90 percent of the fair value.

To ensure that lessees and lessors treated leases symmetrically, the FASB used the same three criteria to determine when a lease should be classified as a sales-type lease or a direct financing lease by a lessor. It imposed two additional criteria, though.

1. The collection of minimum lease payments should be reasonably predictable.
2. The unreimbursable costs to be incurred by the lessor under the lease other than for insurance, maintenance, and taxes should be measurable and not be surrounded by important uncertainties.

Neither of these criteria change the basic approach to recognizing leases. They simply add the usual caveat of conservatism. On the other hand, they do change the approach to defining a lease in that, in addition to classifying the lease according to whether or not it transfers risk and benefits of ownership, the classification, not just the recognition, is also determined by the measurability of the net receivable to the lessor. In principle, this allows for asymmetry, but in practice this appears to be rare.

Leases Involving Real Estate.   Matters are made more complex when real estate is involved because of the potential conflicts between *SFAS 13* and *SFAS 66*. For instance, it became apparent early that an owner of property could structure the transfer of property as a sales-type lease and recognize a profit under *SFAS 13*. The same transfer structured as an installment sale fell under *SFAS 66,* which would not permit the immediate recognition of profit. The FASB has since made all leases involving real estate subject to the overall provision of *SFAS 66*.[5]

Leases involving land only are generally operating leases, because land has an indefinite life. If the lease includes a bargain purchase option or a stipulation that title will be transferred, the lease is an installment sale in substance and should be capitalized subject to the rules of *SFAS 66.* Leases in which land is less than 25 percent of the total fair value are treated as any normal property and equipment lease. When land constitutes more than 25 percent of the total fair value, the land should be treated separately. Each portion will then be accounted for in accordance with the normal rules of land leases and property and equipment leases.

Owning Assets versus Owning Rights

The analogy that is drawn here between a lease and purchase is not strictly accurate, though, and for a number of reasons. The purchase of an asset provides one with a number of ownership rights. These generally include the right to hold, use, and dispose of property within certain restrictions of the law and the rights of others. A long-term noncancelable lease has some of these rights of ownership, but not all. It generally does not include the right of disposal, for instance. More broadly, leases give one the rights to the use of the property without giving one rights to the property itself. In this, leases are somewhat like intangible assets.

The characteristics of ownership of plant and equipment present in the lease include the right of the lessee to use the property during the life of the lease with, generally, obligation to pay a fixed price in the form of installments. Thus, the lessee has a nonmonetary asset in the form of a right to receive benefits from the use of the plant and equipment. The lessor, even though it holds the equity in the property, has a receivable that is a monetary asset representing the right to receive a specified number of dollars over the life of the contract. However, the rights held by the lessee and the receivable of the lessor differ from those arising from usual sales/purchase transactions in several respects.

In many cases, the lessor, not the lessee, may be required to provide for the maintenance of the equipment and pay for the expenses, such as taxes and insurance, relating to the property leased. The residual equity is held by the lessor rather than the lessee who receives the benefits, although it may be transferred to the lessee at the end of the contract or during the lease period under option terms. In addition, special tax benefits may accrue to the lessor, rather than to the lessee who holds the property. On the other hand, leases are often structured to include certain benefits that would not normally be available to an owner. For example, the lessor often transfers to the lessee certain specific tax advantages, which accrue to the lessor only. In short, while leases and purchases share some characteristics, they do not share all.

The analogy is imperfect at the legal level too. When one defaults on installment payments, one is still liable for the remaining payments. When one defaults on a lease, one is not liable for the remaining lease payments. The lessor is entitled only to the residual loss after selling the asset or releasing it to someone else. In other words, the law treats leases as though they were executory contracts. As noted, though, in Chapter 1, accountants have not always followed legal precedent in setting standards.

A basic criticism, then, of all criteria that emphasize the similarities of leases to purchases is that they fail to recognize that a lease has characteristics of its own. It is not necessary that all new forms of economic relationships be molded to fit the traditional accounting classification. A similar criticism applies to the additional criteria that apply to the classification of the lease as a sales-type or a direct-financing lease by the lessor. It is not uncommon to defer the reporting of a sale (and the presentation of the receivable) until there is a relative degree of certainty regarding the collectibility of the receivable. However, the existence of uncertainty should not determine the classification of the lease, and whether or not a receivable exists. Instead, the degree of uncertainty should be reported by presenting a range of measurements, or by the use of probabilities.

An analogy may be drawn at this point to convertible bonds. These fall somewhere between pure liabilities and pure owners' equity. They share some characteristics of both. Accounting proceeds by forcing convertible bonds into the liability category for balance sheet purposes. It then forces them into the owners' equity category to compute earnings per share. It might be better to simply acknowledge them as a third form of equity.

Because of the complex nature of most leases, it is not sufficient to assume that they represent in substance sales/purchase contracts and normal debt instruments. They should be reported in a way that describes their nature and characteristics as completely as possible, rather than attempting to incorporate all of the information in the traditional form of assets and liabilities. This is not to say that the measurement of the resources and obligations is not meaningful; it is not meaningful, though, if it captures only *some* of the relevant characteristics of leases. Other characteristics, such as the patterns and terms of cash flows and purchase rights, should be described by other methods.

Capitalization of All Long-Term Noncancelable Commitments

An alternative approach to these methods of handling long-term leases is to consider them a part of the broader problem of long-term noncancelable commitments. Whenever a firm enters into a long-term contract to acquire goods or services and to make appropriate payment, certain specific rights and obligations arise. If these goods and services are acquired on a year-to-year basis or under contracts that are cancelable on short notice, the rights and obligations are generally not material regarding their effect on the balance sheet, and it is appropriate to record the transactions when the goods and services are received or accrued or when payment is made. No capitalization is necessary. But if the contract is noncancelable by either party and if each has a valid and material claim against the other, the contract should be capitalized, and the discounted value of both the rights and obligations should be disclosed.

While this position does not have the support of currently accepted accounting practice, it does have considerable merit in its favor. A contract to purchase a given quantity of goods gives rise to a liability just as much as an obligation to pay for goods already acquired. The main difference is that in the first case the firm has an obligation to pay for goods when they are received, but in the latter case the obligation is to pay for goods that have already been received. In the case of the noncancelable contract to purchase, there is not an unconditional right of offset. The purchasing firm has an obligation to pay for the merchandise to be acquired under the contract, even though it should decide later that the goods are not wanted. The going-concern postulate assumes that the firm intends to carry out its commitments, and it also assumes that other firms will normally carry out theirs. The nature of the obligation is not different simply because of a possible default on the part of the seller. Of course, if the seller does default, a right of unconditional offset does arise and the obligation to pay for the unperformed part of the contract may be canceled. But default is not the normal pattern, and the best expectation is that both sides of the contract will be carried out.

The asset arising from the long-term commitment is the right to receive goods and services, and this claim should be recorded on the basis of the discounted amount of its expected values. As with receivables, the value of the claim depends on the expectations that they will materialize. The possibility of default is the exceptional case rather than the rule, and this possibility should be taken into consideration only in the determination of the valuation of the rights and obligations.

It should be realized that the suggestion being made here to capitalize certain long-term commitments goes well beyond that of leases, and more particularly leases as defined in *SFAS 13*. In that statement, leases are confined to contracts involving land and depreciable assets. But one can also lease intangible assets, such as the right to use the name of a franchiser. Also excluded by *SFAS 13,* but included in this discussion, are long-term contracts for the supply of heat and electricity and other contracts known as *take-or-pay agreements.*

In all these contracts, the distinction between long-term and short-term obligations is not as important in the decision whether or not to capitalize the rights and obligations as the question of cancelability. The materiality of the discounted value is also an important criterion. But there are many other considerations that must be studied thoroughly before a definite broad principle of capitalization can be established. Employment contracts probably should not be capitalized because they are usually cancelable by the employee. Other types of contracts may also be cancelable with a penalty. Capitalization should be necessary only if the penalty is sufficient to act as a deterrent to unilateral default.

In general, the arguments for capitalization of long-term commitments other than leases are not as compelling as the arguments for capitalization of long-term leases. The similarity to property rights is not generally present. The obligation is not generally an alternative to other forms of financing. And the asset or right received is not generally amortized over its useful life. But one advantage of capitalization of long-term commitments in general is that the valuation of the rights can then be treated separately from the valuation of the obligations. A contract to purchase a given quantity of merchandise over a long period of time at a predetermined price, that is, a take-or-pay contract, results in an obligation that is monetary in nature but has rights or claims that are nonmonetary. If the value of the goods to be acquired should change materially, capitalization would permit showing the valuation of the asset differently from the value of the liability. Therefore, holding gains and losses could be recorded conveniently. The current practice of recording losses on long-term commitments requires setting up a partial liability or a reserve.* Capitalization permits the valuation of the asset and the valuation of the liability to be treated separately.

The application of this general principle to long-term leases has the effect of extending the amount to be capitalized. The principle does not limit the amount to the property rights. If the lease requires a fixed payment that is noncancelable, the entire amount should be capitalized regardless of whether it represents payment for property rights or for additional services, including repairs, maintenance, and taxes, and other services related to the use of the property. On the other hand, if the lessee is required to take care of the maintenance and repairs and pay the property taxes and insurance, these amounts should also be capitalized as long-term commitments—if they require unconditional payments regard-

---

* For more details, see Chapter 18 on executory contracts and unconditional rights of offset. Rights of offset are also discussed in Chapter 13.

less of whether or not the property is used. But payments for utilities and other related costs should not be capitalized if they can be avoided by not using the property.

One of the main arguments against the capitalization of long-term commitments other than long-term leases is that, since capitalization is not a common practice in this case, there is no lack of comparability among firms. But, in the case of long-term leases, there is a lack of comparability, because those firms that own property do show the assets and related obligations, and those that lease the property traditionally have failed to show either the asset or the liability in the balance sheet. Thus, many financial ratios computed from the statements of property owners cannot be compared with similar ratios computed from the statements of firms that lease property. It is also claimed that, generally, the payments under long-term commitments other than leases are more related to the associated expenses than is generally the case with long-term leases. It may also be argued that the reporting of current payments better discloses the actual cash flows of the firm. However, the capitalization of noncancelable commitments should not preclude the disclosure in financial statements of current cash payments and the amount and timing of future cash requirements under the contracts.

Reporting Leases

Deciding the most appropriate way in which to report on leases has proven complex partly because of the many types of leases that have to be considered. The following paragraphs lay out some of the considerations affecting:

Lessee reporting of capital leases.

Lessor reporting of financing-type and sales-type leases.

Operating leases.

Leveraged leases.

Sale-and-leaseback arrangements.

The next section briefly discusses some of the disclosure-related issues. These are illustrated in Exhibit 17-2.

Leases Reported by the Lessee. The classification of the lease as a capital lease requires that the lessee report in the financial statements both the asset and the liability. The FASB states that the amount capitalized at the inception of the lease should be the sum of the present value of what are termed *minimum lease payments*—subject to a ceiling of the fair value of the asset. These are the lease payments after deducting the amounts that represent expenses, such as maintenance, insurance, and taxes, that is, those amounts that are termed *executory* costs. The present value of the amount to be paid in a bargain purchase option, if any, should be included in the minimum lease payments.[6] In the absence of a bargain purchase option, the minimum lease payments will also include any residual values guaranteed by the lessee to the lessor, and any payments that will be due on failure to renew or to extend the lease.

The determination of what constitutes minimum lease payments is based on an analogy between leases and purchases. When property is owned, the value of the property rights is capitalized by setting up an asset equal to its cost when acquired. However, the cost of maintenance and periodic payments for insurance and taxes are charged to expense only as they are incurred or accrued. No asset or obligation is generally shown in the balance sheet for the cost of services and other expenditures necessary to provide proper use of the property during its lifetime. Similarly, only the property rights being acquired under the terms of a lease should be capitalized.[7] That is, where the terms of the lease require the lessor to provide necessary repairs and to pay taxes, insurance, and other costs of making the property available and useful to the lessee, that portion of the periodic lease payments representing the payment for these services should be excluded from the amount capitalized in the balance sheet. The payments for these services should be recorded as expenses in each period of payment, as with owned property.

Amortization of the lease is affected by assumptions about the transfer of title. Whenever title moves to the lessee at the end of the lease, or when one can assume that it will, such as when the lease contains a bargain purchase option, then the leased asset is amortized over its life. Failing this, amortization is over the life of the lease.

One of the advantages of capitalization of the property rights inherent in lease contracts is that it presents a clearer picture in the financial statements of the rights and obligations of the firm. It also permits comparability with firms that own property and with other firms with long-term leases. The capitalization, however, does not eliminate the necessity for additional disclosure, by footnote or otherwise, of the annual payment and other material terms of the lease contract. Finally, a major advantage of capitalization is that it permits separation of the property rights and the lease obligations. Thus the value of the property can be amortized independently of the timing of the contractual payments, in a manner similar to the depreciation of owned plant and equipment. Capitalization of property rights is not without its problems, though. Two of these are:

1. The difficulty in separating that portion of the rentals considered to be payment for property rights and that considered to be payment for services yet to be performed.
2. The selection of a proper rate of interest for capitalization.

The value of the property rights can be computed either by estimating the value of property without the additional services provided and subtracting the discounted value of the property at the termination of the lease, or by estimating the value or cost of the services to be provided by the lessor annually. In the latter method, the annual payment for the property rights can be estimated by subtracting the value of the annual services from the total annual lease payments. The FASB states that the discount rate should be the incremental borrowing rate available to the firm currently for long-term credit with similar risk and terms.* This rate emphasizes

---

EXHIBIT 17-2 Footnote Disclosure of Fixed Asset Policies

SUNRISE MEDICAL INC. (June) *($000)*

	1988	1987
Current liabilities:		
Current installments of obligations under capital leases and long-term debt	$ 1,873	$ 2,325
Trade accounts payable	9,870	8,920
Accrued compensation and other expenses	9,921	8,597
Income taxes	1,564	1,397
Total current liabilities	23,228	21,239
Obligations under capital leases, less current installments	$ 2,753	$ 3,199

NOTES TO CONSOLIDATED FINANCIAL STATEMENTS
(Dollars in thousands, except per share amounts)
Summary of Significant Accounting Policies (In Part)
Property, Plant, and Equipment

Property, plant, and equipment is recorded at cost and depreciated over its estimated useful life by use of the straight-line or declining balance methods. Assets recorded under capital leases and leasehold improvements are amortized over the shorter of their useful lives or the term of the related leases by use of the straight-line method. The estimated useful lives of property, plant, and equipment are 3–40 years.

	July 1, 1988	June 26, 1987
Land	$ 160	$ 160
Improvements	2,058	2,058
Property and equipment	2,111	2,309
Assets under capital lease	4,329	4,527
Accumulated amortization	1,676	1,360
Assets under capital lease, net	$2,653	$3,167

---

* The implicit rate used by the lessor should be used if it is known and is less than the incremental borrowing rate.

EXHIBIT 17-2 *(continued)*

Capital lease obligations are summarized as follows:

	July 1, 1988	June 26, 1987
Subleases of an operating facility and certain equipment with lease periods expiring through 1998, at interest of approximately 7% and 15%. Leases contain options to purchase the assets	$2,863	$3,097
Leases of automobiles with lease periods expiring at various dates through 1990, at interest of approximately 10%	196	378
Leases of office equipment with lease periods expiring in 1991, at interest of approximately 11% and 13%	88	112
Total obligations under capital leases	3,147	3,587
Less current installments	394	388
Obligations under capital leases, less current installments	$2,753	$3,199

Sunrise also leases office and operating facilities, machinery and equipment, and automobiles under operating leases with unexpired terms ranging from one to fifteen years. Rental expense for operating leases amounted to $1,349, $1,515, and $1,001 for fiscal 1988, 1987, and 1986, respectively.

Minimum lease payments under leases expiring subsequent to July 1, 1988 are:

Fiscal Years Ending	*Capital Leases*	*Operating Leases*
1989	$ 583	$ 2,087
1990	534	1,803
1991	436	1,504
1992	387	1,252
1993	382	997
1994–2003	1,918	2,806
Total minimum lease payments	4,240	$10,449
Less amount representing interest.	1,093	
Present value of net minimum lease payments	$3,147	

---

measurement of the liability, which in turn determines the amount that represents the historical cost of the asset. The procedures for estimating the minimum lease payments, and the discount rate used, can be criticized:

1. Capitalization of only the minimum lease payments for the benefits of ownership of property assumes that the lease is directly comparable to

the owning of property. As stated above, instead of trying to mold the reporting of leases into the traditional property classification, it would be better to recognize that the lease has individual characteristics. These characteristics might be captured better by capitalizing all expected payments, not just the amounts that represent property rights.

2. Use of the incremental borrowing rate at the inception of the lease is based on the historical cost tradition. This is one situation in which the current value can be computed quite easily each year by using the current incremental rate and the expected remaining payments.

Financing-Type Leases Reported by Lessors.   From the point of view of the lessor, a lease may be either a direct financing or a sales-type lease. In the direct financing lease, the finance or leasing company holds a secured installment note receivable. The FASB states that the net value of this receivable should be stated at the net present value of the minimum lease payments. This should include the residual value whether or not it is guaranteed. This is computed similarly to the way in which the lessee computes the payable except that an unguaranteed residual must be included. The receivable is often stated in terms of the gross amount, less a valuation account labeled unearned income, to yield the net present value. This presentation has no theoretical justification. A problem arises with inclusion of the residual value in the receivable. Recall that receivables are monetary assets. Residual values, if they are not guaranteed by the lessee, are more in the nature of a nonmonetary asset than a receivable.*

Lease income is reported by the lessor using the interest method. All this income is assumed to represent investment income; none is associated with the precontract arrangements, signing of the contract, or the supervision and accounting for the collections, which may be constant over the life of the lease. This presupposes that the investment of funds is the critical function of a finance company. An allocation of gross income to other functions would be arbitrary and would not improve reporting.

Sales-Type Leases Reported by the Lessor.   When manufacturers use the leasing method to report the financing of their own products transferred to customers under long-term lease contracts, income should be reported separately for the two basic functions:

1. The manufacture and sale of the product.
2. The investment in the lease contract during the life of the lease.

---

* The lease must be refigured whenever there are permanent, downward changes in estimates of the residual value. Upward changes in residual value estimates are ignored.

The manufacturing revenues can be reported when the lease is signed by reporting the value of the lease contract receivable equal to the normal selling price of the product.

The FASB states that the manufacturing revenues should be equal to the discounted amount of the future minimum lease payments (net of executory expenses) using the rate implicit in the lease. However, the implicit rate cannot be known without estimating the sales price. If a normal sales price is not well established or readily available, the lessor has considerable discretion regarding the amount to be reported as gross profit from sales and the amount to be reported as interest income. But this does not necessarily result in poor information because any procedure would represent an arbitrary allocation of the gross rental income between the manufacturer and investment functions.

The FASB does not specifically forbid the use of the installment method of reporting the income from manufacturing and selling. However, the denial of such a procedure is implied by the recommendation that if the conditions that would normally support the use of the installment method exist, the lease be classified as an operating lease. These conditions include:

1. Unpredictable credit risks.
2. Material uncertainties regarding the amount of additional costs relating to the lease.

That is, those conditions that must be fulfilled for the lessor to capitalize a lease as noted above.

The Operating Lease.   For the lessee, a long-term lease is classified as an operating lease if it does not meet the criteria for a capital lease. For the lessor, the lease is an operating lease if it does not meet the criteria for direct financing leases or sales-type leases. That is, if the lease does not have the basic characteristics of a purchase or a sale/financing transaction, it is assumed that the lease is a long-term executory rental contract. Thus, rental payments will normally represent rent expenses to a lessee. However, the FASB states that, if the payments are not constant, the rental expenses should be recognized on a straight-line basis unless some other method can be justified. But, like depreciation, no allocation method can be justified on economic grounds alone, and information is lacking to justify any allocation method on the basis of behavioral effects.

For the lessor, the FASB has recommended that the asset be classified as plant and equipment, that it be valued at cost or cost less accumulated depreciation, and that the rental receipts be reported as the gross revenues unless they depart radically from a straight-line basis or from the economic usefulness of the property in each period. The result is that the cash basis of reporting is used for rental receipts and most operating expenses except depreciation and initial direct costs, which should be allocated over the life of the lease if material.

Leveraged Leases.   A leveraged lease is one in which the asset, although owned by the lessor, is largely financed by a creditor. The essence of this arrangement is that it enables "the lessor to recover his investment in the early years of the lease and thereafter affords him the temporary use of funds from which additional income can be derived."[8] In some respects, many two-party leases are leveraged leases. That is, if the lessor is entitled to an investment tax credit and uses accelerated depreciation on the property being leased, the net cash flows (including the effects on tax payments) will be larger in the early years of the lease and less in later years, giving the lessor leverage in increasing the rate of return on investment. When a substantial part of the financing is provided by a long-term creditor in the form of debt that is nonrecouse to the general credit of the lessor, then the leverage to the lessor is increased substantially.

The effect of a leveraged lease is that the net cash flows and net investment, defined as the equity that the lessor has in the asset, each have three phases. Initially, mainly as a result of tax credits, the lessor experiences cash inflows; then, as tax credits decrease and become tax payments, so the cash inflows become increasing cash outflows; finally, a cash inflow is received from the sale of the residual asset value. The net investment is positive although decreasing during the initial period; it then becomes negative, implying that the lessor has recouped his investment in the asset and has a cash surplus; finally, as the cash outflows increase again, the net investment returns to a positive position until it reaches the residual value of the asset at the end of the lease.

The FASB states that the income from the lease should be recognized on the basis of the net investment and the implicit rate of return while the net investment is positive. Although secondary earnings from the investment of funds held temporarily are also a part of the economic advantages of a leveraged lease to the lessor, the FASB stated that these earnings should be reported as they occur. The Board supported this position on the basis of a lack of support for the anticipation of future interest on temporarily held funds in present generally accepted accounting principles.

Ignoring the secondary earnings, the effect of the above procedures is to report a constant rate of return on the book value of the net investment while it is positive and no return when it is negative. Because a constant implicit rate is used instead of an opportunity rate, the net investment in any year represents only the unallocated portion of the original computed value of the investment. A current value of the investment is presented only at the inception of the lease. An exception is made when a revision of the basic assumptions results in a reduction of the net investment balance; in this case, the net investment balance is reduced and a loss is reported. This is similar to the lower-of-cost-or-market rule. Therefore, it is not likely that the reported book value of the lease investment can necessarily be interpreted as a market value or as a value to the firm.

Sale-and-Leaseback Arrangements.   In a sale-and-leaseback arrangement, the original owner of the property sells the property and then leases it back from the new owner. The original owner is thus the seller-lessee, while the new owner is the purchaser-lessor. The new lessee and the new lessor classify their leases in normal accordance with *SFAS 13*. The only new theoretical question to arise from this arrangement is what to do with the profit that arises from the sale of the property. One argument is that there are two transactions here: (*a*) a sale and (*b*) a lease. If this is so, the profit should be recognized at the time. The counterargument is that there is really only one transaction. The lessee once controlled the benefits of the asset through ownership; the lessee now controls exactly the same benefits through a lease. From the point of view of benefits, nothing has changed. Recognizing profit at the time of the sale would be like recognizing profit on a sale to oneself. If one accepts the counterargument, as the FASB did in *SFAS 13,* then the profit should be deferred and recognized over the term of the lease.

Sale-and-leaseback arrangements become particularly complex when real estate is involved because of the potential conflicts between the recognition requirements of *SFAS 13* and those of *SFAS 66. SFAS 98,* "Sale-Leaseback Transactions Involving Real Estate," "Sales-Type Leases of Real Estate," "Definition of the Lease Term," and "Initial Direct Costs of Direct Financing Leases," address this conflict. It essentially makes *SFAS 66* the controlling document. In the words of the FASB:

Sale-leaseback accounting shall be used by a seller-lessee only if a sale-leaseback transaction includes all of the following:

1. A normal leaseback (as described above).
2. Payment terms and provisions that adequately demonstrate the buyer-lessor's initial and continuing investment in the property (refer to . . . *SFAS 66*).
3. Payment terms and provisions that transfer *all* of the other risks and rewards of ownership as demonstrated by the absence of any other continuing involvement by the seller-lessee described in . . . *SFAS 66*.

Note the heavy emphasis on *SFAS 66,* "Accounting for Sales of Real Estate" here. It should not go unnoticed that *SFAS 98* was passed by only four votes to three. Under the new voting requirements, the statement would not have passed.

Disclosure of Leases

It is frequently argued by management that the capitalization of leases, particularly operating leases by lessees, presents misleading information because the lease obligation is different from other debt instruments. They believe that reporting the lease obligation in the balance sheet distorts their debt ratios. Others argue that it is the omission of the lease obligation that distorts the debt ratios. Management's argument is driven, in part, by their belief that their advantages lie in "off-balance sheet financing." However, Standard & Poors and other credit agencies and other financial intermediaries stress that they make a point of adjusting financial statements for omitted leases. In other words, the advantage of off-balance sheet financing may be more imagined than real.

To satisfy all parties, and in order to avoid the provision of misleading information, the FASB requires that the minimum lease rental payments for operating leases should be disclosed in notes to financial statements in the aggregate and for each of the succeeding five years. Additional lease payments contingent on the amount of use or total revenue or other activity should be presented for the current past year with a disclosure of the basic characteristics relating to contingent lease rentals. Thus, one is able to make any adjustments one wishes to the financial statements. The disclosure of information relating to cash flows is at least an attempt to meet the assumed needs of investors and creditors. How well these needs are met awaits the results of empirical research. According to Stanford professor George Foster, "At present, the literature is long on anecdotes (e.g., as to the extreme lengths to which management will go to avoid transactions qualifying as debt) and short on detailed research analysis."[9]

CHECKPOINTS

1. List the four criteria for classifying capital and operating leases provided in *SFAS 13*.
2. List the additional criteria that must be applied to leases by lessors.
3. Distinguish a financing-type lease from a sales-type lease.
4. What is unique about leveraged leases?
5. What additional analyses must be performed when classifying leases involving real estate?
6. What is a sale-and-leaseback arrangement? When can profit be recognized by the seller-lessee?

CAPITAL AND REVENUE EXPENDITURES

Once plant and equipment are installed ready for use, no further costs (historical or current) should be capitalized. All maintenance expenditures and anticipated or normal replacements of parts of the asset should also be charged to operations during the normal life of the asset. The total cost of obtaining a given amount of service from the asset during its expected life, therefore, should include the initial acquisition costs and all maintenance and normal replacement expenditures. How these costs should be allocated to the individual years or periods is a separate problem, which was treated in a preceding section on depreciation, where it was seen that repairs, normal replacements, and depreciation are interrelated. The repair and normal replacements should be charged to the expenses or operations of one or more years, depending on the depreciation method used and the distribution of the expected benefits to be received from the asset or other bases of allocation.

Certain types of expenditures, however, are incurred to obtain greater future benefits, rather than to maintain a given quantity of services. These increases in future benefits may arise from expenditures that may be classified as either additions, improvements and betterments, or major replacements. Since these expenditures affect future periods, they should be capitalized and allocated to those future periods benefiting from them. This increase in future benefits can arise in one of three ways:

1. An increase in the life of the asset—that is, an increase in the number of years over which services will be obtained.
2. An increase in the quantity of services to be obtained in each year during the remaining life of the asset.
3. An increase in the quality of the service to be obtained in each year during the remaining life of the asset.

In the first case, the term of which depreciation is being calculated will need revision—the result might be an unchanged depreciation expense. The depreciation term should not be extended in the other two cases. This will have the effect of increasing the depreciation expense. Where the property involved is being leased, the amortization of any improvements to the leasehold should be over the remaining useful life of the asset or the remaining term of the lease, whichever is the shorter.

There is little doubt that additions should be capitalized. By definition, additions increase the productive or service capacity of the plant and equipment. But what about the costs of tearing out parts of an old building to make room for the new facilities or to integrate the new with the old facilities? The answer depends on the circumstances. Usually, if the need for the addition could not have been anticipated or if it was not practical to include it in the original construction, all costs of tearing out should be included in the cost of addition and none of the costs of the old facilities should be removed from the accounts except to the extent that these costs exceed the service value of the old asset before adding the new facilities. The additional services cannot be obtained without incurring these costs, and the construction of the addition at an earlier date, before the services were needed, would probably have added more to the total costs of the firm. But this does not mean that such costs should be capitalized in every case. It is possible that the necessity for tearing out and reconstruction is due to inefficiencies in planning or in construction. In these cases, such costs represent losses, rather than costs chargeable to operations.

Improvements and betterments are more difficult to define than additions, but the treatment is very similar. If the result is an increase in the quantity of service provided by the assets, it may, in fact, be difficult to distinguish improvements from additions. A truck may be improved by adding overload springs and a larger bed, thus permitting heavier payloads. The result may be little different from the acquisition of a trailer, which would be considered an addition. On the other hand, many improvements may result in an increase in the quality of the service provided by the asset. The installation of an improved lighting system in a factory building improves the services provided by the building. One of the greatest difficulties in accounting for improvements arises when they are made as a part of a normal repair and replacement program. An attempt should be made to capitalize only those costs resulting in an increase in the future services of the asset, as opposed to the expenditures necessary to maintain a given level of services. To the extent that an improvement involves the replacement of major components, the discussion in the following paragraph is also relevant.

Major replacements are the most difficult to define and treat properly because the effect is similar to that of minor replacements and normal repairs. If an asset is made up of a single unit, a replacement involves the entire asset; in this case the solution is simple—the old asset is retired and the replacement asset is recorded as a new asset. But in most cases, plant and equipment items are made up of several units that wear out at different rates. Recurring replacements of parts of the asset can be charged to operations in the years in which they occur because they are necessary to obtain the expected service life of the composite asset. No advantage would be obtained by capitalizing these items, because it is not possible to associate the outlays directly with the benefits to be received from them. Since all periods are charged with some replacement costs, an allocation to each period by a depreciation method would not necessarily improve the computation or meaning or net income. However, as we saw in Chapter 15, if repairs vary in a predictable manner, they can be taken into consideration in the selection of a depreciation method for allocating the initial cost of the asset in order to obtain the desired results.

Major replacements that occur infrequently, however, need to be capitalized so that all periods will be charged with a portion of the replacement cost. This can be accomplished by including the costs of major replacements in the depreciation charge in one of two ways:

1. If the life of the asset is determined by the maximum life of the most durable major component, replacements should be charged to the asset or set up as a separate account and allocated over its separate life.
2. The depreciation can be computed on the basis of the average composite life of all the components of the asset, in which case the replacements should be charged to accumulated depreciation.

By using the maximum life of the most durable component, the replacements are not included in the depreciation based on the original life alone. Since they occur infrequently, it would not be correct to charge the entire amount of the replacement to operations in the year that it is made. The best solution in this case would be to set the amount up as a separate account (or debited to the main asset account) and allocate it over the period from the date of replacement, of the same component. For example, if major redecorating is necessary every three years, the redecorating costs can be capitalized and allocated over a three-year period. Care must be taken, however, to be sure that the original decorating costs are charged through depreciation to the first three years; if they are not, subsequent years will be charged twice with decorating costs, once through the depreciation based on the original total costs and a second time through the allocation of the redecorating costs.

The second treatment of major replacements bases the depreciation on the average composite life of all the components. For example, if the maximum life of a building is 50 years, the average composite life could be 30 years. The original cost of the building would then be allocated on the basis of a 30-year life but, by carrying the depreciation over 50 years, the total depreciation for the 50 years would be equal to the original cost of the building plus the cost of all major repairs minus the ending scrap value. When replacements occur, they are then charged to the accumulated depreciation amount. The effect is to increase the net carrying value at the time of the replacement without increasing the original cost basis. This procedure has the same effect as writing off the replaced asset and debiting the asset account with the replacement cost if two basic conditions exist:

1. The cost of the replacement must be the same amount as the original cost of the component that it replaces.
2. The total cost of all replacements must have been anticipated with some fair degree of accuracy, so that the depreciation charge will be adequate to include all replacements.

Because of the extreme difficulty of finding allocation procedures with economic significance, the procedure of capitalizing costs and allocating them to subsequent periods is of dubious value from either a semantic point of view or from the point of view of relevance to the users. An alternative might be to classify and report the capital expenditures according to their recurring or nonrecurring behavior and the approximate remaining useful lives as well as the current market prices of the assets in used capital asset markets.

CHECKPOINTS

1. Distinguish minor repairs from betterments.
2. Distinguish between revenue and capital expenditures, and explain why this distinction is important.
3. List two ways in which major repairs can be capitalized.
4. When should the cost of repairs be charged to an asset?

SUMMARY

Previous chapters have provided the basic definition of assets, discussed the broad classification of assets, how to measure them, and when to recognize them. This chapter treats the recording of particular assets: specifically plant and equipment, both purchased and leased. The next chapter treats intangible assets and noncurrent investments.

As the last chapter noted, the general rule for recording all assets is to enter them at the present value of their maturity value adjusted for uncertainty. This is subject to the usual caveats of materiality and conservatism—specifically, assets should not be entered above their net realizable values. Cost accumulation ceases once an asset is available for sale or use.

Plant and equipment differs from the assets discussed in the previous chapter in that their services are received over a period longer than one year or the operating cycle of a business. Nevertheless, they follow the general rule for entry. The cost of a self-constructed asset is accumulated much as one would with inventory. This includes the cost of overhead. In addition, interest costs are generally included in self-constructed plant and equipment, but not in inventory. No further costs are accumulated once plant and equipment has been installed. The exception to this rule involves situations where the services of the asset have been increased or extended due to betterments or rearrangements.

Long-term, noncancelable leases which pass title to the lessee before expiration of the lease, or offer the lessee a bargain purchase option, or which have terms greater than 75 percent of the useful life of the asset, or payment agreements that account for more than 90 percent of the fair value of the asset, should be entered on the lessee's books at the present value of the minimum lease payments, but not more than their fair value. Lessors are required to apply similar criteria for entering either sales-type or financing-type leases.

Subsequent to installation, all normal, recurring costs associated with the plant or equipment should be expensed. Exceptions involve additions, improvements, and betterments that increase the service potential of the asset.

MULTIPLE CHOICE QUESTIONS

Initial Recognition

1. [N87#11] For a capital lease, the amount recorded initially by the lessee as a liability should
a. Exceed the present value at the beginning of the lease term of minimum lease payments during the lease term.
b. Exceed the total of the minimum lease payments during the lease term.
c. Not exceed the fair value of the lease property at the inception of the lease.
d. Equal the total of the minimum lease payments during the lease term.

2. [M87#14] Lease Y does not contain a bargain purchase option, but the lease term is equal to 90 percent of the estimated economic life of the leased property. Lease Z does not transfer ownership of the property to the lessee by the end of the lease term, but the lease term is equal to 75 percent of the estimated economic life of the leased property. How should the lessee classify these leases?

	Lease Y	*Lease Z*
a.	Capital lease	Operating lease
b.	Capital lease	Capital lease
c.	Operating lease	Capital lease
d.	Operating lease	Operating lease

3. [N86#10] Theoretically, which of the following costs incurred in connection with a machine purchased for use in a company's manufacturing operations would be capitalized?

	Insurance on Machine While in Transit	Testing and Preparation of Machine for Use
a.	No	No
b.	No	Yes
c.	Yes	No
d.	Yes	Yes

4. [M86#17] An asset is being constructed for an enterprise's own use. The asset has been financed with specific new borrowing. The interest cost incurred during the construction period as a result of expenditures for the asset is

a. Interest expense in the construction period.

b. A prepaid asset to be written off over the estimated useful life of the asset.

c. A part of the historical cost of acquiring the asset to be written off over the estimated useful life of the asset.

d. A part of the historical cost of acquiring the asset to be written off over the term of the borrowing used to finance the construction of the asset.

5. [M85#9] A donated plant asset for which the fair value has been determined, and for which incidental costs were incurred in acceptance of the asset, should be recorded at an amount equal to its

a. Incidental costs incurred.

b. Fair value and incidental costs incurred.

c. Book value on books of donor and incidental costs incurred.

d. Book value on books of donor.

Repairs and Betterments

6. [M89#5] A lessee incurred costs to construct office space in a leased warehouse. The estimated useful life of the office is 10 years. The remaining term of the nonrenewable lease is 15 years. The costs should be

a. Capitalized as leasehold improvements and depreciated over 15 years.

b. Capitalized as leasehold improvements and depreciated over 10 years.

c. Capitalized as leasehold improvements and expenses in the year in which the lease expires.

d. Expensed as incurred.

7. [M88#8] An expenditure to install an improved electrical system is a

	Capital Expenditure	*Revenue Expenditure*
a.	No	Yes
b.	No	No
c.	Yes	No
d.	Yes	Yes

8. [M84#11] A machine with an original estimated useful life of 10 years was moved to another location in the factory after it had been in service for 3 years. The efficiency of the machine is increased for its remaining useful life. The reinstallation costs should be capitalized if the remaining useful life of the machine is

	Five Years	*Ten Years*
a.	No	No
b.	No	Yes
c.	Yes	No
d.	Yes	Yes

9. [N84#14] Which type of expenditure occurs when a company installs a higher capacity boiler to heat its plant?
a. Rearrangement.
b. Ordinary repair and maintenance.
c. Addition.
d. Betterment.

Amortization

10. [N88#13] A six-year capital lease expiring on December 31 specifies equal minimum annual lease payments. Part of this payment represents interest and part represents a reduction in the net lease liability. The portion of the minimum lease payment in the fifth year applicable to the reduction of the net lease liability should be
a. Less than in the fourth year.
b. More than in the fourth year.
c. The same as in the sixth year.
d. More than in the sixth year.

11. [N87#10] In a sale-leaseback transaction, the seller-lessee retains the right to substantially all of the remaining use of the equipment sold. The profit on the sale should be deferred and subsequently amortized by the lessee when the lease is classified as a (an)

	Capital Lease	Operating Lease
a.	No	Yes
b.	No	No
c.	Yes	No
d.	Yes	Yes

12. [M86#19] The lessee should amortize the capitalizable cost of the leased asset in a manner consistent with the lessee's normal depreciation policy for owned assets for leases that

	Contain a Bargain Purchase Option	Transfer Ownership of the Property to the Lessee by the End of the Lease Term
a.	No	No
b.	No	Yes
c.	Yes	Yes
d.	Yes	No

DISCUSSION QUESTIONS

Self-Constructed Assets

1. In your view, should *all* overhead or only *variable* overhead be charged to special projects? Why?

2. Alexander Hamilton Church was an English electrical engineer who later settled in the United States around the turn of the century. In an article that he wrote in 1913 he emphasized that:

> Wherever capital is made use of, whether in the power plant, in the erection of buildings, or in the purchase of costly special machinery, the use of such capital has to be paid for, somehow and somewhere. *It is only rational that it should be paid for by just those processes (and therefore those jobs) which involve its use. To exclude interest charge from cost of these jobs is to ignore one of the most*

important matters that we should know, namely—how far this use of capital is economically justified.[10]

Almost 80 years later, we still capitalize interest only on major assets that are constructed for the use of the firm or for sale or lease. *SFAS 34,* paragraph 10, specifically excludes inventories on grounds that "in the Board's judgment, the informational benefit does not justify the cost of so doing."

Required:

a. Take Mr. Church's side and argue why the FASB might not be right. In your answer examine the case of an item produced by a highly automated process. Contrast the cost of labor, that is included, with the cost of capital, that is excluded.
b. Pursue the FASB's argument further. Does it lead to the exclusion of labor costs on grounds of a lack of a favorable cost-benefit ratio?

   3. (November 1969) Jay Manufacturing, Inc., began operations five years ago producing probos, a new type of instrument it hoped to sell to doctors, dentists, and hospitals. The demand for probos far exceeded initial expectations, and the company was unable to produce enough probos to meet demand.

   The company was manufacturing its product on equipment that it built at the start of its operations. To meet demand, more efficient equipment was needed. The company decided to design and build the equipment, since that currently available on the market was unsuitable for producing probos.

   In 1982 a section of the plant was devoted to development of the new equipment, and a special staff of personnel was hired. Within six months and at a cost of $170,000, a machine was developed that successfully increased production and reduced labor costs substantially. Sparked by the success of the new machine, the company built three more machines of the same type at a cost of $80,000 each.

Required:

a. In addition to satisfying a need that outsiders cannot meet within the desired time, why might a firm construct fixed assets for its own use?
b. In general, what costs should be capitalized for a self-constructed fixed asset?
c. Discuss the propriety of including in the capitalized cost of self-constructed assets:
   1. The increase in overhead caused by the self-construction of fixed assets.
   2. A proportionate share of overhead on the same basis as that applied to goods manufactured for sale.
d. Discuss the proper accounting treatment of the $90,000 ($170,000 − $80,000) by which the cost of the first machine exceeded the cost of the subsequent machines.

Historical Cost

4. **(November 1980)** Among the principal topics related to the accounting for the property, plant, and equipment of a company are acquisition and retirement.

Required:

a. What expenditures should be capitalized when equipment is acquired for cash?

b. Assume that the market value of equipment acquired is not determinable by reference to a similar purchase for cash. Describe how the acquiring company should determine the capitalizable cost of equipment purchased by exchanging it for each of the following:

1. Bonds having an established market price.
2. Common stock not having an established market price.
3. Similar equipment having a determinable market value.

c. Describe the factors that determine whether expenditures relating to property, plant, and equipment already in use should be capitalized.

d. Describe how to account for the gain or loss on the sale of property, plant, and equipment for cash.

5. **(May 1976)** A company may acquire plant assets (among other ways) for cash, on a deferred-payment plan, by exchanging other assets, or by a combination of these ways.

Required:

a. Identify six costs that should be capitalized as the cost of land. For your answer, assume that land with an existing building is acquired for cash and that the existing building is to be removed in the immediate future in order that a new building can be constructed on that site.

b. At what amount should a company record a plant asset acquired on a deferred-payment plan?

c. In general, at what amount should plant assets received in exchange for other nonmonetary assets be recorded? Specifically, at what amount should a company record a new machine acquired by exchanging an older, similar machine and paying cash?

Leases of Plant and Equipment

6. **(November 1975)** Wright Aircraft Company manufactures small single- and multiple-engine aircraft primarily for sale to individuals, flying clubs, and corporations. Wright is one of the pioneers in the industry and has developed a reputation as a leader in small-craft engineering and marketing innovations.

During the last few years, Wright has profitably leased an increasing number of its aircraft to flying clubs. The leasing activity currently represents a significant portion of Wright's annual volume. Details of the leasing arrangements with flying clubs follow:

The flying club signs a long-term lease agreement with Wright for the aircraft.

The lease has a noncancelable term of 6 to 18 years, depending upon the aircraft's useful life. The lease term is set to be three-fourths of the normal life of the aircraft leased.

The club is required to deposit with Wright an amount equal to 10 percent of the total lease rental for the term of the lease. The deposit is not refundable, but it is used in lieu of rent during the last one-tenth of the lease term.

A bank loans Wright an amount equal to the remaining 90 percent of the total lease rental, after deducting a discount of 14 percent per year. The net discounted amount is immediately paid to Wright. The bank-loan agreement requires Wright to use the lease rental payments from the flying club to pay off the loan to the bank.

As a condition for the loan, the bank requires Wright to insure the leased aircraft for an amount equal to the loan.

The flying club signs Wright's bank-loan agreement as a surety, thus obligating itself if Wright should default on the loan.

When the bank loan is paid in full at the end of the lease term, the flying club can purchase the aircraft and receive title to it by paying Wright $100.

Required:

Discuss the criteria and other aspects of Wright's leasing activities that it should consider in determining whether to account for its flying club leases as operating leases or as sales-type leases. In your discussion, identify criteria that are clearly met in the facts presented in the question. For criteria that are *not* clearly met, indicate what additional information is needed to reach a conclusion with respect to each criterion.

7. **(November 1975)** Cannon, Inc., was incorporated in 1980 to operate as a computer software service firm with an accounting fiscal year ending August 31. Cannon's primary product is a sophisticated on-line inventory-control system; its customers pay a fixed fee plus a usage charge for using the system.

Cannon has leased a large, BIG–I computer system from the manufacturer. The lease calls for a monthly rental of $30,000 for the 144 months (12 years) of the lease term. The estimated useful life of the computer is 15 years.

Each scheduled monthly rental payment includes $5,000 for full-service maintenance on the computer to be performed by the manufacturer. All rentals are payable on the first day of the month beginning with August 1, 1981, the date the computer was installed and the lease agreement was signed.

The lease is noncancelable for its 12-year term, and it is secured only by the manufacturer's chattel lien on the BIG–I system. On any anniversary date of the lease after August 1986, Cannon can purchase the BIG–I system from the manufacturer at 75 percent of the then current fair value of the computer.

This lease is to be accounted for as a capital lease by Cannon, and it will be amortized by the interest method. Borrowed funds for this type of transaction would cost Cannon 12 percent per year (1 percent per month). Following is a schedule of the present value of $1 for selected periods discounted at 1 percent per period when payments are made at the beginning of each period.

Periods (months)		Present Value of $1 per Period Discounted at 1% per Period
1	. . . .	1.000
2	. . . .	1.990
3	. . . .	2.970
143	. . . .	76.658
144	. . . .	76.899

Required:

Prepare, in general journal form, all entries Cannon should have made in its accounting records during August 1981 relating to this lease. Give full explanations and show supporting computations for each entry. Remember, August 31, 1981, is the end of Cannon's fiscal accounting period, and it will be preparing financial statements on that date. *Do not prepare closing entries.*

8.   (November 1978) Milton Corporation entered into a lease arrangement with James Leasing Corporation for a certain machine. James's primary business is leasing, and it is not a manufacturer or dealer. Milton will lease the machine for a period of three years, which is 50 percent of the machine's economic life. James will take possession of the machine at the end of the initial three-year lease and lease it to another smaller company that does not need the most current version of the machine. Milton does not guarantee any residual value for the machine and will not purchase the machine at the end of the lease term.

Milton's incremental borrowing rate is 10 percent, and the implicit rate in the lease is 8½ percent. Milton has no way of knowing the implicit rate used by James. Using either rate, the present value of the minimum lease payments is between 90 percent and 100 percent of the fair value of the machine at the date of the lease agreement.

Milton has agreed to pay all executory costs directly, and no allowance for these costs is included in the lease payments.

James is reasonably certain that Milton will pay all lease payments, and because Milton has agreed to pay all executory costs, there are no important uncertainties regarding costs to be incurred by James.

Required:

a. With respect to Milton (the lessee) answer the following:
   1. What type of lease has been entered into? Explain the reason for your answer.
   2. How should Milton compute the appropriate amount to be recorded for the lease or asset acquired?
   3. What accounts will be created or affected by this transaction and how will the lease or asset and other costs related to the transaction be matched with earnings?
   4. What disclosure must Milton make regarding this lease or asset?
b. With respect to James (the lessor) answer the following:
   1. What type of leasing arrangement has been entered into? Explain the reason for your answer.
   2. How should this lease be recorded by James, and how are the appropriate amounts determined?
   3. How should James determine the appropriate amount of earnings to be recognized from each lease payment?
   4. What disclosures must James make regarding this lease?

KRESGE VERSUS MAY*

Kresge and May are two major department stores in the United States of America. Known to some by their original names, others will know them by their subsidiaries. Kresge, for instance, founded in 1916, changed its name to K mart in 1977. It also owns and operates WaldenBooks. May goes back even further—to 1866—and today owns Filene's, Foley's, and Lord & Taylor's, to name but a few of its subsidiaries.

---

* The article on which this case is based was first cast in case format by Robert N. Anthony. The data in the case come from public sources.

FIGURE 17-1   Balance Sheets (Kresge versus May) (millions of dollars)

| Kresge 1/29/75				May 2/1/75	
W/L	*Wo/L*			*Wo/L*	*W/L*
		Assets			
156	156	Cash and marketable securities		13	13
157	157	Receivables		407	407
1,073	1,073	Inventories		193	193
32	32	Other current assets		18	18
$1,418	$1,418	Current assets		$ 631	$ 631
60	60	Investments and other assets		54	54
418	418	Fixed assets		521	521
1,283	——	Rights to use of leased property		——	115
$3,179	$1,896	Total assets		$1,206	$1,321
		Liabilities			
$ 779	$ 613	Current liabilities		$ 287	$ 298
212	212	Long-term debt		356	356
1,117	——	Rental obligations		——	104
50	50	Deferrals		61	61
1,021	1,021	Owners' equity		502	502
$3,179	$1,896	Total liabilities and equity		$1,206	$1,321
$1,283		Present value of leases*			$ 115
$ 166		Current portion due 1975			$ 11

* Present value of leases was found by discounting Kresge's obligations at 7.7 percent and May's obligations at 5.7 percent, respectively.

In 1975 the two companies had completely different approaches to acquiring retail sales space. Kresge leased many of its stores; May purchased most of its stores. The result was two sharply different sets of financial reports even though the two companies were similar in other respects. Sparked by the promulgation of *SFAS 13,* the difference between the two companies caught the attention of three practitioners: John J. Kalata, controller of Schuykill Chemical Corp.; Dennis G. Campbell of Philadelphia Savings Fund Society; and Ian K. Shumaker of the Veterans

FIGURE 17-2   Income Statements (Kresge versus May) (millions of dollars)

Kresge Year Ended 1/29/75		*May* Year Ended 2/1/75
$5,536	Revenues	$1,697
4,248	Cost of sales	2,432
195	Pretax income	94
105	Net income	47

FIGURE 17-3   Key Financial Ratios (Kresge versus May)

1/29/75 Kresge			2/1/75 May	
W/L	Wo/L		W/L	Wo/L
		Working Capital Analysis		
	2.31	Current ratio		2.12
	0.56	Acid test ratio (quick ratio)		1.47
	3.96	Inventory turnover		7.42
	35.26	Receivables turnover		4.17
		Long-Term Financial Analysis		
	0.54	Owners' equity to total assets		0.38
	1.62	Current assets to total liabilities		0.77
	1.97	Long-term debt to fixed assets		0.72
	0.21	Long-term debt to owners' equity		0.92
	0.17	Long-term debt to invested capital		0.48
	0.83	Owners' equity to invested capital		0.52
		Profitability Analysis		
	3.52	Pretax margin		5.54
	10.28	Pretax return on assets		7.12
	10.28	New return on equity		9.36

Administration, Philadelphia Regional Office.[11] They noted that when one compares the two companies without leases:

> Kresge is a company which leases approximately 40 percent of its "available assets" ($3.2 billion), while May, on the other hand, leases 8.7 percent of their "available assets" ($1.3 billion). Kresge's sales in 1974 were 5.6 billion (5th in terms of sales) and May's were 1.7 billion (18th in sales). Kresge's average annual growth rate (earnings per share) over the last five years was 10.84 percent, while May's was 10.38 percent per annum.
>
> Kresge's profits, while higher than May's, are based on higher sales volume and as such, Kresge's pretax margin is over 2 percent less than May's. Given that the growth rates of the two companies are roughly equal, the balance sheet is the only other deciding factor to show why Kresge has an AA rating and sold for 29 times earnings, while May has a split rating—AA (S&P) and A (Moody's)—and sold for only 11 times earnings.

They go on in their article to note that:

> The balance sheet, in its present form, makes Kresge appear to be a good stable company to invest in. It exhibits a superior financial base and operating record.

This in large part explains the premium multiple of 29× earnings assigned Kresge. What this means, in essence, is that investors are willing to pay a much higher price for Kresge's financial stability and earnings growth potential. In addition, the company's relatively low leverage and its ability to more than adequately cover its fixed charges have significantly influenced their AA credit rating assigned by both major services. On the other hand, May Department Stores' multiple of 11× earnings and its A rating by Moody's reflect a more extensive use of debt financing (higher leverage), less favorable growth potential, and generally higher risk characteristics.

Required:

a. Satisfy yourself that you know how the authors computed the financial ratios in the case. Be prepared to explain the meaning of each ratio.

b. For each company insert the leases using the present values shown at the bottom of the balance sheet.

c. Rework all the ratios.

d. Comment on the outcome of your new financial analysis. You might want to reflect on the potential implications, if any, of your findings on issues such as market efficiency.

PRIMARY SOURCES

Those interested in learning more about the topics covered in this chapter might begin by consulting the following sources:

Anthony, Robert N. *Accounting for the Cost of Interest* (Lexington, Mass.: Lexington Books, 1975).

Beidelman, Carl R. "Valuation of Used Capital Assets." *Studies in Accounting Research No. 7* (AAA, 1973).

Financial Accounting Standards Board, *FASB Discussion Memorandum: An Analysis of Issues Related to Accounting for Leases* (Stamford, Conn.: FASB, 1974).

Myers, John H. "Reporting of Leases in Financial Statements." *Accounting Research Study No. 4* (New York: AICPA, 1962).

SELECTED ADDITIONAL READINGS

In addition to the works cited above and in the Endnotes to this chapter, the reader is referred to the following authors:

Bases of Valuation of Plant and Equipment

McKeown, James C. "Comparative Application of Market and Cost-Based Accounting Models." *Journal of Accounting Research,* Spring 1973, pp. 65–78.

NAA Committee on Management Accounting Practices. "Fixed Asset Accounting: The Capitalization of Costs." *CPA Journal,* March 1973, pp. 193–207.

Snavely, Howard J. "Current Cost for Long-Lived Assets: A Critical View." *The Accounting Review,* April 1969, pp. 344–53.

Nonmonetary Exchanges

Arnett, Harold E. "*APB Opinion No. 29:* Accounting for Nonmonetary Transactions—Some New Perspectives." *Management Accounting,* October 1978, pp. 41–48.

Capettini, Robert, and Thomas E. King. "Exchange of Nonmonetary Assets: Some Changes." *The Accounting Review,* January 1976, pp. 142–47.

Imhoff, Eugene A., and Paul A. Janell. "Opinion No. 29: A New Valuation Method." *Management Accounting,* March 1979, pp. 50–53.

Interest on Construction

Bierman, Harold, Jr., and Thomas R. Dyckman. "Accounting for Interest during Construction." *Accounting and Business Research,* Autumn 1979, pp. 267–72.

Frazer, Robert E., and Richard C. Ransom. "Is Interest during Construction Funny Money?" *Public Utilities Fortnightly,* December 21, 1972, pp. 20–27.

Means, Kathryn M., and Paul M. Kazenki. "*SFAS 34:* A Recipe for Diversity." *Accounting Horizons,* September 1988, pp. 62–67.

Long-Term Leases

Abdel-khalik, A. Rashad; Robert B. Thompson; and Robert E. Taylor. "The Impact of Reporting Leases off the Balance Sheet on Bond Risk Premiums: Two Exploratory Studies." *Economic Consequences of Financial Accounting Standards* (FASB, 1978), pp. 103–55.

Abdel-khalik, A. Rashad. *The Economic Effects on Lessees of FASB Statement No. 13, Accounting for Leases* (Stamford, Conn.: FASB, 1981).

Bowman, Robert G. "The Debt Equivalence of Leases: An Empirical Investigation." *The Accounting Review,* April 1980, pp. 237–53.

Coughlan, John W. "Regulation, Rents and Residuals." *Journal of Accountancy,* February 1980, pp. 58–66.

DeFliese, Philip L. "Accounting for Leases: A Broader Perspective." *Financial Executive,* July 1974, pp. 14–23.

Elam, Rick. "Effect of Lease Data on the Predictive Ability of Financial Ratios." *The Accounting Review,* January 1975, pp. 25–43.

Finnerty, Joseph F.; Rick N. Fitzsimmons; and Thomas W. Oliver. "Lease Capitalization and Systematic Risk." *The Accounting Review,* October 1980, pp. 631–39.

Goodman, Hortense, and Leonard Lorensen. *Illustrations of Accounting for Leases: A Survey of the Application of FASB Statement No. 13* (AICPA, 1978).

Hawkins, David, and Mary M. Wehle. *Accounting for Leases* (New York: Financial Executives Research Foundation, 1973).

Myers, John H. "Reporting of Leases in Financial Statements." *Accounting Research Study No. 4* (AICPA, 1962), pp. 63–67.

Richardson, A. W. "The Measurement of the Current Portion of Long-Term Lease Obligations—Some Evidence from Practice." *The Accounting Review,* October 1985, pp. 744–52.

Ro, Byung T. "The Disclosure of Capitalized Lease Information and Stock Prices." *Journal of Accounting Research,* Autumn 1978, pp. 315–40.

Wilkins, Trevor, and Ian Zimmer. "The Effect of Leasing and Different Methods of Accounting for Leases on Credit Evaluations." *The Accounting Review,* October 1983, pp. 749–64.

Wyatt, Arthur R. "Leases *Should* Be Capitalized." *CPA Journal,* September 1974, pp. 35–38.

Leveraged Leases

Anton, Hector R. "Leveraged Leases—A Marriage of Economics, Taxation and Accounting." In *DR Scott Memorial Lectures in Accountancy,* vol. 6. Edited by Alfred R. Roberts (Columbia: University of Missouri, 1974), pp. 81–113.

Bullock, Clayton L. "Accounting Conventions and Economic Reality." *CPA Journal,* July 1974, pp. 19–24.

Shanno, David F., and Roman L. Weil. "The Separate Phases Method of Accounting for Leveraged Leases: Properties of the Allocating Rate and an Algorithm for Finding It." *Journal of Accounting Research,* Autumn 1976, pp. 345–56.

ENDNOTES

1. The term *prudent cost* is defined in Chapter 14.
2. *APB 29,* par. 18.
3. *ARB 43,* Ch. 14, par. 7.
4. *SFAS 13,* par. 7.
5. See *SFAS 98.*
6. *SFAS 13,* par. 5 as amended.
7. See John H. Myers, "Reporting of Leases in Financial Statements," *Accounting Research Study No. 4* (New York: AICPA, 1962), p. 38.
8. *SFAS 13,* par. 108.
9. George Foster, *Financial Statement Analysis,* 2nd ed. (Englewood Cliffs, N.J.: Prentice Hall, 1986), p. 76.
10. A. Hamilton Church, "On the Inclusion of Interest in Manufacturing Costs," *Journal of Accountancy,* April 1913. Reprinted in *Significant Accounting Essays.* Edited by Maurice Moonitz and A. C. Littleton (Englewood Cliffs, N.J.: Prentice Hall, 1965).
11. J. J. Kalata, Dennis G. Campbell, and Ian K. Shumaker, "Lease Financing Reporting," *Financial Executive,* March 1977, pp. 34–40.

Chapter 18

Intangibles and Noncurrent Investments

CHAPTER OBJECTIVES

After studying this chapter, you will be able to:

Differentiate between tangible and intangible assets, identifiable and unidentifiable assets, and intangible assets and deferred costs.

Apply the general rule for the recognition, measurement, and amortization of assets to the class of intangible assets.

Apply the general rules for the recognition, measurement, and amortization of intangible assets to specific examples, such as research and development.

Discuss the significance of rules of investment accounting for the measurement of intangibles, especially goodwill.

CHAPTER OVERVIEW

The Nature and Recognition of Intangibles

Intangibles are assets that lack substance. As such, they should be recognized whenever they satisfy the criteria for recognizing all assets, that is, they should meet the definition of an asset, they should be measurable, and they should be relevant and reliable.

Measurement and Amortization

Intangibles are difficult to measure. This characteristic is particularly true of intangibles that cannot be separately identified, such as goodwill. Cost is the usual basis, chosen on pragmatic grounds. All intangibles are amortized over a period not to exceed 40 years.

Issues and Applications

A number of particular intangibles are discussed in an attempt to highlight some of the conceptual issues presented in the chapter.

Noncurrent Investments

Purchased goodwill results from the investment of one company in another. As an accompaniment to the specific concerns of goodwill, this section lays out the basic rules for investment accounting.

Intangible assets present one of the more difficult areas in accounting theory, partly because of difficulties of definition, but mainly because of the uncertainties regarding the measurement of their values and the estimation of their useful lives. To illustrate, consider King World Production, Inc., the syndicators of *Jeopardy, Wheel of Fortune,* and *Oprah Winfrey.* The company reported negative equity of $30 million in 1988, but estimated profits for the year of $58 million. Is it, as *Forbes* asked, a healthy company or is it at death's door?[1] The company's dilemma is that it is not in the business of constructing bricks and mortar. Instead, it deals in rights to TV shows. The rights to these shows appear on their books at only $3 million. According to *Forbes,* King World has contracts on these same shows worth $700 million. Accountants' failure to report the true value of these intangibles leaves the impression of a troubled company. The reality is far different. This result means, as Northwestern University professor Alfred Rappaport said in the article: "As we become a more information-intensive society, shareholders' equity is getting further away from the way the market will value a company."

What to do? First, it is necessary to define intangibles and then to find ways to measure them reliably. The objective of this chapter is to discuss the nature of intangibles and evaluate the alternative methods of reporting them. The chapter begins by discussing their nature and when intangibles should be recognized. Questions of measurement and amortization follow. These general results are applied to some particular examples of intangibles. The chapter concludes with a discussion of investments, which, apart from being intangibles themselves, are also the generators of goodwill, the most discussed of all intangibles.

THE NATURE AND RECOGNITION OF INTANGIBLES

Intangibles are sometimes defined as the excess of the cost of an acquired company over the sum of its tangible net assets. But this is to mistake measurement for definition. Also, the purchase of a company merely brings intangibles, like "goodwill," to light; it does not create them. What does create intangibles, then? More precisely, what are intangibles?

The word *intangible* derives from the Latin *tangere,* meaning "to touch." Intangible property, therefore, is property which cannot be touched because it lacks body. More formally, intangibles are said to be incorporeal (corpus = corpse = body).[2] A wide variety of assets are, strictly speaking, intangible. Besides the familiar goodwill, the list includes accounts receivable, prepaid expenses, and stocks and bonds held as investments. None of these examples, except goodwill, are what accountants usually mean by intangibles, though. Accountants have sought to tighten the definition of intangibles by limiting them to capital assets, that is, to assets that are noncurrent.[3] This restriction enables accountants to exclude items such as accounts receivable and prepaid expenses. This approach fails to solve the problem completely, though, because accountants usually do not classify many noncurrent incorporeal assets, such as long-term receivables and long-term investments, as intangibles, even though, in a strict sense, they are intangibles.

The approach adopted in this text is to broaden the definition rather than to narrow it. Most assets result from situations where cash (or its equivalent) has been expended, but the related expense has not appeared in the income statement. The expenditure has been deferred, in other words. Inventory and prepaid expenses are classic examples of deferred costs. Intangible assets, as that term is used here, are the result of deferrals of expenditures on services as opposed to expenditures on property. In other words, intangibles arise when cash (or its equivalent) is expended on services. Some of the assets that result are known as *deferred charges* in the accounting literature; others are the traditional intangibles. In the

---

EXHIBIT 18-1   Intangibles

Traditional Intangibles	*Deferred Charges*
Brand names	Advertising and promotion
Copyrights	Authors' advances
Covenants not to compete	Computer software development costs
Franchises	Debt issuance costs
Future interests	Legal costs
Goodwill	Marketing research
Licenses	Organization costs
Operating rights	Preopening costs
Patents	Relocation and rearrangement costs
Record masters	Repair
Secret processes	Research and development costs
Trademarks	Start-up costs
Trade names	Training costs

discussion that follows, the term *intangible* will be used to cover both categories unless otherwise noted. Exhibit 18-1 lists some examples of the two kinds of intangibles. The fact that a name can be given to an intangible asset generally signals that it is an *identifiable asset*.[4] The most common example of an unidentifiable intangible asset is goodwill.[5] The point at which a resource becomes identifiable is a matter of some judgment. Of great current interest, for example, is whether brand names are sufficiently identifiable to warrant recognition on a balance sheet.

Recognition

Intangibles are no less assets just because they lack substance. Their recognition should follow, therefore, the same rules as all assets. *SFAC 5,* par. 63, says that an item should be recognized when it (*a*) meets the appropriate definition, (*b*) is measurable, (*c*) is relevant, and (*d*) is reliable. *SFAC 6,* par. 25, defines assets as probable future economic benefits obtained or controlled by a particular entity as a result of past transactions or events. Anytime, therefore, that an intangible resource meets these criteria it should be recognized as an asset just as one would a tangible resource.

Capitalization (the recognition of an item as an asset) should be considered for a number of items that are often treated automatically as expenses. For instance, advertising should be expensed only if it fails one of the four criteria. Whenever advertising can be demonstrated to have probable future benefits, it should appear as an asset. In the words of the FASB:

> Costs incurred for services such as research and development, relocation, repair, training, or advertising relate to future economic benefits in one of two ways. First, costs may represent rights to unperformed services yet to be received from other entities. For example, advertising costs incurred may be for a series of advertisements to appear in national news magazines over the next three months. Those kinds of costs incurred are similar to prepaid insurance or prepaid rent. They are payments in advance for services to be rendered to the entity by other entities in the future. Second, they may represent future economic benefit that is expected to be obtained within the entity by using assets or in future exchange transactions with other entities. For example, prerelease advertising of a motion picture may increase the future economic benefits of the product, or repairs may increase the future economic benefits of a piece of equipment. Those kinds of costs may be accounted for as assets either by being added to other assets or by being disclosed separately.

In short, advertising can be treated as an asset despite the fact that it is commonly expensed in practice. The same holds true for all intangibles.

It is sometimes argued that intangible deferred costs such as the start-up costs of a new business, the initial advertising costs of a new business, or the costs associated with opening a new store should be capitalized and amortized over time. The reason generally given is that these are large costs which would otherwise distort the income in the early years. A related argument is that in the early years the company generates no revenue against which to match expenses. It is thus not uncommon for these costs to be capitalized and amortized over a period of time that is typically five years, because this is the period allowed by tax law. Despite common practice and the provisions of the tax code, there is no theoretical justification for this usage. Assets should be recognized only when they meet the four criteria presented above. Smoothing of income is not grounds for deferral of costs.

The FASB underlined this point in *SFAS 7,* "Accounting and Reporting by Development Stage Enterprises," which brought accounting for development-stage companies into line with the accounting for established companies. In the statement, the FASB noted the common practice at the time of deferring start-up costs and amortizing them over time. It disallowed this practice unless the deferrals were based on the same assessment of recoverability as established operating companies. Stated otherwise, *SFAS 7* permits all deferrals that meet the normal recognition tests of all assets.

The practice of capitalizing legal expenses on patents and copyrights also gives implicit recognition to the point that is being made here. The costs of a successful defense of a patent can be capitalized on grounds that they ensure that the patent will be revenue-generating. It is slightly absurd then to not recognize the costs of developing that patent on grounds that the research and development costs that went into that patent were too uncertain.

Despite what has just been said, some claim that intangibles have several particular characteristics that distinguish them from tangible assets and that demand that intangibles be treated differently from tangibles. Three of these supposed distinguishing characteristics are said to be no alternative uses, lack of separability, and great uncertainty of recoverability.

Alternative Uses.   All agree that both tangible and intangible nonmonetary assets derive their economic value from the expectations of future earning power. Tangible assets also have value in alternative uses, and their value to the firm can, at least in part, be compared with their physical condition, their replacement cost, the market value for used assets, and the market for the product of the enterprise. On the other hand, some say that most intangible assets represent the development of exclusive processes or products, or the protection of marketing superiority, none of which can be transferred to alternative uses. While the argument is true for some intangibles, there are important exceptions.

Most notable are brand names. The manner in which the Disney Company has exploited Mickey Mouse is known universally. Less well known, perhaps, is the story of the Coleman lamp.[6] At the turn of the century, William C. Coleman saw the gas-powered lamp in the window of a drugstore, realized its potential, and contracted to produce and sell these lamps. Since their introduction in 1903, more than 40 million have been sold. Among other things, they are reputed to have lit the first night football game. Their fine quality built a reputation for the Coleman Company, which the firm was able to transfer to other products including camp stoves, coolers, jugs, and even trailers. Both Coleman and Disney, therefore, are examples of where intangibles have been put to many alternative uses.

Separability.   Another supposedly distinguishing characteristic of intangibles is that they cannot be separated from the firm or the physical property of the firm. They exist and have value only in combination with the tangible assets of the firm. Because of this characteristic, some say that they should be considered to represent only residual benefits after all tangible assets are specifically identified. Australian professor Raymond Chambers is one who has argued that, because intangibles are not severable from the firm and cannot be measured in terms of a current cash equivalent, they are not assets and should not be included in the statements of the firm.[7] He would charge all intangibles to expense immediately upon their acquisition.

Two counterarguments can be made. First, many intangible assets are severable. Copyrights, for instance, can be bought and sold. So can brand names and trademarks. Second, Chambers' argument can be reversed to say that tangible assets derive value only from their association with intangibles. The script of a play, for instance, has no value unless one has the right to stage it. One might argue that tangible assets are the residuals. By this argument, tangibles should be expensed, and not intangibles. In truth, both are jointly responsible for value, and both should be recognized, whenever possible, to signal that fact.

Uncertainty.   The third characteristic that is said to distinguish intangibles is the high degree of uncertainty regarding the value of the future benefits to be received. Possible values may range from zero to very large amounts. Some intangibles relate to the development and manufacture of a product, and others relate to the creation and maintenance of the demand for the product. Patents and copyrights reflect primarily the former; trademarks and trade names reflect primarily the latter. Goodwill may represent either or both. All, however, represent benefits that are said to be highly uncertain and difficult to associate with specific revenues or specific periods. The result, many conclude, dictates a very conservative treatment of intangibles. Once again, uncertainty may be high for some intangibles, but it is not true for all. The value of a college education is considerably less uncertain than the specialized equipment in a new research laboratory. We capitalize the cost of the latter. Why not the former?

Recognizing Goodwill

The major example of an intangible that lacks alternative uses, is not separable, and whose benefits are highly uncertain, is goodwill. Should it, therefore, be recognized at all? One could, in principle, recognize goodwill at any point in time by comparing the market value of a company with the value of its net assets. Equity could be marked up to market by a valuation account, and a goodwill account could be entered among the assets. It seems, though, that little would be achieved by this treatment. Goodwill represents advantages that are not specifically identifiable. One lacks, therefore, any logical method of associating these costs with any specific revenue in future periods. *APB 17* concluded on these grounds that expenditures for "nonpurchased" goodwill should be deducted from income when incurred. The authors agree with this practice because no apparent advantage would be obtained by attempting to capitalize goodwill acquired in this fashion. The lack of advantage follows because capitalization does not determine changes in the value of the firm. Value changes occur for other reasons, such as exogenous changes in the demand for the product and fortuitous discoveries of previously unknown resources. However, a disclosure of such expenditures may be relevant for a valuation of the firm by investors.

On the other hand, when a company is purchased, the price paid must be allocated in some fashion in the accounts of the company. American practice is to allocate as much of the purchase price to specific assets as possible and to denote the residual as goodwill. Goodwill is recognized, therefore, by default. Sometimes, no attempt is made to allocate to specific assets the excess of the market value of the business over the carrying value of the specific assets. Even though this residual may be called goodwill, it has few attributes of an intangible asset. Instead, this excess simply represents unallocated costs of tangible assets and some specific intangibles. This kind of goodwill is not an adequate substitute for the careful determination of the cost of specific assets, based as closely as possible on their value to the firm at the date of acquisition. More generally, given the lack of alternative uses for goodwill, its lack of separability, and the uncertainty attaching to its benefits, one can reasonably question whether it should be recognized at all.

Conclusion

In short, intangible assets should be required to pass the same tests of recognition as tangibles—no more, and no less. If they pass that test, intangibles should appear in the financial statements. The list of intangibles so determined could include items that are often currently expensed, such as research and development costs and advertising.

The treatment of unidentifiable intangibles is less clear. Unidentifiable assets lack semantic interpretation. They fail, therefore, the test of relevance and, by right, they should not be recognized. However, according to the traditional accounting structure, if resource outlays are incurred in order to benefit future periods, the cost should be capitalized and allocated to the future periods. In other words, all purchased intangibles tend to be capitalized in practice, whether they meet the criterion of relevance or not.

CHECKPOINTS

1. Define in your own words what is meant by an intangible asset.
2. What is the difference between an identifiable and an unidentifiable intangible?
3. When should an asset be recognized?
4. What three characteristics make intangible assets less likely to be recognized than tangible assets?

MEASUREMENT AND AMORTIZATION

Intangibles can be extremely difficult to measure. This is especially true when they are not identifiable or separable. By definition, these intangibles are then associated with other assets with the result that one has a joint cost problem. The usual solution is to treat the intangible as a residual. That is, one computes some value for the tangible assets and ascribes the difference between this value and the total value ascribed to the asset as a whole to the intangible. This approach is discussed in more detail below in connection with goodwill. In cases where the intangible is identifiable and separable, such as patents and copyrights, an independent measurement of the intangible is possible. In principle, the most informative measure is the present value of its projected benefits. As with all assets, though, accountants have preferred to use transaction costs because of their greater perceived reliability. Even when intangible assets are donated to the firm, there is a general reluctance to record any value in the accounts because of the high degree of uncertainty regarding whatever valuation may be chosen. This led the AICPA to state in *Accounting Research Bulletin No. 43:*

> The initial amount assigned to all types of intangibles should be cost. . . . In the case of non-cash acquisitions, as, for example, where intangibles are acquired in exchange for securities, cost may be considered as being either the fair value of the consideration given or the fair value of the property or right acquired, whichever is the more evident.

The authors of *ARS 3* also recommend the use of cost for intangibles in spite of their general preference for current values or replacement cost. They state:

> these items are notoriously difficult to evaluate and therefore should probably be carried at acquisition cost in the absence of compelling evidence that their value is markedly different.[8]

Despite these recommendations, whenever compelling evidence exists that some other valuation is more appropriate, it should be used. For instance, using the value of the signed contracts as a measure of the TV rights of King World Productions would not seem unreasonable.

When intangibles are acquired by purchase, individually or as a part of a basket purchase, the determination of cost is similar to the computation of the cost of plant and equipment under like circumstances. When intangibles are developed within the company, however, the computation of their cost involves all the difficulties of self-constructed assets plus some additional problems of their own. Most of the costs of patents, trademarks, and trade names are joint costs. Many patents may emerge from joint research and development expenditures, and several trademarks and trade names may be advertised jointly. These problems can be solved by the use of known costing methods, but the results are likely to be arbitrary if they include allocated joint costs. To the extent that they do, the valuations are likely to be almost meaningless—but no more so than the acquisition of joint tangible assets such as land and buildings.

In many start-up situations, founders' stock is issued in return for the expertise of an individual. This expertise is then capitalized as an intangible. The determination of cost in these situations is an especially difficult problem, because stock may not be traded at the development stage. At best it will be thinly traded. The fair value of the rights may have to be estimated directly. Sometimes, the fair value of the stock given can be estimated on the basis of the price paid for other stock. It is inappropriate, however, to assume that cost is equal to the par value or stated value of the shares issued in exchange.

Measuring Goodwill

Goodwill is the largest intangible of most companies. It is often the most complex to handle because it lacks many of the characteristics associated with assets such as identifiability and separability. As a result, its measurement has received particular attention. Three major approaches for valuing goodwill have resulted:

1. Through the valuation of favorable attitudes toward the firm.
2. Through the present discounted value of the excess of expected future profits over that considered a normal return on the total investment, not including the goodwill.
3. Through a master valuation account—the excess of the value of the business as a whole over the valuations attaching to its individual tangible and intangible net assets.

All three approaches have been applied to some extent to other intangibles.

The Valuation of Favorable Attitudes toward the Firm.   Goodwill is frequently thought to arise from advantageous business relationships, good relations with employees, and favorable attitudes of customers. These favorable attitudes may be due to an advantageous location, an excellent reputation and name, monopolistic privileges, good business management, and other factors. When the purchase price of a going business exceeds the sum of the valuations of all individual assets other than goodwill, the excess is assumed to represent the payment for these specific intangible attributes generated by the previous owners. This approach assumes that these attributes can be listed and then valued independently of the tangible assets of the firm. In other words, the approach suggests, in effect, that the factors making up goodwill are as identifiable as, say, a brand name.

Critics of this approach argue that most of these attributes attach to specific assets, including other intangible assets. A favorable location, for example, means that the land and buildings are worth more than similar property elsewhere. The value of excellent reputation and name attach to the valuation of trade names and brand names. Goodwill, to the extent that any remains, represents only the residual benefits that cannot be associated with specific assets. It is the result of good business management and monopolistic privileges—attributes of the firm as a whole.

The Present Value of Superior Earnings.   The approach to measuring goodwill that appears most frequently in accounting textbooks is to assume that goodwill represents the present discounted value of expected future earnings (or cash payments to equity holders) in excess of that which may be considered a normal return. For example, consider an enterprise with a net book value of $240,000. Its annual net income is $60,000. This gives a return on investment of 25 percent. If the normal return in the marketplace is 10 percent, an income of $60,000 suggests that the assets are really worth $600,000 in total. The excess return of 15 percent over the normal rate of return is ascribed to intangibles. Stated otherwise, intangibles are valued at $360,000. Some of these intangibles may be identifiable. Some may be associated with specific tangible assets. Some of the gap may be due to the fact that tangible assets are undervalued. The residual, after subtracting all the identifiable causes of the difference, is said to be goodwill. If one attributes $240,000 to identifiable intangible assets and undervalued tangible assets, the goodwill would be valued at $120,000.

As indicated in Chapter 11, the value of the firm as a whole to individual investors can only be determined subjectively by investors, because it depends upon their expectations of future cash flows, the expected opportunity rates of return, and personal utility risk functions. As Chambers stated, "the goodwill of a going concern runs to the constituents, not to the firm."[9] Therefore, neither management nor the accountants can place a correct valuation on goodwill. But neither can the investor allocate this total value of the firm logically to specific tangible and intangible assets and to goodwill. The assumption that the tangible assets can earn only a "normal" rate while other factors are responsible for the excess is pure fiction. Tangible assets may have value in their specific use because of imperfect competition and changes in demand for the products as well as efficient utilization. All factors interact in the production of the final service or product and in permitting cash distributions to stockholders. Any attempt to allocate a portion of the total value of a firm on the basis of the capitalization of superior earnings is, therefore, completely artificial.

Goodwill as a Master Valuation Account. Stanford professor John Canning was one of the early writers who questioned whether goodwill is an asset at all in the usual sense. He preferred to view goodwill as a straight plug—what he termed a *master valuation account*.[10] All assets have value to the firm because of their expected contribution to the firm's stream of future earnings and cash flows. Therefore, the value of the firm should be associated with all the assets giving rise to this stream of cash flows. If expectations of cash flows should increase (for instance, after making an additional payment for superior management skills), all assets contributing to this increase are now worth more than before.

Receivables can be valued in terms of the discounted expected cash receipts; inventories can be valued in terms of net realizable value; other assets, such as land, plant and equipment, and patent rights, can also be valued at their net realizable values. Whatever value remains unallocated is recorded as goodwill. The more assets that are identified, the smaller the goodwill residual. In the limit goodwill disappears, to be replaced by identifiable tangible and intangible assets. Goodwill, according to this view, is simply the company value that we are unable to associate with particular assets. In and of itself, it has no meaning. That is to say, goodwill is not associated with any specific attributes independent of tangible assets; it is not the firm's excess earning power—it is purely and simply a plug.

Measuring "Negative" Goodwill

Can goodwill be negative? However goodwill is defined, conceiving of it with a negative value is difficult. For, if the firm is worth less than the supposed value of its assets sold separately, the previous owners surely would have sold them separately, rather than as a whole. This argument suggests that the real value of the identifiable assets is less than claimed. An appropriate response would be to allocate the net worth of the firm to the identifiable assets so that they appear at lower numbers than presently shown. In this way negative goodwill would be eliminated.

This view is the position taken in *APB 16*, which recommends that, when a combination is deemed to be a purchase, the assets acquired should be recorded at their fair value, or the fair value of the consideration given in the exchange.[11] This view is also consistent with the historical cost concept, which states that assets should always be recorded at their current value if the consideration given is not as clearly measurable as the assets received. *APB 17* also suggests that, when the cost of an acquired company is less than the sum of the market, or appraised values, of identifiable assets less liabilities, the difference should be allocated to reduce the values of the noncurrent assets. Only if an unallocatable difference remains (after the noncurrent assets are reduced to zero) is negative goodwill shown. This is relatively rare.

The British Accounting Standards Committee, on the other hand, suggests that negative goodwill is the result of a bargain purchase as a consequence of a "forced sale, negotiating skills or market imperfections, or where disadvantages exist which are part of the business but are not attributable to any particular asset or class of asset; a badly motivated work force, unfavorable customer perceptions."[12] The implication is that the same identifiable assets in a more favorable location would produce more benefits for the purchaser. Their conclusion is that negative goodwill is simply the mirror image of positive goodwill. The value of the identifiable assets should not be written down because that is their fair value. The negative goodwill is an intangible that might be called *Unfavorable Location*.

Amortization

Most intangibles that are generated gradually by the firm through annual expenditures are charged immediately to expense. However, intangibles that are acquired through a lump-sum purchase or that are developed through extraordinary identifiable expenditures are frequently capitalized and amortized similarly to the depreciation allocations of plant and equipment. Once the initial valuation to be amortized is determined, the major factors to be estimated are:

1. The useful life of the asset.
2. The pattern of allocation to the several periods of the life of the asset.

The residual or scrap value is generally nonexistent or immaterial.

Intangibles with Limited Life.   Patents, copyrights, and some franchises have a maximum legal life, and only rarely will the economic life exceed this legal life.* If circumstances permit the value to extend beyond the legal life, the cost or other value should be amortized over this economic life. Many use the legal life, though, in the belief that without the legal protection, the value beyond the legal life is too uncertain to include in the amortization schedule. More commonly, the economic life is shorter than the legal life because of either market demand conditions, or obsolescence. When this is the case, the economic life should definitely be the controlling factor. For example, it is unusual for copyrights to provide benefits to the firm for the entire period of the copyright. Textbooks, for example, frequently become obsolete in five years or less. But if the book is revised, some of the initial value may carry into the second, third, and possibly the fifth editions. In no case, though, may assets acquired after November 1, 1970 be amortized over more than 40 years. This is true even of trademarks, which can be renewed every 20 years indefinitely.

Determining the useful life of intangibles is difficult. Each intangible is more or less unique, so experience is of little help. Also, the capital expenditure decision is generally not so precisely formulated as with tangibles. As a result, the amortization procedure tends to result in a method of smoothing income to prevent fluctuations of income due to the irregular acquisition of intangibles that related to more than just current operating activities. If the net income figure is used as the major item for prediction, the smoothing process may be of some assistance; however, arbitrary

---

* Patents have a maximum legal life of 17 years; copyrights have a legal life of 50 years beyond the death of the author. This life can be extended a further 50 years. Trademarks have a life of 20 years, but are renewable as long as the trademark is in continuous use. The life of a franchise is determined by the contract.

allocations are highly unlikely to provide relevant information for investors and creditors.

Like depreciation, the pattern of amortization of intangibles is generally thought to be appropriate if it is related to the expected associated revenue contributions or benefit patterns. The benefit pattern for patents may depend on many economic considerations, including the effect of subsequent supporting or competing developments. Each case must be judged on its own circumstances and expectations. In the case of copyrights, the benefits frequently increase during the first few years and then drop off substantially. If frequent revisions are expected, some of the initial acquisition costs should be amortized over the lives of subsequent editions. Since such associations are not likely to be apparent with most intangibles, partly because of the many interactions of the resources of the firm, *APB 17* suggests that the straight-line method be used unless other systematic methods can be demonstrated to be more appropriate.

Because of the high degree of uncertainty regarding the periods to be benefited, changes in expectations are more likely to occur for intangibles than for plant and equipment. Therefore, *APB 17* recommends that when changes in expectations of useful lives occur, the unamortized cost should be allocated to the remaining periods in the revised useful life, but not to exceed 40 years. If the value itself is reduced significantly, a partial write-down should be made by reporting an extraordinary loss in the income statement. These recommendations are in accordance with *APB 20* on accounting changes.

Note that a write-up of an intangible is not permitted. The inability to restore an asset to its market value can lead to distortions of income. For instance, if excessive amortization occurs in the early years, one cannot correct this by writing up the intangible. Instead, amortization to subsequent periods must be reduced by an amount large enough to offset the earlier overamortization. This procedure results in a material reduction in the reported expense in the later years—and an overstatement of income. This situation is a major inconsistency in the traditional accounting structure.

Intangibles with Indefinite Lives.   Trademarks, trade names, organization costs, and goodwill are examples of intangibles generally considered to have no limited term of existence and no natural limited life. Should they then be amortized? Some argue that, as a result of the nature of these intangibles, both the life and the pattern of amortization must by necessity be arbitrary, and thus without a logical basis. Without this logical basis, the resulting reported net income figures are highly unlikely to be any more meaningful than if the amortization had not been taken.*

---

* This argument excludes most depreciation on tangible fixed assets as well.

Systematic amortization is supported on the ground that all intangibles represent benefits to be matched with future revenues over a reasonable period of time. In the specific case of goodwill, many argue that if it represents a payment for superior earnings, the purchase price was based on expectations regarding a limited period during which the superior earnings would be received. If goodwill does continue beyond this reasonable period, then it is assumed to represent benefits accumulated since the acquisition of the property. Therefore, it is argued, purchased goodwill should be accounted for consistently with other nonpurchased goodwill. Thus, the amortization of goodwill is supported on the ground that the value of the purchased goodwill declines over time.

This is the position of *APB 17,* which claims that all intangibles eventually lose their value and, therefore, that they should be amortized over the period estimated to be benefited, but not exceeding 40 years. This 40-year period is arbitrary and can be defended only on the basis that it is long enough so that the income of no period is significantly affected. The effect is to neutralize or sterilize the allocation of goodwill with respect to the information presented to investors and creditors. In other words, while the amortization of intangibles does not provide useful information, it does not harm or distort other information being presented.

Not everyone has agreed with the 40-year term for the amortization of goodwill. For instance, banking authorities and the SEC require banks and thrifts to write off unidentified intangibles, such as goodwill, over a period not to exceed 25 years.[13] Identified intangibles must be amortized over an even shorter period: no more than 10 to 15 years. The Australian Accounting Research Foundation has proposed a maximum of 20 years for goodwill. Businesses, on the other hand, have argued that 50 to 100 years would be more appropriate. Since no theory exists to guide the choice, whatever period is selected is inherently arbitrary.

Write-Offs of Intangibles. *ARS 10* suggested that goodwill should be accounted for as a reduction of stockholders' equity. The reasoning given for this suggestion is that the amount paid for the goodwill represents a decrease of the firm's current resources in anticipation of future earnings. The remaining equity then represents the values of the separate resources and property rights consistent with the reporting for enterprises that have not engaged in purchasing other entities. A fallacy of this argument, however, is that the entire purchase price is a payment for future cash flows and earnings; the amount paid for the acquired enterprise represents invested capital just as does an amount paid to acquire an addition to an existing plant.

The authors are sympathetic with the recommendations of *ARS 10* for other reasons, however. After the date of acquisition, there appears to be little evidence that the continual presentation of the goodwill as an asset provides useful information to investors or other interested readers of financial statements. For one thing, goodwill lacks semantic interpretation. Furthermore, the amortization of goodwill to income by the use of arbitrary procedures seems of doubtful validity because of the homogeneity problem and interactions mentioned in Chapter 15.

APB 17 is very clear in prohibiting write-offs immediately after acquisition. The assumption is that, if the intangible has been acquired at a cost, it must be worth this price at the time of purchase. The main purpose of this restriction was to prevent undue conservatism in asset valuation and overstatement of the incomes of subsequent periods. The opinion does permit a lump-sum write-off of intangibles when reasonable evidence emerges that they have become worthless.* The intangible may have become worthless because an error was made in the acquisition of the asset, leading to an overstatement of the value of the intangible. As soon as this situation is recognized, the loss should be recorded; there is no justification for carrying forward the loss to future periods. Immediate write-offs of overstatements of an intangible should also occur when there has been an error in the valuation of a nonmonetary asset exchanged for the intangible.

Maintaining Goodwill.   Many argue that the economic life of all intangibles, as with all tangible assets, is limited unless expenditures are continually made for maintenance and replacement. Even initial organization costs require periodic reorganization expenditures, most of which are interrelated with goodwill and current operations. However, the time at which the original asset value is completely replaced by additional expenditures cannot be determined, even in retrospect. This suggests that the original cost should remain on the books and the costs of maintenance or replacement should be charged against current income. No amortization should be made because the value of the original asset continues if proper maintenance expenditures are made.

A closely related argument points to another major difficulty of amortizing intangibles. If allocation is required in addition to expensing the current expenditures for the maintenance of their value, a double charge against income results during the amortization period. The process is similar to charging the cost of replacement equipment against income while at the same time depreciating the cost of the original equipment. If expensing replacements is acceptable, the amortization of the original cost is not also appropriate; if amortization is proper, the cost of replacements should be capitalized.[14]

---

* This procedure was still permissible in the United Kingdom at the time of writing, but standards are being changed to harmonize with the EEC, where immediate write-offs are not permitted.

Capitalizing replacements while amortizing the total cost of intangibles provides a practical method for charging the cost of benefits received to expenses. Difficulties in the measurement of replacements, however, indicate that expensing replacements without amortizing the original cost may be the most appropriate, or at least the most convenient, method. The procedure of carrying the intangible asset at its original cost and charging maintenance and replacement expenditures to current income accounts is similar to the replacement method of depreciation. However, its application to intangibles is more appropriate than its use for the depreciation of plant and equipment, because replacement is a continual process with some intangibles and is sporadic and infrequent for plant and equipment. Thus, the replacement expenditures are charged fairly evenly against the incomes of all periods. This method is also advantageous because it provides for an income charge based on current costs, like LIFO. There are some major disadvantages:

1. If the value of the intangible is being increased through current expenditures, the charge against current income is excessive, and the reverse is true if the value of the intangible is not maintained.
2. As with LIFO, the value of the intangible soon becomes out of date and not representative of the value to be charged to future periods.
3. The current charge against income is subject to manipulation by management.
4. The method does not result in a systematic matching of expenses with benefits received or with current revenues.

Amortizing Negative Goodwill.   *APB 16* suggests that negative goodwill, when recognized, be taken into income in future periods by systematic amortization. The British Accounting Standards Committee has made the same recommendation. *ARS 10* refined this approach by suggesting that negative goodwill indicates the necessity for future expenditures to improve the organization and efficiency of the firm. They would classify negative goodwill as a liability and would reduce that liability by charging these future expenditures to the goodwill account and not to expense. But the need to improve the efficiency of a firm does not fall into the usual definition of a liability. Also, since any costs could be charged against this "liability," the result would be capricious and arbitrary.

Since the excess of the amount assignable to net assets over the cost to the parent represents either an advantageous purchase or an overvaluation of all net assets as a whole, there is no logic in any allocation of this amount to income on a "reasonable and systematic" basis. Without knowing the meaning of the credit, no allocation can be reasonable. Furthermore, since most firms report this deferred credit as neither a liability nor stockholders' equity, it is a meaningless item in the balance sheet. Thus, the allocation to income appears to be only a method of smoothing the effect of the acquisition. Since both the classification of the deferred credit and its amortization are uninformative to users of financial statements, they create more questions than answers.

This suggests that a better alternative than allocation is simply to write it off immediately either to retained earnings or to capital surplus. This alternative was also suggested in *ARS 10*. Although the theoretical justification for this method is slim, it creates no more misinformation than any other method, so long as the net purchase price is disclosed at the date of acquisition. If the reason for the difference cannot be identified, it should not be taken into income merely to stay within the double-entry reporting system.

CHECKPOINTS

1. Distinguish the three bases for measuring goodwill.
2. What value does *ARB 43* suggest one should give to an identifiable intangible?
3. What value do current standards give to a patent developed by a company and successfully defended in court?
4. Over what period should one amortize the cost of a patent? Briefly explain why.
5. Over what period should one amortize purchased goodwill? Briefly explain why.

ISSUES AND APPLICATIONS

Applying the general rules of accounting for intangibles to specific situations requires a great deal of judgment on the part of management and their accountants. Whenever practice is left to the judgment of producers of financial information, the financial reports should be accompanied by full disclosure of the method chosen and its justification. Unfortunately, as Chapter 8 noted, management has been reluctant to make full disclosure of the reasons for their reporting choices. The inevitable result has been the imposition of arbitrary rules to enforce uniformity. Some of these rules are discussed below.

Program License Agreements

SFAS 63 deals with the special accounting problems of broadcasters. Broadcasters typically enter into license agreements that give them the right to broadcast a number of programs such as a cartoon series, or a season of football games, for a fee established up front. The FASB requires that the license be entered as an intangible asset, not unlike prepaid expenses, if:

1. The cost of each program is known or reasonably determinable.
2. The program material has been accepted by the licensee in accordance with the conditions of the license agreement.
3. The program is available for its first showing or telecast.

The FASB compromised by allowing the asset to be entered at either its discounted or its gross value, even though the latter is a direct contravention of *APB 21*. The capitalized value is amortized over the number of programs broadcast, ideally in accordance with the value received, but failing that, pro rata to the number of showings. Like all assets, the value of program licenses should be reviewed periodically. They should be written down if below their amortized cost.

Sports Franchises

Most sports franchises are private, so discovering how they do their financial reporting is not easy. Nevertheless, from research that has been done and from the financial reports of the Boston Celtics, which are now public, several things have become apparent. First, when clubs change hands as much as 50 percent of the purchase price is attributed to the players. The amount attributable to players is the equivalent of goodwill and, like goodwill, it must be amortized or depreciated. The result is known as *initial-roster depreciation*. Second, when a contract is entered into with a new player, the value of this contract is typically entered onto the books at its present value. This is known as the *deferred compensation fund*. This fund is amortized over the playing life of the player using the interest-rate method, if it has been entered at present value.[15]

The franchise itself is a purchased right. In the case of football, the National Football League grants the franchise and permits the owner of the team, the franchisee, the sole right to operate a football team in a particular area. Franchises (think of those given to owners of MacDonald's fast-food outlets) also entitle the franchisee to use the franchisor's products, brand names, and trademarks, and to benefit from its reputation. The initial amount paid for a franchise is typically capitalized and amortized over a period of less than 40 years, even though the franchise may have been granted in perpetuity. Sports franchises, being private, are not obliged to follow GAAP. For instance, the previous owner of the Dallas Cowboys, Mr. Bum Bright, was reported to have paid $8 million for the franchise—but not to have amortized it on grounds that it was a perpetuity.

Research and Development Costs

To the extent that research and development activities (R&D) are carried out to develop new products, improve old ones, or reduce future operating costs, they are expected to benefit future periods, rather than only the current period. Because future periods are expected to be benefited, the knowledge gained is either an asset of the firm, or an increase in the value of existing assets or of the firm as a whole. Therefore, according to the matching concept, the research and development costs should be capitalized and amortized over the period benefited. Even though the length of the period and the timing of the benefits are highly uncertain, proponents of the matching concept claim that an appropriate allocation is better than an immediate write-off, because a subjective estimate of the value is better than an arbitrary valuation of zero.[16] Allocation is also assumed to be better because an immediate write-off may result in lower net earnings now. This would indicate an adverse situation, even though the reverse might be true. That is, a firm that sponsors a large amount of research may have a very favorable future, and one that carries out no research may be doomed to failure. Thus, if all R&D is required to be expensed, there may be a short-term incentive for management to cut back research to boost earnings just when research is needed to maintain market position or efficiency.

An alternative to full capitalization and amortization is the common practice of expensing general research and development costs and capitalizing only research costs that relate to specific projects with expected net revenue contribution streams.[17] These special projects are treated like investments in plant and equipment, and the amortization is similar to the depreciation concepts related to net revenue contributions discussed in Chapter 15.

The position of the FASB in *Statement No. 2* is that all research and development costs should be charged to expense when incurred, except when R&D is conducted for others under contract. This recommendation was based on the claim that no causal relationship can be found between R&D expenditures and future benefits. It is also based on the lack of interpretation of the asset (arising from capitalization of expenditures) on grounds that it does not reflect the value of any specific future benefits and, even if those benefits do exist, their value is not measurable. The conclusion of the FASB was also based on the lack of usefulness of the information arising from capitalization. The Board was influenced by the fact that a survey of security analysts and investors showed that capitalization was not useful to them in assessing the earnings potential of the enterprise. Further, no evidence was given that capitalization improves the ability to predict either the amount or variability of future rates of return. In addition, the expensing of R&D is consistent with the efficient-market hypothesis—so long as the firm fully discloses the amount and types of expenditures.

Unfortunately, disclosure of research and development is limited to its cost. The FASB had suggested originally that disclosure might include:

1. The nature, status, and costs of individual research and development projects.
2. The nature and status of patents.
3. Projections about new or improved products or processes.
4. An enterprise's philosophy regarding research and development.

This suggestion was abandoned in light of business's claim that this information was private, confidential, and beyond the scope of financial information.[18] In reality, most of this information is almost certainly available to a company's competitors through scientific networks. The only people deprived of this information are the owners of the enterprise.* This is yet another example of where unsatisfactory regulation by uniformity has replaced the more satisfactory regulation by disclosure. It is also an example of where the public's right to know might have to override business's penchant for secrecy.

The expensing of research and development costs leads to a curious situation in the computation of goodwill. Purchased goodwill, it will be recalled, is usually computed as the residual after all identifiable assets have been valued. Research and development is an identifiable asset in this context. The purchaser of a company, therefore, is obliged to establish the value of research and development done by that company. Once that value is established and the residual goodwill computed, the research and development asset is immediately written off so as to be in accordance with *SFAS 2*.†

The international accounting community has not followed the FASB. They have argued in *International Standard No. 9 (IASC 9)*, correctly in the opinion of the authors, that if a firm can demonstrate ''that the product or process is technically and commercially feasible and that the enterprise has adequate resources to enable the product or process to be marketed . . . (then) . . . it may be appropriate to defer the costs of development activities to future periods.''[19] One of the arguments for capitalizing research and development costs is that it encourages management to look upon R&D as a strategic asset and not just as a cost of doing business. Many claim that expensing R&D deters management from spending more on research, but as yet, no one has demonstrated that conclusively.

---

* Recall that models, admittedly slightly inaccurate, of the top-secret Stealth bomber were on sale before the bomber itself was made public.

† The Genentech case at the end illustrates the procedure.

Software

In the specific case of software, the FASB has contradicted its own stand against capitalizing research and development costs, and is much closer to the position of the international accounting community. In *SFAS 86*, the FASB allowed the capitalization of costs for computer software that is "to be sold, leased, or otherwise marketed as a separate product or as a part of a product or process." The condition for capitalization is that the company has established the technological feasibility of the product.[20] These words echo almost identically the quote from *IASC 9* above.

The statement covers computer software only, but the principle can be applied to other intangible assets involving information. Consider, for instance, the development of large databases such as those used by the airlines regarding their flight times. Consider, also, the development of education materials. Currently, most companies expense the costs associated with the development of these information sources on the grounds that they fall under the rubric of *SFAS 2*, requiring all development costs to be expensed. Theory suggests, and *SFAS 86* allows, that these costs might be more appropriately deferred.

Further confirmation of the general desirability of capitalizing the costs of identifiable intangible assets comes from *SFAS 61*. This statement deals with reporting for title companies. These companies establish a database called a *title plant* which "constitutes a historical record of all matters affecting title to parcels of land in a particular geographic area." The statement permits capitalization of all development costs. (In this and all other cases of deferral, capitalization stops when the asset is taken into use.) *Statements 61* and *86* suggest, therefore, that the FASB could easily reconcile its standards on research and development with those of the IASC.

Brand Names

Statements 61 and *86* shatter another taboo, namely that intangibles may be recognized only if they are purchased. Both involve situations where an internally developed resource is recognized as an asset. This raises the question of whether other internally generated resources may not be recognized. Most prominent among those resources in current debate are brand names such as *Coca Cola* and *Pepsi Cola*. These names are recognizable across the world because of millions of dollars of advertising. Currently, those advertising dollars are expensed. The Australian Accounting Research Foundation has proposed to change that practice and to allow the cost of developing brand names to be capitalized under the heading of the brand name.[21] The proposal is controversial but clearly follows developing practice in recognizing all intangible assets—when they meet the criteria for recognition of assets.

The valuation of brand names arose in the context of minimizing goodwill. To avoid large unidentified goodwill accounts, some consultants suggested that brand names be recognized as identifiable intangible assets. Proponents of recognizing brands argue that a brand is "a separately identifiable asset with independent legal status capable of conferring considerable benefit on its owner. A brand can be transferred between brand owners by simple transfer of the trade mark certificate that governs the brand's legal status."[22] In short, a brand name has many of the characteristics of tangible assets: a market due to alternative uses, separability, and reasonable certainty of return. Given that brand names are assets by definition and that some experts claim they are able to measure their value, there seems to be little reason not to recognize them.

Once the brand name is developed, capitalization ceases and amortization of the brand name begins. The effect, therefore, is to move the expensing of advertising from the period in which it is incurred to the presumed period in which that benefit is received. Exactly when the benefit is received is unclear though. The Foundation's solution is to amortize the brand name over an arbitrary 20 years. Given that brand names are in constant development and use, one can foresee a situation where advertising dollars would be debited to the brand name and a 20-year amortization of those dollars would proceed simultaneously. Where brand names already exist, the Foundation proposes to simply enter them into the balance sheet at a value determined by independent assessors. These values would also be amortized over a maximum of 20 years.

Push-Down Accounting

When one company acquires another, an investment account, in the amount paid, appears in the books of the acquiring company. Traditionally, the books of the acquired company are unchanged. When the companies are consolidated for financial reporting purposes, the investment account is replaced by the fair value of the individual assets. The difference between the investment account and the fair value of the identifiable net assets is the residual goodwill. Therefore, it is only at the point of consolidation that goodwill is computed.

The case has been made that, when a company is acquired, the assets and liabilities of the acquired company should be restated at their fair values. In other words, one would not wait until consolidation to do these restatements, but would keep the acquired company permanently at its newly established values. This procedure is known as *push-down* accounting. "Pushing fair values down" is relevant to users only if the statements of the acquired company are made public. If it is always consolidated into the acquirer, the issue is irrelevant.

The situation was brought to a head by the SEC's concern over the way in which a parent offered investors a minority interest in companies that had been acquired at a premium. By not restating the assets of the subsidiary at fair value, the parent was able to allow its subsidiary to show a superior rate of return. The SEC believed this practice could be misleading to prospective investors. *Staff Accounting Bulletin No. 54* and *Staff Accounting Bulletin No. 73* require SEC registrants to use push-down accounting in situations where the subsidiary is substantially owned by the parent. Still unresolved is whether the amount to be pushed down should be the full revision of the net assets to fair value or just a fraction proportional to the common stock holdings of the parent. A similar question arises in connection with consolidations and is addressed there.

CHECKPOINTS

1. Are program licence agreements executory contracts? If so, should they be recognized?
2. Are leases tangible or intangible assets? Explain your answer.
3. On the basis of the rules for recognizing computer software, draw up a brief standard that would justify a company's recognizing their investment in your education.
4. Why can one capitalize the legal cost of defending a patent but not the research and development that produced the patent?
5. If the lifetime contracts of football players are capitalized, over what period would you amortize them?
6. Over what period must a franchise granted in perpetuity be amortized? What is the justification?

NONCURRENT INVESTMENTS

Investments in securities of other firms not held for current purposes are generally classified and accounted for on the basis of the intent of holding the securities and the relationship with the investee firm. Investments that represent a controlling interest in the voting stock of a firm (generally in excess of 50 percent) should be included in the consolidated financial statements. More is said on the subject of consolidations in Chapter 22. When less than a controlling interest is present but the investor is able to exercise significant influence over the operating and financial policies of the investee (generally representing 20 to 50 percent of outstanding shares), the investment should be accounted for on the equity basis. Noncurrent marketable securities should be reported at the lower of cost or market for the noncurrent portfolio. Noncurrent investments not included in the above classifications are normally reported at cost. Noncurrent investments not involving any issue of control are discussed in Chapter 16.

Noncurrent Marketable Equity Securities

As noted in Chapter 16, *FASB Statement No. 12* requires that a separate portfolio be set up for noncurrent marketable equity securities. As with current marketable securities, the noncurrent portfolio would be valued on a lower-of-cost-or-market basis. Unlike current marketable securities, however, the reduction from cost to market that results in a valuation allowance offsetting the original cost of the portfolio is reported as an offset to stockholders' equity—not as an unrealized loss in the income statement.

The purpose of this procedure is to avoid reporting losses on the noncurrent portfolio until those losses are realized. Realization is assumed to occur when securities are either transferred to the current portfolio, are sold, or when the decline in market price is considered to be permanent. The result is that all gains and losses on the investments are included in income at or before the sale of the investment, that is, the procedure simply delays the reporting of losses and recoveries.

The main difficulty with this procedure is its lack of consistency with the comprehensive concept of income, which includes all changes in asset valuations, other than those arising from equity transactions. In addition, it uses an offset to stockholders' equity as a means of deferring the reporting of losses. Thus, the method has all of the deficiencies of deferred charges when used for the same purpose. Also, these procedures have all of the disadvantages of the lower-of-cost-or-market method discussed in Chapter 14.

The Equity Method for Unconsolidated Subsidiaries

APB 18, as amended by *SFAS 94,* requires the use of the equity method for investments in which the investor is able to exercise considerable influence over the company, but in which the investor does not have the controlling interest. Considerable influence is usually assumed to start when an investor owns about 20 percent or more of the voting stock. Full control is assumed when the investor has 50 percent or more of the voting stock. Under the equity method, the initial cost of the investment is adjusted each period to include the investor's share of the earnings or losses of the subsidiary. Dividends are viewed as liquidations of the investment and thus reduce the amount of the investment. The excess of cost over the investor's equity in the book value of the investee at the date of acquisition is allocated to specific assets and goodwill. Depreciable assets and goodwill are allocated systematically to expense. Intercompany profits and losses are eliminated and other adjustments are made as in consolidation. The result is that the investment and income each year are accounted for as if the investment had been reported as a consolidated subsidiary.

A major advantage of the equity method is that, at the structural level, it provides some consistency between the reporting of consolidated subsidiaries and the reporting of investments that are not included in the consolidation, but which have some of the characteristics of subsidiaries. However, this method also has all of the limitations of consolidations discussed in Chapter 22. In addition, there is inadequate information regarding what the investment valuation means, as it does not represent either the investor's equity in the book value of the investee or the market price of the stock. Also, the specification of a minimum of 20 percent of voting stock is arbitrary, and the criterion of significant influence is vague.

On *a priori* grounds, the market value method appears to serve the needs of investors and creditors better than the equity method, in addition to permitting better real-world interpretation. Lloyd and Weygandt confirmed that market value information provides useful information for investors.[23] Copeland, Strawser, and Binns also suggest that the equity method does not provide an adequate surrogate for market value.[24] Financial information would be improved further if there were a disclosure of the dividends received over several periods as well as the firm's share of the investee's reported income. Such information would likely be helpful to investors in evaluating the firm as a whole and in predicting future cash flows.

SUMMARY

An intangible asset has been defined as "a capital asset having no physical existence, its value being dependent on the rights that possession confers upon the owner."[25] Intangibles arise from the acquisition of rights or services. The cash, or its equivalent, that is expended in their acquisition is typically expensed. Advertising, research and development, and training costs are just three examples of costs incurred in the acquisition of rights or services that are usually expensed.

Intangibles, though, are assets. Therefore, intangible costs should be capitalized and not expensed when they meet the criteria for asset recognition. Those criteria are that the item in question meet the definition of an asset, be measurable, and be relevant and reliable. Most identifiable intangibles meet the definition of an asset and are arguably relevant. Intangibles, like many tangible assets, are often difficult to value. Their historical cost, though, can be established as reliably as that of many tangible assets. Unidentifiable intangible assets, of which goodwill is the prime example, may not be relevant, given the difficulty of defining goodwill. Purchased goodwill is recognized automatically as the difference between the amount paid for a company and the fair value of its net assets. Even though it is shown, many argue that purchased goodwill does not meet the definition of an asset, and that it has no relevance to users.

Intangibles are amortized much as tangibles are depreciated. The life used should be their estimated economic life. This is usually less than their legal life and should in all cases be less than 40 years. Revisions of their useful life should be treated prospectively as changes in estimates. Downward revisions in estimates of their value should be treated as extraordinary expenses.

To illustrate these general rules, some major categories of intangibles were treated in the chapter. Specifically, the chapter dealt with licenses, franchises, research and development, and software costs. The chapter also introduced the controversial topic of push-down accounting and asked whether the statements of acquired companies should be restated at their fair values. In addition, the chapter briefly discussed accounting for investments which, apart from being intangibles in their own right, are also the vehicles for generating the major intangible, goodwill.

MULTIPLE CHOICE QUESTIONS

1. [M89#6] Which of the following costs of goodwill should be capitalized and amortized over their estimated useful lives?

	Developing Goodwill	Restoring Goodwill
a.	Yes	Yes
b.	Yes	No
c.	No	No
d.	No	Yes

2. [M86#12] Legal fees incurred in successfully defending a patent suit should be capitalized when the patent has been

	Internally Developed	Purchased from an Inventor
a.	Yes	No
b.	Yes	Yes
c.	No	Yes
d.	No	No

3. [N85#7] Which of the following should be expensed as incurred by the franchisee for a franchise with an estimated useful life of ten years?

a. Amount paid to the franchisor for the franchise.
b. Periodic payments to a company, other than the franchisor, for that company's franchise.
c. Legal fees paid to the franchisee's lawyers to obtain the franchise.
d. Periodic payments to the franchisor based on the franchisee's revenues.

4. [N84#18] Which of the following amounts incurred in connection with a trademark should be capitalized?

	Costs of a Successful Defense	Registration Fees
a.	Yes	No
b.	Yes	Yes
c.	No	Yes
d.	No	No

DISCUSSION QUESTIONS

Nature and Measurement of Intangibles

1. Some argue that intangible assets arise only from conditions of imperfect competition.[26] Patents, copyrights, and franchises grant the firm special partial monopolistic powers or rights to limit direct competition. Therefore, they say, these rights do not add directly to the wealth of the economy and are differentiated from plant and equipment, which are productive assets. They conclude that intangibles should not be recognized at all.

Required:

How would you vote?

2. *SFAS 63* records two issues that were addressed with regard to financial reporting by broadcasters:

a. Should a license agreement for television program material be treated by a licensee as a purchase of a right or as an operating lease?
b. If the license agreement is treated as a purchase of a right, and an asset and a liability are reported, should the liability be reported in accordance with *APB 21,* that is, at its present value determined by discounting future license payments using an imputed rate of interest?

Required:

How would you have responded to the concerns of the FASB?

3. Paul Stobart, managing director of Interbrand UK Ltd. argues that his company is able to provide true and fair values for brand names. He writes:

> So how then do we value a brand to give it the credit it deserves as one of a company's most important assets. Interbrand computes the value of a brand by the application of a multiplier to the earnings stream derived from ownership of the brand. Its ability to generate an independent stream of earnings is the overwhelmingly important factor in determining valuation. However, to arrive at a balance sheet value it is not enough merely to apply a simple multiplier to posttax profits. First, not all of a brand's profitability can necessarily be applied to a valuation of the brand. It may be essentially a commodity product, or may derive much of its profitability from the distribution system. The elements of profitability which do not result from the brand's identity must therefore be excluded. Second the value may be materially affected by using a single, possibly unrepresentative year's profit. Consequently historical brand profit data must be scrutinized before settling for an adjusted brand earnings stream.[27]

Required:

On the basis of this description of their methodology, would you advise the FASB to permit brand valuation in the United States? What arguments can you make for and against the methodology?

4. **(November 1970)** On June 30, 1980 your client, The Vandiver Corporation, was granted two patents covering plastic cartons that it has been producing and marketing profitably for the past three years. One patent covers the manufacturing process, and the other covers the related products.

Vandiver executives tell you that these patents represent the most significant breakthrough in the industry in the past 30 years. The products have been marketed under the registered trademarks Safetainer, Duratainer, and Sealrite. Licenses under the patents have already been granted by your client to other manufacturers in the United States and abroad and are producing substantial royalties.

On July 1, Vandiver commenced patent infringement actions against several companies whose names you recognize as those of substantial and prominent competitors. Vandiver's management is optimistic that these suits will result in a permanent injunction against the manufacture and sale of the infringing products and collection of damages for loss of profits caused by the alleged infringement.

The financial vice president has suggested that the patents be recorded at the discounted value of expected net royalty receipts.

Required:

     a. What is an intangible asset? Explain.

     b. 1. What is the meaning of "discounted value of expected net receipts"? Explain.

       2. How would such a value be calculated for net royalty receipts?

     c. What basis of valuation for Vandiver's patents would be generally accepted in accounting? Give supporting reasons for this basis.

     d. 1. Assuming no practical problems of implementation and ignoring generally accepted accounting principles, what is the preferable basis of evaluation for patents? Explain.

       2. What would be the preferable theoretical basis of amortization? Explain.

     e. What recognition, if any, should be made of the infringement litigation in the financial statements for the year ending September 30, 1980? Discuss.

Research and Development Costs

     5. **(May 1978)** The Thomas Company is in the process of developing a revolutionary new product. A new division of the company was formed to develop, manufacture, and market this new product. As of year-end (December 31, 1977) the new product has not been manufactured for resale; however, a prototype unit was built and is in operation.

     Throughout 1977 the new division incurred certain costs. These costs include design and engineering studies, prototype manufacturing costs, administrative expenses (including salaries of administrative personnel), and market research costs. In addition, approximately $500,000 in equipment (estimated useful life—10 years) was purchased for use in developing and manufacturing the new product. Approximately $200,000 of this equipment was built specifically for the design development of the new product; the remaining $300,000 of equipment was used to manufacture the preproduction prototype and will be used to manufacture the new product once it is in commercial production.

Required:

     a. What is the definition of *research* and of *development* as defined in *Statement of Financial Accounting Standards No. 2?*

     b. Briefly indicate the practical and conceptual reasons for the conclusion reached by the Financial Accounting Standards Board on accounting and reporting practices for research and development costs.

     c. In accordance with *Statement of Financial Accounting Standards No. 2,* how should the various costs of Thomas described above be recorded on the financial statements for the year ended December 31, 1977?

Goodwill

6. (May 1977) Accounting practitioners, accounting authors, and the courts have proposed various solutions to the problems of accounting in terms of historical cost for goodwill and similar intangibles.

Required:

a. In comparing the problems of accounting for goodwill and similar intangible assets to those for other plant assets,
    1. What problems are similar? Explain.
    2. What problems are different? Explain.
b. 1. What are the possible accounting treatments subsequent to the date of acquisition for the cost of goodwill and similar intangible assets? Explain.
    2. What is the logic in requiring a maximum life of 40 years for goodwill?

7. (November 1970) After extended negotiations Beach Corporation bought from Cedar Company most of the latter's assets on June 30, 1980. At the time of the sale Cedar's accounts (adjusted to June 30, 1980) reflected the following descriptions and amounts for the assets transferred:

	Cost	Contra (valuation) Account	Book Value
Receivables.	$ 83,600	$ 3,000	$ 80,600
Inventory	107,000	5,200	101,800
Land.	20,000	—	20,000
Buildings	207,500	73,000	134,500
Fixtures and equipment	205,000	41,700	163,300
Goodwill	50,000	—	50,000
	$673,100	$122,900	$550,200

You ascertain that the contra (valuation) accounts were allowance for doubtful accounts, allowance to reduce inventory to market, and accumulated depreciation.

During the extended negotiations Cedar held out for a consideration of approximately $600,000 (depending upon the level of the receivables and inventory). However, as of June 30, 1980, Cedar agreed to accept Beach's offer of $450,000 cash plus 1 percent of the net sales (as defined in the contract) of the next five years with payments at the end of each year. Cedar expects that Beach's total net sales during this period will exceed $15 million.

Required:

    a. The term *goodwill* often appears in connection with business combinations.
        1. What is goodwill? Explain.
        2. What is "negative" goodwill? Explain.
    b. 1. How should Beach Corporation record this transaction? Explain.
        2. Discuss the propriety of recording goodwill in the accounts of Beach Corporation for this transaction.

Noncurrent Investments

    8. (November 1974) Hawkes Systems, Inc., a chemical processing company, has been operating profitably for many years. On March 1, 1984 Hawkes purchased 50,000 shares of Diversified Insurance Company stock for $2 million. The 50,000 shares represented 25 percent of Diversified's outstanding stock. Both Hawkes and Diversified operate on a fiscal year ending August 31.

    For the fiscal year ended August 31, 1984, Diversified reported net income of $800,000 earned ratably throughout the year. During November 1983, February, May, and August 1984, Diversified paid its regular quarterly cash dividend of $100,000.

Required:

    a. What criteria should Hawkes consider in determining whether its investment in Diversified should be classified as (1) a current asset (marketable security) or (2) a noncurrent asset (investment) in Hawkes' August 31, 1984 balance sheet? Confine your discussion to the decision criteria for determining the balance sheet classification of the investment.

    b. Assume that the investment should be classified as a long-term investment in the noncurrent-asset section of Hawkes' balance sheet. The cost of Hawkes' investment equaled its equity in the recorded values of Diversified's net assets; recorded values were not materially different from fair values (individually or collectively). For the fiscal year ended August 31, 1984, how did the net income reported and dividends paid by Diversified affect the accounts of Hawkes (including Hawkes' income tax accounts)? Indicate each account affected, whether it increased or decreased, and explain the reason for the change in the account balance (such as Cash, Investment in Diversified, etc.). Organize your answer in the following format:

Account Name	Increase or Decrease	Reason for Change in Account Balance

9. **(May 1979)** *Part a.* The most common method of accounting for unconsolidated subsidiaries is the equity method.

Required:

Answer the questions shown below with respect to the *equity* method.
1. Under what circumstances should the equity method be applied?
2. At what amount should the initial investment be recorded, and what events subsequent to the initial investment (if any) would change this amount?
3. How are investment earnings recognized under the equity method, and how is the amount determined?

Part b. For the past five years Herbert has maintained an investment (properly accounted for and reported upon) in Broome amounting to a 10 percent interest in the voting common stock of Broome. The purchase price was $0.7 million, and the underlying net equity in Broome at the date of purchase was $620,000. On January 2 of the current year, Herbert purchased an additional 15 percent of the voting common stock of Broome for $1.2 million; the underlying net equity of the additional investment at January 2 was $1 million. Broome has been profitable and has paid dividends annually since Herbert's initial acquisition.

Required:

Discuss how this increase in ownership affects the accounting for and reporting upon the investment in Broome. Include in your discussion adjustments, if any, to the amount shown before the increase in investment to bring the amount into conformity with generally accepted accounting principles. Also include how current and subsequent periods would be reported upon.

GENENTECH

Genentech describes itself as "a biotechnology company focusing on the development, manufacture, and marketing of pharmaceutical products produced by recombinant DNA technology." The company was founded in 1976 to take advantage of scientific breakthroughs in the field of genetic engineering that occurred in 1973. Among the company's major products it lists Activase, which is used in preventing heart attacks by dissolving blood clots, and Protropin, which is a growth hormone. The rise in product sales as the accompanying consolidated statement of operations shows has been phenomenal.

Required:

a. Discuss the treatment of research and development costs in the financial statements of Genentech. In particular, is this not a case where a good argument could have been made for the capitalization of a purchased intangible in 1986 as described in footnote 11 (Exhibit 18–2).

b. Do a literature search of the financial press for details on what has happened to Genentech since 1988. Does their ongoing success, or lack thereof, confirm or weaken your first arguments?

c. Is it fair to look back like this? In your opinion, to what extent, if any, are court cases brought by disgruntled investors affected by hindsight?

EXHIBIT 18-2

GENENTECH, INC.
Consolidated Statements of Operations
(In thousands except per share amounts)

	Year Ended December 31		
	1988	*1987*	*1986*
Revenues:			
Product sales.	$262,476	$141,416	$ 43,563
Contract (including amounts from related parties:			
1988—$2,394; 1987—$6,441; 1986—$30,740).	60,283	77,273	83,749
Interest	12,081	11,854	6,642
Total revenues	334,840	230,543	133,954
Costs and expenses:			
Cost of sales	46,897	23,800	10,815
Special charge (principally inventory related)	23,349	—	—
Research and development (including contract related:			
1988—$21,001; 1987—$28,856; 1986—$47,597).	132,682	96,509	79,834
Marketing, general and administrative.	101,898	59,496	27,273
Interest	6,906	6,801	—
Charge for purchase of in-process research and			
development	—	—	366,640
	311,732	186,606	484,562
Income (loss) before taxes	23,108	43,937	(350,608)
Income tax provision	2,543	1,707	2,375
Net income (loss).	$ 20,565	$ 42,230	$(352,983)
Net income (loss) per share	$ .24	$ .50	$ (5.10)
Weighted average number of shares used in computing per			
share amounts	84,459	84,418	69,269

See notes to consolidated financial statements.

EXHIBIT 18-2 *(continued)*

NOTE 11: Acquisition of Research and Development Partnerships

In December 1986 the Company recorded the purchase of substantially all of the assets of GCP and GCP II, subject to their liabilities, for 6,600,000 and 3,385,000 shares, respectively, of the Company's Common Stock. The acquisitions have been accounted for as purchases of assets for an aggregate consideration of $458 million consisting of the 9,985,000 shares of Common Stock issued at the fair market value of the stock at issuance (January 2, 1987) and the value of liabilities assumed and incurred, less the amount of cash in the Partnerships on the closing date. The assets acquired consist principally of the Partnerships' United States rights to, and the technology resulting from the research and development performed on, tissue plasminogen activator, human growth hormone and gamma interferon. The aggregate purchase price has been allocated on the basis of relative fair market values to the individual rights acquired. To the extent that these rights represented completed products for which FDA marketing approval had been received, the amounts ($91.3 million) were capitalized and the intangible assets are amortized over their estimated useful lives. To the extent that the purchase price was allocated to research and development projects in-process, the amounts ($366.6 million) were charged to expense in the fourth quarter of 1986.

The liabilities assumed and incurred included the outstanding long-term debt of GCP and GCPII, which consisted of term loans totaling $21.0 million. During 1988 and 1987 the Company repaid $11.5 million, including interest, and $10.0 million, respectively, related to the term loans. Other long-term liabilities at both December 31, 1988 and 1987 include other transaction costs related to the acquisition of the Partnerships.

PRIMARY SOURCES

Those interested in pursuing the topics raised in this chapter might begin by consulting the following sources.

Catlett, George R., and Norman O. Olson. "Accounting for Goodwill." *Accounting Research Study No. 10* (AICPA, 1968).

Financial Accounting Standards Board Discussion Memorandum, *An Analysis of Issues Related to Accounting for Business Combinations and Purchased Intangibles* (Stamford, Conn.: FASB, August 1976).

Gellein, Oscar S., and Maurice S. Newman, "Accounting for Research and Development Expenditures." *Accounting Research Study No. 14* (AICPA, 1973).

Storey, Reed K., and Maurice Moonitz. "Market Value Methods for Intercorporate Investments in Stock." *AICPA Accounting Research Monograph No. 1* (AICPA, 1976).

SELECTED ADDITIONAL READINGS

Accounting for Intangibles

Abdel-khalik, A. Rashad. "Advertising Effectiveness and Accounting Policy." *The Accounting Review,* October 1975, pp. 657–70.

Falk, Haim, and Joseph C. Miller. "Amortization of Advertising Expenditures." *Journal of Accounting Research,* Spring 1977, pp. 12–22.

Picconi, Mario J. "A Reconsideration of the Recognition of Advertising Assets on Financial Statements." *Journal of Accounting Research,* Autumn 1977, pp. 317–26.

Goodwill

Gynther, Reg S. "Some Conceptualizing on Goodwill." *The Accounting Review,* April 1969, pp. 247–55.

Lee, T. A. "Goodwill: An Example of Will-o'-the-Wisp Accounting." *Accounting Business Research,* Autumn 1971, pp. 318–28.

Miller, Malcolm C. "Goodwill—An Aggregation Issue." *The Accounting Review,* April 1973, pp. 280–91.

Tearney, Michael G. "Accounting for Goodwill: A Realistic Approach." *Journal of Accountancy,* July 1973, pp. 41–45.

Weinwurm, Ernest H. "Modernizing the Goodwill Concept." *Management Accounting,* December 1971, pp. 31–34.

Research and Development

Dukes, Roland E. "An Investigation of the Effects of Expensing Research and Development Costs on Security Prices." In *Proceedings in the Conference on Topical Research in Accounting.* Edited by Michael Schiff and George Sorter (New York: New York University, 1976), pp. 147–93.

Gridley, F. W. "Accounting for R&D Costs." *Financial Executive,* April 1974, pp. 18–22.

Johnson, Orace. "Contra-Equity Accounting for R&D." *The Accounting Review,* October 1976, pp. 808–22.

Noncurrent Investments

Barrett, M. Edgar. "Accounting for Intercorporate Investments: A Behavioral Field Experiment." *Journal of Accounting Research,* 1971, pp. 50–65.

Barrett, M. Edgar. "APB Opinion No. 18: 'A Move toward Preferences of Users.'" *Financial Analysts Journal,* July–August 1972, pp. 47–50, 52–55.

Copeland, Ronald M.; Robert Strawser; and John G. Binns. "Accounting for Investments in Common Stock." *Financial Executive,* February 1972, pp. 36–38ff.

Lloyd, B. Michl, and Jerry Weygandt. "Market Value Information for Nonsubsidiary Investments." *The Accounting Review,* October 1971, pp. 756–64.

Lynch, Thomas Edward. "Accounting for Investments in Equity Securities by the Equity and Market Value Methods." *Financial Analysts Journal,* January–February 1975, pp. 62–69.

O'Connor, Melvin C., and James C. Hamre. "Alternative Methods of Accounting for Long-Term Nonsubsidiary Intercorporate Investments in Common Stock." *The Accounting Review,* April 1972, pp. 308–19.

ENDNOTES

1. Richard Greene, "Inequitable Equity," *Forbes,* July 11, 1988, p. 83.
2. *Webster's Third New International Dictionary* (Springfield, Mass.: G. & C. Merriam Co., 1961), p. 1173.
3. Eric L. Kohler, *A Dictionary for Accountants,* 3rd ed. (Englewood Cliffs, N.J.: Prentice Hall, 1963), p. 629.
4. See *APB 17,* par. 1.
5. *APB 7,* par. 1.
6. Michael Selz, "Coleman's Familiar Name Is Both Help and Hindrance," *The Wall Street Journal,* May 17, 1990, p. B2 (Western edition.)
7. Raymond J. Chambers, *Accounting, Evaluation and Economic Behavior* (Englewood Cliffs, N.J.: Prentice Hall, 1966), p. 209.
8. Robert T. Sprouse and Maurice Moonitz, "A Tentative Set of Broad Accounting Principles for Business Enterprises," *Accounting Research Study No. 3* (New York: AICPA, 1962), p. 36.
9. Chambers, *Accounting, Evaluation,* p. 211.
10. John B. Canning, *The Economics of Accountancy* (New York: Ronald Press, 1929), p. 42.
11. *APB 16,* par. 67.
12. Accounting Standards Committee, *Accounting for Goodwill ED 47* (London: ASC, 1990), par. 30.
13. This is an override of *SFAS 72,* which still permits a 40-year maximum.
14. George R. Catlett and Norman O. Olson, "Accounting for Goodwill," *Accounting Research Study No. 10* (AICPA, 1968), p. 89.
15. For a most illuminating discussion of some of the issues in sports accounting, see George Sorter, "Accounting for Baseball," *Journal of Accountancy,* June 1986, pp. 126–33.
16. See, for example, Allan R. Drebin, "Accounting for Proprietary Research," *The Accounting Review,* July 1966, p. 425.
17. See, for example, J. A. Milburn, "A Look at Problems in Research and Development Accounting," *Canadian Chartered Accountant,* June 1968, pp. 404–8.
18. *SFAS 2,* par. 62.
19. *IASC 9,* par. 9. Also see par. 17 for a full list of stipulations for recognition of an asset.
20. For an illuminating discussion of when technological feasibility is achieved, see Terry L. Fox and Reagan M. Ramsower, "Why FASB 86 Needs Revision," *Journal of Accountancy,* June 1989, pp. 94–98.
21. ED 49, *Accounting for Identifiable Assets.*

22. Paul Stobart, "Brand Valuation: A True and Fair View," *Accountancy,* October 1989, p. 27.
23. B. Michl Lloyd and Jerry J. Weygandt, "Market Information for Nonsubsidiary Investments," *The Accounting Review,* October 1971, pp. 756–64.
24. Ronald M. Copeland, Robert Strawser, and John G. Binns, "Accounting for Investments in Common Stock," *Financial Executive,* February 1972, p. 46.
25. Eric L. Kohler, *A Dictionary for Accountants,* 3rd ed. (Englewood Cliffs, N.J.: Prentice Hall, 1963), p. 269.
26. See, for example, J. E. Sands, *Wealth, Income, and Intangibles* (Toronto: University of Toronto Press, 1963), p. 28.
27. Paul Stobart, "Brand Valuation: A True and Fair View," *Accountancy,* October 1989, pp. 27–28.

Chapter 19

Recording Liabilities

CHAPTER OBJECTIVES

After studying this chapter, you will be able to:

Define liabilities so as to distinguish them from owners' equity.

Define the essential characteristics of accounting liabilities as a distinct subset of a broader set of economic obligations.

Discuss the treatment of unconditionally offset contracts.

Outline the measurement of liabilities in accounting statements and their valuation in the marketplace.

Discuss the nature and complications of hybrid securities.

CHAPTER OVERVIEW

The Nature of Liabilities

Liabilities are probable future sacrifices of economic benefits arising from present obligations. Owners' equity is the residual after liabilities are subtracted from assets. Some of the complications in applying the definition of a liability in practice are illustrated by unconditionally offsetting contracts and by off-balance sheet financing.

Measuring Liabilities

Liabilities are recognized when they meet the definition, are measurable, relevant, and reliable. In general, they are measured by the present value of the expected, future cash outflows.

Terminating Liabilities

Liabilities may be terminated by extinguishment, for instance, by repayment; by restructuring, that is, by replacement of one debt by another; or by conversion, that is, by swapping debt for equity.

Hybrid Securities

The distinction between liabilities and owners' equity has been clouded in recent years by the emergence of a wide range of financial instruments having characteristics of both liabilities and equities. Convertible debentures are used as an example of the difficulties encountered.

Liabilities were for many years the neglected offspring of accounting. One purchased an asset—what one did not pay in cash was recorded as a payable. One borrowed money—the cash received was recorded as a debt. One charged the income statement with a wage expense—an accrued liability resulted. Credits, in other words, followed debits. Where there was no debit, there was no credit. Circumstances have forced a major shift in attitude. Liabilities today stand in their own right as direct measures of corporate obligations.

One reason for the shift in attitude may be found in the public's increasing awareness of the size of these huge and growing economic obligations. For instance, companies have long offered pension benefits to employees. Since payments were in the future, pension obligations were initially left unrecorded. As the size of the obligation became increasingly apparent, the government and accounting authorities stepped in to ensure that the liability was recorded—regardless of whether payment was being made. Pension liabilities now appear routinely in company balance sheets. Soon obligations for postretirement benefits, which at present are not recorded as accounting liabilities, will require treatment similar to that of pensions. Leases, income taxes, and frequent flier bonuses are just a few of the other areas that have yielded to the new approach to liabilities.

Simultaneous with a growing awareness of the need to recognize more obligations on balance sheets, there has been an explosion of different types of liabilities. This explosion has been fueled in part by the use of leveraged buyouts to finance takeovers and mergers. These liabilities, also known as *financial instruments*, pose a number of problems for accountants. Bonds, for instance, were stripped of their coupons enabling one person to purchase the capital portion and another to purchase the interest portion. Should these two financial instruments be classified together, or should there be two classifications on the balance sheet? Interest rates, which previously were fixed, are now allowed to fluctuate. How does one build this variability into the measurement of the variable rate bond? And, if the interest rate varies with the profitability of the enterprise, has an equivalent of equity now been created? The FASB has responded to these questions by establishing an ongoing study to examine how, if at all, these financial instruments should be recognized. The first fruit of that endeavor was *SFAS 105*, which requires companies to make footnote disclosure of the cash flow effects of these instruments over time.

This chapter begins with a review of the FASB's definition of liabilities. The FASB's three essential characteristics of liabilities are reviewed before moving into a treatment of the new financial instruments. This is followed by a discussion of the measurement and recognition of liabilities. The termination of liabilities through extinguishment, restructuring, and conversion is handled after the complications created by unconditionally offsetting contracts and off-balance sheet financing are discussed. The next two chapters treat specific aspects of liability accounting, namely income taxes and pensions.

THE NATURE OF LIABILITIES

Chapter 13 noted that the FASB defined liabilities as probable future sacrifices of economic benefits arising from present obligations of a particular entity to transfer assets or services to other entities in the future as a result of past transactions and events."[1] Specific characteristics of liabilities include the following:

1. The obligation must exist at the present time. Currently, that is seen to arise out of some past transaction or event. This may be from the acquisition of goods or services, from losses already sustained for which the firm is liable, or from the expectation of losses for which the firm has obligated itself.

2. Equitable and constructive obligations or duties should be included if they are based on the necessity of making future payments to maintain good business relationships or if they are in accordance with normal business practice.

3. There should be little or no discretion to avoid the future sacrifice. It is not necessary that the amount of the obligation be known with certainty so long as a future sacrifice is probable.

4. Normally there should be a determinable maturity value or the expectation that payment of an amount determined by reasonable estimation will be required at some specific time in the future, even though the exact timing is not known at the present. The time of payment may be extended by substituting new liabilities, or the obligations may be terminated by their conversion into stockholder equities. The repeated extension or conversion of the debt does not deny its initial classification as a liability.

5. Normally, the payee would be known or be identifiable either specifically or as a group. However, so long as the payee will become identifiable by the settlement date, it is not necessary that the payer know the identity of the payee or that the creditor profess the claim or have knowledge of it at the present time.

Unconditionally Offsetting Contracts

Numerous complications have been encountered in attempting to apply definitions of liabilities. One set arose in regard to obligations arising out of current contracts for the future acquisition of goods and services. For example, a company may sign an agreement with its supplier to deliver raw materials in three months, at which time payment will be made. The signing of such a contract is a financial event arising from business dealings. It gives rise to obligations to make payment in the future when the goods or services have been received. However, there has been no "performance" on either side—the supplier has not delivered, and the buyer has not paid.

Traditionally, accountants have refrained from recording contracts such as these, where neither party has performed, often termed *executory contracts*. The reasoning is that, until the goods are made available, the buyer's obligation is offset by the buyer's rights to receive the goods.[2] Until the goods are brought into existence and committed to the contract, there is an unconditional right of setoff. But when goods or services are committed under the contract, the buyer may not be able to cancel the contract without paying for the goods and services committed, even though they have not as yet been received.

An exception to the practice of not reporting unconditionally offsetting contracts for the purchase of goods and services is made when the obligation of the purchase commitment exceeds the value of the goods to be acquired. For example, if a material decline in the price of the goods occurs subsequent to the signing of a long-term purchase contract, the obligation exceeds the value of the rights under the contract, and a loss has occurred. A liability equal to the amount of the loss is recorded. This liability results from the need to record a credit equal to the loss's debit under the double-entry system.

Pension accounting is another example of where liabilities are offset by assets. In *SFAS 87,* the FASB has allowed the pension obligation to be offset by the pension fund in the balance sheet of the sponsoring company. At best, a differential appears.

In the authors' opinion, the practice of recording only the differential amount is deficient because it assumes that the total amount of the firm's rights and obligations are not relevant to the predictions and decisions of investors and creditors. But these total amounts are relevant, because the users of the statements may place different expectations on the values of the rights under contracts or on the effect of committed cash disbursements.

In our opinion, then, all unconditionally offsetting contracts should be recognized. Apart from being offset by an asset, these contracts typically meet all the conditions for liability recognition. They arise from a past event and, in many cases, there is little uncertainty regarding the existence of the obligation. Since offsetting contracts invariably affect future cash flows, their disclosure is relevant to investors and creditors. Furthermore, they often arise from some of the more controversial activities of management such as the signing of executive management contracts. In addition, given the information that is contained in the disclosure of both the debit and the credit sides of unconditionally offsetting contracts, we argue that both the liability and the associated asset should be recognized in full.

One example of where this is done is leases, which are often quoted as an example of unconditionally offsetting contracts. The lessor agrees to provide the services of an asset for a specified period of time. The lessee agrees to transfer to the lessor specified sums of cash in exchange for the use of the asset. At the outset of the lease neither party has performed. At any point during the lease, it may be argued, the performance of the lessee and lessor is equally balanced. Yet, as Chapter 17 discusses in more detail, the FASB has held that where the lease is in substance a purchase, the lessee should recognize both a liability and the asset. Leases of this type, therefore, are an exception to the general rule of not recognizing offsetting contracts.

Off-Balance Sheet Financing

Another set of complications in applying the definition of liabilities arises from a desire on the part of management to keep the debt-equity ratio of the company in line with expectations. The ratio of liabilities to owners' equity, also known as the *financial leverage* of the company, is tracked by many financial analysts. The real significance of this ratio has been the subject of considerable debate over the years. Arguments aside, many fear that because interest is a fixed cost, a financial leverage ratio that is too high can expose a company to excessive financial risk: when income falls, dividends can be lowered, but interest must still be paid. Often creditors of a company will seek to prevent high financial leverage ratios by requiring a debt covenant of the company. The company undertakes in these covenants to keep its leverage below prespecified limits. To avoid undue increases in financial leverage and to avoid violating their debt covenants, many companies attempt to finance their operations with debt that does not appear on the balance sheet.

Leases are a classic example of off-balance sheet financing. Instead of purchasing an asset and showing the unpaid balance as a liability, companies lease assets. If the deal can be so structured that it does not fall foul of the FASB's stipulations for capitalizing leases in *SFAS 13*, the company can avoid showing a lease liability. Even more creatively, perhaps, companies have formed wholly owned subsidiaries whose sole purpose is to buy assets on behalf of the company and then to lease them to the parent. If the argument could be sustained that the subsidiary's business was financing and, therefore, distinct from the parent's business, consolidation was not required. Instead of a liability, the parent showed an investment asset equal to the net worth of the subsidiary! *SFAS 94* has effectively ended this practice for private enterprises—but not for the federal government!

Consider the sleight of hand planned by the federal government in raising money to address the savings and loan crisis. To avoid the appearance of an increase in its borrowing, the government proposed to create a private company, the Resolution Trust Corporation, whose sole function was to borrow money to lend to the government. The monies received from the company would have been treated by the government as a receipt. The net effect would have been to avoid showing any additional liabilities and, in addition, the budget deficit would have been reduced! As the director of the bipartisan Citizens for a Responsible Federal Budget said, "Would you believe that the thrift crisis is going to save us money and reduce the deficit? Well that's just what the budget says!"[3]

A further twist to the treatment of liabilities for the benefit of financial analysts is provided by the attempt to reduce the existence of short-term liabilities on the balance sheet. Apparently, firms consider current liabilities to be even less desirable than long-term liabilities. One practice was to undertake to refinance the short-term liability with long-term debt after the year-end but prior to the issuance of the balance sheet. The argument was then made that the imminent appearance of the new debt along with the stated intent to refinance the old made it unnecessary to report it as a short-term liability. *SFAS 6* closed this loophole by insisting that companies (*a*) have an intent to refinance the obligation on a long-term basis and

---

CHECKPOINTS

1. Define the term *executory contracts* and explain briefly why they usually do not appear on statements of financial position.
2. What theoretical argument might be made for excluding leases from a statement of financial position? Use the concept of executory contracts to make your argument.
3. In what circumstances can a current asset be offset against a current liability? How does this relate to executory contracts? (Hint: Begin by reviewing the discussion of offsetting liabilities against assets in Chapter 13.)
4. In what way do contingent liabilities provide a means of off-balance sheet financing? (Hint: Begin by reviewing the discussion of contingent liabilities in Chapter 13.)
5. Can an argument be made for recognizing all contingent liabilities?

(*b*) demonstrate that intent by either issuing the new liability before the issuance of the balance sheet or by entering into a noncancelable agreement to issue the new liability within a year.[4]

MEASUREMENT AND RECOGNITION

For a liability to appear on a statement of financial position, it must be recognized and measured. Recognition follows the standard rules of *SFAC 5* as laid out in Chapter 13. These rules state that an obligation should be recognized as a liability when it meets four general criteria:

1. It meets the definition of a liability.
2. It is measurable.
3. It is relevant.
4. It is reliable.

The objectives of liability valuation are similar to the objectives of asset valuation discussed in Chapter 14. Traditionally, the most important of these objectives has been the desire to record expenses and losses in the determination of current income. Today, it is realized that an equally important objective is that the measurement of liabilities should permit the presentation to investors and creditors of information useful as a means of predicting cash flows. Other objectives include valuation as a basis for interperiod and intercompany comparisons of income, and as a comparison of the claims of the several equity holders.

Recognizing Liabilities

For most liabilities, the point at which recognition occurs is quite definite because the obligation arises from a contract where the amount and time of payment of the obligation are specified or determinable from the conditions of the contract. However, in some cases, the amount to be paid is dependent upon future events, such as future gross sales from the use of leased property. In these cases, the liability does exist, even though the amount must be expressed in terms of certainty equivalents, or as a range of probable amounts. In the case of loss contingencies, *SFAS 5* implies that a liability exists and should be recorded if the amount of the loss can be reasonably estimated. Therefore, from a semantic point of view, and from the point of view of users of financial statements, an obligation should be classified as a liability if it can be reasonably measured, or if a meaningful range of values or probabilities can be assigned to it.

But the point in time when the transaction takes place is not always clear. As indicated in Chapter 11, an expense should be recognized when the goods or services are consumed or used in the process of obtaining revenue. If the obligation to pay for these goods and services has not already been recorded, it must be done no later than the time the expenses are recognized. In many cases, however, the goods or services are received before they are used. In this case, the asset and liability should be recorded, unless, of course, payment is made immediately. The obligation arises when the right to use the goods and services is obtained.

The recognition of accrued liabilities is no different from that of other liabilities. Accrued liabilities arise from the use of services by the firm and the obligation to pay for them under the terms of a formal or informal contract. Because the services are received continuously, recording the expense and the accrual is usually done at the end of the accounting period. Failure to record the accrual would misstate current income and the amount of current liabilities in the balance sheet. However, unless a contract or market price is available, an accrual is the result of an allocation and as such is arbitrary in nature.

In the above cases, recognition of the current liability is dependent upon the simultaneous recognition of an asset or expense. In fact, the necessity to recognize the asset or expense is often the impelling reason for recognition of the liability. But, in the case of a loss arising from a claim against the firm without a current or future benefit to the firm, the focus of recognition must come from the liability itself. The amount of obligation and the timing of its recognition determine the amount and timing of the loss recognition. As soon as the obligation becomes definite and capable of being estimated, it should be recognized, therefore, and the loss recorded.

Measuring Monetary Liabilities

Monetary liabilities are obligations denominated in nominal terms. In other words, they typically involve the payment of set amounts of cash. In most cases, the amount payable is determined by contract or agreement. In all cases, the current valuation of the debt is the present discounted value of the amounts payable in the future. Since current liabilities are generally payable within a short period of time, the amount of discount is usually immaterial and the amount of the liability can be presented at its face value (amount payable in the future). In the case of notes, what is sometimes termed *prepaid interest* should be deducted from the face value of the note to present the current discounted value.

If the debt can be satisfied by two or more alternatives, the discounted value of the lowest is the current value of the liability. For example, if the credit terms permit a discount of 2 percent if payment is made within 20 days and require a penalty if payment is made after 60 days, the correct value of the liability is the invoice price less the 2 percent discount. The other alternatives require an excess payment that need not be made and should not be made under good business practice. If the higher price is paid, the excess should be recorded as purchase discounts not taken and treated as a loss arising from inefficiency.

In the case of long-term liabilities, the amount of discount is generally significant and, therefore, the current valuation should be the discounted value of all future payments to be made under the contract.[5] In the case of bonds, the contractual interest payments, the amount to be paid at maturity, and any serial payments of principal should all be discounted to the present. The appropriate discount rate at the time the debt is incurred is the current yield rate determined by the market for bonds of similar risk and term.

In the case of bonds, if the stated interest rate, also termed the *coupon rate,* is lower than the discount rate, the present value of the bond will be less than its face value, and the bond is said to trade at a *discount*. If the stated interest rate equals the discount rate, the present value of the bond will equal its face value, and the bond is said to trade at *par*. If the stated interest rate exceeds the discount rate, the present value of the bond will be above the face value, and the bond is said to trade at a *premium*.

It is common practice to record the bond at its face value and to create a separate valuation account containing the premium or discount. One then speaks of amortizing the valuation account over the life of the bond. The practice goes back to earlier days in accounting when the concept of the time value of money was new and unusual. Managers and investors thought in terms of the face value as the "real" liability, or the "real" investment of a bond receivable, which was offset by "unearned interest" or something similar. Today, now that the concept is completely familiar to almost all, it is time to focus on the present value as the "actual" debt, or "actual" investment, at whatever point it is computed. One result is a huge gain in simplicity. Instead of all the paraphernalia of amortization of premiums or discounts, one can simply compute the interest expense or income as the value of the debt at the beginning of the period times the yield rate. The difference between the interest expense or income and the stated interest or coupon amount is charged to the bond account. The result is a new present value. Exhibit 19-1 illustrates the process. Notice that there is no mention in this exhibit of premiums, discounts, or amortization.

The effect of the interest method is to report a periodic interest expense that represents a level effective rate on the book value of the debt. The interest method also ensures that the carrying value of the debt is always equal to the present value of the future payments discounted at the original yield rate.

One dilemma in using the interest method is that interest rates tend to fluctuate. Changing circumstances might persuade bondholders that the risk has changed and that another discount rate is more appropriate. Even more commonly, perhaps, inflation expectations change. The discount rate is a nominal rate which is the sum of a real rate of interest appropriate

---

EXHIBIT 19-1   Bond Computations Using the Interest Method

Assume the issuance of a bond with a face value of $1,000 and a coupon rate of 10 percent per year payable semiannually for eight years. The rational price investors will pay for this bond, if market rates of interest for equivalent bonds are 12 percent per year payable semiannually, is

$$\$898.84 = 50 \times 10.105895 + \$1,000 \times 0.393646$$

where

    10.105895 = discount rate on an annuity at 6 percent per period for
                16 periods
     0.393646 = discount rate on a single amount at 6 percent per period for
                16 periods.

Thus, $898.84 will be the cash received by the company and credited to Bonds Payable (net). At the end of the first six months, the following computations will be done and the following journal entry made.

$$\text{Interest expense} = 6 \text{ percent} \times \$\ 898.84 = \$53.92$$

$$\text{Coupon payment} = 5 \text{ percent} \times \$1,000.00 = \$50.00$$

Interest expense 53.92

Cash   50.00
Bond payable (net)   3.92

Thus, the bond payable account will now be at $902.76. It is simple to show that this is the present value of the remaining payments based on the 12 percent discount rate.

---

to the level of risk involved and the expected rate of inflation. When expectations of inflation increase, interest rates increase, and bond prices fall. Using a current yield rate produces a current value, whereas the use of the yield rate at the date of issue produces a value similar to historical cost.

The advantage of keeping to the yield rate at the date of issue is that it can be assumed to be the effective rate for which the firm is committed. The resulting value at the date of issue was the current value at that time and is objectively determined. The disadvantage is that, by continuing to use the original yield rate, the periodic holding gains and losses are not recorded. However, the total interest expense recorded under the historical interest method will always be equal to the sum of the interest expense, using current yield rates and the holding gains and losses. If the debt is held until maturity, and changes in the yield rate are not material, the hidden gains can be ignored. If changes in the yield rate are large, the accumulation of holding gains and losses provide management with an incentive to manipulate earnings.

Measuring Nonmonetary Current Liabilities

Nonmonetary current liabilities are those obligations to provide goods or services of specified quantity and quality. They usually arise from the advance payment for services by customers. Subscriptions to periodicals and season tickets are good examples. Other obligations arise from advances by customers for special merchandise. It should be noted, however, that not all advances are nonmonetary in nature. Some advances represent a given number of dollars that may be applied against a future purchase or purchases at the prices existing when the advance is liquidated. These are monetary advances because they represent the obligation to repay a given number of dollars or the equivalent in goods or services at a future date. The nonmonetary obligations are expressed in terms of predetermined or agreed-on prices for specific goods or services. Thus, the monetary value of the goods and services might change, but the quantity and quality would not.

Income or Credits?   These nonmonetary obligations have frequently been classified as deferred income or deferred credits. Technically, *deferred income* represents income items received by the firm, but not yet reported as income. However, it is also used to refer to revenue that normally would have been included in income, but where the recognition is deferred until later expenses can be matched with it—more correctly referred to as *deferred revenue*. The term *deferred credit* is frequently used synonymously with deferred income and deferred revenue, but it is also used in a broader sense, including monetary advances by customers.

These terms do not have clear meanings because they include a heterogeneous group of items and they are not consistently classified in the balance sheet. Some of the deferred income and deferred credit items found in published annual reports are classified as current liabilities; others are classified as noncurrent liabilities; a few are reported as unearned revenue in the stockholders' equity section; and a majority are found listed as an unclassified item between the liabilities and the stockholders' equity section of the balance sheet. The latter presentation is partly a carry-over from a former classification in a reserve category. However, its placement is frequently rationalized on the ground that it represents amounts that will be added to income in a subsequent period but excluded in the current period, for one of several reasons.

The deferred income concept apparently arose from the idea that the "realization" of income is closely related to the receipt of cash, but that when the services have not yet been performed, or when the amount is likely to be reduced because of subsequent related expenses or losses, the income reporting should be deferred. However, the separate classification of deferred income does not indicate the nature of the items included in the classification and it is subject to abuse, just as was the former reserve classification.

Monetary Advances.   Frequently, the advance payments for goods or services by customers have been considered to represent a mixture of liabilities and profit. If cost is the predominant element, the entire amount could be considered a liability; but if cost is only a small part of the total, it is argued that the whole may be considered a deferred credit to income (gross income) rather than a current liability, presumably classified as unearned income in the stockholders' equity section of the balance sheet. If the advance payment represents both costs and income, it is argued that it may be divided between the amount of prospective cost that should be included among the current liabilities and the amount representing prospective income, which should be classified as unearned income.

This separation of the advance payment into a cost element and an element representing prospective profit stems from two customs. One is the traditional reliance upon the cost concept. The other is the reporting of revenue only after all services have been performed and when all expenses can be measured and matched with the associated revenues. However, it may be more relevant to report the obligation to perform services or provide goods in terms of the output (sales price) of such goods or services. The important consideration is that, unless the funds are returned to the customer, the advance payment does not represent an outflow of cash in the future. Regardless of how it is measured, it cannot be identified with specific goods or services to be acquired in the future and used in operations. Some of the services will have been acquired in the past in the form of plant and equipment and thus will be classified as noncurrent assets; others will represent inventories and prepaid expenses classified as current assets; and many of the associated expenses will represent goods and services not yet acquired at the time of the receipt of the advance. Therefore, the advance cannot be associated with costs incurred or to be incurred.

ARB 43, Chapter 3A, as amended, specifically includes among the current liabilities advances for the delivery of goods or the performance of services in the normal course of operations. This treatment of the advance as a current liability is correct for two reasons:

1.   The advance is a current financing transaction rather than a revenue producing one.[6] Although other reasons may give rise to the advance, such as an attempt to avoid bad debt losses, the result is an aid in the financing of the operations of the enterprise.

2.   The obligation to provide goods or services is generally a part of current operations. Only in the case of incidental transactions would the advance generally represent an obligation extending beyond the normal operating cycle of the business.

Value is added to the firm during the entire process of production, selling, and collection, but revenue is generally reported at a single point in time, as discussed in Chapter 11. If the critical event in the operations is the providing of goods and services, rather than the collection of the cash, no profit, deferred or current, should be reported at the time of the receipt of the advance. The entire amount is a liability, regardless of whether it is to be repaid in cash or in goods or services. Accounting terminology, therefore, would be improved if the term *advances from customers* were substituted for the term *deferred income*.

Uncertain Realization.   There are a few cases, however, where the reporting of deferred income arises for reasons other than advance from a customer. In these cases, the services have been provided and the revenue-producing operations have been completed, but the reporting of the income is deferred because of uncertainties in the collection of receivables, or because of uncertainties regarding additional expenses. One example involves real estate sales in which the initial deposit has not reached the minimum required by *SFAS 66*. These so-called *deferred credits* are not liabilities, as there is no obligation to the customers. They should be included in the income of the current period, less the estimated additional expenses and uncollectible receivables. But, as indicated in the discussion in Chapter 16 on installment sales, if the deferral of income is at all justified, the deferral can be accomplished by carrying the receivables at the input (cost) values. That is, the "deferred gross profit" can be used as an asset valuation account deducted from the receivables in the balance sheet. However, in almost all cases, the uncertainties are not so great that estimates are impossible. Therefore, the income should be reported on the basis of the best estimates, with an indication of the probabilities of expected values. The expected future related costs should be reported as liabilities. In all too many cases, the existence of uncertainties is used as an excuse for the deferral of income reporting, with the goal or result being the smoothing of income artificially. For these many reasons, the deferred income concept should be ousted from the kit of tools for financial reporting.

CHECKPOINTS

---

1. Distinguish monetary from nonmonetary liabilities. Give two examples of each.
2. What are deferred credits? How do they arise? Why has the FASB attempted to limit their recognition in financial statements?
3. Why is the term *deferred income* misleading?

TERMINATING LIABILITIES

Liabilities remain on the books until "a transaction or other event" occurs to remove them. What, though, defines an event? The question was asked earlier and continues to haunt us in questions regarding the retirement. In the simplest case, the event consists of a debtor paying the creditor what is owed. The debtor is relieved, thereby, of all further obligations. This is known as an *extinguishment* of debt. In the most common case, debt is repaid at its maturity date. In other cases, the debt is called or repaid ahead of maturity. Debt may also be forgiven wholly or in part by the creditor. These situations are discussed in the section on debt *restructuring*. In what is known as *defeasance*, the debtor is legally released from being the primary obligor under the debt either judicially or by the creditor. In such a case, consistent with *SFAS 5*, it must be probable that the debtor will not be required to make future payments with respect to that debt under guarantees. An *in-substance defeasance* occurs when a debtor irrevocably places cash or other assets in a trust to be used solely for satisfying scheduled payments of both interest and principal of a specific obligation. The possibility that the debtor will be required to make future payments with respect to that debt must be remote.

Extinguishing Debts

Market values of bonds and other debt instruments rise and fall with interest rates. Typically, and regrettably, these changes are not recognized by the accounting system. At the point, therefore, when a debt is extinguished, for whatever reason, it is often necessary to account for the difference between the market value of the debt and its book value. Consider the simplest case, where a company buys back its bonds in the open marketplace. How does one account for the difference between the price it pays for them and their carrying value on the company's books?

The difference arises at the point of retirement only because in this, or previous periods, the changes in market values of the bond were not recognized. If interest rates were adjusted each period to current yields, holding gains and losses would be reported each period, and no difference would exist at the time the bonds were retired. *APB 26* ruled that in all cases of debt retirement, the difference should be treated as a gain or loss of the period. *SFAS 4*, partly in response to concerns that companies were retiring debt for the sole purpose of achieving increases in net income, added that these gains (and losses) should be treated as extraordinary items. This clashes, unfortunately, with the definition of extraordinary items as unusual and infrequent. If these differences were treated as the holding gains and losses that they are, and recognized in the periods in which they occur, there would be no need to force them into an incorrect classification.

One exception to the extraordinary rule is permitted. This concerns debt which is retired by means of a sinking fund. The mechanics of a sinking fund are that monies are set aside in accordance with a prespecified contract to periodically retire a portion of the loan and, ultimately, to retire the entire debt. When debt is retired to comply with the requirements of the sinking fund, gains or losses may occur. The existence of a plan convinced the Board in *SFAS 4* to permit these to be recognized as ordinary gains or losses. Later, in *SFAS 64*, the Board limited the retirements to those made within one year of the relevant requirements of the sinking fund. Early retirements, being discretionary, are treated as extraordinary items.

In-substance defeasance, treated in *SFAS 76* (an amendment to *APB 26*) is the most controversial method of extinguishing debt. Three of the seven board members dissented from allowing it as an extinguishment of debt. Their grounds were that the fund, even though dedicated to the repayment of the debt, remained an asset of the company since it provided probable future economic benefit to the company. Moreover, they said, a debt could not be considered extinguished until it was indeed satisfied in "another transaction or other event or circumstance affecting the enterprise." The majority response was that placing assets in an irrevocable trust fulfilled the requirement of "another transaction or other event." This response is further evidence that the term "other event" is too broad to serve as a useful defining characteristic of a liability.

A variant on in-substance defeasance is known as *instantaneous defeasance*. In an instantaneous defeasance, the company issues debt and sets money aside immediately to retire that debt in due course. The intent is to take advantage of interest differentials existing in major money markets without impacting the balance sheet. *Technical Bulletin 84–4* disallows this procedure on grounds that it is a borrow-and-invest activity, not a defeasance. This raises the immediate question of how long one should wait before one becomes the other. It also serves as a good illustration of how companies can and do exploit gray areas in financial reporting standards.

Calling Bonds. Bonds typically contain a provision permitting a company to recall the debt at a predetermined percentage of its face value. The firm typically will exercise this provision if, and when, the market value of the bonds becomes greater than the call price. If the call involves cash only, it is called a *retirement*. If it involves the issuance of new bonds to replace the old, it is called a *refunding*. In either case, the difference between the carrying value of the old bonds, including any unamortized bond issue costs, and the call price is treated as an extraordinary gain or loss in the period in which the call is made.

The argument has been made that the gain or loss should be recognized over time: either the remaining life of the old bond, or the life of the new bond. The justification for the first option is that the gain or loss results from the call provisions of the old bond and should remain, therefore, within the terms of the old bond. The justification for the second option is that the amortization of the gain or loss over the life of the new bond results in better matching.

The case for current recognition rests on the nature of the gain or loss. If current values had been recorded each period, the holding gains or losses would have been recorded over time each time the market rate of interest changed. The current value of the bonds at the time of a call would have approximated the call price, therefore. The only remaining difference would have been the cost of obtaining the necessary funds—unless the firm failed to take advantage of the call opportunity. In short, the gain or loss on a call is primarily due to holding, which should have been recognized prior to the call. Historical cost accounting typically does not recognize holding gains or losses until an event such as a retirement occurs. When that event occurs, the entire accumulated holding loss or gain should be recorded. Additionally, the remaining costs, such as the unamortized bond issue costs and the call premium, represent the cost of terminating a disadvantageous contract and should be written off immediately. This view is consistent with both *APB 26* and *SFAS 4*.

Restructuring Debts

As noted earlier, the forgiveness of part or the whole of a debt by a creditor is yet another way in which debt can be extinguished. One can imagine cases in which a creditor might permit a debtor to extinguish a debt for less than its current value computed at current yield rates. The creditor might be short of cash and be willing to take a lesser amount immediately. The gain which would result to the debtor would be treated in accordance with the regular rules for extinguishment of debt, that is, it would be an extraordinary gain. When the debtor is financially troubled and the creditor offers a concession intended to recover as much money as possible, one enters the particular aspect of debt extinguishment called *troubled debt restructuring*.

Troubled debt restructuring can occur in several ways. The debtor can offer cash or other assets in part payment of the loan. The debtor can offer equity in exchange for the liability. Alternatively, the creditor can modify the terms of the loan by lowering interest rates, extending payment schedules, or decreasing the amount to be repaid. More commonly, debt restructuring consists of a combination of these approaches. In a combination restructuring, transfers of cash, assets, or equity are treated first, and the balance of the debt is subjected to a modification of terms.

The transfer of assets or the issuance of equity to satisfy the debt is handled without controversy where debtors are concerned. The fair, or market, value of the item transferred is charged to the liability account of the debtor. The debtor will treat the difference between the debt and the fair value of the item as an extraordinary gain in line with the general provisions of debt extinguishment. In the case of assets, the difference between the fair value of the asset surrendered and its carrying value is treated as an ordinary gain (or loss) before entering it into the restructuring computation.

Journal entries for the creditor generally mirror those of the debtor. However, in accordance with *SFAS 5,* given that the debt constitutes an asset to the creditor, contingent receipts are excluded from the receivable unless they are probable and estimatable. Also, gains on restructuring are required to be classified as ordinary, not extraordinary. A subsequent technical bulletin requires that excluded future cash payments be treated as interest income when received, even though this might yield an absurdly high interest rate.[7] Little of this makes theoretical sense; at best it ensures a certain consistency with the concept of conservatism.

The accounting treatment of a modification of terms is considerably more controversial. The approach required by *SFAS 15* is to compare the revised cash flow stream with the current carrying cost of the liability. If the total cash flow is greater than the carrying cost, an interest rate should be found that will discount the future cash flow to the carrying cost.[8] This becomes the new effective interest rate. Should the total cash flow be lower than the carrying cost, the sum of the future cash flows should be recorded as the new carrying cost of the debt, and an extraordinary loss recorded for the difference. No interest income should be recorded. All cash payments should be used to amortize the new carrying cost.[9]

The argument made in favor of this procedure is that a modification of terms should not be perceived as a reduction in the face value of the debt but in the interest payments that will be made on that debt. Furthermore, since no transaction had occurred, in the sense of a transfer of assets or equity, the carrying value of the liability should not be changed so long as the future cash flows were sufficient to support it. In other words, although the creation of an irrevocable trust is an "other event," the modification of terms is not considered to fall under the rubric of "other events."

The stated ideal of the FASB is to put onto the balance sheet numbers which indicate the amount, timing, and uncertainty of probable future cash flows. The best measure of this is the present value of those flows or, equivalently, the future cash flows discounted at the current appropriate yield for bonds of this sort. The carrying value of the old debt is quite irrelevant; the undiscounted sum of future cash flows is most misleading to users; the equation of future cash flows with an irrelevant number results in an equally irrelevant interest rate. In short, the FASB's argument makes no sense and appears to have been driven by the political pressure of banks reluctant to face up, at the time, to the enormous losses they had sustained in loans to Third World countries and to the real estate and energy sector. With the hindsight gained from the collapse of the savings and loan industry one wonders whether this rule has not had enormous negative economic consequences for us as a nation.

CHECKPOINTS

---

1. Define in your own words the term *in-substance defeasance* and distinguish it from ordinary defeasance.
2. What causes the gain or loss when a bond is called?
3. Distinguish the two kinds of troubled debt restructuring.
4. In what ways does the accounting treatment of restructuring for debtors mirror that of creditors? Where does it differ?

HYBRID SECURITIES

In recent years there has been an explosion in the number and the kinds of "liabilities" in the marketplace. The old bank loan familiar to most in which a company promises to pay the bank interest at a fixed rate of interest with a final repayment of the capital still exists, but numerous variations are now seen. For example, many loans now contain a feature which enables those who have loaned the money to convert it, given certain restrictions, into common stock. The loan itself may be traded from one bank to another. Indeed its separate parts are each tradable. For instance, one person may purchase the right to receive the interest payments, while another receives the right to repayment of the final repayment of capital. Other changes include making the interest rate vary by letting it depend on underlying economic variables such as the prime rate or the rate of inflation.

All these new "liabilities" are known generically as *financial instruments,* which the FASB defines as:

cash, evidence of an ownership interest in an entity, or a contract that both:

a. imposes on one entity a contractual obligation (1) to deliver cash or another financial instrument to a second entity or (2) to exchange financial instruments on potentially unfavorable terms with the second entity.

b. conveys to that second entity a contractual right (1) to receive cash or another financial instrument from the first entity or (2) to exchange other financial instruments on potentially favorable terms with the first entity.[10]

At current count, there are literally hundreds of these new financial instruments.* They include intriguing names such as:

BITS	CIRCUS'S	JETS	STARS
CAMPS	COINS	LYONS	STILTS
CARS	DARTS	SCOUTS	TIGRS

This vast number of instruments is causing an enormous problem for the FASB, because the line between equity and liabilities has become extremely gray.

The difficulty that these securities cause for accountants is that many of them have characteristics of both debt and equity. One instance is mandatory redeemable preferred stock in which the company must repay the stockholders' capital at a set point in time. Ordinary preferred stock has a fixed dividend, which made it look to some like an interest payment. One argument against classifying ordinary preferred stock as a liability is that, despite the similarity of the dividend to interest, there is no date for repayment as there is with a bond. This argument appears to collapse in the face of mandatory redeemable preferred stock. Does that mean that this class of preferred stock is really a kind of liability?

Another instance is convertible debt. In this case, the holder of the debt has an option to exchange the debt for shares in the company. The value of the option depends on the price of the shares, making the option, strictly speaking, a part of owners' equity. Should the debt be split, therefore, over two sections of a balance sheet? If one does make this split, how does one link the two pieces again so that users will know that these two parts belong together? If one does not split them, should one open a new section on the balance sheet labeled "part-debt; part-equity?" The next section attempts to identify some of the many issues involved.

Convertible Debt

Debt securities are frequently issued with a convertible feature. This feature permits the holder to convert the bond certificates into a determinable number of shares of common stock at any time before the conversion privilege expires. The convertible feature generally permits the issuer to sell the bonds initially at a price considerably above what could be obtained for nonconvertible bonds with the same contractual interest rate. Although many possible alternative features and relationships may be found in connection with convertible bonds, generally the following holds:

---

* Estimates of the number of different financial instruments on the market range from as few as 150 to as many as 700.

1. The contractual interest rate is considerably below the market rate for nonconvertible bonds.
2. The initial conversion price is greater than the market price of the common stock.
3. The conversion price does not decrease over time except to the extent necessary to protect the bondholder from the dilution of the common stock rights (such as a stock split or a stock dividend).

Two views have been proposed for the accounting treatment of convertible debt at the date of issuance and for the subsequent reporting of interest expense. One view is that convertible debt possesses the characteristics of both debt and equity. A portion, therefore, of the proceeds from the sale of the securities should be allocated to the conversion privilege and credited to paid-in capital. The remainder should be allocated to the debt, resulting in the presentation of debt discount or a reduction of debt premium. The amount assigned to paid-in capital can be measured as the excess of the amount received for the securities over the estimated price that could have been obtained for similar securities without the conversion feature. A second view is that the convertible debt should be treated solely as debt with no portion of the proceeds being allocated to the conversion feature. This was the recommendation of *APB 14*.

The main arguments for the allocation of the proceeds between the debt and the equity characteristics are twofold. One is that the economic value of the conversion feature exists as a distinct element of the contract, as opposed to the debt. The second is that the measurement of interest expense should be based on the debt characteristics only. Although these two arguments are related in the accounting treatment, they are discussed separately. The argument for a separate reporting of the debt and equity portions is based on the premise that the classification of the proceeds from the sale of the securities should be comparable to the traditional debt and equity classifications. If an amount is actually paid for the right to become a holder of common stock at some time in the future, this is similar to the sale of an option or warrant for the purchase of common stock in the future at a fixed price. Therefore, the amount paid for the conversion privilege should be accounted for consistently with the treatment of stock options or warrants. Likewise, valuation of the portion classified as debt should reflect the market yield for similar debt when the securities are issued, which would then be consistent with the reporting of nonconvertible bonds. The disclosure of a material discount on bonds would be relevant to make the presentation similar to other securities classified as long-term debt. Note, however, that in this case an adjustment should be made for the fact that the discount arising from the allocation to the conversion feature may not be deductible in arriving at taxable income.

A major difficulty with the allocation of the issue price between the debt and equity portions is that valuation and classification similar to nonconvertible issues gives the reader of the financial statements the impression that the face amount is expected to be paid at maturity. However, if the market price of common stock increases above the conversion price, the normal expectation is that the bonds will not be paid at maturity. Until the bonds are converted, the face value is a protection for the holders of the securities against loss through bankruptcy or reorganization; it is therefore similar to the liquidation value of preferred stock, although with a different degree of priority. Another difficulty is that the interest expense reported by this method is not related to the contractual cash outflows, whether conversion takes place or not. If the bonds are not converted but paid at maturity, the cash outlays include the contractual annual payment and the face value at maturity. If the bonds are converted, the cash outlay for interest also turns out to be the amount specified in the contract until the period of conversion. It may be argued that treating the convertible bonds as if they were nonconvertible does not disclose the cash flow attributes of the bonds under either potential alternative.

The arguments for treating the bond issue only as debt are that the debt and conversion privilege are inseparable and that the practical problems of computing valuations for the conversion feature and the debt portion are too subjective to be meaningful. The valuation of debt that is nonconvertible but similar in other regards is difficult because of the many different features possible in the bond contract and because the valuation in the market may be unique to the special risks of the specific firm. However, the Accounting Principles Board, in *APB 14*, placed greater weight on the inseparability of the debt and the conversion option. The convertible bond is a hybrid form of security because under one set of conditions the conversion feature may be the more relevant attribute, but under another set of conditions the debt form may become the more important.

Treatment of the convertible bonds solely as debt, however, has some major weaknesses. Including the proceeds of the securities in the long-term debt classification may be misleading because generally, in a viable concern, it is not anticipated that they will ever be repaid as debt. In many cases, it may be the intent of the firm to force conversion at some time in the future by calling the bonds when the market price is above the conversion price. In most other cases, the attractiveness of the security rests primarily on the expectation that the market price of the common stock will increase significantly above the conversion price. The debt feature is regarded more as a protection under adverse conditions. Accordingly, the convertible debt security is more in the form of stockholders' equity than long-term debt. Therefore, the recommendation of *APB 14* to treat the securities solely as debt is inconsistent with the recommendation made in *APB 15* that they should be treated as common stock in the computation of primary earnings per share. It is also inconsistent with the additional recommendation in *APB 14* that, if convertible debt is issued at a substantial premium, there is a presumption that the premium represents the value of the conversion feature and should be allocated to paid-in capital.

The recommendation of *APB 14* regarding convertible debt is also inconsistent with its recommendation regarding accounting for debt with detachable warrants to purchase stock. In the latter case, it recommends that the proceeds of the debt securities issued with detachable warrants should be allocated to the debt and to the warrants separately and that the amount allocated to the warrants should be treated as paid-in capital. However, convertible debt and debt issued with detachable warrants are in substance the same. The holder of convertible bonds may sell these securities and buy similar nonconvertible bonds, just as the holder of the debt with the detachable warrants may sell the warrants and continue to hold the bonds. Likewise, if the investor wishes to hold stock, the convertible bonds may be converted, or if bonds with detachable warrants are held, the proceeds from the sale of the bonds may be used to purchase stock with the warrants. From the firm's point of view, they are also similar in substance because, if the detachable warrants are exercised, it may use the proceeds to call or repurchase the bonds. Therefore, the two types of securities should be treated alike. It is inconsistent to treat one solely as debt while treating the other as both debt and equity.

An alternative to the two solutions discussed above is to create a new classification between the long-term debt and the stockholders' equity for both convertible bonds and debt with detachable warrants. A major difficulty in accounting is the continual attempt to fit new circumstances into the same old molds. A new classification, however, would also require a new type of disclosure of the interest expense in the income statement. But a clear disclosure of the several attributes of convertible debt securities and debt with detachable warrants would present a more informative picture of the possible outcomes. It would permit investors and creditors to predict the future cash disbursements likely to be required and the potential relationship of the securities to existing securities of the firm, as well as the potential dilution of earnings per share.

Accounting for Hybrid Securities

The treatment of convertible debt sets the scene for asking whether a financial instrument which pays no coupons and relies for its value on its ability to be converted into owners' equity is truly a "liability." Or the even more basic question of whether the distinction between liabilities and owners' equity serves any purpose today. Should one simply speak of equity holders with various rights and compute the present value of those rights? If one accepts that approach, then what does one do with the income statement which measures a residual amount going to the holders of owners' equity? Should one provide a value-added statement rather than an income statement? This section does not provide answers. It merely suggests that these are questions that we should be asking.

How difficult it has been to answer questions like these may be gauged from the mere fact that a bond issued with separable warrants, which in economic terms is identical to a convertible bond, is treated differently from a convertible bond, which contains an inseparable warrant. The problem might have been easier to solve if one had a definition of owners' equity. But owners' equity is not, and probably cannot be, defined independently of assets and liabilities because it is no more than a residual. It is simply the difference between the assets and the liabilities. In a more general formulation, it is the difference between resources and obligations.[11]

One solution that this text recommends is to drop the distinction between "equity" and "debt." Companies would recognize all obligations as "equities" in the broadest sense of that word. Each class of equity, such as equity deriving from common stock, or equity deriving from convertible debt, or equity deriving from straight debt, would be distinguished by the various rights that accompany it. This point was made in Chapter 9 on cash-based income and is revisited in Chapter 22 on the entity theory of the corporation, which was embraced as early as 1922 by Michigan professor William Paton.

Another approach, the one that the FASB is currently taking, is to seek to divide the new financial instruments into their component parts, much as physicists sought to split the atom into protons, neutrons, and electrons. They have tentatively identified six fundamental financial instruments:

1. Unconditional receivable-payable contracts.
2. Conditional receivable-payable contracts.
3. Financial option contracts.
4. Financial guarantees or other conditional exchange contracts.
5. Financial forward contracts.
6. Equity instruments.[12]

Whether this approach will lead to a few elementary building blocks or whether, as the physicists discovered, it will be found eventually that there are numerous blocks, remains to be seen.

In the meantime, until the details of recognition and measurement can be settled, the FASB has required in *SFAS 105,* "Disclosure of Information about Financial Instruments with Off-Balance Sheet Risk and Financial Instruments with Concentrations of Credit Risk" that companies disclose the cash-flow effects of their financial instruments. In effect, companies are asked to make disclosures for all their liabilities like those currently made for lease payables.

CHECKPOINTS

1. Use the three essential characteristics of liabilities to distinguish convertible debt from owners' equity.
2. List the weaknesses of treating convertible debentures as a liability.
3. Contrast the treatment of convertible bonds with that of bonds issued with separable warrants.
4. List the six fundamental financial instruments identified by the FASB.

SUMMARY

This chapter reviewed the FASB's definition of liabilities and discussed three supposedly essential characteristics of liabilities. The chapter also noted the changing view of liabilities from a balance sheet credit dependent on prior debits to an element that had meaning in its own right. That meaning was derived from a view of liabilities as obligations to deliver cash or other assets over a period of time. But what, it may reasonably be asked, have all these definitions really achieved for us? It appears that at the end of the day at least two major questions still lie unresolved. First, what does one do about those financial instruments which are neither pure liabilities nor pure owners' equity? Second, was the definition of a liability designed to justify what had been decided on other grounds or has it really been determinative of FASB standards? These questions have not yet been resolved.

MULTIPLE CHOICE QUESTIONS

1. [M87#11.] Which of the following is classified as an accrued liability?

	Liability for Federal Unemployment Taxes	Liability for Employer's Share of FICA Taxes
a.	Yes	Yes
b.	Yes	No
c.	No	No
d.	No	Yes

2. [M86#13.] A returnable cash deposit should be classified as a liability when the deposit is from

	A Customer	An Employee
a.	Yes	No
b.	Yes	Yes
c.	No	Yes
d.	No	No

3. [N88#14.] The issue price of a bond is equal to the present value of the future cash flows for interest and principal when the bond is issued

	At Par	At a Discount	At a Premium
a.	Yes	No	Yes
b.	Yes	No	No
c.	No	Yes	Yes
d.	Yes	Yes	Yes

4. [M88#14.] A five-year term bond was issued by a company on January 1, 1986, at a discount. The carrying amount of the bond at December 31, 1987, would be

a. Higher than the carrying amount at December 31, 1986.
b. Lower than the carrying amount at December 31, 1986.
c. The same as the carrying amount at January 1, 1986.
d. Higher than the carrying amount at December 31, 1988.

5. [M88#16.] When bonds are issued with stock purchase warrants, a portion of the proceeds should be allocated to paid-in capital for bonds issued with

	Detachable Stock Purchase Warrants	Nondetachable Stock Purchase Warrants
a.	No	Yes
b.	No	No
c.	Yes	No
d.	Yes	Yes

6. [N85#11.] The lessee's balance sheet liability for a capital lease would be periodically reduced by the total

a. Minimum lease payment plus the amortization of the related asset.
b. Minimum lease payment less the amortization of the related asset.

c. Minimum lease payment less the portion of the minimum lease payment allocable to interest.

d. Minimum lease payment.

7.   [N85#9.] Magazine subscriptions collected in advance are reported as

a. A contra account to magazine subscriptions receivable in the asset section of the balance sheet.

b. Deferred revenue in the liability section of the balance sheet.

c. Deferred revenue in the stockholders' equity section of the balance sheet.

d. Magazine subscription revenue in the income statement in the period collected.

DISCUSSION QUESTIONS

1.   Increasingly, financial theorists are treating liabilities as just another equity distinguished only by differences in rights from that of owners' equity. Do you agree with this approach? Discuss.

2.   What factors will cause the market price of debt to rise and fall? Should accountants disclose the market price of liabilities? Structure your argument in terms of relevance and reliability and their subcomponents.

3.   Retailers who deal in household appliances often offer service contracts. How would you account for the service contract at the time of sale? How would you account for it subsequently? How would you account for those monies received from customers who never make use of their service contracts? In your answer be sure to trace the various events that trigger your journal entries.

4.   All employees are entitled to several weeks of vacation each year. Employers typically pay employees while they are on vacation even though they may not be legally obliged to do so. Such periods are known as compensated absences. *SFAS 43* held that a liability for future compensated absences should be accrued if all of the following conditions are met:

> *a.* The employer's obligation relating to employees' rights to receive compensation for future absences is attributable to employees' services already rendered.
>
> *b.* The obligation relates to rights that vest or accumulate.
>
> *c.* Payment of the compensation is probable.
>
> *d.* The amount can be reasonably estimated.

Each of these conditions derives from the more general definition of liabilities. Trace their origin. Are any of the essential characteristics of liabilities not included here?

5. Standard costing systems are intended to produce a standard or average cost for each product. To achieve this, some enterprises each month charge to work-in-process inventory one-twelfth of their annual repair and maintenance costs. The credit is made to a liability account called the Operating Reserve. Discuss the pros and cons of this procedure.

6. Explain why convertible debt is treated as a pure liability. Draw on the classes you have had in finance to suggest alternative ways in which one might report convertible debt. Which of your choices do you prefer?

7. **(November 1972)** Business transactions often involve the exchange of property, goods, or services for notes or similar instruments that may stipulate no interest rate or an interest rate that varies from prevailing rates.

Required:

a. When a note is exchanged for property, goods, or services, what value should be placed upon the note
   1. If it bears interest at a reasonable rate and is issued in a bargained transaction entered into at arm's length? Explain.
   2. If it bears no interest and/or is not issued in a bargained transaction entered into at arm's length? Explain.
b. If the recorded value of a note differs from the face value,
   1. How should the difference be accounted for? Explain.
   2. How should this difference be presented in the financial statements? Explain.

8. **(November 1978)** Gains or losses from the early extinguishment of debt that is refunded can theoretically be accounted for in three ways:

Amortized over remaining life of old debt.

Amortized over the life of the new debt issue.

Recognized in the period of extinguishment.

Required:

a. Discuss the supporting arguments for each of the three theoretic methods of accounting for gains and losses from the early extinguishment of debt.
b. Which of the above methods is generally accepted, and how should the appropriate amount of gain or loss be shown in a company's financial statements?

9. **(May 1971)** On January 1, 1971 Guadagno Corporation issued for $1,106,775 its 20-year, 8 percent bonds, which have a maturity value of $1 million and pay interest semiannually on January 1 and July 1. Bond issue costs were not material in amount. The following are three presentations of the long-term liability section of the balance sheet that might be used for these bonds at the issue date:

1. Bonds payable (maturing January 1, 1991) $1,000,000
   Unamortized premium on bonds payable   106,775

   Total bond liability $1,106,775

2. Bonds payable—principal (face value $1,000,000,
      maturing January 1, 1991)   . . . . $ 252,572*
   Bonds payable—interest (semiannual payment
      $40,000)   . . . .   854.203†

   Total bond liability $1,106,775

3. Bonds payable—principal (maturing January 1, 1991) $1,000,000
   Bonds payable—interest ($40,000 per period for 40
      periods)   1,600,000

   Total bond liability $2,600,000

*The present value of $1,000,000 due at the end of 40 (six-month) periods at the yield rate of 3½ percent per period
† The present value of $40,000 per period for 40 (six-month) periods at the yield rate of 3½ percent per period

Required:

a. Discuss the conceptual merit(s) of each of the date-of-issue balance sheet presentations shown above for these bonds.

b. Explain why investors would pay $1,106,775 for bonds that have a maturity value of only $1 million.

c. Assuming that a discount rate is needed to compute the carrying value of the obligations arising from a bond issue at any date during the life of the bonds, discuss the conceptual merit(s) of using for this purpose

1. The coupon or nominal rate.
2. The effective or yield rate at date of issue.

d. If the obligations arising from these bonds are to be carried at their present value computed by means of the current market rate of interest, how would the bond valuation at dates subsequent to the date of issue be affected by an increase or a decrease in the market rate of interest?

10. (May 1974) Incurring long-term debt with an arrangement whereby lenders receive an option to buy common stock during all or a portion of the time the debt is outstanding is a frequently used corporate financing practice. In some situations the result is achieved through the issuance of convertible bonds; in others the debt instruments and the warrants to buy stock are separate.

Required:

 a. Describe the differences that exist in current accounting for original proceeds of the issuance of convertible bonds and of debt instruments with separate warrants to purchase common stock.
 b. Discuss the underlying rationale for the differences described in *a*.
 c. Summarize the arguments that have been presented for the alternative accounting treatment.

 11. (November 1970) The equity holders of a business entity usually are considered to include both creditors and owners. These two classes of equity holders have some characteristics in common, and sometimes it is difficult to make a clear-cut distinction between them. Examples of this problem include (1) convertible debt and (2) debt issued with stock purchase warrants. Both examples represent debts of a corporation, but there is a question as to whether there is an ownership interest in each case that requires accounting recognition.

Required:

 a. Identify
  1. Convertible debt.
  2. Debt issued with stock purchase warrants.
 b. With respect to convertible debt and debt issued with stock purchase warrants, discuss
  1. The similarities.
  2. The differences.
 c. 1. What are the alternative accounting treatments for the proceeds from convertible debt? Explain.
  2. Which treatment is required by the FASB? Explain the logic of this method.
 d. 1. What are the alternative accounting treatments for the proceeds from debt issued with stock purchase warrants? Explain.
  2. Which treatment is required by the FASB? Explain the logic of this method.

 12. (November 1980) One way for a corporation to accomplish long-term financing is through the issuance of long-term debt instruments in the form of bonds.

Required:

 a. Describe how to account for the proceeds from bonds issued with detachable stock purchase warrants.
 b. Contrast a serial bond with a term (straight) bond.
 c. For a five-year term bond issued at a premium, why would the amortization in the first year of the life of the bond differ using the interest method of amortization instead of the straight-line method? Include in your discussion whether the amount of amortization in the first year of the life of the bond would be higher or lower using the interest method instead of the straight-line method.

d. When a bond issue is sold between interest dates at a discount, what journal entry is made and how is the subsequent amortization of bond discount affected? Include in your discussion an explanation of how the amounts of each debit and credit are determined.

e. Describe how to account for and classify the gain or loss from the reacquisition of a long-term bond before its maturity.

SILVERSTONE INC.

Silverstone Inc., issued bonds with a face value of $1 million and a coupon rate of 8 percent payable semiannually.

a. If the market rate of interest at the time was 6 percent, what would a rational investor pay for the bonds?

b. Compute the interest expense in the first and second half years. Also compute the carrying value of the bonds at the end of the first year.

c. Assume that at the end of the first half-year market rates of interest rose to 8 percent. Now what would a rational investor pay for the bonds? If the bonds had been called at this point, what would the gain or loss have been?

d. Compute the interest expense that would have been shown in the second half-year had the discount rate been adjusted to the current level. Account for the difference between the reported interest expense and the interest expense based on current or market values of the debt.

e. Discuss the conceptual merits of discounting at the coupon rate, the historical market rate, and the current market rate.

MAKI ENTERPRISES

Maki Enterprises was unable to meet the interest payments on its debts, which had accumulated by the end of December 1988 to $1,854,554. The bank, rather than force the company into bankruptcy, made concessions to the company consisting of (*a*) a transfer of land valued at $560,000, (*b*) the issuance of shares with a market value of $600,000, and (*c*) an extension of the remainder of the debt over five years to be paid in equal annual installments of $150,000.

a. Show how this transaction would be accounted for.

b. Discuss the conceptual merits of this treatment.

PRIMARY SOURCES

Those interested in pursuing the topics raised in this chapter in more depth might begin by consulting the following texts:

Brealey, Richard A., and Stewart C. Myers. *Principles of Corporate Finance,* 3rd ed. (New York: McGraw-Hill, 1988). See especially Chapters 20–22 and Chapter 24.

Financial Accounting Standards Board, *Distinguishing between Liability and Equity Instruments and Accounting for Instruments with Characteristics of Both* (FASB Discussion Memorandum, 1990).

Paton, William A. (1922) *Accounting Theory* (Accounting Studies Press, 1962).

Walmsley, Julian. *The New Financial Instruments* (New York: John Wiley & Sons, 1988).

SELECTED ADDITIONAL READINGS

The Nature of Liabilities

Carpenter, Charles G., and Joseph F. Wojdak. "Capitalizing Executory Contracts: A Perspective." *New York CPA,* January 1971, pp. 40–47.

Henderson, M. S. "Nature of Liabilities." *Australian Accountant,* July 1974, pp. 328–30, 333–34.

Hughes, John S. "Toward a Contract Basis of Valuation in Accounting." *The Accounting Review,* October 1978, pp. 882–94.

Kulkarni, Deepak. "The Valuation of Liabilities." *Accounting and Business Research,* Summer 1980, pp. 291–97.

Ma, Ronald, and Malcolm Miller. "Conceptualizing the Liability." *Accounting and Business Research,* Autumn 1978, pp. 258–65.

Long-Term Debt

Clancy, Donald. "What Is a Convertible Debenture? A Review of the Literature in the USA." *Abacus,* December 1978, pp. 171–79.

Falk, Haim, and Stephen L. Buzby. "What's Missing in Accounting for Convertible Bonds?" *CA Magazine,* July 1978, pp. 40–45.

Miller, Jerry D. "Accounting for Warrants and Convertible Bonds." *Management Accounting,* January 1973, pp. 26–28.

Moonitz, Maurice. "The Changing Concept of Liabilities." Reprinted in *Financial Accounting Theory: Issues and Controversies.* Stephen A. Zeff and Thomas F. Keller (New York: McGraw-Hill, 1973), pp. 426–34.

Stephens, Matthew J. "Inseparability of the Valuation of Convertible Bonds." *Journal of Accountancy,* August 1971, pp. 54–62.

Hybrid Securities

Brooks, D. E., and B. Bhave. "New and Innovative Financial Instruments, Part I." *CPA Journal,* July 1987, pp. 32–37; Part II, August 1987, pp. 38–45.

Hynes, L. C., and H. G. Bullen. "Financial Instruments: What Should Be Disclosed." *Management Accounting,* February 1988, pp. 55–59.

Jarzombek, S. M. "What You Should Know about Accounting for Financial Instruments." *Financial Management,* November/December 1989, pp. 46–50.

Jones, J. C. "Financial Instruments: Historical Cost vs. Fair Value." *CPA Journal,* August 1988, pp. 56–63.

Stewart, John E., and Benjamin S. Neuhausen. "Financial Instruments and Transactions: The CPA's Newest Challenge." *Journal of Accountancy,* August 1986, pp. 102–12.

Woods, C. C., and H. G. Bullen. "The FASB's Financial Instruments Project." *Journal of Accountancy,* November 1989, pp. 42–47.

ENDNOTES

1. *SFAC 6,* par. 35.
2. Scott Henderson and Graham Peirson, "A Note on Accounting and Executory Contracts," *Abacus,* 1983, pp. 96–98.
3. Allan Murray, "Bush S&L Bailout Creates Illusion of Deficit Cut That Congress Questions but Wants to Believe," *The Wall Street Journal,* February 22, 1989, p. A18.
4. *SFAS 6,* par. 11.
5. See *APB 21.*
6. See William Paton, "'Deferred Income'—A Misnomer," *Journal of Accountancy,* September 1961, p. 38; and for a criticism, see Robert W. Hirschman, "A Look at Current Classifications," *Journal of Accountancy,* November 1967, p. 55.
7. *FTB 79–7.*
8. *SFAS 15,* par. 16.
9. *SFAS 15,* par. 17.
10. *SFAS 105,* par. 6.
11. *SFAC 6,* par. 49.
12. Financial Accounting Standards Board, *Distinguishing between Liability and Equity Instruments and Accounting for Instruments with Characteristics of Both* (FASB Discussion Memorandum, 1990).

Chapter 20

Deferred Taxes

CHAPTER OBJECTIVES

After studying this chapter, you will be able to:

Define and distinguish permanent from temporary differences.

Develop the case both for and against interperiod tax allocation.

Develop the conceptual underpinnings of the three methods of interperiod tax allocation.

Discuss the appropriate treatment of net operating losses in the light of the Conceptual Framework.

Explain the reasons for the disclosure requirements of income tax accounting and the nature of intraperiod tax allocation.

CHAPTER OVERVIEW

Taxable versus Reported Income

The rules for the computation of taxable income differ from those of GAAP. Congress permits certain items to be permanently excluded from tax computations, others to be temporarily excluded, and still others to be valued differently from GAAP. Each creates a difference between taxable and pretax reported income.

The Case for and against Allocation

Many argue, and currently GAAP requires, that the effect of the difference between taxable and pretax reported income on tax be allocated over time. The effect is that tax expense in any period does not necessarily equal taxes paid. Others argue that allocation is confusing and potentially misleading.

Deferred Taxes and the Conceptual Framework

Allocation of taxes leads to a Deferred Tax account in the statement of financial position. There are arguments, for and against, as to whether these deferrals are indeed liabilities or assets.

Presentation of Results

The requirement of GAAP that total tax expense be allocated to the various parts of the income statement is discussed.

In 1984 a labor-supported organization called Citizens for Tax Justice produced a report called *Corporate Income Taxes in the Reagan Years: A Study of Three Years of Legalized Corporate Tax Avoidance.* The study expressed outrage that out of a group of 250 profitable American companies, 128 of them had paid no taxes in at least one of the years 1981 through 1983. For instance, General Electric had earned $6,527 million in this period and received a tax refund of $283 million. Boeing had earned $1,520 million and been refunded $267 million. To add insult to apparent injury, each company had reported large tax expenses in that period. General Electric, for example, had reported tax expenses of approximately $2,837 million. Boeing had reported tax expenses of $410 million.

The source of the outrage expressed in the study lies in the fact that taxable income is computed differently from accounting income. The taxes that they complained about were based on taxable incomes; the incomes they complained about were accounting net incomes. The difference between the two definitions of income leads to the phenomenon called *interperiod tax allocation* in which a deferred tax account is set up to account for the discrepancies.

Some have suggested that income tax be based on reported income. That would have prevented the cases already cited or a company like U.S. Homes from receiving a refund of $53.6 million when it reported profits of $54.3 million. Congress moved in this direction when it proposed the alternative minimum tax. However, as Chapter 1 noted, the objectives of taxable income and those of reported net income are very different so that this is not a viable solution.

Others have suggested that the apparent confusion in the public's mind caused by the differences might be reduced if corporations simply reported the taxes that are due to the Internal Revenue Service each year, presumably as a lump sum, as the tax expense for that year.* In other

---

* This was, in fact, the typical manner of reporting income taxes prior to the issuance of *APB 11* in December 1967.

words, why do interperiod allocation? Would nonallocation not be clearer to readers? Might it not constitute more truthful disclosure?

The chapter attempts to sort out some of the issues raised by these questions. It begins with a discussion of the differences between taxable and reported income. It then deals with the question of interperiod tax allocation, exploring the arguments both for and against and noting how the APB and the FASB have each attempted a solution to the problem. This discussion closes with a comparison of the methods proposed by these two regulatory bodies. A discussion of intraperiod tax allocation ends the chapter.

TAXABLE VERSUS REPORTED INCOME

The major differences between taxable income and the income reported to shareholders can be classified under two main headings:

1. *Permanent differences* arising from special legislative allowances or restrictions permitted or required for economic, political, or administrative reasons not related to the computation of accounting net income.
2. *Temporary differences* resulting from
   a. Differences in timing of charges and credits to income, also called *interperiod differences*.
   b. Differences arising from alternative measurement bases in financial and tax accounting also called *valuation differences*.

Each of these types of differences is discussed in more detail below.

When the differences between taxable and accounting income are due to temporary differences, the recording of a tax expense (or equivalent effect on income) based on pretax reported income requires *interperiod allocation*. The basic principle of interperiod allocation is to let the tax follow the income on which it is based. Income taxable in the current period but recognized or reported in a later period requires a *deferral* of tax expense; income recognized for accounting purposes and reported in the current period but taxable in a later period requires an *accrual* of tax expense. That is to say:

Income	*Taxable*	*Reported*
Tax expense:		
Deferred	This year	Next year
Accrued	Next year	This year

The desire to report direct charges to retained earnings or extraordinary gains and losses and similar nonoperating items net of tax gives rise to a procedure called *intraperiod allocation* in which the total tax expense of the enterprise is allocated to the various sections of the income statement and the statement of changes in retained earnings. Little opposition is found to intraperiod allocations because only the income and retained earnings statements of the same period are affected; the balance sheet and income statements of other periods are unaffected.

Furthermore, it is not a source of difference between taxes paid and taxes expensed. Its effect on presentation, its only effect, is discussed at the end of the chapter.

Permanent Differences

Permanent differences reflect the computation of the total tax to be paid by the corporation during its lifetime. Interest on municipal bonds is one example of such a difference—it appears as part of reported income, but it is generally not taxable in the United States. The amortization of goodwill in the United States is another example. It is an operating expense for reporting purposes, but nondeductible for tax purposes. Permanent differences affect total taxes only and do not give rise to tax allocation problems. They, therefore, create no theoretical issues in accounting. Short of abandoning financial accounting, they are not subject to the control of accountants, so they are not discussed further in this chapter. In all that follows, it is assumed that permanent differences have been adjusted out of the pretax book income before any of the temporary differences are treated.

Despite their lack of theoretical importance, permanent differences are of considerable practical importance since they are a major source of the gap between what the public believes should be paid and what is being paid in taxes by corporations. Congress responded to the public's concerns regarding permanent differences by including an alternative minimum tax in the 1986 Tax Reform Act. Essentially this tax is computed by withholding many of the tax benefits Congress had legislated in the first place and then taxing the resulting income number at a flat rate of 20 percent. The higher of the two tax numbers is then paid. To close the gap between book and taxable income still further, Congress decreed that 50 percent of the difference between the two had to be added to the adjusted taxable income before applying the flat rate tax. Realizing the pernicious effect this would have on the computation of book income, Congress has repealed this last from 1990 on and substituted an alternative adjustment, the Adjusted Current Earnings (ACE) number. The alternative minimum tax system is equivalent to a second system of tax, but apart from that it creates absolutely nothing new at the theoretical level.

Temporary Differences

Temporary differences are more easily illustrated than explained. Consider a situation where a company's reported income before tax is $100,000. Assuming a tax rate of 34 percent, a tax expense of $34,000 will be reported. Included in the sales for the year are transactions that will not be reported for tax purposes until next year. For instance, the firm might use accrual accounting for financial reporting and cash accounting for tax purposes. Taxable income, therefore, might be $20,000 only. A current tax liability of only $6,800 results. That is:

$$\text{Tax expense} = 34 \text{ percent} \times \$100,000 = \$34,000$$

$$\text{Tax payable} = 34 \text{ percent} \times \$\ 20,000 = \$\ 6,800$$

The difference between these two is accounted for by a deferred tax liability of $27,200. Stated otherwise, the company owes $6,800 in taxes now and, all other things being equal, owes $27,200 in the future. One might expect taxable income to exceed reported income next year in the amount of $80,000 when the deferred tax liability would be eliminated by a payment of $27,200 to the Internal Revenue Service.

Temporary differences form the core of accounting theory regarding accounting for income tax since accountants have some control over how they are handled. They are a major source of the gap between taxable and reported income in a particular period but, unlike permanent differences, they do not create a gap over the life of the corporation.

Temporary differences exist between reported income and the regular taxable income, and between reported income and the alternative taxable income. Each set of temporary differences must be computed each year; the set related to the tax computation that produces the highest tax payment is the set that applies for that year and for which accounting must be done. As a practical matter, this is extremely complicated. Fortunately, at the theoretical level one has simply to note the existence of temporary differences regardless of how they are computed.

Timing Differences.   As already noted, when transactions affect taxable income in one period and pretax accounting income in another, interperiod allocation of taxes is necessary. These were defined as *timing* differences in *APB 11*. Four situations are possible.

1. A deduction taken for tax purposes but deferred in the accounting statements. Common examples are the use of accelerated depreciation for tax purposes while using the straight-line method in the accounts.

2. Revenue recorded currently in the accounts but reported for tax purposes at a later date. Use of the installment basis for tax purposes and the sales basis for accounting purposes is a common example.

3. Income included in a tax calculation but deferred in the accounting statements. An example is rent received in advance and taxable when received but reported as income for accounting purposes when the services are incurred.

4. Expenses deducted in the income statement but deductible for tax purposes only in a later period. An example is estimated warranty expense which is deductible for tax purposes in the period of payment only.

Cases 1 and 2 require the use of an income tax liability, or other credit account, because the tax expense related to the current accounting income is greater than the tax to be paid currently. Cases 3 and 4 require the use of a prepaid tax, or other debit account, because the amount of the tax paid currently is greater than the reported tax expense allocated to the income of the current period.

Valuation Differences.   Less often quoted examples of temporary differences, partly because they had not affected deferred taxes under *APB 11*, include:

1. A reduction in the tax basis of depreciable assets because of tax credits. One source of this difference is the Tax Equity and Fiscal Responsibility Act of 1982, which provides taxpayers with the choice of either taking the full amount of Accelerated Cost Recovery System (ACRS) deductions and a reduced tax credit or taking the full tax credit and a reduced amount of ACRS deductions.

2. Foreign operations for which the reporting currency is the functional currency. Under *SFAS 52*, after a change in exchange rates the foreign tax basis of certain assets and liabilities can differ from their equivalent U.S. dollar historical costs.

3. An increase in the tax basis of assets because of indexing for inflation. Certain tax jurisdictions might require indexation of certain assets for tax purposes that would cause their bases then to differ from the historical costs found in financial reports.

4. Business combinations accounted for by the purchase method.

There are often differences in the amounts assigned to assets in a combination and their corresponding tax bases.*

These cases are caused by differences in tax accounting and financial accounting valuation bases and are sometimes described as *valuation* differences. The term *temporary* differences covers both timing and valuation.

Balance Sheet Approach

An alternative approach to the one used above for computing temporary differences relies on the fact that, given articulated statements, all transactions giving rise to temporary differences leave recognizable imprints in the balance sheet. For instance, different depreciation schedules result in different book values. The difference between the book values in the accounts used for financial reporting and those used for tax reporting must equal the cumulative sum of the temporary differences to that point. The difference in book values, therefore, enables one to compute the remaining temporary differences. In each case, the temporary differences, when multiplied by the appropriate tax rate and then summed, yield the deferred tax. The balance sheet approach, therefore, adds a second computational device, but does not add anything at the theoretical level.

CHECKPOINTS

1. Distinguish permanent differences from temporary differences. Give examples of each.
2. Distinguish timing differences from valuation differences. Give examples of each.
3. What is intraperiod tax allocation and how does it differ from interperiod tax allocation?

THE CASE FOR AND AGAINST ALLOCATION

Interperiod tax allocation has stirred a vigorous and, at times, even emotional debate over the years. The controversy can be traced back to disagreement on several basic premises which are at the root of much of

---

* For many companies, this was a permanent difference under *APB 11*.

the conflict in the accounting literature. One group believes that the matching concept is fundamental to accounting. They argue that the reporting of net income should override any effects on the balance sheet. Another group argues that asset and liability valuations that permit economic interpretation both as to the item and its measurement are key. A third group bases its preferences on the belief that predictions of future cash flows are more important than predictions of reported net income. For them, financial statements should reflect cash flows as closely as possible in order to permit predictions of future cash flows. These premises will be seen to surface and resurface in the paragraphs that follow describing the debate.

The Case for Comprehensive Allocation

A number of arguments have been made in favor of interperiod tax allocation at different times. Three are presented here: one based on the concept of matching, another based on the concept of the going concern, and the third based on managerial practice.

Matching.   The traditional case for full or comprehensive interperiod tax allocation relies on the notion of matching. As indicated in Chapter 11, matching is the process of reporting expenses on the basis of a cause-and-effect relationship with reported revenues. Direct matching requires the reporting of expenses in the same period as the associated revenues. Application of the matching concept to accounting for income taxes is found in *APB 11* where the Board recommended that the reported income tax expense for a period should include the tax effect of all revenue and expense transactions included in the measurement of pretax income. Since the tax effects of all revenues and expenses are included, the approach is called *comprehensive* tax allocation.

The tax effects are reported in an originating entry in the period during which the timing differences arise and also in reversing entries in the periods during which the differences reverse. Between these two dates, the APB recommended that the differences should be reported as deferred charges or deferred credits, hence the title of the *deferred method* of interperiod tax allocation. The tax effect is based on the tax rate at the time of reporting the initial difference, and no adjustment is made for changes in tax rates in accordance with the historical cost tradition.

APB 11 was severely criticized on grounds that the deferred method was not supported by logic. First, matching is being done not with revenues, but with before-tax income. This concept of matching is very different from that in Chapter 11. Second, the deferred charges and deferred credits are intended to represent neither assets and liabilities nor stockholders' equity.* Therefore, they represent merely a method of shifting the tax effect from one period to another. Even if the method is supported on the basis of the matching concept alone, the amounts carried forward should represent measurements of resources or obligations if the double-entry system is to be maintained. The use of undefined debits and credits made the entire method suspect. *SFAS 96*, with its emphasis on balance sheet measurement, is the FASB's response to this criticism.

Going Concern.   The FASB's case is based on the concept of a going concern. It begins with the assertion that the tax consequences of an event are inherent in that event. The tax payment itself is merely a matter of cash, subject only to a question of when it will be paid, not whether. If the taxes actually paid in the period in which the event occurs are less than the tax inherent in the event, that is to say the related tax expense, an income tax payable should be set up. By the same token, if taxes paid in the period of the event exceed the related tax expense then, all other things being equal, a prepaid tax or other debit account should be set up. Both statements are subject to normal recognition criteria.

Consider, for example, an installment sale. Assume that the sale is recognized for financial reporting purposes at the moment of delivery of goods. When cash comes in it is credited to an accounts receivable, not to revenue. The FASB now argues that coincident with that sale is a tax obligation arising from that sale, to be recognized with that sale, and like it, relatively independent of the cash flow. At the moment of the sale a tax expense should be recognized and with it a tax liability, deferred if necessary. When the tax is ultimately paid in cash, it will reduce the liability, but it will not, and should not, affect the expense. To recognize the sales revenue at the time of delivery but not the related tax expense is inconsistent, says the Board.

Managerial Practice.   Another argument against simply reporting income taxes paid as the expense of the period is that it is common practice to define tax as an expense of doing business. Also managements generally make decisions on the basis of an aftertax expected net income. Additionally, tax must be taken into consideration in investment and dividend decisions. Practice, however, does not determine the logic of the classification. Expense classifications have no clear definitions other than what accountants choose them to be. The argument that tax allocation is

---

* *APB 11*, paragraph 57, noted that: Deferred charges and deferred credits relating to timing differences represent the cumulative recognition given to their tax effects and as such do not represent receivables and payables in the usual sense.

appropriate because tax is treated as an expense is difficult to support, therefore.

Some have attempted to refute the "cost of doing business" case for tax allocation by pointing out that taxes are not directly related to revenues or revenue-seeking functions. Expenses, however, are not homogeneous in nature; some are variable with output or sales, and others are fixed. Most expenses are incurred deliberately, with the objective of increasing revenues or decreasing costs, but some result from expected or unexpected outside influences beyond the control of the firm. This argument is, therefore, inconclusive.

The Case against Allocation

As many, and possibly more, arguments have been made against allocation as for it. A number are discussed here. Despite the plethora of arguments, none has proven sufficiently convincing to overturn the use of interperiod tax allocation in the financial statements of American corporations.

Lack of Understandability. The first argument against tax allocation relates to the audience. The claim is made that reporting a tax expense that is not equal to the actual tax paid confuses the public. This claim is implicit in the report done by the Citizens for Tax Justice. It appears, though, to assume a naive group of annual report consumers. One is introduced fairly early in one's accounting education to the fact that accounting accrues revenues and expenses and that income is not cash flow. If our audience does have "a reasonable understanding of business and economic activities and are willing to study the information with reasonable diligence," then one can reasonably expect them to understand that tax expense is not a cash payment.[1]

A Distribution, Not an Expense. A deeper argument in favor of reporting the actual taxes paid as the tax expense for the period is that taxes are like the payment of dividends and, therefore, a distribution of income. This view suggests that there is no legal liability beyond that shown on an income tax return. The proponents of this view note that, like dividends and unlike payments for wages and supplies, taxes are paid only if income is earned. Future taxes will become payable only if income is earned in future years. Assuming a deferred tax liability implies an assumption of events which have yet to occur.

The government, however, is a beneficiary of the corporation only in a broad sense, in the same way that employees and suppliers are beneficiaries and receive payment for the services they render. The main difference is that the federal government does not provide services to the corporation in direct proportion to the amount of the tax. But there is no question that services are provided. The payment of the corporate income tax (like a franchise tax) is associated with the right to conduct a profitable corporation in a favorable economic climate provided by the government. And the classification of this payment is independent of its calculation.

A related argument against tax allocation is that the impact of the tax is really on the shareholder and should be reported as such. The corporation, they say, is really just an intermediary in this regard, paying taxes on behalf of shareholders. But, even if the final incidence of the tax is on the shareholders, this does not necessarily change the nature of the tax as an expense of the corporation. Also, there is evidence that shareholders are not the only ones impacted by corporate taxes; consumers are too.

Lack of Relevance.   Another line of argument against income tax allocation is that financial statements should reflect as clearly as possible the cash flows of the firm to permit predictions of future cash flows. Since the tax obligation is not necessarily functionally related to reported net income, critics of current procedures claim that the tax levied each year is more relevant to investors and creditors than some artificially allocated tax expense. Some supporters of this view would eliminate all accrual accounting; others would continue the accrual basis for other items. They are united in doubting whether reported net income is made more relevant by the allocation of taxes to expense or income items that are themselves the result of allocation unsupported by theory.

One counterargument to this is that predictions and evaluations should be made on the basis of pretax income and expectations regarding changes in the amount of tax, rather than upon a single aftertax net income. However, in the final analysis pragmatic arguments can be answered only on pragmatic grounds. Unfortunately, currently available empirical evidence does not permit a definitive answer to the question of relevance.

Uncertainty.   Tax allocation is also opposed on the ground that the uncertainties in making estimates of future tax obligations and future tax effects are too great to make allocation meaningful. Since the tax is payable only when taxable income is earned, tax "savings" of one period may result in permanent savings if the corporation incurs losses for several years. Likewise, expenses deductible for tax purposes only in a later period may never reduce taxes if losses are incurred beyond the carry-back and carry-forward periods. Also, it is claimed, future tax rates and tax regulations are uncertain and subject to change by Congress, and the method of application of the regulations may be subject to change by administrative decisions. However, it is not clear that uncertainties affecting tax allocations are any greater than they are in other areas of financial reporting.

The Case for Partial Allocation

Some argue that, while it might be appropriate to allocate certain taxes, it is another matter altogether to allocate all taxes. Proponents of this view point out that at the aggregate level the deferred tax account simply rolls over. For instance, if accelerated depreciation is used for tax purposes while straight-line is used in the financial statements, the tax difference will not be paid so long as the firm continues to replace its assets; and in a growth firm, the aggregate difference will continue to increase indefinitely. Under partial allocation, taxes would be deferred only in those cases in which tax benefits or tax obligations are likely to be reversed in the aggregate within a reasonable time in the future. In particular, tax allocation would not be done on depreciation related differences. In their view, there is no legal liability in this case.

Their argument is based on the correct observation that, as long as a company is growing, its receivables and payables will grow. Once that company moves into a steady state, its receivable and payables will be stable. In particular, its net income will be the same no matter what kind of accounting it employs. In this case, whether one accounts for taxes on a cash or an accrual basis, in a steady state situation the tax expense will be identical. Only if the company slowly and steadily shrinks away to nothing will the deferred taxes be reduced and, thereby, be paid off.

One counterargument is that there is a continual rollover of the liability, so that each year a part is paid and an additional amount accrued. Like accounts payable, the liability cannot be denied just because the aggregate does not decrease over time. However, taxes payable and accounts payable are not quite the same. If the firm ceased profitable operations, the tax payable would not have to be paid, but the creditors represented by the accounts payable would maintain their claims. The rollover concept is not as applicable to the tax liability as it is to the accounts payable, therefore.

An alternative counterargument notes that the only reason that deferred taxes payable at the aggregate level can remain steady and even continue to grow is because the originating entries on new events are greater than or equal to the reversing entries on old events. The taxes on each event individually will reverse even if they do not reverse at the aggregate level. Since, say the proponents of the full allocation approach, we are concerned with measuring the tax consequences of each event, partial allocation is inappropriate.

The Case for Discounting

A final argument against showing the full amount of the tax liability or prepaid tax is that, since the obligations will be paid and the tax benefit received only at some time in the future, they should be discounted at some positive rate of interest. If the time period is long or infinite, the present value would be close to zero. The purely theoretical argument appears to be unassailable. There are, though, numerous practical difficulties with the suggestion, such as the choice of discount rates and the determination of the future years in which amounts will become taxable or deductible. Also, it would add considerable complexity to tax accounting. For these reasons, and for the reason that discounting raises much broader issues than those in tax accounting, the FASB decided not to address the issue in the context of *SFAS 96*. The desirability of discounting, therefore, remains an open question at the practical, although not at the theoretical, level.

Empirical Studies

Empirical studies to date have not been strongly supportive of tax allocation. Beaver and Dukes, for example, concluded in a preliminary study that tax allocation is a correct decision if one accepts market efficiency.[2] However, in a later study, they concluded that the premise on which tax allocation is based is open to serious question and that current tax allocation procedures are not necessarily optimal.[3] The lack of basic supporting theory and the many complications involved in the tax allocation process, therefore, make it doubtful as a relevant accounting procedure. Part of the difficulty, however, is not with the tax allocation itself, but with the entire accounting process, which stresses the reporting of a single net income figure, which is then used as a predictive indicator. Alternative theoretical structures should be investigated, and empirical studies should be made to find better methods of communicating the effects of corporate income taxation.

CHECKPOINTS

1. List the arguments for interperiod tax allocation.
2. List the arguments against interperiod tax allocation.
3. What are the arguments for and against partial as opposed to comprehensive tax allocation.

DEFERRED TAXES AND THE CONCEPTUAL FRAMEWORK

After comparing the various methods for computing the deferred tax liability, the FASB opted for the so-called *asset/liability* method of interperiod tax allocation on grounds that it fits most closely with the Conceptual Framework; that it produces the most useful and understandable information; and that it is no more complex than any of the other methods. The asset/liability method differs from the deferred method in that:

1. It shifts the analysis away from matching, replacing it with definitions of assets and liabilities from *SFAC 6* to justify interperiod tax allocation.
2. It requires one to estimate the effect of temporary differences in the future rather than use the results of the known past.

In other words, using our earlier example, if current reported pretax income is $100,000 and current taxable income is $20,000, then a *future* reversal of $80,000 is expected. This future income will require a tax payment of $27,200, given a tax rate of 34 percent. Thus, inherent in the present transaction is a future or deferred tax liability of $27,200. The key here is the emphasis on the future tax consequences.

In a pure application of the asset/liability method, reversing the income streams would lead to a deferred tax asset. For instance, warranty expenses may make current reported pretax income $20,000 and current taxable income $100,000. This situation ensures an expected *future* reversal of $80,000 which may now be interpreted as a loss. The present tax payment of $34,000 is accompanied, therefore, by a future expected refund of $27,200 which should be shown, strictly speaking, as a deferred tax asset.

In practice, companies by their actions in any given year generate a stream of future expected "incomes" and "losses." Losses in this stream may be offset against incomes to the extent permitted by the tax code in its treatment of net operating losses. Current tax rules permit operating losses to be carried back 3 years and carried forward 15 years.

The difference between the deferred tax account at the start and end of the year yields the net deferred tax debit, or credit, for the year. In our example, the opening deferred tax was zero; the ending deferred tax account was $27,200; the change is a credit of $27,200 to the liability account, indicating a debit to the tax expense account. Combining this with changes in any other tax-related accounts and the tax paid to the authorities yields the tax expense for the year. Thus, with tax paid being $6,800, the full tax expense is $34,000. In the second year of the example, the tax paid was $34,000, so tax expense was $6,800 (i.e., $34,000 less $27,200). In short, tax expense is the residual in the asset/liability method, whereas deferred taxes are the residual in the deferred method.

	Year 1	*Year 2*
Deferred tax liability:		
Opening balance	$ 0	$27,200
Closing balance	27,200	0
Difference	27,200	(27,200)
Tax paid	6,800	34,000
Tax expense	$34,000	$ 6,800

SFAS 96 added an additional feature that is not a necessary part of the asset/liability method, but does represent a significant change from old GAAP requirements. This feature bases tax related effects on *all* events that have happened, and excludes all events that have not happened. The Board used this feature to include the use of all previously enacted tax rates, even where they involve changes in future periods. This feature was also used to exclude the assumption of income in future years to offset tax losses created by reversing tax differences.

Net Operating Losses

The current tax code permits tax losses to be carried backward and forward to reduce the total tax payable by the corporation. The principle of allocation is the same for both carry-backs and carry-forwards, but more uncertainty regarding the tax benefit exists in the latter case.

When a tax loss can be carried back to reduce the taxes paid in prior years, a claim for refund arises immediately, even though it may be subject to approval by the Internal Revenue Service at a later date. In most cases, the claim for refund is sufficiently certain and can be estimated with reasonable accuracy. Both the APB and the FASB have suggested that the refund be shown as a reduction of the operating loss in the current period, arguing that the refund is a function of tax loss, not the income to which the loss was carried back. In other words, the refund should be shown as a negative tax amount: a contra-income tax expense.

In the case of a loss carry-forward, a tax benefit is incurred in the current year but not actually realized until a future year. If one follows the argument of the previous paragraph, the current tax loss should be reduced and a tax asset recognized. This tax asset is not the same as the deferred tax asset which arises from interperiod tax allocation. On the other hand, it is not exactly a true receivable, since there will seldom be a direct claim against the government. However, it does represent an anticipated future benefit to the firm in the form of a reduction in a future liability. Although this benefit may not have all the characteristics of normal assets, it does reflect the possibility of greater aftertax income than would otherwise occur. Other things being equal, a firm with a carry-forward tax loss is worth more than a firm without it.

The other alternative is to defer recognition of the asset until sufficient income has been earned to enable the corporation to realize the benefit of the tax loss. At that point the refund could be reported as a reduction of the taxes which would otherwise have been paid. Instead, it could be reported in the year realized but as a prior period adjustment to the financial statements of the year in which the loss was incurred. This last approach is consistent with the assertion that the source of the refund is the loss and not the subsequent income—the latter merely permits its realization.

APB 11 requires that the benefit should be reported only in the year to which the loss is carried forward. This opinion states further that the amount of the tax refund arising from the carry-forward of the loss should be reported in the income statement of the year realized as an extraordinary item, unless it has been reported in the year of the loss. The result may be interpreted as a correction of the income or loss of the prior period, but it is not clear why the Board did not recommend that it be excluded from income of the carry-forward period, which would then be consistent with the recommendations of *APB 9* and *APB 30* regarding prior-period adjustments. However, the inclusion of the tax refund in the income statement is consistent with the more recent *SFAS 16*. But this treatment of carry-forwards is not consistent with the treatment of carry-backs. The benefit should be treated consistently as relating to the operations of the loss year in both cases, in accordance with income tax allocation procedures.

This inconsistency in treatment continued into *SFAS 96,* which introduced the asset/liability method. The FASB permits the full benefit of carry-backs to be reported as current tax receivables and offset by reductions in the current operating loss. Carry-forwards are permitted to reduce future positive temporary differences—in effect to reduce the deferred tax liability account to zero. The balance, if any, is not recognized until income is earned in future years, when it will be included as part of the ordinary tax expense—not as a prior-period adjustment. The existence of an unrecognized carry-forward is, however, required to be reported in the footnotes.

The position of the FASB regarding loss carry-forwards differs from the position taken regarding carry-backs, apparently because of the greater uncertainty of the benefits under a loss carry-forward than under a loss carry-back. If income is not earned during the permitted period, the tax benefit may be lost. But this uncertainty is always present when the allocation of taxes depends on future taxable income. There is some merit in the argument that a firm that has incurred losses is more likely to incur additional losses than a firm that has a long record of profitable operation;

however, it can be argued that each case should be treated on its merits. If there is a good probability of future income within the carry-forward period, the anticipated tax benefit should be recorded in the period in which the loss is incurred. To do otherwise is to be unnecessarily conservative.

Another criticism of the current handling of carry-forwards derives from the stated objective of accounting as permitting predictions of future cash flows. One of the presumed advantages of tax allocation is that it permits a better matching of the tax payments with the associated pretax income items, and thus permits a better prediction of reported net income in the future, and hence of future cash flows. If a loss in one year gives rise to a refund arising from the carry-back provisions, but a subsequent loss is dependent on carry-forward provisions, then the failure to adjust the loss for a potential future refund will result in reported net income or loss figures for the two years that are not indicative of the operations of the two periods. If the pretax reported income or loss amounts are the same for the two years, the failure to allocate any potential refund to the second year could give the impression that the outlook for the firm is rapidly becoming worse.

At the same time it must be added that a loss by itself does not create a tax refund; the refund is associated with the taxable income as well as with the loss. The functional relationship is not clear-cut. As with all interperiod tax allocations, the allocation of refunds, no matter how it is done, does not necessarily improve the communication of information. Full disclosure of tax effects is necessary because income taxes do not behave in the same way as other expenses; the reliance on a reported aftertax net income is not adequate for the decisions and predictions of investors and creditors.

Are These Really Assets and Liabilities?

The asset/liability approach adopted by the Board in *SFAS 96* has been severely challenged on the ground that the deferred taxes do not have the usual characteristics of assets and liabilities. For instance, some claim that the deferred tax asset, which represents "prepaid tax" arising from the allocation of income taxes, is not an unconditional right for future benefits. In particular, they argue, it is not a claim that would be recognized by the Internal Revenue Service. Therefore, the argument goes, it does not have the usual characteristics of assets.

There are circumstances, however, where under normal expectations of future corporate income and the continuation of current income tax regulations, the item may have many of the normal characteristics of an asset. For example, the tax paid on rent received in advance gives the firm the right to provide services in the future without incurring a tax obligation in doing so. The benefit is less real when it results from differences in methods of depreciation of other allocations, rather than from timing of cash flows. This conclusion is particularly true when the tax allocation is looked at from the point of view of the entire firm, rather than looking at each item separately, because of the many interactions, even in the computation of the income tax payable.

The deferred tax payable, which represents "income taxes payable in the future" arising from tax allocation, has likewise been accused of possessing few of the normal characteristics of liabilities. An obligation to the government does not really exist. If it did, the Internal Revenue Service would press its claim for payment of these deferred taxes. The future obligation arises only in part from the past transaction—the earning of the income not reported for tax purposes or the deduction for tax purposes of an expenditure carried forward in the accounts. The main transaction—the levying of the tax—is a future transaction.

In some circumstances, however, there is an obligation to pay a tax in the future based on past or current activities. For example, income reported on the basis of the percentage-of-completion method for long-term contracts should take into consideration the fact that a tax obligation will arise when the contract is completed. But the "liability" arising from the use of the accelerated method of depreciation for tax purposes while using the straight-line method of depreciation for reporting purposes is an obligation only under some very limited assumptions regarding the validity of the depreciation method used for accounting purposes. Critics conclude that, because of the lack of theoretical logic behind such methods, the tax liability is of doubtful validity.

The FASB effectively conceded the argument against the recognition of deferred tax assets. It does not permit, except in certain specified circumstances, a deferred tax asset to be reported. The Board did not concede, though, the argument against the recognition of deferred tax liabilities. They based their argument on the definition of liabilities appearing in paragraph 25 of *SFAC 6*, namely:

> Liabilities are probable future sacrifices of economic benefits arising from present obligations of a particular entity to transfer assets or provide services to other entities in the future as a result of past transactions or events.

The Board concluded that, in general, taxes are a legally binding obligation to the government. Temporary differences result from past transactions or events whose effects are already in the financial statements. Since no further event need occur for the temporary difference to be recognized, the Board concluded that a probable future transfer or use of assets would occur. The Board also argued that, given the assumption of a going concern, there was a virtually certain obligation to tax authorities, involving little or no discretion, to transfer assets to them. The Board concluded that temporary differences do give rise to liabilities and not just deferred credits. In particular, the Board rejected the claim that the levying of a tax payable had to occur before recognizing a deferred tax liability. In their view, the critical point is the moment of recognition of the underlying event; thereafter, it is merely a matter of payment.

As already noted, the Board did not conclude that temporary differences give rise to deferred tax assets except in one special case. This exception occurs when a negative net temporary difference in the future is carried back against current or prior taxable income. The ground for this hotly disputed conclusion was that a tax benefit could be realized only if income were earned; this second event had not yet occurred, nor was it an inherent assumption of accrual accounting or the going-concern principle.

At least one member of the Board continued to maintain that the mirror image to the arguments in favor of deferred tax liabilities were arguments in favor of deferred tax assets. He claimed that in the going-concern assumption there is an implicit assumption that the company would make an operating profit in years ahead at least sufficient to cover negative temporary differences which could then be folded into that profit. The rest of the Board denied this implication of the going-concern concept. They saw future operating profits as events that had not yet occurred. To the argument that this creates an inconsistency between the handling of deferred liabilities and deferred assets, the Board responded that this was appropriate because it was representationally faithful to the operation of the tax code.

A Comparison of *SFAS 96* and *APB 11*

Much has been said to this point about the different arguments for and against the various methods of tax allocation. But what are the practical consequences of a switch from a deferred method such as that in *APB 11* to an asset/liability method such as that in *SFAS 96*? It turns out that they are relatively small. The only real change occurs when one allows for a change in tax rates which is actually independent of the choice between the two methods.

The reason for the similarity in the two methods lies in the nature of temporary differences which, by definition, reverse themselves over their lives. Stated otherwise, the sum of the temporary differences over their lives is zero. Now, if any series that sums to zero is split at any point along its length, the absolute sum up to the split must equal the absolute sum after the split. If the split is the current year, the origin is the point at which the temporary difference series begins, and the end is the point at which the temporary difference closes, the sum of the temporary differences from the origin up to the split is equal to the sum from the split to the end (ignoring signs).

Consider, for example, a company using straight-line depreciation for reporting purposes and some form of accelerated depreciation for tax purposes. In particular, assume the following pattern:

Year	1	2	3	4	5
Reported depreciation	100	100	100	100	100
Tax depreciation	200	150	75	50	25
Temporary difference	(100)	(50)	25	50	75

The total of the temporary differences is zero. The sum of the first two years is $150 (negative); the sum of the last three terms is $150.

There are two means of totaling temporary differences, therefore. One can sum forward from the origin to the split or one can sum backward from the end to the split. Summing forward to the split is what one does in the deferred method; summing backward to the split is what one does in the asset/liability method. *APB 11* focused on the temporary differences that had occurred; *SFAS 96* focuses on the temporary differences that will occur. The two methods must, subject to only a few exceptions, give exactly the same result. For instance, assume income of $200 per year before depreciation and a tax rate of 20 percent. Then, given the above depreciation schedules, the following table results:

Year	1	2	3	4	5
Pretax income	100	100	100	100	100
Taxable income	0	50	125	150	175

Following the provisions of *APB 11*, one computes the tax expense by applying the tax rate to the pretax income. One computes the tax payable by applying the same tax rate to the taxable income. The difference between the two is the credit, or debit, to the deferred tax account. The entry in the second year, for instance, would be:

Tax expense	20	
Tax payable		10
Deferred tax		10

Tabulating the journal entries for the five years yields:

Year	1	2	3	4	5
Tax expense	20	20	20	20	20
Tax payable	0	10	25	30	35
Deferred tax	20	10	(5)	(10)	(15)
Deferred tax liability	20	30	25	15	0

Note that the deferred tax liability in any year is obtainable by summing the temporary differences from left to right and multiplying the sum by the tax rate. For instance, in the second year, the temporary differences sum to $150. Multiplying this by 20 percent gives the deferred tax liability of $30.

SFAS 96 begins with the balance sheet. More specifically, it begins with the future temporary differences. In the second year, the future temporary differences sum to $150. Multiplying this result by 20 percent gives the deferred tax liability. In the first year, the future temporary differences sum to $100, yielding a deferred tax liability of $20. The difference added to the tax payable of $10 results in a tax expense of $30. This is summarized in the next table.

Year	1	2	3	4	5
Future temporary differences	100	150	125	75	0
Deferred tax liability	20	30	25	15	0
Change in liability	20	10	(5)	(10)	(15)
Tax payable	0	10	25	30	35
Tax expense	20	20	20	20	20

It should be readily apparent from these tables that *APB 11* and *SFAS 96* give the same answers if based on the same assumptions.

One exception to the general rule of equality is changes in tax rates. If changes in tax rates are handled in the deferred method comparably with their handling in the asset/liability method, they are not a source of a difference between the two methods. To the extent that changes in tax rates are ignored in the one method and recognized in the other, one has a distinct arithmetical shift in computations.

Another exception lies in the asymmetric treatment of negative temporary differences between *APB 11* and *SFAS 96*. In general, negative temporary differences are offset by positive temporary differences. As long as the offset is complete, there is no difference between the two standards. However, there are occasions when tax laws regarding carries do not permit one to eliminate one or more negative temporary differences in future years. *SFAS 96* requires these residual negative differences to be treated as unrecognized losses, albeit disclosed in the footnotes. *APB 11*, on the other hand, recognizes them.

The conclusion to all this is that the deferred method and the asset/liability method, as interpreted in *APB 11* and *SFAS 96*, respectively, will produce identical tax expenses provided:

1. Changes in tax rates are handled comparably.
2. There is no unrecognized deferred tax asset shown in the footnotes under the asset/liability method.

Much has been made of the apparent shift the FASB is making from an income statement to a balance sheet approach. Clearly, there are conceptual differences in arguing whether the deferred tax appearing on a balance sheet is derived directly as a liability or as the result of the sum of differences in reported and taxable income. Equally clearly, the balance sheet and the income statement, articulated as they currently are, are simply mirror images of one another. The results of income statement and balance sheet approaches, therefore, must lead to similar results. This conclusion follows even in the case of the alternative minimum tax. The minimum tax is no more than a second tax system which creates a second set of differences against reported income. Either these differences are permanent when they do not figure into either approach or they are reversing when they yield to the identical analysis as done with regular taxes above.

The emphasis on book values in *SFAS 96*, which appears at first glance to create a completely new system of deferring taxes, turns out to be no more than the mirror image of already familiar temporary differences. If one knows what impact there was on the income statement under *APB 11*, one should be able with only clerical effort to translate this into the related impact on the balance sheet. The reverse is equally true. And, as long as the two statements articulate, this has to continue to be true.

Most of the complexities which appear to be in *SFAS 96* are really a function of the Tax Reform Act of 1986 with its subsequent amendments. Were Congress to settle on a stable corporate tax rate, most of the differences encountered in practice would vanish. The one source of remaining difference between *APB 11* and *SFAS 96* can be resolved by the unrecognized deferred tax asset appearing in the footnote.

CHECKPOINTS

1. What are the three characteristics of a liability? Explain how the FASB concluded that "future income taxes payable" is a genuine liability.
2. What are the three characteristics of an asset? Explain how the FASB concluded that "future income taxes refundable" is not a genuine asset.
3. What are the objectives of the method for handling operating losses?
4. Explain the basic difference between the revenue-expense and the asset-liability methods.
5. Define the concept of "matching" in the context of tax allocation and explain why the FASB has moved away from its use.
6. In what circumstances does a carry-back produce a tax asset and in what circumstances does it produce a deferred tax asset?

PRESENTATION OF RESULTS

It remains only to discuss how to present the various tax-related income statement and financial statement accounts. The material covers three areas: intraperiod tax allocation, the net-of-tax method of interperiod tax allocation which really deals with matters of presentation, and the current presentation requirements of *SFAS 96.*

Intraperiod Tax Allocation

If the all-inclusive concept of income were fully accepted, allocations of the tax between the income statement and the retained earnings statement would not be necessary. However, according to *APB 9,* extraordinary gains and losses should be reported separately in the income statement. According to *SFAS 16,* some adjustments of prior periods should be reported as adjustments of retained earnings. In these cases, and others like them, intraperiod allocation within the income statement, or between the income statement and the retained earnings statement, may make the reported operating net income before extraordinary items more meaningful.

For example, if the net operating income before tax is $1,000, a 34 percent income tax rate would result in a tax of $340 and a net income before extraordinary items of $660. But if, in addition, a nonrecurring taxable gain of $600 is reported during the year, the total tax payable becomes $544 (34 percent × $1,600). Without allocation, the net operating income would be $456, and the $600 would be reported as an extraordinary gain. With allocation, the tax assignable to current operations would be $340, and that assignable to the extraordinary gain would be $204.

	With Allocation	Without Allocation
Net operating income	$1,000	$1,000
Income tax	340	544
Income before extraordinary items	$ 660	$ 456
Extraordinary gain		600
Extraordinary gain net of tax	396	
Net income	$1,056	$1,056

Thus, the operating net income before extraordinary items would not be disturbed by the recording of the gain and the gain (net of the associated tax) would be reported separately.

The argument for intraperiod allocation rests primarily on the usefulness of the reported figure of net income before extraordinary items. Some believe that, for financial reporting purposes, an operating net income figure might be more useful to investors in making predictions regarding future income and making comparisons of the net incomes of several periods. Without allocation, the net income figure before extraordinary items is subject to misinterpretation. If operating revenues and expenses are the same in a second year and following years, but the nonoperating gains or losses do not recur, the failure to allocate tax in the first year would result in an erroneous prediction and a poor comparison of the efficiency of management in conducting normal operations. It might also lead to misinterpretation of the net effect on the firm of the nonrecurring gains or losses reported as extraordinary items.

This argument assumes, though, that operating income is more predictable than net income or, indeed, comprehensive income. More broadly still, this assumes that accounting earnings are predictable. The results of empirical research have not been hopeful. As mentioned in Chapter 10, earnings numbers tend to follow a random walk with a fairly wide dispersion. There seems to be little to choose in this regard between income of continuing operations excluding extraordinary items, and net income including extraordinary items.

A simpler argument might assert that tax consequence should be associated with the pretax consequences of an event. If one is to break out the details of the underlying event, one should break out its tax consequences. The result is more disclosure or, equivalently, a finer information set. In a costless world, a finer information set is always preferable.

Given that the marginal cost of producing the finer set is probably quite low, this is almost certainly a desirable approach.

The method of handling intraperiod tax allocation recommended in *SFAS 96* is to compute taxes on continuing income independently of any other items such as discontinued segments or extraordinary items. These latter are computed separately at their appropriate, incremental rates.* The resulting sum is then compared to the result that one obtains by figuring the tax on comprehensive income as a whole. Almost inevitably, the sum of the parts will not equal the whole. To resolve this, the various items other than continuing income are allocated a portion of the difference between tax on continuing income and tax on comprehensive income in proportion to their tax burdens computed individually.

The Net-of-Tax Method

An alternative to reporting deferred tax assets and liabilities as independent accounts, called the *net-of-tax* method, is to treat them in close relationship to the items giving rise to them. Thus, the prepaid taxes may be considered valuation accounts to the related liabilities, and the taxes payable in the future may be considered contra asset accounts, or the assets and liabilities may be reduced directly. For example, if a capital asset in the amount of $10,000 is written off for tax purposes but carried forward in the accounts, the net valuation to the firm is only $6,600 (assuming a 34 percent tax rate).

The net-of-tax method is based on the assumption that an adjustment of the historical cost of an asset for the tax effect results in a current valuation of the asset. The difficulties with this assumption are twofold. First, many other factors should be considered in measuring the value of the firm to investors. Second, it is questionable whether the objective of accounting is to measure and report the value of each asset or liability. A third problem with the method is that some temporary differences cannot be identified with specific assets and liabilities. One example is the use of cash basis accounting for tax purposes and accrual accounting for financial reporting purposes. Another example is the use of completed-contract accounting for tax purposes and percentage-of-completion accounting for financial reporting.

The FASB, after considering and rejecting its use, expressed the belief that the asset/liability method provided a finer information set than combining the tax effects with other assets and liabilities. They did nod, however, in the direction of the net-of-tax method when they ruled that

---

* The current tax rates are 15 percent on the first $50,000 of taxable income, 25 percent on the next $25,000, and 34 percent on the remaining balance with a surcharge of 5 percent on taxable income in excess of $100,000, but not to exceed $11,750.

deferred taxes should follow the current/noncurrent deferred classification of the underlying events. For example, the tax consequences associated with inventory should be shown as a current deferred if the associated inventory is a current asset.

CHECKPOINTS

---

1. Distinguish intraperiod tax allocation from interperiod tax allocation.
2. How are the details of tax accounting disclosed to stockholders? Would the net-of-tax method be preferable?

SUMMARY

Differences in tax and financial accounting lead to differences in pretax incomes. Two kinds of differences exist: those due to permanent differences between the two methods and those due to temporary differences. These differences create a dilemma for accountants. Should they report the tax actually paid or should they attempt to accrue taxes as one might any other expense? Most accountants have settled for the latter approach and favor some form of interperiod tax allocation. This procedure involves first eliminating permanent differences from the pretax book income and then allocating taxes over the remaining temporary differences.

Two methods for doing interperiod tax allocation have gained particular favor. The deferred method which attempted to match tax expense with pretax book income was required by *APB 11*; the asset/liability method which attempts to compute the deferred tax liability directly is required by *SFAS 96*. In the latter approach, at the end of each period the tax consequences of all events occurring during the year are scheduled over the future periods which they will affect. No income or loss is assumed in these future periods so that the temporary differences themselves become the only taxable income and loss available. After carrying losses backward and forward as tax law permits, taxes are computed for each year. The taxes owing in this year are the current taxes payable; the sum of the taxes owing in future years is the deferred tax payable. In the event that a negative temporary item is carried back into the current or prior years, a deferred tax asset is possible. If a net operating loss occurs in the current year, a tax recoverable account can be established. Under these constructs, deferred tax expense (or benefit) represents the net change in the various tax-related accounts in the enterprise's balance sheet. It is always a derived number.

Many conceptual arguments for and against each method exist but the practical implications are that in most circumstances the two methods will give identical tax expense amounts. Exceptions to this general rule are the result of the *SFAS 96* mandate that tax changes be taken into account as soon as enacted and their asymmetric treatment of deferred tax losses. (A number of practical issues such as the choice of tax jurisdictions will cause further differences but these are not important here.)

The resulting tax expense is allocated among the various sections of the income statement to indicate where it was generated. The footnotes will contain an explanation of how the tax expense was computed and a reconciliation of this amount to the tax actually paid. Whether this presentation of the results along with the introduction of the alternative minimum tax by Congress will satisfy the general public that corporations are paying what they perceive to be their fair share of tax is yet to be discovered.

DISCUSSION QUESTIONS

1. Companies are often accused of keeping two sets of books. In one, they take advantage of every break in the tax code that they can to reduce their taxable income. In the other, it is claimed, they extend the lives of assets, recognize revenues as early as possible, and defer expenses in order to puff up earnings reported to shareholders. This was the situation described by Citizens for Tax Justice.[4]

Required:

Write a letter to your local newspaper explaining your position on the subject of tax allocation and why business should, or should not, be permitted to keep two sets of books.

2. Imagine you are writing a speech for your local Congressperson to deliver on the debate on an Alternative Minimum Tax. Put your case for or against the effective elimination of permanent differences.

3. (May 1985) The Primrose Company appropriately uses the deferred method of interperiod income tax allocation.

Primrose reports depreciation expense for certain machinery purchased this year using the accelerated cost recovery system (ACRS) for income tax purposes and the straight-line basis for accounting purposes. The tax deduction is the larger amount this year.

Primrose received rent revenues in advance this year. These revenues are included in this year's taxable income. However, for accounting purposes, these revenues are reported as unearned revenues, a current liability.

Required:

a. What is the theoretical basis for deferred income taxes?
b. How would Primrose determine and account for the income tax effect for the depreciation and rent? Why?

   c.   How should Primrose classify the income tax effect of the depreciation and rent on its balance sheet and income statement? Why?

   4.   (May 1982) *Part a.*
This year Lorac Company has each of the following items in its income
statement:

- Gross profits on installment sales.
- Revenues on long-term construction contracts.
- Estimated costs of product warranty contracts.
- Premiums on officers' life insurance with Lorac as beneficiary.

Required:

   a.   Under what conditions would deferred income taxes need to be
reported in the financial statement?
   b.   Specify when deferred income taxes would need to be recognized
for each of the items above, and indicate the rationale for such recognition.
   Part b.
Eneri Company's president has heard that deferred income taxes can be
variously classified in the balance sheet.

Required:

   Identify the conditions under which deferred income taxes would be
classified as a noncurrent item in the balance sheet. What justification
exists for such classification?

   5.   (May 1976) *Part a.* Income tax allocation is an integral part of
generally accepted accounting principles. The applications of intraperiod
tax allocation (within a period) and interperiod tax allocation (among
periods) are both required.

Required:

1. Explain the need for *intraperiod* tax allocation.
2. Accountants who favor *interperiod* tax allocation argue that income
   taxes are an expense, rather than a distribution of earnings. Explain
   the significance of this argument. *Do not explain the definitions of
   expense or distribution of earnings.*
3. Indicate and explain whether each of the following *independent* situations should be treated as a timing difference or a permanent difference.
   a.   Estimated warranty costs (covering a three-year warranty) are expensed for accounting purposes at the time of sale, but deducted for
   income tax purposes when incurred.
   b.   Depreciation for accounting and income tax purposes differs because of different bases of carrying the related property. The different bases are a result of a business combination treated as a pur-

chase for accounting purposes and as a tax-free exchange for income tax purposes.

c. A company properly uses the equity method to account for its 30 percent investment in another company. The investee pays dividends that are about 10 percent of its annual earnings.

4. Discuss the nature of the deferred income tax accounts and possible classifications in a company's statement of financial position.

Part b. The investment tax credit can be accounted for by one of two generally accepted methods for accounting purposes.

Required:

Identify and explain these two accounting methods for the investment tax credit. *Do not discuss income tax computations of the investment tax credit.*

6. **(May 1973)** *Part a.* In preparing financial statements a corporation is expected to follow the practice of comprehensive income tax allocation. At various times three methods of allocation have been used: the deferred method, the liability method, and the net-of-tax method.

Required:

1. Discuss the theoretical justification for interperiod income tax allocation. (Do not discuss the theoretical aspects of intraperiod tax allocation.)
2. Describe briefly each of the above three methods of tax allocation and give reasons why each method is acceptable or unacceptable.

Part b. The following differences enter into the reconciliation of financial net income and taxable income of A. P. Baxter Corp. for the current year.

1. Tax depreciation exceeds book depreciation by $30,000.
2. Estimated warranty costs of $6,000 applicable to the current year's sales have not been paid.
3. Percentage depletion deducted on the tax return exceeds cost depletion by $45,000.
4. Unearned rent revenue of $25,000 was deferred on the books, but appropriately included in taxable income.
5. A book expense of $2,000 for life insurance premiums on officers' lives is not allowed as a deduction on the tax return.
6. A $7,000 tax deduction resulted from expensing interest during construction for tax purposes while such costs were capitalized for financial reporting.
7. Gross profit of $80,000 was excluded from taxable income because Baxter had appropriately elected the installment sale method for tax reporting, while recognizing all gross profit from installment sales at the time of the sale for financial reporting.

Required:

Consider each reconciling item independently of all others, and explain whether each item would enter into the calculation of income taxes to be allocated. For any that are included in the income tax allocation calculation, explain the effect of the item on the current year's income tax expense and how the amount would be reported on the balance sheet. (Tax allocation calculations are not required.)

GRAND METROPOLITAN

Grand Metropolitan Ltd., a London-based brewery, liquor, and food corporation acquired the Ligget Group in 1980. The acquired company had $5.7 million of deferred tax liabilities in its balance sheet which, if Grand Metropolitan Ltd. had been an American company, would have appeared on the books of the consolidated company. British accounting permits companies to eliminate deferred tax liabilities if the company can demonstrate that, as a result of their capital investment plans, it is improbable that the tax will become due. This was done in this case, enabling the $5.7 million to be shown as part of the acquiring company's equity.[5]

Required:

Build a case both for and against the British method of accounting for deferred tax liabilities. Do you believe, as did the author of the article from which this case was drawn, that the results for the British are far healthier looking companies? Does this give British companies an unfair advantage over American companies?

PRIMARY SOURCES

Those interested in pursuing the issues raised in this chapter might begin by reviewing the following sources:

Beresford, D.; L. Best; P. Craig; and J. Weber. "Accounting for Income Taxes: A Review of Alternatives." *FASB Research Report* (Stamford, Conn.: FASB, 1983).

Black, Homer A. "Interperiod Allocation of Corporate Income Taxes." *Accounting Research Study No. 9* (New York: AICPA, 1966).

Financial Accounting Standards Board. *Discussion Memorandum Accounting for Income Taxes* (Stamford, Conn.: FASB, 1983).

SELECTED ADDITIONAL READINGS

Income Tax Allocation

Beresford, Dennis. "Deferred Tax Accounting Should Be Changed." *The CPA Journal*, June 1982, pp. 16–23.

Bevis, Donald J., and Raymond E. Ferry. *Accounting for Income Taxes* (New York: AICPA, 1969).

Bierman, Harold, and Thomas R. Dyckman. "New Look at Deferred Taxes." *Financial Executive,* January 1974, pp. 40ff.

Dopuch, Nicholas, and Shyam Sunder. "FASB's Statements on Objectives and Elements of Financial Accounting: A Review." *The Accounting Review*, January 1980, pp. 1–21.

Drummond, C., and S. Wigle. "Let's Stop Taking Comprehensive Allocation for Granted." *CA Magazine,* October 1981, pp. 56–61.

Hawkins, David F. "Controversial Accounting Changes." *Harvard Business Review,* March–April 1968, pp. 20–41.

Hope, Tony, and John Briggs. "Accounting Policy Making—Some Lessons from the Deferred Taxation Debate," *Accounting and Business Research,* Spring 1982, pp. 83–96.

Jeter, Debra C., and Paul K. Chaney. "A Financial Statement Analysis Approach to Deferred Taxes." *Accounting Horizons,* December 1988, pp. 41–49.

Jeter, Debra C., and Paul K. Chaney. "Accounting for Deferred Income Taxes: Simplicity? Usefulness?" *Accounting Horizons,* June 1989, pp. 6–13.

Levy, Gregory H. "'TEFRA': Its Accounting Implication." *Journal of Accountancy,* November 1982, pp. 74–82.

Maloney, David H., and Robert H. Sanborn. "Interactions between Financial and Tax Accounting Caused by the Tax Reform Act of 1986." *Accounting Horizons,* December 1988, pp. 21–28.

Moore, Carl L. "Deferred Income Tax—Is It a Liability?" *New York CPA,* February 1970, pp. 130–38.

Nair, R. D., and Jerry J. Weygandt. "Let's Fix Deferred Taxes." *Journal of Accountancy,* November 1981, pp. 87–102.

Nurnberg, Hugo. "Discounting Deferred Tax Liabilities." *The Accounting Review,* October 1972, pp. 655–65.

Revsine, Lawrence. "Some Controversy concerning Controversial Accounting Changes." *The Accounting Review,* April 1969, pp. 354–58.

Ritchie, P. C.; J. E. Rowcroft; and B. A. Trenholm. "An Analytical Basis for the Treatment of Corporate Income Tax." *Accounting Horizons,* December 1988, pp. 29–40.

Rosenfield, Paul, and William C. Dent. "No More Deferred Taxes." *Journal of Accountancy,* February 1983, pp. 44–55.

Thomas, Arthur. "The Allocation Problem: Part Two." *Studies in Accounting Research No. 9* (AAA, 1974).

Van Breda, Michael F., and Kenneth R. Ferris. "Accounting for Deferred Income Taxes: Understanding the New Approach." *Journal of Managerial Issues,* Fall 1989, pp. 76–85.

Watson, Peter L. "Accounting for Deferred Tax on Depreciable Assets." *Accounting and Business Research,* Autumn 1979, pp. 338–47.

Weber, Richard P. "Misleading Tax Figures: A Problem for Accountants." *The Accounting Review,* January 1977, pp. 172–85.

Wolk, Harry I.; Dale R. Martin; and Virginia A. Nichols. "Statement of Financial Accounting Standards No. 96: Some Theoretical Problems." *Accounting Horizons*, June 1989, pp. 1–5.

Tax Allocation—Empirical Studies

Beaver, William F., and Roland E. Dukes. "Interperiod Tax Allocation: Earnings Expectations and the Behavior of Security Prices." *The Accounting Review*, April 1972, pp. 320–22.

Beaver, William F., and Roland E. Dukes. "Interperiod Tax Allocation and Delta-Depreciation Methods: Some Empirical Results." *The Accounting Review*, July 1973, pp. 549–59.

Davidson, Sidney; S. R. Rasch; and R. L. Weil. "Behavior of the Deferred Tax Credit Account, 1973–82." *Journal of Accountancy*, October 1984, pp. 138–42.

Dawson, J. P.; P. M. Neupert; and C. P. Stickney. "Restating Financial Statements for Alternative GAAPs: Is It Worth the Effort?" *Financial Analysts Journal*, November–December 1980, pp. 38–46.

Leftwich, R. "Accounting Information in Private Markets: Evidence from Private Lending Agreements." *The Accounting Review*, January 1983, pp. 23–42.

Livingstone, John L. "Accelerated Depreciation and Deferred Taxes: An Empirical Study of Fluctuating Asset Expenditures." *Empirical Research in Accounting: Selected Studies*, 1967, Supplement to the *Journal of Accounting Research*, pp. 93–105.

Livingstone, John L. "A Behavioral Study of Tax Allocation in Electric Utility Regulation." *The Accounting Review*, July 1967, pp. 544–552.

Livingstone, John L. "Accelerated Depreciation, Tax Allocation, and Cyclical Asset Expenditures of Large Manufacturing Firms." *Journal of Accounting Research*, Autumn 1969, pp. 245–56.

Robbins, Barry P., and S. O. Swyers. "Accounting for Income Taxes: Predicting Timing Difference Reversals." *Journal of Accountancy*, September 1984, pp. 108–18.

Sharp, William M. "An Analysis of Corporate Transactions Involving Net Operating Loss Benefits." *Indiana Law Review*, 1977, pp. 981–1007.

Skekel, Ted, and C. Fazzi. "The Deferred Tax Liability: Do Capital-Intensive Companies Pay It?" *Journal of Accountancy*, October 1984, pp. 142–50.

Allocation of Carry-Backs and Carry-Forwards

Laibstain, Samuel. "New Look at Accounting for Operating Loss Carry-Forwards." *The Accounting Review*, April 1971, pp. 342–51.

Wolk, Harry I., and Michael G. Tearney. "Income Tax Allocation and Loss Carry-Forwards: Exploring Unchartered Ground." *The Accounting Review*, April 1973, pp. 292–99.

Investment Tax Credit

Moonitz, Maurice. "Some Reflections on the Investment Credit Experience." *Journal of Accounting Research*, Spring 1966, pp. 47–61.

Stamp, Edward. "Some Further Reflections on the Investment Credit." *Journal of Accounting Research*, Spring 1967, pp. 124–28.

Throckmorton, Jerry J. "Theoretical Concepts for Interpreting the Investment Credit." *Journal of Accountancy,* April 1970, pp. 45–52.

Discounting

Findlay, M. Chapman, and E. E. Williams. "Discounting Deferred Tax Liabilities: A Reply." *Journal of Business Finance and Accounting,* Winter 1981, pp. 593–97.

Lemke, Kenneth, and Paul Graul. "Deferred Taxes—An 'Explicit Cost' Solution to the Discounting Problem." *Accounting and Business Research,* Autumn 1981, pp. 309–15.

Nurnberg, Hugo. "Discounting Deferred Tax Liabilities." *The Accounting Review,* October 1972, pp. 655–65.

Stepp, James O. "Deferred Taxes: The Discounting Controversy." *Journal of Accountancy,* November 1985, pp. 98–108.

Wolk, Harry I., and M. G. Tearney. "Discounting Deferred Tax Liabilities: Review and Analysis." *Journal of Business Finance and Accounting,* Spring 1980, pp. 119–33.

ENDNOTES

1. *SFAC 1*, par. 34.
2. William H. Beaver and Roland E. Dukes, "Interperiod Tax Allocation, Earnings Expectations, and the Behavior of Security Prices," *The Accounting Review,* April 1972, pp. 302–32.
3. William H. Beaver and Roland E. Dukes, "Interperiod Tax Allocation and Delta-Depreciation Methods: Some Empirical Results," *The Accounting Review,* July 1973, pp. 549–58.
4. Craig C. Carter, "A Tax Study Business Doesn't Like," *Fortune,* November 26, 1984, p. 33.
5. Janet Bamford, "Try It, You'll Like It," *Forbes,* June 6, 1983, p. 162.

Chapter 21

Pensions

CHAPTER OBJECTIVES

After studying this chapter, you will be able to:

Contrast the economic liability of the company with the accounting liability recognized in its financial statements.

Compute the net periodic interest cost, given the various components disclosed in the financial statements of a corporation.

Apply the concepts of assets and liabilities to other situations similar to pensions, such as postretirement benefits.

CHAPTER OVERVIEW

Determining the Pension Obligation

Pensions are promises to pay amounts to retirees. The obligation is defined by the amount to be paid, the length of time over which it is expected to be paid, and the length of time before it will be paid. Uncertainties such as date of retirement, salary increases, possible death before retirement, and the expected date of death after retirement are handled by actuaries in determining the pension obligation.

Funding the Obligation

Most companies set aside monies into a pension fund to meet the pension obligations when they come due. It is common to net the value of the fund's assets against the pension obligation to arrive at a net figure. Pension plans are accordingly said to be under-, over-, or fully funded.

Accounting Liabilities

Accountants recognize only the earned portion of the total pension obligation and show this netted against the pension fund as the unfunded pension liability of the company. The change in the pension liability is the basis for computing the net periodic pension cost each year.

Pensions, until well into this century, were thought of as gratuities. Individuals served their king and country for as long as their health permitted them to do so. Once that health failed, the state provided them with a pension. The pension had little connection with what the individual had earned. It was simply a grant or a reward for good service. Today there still are owners of small businesses, homeowners, farmers, and others who treat pensions as gifts made to ease the last years of elderly and often respected servants.

The word itself has an interesting history. Before the days of refrigerators, food spoiled quickly and easily unless it was heavily salted. Salt, therefore, was an essential commodity and was paid by the Romans to their soldiers in lieu of cash wages. These salt wages give us our word *salary*. Once one retired, if one was favored, one received a fixed weight of salt on a regular basis—the amount of salt measured out has given us words like *pound avoirdupois*, a measure of weight; *pound sterling*, the value of that weight; *pendant*, the weight one hangs around one's neck; *ponder*, the weight that hangs on one's head as one thinks; and *pension*, the regular weight of salt provided in one's old age.

Much has changed since those early days. Many of those changes have been driven by the increase in life expectancy. For instance, in the United States in this century alone, life expectancy at birth has risen from 47 to 74. One result has been an increase in the population over the age of 65 in both absolute and relative terms. In 1900 it stood at 3 million. By 1980 it had climbed to 25 million. By the year 2000, the number of people over the age of 65 is expected to exceed 32 million. That means that currently about 11.5 percent of the population is in, or near, retirement as against 4 percent in 1900. Finding ways to care for this growing population of elderly citizens has become increasingly urgent. Consequently, pensions and other postretirement benefits have become more and more important.

One of the first major steps in providing security to retirees came in 1935 with the Federal Insurance Contribution Act, which created what is commonly called Social Security. This was intended to supplement people's retirement benefit plans only, but for some retirees it is their sole means of support. For the majority of Americans, though, private pension plans of many different kinds provide the bulk of the financial support.

In most of these private pension plans, until quite recently, companies simply paid pensioners out of the company's cash flow. Such plans were known as *pay-as-you-go*. One argument for this approach was that if one looked at pensions on an aggregate basis the employees of a firm would always pay for the pensioners of that firm. This works as long as employees are not outnumbered by pensioners. Another argument was that pensions were a favor, not a right. Today, given the increase in the elderly, and the sense that pensions should be part of one's normal compensation package, neither argument can be sustained.

Pension funds have replaced pay-as-you-go schemes. It is now estimated that as much as $1.2 trillion has been invested in these funds.[1] To ensure that these private pension funds were appropriately managed, Congress passed the Employee Retirement Income Security Act (ERISA), also known as the Pension Reform Act, in 1974. Compliance with the Act is encouraged by making payments into a qualified pension plan tax-deductible. Among other things, the Act recognizes that a right to a pension is earned each year of one's employment. Today, every employee in a qualified pension plan is guaranteed a pension from a firm after working for that firm for five years. The pension is said to *vest* at that point. Pension obligations can be split, therefore, into a vested and an unvested component.

Both the APB and the FASB have issued rulings on how to account for these pension obligations. The difficulty that they encountered stems from the fact that, while employee pension plans are a type of long-term commitment, they possess some special characteristics not found in other types of commitments. For one thing, they tend to be more open-ended—in many cases, companies do not know for how many years they will be obliged to make pension payments to a retiree. They are also relatively unique in being accompanied by a pension trust fund which, with the income from the investment of the fund, will be adequate to ensure continued payments under the terms of the plan. The firm itself may manage the trust fund, or the amounts funded may be transferred periodically to a trustee or agent who in turn manages the investments and makes the retirement payments. The basic accounting problems are:

1. Allocation of the pension costs to periods.
2. Reporting appropriate amounts for the rights and obligations existing at different points in time.
3. Disclosure of major terms of the plan, including the amount and timing of cash disbursements required or intended to be paid into the fund.
4. The presentation of financial statements of the fund or plan.

The chapter begins by laying out the theoretical foundations of pension accounting, namely, how to determine the economic obligation incurred in a defined benefit plan and how this is offset by a pension fund. The chapter then moves to the determination of the accounting liability and notes how political compromises resulted in a number that is complex to compute and difficult to interpret. The chapter attempts to guide the reader through the shoals of pension accounting by means of an extended example. To gain a full understanding of the complexities of the subject, it is essential to work this example.

In reading this chapter, the reader should remain aware that other postemployment benefits, known by their acronym as OPEBs, are handled both theoretically and practically virtually identically to pensions. All that the reader needs to do is substitute the word OPEB wherever the word pension appears. *SFAS 87* on pensions and *SFAS 106* on postemployment benefits are, therefore, very close.

DETERMINING THE PENSION OBLIGATION

A *pension plan* may be defined as a scheme to provide income to employees after they retire. Usually, this involves a series of payments, but the term does not exclude a lump-sum payment. The FASB did exclude, however, the payment of postretirement medical benefits from its statement on pensions. These have been treated separately, but in a manner very similar to pensions. While there are many different kinds of pensions, they all fall into one of two basic categories: defined contribution plans and defined benefit plans.

In a *defined contribution* plan, retirement income is limited to the income that can be derived from those monies set aside by the employer (and often the employee) during the working life of the employee. Typically, both employer and employee, under a defined contribution plan, will contribute a set percentage of the employee's salary to a fund which will accumulate interest over the years. On retirement, the funds so invested will buy an annuity for the now retired employee which will pay out a fixed amount each month until the death of the employee. In many cases, the annuity will also provide for the employee's spouse.

By contrast, a *defined benefit* plan promises certain amounts to the employee on retirement. For instance, the plan might state that employees will receive a pension equal to 1 percent of their final salary for each year they were with the company. Employees who had worked for 30 years for the company and ended with a salary of $40,000 would get a pension equal to 30 percent of their final salary, or $12,000 per year. The plan might go on to state that these benefits will be adjusted for inflation. Should inflation of 5 percent subsequently be experienced, that pension would rise by 5 percent to $12,600.

The key difference between the two categories is associated with risk: who bears it. In the defined contribution plan, the company (and the employee) puts money away. Whatever is available at retirement age is for the retiree to spend—however the retiree chooses. The company has no further responsibility. The retiree has to guess whether he or she will live to 100 or only to 70; how much inflation to allow for; and so on. In the defined benefit plan, these questions have to be addressed by the company, because it is the company that pays the pension until the retiree and the retiree's beneficiaries die. It follows that defined contribution plans are no more complex from the company's point of view than a savings account. Accordingly, this chapter focuses on defined benefit plans, where the difficult accounting and actuarial problems from the standpoint of the company are to be found.*

The Economic Obligation

We begin our analysis of defined benefit plans by analyzing in slightly more depth the example begun above. We do this from an economic standpoint. We examine the accounting for the obligation later.

Assume that the individual mentioned in the last paragraph has worked for 6 years, is expected to work another 24 years, and to retire with a final salary of $40,000. Assume that no inflation benefits have been promised and that the retiree is expected to live 15 years beyond retirement. Assume, further, that the discount rate appropriate to these computations is 6 percent. Then it can be shown that the expected present value of the pension at retirement is:

$$\$116,546 = 12,000 \times 9.7122$$

where 9.7122 = factor for a 15-year annuity at 6 percent per year.

The present value of that annuity today, assuming the same discount rate is:

$$\$28,787 = 116,546 \times 0.2470$$

where 0.2470 = factor for a single amount 24 years hence at 6 percent per year.

```
<--    6 years    -->*<--        24 years        -->*<--  15 years    -->
|------------------|----------------------------|------------------|
Start              Now                          Retirement          Death
                 $28,787                        $116,546
```

In diagrammatic form, the actuarial obligation appears as above. The amount of $28,787 is the actuarial obligation of the company based on

---

* The complexity is completely reversed from the individual's standpoint.

no final pay. It grows by 6 percent each year as the employee gets closer to pensionable age, when it reaches $116,546. The journal entries, were this approach in use, are simple. The entry in the first year of the pension would be:

Pension expense	28,787	
Pension obligation		28,787

Each year the company would simply add interest to the amount owed. This would be the sole pension-related expense. Thus, in the seventh year, given interest of 6 percent on $28,787, equalling $1,727, the entry would be:

Pension expense	1,727	
Pension obligation		1,727

This would increase the pension obligation to $30,514. Eventually, the obligation reaches $116,546: the sum the company has estimated it needs to pay this individual a pension over 15 years. Should the individual live longer than 15 years, the company will have to add to that pension; should the individual live less than 15 years, the company will save money. The company hopes that on average its pension promises will balance out.

Actuarial Science

Since the individual's final salary and future life span are currently unknown, the pension benefit can be an estimate only. This estimate will have to be adjusted each period until the individual retires. Also, since the pension lies in the future, the amount owed now is the present value of the amount it is estimated will be paid from the individual's retirement to the individual's death. This amount should also be adjusted by the probability that the individual will continue with the company to full retirement age. Computations of these benefits are done by highly skilled professionals known as *actuaries*. A simple example illustrates the work of actuaries.

Assume that there is a 70 percent chance that this individual will live to 80, a 10 percent chance that this individual will live to 79, and a 20 percent chance that the individual will live to 81. The company can then expect to have to pay out:

$$12,000 \times \ \ 9.2949 = \$111,539 \text{ with a } 10\% \text{ probability}$$

$$12,000 \times \ \ 9.7122 = \$116,546 \text{ with a } 70\% \text{ probability}$$

$$12,000 \times 10.1058 = \$121,270 \text{ with a } 20\% \text{ probability}$$

The expected amount that the company will pay out is therefore:

$$111,539 \times 10\% + 116,546 \times 70\% + 121,270 \times 20\% = \$116,990$$

An alternative way of deriving this same number is by attaching the probabilities to the annuity factors and then multiplying the result by $12,000, that is:

$$12,000 \times (9.2949 \times 10\% + 9.7122 \times 70\% + 10.1058 \times 20\%)$$
$$= 12,000 \times 9.74919$$

$$= \$116,990$$

The 9.74919 is the present value factor for an annuity adjusted for the possibility of death—or, as actuaries say, the annuity as adjusted for mortality.

This combination of present value factors with mortality factors is the heart of actuarial science. Actuaries keep careful statistics on births and deaths, health and illness, trends in retirement age, and so on. They must also consider, in this context, the likelihood of an individual being fired or leaving the firm for his or her own reasons. Based on these statistics, they are able to compute the appropriate adjusted present value factors to use in estimating the likelihood of retiring at the normal age and of living beyond that time. It is these factors that establish the actuarial value of the pension obligation at any point in time.

Components of the Obligation

The total pension obligation may be divided into several components that shed further light on the precise nature of pension costs. The main split is between the pension that has been earned, the pension which is currently being earned, and the pension that will be earned. To continue our earlier illustration, assume that the pension plan was adopted after an employee had been with the company for five years and that the employee was awarded an immediate pension benefit at the date of adoption of the plan equal to 5 percent of the employee's estimated final salary. The pension that the employee has *earned* at the end of the sixth year is a total of 6 percent of the employee's estimated final salary. In dollar terms, this amounts to $5,757 (= 6/30 × $28,787). This $5,757 is known as the *projected benefit obligation* (PBO). The balance of $23,030 is the unearned portion.

The earned portion can be split into two further components: the portion due to prior service and the portion due to service in the current year. For the projected benefit obligation, one has:

$$\text{Prior service costs (PSC)} = (5/6) \times 5{,}757 = \$4{,}798$$

$$\text{Current service costs (CSC)} = (1/6) \times 5{,}757 = \$\ \ 959$$

These numbers can be computed directly. For example, the portion of the projected pension obligation that is due to this year's service is:

$$\text{CSC} = 1\% \times 40{,}000 \times 9.7122 \times 0.2470 = \$959$$

and the portion that is due to prior service is:

$$\text{PSC} = 5\% \times 40{,}000 \times 9.7122 \times 0.2470 = \$4{,}798$$

Each year the employee continues with the company, the current service cost is added to the company's earned portion of the obligation. That same amount is then deducted from the future unearned portion of the obligation. In the sixth year, for instance, after taking interest into account, the earned portion will grow by $959 while the unearned portion will shrink by $959. Ultimately, at the point of retirement, the unearned portion will have shrunk to zero and the earned portion will have grown to equal the total obligation.

More specifically, the earned portion of the projected benefit obligation will grow each year by the rate of interest and by the current service cost. Formally, one has:

$$\text{PBO}_t = \text{PBO}_{t-1} (1 + i) + \text{CSC}_t$$

Thus, another way to derive the projected benefit obligation in the sixth year is to start with the obligation in the fifth year, which one can show to be $4,526. Hence:

$$\text{PBO}_6 = 4{,}526 \times 1.06 + 959$$

$$= \$5{,}757$$

Moving our attention to the seventh year, we have:

$$\text{CSC}_7 = 1\% \times 40{,}000 \times 9.7122 \times 0.2618$$

$$= \$1{,}017$$

where $0.2618 = $ factor for a single amount 23 years hence at 6 percent per year.

Note that this is 6 percent larger than the current service cost in the sixth year. It now follows that

$$\text{PBO}_7 = \text{PBO}_6 \times 1.06 + \text{CSC}_7$$

$$= 5{,}757 \times 1.06 + 1{,}017$$

$$= \$7{,}120$$

The projected benefit obligation in year seven could also have been derived by noting that the actuarial obligation at the end of year seven is 6 percent higher than the previous year, that is,

$$\$30,514 = \$28,787 \times 1.06$$

The projected benefit obligation would then be:

$$PBO_7 = (7/30) \times 30,514 = \$7,120$$

Similarly, the current service cost in year seven of \$1,017 can be derived by noting that it is one-seventh of the pension benefit obligation of \$7,120. We can summarize all the above diagrammatically as shown in Exhibit 21-1.

EXHIBIT 21-1   Accruing Pension Obligations

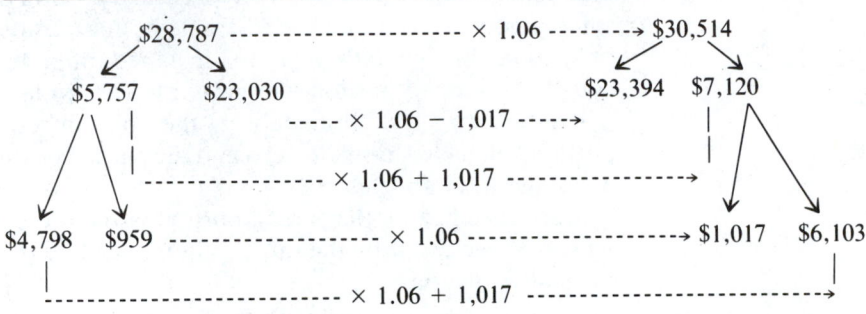

All these computations can be repeated by substituting the employee's *current* salary for the employee's estimated *final* salary. Assume that this is \$30,000. The effect is to reduce all the amounts by 75 percent in this example. The earned obligation based on current salary is known as the *accumulated benefit obligation* and may be shown in this example to be \$4,318 (= 75% × \$5,757) at the end of year six and \$5,340 (= 75% × \$7,120) at the end of year seven. Alternatively, note that at retirement the annual benefit will be 30 percent of \$30,000 or \$9,000. The total pension obligation based on current salary is, therefore:

$$ABO_6 = \$9,000 \times 9.7122 \times 0.2470 \times (6/30)$$
$$= \$21,590 \times (6/30)$$
$$= \$4,318$$

The relationship between one year and the next follows exactly the same rules as that for the projected benefit obligation. These results are summarized in Exhibit 21-2 for the end of year six.

EXHIBIT 21-2 Projected versus Accumulated Obligations

	Prior	*Current*	*Earned*	*Unearned*
Accumulated	$3,598	$720	$4,318	$17,272
Projected	$4,798	$959	$5,757	$23,030

The accumulated obligation will grow toward the projected obligation as time passes and as estimates of salary increases become realized salary increments.

CHECKPOINTS

1. What is a pension plan?
2. Why are defined contribution plans not as important for accounting theory as defined benefit plans?
3. Define, in your own words, the total pension obligation a corporation has to an employee in a defined contribution plan.
4. Distinguish the accrued benefit obligation from the projected benefit obligation.

FUNDING THE OBLIGATION

It is important to remember that the existence of an obligation does not automatically imply that there is any cash to meet that obligation. And indeed, strictly speaking, until an employee retires there is no need for cash to be set aside. However, for both tax-related reasons and as a result of rules in ERISA, most companies that provide pension benefits have established a separate pension fund into which regular payments are made, and from which pensions are drawn. The obvious question is how much to pay into the fund. Various rules, generally flowing from the various tax acts, govern the funding of prior service costs. The details of these rules are neither here nor there at this particular point. Our understanding of the nature of liabilities suggests a conceptual framework sufficient for our purpose.

At the extreme, one could argue that the company should pay into the fund an amount equal to the pension obligation. The amount this would equal would depend on the way that the pension obligation was defined. Assume first that the pension obligation was defined as the total pension benefit. Funding this entire amount would ensure sufficient money to meet all future expected pension costs.

Few companies fund their pension funds, at least not initially, to this extent. A number of actuarial methods exist to determine the appropriate size of the funding each year. At one extreme, a company could simply deposit the amount required to pay the full pension at the start of retirement. More precisely, they would deposit $116,546 over 24 years. Alternatively, a company could set aside the present value of the full amount required now so that it would accumulate to the amount required at the start of retirement. In other words, they would deposit $28,787 now. The most common method is to set amounts aside regularly, that is, to fund the pension over the working life of the employee. Two distinctly different methods illustrate the possibilities.

The first sets aside a fixed amount each year. In our example, this would be $2,294 (= $116,546 × 0.247/12.551), where 12.551 is the present value of $1 per year for 24 years and 0.247 is the present value of $1 to be received 24 years hence. The effect of this approach is that amounts set aside in early years, through the power of compound interest, provide a greater proportion of the pension than equal amounts set aside in later years. In other words:

$$2{,}294 \times (1.06)^{24} = \$9{,}288$$

$$2{,}294 \times (1.06)^{23} = 8{,}762$$

$$\cdots$$

$$2{,}294 \times (1.06) = 2{,}432$$

where $9,288 + 8,762 + . . . + 2,432 = $116,546.

The other extreme is to set aside an amount each year that will accumulate, at retirement age, to the same amount. Given 24 payments, this would mean that each year the amount should accumulate to $4,856 (= $116,546/24). This would mean smaller amounts to be set aside in early years and larger amounts in later years. In other words:

$$1{,}199 \times (1.06)^{24} = \$4{,}856$$

$$1{,}271 \times (1.06)^{23} = 4{,}856$$

$$\cdots$$

$$4{,}481 \times (1.06) = 4{,}856$$

where $4,856 + 4,856 + . . . + 4,856 = $116,546.

The methods are illustrated in Exhibit 21-3.

Variations on these methods are in actual use. The choice between them is a function of tax laws and pension laws. The key point is that the choice between them is not affected by accounting standards—nor are accounting standards affected by the choice of funding method.

EXHIBIT 21-3 Funding Possibilities

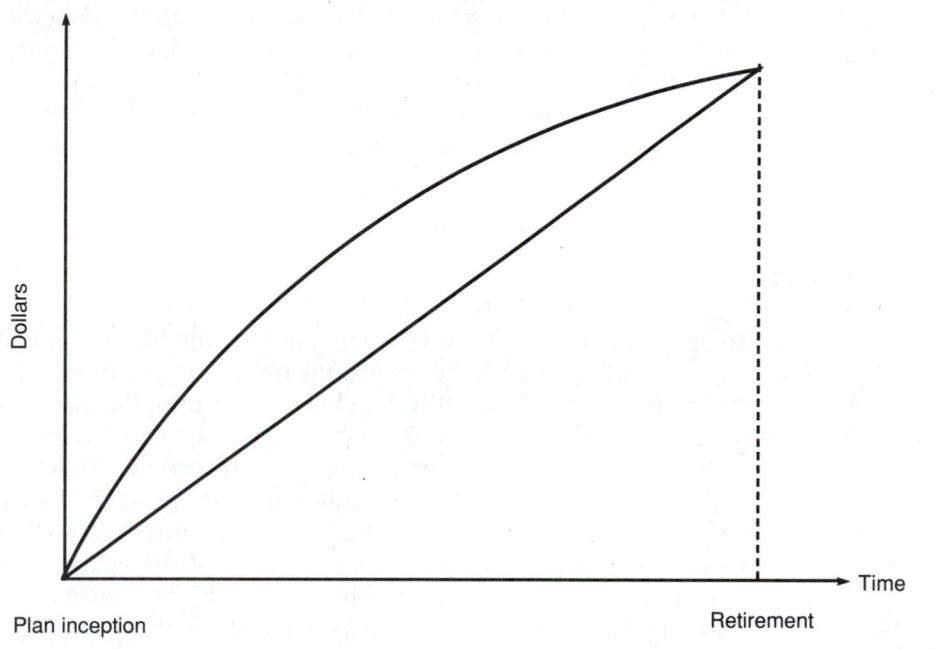

Stocks and Flows

The preceding examples have been done at the individual level. One can also look at pensions at an aggregate level. Consider first the steady state or stationary case. Here, as many people take employment with a firm each year as move into retirement. As a result, the cash paid into the pension fund by currently hired employees exactly equals the cash drawn from the fund to pay the pensions of retirees. We are then in a perfectly steady state in which, strictly speaking, we need no pension fund at all. When the streams running into a reservoir are equal to the flow of water from the reservoir, there is no need for the reservoir. The sole purpose of the reservoir is to provide a buffer in the event the inflow in a particular year is unequal to the outflow. The same is true for a pension fund.

Many have used this analogy to argue against the need for recognizing a pension liability, but this is to confuse the desirability of recognizing the obligation with the funding of that obligation. Whether that obligation is met by deductions from current employees, from the sale of stock, or from other reserves is irrelevant to the recognition of the obligation itself.

The size of the obligation is as important a piece of information as the cash flows in and out of a pension fund.

The pattern of growth also affects the total pension expense and the total funding of the pension. If one assumes a stationary company, then all methods aggregate to a constant. On the other hand, if the company is growing or declining, the different methods of funding shown in the previous section will give different aggregates. Different methods of computing the pension expense will also yield different results.

The Net Obligation

Given the existence of an investment pool to fund the pension obligation, it is common to net the fund against the obligation and to speak of the net obligation. In cases where the net obligation is zero, the plan is said to be *fully* funded. Where the obligations are greater (less) than the investments, the plan is said to be *underfunded (overfunded.)* As a practical matter, pension plans at their inception tend to be underfunded because the prior service costs are not fully funded. As time passes and the company catches up on funding the prior service costs, the plan becomes fully funded. Thereafter, whether the plan is under- or overfunded depends partly on the behavior of the investment portfolio as a function of the market and partly on how accurate the actuarial estimates were.

Fluctuations in the net obligation occur for many reasons. Rates of interest can change as a result of new estimates of expected inflation; salaries can rise unexpectedly as a result of unanticipated inflation; mortality rates can rise and fall. Each of these events falls under the heading of actuarial gains and losses. The net pension obligation should be adjusted accordingly, with the adjustments forming part of the pension expense for the period.

Summary

The economics of pensions can now be summarized quite simply. On the one side one has a pension obligation established by actuaries. On the other side one has a fund whose size is largely determined by tax and pension laws. The difference between the two is the net obligation of the company to its pensioners. Accounting for the two is relatively straightforward: the fund grows by the monies deposited into it and by interest earned; the obligation grows by additional obligations incurred and by interest incurred. Periodically, the balance needs adjusting for actuarial gains and losses. All the remaining complexities in the area are created by political compromises.

CHECKPOINTS

---

1. How do the two basic methods of funding a pension plan differ?
2. What is meant by a fully funded pension plan?
3. Explain, in your own words, why a fully funded pension plan is not necessary for a stationary company.

ACCOUNTING LIABILITIES

Since a pension plan is a form of long-term commitment, there is much merit in the capitalization of the discounted amount of the *entire* retirement benefit to employees. However, economic obligations are not necessarily accounting liabilities, either by definition, as a matter of recognition, or as a politically feasible act.

Many respondents to the FASB's call for comments on *SFAS 87* argued that no accounting liability for pensions should appear at all. Their arguments are summarized in Exhibit 21-4. Students should have enough background in accounting theory to be able to supply arguments against these positions. If in doubt one can consult the relevant paragraphs in *SFAS 87* where the FASB supplies its own counterarguments. These counterarguments were based on the FASB's definition of liabilities, discussed in Chapters 13 and 19. This stated that liabilities are:

> probable future sacrifices of economic benefits arising from present obligations of a particular entity to transfer assets or provide services to other entities in the future as a result of past transactions or events.[2]

The definition suggested to the FASB that a liability should be recognized, but the last phrase in this definition, namely that liabilities are the "result of past transactions or events," suggested to the FASB that the accounting liability should be limited to the earned portion and not include the unearned portion.

One reason for recognizing the earned portion only is that the rights under the pension plan are not unconditional. Furthermore, they represent only part of the benefits to be received from employees during their remaining years of service. The obligation under the pension plan is only a small part of the total obligation to employees for services to be performed. Therefore, since there is little justification for the capitalization of future wage commitments, there is also little justification for the capitalization of all future pension benefits and obligations.

The argument that the critical event in the establishment of a pension liability occurs when the employee earns the pension enabled the FASB

EXHIBIT 21-4   Objections to *SFAS 87*

Paragraphs	Objections
79	Pensions are a gratuity, not an obligation.
80, 87, and 109	The liability belongs to the pension fund, not to the company. Only the cash flows to the fund, not the obligation of the fund, are relevant to a company's shareholders.
103	Only the unfunded accrued expense is a liability. Only current funding is relevant to a company's shareholders. This was the position of *APB 8.*
109, 138, 143, 145	Part or all of the obligation lies in the future and is, therefore, not an accounting liability. Specifically, future contributions (109), future salary increases (138), final pay (143), and plan amendments (145) are not present obligations.
111	The liability should be examined at a fund level. At this level, the obligation can be met from the fund without need of establishing a liability. This is the stationary argument discussed above under funding.
116	The cost of providing this information greatly exceeds its benefits.
120	The obligation induces too much volatility in accounting earnings. This obscures the current operating performance of the company.
146	The liability cannot be measured reliably.
148	Only the vested portion is a liability.

to fend off the argument that only the vested obligation should be recognized. The FASB argued that the legal date of vesting serves merely to confirm an event which in substance occurred some years before. The Pension Reform Act of 1974 encourages one to take this view. Following this line of reasoning, accountants ignore the distinction between vested and nonvested benefits.

The definition of a liability provides less help on how to treat future salary increases, an issue which split the Board. The minority argued that these should be excluded since they are events which have yet to occur. The majority countered that pensions that are based upon a person's final pay include an implicit promise, already made, to pay an amount that assumes salary increases. So those salary increases should not be ignored when computing current service costs. The majority then bent to the minority by allowing companies to exclude salary increases when computing the minimum liability to be shown in the balance sheet.

Prior Service Costs

Even limiting the obligation to the earned portion was too much for many companies to handle. They argued that the FASB should not require employers to show the previously earned obligation immediately—if at all. The immediate justification for this was the size of the earned obligation. A more theoretical justification was provided by the nature of expenses. All agree that expenses should represent the cost of benefits received in a period. However, so the argument goes, the charge to retained earnings or to current income of the *prior service costs* as either an operating charge or an extraordinary item is not an expense of this period, because these costs will benefit both this and future periods. Furthermore, since there was no benefit received by the firm in the prior periods, it cannot be a correction of prior years' income. And since the firm hopes to enjoy better employee relations in the future, there is no loss or gain to be recognized when the plan is adopted. Thus, one concludes that prior service costs should be amortized over future periods.

Part of the problem in dealing with the concept of prior service costs is that the name is a misnomer. It is really just an unallocated cost that emerges from the way the pension benefits of an employee have been computed. Consider, by way of illustration, one of the other actuarial cost methods that exist. Take one that assumes all the benefits accrue from the inception of the plan not, as we did, from when the employee would have been eligible. In such a method, no prior service cost arises; the entire projected cost, less the assumed interest on the pension fund, is allocated over the period after the inception of the plan. The result is that total normal pension costs will be greater for several years after starting the plan than after the plan matures because the costs per year for employees who have been with the firm for many years will be greater than the costs allocated to new or younger employees.

Others have taken these arguments further and suggested that there should be no recognition of the prior service costs at all. This argument is based on the assumption that, if the plan is to continue indefinitely into the future, the accrual of normal costs plus interest on unfunded prior service costs will be adequate at all times to provide for current retirement benefits. But this is a confusion of the costs of a retirement plan and the funds necessary to carry out the plan. The costs do exist even though full funding may not be necessary from a financial point of view.

The above arguments are based on the centrality of the income statement and on a desire to make the income statement articulate with the balance sheet. An alternative argument begins with the balance sheet and notes that at the inception or the subsequent revision of the plan, the prior service costs are part of the pension obligation. Full disclosure of this amount should be made to users of financial statements. The preceding arguments that suggest nonrecognition of the obligation or the allocation of the prior service cost over arbitrary periods appear to have as their real objective the smoothing of net income. The results may be politically acceptable, but they lead to semantically unintelligible results.

Unfortunately, the FASB was unable to persuade its constituents of the virtues of full and immediate recognition of economic realities. *SFAS 87*, therefore, permits corporations to amortize the prior service costs over the average remaining period of employment of the employees. Alternative amortization schemes are permitted provided they lead to swifter amortization. The prior service costs that are amortized are based on the projected benefit obligation. To ensure that amortization does not produce too small a liability number, the FASB requires that the pension liability be the accumulated benefit obligation as a minimum.

Periodic Pension Costs

The complications that have ensued from the compromises the FASB felt constrained to make are best explained by continuing the example used earlier to explain the economics of pensions. That example, it will be recalled, showed a total actuarial obligation of $28,787 at the end of year six. The projected benefit obligation was $5,757 at that point. The current service cost in that year was $959 ($5,757/6). The accumulated obligation was $4,318 ($5,757 × 0.75).

The Board decided unanimously to recognize only the earned portion of the pension obligation. A majority on the Board decided that the projected benefit obligation was the most appropriate amount to recognize as an accounting liability. The growth in the projected benefit obligation from one year to the next was defined as the basic pension expense—the Board preferred the term *periodic pension cost*. As we have already shown, in year seven the projected obligation grew to $7,120 with a current service cost of $1,017 and an interest cost of $345 (6% of $5,757). The periodic pension cost, therefore, totals $1,362 ($1,017 + 345). This yields the journal entry:

Pension expense	1,362	
Pension liability		1,362

This was fine for the second year of the plan onward, but what did one do about the first year? The Board felt that bringing the entire $5,757 onto the balance sheet in one fell swoop would be too dramatic. The Board, therefore, permitted the prior service cost portion, $4,798 in this example, to be amortized over the average remaining service life of the employees.

This would be 24 years in this example. To shorten the example, we will assume a two-year amortization policy! This produces an additional pension expense of $2,399 ($4,798/2) for two years. In other words, the periodic pension cost in the two years now totals:

$$\text{Year } 6 = \$3,358 = \$\ \ 959 + \quad 0 + 2,399$$

$$\text{Year } 7 = \$3,761 = \$1,017 + 345 + 2,399$$

The journal entry in year seven would be:

Pension expense	3,761	
Pension liability		3,761

Or, if one wanted to write this out more fully:

Current service cost	1,017	
Interest costs	345	
Amortization of prior period costs	2,399	
Pension liability		3,761

Similarly, the full entry for year six would be:

Current service cost	959	
Amortization of prior period costs	2,399	
Pension liability		3,358

The pension liability at the end of year seven is, therefore, $7,119 or $3,358 plus $3,761. Allowing for rounding error, the pension liability at the end of year two, because of the choice of a two-year amortization period, equals the projected benefit obligation, shown earlier to be $7,120.

The pension liability at the end of each year, per *SFAS 87,* is then subject to the accumulated benefit obligation (ABO) as a minimum. The ABO at the end of year six, as noted above, is $4,318. A further amount of $960 ($4,318 − 3,358) must be recognized in year six, therefore. The FASB recommends that this be done by the creation of an intangible asset.

Intangible asset (4,318 − 3,358)	960	
Pension liability		960

Many have criticized this intangible asset as lacking substance and of being confusing. Its sole virtue appears to be that it enables the balance sheet to articulate with the income statement.

A similar procedure occurs at the end of year seven when the pension liability, as a result of the two journal entries above, equals $7,119. The accumulated earned obligation at this point is 75 percent of the projected benefit obligation or $5,340. The ABO in year seven is less than the pension liability, therefore. The alternative minimum liability, therefore, is no longer required and an entry to reverse the intangible asset and the minimum from last year is made:

Pension liability	960	
Intangible asset		960

Note again that $7,120 is the projected benefit obligation at the end of year seven. In other words, what the example also shows is that the accounting liability for pensions will equal the projected benefit obligation when the prior service costs are fully amortized. Getting to the point of equality, though, is made unnecessarily complicated by the need to accommodate various political realities. In that transition phase, the accounting liability has little semantic content. It is determined largely by syntactics. In practice, this period in which relatively meaningless pension numbers are being presented to the public can last 20 years or more.

Adjustments

The preceding example assumes that $7,120 is the correct projected benefit obligation at that point. Stated otherwise, it is possible that interest rate changes, or changes in mortality experience, or any of a myriad of other factors might have led actuaries to conclude that the real projected liability at this point was something other than $7,120. The simplest way of dealing with this is to adjust to the new figure by including these so-called actuarial gains and losses in the pension expense number.

Companies complained that there was the potential that these actuarial gains would cause net income to fluctuate by amounts unacceptably large to management. There is no empirical evidence that shareholders are disturbed by these fluctuations, however. To the extent that they affect the beta of a company's shares, prices seem to adjust quite normally. Nevertheless, management finds the potential fluctuations unacceptable. A complex corridor system was therefore established in which actuarial gains and losses would not be included until they were large enough to break outside this corridor. The corridor was defined as 10 percent of the greater of the projected benefit obligation and the value of the plan assets. At the point at which the gain or losses broke through this corridor, the excess would be amortized over the average remaining service lives of employees to bring the syntactically defined pension obligation in line with the semantically defined obligation. Since this procedure lacks all theoretical merit, it is not further analyzed here.

CHECKPOINTS

1. Define the term *prior service costs*.
2. Define the term *current service cost*.
3. What are the four components of the net periodic pension cost?

Offsetting

As already noted, it is common practice to offset whatever pension liability is recognized by the funds available to meet it. The basis for this practice is partly historical. Until *SFAS 87*, no liability of the pension fund was recognized in the books of the sponsoring company. The argument for this was that the fund was responsible for all pension obligations. The company, it was claimed, was responsible only for paying into the fund an amount equal to the current service cost plus a portion of the unfunded prior service cost. These two amounts constituted the company's pension expense. Should the company not have paid into the fund the full pension expense, it recognized a pension fund liability for the difference. The liability was to the fund, though, and not to the retiree.

This ability to offset the pension liability against the assets of the fund has continued into *SFAS 87*. The result is that, in the body of the financial statements of the company, a net liability will appear only in the event that the assets of the fund are less than the pension obligation. If the assets are greater than or equal to the pension obligation, no (net) pension liability will appear in the books of the company.

As a result of netting the pension fund against the pension obligation, the return earned on the fund is also netted against the pension expense incurred in building up the pension obligation. In some cases, the interest on the fund exceeds the pension expense, giving rise to pension income. In the extreme, if the fund equals the obligation and if the interest earned on the fund equals the expenses incurred in the plan, a company will show neither pension expense nor a net pension liability. Vast sums of money may have been transmitted to a giant pension plan, but no track of it will remain in the financial statements.

Net Pension Liabilities

The points being made here regarding funding and its interaction with expensing are best illustrated by continuing the chapter's numerical example. Recall first that the funding is determined by ERISA and the IRS; its determination has nothing to do with accountants. Now assume funding at $3,000 per year beginning in year six, so that:

$$\text{Pension fund at end of year } 6 = \$3,000$$

$$\text{Pension fund at end of year } 7 = \$3,000 \times 1.06 + 3,000$$

$$= \$6,180$$

Now consider how this funding interacts with the liability. In other words, consider the netting that *SFAS 87* permits. At the end of year 6, there is an asset of $3,000 and an accrued pension liability, as shown previously, of $3,358. Other things being equal, the company will show a net unfunded accrued liability or cost in the amount of $358.

An examination of the accumulated earned obligation at this point revealed that it stood at $4,318. The FASB requires that a minimum net liability in the amount of $1,318 ($4,318 − 3,000) be recorded. To achieve all this, the company is required to put through three entries. The first records the pension expense:

Net pension expense	3,358	
Net pension liability		3,358

The second records the funding:

Net pension liability	3,000	
Cash		3,000

To that net pension liability must now be added $960 to bring the net pension liability up to the required $1,318. The FASB recommends that this be done by the creation of an intangible asset.

Intangible asset (1,318 − 358)	960	
Net pension liability		960

This journal entry is identical to the one shown in the previous section where pension liabilities were shown on a gross basis.

A similar procedure occurs at the end of year seven when the pension fund has assets of $6,180 and the pension liability stands at $7,119, leaving a net unfunded pension liability of $939. The accumulated benefit obligation is $5,340, which is now fully funded so an alternative minimum liability is not required. An entry to reverse the intangible asset and the minimum pension liability from last year is required:

Net pension liability	960	
Intangible asset		960

A second entry is required to record the payment of $3,000 into the pension fund.

Net pension liability	3,000	
Cash		3,000

This sets the net pension liability account to a debit balance of $2,642 ($3,000 − 358). A third entry is required, therefore, to bring the net pension liability back up to $939. This entry defines the pension expense.

Pension expense (939 + 2,642)	3,581	
Net pension liability		3,581

Writing this out more fully:

Current service cost	1,017	
Interest costs	345	
Amortization of prior period costs	2,399	
Cash		3,000
Return on fund		180
Net pension liability		581

The net pension liability is also termed the *unfunded accrued liability*.

Disclosure

Pensions are inherently complex. Inevitably, then, it is necessary to make supplemental disclosures in the footnotes to explain the details. Such descriptions should disclose at a minimum the extent to which the pension plan is being funded, including an amount for prior service costs if the actuarial method used treats them separately. Furthermore, the annual cash disbursements required or expected to be made into the pension fund should be disclosed in cash flow or funds flow statements or in footnotes to the financial statements. The FASB mandated the following disclosures:

a. A description of the plan including employee groups covered, type of benefit formula, funding policy, types of assets held and significant nonbenefit liabilities, if any, and the nature and effect of significant matters affecting comparability of information for all periods presented.

b. The amount of net periodic pension cost for the period showing separately the service cost component, the interest cost component, the actual return on assets for the period, and the net total of other components.

c. A schedule reconciling the funded status of the plan with amounts reported in the employer's statement of financial position, showing separately:
1. The fair value of plan assets.
2. The projected benefit obligation identifying the accumulated benefit obligation and the vested benefit obligation.
3. The amount of unrecognized prior service cost.
4. The amount of unrecognized net gain or loss (including asset gains and losses not yet reflected in market-related value).
5. The amount of any remaining unrecognized net obligation or net asset existing at the date of initial application of this Statement.
6. The amount of net pension asset or liability recognized in the statement of financial position . . . (which is the net result of combining the preceding six items).

    d. The weighted-average assumed discount rate and rate of compensation in-crease (if applicable) used to measure the projected benefit obligation and the weighted average expected long-term rate of return on plan assets.

    e. If applicable, the amounts and types of securities of the employer and related parties included in plan assets, and the approximate amount of annual bene-fits of employees and retirees covered by annuity contracts issued by the employer and related parties. Also, if applicable, the alternative amortiza-tion methods used. . . .[3]

The level of disclosure is quite extraordinary, enabling the sophisticated reader to make many adjustments. However, as the FASB itself has stated, footnote disclosure is no substitute for correct recognition in the first place.

CHECKPOINTS

1. Distinguish the gross pension liability from the net pension liability.
2. How, if at all, is funding related to expensing?
3. Where, if at all, is the projected pension benefit obligation disclosed?
4. Where, if at all, is the accumulated pension benefit obligation disclosed?
5. In what circumstances will a net pension liability appear in a financial statement?

SUMMARY

Pension accounting is a magnificent example of all that is right and wrong with accounting. On the side of right, there is the careful handling of present values and the continued evolution of the standard as understand-ing of pension accounting develops. On the negative side, there are all the political compromises that have taken what was a relatively straightfor-ward economic exercise and turned it into a complex and, at times, ob-scure set of accounting requirements.

SFAS 87 begins well enough with its definitions of pension obligations and the funds to support those obligations. Unfortunately, the balance of the statement consists of a series of practical compromises. Constituents felt, without providing evidence, that users would be dismayed if the entire obligation were to appear on the company's financial statements all at once. The FASB obliged, therefore, by allowing the obligation for prior service to be added to over time. Constituents also felt, and again without providing evidence, that users would be dismayed by the potential volatil-ity. The FASB obliged, therefore, by allowing smoothing.

It is questionable whether these complexities add understanding. The basic notion, as we have seen, is quite straightforward. An obligation is earned and, based upon final terms, monies are paid into a fund. The difference is the unfunded portion of the pension obligation. The fund grows by contributions and interest and declines by pensions paid. The obligation grows by interest and service rendered and declines by pensions and deaths. This much is simple to understand and comparable from one corporation to another. It is sad that corporate politics have forced complexities which obfuscate the situation.

The arguments made in favor of permitting corporations to hold such power over standard setters suggest that to do otherwise would affect their economic interests. This misses the point, though. There is a national interest in disclosing the full extent of all obligations. There is often an individual interest in hiding these facts. In situations like these the national interest should override the interest of individual managers in concealing the parlous state into which they may have driven their companies.

MULTIPLE CHOICE QUESTIONS

1. [M89#35] An employer sponsoring a defined benefit pension plan should disclose the

	Amount of Unrecognized Prior Service Cost	Projected Benefit Obligation
a.	Yes	Yes
b.	Yes	No
c.	No	No
d.	No	Yes

2. [N87#36] An employer sponsoring a defined benefit pension plan should

a. Disclose the projected benefit obligation, identifying the accumulated benefit obligation and the vested benefit obligation.

b. Disclose the projected benefit obligation, identifying the accumulated benefit obligation but *not* the vested benefit obligation.

c. Disclose the projected benefit obligation, identifying the vested benefit obligation but *not* the accumulated benefit obligation.

d. Not disclose the projected benefit obligation.

DISCUSSION QUESTIONS

1. (May 1978, amended) The accounting for prior service cost has been a controversial issue. Some members of the profession advocate the accrual of prior service cost only to the extent funded, and others advocate the accrual of past service cost regardless of the amount funded.

Required:

a. What are the arguments in favor of accruing prior service cost only to the extent funded?

b. What are the arguments in favor of accruing prior service cost regardless of the amount funded?

2. (May 1976, amended) *Part a.*

Pension plans have developed in an environment characterized by a complex interaction of social concepts, legal considerations, actuarial techniques, income tax laws, and accounting principles. *SFAS 87* delineates acceptable accounting practices for the cost of pension plans.

Required:

a. The following terms are relevant to accounting for the cost of pension plans. Define or explain briefly each of the following:

1. Net periodic pension cost
2. Current service cost
3. Prior service cost
4. Funded plan
5. Vested benefits
6. Actuarial gains and losses
7. Interest

b. Identify the disclosures required in financial statements regarding a company's pension plan.

Part b.

Liberty, Inc., a calendar-year corporation, adopted a company pension plan at the beginning of 1988. This plan is to be funded and noncontributory. Liberty used an appropriate actuarial cost method to determine that its current service cost for 1988 and 1989 was $15,000 and $16,000, respectively, which was paid in the same year.

Liberty's actuarially determined prior service costs were funded on December 31, 1988 at an amount properly computed as $106,000. These prior service costs are to be amortized over five years. The interest factor assumed by the actuary is 6 percent.

Required:

Prepare journal entries to record the funding of prior service costs on December 31, 1988 and the pension expenses for the years 1988 and 1989. Under each journal entry give the reasoning to support your entry. Round to the nearest dollar.

3. Many accountants were critical of the FASB's proposals for reporting on pensions. Some samples of their criticisms follow.

A. Coopers & Lybrand produced a supplement to their Executive Alert in June 1985 entitled Pension Accounting: An Analysis of the FASB Exposure Draft. Among their criticisms were the following comments found on page 24:

> We believe that the unfunded accumulated benefit obligation is not an accounting liability. Our view is founded on these arguments:
>
> Employer pension accounting should be based on a company's responsibility toward its work force—an obligation to make adequate annual contributions to the plan—rather than on recognition of a liability to individual employees.
>
> The determination of prior service cost or the unfunded actuarial liability is an actuarial technique used to allocate future pension costs. The terms, as used by actuaries, are not meant to define an accounting liability, but are used to determine the amounts of future contributions.
>
> A company's pension plans should be viewed as executory contracts, similar to other employee compensation arrangements. Accordingly, we believe that the cost of plan amendments, referred to as prior service cost, is given in exchange for future employee services, not for past services rendered.

B. Peat Marwick in their *Executive Newsletter* dated December 26, 1983, agreed with Coopers & Lybrand, arguing that the pension obligation did not "meet the board's own definition of a liability." In addition, they said:

> The board's proposals, if adopted, would confuse many readers of financial statements. The amounts to be reported on the balance sheet would be complex; an involved explanatory footnote would be required; the volume of information given would be disproportionate to other data in the financial statements in terms of relevance; and the information might tend to obscure other important information.

C. Deloitte Haskins+Sells in their newsletter *The Week in Review* dated September 30, 1983 announced that their firm had concluded that the Board:

> Should not issue a pension accounting standard that would require an employer to recognize the actuarial present value of accumulated plan benefits as a liability in its balance sheet.

They added that:

> In developing the tentative conclusions in the Preliminary Views, the Board has relied heavily on the asset and liability view of earnings. This reliance is evi-

denced by the emphasis given to defining the pension benefit obligation and to evaluating that obligation in relation to the definition of a liability in [*SFAC 6*], and by the decision to measure periodic pension cost based on the change during the period in the net pension liability. This approach is a substantial departure from the emphasis in present practice on the revenue and expense view of earnings.

D. Ernst & Whinney supported the views of the other firms in its comments on Pension Accounting dated 1983. It also disagreed with the Board's decision to impose a single method on expense measurement, saying:

> We see a significant advantage of present practice—pension expense generally is the same as cash flow because most companies fund the amount of expense determined under their actuarial cost method. Assessing future cash flows, *a primary objective of financial reporting*, is significantly easier under current practice (particularly if disclosure requirements are expanded) than it would be if all companies use the same method of determining expense but many use different methods for funding.

Required:

In each case, you are asked to state whether you agree or disagree, stating why. You should also comment, where appropriate, on whether the fears, explicit or implicit, in the criticism have been realized.

4. Some of the more visible users of financial reporting are the organizations who rate the bonds issued by companies. Using financial and other data, they regularly evaluate the debt issues of companies in terms of their risk. In a move that was labeled as highly unusual, one of the major bond rating agencies, Standard & Poors, announced that it would ignore any proposal by the Financial Accounting Standards Board to recognize postretirement medical benefits on the balance sheet. In an article appearing in *The Wall Street Journal,* "Mr. Sprinzen, an assistant vice-president for corporate finance for S&P, said that 'the FASB approach could result in huge distortions to finance statements in the most extreme cases, severely reducing operating earnings, giving rise to liabilities that could dwarf other financial liabilities on the balance sheet, and substantially eroding equity.' "

He went on to say that "the FASB's approach is 'flawed, due to the highly speculative assumptions that would be necessary' to accrue insurance expense, setting up a reserve for the retiree's medical expenses. S&P said if the proposal is adopted, S&P would 'reverse the accounting changes.' "[4]

Required:

a. Compare and contrast Mr. Sprinzen's concerns with those expressed almost a decade earlier regarding the recognition of pension obligations.

b. What impact do you think the rejection of an accounting standard by a major organization, like Standard & Poors, has on the FASB?

c. If the FASB is simply giving recognition to an already existing economic obligation, how can Mr. Sprinzen justify his position?

d. Are statements like *SFAS 87* and *SFAS 106* neutral? [Hint: Reexamine the meaning of the word *neutral* in Chapter 5.]

PRIMARY SOURCES

Those interested in pursuing the topics raised in this chapter in more depth might begin by consulting the following texts.

Allen, Everett T., Jr.; Joseph J. Melone; and Jerry S. Rosenbloom. *Pension Planning* (Homewood, Ill.: Richard D. Irwin Series in Insurance and Economic Activity, 5th ed., 1984).

Financial Accounting Standards Board. *FASB Discussion Memorandum: An Analysis of Issues Related to Employers' Accounting for Pensions and Other Postemployment Benefits* (FASB, 1982).

Miller, P. B. W. "The New Pension Accounting (Part I)." *Journal of Accountancy,* January 1987, pp. 98–109.

Miller, P. B. W. "The New Pension Accounting (Part II)." *Journal of Accountancy,* February 1987, pp. 86–95.

SELECTED ADDITIONAL READINGS

Conceptual Framework

Accountants International Study Group. *Accounting for Pension Costs* (AIS Group, 1977).

Danker, Harold; Michael P. Glinsky; John H. Grady; Murray B. Hirsch; and Richard M. Steinberg. *Employer Accounting for Pension Costs and Other Post-Retirement Benefits* (Financial Executives Research Foundation, 1981).

Dewhirst, John F. "A Conceptual Approach to Pension Accounting." *The Accounting Review,* April 1971, pp. 365–73.

Financial Accounting Standards Board. "Accounting for the Cost of Pension Plans Subject to the Employee Retirement Income Security Act of 1974." *FASB Interpretation No. 3,* 1974.

Financial Accounting Standards Board. *FASB Discussion Memorandum: An Analysis of Issues Related to Accounting and Reporting for Employee Benefit Plans* (FASB, 1975).

Financial Accounting Standards Board. *Preliminary Views of the Financial Accounting Standards Board on Major Issues Related to Employers' Accounting for Pensions and Other Postemployment Benefits* (FASB, 1982).

Financial Accounting Standards Board. *FASB Discussion Memorandum: An Analysis of Additional Issues Related to Employers' Accounting for Pensions and Other Postemployment Benefits* (FASB, 1983).

Financial Accounting Standards Board. "Disclosure of Postretirement Health Care and Life Insurance Benefits." *SFAS 81* (FASB, 1984).

Financial Accounting Standards Board. "Employers' Accounting for Settlements and Curtailments of Defined Benefit Pension Plans and for Termination Benefits." *SFAS 87* (FASB, 1985).

Financial Accounting Standards Board. *Preliminary Views—A Field Test: Employers' Accounting for Pensions* (FASB, 1983).

Hall, William D., and David L. Landsittel. *A New Look at Accounting for Pension Costs* (Homewood, Ill.: Richard D. Irwin, 1977).

Hicks, Ernest L. "Accounting for the Cost of Pension Plans." *Accounting Research Study No. 8. AICPA* (1965).

Smith, Jack L. "Actuarial Cost Methods—Basics for CPA's." *Journal of Accountancy,* February 1977, pp. 62–66.

Empirical Studies

Bodie, Z., and J. Shoven, eds. *Financial Aspects of the U.S. Pension System* (National Bureau of Economic Research, 1983).

Bulow, Jeremy. "What Are Corporate Pension Liabilities?" *Quarterly Journal of Economics,* August 1982, pp. 435–52.

Clark, Hal G., and Leonard Lorensen. *Illustrations of Accounting for Pensions and for Settlements and Curtailments of Defined Benefit Pension Plans* (AICPA, 1987).

Daley, Lane Alan. "The Valuation of Reported Pension Measures for Firms Sponsoring Defined Benefit Pension Plans." *The Accounting Review,* April 1984, pp. 177–98.

Deaton, William C., and Jerry J. Weygandt. "Disclosures Related to Pension Plans." *Journal of Accountancy,* January 1975, pp. 44–51.

Dhaliwal, Dan S. "Measurement of Financial Leverage in the Presence of Unfunded Pension Obligations." *The Accounting Review,* October 1986, pp. 651–61.

Feldstein, Martin, and Stephanie Seligman. "Pension Funding, Share Prices, and National Savings." *Journal of Finance,* September 1981, pp. 801–24.

Francis, Jere R. "Lobbying against Proposed Accounting Standards: The Case of Employers' Pension Accounting." *Journal of Accounting and Public Policy,* Spring 1987, pp. 35–57.

Francis, Jere R., and Sara Ann Reiter. "Determinants of Corporate Pension Funding Strategy." *Journal of Accounting and Economics,* March 1987, pp. 35–59.

Hamdallah, Ahmed El-Sayed, and William Ruland. "The Decision to Terminate Overfunded Pension Plans." *Journal of Accounting and Public Policy,* Summer 1986, pp. 77–92.

Leo, Mario; Preston C. Basset; and Ernest S. Kachline. *Financial Aspects of Private Pension Plans* (Financial Executives Research Foundation, 1975).

Moonitz, Maurice, and Alexander Russ. "Accrual Accounting for Employers' Pension Costs." *Journal of Accounting Research,* Autumn 1966, pp. 155–63.

Stone, Mary, and Robert W. Ingram. "The Effect of 'Statement No. 87' on Financial Reports of Early Adopters." *Accounting Horizons,* September 1988, pp. 48–61.

ENDNOTES

1. "How Safe Is Your Pension?" *Fortune*, October 27, 1986, p. 52.
2. *SFAC 6*, par. 35.
3. *SFAS 87*, par. 54.
4. Lee Berton, "S&P Will Ignore Proposed FASB Rule Raising Firms' Deductions for Retirees," *The Wall Street Journal*, September 5, 1989, p. A11.

Chapter 22

Ownership Equities

CHAPTER OBJECTIVES

After studying this chapter, you will be able to:

Distinguish between proprietary, entity, residual, enterprise, and fund theories of equity.

Justify the appropriate treatment of owners' equity using equity theories.

Do a simple consolidation of two companies, explaining the basic method in use.

CHAPTER OVERVIEW

Nature of Equities

Equities are essentially an individual's fair share in an enterprise. Their precise nature has been the subject of much debate and has produced a number of theories.

Classifying Equities

A number of classifications are possible within the category of owners' equity. Which elements should be displayed is determined in large measure by one's choice of theory regarding the nature of equity.

Consolidated Financial Statements

When one company takes a majority ownership position in another, the parent company is required to consolidate its financial statements with those of the subsidiary. Ideally, the consolidation method used would be consistent with one's preferred theory of equity.

The rights of owners of business firms are many and varied, but those rights of greatest interest to accountants are the rights to share in the cash or property distributions of the firms, the residual rights to assets in the case of final liquidation, and the equity (proprietary) rights in a going concern—the right to sell or transfer all equity rights in the enterprise. The disclosure of these economic rights and any abridgment of them is an important objective in the presentation of financial statements.

In this chapter, the nature of ownership equities is explored and viewed from the perspective of several equity theories—the proprietary theory, the entity theory, the residual equity concept, the enterprise theory, and the funds theory. Each of the several equity theories interprets the economic position of the enterprise in a different way and thus presents a different emphasis on the method of disclosure of the interests of the several equity holders or interested groups. They also lead to different concepts of income or different methods of disclosing the equity interests in the income of the enterprise. The different concepts lead to two main questions:

1. Who are the beneficiaries of net income?
2. How should the equity relationships be shown in the financial statements?

These questions are closely related to the objectives of accounting.

There is some evidence that the proprietary concept requires an emphasis on current valuations of assets, that the entity and funds theories are neutral with respect to asset valuation, and that the enterprise theory emphasizes the need for a market output valuation concept. However, it will be argued that the associated valuation method and the associated concept of income are primarily the result of the way the several concepts have been developed. If one accepts this argument, then the problem of valuation and the most relevant concept of income are basically independent of the equity theory selected.

The objectives and logic of the classification of partnership and stockholder equities are then discussed in the general framework of the various equity theories. The classification of equities in consolidated statements concludes this chapter. The next chapter is concerned with changes in the composition of stockholder equities due to stock dividends and treasury stock. Changes arising from business combinations and the potential dilutive effect of convertible securities and warrants are also treated in the next chapter.

THE NATURE OF EQUITIES

The term *equity* has a variety of meanings. It derives from the same root as the word equal and came to have the connotation of fairness. In other words, equity can be interpreted as one's fair share. In the case of people who lend money to a corporation, they gain a fair share in the assets of that corporation. Many use the term equity to cover all who lend money to a corporation. They see the fundamental equation of accounting to be:

$$\text{Assets} = \text{Equities}$$

They would speak, therefore, of creditors' equity and owners' equity as two kinds of equity. Others use the term equity in a narrower sense to cover only owners' equity and refer to creditors' equity as liabilities. They see the fundamental equation of accounting to be:

$$\text{Assets} = \text{Liabilities} + \text{Equities}$$

Still others seem to equate equity with the interests of common stockholders.

All this might seem like semantics, but with the explosion in hybrid securities, such as convertible bonds that are neither liabilities nor owners' equity, it is increasingly difficult to classify various securities. One solution might be to return to the broader usage and simply acknowledge that there is a spectrum of equity holders, each of whose rights vary slightly. These rights can be described in terms of the time to maturity, the nature of the period payments, the nature of the final payment (if any), the extent to which the equity holder shares in the profits of the company, and the extent to which the equity holder can participate in the management of the company. These are summarized in Exhibit 22-1, where the shading indicates that the equity has the feature, while the partly shaded area indicates that it has the feature in part. In what follows we focus our attention on the traditional definition of owners' equity.

Owners' Equities

Individual assets and liabilities of a business enterprise can be defined and measured independently of other elements in the accounting equation. This is not so with *owners' equities,* also commonly known as *proprietorship* or *stockholder equities* in a corporation.* Owners' equities are simply the difference between the assets of the corporation and its liabilities. These are often termed the *net assets* of the corporation.

Owners' equity is traditionally split into two categories, *invested capital* (also called *contributed* or *paid-in capital*) and retained earnings. Invested capital also includes capitalized retained earnings. The invested capital is traditionally split into two further categories, the *capital stock,* which includes both the common and the preferred stock at the par or stated value, and the *paid-in capital in excess of par,* which may be

---

* An absence of an independent definition also affects hybrid securities such as convertible stock, because they are partly owners' equities.

EXHIBIT 22-1   Key Features of Traditional and Newer Market Instruments[1]

	Fixed maturity	Fixed rate	Guaranteed principal	Profit participation	Management control	Known maturity value
Bank deposit	■	■	■			■
Bond	■	■				■
Preferred		▨				
Convertible	■	▨		■		■
Equity				■	■	
Warrant	■			■		
Certificate of deposit (CD)	■	▨				■
Convertible preferred	■	▨		■		■
Floating-rate preferred						
Floating-rate note (FRN)	■					■
Warrant bond	■	■		■		■
Indexed bond	■	▨				
Puttable equity	■			■	■	■
Perpetual		▨				

broken out according to source. Shares repurchased by a company are typically segregated in an account labeled *treasury stock.*

Generally there is no pretense that owners' equities, as presented in the balance sheet, represent either the current market value or the subjective value of the enterprise to the owners. The total amount presented in the statements is simply a result of the methods employed in measuring the specific assets and liabilities and from traditional structural accounting procedures. Since, as Chapter 14 showed, the total value of the firm to its owners cannot be measured from the valuation of specific assets and liabilities, the reported amount of proprietorship cannot represent the current value of the rights of the owners. Instead, therefore, of looking at specific rights to future benefits, as with assets, or at specific obligations of the enterprise, as with liabilities, accounting theory views the rights, priorities, and restrictions of owners' equities from an aggregate point of view.

In some cases, the rights and priorities of some classes of corporate stock are similar to those of some types of long-term debt. In general, though, there are notable differences between stockholder equities and liabilities. These include:

1. The extent to which other equity holders have priority rights.
2. The degree of certainty in the determination of amounts to be received by the equity holders.
3. The maturity dates of the payments of final rights.

In normal circumstances, creditors and debt holders have priority over stockholders for the payment of periodic interest and in the repayment of principal. Preferred stockholders may have priorities over common stockholders, but both are residual claimants in relationship to the claims of creditors. In a viable concern, the amounts payable to creditors are usually determinable in advance, the amount to be paid at maturity is usually a fixed number of dollars, and the interest payments are usually expressed as a percentage of a face value. Dividend payments to stockholders are generally dependent on reported income or retained earnings, the availability of cash, and a formal declaration by the board of directors. The maturity date of creditors' claims is generally fixed or determinable, but stockholders' equities do not represent legal obligations of the enterprise. Dividends become liabilities only upon declaration by the board of directors. Generally, stockholders cannot expect repayment of capital at definite, or determinable, dates.

The Proprietary Theory

The notion of proprietorship originated with an attempt to place logic into the exposition of double-entry bookkeeping. In the accounting equation $\Sigma A - \Sigma L = P$, the proprietor is the center of interest. The assets are assumed to be owned by the proprietor and the liabilities are the proprietor's obligations. One early author treated liabilities as negative assets and stated that capital, ". . . in the initial bookkeeping equation, represents the net wealth of the proprietor."[2] Regardless of the treatment of liabilities, the proprietorship is considered to be the net value of the business to the owners. When the business is begun, this value is equal to the investment of the owners. During the life of the enterprise, it is equal to the original investment and additional investments plus the accumulated net income in excess of that withdrawn by the proprietors (or minus net losses and withdrawals). It is, therefore, a wealth concept.

Under the proprietary theory, revenues are increases in proprietorship and expenses are decreases. Thus, net income, the excess of revenues over expenses, accrues directly to the owners; it represents an increase in the wealth of the proprietors. And since income is an increase in wealth, it is immediately added to the owner's capital or proprietorship. Cash dividends represent withdrawals of capital, and retained earnings are a part of total proprietorship. Interest on debt, however, represents an expense of the proprietors and should be deducted before arriving at net income to the owners. Corporate income taxes are likewise expenses in the proprietorship theory; however, some argue, as Chapter 20 points out, that the corporation is acting as an agent of the stockholders in paying the tax that is really a tax on the income of the stockholders.

The proprietary theory is adapted best to the single proprietorship form of organization because in this form there is generally a personal relationship between the management of the business and the ownership. The proprietary theory is also a logical framework for the partnership form of organization, particularly when it is organized under common law. In accounting for both the single proprietorship and the partnership forms, the proprietary theory appears to dominate. This is largely because net income is added each period to the personal capital accounts of the owners even though the traditional computation of income really does not measure net increases in wealth.

The proprietary theory is not so readily applicable to the corporate form of organization as it is to the single proprietorship and the partnership. However, many writers have chosen to look through the veil of the corporate form and describe the total of the invested capital stock and retained earnings as the net wealth of the stockholders, implying the proprietary theory.[3] The *comprehensive income* concept adopted by the FASB, for instance, is based on the proprietary theory. It includes all items affecting proprietorship during the period except dividend withdrawals and capital transactions.

The proprietary theory is also implied in many accounting practices and in accounting terminology relating to corporations. For example, the net income of the firm is often referred to as net income to the stockholders. Furthermore, financial statements must make reference to earnings per share and occasionally refer to book value per share. However, these computations are not necessarily meaningless without the proprietary concept. "Net income to stockholders" can be interpreted as the residual net income allocable to the stockholders' equity, and "book value per share" can be interpreted as the book equity per share under the entity approach.

The equity method for accounting for nonconsolidated investments in subsidiaries also implies a proprietary concept. The parent's proportionate share of each year's income is added to the investment account on the theory that the income of the subsidiary accrues to the stockholders, including the parent corporation as the major stockholder. It may be argued, however, that this accrual is merely a reflection of an increase in the value of the stock held by the parent and is, thus, in accord with the entity view. However, there is little merit in this view, since the proportionate share of the recorded income of the subsidiary is at best a poor indicator of an increase in the value of the stock to the parent.

The Entity Theory

The existence of a business entity separate from the personal affairs and other interests of the owners and other equity holders is recognized in all concepts of owners and equities. In the entity theory, however, the business firm is considered to have a separate existence, even personality, of its own. The founders and owners are not necessarily identified with the existence of the firm. This relationship finds legal and institutional support in the form of the corporation, but it is also found in other forms of business enterprises. Indeed, the entity theory is said to have actually preceded the corporate concept. This separate existence is not unique to business enterprises; universities, hospitals, governments, and other organizations have a continuity of existence separate from the lives of the organizers and even separate from the individuals directly associated with the organization.

The entity theory is based on the equation: $\Sigma A = \Sigma L + SE$, or Assets = Equities (Liabilities plus Stockholders' Equity). The items on the right side of the equation are occasionally called liabilities, but they are really equities with different rights in the enterprise. The main difference between the liabilities and the stockholder equities is that the rights of the creditors can be valued independently of other valuations if the firm is solvent, while the rights of the stockholders are measured by the valuation of assets originally invested plus the valuation of reinvested earnings and subsequent revaluations. But the rights of the stockholders to receive dividends and share in net assets upon liquidation are rights as equity holders, rather than as owners of the specific assets.

The liabilities, therefore, are the specific obligations of the *firm*, and the assets represent the rights of the *firm* to receive specific goods and services or other benefits. The valuation of assets, therefore, should reflect a measurement of the benefits to be received by the enterprise.

The net income of the enterprise is generally expressed in terms of the net change in the stockholders' equity, not including changes arising from dividend declarations and capital transactions. This is not the same as saying that the net income is the income to the stockholders, as is implied in the proprietary theory. Net income, in the entity view, simply represents a residual change in equity position after deducting all other claims, including interest on long-term debt and income taxes. It is personal income to the stockholder only if the value of the investment has increased or to the extent of a dividend declaration.

A strict adherence to the entity concept requires that interest on debt should be considered a distribution of entity income rather than an expense. That is, all distributions or allocations to equity holders should be considered allocations of corporate income. This was the position taken in Chapter 9 in defining entity income. Income taxes, however, in the opinion of the authors and as discussed in Chapter 20, are not a distribution of income, but rather an expense of the business.

Since corporate net income is not considered to be directly the net income of the stockholders, revenues and expenses are not increases and decreases in the stockholders' equity. Revenue is the product of the enterprise, and the expenses are the goods and services consumed in obtaining the revenue. Therefore, expenses are deductions from revenue, and the difference represents the corporate income to be distributed to stockholders in the form of dividends or reinvested in the business.

The entity theory has its main application in the corporate form of business enterprise, but it is also relevant to unincorporated firms that have a continuity of existence separate from the lives of individual owners. The entity theory is also relevant to the preparation of consolidated financial statements; however, in this case, the economic entity, rather than the legal entity, is the relevant accounting unit. The classes of equity holders are increased to include the minority stockholders as a separate class in addition to the stockholders of the parent corporation and all creditors of the parent and its subsidiaries.

Several authors have proposed or implied that the proprietary and entity theories lead to different bases for asset valuation. Under the proprietary theory, it is claimed that the assets should be valued in terms of current values because the owners' equity is considered to be their net worth or net wealth. Under the entity theory, the firm is not concerned with current values because the emphasis is on the accountability of cost to the owners and other equity holders.[4] However, recent discussions of valuation have stressed the importance of current values as relevant in determining the income of the enterprise, as a measure of the future services to the firm, and as a basis for future decisions of management. Even in meeting the objective of accountability to equity holders, it may be argued that current values are just as important as costs. Therefore, in the authors' opinion, the proprietary and entity theories do not necessarily dictate different valuation bases.

The Residual Equity Theory

Accounting theorist William Paton referred to the residual equity as one of the several types of equity under the entity theory.[5] In the entity theory, the stockholder has an equity in the firm like other equity holders, but the stockholder is not considered to be the owner. Paton emphasized the special relationship of the residual equity holder to the work of the accountant "because it is in such an equity that much of his work comes to a focus."[6] Changes in asset valuation, changes in income and in retained earnings, and changes in the interests of other equity holders are all reflected in the residual equity of the common stockholders. But even though the equities of creditors, preferred stockholders, and common stockholders should be classified separately, they are all equities under the entity theory.

The residual equity point of view is a concept somewhere between the proprietary theory and the entity theory. In this view, the equation becomes Assets − Specific equities = Residual equity. The specific equities include the claims of creditors and the equities of preferred stockholders. However, in certain cases where losses have been large or in bankruptcy proceedings, the equity of the common stockholders may disappear and the preferred stockholders or the bond holders may become the residual equity holders.

The objective of the residual equity approach is to provide better information to common stockholders for making investment decisions. In a corporation with indefinite continuity, the current value of common stock is dependent primarily upon the expectation of future dividends. Future dividends, in turn, are dependent upon the expectations of total receipts less specific contractual obligations, payments to specific equity holders, and requirements for reinvestment. Trends in investment values can also be measured, in part, by looking at trends in the value of the residual equity measured on the basis of current values.

Common stockholders are generally thought to have a residual equity in the income of the firm and in the net assets upon final liquidation. Since financial statements are not generally prepared on the basis of possible liquidation, the information provided regarding the residual equity should be useful in predicting possible future dividends to common stockholders, including liquidation dividends. The income statement or combined income statement and statement of retained earnings should show the income available to the residual equity holders after all prior claims are met, including the dividends to preferred stockholders. The equity of the common stockholders in the balance sheet should be presented separately from the equities of preferred stockholders and other specific equity holders. The cash flow statement should also show the cash available to the firm for the payment of common dividends and other purposes.

An alternative approach to the residual equity concept is that, since under the usual assumption of enterprise continuity the common stockholders' only claim against the corporation is to receive dividends when and if declared, the residual equity in capital is not assigned to the residual equity holders. Both the initial capital supplied by the common stockholders and the retained earnings are, therefore, the equity of the corporation in itself. Note that this is similar to the strict entity approach discussed below under stock dividends.

The residual concept has a different meaning in the context of the earnings per share computations; however, it can be considered an extension of the residual equity theory. A *residual security* is defined as a common stock equivalent, which would include debt or preferred stock convertible into common stock, and warrants for the purchase of common stock. Under certain conditions, holders of these securities may obtain the rights of common stockholders, thus giving them residual rights. The disclosure of these potential residual rights and the potential dilution effect is discussed in Chapter 23 in the section on earnings per share.

The Enterprise Theory

The enterprise theory of the firm is a broader concept than the entity theory, but less well defined in its scope and application. In the entity theory the firm is considered to be a separate economic unit operated primarily for the benefit of the equity holders, whereas in the enterprise theory the corporation is a social institution operated for the benefit of many interested groups. In the broadest form these groups include, in addition to the stockholders and creditors, the employees, customers, the government as a taxing authority and as a regulatory agency, and the general public. Thus, the broad form of the enterprise theory may be thought of as a social theory of accounting.

This concept of the firm is most applicable to the large modern corporation that has been obliged to consider the effect of its actions on various groups and on society as a whole. From an accounting point of view, this means that the responsibility of proper reporting extends not only to stockholders and creditors, but also to many other groups and to the general public. The large corporation can no longer operate solely in the interests of the stockholders, and it cannot be assumed that the forces of competition will necessarily protect the interests of other groups. Employees, particularly through labor unions, utilize accounting data in presenting their claims for wage increases or increases in other benefits. Customers and regulatory agencies have been interested in the fairness of price changes, and the government has been interested in the effect of price changes on the general state of the economy.

The most relevant concept of income in this broad social responsibility concept of the enterprise is the value-added concept discussed in Chapter 10. The total value added by the enterprise is the market value of the goods and services produced by the firm less the value of the goods and services acquired by transfer from other firms. Thus, value-added income includes all payments to stockholders in the form of dividends, interest to creditors, wages and salaries to employees, taxes to governmental units, and earnings retained in the business. The total value-added concept also includes depreciation, but this is a gross product concept rather than a net income concept.

The term *enterprise net income*, as used by the 1957 AAA statement, is a narrower concept than the value-added concept.[7] In addition to the traditional net income to stockholders, this concept of enterprise net income includes interest charges and income taxes. Therefore, it is closer to the entity concept. The inclusion of income taxes in enterprise net income apparently stems from the idea that this is paid to the government on behalf of the stockholders. If income taxes are an expense under the entity theory, as proposed earlier, they should not be included in enterprise net income. If a broader concept of income is intended, the enterprise net income should also include payments to other beneficiaries of the corporation.

The position of retained earnings in the enterprise theory is similar to its position in the entity concept. It either represents part of the equity of the residual equity holders, or it represents undistributed equity—the equity of the corporation in itself. In the entity theory there is considerable merit in the former position; but in the enterprise theory the earnings reinvested in the business do not necessarily benefit the residual stockholders only. Capital employed to maintain market position, to improve productivity, or to promote general expansion may not necessarily benefit the stockholders only. In fact, it is possible that the stockholders may not be benefited at all if future dividends are not increased.

The Fund Theory

The fund theory abandons the personal relationship assumed in the proprietary theory and the personalization of the firm as an artificial economic and legal unit under the entity theory. Instead, the fund theory substitutes an operational, or activity-oriented, unit as the basis for accounting. This area of interest, called the fund, includes a group of assets and related obligations and restrictions representing specific economic functions or activities.

The fund theory is based on the equation Assets = Restrictions of assets. Assets represent prospective services to the fund or operational unit. Liabilities represent restrictions against specific or general assets of the fund. The invested capital represents either legal or financial restrictions on the use of assets; that is, the invested capital must be maintained intact unless specific authority has been obtained (with few exceptions) for partial or complete liquidation. Even partial liquidation of invested capital, however, requires full disclosure. Appropriations of retained earnings represent restrictions imposed by management, by creditors, or by legal requirements. Unappropriated retained earnings also represent restrictions—a residual overall restriction that the assets be used for the purposes for which they are devoted. Thus, all equities represent restrictions imposed by legal, contractual, managerial, financial, or equitable considerations.

The fund concept has found its greatest usefulness in governmental and nonprofit institutions. In a university, for example, the most commonly used funds are the special funds for endowments, student loan funds, plant funds, auxiliary enterprises, and current educational activities. Each of these funds has its specific assets restricted for particular purposes. But the fund concept is also relevant to specific areas of interest within the corporation, or even for areas of interest greater than the single legal form of enterprise. Examples of direct applicability are the sinking fund in financial reporting, branch or divisional accounting, and accounting for estates and trusts. The preparation of consolidated statements is also an application of the fund theory just as much as it is an extension of the theory of the economic entity. The fund theory can also be applied in other areas of financial accounting; for example, the fund theory can find usefulness in the distinction between current and fixed assets and equities.

Although the income concept can be retained under the fund theory, it is not the central concept in financial reporting. Instead, the description of the operation of the fund is presented more clearly in the funds statements. The major financial statements are statistical summaries of the sources and dispositions of funds. An income statement, if it appears at all, is an adjunct of the funds statement—a description of the funds provided from operations. Although the funds theory is not oriented toward the interests of any specific equity holder, all interested parties should be able to find the information they want in the financial statements. Like the enterprise theory, it is neutral with respect to the interests of any specific group.

The FASB's Position

The FASB took a strong stand in favor of the residual equity theory when it came to owners' equity, which it defined as "the residual interest in the assets of an entity that remains after deducting its liabilities."[8] It termed the difference between assets and liabilities as "net assets" in the case of not-for-profit organizations and claimed that the two terms were interchangeable.[9] As it noted in the earlier Discussion Memorandum "capital (which equals net assets) has no existence apart from assets and liabilities because it is a residual interest."[10]

This approach is not surprising given the FASB's earlier statement of objectives as the provision of information primarily to investors or, more specifically, common shareholders. It did note that this approach created problems in dealing with hybrid securities that were part liability, part equity and quoted *APB 14* "Accounting for Convertible Debt and Debt Issued with Stock Purchase Warrants," and *APB 15* "Earnings per Share" as examples of where such issues had cropped up. It concluded that "securities with dual characteristics present practical problems of separating and disclosing diverse characteristics—that is, they involve primarily problems of applying, rather than problems of determining, the basic concepts of a conceptual framework."

Summary of the Equity Theories

The several theories or approaches to the nature of an enterprise and the relationships or activities to be reported are all relevant under different circumstances of organization, economic relationships, and accounting objectives. Therefore, accounting theory and practice should take an eclectic approach to these theories. All help to explain and understand accounting theory and to develop logical patterns for the extension of theory. However, care must be taken to apply the most logical equity theory in each case and to use a single theory consistently in the same circumstances. For example, it is inconsistent to argue that a subsidiary's income should be added to the parent company's investment account (a proprietary approach), and also to argue that the parent should capitalize the market value of shares issued by a subsidiary in a stock dividend (a narrow entity approach). It is not inconsistent, however, to apply the proprietary concept to a small single proprietorship, the entity concept to a medium-size corporation, and the enterprise theory to a very large corporation.

CHECKPOINTS

---

1. Where did the proprietary theory originate?
2. How does the residual equity theory relate to the entity theory?
3. In what ways is the enterprise theory broader than the entity theory?
4. How does the fund theory differ from the enterprise theory?
5. Which theory do you prefer? Why?

THE CLASSIFICATION OF SINGLE PROPRIETORSHIP AND PARTNERSHIP EQUITIES

In the single proprietorship, the entire ownership equity is generally presented in one amount. In accordance with the proprietary theory, this equity represents the ownership of the business by the proprietor. There is no need to present subclassifications of this equity because the owner is not restricted regarding how much to invest or take out of the business. Also, there are no superior claims other than those held by the creditors of the business. In case of liquidation or insolvency, the creditors can reach the personal assets of the owner, making the distinction between permanent invested capital and reinvested earnings of little importance for this purpose. This does not mean, however, that a distinction is not made between capital and income. Income is computed periodically and added to the capital account at the end of each period; capital transactions (withdrawals and additional investments) are recorded directly in the capital account; and all changes are generally summarized in a separate statement of the proprietorship.

The ownership equity of the partnership is similar to the equity of a single proprietor, except that it is classified according to the interests of each of the partners. Separate drawing accounts may be used to establish control over withdrawals or to force compliance with a withdrawal agreement. But even these accounts are generally closed into the capital account at the end of each period, so that no classification according to source of the equities is maintained.

What, then, is the value of the classification according to the several partners' interests? First, it should be recognized that this classification shows only the interest in the net assets of the business; each partner's interest in the income of the enterprise may be entirely different according to the terms of the partnership agreement. But the capital accounts do not show the specific rights of the partners in liquidation (except in the unusual case where there are no gains or losses in the liquidation process). If the gains and losses are allocated to the partners' capital accounts in a ratio other than the ratio of the capital balances, the final distribution to partners may be entirely different from the apparent interests in the business before starting liquidation. Therefore, the capital accounts serve primarily as a starting point in determining the distribution of assets in final liquidation and dissolution—unless all, or a part of, the income is allocated on the basis of capital balances. Creditors are not as interested in the capital balances of the partners as they are in the total ownership equity and the personal assets of the partners because any partner may become personally liable for any or all of the debts of the partnership.

CLASSIFICATION OF STOCKHOLDER EQUITIES

The relationships between a corporation, the stockholders, and the creditors are much more involved than the relationships in a single proprietorship or in a partnership. Therefore, the financial statements should present more information regarding these relationships than is expected in the financial statements of the less formal types of organization. However, the information that is traditionally presented is an outgrowth of certain assumed legal and economic relationships, rather than being a result of a complete analysis of the needs of the various users of financial statements. As a result, traditional stockholders' equity classifications often attempt to meet several objectives and, therefore, meet none adequately.

The most basic objective of stockholder equity classifications is to provide information to stockholders, investors, creditors, and other interested groups regarding the efficiency and stewardship of management. The classifications should also provide information regarding the historical and prospective economic interests of the groups holding specific equities and the groups (such as employees, customers, and the government) that have a general economic interest in the corporation. In meeting these objectives, the information in the financial statements should disclose some or all of the following:

1. The sources of capital supplied to the corporation.
2. The legal restrictions on the distribution of invested capital to stockholders.
3. The legal, contractual, managerial, and financial restrictions on the distribution of dividends to current and potential stockholders.
4. The priorities of the several classes of stockholders in partial or final liquidation.

Each of these specific objectives of classification will be discussed and evaluated in the following paragraphs.

Classification by Source of Capital

Classification of stockholders' equity by source is generally considered to be the major classification objective in balance sheet presentation in the traditional accounting structure. The main sources of corporate stockholder equity are:

1. Amounts paid in by stockholders.
2. The excess of net income over dividends paid to stockholders (earnings retained in the business).
3. Donations from other than stockholders.

A description of the sources of capital is valuable because it provides information regarding the historical development of the corporation. It also indicates whether the firm has financed its growth internally or through external financing.

The traditional fourfold classification of stockholder equities—capital stock, paid-in capital in excess of par or stated value, revaluation capital, and retained earnings—only partially meets the objective of classification by source. The capital stock and additional paid-in capital categories generally represent the amounts paid in by stockholders. One exception is that donations are usually included in the additional paid-in capital classification.

A main disadvantage of the conventional classification is that the classification by source is lost whenever transfers are made from retained earnings to capital stock and additional paid-in capital by issuing stock dividends or other means. The original classification by source is also lost in a recapitalization and in some treasury stock transactions.

The Disclosure of Legal Capital

In a corporation, stockholders generally have no personal liability for the debts of the business; creditors must look only to the assets of the enterprise. Without this provision, corporate stock would not be so readily transferable as it is today. To obtain this provision, however, the legislatures felt a need to provide some protection to creditors from unscrupulous promoters, stockholders, or directors. To provide this protection to creditors, the courts and legislatures placed restrictions on the amount of assets that can be distributed legally to the stockholders under normal circumstances prior to final liquidation.[11]

Most states define *legal capital* or *stated capital* as the aggregate par value of all par value shares issued (not subsequently canceled) and the aggregate consideration received for all shares issued without par value. In the case of no-par value shares, however, many states permit the directors or stockholders to designate how much of the consideration received shall be classified as stated capital and how much shall be classified as additional paid-in capital. A few states also require the excess of the amount paid in over the par value of par value shares to be included in stated capital. As a result, it is difficult to determine the exact amount of legal capital in specific situations. In general, it may be assumed that the legal capital is at least equal to the par value of par value shares plus the stated value of no-par value shares. But there are exceptions to this (e.g., in the case of wasting asset corporations. These are companies owning assets such as gold mines or oil wells that deplete over time).

Current financial statements do not disclose the amount of legal capital, although there are usually separate classifications for capital stock and additional paid-in capital. But, because of the many differences from one state to another, even a disclosure of the number of shares issued and outstanding of each class and the par value of shares in each class is not sufficient in many cases to permit the informed reader to compute the total legal capital.

As a result of the differences between legal capital and invested capital for accounting and financial purposes, the separation of invested capital into capital stock and additional paid-in capital is probably more misleading than helpful. An alternative would be to disclose in a footnote what the accountants consider to be the legal or stated capital, making it clear that a final determination of stated capital is a legal decision subject to court interpretation and not basically an accounting problem.

In the authors' opinion, the disclosure of legal capital is probably unnecessary in all cases except in small or incipient corporations. In large and profitable concerns, the legal capital is generally a small part of the total stockholders' equity. In these cases, it is usually apparent that the amount of current and future dividends is not dependent on the amount of legal capital. Therefore, the entire stockholders' equity acts as a buffer for the protection of creditors, and the creditors rely more on the total resources, profitability, and financial policies of the firm than on the status of legal capital.

The Disclosure of Restrictions on the Disposition of Income

A disclosure of the *intended* distribution or disposition of the income of a corporation is not the same as a disclosure of the *restrictions* on the disposition of income. Frequently, the former is assumed from the latter, but generally this is unwarranted. Therefore, the classification of stockholder equities and footnotes to the financial statements should make a clear distinction between these two.

A first general assumption is that cash dividends should not be paid if the result will be to reduce net assets below the total paid-in capital of the firm, even though a part or all of the paid-in capital in excess of par value may be distributed legally. This is a self-imposed restriction influenced by the accounting distinction between invested capital and income. If a dividend should be paid "out of" additional paid-in capital, accounting principles require that this be disclosed as a liquidating dividend—a return *of* capital rather than the usual assumption that a dividend is a return *on* capital. This disclosure is also required by the Model Corporation Act adopted by many states.

It cannot be assumed, however, that any or all of the retained earnings will be made available for distribution to stockholders as cash dividends. In fact, the current titles for this amount of accumulated earnings deny this. "Earnings Retained for Use in the Business" or simply "Retained Earnings" implies that the income not already distributed as dividends has been invested permanently in the business. This implication is supported by two general observations:

1. The dividend distributions of most large firms are correlated highly with the current year's income, the prior year's income, and the prior year's dividends. With a short lag and with minor deviations, there appears to be an attempt to limit dividends to income of the firm for the current year, rather than pay dividends out of the earnings retained in prior years.

2. In most mature firms, the amount of retained earnings is larger than the capital invested directly by the stockholders. At the very least it is a large percentage of total stockholders' equity. Therefore, corporate financial policy would not permit the payment of dividends equal to retained earnings; to do so would be tantamount to a distribution of the capital of the corporation. One might ask what the logic then is behind the capitalization of stock dividends in excess of the legal or stated capital.

Since the classification of a part of stockholders' equity as retained earnings does not indicate the amount that is likely to be paid out as dividends in the future nor even the intent of the firm, an alternative is to show the legal, contractual, or financial restrictions on the payment of dividends. Care must be taken, however, not to leave the impression that unrestricted retained earnings will be, or are likely to be, distributed as dividends. The appropriation of retained earnings and the labeling of the residual as "Unappropriated" or "Free" is, therefore, misleading. It may still be restricted by managerial or financial policy. A footnote disclosure may be less misleading. But even here, the restriction may be meaningless from the point of view of possible dividend distributions, particularly if only a small part of the total retained earnings is restricted. Therefore, classification of stockholders' equity according to the probable distribution of income or retained earnings should not be an objective. It should not be permitted to influence or distort the classification according to source. In that light, the authors believe that when amounts are transferred from retained earnings to permanently invested capital, a separate classification entitled "Retained Earnings Transferred to Paid-in Capital" should be used. This would aid in maintaining the classification according to source and still disclose the restriction on dividend payments.

Dividend payments to common stockholders are also restricted by contractual preferences granted to preferred stockholders or other stockholder groups given priority rights above those of the residual stockholders. The traditional classification of stockholders' equity does not provide for disclosing these restrictions. Cumulative preferred dividends in arrears are not generally shown as appropriated retained earnings because, under the entity theory, all stockholders are treated as a group. Under the residual equity theory, an appropriation would be acceptable to disclose the restriction on the payment of dividends to common stockholders. But, as argued above, all such restrictions can be disclosed more fully by parenthetical explanations or by footnotes.

The Disclosure of Restrictions on Liquidation Distributions

Creditors always have priority in liquidation over stockholders, and certain classes of stockholders have priority over other classes by the terms of the corporate charter or by contractual arrangements. This liquidation preference of preferred stock may be equal to the par value or stated value per share or it may include a premium. Usually the preferred dividends in arrears are included if the preferred dividends are cumulative.

Liquidation preferences, therefore, are not the same as legal or stated capital. An entirely different classification than that used to disclose legal capital would be needed to disclose these preferences. But how important is it that they be disclosed? If a profitable corporation has no intent to liquidate, the liquidation preference may be relatively unimportant. And even if the corporation has incurred losses for one or several years, the liquidation preference may still be unimportant if the net assets of the firm exceed the amount of the liquidation preference by a wide margin. In these cases, the shareholders can determine their rights by reading the fine print on the back of their share certificates or by other means. But if the total liquidation preferences become large in proportion to total net assets or if partial or final liquidation appears likely, disclosure should be made in the financial statements.

Even the necessity for full disclosure of liquidation priority rights does not mean that classification is the best method of achieving this disclosure. Parenthetical and footnote disclosure will usually be adequate. However, if the firm is in final liquidation or liquidation is being planned, the original source of the capital is unimportant and the final disposition is most relevant. Thus, since the objective of reporting has changed in this case, the classification objectives should also be changed. The residual equity theory should now dominate the reporting of stockholders' equities.

Summary

In the authors' opinion, it is not possible to maintain consistent classification of stockholders' equity according to source, legal restriction, disposition or restrictions of earnings, and the partial or final distribution of invested capital. The FASB went so far as to wonder aloud whether classification should be abandoned altogether. It left as "a question for later consideration . . . whether owners' interests should be classified in financial statements and, if so, the kind of classification that is most useful to investors, creditors, and others who use the statements."[12]

As the prior discussion of the problem has revealed, the classification of invested capital and retained earnings on the basis of committed and uncommitted capital appears logical from an accounting point of view alone; but in reality, in most large corporations, retained earnings have become a very significant part of invested capital without formal action by the board of directors. Therefore, it is the authors' recommendation that the primary basis for classification should be source, to maintain logic within the traditional accounting structure. And this source should not be disturbed by transfers of retained earnings to invested capital. The amounts so transferred should be designated as retained earnings formally capitalized.

Legal capital may be shown, if it does not thereby disturb the classification according to source. Restrictions regarding the distribution of earnings and the priorities of assets in liquidation can generally be disclosed properly by parenthetical notes or in footnotes. This major emphasis on classification according to source permits a disclosure of the source of all distributions to stockholders. That is, payment should be designated as either:

1. Distributions of current income.
2. Reductions of uncommitted retained earnings.
3. Reductions of retained earnings capitalized.
4. Distributions of capital invested by stockholders or from other sources.

The sources of invested capital, however, can be disclosed more clearly in a cash flow statement. As suggested by the Committee on External Reporting of the American Accounting Association, the stockholders' equity section of the balance sheet is fairly sterile with respect to its relevance to the needs of investors and creditors.[13] A major difficulty with this classification is that it is a residual, its amount being determined by the measurements of assets and liabilities. However, information regarding the current and potential relationships of the several classes of long-term equity holders is relevant for an evaluation of the current and prospective rights of each of the creditors and stockholders.

CHECKPOINTS

1. What is generally believed to be the major objective of classifying equity?
2. List the three potential disclosures that classifications of equity might achieve.
3. Define the term *legal capital*.
4. Distinguish between the disclosure of intended distributions and disclosure of restrictions in the context of dividend payments.

CONSOLIDATED FINANCIAL STATEMENTS

When one corporation has a majority ownership and control in one or more related subsidiary firms, valuable information can be obtained and presented by combining the financial data and preparing consolidated financial statements for the entire group. Until recently, the requirements for consolidation were governed by the original paragraphs 2 and 3 of *ARB 51* established in 1959. The first of these paragraphs stated that:

> The usual condition for a controlling financial interest is ownership of a majority voting interest, and, therefore, as a general rule ownership by one company, directly or indirectly, or over fifty percent of the outstanding voting shares of another company is a condition pointing toward consolidation.

The second of those paragraphs then added the caveat that:

> separate statements or combined statements would be preferable for a subsidiary or group of subsidiaries if the presentation of financial information concerning the particular activities of such subsidiaries would be more informative to shareholders and creditors of the parent company than would the inclusion of such subsidiaries in the consolidation. For example, separate statements may be required for a subsidiary which is a bank or insurance company and may be preferable for a finance company where the parent and the other subsidiaries are engaged in manufacturing operations.

This so-called nonhomogeneous clause enabled a number of companies to avoid consolidating certain of their subsidiaries. For example, General Motors did not consolidate its accounts with General Motors Acceptance

Corporation on grounds that the parent GM was a manufacturing company and the wholly owned subsidiary GMAC was a finance company. *SFAS 94* changed that by amending paragraph 3 of *ARB 51* to eliminate the nonhomogeneous exception. Effectively now, all companies in which a parent has a 50 percent or more interest are consolidated with the parent. The only exceptions involve temporary situations and situations where, due to circumstances such as government control in a foreign country, the parent has no effective control over the subsidiary.

Although the consolidated group is generally thought of as a single economic unit, the accounting procedures of consolidation frequently deny this in their treatment of minority interests. There does not appear to be reliance on a single theory, such as the proprietary theory, the entity theory, or the funds theory to serve as a guide in the establishment of consistent logical procedures of consolidation. Furthermore, the classification of stockholders' equity has not developed into a logical, consistent pattern. In fact, accounting practice is far from uniform in this area, reflecting either a lack of a logical basis for classification or a failure to agree on the basic objectives of classification. These areas are discussed at greater length in the following paragraphs.

Consolidation Procedures

Full details of how consolidations are performed are typically found in Advanced Accounting textbooks. This section provides a brief survey only. Its sole intent is to motivate the discussion of consolidations that follows.

The consolidation of a parent company with its subsidiaries is relatively straightforward in principle. The many complications that arise lie in the details. At the broad level, two or more companies are consolidated by adding together their assets and their liabilities. The difference between the two sums constitutes the equity of the consolidated company. Exhibit 22-2 illustrates the process.

The exhibit assumes that one parent company has bought a portion of the shares of another company. Assuming that it has purchased more than 50 percent of the shares of the other company, it establishes a parent-subsidiary relationship. If it does not own all the shares, there will also be minority shareholders holding the balance. The majority holding is designated by *MI* in the exhibit; the minority holdings are designated *mi*. The parent's investment in the subsidiary is the price paid for these shares. This is the book value of its holdings (*MI*) plus a premium (*PR*). With this by way of introduction, several points can be made. We focus initially on columns 1 through 3.

First note, as column (3) shows, that *all* the assets of the subsidiary are added to *all* the assets of the parent, regardless of the relative holding of

EXHIBIT 22-2 The Process of Consolidation

	(1) Parent Co.	(2) Subsidiary	(3) Consolidated (unadjusted)	(4) Consolidated (adjusted)
Assets other than investment	$A + r$	a	$A + a + r$	$A + a$
Investment in subsidiary	$MI + Pr$		$MI + Pr$	
Goodwill				Pr
Liabilities	L	$l + r$	$L + l + r$	$L + l$
Minority interest				mi
Owners' equity	OE	$MI + mi$	$OE + MI + mi$	OE

the parent in the subsidiary. Similarly, *all* the liabilities of the subsidiary are added to *all* the liabilities of the parent, regardless of the relative holding of the parent in the subsidiary. There are only two exceptions to this general rule.

One is that assets and liabilities representing transactions between the companies being consolidated are canceled. In this case, we have assumed that the parent made a loan to the subsidiary in the amount of $r. The result of canceling these intercompany transactions is the assets and liabilities shown in column (4).

The other is that the parent's investment of *MI*, that is, the book value portion of the investment, is canceled against the subsidiary's equity of *MI*, that is, the equity of the majority ownership of the subsidiary. The result is a consolidated equity account of *OE* plus *mi*. Also, the excess of the cost of the investment over its book value (i.e., *Pr*) appears in an account in the consolidated entity labeled goodwill. As noted in previous chapters, goodwill is amortized over a period not to exceed 40 years, so that eventually this premium will disappear.

Note now that the equity of the consolidated company at this first level, that is, *OE* plus *mi*, represents the ownership interests of *all* parties involved. In particular, it combines the ownership interest of the majority shareholders with that of the minority shareholders. It is standard practice to separate the equity of the consolidated company into a majority interest and a minority interest. Practice varies considerably as to where the minority interest is then shown on the balance sheet. Some show it as part of equity, others as a liability, and still others as an entry on the balance sheet between owners' equity and liabilities. This is the way it is shown in column (4). More is said on this later.

The result of this consolidation is to create the combined asset/liability picture shown in column (4). Not shown in the exhibit is a further adjustment to the excess cost amount. On grounds that one should enter assets at their purchased value, it is standard practice to revalue the identifiable assets of the subsidiary to take into consideration that their fair value at the time of acquisition exceeds their book value. The revaluation in years subsequent to the acquisition is based on the amortized excess cost. An example of how the revaluation is done at the time of acquisition is the easiest way to explain the process.

Assume, for simplicity, a one-asset subsidiary. The asset, a building, has a book value of $50,000. This is also the owners' equity of the subsidiary. Assume further that the subsidiary is wholly owned by the parent. The parent purchased the subsidiary for $120,000, say, and estimates the fair value of the building to be $90,000. The excess of the fair market value of the building over its book value, in the amount of $40,000, should be moved to the asset account leaving $30,000 as goodwill. This residual amount can be thought of as representing an intangible, such as a good location.*

Now assume that the parent's $120,000 investment purchased only a 60 percent interest in the subsidiary. This suggests that the value of the subsidiary as a whole was $200,000. As before, the building has a book value of $50,000 and an estimated fair value of $90,000. But the parent owns only 60 percent of the building. Its pro rata share of the book value is $30,000. Therefore, it is argued, only 60 percent of the excess of fair value over book value should be added to the asset. In other words, the parent's share of the building is adjusted to $30,000 plus 60 percent of $40,000; that is, to $54,000. To that must be added the portion held by minority shareholders, which has a $20,000 book value. The building thus is shown at a total of $74,000. This leaves residual goodwill of $66,000 equal to the investment of $120,000 less the parent's investment in the book value of the subsidiary of $30,000, less the allocated $24,000. The two cases are illustrated in Exhibit 22-3.

There are two key points to notice in Exhibit 22-3. The first is that the consolidated owners' equity account is unaffected by the degree of ownership of the majority shareholder. The second is that the value of the assets of the subsidiary is affected by the degree of ownership of the majority shareholder. Algebraically, where f stands for the fair value of the assets:

Value of subsidiary's assets in a consolidated statement

$$= \text{Book value of assets}$$

$$+ \text{Percentage majority interest} \times (\text{Fair value} - \text{Book value})$$

---

* See Chapter 18 on intangibles for more detail on the nature of goodwill.

EXHIBIT 22-3 Revaluing the Subsidiary

	(1) Parent Company	(2) Subsidiary	(3) Consolidated (100 percent)	(4) Consolidated (60 percent)
Assets other than investment	$500,000	$50,000	$590,000	$574,000
Investment in subsidiary	$120,000			
Goodwill			$ 30,000	$ 66,000
Liabilities	0	0	0	0
Minority interest				$ 20,000
Owners' equity	$620,000	$50,000	$620,000	$620,000

Alternatively:

$$\text{Adjusted value} = a + \frac{MI}{(MI + mi)} \times (f - a)$$

Whether any of this makes sense or not is the topic of the next section.

Purpose and Nature

Accounting Research Bulletin No. 51, the original and still controlling standard on consolidations, states that:

> the purpose of consolidated statements is to present, primarily for the benefit of the shareholders and creditors of the parent company, the results of operations and the financial position of a parent company and its subsidiaries essentially as if the group were a single company with one or more branches or divisions.[14]

This objective implies that we should look through the legal relationships of the corporations and view the enterprise as a single economic unit. But the emphasis on the interests of the shareholders and creditors of the parent company to the exclusion of the minority shareholders is inconsistent with this major objective. If the entire enterprise is really one economic unit, all interested parties should be given equal consideration, as in the enterprise theory; or the entity theory should be expanded to include the entire economic entity rather than merely the legal entity of the parent corporation.

Consolidated Balance Sheet.   In the balance sheet, the practice of adding together the separate classifications of assets and liabilities of the parent corporation and the subsidiaries is in keeping with the idea of presenting a financial statement of the enterprise as a whole. By eliminating all intercompany obligations and adding together all other assets and liabilities, a picture of the group as a single enterprise is obtained. However, to be consistent with the entity approach to consolidated statements, the revision of the asset valuation of the subsidiary should include not only the excess amount paid by the parent company, but also the minority interest's share in this increased valuation.[15]

Cost is relevant at the time of acquisition only because it is the best evidence of value. When only a fractional interest is obtained, the cost of the partial interest should be used as evidence of the value of the whole. To continue the example used earlier, if a 60 percent interest in a subsidiary is obtained by a parent company for $120,000, the total value to the consolidated enterprise, as evidenced by the payment of the parent, is $200,000. The fair value of the building is a known $90,000. Why not then record the full fair market value of the building? This would set the asset account at $590,000, reflecting the full fair value of the acquired assets. The goodwill account would stand at $110,000, reflecting the residual intangible of the majority shareholder of $66,000 (i.e., $120,000 − 30,000 − 24,000) and the residual intangible of the minority shareholder of $44,000 (i.e., $80,000 − 20,000 − 16,000). The assets of the enterprise would be split $620,000 for the majority shareholder and $80,000 for the minority. The result would be consistent with the general policy of including the full value of all assets and liabilities in the consolidated statements.

Consolidated Income Statements.   The enterprise theory is also followed in the preparation of consolidated income statements. Intercompany sales and intercompany profits are eliminated in their entirety, and other sales and expenses are combined to show the activities of the enterprise as a whole. However, the occasional practice of allocating the entire intercompany profit or loss to the majority interest alone is not consistent with this position. An alternative is to allocate these intercompany profits or losses proportionately between the majority and minority interests when reported by the subsidiary, although this also is arbitrary.

The consistent application of the enterprise theory again breaks down in conventional practice because most firms subtract the minority interest in the total income to arrive at consolidated net income. Thus, the net income is not the income of the enterprise as a whole, but only that portion allocated to the majority interest. But it is difficult to interpret just what this final income really represents, particularly if the minority interest is a negative figure arising from a net loss of the subsidiary. It is not in the nature of a residual equity in net income, because there is no consideration for the preferred equities in either the majority or minority groups.

And it does not provide useful information regarding the amount available for dividends to the majority interest because the parent firm may be able to pay dividends even though the subsidiaries are operated at a loss and vice versa. Therefore, the implication is that the consolidated net income represents the proprietary equity of the stockholders of the parent company in the income of the entire enterprise. But this is inconsistent with the entity or enterprise theories. It would be better to show the net income of the enterprise as a whole and then disclose separately the relative interests of the majority and minority interests.

Classification of Consolidated Equities

In the classification of consolidated equities in published statements, there is not only a lack of uniformity, but also a lack of understanding of the specific objectives. Is the objective to disclose the legal stated capital, the sources of capital, or the possible disposition of either income or invested capital? The next few paragraphs highlight the problems of settling on an appropriate objective for classification.

Disclosing Legal Capital.   There is little doubt that the disposition of legal capital and the extent of the legal protection to creditors can be presented more clearly in the separate financial statements of each corporation than in the consolidated statements. The creditors of a subsidiary firm must look at the individual statements of the subsidiary to determine the relevant legal capital (if indeed, it can be found even there) and their relationships to other creditors. For they, of course, have no claim against the assets of the parent corporation. But the creditors of the parent must also look at the separate statements of the parent firm to establish their specific relationship to stockholders and other creditors because they have only a secondary claim against the assets of the subsidiary, but a primary claim against the assets of the parent. Therefore, the presentation of legal capital and the rights of creditors cannot and should not be a major objective in the classification of the equities of a consolidated enterprise. Despite this, many firms, through tradition, show on the consolidated balance sheet the par value of shares issued separately from the capital received in excess of par value as though this had some meaning.

Disclosing Sources of Capital.   Probably the most common objective in the classification of consolidated equities is to disclose the sources of capital. It is not uncommon to find captions designating the stockholders' equity section of the consolidated balance sheet as ''Sources from Which Capital Was Obtained'' or ''Derived from.'' In practically all of these cases, however, the classification is not strictly according to source. The limitations of this method of classification are similar to the limitations of attempting to maintain a classification by source in unconsolidated corporations. But there are several additional limitations in consolidated statements.

First, the capital obtained from the majority stockholders is represented by the capital stock and additional paid-in capital of the parent firm in most cases. However, the minority interest is generally included among the liabilities or as a separate item between the liabilities and the stockholders' equity. This item generally represents the minority stockholders' interest in the total equities of the subsidiaries; but it is just as much a source of capital for the entire enterprise as is the capital contributed by the stockholders of the parent firm.

A second limitation on the conventional practice of classification by source is that the amount of capital derived from retained earnings is not clearly presented. For one thing, the minority interest is usually not classified according to the separate sources of capital invested by stockholders and earnings retained by the subsidiary. Also, there is no distinction between the minority stockholders' interest in the retained earnings at the date of consolidation, and the minority interest in the earnings retained since consolidation. For another, the consolidated retained earnings amount represents the total earnings of the parent firm retained since its incorporation (except for transfers to capital stock and additional paid-in capital), but only the majority interest in the earnings of the subsidiaries retained since the date of consolidation. Thus, the consolidated retained earnings does not represent a homogeneous source of invested capital.

A suggested remedy to give the source objective a better role in the classification of consolidated equity is to include in the consolidated invested capital the minority interest in the total stockholders' equity at the date of consolidation, and to classify the retained earnings as either:

1. That obtained from the earnings retained by the parent company since its organization.
2. That retained by the subsidiary firms since the date of consolidation (without consideration of the majority's and minority's separate interests in the subsidiaries' retained earnings).[16]

Disclosing Possible Distributions.   By stating that consolidated statements are presented primarily for the benefit of the shareholder and creditors of the parent company, *ARB 51* implies that the objective is to show the relative equities of the beneficiaries in the consolidated enterprise. But information regarding ownership equities is relevant only if it provides some information about the possible distribution of income and capital. That is, it should show some information regarding the relative rights of the several classes of equity holders in any distributions that may be made. However, the conventional classification of equities of consolidated enterprises fails to disclose the possible distribution of income to majority and minority stockholders. If the subsidiaries are operating at a loss, the consolidated income may be distributed entirely to the majority stockholders without paying any dividends to the minority group. On the other hand, if the consolidated net income is obtained entirely from the operations of subsidiaries, substantial dividends may be required to be paid to the minority stockholders before the stockholders of the parent may be able to receive any dividends.

The conventional classification also fails to disclose the rights of the various classes of equity holders in the possible distribution of capital. Creditors, in general, have preference in liquidation over stockholders. The creditors of the subsidiaries, however, have no claim to the separate assets of the parent and, therefore, the bonded indebtedness of subsidiaries and of the parent should not be combined if the objective is to disclose this priority. The creditors of the parent have only a secondary claim against the assets of a subsidiary, on the same level as the claim of the minority interest. This fact is probably the strongest justification for classifying the minority interest among the liabilities, or as a separate item between the liabilities and capital on the consolidated balance sheet.

Conclusion. We see, therefore, that although the disclosure of the possible distribution of income and capital appears to be the major objective in the conventional classification of the equities of a consolidated enterprise, the interrelationships of the several groups place severe limitations on the usefulness of this classification. The difficulties in disclosing legal capital are even greater. This suggests that, except when dissolution or reorganization seems probable or imminent, a strict classification by source seems to be most consistent with traditional accounting structures.

CHECKPOINTS

1. What exception did *ARB 51* permit for consolidations and why?
2. Company A has a 60 percent interest in Company B. If both A and B have $10 million of fixed assets, what value will be shown in the consolidated company for fixed assets?
3. In what way does consolidation produce results that are not necessarily consistent with the aims of equity classification?

SUMMARY

Equities are essentially an individual's fair share in an enterprise. Liabilities represent the equity of creditors in an enterprise, while the holdings of stockholders represent the equity of shareholders. However, conventional practice is to associate the term equity with owners' equity only.

The nature of the equities has been a matter of much debate in this century and more especially in recent years. The debate comes from several quarters. Managerial writers have stressed the importance of the broader concept of a stakeholder as opposed to the narrower concept of the shareholder. This leads one to question whether shareholders really own the enterprise or whether it would be more appropriate to define equity more broadly. Financiers have produced a vast range of hybrid securities, which have also broken down the clear distinctions between debt and equity. Again, this raises the question of whether, in the context of the financial markets of the 20th century, one should not use the enterprise rather than the proprietary theory of equity.

In one sense, the choice of theory is arcane. In another sense, it is very practical, because it raises many questions as to how one should account for interest, cash dividends, stock dividends, treasury stock, and the like. Stated otherwise, the definition of what goes into net income depends critically on whose net income it is. In the extreme, income statements merge with the value-added statements addressed in Chapter 10.

MULTIPLE CHOICE QUESTIONS

1. [M88#3] A subsidiary was acquired for cash in a business combination on January 1, 1987. The purchase price exceeded the fair value of identifiable net assets. The acquired company owned equipment with a market value in excess of the carrying amount as of the date of combination. A consolidated balance sheet prepared on December 31, 1987, would

a. Report the unamortized portion of the excess of the market value over the carrying amount of the equipment as part of goodwill.

b. Report the unamortized portion of the excess of the market value over the carrying amount of the equipment as part of plant and equipment.

c. Report the excess of the market value over the carrying amount of the equipment as part of plant and equipment.

d. Not report the excess of the market value over the carrying amount of the equipment because it would be expensed as incurred.

2. [N81#17] Goodwill represents the excess of the cost of an acquired company over the

a. Sum of the fair values assigned to identifiable assets acquired less liabilities assumed.

b. Sum of the fair values assigned to tangible assets less liabilities assumed.

c. Sum of the fair values assigned to intangible assets acquired less liabilities assumed.

d. Book value of an acquired company.

3. [N82#4] Consolidated financial statements are typically prepared when one company has

a. Accounted for its investment in another company by the equity method.

b. Accounted for its investment in another company by the cost method.

c. Significant influence over the operating and financial policies of another company.

d. The controlling financial interest in another company.

DISCUSSION QUESTIONS

Equity Theories

1. The concept of the accounting entity often is considered to be the most fundamental of accounting concepts, one that pervades all of accounting.

Required:

a. 1. What is an accounting entity? Explain.

2. Explain why the accounting entity concept is so fundamental that it pervades all of accounting.

b. For each of the following indicate whether the accounting concept of entity is applicable. Discuss and give illustrations.

1. A unit created by or under law.
2. The product-line segment of an enterprise.
3. A combination of legal units and/or product-line segments.
4. All of the activities of an owner or a group of owners.
5. An industry.
6. The economy of the United States.

2. **(May 1967)** The Roz Corporation, a client, is considering the authorization of a 5 percent common stock dividend to common stockholders. The financial vice president of the corporation wishes to discuss the accounting implications of such an authorization with you before the next meeting of the board of directors.

Required:

a. The first topic the vice president wishes to discuss is the nature of the stock divided to the recipient.

1. Discuss the case *for* considering the stock dividend as income to the recipient.

2. Discuss the case *against* considering the stock dividend as income to the recipient.

b. The other topic for discussion is the property of issuing the stock dividend to all "stockholders of record" or to "stockholders of record exclusive of shares held in the name of the corporation as treasury stock."

1. Discuss the case *for* issuing stock dividends on treasury shares.

2. Discuss the case *against* issuing stock dividends on treasury shares.

c. These topics raise several issues about the nature of the accounting entity and the equities for which it is accountable. Of the theories that explain accounting equities, describe the

1. Proprietary theory.
2. Entity theory.
3. Residual equity theory.
4. Fund theory.

Equity Classifications

3.   (November 1980) Problems may be encountered in accounting for transactions involving the stockholders' equity section of the balance sheet.

Required:

a. Describe the accounting for the subscription of common stock at a price in excess of the par value of the common stock.

b. Describe the accounting for the issuance for cash of no-par value common stock at a price in excess of the stated value of the common stock.

c. Explain the significance of the three dates that are important in accounting for cash dividends to stockholders. State the journal entry, if any, needed at each date.

d. Assume retained earnings can be used for stock dividends distributable in shares. What is the effect of an ordinary 10 percent common stock divided on retained earnings and total stockholders' equity?

4.   (May 1976) *Part a*. A corporation's capital (stockholders' equity) is a very important part of its statement of financial position.

Required:

Identify and discuss the general categories of capital (stockholders' equity) for a corporation. Be sure to enumerate specific sources included in each general category.

Part b. Stock splits and stock dividends may be used by a corporation to change the number of shares of its stock outstanding.

Required:

1. What is meant by "a stock split effect in the form of a dividend?"
2. From an accounting viewpoint, explain how the stock split effected in the form of a dividend differs from an ordinary stock dividend.
3. How should a stock dividend that has been declared but not yet issued be classified in a statement of financial position? Why?

Part c. Jones Company has adopted a traditional stock option plan for its officers and other employees. This plan is properly considered a compensatory plan.

Required:

Discuss how accounting for this plan will affect net earnings and earnings per share. *Ignore income tax considerations and accounting for income tax benefits.*

Consolidations

5. **(May 1968)** Because of irreconcilable differences of opinion, a dissenting group within the management and board of directors of the Algo Company resigned and formed the Bevo Corporation to purchase a manufacturing division of the Algo Company. After negotiation of the agreement, but just before the closing and actual transfer of the property, a minority stockholder of Algo notified Bevo that a prior stockholders' agreement with Algo empowered him to prevent the sale. The minority stockholder's claim was acknowledged by Bevo's board of directors. Bevo's board then organized Casco, Inc., to acquire the minority stockholder's interest in Algo for $75,000, and Bevo advanced the cash to Casco. Bevo exercised control over Casco as a subsidiary corporation with common officers and directors. Casco paid the minority stockholder $75,000 (about twice the market value of the Algo stock) for his interest in Algo. Bevo then purchased the manufacturing division from Algo.

Required:

a. What expenditures are usually included in the cost of property, plant, and equipment acquired in a purchase?

b.

1. What are the criteria for determining whether to consolidate the financial statements of Bevo Corporation and Casco, Inc.?
2. Should the financial statements of Bevo Corporation and Casco, Inc., be consolidated? Discuss.

c. Assume that the unconsolidated financial statements are prepared. Discuss the propriety of treating the $75,000 expenditure in the financial statements of the Bevo Corporation as

1. An account receivable from Casco, Inc.
2. An investment in Casco, Inc.
3. Part of the cost of the property, plant, and equipment.
4. A loss.

6. (May 1984, amended) Selected information from the balance sheets of Golden Company and Bridge Company at December 31, 1982 follows:

	Golden Company	Bridge Company
	(000s omitted)	
Assets:		
Current assets:		
Cash	$103,500	$ 800
Marketable equity securities, at cost which approximates market	13,000	—
Accounts receivable, net of allowance for doubtful accounts	55,000	24,700
Inventories, at lower of cost or market	76,000	25,000
Prepaid expenses	2,500	500
Total current assets	250,000	51,000
Property, plant, and equipment, net of accumulated depreciation	311,000	62,000
Other assets	29,000	6,000
Total assets	$590,000	$119,000
Liabilities:		
Total liabilities (condensed)	$327,000	$ 65,000
Stockholders' Equity:		
Common stock, par value $1.00 per share	10,000	2,000
Additional paid-in capital	111,000	23,000
Retained earnings	142,000	29,000
Total stockholders' equity	263,000	54,000
Total liabilities and stockholders' equity	$590,000	$119,000

Additional facts are as follows:

- On January 1, 1983, Golden acquired for cash of $101 million all of the shares of outstanding stock of Bridge. The market (fair) values of

Bridge's assets and liabilities on January 1, 1983, were the same as the book values on December 31, 1982, except property, plant, and equipment, net of accumulated depreciation, which had a market value of $93 million on January 1, 1983. Golden and Bridge are in similar lines of business.

Required:

a. Should consolidated financial statements for Golden and Bridge be presented for 1983? Explain why or why not.

b. If consolidated financial statements were prepared for the year ended December 31, 1983, how should the excess of the cash paid by Golden over the book value of Bridge be accounted for in those consolidated financial statements? Why? Ignore income tax considerations.

GENERAL MOTORS

General Motors Corporation (GMC) founded a wholly owned finance house, called General Motors Acceptance Corporation (GMAC), whose sole purpose was to provide credit facilities to those customers who wished to purchase General Motors automobiles. Despite being a wholly owned subsidiary, GMAC was not consolidated into GMC on grounds that it would be misleading to users of financial statements if that were done. Instead, the financial statements of GMAC were provided as a footnote to GMC's statements. The net worth of GMAC appeared as an investment in the GMC balance sheet. A condensed version of the 1978 balance sheets follows (all numbers are in millions of dollars):

	GMC	*GMAC*
Accounts receivable from GMAC	2,893.0	0.0
Other current assets	15,106.0	26,903.4
Investment in GMAC	2,005.8	0.0
Other investments	806.3	0.0
Fixed assets (net)	9,605.6	0.0
Other assets	181.1	0.0
Total Assets	30,598.3	26,903.4
Accounts payable to GMC	0.0	2,893.5
Other current liabilities	10,050.6	12,058.4
Long-term liabilities	978.9	9,945.7
Other liabilities	1,999.0	0.0
Owners' equity	17,569.9	2,005.8
Total Equities	30,598.3	26,903.4

a. Compute leverage and liquidity ratios for the two companies as reported. Consolidate GMC and GMAC and compute leverage and liquidity ratios for the consolidated company.

b. Using these ratios, and whatever other information you deem desirable, discuss the pros and cons of the FASB's decision to require that all majority-held subsidiaries be consolidated. (Note that GMAC's income statement was not provided in the footnote. GMAC's net income, though, for 1978 was reported in the body of its statement at $229.6 million compared to GMC's net income of $3,508.0 million.)

PRIMARY SOURCES

Those interested in learning more about the topics covered in this chapter might begin by consulting these sources. Each has numerous excellent citations.

Anthony, Robert N. *Tell It Like It Was* (Homewood, Ill.: Richard D. Irwin, 1983), esp. Ch. 4.

Financial Accounting Standards Board, *Distinguishing between Liability and Equity Instruments and Accounting for Instruments with Characteristics of Both* (FASB Discussion Memorandum, 1990).

Goldberg, Louis. *An Inquiry into the Nature of Accounting. American Accounting Association Monograph No. 7* (AAA, 1965), esp. pp. 162–74.

Kam, Vernon. *Accounting Theory,* 2nd ed. (New York: John Wiley, 1990).

Staubus, George A. (1961) *A Theory of Accounting to Investors* (Houston: Scholars Book Co., 1971).

SELECTED ADDITIONAL READINGS

Equity Theories

AAA Committee on Concepts and Standards Research—The Business Entity. "The Entity Concept." *The Accounting Review,* April 1965, pp. 358–67.

AAA Committee on Tax and Financial Entity Theory. "Report of the Committee on Tax and Financial Entity Theory." *The Accounting Review,* Supplement to vol. 48, 1973, pp. 187–92.

Bartlett, J. W., and L. F. Davidson. "The Entity Concept and Accounting for Interest Costs." *Accounting and Business Research,* Summer 1982, pp. 175–87.

Bird, Francis A.; Lewis F. Davidson; and Charles H. Smith. "Perceptions of External Accounting Transfers under Equity and Proprietary Theory." *The Accounting Review,* April 1975, pp. 233–44.

Moores, K., and G. T. Steadman. "The Comparative Viewpoints of Groups of Accountants: More on the Entity-Proprietary Debate." *Accounting, Organizations, and Society,* 1986, pp. 19–34.

Classification of Stockholder Equities

Melcher, Beatrice. "Stockholders' Equity." *Accounting Research Study No. 15* (AICPA, 1973).

Roberts, Michael L.; William D. Sampson; and Michael T. Dugan. "The Stockholders' Equity Section: Form without Substance?" *Accounting Horizons,* December 1990, pp. 35–46.

Scott, Richard A. "Owners' Equity, the Anachronistic Element." *The Accounting Review,* October 1979, pp. 750–63.

Consolidated Financial Statements

Accountants International Study Group. "Consolidated Financial Statements," 1973.

Baxter, George C., and James C. Spinney. "A Closer Look at Consolidated Financial Statement Theory." *CA Magazine,* January 1975, pp. 31–36.

Colley, J. Ron, and Ara G. Volkan. "Accounting for Goodwill." *Accounting Horizons,* March 1988, pp. 35–41.

Frances, Jere R. "Debt Reporting by Parent Companies: Parent-Only versus Consolidated Statements." *Journal of Business Finance and Accounting,* Autumn 1986, pp. 393–403.

Heian, James B., and James B. Thies. "Consolidation of Finance Subsidiaries: $230 Billion in Off-Balance Sheet Financing Comes Home to Roost." *Accounting Horizons,* March 1989, pp. 1–9.

Mohr, Rosanne M. "Unconsolidated Finance Subsidiaries: Characteristics and Debt/Equity Effects." *Accounting Horizons,* March 1988, pp. 27–34.

Petri, Enrico, and Roland Minch. "The Treasury Stock Method and Conventional Method in Reciprocal Stockholdings—An Amalgamation." *The Accounting Review,* April 1975, pp. 330–41. See also Raymond S. Chen. "A Comment." *The Accounting Review,* April 1975, pp. 359–64, and Enrico Petri and Roland Minch. "A Reply." *The Accounting Review,* April 1975, pp. 365–69.

Thomas, Paula B., and J. Harry Hagler. "Push Down Accounting: A Descriptive Assessment." *Accounting Horizons,* September 1988, pp. 26–31.

Walker, R. G. "An Evaluation of the Information Conveyed by Consolidated Statements." *Abacus,* December 1976, pp. 116–24.

ENDNOTES

1. Julian Walmsley, *The New Financial Instruments* (New York: John Wiley & Sons, 1988), p. 58.
2. Henry Rand Hatfield, *Accounting, Its Principles and Problems* (New York: Appleton-Century-Crofts, 1927), pp. 171, 221.

3. See, for example, ibid, p. 172.

4. See, for example, Stephen Gilman, *Accounting Concepts of Profit* (New York: Ronald Press, 1939), p. 74.

5. William Andrew Paton, *Accounting Theory* (New York: Ronald Press, 1922), pp. 84–89.

6. Ibid, p. 85.

7. AAA Committee on Accounting Concepts and Standards, *Accounting and Reporting Standards for Corporate Financial Statements and Preceding Statements and Supplements* (AAA, 1957).

8. *SFAC 6,* par. 49.

9. *SFAC 6,* par. 49, fn. 26.

10. FASB Discussion Memorandum, *Conceptual Framework for Financial Accounting and Reporting* (Conn: FASB, 1976), par. 188.

11. This is called the trust-fund theory. The title is something of a misnomer because there is no fund and no real "trust" in any legal sense of the word.

12. FASB Discussion Memorandum, *Conceptual Framework,* par. 191.

13. Committee on External Reporting, "An Evaluation of External Reporting Practices," *The Accounting Review,* Supplement to vol. 44, 1969, pp. 103–4.

14. *ARB 51,* par. 1.

15. Maurice Moonitz, *The Entity Theory of Consolidated Statements* (Brooklyn: Foundation Press, 1951), pp. 58–59.

16. See S. R. Sapienza, "The Divided House of Consolidations," *The Accounting Review,* July 1960, pp. 503–10.

Chapter 23

Changes in Stockholders' Equities

CHAPTER OBJECTIVES

After studying this chapter, you will be able to:

Justify the accounting for conversions of debt and preferred stock to common stock and the issuance of stock dividends.

Account for stock options and warrants, especially compensating stock option plans.

Compare the single-transaction from the double-transaction approach in the treatment of treasury stock.

Contrast the treatment of owners' equity in a purchase transaction with that in a pooling transaction.

Evaluate the information content of primary and fully diluted earnings-per-share computations.

CHAPTER OVERVIEW

Increases in Invested Capital

Invested capital may be increased by a variety of strategies: capital stock subscriptions, conversions of debt or preferred stock, stock dividends, stock options, or warrants. Each affects the classification of invested capital differently.

Decreases in Invested Capital

Invested capital may be decreased by repurchasing shares and creating, as a result, treasury stock. Treatment of a subsequent resale of treasury stock depends on whether one considers the sale and purchase a single or a double transaction.

Business Combinations

The purchase of another company's stock for cash or other assets does not lead to an increase in invested capital. On the other hand, when two companies pool their resources, invested capital does increase to reflect the net assets of the combined companies.

Earnings per Share

Manipulations of earnings per share during the bull market of the 1960s led accountants to require the disclosure of primary and fully diluted earnings per share computations to reflect the potential impact of converting debt and preferred stock.

The original classification of stockholders' equity is generally considered to be descriptive of its source; however, changes and reclassifications of equities make it difficult to retain this information. For example, in the case of stock dividends or other transfers to invested capital, the identity of the original source is lost.

The main reason for the loss of the source information is that the conventional procedures to record changes and reclassifications of stockholders' equity are based primarily on other objectives. Generally, these procedures attempt to maintain a distinction between invested capital and retained earnings, disclose legal capital, and indicate the amount available for distribution as dividends. As a result, none of the objectives is met adequately. In this chapter, the procedures for recording changes and reclassifications, and the reporting of earnings per share are analyzed critically in terms of the relevant objectives and on the basis of consistent equity theories.

INCREASES IN INVESTED CAPITAL

Invested, or contributed, capital is the investment in an enterprise of its owners. In the case of a corporation, invested capital includes the total amount paid for shares plus capitalized retained earnings. It may be increased by the subscription or sale of additional shares of stock, by the acquisition and resale of treasury shares, by the conversion of indebtedness into stockholder equities, and by the transfer of retained earnings into invested capital. However, a basic principle widely held at least since the early 1930s is that retained earnings should include no credits from transactions in the company's own stock or transfers from paid-in capital or other capital accounts.[1] Therefore, the apparent basic objective in the classification of these increases in capital is to prevent the showing of equity arising from capital transactions as income or retained earnings and to prevent the implication that these amounts are available for ordinary dividends.

Capital Stock Subscriptions

When shares of previously unissued stock are sold for cash or other consideration, the total increase in equity is included in invested capital. Although it is still common practice to separate this amount into two parts—par or stated value, and the excess over par or stated value—the entire amount represents capital invested by stockholders for an indefinite period. Whether subscriptions for shares received by the corporation are part of invested capital, or merely a promise to increase the capital, is less clear. In some states, the codes regulating corporations treat stock subscribed, but not issued, as a part of legal capital. However, the Model Business Corporation Act includes in stated capital only shares that have been issued.[2] But, whether or not the subscribed shares are considered legal capital, accounting practice is to include the subscriptions in invested capital if:

1. The subscriptions represent legal claims against the subscribers.
2. The corporation intends to collect the subscriptions within a reasonable and definite period of time.

If the subscriptions are not intended to be called, or if the time of call is indefinite, the subscriptions do not really represent invested capital. But a valid commitment to invest and a reasonable expectation that the amounts will be paid in to the corporation in due course should be sufficient to consider the subscriptions to be permanent investments. Reports filed with the SEC are required to treat the Subscriptions Receivable account for the unpaid balance on the shares as a valuation account in the stockholders' equity section.

Conversion of Debt

When convertible bonds are exchanged for stock, two methods have been suggested for treating the conversion:

1. The *book value* method in which the book value of the long-term debt is simply reclassified, when the new shares are issued, as capital stock and additional paid-in capital. No gain or loss is recognized on the transaction; the book value of the debt is merely converted into stockholder equity.

2. The *market value* method in which the current market price of the bonds is capitalized as stockholder equity. Any excess of the current price over the book value of the bonds is shown as an extraordinary loss on conversion. If the book value of the bonds exceeds the current market price of the bonds or stock, an extraordinary gain on conversion results.[3]

A preference for method 1 is implied in *APB 14*, which recommends that the entire proceeds from the sale of convertible debt be classified as debt.* Since none of the initial proceeds is allocated to the conversion privilege, a gain or loss cannot be measured by comparing either the book value of the securities with their market value, or the market value of nonconvertible debt (with similar characteristics) at the time of the conversion. This method is consistent with entity theory because all long-term equities are treated as interests in the enterprise. A transfer from one type of equity to another does not change the capital invested in the enterprise so it should not result in enterprise income.

Method 2 was preferred by the American Accounting Association.[4] It is consistent with proprietary theory because changes in the valuation of liabilities are considered from the point of view of their effect on the stockholders. However, to follow this concept through clearly, the gain or loss should be measured from the change in the investment value of the debt only. The investment value of interest here is the value of nonconvertible debt with characteristics similar to the convertible securities, except for the conversion feature. A portion of the proceeds, therefore, should be allocated to the conversion privilege. It is the portion allocated to debt that should be compared with the investment value at the time of conversion. The market value of the convertible securities is not relevant at either date because the securities derive part of their value from the conversion feature.

Conversion of Preferred Stock

The conventional procedure for the conversion of preferred stock into common stock is to follow method 1 for converting bonds. That is, the par value of the preferred plus the pro rata share of paid-in surplus on preferred shares is transferred to common stock and paid-in surplus on common. No gain or loss is shown on this transaction because both are included in the stockholders' equity classification.

The sum of the par value of the preferred stock and the pro rata portion of the additional paid-in capital from the original sale of the preferred

---

* See Chapter 19 for a discussion of the recording of convertible debt.

stock represents the source of the original invested capital. Note that it does not represent the amount of book equity of the preferred stock since, in the case of dissolution, preferred stockholders are entitled to the par value, or liquidation value, of the preferred stock. But there is some merit in reclassifying the additional paid-in capital because, if all of the preferred stock is finally converted, it may be misleading to show paid-in capital from the sale of preferred stock when there is no preferred stock outstanding. The transfer of these amounts from a preferred stock to a common stock classification does not violate the source objective because it all represents capital invested by stockholders. The reclassification represents mainly a change in the rights of the several classes of stockholders. The original source classification is lost only if a transfer from retained earnings is required; and in this case, the reclassification of retained earnings is similar to a stock dividend, discussed below.

An alternative is to transfer to common stock an amount equal to the current market value of either the preferred shares retired, or the new common shares issued, although these amounts should be fairly close. If this amount is in excess of the contributed capital of the retired preferred stock, the excess must be transferred from retained earnings. The result is that the original source classification is lost. This procedure also has some interesting implications. First, it implies an acceptance of this strict entity theory since it interprets retained earnings as the firm's equity in itself. Second, it implies that the current market price of the common stock does not reflect an interest in the retained earnings; if it did, there would be double counting. It also implies that there are two transactions. The first is a retirement of preferred shares, resulting in a partial distribution of retained earnings. The second is the sale of new shares of common stock at the current market value. Since the convertible preferred shares are generally issued originally with the convertible feature, treating the conversion as a single transaction seems more logical.

Stock Dividends and Stock Splits

Both stock dividends and stock splits are basically financial maneuvers that have nothing to do with the accounting principles of income determination and balance sheet valuation. In fact, if accountants held strictly to the classification of equities by original source, there would be no need for equity reclassifications as a result of these types of transactions. The only requirement would be to disclose the change in the number of shares outstanding and any change in par value or stated value. It would be necessary also to recompute the reported earnings per share for the current and prior periods. This is the case with a pure stock split. Since there is no change in either the legal or stated capital, no reclassification of equity is necessary. The number of shares outstanding is increased in inverse proportion to the decrease in par value or stated value per share. If the increase in the number of shares is accompanied by an increase in the total capital stock (total par value or stated value of shares outstanding), a partial stock dividend is also present. On the other hand, a 100 percent (or other large percentage) increase in the number of shares held by the same stockholders without an increase in total stockholders' equity, or a decrease in par value per share, is considered to be a stock split effected in the form of a stock dividend.

When accountants recognize classification objectives other than by the original source of capital, stock dividends present a problem in the treatment and disclosure of the transaction. Basic questions arise regarding the nature of the transaction and the amount to be capitalized. The nature of the transaction depends, in large part, on the equity theory selected as the most relevant. The amount to be capitalized depends on the objectives of classification and the assumed nature of the transaction. The amounts most commonly suggested for capitalization are:

1. The par value or stated value (or other legal capital amount) of the shares issued as a dividend.
2. The current market value of the shares issued.
3. The paid-in capital per share prior to the dividend times the number of shares issued.

The merits of each are discussed below.

The Nature of Stock Dividends.   Most accountants agree that stock dividends are not income to the recipients, but they differ in the reasoning leading to this conclusion. The AICPA Committee on Accounting Procedure (CAP) based its belief that stock dividends are not income to the recipients on the entity theory.[5] It argued that the corporation is a separate entity and that there can be no income to the stockholders until there is a severance of corporate assets. The income of the corporation is corporate income, not income to the stockholders. Cash dividends represent a transfer of assets to stockholders and, therefore, represent income to the recipients; stock dividends may result in unrealized appreciation, but it is not income to the stockholders until it is realized by them as a result of a division, distribution, or severance of corporate assets. Note that a rigid adherence to the realization concept rather than the entity theory is the controlling feature of this argument.*

Another interpretation of the entity theory that leads to different conclusions is that retained earnings represent a part of the total equity of the stockholders. Therefore, corporate income resulting in an increase in

---

* Chapter 1 recounts the details of Eisner *v.* Macomber in which a similar argument was made.

retained earnings is also an increase in stockholders' equity. Income is earned by stockholders when the value of their equity has increased either because of the reinvestment of corporate income, because of unrecorded increases in the value of the firm, or because of the transfer of equity from other equity holders for reasons such as price-level changes. In this interpretation, neither cash dividends nor ordinary stock dividends are income to the common stockholders since they do not result in an increase in the value of the stockholders' assets, including their equity in the firm.

A much narrower view of the entity theory was expressed by accounting theorist George Husband in his proposal of the proprietary or agency viewpoint as a logical alternative to the entity theory. In his strict interpretation of the entity theory, the "income earned by the corporate endeavor is the property of the corporation, per se."[6] According to him, retained earnings represent the *corporation's proprietary equity in itself*.[7] Therefore, cash dividends alone should be considered income to the stockholders. Only then do stockholders have something that they did not have before. It also follows logically from this view that, since the corporate income is not added to the stockholders' equity, a stock dividend represents income to the stockholders. Stated otherwise, a stock dividend increases the stockholders' equity by transferring to the stockholders a portion of the undivided corporate equity in itself. This interpretation does have some merit, but the generally accepted view is that, although corporate income accrues to the corporation rather than directly to the stockholders, the retained earnings represents an allocation of the undistributed income to the stockholders' equity. That is, the entity theory is based on the equation Assets = Equities; no portion of the total equities remains unallocated. Therefore, a stock dividend is not income to the stockholders but rather a reclassification of the stockholders' equity.

The proprietary theory leads to the same conclusion as the first two interpretations—that stock dividends are not income to the recipients—but for different reasons. The income of the corporation is also income to the owners. Therefore, cash dividends represent withdrawals by the owners of what already belongs to them. Stock dividends represent a reclassification of equity, but they are not income to the owners, since there is no increase in total proprietorship.

The Capitalization of Par or Stated Value. Under the prevalent interpretation of the entity theory, that stock dividends are not income to the recipients, the question becomes that of determining how much, if any, of corporate equity should be reclassified. If the objective of equity classification is to show the source of capital, the answer is that no reclassification should be made, since the original source has not changed. All that would be required is that proper disclosure should be made of the change in the number of shares outstanding. However, if we also wish to show the total amount of legal capital, it is necessary to transfer from retained earnings, or additional paid-in capital, to capital stock an amount equal to the stated value of the shares issued as required by the state of incorporation. In most states and in the Model Business Corporation Act, this amount is the par value of par value shares or the stated value of no-par shares.

Most writers agree that the par or stated value is the minimum amount that should be capitalized because of the legal considerations involved. While CAP recommended the capitalization of fair value in certain circumstances, as indicated below, it clearly recognized the showing of legal capital as one of the objectives of classification.[8] This is reflected in its statement to the effect that the minimum amount capitalized should be, in all cases, that necessary to meet legal requirements, but this does not prevent the capitalization of a larger amount per share. It also recommended that there is no need to capitalize more than that necessary to meet legal requirements in two special cases:

1. When the number of additional shares issued is so great that it may reasonably be expected that the market price per share will be reduced materially.
2. In the case of closely held companies where it may be expected that intimate knowledge of the corporation's affairs would preclude any implication by the stockholders that the stock dividends represent a distribution of corporate earnings.

If the objective of classification is to show the legal capital, it should be recognized that the classification by source is destroyed. It is possible to meet both objectives only by a dual classification, by showing the legal capital in a footnote, or by maintaining a separate item in the balance sheet for the retained earnings capitalized equal to the par value (or stated value) of the shares issued as a stock dividend.

The Capitalization of Market Price.   Only in the very strict interpretation of the entity theory can a stock dividend be considered to be income to the stockholders. But in this interpretation the amount of the dividend is considered to be the current market price of the shares. It is claimed that stockholders could sell these additional shares at this price and be as well off as they were before. Well-offness is interpreted here as the number of shares held. A stock dividend increases this number; it remains the same if the additional shares are sold. Thus, it is interpreted as a distribution of undivided retained earnings by an allocation to the stockholders' permanent equity.[9]

Although CAP did not recognize that a stock dividend is income to the recipient, it recommended that the amount to be capitalized (transferred to capital stock and additional paid-in capital) should be an amount equal to the fair value (market value) of the shares issued in all cases where the amount of stock issued is so small in comparison with the total shares outstanding that it has no apparent effect on the market price per share.[10] The reasoning for this recommendation is that, because of general representations, the recipients look on the stock dividend as distributions of corporate earnings equal to the market price of the shares issued. Therefore, if less than the market price were capitalized, an amount of the retained earnings thought to have been distributed to the stockholders would be available for additional stock dividends or cash distributions.

In those cases where the number of additional shares issued is large enough to materially influence the market price per share of the stock, CAP recommended that there is no need to capitalize more than that necessary to meet legal requirements (usually par or stated value).[11] Although the situations where this condition is met are assumed to arise for varying percentages of new shares, depending upon differing market conditions for individual firms, an arbitrary rate of 20 to 25 percent of shares previously outstanding was suggested as the dividing line between a small and a large stock dividend. Subsequently, the SEC adopted an arbitrary rate of 25 percent as the upper percentage requiring a transfer from retained earnings to paid-in capital accounts.[12]

As noted above, the capitalization of retained earnings results in an abandonment of the objective of classification by source of stockholders' equity. In its place is substituted the objective of showing the possible disposition of equity. Retained earnings is presumed to show the amount available for distribution in the future as either stock dividends or cash dividends. However, since most states permit at least stock dividends, and in many cases both cash and stock dividend distributions, out of paid-in capital in excess of par value, this restriction on future distributions is purely a financial and accounting restriction. The main argument against this line of reasoning is that most firms do not intend to make cash distributions out of earnings retained in prior years except in emergency situations. Retained earnings generally represent earnings reinvested in the business without formal action. However, it is erroneous to assume that just because there has not been a formal transfer to permanent invested capital, they are then intended to be used for future distributions.

Two other arguments for the use of market value in the capitalization of stock dividends are the following:

1. The stock dividend can be thought of as two transactions— a cash dividend to stockholders and a subsequent sale to them of stock at the current market price. Therefore, the cash dividend would reduce retained earnings by the market value of the shares. The subsequent sale of stock would increase invested capital by this same amount.

2.   The cost to the corporation of the stock dividend is assumed to be the opportunity cost of giving the shares to stockholders rather than selling them in the market. That is, since the corporation could have sold the shares at market price, this is the best evidence of the amount of the dividend and the amount that should be capitalized.

Both of these arguments are weak in that they assume situations that do not really exist. The corporation has a right to sell shares to its common stockholders at amounts less than the market price (with some exceptions), and this action does not generally injure any class of equity holder.

The main argument in opposition to the use of market values is that, if a stock dividend is not income to the stockholders, it is misleading to act as if it were, even if some people may believe that it is so. Capitalization of the market value of the stock issued only helps to continue the illusion that the stockholders are receiving something comparable to a cash dividend, or that they are receiving something they did not have already. This illusion is generally strengthened by the fact that most firms continue the same cash dividend per share after the stock dividend as before, resulting in an increase in the total dividends declared.

Another argument in opposition to the use of fair value is that market value represents the total equity of the stock in the firm, including both invested capital and retained earnings. Therefore, it is illogical to transfer from retained earnings to invested capital that which represents both of these. It is better to present the transaction as a partial *stock split* with an accompanying increase in legal capital. In other words, the original source of capital should not be disturbed; disclosure of the increase in legal capital can be made in footnotes or by other means. This procedure has the additional advantage of presenting a proper interpretation of retained earnings—as income reinvested permanently in the business.

It may appear that the widespread use of automatic dividend investment plans provides credence to the market value method. However, in these plans, the stockholders have the option to receive cash dividends, or an equivalent number of shares computed on the basis of the current market price of the stock. Since stockholders are not required to receive shares, this represents two transactions—the issue of a cash dividend and a simultaneous reinvestment by the stockholder in exchange for additional shares. The effect is merely a convenient method of issuing additional shares in small lots at a low cost to the stockholders and to the issuing firm.

The distinction between a stock dividend and a stock split based on market reaction to the new shares is not supported by empirical research. Several studies of market behavior suggest that the requirement of the capitalization of market value in specific cases is based on a spurious premise.[13] This distinction also fails to find support in the efficient-market thesis. If the market is efficient, any dilution of shares by either stock dividends, or stock splits, should be reflected immediately in share prices.

Stock Options and Stock Warrants

Stock rights are frequently granted to current stockholders, permitting them to purchase shares of stock (in proportion to the shares held) at a price less than the market price, or less than the price at which the shares are offered to others. Generally, the granting of these stock rights does not result in an increase in invested capital because no new capital is brought into the enterprise until the stock is sold. According to the objective of classification by source, this solution is correct. But it is inconsistent with the procedure recommended above by CAP for the handling of stock dividends.

A stock dividend is an extreme form of a stock right—a right to acquire shares with no additional cost. Therefore, the main difference between a stock dividend and a stock right is the amount to be paid by the stockholders for the additional shares received by them. Turning the analogy around, a stock right is a stock dividend in the amount of the value of the right—the excess of the market value of the shares over the purchase price to the stockholders. To be consistent with the recommendations for the treatment of stock dividends, this amount should be capitalized by a transfer from retained earnings to invested capital, usually "contributed capital in excess of par or stated value." But, in the opinion of the authors, the capitalization of market value is illogical in both situations because neither is a source of invested capital.

When stock warrants are sold by the firm, however, the proceeds represent invested capital whether or not the warrants are exercised. If the warrants are exercised, the original proceeds plus the additional amount paid by the holders to acquire the shares represent the total amount invested by the new stockholders, and that amount should be classified accordingly as invested capital. Before the warrants are exercised, however, a potential dilution of dividends and earnings per share exists. The effect of this dilution is discussed below in the section on earnings per share.

Rights Granted to the Purchasers of Other Securities.   Detachable warrants are frequently granted to purchasers of bonds giving them the right to purchase common stock at a fixed price (frequently less than the market price of the stock when the rights are granted). As discussed in Chapter 19, *APB 14* recommended that the market prices of the bonds and the warrants be used to allocate the proceeds from the sale of the securities to debt and to stockholders' equity. When the warrants are exercised, the amount allocated to the warrants plus the additional amount paid for the shares is treated the same as proceeds from the sale of new stock issues. However, since bonds with detachable warrants do not differ in substance from convertible debt, both should be accounted for in the same way as discussed previously.

An allocation is even less important when common stock options are granted to purchasers of preferred stock (or vice versa). In this case, the entire amount paid in by the stockholders represents invested capital. There is little advantage in showing the source from preferred stockholders separately from that obtained from common stockholders, particularly when the two sources are not independent of each other. A separation of the invested capital into the two classes does not change the rights of the two classes of stockholders nor does it aid in disclosing these rights. However, if legal capital is also to be shown, an allocation may become necessary if the option price is below legal or stated capital.

Noncompensatory Employee Stock Purchase Plans.   Frequently, stock options are granted to employees as a means of raising capital and as a means of gaining widespread ownership among the officers and other employees of the enterprise. In these cases, no compensation need be presumed and, therefore, only the amounts paid in by the employees should be included in stockholders' equity. Four characteristics are considered essential in a noncompensatory plan:

1. Substantially all full-time employees meeting limited employment qualifications may participate.
2. The stock offer applies equally to all eligible employees or in the ratio of their salaries or wages.
3. The option period is short or reasonable in length.
4. The purchase price should not be lower than would be reasonable if the stock were offered to others.[14]

It is also assumed that granting the option does not impose additional obligations on the employees.

Compensatory Stock Option Plans.   Granting stock options to executives has been a popular method of providing compensation because of the potential tax advantages at different periods of time to the recipient. Prior to the Tax Reform Act of 1976, for instance, any taxes related to *qualified stock option plans* were deferred until the recipient sold the stock. Taxes were then computed at a capital gains rate which was lower than the rate for income. These advantages were eliminated by the 1976 Act but reinstated by the Economic Recovery Tax Act of 1981, which introduced the concept of *incentive stock options*. The Tax Reform Act of 1986 removed some of the benefits of stock options by raising the capital gains rate again. However, in 1991 the maximum marginal rate on capital gains will again be lower than the maximum marginal rate on income. A major issue throughout this period has been whether or not any compensation expense should be recorded and, if so, when and how much.

One view, applying the strict entity approach to accounting, is that the services received for which the stock options are granted do not cost the corporation anything and, therefore, should not be recorded at all. However, this argument is weak because it is based on the assumption that costs to the entity must result in a decrease in its net assets. If this were true, there would be no reason to record nonmonetary assets acquired by the issuance of stock. But it is possible to invest services in the business just as it is possible to invest nonmonetary assets. The main difference is that the services benefit the current period while the nonmonetary assets may benefit a future period or periods.

APB 25 clearly recognizes the possibility of compensation arising out of stock option contracts. Under compensatory stock option plans, the consideration the corporation receives for the stock issued "consists of cash or other assets, if any, plus services received from the employee."[15] Those accountants who recognize the existence of compensation generally agree that the amount of the compensation should be apportioned over the period that the services are received by the corporation. The main area of disagreement is in the valuation of the services and the determination of the resulting increase in invested capital arising from the stock option grant. The most commonly proposed valuation methods are:

1. The excess of the fair value of the stock over the option price at the date of the option grant.
2. The excess on the date the option becomes the property of the employee.
3. The excess of the fair value over the option price at the date that the option is first exercisable.
4. The excess on the date that the option is actually exercised.
5. The cost to the corporation at the date of exercise adjusted for the income tax effect to the firm.
6. The probable value of the option to the recipient at the date of grant.

More is said on each of these valuation methods in the following paragraphs. Also, a discussion of modern option pricing methods may be found in Chapter 6.

1.   The excess value at date of grant.   *APB 25* recommends that the value of the compensation should be the excess of the quoted market price of the stock over the option price at the date that the option is granted. An exception to measurement at the date of grant is necessary when a plan may contain variable terms contingent on events after the date of grant. In this case, the measurement date is the first date that both the number of shares and the option price are known. The main reasons for the choice of the date of grant or the above alternative are summarized as follows:

a.   The value at this date is assumed to be measurable and meaningful to both the employee and the employer. Although an option would have some value even if the option price were the same as or greater than the market value of the shares, the Board considered it impracticable to measure this value.

b. The value at the date of grant is assumed to be the value that both parties had in mind when the option was granted. Any additional value of the option to the employees is assumed to be offset by the restrictions imposed. From the point of view of the corporation, the value of the options at the date of grant must be estimated in order to determine the number of options to grant as just compensation for the services received.

c. The excess value at the date of grant represents the costs of restricting such shares to this purpose, because the principal alternative use of the shares is to sell them in the currently prevailing market.

d. Once an option is granted to an employee, the decision when to exercise the option, if at all, rests largely with the employee. Thus, changes in the market value of the shares are assumed to represent changes in the value of the option to the employee but not in the cost to the corporation.

The most important of these reasons is the inability to measure the true value of the option to the employee or the real cost to the corporation except for that portion of the value represented by the excess of the value at the date of grant over the option price. This reason is beginning to yield to recent theoretical advances in the pricing of options.

2. Excess value on vesting. Vesting is the date on which the option right becomes the property of the grantee. The main argument for this alternative is that only at this date does the corporation have an unqualified obligation under the agreement. The employee can exercise the option only after fulfilling certain conditions; but when these conditions are met, the option belongs to the employee, and even though he or she must wait to exercise the option, the employee holds the property rights. This situation is compared with the granting of bonus shares to be issued at the end of the period of service, at which time the compensation is determined by the value of the bonus shares.

3. Excess value on date the options are first exercisable. Although the options may be exercisable as soon as the employee obtains the property right, a waiting period is frequently required before the options may be exercised. From this date on, the grantee may speculate on the option by either exercising it or holding it as long as possible before it expires. Therefore, it is argued, changes in the market value of the shares after this date are irrelevant to the corporation. It is also argued that the value of the option cannot be known before it can be exercised.

4. Excess value on the date the options are exercised. The argument that the amount of compensation is the excess of the market value over the option price at the date the option is exercised is based on the fact that only at this time does the grantee become a stockholder. Upon purchasing the shares, the employee acquires an interest in the enterprise that is worth more than the current cash outlay. This excess value is compensation because only as a stockholder could the employee obtain a capital gain due to the increase in the value of the shares. It is also assumed that this is the cost of the option to the corporation because before this date the option is only a contingency. Any valuation before this date is only an estimate of the final cost to the corporation, and any valuation subsequent to this date is irrelevant because the grantee has then become a stockholder.

5.   Cost adjusted for income tax effect.   A modification of the above method is to include in the cost of the compensation the amount of the income tax foregone, if any, by the corporation. How appropriate this modification is will depend on the tax code at the time. Assume, for example, that the tax code at the time does not permit stock options to be tax-deductible. Then, if the value of the stock exceeds the option price by $60,000 at the time the options are exercised, and if we assume a corporate tax rate of 40 percent, this would be equivalent to a cash salary of $100,000. This, it is argued, represents the actual cost of the stock options to the corporation.

6.   The cash value of the services at the time of option grant.   When property is received by a corporation in exchange for stock, the amount of the invested capital is generally measured by the current value of the property received. If it is not possible to obtain a current value for the property, it may be assumed that the property value is equal to the current market value of the stock given in exchange. In a stock option contract, the employee makes an investment in the firm in an amount equal to the value of his services being compensated. However, since it is not generally possible to determine the value of the services received, it may be assumed that the compensation is equal to the current value of the stock options. But since the restricted stock options are not transferable, they have no market price and their current value is difficult to estimate. Nevertheless, a current value does exist, and some writers propose that a bargained price for the services can be obtained.

By accepting stock options rather than cash compensation, the executive is making an investment in the firm of an amount equal to the excess of the bargained value of his or her services over the cash salary received. Between the date of option grant and either the date that the option is exercised, or the date it expires, the market price of the stock may increase substantially or moderately, or it may decline. Therefore, the final value of the option to the grantee may possibly be very large, or it may be zero. At the date of the option grant, the expected value is between these two extremes. But note that it is always positive if there is some possibility of the market price rising above the option price; it would never be negative, and would be zero only if the option price were equal to, or greater than, the market price of the stock at the date of grant and if there were no expectation of an increase in the market price above the option price. The net aftertax value of the option to the executive should then be converted into the equivalent of a cash salary before consideration of the personal income tax effect.

An Appraisal of Valuation Methods.   In the opinion of the authors, the most logical method of valuation is the cash value of the services as measured by the value of the option at the date of grant. However, most accountants shy away from this solution because it is highly subjective and depends upon speculation regarding the future. But in this case there is no bargained price nor any marketable value, so that there is no alternative to the use of estimates. The position of the APB in *Opinion No. 25* was that only the obvious value at the date of grant—the excess of the market value at date of grant over the option price—should be recorded as the compensation. It did not deny that additional value exists; rather, it claimed only that it cannot be measured.

All other methods are attempts to find some objective measure of the value of the compensation based on either the benefit received by the employee or the final cost to the corporation. The excess of market price over option price at any specific date is based on a cost concept, rather than on a concept of service value invested by the employee. In the cost concept, we forget that invested capital is measured by the value of the consideration received by the firm and not the reverse. Even though the value of the option should be used in estimating the value of the services received, the value of the services is invested by the employee and this value should be determined by taking into consideration all possible outcomes and the risk taken by the grantee in receiving the option. The result is that the excess value of the market price over the option price at the time of property right, or the date the option becomes exercisable, is an incomplete valuation and probably understates the value of the option, particularly if it may be held by the grantee for several additional years before expiring. Even if the market price were equal to the option price at this date, the option would have a value to the grantee because of the possible increase in the market price before the option expires.

The excess of the market price over the option price at the date the option is exercised does represent the final gain to the employee, but this total gain is made up of two basic parts —the compensation to the employee and the gain or loss on the investment of the employee's services. The value of the compensation should be measured by the most probable change in market price; if the increase in market price exceeds this expectation, the grantee has a gain on the investment, and if it falls short of this expectation, there is a loss.

Regardless of which method one might prefer in valuing stock options, full disclosure should be made of the terms of the stock option contracts, the situation at the date of the balance sheet, and the method of valuation.

CHECKPOINTS

---

1. Define the term *invested capital*.
2. Which of the two methods for handling conversions of debt was preferred by the American Accounting Association? State briefly why they preferred it.
3. Distinguish between a stock dividend and a stock split.
4. Provide two reasons why stock dividends are not considered income to the recipients.
5. In what circumstances might one capitalize the market price of shares in a stock dividend transaction?
6. Briefly contrast the capitalization of stated value with the capitalization of market value approach to handling stock dividends.
7. Draw a time line of the six dates mentioned in regard to a compensating stock option plan, labeling what happens at each point.

DECREASES IN INVESTED CAPITAL

Normally, the invested capital of a firm is thought to represent the permanent capital of an enterprise. Deliberate reductions in invested capital should not be made by payments to stockholders unless these payments are specifically disclosed as liquidating dividends. But partial liquidation also occurs when a specific class of stock is called and redeemed. The purchase of treasury shares is similar to the redemption of preferred stock, with the exception that few stockholders of any class may be involved and the purchase price is not usually prearranged. If the treasury stock is reissued, the net result may be either an increase, a decrease, or no change in stockholders' equity. Invested capital may also be reduced by a recapitalization in recognition of the fact that accumulated losses have caused an effective reduction in capital without any distributions to shareholders.

Treasury Stock

When stockholders' equity is increased as a result of transactions with shareholders, accountants are generally agreed that no gain results and no part of the increase should be added to income or retained earnings; it all represents invested capital. But when stockholders' equity is reduced as a result of the acquisition of the corporation's own shares, accountants are not in agreement regarding the effect on invested capital and retained earnings. Two basic questions relating to this controversy are these:

1. How much of the payment to stockholders should be treated as a return of invested capital, and how much should be considered a distribution of retained earnings?
2. How should the effect on legal capital be shown?

When a firm acquires its own shares and holds them for reissuing or subsequent cancellation, the acquisition and disposition can be treated as either a single transaction or two separate and distinct transactions. The former is commonly referred to as the cost method and the latter is generally referred to as the par value method; however, it is possible to record the treasury stock at either cost or par value and still treat the purchase and sale as either a single transaction or as two separate transactions.

The Single-Transaction Concept.   If a firm acquires its own shares and then sells them to other stockholders at a price equal to cost, it does not seem logical that the classification of stockholders' equity should be disturbed merely because the corporation handled the shares. If the shares are purchased and sold merely for the convenience of the stockholders, the transaction is equivalent to the sale of shares by one stockholder to another. If the stock is sold by the corporation in excess of its cost, the excess represents an increase in invested capital in excess of par value. Therefore, the classification by source is maintained and the legal capital is not disturbed.

When treasury stock is sold at less than its cost to the firm, the excess of cost over sale price represents either a repayment of invested capital or a distribution of retained earnings. Although accountants are not in general agreement as to the accounts to be charged for this excess, three proposals are frequently made:

1.   Following the suggestion in *APB 6*, many writers maintain that the excess represents a return of invested capital. They conclude that it should be charged to capital surplus arising from other treasury stock transactions, or to contributed capital in excess of par value related to the same class of stock.[16] Only if the excess is greater than the total of these capital surplus accounts do these writers recommend that retained earnings should be reduced.

2.   An alternative is to reduce contributed capital in excess of par from the original sale of this class of stock by a pro rata amount and to treat the remainder as a distribution of retained earnings. The capital stock account is not disturbed because of a desire to show the amount of legal capital, which has not been reduced (in most cases) by the transaction.

3.   A third solution is to treat the entire excess as a distribution of retained earnings. This alternative is popular because of its simplicity and conservatism. It is also frequently recommended for use in those states that include contributed capital in excess of par value as a part of legal capital, with the result that the presentation of legal capital is not disturbed by the transaction. However, in the opinion of the authors it has considerable merit from a theoretical point of view. If the purchase and sale of treasury stock are treated as a single transaction, the net effect is a selective distribution of the firm's assets to one or more stockholders. Any distribution to stockholders that does not reduce the number of shares outstanding should be treated as a distribution of retained earnings if such is available. Invested capital should not be disturbed.

A major difficulty of the single-transaction concept and the application of the cost basis occurs when the treasury stock is not sold immediately or when it is subsequently canceled. While the stock is held in the treasury, the cost represents an unallocated reduction of stockholders' equity held in suspense until completion of the transaction. Therefore, both invested capital and retained earnings are overstated and this may result in a misleading interpretation, particularly if the shares are later canceled or sold substantially below cost.

The Two-Transactions Concept. In the two-transactions approach to treasury stock, the acquisition of a corporation's own shares is assumed to represent a contraction in its capital structure. If the shares are subsequently reissued, the issuance of the reacquired shares is accounted for in the same way as the issuance of previously unissued shares.

When the outlay for the reacquired stock exceeds the pro rata portion of contributed capital, the excess is considered a distribution of retained earnings. This is the view of *APB 6* for those cases in which the stock was purchased for constructive retirement. *APB 6* also allows the excess of purchase price over par or stated value to be charged entirely to retained earnings as a capitalization of retained earnings and credited to contributed capital in excess of par value.[17]

If the treasury shares are acquired at a cost in excess of the pro rata amount of invested capital, the effect of this recommendation would be to transfer a portion of retained earnings to additional contributed capital as a result of the acquisition and resale of a firm's own shares. Retained earnings are reduced when the shares are purchased, and additional contributed capital is increased when the shares are sold, even though the purchase and sale prices may be the same. On the other hand, if the stock is acquired and resold at a price less than the par or stated value, additional contributed capital would be increased at the time of purchase, and a discount on stock or similar account would be established when the stock is resold.

Evaluation of the Single-Transaction and Two-Transactions Concepts.
Both the single-transaction and two-transactions concepts have some logic in their favor. The former is based on the premise that substance is more important than form and that a corporation should not transfer

amounts from retained earnings to invested capital merely because it happens to handle the transfer of shares from one stockholder to another. The two-transactions concept is based on the idea that there is little difference between the purchase and sale of treasury shares and the acquisition and retirement of shares with a subsequent sale of new shares. In the opinion of the authors, each concept is appropriate for different circumstances. If shares are acquired by purchase with the express purpose of reselling to employees, executives, or other special groups, the single-transactions concept is relevant. On the other hand, if the objective of the acquisition is to purchase the shares of dissident stockholders or to effect the eventual retirement of certain classes of stock, the two-transactions concept should apply, even though these shares might be resold at a later date. Of course, if eventual cancellation is the objective, the two-transactions approach is clearly appropriate.

This suggested solution has the disadvantage that it is not always possible to determine the intent of the corporation. Therefore, accountants are not likely to treat similar situations uniformly. If the objective is not clear, a suggested solution is to require application of the two-transactions concept.

CHECKPOINTS

---

1. Define the term *treasury stock*.
2. Distinguish the single-transaction concept from the two-transactions concept in the context of treasury stock.

BUSINESS COMBINATIONS

When the assets of one firm are acquired by a second firm as a result of a purchase transaction involving the payment of cash or the exchange of other assets, the purchased assets are generally recorded in the accounts of the acquiring firm at their cost (the value of assets given in exchange), which may be assumed to represent their current value. The historical cost to the selling firm is no longer relevant. And the stockholders' equity of the acquiring firm is not increased or reclassified because of the transaction.

If the acquisition is carried out by the purchase (for cash or other assets) of the entire capital stock of a second firm, the situation is similar to the above purchase. In fact, if the acquired firm is dissolved, the net result of the transaction may be the same as a purchase of the assets, with the possible exception that the acquiring firm may assume the liabilities of the purchased firm. Even if the acquired firm is not dissolved, the consolidated statement should show the acquired assets at their current cost, including the cost of intangibles; and no change in stockholders' equity occurs as a result of the acquisition of the shares or the consolidation of the parent and subsidiary firms. Only if a minority interest remains is there an increase in the total equity of the consolidated enterprise. As indicated in the previous chapter, however, the minority interest is not always shown as a part of the total equity in the consolidated balance sheet.

In the above cases, the acquisition of additional nonmonetary assets or stock of another firm for cash leads to a clear-cut treatment of the transaction as a purchase, even though several problems of consolidation remain unresolved. But when two or more firms combine by the exchange of the stock of one for the assets or stock of others, or when a new corporation is formed for this purpose, a question arises as to whether the transaction is a purchase or, in fact, only a "pooling of interest" of two or more firms. The nature of the transaction and the resulting enterprise rather than the legal form should dictate the accounting procedure to be followed.

Both the purchase and the pooling methods are consistent with different concepts of the traditional historical cost structure. However, neither method permits a good semantic interpretation of the economic situation and the resulting relationships. Therefore, the appearance of the financial statements resulting from the combination and the expected reaction of investors and creditors have usually been the determining factors in the choice of reporting method, and in many cases the determining factors in the decision whether or not to combine. Because of this emphasis on the accounting result rather than on providing interpretive information for investment decisions, the rule-making bodies in both the United States and other countries have found it difficult to establish rules that cannot be circumvented in spite of their continual revision.

Combinations Treated as Purchases

Whenever assets are acquired by the exchange of capital stock, the valuation of the assets is assumed to be equal to the value of the stock given in exchange unless the current value of the assets can be obtained by other verifiable means. Similarly, when all of the assets of a firm or its stock are acquired by giving capital stock in exchange in a purchase transaction, the accounting treatment involves two parts:

1. The net assets are valued in terms of total market value of the stock issued in exchange. This total cost should be allocated to specific assets whenever possible, and any excess should be considered purchased goodwill or other intangibles.

2. The total value of the stock issued is credited to invested capital with a possible division between legal capital and capital in excess of par or stated value. The former classification of the stockholders' equity of the acquired corporation has no effect on the classification in the acquiring firm.

A purchase transaction is based on the traditional structural concept that the valuation of assets and liabilities received should be recorded in the amount of the valuations of the assets or equities given in the exchange. These values then become the historical costs reported in subsequent periods. However, there is strong support for the position that some combinations are not the result of purchase transactions, but rather the result of a mutual joining together where neither firm purchases the other. The distinction between a purchase transaction and a mutual joining together cannot be settled on either structural or semantic grounds. Therefore, the rule-making bodies have attempted to legislate this distinction, but without success.

Because of this failure to establish workable criteria, and because of the abuses of accounting for acquisitions permitted by this failure, the pooling method has come under severe criticism from many sides and the purchase method has been claimed to be appropriate in all cases. For example, author of *ARS 5* and recent FASB board member Arthur Wyatt concluded that a business combination "is basically an exchange event in which two economic interests bargain to the consummation of an exchange of assets and/or equities."[18] Therefore, it follows that almost all combinations are purchases and should be accounted for as such. This was also the conclusion of the authors of *ARS 10*, George Catlett and Norman Olsen.[19] Likewise, the AAA recommended in ASOBAT the adoption of the purchase method as opposed to the pooling concept because of greater relevance.[20]

One of the main advantages of the purchase method is that it permits a "fresh start" from an accounting point of view, at least for the acquired firm. If the assets of the acquired firm are overvalued, they can be adjusted to a fair value at the time of combination. However, the purchase method is claimed to be disadvantageous if the fair value of the assets is greater than the previous book value, because recording these higher values will necessitate higher depreciation and amortization charges, resulting in lower reported net income for several years. This is compounded by the fact that, if the combination is a tax-free combination, this extra depreciation and amortization is not deductible for income tax purposes. It is also assumed to be disadvantageous because it eliminates the retained earnings of the acquired corporation, thereby reducing the amount available for dividends out of accumulated income, although the legal amount available may not be altered. These arguments are discussed more fully below.

Pooling of Interests

A pooling of interests is assumed to occur when two or more firms combine to carry out their business functions as a single economic enterprise. The enterprise may take the form of one of the existing corporations, a new corporation organized for the purpose, or a continuance of the previous corporations with one being the parent and the others the subsidiaries. In the absence of general principles to determine when a pooling of interests occurs, rule-making bodies have chosen to define specific conditions where pooling-of-interest accounting is permitted and have concluded that all other combinations should be treated as purchases. In spelling out the specific conditions, emphasis has been placed on the attendant circumstances surrounding the combination and the nature of the exchange transaction rather than the legal form. Among the attendant circumstances are the conditions that the firms being combined should be autonomous and without significant intercorporate investments. Earlier rules also emphasized the need for continuity of management and business activities, although these conditions were difficult to define and control. An additional factor complicating the enforcement of rules is the ability of firms to manipulate stockholdings and other circumstances to give the appearance of meeting the rules at the time of combinations. As a result, the rule-making bodies were forced to establish rules relating to exchanges occurring both before and after the combination transaction.

The emphasis on the exchange has focused on the requirement that pooling-of-interest accounting can be used only when common stock of the acquiring firm is exchanged for substantially all of the voting common stock of the acquired firm. The emphasis on this form of the transaction is assumed to provide evidence of a continuance of ownership interests assumed to be necessary in a pooling of interests. However, firms have manipulated stockholdings before and after the combination to give the appearance of a continuance of ownership interests at the time of the combination transaction. Thus, rules are necessary to prevent certain types of transactions both before and after the effective date of the combination.

In a pooling of interests, the accounting treatment involves two basic differences from the treatment as a purchase:

1. The assets and liabilities of the several combining enterprises are brought into the new enterprise at their book value in the accounts of the former separate organizations, with the exception that adjustments may be made to provide for uniform treatment.
2. The retained earnings of the several corporations should be added together in the surviving corporation or in consolidation, except for that amount that must be transferred to invested capital to present the proper legal capital.

Pooling-of-interest accounting has been popular in business combinations for several reasons:

1. When the fair value of the assets combined is greater than the book value, the depreciation and amortization would be increased if the combination were treated as a purchase. Also, the net income of the new combination would be less than the summation of the net incomes of the former enterprises.
2. The pooling-of-interests treatment avoids the dilution of earnings per share arising from the revaluation of assets.
3. It avoids the necessity of recording goodwill and other intangibles that present problems of amortization and interpretation.
4. Combining the retained earnings of the several enterprises does not reduce the amount available for dividends as income distributions.

These so-called advantages, however, are illusory and deceptive and should not be controlling factors in the decision to apply purchase or pooling-of-interest accounting.

An additional objective of the pooling-of-interests method is to present the effect of the combination for prior periods as if the firms had been combined at the earlier date. The apparent objective is to show meaningful trends of income and earnings per share data that can be used for predictive purposes. However, this is a misuse of comparative data, because a discontinuity has occurred. The combined firm is not the same as a group of separate firms. It is misleading to assume that nothing has happened. Furthermore, the combination generally results in a new capitalization and new relationships among the equity holders. It is misleading to assume that these new capitalization relationships existed in an earlier period, under entirely different circumstances. Comparative data should be prohibited in this case unless the nature of the discontinuity is clearly disclosed.

An Evaluation of Purchases and Poolings of Interests

The distinction between a purchase and a pooling of interests rests primarily on the selection and interpretation of the relevant surviving entity. In a purchase, only one combining enterprise survives; the others die both in form and in spirit. However, in a pooling of interests, the surviving corporation is really a combination of two or more viable economic enterprises. The fact that one of the legal organizations is chosen to house the new entity is not sufficient evidence that it has purchased the others. The evidence must rest in the attendant circumstances, rather than in the legal form of the combination.

Once a combination is decided to be either a purchase or a pooling of interests, the specific accounting treatment is then thought to be determined. The two major accounting problems are the valuation of the assets acquired or combined and the classification of the increased or combined equity of the stockholders. However, these two aspects of the combination should be analyzed and treated separately. There is no clear evidence in accounting theory that the classification of stockholders' equity in a combination is dictated by the method of asset valuation or vice versa.

The Valuation of Assets in a Combination.   When a combination is treated as a purchase, the net assets are acquired at their cost as measured by the market value of the stock given in exchange. This treatment is correct, not because it complies with the traditional cost basis of accounting, but because this cost represents the best measure of the current value of the assets to the combined enterprise. If the total cost cannot be allocated to specific assets as part of their current value, the difference represents the cost of unidentified goodwill or other intangibles to be reported, as discussed in Chapter 18.

The decision to treat a combination as a pooling of interests is generally assumed to dictate that the assets be carried forward at the book value in the accounts of the previous enterprise. This treatment is based upon the tradition that historical cost is the most objective and the most relevant valuation basis when there is continuity of ownership interests. However, current values are probably more relevant for most decisions to be made by external investors and for most decisions of management.

The authors believe that even though a combination is considered to be a pooling of interests, it is a significant event in the history of the enterprise, and the assets should be recorded at their current value or current replacement cost, rather than the historical costs in the accounts of the former enterprises. Because the current value of the assets can be obtained by objective means if the stock given in exchange has a market value, the revaluation obtains greater reliability than an independent revaluation. However, a serious difficulty arises when one of the combining firms continues in its legal form and its assets cannot be revalued in terms of the market value of any stock given in exchange for it. A difficulty also arises when a new corporation is formed for the purpose of the combination, because the stock may not have a current market value. But in each of these cases, there is good reason to revalue all of the assets of the new combined enterprise by using available evidence, such as replacement costs and the market price of the stock of the combining corporations.

Classification of the Stockholders' Equity of the Combination.   When a new corporation is organized to purchase the assets or stock of two or more firms, a new enterprise is formed and the entire stockholders' equity at the inception of the new enterprise is invested capital. As indicated earlier, subclassifications may be made to disclose the interest of different classes of stockholders and to disclose the amount of legal capital. But since the firm is a new entity, none of the equity is derived from the retention of earnings. If an existing firm purchases the assets or stock of another firm, a situation similar to the acquisition by a new firm is encountered insofar as the acquired firm loses its identity; but the stockholders' equity of the acquiring firms is not affected because the transaction involves only an exchange of assets (or net assets).

When the acquiring firm issues common stock for the assets or stock of another firm, however, the classification of the stockholders' equity in the acquiring firm (or in a new firm organized for the purpose) depends upon the interpretation of the new enterprise as:

1. An entirely new accounting entity.
2. An accounting entity comprised of the acquiring corporation only.
3. A continuation of all combining enterprises as a single accounting entity.

In the first interpretation, the new enterprise obtains a fresh start and all of the stockholders' equity is invested capital. The second case is assumed to represent a fresh start for the acquired firm, but not for the continuing corporation.

The idea of a fresh start is derived from the concept of a quasi-reorganization. But this analogy is weak, because in a quasi-reorganization there is continuity of interests, with a reclassification of stockholders' equity at the time of the fresh start, while in a combination treated as a purchase, the acquired firm or firms are assumed to disappear entirely. Therefore, rather than being a "fresh start," the entire net assets of the acquired firm or firms are *invested* in the new firm or the surviving firm. Therefore, all of the stockholders' equity arising from the exchange of shares for the net assets or stock of the acquired firms should be treated as invested capital.

What justification is there, then, for carrying forward the retained earnings of the combined firms when the combination is treated as a pooling of interests? If classification of stockholders' equity by source is considered to be the major objective of classification, the question is one of determining the relevant entity and the relevant sources of the equities of this entity. If several firms combine without changing the ownership interests, the source of the equity in the new firms is the summation of the sources in the predecessor corporations. However, if the ownership interests of the acquired firm changed from residual interests to preferred interests, the retained earnings of the corporation dissolving in form should not be carried forward into the combined enterprise. To do so would lead to a misinterpretation regarding the nature of this equity as being obtained from the retention of earnings that would otherwise have been distributed to the current residual equity holders.

If the ownership interests of the several firms are continued in the combined enterprise, however, a distinction between the capital originally invested by these stockholders and the capital obtained by the retention of earnings is relevant in the description of the combined firm. If the equities of the several firms are all material in relationship to the stockholders' equity of the combined enterprise, it would be misleading to carry forward the retained earnings of only one of the firms because this would distort the ratio between capital originally invested and that derived from the retention of earnings. There is considerable merit in disclosing the retained earnings of the several firms at the date of combination and making a separate disclosure of the earnings retained after the combination, unless the continuing firm is so large in relationship to the others that there is no material change in the total retained earnings resulting from the combination.

In summary, continuation of the same classifications of stockholder equities in a combined enterprise as in the former firms is logical if the ownership interests continue with similar equity rights in the combined firms as in the predecessor corporation. Other criteria, such as relative size, continuity of management, and the basis of valuation of the assets of the combined enterprise, are not relevant in determining the classification of stockholders' equity. However, a major difficulty in a classification by sources originating in the former corporations is that a reclassification may be necessary if legal capital is to be disclosed in the classification. The important point is that the rights in both liquidation and dividend distributions of all stockholders in the combined firm should be clearly disclosed.

CHECKPOINTS

1. Distinguish a purchase from a pooling.
2. Contrast the treatment of asset values in a purchase from their treatment in a pooling.
3. Contrast the treatment of retained earnings in a purchase from their treatment in a pooling.

EARNINGS PER SHARE

Earnings per share ratios are probably the most frequently published summaries of accounting data. One reason for their popularity is that they are thought to contain information useful in making predictions regarding future dividends per share and future share prices. They are also thought to be relevant in an evaluation of management effectiveness and dividend policy. The main difference of opinion, however, is whether earnings per share data should reflect historical information only, or whether they should reflect pro forma and predictive information. The APB in *Opinion*

No. 15 chose an emphasis on the pro forma concept because it was thought to be more useful for investment decisions and for evaluating the potential of a firm for credit purposes. Accordingly, it required the presentation of two earnings per share computations (when materially dilutive), both of which are pro forma in nature and are assumed to have predictive qualities.

As discussed in Chapter 9, cash flow data and other information relevant to a prediction of dividends may be more significant for investment decisions than net income and earnings per share data. If this is the case, more emphasis should be placed on the computation of dividends per share and total dividend requirements on a pro forma basis than on the computation and presentation of earnings per share.

Computation of Number of Shares

The computation of an earnings per share ratio requires a computation with net income to common stockholders as the numerator and the related number of common shares as the denominator. In a simple case in which there have been no significant changes in capitalization during the year and no obligations to issue additional shares, the relevant denominator is the number of shares outstanding at the end of the year. However, if additional shares have been issued during the year, an average of the number of shares weighted by the number of months outstanding is assumed to be more relevant because the capital invested through the sale of the additional shares was available to the firm to increase its earnings during the year. Therefore, the use of the weighted average of the shares outstanding during the year is assumed to reflect the historical conditions as well as to permit comparisons with other years.

When other securities that have some characteristics of common stock are outstanding, usefulness of earnings per share data may be increased if these securities are counted as common stock. For example, if preferred stock is fully participating with respect to dividends, the preferred stockholders have the same rights as common stockholders to share in dividend distributions in excess of the preferred rate. Therefore, if such securities have the right to share in future dividends on the same basis as common stock, they should be included in the computation of earnings per share. Convertible debt, convertible preferred stock, options, and warrants do not share in dividends on the same basis as common until they become common shares; but they have *potential* rights to share in future distributions. Therefore, from the point of view of using the earnings per share figure as a predictive indicator, they should be included in the computation if they are likely to gain the rights of common stockholders. If these security holders exercise their rights, the earnings per share figure based on outstanding shares is likely to decrease.

Although there are many ways to compute earnings per share if these different types of securities are present, *APB 15* recommended two separate computations called "primary earnings per share" and "fully diluted earnings per share," respectively. These two computations are based on neither the probability of conversion or exercise nor on their imminence. They are, rather, computations based on arbitrary rules and assumptions, without evidence that either computation is necessarily relevant for investment decisions.

Primary Earnings per Share. The primary earnings per share (EPS) computation includes the weighted average number of shares outstanding during the year plus the number of shares represented by securities that are considered to be common stock equivalents and have a dilutive effect. A dilutive effect is assumed to occur if the earnings per share figure would be reduced if the common stock equivalents were included. Securities considered to be common stock equivalents include all stock options and warrants, participating securities, convertible securities that come within the limits of a specific formula at the time of issuance, and other securities having current or potential common stock equivalents if the effective yield at the time of issuance is less than two-thirds of the current average Aa corporate bond yield.[21]

The use of "primary earnings per share" can be criticized for the following reasons:

1. The use of the term *primary* implies that the computation is of greatest significance, whereas any one of a family of earnings per share computations may be the more relevant under different assumptions and expectations.

2. Convertible debt and convertible preferred stock are treated differently from debt and preferred stock with detachable warrants. Convertible securities are classified as common stock equivalents only at the date of issuance. Warrants, however, are included in the computation according to the conditions in each period. The methods of adjusting income are also different.

3. Convertible securities are classified as common stock equivalents only at the time of issuance, rather than reflecting the conditions current in each year.

4. It is inconsistent to say that convertible debt should be classified solely as debt in the balance sheet (as required in *APB 14*) and to classify it entirely as a common stock equivalent in computing the earnings per share.

5. The primary earnings per share is a pro forma computation, but the title does not indicate its significance. Without full disclosure, the reader would not be able to determine which securities have been treated as common stock equivalents.

Fully Diluted Earnings per Share.   A fully diluted earnings per share should be computed by including all potentially dilutive convertible securities, whether classified as common stock equivalents or not. Warrants and options should also be included but their effect may differ from the primary EPS computation if the closing market price of common stock exceeds the average price. Neither primary nor fully diluted EPS computations should be shown if the fully diluted effect is not greater than 3 percent.

The alleged purpose of the fully diluted computation is to show the maximum potential dilution of current earnings per share on a prospective basis.[22] However, this computation does not include the *maximum* potential dilution, because the treatment of warrants is dependent upon the market price at the end of the period while expected dilution depends upon expectations of *future* market prices. Thus, actual dilution may be considerably greater than that reported for two reasons:

1.   Warrants are not included if the market price of common stock at the end of the period does not exceed the exercise price. This is similar to the assumption made with executive stock options that no compensation is involved if the market price does not exceed the exercise price at the date of the grant. However, if the market price increases in a later period, dilution will occur when the warrants are exercised.

2.   The elimination of warrants from the computations on the basis of the market price of the stock at the end of the period assumes that the proceeds from the exercise of the warrants can be used to purchase stock at that price. But if the warrants are exercised at a later date, when the market price of the stock has increased, the proceeds will not permit the acquisition of the same number of shares.

The fully diluted earnings per share computation can also be criticized on the basis that it is likely to be interpreted as the most probable result. Experience is likely to indicate that not all conversion rights nor warrants are exercised or are likely to be exercised. The computation, therefore, may reflect a worse situation than is probable under any circumstances.

Computation of the Earnings

The numerator in the computation of earnings per share must be adjusted, even on an historical basis, if there are senior stock equity issues outstanding. Since the earnings relate only to common stock securities with residual rights, dividends paid or payable on senior securities should be deducted from the net income figures shown on the income statement. If an addition is made to the common stock shares in the denominator to represent convertible debt outstanding, the interest expense for the year adjusted for the income tax effect should be added to the reported net income. Convertible preferred stock included in the denominator, however, does not require an adjustment of reported net income because the net income amount must be allocated to these shares as well as to common stock.

Stock options and warrants require, upon exercise, payment to the firm of an amount referred to as the *exercise price*. Since the equivalent number of shares are included in the denominator on the assumption that the options and warrants have been exercised since the beginning of the period or date of grant, the net income should include an amount equal to the net income effect of utilizing the cash proceeds from the exercise of the warrants. Since this is a pro forma assumption, there is no way of knowing what the income effect would have been. One assumption is that the firm could have earned at least an amount equivalent to the interest on government securities or commercial paper adjusted for the income tax effect. An alternative assumption is that the firm could reacquire its long-term debt and thereby save interest expense. The assumption of *APB 15*, however, is that the proceeds could have been used by the firm to reacquire its own shares at the average market price during the year. Under this so-called treasury stock method, the number of shares added to the denominator would be reduced by the number of shares that could have been purchased with the proceeds from the exercise of the warrants, and the net income in the numerator is not increased. Thus, no dilution is assumed to occur if the average market price of the common stock is equal to or less than the exercise price. *APB 15*, however, suggested that, if the number of shares obtainable upon exercise of the warrants exceeds 20 percent of the outstanding common shares, the proceeds from the shares in excess of 20 percent should be assumed to be used to repay debt, or be invested in government securities or commercial paper. In this case, the net income should be increased by the net income effect of the interest that could have been saved or earned.

Criticisms of the recommendations of *APB 15* regarding the adjustment for the income effect of the proceeds from the exercise of warrants are:

1. The treasury stock method may not reflect the best use of the funds or even the most likely use.
2. The use of a current market price to determine the number of shares that could be purchased does not reflect the potential of the firm to reacquire such shares in the future, particularly if the market price is increasing each year.
3. The 20 percent limitation is arbitrary and therefore does not necessarily lead to meaningful measurements.
4. The market price of the stock generally reflects expectations regarding future earnings and is not related to the current opportunities available to the firm for investment of the proceeds from the exercise of warrants.

The authors conclude that the earnings per share computations recommended by *APB 15* are based on unsupported assumptions. Instead of presenting only two ratios that are assumed to be most relevant, the financial statements should present a full disclosure of all relevant information to permit investors to make their own evaluations of the potential dilution of earnings per share by the firm. Furthermore, since future dividend distributions may be more significant than reported earnings per share computations, the information should be presented in such a way that alternative dividends per share computations can also be estimated under different assumptions.

CHECKPOINTS

1. Define the term *common stock equivalents*.
2. Define the term *primary* earnings per share.
3. Define the term *fully diluted* earnings per share.
4. What is the purpose of computing primary and fully diluted rather than ordinary earnings per share?

SUMMARY

Invested capital was defined as all purchased capital, including capitalized retained earnings. There are a variety of ways in which this capital can be increased. The most traditional way is by the simple issuance of new shares of capital by the company. Other ways include the conversion of debt or preferred stock into common stock. Another alternative is by the exercise of stock options. Invested capital may also be decreased by the company through repurchase from stockholders, and subsequent retirement, of shares of common stock.

In each of these cases, the question arises as to whether any gain or loss should be registered on the increase or decrease in invested capital. For example, if preferred stock is converted to common stock at a value other than its book value, an accounting gain or loss is possible. Whether to recognize an income-related element or not depends on the view one has of the corporation. Those who hold to the entity view generally feel that these transactions should not involve income. Those who hold to the proprietary view are much more comfortable with the recognition of gains and losses in these circumstances.

Business combinations also lead to possible changes in stockholders' equity. The nature of the changes depends on whether the combination is perceived to be the purchase of one company by another, or a pooling of their interests. The nature of the changes is also affected by whether some or all of the assets of the new corporation are revalued, giving the new corporation a partial or a wholly fresh start.

Each of the changes alluded to above affects the computation of earnings per share. *APB 15* requires that earnings per share be based on a weighted average number of shares outstanding over the year. That statement also requires that hybrid securities be examined for potential conversion and be partly or wholly included in the computation of earnings per share for the year.

MULTIPLE CHOICE QUESTIONS

Retained Earnings Dividends

1. [M86#14] When a property dividend is declared and the book value of the property exceeds its market value, the dividend is recorded at the
a. Market value of the property at the date of distribution.
b. Market value of the property at the date of declaration.
c. Book value of the property at the date of declaration.
d. Book value of the property at the date of distribution if it still exceeds the market value of the property at the date of declaration.

2. [N87#15] How would the declaration of a liquidating dividend by a corporation affect each of the following?

	Contributed Capital	Total Stockholders' Equity
a.	No effect	Decrease
b.	Decrease	Decrease
c.	Decrease	No effect
d.	No effect	No effect

3. [M87#20] A company declared a cash dividend on its common stock in December 1986, payable in January 1987. Retained earnings would
a. Increase on the date of declaration.
b. Not be affected on the date of declaration.
c. Not be affected on the date of payment.
d. Decrease on the date of payment.

4. [M87#21] How would retained earnings be affected by the declaration of each of the following?

	Stock Dividend	Stock Split
a.	Decrease	Decrease
b.	No effect	Decrease
c.	No effect	No effect
d.	Decrease	No effect

Treasury Stock

5. [M89#10] The par-value method of accounting for treasury stock differs from the cost method in that

a. Any gain is recognized upon repurchase of stock but a loss is treated as an adjustment to retained earnings.

b. No gains or losses are recognized on the issuance of treasury stock using the par-value method.

c. It reverses the original entry to issue the common stock with any difference between carrying value and purchase price adjusted through paid-in capital and/or retained earnings and treats a subsequent reissuance like a new issuance of common stock.

d. It reverses the original entry to issue the common stock with any difference between carrying value and purchase price being shown as an ordinary gain or loss and does not recognize any gain or loss on a subsequent resale of the stock.

6. [M88#20] Treasury stock was acquired for cash at a price in excess of its original issue price. The treasury stock was subsequently reissued for cash at a price in excess of its acquisition price. Assuming that the par value method of accounting for treasury stock transactions is used, what is the effect on total stockholders' equity?

	Acquisition of Treasury Stock	Reissuance of Treasury Stock
a.	No effect	No effect
b.	Increase	Decrease
c.	Decrease	No effect
d.	Decrease	Increase

7. [N88#19] Treasury stock was acquired for cash at a price in excess of its par value. The treasury stock was subsequently reissued for cash at a price in excess of its acquisition price. Assuming that the cost method of accounting for treasury stock transactions is used, what is the effect of the subsequent reissuance of the treasury stock on each of the following?

	Additional Paid-In Capital	Retained Earnings	Total Stockholders' Equity
a.	Decrease	Decrease	No effect
b.	Increase	Increase	Increase
c.	Increase	No effect	Increase
d.	No effect	No effect	No effect

Stock Options, Warrants, and Rights

8.   [M89#11] A company issued rights to its existing shareholders without consideration. The rights allowed the recipients to purchase unissued common stock for an amount in excess of par value. When the rights are issued, which of the following will be interested?

	Common Stock	Additional Paid-In Capital
a.	Yes	Yes
b.	Yes	No
c.	No	No
d.	No	Yes

9.   [M87#34] A company issued rights to its existing shareholders to purchase, for $30 per share, unissued shares of $15 par value common stock. Additional paid-in capital will be credited when the

	Rights Are Issued	Rights Lapse
a.	Yes	No
b.	No	No
c.	No	Yes
d.	Yes	Yes

Business Combinations

10. [M88#35] Company L acquired all of the outstanding common stock of Company M in exchange for cash. The acquisition price exceeds the fair value of net assets acquired. How should Company L determine the amounts to be reported for the plant and equipment and long-term debt acquired from Company M?

	Plant and Equipment	Long-Term Debt
a.	Fair value	M's carrying amount
b.	Fair value	Fair value
c.	M's carrying amount	Fair value
d.	M's carrying amount	M's carrying amount

11. [N87#29] A business combination occurs in the middle of the year. Results of operations for the year of combination would include the combined results of operations of the separate companies for the entire year if the business combination is a

	Pooling of Interests	Purchase
a.	Yes	No
b.	Yes	Yes
c.	No	Yes
d.	No	No

Earnings per Share

12. [M89#25] Antidilutive stock options would generally be used in the calculation of

	Primary Earnings per Share	Fully Diluted Earnings per Share
a.	Yes	Yes
b.	Yes	No
c.	No	No
d.	No	Yes

13. [N86#32] In determining earnings per share in a complex capital structure, which of the following is a common stock equivalent?

	Nonconvertible Preferred Stock	*Stock Option*
a.	Yes	No
b.	Yes	Yes
c.	No	Yes
d.	No	No

DISCUSSION QUESTIONS

Stock Options

1. **(May 1972)** *Part a.* Stock options are widely used as a form of compensation for corporate executives.

Required:

1. Identify five methods that have been proposed for determining the value of executive stock options.
2. Discuss the conceptual merits of each of these proposed methods.

Part b. On January 1, 1980, as an incentive to greater performance in their duties, Recycling Corporation adopted a qualified stock option plan to grant corporate executives nontransferable stock options to 500,000 shares of its unissued $1 par value common stock. The options were granted on May 1, 1980 at $25 per share, the market price on that date. All of the options were exercisable one year later and for four years thereafter providing that the grantee was employed by the Corporation at the date of exercise.

The market price of this stock was $40 per share on May 1, 1981. All options were exercised before December 31, 1981 at times when the market price varied between $40 and $50 per share.

Required:

What information on this option plan should be presented in the financial statements of Recycling Corporation at (1) December 31, 1980 and (2) December 31, 1981? Explain why this is acceptable.

2. **(November 1986)** Wesley Company granted compensatory common stock options to its executives on January 1, 1983, the measurement date, for services to be rendered during 1983 and 1984. The quoted market price of Wesley's par value common stock exceeded the option price on January 1, 1983.

The stock options were exercisable beginning on January 1, 1985, and they lapsed on December 31, 1985. Half of the stock options were exercised in 1985 and half were allowed to lapse.

Required:

a. How should Wesley determine the amount of compensation expense related to the compensatory stock options, if any, that should be recognized in its income statements for 1983, 1984, and 1985? Why?

b. How should Wesley account for the exercise of the stock options? Justify the accounting recommended.

c. How should Wesley account for the lapse of the stock options? Justify the accounting recommended.

Treasury Stock

3.   (November 1979) For numerous reasons a corporation may reacquire shares of its own capital stock. When a company purchases treasury stock, it has two options as to how to account for the shares: (1) cost method and (2) par value method.

Required:

Compare and contrast the cost method with the par value for each of the following:

a. Purchase of shares at a price less than par value.

b. Purchase of shares at a price greater than par value.

c. Subsequent resale of treasury shares at a price less than purchase price, but more than par value.

d. Subsequent resale of treasury shares at a price greater than both purchase price and par value.

e. Effect on net income.

4.   (November 1985) Brady Company has 30,000 shares of $10 par value common stock authorized and 20,000 shares issued and outstanding. On August 15, 1984, Brady purchased 1,000 shares of treasury stock for $12 per share. Brady uses the cost method to account for treasury stock. On September 14, 1984, Brady sold 500 shares of the treasury stock for $14 per share.

In October 1984, Brady declared and distributed 2,000 shares as a stock dividend from unissued shares when the market value of the common stock was $16 per share.

On December 20, 1984, Brady declared a $1 per share cash dividend, payable on January 10, 1985, to shareholders of record on December 31, 1984.

Required:

> *a.* How should Brady account for the purchase and sale of the treasury stock, and how should the treasury stock be presented in Brady's balance sheet at December 31, 1984?
>
> *b.* How should Brady account for the stock dividend, and how would it affect Brady's stockholders' equity at December 31, 1984? Why?
>
> *c.* How should Brady account for the cash dividend, and how would it affect Brady's balance sheet at December 31, 1984? Why?

Business Combinations

> **5.** **(May 1973)** The boards of directors of Kessler Corporation, Bar Company, Cohen, Inc., and Mason Corporation are meeting jointly to discuss plans for a business combination. Each of the corporations has one class of common stock outstanding; Bar also has one class of preferred stock outstanding. Although terms have not as yet been settled, Kessler will be the acquiring or issuing corporation. Because the directors want to conform to generally accepted accounting principles, they have asked you to attend the meeting as an advisor.

Required:

> Consider each of the following questions independently of the others, and answer each in accordance with generally accepted accounting principles. Explain your answers.
>
> *a.* Assume that the combination will be consummated August 31, 1983. Explain the philosophy underlying the accounting and how the balance sheet accounts of each of the four corporations will appear on Kessler's consolidated balance sheet in September 1, 1983 if the combination is accounted for as a
>
> > 1. Pooling of interests.
> > 2. Purchase.
>
> *b.* Assume that the combination will be consummated August 31, 1983. Explain how the income-statement accounts of each of the four corporations will be accounted for in preparing Kessler's consolidated income statement for the year ended December 31, 1983 if the combination is accounted for as a
>
> > 1. Pooling of interests.
> > 2. Purchase.
>
> *c.* Some of the directors believe that the terms of the combination should be agreed upon immediately and that the method of accounting to be used (whether pooling of interests, purchase, or a mixture) may be chosen at some later date. Others believe that the terms of the combina-

tion and the method to be used are very closely related. Which position is correct?

d. Kessler and Mason are comparable in size; Cohen and Bar are much smaller. How do these facts affect the choice of accounting method?

e. Bar was formerly a subsidiary of Tucker Corporation, which has no other relationship to any of the four companies discussing combination. Eighteen months ago Tucker voluntarily spun off Bar. What effect, if any, do these facts have on the choice of accounting method?

f. Kessler holds 2,000 of Bar's 10,000 outstanding shares of preferred stock and 15,000 of Cohen's 100,000 outstanding shares of common stock. All of Kessler's holdings were acquired during the first three months of 1983. What effect, if any, do these facts have on the choice of accounting method?

g. It is almost certain that Mrs. Victor Mason, Sr., who holds 5 percent of Mason's common stock, will object to the combination. Assume that Kessler is able to acquire only 95 percent (rather than 100 percent) of Mason's stock, issuing Kessler common stock in exchange.

   1. Which accounting method is applicable?

   2. If Kessler is able to acquire the remaining 5 percent at some future time—in five years, for instance—in exchange for its own common stock, which accounting method will be applicable to this second acquisition?

h. Since the directors believe that one of Mason's major divisions will not be compatible with the operations of the combined company, they anticipate that it will be sold as soon as possible after the combination is consummated. They expect to have no trouble in finding a buyer. What effect, if any, do these facts have on the choice of accounting method?

6. **(May 1977)** Hanover Company and Case Company, both of which have only voting common stock, are considering a merger whereby Hanover would be the surviving company. The terms of the combination provide that the transaction would be carried out by Hanover exchanging one share of its stock for two shares of Case's stock. Before the date of the contemplated exchange, Hanover had purchased 5 percent of Case's stock, which it holds as an investment. Case, at the same date, owns 2 percent of Hanover's stock. All of the remaining outstanding stock of Case will be acquired by Hanover in this contemplated exchange. Neither of the two companies has ever had an affiliation as a subsidiary or division of any other company.

Required:

a. Without enumerating specific criteria, how is a determination made as to whether a business combination is accounted for as a pooling of interests or as a purchase?

b. Based only on the preceding facts, discuss the specific criteria that would qualify or disqualify this business combination as being accounted for as a pooling of interests.

c. What additional requirements (other than those discussed in *b* above) must be met in order to account for this business combination as a pooling of interests?

7. (May 1987) There are two methods of accounting for business combinations, purchase and pooling of interests.

Required:

a.
1. What is the rationale for accounting for a business combination as a purchase? **Do not discuss the specific criteria for accounting for a business combination as a purchase.**
2. In a business combination accounted for as a purchase, how should the amount of goodwill at acquisition be determined?
3. In a business combination accounted for as a purchase, how should goodwill be amortized?

b.
1. What is the rationale for accounting for a business combination as a pooling of interests? **Do not discuss the specific criteria for accounting for a business combination as a pooling of interests.**
2. In a business combination accounted for as a pooling of interests, when both companies use the same methods of accounting, how should the stockholders' equity be accounted for?

Earnings per Share

8. (November 1978) The earnings-per-share data required of a company depend on the nature of its capital structure. A corporation may have a simple capital structure and only compute earnings per common share or may have a complex capital structure and have to compute primary earnings per share and fully diluted earnings per share.

Required:

a. Define the term *common stock equivalent* and describe what securities would be considered common stock equivalents in the computation of earnings per share.

b. Define the term *complex capital structure* and discuss the disclosures (both financial and explanatory) necessary for earnings per share when a corporation has a complex capital structure.

9. (May 1970) *APB Opinion No. 15* discussed the concept of common stock equivalents and prescribes the reporting of primary earnings per share and fully diluted earnings per share.

Required:

a. Discuss the reasons securities other than common stock may be considered common stock equivalents for the computation of primary earnings per share.

b. Define the term *senior security,* and explain how senior securities that are not convertible enter into the determination of earnings-per-share data.

c. Explain how convertible securities are determined to be common stock equivalents and how those convertible senior securities that are not considered to be common stock equivalents enter into the determination of earnings-per-share data.

d. Explain the treasury stock method as it applies to options and warrants in computing primary earnings-per-share data.

10.   (May 1974) Earnings per share (EPS) is the most featured single financial statistic about modern corporations. Daily published quotations of stock prices have recently been expanded to include a times earnings figure for many securities, which is based on EPS. Often the focus of analysts' discussions will be on the EPS of the corporations receiving their attention.

Required:

a. Explain how dividends or dividend requirements on any class of preferred stock that may be outstanding affect the computation of EPS.

b. One of the technical procedures applicable in EPS computations is the treasury stock method.

1. Briefly describe the circumstances under which it might be appropriate to apply the treasury stock method.

2. There is a limit to the extent to which the treasury stock method is applicable. Indicate what this limit is, and give a succinct indication of the procedures that should be followed beyond the treasury stock limits.

c. Under some circumstances convertible debentures would be considered common stock equivalents, and under other circumstances they would not be.

1. When is it proper to treat convertible debentures as common stock equivalents? What is the effect on computation of EPS in such cases?

2. In case convertible debentures are not considered as common stock equivalents, explain how they are handled for purposes of EPS computations.

SELECTED ADDITIONAL READINGS

Single texts covering the topics raised in this chapter do not exist. Readers interested in pursuing these topics in more depth are advised, therefore, to consult the following articles:

Stock Dividends and Stock Splits

Asquith, P.; P. Healey; and K. Palepu. "Earnings and Stock Splits." *The Accounting Review,* July 1989, pp. 387–403.

Foster, Taylor W. III, and Don Vickrey. "The Information Content of Stock Dividend Announcements." *The Accounting Review,* April 1978, pp. 360–70.

Liljeblom, E. "The Informational Impact of Announcements of Stock Dividends and Stock Splits." *Journal of Business Finance and Accounting,* Winter 1989, pp. 681–98.

Millar, James A. "Split or Dividend: Do the Words Really Matter?" *The Accounting Review,* January 1977, pp. 52–55.

Pusker, Henri C. "Accounting for Capital Stock Distributions (Stock Split-Ups and Dividends)." *New York CPA,* May 1971, pp. 347–52.

Stock Options

Alvin, Gerald. "Accounting for Investment and Stock Rights: The Market Value Method." *CPA Journal,* February 1973, pp. 126–31.

Boudreaux, Kenneth J., and Stephen A. Zeff. "A Note on the Measure of Compensation Implicit in Employee Stock Options." *Journal of Accounting Research,* Spring 1976, pp. 158–62.

Milne, R. A.; G. A. Vent; and R. Neumann. "Accounting for Variable Stock Options." *Journal of Accounting,* Fall 1987, pp. 333–38.

Noreen, E., and M. Wolfson. "Equilibrium Warrant Pricing Models and Accounting for Executive Stock Options." *Journal of Accounting Research,* Autumn 1981, pp. 384–98. See also, D. Galai. "A Note on 'Equilibrium Warrant Pricing Models and Accounting for Executive Stock Options.'" *Journal of Accounting Research,* Fall 1989, pp. 313–15.

Rogers, Donald R., and R. W. Schattke. "Buy-Outs of Stock Options: Compensation or Capital?" *Journal of Accountancy,* August 1972, pp. 55–59.

Smith, Clifford W., and Jerold L. Zimmerman. "Valuing Employer Stock Option Plans Using Option Pricing Models." *Journal of Accounting Research,* Autumn 1976, pp. 357–64.

Smith, Ralph E., and Leroy F. Imdieke. "Accounting for Stock Issued to Employees." *Journal of Accountancy,* November 1974, pp. 68–75.

Wallace, W. "The Effects of Delays by Accounting Policy-Setters in Reconciling the Accounting Treatment of Stock Options and Stock Appreciation Rights." *The Accounting Review,* April 1984, pp. 325–41.

Weygandt, Jerry J. "Valuation of Stock Option Contracts." *The Accounting Review,* January 1977, pp. 40–51.

Business Combinations

Anderson, John C., and Joseph G. Louderback III. "Income Manipulation and Purchase-Pooling: Some Additional Results." *Journal of Accounting Research,* Autumn 1975, pp. 338–43.

Brenner, Vincent C. "Empirical Study of Support for APB Opinion No. 16." *Journal of Accounting Research,* Spring 1972, pp. 200–208.

Defliese, Philip L. "Business Combinations Revisited." *D. R. Scott Memorial Lectures in Accountancy,* vol. 6 (Columbus: University of Missouri, 1974).

Emanuel, David M. "Accounting for Business Combinations." *Australian Accountant,* October 1973, pp. 518–22, 525–26.

Foster, William C. "Illogic of Pooling." *Financial Executive,* December 1974, pp. 16–21.

Gaertner, James F. "Proposed Alternatives for Accounting for Business Combinations: A Behavioral Study." *Abacus,* June 1979, pp. 35–47.

Gagnon, Jean-Marie. "Purchase-Pooling Choice: Some Empirical Evidence." *Journal of Accounting Research,* Spring 1971, pp. 52–72.

Hong, Hai; Robert S. Kaplan; and Gershon Mandelker. "Pooling vs. Purchase: The Effects of Accounting for Mergers on Stock Prices." *The Accounting Review,* January 1978, pp. 31–47.

Mian, S. L., and C. W. Smith, Jr. "Incentives for Unconsolidated Financial Reporting." *Journal of Accounting and Economics,* January 1990, pp. 141–72.

Mohr, Rosanne M. "Unconsolidated Finance Subsidiaries: Characteristics and Debt/Equity Effects." *Accounting Horizons,* March 1988, pp. 27–34.

Whittred, G. "The Derived Demand for Consolidated Financial Reporting." *Journal of Accounting and Economics,* December 1987, pp. 259–86.

Earnings per Share

Arnold, Donald F. "Earnings per Share: An Empirical Test of the Market Parity and Investment Value Methods." *The Accounting Review,* January 1973, pp. 23–33.

Coughlan, J. W. "Anomalies in Calculating Earnings per Share." *Accounting Horizons,* December 1988, pp. 80–88.

Ellon, Samuel. "Earnings per Share Can Be Misleading." *Journal of Business Finance and Accounting,* Summer 1975, pp. 239–42.

Gibson, Charles H., and John Daniel Williams. "Should Common Stock Equivalents Be Considered in Earnings per Share?" *CPA Journal,* March 1973, pp. 209–13.

Mautz, R. D., and T. J. Hogan. "Earnings per Share Reporting: Time for an Overhaul." *Accounting Horizons,* Spring 1989, pp. 21–27.

Parker, James E., and Barry E. Cushing. "Earnings per Share and Convertible Securities: A Utilitarian Approach." *Abacus,* June 1971, pp. 29–38.

Rice, Steven J. "The Information Content of Fully Diluted Earnings per Share." *The Accounting Review,* April 1978, pp. 429–38.

Shank, John K. "Earnings per Share, Stock Prices, and APB Opinion No. 15." *Journal of Accounting Research,* Spring 1971, pp. 165–70.

Tritschler, Charles A. "Dilution and Counter-Dilution in Reporting for Deferred Equity." *Accounting and Business Research,* Autumn 1971, pp. 274–83.

Vigeland, R. L. "Dilution of Earnings per Share in an Option Pricing Framework." *The Accounting Review,* April 1982, pp. 348–57.

Wiseman, Donald E. "Holding Loss/Gain as an Alternative to EPS Dilution." *Accounting Horizons,* December 1990, pp. 18–34.

ENDNOTES

1. Executive Committee of the American Accounting Association, "A Tentative Statement of Accounting Principles Underlying Corporate Financial Statements," *The Accounting Review,* June 1936, p. 191. Reprinted in AAA Committee on Accounting Concepts and Standards, *Accounting and Reporting Standards for Corporate Financial Statements and Preceding Statements and Supplements* (AAA, 1957), p. 63. Also see *APB 9,* par. 28.
2. Committee on Corporate Laws of the American Bar Association, *Model Business Corporation Act* (1962 and subsequent revisions), Sec. 2(j). The Committee has since issued the *Revised Model Business Corporation Act* (1984) from which many terms, such as stated capital, are dropped or redefined. The Model Act, however, remains under adoption by more states than the Revised Act and continues, therefore, to be the focus of the CPA examination. A copy of the Act may be found in the appendix of many business law texts.
3. *SFAS 4.*
4. AAA Committee on Accounting Concepts and Standards, *Accounting and Reporting Standards* (1957), p. 7.
5. *ARB 43,* Ch. 7B, as amended, par. 6.
6. George R. Husband, "The Entity Concept in Accounting," *The Accounting Review,* October 1954, p. 554.
7. Ibid.
8. *ARB 43,* Ch. 7B as amended, par. 11.
9. See, for example, George R. Husband, "The Entity Concept in Accounting," *The Accounting Review,* October 1954, p. 555.
10. *ARB 43,* Ch. 7B, as amended, par. 10.
11. *ARB 43,* Ch. 7B, as amended, par. 11.
12. SEC *Accounting Series Release No. 124.*
13. See, for example, Taylor W. Foster III and Don Vickrey, "The Information Content of Stock Dividend Announcements," *The Accounting Review,* April 1978, pp. 360–70.
14. *APB 25,* par. 7.
15. *APB 25,* par. 9.
16. *ARB 43,* Ch. 1B, as amended, par. 13.
17. Also see *Accounting Standards Current Text,* par. C23.103.
18. Arthur R. Wyatt, "A Critical Study of Accounting for Business Combinations," *Accounting Research Study No. 5* (AICPA, 1963), p. 104.

19. George E. Catlett and Norman O. Olsen, "Accounting for Goodwill," *Accounting Research Study No. 10* (AICPA, 1968), p. 110.
20. AAA Committee to Prepare a Statement of Basic Accounting Theory, *A Statement of Basic Accounting Theory* (AAA, 1966), p. 19.
21. *SFAS 85,* par. 3, and emendation of *SFAS 15* and *SFAS 55*.
22. *APB 15*, par. 40.

Chapter 24

Disclosure of Financial Information

CHAPTER OBJECTIVES

After studying this chapter, you will be able to:

Distinguish various forms of disclosure within and without the annual report.

Evaluate a given level of disclosure in light of standards such as those laid down by the FASB.

Contrast the disclosure requirements of the SEC, the IASC, the FASB, and other financial regulatory bodies.

Discuss the virtues of the various forms of disclosure.

Describe the different methods of disclosure.

CHAPTER OVERVIEW

Disclosure to Whom?

Shareholders are the primary group to whom financial disclosure is made. However, particularly in Europe, other stakeholders such as employees are seen as equally important recipients of financial information.

Levels of Disclosure

Establishing the appropriate level of disclosure depends ideally on the level of social welfare induced by disclosure. In the absence of an ethical theory permitting the measurement of social welfare, accounting regulators are obliged to rely on criteria such as relevance and reliability.

Forms of Disclosure

Many have suggested that disclosure should be made in addition to the standard balance sheets and income statements. Examples include forecasts of future financial results, statements of accounting policies, and financial analysis by segment.

Methods of Disclosure

A number of disclosure methods are available to managements. They include the formal financial statements, parenthetical information in these statements, and a wide variety of narrative forms.

What information should the senior management of a company disclose to people outside that small circle? This is the question that has dominated this book from its first page and will continue to dominate it to its last. Given that the topic of disclosure is broad enough to encompass almost the entire area of financial reporting, a question regarding disclosure serves as an appropriate final chapter to a book on accounting theory.

As we enter this, the last chapter of this book, and ask that question one last time, we have to admit that we do not have an answer—at least, not one that we can prove to everyone's satisfaction. This does not mean that we have no opinions—the problem is that others have their own opinions. There are many who claim to have all the answers. Unfortunately, their answers contradict one another—sometimes quite sharply. No one has managed to convince everyone of the rightness of a particular solution.

At first glance, this is discouraging, but reflection reveals that this is the normal state of affairs in any living, growing discipline. The law is constantly evolving. Medicine is still struggling to find answers. Science is continually making new discoveries. So it is with accounting. The controversies that swirl around it at times reveal its life. Agreement on everything would signal its death. In short, there will always be disagreements over what should be disclosed and in what form. Those disagreements are right, proper, and exciting—they make accounting the vital, fascinating subject that it is.

The lack of consensus about the most appropriate level of disclosure reflects, in part, the state of research in economics, finance, accounting, and other related disciplines such as psychology and political science. Much has been discovered. Much more still awaits discovery. We can say with some certainty, based on current research, some things about disclosure. There are many other things, though, that we intuitively feel are appropriate to disclose, but for which we lack solid evidence.

This chapter attempts to distinguish between those things that we can say about disclosure on theoretical grounds and those that we merely think are right. It notes that one of the major objectives of financial reporting is to supply information for decision making. This requires a proper disclosure of financial data and other relevant information. To achieve proper disclosure, three major questions need answering:

1. For *whom* is the information to be disclosed?
2. What is the *purpose* of the information?
3. How *much* information should be disclosed?

The question of how and when the information should be disclosed is, of course, also important, as the method and timing of disclosure determine the usefulness of the information; but the question of method is less important than the question of the choice and timing of financial disclosure.

DISCLOSURE TO WHOM?

The question: "For whom?" is traditionally answered in the United States by the assertion that financial reports are directed to stockholders, other investors, and creditors. To quote the FASB:

> Financial reporting should provide information that is useful to present and potential investors and creditors and other users in making rational investment, credit, and similar decisions.[1]

Allowance is made for disclosure to employees, customers, governmental agencies, and the general public, but these are seen as secondary recipients of annual reports and other forms of disclosure only. Part of the reason for this lack of emphasis on users other than investors is a lack of knowledge about their decisions. The decisions to be made by investors and creditors are relatively straightforward and well defined: investors primarily make buy-sell-hold decisions, and the decisions of creditors are primarily related to the extension of credit to the enterprise. Stockholders, and sometimes creditors, may also make decisions regarding the hiring, firing, and compensation of management and the approval or disapproval of major changes in firm policy. The objectives of financial reporting relative to these users can be fairly clear, therefore. The objectives of presenting information to employees, customers, and the general public, on the other hand, have not been as well formulated. Failing more specific knowledge, the general assumption is that information useful to investors and creditors will be useful to others.

If one defines stockholders and other investors as the appropriate focal group for accounting, then disclosure in financial reporting may be de-

fined as the presentation of information necessary for the optimum operation of efficient capital markets. This implies that sufficient information
should be presented to permit the prediction of future dividend trends and
variability and the covariability of future returns with the market. Emphasis should be placed on the preferences of sophisticated investors and
financial analysts. However, all investors need information to evaluate
the relative risks of individual firms in order to obtain diversified portfolios and combinations of investments that meet individual risk preferences. Creditors and governmental agencies generally have the power to
obtain additional information for their needs.

Disclosure to Stakeholders

Other parts of the globe, particularly Europe, tend to give a broader
answer to the question, ''For whom?'' In particular, they tend to place
the interests of employees and the state on a par with the interests of
shareholders. The importance of stockholder ownership is discounted in
favor of the broader concept of stakeholder concerns.* The effect is to
alter the nature of disclosure. French corporations, for instance, are required to present a *social balance sheet* to a *company works council* each
year. These councils are made up of labor and management. Every social
balance sheet must provide information regarding:

1. Employment.
2. Wage-related costs (benefit packages).
3. Health and safety protection.
4. Other conditions of work.
5. Employee training.
6. Industrial relations.
7. Other conditions of life relating to the undertaking, including housing
   and transportation provided to employees by the company.[2]

Clearly, this goes beyond anything required of American corporations.

There has been considerable debate in the United States over the years
regarding the desirability of *human resource accounting*. Proponents argue that corporations train employees because, on average, training ensures increased future benefits from the services of the employee. That
being the case, the cost of training should be capitalized and not expensed
as is current practice. At a minimum, the costs associated with human
resources should be spelled out in detail so that users might see where a
company has invested its resources.[3]

---

* More was said on the subject of stakeholders in the opening chapter.

Some corporations have begun to prepare financial reports specifically tailored to their employees. For instance, Anglo American, the giant South African mining house, has attempted to forestall future nationalization by encouraging shareholding among its employees. A financial report is prepared specifically for them. Extracts from that report appear in Exhibit 24-1.

EXHIBIT 24-1   Anglo American: The Financial Report

	1988 (Millions of Rands)	1987 (Millions of Rands)
Anglo's income was earned from these sources		
Dividends from investments	923	853
Anglo's share of trading profits of its subsidiary companies	199	319
Interest and fees earned after deducting Anglo's operating expenses	420	478
	1,542	1,650
Anglo paid out		
Interest on money lent to us	191	231
Prospecting expenditure on the search for new mining ventures	108	72
Taxes	206	316
	505	619
	1,037	1,031
Leaving a profit of		
Anglo also accounts for its share of the profits of its associate companies not paid out as dividends	772	472
Giving a total profit of	1,809	1,503
The profit was used		
By Anglo to pay dividends to its shareholders	516	514
By Anglo to provide for future business expansion	521	517
	1,037	1,031
By Anglo's associate companies to provide for future business expansion	772	472
	1,809	1,503

Anglo's business year (this is normally called the financial year) begins on April 1 of one year, and ends on March 31 of the next. The profit statement of Anglo for the financial year which began on April 1, 1987 and ended on March 31, 1988 is set out above, with the figures for the previous year shown in the right-hand column.

The profit of R1,037 million earned by Anglo and its subsidiaries was only slightly better than the profit earned in the previous year. This was mainly because of the lower trading profits from the subsidiary companies, which were due in part to lower profits earned by the gold mines arising from the strike of last year. However, the profits of Anglo's associate companies improved compared with the previous year.

Of this profit, R516 million will be paid out in dividends to those people who own shares in Anglo. The rest of the profit will be kept in Anglo to pay for future expansion, thus helping to increase the value of Anglo to the benefit of all its shareholders. After paying dividends to their own shareholders, Anglo's associate companies also retained R772 million of profits which will be used to finance expansion of their own businesses.

However, even where the case is made for necessary disclosures to a broader audience than shareholders, such as in the British *Corporate Report*, emphasis is still placed on *general-purpose* statements. As they note:

> The reporting responsibility we identify is an all-purpose one, intended for the general information of all users outside those charged with the control and management of the organization. In short, we are concerned with general-purpose reports designed for general purpose use.[4]

In other words, disclosure may broaden, but it does not become more specific.

CHECKPOINTS

---

1. Who are the users of financial statements?
2. Why is it important to know who the users of financial statements are?
3. Are investors a homogeneous group? If not, list as many kinds of investors that you can.

LEVELS OF DISCLOSURE

In the broadest sense of the word, *disclosure* simply means the release of information. Accountants tend to use the word in a slightly more restrictive sense to mean the release of financial information about a company within a financial report, generally the annual report. The term is sometimes further restricted to mean the information not contained in the financial statements themselves. Questions regarding the release of information in the balance sheet, income statement, and cash flow statement fall under the rubrics of *recognition* and *measurement*. Disclosure, in its narrowest sense, covers such things as managements' discussion and analysis, footnotes, and supplementary statements.

Exhibit 24-2, drawn from *SFAC 5*, provides a useful summary of the various levels of disclosure. Note how financial statements are only one component of a larger disclosure system. Note, too, how disclosure about a firm coming from sources outside a firm is also part of the total disclosure system.

Disclosure outside the financial statements themselves serves a very important role in today's global marketplace. There remains a great deal of disagreement as to how certain items should be measured. For example, the treatment of goodwill differs quite widely from one country to another. In such circumstances, simple disclosure of the facts enables a

EXHIBIT 24-2[5]   Financial Disclosure

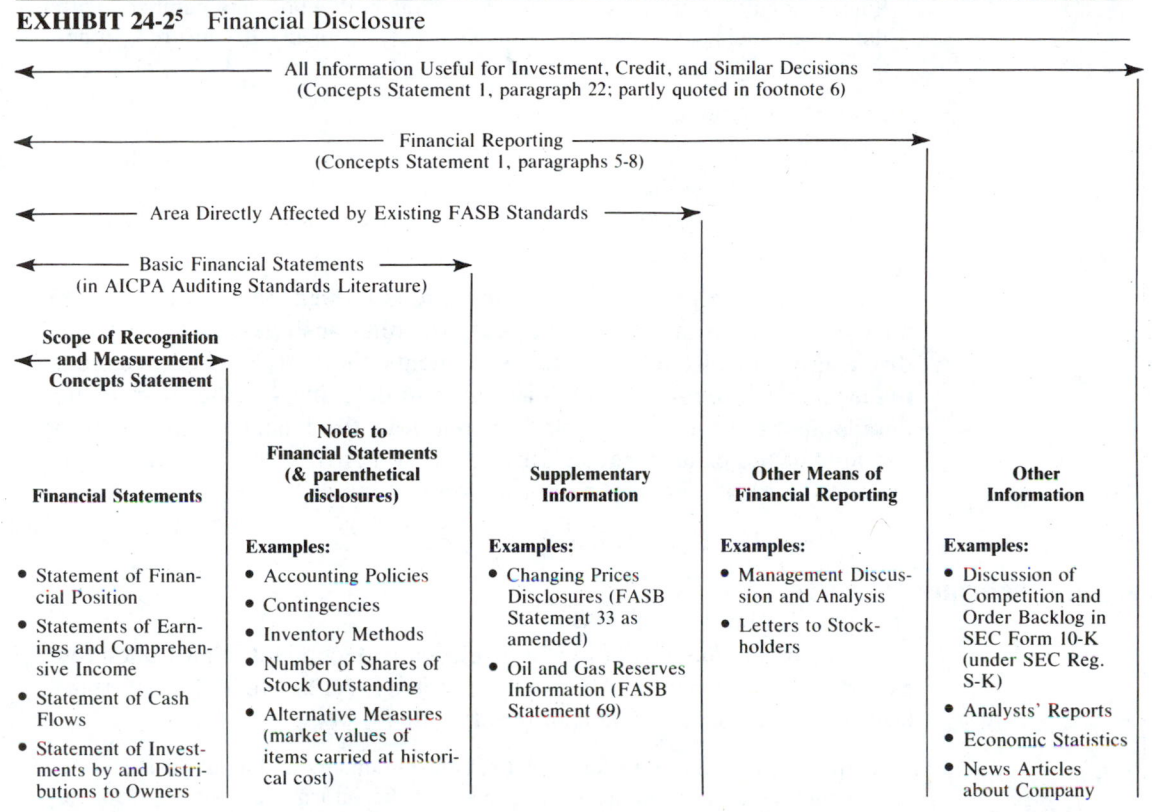

Recognition and Measurement in Financial Statements CON5
of Business Enterprises

reader to determine to his or her own satisfaction the appropriate treatment. Where the items are recognized in the body of the financial statements, it remains important to disclose the accounting policies followed in their measurement. As the International Accounting Standards Committee (IASC) put it:

> Financial statements must be clear and understandable. They are based on accounting policies which vary from enterprise to enterprise, both within a single country and among countries. Disclosure of the significant accounting policies on which the financial statements are based is therefore necessary so that they may be properly understood.[6]

This statement is in line with *APB 22*, "Disclosure of Accounting Policies," published in 1972.

However, the two levels at which financial information can be released, in the financial statements and in material accompanying the financial statements, are not considered equal by accounting authorities. The FASB, for instance, has held that:

Since recognition means depiction of an item in both words and numbers, with the amount included in the totals of the financial statements, disclosure by other means is not recognition.[7]

The IASC has made the same point:

Sometimes a wrong or inappropriate treatment is adopted for items in balance sheets, income statements or profit and loss accounts, or other statements. Disclosure of the treatment adopted is necessary in any case, but disclosure cannot rectify a wrong or inappropriate treatment.[8]

Aside from these fairly general observations though, there is little guidance in the authoritative literature as to the relationship between footnote disclosure and disclosure in the statements themselves. For instance, management has considerable discretion in deciding whether to provide details about the various capital accounts in the balance sheet or in a footnote to the balance sheet. Currently, the FASB has not taken a position on the ideal location of information in general.

Level of Disclosure

How much information should be disclosed is dependent in part upon the expertness of the reader. The FASB, for instance, has held that information being disclosed in financial reports should be:

comprehensible to those who have a reasonable understanding of business and economic activities and are willing to study the information with reasonable diligence.[9]

The level of disclosure also depends upon the standard deemed most desirable. Three concepts of disclosure generally proposed are *adequate*, *fair*, and *full* disclosure.

The most commonly used of these expressions is adequate disclosure, but this implies a minimum amount of disclosure congruous with the negative objective of making the statements not misleading. Fair and full are more positive concepts. Fair disclosure implies an ethical objective of providing equal treatment for all potential readers. Full disclosure implies the presentation of all relevant information. To some, full disclosure means the presentation of superfluous information and is, therefore, inappropriate. Too much information, they say, is harmful in that the presentation of unimportant details hides the significant information and makes the financial reports difficult to interpret. However, appropriate disclosure of information significant to investors and others should be adequate, fair, and full. There is no real difference among those concepts if they are used in the proper context. A positive objective is to provide the users of financial statements with significant and relevant information to aid them in making decisions in the best possible way with the limitation that the benefits should exceed the costs.* This implies that information that is not material or relevant is omitted to make the presentations meaningful and understandable.

In addition, the level of disclosure made by a company should depend on the level of disclosure available from other sources. In many of the developed countries there is a very sophisticated system of financial reporting. For example, in the United States one thinks of publications such as *Business Week, Forbes, Fortune, Inc.,* and *The Wall Street Journal,* to quote but a few well-known names. In addition, there are numerous specialist and trade publications covering industries in depth. Contrast this with smaller countries where the market for financial publications may not be as active. Investors in countries with a less active financial press are far more dependent on the company for news about its activities than in a country where the news is made public in a plethora of publications almost the day before they occur. In such situations, the question is not so much what to disclose, but what is the most efficient way of disclosing.

A similar question about the level of disclosure arises in regard to smaller companies who often make an argument for being exempted from FASB rulings on grounds that they are too onerous. One example of *differential disclosure* is *SFAS 21* which suspends the reporting of earnings-per-share disclosures for nonpublic enterprises. The problem with differential disclosure is that there are relatively few financial analysts who follow small companies. A recent paper concluded that "the body of evidence indicates that small companies' reported earnings are especially important to investors, presumably due to the limited availability of alternative sources of information."[10]

Standards for Disclosure

In an ideal world, decisions regarding the appropriate level of disclosure would be based on the increase in social welfare that any additional disclosure would produce. However, as Chapter 6 noted, the world of neoclassical economics is dominated today by an individualistic, utilitarian approach to ethics. In this approach, the possibility of comparing the welfare of two individuals is denied and, therefore, the aggregation of individual welfare is said to be infeasible. The result is that modern accountants are reluctant to make any social welfare statements. Take the issue of disclosure by small businesses as an example. On the surface, one is tempted to say that while disclosure might cost small businesses, the

---

* In a cost-free world, as Chapter 6 pointed out, more information is always better than less. Irrelevant information can always be discarded.

benefits to the public at large outweigh the costs. Such claims, though, are not possible within the neoclassical framework.

The FASB, who is obliged to make decisions affecting society's welfare, attempts—unsuccessfully in the eyes of their critics—to finesse this problem by resorting to qualitative characteristics, which it believes useful information ought to have. Information, the FASB says, should be relevant, timely, and understandable. It should also be reliable, neutral, and representationally faithful. (Each of these terms was discussed in Chapter 5.) The assumption is that, when information has these characteristics, it will be of benefit to society. Furthermore, if the specific and general preferences of sophisticated investors are emphasized, one of the objectives should be the presentation of sufficient information to permit comparisons of expected results. Comparability, however, can be applied in at least two different ways. One is to provide sufficient disclosure of how accounting numbers are measured and computed to permit investors to convert the amounts from different firms into measurements that are directly comparable. That is, it is assumed that adjusted accounting numbers for the several firms can be used by investors to determine the degrees of difference, for example, in the rates of growth of net income or dividends. A second way of applying comparability is to permit the investor to make ordinal rankings of the several inputs into the decision models. For example, an investor might compare the risks of two firms and conclude merely that one is more or less risky than the other.

Quantitative Data.   In selecting criteria for deciding what quantitative data are material and relevant for investors and creditors, emphasis should be placed on financial or other information that might be of use in decision models. Not all quantitative data, though, have the same reliability. For example, it is generally thought that cash and related items can be measured relatively accurately; the current value of receivables is somewhat less accurate; and intangibles can be measured only within a relatively wide range of reliability. Informed readers, therefore, place greater reliance on some items in the financial statements than on others. They should be able to expect full disclosure if their assumptions regarding reliability are not justified. Therefore, any uncertainties in the measurement of cash items, such as deposits in closed banks or in foreign currencies, would be material and relevant and should be fully disclosed. On the other hand, uncertainties regarding an intangible item are expected and so disclosure may not be necessary. Research in accounting should focus on the method of measuring and reporting probabilistic data rather than deterministic amounts.

Nonquantitative Information.   Information that cannot be expressed in quantitative terms is more difficult to evaluate as to its materiality and relevance because it is given various weights by those using the information in decision making. In general, information that is given greater weight in decision making is more relevant than information given less weight. Therefore, the point should be sought where it can be said that the information is important enough in decision making that it should not be omitted.

The relevance of certain types of nonquantitative information can be determined by the relevance of the quantitative data to which they relate. For example, if certain assets are pledged as security to specific creditors, the pledging is a relevant fact if the assets themselves are material in amount. If the assets are not material, the descriptive or qualifying information is not likely to be relevant. In a few cases, however, this may not be true; for example, the loss of an immaterial amount of inventory or cash may become a relevant fact if it is due to a fraudulent management.

Nonquantitative information is relevant and worthy of disclosure only if it is useful in the decision-making process. It is relevant only if it adds more to the total information than it detracts by making the statements overly detailed and difficult to analyze. The question should always be asked: Is the addition of the information likely to improve most decisions made on the basis of the financial reports?

Voluntary versus Enforced Disclosure

There is a large body of opinion today which holds that companies will disclose all the information that is necessary for the optimal functioning of capital markets. Proponents of this view argue that if information is not disclosed, it is only because it is irrelevant to investors or available to them elsewhere. The argument shifts, therefore, from information supplied by accountants through financial information to supplementary information.

There is some evidence to show that, as companies become more reliant on international capital, they tend to make financial disclosures appropriate to the financial markets in which they hope to raise capital. For instance, a 1977 study which compared the financial reports of the 15 largest publicly held firms in the United States, the United Kingdom, Japan, France, West Germany, The Netherlands, and Sweden concluded that there was evidence of "a relationship between the extent and quality of financial disclosure and the degree of efficiency of national equity markets."[11] NYU professor Fred Choi also concluded that there was "evidence of a direct relationship between improved financial disclosure and entry into the international capital markets."[12] However, whether increased disclosure is due solely to competition for funds alone, or whether it is also a function of seeking those funds in markets such as the United States and the United Kingdom, where disclosure is strictly regulated, is less clear.[13]

Others argue that evidence shows that corporations are reluctant to increase the extent of financial disclosure without pressure from the accounting profession or the government. They attribute the reluctance of companies to disclose more financial information to the following arguments, among others (responses to each are included):

1. Disclosure will aid competitors to the disadvantage of stockholders. This argument, however, has little merit, since competitors generally obtain their information through other sources.

2. Unions are said to gain an advantage in wage bargaining by a complete disclosure of financial information. However, full disclosure will generally improve the general climate for bargaining.

3. It is frequently claimed that investors cannot understand accounting policies and procedures and that full disclosure will only mislead, rather than enlighten. This claim is also unsupported because financial analysts and investment managers are well educated in accounting, and other investors either benefit from the use of financial information in an efficient market or they are able to learn through the study of reported financial information.

4. One argument that has some merit is that frequently other sources of financial information may be available to provide the information at a lower cost than if it were provided by the firm in its financial statements.

5. A lack of knowledge of the needs of investors is also given as a reason for limiting disclosure. Given the possibility of many investment models and an increasing reliance on information intermediaries, this reason should not be a restricting factor.

Regulating Disclosure

The claim that companies fail to disclose sufficient information and the reasons for this claim have already been encountered in Chapter 8, where it was pointed out that one result of a lack of disclosure is a failure of the market. The potential failure of the market has been used to justify government intervention in the market to ensure that sufficient information is disclosed. The primary authority in the United States in this regard is the Securities and Exchange Commission (SEC) created, as noted in Chapter 3, in 1934. It is often said, with a certain degree of truth, that the SEC is responsible for the level of disclosure, while the FASB is responsible for the format of that disclosure. The Advisory Committee on Corporate Disclosure described the SEC's mission in these terms:

> The Commission's function in the corporate disclosure system is to assure the public availability in an efficient and reasonable manner and on a timely basis of reliable, firm-oriented information material to informed investment and corporate suffrage decision-making.[15]

It achieves its purposes primarily through Regulation S-X, Accounting Series Releases (ASRs), and Staff Accounting Bulletins (SABs).

Regulation S-X, which governs the form and content of financial statements, notably the annual report known as the 10-K, submitted to the SEC, was promulgated in 1940 at a time when GAAP was relatively sparse. The disclosure requirements of Regulation S-X appear in Exhibit 24-3.

Regulation S-X differed in significant respects from GAAP so that the form and content of the 10-K deviated from the form and content of the annual report sent to shareholders. In 1980, the SEC revised Regulation S-X to bring the basic information package into line with the corporate annual report. Accounting theorist Kenneth Most notes that one effect of this is to permit "the SEC to dictate the form and content of financial reporting."[16]

Other countries have also found it necessary to enforce disclosure of accounting information. Canada, for instance, led the way on the North American continent. As early as 1907 the Canadian province of Ontario enacted a Companies Act, modeled on the British Companies Act of 1862, mandating the disclosure of income statement and balance sheet informa-

---

EXHIBIT 24-3   SEC's Form 10-K Requirements[14]

General instructions

Part I
 1. Description of the business
 2. List of properties
 3. Report of any significant legal proceedings
 4. Ownership of securities—special features

Part II

5. Market for the registrant's stock 6. Selected financial data 7. Management's discussion and analysis of financial condition and results of operations 8. Financial statements and supplemental (e.g., quarterly) data	Basic information package

Part III
 9. Directors and executive officers
10. Management remuneration and transactions

Part IV
11. Exhibits, financial statement schedules, and form 8-K reports
Signatures
Supplemental Information

tion to shareholders. The early date has been attributed in part to the creation of the Institute of Chartered Accountants of Ontario in 1879, eight years before the creation of the American Institute, and its subsequent vigorous growth.[17]

More recently, in 1978, the European Economic Community (EEC) issued their *Fourth Directive* which deals with the content and format of financial reports and also has some specific provisions relating to disclosure. One of the more significant aspects of the Directive from a North American perspective is that it applies to both public and private companies. This stands in sharp contrast to U.S. practice where only public companies are subject to SEC regulation. Also of interest is that exemptions are granted to small and medium companies regardless of whether or not they are public.

One of the earliest statements issued by the IASC dealt with the subject of disclosure and was entitled, "Information to Be Disclosed in Financial Statements."[18] This specifies particular items to be disclosed. For example, it requires that payables in the current liability section show at least the following detail:

Accounts and notes payable—trade.

Payable to directors.

Intercompany payables.

Associated company payables.

Taxes on income.

Dividends payable.

Other payables and accrued expenses.

As the IASC notes, financial statements prepared in conformity with U.S. Generally Accepted Accounting Principles will comply with this standard in all material respects.

CHECKPOINTS

1. What factors influence the most desirable level of disclosure by a corporation?
2. What standards govern disclosure?
3. What forces encourage voluntary disclosure? What forces impede it?
4. Which bodies regulate disclosure?
5. What is Regulation S-X?

FORMS OF DISCLOSURE

In addition to the quantitative data usually presented in traditional financial statements, there is considerable merit in the presentation of greater detail regarding the several segments of a business enterprise representing product or geographical diversifications arising from normal growth or from mergers in the development of conglomerate firms. This will be discussed at greater length in a special section below. Considerable pressure has also arisen to require the reporting of forecast data.

Financial Forecasts

The historical cost accounting structure has been thought to be a review of past events. Investors, on the other hand, are primarily interested in the future prospects of the firm. One view is that accountants should present only historical and current information that will permit investors to make their own predictions of the future. That is, the process of forecasting requires subjective evaluations in addition to an analysis of a large number of variables and assumptions; it is thought that the investor can understand the subjective evaluations and assumptions only by making the forecast. Another view is that management has far superior resources for making reliable forecasts and that the public availability of its forecasts increases the efficiency of the financial markets.

Deciding between these views is difficult because, as noted on several occasions before, we lack a good understanding of how investors and others process financial information. Also, one has to take into consideration the findings of efficient-market theory with regard to how much and how quickly stock prices capture information. These findings suggest that most publicly available forecasts may be based on information that has already been impounded in stock prices by the activities of market specialists.

Some early studies on forecasting concluded that forecasts are indeed useful to stockholders.[19] Others were less convinced. For instance, another early study showed that forecasts tended to be simple extrapolations of current and past trends. The result is that the forecasts are less useful in the area that would be of the greatest assistance to investors, namely, determining turning points in the economy.[20] That study also found some evidence that forecasters tend to be overly optimistic, particularly for a period following a long expansion. There is also some quite understandable evidence that more managements make disclosures when there is "good news" to report than when there is "bad news."[21] Despite the lack of confirming evidence, most observers believe that the regular publication of management's forecasts is likely to aid rather than hinder investment decisions.

The basic questions that remain are what information should be forecast and how its reliability can be measured. The most frequently mentioned forecast accounting numbers are probably net income and earnings per share, but these are probably more difficult to predict and also the least reliable. This results from the fact that a projection of accounting income depends on many subjective variables and many assumptions regarding the firm and the economy. Items that may be more reliable and easier to predict include expected sales, budgeted receipts and disbursements, and measurements relating to expected changes in the prices and demand for the product of the firm, and expected changes in the costs of labor and goods generally acquired by the firm. These items also have more semantic content than accounting income.

With publication of the forecast of financial accounting information and other information relating to the firm, it is necessary that the basic assumptions relating to the economy and external factors be disclosed so that the users of the forecasts can better evaluate its reliability. Such assumptions should include expectations regarding the industry as well as assumptions regarding changes in economic conditions.

The lack of reliability in making forecasts has been a matter of much concern to managements who fear litigation as a result of unfulfilled expectations. This concern has been mitigated by *SEC Release No. 6084* issued in 1979, which provided management a "safe harbor" if their forecasts were made in "good faith." This release covers analyses of trends as well as projections. Despite the safe harbor, managements are still reluctant to make specific projections in public for a number of reasons:

1. Projections may convey an unwarranted impression of accuracy.
2. Projections are virtually certain to become outdated very quickly. Therefore, to be useful and to avoid misleading the public, they would almost inevitably require frequent updating.
3. Forecasts and projections may be used by competitors to the detriment of the reporting entity.
4. Managements may feel compelled to meet published forecasts to the point of making short-run decisions that are not in the shareholders' best interests.
5. Failure of the enterprise to meet its projections could generate stockholder dissatisfaction and possibly litigation.[22]

There has been less reluctance to discuss broad trends, though. These discussions are typically found in Management's Discussion and Analysis, discussed below.

Accounting Policies

With the proliferation of accounting procedures in use by different firms and even within the same firm, direct comparability of financial statements has become more difficult. One suggested solution has been an attempt to reduce the number of alternatives in the hope that uniformity would automatically permit comparability. However, selecting one procedure for all firms is not only a difficult choice but one that may not achieve its goal under conditions of differing circumstances. The argument for diversity on the grounds of differing circumstances has, however, been too often used as a rationalization for the prerogative of management to choose whatever methods it wishes, frequently those methods that present the firm in the best light.

An alternative solution to the reduction of available alternatives is to disclose in each case the specific methods used under the assumption that the reader will then be able to restate the accounting reports in order to gain comparability. Empirical evidence has shown that this is possible in

---

EXHIBIT 24-4   Disclosure of Accounting Policies (selection only)

The Walt Disney Company and Subsidiaries

Revenue Recognition

Revenues from the theatrical distribution of motion pictures are recognized when motion pictures are exhibited domestically and when revenues are reported from foreign distributors; revenues from television licensing agreements are recorded when the program material is available for telecasting by the licensee and when certain other conditions are met.

Revenues from participant/sponsors at the theme parks are recorded over the period of the applicable agreements commencing with the opening of the attraction.

Merchandise Inventories

Costs of merchandise, materials and supplies inventories are generally determined on the moving average basis and the retail method and are stated at the lower of cost or market.

Film Production Costs

Film production costs are amortized and participation expense is accrued in the ratio that the current period's gross revenues bear to estimated total gross revenues from all sources on an individual production basis. Estimates of total gross revenues are reviewed periodically and amortization is adjusted accordingly. Programming costs for The Disney Channel are amortized primarily on a straight-line basis over the estimated useful lives of the programs.

Entertainment Attractions and Other Property

Depreciation is provided principally on the straight-line method using estimated service lives ranging from three to fifty years.

Other Assets

Rights to the name, likeness, and portrait of Walt Disney are being amortized over forty years.

some circumstances, such as when the investment credit is reported as a direct reduction of the tax, rather than being allocated to income over a period of time. But, in most cases, there is no evidence that investors can gain comparability by converting various statements into uniform methods. For example, one research study showed that functional fixation on reported income prevented the decision makers participating in the study from adjusting for the effects of LIFO and FIFO inventory methods, even though they had the information and knew how to make the adjustment.[23]

Disclosure of accounting policies, nevertheless, may provide assistance in permitting better interpretation of the financial statements of any particular firm and, therefore, influence investment decisions. On the basis of this assumption, the Accounting Principles Board in *Opinion No. 22* concluded that information about accounting policies in use is necessary for a fair presentation of financial statements. This assumption is also given support by the results of an empirical study which found that investors did react to both the content and the art of disclosure itself.[24] An example of the disclosures made in accordance with *APB 22* is shown in Exhibit 24-4.

Accounting Changes

The consistent use of accounting principles and procedures has long been considered essential in the evaluation of a firm's activities and in the projection of future activities. *APB 20* supported this view but stated that, when justified, such changes should be disclosed in the financial statements when the change is made. This should be accompanied by a justification for the change. Accounting changes include changes in accounting principles, in accounting estimates, and in the reporting entity. The disclosure of these changes, like the disclosure of accounting policies, is essential for optimal investment decisions.

Empirical evidence has supported the view that changes in reported net income resulting from changes in accounting methods have not materially affected the market price of stock when disclosure of the change has been made.[25] However, contrary to the opinion of the APB, there appears to be some logic in the restatement of financial statements of prior periods when they are included for comparative purposes. The efficient-markets hypothesis, on the other hand, supports the conclusion that disclosure itself is sufficient if sophisticated investors or investment analysts can interpret the financial information correctly.

Disclosure of Poststatement Events

The income statement is a summary of certain types of changes during the period reported on, and the balance sheet summarizes the resource measurements and financial relationships at the end of this period. However, almost all of the figures included in these statements are tentative in nature because of uncertainties regarding the future. As time passes and additional information is obtained, many of these uncertainties are resolved. Therefore, many of the events occurring after the statement date affect the validity or the interpretations of the statements and the resulting decisions based on the information presented in them. To the extent that material events occur or become known after the statement date and before the report is completed, the objective of disclosure requires that this information be properly revealed in the report.

Two types of relevant events that may occur after the statement date and before the completion of the report are:

1. Events that affect directly the amounts reported in the financial statements.
2. Events that alter materially the continuing validity of balance sheet valuations or the relationships among equity holders or materially affect the usefulness of the prior year's reported activities as a prediction of the current period.

Events of the first type arise from inadequate knowledge during the accounting period and result in changes in estimated valuations because of knowledge gained subsequent to the balance sheet date. For example, if a major customer goes into bankruptcy during this period, the receivables included in the balance sheet and not collected at the date of the bankruptcy are likely to be overvalued, and the related bad debt expense would probably be understated. If knowledge of this type of information is obtained early enough, the financial statements should be adjusted appropriately before they are published. If knowledge is obtained too late to make a complete correction of the statements, the information can be disclosed by some other means unless the statements would be completely erroneous if direct correction is not made. The Auditing Standards Board recommended that this type of event should be recognized by an adjustment directly in the financial statements if the information would have been utilized had it been available at the balance sheet date.[26]

Events of the second type have no direct effect on the financial statements of the prior year, but are likely to materially affect decisions based on these statements. These include:

1. Events that affect materially the financial structure of the firm or current or future relationships among equity holders.
2. Events that affect the income or potential dividend distributions of the period following the period included in the report or in later periods.

Thus, a relatively large sale of capital stock or bonds or the purchase or sale of assets representing a large part of the total assets of the firm is assumed to be relevant for investment or credit decisions regarding the firm. Events that may result in abnormal and nonrecurring gains or losses may also affect decisions by influencing predictions of the future economic health of the firm. The Auditing Standards Board stated that these events do not require adjustment, but it did say that disclosure is advisable.[27] In the opinion of the authors, the recommendation should be much stronger than this. Appropriate disclosure is just as important for these events as for similar events occurring during the reporting period. For example, the disclosure of a new stock option plan, or an agreement to negotiate a merger, is just as important if the event occurs after the balance sheet date as it is if it occurred before. Partial recognition is given to this in *APB 16*, which recommends that in the case of a combination accounted for as a pooling, consummated after the close of the period but before the financial statements are issued, the financial statements should be restated to give effect to the pooling for the entire period.

Other subsequent events which reflect "a concurrent evaluation of new conditions" lead typically neither to disclosure nor to adjustments of the financial statements.[28] Examples of such events include changes in specific market conditions or in prices affecting the firm; new management policies; the signing of major contracts; and such external events as wars, legislation, and economic conditions.

These recommendations, however, apply to disclosure in audited statements. Disclosure of the events of the third type, or of all types, may be made in the president's letter, or in a separate section of the annual report, without any implication that the auditors consider this information a qualification of the statements. A broader and more positive viewpoint is that events of all three types, including their effect on the expectations of management, should be disclosed directly in the financial report reviewed by the auditor. The authors agree with this position as a long-run goal to provide the best possible information for making investment decisions.

DISCLOSURE OF SEGMENTS OF A BUSINESS ENTERPRISE

The growth of diversified businesses and the expansion of firms into foreign markets has resulted in the aggregation of financial information that includes nonhomogeneous elements. This problem of aggregation has become more acute with the development of large conglomerate firms that obtain their diversification through mergers or acquisitions of a wide variety of unrelated businesses. With each combination, there is a loss of information to the investor community and to the general public, since firms previously reporting separately report only a single firm after the combination. Also, because of the diversification of activities, evaluation of these conglomerate firms and the prediction of their future activities and successes have become more difficult with only aggregated data available.

SFAS 14 requires the presentation (in specific cases) of information regarding a firm's operations in different industries, its foreign operations and export sales, and its major customers. *IAS 14* has similar requirements to that of the FASB and notes that "financial statements prepared in accordance with U.S. Generally Accepted Accounting Principles will comply with International Accounting Standard 14 in all material respects."[29] The EEC's *Fourth Directive* is not as comprehensive: it requires only that sales be analyzed by industrial (or product) and geographical segments.[30]

Need for Segment Disclosures.   The need for disclosure of the operations of the major segments of diversified firms and firms with geographical or customer-segmented markets arises because growth trends, variability of operations, and risk cannot be evaluated adequately from aggregated data. Disaggregation of the financial data is necessary to permit the prediction of future cash flows and risk for use in investment decision models. In estimating the value of a firm and in evaluating the risk, investors need to make predictions regarding the future operations of the enterprise. Predictions that are based on or supported by extrapolations of historical data are likely to be more reliable if they are made from information regarding the various segments of a business that have different characteristics.

Whether the objective should be to permit comparability or to permit predictability has a bearing on the minimum size of a business segment that should be reported separately. To obtain comparability among firms for similar types of operations, the selection criterion should be the absolute size of the operations. If a criterion is based on a percentage of total revenues of the firm, one type of operation representing 50 percent or more of the revenues of a small firm would require disclosure; but if it represents less than, say, 10 percent of the total revenues of a large firm, it would not be reported, even though an operation of this type may be considerably larger than the similar operation of the smaller firm. For this reason, recommendations have been made that segments as small as 5 percent of the total operations of a diversified firm should be reported separately, with a minimum absolute dollar criterion. However, if predictability is the objective, a higher minimum percentage may be adequate in order to provide relevant information regarding the contribution of a segment to the firm's revenue and net income. The FASB has suggested that an industry segment is significant if it represents 10 percent or more of the firm's revenues, operating profit, or identifiable assets.

Information regarding segments of a business is also thought to be relevant in external reports to prevent management from hiding information that it does not want published. For example, managements may wish to hide the fact that certain segments of the business are being operated at a loss for fear that they will be criticized by the stockholders for their managerial inefficiency. If some segments are quite profitable, they can be used to cover up the fact that other segments are unprofitable. This ability to hide losses has also been used by large firms as a way to finance their entry into a new line and to compete with established firms without being accused of underpricing to gain monopolistic control in markets.

Accounting Difficulties.   One of the first problems in reporting on divisions or segments of a business is the decision regarding how logical breakdowns should be made for reporting purposes. Product lines may be relevant in some cases but not in others. Geographical divisions may be particularly relevant with respect to foreign operations, and in other cases, classification by type of customer may be relevant. That is, predictability requires the grouping of activities that have similar behavioral characteristics over time.

A second important problem in the reporting of profit for separate segments of a business is the allocation of joint costs. If the segments are autonomously operated divisions, the amount of joint costs may be small; but in relation to the net incomes of the segments, it may be significant. Since accountants make allocations in many areas of reporting (such as the computation of depreciation), it has been suggested that one more allocation might make little difference.[31] But since such allocations are arbitrary, it is unlikely that relevant information can be obtained by their use. An alternative is to report only the ''defined profit'' or contribution to each division, computed from only the revenues and expenses that can be directly associated with the reporting segment. However, some firms may fear that such contribution may be interpreted as the net income of the division and as being excessive.

Another accounting problem is the treatment of interdivisional transfer pricing. The final product of one division may be the raw material of another within the same firm, so that if transfers are made in excess of cost, income will appear at the time of the transfer rather than when the final product is sold to a customer outside the firm. Wharton professor David Solomons suggested that the best procedure would seem to be to eliminate interdivisional cost.[32] From the point of view of the objective of attaining predictive ability, this seems to be the best solution because a prediction of the cash to be received from customers is more important to investors than the amount of product transferred from one division to another. However, comparability among firms is not attained because in some cases the semifinished product may be the final product of the firm, whereas in other cases the output of the semifinished product would not be reported prior to the sale of the final product of which it becomes a part.

Since the profitability of a firm is frequently measured in terms of the net income in relationship to the amount of net assets invested in the firm, it seems logical that divisional reporting should also require the separate reporting of the net assets used by each segment of the business. This separate reporting of assets was included in the proposed rules of the SEC to the extent that it is practicable and in *SFAS 14*. However, the measurement of assets is a difficult problem even for an entire enterprise. The assignment of physical assets to segments of a business may be possible in some cases, but accounting has not yet devised a consistent method of measuring these assets in a meaningful way so they can be related to the revenue contribution derived from them. Even if physical assets could be assigned to segments and measured in a meaningful way, the intangible assets—which may be more important in many cases—are most likely to be omitted. Furthermore, the liabilities of the enterprise cannot usually be designated in a meaningful way to represent the financing of specific assets.

CHECKPOINTS

1. Are financial forecasts audited? If not, why not?
2. Why do companies disclose their accounting policies?
3. What level of disclosure would you want in a footnote announcing a change in accounting policy?
4. What two kinds of subsequent events are there? How do they differ in treatment?
5. In what ways does U.S. regulation of segment disclosure differ from European regulations?

METHODS OF DISCLOSURE

Disclosure involves the entire process of financial reporting. However, several different methods of making disclosure are available. The selection of the best method of disclosure in each case depends on the nature of the information and its relative importance. The common methods of disclosure can be classified as follows:

1. Form and arrangement of formal statements.
2. Terminology and detailed presentations.
3. Parenthetical information.
4. Footnotes.
5. Supplementary statements and schedules.
6. Comments in the auditors' report.
7. The letter of the president or chairman of the board.

Form and Arrangement of Formal Statements

The most relevant and significant information should always appear in the main body of one or more of the financial statements if it is possible to include it there. Assets and liabilities and the resulting effect on net income, and stockholders' equity should be disclosed in the statements as soon as transactions and other changes can be measured reliably and with a fair degree of accuracy. But the form and arrangement of the statement can be altered effectively to bring out certain types of information not readily disclosed by traditional statements.

Position Statement. In the position statement or balance sheet, relevant relationships can be disclosed by rearranging the basic classifications. For example, current liabilities are frequently subtracted directly from current assets to show working capital, although this procedure has some deficiencies (as discussed in Chapter 16). Alternative classifications may separate monetary from nonmonetary assets and liabilities, or group the firm's resources according to the several segments of the business in which they are used. The classification of assets and liabilities was discussed in Chapter 13, several alternative methods of classification and presentation of stockholders' equity were discussed in Chapter 22, and the problems of divisional reporting were discussed earlier in this chapter.

Income Statement. In the income statement, different forms of presentation can emphasize different concepts of income or different interpretations of the data. The single-step income statement, for example, associates all items of expense with all items of revenue; gross profit and other preliminary net figures are considered to be more misleading than helpful to the readers of the statement. In a suggested alternative, expenses are classified as either fixed or variable in order to aid the reader in making predictions of future outcomes with changes in sales volume. The disclosure of other income concepts and relationships was discussed in Chapter 10. The disclosure of earnings-per-share data in the income statement was discussed in Chapter 23.

Cash Flow Statements. As discussed in Chapter 9, considerable relevant information can be presented in cash flow statements, particularly if care is taken to provide relevant classifications. For example, classifications of cash disbursements are more relevant for predictive purposes if the disbursements are grouped according to their functional behavior, such as fixed and variable characteristics. Additional groupings according to the major segments of the business are also likely to be relevant to the decisions of investors and other interested parties.

Terminology and Detailed Presentations

Just as important as the form of the statements in disclosure are the descriptions used in the statement and the amount of detail shown. Appropriate captions and descriptions of the items in the statements can be enlightening to the reader, but obscure terms can lead only to confusion or misunderstanding. Technical terms may be useful if they have precise meanings that are generally well known, but many technical terms in accounting lack this preciseness. In these cases, accountants should apply descriptive terms generally used by financial analysts and other informed readers. Uniformity of terms throughout all accounting reports are helpful if the meanings are clear and if the items are similar in all cases where the term is applied.

Because of the limitations of human spans of attention and comprehension, accounting data must be summarized to be meaningful and useful. The choice of how much information to present and the selection of what items to list separately are dependent on the objectives of the reports and on the materiality of the items. Brevity is a desirable goal in financial reports, but appropriate disclosure of detailed information should take precedence if it is necessary to make the reports valuable for decision making.

Parenthetical Information

The most significant information should be presented in the body of a financial statement, rather than in footnotes or supplementary schedules. If the titles of items in the statements cannot be made fully descriptive without being overly long, additional explanations or definitions can be presented as parenthetical notes following the titles in the statements. These notes, however, must not be long or they will detract from the main data summarized in the statement.

Other nonquantitative data that can be presented in parenthetical notes include:

1. An indication of the specific procedure or valuation method used, to give the reader a better understanding of the meaning of the data.
2. The special characteristics that give greater meaning regarding the relative importance of the item, such as the fact that certain assets are pledged or that certain liabilities have prior rights.
3. Detail regarding the amount of one or more items included in the broader classification listed.
4. Such alternative valuations as current market price.
5. Reference to related information in other statements or elsewhere in the report.

Footnotes

Current financial reports have given rise to what may be called the foot-note era. On the one hand, this is an improvement in reporting because it has resulted in a fuller disclosure of financial events and relevant financial data. On the other hand, the extensive use of footnotes has hindered the proper development of the statements themselves because it has resulted in the substitution of footnotes for better information in the body of the statement. Footnotes have an appropriate place in financial reporting, but there is danger in placing too much reliance on footnotes as a method of disclosure or in using footnotes as an apology for inadequate formal statements. Although it is difficult to set forth clear principles of footnoting based on accounting theory, some basic rules of footnoting can be formulated to tie in with the basic postulates and principles of accounting.

Nature and Purpose of Footnotes. The objective of using footnotes in financial statements should be to disclose information that cannot be presented adequately in the body of a statement without detracting from the clarity of the statement. Footnotes should not be used as a substitute for proper classification or valuation and description in the statements, nor should they contradict or repeat the information in the statements. The main advantages of footnotes are their uses:

1. To present nonquantitative information as an integral part of the financial report.
2. To disclose qualifications and restrictions to items in the statements.
3. To disclose a greater amount of detail than can be presented in the statements.
4. To present either quantitative or descriptive material of secondary importance.

The main disadvantages of footnotes are:

1. They tend to be difficult to read and understand without considerable study and thus they may be overlooked.
2. The textual descriptions are more difficult to use in decision making than the summarizations of quantitative data in the statements.
3. Because of the increasing complexity of business enterprises, there is danger of an overuse of footnotes rather than proper development of principles to incorporate new relationships and events into the statements themselves.

The most common types of footnotes can be classified as follows:

1. Explanations of techniques or changes in methods.
2. Explanations of rights of creditors to specific assets or priorities of rights.

3. Disclosure of contingent assets or contingent liabilities.
4. Disclosure of restrictions to dividend payments.
5. Descriptions of transactions affecting capital stock and rights of equity holders.
6. Descriptions of executory contracts.

Footnotes are also used to present detailed quantitative data that are not significant enough to include in the body of a statement, but these are in the form of supplementary schedules and, therefore, are discussed at greater length below as a separate form of disclosure.

Accounting Policy and Accounting Changes.   As discussed above, a proper interpretation of the income statement and the balance sheet requires an understanding of the accounting methods used and the effect of changes in methods. Because most valuation and allocation techniques affect the income statement and the balance sheet, a footnote disclosure of the methods used may be better than parenthetical notes in each statement. And, with a footnote, the methods used can be given fuller treatment than if parenthetical notes are used. This fuller disclosure is important where the differences among the several accepted methods are material—that is, where an assumption of a different method would be a significant factor in the making of decisions. Where such an item as cost of goods sold is a summary of several items computed by different methods, the footnote disclosure should show the amount computed by each of the methods if material. In the case of LIFO, the year the method was started might also be relevant. Since depreciation is generally a major item in most income statements, *APB 12* recommended that the methods used in computing depreciation should be presented for the major classes of depreciable assets.

Changes in methods may be more significant than the methods themselves, particularly when comparative data are presented. The postulate of consistency requires that financial reports should be comparable from period to period and that, when changes are made, the effect of the change should be disclosed. In most cases, this disclosure can be made appropriately in footnotes. However, if the effect of the change is to make a comparison of the data completely misleading, a footnote would be inadequate. In this case, the data for prior years should be computed on the new basis to permit proper comparisons.

Prior Right of Creditors.   The usual types of priorities, such as those granted to mortgage bondholders, can generally be explained succinctly in the balance sheet by a brief reference to the mortgage or to the specific property granted as security. But when the prior claims are unusual or more complex than normal, a footnote disclosure is necessary. For example, in 1989 Litton Industries disclosed that:

Under the terms of a $100 million line of credit agreement between a group of banks and Western Atlas International, Inc., a subsidiary of the Company, this subsidiary is prohibited from making advances or loans which are not in the ordinary course of business.

Such contract provisions are relevant and material if knowledge of them would affect the decisions of other creditors or investors. Generally, it can be assumed that knowledge of these provisions would affect credit or investment decisions if the provisions affect the risk of other creditors or stockholders. These contract provisions may also be relevant if they restrict the freedom of management and the board of directors in the general operations of the firm or in the financing of expansions or replacements.

Contingent Assets and Contingent Liabilities. All assets and liabilities should be estimated, if at all possible, and included in the balance sheet and the effect, if any, on net income should be reflected in the income statement. Only if the most probable value of the asset or liability is likely to be zero, or if the best estimate of current or future value is very likely to be highly erroneous and misleading, should the asset or liability be omitted from the statements. But, if the probable occurrence of a gain or loss, resulting from the failure to recognize the asset or liability, would be a significant element in decision making, the relevant facts should be disclosed in a footnote.

In the case of a pending lawsuit, the amount of the claim and any other relevant information, such as the decisions of lower courts or decisions in other similar cases, should be disclosed to permit the reader to form some judgment regarding the possible effect of the case. Expectations regarding the outcome of the case and the probable damages to be awarded by the court are not generally meaningful unless the reason for the estimate is also given.

Restrictions on Dividend Payments. From a legal point of view, dividends can usually be paid to the extent of total retained earnings and, in many states, additional paid-in capital. But, as explained in Chapter 22, the classification of stockholders' equity in the balance sheet does not disclose the extent of the legality of dividends, nor does it show the intent of the board of directors regarding future dividend payments. However, according to traditional textbook treatments, legal, contractual, and managerial restrictions on dividends may be shown by means of appropriations of retained earnings. Since the stockholders' equity section of the balance sheet is classified primarily by its source, rather than by intended distribution, this use of appropriations is more confusing than enlightening.

A positive statement of the policy of the board of directors regarding dividend distributions is helpful to investors and other users of financial reports. Most dividend payments by large corporations are related to current earnings, past earnings, past dividends, and available cash resources. There is generally no intent to pay dividends to the full amount legally permitted or even to the extent of retained earnings. Therefore, a footnote explanation of dividend restrictions based on retained earnings may not be very relevant to investors who can expect that future dividends will probably not exceed future earnings. However, if current earnings are at all restricted for dividend payments, these restrictions should be disclosed. Because of the nature of the information, all relevant restrictions of either retained earnings or current earnings can be disclosed appropriately in footnotes. For example, ITT Corporation made the following footnote disclosure:

> Under the Corporation's long-term debt agreements, approximately $4.1 billion of consolidated retained earnings as of December 31, 1988 was unrestricted as to the payment of dividends. Subsidiaries are subject to various restrictions, such as regulatory and borrowing restraints on transfers of funds to the Corporation in the form of cash dividends, loans or advances. The restricted net assets of subsidiaries amounted to $1.3 billion as of December 31, 1988.

Not incidentally, note how ITT focused on unrestricted earnings to present the restriction in as positive a light as it could.

Rights of Equity Holders.   Some of the rights of equity holders are apparent in the balance sheet classifications and descriptions, and others can be disclosed by appropriate parenthetical notes in the statements. Significant changes in these rights to share in income and the net assets of the firm arising from transactions or events during the period should be disclosed specifically in the balance sheet or in footnotes, even though the results of the transactions are reflected in the related items in the balance sheet. Several types of transactions, however, are not immediately reflected in the equity accounts, but affect the future rights of equity holders. It is particularly important that these types of transactions and events be disclosed appropriately in the footnotes to the statements. However, *APB 10* recommends that liquidation preferences of preferred stock be disclosed in the aggregate in the balance sheet either parenthetically or "in short," rather than in footnotes.

One of the common types of transactions affecting the future rights of stockholders is the granting of executive stock options. As discussed in Chapter 23, the conventional method of disclosing these contracts does not show the true effect on income or the true effect on the rights of equity holders. Possibly, because of the uncertainties involved, the true effect cannot be anticipated, and therefore cannot appropriately be shown by merely recording the transaction in the formal accounts. Footnotes showing the nature of the options, the requirements of the contract, and the possible effects on income and stockholders' equity should supplement whatever information can be presented in the formal statements. These disclosures are usually quite extensive. For example, Warner Lambert had the following footnote in 1989:

Note 10—Stock Options:

Warner-Lambert has stock option plans established in 1987, 1983 and 1974 which provide for the granting of options to officers and key employees to purchase stock at its market value on the date the options are granted. Three million shares of common stock have been reserved for each of the 1987 and 1983 plans for the granting of options until April 28, 1992 and April 25, 1993, respectively. There are outstanding options under the 1974 plan; however, no additional options can be granted under this plan. All plans contain provisions for the granting of options with rights which permit the optionee to exercise the right and receive payment in shares of common stock, cash or a combination of both, equivalent to the value of the rights being exercised. The value of the rights depends upon the fair market value of the common stock at the time the rights are exercised. Options and rights granted generally become exercisable after one year in 25 percent increments per year and expire 10 years from the date of grant. The value of rights granted is charged to income over the vesting period from the date the market price first exceeds the option price with adjustments made based on market fluctuations to the date of exercise. At December 31, 1988, options outstanding with respect to 626,625 shares of common stock have rights attached.

Transactions involving options with and without rights are summarized as follows:

	Number of Shares	Option Price per Share
Options outstanding, December 31, 1986	2,981,305	$17.31–$56.50
Granted	697,138	60.13– 76.13
Exercised	(236,755)	17.31– 56.50
Cancelled or surrendered	(503,460)	17.31– 76.13
Options outstanding, December 31, 1987	2,938,228	17.31– 76.13
Granted	542,215	60.13– 77.56
Exercised	(185,109)	17.31– 76.13
Cancelled or surrendered	(310,313)	18.94– 76.13
Options outstanding, December 31, 1988	2,985,021	$17.31–$77.56
Exercisable, December 31, 1988	953,504	$17.31–$76.13
Shares reserved for future grants:		
December 31, 1987	3,106,343	
December 31, 1988	2,657,689	

Other types of disclosure affecting the rights of stockholders include the potential rights of holders of stock warrants, convertible debt, or convertible preferred stock. Footnote disclosures should include information regarding the period of conversion or exercise of warrants, the conversion price or exercise price, and other relevant terms of contracts relating to these securities.

Executory Contracts.   Traditional accounting does not recognize assets or liabilities arising from executory contracts. One of the reasons for the failure to record these assets and liabilities is that their valuations are not easily estimated. Another reason is that the effect on income arises from later events rather than from the signing of the contract. However, in most cases, because the contracts represent commitments for the future, their disclosure is very relevant for investment and other decisions relying on some prediction of future cash flows. If this disclosure cannot be made appropriately in the formal statements, the information should be disclosed in footnotes.

Included in the executory type of contracts are long-term leases and purchase commitments. Although the capitalization of these commitments and the inclusion of them among the assets and liabilities of the balance sheet may improve the statement, the nature of these contracts usually requires supplementary information also. In addition to the capitalized valuation, the reader of the report would probably be interested in knowing the terminal date of the contract, the amount of annual payment, the annual charge of expense, and other features. Therefore, footnote disclosure may be desirable to provide supplementary information regarding the long-term contracts; it should not be viewed only as an alternative to capitalization.

Related Parties.   An important use of footnotes is to provide details regarding the nature of transactions between *related parties*. The basic assumption in accounting is that transactions are occurring at *arm's length*. This provides some assurance that the price paid represents the value of the item of service exchanged. In the case of transactions between related parties, such as those between subsidiaries of a company, or between companies controlled by one individual, or between family members, there can be no such assurance. Ideally, one would replace the amount paid by the fair value of the item purchased. However, often the fair value is too difficult to establish. Accountants, therefore, content themselves by disclosing the details of the transaction in accordance with *SFAS 57* so that users might be alerted to its nature. An example of the disclosure required involves Electro-Nucleonics, Inc.:

(13) Related Party Transactions

Pharmacia Inc., a wholly-owned subsidiary of Pharmacia AB, owns 20% of the Company's common stock. Purchases from Pharmacia, relating primarily to its allergy product line which is distributed by the Company in the U.S. were $4,129,000 in 1988 and $4,951,000 in 1987. The Company is involved in research and development related to various allergy and diagnostic products for which it invoices Pharmacia. Such billings amounted to $2,607,000 and $1,570,000 in 1988 and 1987, respectively. Included in trade accounts receivable are $1,763,000 and $342,000 at June 30, 1988 and 1987, respectively, representing amounts receivable under the above noted research and development activities.

Note that there is no claim here that these transactions were carried out at prices that would have obtained in an arm's-length transaction.

Supplementary Statements and Schedules

In order that financial data may be summarized and presented in a statement brief enough to be understandable to reasonably informed readers, some of the significant detailed information must be taken out of the statements and presented in supplementary schedules. These schedules are sometimes included among the footnotes and sometimes in a section following the statements and footnotes. In many current annual reports, the supplementary schedules are included in a separate section of the report called financial highlights or some similar section in the report preceding the formal financial statements. By using a separate section in the report, the information presented there is placed in a position secondary to the statements and footnotes and, therefore, it is often assumed to be of lesser importance than the information in the statements and footnotes. But this separation of information is not intended to indicate relative importance—it is used solely to make the statements readable and understandable.

Supplementary statements perform a different function than supplementary schedules. Generally they present additional information or information arranged in a different fashion, rather than just more detailed information. Since they are not necessarily included in the statements covered in the report of the independent accountant, they can be used as methods of developing and experimenting with new exhibits and statements. An example of a supplementary statement frequently recommended for inclusion in the financial reports is a statement disclosing the effect of price-level changes or specific price changes on the financial condition and financial operations of the enterprise.

The Auditor's Report

The auditor's report is not the place to disclose significant financial information regarding the firm. But it does serve as a method of disclosure for the following types of information:

1. A material effect from using accounting methods different from those generally accepted.

2. A material effect of changing from one generally accepted accounting method to another.
3. A difference of opinion between the auditor and the client regarding the acceptability of one or more accounting methods used in the reports.

The first two types of information should be disclosed in the reports themselves. The duplication of disclosure is required to be sure that the reader is not misled regarding the comparability of the reports with those of other firms or the consistency with other periods.

The financial statements are the report of management and not of the auditor. However, the auditor as a member of the AICPA, and subject to its ethical requirements, cannot express an opinion that the financial statements are in conformity with generally accepted accounting principles if they contain any departures from the opinions of the FASB and former bodies. If a departure is made on the basis that the statements would otherwise have been misleading, the auditor must state in the auditor's report the reasons for the departure and its effects.

Management's Discussion and Analysis and the President's Letter

The formal financial statements with the footnotes and supplementary schedules and statements and the auditor's certificate complete the accountant's financial report. All relevant and significant financial data should appear in this report. However, insight into the significance of this information can best be presented in narrative form by management itself. As the FASB said:

> Management knows more about the enterprise and its affairs than investors, creditors, or other "outsiders" and can often increase the usefulness of financial information by identifying certain transactions, other events, and circumstances that affect the enterprise and explaining their financial impact on it.[33]

Items that management might identify, according to the FASB, include:

1. Arbitrary results caused by the convention of dividing continuous operations into fixed accounting periods.
2. Estimates, judgments, and assumptions that they used in their financial reporting.
3. Significant uncertainties underlying estimates or assumptions.

The place for this kind of narrative explanation is in the letter of the president or chairman of the board or in another section of the annual report such as Management's Discussion and Analysis (MD&A). This last was required for the first time by the SEC in *ASR 159*. These requirements were restructured in *ASR 279*, which appeared in 1980. Ideally information in the MD&A will include items such as:

1. Nonfinancial events and changes during the year that affect the operations of the firm.
2. Expectations regarding the future of the industry and the economy and the role of the firm in these expectations.
3. Plans for growth and changes in operations in the following period or periods.
4. The amount and expected effect of current and anticipated capital expenditures and research effort.

The nonfinancial events and changes include shifts in top management and major policies; significant technological improvements in the firm or industry; shifts in the demand for the product of the firm or changes in prices of either major factors of production or of the product; and such events as strikes, wars, political actions, and natural disasters that may have a material effect on future operations of the firm. If any of these nonfinancial events is likely to have a material effect on the valuation of assets or liabilities at the end of the period or on the income of future periods, it should be reported in the financial statements, rather than being left for management to report. But the effect of many of these items is difficult to evaluate, and even though they are taken into consideration in the financial statements, a more complete disclosure by management is desirable.

EXHIBIT 24-5   Management's Discussion and Analysis (selected portion only.)

Borg-Warner Corporation

For Borg Warner, 1981 was an excellent year in many respects. We improved earnings in the face of weak markets. The stock was split 2 for 1, and the dividend was raised 13%.

Yet, as we celebrate our accomplishments, it's good that we keep them in perspective. For some of them pale when adjusted for inflation. Even though the rate was lower than in either of the prior two years, inflation is still an insidious burden that gnaws at our financial underpinnings and benefits no one.

Another sobering fact was the general weakness of our consolidated manufacturing operations in 1981. While 1981 earnings from consolidated manufacturing operations, at $64 million, improved a little from a dismal 1980, they remained far below the record $120 million in 1979. If adjusted for inflation, the comparison is even worse.

Clearly, we have reduced, but in no way eliminated, the impact of the cyclical nature of our largest markets on overall results. The automotive and construction markets remained firmly in the grip of recession, spending by industry was down, the economy in general was weak.

We did as well as we did in that environment because there is a new Borg-Warner emerging.

Expectations are more difficult to disclose and evaluate than nonfinancial events. Management has a tendency to present only optimistic expectations and, therefore, make them somewhat meaningless. A common expression found in these letters of the president is "We are confident that the prospects for profitable operations will continue to improve." Expressions such as this are too vague to be useful in making predictions regarding the future of the enterprise.

Exhibit 24-5 provides an example of a managerial discussion. Its virtue is that it alerts the user to issues that management believes are key. In this case, inflation is clearly seen to be a problem for the company. At the same time, the discussion enables management to mitigate the worst of the numbers by assuring investors that a new company is emerging.

CHECKPOINTS

1. How, if at all, can the format of financial statements affect disclosure? Give examples.
2. What is the relationship between footnotes and the formal financial statements?
3. Do supplementary statements and schedules contain information that is of lesser importance than that in the main statements? If not, why is important information placed in supplements?
4. What is the purpose of management's discussion and analysis?

SUMMARY

Financial disclosures are made to a wide circle of users including government, creditors, investors, and employees. Traditionally, investors are considered the primary focal group for corporate disclosures. Disclosure is vital for the optimum decisions of investors and for a stable capital market. Timely disclosure of relevant information tends to prevent surprises that may completely alter the outlook for the future of the firm. It also tends to give investors greater confidence in the financial information available to them. The nature of the data to be disclosed depends in part on the nature of investors' decision models. The amount of data disclosed tends to be determined by standards such as relevance and reliability.

Many forms and methods exist through which managements can disclose information to users. The most prominent of these methods are the formal financial statements, but footnotes, supplementary statements, and narrative discussions are also key ingredients. No overarching theory, accepted by all, exists to determine the appropriate means for disclosure. Accountants are engaged in an active search for new ways in which users might become better informed. It is this ongoing search that defines accounting as the enormously exciting field that it is.

DISCUSSION QUESTIONS

1. Compare and contrast the following two statements. (Your instructor might ask you to take one side and argue it in class.) The first comes from Henry O. Havemeyer, president of The American Sugar Refining Company, who said in 1899:

> I cannot but regard corporate publicity of the kind and to the extent advocated by many as a certain and serious hindrance to effective competition.[34]

The second comes from Ray Garrett, Jr., chairman of the Securities and Exchange Commission, who said:

> There is no doubt that a major underlying premise of the Federal securities laws is that full and prompt disclosure will best serve the purposes of both investors and corporate issuers.[35]

2. Comment on the following statement by Dean E. Miller, Deputy Comptroller of the Currency, made in 1975:

> A company with problems—including one which came by them without fault—will only be hurt by the securities laws. Their application tends to have the effect of driving companies in trouble out of business. Anyone trying to save a company has to contend with the securities laws, rather than utilize them. Thus it is that what has become regarded by some as our principle means of Federal regulation of business is oriented toward destruction, rather than preservation.[36]

3. As a class project, choose a topic about which a number of companies might reasonably be expected to disclose information. A recent example might be the rise of the price of fuel as a result of the Gulf crisis. Another might be political changes in overseas markets. Other examples are new reporting standards such as for pensions, deferred taxes, consolidations, and financial instruments.

Go to your library singly or in pairs, as preferred by your instructor, and pick out an annual report. Examine its disclosure of that particular topic from cover to cover. Does it appear in the letter to stockholders? Does it appear in a footnote? Does management discuss it in the section labeled MD&A?

Compare your finding with your colleagues. How does disclosure differ? Can you relate the level and kind of disclosure to the industry in which the firm finds itself, or to the size of the firm?

Are you satisfied with the level of disclosure? Do you feel that the average reader will be able to understand the material disclosed? What recommendations, if any, would you make to the FASB and the SEC regarding disclosure of this particular issue?

Accounting Changes

4. *Accounting Principles Board Opinion No. 20* is concerned with accounting changes.

Required:

a. Define, discuss, and illustrate each of the following in such a way that one can be distinguished from the other.

1. An accounting change.
2. A correction of an error in previously issued financial statements.

b. Discuss the justification for a change in accounting principle.

c. Discuss the reporting (as required by *Accounting Principles Board Opinion No. 20*) of a change from the LIFO method to another method of inventory pricing.

5. Sometimes a business entity may change its method of accounting for certain items. The change may be classified as a change in accounting principle, a change in accounting estimate, or a change in reporting entity.

Listed below are three independent, *unrelated* sets of facts relating to accounting changes.

Situation 1

A company determined that the depreciable lives of its fixed assets are presently too long to fairly match the cost of the fixed assets with the revenue produced. The company decided at the beginning of the current year to reduce the depreciable lives of all of its existing fixed assets by five years.

Situation 2

On December 31, 1976, Gary Company owned 51 percent of Allen Company, at which time Gary reported its investment using the cost method due to political uncertainties in the country in which Allen was located. On January 2, 1977, the management of Gary Company was satisfied that the political uncertainties were resolved and the assets of the company were in no danger of nationalization. Accordingly, Gary will prepare consolidated financial statements for Gary and Allen for the year ended December 31, 1977.

Situation 3

A company decides in January 1977 to adopt the straight-line method of depreciation for plant equipment. The straight-line method will be used for new acquisitions as well as for previously acquired plant equipment for which depreciation had been provided on an accelerated basis.

Required:

For each of the situations described above, provide the information indicated below. Complete your discussion for each situation before going on to the next situation.

   a.   Type of accounting change.

   b.   Manner of reporting the change under current generally accepted accounting principles including a discussion, where applicable, of how amounts are computed.

   c.   Effect of the change on the statement of financial position and earnings statement.

   d.   Footnote disclosures that would be necessary.

Segment Reporting

   6.   Many companies are against disclosing information to the general public. Make up as many arguments as you can in favor of nondisclosure. Can you knock them down again?

   7.   (May 1979)   *Part a.*   In order to properly understand current generally accepted accounting principles with respect to accounting for and reporting upon segments of a business enterprise, as stated by the Financial Accounting Standards Board in its *Statement 14,* it is necessary to be familiar with certain unique terminology.

Required:

With respect to segments of a business enterprise, explain the following terms:

   1. Industry segment.
   2. Revenue.
   3. Operating profit and loss.
   4. Identifiable assets.

Part b.   A central issue in reporting on industry segments of a business enterprise is the determination of which segments are reportable.

Required:

   1. What are the tests to determine whether or not an industry segment is reportable?
   2. What is the test to determine if enough industry segments have been separately reported upon and what is the guideline on the maximum number of industry segments to be shown?

EXXON VALDEZ

Two faculty members, Mike Roohan and Susan Dillon, were recently overheard discussing the Alaskan oil spill caused by the Exxon Valdez. Mike is a well-known activist on campus while Susan is relatively conservative.

Mike (rather angrily): We really have to find a way to bring these big companies to heel. I think we should make them pay for all the costs of the cleanup!

Susan (in conciliatory tones): I don't know. Isn't that a bit radical? I mean it was an accident you know and accidents can happen to anyone.

Mike (not mollified): Well, at the very least they should be required to disclose an estimate of the financial burden they have placed on fishermen and others in the Sound, as a result of the accident. That way shareholders will know what their actions have cost others.

Susan (a little intrigued by the idea): That's not necessarily a bad idea, Mike. But I wonder now. Would you be willing to let them put in an estimate of the financial benefits they have brought to Alaska in the past by their actions? After all, these past many years they have been spending monies on safety related activities which just showed up as an expense with no offsetting benefit.

Required:

What do you think of Mike's suggestion? How do you feel about Susan's modification of the idea?

CENTEX CORPORATION

Centex Corporation describes itself as among the nation's largest multimarket home builders and general building contractors. The company also produces and distributes cement, ready-mix concrete, aggregates, and gypsum wallboard. During fiscal 1989, Centex expanded the financial services aspect of its operation by establishing a savings bank.

Management's discussion and analysis reported that, in 1989, Centex had record revenues as well as all-time earnings per share from operations. Revenues climbed to almost 2 billion, a 24 percent increase over the fiscal 1988 level. In addition, earnings from operations were up 66 percent to $40 million from $24 million in 1988.

Among Centex's subsidiaries is a full-service mortgage company which originates mortgage loans for Centex homebuyers and others. During fiscal 1989, the company's financial service operations were expanded through the investment of $26.3 million to establish a savings and loan association, Texas Trust, to acquire certain assets and assume certain liabilities of four central Texas savings and loan associations in a FSLIC-assisted transaction. Centex reported, among many other things, that:

> FSLIC provided assistance to Texas Trust in the form of a note representing the aggregate negative capital (as defined) of the insolvent associations as of December 29, 1988. This note is due in full on December 29, 1998 and bears interest at a designated spread above the Texas Cost of Funds, adjusted quarterly.
>
> Certain of the acquired assets (Covered Assets) are subject to FSLIC assistance for a 10 year period. The FSLIC will reimburse Texas Trust for any losses or costs incurred in connection with the operation and disposition of these assets . . . In addition, the FSLIC will supplement the actual yield on these assets

Centex Corporation and Subsidiaries
CONSOLIDATED BALANCE SHEETS

| | March 31, | | | |
| | 1989 | | 1988 | |
	Supplemental	*Fully Consolidated*	*Supplemental*	*Fully Consolidated*
	(dollars in thousands)			
Assets				
Cash	$ 8,053	$ 21,673	$ 9,443	$ 12,059
Receivables				
Residential mortgage loans	—	127,249	—	101,173
Construction contracts	152,987	152,987	154,791	154,791
Trade	41,116	58,258	23,765	26,310
Notes	22,331	23,412	17,853	24,626
Inventories				
Housing projects	466,056	466,056	457,127	457,127
Land held for development and sale	105,545	105,545	76,458	76,458
Construction products	14,736	14,736	16,408	16,408
Investments				
Joint ventures and unconsolidated subsidiaries	68,703	53,376	45,758	37,697
Centex Development Company, L.P.	76,843	76,843	76,573	76,573
Property and equipment, net	112,587	114,689	133,736	134,990
FSLIC note and receivables ($217,595) and assets covered by FSLIC assistance ($336,099)	—	553,694	—	—
Other assets and deferred charges	27,271	32,004	26,640	29,886
	$1,096,228	$1,800,522	$1,038,552	$1,148,098

Centex Corporation and Subsidiaries
CONSOLIDATED BALANCE SHEETS (*continued*)

	March 31,			
	1989		1988	
	Supplemental	Fully Consolidated	Supplemental	Fully Consolidated
	(dollars in thousands)			
Liabilities and Stockholders' Equity				
Accounts payable and accrued liabilities	$ 358,129	$ 373,426	$ 310,977	$ 319,698
Deposits ($452,135) and FHLB advances ($135,970)	—	588,105	—	—
Notes payable	100,265	200,068	44,100	144,100
Long-term debt				
Subordinated debentures	119,162	119,162	119,144	119,144
Other	21,030	21,030	59,718	59,718
Deferred income taxes	74,487	75,576	139,767	140,592
Negative goodwill	38,981	38,981	—	—
Stockholders' equity				
Common stock, $.25 par value; authorized 50,000,000 shares; issued 14,466,493 and 15,048,264 shares, respectively	3,617	3,617	3,762	3,762
Capital in excess of par value	205	205	—	—
Retained earnings	380,352	380,352	361,084	361,084
Total stockholders' equity	384,174	384,174	364,846	364,846
	$1,096,228	$1,800,522	$1,038,552	$1,148,098

See Note A for discussion of the above dual presentation. The "Supplemental" presentation includes the mortgage company and the savings and loan on the equity method, whereas the "Fully Consolidated" presentation includes all assets and liabilities of these entities. Also see notes to consolidated financial statements.

to provide a guaranteed yield equal to the Texas Cost of Funds plus a designated spread until December 29, 1998.

In earlier years, such subsidiaries would have been accounted for on the equity method because its character differed materially from the rest of Centex's business. The FASB, however, in *SFAS 94* mandated that all subsidiaries in which a parent has at least a 50 percent interest should be consolidated.

Centex noted in its MD&A that the savings and loan operations were consolidated as required, thereby resulting in an increase in consolidated assets and liabilities. They then commented:

We believe that the consolidation mandated by *SFAS No. 94* is confusing because the resulting presentation of the balance sheet does not adequately reflect either the actual or historical financial condition of the company. Centex is not liable for the newly consolidated debt of the mortgage company or of the savings and loan; instead, only our equity in these subsidiaries is at risk. In an effort to clarify the confusion, Centex's balance sheet presents our financial condition as it has traditionally been reported as well as in a format which consolidates the finance subsidiaries. Disregarding the newly consolidated debt, our debt-to-equity ratio is just slightly higher than last year and remains well within an acceptable range for our industry.

A copy of their balance sheet is attached.

The auditors commented in their report that the financial statements present fairly, in all material respects, the financial position of Centex. They then added:

The supplemental balance sheets as of March 31, 1989 and 1988 are presented for purposes of additional analysis and are not a required part of the basic financial statements. These statements are based on the financial statements referred to above [i.e., the statements in conformity with GAAP], adjusted to present the company's mortgage company and the savings and loan on the equity method of accounting as opposed to consolidation. We have reviewed the entries prepared to reflect such adjustments and, in our opinion, the entries have been properly applied to the basic financial statements.

Required:

a. Why, in your opinion, did management make this additional voluntary disclosure?
b. Have you, personally, found it helpful or confusing? How do you think the average reader will react?
c. Do you approve or disapprove of allowing management to make additional disclosures like this? Are there any dangers?
d. Try to find examples of how other companies have dealt with *SFAS 94*. For instance, since each automobile manufacturer has a large finance subsidiary, what additional information do they disclose?
e. Try to find examples of how other companies have accounted for FSLIC-assisted purchases. These purchases clearly cloud any analysis one might want to do on a company. How would you recommend dealing with this?

PRIMARY SOURCES

Those interested in pursuing the topics in this chapter in more depth might begin by consulting the following texts.

Arpan, Jeffrey S., and Lee H. Radebaugh. *International Accounting and Multinational Enterprises* (Boston: Warren, Gorham & Lamont, 1981), esp. Ch. 9.

Most, Kenneth S. *Accounting Theory,* 2nd ed. (Columbus, Ohio: Grid Publishing Inc., 1982), esp. Ch. 7.

Mueller, Gerhard G.; Helen Gernon; and Gary Meak. *Accounting, An International Perspective* (Homewood, Ill.: Richard D. Irwin, 1987), esp. Ch. 4.

Watts, Ross L., and Jerold L. Zimmerman. *Positive Accounting Theory* (Englewood Cliffs, N.J.: Prentice Hall, 1986), esp. Chs. 11 and 12.

SELECTED ADDITIONAL READINGS

Nature of Disclosure

Abdel-khalik, A. Rashad. *Financial Reporting by Private Companies: Analysis and Diagnosis* (FASB, 1983).

Beaver, William H. "What Should Be the FASB's Objectives?" *Journal of Accountancy,* August 1973, pp. 49–57.

Bedford, Norton M. *Extension in Accounting Disclosure* (Englewood Cliffs, N.J.: Prentice Hall, 1973).

Benjamin, James J., and Keith G. Stanga. "Differences in Disclosure Needs of Major Users of Financial Statements." *Accounting and Business Research,* Summer 1977, pp. 187–92.

Birnberg, Jacob G. "Human Information Processing and Financial Disclosure." In *Financial Accounting Theory.* Edited by Stephen A. Zeff and Thomas F. Keller (New York: McGraw-Hill, 1985), pp. 211–20.

Brownlee, E. Richard III, and S. David Young. "The SEC and Mandated Disclosure: At the Crossroads." *Accounting Horizons,* September 1987, pp. 17–24.

Buzby, Stephen L. "Nature of Adequate Disclosure." *Journal of Accountancy,* April 1974, pp. 38–47.

Buzby, Stephen L. "Selected Items of Information and Their Disclosure in Annual Reports." *The Accounting Review,* July 1974, pp. 423–35.

Buzby, Stephen L. "Company Size, Listed versus Unlisted Stocks, and the Extent of Financial Disclosure." *Journal of Accounting Research,* Spring 1976, pp. 16–37.

Chandra, Gyan. "Study of the Consensus on Disclosure among Public Accountants and Security Analysts." *The Accounting Review,* October 1974, pp. 733–42.

Garrett, R. "Disclosure Rules and Annual Reports: Present Impact." *Financial Executive,* April 1975.

Nelson, Carl L. "Case for Accounting Disclosure." *CA Magazine,* March 1975, pp. 35–38.

Pastena, Victor. "Some Evidence on the SEC's System of Continuous Disclosure." *The Accounting Review,* October 1979, pp. 776–83.

Pastena, Victor, and Joshua Ronen. "Some Hypotheses on the Pattern of Management's Informal Disclosures." *Journal of Accounting Research,* Autumn 1979, pp. 550–64.

Sommer, A. A., Jr. "The Limit of Disclosure." *Financial Executive,* October 1975.

Spicer, Barry H. "Investors, Corporate Social Performance and Information Disclosure: An Empirical Study." *The Accounting Review,* January 1978, pp. 94–111.

Disclosure of Company Segments

Ajinkya, Bipin B. "An Empirical Evaluation of Line-of-Business Reporting." *Journal of Accounting Research,* Autumn 1980, pp. 343–61.

Barefield, Russell M., and Eugene E. Comiskey. "Segmental Financial Disclosure by Diversified Firms and Security Prices: A Comment." *The Accounting Review,* October 1975, pp. 818–21.

Collins, Daniel W., and Richard R. Simonds. "SEC Line-of-Business Disclosure and Market Risk Adjustments." *Journal of Accounting Research,* Autumn 1979, pp. 353–83.

Emmanuel, C. R., and S. J. Gray. "Segmental Disclosures and the Segment Identification Problem." *Accounting and Business Research,* Winter 1977, pp. 37–50.

Kochanek, Richard Frank. "Segmental Financial Disclosure by Diversified Firms and Security Prices." *The Accounting Review,* April 1974, pp. 245–58.

Ortman, Richard P. "The Effects on Investment Analysis of Alternative Reporting Procedures for Diversified Firms." *The Accounting Review,* April 1975, pp. 298–304.

Disclosure of Forecast Data

AICPA: The Financial Forecasts and Projections Task Force. *Guide for Prospective Financial Statements* (New York: American Institute of CPAs, 1986).

Basi, Bart A.; Kenneth J. Carey; and Richard D. Twark. "A Comparison of the Accuracy of Corporate and Security Analysts' Forecasts of Earnings." *The Accounting Review,* April 1976, pp. 244–54.

Beaver, William; Roger Clarke; and William F. Wright. "The Association between Unsystematic Security Returns and the Magnitude of Earnings Forecast Errors." *Journal of Accounting Research,* Autumn 1979, pp. 316–40.

Cameron, Alex B. "A Review of Management's Earnings Forecast Research." *Journal of Accounting Literature,* 1986, pp. 57–83.

Hagerman, R. L., and W. Ruland. "The Accuracy of Management Forecasts and Forecasts of Simple Alternative Models." *Journal of Economics and Business,* Spring 1979, pp. 172–79.

Imhoff, Eugene A., Jr., "The Representativeness of Management Earnings Forecasts." *The Accounting Review,* October 1978, pp. 836–50.

Jaggi, Bikki. "A Note on the Information Content of Corporate Annual Earnings Forecasts." *The Accounting Review,* October 1978, pp. 961–67.

Jaggi, Bikki. "Further Evidence on the Accuracy of Management Forecasts vis-a-vis Analysts' Forecasts." *The Accounting Review,* January 1980, pp. 96–101.

Nichols, Donald R., and S. Michael Groomer. "A Study of the Relative Accuracy of Executives' Estimates of Earnings." *Abacus,* December 1979, pp. 113–27.

Nichols, Donald R.; Jeffrey J. Tsay; and Paula D. Larkin. "Investor Trading Responses to Differing Characteristics of Voluntarily Disclosed Earnings Forecasts." *The Accounting Review*, April 1979, pp. 376–82.

Ruland, William. "The Accuracy of Forecasts by Management and by Financial Analysts." *The Accounting Review*, April 1978, pp. 430–47.

Schreuder, H., and J. Klaassen. "Confidential Revenue and Profit Forecasts by Management and Financial Analysts: Evidence from the Netherlands." *The Accounting Review*, January 1984, pp. 64–77.

ENDNOTES

1. *SFAC 1,* par. 34.
2. Jeffrey S. Arpan and Lee H. Radebaugh, *International Accounting and Multinational Enterprises* (Boston: Warren, Gorham & Lamont, Inc., 1981), p. 224.
3. Eric G. Flamholtz, D. Gerald Searfoss, and Russell Coff,"Developing Human Resource Accounting as a Human Resource Decision Support System," *Accounting Horizons,* September 1988, pp. 1–9.
4. Tom Climo, "What's Happening in Britain?" *The Journal of Accounting,* February 1976, p. 57.
5. See *SFAC 5*.
6. International Accounting Standards Committee, "Disclosure of Accounting Policies," *International Standard No. 1* (London: IASC, January 1975), par. 10.
7. *SFAC 5,* par. 9.
8. *IAS 1,* par. 10.
9. *SFAC 1,* par. 34.
10. Rowland K. Atiase, Linda S. Bamber, and Robert N. Freeman, "Accounting Disclosures Based on Company Size: Regulations and Capital Marketing Evidence," *Accounting Horizons,* March 1988, pp. 18–25.
11. M. Edgar Barrett, "The Extent of Disclosure in Annual Reports of Large Companies in Seven Countries," *The International Journal of Accounting,* Spring 1977, p. 19.
12. Frederick D. S. Choi, "European Disclosure: The Competitive Disclosure Hypothesis," *Journal of International Business Studies,* Fall 1974, pp. 15–23.
13. Arpan and Radebaugh, *International Accounting,* p. 204.
14. Drawn from Kenneth S. Most, *Accounting Theory,* 2nd ed. (Columbus, Ohio: Grid Publishing Company, 1982), p. 178, where an excellent description of the details may be found.
15. *Report of the Advisory Committee on Corporate Disclosure to the Securities and Exchange Commission,* vols. 1 and 2 (Washington, D.C.: U.S. Government Printing Office, November 3, 1977).
16. Most, *Accounting Theory,* p. 197.
17. George J. Murphy, "Early Canadian Financial Statement Disclosure Legislation," *The Accounting Historians Journal,* Fall 1984, pp. 39–59.
18. *IAS 5*.

19. Charles A. Nickerson, Larry G. Pointer, and Robert H. Strawser, "Published Forecasts: Choice or Obligation?" *Financial Executive,* February 1974, pp. 70–73.

20. William S. Gray, "The Role of Forecast Information in Investment Decisions," in *Public Reporting of Corporate Financial Forecasts.* Edited by Prem Prakash and Alfred Rappaport (Chicago: Commerce Clearing House, 1974), pp. 53–54.

21. See Stephen H. Penman, "An Empirical Investigation of the Voluntary Disclosure of Corporate Earnings Forecasts," *Journal of Accounting Research,* Spring 1980, pp. 132–60.

22. Robert S. Kay and D. Gerald Searfoss, *Handbook of Accounting and Auditing,* 2nd ed. (Boston: Warren, Gorham & Lamont, Inc., 1989), Ch. 27.

23. A. Rashad Abdel-khalik and Thomas F. Keller, "Earnings or Cash Flows: An Experiment on Functional Fixation and the Valuation of the Firm," *Studies in Accounting Research No. 16* (American Accounting Association, 1979).

24. Haim Falk and T. Ophir, "Influence of Differences in Accounting Policies on Investment Decisions," *Journal of Accounting Research,* Spring 1973, pp. 108–16.

25. See T. Ross Archibald, "Stock Market Reaction to the Depreciation Switch-Back," *The Accounting Review,* January 1972, pp. 22–30.

26. AICPA Professional Standards, AU 560.03. (Also see *SFAS 16.*)

27. Ibid., par. 560.05.

28. Ibid., par. 560.07.

29. *International Accounting and Auditing Standards,* Section 9014.26 (New York: AICPA, 1988).

30. Arpan & Radebaugh, *International Accounting,* p. 218.

31. See, for example, Sidney Davidson, "Implications of Conglomerate Reporting for the Independent CPA—Comments," in *Public Reporting by Conglomerates.* Edited by Alfred Rappaport, Peter A. Firmin, and Stephen A. Zeff (Englewood Cliffs, N.J.: Prentice Hall, 1968), p. 88.

32. David Solomons, "Accounting Problems and Some Proposed Solutions," Ibid., p. 100.

33. *SFAC 1,* par. 54.

34. Richard P. Brief, "Corporate Financial Reporting at the Turn of the Century," *Journal of Accountancy,* May 1987, p. 144.

35. R. K. Mautz and William G. May, *Financial Disclosure in a Competitive Economy* (New York: Financial Executives Research Foundation, 1978), p. 143.

36. Ibid., p. 142.

Index